Baedeker

France

www.baedeker.com

Verlag Karl Baedeker

SIGHSEEING HIGHLIGHTS ✶ ✶

There are innumerable sights worth visiting in France, not to mention the hidden gems found all over the country. Here, we offer an initial overview of the most important regions and towns highlighted individually in this volume.

The Loire valley is also a paradise for cyclists – seen here at Chateau Ussé

Deauville
»Grand Dame« of the Normandy coast

Arles
The Place du Forum is the place to be

BAEDEKER'S BEST TIPS

We have put the most interesting Baedeker tips in this book together for you below. Experience and enjoy France at its very best!

■ Café des Deux Garçons
This café dates from 1792 and served as the meeting place for artists such as Cézanne. ► **page 199**

■ Voix et Route Romane
Concerts make the churches along the Route Romane in Alsace even more appealing. ► **page 209**

■ Fermes auberges
Good hearty food and basic accommodation in an Alsatian country idyll ► **page 219**

■ Little paradise
The area around Les Baux is a Mecca for bons vivants, with an unusually high number of excellent, renowned hotel restaurants. ► **page 249**

■ Papal pleasures
Head through the secret passageways of the Papal Palace to brunch on the terrace of the high dignitaries. ► **page 263**

■ Loire from the air
The gentle Loire valley landscape is even more beautiful from a bird's-eye view, either by hot air balloon, light aircraft or helicopter. ► **page 273**

■ Gregorian chants in Vézelay
A wonderful four-part choir accompanies Mass in the basilica of Vézelay. ► **page 313**

■ Traditional tripe
Be brave and try it: »tripes à la mode de Caen« is famous among gourmets. ► **page 327**

■ Vélosolex
Amazing what this most French of transportation methods can achieve… ► **page 357**

■ Rail adventures
Pleasant expeditions into the mountains of Haute Provence and the Maritime Alps on the »Pine Cone Express« and the Tenda line ► **page 386**

■ Green and yellow Chartreuse
The legendary liqueurs of Chartreuse have been manufactured since 1605 to secret recipes. ► **page 401**

■ Moutarde et Pain d'Épice
Traditional products from Dijon presented in lovely surroundings ► **page 406**

■ Wine and chocolate
Have you tasted Jura wines? You can make some delicious discoveries in Arbois. ► **page 416**

■ Pruneaux d'Agen
Amazing what can be made from the plums of Agen ► **page 422**

■ Music in the park
On a balmy summer evening after a visit to Paris, the park at Sceaux is the perfect place to relax while listening to classical music. ► **page 438**

■ Café de la Paix
A wonderful brasserie from the belle époque ► **page 458**

Braderie de Lille
200km/125mi of passages lined with both
bric-a-brac and quality antiques – with
moules-frites as sustenance
► page 471

Tomatoes fit for a king
Botanical and culinary rarities in Château
La Bourdaisière on the Loire
► page 498

Candlelit gardens
Thousands of candles magically light up
the famous gardens of the Chateau de
Villandry. ► page 499

Saumur Brut
It doesn't always have to be
champagne! ► page 505

Laguiole
Fine pocket knives and a spectacular
modern hotel set in impressive scenery
► page 520

Modern Montpellier
See the sights on the ultra-modern
tramway. ► page 554

Art Nouveau tour
Experience Art Nouveau in a splendid
museum. ► page 566

The finest brasserie in the world
Find out for yourself if the claims are
exaggerated.
► page 571

Let's go fly a kite
On Dieppe's beach many a brightly
coloured kite dances in the stiff sea
breeze. ► page 589

Open doors
Would you like to see where the most
powerful men in France – the president
and the prime minister – reside?
► page 631

La Cigale in Nantes
The full splendour of the belle époque
unfolds in this brasserie, opened in 1895

Cathedrals of luxury
Go shopping or just dream a little in the
most beautiful of Paris's department
stores. ► page 633

Train Bleu
The luxurious atmosphere of travel from a
bygone age ► page 638

Savon de Marseille
Real Marseille soap is still made in
traditional fashion. ► page 710

Casals-Festival
Concerts in old abbeys in the East
Pyrenees recall the works of the great cello
virtuoso. ► page 720

Champagne in Reims
Visit the champagne companies and get to
know the world of the precious bubbly a
little better. ► page 734

Factory outlets
Even Parisian bargain hunters come to
Troyes by the bus-load to shop at its
factory-outlet shops. ► page 788

Royal feasts in Versailles
Experience how the Sun King threw a
garden party. ► page 808

France, a seafaring nation: grand festival of windjammers at Douarnenez in Brittany
► page 300

BACKGROUND

PRACTICALITIES

»La Gioconda« or the »Mona Lisa«, the major attraction at the Louvre in Paris
► page 627

A trip to France just wouldn't be the same without investigating its wine. The »Rosacker« belongs to the Grands Crus of Alsace
▶ page 205

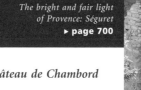

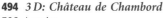

*The bright and fair light
of Provence: Séguret*
► **page 700**

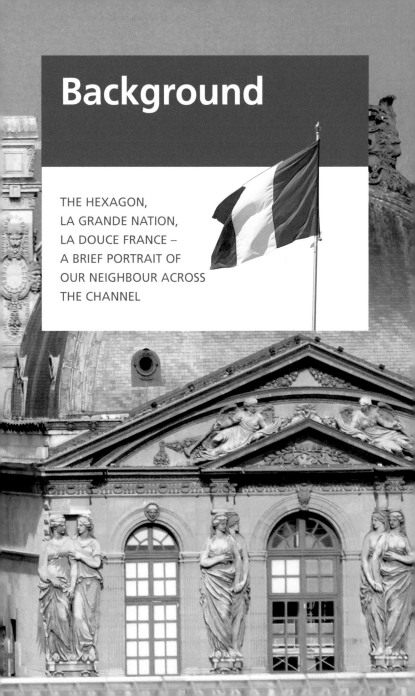

Background

THE HEXAGON,
LA GRANDE NATION,
LA DOUCE FRANCE –
A BRIEF PORTRAIT OF
OUR NEIGHBOUR ACROSS
THE CHANNEL

L'ART DE VIVRE

A vast land with a grand history, delightful landscapes and a culture well served by the motto »vivre comme Dieu en France«, or »live like God in France«. Holidaymakers will find that there could hardly be a more apposite expression for the finest weeks of the year.

»Fascinating variety« is the common response of so many visitors to France when asked for the most striking aspect of our close neighbour. Charles de Gaulle summed it up rather nicely with a tongue-in-cheek culinary reference: »How should one govern a country that produces more than 370 types of cheese?«. The range of scenery in the country is indeed huge. Bordered by two seas and two mountain ranges, the second largest European country belongs to western Europe in geographical terms, but with its wealth of natural landscapes it is western, central and southern Europe in one, as it were.

Paris
The elegant heart of France – a legend that never dies

The Hexagon

The French mainland is hexagonal in form, hence it is sometimes known as the »hexagon«. Covering an area of 535,285 sq km/206,675 sq mi (excluding the Mediterranean island of Corsica and the overseas territories, which are not featured in this guide for practical reasons), the country stretches from Dunkirk on the English Channel in the north to Coma Negra at Prats-de-Mollo in the Pyrenees, and from the Pointe de Corsen in Brittany to Lauterbourg, which lies close to Karlsruhe in Germany. The north to south axis measures some 973km/605mi, while the distance from east to west is 945km/587mi. Contained within this hexagon are seemingly endless plains, contemplative rivers, lakes and swamps, hilly regions with dense woodland, extinct volcanoes and rugged mountains with snow-capped peaks; flat, sandy beaches stretch for miles, chalk cliffs rise perpendicular to the coastline, and hidden bays look out onto sun-drenched or storm-tossed, gentle or wild waters. Yet France's cultural variety is of even greater significance – Europe's oldest nation was born out of a long, tempestuous history of independent regions. Today it is still (or, perhaps more accurately, is again) dominated by a »provincial« mentality. There are

Noble estates
Few countries have seen the aristocracy play such a defining role as has France. Thousands of splendid chateaux, such as Vaux-le-Vicomte in the Ile-de-France, bear witness to its legacy.

Food & drink
Whether in a village inn or a starred gourmet restaurant, culinary pleasures are afforded ample attention.

Pointe-du-Raz
A quite inexhaustible array of impressive landscapes awaits the visitor, from (as here) the rocky cliffs of Brittany to the vineyards of Alsace.

Beach holiday tradition
The beaches of France invariably awaken memories of »M. Hulot's Holiday«

The best seat in the house
Part of the very essence of France, cafés like the Deux Magots in Paris are urban retreats from which you can observe the comings and goings.

Windsurfing at Cap d'Antibes
The hexagon offers everything a sports enthusiast could wish for.

many whose first allegiance is to Brittany, Provence, Gascony or Alsace, with the sense of being French coming a clear second. Their regional languages are, in some instances, also alive and well.

La Douce France

Nevertheless, they do have one thing in common: the »typically French« way of life, a certain lightness of being, coupled with an acute awareness of all the things which make life more attractive – the French like to speak of »Douce France«. It is no coincidence that Paris is the mecca of Haute Couture, nor that fresh victuals are available in healthy abundance both on market stalls and in supermarkets. It may be a cliché, but food and drink really do occupy centre stage in French culture. Even in the modern age of fast food, the French devote time to the purchase, preparation and enjoyment of their food. French civilization is, above all, evident in the testaments to its glorious history that are to be found all over the country: castles and chateaux, monasteries and cathedrals, historic towns – numerous monuments created by master craftsmen, rightfully amongst the most famous in the world. Paris is in a league of its own, and not only for lovers of life in grand cities. Those who are interested in art, museums or festivals will find themselves equally well rewarded in France as those in search of elegant bathing resorts or family beaches, a rural idyll or sporting challenges – on land, in the water or in the air. This »fascinating variety« is not, however,

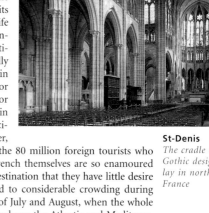

St-Denis
The cradle of Gothic design lay in northern France

without its price: in addition to the 80 million foreign tourists who come to France each year, the French themselves are so enamoured with their country as a holiday destination that they have little desire to travel elsewhere. This can lead to considerable crowding during the high season – in the months of July and August, when the whole of France is on holiday – particularly on the Atlantic and Mediterranean coasts and also in the Alps and Pyrenees. Anyone intent on visiting the »star attractions« such as the castles in the Loire valley, Mont St-Michel, the Eiffel Tower in Paris or the Château de Versailles during this period will require ample reserves of patience. Meanwhile, those who prefer individual attention, calm and seclusion will not be disappointed – especially if they head inland, but, with luck, in coastal areas as well.

Facts

Where and what is the Massif Central? What is the Mistral exactly and what are the lyrics of the *Marseillaise*? How should the »cohabitation« of President and Prime Minister be understood? Facts worth knowing about the country, its people, the economy, politics, society and daily life.

Natural Environment

Apart from approximately 3120km/1939mi of coastline, mainland **Basic landscapes**
France can be divided into three principal types of landscape: large,
virtually flat basin landscapes (Paris basin, Aquitaine or Garonne basin and the Rhône-Saône corridor), old, eroded highlands (Massif
Central, Vosges, Ardennes) and young mountain ranges (Pyrenees,
Alps, Jura). These landscapes combine to offer a mosaic of basins,
plateaus, mountain ranges and peaks.

The core landscape of France – not only geographically, but also in **Basin**
historical and economic terms – is the Paris basin (Seine basin) with **landscapes**
the capital city at its centre, a broad, gradually layered landscape encompassing the Ile de France, Champagne, Lorraine, Burgundy, Picardy and eastern Normandy. The Aquitaine or Garonne basin, with
its limestone plateaus and fertile valleys, lies in the southeast of the
country. The third basin, the Rhône-Saône furrow, spans some
450km/280mi from Dijon to the Mediterranean in the south. It belongs to the continental graben system, stretching across the Belfort
Gap and the Upper Rhine basin to Scandinavia.

The Paris basin is surrounded by four ancient mountain ranges: the **Ancient moun-**
Vosges, the Ardennes, the Massif Central and the Armorique. The **tain ranges**
Grand Ballon (1424m/4672ft) marks its conclusion to the east, where
the corridor of the Rhine Valley meets the lush woodlands of the
Vosges. The foothills of the Ardennes on Belgian soil (part of the
Rhine Slate Mountains) reach into France. In the south, the sparsely
wooded Massif Central is a dormant volcanic region with character-
istically prominent peaks (Puy de Sancy 1886m/6187ft), and plateaus
riddled with river valleys. Its 90,000 sq km/34,750 sq mi cover one
sixth of the area of France. All of the rivers between the Loire in the
north and Tarn/Garonne in the south have their origins here. In the
northwest, the peaks of the Massif Armoricain (Brittany, the Cotentin Peninsula, parts of Normandy, Maine, Anjou, Vendée) barely
reach 400m/1310ft in height (Mont St-Michel, 391m/1279ft). The
rugged cliffs and numerous outlying islands of Brittany are testimony
to the might of the raging sea.

In the southwest and southeast, France is cut off from its neighbours **The Alps and**
by high mountains: towards Switzerland and Italy – between Lake **Pyrenees**
Geneva and the coast of Provence – by the Western Alps with Mont
Blanc, Europe's highest peak (measured in 2004 at 4792m/15,722ft,
with its ice peak at 4808m/15,770ft); on the Spanish frontier by the
Pyrenees, a mountain range 430km/267mi in length and up to
3404m/11,167ft high (Pico de Aneto, on the Spanish side). The Jura,

← *The national holiday is celebrated with military pomp in Paris*

The spectrum of French landscapes: from the Cantal mountains of the Auvergne...

which provides a foretaste of the Alps, is a range of fold mountains rising to 1717m/5633ft with the peak of Le Crêt de la Neige, close to Geneva.

Origins France's landscape can be understood by briefly examining the geology of the country. Although the higher mountains were packed in ice during the Ice Age, the glaciers and their deposition did not penetrate further into the land. The Scandinavian ice masses stopped short of France. The older mountain ranges (Massif Armoricain, Massif Central, Vosges and the Ardennes) came into existence 600 million years ago and belong to the Late Palaeozoic Variscan-Armorique fold belt. As they subsequently broke up, they began to shift or were raised higher. Between these mountain ranges lie broad basin landscapes where sediments collected from the Triassic up to the Tertiary period some 225 to 60 million years ago and, for the most part, remained undisturbed in the years that followed. As little folding or tilting took place, they are predominantly flat; the transition from the Paris basin to the Aquitaine or Garonne basin is barely perceptible. In the latter, deposition from the Pyrenees accumulated in vast pockets which folded out much like the Alps in the Tertiary period. The coastal regions of the south and southwest represent the youngest environs of France in geological terms. The shifting of river currents and the tides created the alluvial land and the coastal lagoons of Gascony in the Atlantic region and of Languedoc on the Mediterranean, as well as the Camargue in the Rhône delta.

Thanks to the valuable deposits of raw materials stored there, the **Mineral** cavernous hollows between the old mountain ranges and the young **resources** fold mountains took on great economic significance. Coal and ores at the edges and inner reaches of the Variscan mountains proved to be the catalysts for the foundation of the old industrial areas such as Artois (coal) in northern France and Lorraine (coal, iron ore) in the northeast. The industries of St-Etienne and Le Creusot on the perimeter of the Massif Central also owe their existence to the presence of coal. South of Caen, ore from the Massif Armoricain was also extracted, but to a lesser degree. The Garonne basin offered favourable conditions for the extraction of natural gas and crude oil; the bulk of French production is located at the base of the Pyrenees in Lacq (gas), St-Marcet (gas) and Parentis (oil). Oil is also extracted in the Paris basin (for example at Coulommes, Chailly, Chateaurenard). Uranium extraction (above all in the Vendée, Limousin, Forez) has a certain economic role to play in what is otherwise a less industrialized region.

The largest rivers in France follow a radial course, beginning in the **Rivers** Massif Central. The longest of these, and of the greatest historical significance, is the Loire (1020km/634mi), rising in the Cevennes, followed by the Seine (775km/481mi) in the north, the Garonne (650km/404mi, rising from the Pyrenees with the Massif Central tributaries the Tarn, Lot and the Dordogne) and the Saône-Rhône waterways; the 482km/299mi-long Saône stems from the Vosges, while the 812km/504mi-long Rhône, a 522km/324mi stretch of

...to the Ile de Batz off the Breton coast

France Major Regions

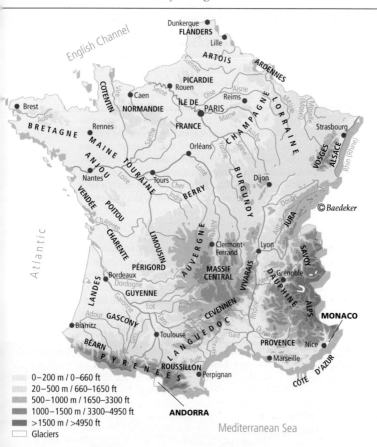

0–200 m / 0–660 ft
20–500 m / 660–1650 ft
500–1000 m / 1650–3300 ft
1000–1500 m / 3300–4950 ft
>1500 m / >4950 ft
Glaciers

© Baedeker

which runs through France, rises in the Alps. A 200km/124mi section of the Rhine demarcates the border to the east in Alsace. The valleys of the smaller rivers are at least as enchanting as the Loire itself. The Lot and Dordogne, Allier and Ardèche, Meuse and Tarn, Aude and Indre, Saône and Aisne are all worthy of note. Nor should the impressive estuary landscapes of some rivers such as the Rhône with the Camargue or Garonne / Dordogne with the Gironde go unmentioned. As well as these natural waterways, France is also served by an extensive network of canals. Formerly of great economic importance, their idyllic scenery has endeared them to many holidaymakers (►Baedeker Special p.192).

Climate

Thanks to its location between the Mediterranean and the Atlantic and North Sea, France generally enjoys a moderate, mild climate. Neither the extreme temperatures of the southern Mediterranean nor the wintry cold of northern Europe leaves much of an impression here. Three climate zones (maritime, continental and Mediterranean) meet in the low mountain range climate of the Massif Central.

Climate zones

Purely maritime and, consequently, most temperate, is the climate of Brittany and the Atlantic coast. Copious precipitation all year round, especially in autumn, along with moderate temperatures and seemingly tireless winds characterize these regions. A narrow stretch of coast in Brittany falls under the influence of the Gulf Stream, rendering winter as mild as on the Mediterranean. Further inland, the climate rapidly becomes more continental. The Paris basin already registers a much sharper contrast in temperature between summer and winter. August is the rainiest month in Paris. The regions south and southeast of the Massif Central are Mediterranean in character, as reflected by the intense sunshine and dry summer scenery of Provence, the southern Rhône valley and Languedoc. In spring and summer the warm and moist Marin blows here from the Mediterranean. On reaching the southern face of the Cevennes and the Massif Central it can bring about the feared heavy rains known as »averses cévenoles«.

The weather of northern France is typified by a mix of sun and cloud with passages of rain or scattered showers. The least rain falls here in spring and summer, in southern France in summer. From May to October, the Azores High cuts in to bring a stable period of dry and sunny weather. In the peripheral areas closer to the sea, precipitation occurs mostly in late autumn and winter. Further inland, there is little seasonal variation in rainfall. The sunniest regions are southern Brittany, (2000 hours per year), La Rochelle and Ile de Re (2300 hours), the south of France (2500 hours) and the Côte d'Azur (2700–2800 hours). By way of comparison: Leicester has 1570 hours of sunshine per year.

Sunshine and showers

Summer (June–August) on the Brittany coast is coolest, with a daily average of 20°C/68°F. Further south on the Atlantic coast, temperatures rise to 22–24°C/72–75°F, with 23–25°C/73–77°F common inland. On the Mediterranean, in the south of France, the thermometer climbs to 26–29°C/79–84°F. Directly on the coast, a sea breeze takes the edge off the summer heat. Global warming has brought increasingly intense heatwaves, hitting the 40°C/104°F mark – as in the summer of the century in 2003. Autumn in southern France and on the Mediterranean enjoys late summer warmth. 23°C/73°F in mid-

Temperature

France *Climate*

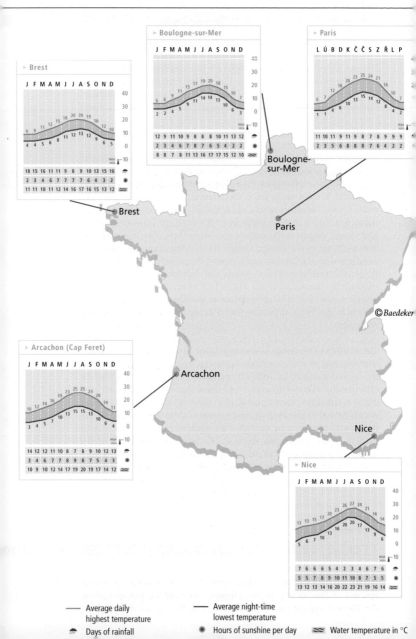

► Brest

J F M A M J J A S O N D

► Boulogne-sur-Mer

J F M A M J J A S O N D

► Paris

L Ú B D K Č Č S Z Ř L P

► Arcachon (Cap Feret)

J F M A M J J A S O N D

► Nice

J F M A M J J A S O N D

Boulogne-sur-Mer

Brest

Paris

© *Baedeker*

Arcachon

Nice

—— Average daily highest temperature

—— Average night-time lowest temperature

☂ Days of rainfall

☀ Hours of sunshine per day

≈ Water temperature in °C

October is a distinct possibility. Winter on the Côte d'Azur is particularly mild, with daytime temperatures averaging 12–14°C/54–57°F. Nevertheless, the palms of Nice have been known to wear a white cloak of snow, albeit briefly.

An important factor in the climate of the Rhône valley is the Mistral, **The Mistral** an extremely brisk, cold north wind, often reaching storm levels. It can occur at any time, although it is most common in the early part of the year, when an area of low pressure lies above the Golfe du Lion. Cold air from the Massif Central and the Alps is propelled south through the Rhône valley between the Cevennes and the Alps. Wherever the Mistral leaves its mark, vegetation suffers. Lines of trees and hedgerows have been planted to protect the earth and plants. Sometimes in summer the hot African Sirocco reaches Provence and makes its presence felt in the Rhône valley up to Lyon.

In the high and low-lying mountains of northern France (Vosges, Jura, Alps, Massif Central), temperatures and precipitation are dependent on the height and location on the luff (heavy precipitation) or leeside (dry) of the range. Alpine winter sports destinations profit from the lengthy snow season, whilst in the Massif Central and the Pyrenees, the snow can last into May. **Mountain regions**

By the end of April, the weather everywhere becomes decidedly sunnier and warmer. This is also true of the holiday resorts on the Mediterranean, still surprisingly cool and wet at this juncture. The Atlantic region struggles to reach higher temperatures in June due to the cooling effect of the sea. At the height of summer, the constant movement of air leads to extremely pleasant conditions. This is a marked contrast to the valleys in the south of France and the Mediterranean, where the lack of wind can mean the days are hot and sticky. Unsettled weather and cooler temperatures make themselves felt on the Atlantic when autumn arrives. Between La Rochelle and Biarritz the bathing season comes to a close in the latter half of September (water temperature approx. 19°C/66°F), whilst in the Mediterranean it is possible to swim until mid-October (water temperature around 20°C/68°F). The ideal period to visit any part of the country is spring, early summer or September, with the Atlantic coast also worth a sojourn in midsummer. **Travel weather**

Flora and Fauna

France's topographical and climatic variety is matched by a wealth of **Flora** different forms of vegetation. Human intervention, particularly in the form of agriculture, deforestation both for the shipbuilding in-

Fields of lavender set the tone in the Provence countryside

dustry and to meet energy requirements, draining wetlands and environmental pollution have all altered the face of the land irreversibly. The dense woodlands which once covered France now occupy about 30% of the area. Thanks to its status as a hunting ground for the nobility, the famous forest of the Ile de France was able to escape deforestation. Les Landes in Gascony, the largest forested area of France, was only created in the 19th century. Covering almost 1 million ha/2.5 million ac at its height in 1939, the current size is only slightly more than half of that area. The northern landscapes of Brittany and Normandy are dominated by oak trees, heath and gorse thickets (Landes, Bruyère). The inlands are green with mixed forests of beech, hornbeam, linden and ash. In the more hilly regions, the vegetation is more typical of higher ground. Coniferous forests come to the fore, giving way to alpine meadows somewhere above 1700m/ 5570ft. The Aquitaine climate allows holm oak and beach pine to thrive, trees more commonly found in the Mediterranean. In the Mediterranean itself, to the south, evergreen oak and stone pine forests cover the lower ground, with woods of sweet chestnut and Scots pine higher up in the mountains.

The olive tree, one of the typical Mediterranean plants, was introduced to France by the Greeks of the eastern Mediterranean 2500 years ago and has spread far up into the Rhône valley. Sclerophyllous evergreens, characterized by their capacity for dealing with a dry climate, are well represented by the maquis and garrigue groups of vegetation. The maquis, a roughly 2m/7ft-high scrubland of trees and bushes, thrives on silicate soils. It advanced in the wake of oak forests lost to deforestation and pasturing. Holm oak, kermes oak, strains of gorse, Judas tree, myrtle and tree heath can all be found here. Moreover, the scent of aromatic shrubs and herbs such as rosemary, thyme, butcher's broom and erica can be noted in the air. The garrigue, commonly found on rocky, calcareous soil and growing little higher than 50cm/20in, is a thorny briar with boxtree, thistle, kermes oak, gorse and aromatic plants such as thyme, lavender, sage and rosemary, as well as hyacinths, iris, tulips and varieties of orchid.

Fauna

The fauna of France is largely typical of central Europe. The French are enthusiastic anglers and hunters, and as a consequence the number of animals that can be hunted has been decimated. Less accessible terrain is home to many reptiles and insects, particularly in the south, where tortoises, lizards, geckos, adders and vipers thrive. Sought-after inhabitants of the water include trout, pike, perch and crayfish; along the coast, mussels, molluscs and crustaceans abound, as well as fish. Admittedly, stocks in the Mediterranean have dwindled as a result of intensive fishing and pollution. Semi-wild horses and flamingo colonies live in the Camargue.

National and nature parks

Six national parks (Vanoise, Port-Cros, Pyrenees, Cevennes, Écrins und Mercantour), cover 1.3 million ha/3.2 million ac, equivalent to 2.3% of the total area of France. Here, efforts are being made to conserve rare flora and fauna. There are also 42 regional nature parks whose total area comes to a further 6.8 million ha/16.8 million ac. The careful use of ecosystems attractive for tourism promotes regional economies (►Practicalities, National Parks).

Environment

France is no stranger to environmental transgressions. The substantial catalogue of faux pas includes gigantic industrial estates, overcrowding on the Mediterranean coast, the destruction of biotopes (the Camargue and Crau for example) for agricultural purposes or for rubbish dumps, the clogging up of entire Alpine valleys with industrial plants, the construction of huge dams and the unbridled exploitation of nuclear energy. Nevertheless, due to the existence of large areas that are still thinly populated and the primarily rural structure of the land, France can claim to have a relatively intact natural environment.

Population

Settlement pattern

Extrapolating from the 1999 census, 61.2 million French citizens (9% of Europe's population) reside in an area measuring 543,965 sq km/210,026 sq mi. With 112 inhabitants per sq km/290 per square mi, France has a significantly lower population density than the UK (249 inhabitants per sq km/644 per sq mi). The settlement pattern is, moreover, quite extreme: approximately 75% of the French live in towns or cities (compared with 81% in the UK), of which only 37 have a population of more than 100,000 and only 7 of these, in turn, have in excess of 250,000 dwellers (compared to figures of 65 and 17 in the UK). The most heavily populated conurbations in the country are Paris with approx. 10.9 million inhabitants, Marseille with 1.3 million, Lyon also with 1.3 million and Lille with 1.1 million. Taken together, these four represent 25% of the entire population, more than the whole of the southwest of France. Around 78% of all communities number less than 1000 inhabitants, accounting for 17% of the population. The most sparsely populated region (after Corsica, with 32 inhabitants per sq km/82 per sq mi) is Limousin (43/111), whilst the départements with the lowest population density are – apart from the Alps – Lozère (14/36), Creuse (23/60) and Cantal (26/67). The overall picture in the country is rural and provincial in character.

Growth and proportion of immigrants

Between 1800 and 1866 the population rose from 27.5 million to 38 million. There was little change up to 1950 (41.6 million), fatalities in the war being balanced out by immigration. It was only after the Second World War that the population explosion took place. The high post-war birthrate was accentuated by the repatriation of French citizens from the colonies in Indochina and North Africa (1.5 million), as well as by the influx of foreign labour. Today, around 5.7 million foreign nationals (9.3%) are registered in France, plus more than 1 million illegal immigrants (»sans papiers«). However, these figures do not include foreigners now recognized as French citizens. Thus approximately one in every five French residents (18%) is either an immigrant or has at least one foreign parent. In the 1999 figures, 13 % of immigrants were Portuguese or Algerian, 12% Moroccan, 9% Italian and 7% Spanish. The highest proportion of foreigners work in the construction and automotive industries in the major industrial regions.

A little chat in a southern French village

Religious denominations

Religious freedom is guaranteed by the constitution. Over 80% of French people have been baptized Catholic, and yet the Catholic Church is losing ground. Only 55% describe themselves as Catholic, less than 10% can be termed practising Catholics and baptisms of newborn babies are down to a mere 60%. The Catholic Church surrendered lands and riches in the Revolution, church and state have been separated since 1905, with the bulk of church buildings handed over to the state at that time. Since then, the church has been financed by donations, through its own financial operations, and by the large land holdings that have been reassigned to it by foundations. The state does not levy a church tax and the state school syllabus does not include religious studies. Yet the Catholic Church is the

principal force behind the private schools which carry considerable weight in France. In the départements of Haut-Rhin, Bas-Rhin and Moselle, as well as Alsace-Lorraine, once German territory, the church enjoys special status. Here, the Concordat of 1801 is still in effect and priests are paid a salary by the state. Religious studies are part of the school curriculum and Strasbourg is home to state theological faculties. The second largest religious denomination comprises approximately 4–7 million Muslims, mostly immigrants from North Africa. They – and the Jews – are the prime target for the extreme right-wing groups, which have been active since the 1980s. Most recently, a »new« form of anti-Semitism has been has been identified, one that stems from Muslims and black people. Other faiths play a less prominent role in public life: 950,000 Protestants, 520,000 Jews and 120,000 Orthodox Christians.

The French language developed out of vulgar Latin, adopted by the **Language** defeated Gauls following the Roman victory over the Celts. Many words of Celtic or Germanic origin have survived, however. Modern French was born in Paris and the Ile de France (Langue d'oïl) as the language of the king and his court. It spread to the remaining regions as the crown conquered and centralized the hexagon step by step. In 1539, the Villers-Cotterêts edict declared French to be the official language. The French Revolution and Napoleon completed the process of nationalization. For centuries, French was the most important language in Europe, the language of diplomacy and of the well educated. Today it is the principal language in 35 countries.

The various groups who live in the »provinces«, i.e. beyond the Ile **Regional** de France, have kept their own languages alive in spite of centuries **languages** of censure: in southern France the Langue d'oc (Occitain or Provençal, although it is difficult to determine actual numbers); to the far west Breton (Ar Brezhoneg approx. 0.2 million); in the French part of Flanders Flemish (20,000); in Roussillon Catalan (200,000); in Alsace and parts of Lorraine Alemannic Alsatian (approx. 0.7 million); Corsican, an Italian dialect, on Corsica (approx. 130,000). Basque (Euskara), a non-Indogermanic language is still spoken by some 70,000 French people; in the autonomous Spanish Basque region it is the official language (570,000).

The revival of regional languages, together with the promotion of local and regional cultural tradition, has been supported since the 1970s primarily by scholars, their students and literary figures. Regional ambitions to conserve local languages different to French coincide with demands for stronger devolution of political and cultural policy and greater independence from the Paris centre. Some groups are going so far as to demand political autonomy, with Corsica to the fore, followed by the Pays Basque and Brittany.

State and Government

Form of government France is a democratic, parliamentary republic with a strong president, as determined by the referendum of 6 October 1958 and the constitution of the Fifth Republic, modified on several occasions (most recently in 1998). The active voting age is 18, the passive 23. The voting system for national elections is first past the post, with proportional representation for regional parliamentary elections.

State emblem Since 1870 France has not really been in possession of an emblem of the state. The one in use today uses symbols of the French Revolution, bordered by the great chain of the Order of the Legion of Honour. On the ribbon are the words »Liberté, Égalité, Fraternité« (»freedom, equality, brotherhood«).

National anthem The Marseillaise was composed by C.-J. Rouget de Lisle in Strasbourg in 1792 and was declared the national anthem in 1795.

Allons enfants de la patrie! / Le jour de gloire est arrivé.
Contre nous de la tyrannie / L'étendard sanglant est levé.
Entendez-vous dans les campagnes / Mugir ces féroces soldats?
Ils viennent jusque dans nos bras, / Egorger vos fils, vos compagnes!
Aux armes citoyens! / Formez vos bataillons,
Marchons, marchons! / Qu'un sang impur abreuve nos sillons.

Arise, children of the fatherland, the day of glory has arrived!
Against us, tyranny's bloody banner is raised.
Do you hear in the countryside the braying of these ferocious soldiers?
They are coming into our midst to cut the throats of our sons, our wives!
To arms, citizens! Form your battalions!
March, march! May tainted blood water our fields!

Important national dates Two events are highlighted as marking the beginning of the nation's history: the division of France in the Treaty of Verdun in 843 and the coronation of Hugo Capet on 3 July 987 as the first French king. The

Facts and Figures France

France

© *Baedeker*

Location
► In western Europe, between the Atlantic and the Mediterranean Sea
► between 42° and 51°N latitude, 5°W and 8°E longitude

Area and National Territory
► Mainland 535,285 sq km/ 206,675 sq mi
Corsica 8680 sq km/3351 sq mi
Overseas territories 88,869 sq km/ 34,313 sq mi
► Neighbouring countries: Belgium, Luxembourg, Germany, Switzerland, Italy, Spain, Andorra.
► Enclave: Monaco

Population
► 61.2 million (mainland and Corsica)
DOM-TOM approx. 1.8 million
Population density (mainland and Corsica) 112 inhabitants/sq km/ 290 per sq mi
► Largest conurbations: Paris (10.9 million), Marseille (1.3 million), Lyon (1.3 million), Lille metropolis (1.1 million)

Comparison to UK
► Area 244,820 sq km/94,526 sq mi
► Population: 60.9 million
Population density: 249 inhabitants/ sq km/644 per sq mi

State and Administration
► Representative presidential democracy
► President: N. Sarkozy (since 2007)
► Parliament: National Assembly and Senate
► Country subdivisions: 22 regions with 96 départements

Economy
► Gross national product: €31,700 per capita (2007)
► In percentages: service sector 72%, industry 26%, agriculture 2%
► Main trading partners: Germany, UK, Italy, Belgium
► Chief exports: machinery, vehicles and accessories, chemical and agricultural products (especially wine)
► Tourism: 79 million visitors per annum; turnover (2006): €37 billion

National flag
► The red, white and blue flag, the tricolore, was the world's first national flag and is its most famous. In 1789,

the members of the National Constituent Assembly created a new »municipality« with its own civic militia led by the Marquis de Lafayette. The militia wore coloured armbands: red and blue for Paris, and white to represent the royal fleurs-de-lys. The red, white and blue cockade became the symbol of the French Revolution and the basis of the French national flag.

France *Administration*

Region	Area	Population	Adminstrative centre
Alsace	8 310 km² / 5 164 miles²	1 734 100	Strasbourg
Aquitaine	41 407 km² / 25 730 miles²	2 908 300	Bordeaux
Auvergne	25 988 km² / 16 149 miles²	1 308 800	Clermont-Ferrand
Bourgogne	593 km² / 369 miles²	1 160 100	Dijon
Bretagne	27 184 km² / 16 892 miles²	2 906 200	Rennes
Centre	31 592 km² / 19 631 miles²	2 440 300	Orléans
Champagne-Ardenne	25 600 km² / 15 907 miles²	1 342 300	Châlons-en-Champagne
Franche-Comté	16 189 km² / 10 060 miles²	1 117 100	Besançon
Ile de France	12 001 km² / 7 457 miles²	10 952 000	Paris
Languedoc-Roussillon	27 448 km² / 17 056 miles²	2 295 600	Montpellier
Limousin	16 932 km² / 10 521 miles²	711 000	Limoges
Lorraine	23 540 km² / 14 627 miles²	2 310 400	Metz
Midi-Pyrénées	45 382 km² / 28 199 miles²	2 551 700	Toulouse
Nord-Pas-de-Calais	12 376 km² / 7 690 miles²	3 996 600	Lille
Basse-Normandie	17 583 km² / 10 926 miles²	1 422 200	Caen
Haute-Normandie	12 258 km² / 7 617 miles²	1 780 200	Rouen
Pays de la Loire	32 126 km² / 19 963 miles²	3 222 000	Nantes
Picardie	19 411 km² / 12 062 miles²	1 857 800	Amiens
Poitou-Charentes	25 790 km² / 16 026 miles²	1 640 100	Poitiers
Provence-Alpes-Côte d'Azur	31 436 km² / 19 534 miles²	4 506 200	Marseille
Rhône-Alpes	43 694 km² / 27 151 miles²	5 645 400	Lyon

First Republic was declared in 1792, the Third in 1870. 14 July, the date of the Storming of the Bastille in 1789, is celebrated as a national holiday.

Head of state

The President of the Republic is elected for seven years in a direct vote and can stand once for re-election. He cannot be dismissed but it lies within his power to dissolve parliament (as occurred in 1962, 1968, 1981, 1988 and 1997). He appoints the prime minister, authorizes or rejects laws and is the commander-in-chief of military forces (including the deployment of nuclear weapons); in a state of emergency, ultimate jurisdiction lies with him alone (right of emergency decree). Executive powers are shared by the president and his cabinet, run by a prime minister who answers to parliament but is, in practice, subordinate to the president. As happened between 1997 and 2002, »cohabitation« is possible, i.e. the president and prime minister need not necessarily belong to the same party. Should this situation arise, the prime minister determines policy, whilst the president has a say in matters of foreign policy and defence.

Parliament

Parliament consists of two chambers, the national assembly (Assemblée Nationale) and the senate. The 577 members of the assembly are elected by direct vote for five years. Should a candidate not obtain an absolute majority in the first vote, a second vote takes place based on a relative majority – the same procedure as for the prime minister. The 321 members of the less powerful senate are elected by delegates for nine years. Every three years, a third of the senators are replaced. Both chambers are involved in legislation, with the national assembly having the final say. It can also bring down a government (with a vote of no confidence).

Administrative structure

Since 1972 mainland France has been divided into 22 régions, subdivided into 96 départements with an elected assembly, the most important regional bodies between the central administration and the communities. The départements are alphabetically numbered, with these numbers providing the last two digits on vehicle registration plates and the first two digits of the postcode. The départements, with a prefect (Préfet) at their head, are divided into (or sous-préfectures; 325), these in turn are split into cantons (3876) and communities (communes, 36,566).

Decentralization

Since the Middle Ages a centralist structure has evolved, with however the king handing over administrative duties for the »gouvernements« to regional nobility and, later, installing directors for the »provinces«. Napoleon perfected the structure of command through prefects as governors in the départements. Up until 1981, political and economic power was concentrated at the centre of the French state in Paris. The régions, similar to the federal states of Germany or Austria, had little power of their own. The administrative councils

The Assemblée Nationale (National Assembly) meets in the Palais Bourbon in Paris

of the départements and communes lacked resources to manage their growing remit. Urgent problems such as the need to modernize the infrastructure of the communities and correct the inflexible monostructure of industrial areas such as Lorraine, rural exodus and land erosion in the Massif Central, and the resurgence of regional culture in Alsace, Brittany, southern France and Corsica, led the Mitterrand government to open the way to decentralization in 1981. Regions gained a degree of independence with their own elected parliamentary bodies, whilst the responsibilities and duties of the central state, region, département and commune were reviewed.

Law Until 1958 judicature was basely largely on the Code Napoléon of 1810 with the Code Civil and Code Pénal, which saw important reforms as time progressed (in 1792, for example, marital divorce was introduced, then annulled in 1816 and reintroduced in 1884. The death penalty was abolished in 1981). Comprehensive reforms to the Napoleonic Penal Code came into effect on 1 March 1994.

Political parties Political parties in France do not have the same constitutional status as their counterparts in the UK. Mistrust of a party state meant that there were no state funds available for election campaigns prior to 1988. Only the communists and, to some degree, the socialists and Gaullists resemble the member-based parties of the British system. If France is characterized by a multipartite landscape, the first past the post voting system has proved beneficial to two particular camps of roughly equal strength: on the right, the Gaullist Rassemblement pour la République (RPR) and the liberal-conservative, non-Gaullist Union pour la Démocratie Française (UDF); on the left the Socialist Party (Parti Socialiste, PS) and the French Communist Party (Parti Communiste Français, PCF). In 2002 the RPR, UDF and the conservative-liberal Démocratie Liberale formed the Union pour un Mouvement Populaire. There are also many more parties less significant in numbers such as the radicals (Parti Radical; founded in 1901, the oldest French political party in existence) and the Christian-democratic Forces Démocrate.

Founded in1972 by Jean-Marie Le Pen, the extreme right-wing Front National (FN) scored their first successes in the communal and European elections of 1983–84 before breaking into parliament in 1986. In the 1998 regional elections he won 20% of the vote in Alsace and as much as 29% in Provence-Alpes-Côte d'Azur. Some towns in southern France have an FN mayor. Immigration, unemployment, crime and the fight against European unification are exploited to foster fears of social collapse. **Front National**

The French Green Party (Les Verts, Confédération Écologiste), had a healthy nine representatives in the European Parliament of 1989 (in the UK, although the Greens received 15% of the vote, no Green Party MEPs were elected), but failed to make a similar impression in the French parliamentary elections. On the one hand, the ecology movement is divided and, on the other, »green« issues such as the careful use of natural resources and nuclear energy are perceived differently in France: the 56 nuclear power stations (and an arsenal of nuclear weapons) are accepted as symbols of the nation's independence. Another important factor is certainly the elitist technocratic mindset of the captains of industry and political managers. Electoral successes for the Greens attest to a growing interest in environmental issues, whilst opposition to environmentally hazardous prestige projects is also on the rise. In 1997 a Green MP became Minister for Environmental Protection. Nevertheless, the cultivation of genetically modified corn was sanctioned in the same year. **Les Verts**

The French unions are not unified in an umbrella organization; instead they are in competition with one another on policy. The most important organizations are the communist CGT (Confédération Générale du Travail, inaugurated 1885), the anti-communist FO (Force Ouvrière, formed by a splinter group of the CGT in 1947), the Christian CFTC (Confédération Française des Travailleurs Chrétiens, founded in 1919) and the socialist CFDT (Confédération Française Démocratique du Travail, which broke with the CTFC in 1964). The unions operate across the board, without being tied to specific industries. The CGC (Confédération Générale des Cadres, founded in 1944) represents professionals and managers on all levels, **The unions** as does the FEN (Fédération de l'Education Nationale, founded in 1947 as the united teachers' union). The unions still hold considerable sway in the public sector, as the SNCF and Paris Métro strikes have shown. They are less influential in trade and industry sectors or with regard to state concerns. Membership is amongst the lowest in the EU, at around 10%). Employers' interests are represented by the Conseil National du Patronat Français (CNFP, founded in 1946), with some 1.5 million members.

Employers' representation

Foreign policy Befitting its international status, France is a member of the following organizations: the UN and its subdivisions, the EU, WEU, European Council, OECD, GATT, IMF. France's rank in world affairs is underlined by its permanent membership of the UN World Security Council (with the right of veto). Paris is the seat of international organizations as UNESCO and the OECD.

France is also a founder member of NATO, although in foreign policy the traditional aspirations of being a world power mean that France tends to see itself in competition with the USA. In the wake of political and economic stabilization in France after the major problems of decolonization and the Indochina and Algerian wars, Charles de Gaulle embarked on his programme to make France an »independent world power« in the late 1950s, leading to the development of the nation's own nuclear capabilities (»force de frappe«) and the withdrawal of France from the NATO executive in 1966. The collapse of the Warsaw Pact saw France grow closer to NATO, taking a part in determining NATO's new responsibilities. A further consequence of the change in protocol for the army was the abolition of military service in 2001. French foreign policy is geared towards securing national independence. This is borne out by the fact that France has been a driving force for European unity since the days of de Gaulle and Konrad Adenauer, first Chancellor of the Federal Republic of Germany, but, for France, the desire for an independent Europe stops short of support for a federal European super-state. The European Union (ratified in the Maastricht Treaty in 1992, economic and monetary union following in 2002) has rendered French ambitions of national grandeur and economic independence barely sustainable. As a legacy of its earlier colonial possessions, France has relationships with numerous Third World states, with a military presence primarily in Africa and in the Mediterranean region.

Education

The French education system is centralized, curricula are determined at state level and teaching staff enjoy civil servant status. The school system is divided into tiers. Since 1959 the minimum age for leaving school has been 16. Primary and secondary schools are free of charge and undenominational. All schools are full-time, from kindergarten through to sixth-form or its equivalent. Some 18% of pupils attend private schools, 93% of which are Catholic (at secondary level II this figure rises to over 20%); they are seen as particularly important institutes of learning for children from conservative, middle-class families. The state also covers salaries and some miscellaneous costs of private schools, meaning that school fees are kept relatively low.

Preschool

Children between the ages of two and six are accepted at the »école maternelle«. Attendance is not compulsory. 99% of three-year-olds and 100% of four and five-year-olds visit these state facilities, where staff are trained as primary school teachers and paid as such. Children younger than two may visit a crèche or participate in the state's childminding programme.

Primary school

Attendance at primary school (école primaire or élémentaire) is for six to eleven-year-olds.

Secondary level I

The »collège« is organized along the lines of a comprehensive school, taking children from eleven to fifteen years of age. In addition to the subjects taught at primary level, the humanities, economics and natural sciences now come into the equation. For pupils intending to leave school at the minimum age of 16, career-orientated courses are offered, with a move to vocational schools also a possibility (Centres de formation d'apprentis). Secondary level I is completed with the B.E.P.C. (Brevet d'Etudes du Premier Cycle).

Secondary level II

At this point, the school system splits into the general studies model of the »lycée« over three years and the vocational »lycée professionel« for a two-year period. The lycée tends to focus on specific disciplines (e.g. social or natural science) with a corresponding qualification (baccalauréat, or »bac«). Grades are stringently awarded, with a fairly high rate of failure (approx. 25 %).

Further education

Further education institutions have been autonomous since 1968. There are 78 universities, 67 technical colleges (Instituts Universitaires de Technologie) and 140 »grandes écoles«. The total number of students in further education currently stands at around 2 million. The sole condition of entry is the Baccalauréat. The bar is raised to a considerable height for examinations, with a mere 30–50 % of students surviving the intermediary exams at the end of their first or second year. Those who continue require a further two years to earn their »licence« or »maîtrise«, both of which may open the way to professional careers. The latter is necessary for students wishing to further their studies in the form of a doctorate.

Grandes écoles

Most prestigious of all are not the universities but the élite grandes écoles, offering a range of subjects from agricultural science to the fine arts. Following the Bac and having attended one or two years of classes préparatoires, some 6% of students go through a rigorous selection process before entering careers in administration, politics, the armed forces, trade and industry. Held in the highest regard are the École Nationale d'Administration (ENA) for top level positions in economics and politics, the four Écoles Normales Supérieures, the École Polytechnique and the Institut d'Etudes Politiques. They are, however, coming in for increasing criticism for their perceived role of protecting the interests of a privileged few (some three-quarters of top managers in the 200 biggest French companies attended a grande école).

Economy

General information
Measured in terms of gross domestic product, France is the sixth largest economy in the world. The most important industries are the automotive industry (approx. 6 million vehicles per year, fourth largest exporter in the world), the agricultural and foodstuffs industries (largest producer and exporter in the EU), telecommunications, the aeronautics and space industries (second only to the USA), the metal industry (third largest exporter worldwide) and chemicals (fourth largest exporter worldwide), as well as the textiles and clothing industries. Service industries (banking, insurance, tourism etc.) represent the largest and fastest growing sector of the French economy.

Structural change
After the Second World War the economy grew rapidly, changing France's economic structure from that of an agricultural nation into one of the leading industrial countries. State intervention in the economy (the nationalization of major companies, especially in the fields of transport, energy, banking/insurance and automobile production; the five year »planification« plans were designed to aid orientation rather than set rigid targets), a concerted effort to encourage modernization and concentration of companies, and technological advancements are the most evident signs of this development. Since the 1970s the realization of a European economic space has been added to the agenda. The division of labour in structural terms has seen a reduction in the numbers employed in agriculture (1946: 40%, 2004: 3.5%) and a marked increase in the number of people working in service industries, trade, transport and the public sector.

Agriculture and Fishing

General information
Although the low revenues generated represent a mere 2.5% of the gross domestic product, agriculture (together with forestry and fishing) is still of great importance. In addition, the food industry contributes 1.8% of the GDP. 50% of the French mainland is used for

Modern production methods dominate French agriculture

agricultural purposes, 58% of which is arable land, 37% pasture and 5% for fruit and wine growing. France has the most woodland of any EU country, covering 15 million ha/37 million ac (30% of the country's total area). France is also the largest agricultural exporter in the EU and the second largest worldwide behind the USA. In grain production, France lies fifth in the worldwide rankings. Two thirds of agricultural exports, mostly grain, dairy products, fruit, vegetables and wine, remain in the EU. The structural evolution in agriculture – mechanization and automation, improved methods in cultivation, land consolidation – with a sharp increase in productivity, has led to a steady rural exodus and reduction in the number of companies or farms in operation (from 1.5 million in 1970 down to 545,000 by the year 2007, with the number of people employed on farms having fallen by more than 50% during this period).

Products

Geographical location, soil quality and climate determine the rich variety of agricultural produce. In the north, medium-sized farms are principally engaged in production of wheat, grain, oats, corn, potatoes and sugar-beet. On just 15% of the land in use, 40% of France's wheat and oats and 90% of its sugar-beet are cultivated here. Dairy and meat production also makes a sizeable contribution. In the western part of Normandy, Brittany, the Vendée and to the south, as far as the beginning of the Massif Central, fodder is grown and livestock reared. The region's landscape is noted for the so-called Bocage, a network of hedgerows similar to those seen in southern and central

England. Not only do the hedges act as a shield against the wind, they also serve to mark land ownership. The Paris basin is best known for grain and corn cultivation by large enterprises (usually over 200ha/494ac), the open ploughed fields referred to as »campagne«. In Aquitaine and the Mediterranean south, the land is put to different use. Initially reserved for wine, grain and olive trees, in more recent times fruit and vegetables, tobacco and rice have been added to the list of crops. On higher ground, sheep and cattle are reared; the animals are either moved back and forth from winter to summer pasture or grazed on mountain pasture in summer and housed in stalls in winter. As mountain farming declines in the Alps and Pyrenees, so the higher grazing lands become increasingly desolate.

Viniculture France is actually the second largest producer of wine in the world with 53 million hectolitres/1.6 billion gallons placing it behind Italy. In terms of quality, however, it is still seen as the number one, in spite of fierce competition. The chief wine regions are Burgundy, the Bordelais, Rhône and Loire valleys, the Mediterranean, Champagne and Alsace. Languedoc-Roussillon focuses heavily on viniculture.

Fishing France owns fishing rights across wide areas but is only the seventh in Europe and 27th worldwide when it comes to size of catch. Key areas are along the Atlantic coast and towards the Channel. One third of all fishing-boats are registered in Brittany. The most important fishing harbours are (in terms of size of catch) are Concarneau, Cherbourg, Boulogne-sur-Mer, Sète, Lorient, Marennes/Oléron, Les Sables d'Olonne, Caen and La Rochelle. The cultivation of oysters and mussels is growing in importance, accounting for roughly 50% of turnover in the fishing sector.

A typical scene: a nuclear power station in a pastoral idyll (Chinon on the Loire)

Energy and Natural Resources

France's geology means that conventional energy sources are negligible. High expenditure on energy imports and the dependence on foreign countries (as underlined by the oil crisis of 1973, for example) have led to huge investment in nuclear energy. In 2007, proportional energy consumption looked like this: 33% oil, 43% nuclear, 14% natural gas, 4% coal and 6% renewable energy sources. 50% was generated through local power supplies. France can produce approximately 30% more energy than it actually requires.

General

In spite of European subsidies, French coal has lost out to far cheaper coal from other countries (South Africa in particular), the same being true of natural gas and oil. The most productive coal mines were to be found in Lorraine, the last of which – indeed, the last in the country – closed down in 2004. The gas fields developed in Lacq below the Pyrenees in the 1950s are almost exhausted. Oil extraction, its centre in Parentis (département of Landes), covers just 3% of energy requirements. With this in mind, Elf-Aquitaine and the Compagnie Française des Pétroles (CFP) are intensifying their activities in other countries and pressing for off-shore drilling. Imported oil is refined in the harbour regions and conveyed to industrial areas via a vast pipeline network.

Fossil fuels

France has iron ore deposits in Lorraine and Normandy and was once amongst the largest producers of iron ore in the world. High prices and worldwide competition saw production shrink rapidly; the last mine was closed in 1997. Bauxite, the aluminium ore discovered in 1821 at Les Baux in Provence, has little role to play. The fairly common uranium deposits found in the Vendée, Limousin and Forez were an important factor in the creation of France's nuclear economy; mining ceased in 2001. Further natural resources worthy of mention are salt, potash and fluoride, as well as some gold and silver.

Further natural resources

Prior to the 1973 oil crisis, France covered 77% of its energy needs with crude oil from abroad. Thereafter, the French nuclear programme was launched by Electricité de France (EDF) – benefiting from the French reserves of uranium – and enjoying a monopoly in the country's energy economy with 96% of the market. Today, approximately 79% of energy used in France comes from the 58 (!) nuclear power stations. France is second only to the USA in worldwide nuclear energy production and the seventh largest exporter of power. The most important customers are Switzerland, Italy, Great Britain and Spain. In Cadarache in Provence, a nuclear fusion experimental reactor, ITER, is being built, and should go into operation in 2018. There are currently three reprocessing plants in France, the first (UP 1) opened in Marcoule near Avignon in 1958, the second (UP 2) fol-

Nuclear energy

lowed in La Hague (Brittany) in 1966, and its capacity was considerably extended in the following years. To ease the burden on the French electricity economy, heavily in debt, reprocessing capacity is also sold to foreign nuclear industries: 80% of the Western world's spent fuel rods are processed in La Hague. Uneasiness with regard to the nuclear industry is no longer unknown in France; the Superphénix fast breeder was decommissioned in 1998, and in recent years here have been numerous »malfunctions«.

Further energy sources Thermal power stations account for approximately 10% of energy requirements, hydroelectric power for about 14%. Hydroelectric power plants are stationed in the Alps (bringing metal and paper industries with them) and the Pyrenees, as well as at the barrages on major rivers such as the Rhône, Durance, Loire, Dordogne and Garonne.

Industry

General information France is one of the most important industrial nations on earth. In 2008, industry accounted for around 24% of the gross domestic product. Some 24% of the working population is employed in industry.

Development since 1945 Since the Second World War, France has developed into one of the leading industrial nations in the world, the French economy boosted by considerable state intervention, nationalization, intensive economic planning (»planification«) and targeted deployment of public funding. Five year plans (»plans quinquennaux«), prepared by the state policy commission (»Commissariat au plan«), are a special feature of French economic policy. These are of a compulsory nature for state companies, taking the form of directives for private industry which carry considerable weight. The areas of highest growth are in capital goods (engineering, automobile and electrical industries) and durable consumer goods. Favoured by support for mergers, the dominance of small and medium-sized family enterprises – typical of the French economy for so many years – has given way to major companies and huge corporations backed, in some cases, by the state. Figures for 1990 show that enterprises with over 500 employees or more – 2.4 % – generated 56.8% of turnover with 46% of the industrial labour force. Thanks to greater specialization, the 1990s actually saw a trend towards smaller companies again.

Paris as an economic area Around three quarters of industrial enterprises have their headquarters in Paris/Ile de France. 21% of those in employment live here, generating 24% of the gross domestic product. At the outset of the 19th century, there were, by way of example, 65 wallpaper manufacturers, 70 cabinetmakers, 166 watchmakers, 108 perfume factories and 72 manufacturers of artificial flowers. Contemporary Paris is both France's largest producer and consumer, with a particular focus on modern branches of industry such as electronics and electrotechnology, aircraft and vehicle construction and service industries (banking, wholesale, and insurance). Many companies, from clothing, costume jewellery, printing and publishing to leather goods, are concentrated in the capital.

Important sites for mining, chemicals, textiles and engineering can be found in northern France. The industrial zones of Lyon, St-Etienne and Clermont-Ferrand are important centres for the automotive industry, whilst suppliers, especially for car parts, are based in Alsace and Lorraine. Toulouse is the second largest location in the world for the aeronautics and aerospace industries. The food production industry is centred on Brittany, Normandy and the Lyon region.

Further economic areas

An interesting feature of the French economy since 1945 has been the existence of state companies steered by the government, based to a degree on structural politics or anti-capitalist principles. Campaigns for nationalization or privatization were dependent on whoever was in power. The first wave of nationalization from 1945 to 1948 encompassed banks (e.g. Banque de France, Crédit Lyonnais, BNP), insurance, transport (SNCF, Air France), energy (EDF, GDF, amongst others) and industrial enterprises such as Renault and SNECMA (aircraft construction). The second wave in 1981 took in almost all of the remaining banks, further insurance companies and large firms in the iron, steel, armaments and electronics branches

Nationalization and privatization

The Airbus is a European success story. This is the assembly plant in Toulouse.

(Usinor, Bull, Thomson, Dassault). Once Chirac came to power, a large number of these companies were reprivatized after 1986 (over 1100 firms with more than half a million employees), at which point the rationalization and restructuring processes carried out with public money made them an attractive proposition for private investors. The socialists put a partial halt to this initiative in 1988, permitting state-private hybrids. Since 1993, conservative governments have set about privatizing important companies such as Crédit Lyonnais, Air France, Elf-Aquitaine, Aérospatiale, Thomson, Rhône-Poulenc and, most recently, France Telecom. The revenues were, or are, earmarked to deliver the promised tax cuts, to support job creation schemes and to ease the national debt.

When Jacques Chirac became president in 1995, there was a move away from state intervention, with European unification also playing a significant part: the Maastricht Treaty does not allow state intervention, although this has by no means put an end to national protectionism. It has gradually become apparent that none of these approaches offers a definitive solution to the problems of French society – the budget deficit, unemployment, immigration and destabilization.

Transport and Tourism

General information
France, a spacious country with a relatively sparse population for its size, has well-developed road and rail networks. Paris is their focal point, as the course of history has determined. The more densely populated regions, Paris in particular, carry the most traffic, with the north-south axis coming in for heavier treatment during holiday periods. The French share their German neighbours' love of cars; some 2 million new vehicles are registered per annum. In 2006 there were 595 vehicles per 1000 citizens, compared to 468 in the UK, 597 in Germany and 813 in the USA.

Road network
The French road network is one of the finest in the world. Even the country lanes are in good condition. By the end of 2007 it covered a total of approx. 1,080,000km/671,080mi. The ratio of 17km/10.5mi per 1000 inhabitants – compared with just over 6km/3.7mi in the UK – reflects the meagre population in large parts of the country. Driving on the 10,492km/6519mi of motorways is usually subject to a toll.

Railways
The French rail network of the Société Nationale des Chemins de Fer Français (SNCF) is one of the most modern in the world, excelling in comfort and speed. **TGV** The pride of the French railways is the TGV (Train à Grande Vitesse, high speed train), connecting Paris to all parts of the country. Top speeds of up to 186mph/300kmh have had a dramatic impact on the economic landscape of the country. Towns like Amiens, Rouen and Orléans, for example, are now within an

hour's reach of Paris, less time than many Parisians need to get to work themselves within the city. The same is true of the relationship between the capital and the provinces; further benefits for the regions have been realized by new connections bypassing Paris. What is more, the high-speed rail network, with trains such as the Eurostar and the Thalys services, is also linked to London (via the Eurotunnel), Brussels, Amsterdam and various cities in Germany and Switzerland.

Shipping

The French coastline extends for more than 3120km/1938mi with many important ports. Military harbours are located at Cherbourg, Brest, Lorient and Toulon, whilst Calais, Toulon and Marseille are busy ferry terminals. Fishing ports include Boulogne, Lorient, Concarneau and La Rochelle.
The French merchant navy consisted of 212 units in 2007 with gross tonnage of 4.7 million (28th in the world). 340 million tons in goods were conveyed in 2007. The largest seaport is Marseille (95.5 million tons of cargo; the fourth largest in Europe and the most important harbour for crude oil on the Mediterranean), followed by Le Havre, Dunkirk (Dunkerque), Nantes-St-Nazaire, Rouen, Calais and Bordeaux.

Inland navigation

The 18th century saw a boom in canal construction in France. A unique network of waterways was developed, the longest in western Europe and still longer than the French motorways of today. Of the approx. 13,200km/8202mi navigable waterways, 6500km/4038mi are still in use, namely 2600km/1615mi of rivers and 3900km/2423mi canals. The most important are the Seine below Paris, the Rhône below Lyon and the Alsatian stretch of the Rhine-Rhône canal. The most important inland harbour is Paris, then Strasbourg and Rouen.

Air travel

French air travel is dominated by Air France, which merged with the Dutch airline KLM (the largest airline in Europe with over 600 aircraft). The aircraft registered in France carry about 160 million passengers and 4.8 million TKT of freight every year. The key international airports are Paris (Charles de Gaulle, Orly), Lyon (St-Exupéry), Marseille (Marignane) and Nice (Côte d'Azur).

Tourism

France as a holiday destination welcomes more visitors than any other country and the numbers are still on the rise: 60 million foreign holidaymakers came in 1992, 70 million in 1998, 76 million in 2002 and 79 million in 2006. The greatest number of visitors come from the UK and Ireland (17.5%), followed by Germany (16.5%); some 22% come from the Benelux countries, and 4% of visitors come from the USA. Tourism is the most important service branch of the French economy, generating more foreign currency than any other sector, including agriculture and the automotive industry. It also secures around one million jobs.

History

France almost became English once – but then Joan of Arc appeared on the scene. Described here are stages in the origins of France, from Stone Age cave paintings via the Romans to Charlemagne, from Hugo Capet via Louis XIV to the Revolution, from Napoleon to Jacques Chirac.

Prehistory and antiquity

30,000 BC	Cave paintings in the south of France
5000 BC	Megalithic culture
800 BC	Immigration of the Celts
600 BC	Founding of Marseille by the Greeks
58–51 BC	Caesar conquers Gaul

Man inhabited the hexagon as early as prehistoric times. Remains of the Terra Amata settlement (now a part of Nice) are 400,000 years old. There are many well-preserved relics from the Stone Age, including Neanderthal and homo sapiens skeletons from the Neolithic period and the world-famous paintings discovered in the caves of southern France (►Baedeker Special p.662). No less renowned is the megalithic culture of Brittany; towards the end of the New Stone Age and the beginning of the Bronze Age, monumental stone structures were erected, their meaning still uncertain today (►Baedeker Special p.306).

Prehistory

From around 1500 BC the Celts moved in from the east. Around 300 BC, the Parisii settled on an island of the Seine, which subsequently became Paris. To the south, the Iberians remained independent north of the Pyrenees, with the Ligurians on the Mediterranean coast.

Celtic colonization

Around 600 BC, Phocaens, namely Greeks from Asia Minor, founded the colony of Massilia (Marseille). Trading posts were established close by, including Nikaia Polis (Nice) around 350 BC.

Greek colony

To secure the stretch of land between Italy and Spain, the Romans founded the province of Gallia in 121 BC, the southern section of the hexagon between Lake Geneva and Toulouse; the main settlement was Narbo (Narbonne, founded in the year 118 AD). Not long afterwards, the Germanic Cimbri and Teutons penetrated Provence (109 BC); the Roman commander Marius defeated the Teutons in 102 BC at Aquae Sextiae (Aix-en-Provence). Victories over the Suebi Prince Ariovistus (58 and 52 BC) and the Gauls under Vercingetorix at Alesia (52 BC) sealed Caesar's conquest of Gaul. In the »Gallo-Roman« era, the local inhabitants adopted the culture and language of the victors, which would later become Old French. Towns and a network of fortified roads were developed; stone buildings took the place of wooden huts. The economy and culture flourished into the 3rd century AD. Significant buildings have survived in Nîmes, Or-

Roman colonization

← *On 20 May 1800 Napoleon Bonaparte crosses the Great Saint Bernard Pass. This heroic portrayal is the work of J.L. David.*

Vercingetorix, the hero of Alesia, was declared the first resistance fighter in the 19th century

ange and Arles. As early as the beginning of the 2nd century AD, the **Christianization** of Gaul was set in motion. Around 300 AD new fortifications were added to the towns; Roman emperors resided in Lutetia (Paris) from time to time.

Around 250 BC Gaul felt the effects of **migration**. Wave after wave of Alemanni, Franks, Vandals, Burgundians and Goths swarmed into the land. From AD 418 to 507 the Visigoth kingdom took root in southern Gaul, with Tolosa (Toulouse) as its capital; the Franks then forced them out to Spain. Defeated by the Huns in Rhineland, in AD 443 the Burgundians founded a kingdom in the Rhône region (Burgundy) under the protection of the Romans. Celts driven out of Brittania moved into Gaul in 449 and settled in Brittany (Bretagne), giving the region its name. The Huns, under Attila, were defeated at the Battle of Chalons (Catalaunian Fields) in 451 by the Roman General Aetius and retreated to Hungary.

The Merovingian and Carolingian Dynasty

482–751	Merovingian rule
751–887	Carolingian rule

France comes into being

The founding of the Frankish dynasty formed the basis of the political, social and cultural development of the territories which would later become France and Germany. From around 250, the Franks – a band of Germanic tribes who had settled in the Lower Rhine region – repeatedly pressed into Gaul as far as the Seine and Loire. The Merovingian king Clovis (on the throne 482–511), grandson of King Merovech (hence the name »Merovingian«), unified the Franks, conquered Gaul and thus founded the Frankish Empire. In 496 the Franks defeated the Alemanni, accepted Christianity and received the support of the church.

Following the death of Clovis in 511, the kingdom was divided into three parts: the Germanic Austrasia with Reims (later Metz) as its capital, the Romanic Neustria with Paris, and Burgundy with Or- léans. Internal and external conflicts undermined the power of the Merovingian kings, their duties progressively usurped by so-called »Mayors of the Palace« from the aristocracy.

Merovingian kingdom

Pippin the Middle, the Mayor of the Palace of Austrasia, reigned as majordomo over the entire Frankish kingdom from 687. In the Bat- tle of Tours and Poitiers in 732, his son Martel (»the Hammer«) de- feated the Arabs who had invaded from Spain. Pepin, or Pippin the Short, pronounced himself king in 751 in front of an assembly in Soissons – the commencement of the highly significant connection of secular and papal power, and furthermore the stylization as »King by the Grace of God« – anointed by the papal legate, St Boniface (»Apostle of the Germans«) following Pope Zachary's consent to the deposition of the last Merovingian king. In return, Pope Stephen II asked for Pippin's aid in 754 against the Lombards. The Carolingians were rewarded with the title »Patricius Romanorum« (Patrician of the Romans).

Rise of the Carolingians

Charlemagne, king from 768–814, expanded the Carolingian king- dom (named after him) by force of arms, entering northern Italy and the regions of the West Germanic tribes (Saxony, Bavaria). The kingdom was subdivided into shires, secured by borderlands on the perimeter. Imperial palaces and monasteries became economic and cultural centres; the cultural continuation of ancient tradition be- came known as the »Carolingian Renaissance«. Charlemagne's coro- nation as emperor by the pope in Rome in the year 800 confirmed his power.

Charlemagne

From the Treaty of Verdun to absolutism

843	Treaty of Verdun: Division of the Frankish kingdom
987	Hugues Capet first »French« king
from 1209	»Crusade« against the Cathari in southern France Annexation of Languedoc by the Crown
1339–1453	Hundred Years' War against England 1429–31 Role of Joan of Arc
1562–98	Religious conflicts between Catholics and Huguenots

The authority of the French kings, supported by the church and the municipalities, gradually established itself. On the one hand, the kingship imposed its will as hereditary monarchy on countless inde- pendent principalities, on the other, English expansion was halted and the perpetrators banished.

Division of the empire
In the Treaty of Verdun, 843, the Frankish kingdom is divided: Charles II (Charles the Bald) received the western, Romanic portion, its eastern border largely marking the frontier between France and Germany into the late Middle Ages. The last Carolingian king, simultaneously ruler of the entire kingdom, was, until 887, Charles III (Charles the Fat).

Normans
From the 7th century the Normans' raids extended into western France; in 845 Paris was plundered. They gradually began to settle and, in 911, Charles the Fat granted them the duchy of Normandy. In 1066 William of Normandy emerged victorious in the Battle of Hastings, conquering England in the process.

The way to the Capetians
The lack of a strong central power favoured the development of strong principalities: Francia (at the heart of the later kingdom), Champagne, Aquitaine, Gascony, Toulouse, Gothia, Catalonia, Brittany, Normandy and Flanders. The king was chosen from amongst the lords' own ranks. In 987 Hugues Capet (»cappa« as in »cloak«) became the first »French« king. His power base consisted of the duchy of Francia, the Paris and Orléans region. Directly descended Capetians ruled until 1328, and their line continued indirectly (with the exception of 1792–1814) until as late as 1848. Royal power was less great than that of the regional princes, but won the church as an ally; the Capetians also succeeded – initially by designating a son as co-king – in re-establishing the hereditary principle of the Crown. The incipient literature of the 11th century shows differences between the Frankish character of the north (langue d'oil) and the Celtic-Romanesque oriented south (langue d'oc).

The Bayeux Tapestry relates the conquering of England by the Norman Duke William

Crusades and monasteries
The main impetus behind the crusades originated in France. French princes and lords were the leaders, paving the way for the spiritual remit of the monks and clerical orders. In 1095, Pope Urban II, who came from France, summoned the First Crusade in Clermont (1096–99). Ideas for monastery and church reform emanated from Cluny abbey (founded in 910) in Burgundy. The Carthusian Order was founded by St Bruno of Cologne in 1084 at Grenoble (Grande Chartreuse). The Order of Cistercians from Cîteaux abbey (1098) furthered technological advancement and architecture, as well as the Christianization and colonization of the German east. St Bernard of Clairvaux, a French abbot of the Cistercian order, was one of the

most important scholars of his time, as well as the catalyst for the Second Crusade. The expeditions to and conquests in the Orient invited contact with the highly sophisticated culture of Islam, facilitating the political, economic and cultural rise of France in the 12th century; the French nobility became the paragon of European chivalry. The Seventh (and final) Crusade ended in 1270 with the death of King Louis IX at Tunis. Around the same time, Gothic architecture and French chivalric poetry come to the fore, their influence felt throughout Europe.

First Anglo-French conflict

In 1137, Eleanor, heiress of Aquitaine, married King Louis VII (1137–80), and after their divorce she wed Henry Plantagenet, Count of Anjou and Duke of Normandy in 1152, who became King of England two years later in 1154. Together with Aquitaine, more than half of the hexagon was English. From around 1160, Henry and Louis en-

Eleanor of Aquitaine was one of the most important female figures of the Middle Ages (tomb in Fontevreaud)

gaged in open conflict. After 1202, Philippe II (1180–1223) won back all of the English king's properties in France with the exception of Guyenne (Poitou, Gascony, Agenais). Philippe's glorious victory over the English and their German ally, Otto IV, at Bouvines in 1214 considerably strengthened the king's position, both at home and abroad, and »Augustus« was added to his name.

Cathar Crusades

The conquest of Béziers and the slaughter of its inhabitants in 1209 marked the beginning of the terrible war with the Albigensiens (Cathars). As the king was engaged in the war with England, the nobleman Simon de Montfort led the battle. In 1226, Louis VIII (1223–26) then conquered Languedoc, Toulouse excepted.

La Sorbonne

The University of Paris was founded in 1215, and in 1253 the theological college La Sorbonne followed, subsequently developing into the acclaimed theological faculty and later lending its name to the university.

Consolidation of royal power

The accession of Louis VIII cemented hereditary monarchy; coronations took place (from 988) in Reims. Under Louis IX, or St Louis (1226–70), France experienced its most glorious period of the Middle Ages (»siècle de St-Louis«). In 1248, Languedoc fell irrevocably into royal hands, and Provençal culture was suppressed as a consequence. The Peace of Paris, 1258 saw the English King Henry III lose all mainland possessions north of the Charente and pledge an oath of fealty for Guyenne. In Paris, a supreme high court was established, the »Parlement«, whose judgements had authority across the whole country. Philippe IV, or Philip the Fair (1285–1314), acquired the Duchy of Champagne and the archbishopric of Lyon. In 1328, the throne was passed to the House of Valois, a cadet branch of the Capetian dynasty (until 1498).

Popes in Avignon With the king winning out in power struggles with the papacy, popes were relocated to Avignon from 1309 to 1377 (the »Babylonian Captivity«).

Hundred Years' War The Hundred Years' War between France and England began with the confiscation of Guyenne in 1337 by Philippe VI and lasted until 1453. Costly campaigns, devastating defeats at the hands of the English, who were far less in number, plague (1347–49), and disputes between the nobility and the bourgeoisie, as well as peasant revolts, all served to destabilize royal authority. The English King Edward III, as grandson of Philip the Fair, had already staked a claim to the French throne in 1328. The first disastrous defeat for the French took place at Crécy in 1346. Edward's son, the »Black Prince«, defeated John the Good at Maupertuis, to the southeast of Poitiers, in 1356. The Treaty of Brétigny in 1360 granted Edward III sovereignty over the southwest of France (plus Calais, which remained English until 1559), as he renounced his claim to the French throne in return. Charles the Wise renewed hostilities against the English in 1369, forcing them back to a handful of strategic positions. In 1415, Henry V of England landed at Harfleur and defeated the French noble army at Agincourt. Supported by Burgundy, the English occupied all of northern France until 1420, Paris included (Henry VI was crowned French king in Notre-Dame in 1430!). The hexagon was a hair's breadth from becoming English, when Joan of Arc appeared on the scene: a vision of God spurred her on as she succeeded in raising the morale of the French troops to break through the English defences at Orléans. She then led Charles VII to Reims for his coronation. Attempting to take Paris, she was captured by the Burgundians who handed her over to the English. Tried and tortured under the jurisdiction of the Bishop of Beauvais, she died at the stake on 30 May 1431 in Rouen. The king made no attempt to intervene. In 1920, »La Pucelle« was canonized. The »taille royale«, a new form of taxation, was introduced in 1439, enabling the formation of a standing army. By 1453, the English had lost all of their mainland territory apart from Calais.

The kingdom expands Philippe VI purchased the Dauphiné in 1349, tenure of which was subsequently given to heirs to the throne; from then on they named themselves »Dauphin«. John II handed over the Duchy of Burgundy to his son, Philip the Bold, in 1363, and the duchy developed into a formidable power over the next few decades. The »Pragmatic Sanction« of 1438 sealed the autonomy of the French church with respect to the papacy; the »Gallican church« came into being. Following the death of the Burgundian Duke Charles the Bold in 1477, Burgundy and Picardy were seized by the Crown, whilst the Duke's remaining possessions (the Netherlands, Flanders, Franche-Comté) fell to Maximilian I of Habsburg. This marked the beginning of the Franco-Habsburg conflict, a series of wars with heavy losses up until 1559. Further acquisitions are Anjou (1480), Provence (1481) and Brittany (1491).

Charles VIII (1483–98) lay an Angevin hereditary claim to the Kingdom of Naples. In 1494 the campaign against Italian city-states was launched, who joined forces with the House of Habsburg, Aragon and the pope in a Holy League (League of Venice); Charles was forced to retreat from Naples as early as 1495. Louis XII conquered the Duchy of Milan in 1500 but was defeated at Novara in 1513. In 1515, François I captured Milan through his victory over the Swiss at Marignano. Setting his sights higher in 1519, François I aimed to become Holy Roman Emperor (succeeding Maximilian I), but without success, in spite of papal support. François fought four wars against the superior Spanish Habsburg might of Emperor Charles V (1521–44); the net result was the loss of Milan and the withdrawal of French politics from Italy. In the course of the Italian campaigns, the ideas of the Renaissance crossed into France, and with extensive cultural impact, from cuisine to philosophy and from art to technology. François I ordered the construction of magnificent castles, whose interiors were no less splendid (Fontainebleau, Louvre in Paris, Chantilly); Leonardo da Vinci was summoned to Amboise. Henri II (1547–59), married to Catherine de Medici since 1533, renewed the war effort against the Spanish Habsburgs. Coming to the aid of German princes against Emperor Charles V, he earned the bishoprics of Metz, Toul and Verdun. In the Peace of Cateau-Cambrésis, 1559, he relinquished Flanders-Artois, Franche-Comté and his Italian claims, but managed to take Calais back from the English.

At war with the Habsburgs

The Reformation, in the form of Calvinism, impacted on a broad tranche of the affluent bourgeoisie and parts of the nobility. Between 1562 and 1598 (Edict of Nantes), eight military campaigns threw the country into chaos and, combined with famine and plague, saw a million lives lost. The religious conflict was only one factor, with the vested interests of sections of the nobility, territorial princes, the Crown and the rising bourgeoisie all at loggerheads, a situation exacerbated by foreign influence. The Catholics were led by the Guise brothers (two Dukes and a Cardinal), the Protestants by the Bourbons. At the wedding of Henri of Navarre (later Henri IV) to Mar-

Wars of Religion

garete de Valois on 24 August 1572, Margarete's mother, Catherine de Medici, had over 3000 Huguenots murdered, along with their leader, Admiral de Coligny, (»The St Bartholomew's Day Massacre«). With Henri IV (1589–1610), the Bourbons were installed on the throne (until 1792). To pacify the land, Henri IV converted to Catholicism in 1593 (»Paris is well worth a Mass«). He restored the balance of power in royal favour: the nobility were no longer permitted to maintain their own troops, administration was centralized to a large degree, finances were brought into order, and the economy recovered. In the Edict of Nantes, 1598, he accorded the Huguenots wide-ranging religious freedom and equal citizenship; some 1.2 million Protestants, almost 10% of the French population, lived in approx. 150 »safe places«.

Canada   The first French colony was founded in Canada as of 1603, Jacques Cartier having claimed the country for France in 1534.

From Absolutism to Revolution

1643–1715	»The Sun King« Louis XIV; France becomes a major power. In 1682 the court moves to Versailles.
1685	Revocation of the Edict of Nantes
1789	Abbé Sieyès, *Qu'est-ce que le Tiers État?*

The era of absolutism represents the pinnacle of royal state power, although at the same time the estates system was swept away by financial and social change. The principles of the Enlightenment, which the French Revolution sought to instil, did not yet lead to a fixed state system in France, but they did point the way for the Europe of the 19th century.

Richelieu   Cardinal Richelieu (1585–1642) assumed control of the state in 1624 under the weak Louis XIII (1610–43). Absolute power for the monarchy (over the Protestants and nobility) and France's hegemony in Europe, especially against Spain Habsburg, were the goals he ruthlessly pursued. Following the conquest of La Rochelle in 1628, he removed the Huguenots' special political status but not their religious freedom. He suppressed the opposition of the high nobility and established a commissariat for stricter provincial administration. On his initiative, the »Académie Française« for the furtherment of art and science was founded in 1635. In the same year, France officially entered the Thirty Years' War; until then it had supported the reformed (!) Swedes.

1643–60   With Louis XIV (*1638) still a minor, his mother Anne and Cardinal Mazarin took control of state affairs on his behalf. In 1648, the Fronde (parliament and people of Paris, joined by the higher nobil-

Courtly splendour: Louis XIV stages a Grand Carrousel in the Tuileries in 1661, an equestrian event with 15,000 participants

ity) rose up against royal power, i.e. the centralization of administration and tax policy (suppressed in 1653). There was a double victory over the House of Habsburg: the Treaty of Westphalia in 1648 transferred Habsburg possessions in Alsace to the French; the Peace of the Pyrenees, 1659, ended the war with Spain, the latter's power broken. Substantial land gains in the south (Roussillon etc.) and the northeast saw France attain the status of a major European power. In 1660, Louis XIV married the Spanish infanta Maria Theresa.

After the death of Mazarin in 1661, Louis XIV, the »Sun King« ruled alone. Under his reign, absolutism reached the height of its power. The Court in Versailles became the model of aristocratic society in Europe. Baroque art and architecture, classical literature (Corneille, Racine, Molière, La Fontaine), philosophy (Descartes, Pascal) and painting (Poussin, Watteau) flourished. Financial and economic policy (mercantilism) under Colbert and the reorganization of the armed forces under Louvois created the necessary conditions for military conquests, commonly under the banner of tenuous hereditary claims.

Reign of the Sun King

In 1664, the French West India Company was founded; in 1682 Louisiana was taken into French hands. 1667–68 saw the »War of Devolution« against the Spanish Low Countries. From 1672 to 1678 there was war against Holland; in the Treaty of Nijmegen France received the Free County of Burgundy and border regions in Flanders. Annexation (»reunion«) by force of parts of Alsace took place from 1679; in 1681 Strasbourg was occupied. The revocation of Edict of

Nantes in 1685 caused half a million Huguenots to take flight. Jansenists were persecuted. The Pfalz was devastated by the Pfalz War of Succession (1688–97). In the Treaty of Ryswick, France gave up its claims to the right banks of the Rhine, the Pfalz and Lorraine. The War of the Spanish Succession, in 1701–14, saw Louis suffer heavy defeats at the hands of the Grand Alliance (the emperor and princes of the empire, Spain, Sweden, England, Holland, Savoy). In the Treaty of Utrecht (1713–14), Philippe V, grandson of Louis XIV, was recognized as King of Spain; the two nations, however, would never be allowed to unite, whilst France also lost large portions of its colonies to England. When Louis XIV died in 1715, constant wars and a profligate lifestyle at court had brought financial ruin (huge state debt and impoverishment of the peasantry).

The road to revolution The flaws of an absolutist system unable to address the pressing issues of the day accelerated the fall of the Ancien Régime. Royal authority diminished under the incapable Louis XV, with miscalculations in foreign policy and further profligacy, in catastrophic financial circumstances, provoking fundamental criticism. The feudal order of things (e.g. tax exemption for the nobility and clergy) was the prime cause of social unrest amongst the classes. A wealthy bourgeoisie, demanding a greater say in political matters to match its economic relevance (Abbé Sieyès, *Qu'est-ce que le Tiers État? – What is the Third Estate?*), led the fight against king, nobility and church. Economic crises, mass unemployment and chronic food shortages due to bad harvests led to the impoverishment of the petit bourgeois and peasant population. Criticism of the Ancien Régime was also intensified by the ideas of the Enlightenment (the Encyclopaedists; Voltaire, Montesquieu, Rousseau et al.) and the Wars of Independence in North America.

Under Louis XV, (* 1710, king 1723–74) the Scot John Law attempted to alleviate the financial situation through currency speculation; the collapse of the banking and monetary systems in 1720 halved the state debt and fuelled inflation. In lengthy periods of peace, trade and commerce recovered, whilst the working population, particularly those in the country, suffered the effects of inflation. Support in the War of the Polish Succession in 1733–38 saw France earn entitlement to Lorraine, which became French on the death in 1766 of Stanisław Leszczyński, the deposed Polish king and last Duke of Lorraine. Between 1745 and 1774, Louis XV's mistresses had a marked influence on his politics. In the Franco-British colonial war of 1754–63 and the Seven Years' War from 1756 to 1763, France lost its colonies in North America as well as almost all of its strategic bases in South and East Asia.

The financial problems escalated under Louis XVI (1774–89). His economic ministers' attempts at reform failed in the face of massive resistance from the privileged classes, the nobility and the clergy. The actual chaos of state finances only then became fully apparent, however. In August 1788, with a view to introducing measures to remove the deficit, Louis XVI convoked the Estates-General for May 1789; on 16 August the state was declared bankrupt.

The French Revolution

14.7.1789	Storming of the Bastille
3.9.1789	Constitutional monarchy
10.8.1792	Arrest of the royal family
21.1.1793	Louis XVI beheaded
6.4.1793	Committee of Public Safety: Reign of Terror
23.9.1795	The Directory

The Estates-General met on 5 May 1789 in Versailles. The Third Estate (bourgeoisie) declared itself the National Assembly on 17 June and on 20 June in a handball court near the Palace of Versailles they took the so-called Oath of the Tennis Court, pledging not to disband before the king accepted a constitution. Scarcity of food, the dismissal of the popular finance minister and rumours concerning the dissolution of the National Assembly led to the Storming of the Bastille on 14 July (dismantled in the ensuing months). Members of the nobility, including Louis XVI's brothers (later Louis XVIII and Charles X), emigrated. In the »Grande Peur« (»Great Fear«) of July and Au-

Creation of the constitutional monarchy

The storming of the Bastille (lithograph from around 1840)

gust, peasants plundered their lords' manor houses, destroying documents listing their taxes and duties. The National Assembly abolished feudal privileges on 4–5 August, including ecclesiastical tithes, and, on 26 August, adopted the Declaration of the Rights of Man and the Citizen. On 5 October, the people of Paris forced Louis XVI to relocate to the Tuileries in Paris, and the National Assembly followed. Political clubs were founded: radical Jacobins (Robespierre, Saint-Just), radical Cordeliers (Danton, Desmoulins, Marat), and moderate Feuillants (Bailly, Lafayette), to name just a few. The property of the church was taken over on 2 November. Moderate »Girondistes« held a majority in the Legislative Assembly. Louis XVI's attempted escape in 1791 (discovered on 20 June in Varennes) and the massacre of a gathering at Champs de Mar by Lafayette led to further radicalization. The constitution of 3 September proclaimed the constitutional monarchy. The declaration of war on Austria in April 1792 heralded the French Revolutionary Wars.

Reign of the Convention and »La Terreur« Mindful of the threat of the armies of the European monarchs, the populace stormed the Tuileries; on 10 August 1792 the royal family was taken captive and the monarchy overthrown. Danton and Marat took justice into their own hands, executing approx. 1200 prisoners (September Massacres). The First Republic was declared by the Convention on 22 September 1792 with a radical majority (Robespierre, Danton et al.). The Prussian army retreated following the Cannonade of Valmy (20 September); the revolutionary army conquered Belgium and occupied the left bank of the Rhine. The trial of »Citizen Capet« (Louis XVI) began on 11 December; his execution was carried out by guillotine on 21 January 1793. Royalist uprisings in the Vendée, Brittany and major towns were crushed in 1793 with hundreds of thousands of casualties. Radicalization escalated: Girondistes were executed, and on 6 April 1793 the »Committee of Public Safety« was created under Robespierre. In the Reign of Terror (»La Terreur«) the Revolutionary Tribunal had thousands of suspects executed, Queen Marie-Antoinette among their number. In the provinces, violent punishments were meted out by the agents of the Convention (such as Nantes, Lyon). Price ceilings for basic foodstuffs were introduced, and Christianity was replaced by the Cult of Reason. After military defeats, Carnot established a militia army (conscription from 23 August, »levée en masse«). The fall and execution of Robespierre in July 1794 ended the Reign of Terror. Moderate Republicans regained the upper hand in the Convention.

Directory In September 1795 the Directorial Constitution was announced and the Convention dissolved. A census franchise secured the power of the rich bourgeoisie. The Directory (5 members) is too weak to resolve the economic and financial crisis (state bankruptcy in September 1797); resistance from the right (Royalists) and the left (Sans-culottes, Babeuf) was crushed by Carnot.

The Rise and Fall of Napoléon Bonaparte

1796	Bonaparte General of the Army of Italy
1799	Coup d'état, First Consul
1804	Emperor Napoleon I
1814	Abdication, exile to Elba
1815	»Hundred Days«, exile to St Helena

Hailing from Corsica, General Napoléon Bonaparte, commander of the Italian army since March 1796, defeated the Austrians and conquered Lombardy (Peace of Campo Formio, October 1797). The Cisalpine Republic (Milan) and Ligurian Republic (Genoa) were instituted, and in 1798 Switzerland was declared the Helvetian Republic, the Papal States the Roman Republic and Naples the Parthenopeic Republic. The »Egyptian Expedition«, against England saw Bonaparte defeat the Mamelukes at the Pyramids; the French fleet was, however, dealt a crushing blow by the British under Admiral Nelson at Abukir in 1798.

First Coalition against France

Following an adventure-ridden flight from Egypt, Bonaparte dissolved the Directory in a coup d'état in 1799 – »the revolution is over« – and was installed by plebiscite as First Consul for ten years. He centralized administration, sanctioned the return of emigrants and bound the Catholic Church to the state through the Concordat of 1801.

Coup d'état

After defeats on the Upper Rhine and in Northern Italy in 1799, France was victorious in battle at Marengo and Hohenlinden in 1800. In the Peace of Lunéville in 1801 between France and Austria, the left bank of the Rhine remained French, and France's junior republics in Italy were acknowledged. In the Treaty of Amiens between France and Great Britain in 1802, the British surrendered the majority of their overseas conquests (with the exception of Ceylon and Trinidad), while the French moved out of Egypt. A referendum extended Bonaparte's consulate for life. On 2 December 1804, he was crowned Emperor Napoleon I in the presence of the Pope. Law was unified in the Code Civil (Code Napoléon). In 1805, Napoleon crowned himself King of Italy in Milan.

Second Coalition against France

Emperorship

When the British Admiral Nelson destroyed the French fleet at Trafalgar in 1805, he confirmed British superiority on the seas and rendered Napoleon's plans to invade the British Isles redundant. Partly motivated through conflicts of interest across the European map, but primarily driven by his boundless hunger for power, Napoleon led aggressive campaigns against virtually all of Europe until 1815. On the back of spectacular successes, he created dependent states, generally under the rule of his brothers, brothers-in-law or generals. In

Conquest of mainland Europe

spite of the introduction of modern administration, he was unable to establish a durable political system; on top of this, the cost of his wars crippled finances. National uprisings developed into the wars of liberation which ultimately see him forced out.

December 1805 saw Napoleon's first major victory over Russians and Austrians at Austerlitz. Under his protectorate, the Confederation of the Rhine was established in 1806. Napoleon's answer to a Prussian ultimatum was to defeat the issuer in the double battles of Jena and Auerstedt in 1806. From Berlin he decreed the continental barrier against Great Britain. In 1807, he achieved victory over the Russians at Friedland. The Kingdom of Westphalia (under his brother Jérôme) and the Grand Duchy of Warsaw were founded. From 1808 resistance occurred in Spain; Napoleon imposed harsh peace terms on Austria in the Treaty of Schönbrunn in 1809, and there is civil Tyrolese rebellion under Andreas Hofer against the French and Bavarians. In 1810, Napoleon (having divorced his childless marriage to Joséphine de Beauharnais) wed Marie Louise, daughter of the Austrian Emperor. The Russian campaign of 1812 brought a reversal of fortunes: defeat after the Fire of Moscow in the early onset of winter, with terrible losses.

Wars of liberation against Napoleon's foreign rule culminated in defeat at the Battle of the Nations at Leipzig in 1813. In 1814, the Allies marched on Paris. Napoleon abdicated on 6 April 1814; he received Elba as a principality. With Louis XVIII the Bourbons returned to the royal throne. The Congress of Vienna (September 1814–June 1815) saw the European powers attempt to redraw the map of Europe as it had looked before the Revolution; they determined the new territorial picture, rejecting calls for independence. The first Treaty of Paris limited France to its borders of 1792.

Hundred Days Napoleon returned to France in 1815 (»the Hundred Days«). He lost the Battle of Waterloo against the British and Prussians and was exiled to the British island of St Helena in the South Atlantic, where he died in 1821. In the second Treaty of Paris (November 1815), France's borders were reduced to those of 1790.

From the Restoration to the First World War

1814–48	Restoration of the monarchy. Following the July Revolution of 1830, reign of the »Citizen King« Louis-Philippe
1848–70	February Revolution 1848 Louis Napoleon President of the Second Republic 1851 coup d'état. Second Empire under Napoleon III until 1870
1870–71	Franco-Prussian War
1870–1914	Proclamation of the Third Republic (until 1940) Paris World's Fair 1889: Eiffel Tower 1894–1906 the Dreyfus affair

In the 19th century, the history of France was dominated by the effects of revolution and sweeping advancements in technology and industry. The revolutions of 1830 and 1848 created movements which changed the political relations of most European countries. After 1850, the French state pursued similar imperialistic and colonial policies to the other major powers.

Restoration

The Restoration period up until 1830 was characterized by the conflict between the adherents of the Ancien Régime, the defenders of revolutionary gains and the increasingly radical lower and working classes. Louis XVIII (1814–24) decreed the Charte Constitutionelle (constitution) in 1814, which sought an equable solution without dispensing with the privileges of the nobility and landed classes. Persecution of the Jacobins and Bonapartistes occurred in the »terreur blanche« (1815). Charles X continued the increasingly reactionary line; in 1825 he offered compensation to the emigrants. The revocation of freedom of the press, dissolution of the Chamber of Deputies and restrictions of suffrage led to the July Revolution of 1830 and the abdication of Charles, and the liberal, grand bourgeois Duke **July Monarchy** Louis-Philippe of Orléans was elected king (the »Citizen King«). As poverty worsened among the proletariat, socialist ideas came to the fore (Fourier, Proudhon, Blanc, Blanqui); between 1843 and 1848 Karl Marx lived in Paris. The conquest of Algeria from 1830 to 1847 was not enough to deflect attention from problems at home. Added to dissatisfaction over disenfranchisement, conditions were set for the February Revolution of 1848 in Paris: Louis-Philippe went into exile and France became a republic (Second Republic). The first general election for the National Assembly took place. The closure of the National Workshops sparked a workers' revolt in Paris, which was bloodily curtailed in June. Prince Louis Napoléon, Napoléon Bonaparte's nephew, was elected President of the Republic. **Second Republic**

Louis Napoléon's coup d'état took place in December 1851. Initially **Second Empire** installed as president for 10 years, he had his status ratified as Emperor Napoleon III a year later by referendum (»plebiscite Caesarianism«). Backed by the army and the Catholic Church, he promoted industrial development and social policies (heavy industry, construction of the railways, urban building programmes, redesign of Paris under Haussmann) and support for the national unification movements in Italy, Germany and in the Balkans.

French foreign policy aspired to that of a major power, with mixed results. In the Crimean War of 1854–56 against Russia, France gained prestige as a leading power. The war with Sardinia-Piedmont against Austria in 1859 brought little: in spite of victories in Magenta and Solferino, France took Nice and Savoy (1860), Piedmont took Lombardy. From 1859 to 1867, colonial additions were made to the Southeast Asian territories, and between 1859 and 1869 the Suez Canal was constructed by F. de Lesseps with French support. The

»Mexican Expedition« of 1861–67 ended in disaster; Emperor Maximilian (the brother of Emperor Franz Joseph I), installed by Napoleon III in 1864, succumbed to resistance led by Juarez and the USA's ultimatum, and was executed in 1867.

Franco-Prussian War The dispute over a Hohenzollern candidacy for the vacant Spanish throne led to the Franco-Prussian War of 1870–71. When Napoleon III was captured by the Germans in the Battle of Sedan on 1 September 1870, the Third Republic was proclaimed in Paris. Besieged and starved, Paris surrendered on 28 January 1871; the German Empire had already been proclaimed in Versailles on 18 January. The uprising of the Paris Commune was halted by MacMahon under the gaze of the German occupiers; some 30,000 inhabitants lost their lives. France lost Alsace-Lorraine to the German Empire in the Treaty of Frankfurt.

Third Republic The Third Republic (1870–1940) was marked by economic consolidation (»belle époque«), the creation of labour organizations, the continuation of colonial policy, a growth in nationalism (retribution for 1871) and a difficult policy of alliances to safeguard foreign interests. World fairs took place in Paris and the Eiffel Tower was erected in 1889 for the centennial celebration of the Revolution.

The Jewish Officer Dreyfus was accused of spying for Germany in 1896 and condemned on the basis of forged documents. He was not rehabilitated until 1906. The »Dreyfus affair«, however, strengthened the »Bloc républicain« against the nationalist-clerical-conservative opposition, forcing through legislation to divide state and church in 1905. Blériot became the first man to fly across the English Channel in 1909.

Foreign policy The colonies were expanded: Central Africa (1879–94), Tunisia (1881), Indochina (from 1887) and Madagascar (1896). As a consequence of the Fashoda Incident with Great Britain in 1898–99, France had to give up on further expansion into North Africa as far as the upper Nile; the »entente cordiale« of 1904 recognized British rule in Egypt and that of France in Morocco. First Morocco Crisis occurred in 1905–06, when the German Empire protested at the French incursion into Morocco. In 1907, the entente was extended into a British-Russian-French triple entente. In 1911 came the second Morocco Crisis; with Cameroon as compensation, the Germans acknowledge the French protectorate over Morocco.

Labour organizations In 1879, the French Workers' Party was founded under Marxist leadership, 1889 saw the founding of the Second International labour association – 1 May is declared as an international holiday for workers – and in 1895 the General Confederation of Labour (CGT) was formed. The socialists united in 1905 under the banner of SFIO (Parti Socialiste, Section Française de l'Internationale Ouvrière).

First World War and between the Wars

1914–18	First World War
1919	Treaty of Versailles
1925	Treaty of Locarno
1930	France cedes the Rhineland
1938	Munich Agreement

France was a principle theatre in both the First and Second World Wars. In the wake of the Treaty of Versailles, the French desire for security and the particular interests of other countries prevented a workable redraft of Europe.

The catalyst was the murder of the Austrian heir to the throne and his wife in Sarajevo (28 June 1914), while the causes were power conflicts in the European state system (in the case of France, especially the claim to Alsace-Lorraine), national delusions of grandeur on all sides, with a corresponding arms race, conflicts in the Austro-Hungarian multi-national empire, Russia's policy on the Balkans as well as excessively zealous mobilization and ultimata. On 3 August 1914, the German Empire declared war on France. In the Battle of the Marne in September, a French rearguard action halted the German advance, marking a transition from mobile to static warfare. From February to July and again from October to December 1916, the Battle of Verdun raged, with approximately 400,000 dead on each side. In July 1918, Marshal Foch launched the counteroffensive; in November the armistice was signed in Compiègne.

First World War 1914–18

The damage to France was immense: over 1.3 million killed, 3 million disabled, whole areas laid to waste, enormous foreign debt, industrial capabilities and infrastructure crippled. The Treaty of Versailles (28 June 1919) did assign the lion's share of German reparations to France, as well as Alsace-Lorraine, economic authority over Saarland and limited occupation of the Rhineland; and yet this was perceived as too little (»l'Allemagne payera«). Clemenceau and Poincaré thus took a hard line on Germany in their foreign policies (in 1921, reparations were set at the absurd figure of 132 billion Goldmarks; the Ruhr region was occupied in 1923 in order to accelerate payments). The USA, in contrast, aimed for a »sensible« peace under President Wilson (»Fourteen Points«), with the League of Nations founded on his initiative in 1919, to which France also signed up. When the French moved out of the Ruhr in 1925, a short period of Franco-German understanding broke out under the foreign ministers A. Briand and G. Stresemann. The 1925 Treaty of Locarno guaranteed Germany the inviolability of the eastern French border. In 1926, Germany was accepted into the League and in 1930 France va-

Versailles and the aftermath

cated the Rhineland prematurely, agreeing to a reduction of German reparations (the Young Plan). Nevertheless, work commenced on the construction of the Maginot Line in 1929 (►Baedeker Special p.510). Hitler came to power in 1933 and marched into the demilitarized Rhineland, without any military response from the French or the British. In the Munich Agreement of 1938, Prime Minister Daladier, hoping to rescue peace, ceded the Sudeten German regions of Czechoslovakia to Germany.

French internal affairs
The economy boomed as demand increased. By 1924, industrial output matched the level of 1913. Those who profited the most from the war are the »200 families«, the 200 biggest shareholders of the French national bank. France, too, experienced the »Roaring Twenties«, particularly in Paris where an intellectual avant-garde and a free-spirited atmosphere were accompanied by jazz and Josephine Baker. The loss of so many men saw more women go to work and gain greater independence. Attempts to encourage women to produce more offspring (e.g. legislation prohibiting contraception and abortion) were less than fruitful; women, after all, obtained legal maturity in 1938 (the right to vote followed much later, in 1945). By 1940 there had been 40 governments featuring the most diverse coalitions. In the parliamentary elections of 1936, the »Popular Front«, an alliance of radical socialists, communists and socialists, emerged victorious. Léon Blum's government introduced progressive social legislation (including the 40-hour working week and paid holidays, which heralded the birth of mass tourism), but had to step down in 1938 in the face of financial problems.

From the Second World War to the Fourth Republic

1940	German troops occupy France
1944	Allied forces' Normandy landings
1945	German capitulation. De Gaulle Prime Minister
1946–58	Fourth Republic
From 1954	Algerian War (Algeria's independence 1962)

Second World War 1939–45
Following Germany's assault on Poland, France, who had issued a guarantee together with Great Britain, declared war on Germany on 3 September 1939. However it was not until 10 May 1940 (»drôle de guerre«) that German tanks – bypassing the Maginot Line – made their way through Belgium, surrounding the Allies at Dunkirk and, on 14 June, occupying Paris, which surrendered without resistance. A ceasefire was agreed at Compiègne on 22 June; France was divided into occupied (north, west) and unoccupied territory. The »collaborating« government of the Verdun hero Pétain took its seat at Vichy

The Allied landings in Normandy, June 1944

in July. General de Gaulle formed a government in exile in London and organized the Forces Françaises Libres; meanwhile, in France, resistance groups (Résistance) fought back against the occupying forces and collaborators. Under the reactionary, anti-Republican Vichy regime, the traditional French anti-Semitism came to the fore; without pressure from the Germans, Jews were singled out for reprisals, interned in camps and handed over to the Nazis. Alsace and Lorraine were turned into German zones and targeted for »nazification«, their menfolk conscripted – not only on the eastern front, but also in France itself. When the Allies arrived in North Africa in November 1942, German troops also occupied Vichy France. On 6 June 1944, the Allies landed in Normandy, on 15 August in the south of France. The Allied forces accorded de Gaulle the honour of marching into Paris in triumph on 25 August; on 8 May 1945, in the Allied headquarters in Reims, the act of military surrender was signed. On 16 May, France joined the United Nations Security Council.

In the stabilization of relations, it was de Gaulle who led the way to integration. In September 1944, he formed, without official legitimation, a »government of unanimity« encompassing the whole spectrum, from the conservative right to the communists. Vengeance on collaborators and Vichy supporters (»épuration«), who at first faced execution without trial, was channelled into legal procedures; some 10,000 death sentences were meted out. The economic situation was catastrophic; the German occupying forces had exploited the country for their war machine, destroying infrastructure such as bridges, rail-

De Gaulle's first government

way lines, and thousands of houses and factories. In October 1945 the left emerged victorious at the polls, the Assembly going on to prepare a constitution (the first in which women participated). De Gaulle headed the government, stepping down, however, in January 1946, when parliament rejected his proposal of a presidential leadership.

Reconciliation with Germany

As early as 1945, de Gaulle, having travelled through the occupied zones, called for the need to »create something new«, and made a point of extending a hand to German representatives. As well as considerations of Franco-German reconciliation, the nation's own security was a significant consideration in the French policy. With both issues in mind, efforts were made to establish a European system (Council of Europe, 1949, European Coal & Steel Community in 1951, European Economic Community, 1957). Great credit in this difficult process must be given to Robert Schuman, Jean Monnet and Pierre Pflimlin, as well as the prime ministers and federal chancellors of the period – de Gaulle/Adenauer, Pompidou/Brandt, Giscard d'Estaing/Schmidt and Mitterrand/Kohl – who set symbolic milestones of friendship. The 1963 Élysée Treaty sealed a close political, economic and social partnership.

Fourth Republic 1946–58

In October 1946, a new constitution was accepted through a referendum, heralding the Fourth Republic. Due to proportional representation and the fractious nature of the groups and coalitions – communists, socialists, Catholic Popular Republicans and so forth, the National Assembly of the Fourth Republic saw 25 cabinets in 13 years; their major topics were economic policy, schools and the colonies. Banks, insurance companies, the automotive industry and energy corporations were nationalized and progressive social assurances introduced. In 1947, de Gaulle founded the rightist conglomerate movement, the Rassemblement du Peuple Français (RPF). In 1948, France received assistance from the Marshall Plan (in return for opening the market to US goods). In 1949, France joined NATO and the Council of Europe. The economy gradually recovered, and reconstruction continued apace; the boom years of the 1950s continued until the oil crisis of 1974. Investment in industrial production was huge, and the birth rate shot up, as did domestic consumption, once heavy industry had consolidated. 1957 saw membership of the European Coal & Steel Community European Economic Community and EURATOM.

Colonies

In the 1950s, France found itself forced to give up its colonial empire. The constitution of 1946 strove to engineer a similar entity to the Commonwealth with the »Union Française« designed to accommodate the aspirations to independence. The Indochina War, beginning in 1946, in which France aimed to regain control following the capitulation of Japan, ended with a crushing defeat at Dien Bien Phu and retreat in 1954. In 1956, Tunisia and Morocco became independent, whilst the remaining African possessions, with the exception of Algeria, gained independence by 1960.

Under French rule since 1830, Algeria's population of 9 million included approximately 1 million Europeans, who, feeling quite at home here, formed the established upper and middle classes. The political parties in the motherland were not in a position to solve the grave problems of decolonization. From 1954 onwards, acts of violence perpetrated by the Algerian liberation front, the FLN, increased, and the war developed into a dirty, gruesome conflict costing approx. 20,000 French and hundreds of thousands of Muslim Algerians their lives. In 1956, France joined Great Britain and Israel in the disastrous Suez War against Nasser, partly on the premise that he was supporting the Algerian rebels. In May 1958, right-wing colonists and the army seized power in Algiers. A state of emergency was declared, with President Coty subsequently naming de Gaulle as president with extraordinary powers on 28 May. The September referendum sanctioned a new constitution: the Fifth Republic.

The Algerian War

Fifth Republic

from 1958	Fifth Republic under president Charles de Gaulle
1966	France leaves NATO
May 1968	Student riots and general strike
1969–74	President Georges Pompidou: »modernization« of France
1973–74	Oil crisis
1981–94	President François Mitterrand
1994–2007	President Jacques Chirac
since 2007	President Nicolas Sarkozy

The 1958 constitution and the direct election of the president, as forced through by de Gaulle in 1962, form the basis of a political structure which is still intact (► p.33). The mix of presidential and parliamentary systems, initially tailored to de Gaulle, has been preserved by his successors to this day. A persistent tendency to vote for personalities rather than agendas is reminiscent of the continuing admiration for Napoleon; the »grandeur« of the nation and its highest representative is still a major factor in self-image and practical politics. Prime minister and president are chosen separately and yet operate side by side, one part of a complex parliamentary history, the other part being a party landscape which is difficult to navigate (► p.34). One notable anomaly is »cohabitation«, when prime minister and president belong to different camps.

Basic political structures

Charles De Gaulle and Konrad Adenauer outside the Elysée Palace on 9 February 1961

Economic development Reconstruction and consumer growth heralded an economic miracle which lasted from 1945 until around the time of the oil crisis of 1974; the 30-year period is known as the »trente glorieuses« (»glorious thirty«). The boom brought prosperity for many to a greater or lesser extent, but there were losers as well, whose living conditions were bleak. Modernization in agriculture saw millions move into industrial labour. At the same time, economic growth attracted many immigrants who were prepared to work for lower wages. Student unrest and the general strike of 1968 were tangible expressions of the problems facing a changing society, which the political establishment failed to manage. The mid-1970s marked the twilight of the growth society; the fight against recession began, with a series of governments taking different approaches. The leap in productivity through automation and computer technology, coupled with the downfall of heavy industry, saw unemployment rise to over 10%. The proportion of the population with ever decreasing incomes was exacerbated by economic globalization, setting a negative trend in motion the effects of which remained unclear.

In spite of violent resistance from the right-wing colonists (1961 military coup, Organisation de l'Armée Secrète OAS), de Gaulle pushed through Algeria's independence (Evian Treaty of 1962), which was given the seal of approval by an overwhelming majority in a referendum. Some 800,000 »pieds noirs« relocated to France. De Gaulle's policy on foreign affairs and national security very much followed the »Grande Nation« line, regardless of causing affront, willing to face the USA and USSR and the rest of Europe on its own terms: in 1960, the French detonated their first atomic bomb in the Sahara and developed a nuclear armoury (»force de frappe«). In 1966, France withdrew its troops from NATO. De Gaulle twice blocked Great Britain's entry into the EEC, in 1963 and 1967. His vision for Europe was a »Europe of fatherlands«, working together in an economic sense but preserving their sovereignty. The student riots in May 1968, particularly in Paris, spread out and provoked a brutal police response and a severe political crisis; 10 million of the workforce began a general strike. Respect for de Gaulle helped to defuse the situation whilst the prime minister, Pompidou, appeased the workers with pay rises, upping the minimum wage and introducing further reforms. The Gaullistes secured an absolute majority at the parliamentary elections. Nevertheless, de Gaulle resigned in connection with the rebuttal of regional reforms in April 1969; he died in 1970.

Charles de Gaulle 1958–69

His successor Georges Pompidou had the goal of developing France into a major industrial nation: ambitious investment programmes – backed by regional expertise – focussed on aeronautics and aerospace (Concorde), telecommunications, nuclear energy, crude oil refineries and tourism (La Grande Motte). Under his aegis, the architectural modernization of Paris began (including the relocation of Les Halles, the Centre Pompidou, La Défense). Pompidou's foreign policy sought greater conciliation and strengthening of Europe; notably, he gave his support to Great Britain's entry into the EEC in 1972. The oil crisis in late 1973 hit France hard: unemployment, inflation and social insecurities grew. Pompidou died on 2 April 1974.

Georges Pompidou 1969–74

The new president Valéry Giscard d'Estaing had to contend with economic recession on one hand and virtual stalemate in the National Assembly on the other. The Gaullistes (RPR since 1976) and the liberal, central and moderate right (UDF since 1978) stood opposed to the socialists, communists etc. He introduced a series of reforms, especially concerning further education and equality of the sexes. A

Valéry Giscard d'Estaing 1974–81

woman was now allowed to open a bank account without her husband's consent. Women were also entitled to equal pay for equal work. In the presidential elections in 1981, he lost out – due in no small measure to his inapproachable manner and to his friendship with the Central African dictator Bokassa – to the socialist François Mitterrand.

François Mitterrand 1981–95 The coming to power of the socialists (in the National Assembly as well) inspired great hope. Comprehensive reforms were set in motion: an increase in the minimum wage, in pensions, housing benefits etc., a reduction in the working week to 39 hours, five weeks paid holiday, abolition of the death penalty; in addition, further decentralization (establishment of the régions). In Paris, monumental building works were begun (including the Grande Arche, Opéra Bastille and a facelift for the Louvre). In 1981, the TGV line from Paris to Lyon was opened. The gravity of the financial situation was underestimated, however; Keynesian policy-making and increases in taxation proved no more effective in funding expenditure than the nationalization of five industrial corporations (including the Usinor and Sacilor-Sollac steel companies), 26 banks and two finance holdings. As soon as 1982, a drastic change of course based on cutbacks became necessary to slow down the rate of inflation, now in double figures. An attempt to integrate Catholic public schools into the state system in 1984 met with massive opposition and inspired the largest rally in French history (over 1 million people). In 1985, the foreign intelligence service – with Mitterrand informed – sank Greenpeace's *Rainbow Warrior* in the port of Auckland, New Zealand. The ship was to have led a protest against the Moruroa Atoll nuclear tests. The parliamentary elections of 1986 saw the RPR and UDF win a majority; for the first time, in a so-called »cohabitation«, a socialist president governed with a Gaullist prime minister (Chirac) and a parliamentary majority for the opposition. Also a first was Le Pen's radical right-wing Front National's entry to the National Assembly with 10% of the vote. To boost the economy, 65 state companies were earmarked for re-privatization, amongst them 41 banks, industrial and armaments corporations and the oil conglomerate Elf-Aquitaine. In September 1992, only 51.5 % of the French voted in favour of the Treaty of Maastricht, in which the decision to create a European currency was taken. In the 1993 National Assembly elections, the right again won a majority; Edouard Balladur (RPR) led the government, and the second cohabitation occurred. The Banque Nationale de Paris (BNP) was privatized.

Jacques Chirac 1995–2007 The Neo-Gaullist Jacques Chirac became president in May 1995. In July, the announcement that nuclear tests would be resumed in the Moruroa Atoll caused outrage, both at home and abroad. Chirac's attempt to reduce state expenditure by reducing the unwieldy public sector met with vehement resistance. In April 1997, Chirac took the surprising step of dissolving the National Assembly, whereupon the socialist L. Jospin became president of a leftist coalition government (the third cohabitation). Against a background of high unemployment and worsening social problems, a new law on immigration was passed and a 35-hour working week introduced. The 2002 presidential election went to a second vote, which Chirac then won with 82%, the Fascist Le Pen having collected 17% in the first ballot. On 1 January 2002, the euro replaced the franc. The 2003 summer heatwave cost some 15,000 people their lives (6000 in Paris alone), uncovering major flaws in the health system. In June 2004, on the 60th anniversary of the Normandy Landings, Gerhard Schröder became the first German chancellor to take part in the remembrance service.

The presidential elections in May 2007 were won by Nicolas Sarkozy, the candidate of the conservative Gaullist UMP. Born in 1955, the son of a Hungarian lawyer and member of the lower aristocracy has enjoyed a steeply rising career: from 1983 to 2002 he was mayor of Neuilly-sur-Seine, a suburb of Paris; from 1993 to 1995 he was the budget minister in the Balladur government; from 2002 to 2004 he was minister of the interior under Raffarin and in the same year he spent some months as »super-minister« for the economy, finance and industry. With his slogan »everything is possible« Sarkozy narrowly beat his socialist rival Ségolène Royal with 53% of the vote, but only a year later two thirds of French people were dissatisfied with him. This however has less to do with his law-and-order ethos – in 2005 he expressed a view that crime in Parisian banlieues was best remedied with a high-pressure industrial cleaning machine – and more with the negative way he is perceived both politically and personally. Observers accuse him of a lack of style that damages the dignity of the office of president (he has already been labelled »Président Bling-Bling«), and point out that his bold reforms and confident promises, for example of higher purchasing power, have until now failed to have the hoped-for effect.

Nicolas Sarkozy since 2007

Sarkozy and his third wife, former model and singer Carla Bruni, visit South Africa (here with Thabo Mbeki)

Art and Culture

France is a land of culture par excellence. Splendid buildings, both old and new, grace the nation's towns and villages or act as marvellous counterpoints to the surrounding countryside. World-famous museums testify to the superlative role played by France in the history of art. Last, but by no means least, the colourful traditions of folklore are alive and well in all corners of the country.

Art History

Prehistory and early history

The roots of art, in their early stages representing both religious and **Cave paintings**
mythical ideas, reach deep into the past in France. They are docu-
mented in caves where the humans of the Palaeolithic or Old Stone
Age painted and etched animals on the walls around 30,000 BC (►
Baedeker Special p.662). The Périgord region with the Vézère valley
has several such caves, including the Lascaux Grotto, discovered in
1940 (a replica can be visited today); the earliest examples of this art
»in natura« can be admired in Font-de-Gaume, Niaux at Tarascon-
sur-Ariège, in Pech Merle at Cabrerets, in Cougnac and in Mas
d'Azil.

The megalithic stone structures of Brittany, particularly around Car- **Megalithic**
nac, were primarily constructed in the Neolithic or New Stone Age **culture**
(from 7000 BC) (►Baedeker Special p.306). Examples of megalithic
culture can also be found in the Cevennes mountains, created by Ligurians at the outset of the Metal Age.

Celtic relics that have survived – above all, those from the Bibracte **Celtic art**
excavations – include beautifully crafted everyday objects with abstract
designs. The most valuable collection of pre-Roman art is housed in
the Musée des Antiquités Nationales in St-Germain-en-Laye.

From the second century BC, the Romans moved into France via **Roman legacy**
Massilia (Marseille). Until the migration of the 5th and 6th centuries,
Roman administration and civilization dominated the country, leav-
ing a lasting impression in many buildings – if not in the language.
The most heavily influenced region is Provence, the Roman »Provincia«, with the arenas of Arles and Nîmes, the Triumphal Arches of
Orange and St-Rémy, the temples of Nîmes and Vienne, and the
Pont du Gard. Further testimonies to the Roman legacy can be seen
in the foothills of the Pyrenees and in more northerly regions, for example in Toulouse, Besançon, Reims and Bordeaux. The thermae of
Aix-les-Bains and Plombières (Vosges) are still in use today. The
most important »Roman« museum is the Louvre in Paris; lapidary
museums exist in Arles, Nîmes and Vienne, whilst the Musée des
Beaux-Arts in Lyon boasts excellent sculptures and mosaics.

Carolingian Art

In Roman times, Christianity reached France via Italy; the earliest re- **Sacral buildings**
maining church buildings are in Lyon and Vienne. It was common

← *The cathedral of Rouen, a French Gothic masterpiece*

The golden reliquary of St Fides from the 9th century in Conques

practice for existing temples to be converted into Christian places of worship, as in Nîmes, for example. The oldest church in France is St-Pierre-aux-Nonnains in Metz (7th century), with foundations dating back to the 4th century; it was completely rebuilt in the Gothic period. Some chapels were given a gloomy, consecrational crypt serving several functions, from community room to a mausoleum for the remains of the church patron saint. Examples from the 7th century can be found in the abbey of Jouarre (near Metz) and in St-Laurent in Grenoble. The baptistery in St-Jean of Poitiers (late 7th century) is also significant. A major development of the period was the highlighting of a part of the church in the crossing, which would become the spiritual and religious centrepiece. The church of Vignory on the river Marne was not consecrated until 1052, but clearly demonstrates this development, which was connected to the emphasis of the longitudinal axis leading to the altar, where pillars or open walls narrowed the space inside the church. In addition to Vignory, churches in Tournus and Nevers display the same characteristic.

Monastic buildings In the Carolingian era from the middle of the 8th to the end of the 9th century, many important monasteries were constructed. The buildings were, however, frequently renovated in the centuries that followed, so that only a few wall fragments recall the original. The finest remaining construction to reflect the original most faithfully is the central-plan building of Germigny-des-Prés on the Loire, consecrated in 806 and featuring splendid mosaics, a perfect example of Carolingian design, in as far as it goes beyond the typical tresses ornamentation.

Romanesque

Main features of architecture From the beginning of the 11th century until the middle of the 12th century the Romanesque style of construction developed, the first monumental architecture since antiquity, in which the Christian occident appears as an architectural unity. Romanesque is the name given to the style because the forms used in the building components go back to Roman-late antiquity and Byzantine-oriental paradigms.

The Romanesque style did not unfold everywhere in equal measure or form; in interior design, the development of façades and the construction of doorways, a great variety of forms of modification became evident in France. The differing characteristics are less obvious in the »grand« monuments, as they learned from one another and were thus closer in style. Hence the churches of St-Etienne and Ste-Trinité in Caen, St-Sernin in Toulouse, St-Gilles in the town of the same name in the Camargue and Ste-Foy in Conques all exhibit traits from beyond their respective regions. Meanwhile, small, rural churches reveal more about the visions of their creators.

Building elements

Romanesque buildings are distinguished by elements based on squares, cubes or spheres: solid, masonry walls, round arches and calottes, barrel and groined vaults. Elements using these basic proportions are grouped in pyramid form around the dominant crossing tower, dividing the building into numerous echeloned parts. The unostentatious monumental character, which lends itself to the Romanesque complexity, finds its counterpoint in a variety of decorative friezes on the walls, doorways and windows, but above all in the unique variations of ornamentation of the capitals (see below).

Burgundy

Burgundy is, without doubt, the centre of the Romanesque. Here, the two faces of medieval art find completion: monkish asceticism and renunciation are juxtaposed with the refinements of civilization and linked to the prerogatives of power, the worldly ways of life. On this basis, the Clunians became the dominant force. In Burgundy,

The church of Ste-Madeleine in Vézelay, Burgundy, was constructed around 1100

Romanesque design displayed the »stringent centralization of the building in the crossing tower and grouped choir chapels in the most compelling form of the nave, long and steep, the uniformity of the wall, all coming together in the rigour of the barrel vault« (Hamann). To the south and west of Burgundy, towards Poitiers, the hall church developed, in which the central nave and side aisles are of the same height.

Normandy In Normandy, the regimented designs of the walls in the galleries and aisles before the arches and columns (St-Etienne in Caen) al-**Périgord** ready corresponded to Gothic architectural thinking. In Périgord **Aquitaine** and Aquitaine Byzantine influences become apparent. St-Front in Périgueux (redesigned in the 19th century) mimics St. Mark's in Venice, which in turn was based on the church of the Holy Apostles in Constantinople. The cathedral of Angoulême documents the Aquitaine style of a single nave with several domes, although the **Provence** dome over the crossing is clearly the focal point. Further south, in Provence, the ceremonial domed crossing is replaced by an assembly room almost secular in character: Rome rather than Byzantium. A good example of this is the 12th-century St-Gabriel chapel southeast of Tarascon. Important works of the Romanesque are the many cloisters, of which the ones in Moissac and Arles (St-Trophime) can be considered among the finest.

Cluny Romanesque style in France goes hand in hand with the Cluniac Reform (Burgundy). The Cluny II church, consecrated in 981, already shows a marked difference to the basilica constructed previously. The transept is given greater prominence and a crossing tower is introduced, the side aisles are extended as side chapels of the choir to the east, and in the west the atrium is converted into a vestibule. Cluny II is the blueprint on which the sacral buildings in Paray-le-Monial, La Charité-sur-Loire and Fleury are modelled, as well as the Normandy churches of Jumièges and Bernay. Work on Cluny III – the largest and most magnificent Romanesque church of all, had it not been dismantled after the French Revolution – commenced in 1088 and surpassed every dimension of architecture to date, with its multiple elements (double towers at the entrance with a large vestibule, a nave and four aisles, two transepts with crossing towers, and a choir subdivided into rows of chapels).

Cistercians The Cistercians developed their own strong abbey design, based on uncompromising asceticism. In Burgundy (Fontenay, Pontigny) and in Provence (Senanque, Le Thoronet, Silvacane) austere buildings with towerless churches in the shape of a cross stand in the remotest of places.

Sculpture Sculpture underwent renewal at the hands of the same force that formed the buildings which house it, with small, detailed sculpture

The Royal Portal of Chartres cathedral

at the forefront. Column figures abound, with animals, mythical creatures and plants gracing dramatic scenes in the smallest of spaces on capitals. Other important creations are the tympanum reliefs and figures above doorways. In St-Denis and Chartres (Royal Portal) the sculpted figures on columns were the forerunners of the Gothic figure. In the Burgundy region, long rows of animal and human figures illustrate the concepts of virtue and vice, heaven and hell. In the south, however, depictions of Christ and his followers were more popular. A typical bridge between the two is manifested in mosaic, where the Burgundian influence is more obvious (Christ as judge of the world). The Ascension of Christ is the dominant theme of the façades in Poitou and Languedoc. The archaic sculpture of the south owes more to the tradition of antiquity, as may be seen in Toulouse, for example. This becomes even clearer in Provence: the façade of

St-Gilles, undoubtedly the most important artistic creation of the south, does without the miracle, opting to depict a version of history in which the Ascension is less important than the story of the Passion.

Painting   Wall paintings dominate the Romanesque. Churches were decorated with paintings by itinerant artists, with scenes from the Old and New Testaments and the lives of the saints. Greater expression allied with strict stylization characterizes the frescoes in the church of St-Savin-sur-Gartempe near Poitiers, begun in 1080, which decorate the walls and vaults. Glass paintings worthy of note may be viewed in Le Mans, Poitiers, Angers, St-Denis and Chartres, their mystic powers of illumination unique to this day. There is no finer example of tapestry than that of Bayeux, a magnificent representation of cultural history (►photo p.50).

Gothic

Main features   Italian artists and art historians of the Renaissance (G. Vasari) proffered the concept of »Gothic« to denigrate a style beyond their comprehension. »Gotico« was simply »barbaric« art. As late as the 18th century, some still believed that Gothic had really been invented by the Goths and imported to France. French art historians use the term »style français« for this school of design, developed in northern France prior to 1150. As an opposing movement to scholasticism, mysticism and the afterlife form the spiritual background. The fertility of the Middle Ages in terms of architecture, sculpture and painting would not, however, have been conceivable without the devoutness of the population and the economic strength of the burgeoning towns, the resident bourgeoisie growing in self-confidence and power. The construction of Notre-Dame in Paris cost an estimated 120 million gold francs, a horrendous sum.

The first early Gothic building is thought to be the abbey of St-Denis, north of Paris. For almost four centuries, Gothic flourished in France, reaching a peak in the 13th century with the construction of many of the great cathedrals of the north (Chartres, Reims, Amiens, Beauvais, Ste-Chapelle in Paris). Without doubt, Chartres conveys the best impression of French Gothic character, in the design of the exterior as well as the interior. Burgundy and the Champagne region also have important churches (Dijon, Nevers, Auxerre, Semur-en-Auxois, Troyes). In Anjou, Gothic style underwent modification, the Romanesque dome of Byzantine origin being combined with the cross-ribbed vault, as may be seen in the cathedral of Angers. In the south, Gothic style, closely linked to the kingship, made little impression; only the cathedrals of Clermont-Ferrand, Albi, Narbonne and St-Maximin-la-Ste-Baume merit inspection. More prominent in the south are secular buildings, fortress-like in design, as exemplified by Carcassonne, the Papal Palace of Avignon and Aigues-Mortes.

The innovative Gothic building style created a new sense of space: mass was no longer a burden; instead it reached up to lofty heights. The architectural means were based on three elements: the ogive, the ribbed vault and the buttress. Together, they created a sense of lightness which Romanesque architecture could not match; the load and support could be separated from one another. Ribbed vaults distribute the weight out to the sides, where it is absorbed by an (open) buttress; the wall areas are set in a stone framework which allows the generous use of glass windows. Closely arranged clustered piers and half columns divide the wall and direct the gaze upwards to the ever higher vault (in the incomplete building of Beauvais almost 50m/ 164ft high!). Moreover, coloured glass lends the inner space a quite magical aura. The most striking example of this is the rose window in the façades, at the same time one of the most obvious signs of the new style. Of course, the exterior appears in demonstrative splendour, with careful attention given to deny a clear view of the church from the alleyways of the houses gathered around it: the believer should not see it as a whole, but be impressed by the way it reaches into the heavens. The richly structured main façade, most frequently to the west, is graced by two mighty towers, thus creating a monumental entrance gate.

Building styles

There were four distinct periods of Gothic art in France. The first saw the construction of magnificent cathedrals in Laon, Paris, Amiens, Reims, Chartres, Bourges, Strasbourg and Beauvais, which also marked the finest hour of Gothic expression and style. This period includes the buildings of the early Gothic phase (around the second half of the 12th century – with clear Romanesque-Gothic hybrids – up until the first quarter of the 13th century) and the actual High Gothic (until the end of the 13th century), which created a space aspiring to lightness, ordered in height and depth, drawing the gaze of the onlooker to one element after another. The 15th century continued this development with the »Rayonnant« style, in which pillars became columns which blend into the arches, although the capitals disappeared. The late Gothic of the 16th century created a space as a stationary whole, visible in its entirety, hence the preference for hall churches over basilica. A further determining feature is the late »Flamboyant« style, with flame-like, lambent tracery. The churches of Brou at Bourg-en-Bresse, the Palace of Justice in Rouen, the choir at Albi cathedral and the side façades of the cathedrals of Senlis, Beauvais, Sens and Limoges belong to this period.

Periods

As the nobility increased its wealth and the urban bourgeoisie moved up in the world, a large number of chateaux, castles, town halls, palaces of justice, hospices and residential buildings sprang up. In the south of France, Aigues-Mortes and Carcassonne have virtually intact (or, respectively, restored) medieval towns.

Secular buildings

Sculpture Church doorways gain their significance largely through the statues, which now stand freely, but are still integrated in the architecture.

The female figure steps into the foreground, as can be seen in Reims, Paris and Amiens for example; the Madonna becomes a lady with a radiant smile of dignity. Sadly, the French Revolution destroyed the figures of the cathedral in Paris (what is left can be seen in the Musée de Cluny). Other typical doorways with an array of figures may be found in the churches of Amiens, Bourges, Auxerre, Le Mans, Rouen and – although from a later era (after 1400) – in Strasbourg. The clearest example of this style is in Chartres, where the stiffer Romanesque figures of the west façade stand in striking contrast to those of the fronts of the transepts constructed after 1200. The grand master of the late period is the Breton Michel Colombe, his masterpiece the tomb in Nantes cathedral. Also significant are ivory sculptures and the art of goldsmithing, examples of which can be found in all of the larger museums and church treasuries.

Labours of the Months: April in the Duc de Berry's »Très Riches Heures«

The enclos paroissiaux (parish closes) of Brittany, created between 1450 and 1650, display, along with triumphal arch, church, ossuary and graveyard, a Calvary »populated« with a host of sculptures.

Painting Evidence of Gothic painting can, above all, be found in the altar works of the 15th century (e.g. in the Louvre in Paris and in Beaune) and the magnificent book illustrations of the popular »Book of Hours« (prayer books). Dutch Masters, such as the Limburg brothers, worked on these. Excellent examples may be inspected in the National Library in Paris and the Musée Condé in Chantilly. Tapestry also exhibits a Gothic influence; the Louvre and the cathedral of Angers (*Tenture de l'Apocalypse*, 14th century) house admirable examples of astounding realism.

Renaissance

Main features The »rebirth« of antiquity in the 16th century, influenced by humanism, the Reformation and the great discoveries at the beginning of the modern age, was no longer expressed in France in sacral buildings but instead in secular architecture, especially castles. The great patron of the arts at the time was King François I, who not only completed the castles of Chaumont, Langeais and Amboise, begun under his predecessor Charles VIII, but also commissioned Châteaudun, Chenonceaux, Blois, Chambord and Azay-le-Rideau. He brought famous Italian artists, such as the genius Leonardo da Vinci, to his court. In St-Denis, he had Philippe de l'Orme construct a tomb in the style of a Roman triumphal arch.

In the Renaissance, the Gothic ogive is supplanted by the round arch **Characteristics** and the basket arch, and the ribbed vault gives way to the coffered ceiling. The breakthrough came in the 16th century with the return to the archetypes of antiquity (Vitruv); the major influence of Italy, providing a model for, amongst other things, the design of steps and stairways, activated the development of a new sense of national awareness and tradition. Most Renaissance castles are constructed around a square courtyard; the wings of the buildings end in pavilions, the roofs raised. The most important edifices are the castles of the Loire, with their clear lines, and Pierre Lescot's new development for the Louvre in Paris (the modern face of which was, admittedly, created over two centuries), begun in 1546 with the section on the

The Hôtel Gouin in Tours, modelled on the Italian Renaissance

Seine and the half wing connected on the west side. Outside Paris, the castles of St-Germain-en-Laye and Fontainebleau were built. As a complete system of urban architecture, the Marais in Paris, created under Henri IV, with the beautiful Place des Vosges, is especially worthy of note – it was the preferred residential area for the noble classes.

Baroque and Classicism

Architecture Whilst in Italy and Germany the path from the Renaissance led to the stirring forms of the Baroque, France chose to revisit »classisist« forms of Greek and Roman antiquity. This was manifested in the various expressions of »classicisme« of the 17th century, and then moved on to classicism in the stricter sense and architecture of the Revolution and the Empire, continuing up until the Historicism of the late 19th century – a period spanning more than 200 years. Regency and Rococo are mere interludes, concerned primarily with interior design.

An early precursor was the Palais du Luxembourg in Paris, completed in 1621 for Marie de Medici. Around the middle of the century, a series of noble castles were built, the most celebrated being Vaux-le-Vicomte (1661). Its creators, the architect Le Vau, the painter Le Brun and the landscape gardener Le Notre, were enlisted by Louis XIV for the magnificent Palace of Versailles (from 1661). Around the same time, the east façade of the Louvre was completed, for which Louis XIV initially engaged Lorenzo Bernini, the most famous master builder in Europe; he then decided against Roman Baroque and C. Perrault made plans for a mighty portico, finished in 1674. In this way classicism, oriented towards Vitruv and Palladio, was established. Only in the interior did »Baroque« pomp emerge triumphant, as celebrated by Le Brun in the splendid rooms of Versailles. Following the death of Louis XIV (1715), de Cotte swept away the heavy legacy of Louis Quatorze, whitewashing walls and adding just a hint of ornamentation (Régence). The Rococo of Louis XV continued the trend, marked by asymmetric, conchiform ornaments (»rocaille«); prime examples are the Salon Ovale in the Parisian Hôtel de Soubise and the decoration of the interior of the Petit Trianon in Versailles. The only great Rococo ensemble in France is the wonderful Place Stanislas in Nancy (around 1755), owing much to the sponsor's interest in German art. The French solution is exemplified by the Place de la Concorde in Paris (A.-J. Gabriel, 1763).

Around 1765, under Louis XVI, leaning towards antiquity, actual classicism came to dominate (e.g. St-Sulpice, Pantheon in Paris, Petit Trianon in Versailles). The representatives of the so-called architecture of the Revolution (C.-N. Ledoux, E.-L. Boullée) devised visionary projects based on pure geometric principles (cube, sphere, cone), strict elements of antiquity. The agitated times of Napoleon I did not, however, lend themselves to realizing such developments.

French Baroque: Rennes town hall by Ange-Jacques Gabriel (around 1740)

In the 17th century, French painting was determined by the historical depictions of Nicolas Poussin, who lived in Rome from 1624, and Claude Lorrain's landscapes of classicist-heroic character. A counterpoint was offered by the Caravaggio-inspired Realism of the Nain brothers and the »Mystic Realism« of George de La Tour. Charles Le Brun was a leading figure in developing the style of wall paintings (Apollo Gallery in the Louvre, Versailles). Rococo was admirably represented by J.-A. Watteau, whose »lower« works of genre painting offer a gracious reflection of the age. Also important were François Boucher, the »painter of Pompadour« and creator of magnificent tapestries, Simon Chardin and, last but not least, Honoré Fragonard. The founder and grand master of French classicism is considered to be J.-L. David, who endeavoured to revive the strict morals of ancient Rome and succeeded in becoming the official painter of the National Convention and the Empire. (In the late 19th century, as with Marées in Germany, the monumental style of classicism was revisited through Puvis de Chavannes; his frescoes adorn the walls of great museums, but primarily those of the Panthéon in Paris.)

19th Century

»Empire« was the name given to the style of the Napoleonic era. It was concerned primarily with interior design, owing much to Egyptian-Pompeian precedents. Such lightness is not, however, evident in the buildings of the day, which are based more on antiquity: above all, the gigantic Arc de Triomphe de l'Etoile, the Arc du Carrousel in front of the Louvre, the Église de la Madeleine, and La Bourse, all in Paris. The orientation towards older styles develops into Historicism. Major examples in Paris are the Opéra, in the style of the Renaissance by Charles Garnier and the Neo-Byzantine Sacré-Cœur in Montmartre, as well as the churches of Notre-Dame-de-la-Garde in Marseille and Notre-Dame-de-la-Fourvière in Lyon. The reconstruction of Paris by G.-E. Haussmann, starting in 1853, was radical to say the least. The largely medieval face of the city was erased and replaced by wide boulevards, squares which formed the centre of radial street plans, and landscaped parks. Around the middle of the century, the industrial technology of iron construction was imported from England. Famous landmarks in Paris are the Bibliothèque Ste-Geneviève and the Eiffel Tower, built in time for the 1889 World's Fair, whilst the railway stations are also fine examples (Gare du Nord, de l'Est etc.).

Rebirth of the Gothic   Classicism was met by a Romantic current, enthusing over the Gothic style, now recognized as a French creation. This led to con-

Auguste Renoir's »Ball at the Moulin de la Galette« is an enchanting play of light and shadow (1876)

struction of »Gothic« buildings once again, although none of particular note; the restoration of medieval structures – with inspector-general of historical monuments Prosper Mérimée (1803–70) and E.-E. Viollet-le-Duc (1814–79) earning great plaudits as master builders – often did more than was strictly necessary.

J.-L. David exaggerated the idea of the French Revolution with themes of antiquity; he departs from classicist discipline, meanwhile, when portraying the coronation of Napoleon (Louvre) in giant format. David was, moreover, an excellent portrait painter. His student, J.-D. Ingres, eclipsed his fame (there is a museum in his hometown of Montauban); he also shows mythological and religious images alongside images of women. Romanticism did not find the same success as in Germany, in spite of marvellous achievements. Exiled from Spain, Francisco Goya came to France (Castres has a museum). The prime exponent in the first half of the 19th century was Eugène Delacroix, trained on Rubens, whose broad brushwork and bright colours created expressive, passionate works (*Liberty Leading the People*, Louvre). Objective, faithful reproductions of reality were no more a part of his work than classicism. One artist did resemble him in style: Honoré Daumier. He found fame as a caricaturist – although he was also an important painter. He happened upon a new theme for his lithographs – the French people, whom he portrayed both compassionately and sarcastically. Romanticism was followed by a strain of Realism which adopted this topic; many works feature the working people on the land and in the towns. The landscapes and portrayals of young girls by Camille Corot span the years from the 18th to the 19th century. Jean-François Millet – like Corot, one of the Barbizon artists – romanticizes the realities of peasant life into a picture of sentimental piety. Gustave Courbet, from a farming family in the Jura region and leader of the French Realism movement, works with an uncompromising faithfulness to reality. His colours, however, are determined by the light in his studio.

From classicism to Realism

The next generation of French painters, leaving the studios to work outdoors, discovered the immense variation in colour according to light conditions and the surroundings; what they record is a subjective »impression«. Claude Monet painted Rouen cathedral some 17 times from the same angle to capture the differences in atmosphere. Alongside Monet, the big names are Edouard Manet, Edgar Degas, Auguste Renoir, Camille Pissarro and Alfred Sisley. Close to Impressionism are Paul Cézanne, Vincent van Gogh and Henri de Toulouse-Lautrec, the painter of the Bohème, who provided great inspiration for poster art (museum in Albi). Impressionism is further advanced with the splitting and mixing of colours according to scientific principles. What began with Pissarro's brush dabs is continued by Georges Seurat and Paul Signac as pointillisme, in which the coloured points together create the impression.

Impressionism

Post-Impressio-nism The Nabis group (Sérusier, Bonnard, Vuillard) countered the impressionistic dissolution of form with clear images in which colour is an important element in its own right. The Symbolists, including Gauguin, Doré, Moreau, worked in a similar way, with irrational themes and fantastic visions contrasted in light and dark. Paul Cézanne's identification of the object of depiction and colour saw a closed system of pictorial arrangement and a new reality emerge. Cézanne's impulses for modern art also influenced Gauguin, who allowed colour to triumph even more categorically. The portraits and landscapes of his friend Vincent van Gogh are awash with captivating colour.

Sculpture In the field of sculpture, two names were of the utmost significance, even if they did continue into the next century: Auguste Rodin and Aristide Maillol. Rodin, whose captivating works are collected in Paris (Musée Rodin), personified a peak in French art; it is no coincidence that he is termed the only master of the 19th century who can hold a candle to Michelangelo. Maillol's predominantly female sculptures helped define a new classicism.

Art Nouveau Towards the end of the 19th century, Art Nouveau opposes Historicism with flowing forms borrowed from nature, particularly from plant life. Aside from Paris, home to H. Guimard's Métro entrances, Nancy is France's Art Nouveau town (Musée de l'École de Nancy).

20th Century

Les Fauves New means of artistic expression were made available in the early 20th century by Fauvism and Cubism. When a group of painters display their works at the 1905 Salon d'Automne in Paris, a critic christens them »Les Fauves« or »the Wild Beasts«. Much influenced by Gauguin and van Gogh, their number includes Matisse, Rouault, Vlaminck, Derain, Dufy and Braque; colour is all important to their representations of nature. The leading figure and creative force of the group is Matisse. Fauvism proved to be highly influential, particularly in the origins of German Expressionism.

Cubism French, Spanish and Russian painters developed Cubism, breaking down objects and other elements of reality into simple forms (cubes, circles and so on) and combining the fragments in new, multiple perspectives. In the vanguard were Georges Braque and Pablo Picasso, subsequently joined by Juan Gris and Fernand Léger. The Spanish painter, sculptor, graphicist and ceramicist Picasso is possibly the most important artist of the 20th century, leaving his mark on eight decades with one new form of composition after another.

Surrealism The movement grew from the literary base of the likes of Breton and Apollinaire and adopted certain ideas from the Dadaists. Everyday realities, dreams and deep psychological stimuli are reconstructed in a striking world of images – some in the style of the Old Masters. Prominent members were F. Picabia, M. Duchamp, A. Masson, Y. Tanguy, H. Arp, R. Magritte, M. Ernst and S. Dalí.

As international participation grew, Paris became the »art capital of the world« after 1920, centre of Surrealism, Constructivism and, after 1931, the »Abstraction-Création« group, who firmly established themselves after 1945 with »Art Informel«, paving the way for op art. Around 1950, the »École de Paris« became the focal

Pablo Picasso's »Demoiselles d'Avignon« is considered to be the first Cubist painting (1907)

point of Informel, particularly Tachism (from the French word for blot, »tache«). Artists such as Jean Dubuffet, Jean Fautrier, Hans Hartung, Wols and Henri Michaux are identified with this new style of painting.

Around 1960, as a countermovement to Informel, »Nouveau Réalisme« appeared on the scene, a parallel to Anglo-American Pop Art. What these movements have in common is a new approach to reality (Y. Klein, B. Vautier). Mundane everyday objects replace paint, canvas and brush (Arman, César).

Nouveau Réalisme

In the 1980s, a movement comparable to the Neue Wilden or New Fauves of Germany and Italy emerges in the form of »figuration libre«, also called Neo-Expressionism (Robert Combas, Hervé di Rosa, J.-C. Blais). Amongst the most important protagonists are Boltanski and Daniel Buren (Place du Palais Royal in Paris). The most relevant museums for modern art are to be found in Paris (Musée d'Art Moderne, Musée Picasso, Musée National d'Art Moderne), Bordeaux, Céret, Lille, Nice, St-Etienne and Strasbourg.

1980s

Architecture after the First World War is dominated by modern construction methods with steel, concrete and glass as its materials. The industrial structures of Tony Garnier (especially in Lyon) are epochmaking. The trend is continued by the »Pope of Concrete« Auguste Perret (the reconstruction of Le Havre being just one of many projects) and Eugène Freyssinet (bridges, airship hangars). One figure

Architecture

who made a worldwide impact was the Swiss Le Corbusier (Ch.-E. Jeanneret); his static system relied on a minimum of supports, rendering surrounding or support walls dispensable and enabling open foundations. The pilgrimage church in Ronchamp, the »Unité d'Habitation« in Marseille and the workers' commune in Firminy near St-Etienne are typical of his idiosyncratic, somewhat sober and rationalist architectural language and his vision of urban development. In the mid-1960s, the »villes nouvelles« in the environs of Paris marked the revival of state urban planning. Key examples are La Défense on the western perimeter of Paris and Marne-la-Vallée (Bofill). No less striking is the Centre Pompidou (Rogers and Piano, 1977) in the centre of Paris, as well as the La Villette science park (1989). Further »grands projets« of the Mitterrand era are the glass pyramid and redevelopment of the Louvre by I. M. Pei, the Opéra de la Bastille (1989), the Bibliothèque de France (1995) and the Ministry of Finances in Bercy (1997). Elsewhere in France, in Arles, Clermont-Ferrand, Evry, Les Eyzies-de-Tayac, Lille, Lyon, Nîmes, Strasbourg and other towns, numerous buildings will go down in architectural history.

La Défense in Paris, an icon of modern French architecture

Traditions

In France, regional traditions – customs, costumes, festivals and music – are rich in number and very much alive; many ethnic groups see themselves as »Bretons« or »Provencals« first, and French second. A list of regional festivals would be never-ending, but some important examples of folk culture are presented here.

Although the country is predominantly Catholic, church festivities play a lesser role than in Spain or Italy. At Christmas (Noël), Alsace and Lorraine, plus some parts of northern France, put up Christmas trees; in Provence a festively decorated creche is more common, typically featuring »santons«, painted creche figures made of china, wood or metal. Christmas in Provence still has an air of mystery and is accompanied by songs that are centuries old. This is also true of the Alemannic parts of eastern France. This apart, Christmas in France is more of a lively family celebration with a large meal (réveillon), wine and champagne, music and dancing. Children usually receive presents either on 6 December (St-Nicolas) or on 6 January (Les Rois Mages, Three Kings). While the Christ Child comes in Alsace, elsewhere on Christmas Eve there are just sweets. Réveillons and presents are also a part of the New Year (Jour de l'An) celebrations.

Christmas

Carnival (carnaval) was frowned upon by the establishment in centuries gone by, in some cases even banned as a sign of revolt. Traditional carnival is seldom celebrated today, although a revival of interest has been registered. Alsace has a Shrovetide along German lines (»Fastnacht«), although usually later in the calendar than in Germany. Some villages in the Languedoc region indulge in revelry, as in Cournonterral near Montpellier, where mud-covered, masked figures (pailhasses) chase the clean »blancs«. Carnival is famous in the north (e.g. in Lille and Dunkirk) and in Nice, with processions, giant figures, confetti battles and fireworks. In Châlons-sur-Saône a doll is cast into the river, in Limoux »goudils« make fun of the public, whilst in Romans and Dunkirk (Dunkerque) there are well-known sailors' festivals.

Carnival

Easter (pâques) is the second most important religious celebration after Christmas. The Easter bunny is only known in Alsace. Grand processions take place in Holy Week in Perpignan and Saugues (Haute-Loire), with medieval passion plays being performed on occasion.

Easter

Many religious festivals and pilgrimages have changed into folkloristic events; their original character is best preserved in small, isolated communities. This is particularly true of the Breton pilgrimages (pardons). Some French places of pilgrimage enjoy great fame, such

Religious festivals

Grand Pardon in La Clarté-Tregastel

as Lourdes, Lisieux, Chartres and Le Puy; many villages celebrate their local saints and conduct processions to secluded chapels.

Historical festivals
The most notable of the secular festivals are 1 May (Labour Day) and 14 July (Quatorze Juillet), the national holiday. On 1 May, lilies of the valley are given as presents. The national holiday is in remembrance of the Storming of the Bastille in the year 1789, an event which does not inspire enthusiasm in all sectors of the population; however, little of the holiday's revolutionary background is in evidence today, and harmless fun is the order of the day everywhere, with parades, music and dancing in most towns and villages.

Other celebrations
Festivals are held for the most diverse of reasons: from wine-making and wine festivals (e.g. »Trois Glorieuses« in Burgundy, cider festival in Normandy) to a lavender festival in Provence; from the lemon blossom festival to cheese days (Cantal, Champagne, Roquefort, amongst others); from festivals in honour of oysters to those for nougat, cherries (Cantal) and sauerkraut (Alsace) – all in all, there are grounds enough to celebrate with good food, drink and music.

Bullfighting
Bullfights, and variations thereof, enjoy special status in southern and southwestern France. In addition to the bloody bullfight, played to Spanish rules with renowned toreros in the strongholds of Nîmes, Arles, Bayonne, Fréjus, Béziers, Dax and Beaucaire, the »course à la cocarde« is also popular, where young men, the »razeteurs«, attempt to snatch a rosette with coloured strands from between the horns of

the bull. The best bulls are accorded the same respect as racehorses, and the local press covers the exploits of the razeteurs and the animals in detail. For amateurs, mostly young people and tourists, less dangerous versions of the sport are practised using calves or young cows with blunted or padded horns. As well as these games, rodeo style events are also widespread in the south and southwest. Typical of the Camargue, for example, are the »ferrades« (marking the bull) and the »concours de Manades« (riding and bull competitions). The »abrivado« sees bulls galloped through the streets by mounted »gardians«. The »bandido« corresponds to the Spanish »encierro«, i.e. bulls are let loose in the town centre and whoever feels lucky can run in front of them.

In Stes-Maries-de-la-Mer, the festival of Marie Jacobé is held at the end of May, and the festival of Marie Salomé in October. They are attended by Sinti and Roma from all over Europe, who come to pay homage to their patron saint, Sara la Noire, whose mortal remains are said to be preserved in the crypt of the church of Stes-Maries. The men don their gardian costume, while the women and girls – except the Sinti and Roma – wear the splendid, intricate dress of the Arlésiennes. Also popular are the Mireille costumes, with their colourfully patterned (usually yellow) skirts.

Camargue

The Fête des Gardians in Arles honours, above all, the town's beautiful women

Merry dancing in Hunspach, Alsace

Arles In and around Arles, the cult of the Arlésiennes – the beautiful women of Arles, about whom so many songs have been sung – is upheld. Vincent van Gogh and Georges Bizet were amongst those who drew inspiration from them. On 1 May, at the gardians' festival in Arles, the »queen« of the town is chosen. This paradigm of traditional beauty must wear the costume with particular grace. Marvellous Arlésienne costumes may be admired in the Museon Arlaten in Arles.

Costume Traditional costume and song alsofeature in festivals in other parts of France, especially in the countryside and areas with ethnic minorities. In Alsace, the girls wear a red skirt with a black pinafore and the men wear black trousers, red waistcoats and white shirts; the girls of the Auvergne dress in colourful, broad skirts, often worn in layers; in Roussillon espadrilles (coloured cloth sandals with woven soles) and red jelly bag caps and waistbands are all part of traditional dress. The women of Brittany wear dark costume with elaborately decorated pinafores and bonnets, some of daunting proportions and joined to a ruff. A beret, usually red for festive occasions, is typical for the men of the Pays Basque.

Folk Songs and Dances

Centuries of traditional songs and dances have embedded themselves in the cultural life of each and every region; old ditties are sung and played at local fairs, as well as on religious or family occasions. Pop music – harking back to the regional identity of the past – has also discovered them and come to love them.

Alsatian brass music sounds familiar to the German neighbours. **Alsace**
One theme addressed by balladeers singing in dialect concerns the
problems facing Alsace as it stands between two great cultural areas.

The songs of Languedoc, which may be of courtly or pastoral origin, **Languedoc**
are most renowned for the »pastorelles« or shepherd's songs. Their
subject matter usually revolves around the romantic adventures of a
shepherdess with a giant knight or, more commonly, a girl's stead-
fastness when faced with a seductive knight, often one of the King of
France's soldiers. The *Lou Bouie*, a kind of partisan song of the Cathars, comes from the Albi region. Five vowels in rapid succession
contrast with a musical phrase dating back to pre-Gregorian times.
Rearranging the vowels created a secret code which enabled the re-
pressed population to communicate with one another.

The merry songs of Provence are generally accompanied by small **Provence**
flute (galoubet) and tambourine. Most popular of all is the farandole,
an up-tempo round dance. Many folk groups keep the music of the
Occitane region alive, and chansonniers sing songs with political
background.

The »sardana« is widespread in Roussillon, as it is in Catalonia. This **Roussillon**
round dance from the Cerdagne is probably Greek in origin and is
accompanied by a cobla, an ensemble of some 11 to 15 musicians
with highly original instruments. Coblas can be heard in many places
during the summer months, particularly in Perpignan (in front of
the loge de mer). Catalonian chansonniers sing songs both traditional and modern, often with political content.

The Basque country is famous for its beautiful, melancholic choral **Pays Basque**
songs. The dances with their acrobatic figures are among the most
spectacular in Europe. The men let out a piercing cry in the process,
not unlike a cock crowing. Typical instruments include the ttun ttun,
a kind of tambourine, and the xirula or txistu, a small flute or pipe
with three holes. Bandas enliven the local streets on festive occasions.
The *Guernikako Arbola*, a song about the fueros – ancient Basque
privileges – is a kind of national anthem in all seven Basque provinces on both sides of the border.

Brittany is home to almost all varieties of Celtic folk music. Lively **Britanny**
festivals and night-time dances (Fest Noz) preserve the link to other
Celtic regions (Ireland, Cornwall, Wales, Scotland, Galicia). Numerous Cercles Celtiques play folk music with typical instruments such
as the bagpipes and Celtic harp.

Famous People

Who was responsible for Foucault's pendulum, and who took the first photograph? What do Louis XIV, Napoleon, de Gaulle and Mitterrand have in common? In the fields of art, science, history and politics, French men and women have made decisive contributions.

André Marie Ampère (1775–1836)

Mathematician and physicist André-Marie Ampère, born in Lyon, developed the theory of electromagnetism, constructed a telegraph and determined the properties of the magnetic field surrounding an electrically charged conductor. The unit of measurement of electric current is named after him.

Founder of electromagnetism

Antoine Henri Becquerel (1852–1908)

The native Parisian was professor at the Musée d'Histoire Naturelle from 1892, and from 1895 at the École Polytechnique there. In 1896 he discovered that uranium salts emitted rays similar to X-rays; three years later he succeeded in providing photographic evidence of the deflection of beta particles, one constituent of this radiation. The SI unit of radioactive decay (Bq) is named after the recipient of the 1903 Nobel Prize.

Discoverer of radioactivity

Bernard of Clairvaux (around 1090–1153)

Of noble Burgundian stock, the monk, abbot and preacher Bernard de Clairvaux, reformer of the Benedictine order in the 12th century, was one of the leading figures of his age. Having joined the Cîteaux mother-abbey of the Cistercians in 1112, he founded a new house as abbot in Clairvaux in 1115. Harnessing his extraordinary powers of will and belief, his great intelligence and eloquence, he initiated the foundation of numerous monasteries. It was he who, in the name of Pope Eugenius III, preached the Second Crusade. In the 15th century, he was given the sobriquet »doctor mellifluus« (Latin for »honey-sweet doctor«); hence the beehive shown in depictions of him. He was elevated to Doctor of the Church in 1830.

Reformer of European monasticism

Louis Blériot (1872–1936)

The pilot Louis Blériot was a pioneer in the history of aviation: on 25 July 1909 he became the first man to cross the English Channel, from Calais to Dover, flying a »Blériot XI« monoplane with 25 horsepower.

Aviation pioneer

← *Louis XIV, the Sun King, painted in 1701 by Hyacinthe Rigaud*

Jean-François Champollion (1790–1832)

Place des Ecritures in Figeac

Born in Figeac in the Lot valley, J.-F. Champollion took part in Napoleon's Egyptian expedition, and in 1822 succeeded, after intensive research, in identifying Egyptian hieroglyphics as an alphabetic script. The key to his achievement was the »Rosetta Stone« (in Arabic »Rashid«, an Egyptian port), a trilingual inscription from the year 196 BC. From 1831, Champollion taught at the Collège de France, as the first professor of Egyptology. Figeac commemorates its famous son in the form of a huge replica of the Rosetta inscriptions.

Jean Cocteau (1889–1963)

Artistic all-rounder

Jean Cocteau, born in Milly-la-Forêt, was a successful author and poet, film director (*La Belle et la Bête*), scriptwriter (*Les Enfants du Paradis*), dramatist (*Orphée*), painter, choreographer and librettist (his libretti for opera and ballet were set to music by Honegger, Stravinsky and Milhaud, amongst others). More than anything, he personified to a great degree what other nationalities admire in the French: the lightness, sharpness and brilliance of French esprit. His work encompasses Futurist and Dadaist experiments, but is best aligned with late Surrealism. In 1955, Cocteau became a member of the Académie Française.

Louis Jacques Mandé Daguerre (1789–1851)

Inventor of photography

L. J. M. Daguerre from Cormeilles was a painter and the inventor of the daguerreotype process of photography. In 1822, he developed the diorama, a way of observing a round horizon. His aim, however, was to fix the camera obscura image by chemical means. Only after his work with J. N. Niepce, who had been working in the same field, did he manage to expose and fixate silver plates with iodine vapour in 1838. While his process was not the first photographic process invented, it was the first one that made photography commercially effective. His invention was rewarded by the French government with an annual pension of 6000 francs.

Alexandre Gustave Eiffel (1832–1923)

With his famous tower in Paris, opened in 1889 for the World's Fair, Eiffel created the definitive landmark of the city on the Seine, perhaps of France itself. Born in Dijon, the engineer founded a metal construction company which operated throughout the country (the Truyère bridge at Garabit, for example). For the idea and construction of the Eiffel Tower, he was indebted to his engineers M. Koechlin and E. Nougier. However Eiffel's enthusiasm for the project only really ignited when the architect Stephen Sauvestre introduced the three tiers and round arch of the lower level, creating a greater sense of harmony. Eiffel also constructed the iron framework for the Statue of Liberty in New York. From 1903 onwards, he concerned himself with the intensive study of aerodynamics. He died in Paris in 1923.

Engineering genius

Léon Foucault (1819–68)

Born in Paris, Léon Foucault became a science editor in 1845, a physicist at the Paris Observatory in 1855, a member of the Bureau des Longitudes in 1862 and, in 1865, a member of the Parisian Académie des Sciences. In 1850, he invented the rotating mirror process to determine the speed of light; in 1862 he helped in the breakthrough of the wave theory of light. He found fame on the strength of his 1850–51 pendulum experiment in Paris, which proved the rotation of the Earth. He also made significant contributions in the fields of thermal and electrical studies.

Distinguished experimenter

Jean Gabin (1904–76)

The famous film actor (real name Jean-Alexis Moncorgé) from Neuilly-sur-Seine starred in numerous films from the 1930s until shortly before his death. He frequently portrayed simple characters from the lower echelons of society; in later years, he took on mature, established male roles. From 1957 onwards, he made the role of Inspector Maigret, Georges Simenon's crime novel hero, his own. More often than not, Gabin played characters marked by life's travails, endearing himself to the audience through his roles as positive figures, rough at the edges but with a certain charm. His finest films include *Pépé le Moko* (1936), *Le quai des brumes* (1938) and *L'Affaire Dominici* (1973).

Icon of French cinema

Jean Gabin in »Le Chat« (1970)

Charles de Gaulle (1890–1970)

Symbol of resistance and reconstruction

Hailing from Lille, the politician and general Charles de Gaulle had a lasting impact on the fate of France since the Second World War, or, more precisely, since 1940. Active in the First World War, he became a lecturer in military history in St-Cyr in 1920 and, from 1925, took his place in the Supreme War Council. In the 1930s, he recorded his political and military ideas in a series of theoretical papers. Promoted to the rank of brigadier general, in 1940 he became Undersecretary of State for National Defence. In his radio broadcast from London on 18 June 1940, he appealed to France to join Britain in continuing the war against the Axis powers and rose to lead the Résistance. He declared himself head of the French government and leader of the Free French Forces (»Nous, Général de Gaulle, Chef des Français Libres«), establishing separate political and military organizations for the Free France movement. Against this background, he formed a provisional government in Paris in 1944 and took up the post of prime minister and the provisional presidency in November 1945, before taking a 12-year break from active politics in January 1946, having failed to push through extended presidential powers. In 1958, he was elected president of the Fifth Republic, pursuing a policy of independence for the »Grande Nation« by relinquishing the French colonies, increasing nuclear capabilities and taking France out of NATO. With tensions in domestic politics growing ever more extreme, the highly controversial patriot with the bearing of an absolute monarch resigned for the last time in 1969.

Henri IV (1553–1610)

Good King Henry

Henri IV, still known today as »le Bon Roi Henri«, became King of Navarra as Henri III in 1562 and leader of the Huguenots in 1581. His marriage to Marguerite de Valois, Charles IX's sister, was intended to effect reconciliation with the Catholic party. This plan was scuppered by the St Bartholomew's Day massacre: in the night of 24 August 1572, the leaders of the Huguenot nobility, in Paris for Henri's wedding, were murdered along with thousands of their fellow believers. The command had been issued by Catherine de Medici, the queen mother. Henri IV was only able to save himself by denouncing his beliefs. He was kept a prisoner of the court until his escape in 1576. On the death of Henri III (1589), he staked a claim to the throne, yet it was not until 1594 – after lengthy negotiation and his conversion to Catholicism (»Paris is well worth a Mass«) – that he was crowned as the first king from the House of Bourbon. As a ruler, Henri IV endeavoured to overcome the effects of civil war, to establish religious peace by proclaiming freedom of beliefs (Edict of Nantes 1598) and equality of faiths, to rehabilitate the country's finances and develop the country by expanding transportation routes. According to legend, he wished that every peasant in his kingdom may have a chicken in the cooking pot on Sundays. During his reign, the colonization of Canada commences (Québec is founded in 1668), and the recentralization of royal power prepared the ground for the absolutist state. Henri IV was assassinated in 1610.

Jeanne d'Arc (around 1410–31)

Joan of Arc, a national hero to the French, was born a peasant's daughter in the Vosges. Raised with strict beliefs, she heard »voices« call her to liberate France from the English, who tried to force a claim on the French throne in the Hundred Years' War (from 1339). In Chinon and Sully-sur-Loire, Jeanne d'Arc persuaded the Dauphin (Charles VII) to crown himself king. Her greatest military success was the relief of the town of Orléans (8 May 1429), besieged by the English, a turning point in the war. As the fighting continued, she was taken captive by the Burgundians, who handed her over to their English allies. She was put before a clerical tribunal and, on 30 May 1431, was burned alive in Rouen. The king however, to whom she had returned power, was relieved to be rid of a troublesome sectarian and awkward »competition«. On her canonization in 1920, she was declared the second patron saint of France.

The liberator of France

Louis XIV (1638–1715)

Louis XIV, born in the castle of St-Germain-en-Laye and titled »le Roi Soleil« (»Sun King«), was the ultimate personification of absolutist principles (»L'Etat c'est moi«, »I am the state«). To unify the country, he revoked the Edict of Nantes in 1685 and also targeted other attempts at religious reform. On the other hand, he defended the privileged status of Gallican Catholicism, even against the pope. Despite political and military successes, he was unable to enforce the yearned for hegemony of France in Europe.

The Sun King

François Mitterrand (1916–96)

Even today, French heads of state – regardless of allegiance – still have something autocratic about them, or aristocratic in more positive instances. This was also true of the socialist François Mitterrand, who left his mark on France in the 1980s and 1990s. He was born in 1916, the son of a stationmaster from Jarnac (Dép. Charente). As a student he joined nationalist groups in Paris. As a POW he escaped German captivity in 1941 and became an official of the Vichy régime, but soon got involved in the Résistance. It was only on meeting de Gaulle in 1943 that Mitterrand moved into the socialist camp, as a deep antipathy existed between the two from the very first moment. After 1945 he passed through many stations of left-wing politics. He was a minister on eleven occasions in changing cabinets of the Fifth Republic. He stood for the highest office three times, first

The secret monarch

Mitterand after his re-election in 1988

elected in 1981, and again in 1988. Notable achievements of his legislative periods include the abolition of the death penalty, the regionalization of France, the liberalization of the media, reconciliation with
Germany and the preparations for a unified Europe. In Paris he ensured his own memorial in the form of spectacular building works,
from the Louvre pyramid to the new National Library. His terms of
office were not, however, free of scandal, from the attack on the
Greenpeace ship *Rainbow Warrior* to illicit fund raising for the Socialists and the illegal telephone tapping of thousands of citizens.
Twice the French disapproved of his policies and presented him with
a Conservative government. At this time, Mitterand displayed his
great skills of integration and, with the nation divided into two political camps, actually managed to ease the situation and make France a
more tolerant place.

The Montgolfier Brothers (18th–19th Century)

**The first
balloonists** Michel-Joseph (1740–1810) and Etienne-Jacques (1745–99) de
Montgolfier from Vidalon-lés-Annonay launched their first test
flights using smoke-filled cloth sacks in their father's paper factory in
1782. On 5 June 1783, their first public demonstration took place, an
unmanned hot-air balloon named the Montgolfière. The air in the
canvas sack lined with paper was heated by glowing coals. In the
same year, on 21 November 1783, the first manned flight took place
close to Paris, with J.-F. Pilâtre de Rozier and F.-L. Marquis d'Ar-
landes as passengers.

Napoléon Bonaparte (1769–1821)

Conqueror and dictator

Corsica's Napoléon Bonaparte, born of a patrician family, rose quickly through the ranks of the French Revolutionary Army. A brigadier general at 24, he took command of the Italian and Egyptian campaigns and cemented his reputation by overthrowing the Directory (the governing body that followed Robespierre's Reign of Terror) and seizing power of France as First Consul.

On the strength of a referendum, he took the opportunity to declare himself Consul for life in 1802, and first Emperor of France in 1804 (Napoleon I). The hereditary enmity with England led him to wage wars against the Grand Coalition led by the English, defeating Austria and Prussia in the process. He invaded Portugal and Spain to create a continental barrier and hurt England through isolation – the first all-out economic war in history. Eventually he declared war on Russia, underlining his ambition of ruling Europe in its entirety. The failure of this campaign, defeat in the Battle of Nations at Leipzig (1813) and the occupation of Paris by the Allies forced Napoleon to abdicate (1814). He was subsequently exiled on Elba. In 1815, in his famous »Hundred Days«, he attempted to regain power, but his troops were unequivocally defeated at Waterloo. He was exiled to the British island of St Helena in the South Atlantic, where he died in 1821. His mortal remains were ceremoniously delivered to Paris in 1840 to be entombed in the Dome Church at Les Invalides. In spite of his un-

Napoléon I by J.L. David, 1812

scrupulous ambition, which saw millions of people suffer or die, Napoleon always remained a hero in the French consciousness, his legend untouchable. His image as saviour of the Revolution was glorified in romanticism (by Victor Hugo, amongst others). In actual fact, Napoleon's Code Civil of 1804, the first civic statute book, held fast the fundamental gains of the Revolution, namely the conditions pertaining to the property and finances of the middle-classes.

Louis Pasteur (1822–95)

Researcher of alcoholic fermentation

Chemist, biologist and physician Louis Pasteur from Dôle in Franche-Comté was, from 1848, professor in Dijon, Strasbourg and Lille, and then Paris from 1857. He developed the process named after him to conserve fermenting drinks (milk, beer, wine) by heating them to temperatures below 100°C/212°F: this process of pasteurization kills off the bacteria or yeasts which cause fermentation. His fundamental discovery was that micro-organisms need air to enter previously bacteria-free substances. Hence he was, indeed, one of the key founders of bacteriology and sterilization technology. In the field of medicine, he did a great service to mankind in discovering various vaccines, the most important of which can be used against rabies transmitted by dogs (establishment of Pasteur Institutes at home and abroad based on the original »Institut Pasteur« in Paris to manufacture and distribute the vaccine). Louis Pasteur is commemorated by several monuments, two of which are in Paris close to where he died.

Marquise de Pompadour (1721–64)

Formidable mistress of the king

The Marquise de Pompadour, born Jeanne Antoinette Poisson, was one of those women who made history as the mistress of a monarch. Single-minded and equipped with a good education, provided by her mother's lover, she found her way to the court of King Louis XV, who brought her to Versailles in 1745. Married to the junior financier Le Normand d'Etiolles, she became the king's official mistress. She also took an initial interest in promoting art and science: spurred on by the success of Meissner porcelain, she established the porcelain manufactory at Sèvres. When, after some years, Louis XV's interest in her waned, her position remained strong enough that she still had influence over him; her reach extended to his ministries as well. She is said to have played an important role in France's pact with Austria against Prussia and England in 1756 and even to have had the power to name the military commanders in the Seven Years' War.

Jean-Paul Sartre (1905–80)

Philosopher of nothingness

The existential author and philosopher Jean-Paul Sartre was born in Paris to a bourgeois family. He also went to school and studied in the capital, before teaching philosophy in Le Havre and Berlin in the 1930s. During the Second World War he joined the Résistance after his time as a prisoner of war in 1940–41. In 1945 he founded the magazine *Les Temps modernes*, and in 1973 he was co-founder of the *Libération* newspaper. He distanced himself from the French Communist Party in 1956 in the wake of Soviet intervention in Hungary, which he criticized vehemently. Towards the end of the 1960s, his involvement in politics grew stronger, and he acted as an agitator against the Warsaw Pact invasion of the CSSR in 1968, became chairman of the Vietnam War Crimes Tribunal initiated by Bertrand Russell, and defended left-wing movements. His essay published in 1943 entitled *L'être et le néant* (*Being and Nothingness*) stands as the core text of French existentialism. Starting out from Kierkegaard, Husserl, Heidegger, Hegel and Jaspers, he developed the basic atheist concept, negating all transcendental beliefs, that existence precedes essence. Hence man lives in a world without sense, in which he strives to find an essence. He is wholly and solely responsible for developing his

Jean-Paul Sartre with his partner Simone de Beauvoir in 1970

freedom. Conscious action, which Sartre terms »engaged freedom« towards a certain goal, reveals itself as a search for illusion-free humanism. In his second main work of philosophy *La Critique de la raison dialectique* (*Critique of Dialectical Reason*; Vol. 1 in 1960), Sartre expands on the idea of individual freedom with collective consciousness and political action, grounded in a modified Marxist dialectic. Sartre's literary output opens up the debate on philosophical-existential questioning, above all addressing the problems of freedom (»littérature engagée«).

Jules Verne (1828–1905)

Born in Nantes, the author Jules Verne came to fame through his many adventure novels. His early interests, however, went in several different directions. He studied law in Paris and wrote libretti for the opera and dramas before turning his attention to the technical, exotic and utopian novel in 1863. With his »journeys of discovery« on and below the earth he became one of the first authors to write in the fashion of popular science and to transpose the technological advances of the industrial age into utopian fiction. For many years, Jules Verne's gripping tales were considered reading material for the younger generation, who did indeed cherish his novels as they do today. As the genre of science fiction has grown in stature however, the works of Jules Verne now find favour with literary critics as well. His most famous novels are *Vingt mille lieues sous les mers* (*20,000 Leagues under the Sea*; 1869–70) and *Le tour du monde en 80 jours* (*Around the World in 80 Days*).

Inventor of the future

Practicalities

WHEN IS THE BEST TIME TO GO TO FRANCE? WHAT IS THE SPEED LIMIT ON THE AUTOROUTES? IMPORTANT INFORMATION AND THINGS WORTH KNOWING FOR AN ENJOYABLE HOLIDAY.

Accommodation

Hotels

Classification and prices
French hotels are classified according to level of comfort and standard of service by the Comité Régional du Tourisme. There are five categories, from one star (lowest category) to four stars, with the additional »L« classification (luxury hotels). The hotels are identified by a hexagonal blue sign with a white letter »H« and the appropriate number of stars.

Early booking is essential for stays during the high season. As a rule, a credit card or advance payment (*arrhes*) will be required. In France itself it is possible to book accommodation in almost all tourist offices (a small charge is normally made).

Prices must be displayed at the entrance to the hotel and in the rooms. In areas where tourism is important, prices are significantly lower (approx. 25–30%) in the off-season as compared to the peak season. Single rooms are seldom available; the use of a double room by a single person only sometimes costs a little less. A third bed can be provided for an additional charge of about 30%. In many areas frequented by tourists, a visitors' tax is imposed (0.50–1 €).

Logis de France
Approximately 3200 small and medium-sized hotels have come together in the Fédération Logis de France. Moderately priced, these family-run establishments aim to provide a friendly atmosphere, a modern level of comfort and good local cuisine. They can be identified by the green sign with a yellow fireplace.
A series of hotels caters especially for families, hikers, cyclists, anglers, winter sports enthusiasts, wine lovers etc.; the »Logis de Caractère« in historical houses are very interesting. The directory appears annually and is available in book shops as well as from the Fédération Logis de France.

Relais & Châteaux
The hotels brought together in the group Relais & Châteaux offers an especially stylish atmosphere, and most have excellent restaurants.

Châteaux & Hôtels de France
Over 500 special hotels and restaurants of different categories – from plain and simple to exclusive, but always enjoying a privileged location – are collected together in the organisation Châteaux & Hôtels de France.

IMPORTANT ADDRESSES

HOTELS

► **Logis de France**
83 Avenue d'Italie, F-75013 Paris
Tel. 01 45 84 83 84
Fax 01 44 24 04 59
www.logis-de-france.fr

► **Relais & Châteaux**
in France
Tel. 08 25 32 32 32
in the UK and Republic of Ireland
Tel. 00800 2000 0002
in the USA and Canada
Tel. + 1 800 735 2478
in Australia
Tel. + 61 2 9299 2280
in New Zealand
Tel. 00 800 254 50066
www.relaischateaux.com

► **Châteaux & Hôtels de France**
84 Avenue Victor Cresson
F-92441 Issy-les-Moulineaux
Tel. 01 72 72 92 02
www.chateauxhotels.com

PRIVATE ROOMS
BED & BREAKFAST

► **Gîtes de France**
see below

► **Bienvenue au Château**
Les Alizés, La Rigourdière
F-35510 Cesson Sevigne
www.bienvenue-au-chateau.com

► **Further websites**
www.bedbreak.com
www.bbfrance.com

HOLIDAY HOMES

► **Gîtes de France**
59 Rue Saint-Lazare
F-75439 Paris Cedex 09
Fax 01 42 81 28 53
www.gites-de-france.com

► **Chez Nous**
Spring Mill, Earby,
Barnoldswick, Lancs, BB94 0AA
Tel. 0870 197 1000
www.cheznous.com

► **Gite.com**
432 Wellington St West
Toronto, M5V 1E3, Canada
Tel. 1-416-932-8015
Fax 1-416-932-8016
www.gite.com

► **Relax in France**
Tel. +33 4 68 78 23 34
info@relaxinfranceonline.com
www.relaxinfranceonline.com

► **Clévacances**
BP 52166
F-31022 Toulouse Cedex 2
Fax 05 61 13 55 94
www.clevacances.com

CAMPING & CARAVANNING

► **FFCC**
78, Rue de Rivoli, F-75004 Paris
Fax 01 42 72 70 21
www.ffcc.fr, www.camping-car.org

► **Les Castels**
Manoir de Terre-Rouge
F-35270 Bonnemain
Tel. 02 23 16 03 20
Fax 02 23 16 03 23
www.les-castels.com

► **The Camping and Caravanning Club**

► **Greenfields House, Westwood Way**
Coventry CV4 8JH
Tel. 0845 130 7631
www.campingandcaravanning
club.co.uk

YOUTH HOSTELS

► **International Youth Hostel Federation (IYHF)**
Trevelyan House
Dimple Road, Matlock
Derbyshire, DE4 3YH
Tel. 0 16 29 / 59 26 00, fax 59 27 02
www.yha.org.uk

► **Hostelling International**
2nd Floor, Gate House
Fretherne Road Welwyn
Garden City, Herts AL8 6RD
Tel. +44 (0) 1707 324170

Fax: +44 (0) 1707 323980
www.hihostels.com

► **Fédération Unie des Auberges de Jeunesse (FUAJ)**
27 Rue Pajol, F-75018 Paris
Fax 01 44 89 87 49
www.fuaj.org

► **Ligue Française pour les Auberges de Jeunesse (LFAJ)**
67 Rue Vergniaud, F-75013 Paris
Fax 01 44 16 78 80
www.auberges-de-jeunesse.com

Relais Routiers The very reasonably priced Relais Routiers on major roads are used primarily by long-distance lorry drivers. They provide mostly simple but good accommodation. The *Guide des Relais Routiers* is available in French book shops (www.relais-routiers.com).

Information Directories of the named organizations as well as numerous hotel chains with branches all over the country (including especially reasonably priced hotels such as Etap, Fasthotel, Formule 1) are also available from Maison de la France, tourist offices (►Information) and in book shops. Local tourist offices also publish hotel directories.

Countryside Holidays · Holiday Apartments

Tourisme rural Within the rubric »tourisme rural«, various possibilities are offered for holidays in the countryside. The Fédération Française des Gîtes de France offers reasonably priced accommodation, ranging from hotels, through simple country inns (ferme-auberge), holiday apartments and homes (gîte rural), and simple accommodation along hiking trials (gîte d'etape), to camping on farms (Camping à la Ferme). Directories are available from tourist offices (►Information) as well as from Gîtes de France. Gîtes de France also publishes the directories *Chambres d'Hôtes*, *Campings et Châlets-Loisirs* and *Gîtes d'Etape*. In addition, a large number of private companies arrange holiday homes and apartments.

Private Rooms · Bed & Breakfast

Private rooms
Bed & breakfast A stay in a bed & breakfast promises an especially personal experience of France, and is normally significantly cheaper than a comparable hotel. The French terms for this type of accommodation are *chambre d'hôte* (room with breakfast) and *table d'hôte* (with meals).

Look out for the green signs on main thoroughfares that indicate the whereabouts of establishments a little off the main drag. Privately rented rooms (meublés) and apartments can be found in many towns (mostly offered for a week or more). Directories are available from Gîtes de France (▶p.107), Clévances and local tourist offices. The AA guide book *Bed & Breakfast France*, produced in association with Gîtes de France, contains detailed information on chambre d'hote accommodation throughout the country.

It is not surprising that in a country as rich in chateaux – whether plain and simple country residences or noble palaces – as France, many owners are happy to welcome guests. The prices, considering what is on offer, are mostly quite moderate. The Association Bienve-nue au Château (www.bienvenue-au-chateau.com) produces a direc-tory for northwestern France (so far) with over 130 addresses.

Bed & breakfast in a chateau

Camping

Camping has an important role to play in France. There are about 10,000 local authority-run or private camp sites (*terrains de camp-ing*), and almost every place of touristic significance has at least one, and often several, sites. They are officially classified according to the amenities on offer, being allocated from one to four stars. One star is granted to those sites of a simple standard (e.g. only cold water showers), while four-star sites have luxurious facilities. During the high season, camp sites along the main holiday routes are mostly full, but it is normally possible to find a site with some room a little off the beaten track in the hinterland. Wild camping (*camping sauvage*) is permitted only with the permission of the landowner or on the very cheap, small *aires naturelles de camping*, untouched natural sites normally without warm water or electricity; on beaches and in pro-tected areas it is strictly forbidden. Outside the holiday season, i.e. from October to May, most camp sites are closed. It is useful to be in possession of the Camping Card International. Available to Camp-ing and Caravanning Club members, this plastic identity card is rec-ognized at camp sites all over France.

Camp sites

Wild camping

Camping card

There are also a large number of parking spaces for motorhomes and campers, ranging from simple spaces with only the most basic amenities and waste disposal services to comfortable sites with shops, sanitary facilities, swimming pool and recreation room. The spaces lie on the edge of towns or in the town itself and can often be used free of charge, with some costing 5–10 € per night.

Motorhome parking spaces

Camping à la Ferme, camping on a farm, is growing ever more pop-ular (▶Countryside Holidays); there are about 2500 at present. Cas-tel campings, peculiar to France, are camp sites in the grounds of country chateaux and seats of the nobility and gentry (Les Castels).

Camping à la Ferme
Castel Camping

Information
The Fédération Française de Camping et de Caravaning (FFCC) publishes a comprehensive guide, the magazine *Camping-car Magazine*, as well as the *Guide des Aires d'Etapes Camping-car* for motorhome parking spaces (in book shops and newsagents). A large selection of camp sites is described in the AA guide book *Caravan and Camping France* and Michelin's *Camping France*. Information is also provided by regional and local tourist offices.

Youth Hostels

In France there are about 190 youth hostels (Auberges de Jeunesse). They are run by two organizations, the FUAJ and the LFAJ, and can be used by those with a YHA membership card, available from the International Youth Hostel Federation. Book early if you are travelling in the peak season; the length of stay is restricted to three days during this time. The international hostel directory is available from book shops and member organizations.

Arrival · Before the Journey

Getting There

By car
The quickest way across the English Channel to France is via the Eurotunnel. Passengers drive their cars onto the train, *Le Shuttle*, which covers the distance from Folkestone to Coquelles near Calais in 35 minutes. At peak times there are four trains every hour (tel. 0870 535 3535; www.eurotunnel.com). Drivers can also take their cars across the Channel by ferry (see below).

There is an extensive network of motorways, or autoroutes, in France. On many of the main autoroutes a toll is payable (▶Transport). Two routes head south from Calais: the A16 (known as »l'Européenne«), via Boulogne, Abbeville and Rouen; and the A26 (»l' autoroute des Anglais«) via Arras and Reims. Traffic for the east and southeast of France should take the latter, joining the A39 at Dijon. The A7 Rhone valley autoroute runs from Lyon south to Marseille.

Those heading for Normandy and northern Brittany are advised to take the A16 and then head for Le Havre, then Caen, on the A 29, which leaves the A28 before Rouen. Travellers to France's southwest can also go via Rouen, joining the A28 and then the A10 to Bordeaux. Another route to central and southern France is via the A71 to Clermont Ferrand and then the A75 down to Beziers. The A20 leads south towards Limoges and then Toulouse. To get to Paris from Calais, take the A16 and then join the A1, the so-called »autoroute du Nord«, which runs from Lille to Paris and is one of the busiest autoroutes in France. The website www.autoroutes.fr (also in English) gives current traffic information and suggests the best route to your destination in France. For further information see ▶p.163.

Taking the car ferry is sometimes cheaper than using the tunnel. P&O operate a service between Dover and Calais (tel. 01304 863000; www.po-ferries-uk.co.uk), as do Seafrance (tel. 0871 22 22 500; www.seafrance.com). It takes 1 hour 30 minutes to make the crossing. LD Lines (tel. 0844 576 8836; www.ldlines.co.uk) and Transmanche (tel. 0800 917 1201; www.transmancheferries.co.uk) provide services between Newhaven and Dieppe, Portsmouth and Le Havre, Dover and Boulogne, Dover and Dieppe, and Rosslare (Republic of Ireland) and Le Havre. Norfolkline (tel. 0208 127 8308; www.norfolkline.eu) offer ferry crossings from Dover to Dunkirk (Dunkerque). Brittany Ferries (tel. 0871 244 0744; www.brittany-ferries.co.uk) run services from Portsmouth to St-Malo, Caen and Cherbourg, from Poole to Cherbourg, and from Plymouth to Roscoff. Speedferries announced its closure in early 2009 and no longer operates its Dover to Boulogne service. There are many ferry ticket operators, such as www.ferrysmart.co.uk or www.directferries.co.uk, where you can hunt for bargains at one single website.

By ferry

Eurolines run several coaches daily from London Victoria to Paris. The journey time is 9 hours 30 minutes. Further Eurolines services head further south and to other destinations in France.

By bus or coach

All rail routes from the UK to France are via the Eurostar to Paris. Some trains stop briefly at Lille International. The main SNCF lines (including the TGV) emerge radially from the capital (▶ Transport, p.164).

By rail

It is also possible to travel from the UK to various French destinations using French motorail (www.raileurope.co.uk/frenchmotorail). There is an overnight service from Calais to Avignon, Fréjus (for St Tropez) and Nice; another runs from Calais to Brive, Toulouse and Narbonne, also overnight. Motorail services operate from mid-May to mid-Sept, southbound on Fri nights (also Sun nights from late July to late Aug), northbound on Sat nights (also Mon nights from late July to late Aug). The website www.seat61.com is a good source of information. With the SNCF motorail service, passengers have the advantage of being able to travel on any other train (▶ Transport, p.167).

Motorail

Many French cities are served by flights from the UK, many of them direct. The **main hub** is Paris Charles de Gaulle airport (CDG 2) 23km/14mi north of the city centre near Roissy; other important connecting airports are Paris Orly, Strasbourg and Lyon. Air France services connect not only Heathrow and London City airports to Paris CDG, but also offer direct flights from Aberdeen, Birmingham,

By air

⬤ BUS AND TRAIN TRAVEL

▶ **Bus / Coach**
Eurolines UK: tel. 0870 514 3219;
www.eurolines.com
Eurolines France: tel. 0 892 89 90
91, www.eurolines.fr

▶ **Train**
Eurostar
St Pancras International
Pancras Road

London NW1 2QP
Tel. 08705 186 186
www.eurostar.com
SNCF / Rail Europe
▶p.167

▶ **Motorail**
Railsavers
Tel. 01253 595555
www.railsavers.com

Bristol, Edinburgh, Manchester, Newcastle and Southampton airports to France's capital. Air France passengers changing planes in CDG 2 to continue their journey into the provinces do not need to check in again; their luggage is transferred directly onto the next plane. British Airways operates frequent flights from London Heathrow to Paris. Look online or ask at travel agents for the latest information on the numerous services offered by budget airlines, including flights from UK airports other than London (as well as Dublin) to French airports other than CDG 2. Air France offer non-stop flights from the USA (e.g. from JFK airport in New York) to CDG 2; in conjunction with Qantas Airways they also operate services from Sydney to Paris, with a stopover in Singapore or Hong Kong. For further information on air travel see ▶Transport p.167.

Immigration and Customs Regulations

Travel documents
Citizens of the European Union require a valid passport or identity card for entry into France. Children under 16 years of age must carry a children's passport or ID card or be entered in the parent's passport. All holders of non European Union passports should check entry requirements to France with the relevant French Embassy.

Car papers
National driving licences and vehicle registration documents of European Union nationals are recognized, and others can also normally use their own driving licences for up to one year, though purchasing an international driving licence is a good idea. In the case of traffic incidents involving damage to vehicles, the **international green car insurance card** is required. Cars without a European Union number plate must carry the oval national identity sticker.

Pets and travel
Those who wish to bring pets (dogs, cats, ferrets) to France require an EU pet pass, which replaced the documentation required by the

individual European states in October 2004. The animal must be fitted with a microchip (transponder) or have an identifying tattoo. It must have had a rabies vaccination at least 30 days and no more than twelve months before travelling.

If papers go missing, it is very helpful to be in possession of photocopies. They assist in reporting the details of the loss to the police and in the provision of temporary replacement papers by the relevant consulate. Keep the copies separate from the documents themselves. *Copies*

Within the EU, including France and the UK, goods traffic for private use is to a large extent duty free. The distinction between private and commercial use is defined by the following guideline amounts: 800 cigarettes, 400 cigarillos, 200 cigars, 1 kilogramme of tobacco, 10 litres of spirits, 90 litres of wine (of which a maximum of 60 litres can be sparkling), and 110 litres of beer. Should a customs inspection occur, a plausible explanation for the intended private use of the goods is needed. *European Single Market*

For travellers from non-EU countries, the allowance for people over 17 entering France is 200 cigarettes (or 100 cigarillos, 50 cigars or 250g/9oz tobacco); 2 litres/0.5 US gal of wine and 2 litres/0.5 US gal of sparkling wine or 1 litre/0.26 US gal of spirits with more than 22% alcohol content, or 2 litres/0.5 US gal of spirits with less than 22% alcohol content; 500g/1.1lb of coffee or 200g/7oz of coffee extract; 100g/3.5oz of tea or 40g/1.4oz of tea extract; 50g/1.75oz of perfume or 0.25 litres/8.5 US fl oz of eau de toilette; plus presents to a value of €175. Returning US citizens who have been away for 48 hours or more are allowed to bring back, once every 30 days, US$800 worth of merchandise duty-free. *Customs regulations for non-EU nationals*

► Money *Foreign currency regulations*

Travel Insurance

The European Health Insurance Card (EU EHIC card), available in the UK from post offices, has replaced the E111 form. Medical care is only provided to card holders for chronic ailments and in the case of an emergency; it is not possible to use the EHIC card to purposely seek treatment in France instead of in your home country. The card must be presented to the French doctor or hospital. The law of the land applies with regard to medical care. In many cases, supplementary charges are imposed. If the EHIC card is not accepted, the charges must be paid and the patient must seek reimbursement at home. Ensure you get a receipt for any payment, and that it is clear what treatment has been given. Since some of the costs for medical treatment and medication typically have to be covered by the patient, *Medical insurance* and the costs for return transportation may not be covered by the normal health insurance, additional travel insurance is recommended. Non-EU citizens should take out private travel insurance.

Beaches

Channel coast Broad beaches with fine sand are found near Calais. Along the 60km/37mi-long coast of Picardy south of the Authie estuary stretches northern France's most extensive area of dunes, the Marquenterre. The dunes are of fine sand, and now and then reach heights of 30m/98ft. Further south, near Ault and Mers-les-Bains, the sandy beach is covered with pebbles and lined by steep, imposing cliffs. The long coast of Normandy has many faces: rugged, steep cliffs, flat, broad, yellow-hued beaches with fine sand as well as shingle beaches. In Brittany, too, the coast is varied: broad, sandy beaches, mudflats, and small protected bays of sand and shingle, even in the west, where the sea exhibits its wilder side and the coast is no longer so inviting for bathers. The difference between high and low tide is however very marked on the coast of Brittany, and at high tide the broad, sandy beaches are flooded with water.

Atlantic The Atlantic coast in the regions Pays de la Loire, Poitou-Charentes and Aquitaine has small bays with fine sand and surrounded by high cliffs, endlessly long beaches with white sand and long dunes lined by pine forest. The almost endless flat sandy beaches between the mouth of the Gironde and the Spanish border are highly prized; many sections are quite deserted.

Miles and miles of sandy beaches attract bathers to the Atlantic coast, like here near Mimizan

Mediterranean

Large holiday centres were created in Languedoc-Roussillon with its miles of flat beaches with fine sand (no tides) between Montpellier and Perpignan. On the Côte d'Azur holidaymakers stumble upon predominantly small sand or shingle bays, surrounded by white or red cliffs.

Water quality

As it is constantly replenished and because of the tides, the water on the Atlantic coast is good quality. The coast of the English Channel and the beaches of Brittany are exposed to the risk of oil pollution due to their proximity to shipping routes used by large tankers. On the Mediterranean coast the burden of industrial effluents has reduced water quality considerably. Every year the French Ministry of the Environment tests water quality both on the coast and in inshore waterways. The current results must be displayed at the town hall and at the official bathing beaches.

Lifeguard

The important bathing beaches are supervised by lifeguards. A warning service indicates whether weather or currents allow risk-free bathing. A coloured pennant indicates the status of the beach:
green: bathing unrestricted
orange: bathing dangerous!
red: bathing forbidden (no lifeguard service!)
Especially on the Atlantic coast there is often a heavy swell even when there is no wind. The considerable tidal range in the region of the English Channel (up to 14m/46ft at Mont St-Michel) demands special care.

Nudist beaches

While it is normal to go topless on all beaches, nudism is only permitted on sections of beach and in bays away from all the hustle and bustle. Information on the popular nudist beaches (»domaines naturistes«) is provided by Maison de la France and the Fédération Française du Naturisme (www.ffn-naturisme.com).

Cycling Holidays

Cycling has come to enjoy great popularity in France. The Loire valley and Brittany are magnets for tourists on two wheels, and river courses such as the Dordogne or the tow paths along the old canals offer almost perfect biking conditions. Sporting souls will find districts in which it is easy to build up a sweat in the Alps and the Pyrenees, the Massif Central and Provence, for the racing bike as well as for the mountain bike (*vélo tout-terrain*, VTT). Along with the extensive network of country roads with little traffic, there is a network of over 3000km/1860mi of cycle paths to explore. The regional and local tourist offices have designed exciting cycle tours, both short and

⊙ INFORMATION FOR CYCLISTS

▶ **Cyclists' Touring Club (CTC)**
Parklands, Railton Rd
Guildford, Surrey GU2 9JX
Tel. 0844 736 8450
Fax 0844 736 8454
www.ctc.org.uk

▶ **CTC Holidays & Tours**
Heather Evans,
Tours Co-ordinator
32 Hawthorn Walk
Newcastle upon Tyne NE4 7HP
Tel. 0191 273 8042 (after 2.30pm)
Email info@cyclingholidays.org
www.cyclingholidays.org

▶ **European
Cyclists' Federation**
Rue Joseph II 166
1000 Brussels, Belgium
Tel. +32 2 234 38 74
Fax +32 2 234 38 75
www.ecf.com

▶ **Useful websites**
www.biketoursfrance.com
www.experienceplus.com
www.veloloco.com
www.loirevalleybreaks.com
www.headwater.com

▶ **Fédération Française
de Cyclisme**
5 Rue de Rome
F-93561 Rosny-sous-Bois Cedex
Fax 01 48 94 09 97
www.ffc.fr

▶ **Fédération Française
de Cyclotourisme**
12 Rue Louis Bertrand
F-94207 Ivry-sur-Seine Cedex
Fax 01 56 20 88 99
www.ffct.org

long, and the hotel industry has adjusted to cater to cyclists; numerous Gîtes d'Etape also offer moderately priced accommodation (▶ Accommodation). The website of the CTC provides detailed information on cycling holidays in France; each tour is graded so that you can choose a suitable route. The Fédération Française de Cyclisme and the Fédération Française de Cyclotourisme are responsible for amateur cyclists.

**Organized
cycling tours**   A large number of British and French travel companies offer everything from suggesting tour routes to arranging an all-inclusive trip. Information is available from travel agents and Maison de la France (▶ Information). The European Cyclists' Federation, an organization devoted to encouraging cycling in Europe, offers maps of the twelve cycle routes that go under the name »EuroVelo«.

**Getting there by
train or bus**   A somewhat tedious but generally unproblematic way of travelling with a bike is to take it on a train, including the TGV (▶ Transport). Specialized companies such as Natours offer a comfortable outward and return journey by bus.

At about 300 stations, the SNCF offer bikes for hire, which can be re-   Cycle hire
turned to a different station. The same applies to the RER in Paris
and the surrounding areas. There are rental firms in practically all
areas and towns frequented by tourists, including for example the
grounds of chateaux such as Versailles.

Electricity

In France the mains supply is 220 volts AC. An adapter (Fr. *adapta-
teur*) is required for devices with British or other non-European plugs.

Emergency

IN FRANCE

Police, emergency doctors and the
fire service can be contacted from
public telephones without the
need for coins or phone cards.

► **Police**
Police de secours tel. 17

► **Ambulance and
emergency doctor**
SAMU tel. 15
(also in English)

► **Fire service**
Sapeurs pompiers tel. 18

► **Breakdown service**
AIT Assistance
Tel. 0800 08 92 22
(round the clock)
Responsible for all roads except
autoroutes (►Transport)

► **SOS Help**
Tel. 01 47 23 80 80
English spoken

IN THE UK

► **RAC**
Tel. 08705 722 722
(customer services)
Tel. 0800 82 82 82
(breakdown assistance in UK)
Tel. +33 (0)4 72 43 52 44
(breakdown assistance in France)

► **AA**
Tel. 0800 028 9018
(European breakdown)
Tel. +44 (0)161 495 8945
(international enquiries)

INTERNATIONAL
AIR AMBULANCE SERVICES

► **Cega Air Ambulance
(worldwide service)**
Tel. +44 (0)1243 621097
Fax +44 (0)1243 773169
www.cega-aviation.co.uk

► **US Air Ambulance**
Tel. 800/948-1214 (US; toll-free)
Tel. 001-941-926-2490
(international; collect)
www.usairambulance.net

Etiquette and Customs

Politeness   The French greet each other not just with »Bonjour« but with »Bonjour Madame / Monsieur«. Don't forget please and thank-you: »S'il vous plait / Merci, Madame / Monsieur«. If you have to squeeze your way through a crowd or bump into someone, apologise by saying »Pardon« or »Excusez-moi«. Men greet each other with a handshake, women with the hint of a kiss to the right and left (the number varies).

Tipping   In general a tip (*pourboire*) is given under the same circumstances as in the rest of Europe, and the amounts involved are comparable. In restaurants and cafés a service charge is almost always included (*service compris*). Nevertheless – as thanks for good service – it is customary to give about 5–10% of the amount on the bill as a tip. Those paying with a cheque or credit card should leave the appropriate amount in cash. In cafés and bars, simply leave the money on the little plate that carried the bill. Taxi drivers (0.50–1 €), tour guides (1–2 €), toilet attendants and room service personnel are always happy to receive a tip.

Smoking ban   An absolute smoking ban applies to all public buildings in France, namely museums, cinemas, public transport, restaurants, cafés, hotels and roofed squares.

Festivals, Holidays and Events

General information   France celebrates an abundance of festivals, large and small, regional and international. Classical and modern music, chanson, theatre, cinema and dance are the most important themes. In addition there is an inestimable number of traditional festivals, wine festivals, sports events, antique markets and much more. Information is provided by Maison de la France (▶Information) and tourist offices.

PUBLIC HOLIDAYS

1 January New Year's Day
(Jour de l'An)
1 May Labour Day
(Fête du Travail)
8 May Armistice 1945
14 July National Holiday
(Fête Nationale, commemorating
the storming of the Bastille in
1789)

15 August Assumption of the
Virgin (Assomption)
1 November All Saints' Day
(Toussaint)
11 November Armistice 1918
25 December Christmas Day
(Noël)

MOVEABLE HOLIDAYS

Easter Monday (Lundi de Pâques)

Ascension Day
(Whit Monday has not been a
holiday since 2004.)

ADDITIONAL HOLIDAYS IN ALSACE

Good Friday (Vendredi Saint)
26 December (second Christmas
holiday)

HOLIDAYS IN MONACO

Corpus Christi (Fête-Dieu)
19 November (national holiday)
8 December
(Immaculate Conception)

CALENDAR OF EVENTS

▶ **January**
Paris: Start of the Rallye Paris-
Dakar
Angoulême: International Comic
Festival (around 20 Jan)
Clermont-Ferrand: International

Short Film Festival (end of Jan)
Gérardmer: Fantastic'Arts (Fantasy
Film Festival, end of Jan)

▶ **February**
Ile d'Oléron: Fête des Mimosas
(Mimosa Flower Festival) in St-
Trojan-les-Bains
Menton: Lemon Festival

▶ **End of January – mid-March**
Côte d'Azur: carnival takes place
in many towns, the best in Nice:
twelve days long with the climax
on Shrove Tuesday with fireworks,
confetti and a large »Battle of
Flowers«.
Nord-Pas-de-Calais: carnival in
many towns, especially impressive
in Dunkirk (Dunkerque).

▶ **March**
Cognac: Detective Film Festival

*On 14 July in Obernai, Alsace, the large »Hans em Schnokeloch« folk festival is
celebrated, inspired by an old song*

Every even year at the end of July hundreds of magnificent old sailing ships gather in Douarnenez, Brittany

▶ **March / April**
Perpignan: Good Friday procession: the Brotherhood of the Holy Cross, with pointed red hats and shrouded in their habits, brings the cross »Dévot Christ« out of the chapel of the cathedral of St-Jean and carries it in celebration through the town.

▶ **April**
Carnac: end of April catamaran competition
Paris – Roubaix cycle race

▶ **April / May**
Orléans: 29 April and 7–8 May Joan of Arc Festival

▶ **May**
On 1 May gifts of lily of the valley are exchanged.
Arles: Fêtes des Gardians (festival of horse herders). At the Mass, conducted in the Provençal language, horses are blessed. There are also bullfights.
Cannes: International Film Festival (mid–end of May)
Chaumont (Loire): International Garden Festival (mid-May–mid-Oct)
La Rochelle: Intl. Sailing Week
Monaco: Gran Prix der Formel 1 (around 20 May)
Stes-Maries-de-la-Mer: 24–25 May Pèlerinage des Gitans (Sinti pilgrimage): Sinti from the whole of Europe celebrate their patron saint, Sara the Black. In a colourful procession her statue is carried to be blessed in the sea. In the evening there is a celebration with music, bull-oriented events and Provençal dancing.
Nîmes: a week before the beginning of Whitsun a two-week féria takes place with bullfights, theatre, folklore events, jazz.

▶ May – September

In Brittany folk festivals and the »Pardons« take place, processions to honour the patron saint of the town. The largest is on 25–26 July in Ste-Anne-d'Auray (on 25th illuminated procession, on 26th large St Anne procession).

▶ June

Le Mans: mid-June 24-hour motor race

Tarascon: On the last weekend four-day Festival of Tarasque with old customs and traditions of Provence.

21 June: Fête de la Musique, introduced in 1982 by culture minister Jack Lang and almost as important as Bastille Day: music is made across the whole country.

Paris: French Open tennis tournament (Stade Roland-Garros, end of June)

▶ July

Tour de France (▶Baedeker Special p.160)

Magny-Cours: beginning of July Grand Prix (Formula 1)

Avignon: beginning of July till beginning of August Festival d'Art Dramatique: theatre, dance, concerts, ballet, street theatre, classical and avant-garde art

Aix-en-Provence: beginning of July till beginning of August Festival International d'Art Lyrique et de Musique (music and opera)

Locronan: 2nd Sunday in July small Troménie (a combination of Pardon and folk festival); every six years a large Troménie takes place (again in 2013).

14 July: the National Holiday is celebrated everywhere – especially splendidly in Paris – with parades, dance and fireworks.

Quimper: in the week before the 3rd Sunday Festival de Cornouaille, a large folklore festival with participants from all Celtic regions in Europe.

Salon-de-Provence: 3rd week in July Festival de Jazz

Beaucaire: 21–28 July Festival (100 bulls race through the town, accompanied by the herders or »gardians«)

Orange: mid-July–beginning of Aug Chorégies (opera, theatre and concerts in the Roman theatre).

▶ August

15 August (Assumption Day); folk festivals everywhere with processions, flower carnival and fireworks.

▶ September

Deauville: 11-day American Film Festival. Many Hollywood stars attend.

▶ October

Toulouse and surroundings: Jazz sur Son 31: concerts by international Jazz greats – not even New York has more on the bill.

Also: circus festival.

▶ November

Of all the numerous wine festivals in France the »Trois Glorieuses« (Three Glorious Days) in Burgundy stand out. On the 3rd Saturday in November the Confrerie des Chevaliers du Tastevin (Brotherhood of the Knights of Tastevin) arrange a ceremonial banquet with wine tasting in Château Clos-de-Vougeot near Nuits-St-Georges. On the following Sunday in the Hospiz von Beaune the wines of the new vintage are put up for auction. On Monday the festival, which is also

celebrated by the general population, ends with the »Paulée«, a large feast in Meursault.
Paris: on 11 November (Armistice Day 1918) there is a large-scale military ceremony at the Arc de Triomphe.

▶ **December**
Marseille: last Sunday in November – 31 December Foire aux Santons (market for clay figures fro nativity scenes).
Christmas markets in many places; they are especially rich in tradition and attractive in Alsace and Lorraine.

Food and Drink

French gastronomic culture French cuisine is world famous, as much for its diversity as for its quality. Eating is an important aspect of everyday life and cookery is an indispensable part of culture. Great emphasis is placed on offering a varied sequence of courses and one or two hours is set aside for a »real« meal. It was through Catherine de' Medici, the wife of King Henri II, in the Renaissance that the enjoyment of good food came to the French royal court from Italy, eventually finding its way to the kitchens of France's citizens. It is reported that Henri IV wished that every farmer could have his chicken in a pot on a Sunday. The French Revolution not only brought freedoms to the people but also spread sophisticated eating habits. In 1825, Anthelme Brillat-Savarin published *The Physiology of Taste*, still considered to be a philosophical underpinning of the joys of eating. In 1986, in Château du Vivier in Ecully, the Paul Bocuse Institute was founded, where the land's most famous chefs contribute to courses dedicated to the culinary arts. However France, too, has developed modern eating habits – many complain of the decline of eating culture generally – a fact to which the large number of fast food outlets, pizzerias etc. and the broad range of ready-to-serve meals in supermarkets testify. Moreover, a lot of French families are imposing drastic limits on the customary meal out as the divide between prices and available income continues to widen for many.

How and when to eat? The French breakfast (*petit déjeuner*) could be described as rather meagre. It consists mostly of a cup of coffee, normally with a large amount of warm milk (*café au lait*), tea or hot chocolate, a *croissant*, a *brioche* (a sweet bread) or a piece of *baguette* with butter and jam. More importance is attached to lunch and dinner however; as a rule the French eat two hot meals a day. At lunch (*déjeuner*) between noon and 2.30pm and dinner (*dîner, souper*) between 7pm and 10.30pm, three to five or even six courses are served.
Working people generally satisfy themselves with a snack at lunchtimes: something like *steak frites* (steak and chips) or a *baguette cru-*

Truffles galore: black diamonds are a speciality of the
»Chez Bruno« restaurant in Lorgues in Provence

dités (a baguette containing lettuce and raw vegetables) is eaten in a
bistro. In the evenings however, dinner is more substantial and time
is taken – two hours or more. A complete menu looks like this:
amuse geule (to whet the appetite), *hors d'œuvre* (also *entrée*, starter),
another entrée, the *menu principal* (main course), *fromage* (cheese),
dessert. An example of such a meal: Pastis, an aniseed liqueur with
added water, or Kir, a white Burgundy with a splash of *crème de cassis*
(blackcurrant liqueur) is served as an aperitif (*apéro*). The hors
d'œuvre consists of soup, a salad (e.g. *salade niçoise*), an omelette,
pâté or a regional sausage speciality (*charcuterie*); the main course is
meat (*viande*) or fish (*poisson*) with a side dish of vegetables. The
cheese course is very important, there being at least 500 types of
hard and soft cheeses in France. Popular desserts are *mousse au
chocolat*, *crème caramel*, ice cream or a *tarte* (e.g. *tarte Tatin*, an apple
tart). Then comes the *digestif*: cognac, Armagnac, calvados or a fruit
schnapps from the locality. A small black coffee (*café noir, café
exprès*) concludes the meal. White bread accompanies the food, in
the form of slices of long, crispy *baguettes*. It is preferable to drink
wine with a meal with several courses, sometimes diluted with water
(wine is almost exclusively drunk with food).

Regional Cuisine

France is a land composed of individual regions, and this is especially
evident in its cuisine. Let us embark on a culinary expedition.

Nord –
Pas de Calais

The far north is the home of Flemish cuisine. The specialities include meat, fish and seafood, potatoes, vegetables, cheese and apples as well as fine confectionery. Almost every restaurant serves *moules frites* (mussels with chips), also popular in Holland and Belgium.

Picardy

With its wide range of vegetables, such as leek, carrots, peas and green beans, Picardy is a land of milk and honey – as it were – for vegetarians. There is hardly another area where chicory is prepared in such a variety of ways. One Picardy speciality is the *ficelle picarde* (pancakes filled with ham and mushrooms). Further delicacies include the duck and goose liver pâtés, often served as a starter, and cheeses such as *maroilles*, a soft cheese with a strong flavour.

Brittany

For lovers of first-class fish, both freshwater and from the sea, of other types of seafood and of shellfish, Brittany is a veritable paradise. For those who like *fruits de mer* (seafood and shellfish), a *plateau* is recommended, namely a platter with the meat of spider crabs (*araignées*), crabs (*crabes*), edible crabs (*tourteaux*), sea urchin (*oursins*), mussels (*moules*), clams (*palourdes* or *praires* if they are smaller), prawns (*crevettes*), lobster (*homard*) and crayfish (*langoustes*). Scallops (*coquille St-Jacques*) are considered a delicacy. Lobsters and oysters (*huîtres*) are quite reasonably priced. The best oysters are found

Seafood is prepared in the most tempting ways along France's coasts

in Cancale, Riec-sur-Belon and in the Bay of Quiberon. Breton meat specialities include *kig ha fars* (flavoursome stew made of vegetables, beef and knuckle of pork), *andouille* sausage (made of tripe and intestines), *saucisse aux choux* (a boiled pork sausage with white cabbage) and *rillettes* (potted meat made of pork). Those who find all that rather heavy going may prefer *canard nantais* (duck Nantes style) or the dish named after the statesman and writer Chateaubriand (double fillet steak with Béarnaise sauce). *Agneau pré-salé*, the lamb from the salt marshes around Mont St-Michel, is famous. Of the wide range of vegetables, the artichokes of Brittany deserve special mention; the region produces the highest quantity of these noble members of the thistle family. The very epitome of Breton dishes are the *crêpes* and *galettes*, wafer thin pancakes in the greatest variety of flavours: spicy with ham, cheese, mussels or shrimps, sweet with jam, fruit, ice-cream or just sugar. The most typical sweet dish is the *far breton*, an egg pancake flavoured with vanilla and served with baked plums or raisins.

This once royal region serves up numerous specialities: game such as pheasant, guinea fowl, venison and wild pig, freshwater fish such as carp, bass and trout, fruit and vegetables, with asparagus and strawberries at the top of the list, and not forgetting the diverse range of confectionery and desserts such as *tarte Tatin* (upside-down apple tart). **Loire valley**

Porcini and nuts are in abundance in autumn, and truffles (*truffes*), the »black diamonds«, are also collected. Foie gras, the »fat liver« of force-fed goose and duck – in a sauce made from jurançon, a naturally sweet white wine from the Béarn region, or as paté on baked rye bread – is the speciality of the region. The Basque region, too, serves up many delicacies, e.g. *zirkiro*, mutton grilled on a skewer, or *urraburua*, a golden bream grilled with garlic; the favourite spice of the Basque region is the gently piquant chilli pepper. **Aquitaine**

In the Ardennes, rustic fare is highly prized: air-dried ham, the white pork sausage from Rethel (*boudin blanc*) and the sugary (*tarte au sucre ardennaise*) as well as turkey, rabbit, wild pig, and also veal and beef.

Alsatian cuisine is hearty food made of local products: *choucroute garni* (mixed grill with sauerkraut), *chou au lard* (white cabbage with bacon), *tarte à l'oignon* (onion tart), *tarte flambée* (a very thin pizza with onions, crème fraîche and bacon), *baeckoffe* (stew made of meat, potatoes, onions, and white wine), knuckle of pork, patés, boiled ham and cheese from Munster. **Alsace**

Moutarde de Dijon (mustard from Dijon, the capital of Burgundy), *bœuf bourguignon*, *pot au feu* (braised steak with vegetables), *Kir* – all these specialities, known beyond the country's borders, originate **Burgundy** from Burgundy. Above all, it is the meat of the local Charolais cattle and the flavoursome Bresse chickens that land on the table most often here, prepared in the traditional cream or mustard sauce. Kir, by the way, was created out of an awkward situation: because white wine did not agree with him, the mayor of Dijon, Felix Kir (1876–1968), mixed it with the blackcurrant liqueur cassis. Kir Royal is cassis with champagne.

Atlantic coast, Charente   Seafood of all kinds is seen on the menu in almost all restaurants here. The particular speciality is *mouclade*, mussels in a stock made of white wine, bay leaves and onions, with added crème fraîche, egg yolk and curry. Gourmets who are not so keen on fish and seafood would do well to order *daube des Charentes*, a tender beef ragout braised with wine and cognac, or *gigot d'agneau*, a leg of lamb peppered with garlic, with which white beans (*mohettes*) are served.

Provence   Provencal cuisine occupies a special place in French cooking. In contrast to the cuisine of other regions, olive oil and tomatoes are used in abundance. The most important spices are garlic and onions, as well as rosemary, thyme, basil, sage and saffron. Among the specialities are *bouillabaisse* (fish soup with garlic, rosemary and saffron), *ratatouille* (braised vegetables with tomatoes) and *salade niçoise* (green salad with tuna, egg, onions and olives).

Languedoc-Roussillon   Hearty food from the mountains like the potato dish *aligot* and offal dishes such as *tripes à l'alésienne* are among the delicacies of the region. Further specialities are *tapenade*, a paste made of olives and anchovies, served as a starter, and *brandade*, a puree of stockfish, dried salted cod. In coastal areas, of course, fruits de mer feature, perhaps oysters, mussels or *zarzuela*, a Spanish ragout made of fish and seafood.

Midi-Pyrenées   Specialities of the largest region in France include: the well-known *cassoulet*, a bean stew, enriched with goose or duck, ham, knuckle of pork garlic sausage and bacon; around Figeac, *estofinado*, a fish puree; gâteau à la broche (spit-roasted cake), baked over an open flame on a wood fire. The Cevennes are home to the famous Roquefort, a sheep's milk cheese with veins of blue mould.

Drinks

Wine   It goes almost without saying that French wine should accompany a meal in France (▶p.128). The open table wines (*un petit blanc, un petit rouge*) are in general perfectly recommendable, and can be ordered as *une carafe* (approx. 0.5l) or *un carafon* (approx. 0.25l). When making your choice of bottled wine, either a full (*entière bouteille*) or half bottle (*demie bouteille*), it is advisable to take the advice of the waiter.

Sweet wine, such as Monbazillac, is the classic accompaniment to foie gras

The beers of the Alsace region (Pêcheur, Kronenbourg, Kanterbräu, Mutzig) are good and enjoy popularity, as do those from Lorraine (Champigneulles, Vézélise) as well as those from the Nord – Pas-de-Calais region, in which two thirds of the country's breweries are situated. A bottle of beer is an *anette*, while beer on tap is *bière pression*. A small glass of beer (0.3 l) is known as a *demi*, a half-litre glass mostly as a *véritable*, and a full litre as a *formidable*. **Beer**

A meal is often concluded with a strong black coffee. Those who order a *café* will be served an espresso. For a coffee with warm milk, ask for a *café crème, grand crème* or *café au lait*. Tea (*thé*) fans may also like to try the popular herbal teas (*tisane, infusion*). **Coffee and tea**

Mineral water is either still (*eau minérale, plat*) or carbonated (*gazeuse*); the brands Perrier, Vichy, Evian, Vittel and Contrexéville are available across the whole country. **Mineral water**

In Normandy and other fruit-growing areas, *cidre* (cider) is very popular. It comes in various forms: *doux* (sweet), *brut* (dry and tangy), *demi-sec* (medium dry), *sec* (dry) etc. In Normandy, calvados, a spirit made from cider, is drunk is the middle of a meal, a custom known as *trou normand* (»Norman hole«). From the Charente regions comes cognac, which is matured in oak barrels and bears names such as Hennessy, Martell or Rémy Martin. Gascony is the home of Armagnac, a brandy many prefer to cognac. In southwest France, Pineau, a mixture of grape juice and brandy, is widespread. **Regional specialities**

The varieties of fruit schnapps that mostly stem from smaller Alsatian distilleries are outstanding, while most people have heard of such liqueurs as Cointreau and Chartreuse, a herbal liqueur brewed in the Dauphiné region by monks. Pastis, an aniseed liqueur diluted with iced water and drunk as an aperitif, is popular in Provence and elsewhere.

Wine

The oldest wine-growing area in France is Provence, where grapes were already thriving in 600 BC when Greek traders from Asia Minor arrived in the town of Massalia (Marseille), founded by the Phoenicians. Today across the whole of France on about a million hectares of land – almost 10% of the total area used for agriculture in the country – approximately a fifth of the world's wine is produced. The leading regions are Bordeaux, Burgundy, Champagne, and the Loire and Rhône valleys. The largest wine region is the Midi (Languedoc, Roussillon), from which about 40% of all French wines come. Only the sparkling wine from the Champagne region, manufactured according to established processes, can call itself »champagne«; bubbly from other parts of France are called »vin mousseux« or »crémant«. Those that are produced using classic Champagne methods are identified with the phrase »méthode traditionelle«. Tourist offices in wine-growing areas provide information on cellars (tours, tastings), wine seminars, guided tours etc.

Pouilly Fumé from the upper Loire, an elegant Savignon Blanc

Most wine-growing areas are in possession of **appellations contrôlées**, designations of origin, allocated by the Institut National des Appellations d'Origine (INAO). At present there are around 320 areas with such designations, representing about 30% of total production. The AOC (or AC) guarantees specific origins, methods of production, grape varieties and production quantities. Wines that are not made in accordance with the AC regulations (including some first-class, very expensive wines) may bear the label VDQS (Vin Délimité de Qualité Supérieure). In addition there is »vin de pays«, which comes from a specific area marked on the label, as well as »vin de table« (»vin ordinaire«, table wine). Table wines from different growing areas can be blended. In addition there are further regional designations of origin and classification: Cru Classé (Premier Cru, Deuxième Cru etc.) and Cru Bourgeois in Bordeaux, Grand Cru and Premier Cru in Burgundy; in the Champagne region, areas are categorized as Grand Cru or Premier Cru, while in Alsace the title Grand Cru is granted to wines from specific vineyards. Some regions also have typical colours of glass and shapes of bottle.

The Language of Wine

Appellation d'origine contrôlée	Monitored designation of origin
Blanc de Noirs / Blancs	White wine (also sparkling wine) from red / white grapes
Cave / Caveau	Wine cellar
Cépage	Variety of grape
Château	Wine-growing estate
Clos	Wine-growing area, vineyard
Cuvée	Blend
Domaine	Wine-growing estate
Méthode traditionelle	Fermentation in the bottle (sparkling wine)
Mis(e) en bouteille	Where the wine was bottled
Nouveau	Young wine
Vendange tardive	Late vintage
Vin délimité de qualité supérieure	Wine of certified origin and quality
(VDQS)	Area of cultivation
Vin de pays	Country wine
Vin de table	Table wine

Wine literature

Burtschy, B., *Guide Malesan des Vins de France*. Solar, Paris 2004 (last edition). Approx. 300 reasonably priced wines.

Friedrich, Jacqueline, *Wines of France: The Essential Guide for Savvy Shoppers*. Ten Speed Press 2006.

Hachette Encyclopédie Touristique des Vins de France. Paris 2002. Wine travel guide with 38 routes.

Guide Hachette des Vins. Famous reference work with over 35,000 wines. Published annually.

Jefford, A., Lowe. J., *The New France: A Complete Guide to Contemporary French Wine*. Mitchell Beazley 2006

Johnson, H., Duijker, H., *The Wine Atlas of France and Traveller's Guide to the Vineyards*. Mitchell Beazley 1997

Ribérau-Gayon, P., *Atlas Hachette des Vins de France*. Paris 2000

Eating Out

Where to eat In France there are restaurants of every kind in abundance: from temples of haute cuisine to familial local restaurants, offering traditional specialities of the region or dishes from all manner of countries. As in all of Europe, there are also fast food places and pizzerias aplenty. It is cheap to eat in self-service restaurants and (tip!) in cafés and restaurants of universities, which are mostly open to non-students. In »real« restaurants it is not really possible to get even a light meal for a moderate price; for this go to a bistro or brasserie.

Menus Most restaurants offer two to three menus at a fixed price (starter, main course, dessert; drinks not included). Otherwise diners eat à la carte, i.e. they choose their own courses, which is somewhat more expensive. In some restaurants it is possible to choose between a *plat du jour* (dish of the day without a starter but mostly with dessert), the *formule* (the main course and a choice between a starter or a des-

Maison de la Graves in La Brède, a typical country restaurant

sert) and the *menu du jour* (three courses), the most lavish and expensive being the *menu gastronomique / menu dégustation*. Many fine restaurants offer reasonably priced menus at lunchtimes; those on a budget who want to live the high life for once should therefore treat themselves to lunch rather than dinner. One to avoid – especially in large cities – is the *menu touristique*, which is often overpriced.

By evening at the latest it is common to drink a good wine with dinner, whereby it is not normal to order just one glass. In the majority of restaurants, open wines are on offer, served in a *pichet* (pitcher or jug, from a quarter of a litre). Those who prefer bottled wines must not necessarily order a whole bottle (bouteille), as half-bottles are often available. In France plenty of water is drunk with a meal, either carbonated mineral water (*eau gazeuse*) or still spring water (*eau naturelle*); it is also possible to order tap water free of charge. A meal is generally concluded with a small black coffee and/or a *digestif* in the form of a cognac, Armagnac or calvados.

Drinks

At lunchtimes the restaurants are open between noon and 2.30pm, in the evenings between 7pm and 10.30pm. In popular places a table should be booked early. After entering the establishment the guest is normally led to a table; of course, it is possible at this juncture to request a specific one. In small, informal restaurants, diners can choose

Restaurant etiquette in brief

For many almost a second home: the bar

a table for themselves, but it is not done to join other guests at their table. Do not attract the attention of waiters and waitresses by calling »Garçon!«; instead, call »Madame!«, »Monsieur!« or »S'il vous plaît«. As in the UK, the bill is for the whole table, not for individual diners. The service charge is included in the price, but it is nevertheless customary to leave a tip of 5–10%. Tip in cash if you pay by credit card.

More places to eat A bar is not somewhere to go at night; instead it is a mixture of café and bar, and often also sells cigarettes, stamps and telephone cards. A bistro (bistrot) is basically comparable to a bar or café, but today can also be a real restaurant. Cafés concentrate on coffee and other drinks, but serve small snacks such as baguettes with ham or cheese or croque-monsieur (toast with ham and cheese). A salon de thé is generally a tranquil place that serves tea, which if desired can be accompanied by cakes or »pâtisserie«. A brasserie, in which beer is served, combines the café and the restaurant; some are rather plain, some more exclusive, and they are open from the morning until late at night. Relais Routiers are reasonably priced transport cafés that are not only popular with long-distance lorry drivers (►Accommodation).

Health

Doctors The addresses of doctors (médecins) and dentists (dentistes) are listed in the »Pages Jaunes« (Yellow Pages) of the local telephone book. Tourist offices can often provide lists of doctors who speak English. Even the police will help in the search for a doctor. Doctors providing emergency services are listed in the local press.

Pharmacies Pharmacies are marked with a green cross. Opening times: 9am–noon, 2pm–6.30pm. Pharmacies providing a service at night and at weekends are indicated on the doors of other pharmacies and listed in the local press.

Health insurance ►Arrival

Emergency numbers ►Emergency

Hiking and Mountain Climbing

Footpaths France is covered with a well-developed network of footpaths of varying levels of difficulty. On the grandes randonnées (GR, long-distance footpaths), whole areas of the country are experienced, while on the petites randonnées (PR) shorter tours can be undertaken.

INFORMATION

▶ **Fédération Française
de la Randonnée Pédestre**
14 Rue Riquet, F-75019 Paris
Tel. 01 44 89 93 93
Fax 01 40 35 85 67
www.ffrandonnee.fr
www.gr-infos.com

▶ **Fédération des
Clubs Alpins Français**
24 Avenue de Laumière
F-75019 Paris
Tel. 01 53 72 87 00
Fax 01 42 03 55 00
www.ffcam.fr

▶ **Fédération Française
de Montagne et d'Escalade**
8–10 Quai de la Marne
F-75019 Paris
Tel. 01 40 18 75 50
Fax 01 40 18 75 59
www.ffme.fr

Wandering through the Pyrenees

Gîtes d'etape (hostels) are plentiful along the hiking routes (▶ Accommodation). Hotels are more comfortable, and many, such as the Rand'hotels (www.rando-accueil.com), Balad'hotels and Logis de France, cater specifically to the needs of hikers. **Accommodation**

The Fédération Française de la Randonnée Pédestre is concerned with the development and maintenance of the network of footpaths. It publishes three series of hiking guides (Topo guides): *Grande Randonnée* (GR routes with information on how to get there, accommodation and shopping), *Proménade et Randonnée* for short tours and *A Pied en Famille* (hiking with the family). Their website contains good links, including those to the Way of St James (see below). English language publishers also produce good hiking guides to France. For hiking maps see ▶Maps. **Hiking guides**

The Ways of St James in France was added to the list of UNESCO World Heritage Sites in 1998 (▶ Baedeker Special p.792). Alison Raju's *The Way of St. James (France)* (Cicerone International Walking) provides practical and historical information on the pilgrimage route.

For mountain walkers and climbers, the high mountain regions of the Alps and the Pyrenees are naturally outstanding areas, but the lower mountain ranges such as the Jura, the Massif Central and the Cevennes also offer many worthwhile routes. Guide books are available in great number. The Fédération des Clubs Alpins Français maintains branches in many towns.

Houseboating

Boat trips on the approximately 8500km/5280mi of canals and rivers in France have become very popular (▶ Baedeker Special p.192). Countless tour operators, including some based outside France, offer houseboats and tours. Some provide the service of driving the holidaymakers' car to the final destination of the trip. Information is provided by travel agents, French tourist offices and Maison de la France (▶Information).

Technical details The motor cabin boats offered for hire have 2–6 berths and a length of 5.5–11m/18–36ft. A boat driving licence is not required for almost all vessels (a technical briefing is given by the boat hire company). The boats are equipped with a fridge, a kitchen, heating and a toilet. Bikes, which can also be hired, improve mobility and enable the crew to set out on day trips, sightseeing expeditions and shopping runs.

Motorboats Those wishing to sail along the coast or inland waterways in a motorboat must have the appropriate boat driving licence as stipulated in the driver's home country.

Information

Tourist Offices

Maison de la France The French government tourist office »Maison de la France« offers a diverse range of services, primarily by providing information and sending brochures from the régions and départements on accommodation, means of transport, sights and attractions, opportunities for sports etc. The regional tourist offices (Comité Régional de Tourisme, CRT) offer extensive material, as do those of the départements **Regional tourist offices ▶** (Comité Départemental de Tourisme, CDT). These brochures provide the addresses of local tourist offices (Office de Tourisme, OdT), which are able to assist further with detailed queries and offer, for example, listings of restaurants and accommodation (they also make reservations, mostly for a small fee), information on sporting and other activities, and details of events, museums, nature parks and so on. The addresses of each responsible Office de Tourisme or Comité Départemental de Tourisme are listed in the »Sights from A to Z« section of this guide.

Internet

The internet is a rich source of information of all kinds on France. Details of towns and cities, regions, sights and attractions, travel agents, hotels and other accommodation, museums, sport, events and so on can be obtained online. There are always plenty of hits when researching France using one of the well-known search engines. In the »Sights from A to Z« section, important addresses are noted where applicable, and the box below contains a listing of websites that provide helpful information on France.

 IMPORTANT ADRESSES

MAISON DE LA FRANCE

► **In the UK**
Lincoln House
300 High Holborn
London WC1V 7JH
Tel. 09068 244 123
(60p a minute)
Fax 020 7061 6646
www.franceguide.com/uk
www.maison-de-la-france.com

► **In Canada**
1800 Avenue McGill College, Suite 1010
Montreal, Quebec
Canada H3A 3J6
Tel. 514 288 2026
Fax 514 845 4868
www.franceguide.com/ca

► **In the USA**
825 Third Avenue, 29th floor
New York, NY 10022
Tel. 514 288 1904
Fax 212 838 7855
The offices in Los Angeles and Chicago can be contacted at:
Los Angeles: tel. 310 271 6665
Chicago: tel. 312 327 0290
www.franceguide.com/us

FRENCH EMBASSIES AND CONSULATES

► **In Australia**
6 Perth Ave , Yarralumla, ACT
Tel. 02-6216 0100
www.ambafrance-au.org

► **In Canada**
42 Sussex Drive
Ottawa, Ont K1M 2C9
Tel. 416-925 8041
www.ambafrance-ca.org

► **In the Republic of Ireland**
36 Ailesbury Rd, Dublin 4
Tel. 1 277 5000
www.ambafrance-ie.org

► **In New Zealand**
13th fl., Rural Bank Building
34–42 Manners St
PO Box 11-343 Wellington
Tel. 04-384 2555
www.ambafrance-nz.org

► **In the USA**
4101 Reservoir Rd
Washington DC 20007
Tel. 212-606 3600
www.ambafrance-us.org

► **In the UK**
58 Knightsbridge
London SW1X 7JT
Tel. 020 7073 1000
www.ambafrance-uk.org

EMBASSIES IN FRANCE

All foreign embassies are situated in Paris.

► **AMERICAN EMBASSY**
2 av Gabriel, 8e, tel. 01 43 12 22 22
www.amb-usa.fr

► **AUSTRALIAN EMBASSY**
4 rue Jean Rey, 15e
Tel. 01 40 59 33 00
www.ausgov.fr

► **BRITISH EMBASSY**
35 rue du Faubourg St-Honoré, 8e
Tel. 01 44 51 31 00
www.amb-grandebretagne.fr

► **CANADIAN EMBASSY**
35 av Montaigne, 8e
Tel. 01 44 43 29 00
www.amb-canada.fr

► **IRISH EMBASSY**
12 av Foch/4 rue Rude, 16e
Tel. 01 44 17 67 00
www.embassyofirelandparis.com

► **NEW ZEALAND EMBASSY**
7ter rue Léonard de Vinci, 16e
Tel. 01 45 01 43 43
www.nzembassy.com

INTERNET

► **www.franceguide.com**
Site of Maison de la France. Rich in content, but a rather unclear layout.

► **www.francetourism.com**
Plentiful information on the country's regions, accommodation, culture and much more, as well as practical tips and links.

► **www.ambafrance-uk.org**
French Embassy in the UK

► **www.diplomatie.gouv.fr/en/**
An overview of France provided by the French foreign ministry (in English)

► **www.about-france.com**
Though not the most attractive looking site on the net, about-france.com has a wealth of information on travel and tourism in France in both English and French.

► **www.discoverfrance.net**
A source of useful information for tourists

► **www.culture.gouv.fr/culture/exp/exp.htm**
Interesting website on France's important cultural sites

► **www.monum.fr**
The Centre des Monuments Nationaux provides information on the nation's great treasures here.

► **www.tourisme.fr**
This French language site presents information on holidays and accommodation (including hotel reservations).

► **www.tripadvisor.com**
Tourism website with plenty of information on France. The newspaper articles and travellers' personal stories are especially interesting.

► **www.concertandco.com**
www.french-music.org
Information on music of all kinds

(including jazz) with concert dates, addresses for tickets etc.

► **www.plusbeauxdetours.com**
Over 90 especially pretty small towns and villages, presented within the context of France's »most beautiful detours«.

► **www.discovering provence.com**
This website promoting a DVD on Provence provides a good overview of the region.

► **www.liberation.fr**
  www.lemonde.fr
  www.lefigaro.fr
  www.leparisien.com
  www.humanite.fr
  www.lexpress.fr
The websites of the big French newspapers.

Language

Those who do not speak much French should take a dictionary and a phrase book. Even if most French people speak English, they welcome visitors who attempt to communicate in the local language. For language courses see ►Sport and Outdoors, p.162..

FRENCH PHRASES

The essentials

Yes / No / Perhaps	Oui / Non / Peut-être
Please / Thank you	S'il vous plaît (s. v. p.) / Merci
You're welcome. / Sorry!	De rien. / Excusez-moi !
Pardon?	Comment ?
I don't understand.	Je ne comprends pas.
I only speak a little French.	Je parle un tout petit peu français.
Can you help me please?	Vous pouvez m'aider, s. v. p.?
Do you speak English?	Vous parlez allemand / anglais ?
I would like …	J'aimerais …
I don't like that.	Ça ne me plaît pas.
Do you have … ?	Vous avez … ?
How much is that?	Ça coûte combien ?
What time is it?	Quelle heure est-il ?

Greetings

Good morning / day !	Bonjour !
Good evening !	Bonsoir !

Hello!	Salut !
What is your name? (polite form)?	Comment vous appellez-vous ?
What is your name? (informal)	Comment t'appelles-tu?
How are you??	Comment allez-vous / vas-tu ?
Goodbye! / See you!	Au revoir ! / Salut!

Finding the way

left / right / straight on	à gauche / à droite / tout droit
near / far	près / loin
Excuse me, where can I find … please?	Pardon, où se trouve … , s. v. p.?
How many kilometres is that from here??	C'est à combien de kilomètres d'ici ?
What is the shortest route to … ?	Quel est le chemin le plus court pour aller à … ?

At the petrol station

Where is the next petrol station??	Où est la station-service la plus proche ?
I would like … litres …please.	Je voudrais … litres …, s'il vous plaît.
… of super	… du super
… of diesel	… du diesel
… of lead-free / with … octane	… du sans-plomb / … octanes.
Fill her up, please.	(Faites) Le plein, s. v. p.

Breakdown

I have broken down.	Je suis en panne.
Can you send me a breakdown truck?	Est-ce que vous pouvez m'envoyer une dépanneuse ?
Is there a garage near here ?	Est-ce qu'il y a un garage près d'ici?
… is broken.	… est défectueux.

Accident

Help !	Au secours !
Watch out !	Attention !
Please quickly call …	Appelez vite …
… an ambulance.	… une ambulance.
… the police.	… la police.

Eating out

Could you tell me where there is …	Pourriez vous m'indiquer …

... a good restaurant? .... un bon restaurant?
... a reasonably priced restaurant? .... un restaurant pas trop cher?
Is there a nice café (bistro)? .... Y-a-t'il un café (bistrot) sympa?
I would like to reserve a table .... Je voudrais réserver une table
  for this evening, ... pour ce soir,
   for four people. .... pour quatre personnes.
Where is the toilet please? .... Où sont les toilettes, s. v. p.?
Cheers! Your good health! .... A votre santé! / A la vôtre!
Can I have the bill please. .... L'addition, s. v. p.
Did it taste good? .... C'etait bon?
The meal was excellent. .... Le repas était excellent.

Accommodation

Could you recommend ... ? .... Pourriez-vous m'indiquer ...
... a good hotel? .... un bon hôtel?
... a guesthouse? .... une pension de famille?
Do you still have ... free? .... Est-ce que vous avez encore ...?
... a single room .... une chambre pour une personne
... a double room .... une chambre pour deux personnes
... with bathroom .... avec salle de bains
... for one night .... pour une nuit
... for a week .... pour une semaine
What does a room with ...cost? .... Quel est le prix de la chambre ...
... breakfast .... petit déjeuner compris?
... half-board? .... en demi-pension?

Medical help

Could you recommend a ..... Pourriez-vous me recommander
  good doctor? .... un bon médecin, s. v. p.?
I have pain here. .... J'ai mal ici.
Where is the next pharmacy? .... Où est la pharmacie la plus proche?

Post office

How much is it to send ... . Quel est le tarif pour affranchir
... a letter .... une lettre
... a postcard .... une carte postale
... to England? .... pour l'Angleterre?

Zahlen

0 .... zéro   1 .... un, une

2	deux	3	trois
4	quatre	5	cinq
6	six	7	sept
8	huit	9	neuf
10	dix	11	onze
12	douze	13	treize
14	quatorze	15	quinze
16	seize	17	dix-sept
18	dix-huit	19	dix-neuf
20	vingt	21	vingt et un, une
22	vingt-deux	23	vingt-trois
30	trente	40	quarante
50	cinquante	60	soixante
70	soixante-dix	80	quatre-vingts
90	quatre-vingt-dix	100	cent
200	deux cents	1000	mille
2000	deux mille	10,000	dix mille
1/4	un quart	1/2	un demi

Petit déjeuner / breakfast

café noir	black coffee
café au lait	coffee with warm milk
décaféiné	decaffeinated coffee
thé au lait / au citron	tea with milk / lemon
tisane	herbal tea
chocolat (chaud)	(hot) chocolate
jus de fruit	fruit juice
œuf mollet	soft boiled egg
œufs brouillés	scrambled egg
œufs au plat avec du lard	fried eggs with bacon
pain / petits pains / toasts	bread / rolls / toast
croissant	croissant
beurre	butter
fromage	cheese
charcuterie	ham and sausage
jambon	ham
miel	honey
confiture	jam
yaourt	yoghurt

Soupes et hors-d'œuvres / soups and starters

bisque d'écrevisses	crab soup
bouchées à la reine	vol-au-vents
bouillabaisse	fish soup from southern France

consommé de poulet	chicken broth
crudités	various vegetables, raw or blanched
galette	crêpe made of buckwheat
pâté de campagne	country pâté
pâte de foie	liver pâté
salade lyonnaise	green salad with fried bacon cubes and croutons
salade niçoise	green salad with tomatoes, egg, cheese, olives and tuna
saumon fumé	smoked salmon
soupe à l'oignon	onion soup
soupe de poisson	fish soup

Viandes / meat

agneau / gigot d'agneau	lamb / leg of eat
bifteck	steak
bœuf	beef
cassoulet	meat and white beans from the oven
confit	potted meat
côte de bœuf	beef cutlet
crépinette	small meat patty wrapped in caul fat
filet de bœuf	fillet of beef
foie gras	fatty liver of force-fed goose or duck
foie	liver
grillades	mixed grill
mouton	mutton
porc	pork
rognons	kidneys
rôti	roast
sauté de veau	veal ragout
steak tatare	tartare (raw beef)
tripes	tripe
saignant	rare
à point / medium	medium-rare / medium
bien cuit	well done

Volailles et gibier / poultry and game

canard à l'orange	duck with orange
cerf	venison
cuissot de chevreuil	haunch of venison

coq au vin	chicken in red wine
faisan	pheasant
lapin chasseur	rabbit »hunter's style«
oie	goose
poulet rôti	roast chicken
sanglier	wild pig

Poissons et crustacés / fish and shellfish

cabillaud	cod
calmar frit	fried squid
daurade	golden bream
lotte	monkfish
loup de mer	wolffish
maquereau	mackerel
morue	dried cod
omble chevalier	char
perche	bass
petite friture	small fried fish
rouget	barbel
sandre	pikeperch
sole au gratin	grilled sole covered with cheese
truite meunière	trout meunière
turbot	turbot
coquilles Saint-Jacques	scallops
crevettes	prawns, shrimps
homard	lobster
huîtres	oysters
moules	mussels
plateau de fruits de mer	seafood platter

Légumes, pâtés, riz / vegetables, pasta, rice

artichaut	artichoke
choucroute	sauerkraut
épinards	spinach
fenouil	fennel
haricots (verts)	(green) beans
nouilles	noodles
oignons	onions
petits pois	peas
poivrons	peppers
pommes dauphine / pommes duchesse	croquette potatoes
pommes de terre	potatoes
pommes de terre nature	boiled potatoes
pommes de terre sautées	fried potatoes

riz au curry . . . . curry with rice
tomates . . . . tomatoes

Desserts

charlotte . . . . sweet made of sponge fingers,
fruit and vanilla cream
crème brûlée . . . . caramelized cream pudding
gâteau . . . . cake
glace . . . . ice-cream
pâtisserie maison . . . . house dessert
profiteroles . . . . cream puffs
sabayon . . . . zabaglione
tarte aux pommes . . . . apple tart
tarte Tatin . . . . upside-down caramelized apple
tart

Fruits

abricots . . . . apricots
cerises . . . . cherries
fraises . . . . strawberries
framboises . . . . raspberries
macédoine . . . . fruit salad
pêches . . . . peaches
poires . . . . pears
pommes . . . . apples
prunes . . . . plums
raisins . . . . grapes

Liste des consommations / list of beverages

coca . . . . cola
eau minérale . . . . mineral water
bière . . . . beer
bière blonde . . . . pale beer
bière brune . . . . dark beer
bière pression . . . . beer on tap
bière bouteille . . . . bottled beer
bière sans alcool . . . . alcohol-free beer
vin . . . . wine
café arrosé . . . . coffee with a shot
café exprès . . . . espresso
un (verre de vin) rouge . . . . a glass of red wine
un quart de vin blanc . . . . a quarter of a litre of white wine

jus de fruit	fruit juice
jus d'orange / jus de pamplemousse	orange / grapefruit juice
lait	milk
limonade	lemonade

Literature

History and culture

Ardagh, J., Jones, C., *Cultural Atlas of France*. Facts On File Inc 1991. An informative illustrated work of cultural studies.

Goubert, Pierre, *The Course of French History*. Routledge 1991. A learned, well-written overview covering a thousand years of French history.

Johnson, James H., *Listening in Paris: A Cultural History*. University of California Press 1996. A witty account of the experience of opera and concert audiences from the Old Regime to the Romantic era, with an analysis of the political, musical, and aesthetic factors in play as audiences were transformed from loud and unruly listeners to the attentive public we know today.

Jones, C., *The Cambridge Illustrated History of France*. Cambridge University Press 1999. French history vividly described.

Jones, C., *Paris: Biography of a City*. Penguin 2006. An entertaining new history of a capital that has witnessed more extraordinary events than any other major city.

Price, Roger, *A Concise History of France*. Cambridge University Press 2005. An eminently readable history.

Robb, Graham, *The Discovery of France*. Picador 2007. A fast-paced historical guidebook full of facts, events, characters and quotations.

Fiction

Balzac, Honoré de, *The Chouans*. Standard Publications 2007. The love between a Republican and an aristocrat during the battles of the Breton royalists against the supporters of the French Revolution.

Barnes, Julian, *Flaubert's Parrot*. Picador 1985. Entertaining musings on the life of Flaubert and the stuffed parrot that once inspired him. Shortlisted for the Booker Prize in 1984.

Bernanos, Georges, *Mouchette*. New York Review of Books 2006. A young girl, neglected by her terminally ill mother and her abusive alcoholic father, meets with a local hunter apparently sealing her tragic fate.

Charef, Mehdi, *Tea in the Harem*. Serpent's Tail 1989. Odd accounts of life in the concrete suburbs of Paris.

Colette, *My Mother's House and Sido*. Farrar Straus Giroux 2002. This novel with an autobiographical streak takes place in Burgundy.

Feuchtwanger, Lion, *The Devil in France – My Encounter with Him in the Summer of 1940* (2007). Diary sketches and letters of the Jewish writer written in 1940 in a French internment camp and after his escape in 1941.

Flaubert, Gustave, *Madame Bovary*. Penguin Classics 2003. Novel about the affairs of the wife of a country doctor with splendid descriptions of the Normandy countryside.

Giono, Jean, *Blue Boy*. Counterpoint 1999. A fictionalized autobiographical tale of a boyhood in Provence.

Hugo, Victor, *Les Miserables*. Vintage Classics 2008. Excellent translation of Hugo's classic.

Maupassant, Guy de, *The Best Short Stories*. Wordsworth Editions Ltd 1997. These stories contain tragedy, satire, comedy and farce.

Orwell, George, *Down and Out in Paris and London*. Penguin Classics 2001. Poverty at close range in two great capitals.

Pagnol, Marcel, *My Father's Glory & My Mother's Castle: Marcel Pagnol's Memories of Childhood*. North Point Press 1986. Empathetic, witty descriptions of the life of a loveable but chaotic family in and around Aubagne, a hymn to Provence.

Proust, Marcel, *Swann's Way*. Penguin Books Ltd 2000. The decline of the belle époque in Paris.

Rabelais, François, *Gargantua and Pantagruel*. Penguin Classics 2006. Satirical fantasy novel with descriptions of the scenery of the Loire.

Rouaud, Jean, *Fields of Glory*. Harvill P. 1998. Family saga spanning three generations with portraits of the landscape of the Loire estuary and its inhabitants.

Sagan, Françoise, *Bonjour Tristesse*. Penguin Classics 2007. The story of Cécile and how her carefree existence becomes clouded by tragedy.

Stendhal, *The Red and the Black*. Penguin Classics 2005. Satirical portrayal of French society after Waterloo. The handsome, ambitious Julien Sorel is one of the most intriguing characters in European literature.

Zola, Émile, *Germinal*. Penguin Classics 2004. This epic tale describes the world of the miners of northern France in the second half of the 19th century and their struggle for their rights.

Maps

More detailed maps are recommended to supplement those in this guide. Maps of France can be found in book shops at home, but are significantly cheaper in France itself.

Shell General and Holiday Maps France 1 : 200,000   **Road maps**
Michelin Régional Road Maps (various scales), local 1 : 150,000
Michelin France Tourist & Motoring Atlas 1 : 200,000, with 75 city maps
IGN Cartes Routières 1 : 140,000 1 : 250,000

Maps for hikers   The Institut Géographique National (IGN) publishes excellent books of maps on a variety of scales:
Cartes des promenades TOP 100 1 : 100,000, road map and map of footpaths including grandes randonnées and as well as tourist information
Rando Editions 1 : 50,000
Topographical maps 1 : 25,000 and 1 : 50,000
TOP 25 / Series Bleue 1 : 25,000: special edition of the topographical maps for tourist areas such as Alsace/Vosges or the Alps.

Maps for cyclists   The Michelin Régional road maps in combination with the IGN TOP 100 for detail are recommended to cyclists.

Military Cemeteries

The Commonwealth War Graves Commission (www.cwgc.org) can supply information on military cemeteries in France. This non-profit-making organization's remit is to pay tribute to the 1,700,000 Commonwealth soldiers who died in the two world wars. Amongst its many activities, the CWGC undertakes renovation work on military cemeteries all over the world. France is also home to eleven American military cemeteries. The cemeteries are operated by an independent government agency, the American Battle Monuments Commission (www.abmc.gov). All cemeteries are open to the public and are meticulously maintained.

Money

Euro   Since 2002 the euro has been legal tender in France. The national faces of French euro and euro-cent coins show a tree of life on the one and two-euro coins, surrounded by the motto »Liberté, Egalité, Fraternité«; on the 10, 20 and 50 euro-cent coins is the Sower (La Semeuse) well known from the old franc coins but in a new design; and the coins for 1, 2 and 5 euro-cents bear the »Marianne«.
Note: because the word »cent« also means »one hundred«, the old word »centime« is mostly used for euro-cents.

Foreign currency regulations   The import and export of foreign and national currency to and from France is not subject to any restrictions. Amounts above 7600 € must be declared when entering or leaving the country.

Exchanging money   Those bringing currencies other than the euro with them into France should note that only post offices and banks with the sign »Change« offer a foreign currency exchange service. Alternatively, go to a bureau de change.

CONTACT DETAILS FOR CREDIT CARDS

In the event of lost bank or credit cards you can contact the following numbers in UK and USA (phone numbers when dialling from France):

► **Eurocard/MasterCard**
Tel. 001 / 636 7227 111

► **Visa**
Tel. 001 / 410 581 336

► **American Express UK**
Tel. 0044 / 1273 696 933

► **American Express USA**
Tel. 001 / 800 528 4800

► **Diners Club UK**
Tel. 0044 / 1252 513 500

► **Diners Club USA**
Tel. 001 / 303 799 9000

Have the bank sort code, account number and card number as well as the expiry date ready.

The following numbers of UK banks (dialling from France) can be used to report and stop lost or stolen bank and credit cards issued by those banks:

► **HSBC**
Tel. 0044 / 1442 422 929

► **Barclaycard**
Tel. 0044 / 1604 230 230

► **NatWest**
Tel. 0044 / 142 370 0545

► **Lloyds TSB**
Tel. 0044 / 1702 278 270

 Exchange rates

- 1 € = 1.33 US$
  1 US$ = 0.75 €
  1 £ = 1.10 €
  1 € = 0.90 £

The banks are open Mon–Fri or Tue–Sat from 8am or 9am to noon or 1pm and from 2pm to 4.30pm or 5pm. In larger cities some stay open the whole day. Banks close at noon before holidays. **Opening times banks**

All over the country it is possible to obtain money from cash machines (distributeur automatique de billets, point d'argent) using a cheque or credit card and the appropriate PIN (charges applied). **Cash machines**

Payment is commonly made with cards in France, be it in a restaurant, hotel, at the petrol station or in the supermarket. That means that you should always carry notes in smaller denominations, as larger amounts can often not be changed. Many retail shops also accept international credit cards. **Credit cards**

Loss of credit cards or cheque cards should be reported immediately. Note your account number, sort code and card numbers before the trip. **Loss of cards**

Autoroute
tolls

Autoroute tolls can be paid either in cash or with commonly accepted credit cards such as MasterCard or Visa.

Museums and Chateaux

Opening times

Municipal museums are normally closed on Mondays, national museums mostly on Tuesdays. Important establishments do not generally have a closing day during the high season. In the winter, from around November to March or April, many museums and chateaux close completely or restrict their opening hours markedly. Note: the last admission is often 30 minutes or an hour before the published closing time.

Admission

On the first Sunday of the month, admission is free to national museums and state-run monuments – apart from those in Versailles – as well as many municipal museums. A reduced admission price applies on other Sundays. For young people up to the age of 18 and students (ID card) admission is normally free; this is definitely the case in state-run Musées Nationaux. Often local and regional museum passes are available, which allow entry to most institutions; some also include the use of public transport. There is not always a saving to be made, as it is not possible to visit all the sights in the time available; however, it is an advantage not to have to join the queues at the ticket office.

Information

Detailed information is provided of course by the local and regional tourist offices. Maison de la France (► Information) produces the brochure *France's cultural sites* with information on chateaux, museums, monuments, interactive centres and historic routes. Maison de la France brochures can be downloaded from the website. For internet addresses see ►p.110. Larousse publishes the museum guide *Le Nouveau Guide des Musées de France* by P. Cabanne, which covers museums in the whole of France (last edition unfortunately in 1997).

Nature Reserves

France's six national parks (Parc National, www.parcsnationaux-fr.com) cover 2.3% of the country's area, while the 42 regional nature parks of the mainland (Parc Naturel Régional, http://parcs-naturels-regionaux.fr) extend over a further 19%. With the exception of Port-Cros and the Cevennes, the national parks lie in high mountain regions and are well-visited in summer. In the uninhabited core areas, vehicles, dogs and hunting are forbidden, and camping heavily

◉ NATIONAL PARKS

▶ **Parc National du Mercantour**
23 Rue d'Italie, BP 316
F-06006 Nice Cedex
www.parc-mercantour.com
Core area: 685 sq km/264 sq mi
North of St-Martin-Vésubie, in the
High Alps near the Italian border.

▶ **Parc National de la Vanoise**
135 Rue Dr Julliand, BP 705
F-73007 Chambéry Cedex
Tel. 04 79 62 30 54
www.vanoise.com
Core area: 528 sq km/204 sq mi
In Savoy between the high-lying
valleys of the Isère and the Arc, at
elevations of 1250–3850m/
4100–12,630ft.

▶ **Parc National des Ecrins**
Domaine de Charance
F-05000 Gap, Tel. 04 92 40 20 10
www.les-ecrins-parc-national.fr
Core area: 920 sq km/355 sq mi
The départements Isère and
Hautes-Alpes with the Pelvoux
hunting reserve, at elevations of
800–4102m/2625–13,458ft.

▶ **Parc National des Cévennes**
Le Château, BP 15, F-48400 Florac
Tel. 04 66 49 53 00
www.cevennes-parcnational.fr
Core area: 913 sq km/353 sq mi
Départements Lozère, Gard,
Ardèche. Barren limestone high-
lands with sparse, very interesting
vegetation.

▶ **Parc National de Port-Cros**
Castel Ste-Claire, Rue Ste-Claire
F-83418 Hyères Cedex
Tel. 04 94 12 82 30
www.portcrosparcnational.fr
6.5 sq km/2.5 sq mi of land, 18 sq
km/7 sq mi of sea
Ile de Port-Cros with the surrounding sea bed.

▶ **Parc National des Pyrénées**
59 Route de Pau, F-65000 Tarbes
Tel. 05 62 44 36 60
www.parc-pyrenees.com
Core area: 457 sq km/176 sq mi
Southwest of Tarbes near the
Spanish border at elevations of
1100–3300m/3610–10,830ft.

regulated; towns, tourist infrastructure, ski areas and so on are found
on the periphery.
The regional nature parks – which lie in rural problem areas that are
experiencing high levels of urban migration – aim to harmonize the
preservation of an intact ecology with the economic development of
the region and tourism. Some nature parks maintain interesting
open-air museums (*ecomusée*).

Information of all kinds – including details on the numerous activ-   Information
ities such as mountain hiking, climbing, ski tours, MTB, parasailing,
gliding, rafting, kayaking, angling, riding etc. – is provided by the administration of the nature park as well as the local and regional tourist offices. The comprehensive websites of the parks also offer the
possibility of booking accommodation, guided tours and so on.

Newspapers and Magazines

Newspapers and magazines are available from the »Maison de la Presse«, present in every town, in stationery shops, book shops, tobacconists, small newsagents and stations. English-language newspapers and magazines are on sale in the larger holiday centres and cities, normally a day after publication.

National newspapers
The most influential daily is the liberal *Le Monde*. The next day's newspaper is on sale from 3pm in the afternoon. There are supplements on Tuesdays (economy), Wednesdays (culture) and Fridays (literature). Another large daily paper is the conservative *Le Figaro*. On Saturdays it contains supplements, the *Figaro Magazine* and *Figaro Madame*, on Wednesdays it is accompanied by the *Figaroscope*, the weekly what's-on guide. Another daily, *France-Soir*, is issued by the same publisher as *Le Figaro*. *L'Humanité* is the mouthpiece of the French Communist Party, and *Libération*, once on the extreme left, has developed into the favourite newspaper of the liberal-left middle classes. On Wednesdays, *Le Canard Enchaîné* hits the newsstands, satirically attacking the political and social events of the week. For internet addresses see ▶p.137.

National magazines
Thursdays see the publication of three news magazines: *Le Nouvel Observateur* (politically centre-left), *L'Express* and *Le Point* (both rather centre-right). The gossipy *Paris Match* provides some entertainment among the veritable forest of magazines on French shelves.

English-language magazines
Paris Voice is an English language magazine and associated website (www.parisvoice.com) with articles on Paris life, book reviews, sections on music, theatre and dance, classified ads and much more. Covering similar ground, *Paris Kiosque* and its website www.paris.org are also in English.

Personal Safety

Theft
In cities and in tourist regions – especially Provence and the Côte d'Azur – the danger of falling victim to pickpockets or car thieves is ever present. Papers, cash, cheque and credit cards and so on should be kept neither in the back trouser pocket nor in a handbag or rucksack. Never leave any kind of article, not just objects of value, in an unattended vehicle. Copies of all documents – from passport and ID card to credit cards and plane tickets – should be kept separate from the originals; it is also advisable to leave a set of copies with a trusted person back home. Those staying in caravans and motorhomes should not spend the night outside camp sites or in remote spots.

On the Côte d'Azur it is not uncommon for car drivers to get mugged in car parks and at red lights. In summer, an air-conditioning system is an advantage, not least because the windows can then remain closed.

During the summer dry season there is the risk of forest fires. **Forest fires** Though this risk is present everywhere, it is greatest in the south. As a consequence it is strictly forbidden to kindle a fire in a forest or within a distance of 200m/220yd of one. Likewise it is not permitted to smoke or to throw away cigarette butts or flammable objects in open countryside. Camping is only allowed at sites expressly set aside for the purpose.

Post and Communications

Post offices are identified with a yellow sign reading »La Poste«. **Post offices** Sometimes the old PTT (Postes, Télégraphes, Téléphones) signs still show the way. Apart from sending letters, parcels and telegrams, it is possible to make telephone calls and often to use a fax machine and the internet. At certain times of day there can be queues, as the post office also provides a banking service.

In large towns and cities, post offices are open Mon–Fri 8.30–6pm/ **Opening times** 7pm with no break for lunch (otherwise 9am–noon 2pm–5pm/6pm) and Sat till noon.

Stamps (timbres) can be purchased singly or in booklets (carnets) of **Postage** ten in post offices, tobacconists (tabacs) and those bars that also sell cigarettes. Postcards and letters to the UK require a 0.65 € stamp (prioritaire); letters bound for further afield need a 0.85 € stamp.

French letter boxes are yellow and as a rule have two slots: one for **Letter boxes** letters destined for the same département, the other, marked »autres destinations«, for the rest of the world.

Public telephones are designed the accept phone cards (télécartes, **Telephone boxes** with 50 or 100 units), available in post offices, offices of France Telecom, tobacconists, and SNCF and Métro stations. The public telephones in cafés, bistros and post offices often still accept coins. It is possible to receive calls in many telephone boxes.

Normal tariffs (tarif rouge) apply to all calls (local/national/interna- **Telephone tariffs** tional) Mon–Fri 8am–7pm, otherwise the reduced tarif bleu applies. Local calls are then approx. 45% cheaper, with long-distance calls within France approx. 30% and international calls almost 50% less.

INTERNATIONAL DIALLING CODES

▶ **To France**
from the UK and Republic of Ireland: tel. 00 33
from the USA, Canada and Australia: tel. 00 11 33
After dialling the country code, the zero that precedes the subsequent local area code is omitted.

▶ **From France**
to the UK: tel. 00 44
to the Republic of Ireland: Tel. 00 353

to the USA and Canada: tel. 00 1
to Australia: tel. 00 61

▶ **To Monaco**
Tel. 00 377
To make international calls from Monaco (France is sometimes on the other side of the road!) use the normal international dialling codes.

▶ **Directory enquiries**
National: 12
International: 3212

Mobiles The French mobile network is run by three providers: Bouygues, Orange and SFR. Ask your provider about roaming charges, which can be pricey, before you leave. Cheap prepaid cards, with a French telephone number, are available in supermarkets, tobacconists, branches of FNAC and post offices.

Internet access It is possible to use the internet in many post offices all over France (Cyberposte, information at www.cyberposte.com). Chip cards are sold at the counter for this purpose (reload cards are cheaper). It is more comfortable but more expensive in one of the many internet cafés; some calculate time of use to the nearest minute, which can reduce costs. Those who want to use their own computer will need an international adapter set. Many hotels offer free W-LAN (Wi-Fi) access to the internet.

Prices and Discounts

Prices Prices are broadly comparable with those in the UK, though the exchange rate of the pound against the euro will of course have an effect. The lower limit for a daily budget –without travel costs and for two people sharing a room – is around 50 euros per head. In Paris hotels and restaurants are more expensive than in the provinces, although prices vary greatly according to location and proximity to the important sights, so that even in the capital it is not necessary to put undue strain on the purse strings. The price of museum visits can mount up; the important institutions charge 5–8 euros for adults, some going up to 16 euros in the high season.

WHAT DOES IT COST?

Simple double room
from €50

Simple meal
€8

Three-course meal
from €18

Petrol 1l Super
€1.50–1.60

Cup of café au lait
€3–3.50

Lemonade or cola
€3–3.50

Saving money

It is advantageous to travel during the off season; in popular holiday areas, the prices are noticeably higher in the peak season. Many towns offer reasonably priced packages including the hotel, use of public transport, museum admission, tours etc. Regionally and locally, it is common practise to offer tickets to visitors covering public transport and museum visits, as well as museum passes and group tickets. There is free admission to many museums on the first Sunday of the month, and reduced admission charges at others. In cafés it is cheaper to sit at the bar; sitting at a table or outside costs more. Those who want a good meal without stretching the budget too much should go out to lunch during the week. It is possible to save money and have a wonderful meal at the same time in a supermarket or at a *traiteur* (delicatessen with ready prepared food).

Shopping

Types of shop

In every village there is a *boulangerie* (bakery) and a *boucherie* (butcher's) and as a rule also an *epicerie* or *alimentation*, i.e. a small grocer's shop. On the edge of larger towns are *supermarchés* (supermarkets), which mostly boast a large and excellent range of fine foods. Larger cities have pedestrian shopping areas with department stores and shops of every kind.

Markets

A visit to a market, with its myriad of colours and scents, is a real pleasure: fruit, vegetable and flower markets, on which also cheese, sausage and other delicatessen, clothing, kitchen utensils, CDs etc.

are offered for sale; fish markets on the coast; arts and crafts markets, antique markets, flea markets, not forgetting those offering stamps and books. One peculiarity takes the form of the auctions for live fish (criées) in port towns; though it is necessary to get up very early for this experience. Local tourist offices can provide information.

Opening times

No laws apply in France governing the hours of trading. For this reason the following is merely a guide to opening hours. Special note should be taken of the fact that in the months of July and August, the main holiday period, many shops either close completely or restrict their opening hours. This does not apply in the holiday areas themselves.

Retail ► Retail shops are normally open from 9am or 10am to 7pm or 8pm. Grocer's shops and bakeries generally open early; the smaller ones often close between 12.30pm and 4pm but then remain open late into the evening. Normally Sunday is the only closing day; bakeries, butcher's shops, wine shops and flower shops are however open on Sundays until noon or 1pm. The shops open on a Sunday are closed on Mondays, from time to time also on Wednesdays.

Department stores, shopping centres ► Department stores and many large shops are open on weekdays from 9.30am to 6.30pm. Large shopping centres (centres commerciaux, supermarchés) are open for business Mon–Sat 9am–7pm, sometimes to 8pm or 9pm. Some are closed on Mondays.

Souvenirs

As regards the craft industry, many regions have appealing products on offer. Among them are: faïence pottery, lace, mouth-blown glass and earthenware from Brittany; wickerwork, ceramics and stoneware from Burgundy; wickerwork, porcelain and enamel from Limousin; leather, faïence pottery and decorated clogs from the Pyrenees; lace from Normandy; pottery and worked gold articles, furniture and mouth-blown glass from Picardy; cloth, made amongst other things into scarves and bags, as well as perfume and scent from Provence. In the port towns, shops selling boating equipment and sailing clothing are good places to find wet-weather gear for holidays on the coast; seaman's jumpers, sailor shirts and fisherman's caps make good gifts for the folks back home.

Petrossian in Paris (18 Boulevard de Latour Maubourg) is a legendary establishment for delicatessen

France is a veritable cornucopia of **culinary specialities**, which are also available in preserved form. Along with the cheeses and sweets, the products include butter biscuits and smoked offal sausage from Brittany, mustard from Dijon, honey from the mountains of Provence, olive oil from Languedoc-Roussillon, rillons and rillettes (potted pork, goose or duck meat), vinegar and quince jelly from the Loire valley, aromatic Provençal herbs (herbes de Provence), and foie gras (force-fed goose or duck liver) from southwestern France.

Visitors to France who wish to stock up the wine cellar at home can collect advice and recommendations from a wine grower, in a cave coopérative (wine producers' cooperative) or at a Maison du Vin (►Wine). For import/export regulations see ►European Single Market. Spirits are highly taxed in France and for this reason not better value than at home.

Drinks

Son et Lumière

The extravagantly designed »Spectacles Son et Lumière« (»sound and light spectacles«) are very popular. They take place in the summer season in particularly attractive touristic locations, primarily in chateaux and old town quarters, mostly starting at 8pm–10pm. Employing magnificent illumination effects (including coloured lasers), music and sometimes actors clad in historical costume, scenes from the past are played out to the visiting public. Whether the performance is or is not pure kitsch – and whether the spectacle is worth the often pricey admission fee – is something each must judge for himself.

Sport and Outdoors

Sports enthusiasts will find a veritable paradise in France. Many spectator sports are enjoyed here, such as tennis, football, horse racing and sailing, and tournaments, regattas and grand prix competitions take place throughout the year. Those keen on participation sports get their money's worth too. Water sports such as sailing, surfing, diving, kayaking and rafting are much in demand – small wonder considering that France has several thousand miles of coastline as well as innumerable rivers and canals. There are countless possibilities, too, to take part in country sports such as riding, as well as golf and hiking. A number of gliding areas enjoy a worldwide reputation, and hang-gliding and paragliding are very popular. It is often possible to hire equipment, and it goes without saying that instruction is included in the price. Courses are available that include accommodation and food, too. Information is provided by Maison de la France and local tourist offices (►Information).

Spectator Sports

Football and rugby

Football is just as popular in France as it is in England and the popularity of rugby, too, is comparable with that in the British Isles. The two largest stadia in the country are to be found in Paris: the Stade de France (capacity 80,000, in St-Denis), in which France became

world champions in 1998, and the Parc des Princes (capacity 48,000, 16th arr.). Tickets for such events as the »Coupe de France« (a competition open to all French football clubs) or the »Grand Tournoi« (Six Nations Rugby Tournament) are available in branches of FNAC and the Virgin megastores, among other places.

France's second national sport played on grass is rugby.

Horse racing and betting number among the greatest passions of the French people. Countless horse races take place in Paris; in no other city in the world can you place as many bets as in the metropolis on the Seine. On the first Sunday in October in the Hippodrome de Longchamp in Paris – the »French Ascot« – the »Prix de l'Arc de Triomphe« is awarded at the most important horse racing competition in the world.

Cycle racing

In July, the three-week Tour de France takes place, ending on the Champs-Elysées in Paris (▶Baedeker Special p.160). Further classics are the Paris–Roubaix and the Paris–Tours races (for dates ▶Festivals, Holidays and Events). Detailed information can be found in the monthly *Vélo-Magazine* and the sports journal *L'Equipe*.

Tennis

The French Open (Les Internationaux de France de Roland Garros) is one of the best known tennis tournaments in the world. It is staged in Paris's Stade Roland-Garros (end of May, www.fft.fr/rolandgarros).

Traditional sports

In some regions traditional sports are still practised. In Brittany these sports involve shows of strength, and can be experienced at many Celtic festivals, sports such as wrestling, throwing the discus or tree trunks, tug-of-war and tire-bâton, in which competitors lift each other up with a stake. The best known Basque sport is pelota, a fast-moving ball game for two teams with up to ten players, in which a leather ball is hurled at a wall (fronton) and caught again. Tests of strength are also typical for the Basque region: tug-of-war (soka tira), carrying straw bales (lasto altxari), sawing wood (arpana) and lifting wheelbarrows (orga jokoa) – disciplines originating in farm work. This archaic world can be experienced at the »Festivals de la Force Basque«.

Bullfighting based on the Spanish model (*corrida*), which always ends in death – normally for the bull – is very popular in Languedoc-Roussillon and southwestern France. There are large arenas in Nîmes, Bordeaux, Dax and Bayonne. Man and beast also face each other in the »course landaise« of Gascony, but this bullfight requires »only« considerable courage and skill: the *écarteur* or *sauteur* stands before the bull without protection and must move out of the charging animal's way (écarter) or boldly leap over him (sauter). A jury judges the acrobatic performance.

Bullfighting

Course landaise

Sport & Leisure

Angling is a popular pastime in France. Enthusiasts take to the numerous streams, lakes and rivers to enjoy coarse fishing, spin fishing and fly fishing. A distinction is made between inshore waters of the first category (predominantly salmon) and the second category (mainly other species). For the second category a basic stamp suffices (*timbre de base*), for the first a supplement (*supplément*) is required. Regulations and the closed season vary according to the region and the category. For inshore waters open to the public (*eaux libres*) a permit from the responsible Société de Pêche is required, while for privately owned stretches (*eaux closes*) the landowner or leaseholder must give permission. Those fishing in the sea from the shore can use a maximum of two rods; be aware that there are areas where this is prohibited. Other regulations apply to fishing from a boat or with nets.

Angling

► Hiking and Mountain Climbing

Mountain hiking

Boule or Pétanque is a national sport, particularly in the south. Two teams play on firm sand or gravel. The game is played with up to 12 metal balls 70–80mm/2¾–3in in diameter. The team whose balls come closest to a smaller wooden target ball (*cochon*) 6–10m/20–33ft away wins.

Boule

Flying, gliding, hang-gliding and paragliding can be learnt in many places in France. Some gliding areas such as Gap in the Dauphiné enjoy an international reputation. Parachuting and hot-air ballooning is on offer in many regions, e.g. on the Loire or in Alsace.

Air sports

As far as golf goes, France is still an insider's tip. The wonderful golf courses across all the regions are anything but crowded (with a few exceptions such as the Côte d'Azur). Perhaps the most marvellous course is Les Bordes southeast of Beaugency on the Loire. Even if the sport is increasingly becoming open to a broader public, it has main-

Golf

▶ IMPORTANT ADRESSES

▶ **Union Nationale pour la Pêche**
17 Rue Bergère, F-75009 Paris
Fax 01 48 01 00 65
www.federationpeche.fr
www.ffpsc.com

▶ **Fédération Nationale Aéronautique**
155 Avenue Wagram
F-75017 Paris
Fax 01 44 29 92 01
www.ff-aero.fr

▶ **Fédération Française de Vol Libre**
4 Rue de Suisse F-06000 Nice
Fax 04 97 03 82 83
www.ffvl.fr

▶ **Fédération Française de Golf**
68 Rue Anatole France
F-92309 Levallois-Perret Cedex
Fax 01 41 49 77 01
www.ffgolf.org

▶ **Fédération Française de Canoë–Kayak**
87 Quai de la Marne
F-94340 Joinville-Le Pont
Fax 01 48 86 13 25
www.ffck.org

▶ **AN Rafting**
Les Iles de Macot
F-73210 Aime-la-Plagne
Fax 04 79 55 61 63
www.an-rafting.com

▶ **Fédération Française d'Equitation**
81 Avenue E. Vaillant
F-92517 Boulogne Cedex
Fax 01 58 17 58 00, www.ffe.com

▶ **Fédération Française de Voile**
17 Rue H. Bocquillon
F-75015 Paris
Fax 01 40 60 37 37
www.ffvoile.org

A bird's-eye view of the volcanoes of the Auvergne

► **Fédération Française de Surf**
Plage Nord, BP 28
F-40150 Hossegor
Fax 05 58 43 60 57
www.surfingfrance.com

► **Fédération Française d'Etudes et de Sports sous-marins**
24 Quai de Rive-Neuve
F-13007 Marseille
Fax 04 91 54 77 43
www.ffessm.fr

► **Ô Chateau**
Several wine-tasting bars in pretty locations in Paris
(1st, 11th, 15th arr.)
Tel. from France 0800 80 11 48
Tel. from abroad 01 44 73 97 80
www.o-chateau.com

► **École du Vin de Paris**
48 Rue Baron Le Roy
F-75012 Paris
Tel. 01 43 41 33 94
www.ecole-du-vin.fr

► **L'École du Vin CIVB**
1–3 Cours du 30 Juillet
F-33075 Bordeaux Cedex

Tel. 05 56 00 22 85
http://ecole.vins-bordeaux.fr

► **Le Cordon Bleu Paris**
8 Rue L. Delhomme
F-75015 Paris
Fax 01 48 56 03 96
www.cordonbleu.net

► **École de Gastronomie Française Ritz Escoffier**
15 Place Vendôme, F-75001 Paris
(Courses: 38 Rue Cambon)
Tel. 01 43 16 30 50
www.ritzparis.com

► **Cours de Cuisine Françoise Meunier**
7 Rue P. Lelong
F-75002 Paris
Tel. 01 40 26 14 00
www.fmeunier.com

► **Lenôtre**
Pavillon Elysée
10 Avenue des Champs Elysées
F-75008 Paris
Tel. 01 42 65 97 60
63 Rue d'Antibes
F-06400 Cannes, www.lenotre.fr

tained its distinguished character. There are over 550 golf courses in France, and about 140 of them have come together to form the »France Golf International Club«, which concerns itself with foreign visitors. Of special interest are the passes, valid for different lengths of time, that permit the holder to play on any golf course in an entire region. Maison de la France (►Information) produces the brochure *Golf en France* with data on all the courses in France; in addition, Club France Golf International provides information.

Along with long, gentle stretches of river there are numerous white water areas across the whole of France. These require a high level of fitness and experience.

Canoeing, kayaking, rafting

►Cycling Holidays

Cycling

THE GREAT SUMMER SPECTACLE

France's legendary president Charles de Gaulle put it like this: »In July, when the tour is under way, it is pointless doing politics in France. No one listens anyway. At this time of year, even a revolution wouldn't interest a soul.«

The gigantic spectacle that winds through France for three whole weeks absorbs our neighbours completely, and in the rest of the world, too, the »grande boucle« arouses a disproportionate level of media interest. Small wonder: after the Olympic Games and the FIFA World Cup, the Tour de France is the third largest sporting event in the world. On top of this, a win in the Tour de France is the greatest thing that can happen in the life of a competitive cyclist, greater even than the title of world champion.

How it all started

At the beginning of the year 1900 a bitter battle for readers was taking place in the French sporting press. The market leader, with 80%, was Le Vélo, four journals sharing the remaining 20%. The success of Le Vélo was attributed to its involvement in the organization of long-distance races such as Paris–Brest–Paris and Bordeaux–Paris. Becoming entangled in the Dreyfus affair cost the publisher readers however. At the same time the tyre manufacturer Clément began an offensive intended to build up a promotional platform. Together with Henri Desgranges, the hour record holder, and Victor Goddet, father of Jacques Goddet, later to become director of the Tour de France, Clément developed a new sporting paper and called it L'Auto. Now they needed ideas to give their fledgling project momentum. They were provided by the young sports journalist Geo Lefèvre, who in 1902 explained his concept: »If we want to rise above the rest, we must introduce a stage race that runs for six full days across France.« Desranges was amazed: »That is like an invitation to commit suicide,« he responded. But sure enough, on 1 July 1903 the first tour began, with the first stage covering 467km/290mi (!) from Paris to Lyon, and with the exceptions of 1915–18 and 1940–46 it has been taking place every year since. Today the »Societé du Tour de France« is the number one cycle race organizer in the world; even the Rallye Paris–Dakar goes back to one of its initiatives. The Tour soon served as a model for a whole range of cycle races in other countries, such as the Ronde de Belgie (since 1908), Giro d'Italia (1909),

In 2003, Lance Armstrong and Jan Ullrich – here in the Pyrenees – were involved in one of the most exciting head-to-head battles in the history of the Tour de France.

Deutschlandrundfahrt (1911), Tour de Suisse (1933) and Vuelta a Espagna (1935). A plaque commemorates the historic meeting in the »Taverne Zimmer« on Rue du Faubourg-Montmartre in Paris (it was later renamed »Madrid« and then »Friday's«) at which the idea of the Tour de France was first discussed. There is also a commemorative plaque on the gable of the restaurant »Le Réveil Matin« in Montgeron, south of Paris, where 60 fearless cyclists gathered in summer 1903 to set out on their big adventure.

Where, how – and how much

The starting point and route of the Tour de France – around 3500km/2175mi – is newly determined each year. Neighbouring countries are included too – thus the 1998 Tour started in Dublin. During the race, the leader wears the yellow jersey, introduced in 1919. In addition, since 1933 the winner of the highest number of climbs, the King of the Mountain, has been recognized (and has worn the polka dot jersey since 1975), and the green jersey is worn by the rider with the most sprint points, a competition introduced in 1953. The finale of the Tour de France is a very special experience, traditionally taking place on the Champs-Elysées in Paris. In 2008, a total of 3.25 million euros in prize money was awarded, and the overall winner received €450,000. The dates and stage routes are published by virtually all large national newspapers as well as the French sports publications *L'Equipe* and *Vélo-Magazine*.

King of the Mountain

Those who know the Tour well consider the mountain stages to be the real measure. In order to make the race harder, Desranges had introduced the Pyrenees (1910) and then the Alps (1911) to the route. Today, the mountain stages are indispensable. The rider who is first to complete a 14–20km/8.5–12mi climb with slopes of up to 17% is a true hero. The most famous of such ascents in the Alps are the Galbier (2646m/8680ft) and Izoard (2360m/7740ft) passes as well as the climb to Alpe d'Huez (1860m/6100ft). In Provence, Mont Ventoux is the destination of thousands of cycling fans. A memorial near the summit recalls Tom Simpson, the English favourite, who suffered heart failure here in 1967. Further into the Pyrenees the Tourmalet (2115m/6940ft) and Aubisque (1709m/5607ft) passes should not be left out. The knowledge that the best racers in the world – such as Coppi, Kübler, Anquetil, Merckx, Hinault, Lemond, Induráin, Armstrong and Ullrich – have battled it out here make the trip into a truly unforgettable experience.

Riding	There are opportunities to go horse riding in virtually every region of the country. Numerous organizations offer lessons and arrange tours lasting several days.
Sailing	Sailing is possible on the lakes and the coast, particularly the Mediterranean. Boat hire, sailing clubs and sailing schools can be found in many places.
Sand yachting	On the coasts – for instance in Brittany or n the English Channel – the miles of broad beaches with hard sand are perfect for sand yachting with three-wheeled sand yachts (char à voile). Speeds of up to 60mph/100kmh are reached.
Surfing and windsurfing	The main region to go surfing »for real« is the Atlantic coast between the mouth of the Gironde and the Spanish border, because only here during the rising tide do the necessary waves build up. Windsurfing is enjoyed almost everywhere, but the winds of Aquitaine and Brittany are especially suitable. Information on the best surfing areas on the Mediterranean and the Atlantic is provided in *Surfing Europe* by Chris Nelson and Demi Taylor (Footprint Handbooks 2008).
Diving	France as a nation is traditionally a leader in diving, marine research and underwater archaeology. The Mediterranean coast is still among the most highly prized areas, even if the fauna has suffered due to water pollution and overfishing. A licence is required for scuba fishing.
Hiking	▶Hiking
Tennis	Almost all larger towns, the holiday regions and the better hotels have tennis courts. Tourist offices can provide information on tennis holidays and courses offered by a variety of suppliers.
Winter sports	▶Winter sports

Further Activities

Language courses	A whole range of language schools both from France and abroad offer courses in French, which sometimes involve staying with a French family. Alongside holiday courses lasting from two to four weeks, there are intensive courses that last only a few days and, at the other end of the scale, long-stay courses. Courses specifically aimed at school children and young people are also available. There are language schools across the whole of then country, with larger numbers in Paris and southern France. Information is provided by Maison de la France (▶Information) and the cultural services of the French embassy (UK: www.ambafrance-uk.org/French-culture-in-Great-Britain.html; USA: www.frenchculture.org).

Courses on the subject of wine – covering the area of cultivation, viniculture, cellar techniques, tasting, history etc. – are offered by the
central organizations of each individual wine-growing area. The most
renowned institution is the Ecole du Vin des CIVB in Bordeaux.

Wine seminars

A world-famous institute for both professionals and ambitious amateurs is the Le Cordon Bleu culinary school, founded in Paris in
1895. It is also possible to perfect one's talents in the famous Hotel
Ritz or under the guidance of the legendary confectioner Gaston
Lenôtre. A friendly informal atmosphere pervades the activities in
the kitchens of the schools of Françoise Meunier, also in Paris. Naturally, there are culinary schools to be found throughout France; for
addresses and further information go to www.goosto.fr/guide.

Culinary courses

Time

France is in the central European time zone (CET), one hour ahead
of Greenwich Mean Time. For the summer months from the beginning of April to the end of October European summer time is used
(CEST = CET+1 hour).

An hour ahead

Transport

By car

The motorways of France (*autoroutes*) are marked by blue and white
signs. Apart from feeder roads and connecting carriageways in the vicinity of larger cities, drivers must pay a toll (*péage*) to use them,
although some stretches are so little used that in order to save on
staffing costs the toll has been dispensed with. The charges can also
be paid by credit card (but not with a Maestro card) at the »CB«
counter.
The toll amounts to 4.50–6.50 € per 100km/62mi; there is a toll cal-
culator at www.saprr.fr (»Préparation/Itineraires/Tarifs«).

Autoroutes

The main carriers of long-distance traffic are the excellently built
trunk roads known as the *routes nationales*, broadly the equivalent of
the UK's A-roads. They are identified by red and white signage
marked with a number (e.g. N 555). The volume of traffic is mostly
quite low; however long traffic jams are not unknown on the main
routes during holiday periods (beginning of July and beginning of
August).

Routes nationales

▶ INFORMATION FOR TRANSPORT

AUTOMOBILE CLUBS

▶ **AA**
Tel. +44 (0)161 495 8945
www.theaa.com

▶ **RAC**
Tel. +44 (0)1922 727313
www.rac.co.uk

▶ **Automobile Club de France**
6 – 8 Place de la Concorde
F-75008 Paris
Tel. 01 42 65 34 70
www.automobileclubdefrance.org

CAR HIRE

▶ **Avis**
Tel. 0844 581 0147
www.avis.com

▶ **Budget**
Tel. 0844 581 9998
www.budget.co.uk

▶ **Europcar**
Tel. 0845 758 5375
www.europcar.com

▶ **Hertz**
Tel. 08708 44 88 44
www.hertz.com

AIRLINES

▶ **Air France**
In France: tel. 36 54, 0820 320
www.airfrance.fr
In the UK: tel. 0871 66 33 777
www.airfrance.co.uk
In the USA: tel. 1-800-237-2747
www.airfrance.us
In Australia: tel. 1300 390 190
(toll free), www.airfrance.com.au

▶ **British Airways**
In the UK: tel. 0844 493 0 787
In France: tel. +33 (0)825 825
Paris CDG 2: tel. 0825 88 5 100
www.britishairways.com

▶ **Low Cost Carriers**
www.aerlingus.com
www.easyjet.com
www.flybe.com
www.germanwings.com
www.jet2.com
www.ryanair.com

SNCF

▶ **Rail Europe Limited (UK)**
Rail Europe House, 34 Tower View
Kings Hill, West Malling
Kent ME19 4ED
Tel. 0844 848 4 064
www.raileurope.co.uk

▶ **SNCF Travel Centre**
1 Lower Regent Street
London SW1
(nearest tube Piccadilly Circus)

▶ **Rail Europe, Inc. (USA)**
44 South Broadway
White Plains, NY 10601
Tel. 1-800-622-8600 in the USA
Tel. 1-800-361-RAIL (7245) in Canada
www.raileurope.com

Traffic builds up at the start of the holiday season, especially on the autoroutes heading south

The *routes départementales* (secondary or B-roads) are identified by numbered yellow and white signs (e.g. D 555); important stretches are not inferior to the routes nationales. Warnings concerning the condition of the roads (e.g. »chaussée déformée«) are not to be taken lightly.

Routes départe-
mentales

The website of the AA (▸p.164) has a section entitled »Driving Requirements by Country«, which gives touring tips for France. Information on the use of autoroutes is to be found at www.autoroutes.fr, traffic bulletins (especially regarding traffic jams and alternative routes during the holiday period) at www.bison-fute.equipement.-gouv.fr. Tune in to UKW on 107.7 MHz for traffic news around the clock – in French every 15 minutes, in English every half hour.

Information for
drivers

▸Arrival

Car documents

French traffic regulations are similar to those in the UK and elsewhere in Europe. The use of seat belts is mandatory, for both driver and passengers; children under ten years of age must sit in the back and be appropriately secure. Motorbike riders must wear a crash helmet and use headlights during the day. Telephoning is only permitted with a hands-free system. At night warnings can be given only by flashing headlights. A warning vest must be kept within easy reach. In the case of an accident personal injury must have occurred for the police to become involved. Take care: there are often speed bumps in the road at the entrance to towns and villages so that drivers stay within the speed limit. Generally the vehicle coming from the right has right of way (signed »Priorité à droite«); at roundabouts those wishing to join the roundabout must wait. Major roads are identified with a sign reading »Passage protégé« before junctions.

Traffic
regulations

Top speed limits for motor vehicles:
on auroroutes 80mph/130kmh (in wet conditions 68mph/110kmh)
on expressways 68mph/110kmh (in wet conditions 62mph/100kmh)
on trunk roads and secondary roads 56mph/90kmh (in wet conditions 50mph/80kmh)
within urban areas 31mph/50kmh.

Speed limits

In spite of frequent radar speed checks, many French drive fast, not to say dangerously. Even if you drive only slightly over the limit, the fine can be hefty – between 90 and 2300 € – and must be paid immediately or the vehicle can be confiscated. No exception is made for foreigners who commit faux pas behind the wheel.

◂ Speed checks

Driving under the influence of alcohol is strictly punished in France. Driving with a blood alcohol level of 0.5 millilitres or above is an offence, and drunk driving with higher levels of alcohol, even without an injury being caused, is viewed as a serious crime.

Drinking and
driving

The Eurostar provides a fast, comfortable connection between Paris, Calais and London

Parking Around the main sights there are usually sufficient parking spaces (mostly liable to a charge, sometimes with attendants). It is permitted to park on either side of the road (in areas marked with white hatching). The side of the road on which parking is permitted frequently changes daily or fortnightly (*stationnement alterné*). Yellow lines along the side of the road indicate that parking is not allowed. The police keenly pursue parking offenders. The return of towed or clamped cars is expensive, not to mention the time involved. In the *zone bleue* (blue zone) in the inner cities, a parking disc (*disque*) **Ticket** must be displayed. Along with conventional parking meters, *horoda-* **machines** *teurs*, parking ticket machines stand centrally in parking areas. Many **Motorhomes** parking spaces, especially in city centres and along coastal roads, cannot be used by motorhomes (barrier with a height limit of 1.90–2m/6ft 3in–6ft 6in at the entrance).

Fuel Fuel prices have also risen in France. The cheapest place to fill up is at supermarkets. Outside towns, the petrol stations are often closed on national holidays and at weekends. With a credit card you can fill up at self-service petrol pumps at supermarkets.

Breakdown on If you break down on the motorway, park the vehicle on the hard **the autoroutes** shoulder, employ the hazard lights, and put on your warning vest. Call for help using only the orange-coloured emergency telephones, not your mobile. The prices for the assistance provide by licensed companies are fixed and can be read in the breakdown vehicles. For emergency numbers see ▶Emergency.

Car hire

Almost all the national and international car rental companies are represented in all large towns and cities, sometimes in various locations (airport, station, inner city). Local suppliers are sometimes more reasonably priced than international firms, though the latter offer flexibility regarding the return of the vehicle. Flat rates for a whole week or weekend are par for the course, mostly with un-limited mileage. It is possible to book from the home country. Booking a package deal with your flight (Fly & Drive) or train ticket is recommended. The Avis company, with branches in 194 SNCF stations, grants special conditions to train travellers. You will need your passport or ID card, a driving licence (which must be at least a year old) and one of the international credit cards. The minimum age is normally 21. Personal liability insurance is included, and other forms of insurance (passenger accident, fully comprehensive, and others) can be arranged for a supplementary fee.

Taxis

It is not always possible to hail taxis in cities (when empty the taxi sign on the roof is illuminated). Only in exceptional circumstances can a passenger sit alongside the driver in the passenger seat. Many taxi drivers refuse to carry more than three people.

The total price is composed of a standing charge (PC) and a charge based on the time taken for the trip and the distance covered. A higher standing charge applies at stations. For journeys to horse race tracks, stations or airports, as well as for carrying luggage, extra charges apply. The daytime tariff (A, approx. 0.70–0.90 €/km) applies outside Paris Mon–Sat 7am–7pm, in Paris 10am–5pm; otherwise the night-time tariff B applies, and for journeys outside the city boundary tariff C or D, which are almost twice as expensive. Taxi drivers expect a tip of 15%. Information on taxi charges is available at www.taxis-de-france.com and www.artisan-taxi.com.

By Air

Domestic air services are provided by Air France and airlines such as Airlinair, CCM, Continental, EasyJet and KLM. Air France connects Paris Charles de Gaulle 2 (CDG 2) and Orly airports with 24 airports on the French mainland. Air France passengers arriving at Paris CDG 2 do not have to check in again. Paris CDG 2 offers a direct connection to the TGV lines, otherwise travellers must reckon on 2½ hours for the journey to Orly or the railway stations in central Paris. Take either the Air France buses or (faster) the RER trains for the transfer.

Transport hub Paris

By Rail

The rail network of the state-owned SNCF (Société Nationale des Chemins de Fer Français) is very well developed; indeed, along with Switzerland, France can lay claim to having the best railways in Europe. Long-distance trains and high-speed services (rapides) ply the main lines to and from the centre of Paris. The TGV (Train à Grande Vitesse, see below) mostly uses its own tracks.

SNCF

Information is available outside France from travel agents. The official SNCF distributor in the UK is Rail Europe (▶p.164) and book-

Information

ings can also be made online to destinations within France (www.sncf.co.uk). On the SNCF's own website (www.voyages-sncf.com) detailed information is given regarding trains, tariffs, discounts, reservations etc. in both French (»Guide du Voyager«) and English (»Passenger's Guide«).

Special tariffs   The SNCF offers a large number of special tariffs for certain groups (young people, families, old-age pensioners etc.).

Tickets and reservations   Outside France, tickets and reservations can be obtained from travel agents and Rail Europe. Tickets can be ordered two months before the date of travel, and written orders can be made up to six months before travelling. It is highly advisable to book TGV and motorail tickets well in advance. A reservation for the TGV can nevertheless also be made just minutes before leaving. Tickets can be ordered online and paid for with a credit card; the tickets can be collected at a French station by using a confirmation code and presenting the credit card in question.

Franking   Tickets must be stamped before boarding the train. Look for the sign reading »Composter votre billet« and the orange box on the platform. If you forget to stamp your ticket, inform the guard immediately.

Train travel with bikes   In many trains, including the TGV, bikes can be stowed free of charge. In trains with a cycle symbol passengers must load and unload their own bikes. On particular trains, including the TGV, it is possible to take a bike only if it is folded together and packaged up in a transport sack like normal luggage. Passengers must stow it in the train themselves. The reservation of storage space is subject to a charge. Detailed information is given in a publication by the European Cyclists' Federation (► Cycling Holidays) entitled *Bicycle Carriage on Long Distance Trains in the European Union*, available as a download, and from SNCF/Rail Europe (Guide du Train et du Vélo).

TGV   France's »Train à Grande Vitesse« (www.tgv.com) is the fastest scheduled train in the world (top speed 186mph/300kmh). It is often quicker and cheaper than a domestic flight. The TGV Sud-Est connects Paris Gare de Lyon with Dijon (Zurich, Brig), Lyon (Geneva, Grenoble, Milan), Avignon and Montpellier/Perpignan and Marseille/Nice/Ventimiglia. There is a direct service between Bordeaux and Narbonne. The TGV Atlantique runs from Paris Montparnasse into Brittany (Rennes, Brest, Quimper, Nantes) and to the Atlantic coast (La Rochelle, Bordeaux, Biarritz, Hendaye) and Toulouse. The TGV Nord travels from Paris Gare du Nord to Lille (Brussels) and Calais. In 2007 the TGV network was extended east from Paris Est to Mannheim/Frankfurt, to Strasbourg/Stuttgart/Munich as well as to **Eurostar**   Basle/Zurich. The high-speed Eurostar runs from London St Pancras

to Paris Nord, Lille, Calais and Brussels through the Channel
Tunnel. Brussels, Amsterdam and Cologne are connected to Paris via
the Thalys service. Thalys trains bypassing Paris (the nearest station
is Roissy) are destined for Avignon/Aix-en-Provence/Marseille
(www.thalys.com).

Thalys

The shuttle service through the Channel Tunnel, known as »Le Shuttle«, transports passengers and motor vehicles between Calais and
Folkestone around the clock. There are 1–5 trains per hour and the
journey time is 35 minutes (www.eurotunnel.com).

Eurotunnel

By Bus or Coach

A bus station (*gare routière*) is normally to be found in the vicinity of
stations and airports. SNCF buses as well as municipal and private
services complete the network. Commuters and school children are
the principal passengers; for this reason the timetables cater to local
demand rather than to tourists. Often country bus services runs only
twice daily, in the early morning and in the evening.

Regional lines

Eurolines coaches run from Paris to destinations throughout France
(►Arrival). In addition there are numerous private bus companies in
both the UK and France offering services to France and day trips to
tourist attractions.

National lines

Travellers with Disabilities

French tourist offices provide information of all kinds for disabled
travellers. An international parking permit is required to use the
parking spaces reserved for drivers with disabilities. A very helpful
brochure, *Touristes quand même!*, is published by the Comité National Français de Liaison pour la Réadaptation des Handicapés
(CNFLRH), which includes descriptions of sights in approx. 90
towns for disabled visitors. The APF has details of hotels and restaurants suitable for those in wheelchairs.

 INFORMATION FOR DISABLED TRAVELLERS

► **RADAR**
12 City Forum, 250 City Road,
London EC1V 8AF
Tel. 020 72 50 32 22
www.radar.org.uk

► **SATH (Society for the
Advancement of Travel for
the Handicapped**
347 5th Ave., no. 610
New York, NY 10016:
Tel. 21 4 47 72 84, www.sath.org

► **CNFLRH**
236 bis, Rue de Tolbiac
F-75013 Paris, tel. 01 53 80 66 66

► **Association des Paralysés
de France (APF)**
17, Boulevard Auguste Blanqui
F-75013 Paris
Tel. 01 40 78 69 00
www.apf.asso.fr

► **Groupement pour l'Insertion
des Personnes Handicapées
Physiques**
10, Rue Georges de Porto Riche
14e, Paris
Tel. 01 43 95 66 36
www.gihpnational.org

Wellness

Health spas France's thermal and mineral springs were already being used in Roman times, and today around 1200 springs bubble up in about 100 medicinal spas, whose names often carry the adjunct »les Bains«, offering relief or a cure for the greatest range of complaints. Many spas, which are often popular holiday destinations, have preserved the nostalgic feel of their heyday in the 19th century.

Thalasso-therapy »Thalassa« was the ancient Greek word for the sea, and they knew how healing salt water is for the body. In the 19th century the healing power of salt water was discovered anew, and today there are numerous thalassotherapy centres (cures based on baths with sea water). Illnesses such as rheumatism, arthritis, circulatory problems, metabolic ailments, disturbances of the autonomic nervous system and the effects of injury, as well as stress and exhaustion, are combated using baths of various temperatures, algae and mud packs, hydromassage, whirlpool baths, gymnastics in seawater pools, strolls in iodine-rich air and dietary, relaxation and fitness programmes.
The thalassotherapy institutes are increasingly developing into rather luxurious and even exclusive pool facilities visited by a well-to-do clientele without acute complaints but, for example, a little too much unwanted padding.

Information Maison de la France (► Information) produces the brochure *Water and Fitness in France*, which is also available for download. Information is also provided by local and regional tourist offices.

Winter Sports

France is also an attractive destination in winter, and there is a wide choice of winter sports areas: the Alps, Jura, Vosges, Massif Central

The Brevent near Chamonix offers breathtaking descents – with a view of Mont Blanc

and Pyrenees. As the development of the infrastructure only began in the 1960s, many of the more than 400 winter sports resorts have been created only in the last 30 years. These ski areas, where snow is assured, boast 3500 funiculars and ski lifts (only Austria has more), and a visit is well worthwhile. The selection is considerable: modern resorts designed on the drawing board, as it were (e.g. Lac de Tignes); huge skiing metropolises like La Plagne, which can accommodate 30,000 holidaymakers; winter sports towns, rich in tradition, that have developed from old settlements, such as the chic towns of Megève and Chamonix; and a number of unassuming ski stations, visited predominantly at weekends. In spite of the long journey to get there, the pistes between Lake Geneva and the Côte d'Azur are growing ever more popular, above all thanks to the spaciousness of the area, the guarantee of snow, the short waiting times at the lifts and the southern sun, especially in the Maritime Alps. The Pyrenees are considerably less popular than the Alps, although they possess good ski areas such as Font-Romeu, Bagnères and Cauterets.

Above all in Vercors, Vosges and Jura, the large number of cross-country ski runs make possible lengthy tours far from the madding crowd.

Cross-country skiing

Information on Alpine ski areas is available at www.thealps.com. Short descriptions of all French ski areas (with links), including those in the Pyrenees and the Massif Central, can be found at www.skifrance.fr and www.goski.com. The latter also features interesting accounts of personal skiing experiences.

Information

When to Go

School holidays During the summer holidays, which last from about the beginning of July until mid-September, economic and political life in France is reduced to a minimum, and many companies and public institutions close; at this time, France takes its annual holiday (*congé annuel*). The main time to travel is mid-July to the end of August. The cities empty then, and in towns and areas that are not important holiday destinations many restaurants, hotels, businesses and so on close. Conversely the holiday towns and camp sites by the sea, in the mountains and other areas of beauty in the country become overcrowded. Autoroutes and the important routes nationales should definitely be avoided on the first weekend in July and the first weekend in August. The same applies to winter sports resorts in the Alps and the Pyrenees in the winter holidays, from mid-December to the beginning of January and from about 10 February to 10 March. Accommodation must be booked well in advance in the popular regions at these times; in the other months it is possible to get by on significantly less.

Spring The best months in France as a whole – regional peculiarities notwithstanding – are May–June and September–October. In Spring a journey to Alsace is particularly rewarding, as are trips to the chateaux of the Loire, to Provence and to the Côte d'Azur; meanwhile, **Summer** in Normandy, the fruit trees are in bloom. Summer is the right time for both the lower and higher mountain ranges, such as the Vosges, Jura, Auvergne, and Cevennes as well as the Tarn Gorges, Pyrenees and Alps. It is of course the season to holiday on the coasts of the English Channel, Atlantic and Mediterranean – for those who enjoy **Autumn** the hurly burly and the high life. Autumn is a good time to go to France's numerous beautiful cities with their art treasures as well as visiting the large wine-growing regions, from Alsace to Burgundy and the Loire valley all the way Bordelais; it is also a pleasure spend- **Winter** ing time in any of the country's landscapes. In winter it is the lower and the higher mountains that attract visitors, especially the Alps and the Pyrenees, but also the French Jura and the Auvergne with their ski resorts and thermal health spas. For climate see ▶p.23.

Paris Paris is an attractive destination at any time of year. In the winter it is all aglitter, and the theatre and concert season offers a diverse range of entertainment (the number of rainy days is not higher than at other times of year). In spring and autumn the city and its surroundings are at their most colourful, the temperatures are pleasant and the streams of visitors relatively modest in size. A tip: take advantage of the period of good weather in mid-spring (around 22 April). In summer half of Paris goes on holiday, so it is particularly quiet at this time; however a large number of shops and restaurants are closed in August, and the main sights are flooded with crowds of visitors. The heat and closeness of the weather can be very unpleasant in Paris – in that case, make the best of it and head for the Seine (»Paris Plage«).

Young Travellers

France is a classic destination for young people, who prefer to spend the school holidays enjoying a variety of activities at the seaside, in the countryside, or in other towns. Tourism institutions are correspondingly well organized with regard to young people and the range of possibilities is extensive. Maison de la France (▶Information) offers a brochure entitled *France for young travellers* (also available for download) which provides information on all aspects of travelling to and in France that is relevant and interesting to young people: transport (discounts, agencies for arranging lifts in cars), accommodation (from youth hostels and camping to international centres and halls of residence), active holidays (language courses, sport, cultural work, also jobs) and all the necessary technical information. For youth hostels see ▶Accommodation.

 ORGANIZATIONS FOR YOUNG PEOPLE

▶ **Accueil des Jeunes en France**
119 Rue St-Martin
F-75004 Paris
Tel. 01 42 77 87 80

▶ **Éthic Étapes**
27 Rue de Turbigo, F-75002 Paris
Tel. 01 40 26 57 64
www.ethic-etapes.fr

Tours

TO THE NORTH OR THROUGH
THE AUVERGNE? ALONG THE
LOIRE OR ACROSS THE ALPS?
SOME OF THE MOST
MEMORABLE ROUTES
THROUGH FRANCE ARE
PRESENTED HERE.

TOURS THROUGH FRANCE

Undecided which route to take? These suggestions of classic and less familiar itineraries through the hexagon will help to make your planning somewhat easier.

From Toulouse, it is worth taking a trip to Carcassonne

Travelling in France

The types of holiday on offer in France are as rich in variety as the landscape itself. Choose between lazy days on the beach, a taste of the urban lifestyle or sporting activities in the countryside. Perhaps you wish to get to know one particular region, but you may want to gather a kaleidoscope of impressions. Anything is possible in France and, what's more, the permutations are endless.

The preferred mode of transport today is a private vehicle, be it a car, a motorbike or a mobile home. These are ideal both for a »nomadic« holiday and for excursions or reconnaissance from a fixed base. If speed is of the essence, France's motorways are excellent; tolls are not insubstantial, but a relaxing drive is usually possible,

Method of transport

and heavy traffic is only a problem at the beginning and end of the French holidays. Trains and planes are also worth considering as a means of getting there in the first place, well suited to city tours or beach vacations. The railways are very well developed and the TGV reaches all corners of the country in just a few hours; the domestic flight network is also extensive, with many local airports flown to from Paris. Buses provide connections to the more rural areas; one's own vehicle is virtually indispensable here, however.

Accommodation As regards a place to stay, visitors to France are spoilt for choice. Hotels in all categories, from basic to the utmost luxury, can be found almost everywhere, even in the remotest of regions. The same goes for holiday homes, apartments and camp sites. Camping is very popular in France, hence there are thousands of sites, private and municipal, in large towns and small villages, often in beautiful surroundings. For lengthy family holidays, holiday homes or apartments are the best choice, at the beach or in the country, many in quaint old farmhouses or noble villas. The *chambres d'hôte*, rooms rented out privately, are well worth investigating. They are a fine way of discovering France from an intimate perspective.

Tour 1 The North

Distance: approx. 1950km/1200mi   **Length:** 2 weeks

Northern France is – unjustly – one of the less popular holiday destinations of the country. It offers pleasant landscapes, and its dignified towns are steeped in history, rich in flair and home to excellent art collections. This impressive variety is enhanced by a windswept coastline of sandy beaches and limestone cliffs.

Starting from ❶✶✶ **Strasbourg**, the wonderful capital of Alsace, the route heads through the densely wooded Vosges region. In Schirmeck (on the N 420), take the picturesque mountain route along the D 392 over the Col du Donon and down to Raon-l'Etape. Beyond Lunéville, with its chateau, lies ❷✶✶ **Nancy**, the former centre of the Duchy of Lorraine, which the exiled Polish king Stanislav Leszczyński turned into one of Europe's most beautiful Baroque towns. Continuing along the Moselle through a more industrial landscape to ❸✶ **Metz**, where the attractive nooks and crannies of the Old Town nestle alongside the waters of the Moselle. The Lorraine capital's cathedral is famous for its stained glass windows.

The next port of call is ❹✶ **Verdun** to the west, the old fortress town standing on a once pivotal crossing over the Meuse. Numerous

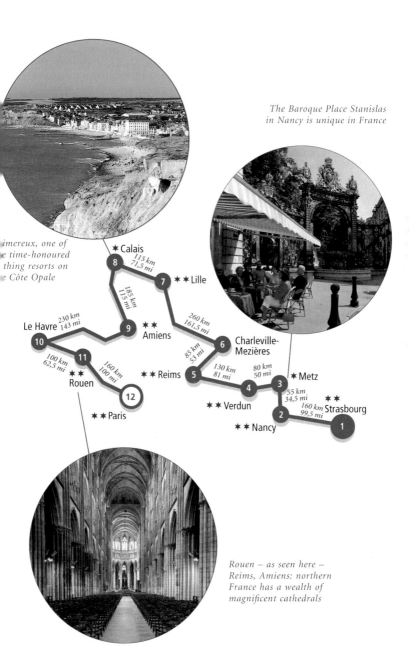

The Baroque Place Stanislas in Nancy is unique in France

imereux, one of
e time-honoured
thing resorts on
e Côte Opale

★ Calais
115 km
71,5 mi
8

7 ★★ Lille

185 km
115 mi

Le Havre
230 km
143 mi
10

9 ★★
Amiens

260 km
161,5 mi

6 Charleville-
Mezières

85 km
53 mi

100 km
62,5 mi
11

160 km
100 mi

130 km
81 mi
5

80 km
50 mi
4

3 ★ Metz

55 km
34,5 mi

Rouen
★★

★★ Reims

12

★★ Verdun

2

160 km
99,5 mi
★★
Strasbourg

1

★★ Paris

★★ Nancy

Rouen – as seen here –
Reims, Amiens: northern
France has a wealth of
magnificent cathedrals

monuments, remnants of fortifications and war cemeteries recall the bloody battle of the First World War. The Voie Sacrée, the French entrance to the fort in 1916, points the way to Châlons-en-Champagne; from here the route continues along the Marne to Épernay. The Montagne de Reims stretches from here to Reims itself, bordered by vines grown for the world-famous champagne. ❺✴✴ **Reims** is, without doubt, a highlight of the tour: for centuries, this is where French kings were crowned, usually in the magnificent Gothic cathedral. A visit to one of the famed champagne producers is a must.

80km/50mi to the northeast is the joint town of ❻**Charleville-Mézières**, a good point of departure for excursions to Sedan – its fort is one of the largest in Europe – and the Vallée de Meuse, where the river twists and turns its way into the Ardennes mountains. The smaller fortified town of Rocroi and Hirson lie on the route to Picardie and St-Quentin (art lovers should take a detour to Laon). The N 43 / N 44 leads, via Cambrai and Douai (with a lofty medieval watchtower and the Lewarde mining museum), to ❼✴✴ **Lille**, the undisputed capital of the north. Lille has undergone a veritable renaissance in recent times, with its lively Old Town and excellent art museum well worth a visit.

The atmospheric little town of Cassel lies on the way to the North Sea coast and ❽✴ **Calais**, which lies at the narrowest stretch of the English Channel, where the Eurotunnel connects France to Great Britain. The Côte Opale features a string of popular seaside resorts, such as Wimereux, Le Touquet and Berck-sur-Mer; an extra trip to Cap Griz Nez is not to be missed. The important fishing port of Boulogne-sur-Mer houses a fascinating Sea Centre and walled upper town. At St-Valéry-sur-Somme, the Somme estuary opens into the English Channel; an interesting bird population inhabits the endless sandy beaches virtually undisturbed. Upriver lies ❾✴✴ **Amiens**, the capital of Picardie, with a famous Gothic cathedral and the Hortillonnages, a system of gardens laced with canals. At Le Tréport, the coast reappears, now in Normandy. Between Dieppe and Le Havre lies the Côte d'Albâtre (Alabaster Coast) with spectacular limestone cliffs, particularly at Etretat. The route to ❿ **Le Havre** is punctuated by busier seaside resorts.

The route now heads upriver through the Seine valley to Rouen in the direction of Paris. The Seine meanders widely to create an idyllic landscape, adorned with many an abbey, chateau and settlement. ⓫✴✴ **Rouen**, the capital of Normandy, is an impressive old town of timber-framed houses with a Gothic cathedral. Of the attractions en route from Rouen to ⓬✴✴ **Paris**, Les Andelys are well worth visiting, with Château Gaillard and Giverny, where Claude Monet lived and worked for over 40 years. Monet's house and gardens are now open to the public.

Tour 2 The Burgundy Tour

Distance: approx. 630km/390mi   **Length:** 1 week

The charming landscapes of Burgundy, marvellous architectural monuments and art treasures, world-famous wines and exquisite restaurants make this the perfect region for bons vivants.

The gloriously historic province of Burgundy marks a thoroughfare between the Rhine, Seine, Loire and Rhône, an especially interesting combination in terms of cultural history. The Ducal Palace in the capital, ❶ ✳ ✳ **Dijon**, houses an art collection amongst the most valuable in France. From Dijon, heading northwest, the N 71 leads to the source of the Seine at St-Seine-l'Abbaye. Switch to the parallel D 10, which leads to Château de Bussy-Rabutin (16th–17th century) and Alise-Ste-Reine; on Mont Auxois, a gigantic statue recollects the defeat of the Celtic prince Vercingetorix against Caesar's troops in the year 52 BC. The neighbouring Flavigny-sur-Ozerain is also worth a look. At Marmagne, shortly before Montbard, take the D 32 to the Abbaye de Fontenay, a former Cistercian abbey. The N 980 leads to ❷ ✳ ✳ **Châtillon-sur-Seine**, famed for its »Trésor de Vix«, the prized find from the grave of a Celtic princess. The beautiful moated chateau of Tanlay from the Renaissance period is situated on the D 965 just before Tonnerre. In the Armançon valley between Montbard and Tonnerre, the chateau of Ancy-le-Franc is of interest. Not far to the west of Tonnerre lies the wine region of Chablis. The next stop is the trade and département capital ❸ ✳ **Auxerre** on the river Yonne.

The Hôtel de Vogüé in Dijon, one of the town's fine Renaissance buildings

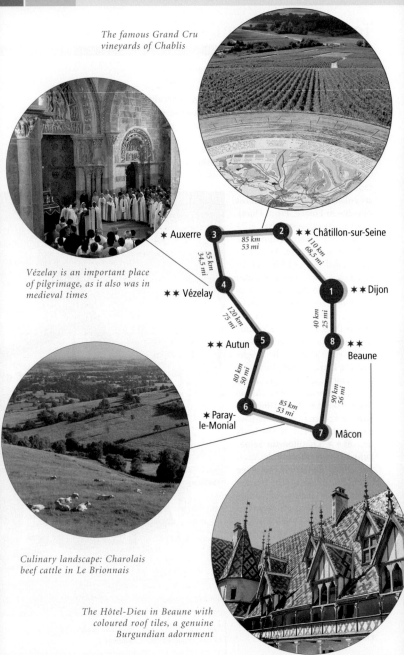

The famous Grand Cru
vineyards of Chablis

Vézelay is an important place
of pilgrimage, as it also was in
medieval times

★ Auxerre   3 ——85 km / 53 mi—— 2   ★★ Châtillon-sur-Seine

55 km
34.5 mi

110 km
68.5 mi

4   ★★ Vézelay

1   ★★ Dijon

120 km
75 mi

40 km
25 mi

5   ★★ Autun

8   ★★ Beaune

80 km
50 mi

90 km
56 mi

6   ★ Paray-le-Monial ——85 km / 53 mi—— 7   Mâcon

Culinary landscape: Charolais
beef cattle in Le Brionnais

The Hôtel-Dieu in Beaune with
coloured roof tiles, a genuine
Burgundian adornment

From Auxerre, head south on the N 6 through the Cure valley – with some of the finest scenery in Lower Burgundy – to ❹✶✶ **Vézelay**, the famous place of pilgrimage, crowned by the mighty Romanesque Ste-Madeleine abbey church. There are many options for the south-bound journey through the hills and mountains of the Morvan, an extension of the Massif Central; one very attractive route takes in Pierre-Perthuis, Bazoches (with a chateau by the famous military architect Vauban) and Lormes, past the barrage de Pannesière-Chaumard (dam), to Château-Chinon. ❺✶✶ **Autun** to the east is another highlight in Burgundy: in addition to relics of the town's 2000-year history, its cathedral is a special treasure of Romanesque architecture and sculpture.

Travelling further south, another side of Burgundy comes into view: Le Creusot and Montceau-les-Mines are the heart of the Burgundian coal and steel industries. A significant work of the Roman age, meanwhile, is the admirable abbey church of Sacré-Cœur in ❻✶ **Paray-le-Monial**. To the east lies the élevage region of the Monts du Charolais; the famous white Charolais cattle are raised in Charolles. The next destination is Cluny with the remains of an abbey church that was once the largest place of worship in Christendom. In Berzé-la-Ville, excellent 12th-century frescos can be seen in the Chapelle aux Moines, whilst Berzé-le-Châtel has a formidable castle. A little further south the striking cliffs of Solutré and Vergisson mark the wine-growing region around Pouilly-Fuissé.
Slightly further to the east lies ❼✶ **Mâcon**, birthplace of the poet Lamartine and centre of Mâconnais viniculture. If time allows, those interested can head for Bourg-en-Bresse, 35km/21mi to the east – at the heart of a region renowned for exquisite poultry – and take a look at the monastery church of Brou, a late Gothic and Renaissance jewel.

Returning north from Mâcon, the mighty Romanesque church in Tournus contains the tomb of Saint Philibert; to the west of the town, in the Monts du Mâconnais, many Romanesque churches and romantic settlements are scattered, such as the medieval Brancion, Chapaize or Cormatin with a splendidly appointed Renaissance chateau. The best road to take from Cormatin is the D 981, leading past Chalon-sur-Saône and through the gentle vineyards of the Côte Chalonnaise.
After Chagny comes the Côte de Beaune with famous wine-growing regions such as Puligny-Montrachet and Meursault. Next on the itinerary is ❽✶ **Beaune**, the centre of the Burgundian wine trade, with an attractive medieval town centre and the impressive Hôtel-Dieu. To the north of Beaune begins an absolute paradise for fans of Burgundy: on the Côte de Nuits a glittering succession of celebrated wine spots can be found, arranged like pearls on a necklace. The walled vineyard of Clos de Vougeot is amongst them. From Nuits-St-

Georges, it is worth taking a slight detour to Cîteaux abbey in the east, the home of the Cistercians, before returning to the departure point of the tour in Dijon.

Tour 3 From Paris to the Atlantic

Distance: approx. 420km/260mi   **Length:** 7–10 days

Combining a trip to Paris with a beach holiday is an enticing prospect, all the more so when the itinerary includes such wonderful places as the lower Loire valley and sights like the famed chateaux and abbeys of Touraine, among them Chartres with its marvellous cathedral, not to mention Bordeaux, the noble centre of the most famous wine region on earth.

Leave the French capital ❶ ✴ ✴ **Paris** and head southwest. If time allows, take the N 906 and take a look at Rambouillet and Maintenon en route. A visit to ❷ ✴ ✴ **Chartres** is an absolute must, its cathedral being one of the most beautiful and significant Gothic monuments in France. There are two ways to reach the Loire, either on the N 154 to Orléans or on the N 10 to Châteaudun and Vendôme, two small towns well worth investigating. The Loire is reached at ❸ ✴ ✴ **Blois**, where the splendid castle, uniting the Gothic and Renaissance periods, was once the residence of Louis XII and François I. Around Blois – on the Loire and the Cher and Indre rivers to the south –opulent noble estates and picturesque towns are so great in number that planning a single route becomes virtually impossible; far better to enjoy a random meander. Further along the Loire from Amboise lies ❹ ✴ **Tours**, the wonderfully atmospheric town of Saint Martin, rich in religious and secular architecture. Attractions abound as the journey continues, such as the fortress of Chinon, the chateau at Azay-le-Rideau and Fontevraud abbey, before reaching ❺ ✴ **Saumur**, also in possession of a beautiful chateau. Saumur is famous for its excellent sparkling wine and as the home of the French Cavalry School and the National Riding School, hence the moniker »horse town«.

From Saumur, continue to Loudun, which lies to the southwest, and take the N 147, a road as straight as an arrow, towards Poitiers. In Neuville-de-Poitou, turn onto the eastbound D 62 in order to visit the Futuroscope, a huge cinema and amusement complex near Jaunay-Clan, and the chateau of Vayres (14th–15th century) with a vast dovecote. In ❻ ✴ **Poitiers**, the former capital of the Poitou region, marvellous sacral works of architecture may be admired, including the church of Notre-Dame-la-Grande, the finest example of Poitou

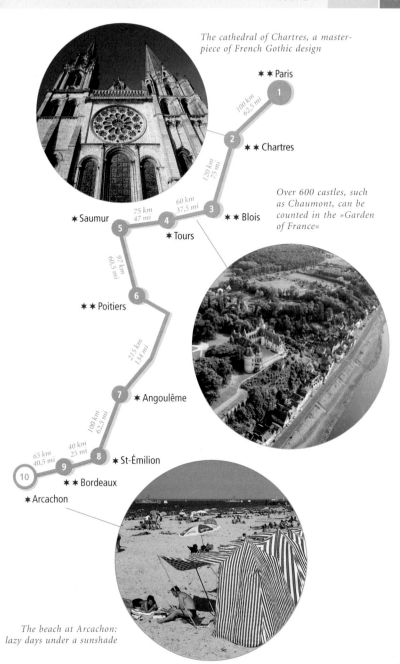

The cathedral of Chartres, a master-piece of French Gothic design

✱✱ Paris
1

100 km
62,5 mi

2
✱✱ Chartres

120 km
75 mi

Over 600 castles, such as Chaumont, can be counted in the »Garden of France«

60 km
37,5 mi
3   ✱✱ Blois

75 km
47 mi
✱ Saumur   4
5   ✱ Tours

97 km
60,5 mi

6
✱✱ Poitiers

215 km
134 mi

7   ✱ Angoulême

100 km
62,5 mi

40 km
25 mi
8   ✱ St-Émilion

65 km
40,5 mi
10   9
✱✱ Bordeaux

✱ Arcachon

The beach at Arcachon: lazy days under a sunshade

Romanesque and the oldest surviving iconic building of Christianity in France. Not far from Poitiers, the abbeys of Ligugé – the oldest in France – and Nouaillé-Maupertuis are worth visiting.

From Poitiers, take the N 151, heading east via Chauvigny (with five castles and renowned capitals in the St-Pierre church) to St-Savin-sur-Gartempe, where an 11th-century church houses wonderful Romanesque frescoes. The idyllic Gartempe valley opens the way south; 16th-century murals adorn the walls of both sacral and secular buildings (for example, in Antigny and Jouhet). South of Montmorillon, the N 54 leads to Lathus (due west, the Portes-d'Enfer, a beautiful gorge in the Gartempe) and crosses the border to Le Dorat in Limousin, boasting a splendid Romanesque church, and Bellac. A slight detour south to Oradour-sur-Glane, where a memorial to the victims of the Nazis in the Second World War stands, is worth considering. From St-Junien, the route leads back to the D 951. An alternative is the N 151, taking in Confolens in a picturesque setting on the Vienne in Charente, and the famous chateau of La Rochefoucauld, before reaching ❼ ✱ **Angoulême**, situated majestically above the Charente. The capital of Angoumois boasts a cathedral with a magnificent Romanesque façade.

A variation on the suggested main route: west of Angoulême, the Charente flows through the hilly Grande Champagne wine-growing region. Worth exploring are Cognac, the famous brandy town, and Saintes. From here, continue along the Atlantic to Rochefort, Marennes or Royan on the Gironde estuary, the Côte de Beauté.

Our route, however, leads from Angoulême along the D 674 via Montmoreau-St-Cybard to La Roche-Chalais. (Yet another detour worth consideration involves taking the D 10 before Montmoreau to Aubeterre, a small old town in a deep curve of the Dronne with an impressive rock-hewn church; continue via St-Aulaye to La Roche-Chalais.) South of La Roche, take the D 21 and cross the Isle before St-Médard to the Libournais, a wine region famous for Pomerol and St-Émilion. The attractive and historic wine town of ❽ ✱ **St-Émilion** itself is reached via Lussac and Montagne or Puisseguin. Leaving the old port and wine trading post of Libourne, on a wide stretch of the Dordogne, join the N 89 to ❾ ✱ ✱ **Bordeaux**, where the Garonne is crossed by means of the Pont de Pierre looking towards the riverfront. Noble, classical buildings give Bordeaux its special flair. On leaving the wine city, take an excursion into the Médoc with its world famous chateaux; the miles of sandy beaches of the Côte d'Argent are no less tempting. ❿ ✱ **Arcachon** is the most attractive holiday destination in the area, its basin used for oyster farming. Cap Ferret lies opposite, as well as the Great Dune of Pilat, the highest in Europe. The beaches of Biscarosse and Mimizan further south are less densely populated.

Tour 4 Through the Auvergne to the Pyrenees

Distance: approx. 700km/435mi   **Length:** 1–2 weeks

**Two of the most impressive mountain landscapes in France domi-
nate this tour. Nevertheless, there are many delights to be discovered along the way: the Lot valley is as pretty as a picture, and
much is offered by the towns on the route, such as Albi and Toulouse, not forgetting the famous Conques abbey-church and the
pleasure-loving Gascony with its bastides.**

Starting out from ❶✷ **Paray-le-Monial** (► Tour 2), the route first
heads in the direction of northernmost Auvergne: in ❷ **Moulins**, the
»Master of Moulins« painted his unmissable triptych. Moving south,
sample the nostalgic charm of the old spa town of ❸✷ **Vichy**. For
the leg of the tour to Clermont-Ferrand, it is worth considering the
longer route through the Gorges de la Sioule, which begins after
Ebreuil (to the west of Vichy). Follow the D 915 / D 109 to Châteauneuf-les-Bains. Then pass through St-Gervais, and under the Fades
viaduct to Les Ancizes. Continue through Châtel-Guyon with its
popular hot springs, and Mozac, with an important Romanesque
church, on to Riom, the capital of the Auvergne in times gone by.
From Clermont-Ferrand, the ideal route passes through Volvic,
famed for its mineral water and the Château de Tournoël, one of the
most beautiful palace ruins of the Auvergne. Some 4km/2.5mi west,
join the D 941 – with views of the Limagne plain, bordered by the
Monts du Forez – to ❹ **Clermont-Ferrand** with its »black« cathedral.

From Clermont, continue to the elegant spa of Royat and Puy de
Dôme, the highest of the Monts Dômes mountains, before heading
southwest to Orcival with one of the most important churches of the
Auvergne and on to Le Mont-Dore, the hot springs and winter
sports haven (cable car on the Puy de Sancy, the highest peak of the
Massif Central) surrounded by the Monts-Dore.
Those with enough time in their schedule should not miss out on
the approx. 75km/47mi circuit around the Puy de Sancy: Col de la
Croix St-Robert – Besse – Lac Pavin – Latour-d'Auvergne – Gorges
d'Avèze – La Bourboule – Le Mont-Dore.
From Le Mont-Dore, take the eastbound D 995 past Lac Chambon
to Murol in the Couze valley. Before going on south to Besse, the delightfully located, diminutive town of Besse-en-Chandesse is worth
exploring, particularly the Rue de la Boucherie, St-André church and
the ski museum. Take a break at Lac Pavin, the most beautiful crater
lake in the Auvergne, before joining the D 978 to ❺ **Condat** in the
Rhue valley.

The peculiar green, volcanic out-crops of the »Puys« dominate the landscape of the Auvergne

★ Paray-le-Monial

1

★★ Moulins

2

75 km
47 mi

55 km
34,5 mi

★ Vichy

3

105 km
65,5 mi

Clermont-Ferrand

4

100 km
62,5 mi

Condat

5

72 km
45 mi

6

72 km
45 mi

Aurillac

7

105 km
65,5 mi

Espalion

★ Auch

10

80 km
50 mi

9

80 km
50 mi

8

★★ Albi

★★ Toulouse

95 km
59 mi

11

★★ Lourdes

50 km
31 mi

12

★★ Gavarnie

The Musée Toulouse-Lautrec in Albi houses the largest collection of works by the artist

Grand corries such as the Cirque de Gavarnie open up in the Central Pyrenees

Continuing from Condat to Pas de Peyrol (1588m/5210ft), the highest pass in the Auvergne, at the heart of the Monts du Cantal, proceed to St-Amandin (D 678) and Riom-es-Montagnes (11th–12th-century church) and through the Vallee de Cheylade (D 62). On leaving the pass, scale the Puy Mary and turn southwest onto the D 17, then south into the Mandailles valley (with a view of the tremendous Cirque du Falgoux) to ⑥ **Aurillac**.

From Aurillac, the D 920 leads to the undulating granite plateau of the Châtaigneraie, its name derived from the chestnut woods, to Montsalvy and quaint old Entraygues in the wonderful Lot valley. An interesting excursion to the Gorges de la Truyère in the north is worth the effort, whilst a trip west to Conques, the famous abbey on the Way of St James, is a must. Take the D 920 from Entraygues through Gorges du Lot to the old and attractive ⑦ **Espalion**. Turning southwest now, follow the D 920 / D 988 to Bozouls, above the »Trou de Bozouls«, the canyon of the Dourdou, and continue on to Rodez, the capital of the département de l'Aveyron.

From Rodez, take the N 88, progressing further southwest. Before reaching Tanus, the deep gorge of the Viaur valley must be negotiated (the late 19th century Viaur viaduct is further upstream). Via Carmaux, the road leads to ⑧ ✱✱ **Albi**, the old town of the Cathars, with mighty medieval brick buildings. In the fertile foothills of the Pyrenees, continue along the river Tarn through the small wine-growing town of Gaillac to ⑨ ✱✱ **Toulouse**, the cultural and financial centre of southern France.

To the southwest of Toulouse, a number of medieval bastides dot the flat hills of the Gascony landscape. One lovely example is Gimont (50km/31mi to the west). The cathedral of ⑩ **Auch** contains magnificent choir stalls; the view of the Pyrenees is similarly impressive. The bastide of Mirande, another fine example, lies on the route to Tarbes, the capital of the county of Bigorre, reached via the N 21. Having arrived here, the short trip to Pau is a worthwhile undertaking. 20km/12mi to the south lies ⑪ ✱✱ **Lourdes**, probably the most famous of all pilgrimage destinations in the Catholic world. Lourdes marks the gateway to the finest stretch of the Pyrenees.
The health resort of Argelès-Gazost leads towards the narrow valley of Gave de Gavarnie and ⑫ **Gavarnie** itself, beyond which the Cirque de Gavarnie opens out, which is enough to impress even those who know alpine scenery well. Those who have experience in the mountains might well consider the hike to the legendary Brêche de Roland. To complete the kaleidoscope of mountain impressions, choose the Col du Tourmalet for the return journey from Luz-St-Sauveur, a cable car connects La Mongie to the Pic du Midi de Bigorre (2872m/9400ft), with a magnificent view rewarding those who make the ascent.

Tour 5 Route des Grandes Alpes

Distance: 650 / 690km/404 / 428mi   **Length:** 3–4 days

This is the ultimate road route through the French Alps. From the gentle banks of Lake Geneva, through the Savoy foothills and into the glacial world of Mont Blanc, the road rises through some of the highest alpine passes and descends into the narrow valleys of the Maritime Alps of Provence to the Mediterranean.

From ❶ **Geneva**, follow the bank of the wonderful Lake Geneva to the renowned spa town of ❷ **Thonon** and continue southwards into the Dranse valley, past the ski resorts of Morzine and Les Gets before arriving at Cluses in the Arve valley. At St-Gervais-les-Bains, take a detour to the famous winter sports resort of ❸ ✶✶ **Chamonix** on

Genf   35 km   ❷ Thonon
❶   22 mi
  100 km
  62.5 mi
  85 km
  53 mi   ❸ ✶✶ Chamonix/
         Mont Blanc

❹

Bourg-
St-Maurice

190 km
118 mi

❺ ✶ Briançon

85 km
53 mi

❻ Barcelonnette

160 km
99.5 mi

✶✶ Nizza ❼

The upper Arve valley at Combloux with Mont Blanc

St-Veran in Le Queyras, the highest village in Europe

Mont Blanc (those wishing to take the shorter route at this juncture should use the Mont Blanc Tunnel to reach Courmayeur and cross the Petit Saint-Bernard to Bourg-St-Maurice). From St-Gervais, the Grandes Alpes route makes a sweeping curve through Megève, Albertville and Moûtiers to Bourg-St-Maurice. More attractive, but with more twists and turns, is the »shortcut« from Flumet over the Col des Saisies into Beaufortin, with the pretty little town of Beaufort, and over the Cormet de Roselend to ❹**Bourg-St-Maurice**.

In the Val d'Isère, passing the ski resorts of Tignes and Val d'Isère, the road climbs to the Col de l'Iseran, with the second highest alpine pass at 2770m/9000ft. Surrounded by the marvellous scenery of the Graian Alps, the descent on the far side leads down to the pictu-

A real high point of the Grande Route des Alpes in every sense: Col du Galibier

resque Bonneval in the upper Arc valley. Follow the river Arc via Lanslebourg to Modane (with the Fort de l'Esseillon coming up just before) and St-Michel-de-Maurienne. The terrain then becomes more alpine again: through the high-lying valley of Valloire up to the Col du Galibier (2646m/8600ft) with a wonderful panorama looking south to the Pelvoux range. From the Col du Lautaret (2058 m/6750 ft) the route continues into the Guisane valley and on to ❺ ✷ **Briançon**, a fortified town at over 1200m/3937ft. The next stretch of mountains is the Col d'Izoard (2360m/7740ft); beyond the high point of the pass lies the desert-like Casse Déserte and the narrow Combe du Queyras which leads to Guillestre (it is worth covering the extra ground to Queyras to see the picturesque little town of Château-Queyras and the beautiful village of St-Véran at 2040m/6690ft). From Guillestre, the route curves upwards to the high-lying valley of the Chagne and Col de Vars (2111m/6925ft), and into the Ubaye valley to ❻ **Barcelonnette**; this is now the (Haute) Provence region.

The final stage, leading to the Mediterranean, initially runs through the Gorges du Bachelard to the barren Col de la Cayolle (2326m/7630ft, tremendous panoramic views) and on to Guillaumes on the upper reaches of the Var. Then come the Gorges du Daluis, a magnificent gulf with 400m/1312ft-high porphyric rock faces, and Entrevaux with its mighty battlements. Follow the Var valley past Puget-Théniers to reach the Pont de la Mescla; finally, pass through the narrow Défilé du Chaudan, the last leg before arriving in ❼ ✷ ✷ **Nice**.

Passing through the locks, such as this one on the Canal du Midi, presents a good opportunity to exchange tips

FRANCE AT FIVE MPH

As Stendhal enthused, »One sees the land better than from a stagecoach«. Houseboating is one of the most charming ways to discover France, and certainly one of the most relaxing.

Gliding in slow motion past meadows and fields, woods and villages, through deep valleys or sprawling vineyards, under bridges or through dark tunnels. Ducks and herons, cattle and horses, ramblers on the towpath and pensive anglers line the route, while poplars and sycamores, cypresses and pines offer cool respite from the sun.

All hands on deck

The heart may beat a little faster at the first lock or docking manoeuvre. Yes, the boat owner explained how to navigate the craft: forwards, reverse, throttle (that's all there is to it), how to negotiate the locks, which hand-holds are required to moor the »pénichette«, as the houseboat is called; moreover, there is plenty of translated information, with lists of all bridges, locks and moorings. Nevertheless, the moment comes when you set sail on your own. The houseboats have a top speed of just five or six mph (10kmh). Apart from in the high season, the canals are not generally crowded. In any case, any other vessels on the waterways are liable to

be houseboats, as the rivers and canals are no longer used for commercial purposes. The craft are easy to manoeuvre; only the flat-bottomed pénichettes, as found on the Saar-Kohle canal, are a little more difficult to steer. Rubber fenders wrapped around the boat mean that even a little scrape along the lock wall cannot do much damage. Muscle power will not go amiss on the voyage, with all the crew lending a hand, as the locks are operated manually. Both lock gates need to be cranked open and closed, a task not to be underestimated. Of course, there is always a lock keeper, or éclusier, who can do the job, but with up to 200 boats passing through per day at the height of the season, amateur sailors are more than welcome to step in themselves. Either way, a friendly chat is always part of the bargain. What's more, this is a fine way to glean tips about the area, its people and good places to eat or drink (a basic command of the French language will come in handy). These days, the wives of the éclusiers can often be found looking after the locks, while their husbands earn a crust – or

baguette – elsewhere. The lockhouse may be rent free, but the job does not pay well.

Comfort and idyll

The boats, with from two to twelve berths, are kitted out with all the comforts of home: a full kitchen, roomy cabins, a shower and toilet. Supplies can be picked up in the villages along the way. Bicycles really come into their own under these circumstances (available for rent from boat stations). Water refills are possible at most locks, with lock keepers often selling their own vegetables, salad and other produce, such as honey or wine. Many boats can be hired one-way only, with the supplier bringing the car to the final destination.

Boredom never comes into the equation. Setting sail, mooring, negotiating the locks, the daily groceries run, all remove the possibility of a dull moment – whilst anglers are quick to gesticulate if the boat sails too close to their fishing rods. Taking turns at the rudder allows other crew members to explore the neighbouring land, to jog or cycle along the towpath or to plan where to moor for the night, perhaps close to a restaurant or in romantic isolation deep into the countryside. Small children may not be quite so enamoured with the houseboat voyage: a pénichette affords little space for frolicking around.

A total of around 8000km/5000mi of canals and rivers are potentially available, covering almost all of France – with the exception of the mountain regions. The most beautiful of the waterways is said to be the Canal du Midi, connecting the Atlantic to the Mediterranean. Yet each region has its own charm: the gentle vineyard hills of Burgundy and Champagne, the flourishing fruit orchards of Aquitaine, the picturesque villages, castles and forts of the Loire, Dordogne and Lot. Here and there, technical achievements can be admired, such as the beautiful canal bridge over the Loire at Briare, or the »inclined plane« of Arzviller, which overcomes a difference in height of 45m/147ft!

Sights
from A to Z

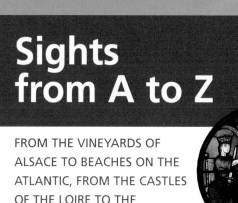

FROM THE VINEYARDS OF
ALSACE TO BEACHES ON THE
ATLANTIC, FROM THE CASTLES
OF THE LOIRE TO THE
MOUNTAIN SCENERY OF THE
PYRENEES – THERE IS SO MUCH TO
DISCOVER IN FRANCE.

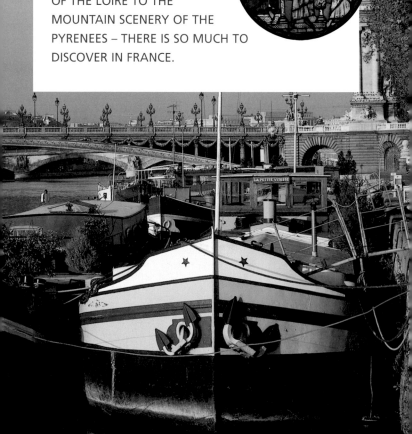

Aix-en-Provence

Région: Provence – Alpes – Côte d'Azur   **Altitude:** 177m/580ft
Département: Bouches-du-Rhône   **Population:** 137,000

Aix, the old capital of ► Provence, is considered one of the most beautiful towns in France with its elegant palaces in Italian Baroque style, majestic boulevards and a vivacious, young atmosphere.

Following the destruction of the Celtic oppidum in 122 BC, the first Roman settlement of Aquae Sextiae Saluviorum was established in Gaul. Aix (pronounced »ex«) became the focal point of Provence, under René of Anjou (»the Good King«, 1409–80) a centre of Provençal poetry, with a university founded in 1409. A flurry of construction in the 17th and 18th centuries gave the town its noteworthy »hôtels particuliers« in Italian Baroque style. The painter Paul Cézanne (1839–1906) hailed from Aix. A bronze plaque at the tourist office marks the »Circuit de Cézanne«, indicating where he lived and worked. Aix has 300 days of sunshine per year and is home to some 30,000 students, many from abroad. It is, however, the most expensive town in all of France.

Aix then and now

What to See in Aix-en-Provence

Cours Mirabeau is a majestic avenue, lined with plane trees and impressive houses from the 17th and 18th centuries; in the middle is the Fontaine Chaude with hot springs at 34°C/93°F, to the west the **Fontaine des 9 Canons** (1691), to the east the Fontaine du Roi René (1819) with a statue commemorating the Good King by David d'Angers. Place de Gaulle in the west is adorned with the Fontaine de la Rotonde (1860).

★
Cours Mirabeau

The Natural History Museum in the Hôtel Boyer d'Eguilles (1675) is famed for its **dinosaur eggs** from the Aix basin. In the church of Ste-Marie-Madeleine (reconstructed 1691–1703, the façade in 1855) the central portion of a triptych from 1444 depicting the Annunciation from the Avignon School is worth viewing.

Muséum d'Histoire Naturelle
Ste-Marie-Madeleine

The town hall square is graced by the post office, formerly used for grain storage (1761) and featuring sculptures in the pediment of Father Rhône and Mother Durance, the Italian Baroque Hôtel de Ville (1668) and the **Tour de l'Horloge**, a gateway to the town constructed in 1510 on Roman foundations with an astronomical clock dating from 1661. North of here are the old noble palais of Rue Gaston-de-Saporta, where the late 17th-century Hôtel d'Estienne-de-St-Jean

Place de l'Hôtel de Ville

← *The lively town hall square in Aix-en-Provence*

Musée du Vieil Aix (no. 17, closed Mon) houses the Musée du Vieil Aix, devoted to civic history.

✶ St-Sauveur The cathedral of St-Sauveur was built between the 5th and the 18th century, with most of the work completed in the 12th and 13th centuries. The wonderful walnut doors carved by J. Guiramand (1510) in the portal are usually concealed behind screens, as is the marvellous 15th-century ***Burning Bush Tryptich*** by N. Froment, showing the Virgin Mary in the centre, with King René depicted in the left wing. The high altar opens onto the Chapelle de St-Mitre (5th century), with a 6th-century baptistery where the font itself dates from the 4th century. Tapestries from Flanders are also on display with scenes from the life of Mary and the Passion (1511). An elegant 11th-century Romanesque cloister adjoins on the south side. The neighbouring archbishop's palace (1648) houses the Musée des Tapisseries with tapestries from Beauvais (closed Tue).

✶ Musée des Tapisseries

Aix-en-Provence Map

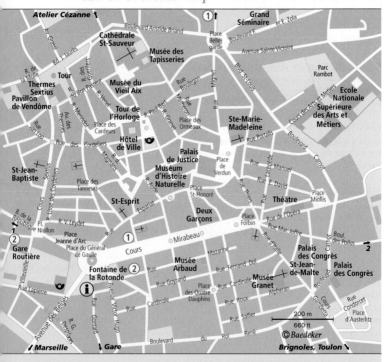

1 Fondation Vasarély
2 Montagne Ste-Victoire

Where to eat
① Clos de la Violette
② Gourmand Passage

Where to stay
① Augustins
② Mas d'Entremont

The cloister of St-Sauveur with slender columns and beautiful capitals

From the cathedral, Rue du Bon Pasteur leads to the hot springs (temperatures reaching 36°C/97°F), which were built on Roman remains. The spa water is used as a health drink and in bathing treatments. Outside the original town walls stands the palais built for the Duc de Vendôme in 1667. It contains furniture and paintings from the 17th and 18th centuries.

Thermes Sextius

Pavillon de Vendôme

The last studio of the great Impressionist lies 1.5km/1mi north of the old town (Avenue Paul Cézanne 9, open daily). There is an audio-visual presentation and a display of various memorabilia.

Atelier Paul Cézanne

On the initiative of Michel Mazarin, Archbishop of Aix and brother of the cardinal und politician, Cours Mirabeau was developed between 1646 and 1653, together with the adjoining district to the south. Its centrepiece is **Place des Quatre Dauphins** with fountains from 1667. One of the most attractive buildings of the district is the 18th-century Hôtel d'Arbaud. It holds the Musée Arbaud with Provençal faiences, paintings and a library. The Musée Granet in the commandery of the Knights of Malta of 1671 displays Celto-Ligurian sculptures from the Oppidum d'Entremont, Greek reliefs, Roman fragments, medieval sculptures and works by painters such as Holbein the Younger, Rubens, Rembrandt and Cézanne. Open Tue–Sun 11am–7pm, Oct–May noon–6pm.

Quartier Mazarin

Musée Paul Arbaud

★
Musée Granet

In the western suburb of Jas de Bouffan (Avenue Marcel Pagnol) a large, unusual black-and-white building greets the eye: the **Fondation Vasarely**. The works of the Hungarian Victor Vasarely (1908–97), the leading exponent of Op Art, are comprehensively documented here (closed Sun, Mon).

! *Baedeker* TIP

Café des Deux Garçons

Cours Mirabeau 53 bis is home to the famous Café des Deux Garçons, dating back to 1792, once the haunt of artists and writers such as Cézanne. It is the place to see and be seen. The prices are accordingly steep.

▶ VISITING AIX-EN-PROVENCE

INFORMATION

Office de Tourisme
2 Place du Gén. de Gaulle
F-13100 Aix-en-Provence
Tel. 04 42 16 11 61
www.aixenprovencetourism.com

FESTIVALS AND EVENTS

June–July: Festival International d'Art
Lyrique (opera). Information and
tickets: www.festival-aix.com, tel. 04
42 17 34 34, fax 04 42 63 13 74
July: Jazz Festival. Sept: Blessing of the
Calissons and Fête Mistralienne
Dec: Bravade Calendale
Events published in *Mois à Aix*

WHERE TO EAT

▶ Expensive

① *Clos de la Violette*
10 Avenue Violette
Tel. 04 42 23 30 71, closed Sun.
Best restaurant in town, in an
elegant villa, modern Provençal
cuisine. Less expensive lunch
menu.

▶ Moderate

② *Gourmand Passage*
6 bis Rue Mazarine
Tel. 04 42 37 09 00
Creative southern French cooking in
a converted chocolate factory. Lively
atmosphere, wine bar and café.

WHERE TO STAY

▶ Mid-range

① *Augustins*
3 Rue Masse
Tel. 04 42 27 28 59
Fax 04 42 26 74 87
29 rooms. Erstwhile 12th-century
cloister in a quiet side street. Large,
luxurious, individually appointed
rooms. No restaurant.

② *Mas d'Entremont*
Montée d'Avignon
Tel. 04 42 17 42 42
www.masdentremont.com
19 rooms. Stylish farm, 3km/2mi to
the northwest (N 7), with garden and
pool. Rustic, old-fashioned ambience,
the bungalows are more modern.
Restaurant with classic cuisine.

**Oppidum
d'Entremont**

The uninspiring excavations of the Celto-Ligurian oppidum are to be
found at Entremont, 3km/2mi north of Aix (access via the D 14,
closed Tue), although a mosaic floor and remains of the ossuaries
are worth a glance. Fine views of Aix and the Ste-Victoire.

Around Aix-en-Provence

Ventabren

Castle ruins tower over Ventabren, a »village perché« 15km/10mi
west of Aix above the Arc valley. Stand on the castle remnants for a
wonderful view of the Etang de Berre. South of Ventabren, the Canal
de Marseille crosses the Arc valley on a replica of the Pont du Gard
(1847). Although larger than the original (83m/272ft high, 375m/
1230ft long), it does not have the same resonance. Further east, the
TGV bridge spans the valley.

**Aqueduc de
Roquefavour**

The brickworks of Les Milles lie approximately 6km/3.5mi southwest of Aix. From September 1939 to mid-1940, as many as 3000 German fugitives were interned here, including a number of important artists and scientists. In 1942, approx. 2000 Jews were transported by the Vichy government to German extermination camps. A cattle wagon has been set up as a museum, and murals by imprisoned artists can be seen in the former officers' mess (closed Sat–Sun). **Les Milles**

The D 10 heads east from Aix through enchanting scenery alongside the Lac du Bimont; there are breathtaking views of the **Montagne Ste-Victoire**. 12km/7.5mi further on is Vauvenargues, where Picasso lived from 1958 onwards in the 17th-century castle; Picasso and his second wife, Jacqueline Roque, are buried in the park (closed to the public). **Vauvenargues**

South of the valley rises the Montagne Ste-Victoire. A lovely path leads from Les Cabassols up to the Croix de la Provence (945m/ 3100ft; return trip 3½ hours, sturdy footwear advisable). At 900m/ 2950ft lie the ruins of the N.-D.-de-Ste-Victoire priory from 1656. There are wonderful panoramic views of the Camargue in the west, the Massif de la Ste-Baume and the Massif des Maures across to the Alps in the east. **✶ ✶ Croix de la Provence**

St-Maximin, a small rural town 40km/25mi to the east of Aix, is famous for its Gothic church (1295– c1530). On the discovery in 1279 of the supposed remains of Mary Magdalene, an 80m/ 262ft-long church, unusual for Provence, was erected. The most notable features of the glorious interior are the high altar (late 17th century), the choir stalls (1692), the **Passion altar by François Ronzen** (1520) and the organ by Isnard (1773); the cope of Louis IX (late 13th century) is also on display. The crypt from the 4th–5th century holds four sarcophagi from the same period, said to contain the remains of Mary Magdalene and saints Maximin, Sidonius, Marcella and Susanne. The convent is now a stylish hotel (Le Couvent Royal). **Saint-Maximin-la-Sainte-Baume**

The church of Ste-Madeleine in St-Maximin is an exceptional sight in Provence

The cathedral of Albi rises like a castle over the town and river Tarn

Albi

Région: Midi-Pyrenées   **Altitude:** 174m/570ft
Département: Tarn   **Population:** 49,000

A symphony in red, the brick town of Albi, home of the Cathars, stands on the banks of the Tarn to the west of the Cevennes. Apart from the cathedral, the main attraction is the museum dedicated to the town's famous son, Henri de Toulouse-Lautrec.

History Between the 11th and 13th centuries, the Cathars spread a doctrine which contradicted church dogma by dismissing the concepts of purgatory and indulgence, amongst others. One of four Cathar bishops had his see in Albi, hence the name given to the followers of this movement: **Albigensians**. Two »crusades« against the Cathars (1209–29) and their persecution during the inquisition by Saint Dominic – in which over 200 wealthy citizens of Albi were burned – ended in 1271 with the annexation of the entire province of Toulouse by the French Crown. This also meant the destruction of Provençal culture (▶Baedeker Special p.450).

What to See in Albi

✱ ✱
Ste-Cécile The townscape – especially beautiful when viewed from the Pont Vieux (1035) – is dominated by the mighty buildings of the cathedral and bishop's palace, constructed in the aftermath of the Albigensian wars as a demonstration of royal power. Some 130m/142yd in length and 50m/50yd in width, the cathedral of Ste-Cécile (begun in 1282, consecrated in 1480, completed 1512) has a highly unusual design. The rounded projections that structure the exterior are circular towers that lie between 5m/16ft thick walls – a genuine fortress. The same method was used to construct the 78m/255ft tower (upper levels built 1485–92). Entry to the cathedral is through the south portal with the Flamboyant Gothic baldachin (1520). The interior, 99m/

108yd long, 19m/21yd wide and 30m/99ft high, is divided by a filigree rood screen of around 1480, although almost all of its 96 statues were lost in the Revolution; the Virgin, John the Baptist, Adam and Eve survived, next to the crucifix. The **murals** are magnificent: vaults and chapels by artists from Bologna (around 1512), the Last Judgement (20×15m/65×49ft) on the west wall by a Burgundian painter (late 15th century, damaged in 1693). The superb organ dates back to 1736. The ornate choir screens are decorated with angels and, on the outside, figures from the Old and New Testaments, Burgundian in style. The glass in the apse is 14th century.

The **Palais de la Berbie** (from the Occitane word »bisbe«, meaning bishop) was constructed from 1265 as a defence against the town; following the Edict of Nantes in 1598, parts of the complex were dismantled. The Musée Toulouse-Lautrec here has over 500 works by the artist as well as by contemporaries such as Degas, Rodin and Matisse (open July–Aug 9am–6pm, June–Sept 9am–noon, 2pm–6pm, April–May 10am–noon, 2pm–6pm, otherwise Wed–Mon 10am–noon, 2pm–5pm).

★ ★
Musée Toulouse-
Lautrec

What else to see in Albi

Construction of the collegiate church of Saint Salvi began in the 11th century on the foundations of a Carolingian church, and was completed after the Albigensian wars in the 13th century. Rue Mariès leads past a 15th-century timber house and meets Rue Timbal, where the Pharmacie des Pénitents is located, a typical piece of 16th-century architecture for Albi. This is also the site of the Hôtel Reynès, a beautiful Renaissance palais (1530, with busts of François I and Eleanor of Austria). The lively centre of the town is Place du Vigan. To the south of the cathedral lies a district with many attractive old houses, such as the Hôtel de Séré de Rivières (15th century), the

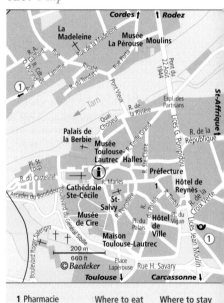

Albi Map

1 Pharmacie
des Pénitents

Where to eat
① Moulin de
la Mothe

Where to stay
① Hostellerie
St-Antoine

Maison du Vieil Alby and the Hôtel Decazes. Alongside is the Maison Lapérouse with a waxworks museum and the 18th-century Hôtel du Bosc, in which Toulouse-Lautrec (1864–1901) was born.

▶ VISITING ALBI

INFORMATION
Office de Tourisme
Palais de Berbie
F-81000 Albi
Tel. 05 63 49 48 80
Fax 05 63 49 48 98
www.mairie-albi.fr

EVENTS
May: jazz festival. July: music festival (classical, opera, jazz)

WHERE TO EAT
▶ **Moderate / expensive**
① *Moulin de la Mothe*
Rue de Lamothe, tel. 05 63 60 38 15
Closed Wed and Sun evenings. Res-
taurant with classic regional fare, in a park with an attractive terrace on the Tarn riverbank.

WHERE TO STAY
▶ **Mid-range / luxury**
① *Hostellerie Saint-Antoine*
17 Rue St-Antoine
Tel. 05 63 54 04 04
www.hotel-saint-antoine.albi.com
High-class accommodation with garden. The building dates back to 1734. Pool and tennis courts at the equally smart sister hotel La Réserve, 3km/2mi outside the town (Route de Cordes, tel. 05 63 60 80 80, closed Nov–April).

Around Albi

Lescure   Approx. 5km/3mi northeast on a bend in the Tarn, the 11th-century Benedictine church of St-Michel stands on the Lescure graveyard, with a beautiful Romanesque portal (12th century).

✱ Cordes-sur-Ciel   Cordes-sur-Ciel (1000 inhabitants), 25km/15mi northwest of Albi, is a jewel: founded in 1222 on a hill in the valley of Cérou, it has maintained its medieval appearance with five encircling walls. Wonderful Gothic residences bear witness to the riches accumulated by the cloth and leather industries. The impressive **Maison du Grand Fauconnier** houses the town hall and a museum with works by Yves Brayer; the cellar contains a museum for embroidery machines. To the north, the market hall stands opposite, with pillars from 1352. Remodelled in Baroque style, the church of St-Michel, at the highest point in town, features a choir and transept from the 13th century. On the Grand'Rue, further to the east, are the Maison Prunet with a museum of confectionery, the Portal Peint lower down and the Musée d'Art et d'Histoire. The **Grand Ecuyer**, the palace of the Grand Squire (Master of Horse to the French monarch) and a Monument Historique, is now a marvellous hotel belonging to the »gastronomic company« of Yves Thuriès (tel. 05 63 53 79 50, fax 05 63 53 79 51, www.thuries.fr), who runs a pâtisserie school, the confectionery museum and two further hotels (Hotel de la Cité, Hostellerie du Vieux Cordes) which are reasonably priced in terms of their quality.

✳ Alsace and the Vosges

Between the Vosges mountains with their thick forests and the valley of the Rhine lies a picture-book landscape of romantic, timber-framed villages, renowned vineyards and wonderful artistic treasures. Along with its magnificent cities of Strasbourg and Colmar, the region enchants visitors time and again.

The Alsace region, the easternmost part of France, borders on Germany and extends south as far as the Swiss border. It is a popular destination for a day trip or a holiday, which means that delightful spots along the Alsatian wine route, in particular, are sometimes like mini-Disneyland, with everything directed to the needs of tourists. The landscape is a mirror image of the country across the Rhine in Germany. The Black Forest and the Vosges were originally part of a single mountain range, which split down the middle in the Tertiary era 65 million years ago to form the Rhine rift valley. For administrative purposes, Alsace consists of the departments Bas-Rhin in the north, with its capital at ► Strasbourg, and Haut-Rhin in the south (capital ► Colmar), with the border between the two running roughly along a line through Sélestat. Strasbourg is the main city and economic centre of the region.

Alsace

The Vosges mountains stretch for some 125km/80mi from the German border in the north to the Trouée de Belfort plateau in the south. The range is 20km/12mi wide at its broadest. The valley of the river Bruche forms its southern boundary. The southern part is made up of volcanic rocks (granite and gneiss) and has the highest

Vosges

Highlights Alsace and the Vosges

Mont Ste-Odile
The »holy mountain of Alsace« with magnificent views
► page 212

Fairy-tale castle
Haut Kœnigsburg is not wholly authentic but impressive nevertheless
► page 214

Monastic life
Murbach Abbey is second only to the abbey at Marmoutier in terms of its importance as Romanesque architecture in Alsace
► page 217/218

Home of humanism
Sélestat has a pretty historic centre and the Bibliothèque Humaniste
► page 213

Higher than a balloon
Fantastic panoramas along the Route des Crêtes, hearty meals in a farmhouse inn
► page 218

Maginot Line
The horrors of war are evident at the forts of northern Alsace
► page 223

► VISITING ALSACE

INFORMATION
CRT Alsace
20 a Rue B. Molly, F-68000 Colmar
Tel. 03 89 24 73 50, fax 03 89 24 73 51
www.tourisme-alsace.com
CRT Lorraine
Abbaye des Prémontrés, BP 97
F-54704 Pont-à-Mousson Cedex
Tel. 03 83 80 01 80, fax 03 83 80 01 88
www.tourisme-lorraine.fr

WHERE TO EAT
► Expensive
Le Cerf
30 Rue Gén. de Gaulle
F-67520 Marlenheim
Tel. 03 88 87 73 73
Closed Tue and Wed. This charming
old staging post between Strasbourg
and Saverne is famous for its modern
Alsatian cuisine. Excellent wine list.
14 rooms for overnight stay. L'Espérance in neighbouring Handschuheim
serves superb tartes flambées from a
wood-burning oven (very busy).

► Moderate / inexpensive
Wistub zum Pfifferhüs
14 Grand'Rue, F-68150 Ribeauvillé
Tel. 03 89 73 62 28
Closed Wed–Thu and for 3 weeks in
June–July. Famous, cosy wine lodge
with Alsace specialities.

Chez Norbert
F-68750 Bergheim, tel. 03 89 73 31
15, closed Thu and 1 week at the start
of July. Bergheim near Ribeauvillé is
well worth a visit, as is this a real
Alsatian restaurant with a lovely
courtyard. Accommodation available.

Les Alisiers
5 Rue Faudé, F-68650 Lapoutroie
Tel. 03 89 47 52 82, fax 03 89 47 22 38
Closed Tue–Wed. Heart-warming regional fare in a farmhouse of 1819
with marvellous views of the Vosges
and Rhine valley. Pretty rooms in a
modern annexe.

WHERE TO STAY
► Mid-range / luxury
Abbaye la Pommeraie
8 Blvd. M.al Foch, F-67600 Sélestat
Tel. 03 88 92 07 84
Conversion of a 17th-century Cistercian monastery to a stylish and
extremely comfortable hotel. Excellent
restaurant and a rustic wine tavern.

► Budget / mid-range
Hostellerie Ville de Lyon
1 Rue Poincaré, F-68250 Rouffach
Tel. 03 89 49 65 51
Excellent accommodation in a former
postal station on the northern edge of
town. Elegant restaurant in rustic
style run by a pupil of Bocuse who
cooked for presidents. Brasserie Chez
Julien, once a cinema, is cheaper.

Hotel de la Tour
1 Rue Mairie, F-68150 Ribeauvillé
Tel. 03 89 73 72 73
Distinguished-looking house right
next to the town hall. Pretty, very
pleasant rooms. The ones facing the
courtyard are quieter.

Les Hirondelles
33 Rue 25 Janvier
F-68970 Illhaeusern Munster
www.hotelleshirondelles.com
Tel. 03 89 71 83 76
Attractive guest rooms in a nicely
converted former farmhouse. A good
base for a visit to the Haeberlin
brothers' world-famous restaurant
Auberge de l'Ill (www.auberge-de-l-
ill.com, tel. 03 89 71 89 00, reserve
well in advance).

peaks, Grand Ballon (1424m/4672ft), Hohneck (1362m/4469ft) and Ballon d'Alsace (1250m/4101ft). The northern mountains are early Triassic sandstone and less high: they reach 1009m/3310ft at Donon, but only 580m/1903ft at Grands Wintersberg near Niederbronn. Numerous valleys cross the Vosges, which greatly assisted human settlement. This meant that the region boasts many attractive castles, monasteries and churches. Nature lovers can find plenty of lonely, untouched landscapes with original flora. In summer the lakes are popular, while in winter the area attracts Nordic skiers, for whom it provides ideal terrain.

The foothills of the Vosges have a characteristic climate. Summers are very warm and the winters are mild, so that there is plenty of sunshine and little rain all year round. 400mm/16in of annual rainfall makes the area around Colmar one of the **driest regions of France**, because it lies in the shadow of the Vosges mountains. Prevailing winds from the west bring rainfall to the peaks and leave the valleys beyond them dry. The western parts of the Vosges and the higher mountains are therefore rather wet: the main ridge gets up to 2000mm/80in of rainfall per year. The best time to visit the area is in spring, when the fruit trees are in blossom, and early summer or autumn, when the leaves redden and the air seems especially clear. It is all the better that fewer visitors come at these times.

Climate and when to visit

Caesar's victory over Ariovistus and his Suebi near Cernay in 58 BC meant that the entire area became part of the Roman province of Germania Superior. Around AD 300 the Romans introduced vines to the region and instigated wine making. The name Alsace emerged in the 5th century from »elisaza«, meaning »the people who live on the other side [of the Rhine]«. This was the name given to the Germanic Alemanni, who were encroaching into the region. They were subdued by the Franks in 496. When the Carolingian Empire was divided in the Treaty of Verdun of 843, Alsace was granted to the middle kingdom of »Lotharingia« under Emperor Lothair I. In 925 it passed to the Duchy of Swabia, which fell to the Hohenstaufen dynasty in 1079. They made it a core component of their territories. When the last Hohenstaufen ruler of the Holy Roman Empire died in 1268, Alsace was split between various secular and ecclesiastical dominions. The landgravate of Lower Alsace came under the control of the Bishop of Strasbourg, while most of Upper Alsace was ruled by the Habsburgs. The free

History

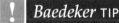

! **Baedeker TIP**

Museum pass

French, German and Swiss provinces on the upper Rhine – Baden, Pfalz, Alsace and the cantons of Switzerland – form a unique cultural region. 150 museums participate in the issue of the Upper Rhine Museum Pass, which can be valid for a whole year or for four days in a month. Information: tel. +33 (0)3 89 33 96 29 (France) or www.museumspass.com.

There are many pretty half-timbered villages and vineyards on the slopes of the Vosges, as here at Hunawihr

cities of the region rapidly gained in importance when ten of them combined to form a union known as the Décapole in 1354. Strasbourg stayed out of the federation, however, and Mulhouse later withdrew. As of 1520 the Reformation made its mark on Alsace via the free cities, leading to a peasant revolt. The Peace of Westphalia in 1648 ceded the Sundgau region and the ten free cities to France, to be joined 25 years later by the rest of Alsace (not including Strasbourg and Mulhouse). Strasbourg was annexed by Louis XIV in 1681, with the exception of its German university. Mulhouse remained part of the Swiss Confederation, as it had been since 1515. The aristocracy and church adapted to the new absolutist monarchy and French culture was fashionable. During the French Revolution, Alsace was subjected to central power from 1793. Certain elements of the regional identity, such as the German language and the Protestant faith, were branded »un-French« and suppressed. In 1798, Mulhouse also came over to France. The Franco-German war of 1870–71 led to the annexation of Alsace by the new German Reich. However the German authorities did not endear themselves to the local populace; their behaviour then, as later in the First and Second World Wars, being the primary reason why Alsace chooses to be definitively French today. After the ceasefire in 1918, French troops occupied the region. It was given back to France by the Treaty of Versailles. The area came under German occupation again during the Second World War from June 1940, but with the ending of hostilities in 1945 it was finally returned to France. Its sovereignty thus changed four times in the space of 75 years. Nowadays Alsace and Strasbourg, seat of the European Parliament and other Europe-wide bodies, play a major role in the new unified Europe.

Alsace has played a major cultural role since the Middle Ages. Gott-fried von Strassburg wrote his epic poem *Tristan and Isolde* here in around 1210, and Strasbourg's cathedral workshop (13th–14th century) had a major influence on medieval sculpture. The mystic Johannes Tauler (1290–1361) lived and died in Strasbourg, and Gutenberg made his first experiments in printing here between 1430 and 1435. Martin Schongauer from Colmar (1450–91), Matthias Grünewald (c1460–1532) and Hans Baldung (aka Grien, 1485–1545) are among the great masters of painting. Humanism and the Reformation made the preacher and writer Geiler von Kaysersberg famous, along with Sebastian Brant (*Ship of Fools/Stultifera Navis*), the Franciscan Thomas Murner and Johann Fischart. In the 19th century the illustrator Gustave Doré (1832–83) and sculptor Frédéric-Auguste Bartholdi (1834–1904, creator of New York's Statue of Liberty) came to prominence. Albert Schweitzer, doctor, theologian, musician and winner of the Nobel peace prize (1875–1965), also came from Alsace. Since the 1970s, its cultural independence has been cemented, as can be seen in the environmental movement, language awareness and dialect poetry concentrating on social and political topics. Part of the population still speaks the local »Elsässer-ditsch«, closely related to the dialect spoken across the river in Germany. Since 1972 schoolchildren as young as nine have been permitted to learn German, and Alsace became the first region in France to be granted a degree of cultural autonomy. However, the German versions of place names are seldom used nowadays.

Art and culture

 Baedeker TIP

Voix et Route Romane

In spring and September there are wonderful opportunities to experience the Romanesque legacy of Alsace in the form of choral concerts in Romanesque churches along the Route Romane. Information: Voix et Route Romane, 43 Rue du Maréchal Foch, F-67003 Strasbourg, tel. 03 90 41 02 02, www.voix-romane.com.

Economy

The Rhine basin is mainly given over to agriculture, while the foothills of the Vosges are dominated by wine cultivation (40% of agricultural production). In the heavily forested Vosges mountains themselves, a wood and paper industry has developed, while the high pastures still support a pastoral system, probably most famous for the production of Munster cheese. In the south, paper, textiles, cars and chemicals are all manufactured, while northern Alsace mainly relies on production of food, luxury goods, metal and shoes. Energy is derived from the river Rhine itself. On the Grand Canal d'Alsace – the man-made navigation canal for the Rhine – there are hydro-electric stations, while in Fessenheim there is a nuclear plant.

Alsatian wine

With vineyards covering some 15,000 ha/58 sq mi, Alsace almost exclusively produces a variety of dry, light **white wine**. The main types of grape, in order of importance, are Riesling, Pinot Blanc, Gewurztraminer, Sylvaner, Pinot Gris (Tokay d'Alsace) and Muscat, while Pinot Noir (Spätburgunder) is used for red and rosé wines. Unlike in the rest of France, the (single-grape) wines are named after the grapes themselves. Edelzwicker wine, however, is a simple blend. 50 selected vines are classified as **Grand Cru**, for which Riesling, Muscat, Gewürztraminer and Pinot Gris are authorized. Stricter rules for yield and quality are applied to these than to ordinary Alsatian wines. Among the most luxurious brands are Vendange Tardive (late vintage, dry to semi-sweet), Sélection des Grains Nobles (sweet wine from noble rot grapes) and the sweeter or less sweet vin de paille. Information on wines and the Route des Vins is available from the Maison des Vins d'Alsace in ▶Colmar.

★★
Route des Vins
A drive along the Alsatian **Route des Vins** is a charming journey through the Vosges foothills. It runs from Marlenheim (west of Strasbourg) via Colmar to Thann (west of Mulhouse), passing through many pretty, traditional wine villages on the way. Along the route, it is possible to visit cellars, and almost all vintners are pleased to sell examples of their produce. The following description of places between Strasbourg and Mulhouse largely follows the Route des Vins, and takes in a few other sights on the Route Romane d'Alsace, the **Alsace Romanesque Road**.

Route Romane d'Alsace

From Strasbourg to Colmar

Strasbourg
▶Strasbourg

Eschau
The country to the southwest of Strasbourg's industrial suburbs is **sauerkraut land** (French: choucroute): the district around the pretty towns of Blaesheim (featuring the restaurant run by choucroute icon Philippe Schadt) and Krautergersheim, where the raw material for Alsace's national dish is cultivated. In Eschau to the east of the N 83 motorway the abbey church of St-Trophime (10th–11th centuries) contains a splendid sculpture featuring the goddess Sophia with her daughters Fides, Caritas and Spes (c1470).

Avolsheim
In Avolsheim, 2km/1.25mi north of Molsheim, the baptismal chapel of St-Ulrich (c1000) with its cloverleaf floor plan and 13th-century frescoes is well worth a visit. In the cemetery to the south, under an ancient linden tree, stands the Dompeter Basilica (from »domus Petri«; 1049). Parts of its apse date back to a church built in the 7th century.

Molsheim
Picturesque Molsheim (7000 inhabitants), still partially encircled by its medieval walls, has a lovely **market place** with its old butchers' guild hall, the Metzig (1554, now a restaurant), and a fountain dating from the same period. On the edge of the old town to the southwest is the Jesuit church, which was built from 1615–18 using the Gothic style, in a kind of architectural Counter-Reformation. Its Silbermann

Tarte flambée, delicious with Alsatian wine

organ dates from 1781. In the Carthusian priory, the Musée de la Chartreuse illustrates the history of the town, while the neighbouring **Fondation Bugatti** is a memorial (including several original vehicles) to the legendary car designer Ettore Bugatti, who founded his Messier Hispano Bugatti factory in Molsheim in 1909. Nowadays the firm is a supplier to the aerospace construction industry, and Volkswagen makes the new 1001-horsepower Bugatti Veyron in Molsheim. In Altorf (Altdorf), southwest of Molsheim, it is worth viewing the Benedictine church, which was given a Baroque makeover by the Austrian architect Peter Thumb in 1724–27. **Altorf**

The old wine town of Rosheim (3900 inhabitants) was once a member of the Décapole league of free cities. Its medieval walls and gatehouse towers are well preserved, as are many timber-framed buildings. The 12th-century church of St-Pierre-et-St-Paul is one of the most important Romanesque buildings in Alsace. Notable features include the frieze of blind arches with sculpted consoles and the half-man/half-beast figures on the front gable. Rosenheim also possesses the only Romanesque house made of stone in Alsace, the 12th-century **Heidehuss**. The town hall (housing the tourist office) dates from 1775, the six-bucket well from 1605. On the weekend nearest the 14th July a big »snail festival« takes place. **Rosheim**

◄ St-Pierre-et-St-Paul

Passing the **picture-book village** of Boersch with its lovely six-bucket well (1617), the route leads on to Ottrott, distinguished by the ruins of two opposing castles, the Lützelburg (12th century) and Rathsamhausen (13th century). In the higher part of the village, one of the few places in Alsace that produces red wine, is a famous wine inn called Ami Fritz, now an upmarket hotel restaurant. At the western perimeter fish from all over the world are on view in the aquarium Les Naïades (open daily). **Boersch Ottrott**

Obernai ✱

The former free city of Obernai (10,000 inhabitants) at the foot of Mont Ste-Odile is the centre of tourism at the northern end of the Route des Vins with its old walls, guarded by towers, and beautiful timber-frame houses. The centrepiece is the Place du Marché with its well-to-do town houses in Gothic and Renaissance styles, its corn market (Ancienne Halle aux Blés, 1554), the well of St Odilia and the town hall (15th–16th centuries). The 60m/200ft Tour de la Chapelle is a remnant of a 13th-century church (and now houses the tourist office). There is a **six-bucket well** (1579), one of the finest in Alsace, in front of Hôtel de la Cloche. The neo-Gothic church of St-Pierre-et-St-Paul (1873) at the northern edge of the old town possesses four windows by Peter Hemmel of Andlau (c1480), which were rescued from an earlier building. The large »Hans em Schnokeloch« **folk festival** takes place on the weekend following the 14th July. There is a wine festival that starts on 15 August as well as a harvest festival in the third week of October.

Mont Ste-Odile ✱

Mont Ste-Odile, 764m/2507ft high, has been dubbed the »holy mountain of Alsace«. The wooded mountain is encircled by a so-called **pagan wall** (mur païen) some 10km/6mi long, up to 3m/10ft high and 2m/7ft thick. It is the most important testament to the prehistory of the area. According to legend, St Odile, daughter of Duke Attich of Alsace, founded a convent here around AD 700. The heyday of the convent was in the 12th–13th centuries, but in 1546 it was destroyed by fire. The **pilgrims' church** (1687) attracts many believers, in particular around 13 December, and is said to be where Odile († 720), the benefactor and patron saint of Alsace, is buried. It is said that she was born blind but gained her sight after being baptized. There is a fabulous view from the terrace, and an even better one a little further southeast from the Männelstein (826m/2710ft). St Odile's Well on the D 33 to St-Nabor is supposed to heal poor eyesight. To the east, at the foot of the steep hillside, the ruins of the convent church, consecrated in 1180, can still be seen.

Barr

The important wine town of Barr (4700 inhabitants) – where the Kirchberg vineyard is classified as Grand Cru – still has many pretty old buildings despite a fire that ravaged the town in 1678. The market place is the site of a Renaissance town hall (1640) as well as some charming houses, some in the Gothic style, from the 14th–15th centuries. The Musée de la Folie-Marco in a magnificent palace dating from 1763 displays aspects of Alsatian domestic life. On the second weekend in July there is a wine market followed by a festival of the grape harvest on the first weekend in October.

Andlau

Two ruins, Spesburg (13th century) and Haut Andlau (14th century, occupied until 1806), tower over the pretty and beautifully situated wine village of Andlau (1650 inhabitants). It grew up around a convent founded by Richardis, wife of Charles the Fat, in around

880. The **abbey church** saw continual alterations and additions from the 12th century (vestibule, crypt) into the 17th century (nave, tower). The figures in the frieze on the façade, the outer wall to the left and the west entrance are some of the most remarkable examples of Romanesque sculpture in Alsace and date from 1130. Noteworthy features inside include the choir stalls and the tomb of the benefactress (both 15th century). Chapelle Ste-Marguerite (11th century) to the east of Epfig (6km/3.5mi southeast of Andlau) has an interesting vestibule and charnel house.

✶
◄ Abbey church

Epfig

The wine and farming village of Dambach (2000 inhabitants) has a wonderfully picturesque old centre. The building containing the Wistub (wine lodge) **Caveau Nartz** on the market place is especially pretty. In Chapelle St-Sébastien amid the vineyard slopes there is a marvellous Baroque altar (1692) and a statue of Our Lady from the Riemenschneider school (15th century). A path leads from the chapel up to the ruins of Castle Bernstein (12th–13th centuries), where there is a magnificent view.

✶
Dambach-la-Ville

Pretty little Châtenois (Kestenholz, 3000 inhabitants) gets its name from the sweet chestnut forests in the vicinity and is renowned for its fruit brandy.

Châtenois

Sélestat (Schlettstadt, 15,000 inhabitants) is situated on the border between Upper and Lower Alsace. Its romantic old quarter is hidden away between large industrial zones. It dates back to a Carolingian royal residence and had the status of a free city between 1217 and 1648. In the 15th–16th centuries, it was known as Schlettstadt and was famed for its school of Latin and the »Literary Society« which made it a centre of the early humanist movement. The most famous student was the reformer Martin Bucer, who was born in the town. The late Romanesque church of **Ste-Foy** (St Faith, 11th–12th century) is one of the best and most typical churches of its time in Alsace. A few paces to the north stands St-Georges (early 13th century) with its 60m/200ft tower, one of the biggest Gothic churches in the Alsace region. The richly decorated pulpit (1619) and stained glass windows are notewor-

✶
Sélestat

The castle at Haut Koenigsbourg

thy. The modern windows in the nave were designed by Max Ingrand. Not far to the west of St-Georges, the corn exchange houses the impressive **Bibliothèque Humaniste**, founded in 1542 (closed Tue). It contains writings dating from the 7th century till the 16th century, as well as the 670 volumes that make up the library of Beatus Rhenanus. Remnants of the town fortifications can be seen in its Tour des Sorcières (Witches' Tower) and clock tower. To the south, the 17th-century walls established under Vauban offer a marvellous view of the »Grosse Ried«, as the Rhine basin is sometimes called here. This pretty village, 9km/5.5mi northeast of Sélestat, possesses the most important Baroque building on the left bank of the upper Rhine. The Austrian **Peter Thumb** of Vorarlberg built his first major monastery here between 1708 and 1712 (façade, towers, dormitories) and from 1721 to 1728 (nave). The pièce de resistance of the expansive interior is the high altar with its unusual crowned dais. There is also a Silbermann organ of 1732.

✷ Ebersmunster

Kintzheim

Further along the Route des Vins, Kintzheim is guarded by a castle dating from the 13th–15th centuries. The attractions here include the birds of prey centre in the castle and the Montagne des Singes, an open-air menagerie with Barbary apes along the road to Haut Kœnigsburg (both April–Oct).

✷ Haut Kœnigsbourg

Haut Kœnigsburg castle is built on an outlier of the Vosges mountains at an altitude of 755m/2477ft. The Hohenstaufen Duke Friedrich, father of Emperor Friedrich Barbarossa, had a castle built here in 1147 but it was destroyed by the Swedes in 1633. The ruins passed into the possession of the town of Sélestat as a gift of **Emperor Wilhelm II** in 1899. In the face of considerable protest he took it upon himself to have the site rebuilt as a romantic, chocolate-box palace by the architect Bodo Ebhard from 1901 to 1908. It is claimed, however, that Ebhard nevertheless stayed close to the original designs. Picturesque St-Hippolyte (1200 inhabitants) at the foot of the Haut Kœnigsburg is known for its splendid red wine. Remnants of its fortifications and its Gothic church (14th–15th centuries) give it a medieval appearance.

Saint-Hippolyte

✷ Ribeauvillé

Ribeauvillé (4900 inhabitants, German: Rappoltsweiler, Alsatian: Rappschwihr) is one of the most visited places in Alsace. It is a pretty little town at the foot of two famous vineyard slopes (Grands Crus Kirchberg and Geisberg), overshadowed by the ruins of three different castles dating from the 11th–14th centuries: Giersberg, Ulrichsburg and Hoch Rappoltstein. In medieval times the counts of Rappoltstein were patrons of the wandering pipers, players and jugglers in the upper Rhine region, who congregated in the town on **Pfifferdaj** (a festival on the 1st Sunday of September). The main spine of the town is formed by the Grand'Rue with its Pipers' House (14th century, now a wine lodge) and the market place with its Baroque town hall (1773–78), Renaissance fountain (1536) and late Gothic monastic church (1412). The Tour des Bouchers (13th century) and some other defensive towers remain from the fortifications. Key dates during the year include the »Kougelhopf« festival on the first Sunday in June and a wine fair on the third weekend in July.

Hunawihr (Hunaweier, 500 inhabitants) is beautifully situated amid the vineyards. Foremost among its attractions is the late Gothic fortified church (15th century) with its dual nave, one for Catholics and one for Protestants. Its beautiful frescoes depict the legend of St Nicholas (*c*1500). On the fourth weekend in July the **Ami Fritz Festival** takes place. Parc des Cigognes to the east of the village has played a major role in reintroducing nesting storks to the Alsace region and has expanded into a major zoological park featuring cormorants, beavers, otters and aquaria. **Hunawihr**

The wine-producing settlement of Riquewihr (Reichenweier, 1000 inhabitants) is another lovely spot. Its walls and towers are beautifully preserved, as are numerous Gothic and Renaissance buildings. However, it attracts some 1.5 million visitors every year and is often full to bursting. At the bottom end of the main thoroughfare, Rue du Général-de-Gaulle, is the town hall. The Dolder gate tower (1291), containing the local museum, stands at the other end. Beyond that there is another main gate. Musée Hansi is dedicated to the popular caricaturist Jean-Jacques Waltz, who called himself **Hansi**. It is on the main street next door to Maison Liebrich (1535) with its lovely courtyard. Further south is a castle (1539), where the dukes of Württemberg-Mömpelgard once resided. Horburg-Reichenweier was part of their domain from 1324 to 1801. Nowadays it houses a postal museum. The Württemberg-Mömpelgard coat of arms can be seen on the well. The Tour des Voleurs (Thieves' Tower, 1300) north of the main gate is part of the local museum and features a torture chamber. A pretty path leads from there to the Grand-Cru Schoenenbourg vineyard. The annual highlights are the Rieslingfest in August and a wine festival that runs for two weekends in September. **✱ Riquewihr**

Sigolsheim is another wine village that has preserved a Romanesque gem in the form of the 12th-century church of St-Pierre-et-St-Paul and its splendid columned entrance.

Ribeauvillé, beneath Ulrichsburg castle

Kaysersberg
Kaysersberg (2700 inhabitants), formerly a free city, is also over-looked by a 13th-century ruined castle alongside the river Weiss. With its remaining walls, a fortified bridge with arrow slits (1514) and fine Gothic and Renaissance houses, it too is a popular destination. The imposing church of Ste-Croix on the main street (1277 to 15th century) has a magnificent **winged altar** by Hans Bongartz of Colmar (1518). Next door is the town hall with its Renaissance oriel (1604), to the rear St Michael's Chapel, featuring frescoes that date back to 1464. Beyond the old white bridge on the main street, the house where **Albert Schweitzer** (1875–1965) was born has been made into a small museum.

Turckheim
This lovely medieval township (3500 inhabitants) lies where the Münstertal opens into the Rhine basin. From May to October, after the clocks strike 10pm, a **night watchman** makes his rounds, singing as he goes. Opposite the town hall (1593–1630), which contains the chamber of the Alsatian Décapole, the 16th-century Hotel des Deux Clefs occupies a marvellous timber-frame building. A nature trail through the Grand Cru Brand vineyards starts from the Porte de Brand heading towards Niedermorschwihr.

Les Trois Epis
For some great views take a quick detour up to Les Trois Epis, a mountain resort since the 19th century and goal of pilgrimages for devotees of the Virgin Mary since the 15th century. The concrete church was consecrated in 1968.

Colmar
▶Colmar

From Colmar to Mulhouse

Munster
The road from Colmar to the Col de la Schlucht (▶ p.218) leads through the Munstertal valley. The main town of Munster (4700 inhabitants) grew up around a Benedictine monastery opened in 630. Its name has been become familiar thanks to the pungent red soft cheese produced from the surrounding mountain pastures. It is protected under European law as an Appellation d'Origine. The town hall dates from 1555, and the Laube store goes back as far as 1503. The remains of the abbey can be found south of the market place along with the visitor centre for the Parc Naturel des Ballons des Vosges.

✱
Neuf Brisach
The fortified township of Neuf Brisach (Neu Breisach, 2100 inhabitants), 17km/11mi east of Colmar, has an unusual appearance. It was laid out by Vauban in 1699–1708 to the orders of Louis XIV. Two of the four town gates are preserved; one of them, the Porte de Belfort, houses a Vauban museum.

✱
Eguisheim
This pretty old township (1500 inhabitants) grew up around an 8th-century moated castle (rebuilt in 1894). A statue of Pope Leo IX, who

is said to have been born here in 1002, adorns the fountain in front of the castle. The 19th-century parish church still has one tower and the west portal of a previous building on the site from around 1230. In late July a Wine Week and Grand Cru Night take place here. There are also another three towers on the castle hill, the **Drei Egsen**: Dagsburg, Wahlenburg and Weckmund, remnants of extended fortifications built in the 12th–13th centuries. They are included in the Route des Cinq Châteaux, which runs from Husseren to Wintzenheim.

This wine village not only has pretty little courtyards leading off its Grande Place, it also has the finest Romanesque church tower in all of Alsace (c1120, 36m/118ft high). The rest of the church of St-Pantaléon is 19th century. What is perhaps the most beautiful choir in any Romanesque church in Alsace can be found in neighbouring Pfaffenheim. The nave dates from the late 19th century.

Guebschwihr

Pfaffenheim

The attractive township of Rouffach (Rufach, 5000 inhabitants) still has parts of its old fortifications. The market place is dominated by the three towers belonging to the unfinished church of **Notre-Dame**, which mainly dates back to the 12th–13th centuries. The corn market (1569) with the town museum is located diagonally across from the church. The old town hall (1581–1617, including the tourist office) is built in two sections along the old town wall. The Tour des Sorciéres (Witches' Tower, 13th–15th centuries) is alongside. Isenburg Castle (now a hotel) is situated on the hill with the local vineyards. It was built in 1880 on foundations dating back to a residence of the Frankish Merovingian dynasty. On the weekend following the feast of the Ascension, a fair for organic food, **Marché Bio**, takes place.

Rouffach

Guebwiller (Gebweiler, 11,000 inhabitants), at the start of the Lauch valley, relied on wine cultivation until well into the 19th century, when textile manufacture and machine production took over. Its main street is Rue de la République, along which there are several interesting buildings. Notre-Dame church (1762–85), one of the few Baroque churches in Alsace, is a marvellous example of French classicism. The **Rococo decoration** inside, created by Swabian artist Fidel Sporer, makes for a startling contrast. The Musée du Florival next door is devoted to archaeology and folklore. Concerts are given inside the plain Gothic church (14th century with frescoes from the 14th–15th centuries) every Friday and Saturday during the summer. Beyond the town hall (Flamboyant, 1514) is the large Romanesque and Gothic church of St-Léger (12th–13th centuries) with its lively west façade. A wine festival takes place in the tithe barn on Ascension Day.

Guebwiller

✴
◄ Notre-Dame

✴

◄ St-Léger

Not far from Guebwiller stands the famous Benedictine abbey of Murbach, which was the spiritual and cultural hub of Upper Alsatian life in the 8th and 9th centuries. Around 800–825, when the abbey

Murbach

✳
Abbey church ►   was one of the powerful political authorities, the »Murbach hymns« were written. Only the towers, transept and choir of the abbey church have survived. They date from the abbey's second heyday in the 12th century, and are among the most important Romanesque remains in Alsace alongside Mauersmünster and Rosheim.

Lautenbach   For devotees of the Romanesque style, it is worth branching off down the Lauch valley to Lautenbach, where the church of St-Michael-et-St-Gingolph (12th century) has a fine western front. The bas-reliefs on the portal are especially notable. The **Ecomusée d'Alsace** (Alsace Open-Air Museum) about 10km/6mi southeast of Guebwiller includes some 70 traditional timber-frame buildings from the 12th to 19th centuries (open daily but closed Jan–Feb). It also provides a home to horses, cattle and poultry while its workshops produce genuine products. Various »fête days« are also held during the year. A hotel and restaurants in the old houses themselves cater for guests. The industrial history of the area can also be discovered in the former potassium mine next to the open-air village. A train runs between the two sites.

Thann   Thann (7700 inhabitants) is the final stop on the Route de Vins d'Alsace (the Route des Crêtes climbs from neighbouring Cernay to Vieil Armand; ►p.219). Thann is a popular resort situated where the Thur valley opens into the Rhine basin. It is grouped around the **collegiate church of** St-Thiébaut, which was built between 1332 and 1516 and is the most important Gothic building in Alsace other than Strasbourg cathedral itself. Its 76m/250ft tower was modelled on that of the minster in Freiburg. The western façade has a double door with 500 separate figures in 150 scenes (14th–15th centuries). Things to see inside include the *Madonna of the Vines* (16th century), stained glass (15th century) and superb choir stalls (15th century). The imposing corn market (1519) to the north on the banks of the Thur houses an art museum and a historical museum. The festival of »burning three pine trees« on 30 June commemorates the founding of the town.

Mulhouse   ►Mulhouse

✳ ✳ Route des Crêtes

The Vosges Route des Crêtes (Road of the Peaks), 75km/45mi of steep, winding roads along the Vosges ridge, was built during the First World War as a supply line to the hard-fought front. It leads from Col du Bonhomme to the west of Kaysersberg over the Col de la Schlucht and Grand Ballon as far as Cernay, and there are some fabulous views along the way. The road is often closed in winter.
The N 415 links Alsace to Lorraine across the 949m/3314ft Col du Bonhomme. Somewhat south of the pass, a side road leads towards

two lakes, Lac Blanc and Lac Noir, both surrounded by pretty scenery (auberge, view from Château Hans). The stretch leading up to the Col de la Schlucht is one of the loveliest – and steepest – routes in the Vosges. At the pass itself (1135m/3724ft) the Route des Crêtes crosses the D 417 road from ▶Colmar to Gérardmer (in ▶Lorraine, p.514). The area is popular with winter sports enthusiasts. The Route des Crêtes reaches its highest point at Hohneck, on the second-highest peak in the Vosges at 1362m/4469ft, where there is a breathtaking panorama. Between 1871 and 1918 the border between

! **Baedeker** TIP

Fermes auberges

»Fermes-auberges« – farmhouse inns – cater for creature comforts from May or June to October, especially in the southerly parts of the Vosges mountains. At least 70% of the fare on offer must have been produced in the farm's own fields. As well as hearty snacks, »repas marcaire« are also served. These »dairymen's lunches« are composed of soup, meat with fried potatoes and a piece of cake. A few of the inns offer some basic accommodation for overnights stays in a country idyll. Information is available from any of the region's tourist offices

France and Germany passed through this point. 18km/12mi further south and 1200m/3937ft high, **Markstein** is a good starting place for a hiking trip. Lac de la Lauch ripples below the peak.

✳ **Hohneck**

Grand Ballon (Grosser or Sulzer Belchen in German), rises to 1424m/4672ft above Guebwiller (▶ p.217), making it the highest summit of the Vosges and a popular place for winter sports. A shrine to the Celtic sun god Bel or Belen was once here. In 1997 a radar station was opened at the summit. More than 400m/1300ft below it is the reservoir Lac du Ballon behind a dam built in 1699 by Vauban, Louis XIV's military engineer.

✳ ✳ **Grand Ballon**

Vieil Armand (Hartmannsweilerkopf) is 956m/3166ft high and was the scene of major struggles during the First World War. A 22m/72ft crucifix on the mountain is dedicated to the estimated 60,000 soldiers who died in the fighting. Other commemorations of the dead include a French cemetery, a martial obelisk, a crypt housing the bones of 12,000 soldiers and a museum. In and around the area, various graves and old bunkers can still be seen. The Route des Crêtes comes to an end at Cernay, 15km/9mi from ▶Mulhouse.

Vieil Armand

Cernay

Ballon d'Alsace (Elsässer Belchen) is 1250m/4100ft high and marks the southwestern tip of the Vosges. The summit of the pass is about 45km/28mi from Cernay, with Thann (▶p.218) and Masevaux in between. The latter is a pretty township with an **abbey** that was once highly renowned (organ recitals July–Sept, Sun). Ballon d'Alsace is not wooded and attracts plenty of visitors in both summer and winter. In theory the view reaches all the way to Mont Blanc. About 35km/22mi southwest of the mountain is Ronchamp, where there is a famous chapel designed by Le Corbusier (▶p.411).

✳ **Ballon d'Alsace**
Masevaux

✴ Sundgau

Route de la
Carpe Frite

The sumptuous scenery of southern Alsace, between Mulhouse and the Swiss border, often gets overlooked as it flashes by on the left of drivers hurtling down the A 36 towards Besançon. Apart from its lush fields, hills and woods with plenty of ponds and small brooks, the Sundgau region has plenty of attractive places and idyllic villages. The **Route de la Carpe Frite** is named after the region's culinary speciality, fillets of carp fried in oil.

Altkirch

Musée Sundgauvien, the Sundgau museum, is housed in the district administration office next door to the town hall in Altkirch (5400 inhabitants), the pretty regional capital nestling above the river Ill. It contains not only exhibits relating to local history and folklore but also paintings by the artist Jean-Jacques Henner (1829–1905), who was born in the town.

✴
Feldbach

The Romanesque basilica of **St-Jacques** in Feldbach is a jewel in the artistic history of Sundgau. It was once part of a Benedictine convent founded in 1144. The difference in design between the nuns' and the congregation's parts of the nave is noticeable.

Ferrette

Ferrette (800 inhabitants), beautifully situated at the edge of the Jura Mountains, is dominated by the ruins of **Hohenpfirt Castle** (1125). In the lower part of the town, the partially Gothic church has a fine statue of the Madonna carrying a figure of the baby Jesus who has three arms. The dark maroon Renaissance town hall 1570 is in the upper section of town. In Vieux Ferrette it is possible to buy some of the exquisite cheeses of the famous »affineur« Antony (Rue de la Montagne 17, Thu to Sat pm).

Northern Vosges and North Alsace

✴
Donon

The N 420 runs southwest from Strasbourg through the Bruche valley to St-Dié. The densely forested Donon massif to the west forms the border between Alsace and Lorraine and marks the southern edge of the sandstone Vosges range. From its 1009m/3310ft peak (2km/1.25mi from the car park) there is a superb view that reaches as far as the Bernese Alps in good weather. The Celts, Romans and Franks all built shrines here, but the »temple« above the TV broadcasting station is a product of the 19th century.

Le Struthof

The German concentration camp of Struthof was located in hills to the east of Schirmeck near Natzwiller. Some 44,000 people were interned there between 1941 and the end of 1944, and 10,000 of them lost their lives. There is a memorial and a small museum.

✴
Château Nideck

The picturesque upland landscape northeast of Donon is sometimes called Petites Vosges. One particularly impressive sight is the castle ruin at Nideck (13th–14th century). There are great views from the ruins of Wangenbourg (13th century), which was once part of Andlau Abbey, and from Rocher de Dabo (16km/10mi to the west ▶Lorraine).

Wangenbourg
Rocher de Dabo

The Romanesque church in Marmoutier (Maursmünster, 6km/3.5mi south of Saverne), one of the loveliest in Alsace, belonged to a monastery founded in 589 and closed in 1792. Its magnificent west façade dates from around 1150–60, while the transept and nave (exhibiting Gothic elements) were built between 1230 and 1300, the aisles from 1519 and the choir up to 1769 (18th-century choir stalls). The **Silbermann organ** (1709) is still used for concerts. The Musée d'Arts et Traditions in its timber-frame Renaissance house, which once had Jewish owners, is well worth a visit. It is devoted not only to local folklore, but also to the Jewish presence in Alsace.

✱
Marmoutier

The Saverne depression, the lowest of the passes between the Rhine valley and Lorraine, is crossed by the Rhine-Marne Canal, a railway and a motorway. At its eastern edge is Saverne (Zabern, 10,500 inhabitants), founded in Roman times as Tres Tabernae (three taverns) and residence of the bishops of Strasbourg between 1414 and 1789. The vast, classical **Château des Rohan**, named after the last bishop to bear the name, was closely involved in the Diamond Necklace Affair, one of the key events that led up to the French Revolution. It was built between 1779 and 1852 on the site of an earlier castle. As well as museums of archaeology, art and the history of the town, the building also houses a youth hostel. The front of the building is 140m/ 153yd long. It faces the canal,

✱
Saverne

Baedeker TIP

Saverne, city of roses
Roses play a major role in the life of Saverne. On the third Sunday in June a rose festival takes place. »Boutons de rose« (rose-flavoured chocolates) are a particular local delight. The garden on the road to Phalsbourg, which was laid out in around 1900, is also well worth a visit.

which is popular with houseboat dwellers and holidaymakers. There are some Renaissance buildings on Grand'Rue, the main street, including Maison Katz from 1605 (wine lodge). The boat lift (plan incliné) at St-Louis-Arzviller opened in 1969 and attracts not only devotees of modern engineering. Situated on the Rhine-Marne Canal, 3km/2mi southwest of Lutzelbourg, it enables ships inside a trough to ascend a 109m/120yd-long ramp, rising 44.5m/146ft in four minutes. Previously this had required a series of 17 locks. Using a brilliantly simple technique it requires only a small amount of power. A boat trip passing through the lift is not to be missed.

✱
St-Louis-Arzviller
boat lift

The hamlet of La Petit-Pierre (700 inhabitants) still has some of its former fortifications and is a popular place to visit. Its castle is delightfully located on the crest of Mount Altenberg with lovely views.

La Petite-Pierre

The 13th-century castle itself houses the visitor centre for the **Parc Naturel Régional des Vosges du Nord** (see below) and its information display. In the choir of the Gothic church at the castle entrance, which has been used by both Catholics and Protestants since 1737, some very fine 15th-century frescoes remain.

Neuwiller-lès-Saverne

The small town of Neuwiller-lès-Saverne (1100 inhabitants, 13km/8mi southeast of La Petite-Pierre) has two impressive Romanesque churches. St-Pierre-et-Paul is a remnant of an abbey founded by St Pirmin in 726. The present church mainly dates from the 12th century, but its crypt goes back to Carolingian times and the western section was added in 1768. A double chapel is built onto the choir (11th century). It has some wonderful capitals and exquisite early 17th-century tapestries. The collegiate church of St-Adelphe was built in the 12th–13th centuries to house relics of St Adelphus, a 4th-century bishop of Metz.

Pfaffenhoffen

Pfaffenhoffen is a pretty little town 14km/9mi west of Haguenau. Its most interesting attractions are the Musée de l'Image Populaire (folk art, closed Mon, Oct–April also Tue) and the synagogue of 1791 – the oldest preserved synagogue and the sole example of a so-called »hidden« synagogue in Alsace. The Protestant church is where Albert Schweitzer gave his first sermon. His grandfather lived here.

Haguenau

Haguenau (Hagenau) has a population of 34,000, making it the fourth-biggest town in Alsace. It is hardly a must-see on the tourist trail, as it has suffered destruction several times in the course of the centuries. There is no longer any trace of its former role as residence of the Hohenstaufen dynasty (Barbarossa established a palace here and it was the birthplace of the minstrel Reimar the Elder) or the glittering meetings of the Reichstag that were held here. Nevertheless its pleasant old quarter has a few points of interest. The church of St-Georges (consecrated in 1189) has a colossal wooden **crucifix** (1488), a splendid sacristy (1523) and the oldest bells in France (1268). The Musée Alsacien in the 15th-century town chancellery exhibits collections of folk art, while the Musée Historique concerns itself with the history of the region. At the northern edge of the old town, close to the Moder Canal, the Gothic church of St-Nicolas (13th–14th centuries) has fine 18th-century choir stalls.

Soufflenheim
Sessenheim

Typical **Alsace pottery** is produced in Soufflenheim, 14km/9mi east of Haguenau. Many of its »poteries« offer souvenirs for sale. Some 5km/3mi southeast of Soufflenheim is Sessenheim, once the home of Goethe's muse Friederike Brion, whom he had met as a student in Strasbourg. There is a museum in the Auberge au Bœuf as well as a Mémorial Goethe in the old guardhouse.

Betschdorf

Betschdorf at the northern edge of the Forêt de Haguenau is the second focus of the Alsace ceramics industry, making a kind of grey earthenware, usually decorated in blue (there is a nice museum). In Surbourg, 5km/3mi to the west, the early Romanesque church is highly significant for the history of art in the region. Some parts of St-Arbogast date back as far as the 9th century.

✱ Surbourg

Hunspach has a reputation as one of the »prettiest villages in France«, overshadowing its near neighbours Seebach and Hoffen. Seebach holds its famous **Streisselhochzeit** festival, a colourful folk celebration centred on the theme of a peasant wedding, on the third Sunday in July.

✱ Hunspach

Visitors can gain a powerful impression of the madness and futility of war in the forts of the Maginot Line (►Baedeker Special p.510), in particular Fort Schœnenbourg (2km/1.25mi west of Hunspach, open daily mid-Apr to early Sept, Sat and Sun only in April and Oct) and Four-à-Chaux near Lembach (15km/9mi southwest of Wissembourg, tours every afternoon mid-March to early Nov; otherwise Sat and Sun).

✱ Maginot Line

The northern part of the Vosges mountains bounded by Saverne in the south, Bitche in the west and Niederbronn in the east was declared a nature reserve in 1976 and a UNESCO biosphere reserve in 1990. In the north the park joins up with Germany's Pfälzerwald reserve.

Parc Naturel Régional des Vosges du Nord

Niederbronn-les-Bains (Bad Niederbronn, 4500 inhabitants) is the leading spa in Alsace. Its thermal springs are rich in common salt and were used as far back as Roman times. The pleasant spa park has a casino and a drinking well, while the Maison de l'Archéologie displays prehistoric and Roman grave relics.

Beyond Philippsbourg, northeast of Niederbronn across the border in Lorraine, the ruins of Château Falkenstein (12th century) loom over the road. Immediately afterwards there is a turn off to Hanau Pond, a popular place for day trippers which has its own ruin, Waldeck Castle.

Château Falkenstein

The N 62 carries on towards the garrison town of Bitche (Bitsch, 7700 inhabitants) with its gigantic citadel, erected in 1681–83 by Vauban (open mid-March–mid-Nov.). A multimedia show and two museums recall the experiences of the war.

✱ Bitche

The impressive ruins in the northern Vosges are those of the Château du Fleckenstein, built in the 12th and modified on several occasions in the 15th century before being destroyed in 1680. It is situated on a narrow sandstone hillock some 20km/12mi west of Wissembourg close to the frontier. There is a great view of the upper Sauer valley from its lookout platform.

✱ Château du Fleckenstein

Wissembourg's »Le Schlupf« quarter on the river Lauter

★
Wissembourg

Wissembourg (Weissenburg, 8400 inhabitants), the northernmost town of Alsace, is just a stone's throw from the German border. The town has a pretty **medieval appearance** and dates back to the founding in 660 of a Benedictine abbey, which was to become a major centre of learning (in 871 Otfried von Weissenburg wrote his *Evangelienbuch* here, the first important book of rhyming poetry to be written in Old High German). From 1719 to 1725 Stanisław Leszczyski, King of Poland, lived here during his first exile in France (► Nancy). The striking abbey church of **St-Pierre-et-St-Paul** (13th–14th centuries) is the largest church in Alsace after Strasbourg's minster. The west tower dates back to an earlier building consecrated in 1074. Notable features include the stained glass painting (12th–13th centuries), a fresco of St Christopher some 11m/36ft high (painted around 1280) and the beautiful 14th-century cloister. Beyond the abbey's tithe barn across the Lauter Canal by the Salt House (Maison de Sel, 1450) is the market place with its town hall of 1752. In the northern part of the old town centre Musée Westercamp, which exhibits collections on archaeology and the history of the town, occupies a 16th-century timber-frame house A walk around the 18th-century fortifications and through the western suburb of Le Bruch is pleasant. There is a large spring festival with a procession, folk events, food etc.

Amboise on the Loire, residence of the Renaissance King François I

✳ Amboise

H 5

Région: Centre
Département: Indre-et-Loire

Altitude: 60m/196ft
Population: 11,000

Amboise, between Blois and Tours on the south bank of the ►Loire, was a resplendent royal residence in the late Middle Ages. This pleasant little town is a good base from which to explore famous castles such as Chenonceau or Chaumont.

Known as Vicus Ambaciensis in Roman times, the town passed into the hands of the Counts of Anjou in the 12th century. Its castle was confiscated by the Crown in 1434; during the reign of Louis XI work began on reconstruction of the residence and continued under his son Charles VIII. Returning from his Naples campaign in 1494–95, Charles brought Italian artists to the Loire, thus introducing France to the Renaissance. François I, king from 1515 onwards, enhanced the grandeur of the castle still further, bringing with him, after the campaign against Milan in 1516, the brilliant artist and technician Leonardo da Vinci, who lived in Amboise until his death in 1519. **History**

What to See in Amboise

The chateau (open all week) was once four times its present size; a lack of funds for renovation saw much of it torn down between 1806 and 1810. Looking towards the river, a richly adorned façade rises above the mighty walls, flanked by the Tour des Minimes, which was accessible by horse and wagon via a ramp. The Chapelle St-Hubert, donated by Charles VIII and his wife Anne de Bretagne in 1491, is an enchanting example of Flamboyant architecture. The famous **door lintel** bears a relief depicting the legend of Saint Hubert (on the **✳ Castle**

✳ ◄ St-Hubert

Logis du Roi ▶

left is Saint Christopher), the tympanum a 19th-century figure of the Virgin, flanked by Charles and Anne. On the northern side of the terrace are the two surviving wings of the Logis du Roi (king's lodge). The Charles VIII wing parallel to the river is Gothic, while the wing of Louis XII and François I dates from the Renaissance period. Armour is on show inside the castle, as well as tapestries from Aubusson and original furniture. There is a wonderful vista of the town and river.

Clos-Lucé ▶

The attractive manor of Clos-Lucé (1477), to the southeast of the castle in Rue V.-Hugo, was home to **Leonardo da Vinci** until his death. Large models based on drawings by the painter, sculptor, architect, engineer, mathematician and musician are displayed in the park; an audio-visual show offers an introduction to the world of Leonardo.

What to see in the town

At the entrance to the town from the Loire stands the erstwhile town hall (c1500) with a small museum. Opposite stands the church of St-Florentin (1484) with a Renaissance tower roof. From here, the rue nationale heads southwest, shortly arriving at the Tour de l'Horloge, the remains of a gateway to the town (1497). Less than half a mile

St-Denis

further the church of St-Denis (around 1110), which was founded by Saint Martin, is a fine example of Anjou Gothic; inside, the Romanesque capitals deserve a look, as do the 16th-century Entomb-

▶ VISITING AMBOISE

INFORMATION

Office de Tourisme
Quai du Gén. de Gaulle
F-37400 Amboise
Tel. 02 47 57 09 28, fax 02 47 57 14 35
www.amboise-valdeloire.com

EVENTS

Easter and mid-August: Foire aux Vins (wine fair)

WHERE TO EAT

▶ **Inexpensive**
Caveau des Vignerons d'Amboise
Place M. Debré, open daily mid-March to mid-Nov, 10am–7pm. Savour the fine wines and crémants of the Loire below the castle walls, with a snack to go with them.

WHERE TO STAY

▶ **Mid-range / luxury**
Château de Pray
F-37530 Chargé, tel. 02 47 57 23 67
http://praycastel.online.fr
2km/1.25mi east of Amboise. Castle of the 13th–17th centuries in a park high above the Loire, antique-furnished rooms, some with magnificent river views, beautiful terrace.

▶ **Budget**
Le Blason
11 Place Richelieu
Tel. 02 47 23 22 41, www.leblason.fr
Pretty 15th-century Gothic house in the town centre. Charming, old-fashioned rooms with raftered ceilings. Pleasant, inexpensive restaurants nearby.

ment scene and a marble grave with the naked figure of a drowned woman, »beautiful Babou«, said to be a mistress of François I. From the bridge to the Ile St-Jean, the view of the town and its castle is wonderful. An original fountain by Max Ernst (1968), who lived close by in Huismes, stands on the Loire dyke. In the northeastern part of town on the Loire, take a look at the interesting Greniers de César, 16th-century granaries set in the tuff stone.

✳ Greniers

Around Amboise

The 44m/144ft-high Pagode de Chanteloup in the Forêt d'Amboise south of town (close to the D 31), erected 1773–78, is an odd structure. It is the only notable surviving part of a Baroque chateau which was expanded after 1760 by the Duc de Choiseul, Louis XV's foreign minister, and dismantled in 1823–25.

Chanteloup Pagoda

✳ Amiens

K 3

Région: Picardie
Département: Somme

Altitude: 27m/88ft.
Population: 139,000

Amiens, the old capital of ►Picardie, boasts a marvellous cathedral and a dignified atmosphere befitting one of the most attractive towns in northern France.

The university town of Amiens, some 120km/75mi north of Paris on the Somme, is the administrative, financial and cultural centre of the region. In medieval times, the linen, wool, cotton and jute industries developed here and the velvets woven here in the 17th century are still known today (»velours d'Amiens«). In Amiens Napoleon and England signed a peace treaty in 1802. In the First World War, the Battle of the Somme raged just a few miles outside the town. Badly destroyed in 1944, Amiens was skilfully reconstructed after the war. Famous sons of the town include Pierre Choderlos de Laclos (1741–1803), author of *Les Liaisons Dangereuses*, and Jules Verne (1828–1905), who wrote many of his novels here and also died in Amiens.

Amiens now and then

✳ ✳ Notre-Dame Cathedral

Notre-Dame Cathedral (UNESCO World Heritage Site) is regarded as the classic prototype of the French Gothic style; built from 1220 to 1288, it stands chronologically between the cathedrals of Reims and Beauvais. Moreover, it is the **largest church in France**: 145m/160yd long, with a nave 42.3m/140ft high and 14.6m/16yd wide, and a transept almost 70m/77yd. The unfinished south tower (65m/

A few facts

Clusters of pillars reach to the heavens from magnificent choir stalls

213ft) dates back to 1366, the northern tower (also unfinished, 66m/216ft) to the beginning of the 15th century. The crossing tower, 112.7m/367ft in height and built of lead-cased chestnut wood, was added in 1529. No less than 3600 figures adorn the inside and outside of the building. In the 1850s, the cathedral was restored by Viollet-le-Duc and survived the Second World War unscathed.

Exterior The three portals of the western face, clearly influenced by Notre-Dame in Paris, primarily depict scenes from the Bible and are amongst the earliest great works of Gothic cathedral sculpture. The serene figure of Christ on the central pillar of the main portal (**Beau Dieu d'Amiens**, from around 1240) is particularly beautiful; on either side are apostles and prophets and, in the tympanum, the Last Judgement. The right door is dedicated to the Virgin Mary, the left to Saint Firmin, the patron saint of Picardie; he brought Christianity to the region and was the first bishop of Amiens. On St Firmin's Door is the »calendar of Picardie« with the signs of the zodiac and Labours of the Months. During restoration of the portals, segments of the original paintwork were uncovered. In the summer months at around 10pm or later, this phenomenon is

Cathedral Plan

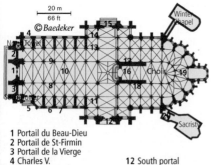

20 m
66 ft
©Baedeker

Winter Chapel

Choir

Sacristy

1 Portail du Beau-Dieu
2 Portail de St-Firmin
3 Portail de la Vierge
4 Charles V.
5 Christophorus
6 Annunciation
7 Woad traders
8 Geoffroy d'Eu
9 Evrard de Fouilloy
10 Labyrinth
11 St. James the Greater defeats the magician Hermogenes
12 South portal
13 Jesus and the traders
14 Font (1180)
15 North portal
16 Choir stall
17 John the Baptist
18 St-Firmin
19 Crying angel
20 Treasury

demonstrated via projection. Above the entrances, the gallery features 22 statues of French monarchs, above these a fine rose window some 11m/36ft in diameter. The similarly grand door of the southern transept depicts the life of Saint Honoré; the central pillar is adorned by the famous Vierge Dorée, which was once gilded.

The interior represents the High Gothic system of northern France in its complete state. In the nave are the tombs of bishops Evrard de Fouilloy († 1222) and his successor Geoffroy d'Eu († 1236), both from the 13th century. The choir, separated by a grand 18th-century **cast-iron grille**, features splendid stalls (1508–19); 3650 figures represent 400 scenes from religious and worldly life. Painted and golden reliefs in the ambulatory feature, amongst other images, the lives of Saint Firmin (1488) and John the Baptist (1531). Behind the high altar, the bowed head of the famous **crying angel**, a Baroque putto of 1628 – a popular image on soldiers' postcards during the First World

Interior

Amiens Map

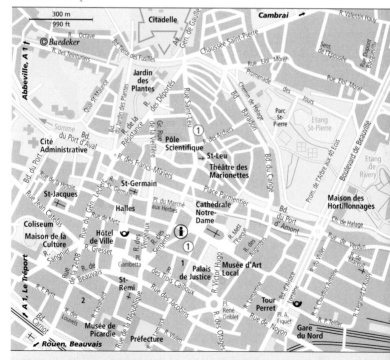

| 1 Maison du Sagittaire | Where to eat | Where to stay |
| 2 Ecole du Cirque | ① La Couronne | ① Prieuré |

▶ VISITING AMIENS

INFORMATION

Office de Tourisme
6 bis Rue Dusevel, F-80000 Amiens
Tel. 03 22 71 60 50, fax 03 22 71 60 51
www.amiens.fr

WHERE TO EAT

▶ **Inexpensive / moderate**
① *La Couronne*
64 Rue St-Leu, tel. 03 22 91 88 57
Popular inn with classic cuisine.
Business guests predominate during
the day. Good-value lunch menu.

WHERE TO STAY

▶ **Budget**
① *Prieuré*
17 Rue Porion, tel. 03 22 71 16 71
www.hotelrestaurantleprieure.com
In a quiet and picturesque street, with
the charm of an old inn.

FESTIVALS

3rd weekend in June: civic festival
with Marché sur l'eau (market on the
water); Mid-Sept: Fete au bord de
l'eau.

War – is above the tomb of Canon Lucas. Pilgrims once shuffled on
their knees across the meander on the floor of the nave (reconstructed). The organ was built in 1442. Treasures of the church include part of the head of John the Baptist, brought to France in 1206
after the Fourth Crusade.

Other Sights in Amiens

Musée d'Art Local Constructed in 1633, the Hôtel de Berny houses the Musée d'Art Lo-
cal et d'Histoire Régionale (mainly crafts and interiors). Opposite the
Palace of Justice are 16th-century patrician houses, including the
Logis du Roi and the Maison du Sagittaire.

✳ **Musée de Picardie** Within the walls of a splendid Second Empire building, the Musée
de Picardie (closed Mon) documents the cultural history of the re-
gion, with an emphasis on local archaeology and fine art from medieval days up to the 20th century.

Tour Perret The Tour Perret, a 104m/340ft-high, 26-storey tower block, was designed by Auguste Perret (1874–1954), as was the railway station.

✳ **St-Leu** A vegetable and flower market is held on Saturdays on Place Par-
mentier. On the far bank of the Somme, the pretty district of St-Leu
is worth a stroll. In the house where **Jules Verne** lived (Bvd Jules
Verne), the author's workplace has been preserved; Verne is buried
in the romantic Madeleine cemetery northwest of town.

✳ **Hortillonnages** On the northeastern border of the old town, 300 ha/740 acres of
marshland have been in use for centuries for the cultivation of fruit

and vegetables. A 55km/35mi network of canals and ditches was created by the removal of peat. Today, just a few hortillons are still operative. Rowing boats can be rented between April and October from the Maison des Hortillonages.

Around Amiens

The southeastern suburb of St-Acheul gave the Acheuléen, a period of the Old Stone Age, its name. The Jardin Archéologique details the archaeology and geology of the region. At Samara, 10km/6mi northwest of Amiens, an archaeological park illustrates the history of man from the Old Stone Age to the Gallo-Roman era. **St-Acheul** **Parc Samara**

In the old village of Naours, 14km/9mi north of Amiens, an extensive system of caves called »grottes-refuges«, or »muches«, can be found, a veritable town dug into the earth since the 11th century, offering a place of refuge (now a museum). **Naours**

Andorra

J 10

Area: 468km/290mi
Altitude: 840–2946m/2756ft–9666ft

Citizens: 29,500
Population: 81,200

The small state of Andorra in the eastern Pyrenees has two faces: a tax and shopping mecca with all the attributes of a new »lifestyle«, and a paradise for nature lovers who are eager to get away from it all.

The Principality of Andorra (in Catalan Principat d'Andorra, French Principauté d'Andorre) can be reached from the Spanish side by a pass road from Seo de Urgel (since 1913), from France since 1931 via the Port d'Envalira (2408m/7900ft) and the 2820m/3100yd-long Tunnel d'Envalira (toll payable) from Ax-les-Thermes or Font-Romeu. The most important settlements are spread through the valleys created by the Valira river and its two headstreams, Valira d'Orient and Valira del Nord.

National flag

Andorra is an independent state with a democratic constitution. Heads of state are the Spanish Bishop of Urgell and the President of France, with sovereignty in the hands of the Andorran people, i.e. a single-chamber parliament. However, only a third of the population are citizens with the right to vote; the rest are mostly Spanish, followed by the French and Portuguese. The official language is Catalan, although Spanish and French are also spoken. The euro is the national currency. Andorra, like other small states, enjoys the reputation of a tax haven. **State and government**

History   People dwelled in the high valleys of Andorra as long ago as the Iron and Bronze Ages. According to legend, Andorra was founded by Charlemagne, its name first mentioned in 839. In 1133, Andorra fell to the Bishop of Urgell and later into the hands of the French counts of Foix through marriage. A long dispute ensued over possession, ending with the signing of the »Pareatges« in 1278, since when the Bishop of Urgell has shared representative power with the Count of Foix, or subsequently his legal heir, the French president. In 1993 Andorra issued its own constitution.

Tourism in Andorra   Where cows grazed and grain or tobacco was cultivated a few decades ago, hotels and restaurants, discount stores and supermarket blocks now stand, frequented by over 10 million tourists each year. Traffic jams clog the narrow valley both in summer and winter. Jewellery, electronic equipment, tobacco goods, alcohol and cheap petrol are the top sellers. Since rates of taxation have been gradually levelled out, turnover has stagnated and Andorra has concentrated its efforts on developing a profile as a holiday destination, complete with mountains over 3000m/9500ft high. The finest ski slopes of the Pyrenees can be found here – skiing is not only popular, but is compulsory for schoolchildren – whilst Andorra offers wonderful routes for hikers and cyclists, as well as ample fish for anglers in the streams and lakes of the mountains.

ANDORRA

Oficina de Tourisme
C/ Dr-Vilanova 13, Andorra la Vella, AD 500
Tel. (00 376) 82 02 14
www.andorra.ad
www.andorramania.com

What to See in Andorra

Andorra la Vella   The capital, Andorra la Vella (1029m/3375ft, population 22,000) lies at the foot of the Pic d'Enclar (2317m/7600ft). The main square, the Plaça del Poble, is also the roof of the Edifici Administratiu Govern d'Andorra (government building). The historic heart of the town and its most important building is the **Casa de la Vall** (around 1580), a former manor house, now the seat of government. The courtroom was once a stable, and the large hall on the first floor, decorated with 16th-century paintings, used to be the dining room; next door, the vast kitchen offers a look into everyday life in the 16th century. The panelled assembly hall contains a famous cabinet which can only be opened with seven keys, each of which symbolizes one of the seven parishes of the country and is held by the parish representative. The council chamber leads into the Capilla Sant Ermengol, where councillors hold prayers before each session. Sant Esteve, the mother church of La Vella (12th century, extended in 1969), features attractive carvings.

✳
Casa de la Vall ►

Adjoining to the east is Escaldes-Engordany (1105m/3625ft). A bizarre glass structure houses the **thermal baths of Caldea**, an opulently appointed fun pool (1994), using spring water at a temperature of 68°C/155°F. Winding its way upwards, a road leads to the Capilla de Sant Miguel d'Engolasters (probably 11th century). From here, a trip to the Estany d'Engolasters reservoir can be undertaken. The ruins of the Capilla Sant Romà are worth seeing, as well as the Pont dels Escalls bridge and a museum containing works by the Catalan sculptor Josep Villadomat.

Casa de la Vall, seat of government

The village of **Encamp** (1315m/4315ft) is home to a Romanesque parish church. Automobile enthusiasts will enjoy the Museu Nacional de l'Automòbil, with over 200 old cars, motorbikes and bicycles. North of Encamp, high up to the right, stands the national treasure of Andorra, the Chapel of Our Lady of Meritxell, patron saint of Andorra since 1873. It was built by Ricardo Bofill in 1976.

Meritxell pilgrimage church

North of the quaint village of Canillo stands the 12th-century Romanesque chapel of Sant Joan de Caselles with a retable dating from 1525 (*Saint John and the Apocalypse*), as well as a decorative choir grille and a Romanesque stucco figure of Christ on the cross.

Sant Joan de Caselles

At Andorra La Vella, the road through the valley of Valira del Nord begins. Beyond the medieval bridge Pont de Sant Antoni lies the picturesque village of Anyòs with the Capilla de Sant Cristofor. The main settlement in the valley is Ordino (1305m/4281ft). The **Casa Plairal d'Areny de Plandolit** is well worth a visit. It was constructed in 1633 and altered in the mid-19th century by the Baron de Senaller. The house has a splendid wrought-iron balcony (1843) and, inside, a copy of the seven-key cabinet, dinner services from Limoges and Sèvres (the latter a gift from the Austrian Habsburg emperors) decorated with the coat of arms of the Baron de Senaller, and a copy of the original Andorran national anthem. The philatelic museum displays Andorran stamps, an important source of income for the principality. Surrounded by tobacco fields, La Cortinada is the site of church of Sant Martí de La Cortinada, with Romanesque frescoes, an ossuary and a lovely old dovecote. The road comes to an end in the attractively situated El Serrat, some 1540m/5050ft above sea level.

Valira del Nord

Anyòs
Ordino

◄ Museu Filatèlic

La Cortinada

El Serrat

Riu Madriu The valley of the Riu Madriu, east of La Vella, is the last large valley in Andorra not to have a road, and presents a unique **man-made landscape** earning a classification as a UNESCO World Heritage Site in 2004. The way (GR 7) is marked by archaic forms or remnants of pasture farming, iron smelting and power generation.

Santa Coloma To the right of the road to Spain, in Santa Coloma, stands the Romanesque church of the same name, with its three-storey round tower. Inside is the fine 12th-century statue of Our Lady of Coloma. The arch at the entrance is painted with Mozarabic frescoes. Look out for a medieval font. The castle of Sant Vicenç, built in the 12th century by the Counts of Foix, overlooks the village.

Sant Julià de Lòria The road continues to the Romanesque bridge Pont de La Margineda and on to Sant Julià de Lòria (939m/3080ft). The church has a Romanesque bell tower, a statue of the Virgin Mary from the same period and a 17th-century crucifix. A small road winds its way from here up to Sant Cerním de Nagol, where there are beautiful Romanesque frescoes.

An archaic sight: Sant Miquel d'Engolasters

Angers

Région: Pays de Loire   **Altitude:** 41m/134ft.
Département: Maine-et-Loire   **Population:** 156,000

Angers is the capital of the historic territory of Anjou on the Loire, with an impressive castle, quaint old town and substantial art treasures.

Anjou, the landscape on the lower reaches of the ►Loire, is a sunny region where fruit, vegetables and fine wines flourish. Angers lies approx. 4km/2.5mi to the north of the Loire on the Maine, a confluence of the Mayenne, Sarthe and Loir, north of the town. The town enjoyed a glorious era with the rise of the Fulks, the ancestors of the mighty house of Anjou, particularly under Foulques Nerra (972–1040). Geoffroi V (1113–51) was the first to use the name Plantagenet, taken from the stylized gorse branch that adorned his helmet; his son married Eleanor of Aquitaine and became king of England as Henry II. Perhaps the most famous figure in the history of Angers is René le Bon, the »Good King« (1409–80; ► Tarascon, p.247). Lacking fortune in politics, he lost Anjou's remaining Italian possessions, but as an educated patron of the arts, he turned his residences into thriving centres of culture.

Old capital of Anjou

Angers Map

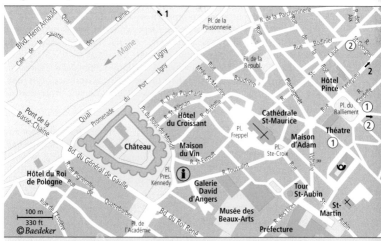

1 Musée Lurçat
2 Jardin des Plantes

Where to eat
① L'Entr'acte
② Le Grandgousier

Where to stay
① Saint-Julien
② Hôtel du Mail

Cathedral and castle are the striking landmarks seen from the Maine

What to See in Angers

✱
Chateau

The strong castle (open May to early Sept, 9.30am–6.30pm, mid-Sept to April 10am–5.30pm), rebuilt by Louis IX in 1228–38, towers above the Maine; its walls are 40–60m (130–200ft) high and consist of layers of slate and limestone with 17 round turrets. In the courtyard are the Chapelle Royale, Logis Royal and the Logis du Gouverneur (from around 1400). Within a modern glass gallery (open from May–early Sept, 9.30am–6.30pm, otherwise 10am–5.30pm) a priceless example of medieval tapestry art is on display: the **Tenture de l'Apocalypse**. 6m/20ft wide, the tapestry series was woven between 1373 and 1380 by the Parisian N. Bataille, based on drawings by Hennequin de Bruges, and originally consisted of seven sections, 168m/550ft in length. Today, six sections (106m/348ft) have survived, 74 scenes in total. Their theme is the Apocalypse of St John. The composition, the attention to detail and dramatic expression are remarkable.

✱ ✱
Apocalypse Tapestry

✱
St-Maurice

Take the narrow Rue St-Aignan with its timber-frame houses and Hôtel du Croissant (1448) to the cathedral of St-Maurice (approx. 1150–1280), where the portal (around 1150) depicts a Majestas Domini (Christ as King) with symbols of the evangelists and Old Testament figures in the archway. The façade is dominated by three towers, the middle one having been renewed in the Renaissance (1540). The 90m/100yd-long, 26m/85ft-high interior features a typically steep **Anjou vault**, dazzling stained glass windows (12th, 13th and 15th century), tapestries and a Rococo organ case (1748). The high altar dates back to 1759, the choir stalls to around 1780 and the magnificent pulpit to 1855.

Behind the cathedral choir stands the Maison d'Adam, a splendid timber-frame house (15th–16th century), with carvings worthy of closer inspection.

Maison d'Adam

Rue Toussaint – with remains of the Gallo-Roman town walls – leads to the 13th-century Eglise Toussaint, where works and replicas by the neo-classical sculptor **P.-J. David d'Angers** (1788–1856) can be seen. On Place Kennedy, pay a visit to the Maison du Vin de l'Anjou to buy or taste wine or to find out more about trips in the region (closed Mon).

Galerie David d'Angers

Maison du Vin

The museum of art housed in the Logis Barrault (1487) exhibits medieval tableaux and crafts, and works by, amongst others, Pisano, Murillo, Watteau, Boucher, Fragonard, David, Delacroix and Corot. Only the 54m/177ft tower remains of the former St-Aubin abbey (11th–12th century); the other sections were integrated into the prefecture: the cloister is in the courtyard and the refectory was turned into a banquet hall.

★
Musée des Beaux-Arts

Tour St-Aubin

Préfecture

VISITING ANGERS

INFORMATION
Office de Tourisme
7 Place Kennedy, F-49000 Angers
Tel. 02 41 23 50 00, fax 02 41 23 50 09
www.angers-tourisme.com

CITY PASS
1–3 days, for museums, the chateau and various discounts.

FESTIVALS AND EVENTS
January: wine market. Late April every second year (2009, 2011 etc): African film festival. June–July: Festival d'Anjou (theatre in the chateaux of Anjou). July–Aug: summer festival, with all kinds of music and theatre.

WHERE TO EAT
▶ Inexpensive
① *L'Entr'acte*
9 Rue L. de Romain
Tel. 02 41 87 71 82
Traditional brasserie behind the theatre, offering hearty fare in the atmosphere of 1953.

② *Le Grandgousier*
7 Rue St-Laud, tel. 02 41 87 81 47
Down-to-earth regional dishes served up a 16th-century hall. Charcoal-grilled meat, extensive, reasonably priced wine list. Patio open for dinner in the summer.

WHERE TO STAY
▶ Budget
① *Saint-Julien*
9 Place Ralliement, tel. 02 41 88 41 62
www.hotelsaintjulien.com.
Centrally located on the theatre square, soundproofed rooms, inexpensive yet elegant. The restaurant Provence Caffé next door is recommended (booking advisable).

② *Mail*
8–10 Rue des Ursules
Tel. 02 41 25 05 25
Elegant 17th-century convent, an oasis of calm in the bustling town centre. Spacious, tastefully appointed rooms. Parking spaces in the courtyard.

Take a close look: the Maison d'Adam

The **Hôtel Pincé**, built from 1523 to 1530 for Jean de Pincé, the mayor, is the finest private residence in town. The Musée Turpin de Crissé displays antique and medieval arts and crafts, as well as pieces from the Far East such as woodcuts by Hiroshige and Hokusai.

Beyond the walls of the medieval town, in Avenue M. Talet, the church of **St-Serge** merits a visit. The choir of 1220 is thought to be the most beautiful and rounded example of the Anjou style. The nave was built in 1445–66, the crossing tower in 1480. Amongst the treasures to be seen here are the three original grisaille windows of the choir and the wonderful corbels and capstones.

La Doutre Across the Maine lies the district of La Doutre (from »d'outre-Maine«). Cross the Pont de Verdun and follow Rue Beaurepaire – taking particular note of number 67, an apothecary's house from 1582 – to **Place de la Laiterie** with its marvellous 16th-century tim-

La Trinité ber-frame houses and a Romanesque church, La Trinité (1080), which belonged to the abbey of Notre-Dame-de-Ronceray (founded in 940). The Ecole des Arts et Métiers in the convent buildings is not open to the public.

Hôpital St-Jean North of Place de la Laiterie stands the Hôpital St-Jean (established
Musée Lurçat in 1174, a hospital until 1854); works by **Jean Lurçat** (1892–1966), famous for revitalizing the art of tapestry weaving, are exhibited here. In the Gothic hospital hall (with a splendid 17th-century pharmacy) hangs a cycle of ten tapestries, woven in Aubusson, depicting Le Chant du Monde (begun in 1957), presenting the problems of mankind today as a riposte to the Apocalypse Tapestry (see above). To the west of the, exhibitions are also held in the hospital warehouse (anciens greniers, late 12th cen-

! **Baedeker** TIP

Rue St-Laud

The atmosphere of Rue St-Laud – running in a northeasterly direction from the cathedral – has a charm all of its own, with old timber-frame houses and cafés, the former Art Nouveau dance hall Alcazar and the restaurant Le Logis with its coveted Michelin star.

tury), whilst the Centre Régional d'Art Textile stands slightly further to the north. Guided tours relate the history of tapestry weaving.

Around Angers

The suburb of St-Barthélemy-d'Anjou (3km/2mi to the east) hosts the famous **liqueur distillery**, founded in 1849 (tours, museum). The chateau beyond St-Barthélemy, to the east, constructed in the 18th century and based on the design of the Petit Trianon in Versailles, played an important role in the Second World War: in 1940 it was the seat of the exiled Polish government and later the headquarters first of Admiral Dönitz, then of General Patton. Today it houses the European Museum of Communications.

Cointreau liqueur distillery Château de Pignerolle

24km/15mi east (take the N 147 towards Mazé) stands a castle built between 1772 and 1777 by L.-G.-E. de Contades, field marshal and governor of Strasbourg, and still preserved in the exact same condition and detail today. The kitchen, chapel and stables (with a collection of coaches) all warrant a closer look.

Château de Montgeoffroy

Le Plessis-Bourré (20km/12mi north of Angers) is a genuine **moated castle**, medieval in character despite its relatively late construction (1468–73). Fascinating rooms contain old furniture and an 18th-century collection of fans. The salle de garde features a splendid wooden ceiling with allegorical, in some cases raunchy and obscene, depictions (late 15th century). Further interesting moated castles are Plessis-Macé (15km/9mi northwest of Angers, 15th century; the Chapelle St-Michel of 1472 boasts a wonderful wooden gallery wall) and Serrant (18km/11mi southwest of Angers), a magnificent Renaissance work of the 16th–18th centuries with a beautiful park.

Le Plessis-Bourré

Antibes · Juan-les-Pins

P 9

Région: Provence – Alpes – Côte d'Azur
Département: Alpes-Maritimes

Altitude
Population: 73,000

With its seaside resorts and suburban villas in Juan-les-Pins and Cap d'Antibes, Antibes is one of the hotspots on the ►Côte d'Azur. It has enjoyed fame and popularity since the early 20th century, thanks to its beautiful sandy beaches and heady nightlife.

Ancient Antipolis – the name meaning »the town opposite Nikaia Polis (Nice)« – was founded from Massalia (Marseille) in the year 5 BC. In 1388, the neighbouring town of Nice passed to Savoy, and Antibes was developed into a border stronghold. Between 1550 and 1578, the Fort Carré north of the harbour was constructed, then expanded in the 17th century by Vauban, Louis XIV's fortress engineer, as were the town defences. Flower growing is an important economic activity, with some 3 sqkm/1.15 sq mi of greenhouses. The Sophia

Antibes now and then

The old town of Antibes with the castle of the Grimaldi

Antipolis technology park lies in the hinterland, with research and production facilities, primarily in the fields of electronics, chemistry, biotechnology and the environment.

What to See in Antibes

Place Nationale The centre of the lively old town, to the south of the Vieux Port, is this pretty, typically Provençal square. The Musée Peynet displays drawings by the »painter of lovers«. Further east is Cours Massena

✱

Musée Picasso with its 19th-century market hall, and, on the seafront, **Grimaldi Castle** (13th–16th century), where Picasso worked in 1946. The Musée Picasso (open mid-June to mid-Sept 10am–6pm, rest of the year from 10am–noon, 2pm –6pm) presents works created here, as well as pieces by famous contemporaries such as Ernst, Miró, Calder, Léger, Modigliani, Saura and Alechinsky; it has a beautiful terrace overlooking the sea.

Cathedral Adjacent on the northern side stands the 12th-century former cathedral. It has a 17th-century façade, an oak door dating from 1710, a **Tour Gilli** polyptych by Ludovico Brea (1515) and a figure of Christ (1447). A museum of folklore is housed in the Tour Gilli, south of the market hall. The coastal promenade runs south to the Bastion St-André, also **Musée d'Histoire** a relic of Vauban's ramparts; here the museum of history shows artefacts from the town's Greek past.

What to See in Cap d'Antibes

Plateau de la Garoupe Villas and gardens grace the landscape of the 4km/2.5mi-long Garoupe peninsula, south of Antibes. The coastline is predominantly in private hands and therefore inaccessible. From the highest point, the Plateau de la Garoupe with its lighthouse, there are splendid views. The pilgrimage church of Notre-Dame-de-la-Garoupe (13th–16th centuries) contains votive plaques, frescoes and a 14th-century icon

● VISITING ANTIBES

INFORMATION
Office de Tourisme
11 Place de Gaulle
F-06600 Antibes
Tel. 04 97 23 11 11
Fax 04 97 23 11 12
www.antibesjuanlespins.com

EVENTS
July: »Jazz á Juan« jazz festival. Tickets available from the Offices du Tourisme Antibes and Juan-les-Pins.

WHERE TO STAY
▶ **Luxury**
Belles Rives
33 Blvd. E. Baudoin
F-06160 Juan-les-Pins
Tel. 04 93 61 02 79
Fax 04 93 67 43 51
www.bellesrives.com
Open March–beginning of Nov.
Former Art Deco residence of Scott Fitzgerald: luxurious, views of the sea and Esterel, two restaurants. Private beach and jetty.

▶ **Budget / mid-range**
Le Pré Catelan
22 Ave. des Palmiers, Juan-les Pins
Tel. 04 93 61 05 11
www.precatelan.com Quiet location in a garden. old villa with attractive rooms, some with a terrace. 200m to the beach.

Relais du Postillon
8 Rue Championnet, Antibes
Tel. 04 93 34 20 77
www.relaisdupostillon.com
Pleasant hotel in the old town, close to the Place des Martyrs de la Résistance. English spoken.

WHERE TO EAT
▶ **Moderate / expensive**
Les Vieux Murs
Avenue Amiral de Grasse, Antibes
Tel. 04 93 34 06 73
Excellent Provençal cuisine and seafood in this busy restaurant which nestles in the town wall. Beautiful terrace opening onto the sea.

---

from Sebastopol. West of the plateau, the botanist G. Thuret began planting exotic trees in 1856 on 4ha/10 acres of land, including the first Australian eucalyptus; today the botanical garden is home to some 3000 varieties. On the southwestern tip of the cape, a maritime and Napoleonic museum is located in the Tour du Grillon. The palace hotel **Eden Roc** (1870), is adjacent on the south side. This exclusive hostelry made its mark in history by appearing in F. Scott Fitzgerald's novel *Tender is the Night* (1934).

Jardin Thuret

Musée Naval et Napoléonien

Around Antibes

The once glamorous villa district of Juan-les-Pins is a popular family resort with a not particularly attractive sandy beach dotted with pines along its 2km/1.25mi length (largely private). The most famous hotels are the Belles-Rives and the Juana, from the 1920s and 1930s. Rudolph Valentino held court in the castle above the harbour. The

Juan-les-Pins

notoriously intense nightlife culminates in the **jazz festival** in Pinède Gould. There is a picturesque walk along the coast to Golfe-Juan.

Biot

✳

Léger Museum

Biot (pronounced »biót«, 5500 inhabitants) is a centre of crafts. The church of Ste-Madeleine (12th–15th centuries) houses beautiful altar paintings from the Nice School and a *Madonna with Rosary* by Louis Bréa. A 20-minute walk southeast leads to the Musée Fernand-Léger (signposted from the D 4, closed Tue), with some 350 works.

✳ ✳ Arles

M 9

Région: Provence – Alpes – Côte d'Azur	**Altitude:** 10m/33ft
Département: Bouches-du-Rhône	**Population:** 52,000

Beautiful old Arles is the gateway to the ▶Camargue. Impressive Roman and medieval buildings, awarded World Heritage status by UNESCO, bear witness to its grand history. Vincent van Gogh painted many of his most famous works here.

Arles then and now

Before the Rhône flows into the Mediterranean, it divides into the Grand Rhône (to the east) and the Petit Rhône (to the west), which enclose the ▶Camargue. Just south of this point lies Arles, the **largest commune** in France, covering an area of 770 sqkm/297 sq (Paris: 105 sqkm/41 sq mi). The Celto-Ligurian Arlath, »town in the swamp«, was a Roman colony from the year 46 BC and succeeded Massilia (Marseille) as the region's most important harbour. In AD 395 the town became the Roman seat of civic administration for Gaul, Spain and Britannia. From the 10th century it belonged to the Kingdom of Burgundy (Arelate) and from 1032 to the Holy Roman Empire. In 1481 it fell to France with Provence.

Vincent van Gogh lived in Arles in 1888–89; he painted the town and its environs over 300 times in this period, and yet there are few reminders of him here now. His »yellow house« on Place Lamartine was destroyed in the Second World War, and none of his pictures hang in Arles.

Café at the Arènes

Arles Map

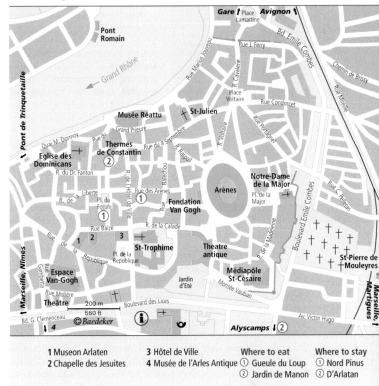

1 Museon Arlaten
2 Chapelle des Jesuites

3 Hôtel de Ville
4 Musée de l'Arles Antique

Where to eat
① Gueule du Loup
② Jardin de Manon

Where to stay
① Nord Pinus
② D'Arlatan

What to See in Arles

The Roman arena, erected around AD 90, an oval measuring 107×136 m/117×149yd had a capacity of 20,000. In medieval times it was made into a fortress, of which three square towers (12th century) and the arcade ramparts have survived; the third row of arcades was removed around 1830. There are wonderful views of the old town and surrounding area from the top. Up to 12,000 spectators gather here from Easter to September to watch **bullfights** in the Spanish tradition (»mise à mort«) and to Camarguaise rules (»courses camarguaises«). Open May–Sept 9am–6.30pm, March, April, Oct until 5.30pm, Nov–Feb 10am–4.30pm.

★★
Arènes

The ancient theatre, built around 25 BC during the reign of Augustus, seated 12,000 spectators on 33 tiers, but was used as a quarry in the early Middle Ages. Fragments of the stage, orchestra and seating

Théâtre Antique

Cloister of St-Trophime

can still be seen. In summer months, it hosts film screenings and concerts.

Further to the west the **Place de la République** is distinguished by a 15m/49ft-high Egyptian obelisk, retrieved from the amphitheatre and erected here in 1676. The town hall on the north side of the square was built in 1673–75 to plans by Hardouin-Mansart, the architect of Versailles. The vaults of the ground floor are worth inspecting and are, indeed, regarded closely by stonemasons as a superlative example of construction. The bell tower was erected from 1543 to 1553, the mausoleum of Glanum (► p.248) providing the inspiration.

★ ★
St-Trophime

Trophimus, a Greek apostle, introduced Christianity to Provence and became the first bishop of Arles. The main **portal** of St-Trophime Cathedral (around 1190) is a masterpiece of Provençal sculpture: the tympanum depicts Christ of the Last Judgement with the symbols of the evangelists around him; the lintel portrays the apostles, to the left the saints, to the right the damned. The two side entrances, smaller than the main one, were added in the 17th century. The basilica, with a 20m/65ft-high nave, was constructed between 1152 and 1180 as the Romanesque gave way to the Gothic style. The cloister also dates from this transitional phase (same opening hours as the Arènes). Pillars alternate with twin columns, and the ornately fashioned capitals depict scenes from the Bible. Lovely tapestries hang in the chapter house.

★ ★
Cloister

Museon Arlaten

Cryptoporticus

The museum of Arles in the 16th-century Palais de Laval-Castellane was founded in 1896 by the Provençal poet and Nobel Prize winner of 1904, **Frédéric Mistral**. It houses the most significant collection of folklore art of Provence. From the former Chapelle des Jesuites (17th century), the Cryptoporticus can be reached. It is a partially subterranean colonnade from the ancient forum (around 40 BC), measuring 89×59m/97×65yd.

Espace Van-Gogh

Vincent van Gogh spent a number of months in this 16th-century hospital with an atmospheric courtyard, also a subject of his paintings. Today it is a bookshop and café.

★
Place du Forum

The charming heart of the old town has a statue of Mistral, remains of the Roman forum and the famous Hotel Nord Pinus.

The small Place du Forum, the charming heart of Arles

From the Roman baths of AD 4, 98×45m/ 107×49yd in size, the caldarium (hot baths), parts of the hypocaust (under-floor heating) and the tepidarium (hot room) have survived. The museum in the adjacent commandery of the Knights of Malta (15th–16th century) presents paintings and drawings from the Provençal School (18th–19th century), a collection of contemporary art (including wonderful drawings by Picasso, paintings by J. Réattu and sculpture by Ossip Zadkine) as well as works by famous photographers.

Thermes de Constantin

★ **Musée Réattu**

Beyond the plane tree-lined Boulevard des Lices, where the town's citizens love to take a stroll and attend the Saturday market, lies the Alyscamps (Elysian Fields), a Roman burial ground which would later become a Christian graveyard, famous far afield in the Middle Ages. The valuable sarcophagi were later given away, sold or destroyed, and some now stand in the Musée Arles Antique. Plain coffins from early medieval times are now all that can still be seen on the Allée des Tombeaux, which ends at the remains of the 12th-century church of St-Honorat.

Alyscamps

Opened in 1995, the Museum of Ancient Arles is a bold, outsized construction approximately 1km/1100yd southwest of the old town. It boasts an excellent **Roman history collection** from the south of France. Open March–Oct 9am–7pm, off-season 10am–5pm.

★★ **Musée Arles Antique**

The famous drawbridge painted by Van Gogh no longer exists. The one on the Ecluse de Montcalde (3km/2mi south, D 35), now shown by tourist operators as Van Gogh's bridge, was actually transported here in 1960 from Fos-sur-Mer. The original stood some 800m/0.5mi further along the canal.

Pont de Langlois

▶ VISITING ARLES

INFORMATION

Office de Tourisme
Boulevard des Lices, F-13200 Arles
Tel. 04 90 18 41 20, fax 04 90 18 41 29
www.ville-arles.fr

FESTIVALS AND EVENTS

1 May: Fêtes des Gardians (Festival of
the Camargue herdsmen), with bullfights and »Queen of Arles« competition. End of May to early July: Fêtes
d'Arles (theatre, music); June–Aug:
bullfights Wed (tickets, tel. 08 91 70
03 70). July: Les Sudas (world music).

PASS MONUMENTS

The Pass Monuments (valid for 3
months) gives access to all museums
and sites of interest.

WHERE TO EAT

▶ Moderate / expensive

① *La Gueule du Loup*
39 Rue des Arènes, tel. 04 90 96 96 69
Small restaurant with a personal
touch and a cosy rustic atmosphere.
Traditional dishes e.g. fillet of beef,
excellent desserts, good value for
money.

▶ Inexpensive/ moderate

② *Jardin de Manon*
14 Av. Alyscamps
Tel. 04 90 03 38 68, closed Wed.
Regional cooking in a pleasant Provençal atmosphere, quiet and attractive
terrace behind the house.

WHERE TO STAY

▶ Mid-range / luxury

① *Nord Pinus*
14 Place du Forum
Tel. 04 90 93 44 44
Fax 04 90 93 34 00
Lots of tradition, an elegant and
intimate hotel on the town's most
celebrated square. Also has a brasserie
and restaurant.

▶ Mid-range

② *D'Arlatan*
26 Rue Sauvage
Tel. 04 90 93 56 66
Fax 04 90 49 68 45
Peaceful, centrally located old palais
with courtyard. Rooms feature Renaissance fireplace and rustic furniture
from Provence, very pleasant atmosphere.

Around Arles

Camargue   Arles is the perfect place to begin a tour of the Camargue, to St-
Gilles and Stes-Maries de la Mer (▶Camargue).

Plaine de la Crau   »Crau« is the name given to the plain created by the rock deposits of
the Durance, southeast of Arles between the Alpilles, Grand Rhône
and Etang de Berre. At first glance, it appears infertile and lacking in
vegetation but closer inspection reveals a fascinating habitat for **rare
animals and plants**. From late winter to June sheep graze here. The
Crau is threatened by fruit-growing (irrigation over 60%) and industry, and is danger of becoming a rubbish tip for Marseilles etc. Hunting and »nature loving« tourists are also a menace. More information
available at the Ecomusée de la Crau in St-Martin-de-Crau.

Round Trip through the Alpilles

Visible from afar, the ruins of the Benedictine abbey stand on a rock ★
outcrop which rises out of the former marshland, some 5km/3mi **Montmajour**
northeast of Arles. An important destination for pilgrims in the Middle
ages, the monastery buildings, the remains of which can still be
seen, were constructed in the 12th–14th centuries and in the 18th
century. From the keep (1369), the Cevennes are within viewing
range. The gigantic Baroque complex (1703–36) was never completed.

Tarascon (11,000 inhabitants) a commercial centre for fruit and veg-   **Tarascon**
etables cultivated in the region, lies on the east bank of the Rhône,
18km/11mi north of Arles. The Château du Roi René on the Rhône,   ★
built after 1400 by Louis II of Anjou, is a real eye-catcher; his son   ◄ Castle
René, Duke of Anjou (»le Bon Roi René«), had it extended between
1447 and 1449 to be his residence, subsequently the centre of Provençal culture. The terrace presents
marvellous views of the Alpilles,
Rhône, Beaucaire and Tarascon.
Next to the castle is the church of
Ste-Marthe (12th and 14th–15th
centuries) with a notable south
door. Inside, a wealth of paintings
(Mignard, Van Loo, Parrocel, to
name just a few) may be seen, as
well as the 1197 sarcophagus of
Sainte Marthe in the crypt. To the
east of the castle (Rue du Château)
stands the elegant 17th-century
town hall; the adjoining **Rue des Halles** is lined with pretty arcaded
houses from the 15th century. The Maison de Tartarin (Blvd. Itam
55) is named after Daudet's fictional character »Tartarin of Tarascon«. This, and the Musée Charles-Deméry (Musée Souleïado, Provence handicrafts) are worth a look.

> **!** *Baedeker* TIP
>
> **Tarasque**
> According to legend, the Rhône was the lair of
> the Tarasque, a man-eating dragon that was
> captured by Sainte Marthe. A four-day festival on
> the last weekend of June is dedicated to the
> heraldic animal of Tarascon, celebrated since the
> days of King René.

Across the Rhône, in Languedoc, lies Beaucaire, once famed across   **Beaucaire**
Europe for its market, inaugurated in 1217. Beyond the castle ruins
(11th–13th centuries, with a museum and great views) the church of
N.-D. des Pommiers (1744) with a Romanesque Passion frieze surviving from its predecessor on the outer east wall and the town hall
(by J. Hardouin-Mansart, 1683) are of interest. During the **Feria du
Toro** in late July, herds of bulls thunder through the streets.

This lively little town (9800 inhabitants) at the foot of the Alpilles,   **Saint-Rémy-**
16km/10mi east of Tarascon, is the birthplace of **Nostradamus**   **de-Provence**
(1503). The sights here are the church of St-Martin (14th century/
1821, with a beautiful and famous organ), the house where Nostra-

Once a fortified town of cultured knights: Les Baux on its rocky outcrop

damus was born just a few yards away, the 18th-century Hôtel d'Estrine with a Van Gogh centre, the 15th–16th century Hôtel de Sade with a lapidarium and the Musée des Alpilles in the Renaissance-style Hôtel Mistral de Mondragon. Approximately 1.5km/1mi south of town the erstwhile St-Paul-de-Mausole monastery with a church and small 12th-century cloister, now a psychiatric hospital, remains as it was in 1889–90 when **Van Gogh** was a patient here. The cloister and a reconstruction of his room are open to visitors.The remains of the Greco-Roman town of Glanum Livii (2 BC to 3rd century AD) south of St-Paul are worth a visit: an 8.6m/28ft-high municipal arch to mark the founding of the town, and an 18m/59ft-high monument built by Augustus for his adopted grandsons Gaius und Lucius, who died young (after AD 4).

St-Paul-de-Mausole

✳ **Glanum**

✳ **Alpilles**

The limestone massif of the Alpilles (»little Alps«) between St-Rémy and Les Baux is a popular hiking and climbing region, thanks to its jagged white rocky terrain. From the highest peak, La Caume (387m/1300ft, track from the D 5), a wonderful panoramic view can be enjoyed, from the Rhône estuary and Camargue in the west to Mont Ventoux in the northeast and the Durance valley in the east.

✳✳ **Les Baux**

Les Baux (or, in Provençal, Li Baus, »the rocks«), is a famous town on the ridge of the Alpilles, in ruins for many years already but the main town of the county in the 12th and 13th centuries with over 3000 inhabitants; today only 450 remain. The »court of love«, where troubadours and court poets would gather to perform or recite their works, was renowned. In 1632, under Louis XIII, it was destroyed as a Huguenot stronghold. Aluminium was discovered in the area in 1822, and the mineral bauxite took its name from the place where it was found. In the **lower town** (swamped by souvenir shops and restaurants) there are houses from the 14th–16th centuries and the church of St-Vincent (10th–15th centuries; window by M. Ingrand, 1962). The adjacent Hôtel des Porcelets (16th century) houses works by the painter Y. Brayer (1907–90). The mayor has his office in the 16th-century Hôtel de Manville, which also contains a museum of modern art. The **upper town** is reached via the Tour du Brau, housing the Musée d'Histoire. The barren rock plateau offers splendid views of the Rhône valley, the Crau and the Alpilles. Little remains of the castle. Perhaps it is inevitable that siege machinery (demonstration every 2 hours, April to Sept) and medieval spectacles of a »tourist-friendly« nature (early June and Sept) set the scene here. The castle is open from 9am until 6.30pm (March–June), 8.30pm (July–Aug), 6.30pm (Sept–Nov), 5pm (Dec–Feb); to avoid the masses, arrive early in the day or late in the evening.

! **Baedeker** TIP

Little paradise

The area around Les Baux is a mecca for bons vivants, with an unusually high number of excellent, renowned hotel restaurants: top of the list is Oustaù de Baumanière, but Riboto de Taven, Cabro d'Or, Régalido and Mas d'Aigret are not far behind. These and other hotels accommodate their guests in wonderful surroundings. Further information from the Office du Tourisme, Maison du Roy, F-13520 Les Baux, tel. 04 90 54 34 39, fax 04 90 54 51 15, www.lesbauxdeprovence.com.

Fontvieille

Approx. 6km/3.5mi southwest of Les Baux, at Fontvieille, is a »place of pilgrimage« for Provence, the Moulin de Daudet. It found fame through Alphonse Daudet's *Letters from my Windmill* (1869), although the book was actually written in Paris. The mill houses a small Daudet museum and offers splendid views towards the Rhône.

** Auvergne

The green, volcanic peaks of the Auvergne represent one of Europe's most unusual landscapes. Pastoral in character, this mountain region has much to offer in terms of impressive natural scenery, as well as old, romantic sites with hot springs and a typical style of church architecture.

Natural and holiday landscape

The extinct volcanoes of the Auvergne, with the close to 1900m/6200ft-high »Puys«, form the core of the Massif Central. Inaccessible for many years, the region is one of the economic problem zones of France, with the départements of Allier and Cantal particularly prone to migration to urban areas. Largely deforested, the mountainous, sparse terrain and bitter climate are not conducive to intensive agriculture, and dairy farming predominates. The famous cheeses Fourme d'Ambert, Cantal and St-Nectaire come from the region. In the few larger towns, such as ►Clermont-Ferrand, ►Le Puy, Mou-

A wonderful view of the unusual landscape from the Puy-de-Dome

lins, Montluçon and Aurillac, some important industries have been established. In the Auvergne, activities like hiking, cycling, kayaking and paragliding are popular, whilst a wide range of Gîtes Ruraux and Gîtes d'Etape provide the infrastructure.

History The Arverni played a crucial role amongst the Gallic tribes; their prince Vercingetorix led the Gauls in combat against Caesar at the Battle of Gergovia in 52 BC. It was in Clermont that Pope Urban II launched the First Crusade in 1095. In the »Grands Jours d'Auvergne« of 1665–66, Louis XIV attacked overly brutal seigneurs. In 1940, Vichy became the seat of Marshal Pétain's government that collaborated with the Nazis.

Landscape structure West of Clermont-Ferrand, the Monts Dômes mark the beginning of the »real« Auvergne, the approx. 100km/60mi chain of volcanic peaks which stretch southwards; it incorporates the Monts Dore and the Monts du Cantal. At the southern end, between the valleys of Truyère and Lot, it connects to the basalt plains of the Monts d'Aubrac. East of the Allier lie the Livradois and the Monts du Forez, to the north of these mountains the Limagne basin, through which the Allier flows, its fertile ground ideal for growing wheat, sugar beet, sunflowers and corn. Up in the north lies the Bourbonnais, a gentle bocage landscape, with the beautiful valley of the Sioule; the wine casks from the oaks of the Tronçais are famous. The destinations are listed in this order.

Natural parks The Parc Naturel Régional des Volcans d'Auvergne, covering 3950 sqkm/1525 sq mi, is the largest natural park in France, encompassing

Highlights Auvergne

Puy de Dôme
The first impression of volcanic Auvergne is also one of the finest.
▶ page 251

St-Nectaire
Auvergnat Romanesque in its purest form, plus a wonderful church treasury.
▶ page 253

Puy Mary
The balcony of the southern »Chaîne des Puys«, remnant of a once giant volcano.
▶ page 255

La Chaise-Dieu
Pope Clemens VI had the abbey of St-Robert built as his burial place.
▶ page 256

Vichy
The somewhat faded glamour of the belle époque can be seen in this famous spa.
▶ page 257

Mont Mézenc
The whole of southeastern France at one's feet.
▶ page 468

the three massifs of the Puys. There are information centres in Aurillac, on the Puy de Dôme and in Issoire. East of the river Allier is the 3000 sq km/1150 sq mi Parc Naturel Régional Livradois-Forez (centre in St-Gervais-sous-Meymont)

Places to Visit in the Auvergne

The Monts Dômes, a roughly 30km/20mi chain of over 100 volcanoes, is the youngest volcanic mountain range (Quaternary) of the Auvergne, with the Puy de Dôme (1465m/4800ft), west of ▶ Clermont-Ferrand, dominating the skyline, some 500m/1600ft above the plateau. Both the Gauls and the Romans considered it sacred; in 1872 the remains of a temple of Mercury were discovered here. From the attractive spa of Royat, a toll road leads upwards. The Col de Ceyssat attains a height of 1078m/3535ft and from its south face (on the D 68) the summit is one hour away on foot. On a clear day, **the fantastic view** reaches as far as Mont Blanc.

★ ★
Puy de Dôme

North of the Puy de Dôme, on the D 941 B between Orcines and Pontgibaud, another »volcano« rises from the verdant scenery: Vulcania, designed by the Viennese architect Hans Hollein, with an interesting multivisual show on volcanoes (open daily April–Aug, otherwise Mon/Tue and closed from mid-Nov.–mid-Feb).

Vulcania

Orcival (400 inhabitants), 23km/14mi southwest of Royat, set in glorious scenery, merits a lengthy stop, primarily to see the 12th-century pilgrimage church of **Notre-Dame**, hewn from volcanic rock and one of the finest examples of Auvergnat Romanesque (pictured overleaf). Typical features are the stepped form of the choir, the »Auvergne pyr-

★
Orcival

amid«, and the high transept with slanted shoulders that forms a transition to the octagonal crossing. In the choir stands a famous votive statue of the enthroned Virgin, fashioned in the 14th century.

Le Mont-Dore

The Monts Dore are a 3 million-year-old volcanic mountain range, formed by erosion in the Ice Age. The health and winter sports resort of Le Mont-Dore (1050m/3444ft, 2000 inhabitants) has a splendid **spa hotel** of 1817 with remnants of Roman thermal baths. A wonderful funicular built in 1898 leads up to the Salon du Capucin. Puy de Sancy, the highest peak of the Massif Central (1886m/6122ft; cable car plus 20 minutes on foot) offers the most beautiful impression of the mountains and lakes. The river Dordogne rises here.

✹ ✹
Puy de Sancy

A trip around the Puy de Sancy (approx. 85km/50mi) is not to be missed. The following points of interest are on the route: Col de la Croix-St-Robert, 1426m/4678ft; Vallée de Chaudefour with interesting granite and lava formations; Besse-en-Chandesse, an old, fortified little town of charming alleys and houses of black lava with the 12th-century church of St-André and its beautiful choir stalls); Lac Pavin (1197m/3927ft), one of the most beautiful volcanic lakes of Auvergne (pathway around the lake); Lac Chauvet; Chastreix with its 14th-century church; La Tour d'Auvergne (990m/3248ft) with a square on basalt prisms.

Trip around the Puy de Sancy

7km/4½mi to the west of Le Mont-Dore lies La Bourboule, a popular spa resort (for children as well) and now a popular haunt of mountain bikers. A cable car leads up to the Plateau de Charlannes (1250m/4100ft). A trip north of the valley to the **Banne d'Ordanche**, a 1512m/4960ft high basalt column, (one hour there and back from the car park) is guaranteed to leave a lasting impression.

La Bourboule

From Le Mont-Dore the route continues past the enchanting Lac Chambon and Murol with its castle (13th–15th centuries) to St-Nectaire. This small settlement (660 inhabitants) comprises hot springs in the valley and the old village higher up. The latter is dominated by the church of St-Nectaire, built in 1160 and one of the most important and beautiful in the Auvergne (restoration work in progress). It features over **100 coloured capitals** carved with scenes from the Old and New Testament and a marvellous **treasury**, including a 12th-century gilded bust of Saint Baudime and the 15th-century arm reliquary of Saint Nectaire. The Maison du St-Nectaire provides information about the eponymous cheese.

✹
Saint-Nectaire

In western Auvergne lies the small town of Bort (4200 inhabitants), beautifully situated in the Dordogne valley. Remains of the old ramparts can be seen by the church (12th–15th century). To the west of town, the **Orgues** (»organ pipes«) can be seen, mighty phonolite col-

✹
Bort-les-Orgues

← *Notre-Dame in Orcival: one from the Auvergne picture book*

► VISITING AUVERGNE

INFORMATION

CRT Auvergne
La Pardieu, 7 Allee P. der Fermat
F-63178 Aubière Cedex
Tel. 04 73 29 49 49, fax 04 73 34 11 11
www.auvergne-tourisme.info

WHERE TO STAY

► Budget / mid-range
Splendid Hotel
5/7 Rue d'Angleterre, F-63140
Châtelguyon
Tel. 04 73 86 04 80
www.splendid-resort.com
The spa resort of Châtelguyon near
Riom is surrounded by marvellous
scenery. This old hotel in the spa
park, where Maupassant often stayed,
offers comfortable rooms and a magnificent restaurant in matching style.

► Budget
Arverna Hôtel
12 Rue Desbrest, F-03200 Vichy
Tel. 04 70 31 31 19
www.hotels-vichy.com. Quiet, comfortable rooms in the town centre.
Breakfast served in a delightful
lounge, looking out onto the small
garden in the courtyard. No restaurant.

WHERE TO EAT

► Inexpensive
La Brasserie du Casino
4 Rue du Casino, F-03200 Vichy
Tel. 04 70 98 23 06, closed Tue–Wed.
Brasserie dating from 1920. In the
early days, singers would relax here
after their performance in the opera.
Large selection of classic dishes.
Tables outside.

umns of volcanic origin 8–10m/26–33ft in diameter and 80–100m/
260–320ft high. The Barrage de Bort (1km/0.5mi to the north) dams
the water of the Dordogne and its tributaries. On its banks stands
Château de Val the 15th-century Château de Val, which owes its picturesque appearance to the lake. Bort makes a good base from which to travel
✴ through the **Gorges de Dordogne** (approx. 85km/50mi): D 127 to
Gorges de St-Nazaire, D 20 to the Barrage de Marèges, D 20 E to the Route des
Dordogne Ajustants, D 982 to Pont de St-Projet, then the D 682 / 105 to the
Barrage de l'Aigle. Continuation: ►Périgord.

✴ This picturesque medieval village sits on a basalt plateau on the west-
Salers ern face of the Monts du Cantal (951m/3120ft, 440 inhabitants),
complete with ramparts and old houses, especially on the Grande
Place, one of the most beautiful squares in France. The church of St-
Matthieu (15th century; porch 12th century) contains 17-century
tapestries from Aubusson and a marvellous tomb from 1495.

Monts du Cantal The Monts du Cantal with the main summits of Puy Mary (1787m/
5862ft), Puy Griou (1694m/5557ft) and Plomb du Cantal (1855m/
6085ft) are what remains of an enormous, 20 million-year-old volcano, once 3000m/9800ft high, which spread lava over a distance of
70km/45mi. It provides the basis for fertile pasture, where the red

Salers cattle graze. From Salers, an attractive route leads over the Maronne and through the Cirque du Falgoux to the **Pas de Peyrol**, the highest pass of the Auvergne at 1582m/5190ft. Continue on foot for 30 minutes up to Puy Mary, which offers a wonderful vista of the mountain range radiating in all directions beneath. Between Murat and Le Lioran, the Gorges de l'Alagnon are worth seeing. The winter sports resort of Super-Lioran serves the Plomb du Cantal (cable car plus 30 minutes on foot) and the Puy Griou (the 2½-hour ascent is rewarded by a fantastic panoramic view).

★ ★
Puy Mary

Plomb du Cantal
Puy Griou

The route to Aurillac leads through the pleasant valley of the upper Jordanne. Alternatively, take a right turn after Mandailles onto the D 46 / D 35 and follow the ridge between the Jordanne and Authre valleys.

Vallée de
Mandailles

The old capital of the Auvergne, now of the département of Cantal (33,000 inhabitants), is famous for its quaint old quarter on the river Jordanne, as well as for umbrella manufacture. A pupil at the abbey church of St-Géraud, Gerbert, a scholar and tutor of the later Emperor Otto II, would become the first French pope (Sylvestre II, 999–1003). Destroyed in 1569, the abbey church was rebuilt by the protestants. A 17th-century Black Madonna in the church of Notre-Dame-aux-Neiges (14th/17th centuries) is worth inspecting, whilst the 19th-century Château St-Etienne (with a 13th-century tower) houses the Musée des Volcans (a museum dedicated to vulcanism and the natural history of Cantal). In the southern part of town (Place des Carmes), the Musée d'Art et d'Archéologie traces the archaeology and traditions of the region.

Aurillac

East of the Monts du Cantal, the fortified town of Saint-Flour (7400 inhabitants) stands majestically on a basalt plateau above the river Ander. In the cathedral of St-Pierre-et-St-Flour, built of basalt between 1400–1466, an impressive **black crucifix** (»Beau Dieu Noir«) from the 13th century can be admired. Next to the cathedral, the 17th-century bishop's palace today houses the Musée de la Haute-Auvergne. On the other side of the cathedral, the pretty Place d'Armes is lined by arcades and is home to the Maison Consulaire (14th–16th century). Further to the west is the Musée Postal d'Auvergne.

Saint-Flour

South of St-Flour, a 564m/1850ft railway bridge, a sleek steel construction built by Gustave Eiffel (1881–84), spans the dammed Truyère. The lessons of engineering learned here were subsequently put to good use in the Eiffel Tower. Standing above the western bank of the Truyère reservoir (D 40 / 48) are possibly the finest castle ruins of the Auvergne (13th century, destroyed in 1405). Up to the point where it flows into the ▶ Lot, the Truyère creates many impressive gullies and dams, only some of which can be reached by car.

Truyère valley
Viaduc de
Garabit
★
Château
d'Alleuze

A 26m/85ft-long »Dance of Death« is the highlight of St-Robert in La Chaise-Dieu

Brioude Brioude (7200 inhabitants), east of the A 75 in the flatlands of the Allier, is in proud possession of the **largest Romanesque church in Auvergne**, the Basilique St-Julien (74m/242ft long; porch dated 1060, choir 1180). The polychrome masonry from soft tufa, the frescoes in the porch and the interior, ornate capitals and an array of stone and wooden statues also render this one of the most beautiful of its kind. As well as lovely old houses, the small town has a lace museum and a Maison du Saumon with aquarium, dedicated to the now rare Allier salmon.

La Chaise-Dieu The most famous church in Auvergne can be found in La Chaise-Dieu (in Latin »casa Dei«, »house of God«), some 40km/25mi east of Brioude. In 1043 a monastery was founded here at 1080m/3543ft and swiftly became one of the most important in France; since 1965, a much-lauded music festival has taken place here in August. The church of St-Robert, built by Pope Clement VI from 1344 to 1352, is divided by a late Gothic **rood screen** (15th century; crucifix 1603). Behind the screen are the resplendent 15th-century **oak choir stalls** with the tomb of Clement' VI (the 44 marble statues were destroyed by the Huguenots in 1562), tapestries from Brussels and Arras (early 16th century) and a 26m/85ft-long three-part Dance of Death in sgraffito (15th century).

Issoire The 12th-century church of St-Austremoine in the industrial town of Issoire (15,500 inhabitants) 30km/19mi southeast of Clermont-

Ferrand is an excellent example of Auvergne Romanesque. Examine the capitals in the choir and transept; the coloured frame dates from the 19th century. The crypt is also worth perusing.

▶ Clermont-Ferrand. The Plateau de Gergovie is also mentioned here.

Clermont-Ferrand

North of Clermont on the western fringe of the fertile Limagne, Riom (19,000 inhabitants) was the wealthy capital of the Duchy of Auvergne in the Middle Ages and from 1531 also an important judicial centre. A series of fine buildings bear witness to this history, particularly on Rue de l'Hôtel de Ville, the town's main street. The Palais de Justice stands on the site of the earlier castle of the Dukes of Berry, of which the Ste-Chapelle has been preserved (1388; beautiful 15th-century windows and splendid 17th-century tapestries). To the west is the Musée Régional d'Auvergne. The Basilica of St-Amable displays the Auvergne Romanesque style in the nave and transept (12th century), and early Gothic forms in the choir (13th century). The church of Notre-Dame-du Marthuret, in the south of the old quarter (14th–15th centuries) has beautiful windows from the 15th and 16th centuries, and the remarkable *Virgin with Bird* a 14th-century statue by the sculptors of Duke Jean de Berry. In the western suburb of Mozac stands an **important abbey church** in Auvergne Romanesque style (12th century; the crypt and tower foundations are pre-Romanesque). In addition to the capitals and an unusual 14th-century crucifix, the shrine containing the reliquary of Saint Calminius (1168) is noteworthy.

Riom

✶
Mozac

Approx. 30–40km/20–25mi northwest of Riom, the river Sioule has carved a beautiful, narrow valley into the granite plateau. From the spa of Châteauneuf-les-Bains to Ebreuil (St-Léger abbey church, 10th–13th centuries, with frescoes from the 12th and 15th centuries), the D 109 and D 915 follow the course of the river. From St-Gervais-d'Auvergne the river Queuille winds its way, with reservoirs and the **Viaduc des Fades**, the highest railway bridge in Europe (132m/433ft, 1901–09, traffic ceased in 2007) marking the landscape.

Gorges de la Sioule

The famous spa town of Vichy (260m/850ft, 27,000 inhabitants) lies on the northern perimeter of the Auvergne on the river Allier. The Romans already reaped the benefits of the thermal baths, alkaline mineral springs with a temperature of 16–43°C/60–109°F, said to alleviate illnesses of the digestive tract. In the grand days of the 17th century through to the mid-20th century, monarchs and famous persons took the waters here. From 1940 to 1944, the town was the seat of government for Marshal Pétain, at which time the 300 plus hotels were of great practical benefit. Today, a trace of the old glamour in **France's largest spa** is still in evidence, even though the retired make up the majority of visitors (hence the relatively moderate

✶
Vichy

prices). The focal point is the Parc des Sources, surrounded by cast-iron pump rooms (1889). The Grand Casino (1865/1903) is to the south with the splendid Opéra, to the north, the Halle des Sources (drinking hall). Beyond the Halle des Sources is the Galerie Napoléon III (1858), along with the Centre Thermal des Dômes in Islamic style (1903), the largest of its kind in Europe. The **spa area** features palatial hotel and marvellous villas, such as the châlets on the Allier, built in 1865 for Napoleon III. Spreading out to the south and west are the beautiful Parcs de l'Allier, across the river the Parc Omnisports with an 18-hole golf course and hippodrome. In the old town, south of the springs park, the Tour de l'Horloge, the remains of a Louis XII castle (15th century), are worth seeing. The Maison du Bailliage (16th century) houses a museum with exhibits on local history and folklore.

Montluçon

The industrial town of Montluçon (44,000 inhabitants, approx. 90km/55mi northwest of Clermont-Ferrand) sits prettily on the banks of the river Cher. It is worth visiting the old town, where a Bourbon castle accommodates a regional museum and a unique **hurdy-gurdy museum**. The 12th- and 13th-century church of St-Pierre contains works of art from the 15th and 16th centuries, including a Mary Magdalene in the style of the Black Madonna, said to have miraculous qualities.

Moulins

Moulins (23,000 inhabitants, approx. 60km/35mi north of Vichy) owes its name to the mills which were so numerous along the Allier. From the early Middle Ages, Moulins was the centre of the Bourbonnais, whose lords, the House of Bourbon, were elevated to the status of dukes in 1327 and later produced eight kings. The centrepiece of the picturesque old town is the town hall square with a clock tower (Jacquemart) from 1455. Old tools and apparatus, costumes and furniture are on display in the Musée de Folklore et du Vieux Moulins. The choir of Notre-Dame Cathedral was built from 1474 to 1507, the nave from 1852. In the ambulatory, beautiful stained glass windows (15th–16th centuries) depict religious themes as well as members of the House of Bourbon.

✷ ✷
Triptych of the Master of Moulins ▶

In the church treasury, the **Triptych of the Master of Moulins** (1499) can be seen. Its creator has been identified as the Netherlandish painter **Jean Hay** (guided tours April–Oct, 9.30am–11.40am, 2pm–5.30pm, out of season 10am–11.40am, 2pm–5pm, Sundays afternoons only). Opposite the cathedral stands the Tour Mal-Coiffée which, like Anne de Beaujeu's Pavilion, belonged to the castle. The pavilion (1497–1503), **the first structure in France in the Italian Renaissance style**, houses a fine museum of art and archaeology.

✷ ✷
Mausoleum of Henri II de Montmorency ▶

Northeast of the cathedral in Rue de Paris, the monumental mausoleum of Henri II de Montmorency is located in the Couvent de la Visitation. It was crafted by the Anguier brothers in Florentine style in 1653.

Pont St-Bénézet and the Papal Palace above the Rhône, the emblems of Avignon

✶ ✶ Avignon

Région: Provence – Alpes – Côte d'Azur **Altitude:** 19m/62ft
Département: Vaucluse **Population:** 22,000

Provence and Avignon are inseparable. The impressive buildings and treasures of the former papal residence – now a UNESCO world heritage site – and the famous festival of theatre are the greatest attractions of the town on the lower Rhône.

During the »Babylonian captivity« of the Church between 1309 and 1376, Avignon – to avoid factional fighting in Rome – became home to the popes and, in the ensuing Great Schism up until 1403, the antipopes. Throughout the entire era, the town was a thriving centre of culture, as well as a swamp of vice and luxury, a »cloaca«, or sewer, as Petrarch described it, in which »the filth of all the universe has gathered«. The important Avignon School of painting derived from the Italian artists engaged by the popes, Simone Martini from Siena in particular. The town and Comtat Venaissin remained in the hands of the Curia in Rome until the French Revolution in 1792, when it was united with France. Busy throughout the summer months, the capital of the Vaucluse département is inundated with visitors during the July festival.

History

What to See in Avignon

✳
City walls
The old quarter is completely enclosed by a 4.3km/2.5mi wall with eight gates and 39 towers, built under the direction of Pope Innocent VI from 1350 to 1368; restoration work carried out in the 19th century under Viollet-le-Duc had a sadly detrimental effect. The most interesting section is between the Pont St-Bénézet and Place Crillon.

✳
Pont St-Bénézet
From the park on the Rocher des Doms, there is a wonderful view of what might be the most famous bridge in France, the Pont St-Bénézet (»**Sur le pont d'Avignon ...**«), which crosses to Villeneuve-lès-Avignon. Constructed between 1177 and 1185, it was closed in 1668 as a result of damage it suffered through wars and flooding.

▶ VISITING AVIGNON

INFORMATION
Office de Tourisme
41 Cours Jean Jaurès
F-84000 Avignon
Tel. 04 32 74 32 74, fax 04 90 82 95 03
www.ot-avignon.fr

FESTIVALS AND EVENTS
July: Festival d'Avignon (theatre, music and dance, staged in or in front of historic buildings). For information and tickets: tel. 04 90 14 14 60, www.festival-avignon.com. In parallel: Festival Off with 500 events and Festival Provençal. Late July: jazz festival.

AVIGNON PASS'ION
This pass, available at the first visit to one of the town's sights, offers reductions in all other places of interest and on the bus network.

WHERE TO EAT
▶ Expensive
① *Christian Etienne*
10 Rue Mons, tel. 04 90 86 16 50
Closed Sun–Mon. One of the best and most attractive restaurants in town, in a 14th-century palais, now modernized. Regional cuisine.

▶ Moderate
② *Fourchette*
17 Rue Racine, tel. 04 90 85 20 93
Closed Sat–Sun and approx. 5–30 August. Bistro with Provençal fare. Also popular with the locals, so advance booking advisable! Excellent value for money.

WHERE TO STAY
▶ Luxury
① *Europe*
12 Place Crillon, tel. 04 90 14 76 76
www.heurope.com
Stately hotel in a fine palais of 1580, with an interior dating back to Napoleon, who stayed here. Those not booked in for the night should still sample the fabulous Sunday brunch in the attractive courtyard. First class restaurant.

▶ Budget
② *Blauvac*
11 Rue de la Bancasse
Tel. 04 90 86 34 11
www.hotel-blauvac.com
Charming, beautifully restored noble palais from the 17th century in a quiet side street at the heart of the old town. Some two-storey rooms.

Avignon Map

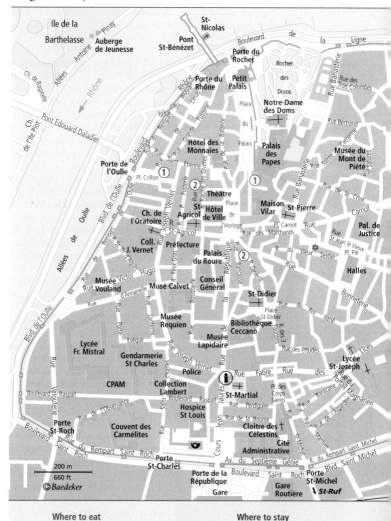

Where to eat
① Christian Etienne   ② Fourchette

Where to stay
① Europe   ② Blauvac

Musée du Petit Palais

★

On the north side of the Place du Palais stands the Petit Palais, a fortified Gothic building (*c*1320, late 15th-century façade) which served as the bishop's seat. Paintings by Italian masters from the 13th to 15th centuries and works of the Avignon School of painting can be seen here (closed Tue).

Hôtel des Monnaies

The 17th-century mint, Hôtel des Monnaies, is now a conservatory. The façade bears the coat of arms of Pope Paul V, from the House of Borghese. Directly behind the Palais des Papes, on the south side, Rue Peyrollerie (tinkers' street) leads to Rue Banasterie (wicker weavers' street); its southern end is marked by the late Gothic Church of St-Pierre (1356 to 15th century) with carved Renaissance doors dating from 1550 and a splendid 17th-century choir.

Rue Banasterie St-Pierre

Palais des Papes

★ ★

The Papal Palace is one of the finest examples of Gothic architecture and evolved from the palace of the Bishop of Avignon. The eastern and northeastern sections (Palais Vieux) were commissioned by Benedict XII (1334–42), the western part (Palais Nouveau) by Clement VI (1342–52). These are still the dominant elements today. Ten towers up to 50m/164ft high underline the fortified character of the whole. Most of the interior furnishings have been lost, apart from some remains of frescoes and sculptures.

The tour commences in the Grande Trésorerie, the treasury; here the **Musée de l'Œuvre** illustrates the history of the palace and its significance in architectural and artistic terms. In the Consistory Hall, frescoes by Simone Martini from the Cathedral of Notre-Dame-des-Doms may be admired. In the Chapelle St-Jean there are frescoes (1348) by Matteo Giovanetti from Viterbo. The Great Banquet Hall (Grand Tinel) adjoins the gallery above the cloister of Benedict XII (1339). The kitchen has a fine view across the town. From the balcony with the »window of the forgiveness of sins« – here the pope would bless the people in the courtyard – a vaulted staircase leads down to the ground floor and the Grande Audience, a double-aisled audience hall for the papal court. The Corps du Garde with a 17th-century tapestry leads back to the entrance.

The town hall square, a pleasant place for a break

A broad flight of steps leads up to the Romanesque **cathedral of Notre-Dame-des-Doms** (12th century, extended in the 14th–16th centuries). The portal features frescoes by Simone Martini. The Baroque-styled interior is notable for its Romanesque dome, Italian bishop's throne in marble (12th century) and the late Gothic tomb of Pope John XXII. The figure of the Virgin Mary on the tower (*c*1430, the base somewhat earlier) was added in 1859.

! *Baedeker* TIP

Papal pleasures

Inside the Papal Palace – accessed directly from Place de la Mirande – the wines of Côte-du-Rhône may be sampled. From September to May, guided tours through the secret passageways and rooms of the palace take place on Saturdays and Sundays, topped off with brunch on the terrace of the high dignitaries (»Palais Secret«, reservations: tel. 04 90 27 50 00).

The atmospheric centre of the old town is the Place de l'Horloge, with a theatre and the town hall (1845). »Jacquemarts« ring the bells on the hour in the 12th-century clock tower. To the east of the square stands the Maison Vilar, headquarters of the festival committee, with an exhibition relating its history. Theatre director Jean Vilar (1912–71) inaugurated the festival in 1947 and led proceedings until his death.

Place de l'Horloge

In the church of St-Agricol, built under Pope John XXII (1326), paintings by Mignard and Parrocel are on display. Just a few yards to the east, the Palais du Roure (1469) houses an institute for the promotion of Provençal culture. Further to the west lies **Rue Joseph Vernet** with fine shops, restaurants and Baroque palais (no. 58, 83, 87). The Hôtel Villeneuve-Martignan (no. 65, *c*1750) contains the Musée Calvet, the most important museum in town, with works of antiquity, sculptures and paintings (closed Tue). Next door, the Muséum Requien (closed Sun–Mon) displays geological and botanical collections.

St-Agricol

Palais du Roure

✱
Musée Calvet
Muséum Requien

The church of St-Didier (Provençal Romanesque, 14th century; late Gothic façade) is notable for the *Way of the Cross* figures (1481) by Francesco Laurana, one of the earliest Renaissance works of art in France. The 14th-century murals in the baptistery are thought to be the work of Florentine artists.

St-Didier

From St-Didier it is recommended to take Rue du Roi René heading east, where the house of King René and splendid palaces of the 17th and 18th centuries stand. Turn right into Rue des Teinturiers; in this romantic little street along the Sorgue (with water wheels) »indiennes« cloth was manufactured until the late 19th century.

Rue du Roi René

Rue des Teinturiers

The Musée Angladon (closed Mon–Tue) is housed in a 17th-century palace and displays Impressionist and modern paintings by the likes of Cézanne, Dégas, Van Gogh and Picasso. In the Musée Lapidaire (closed Tue), inside the Baroque Jesuit church (1620–61), the Celtic

Musée Angladon

Musée Lapidaire

PALAIS DES PAPES

✱ ✱ **For a century, Avignon was the centre of the Catholic Church. The Popes demonstrated their – not unchallenged – power with this well-fortified, splendidly appointed castle.**

⏱ Opening times:
1–14 March: 9am–6.30pm; 15 March to 30 June and 16 Sept to 1 Nov: 9am–7pm;
July and 1–15 Sept: 9am–8pm; Aug: 9am–9pm;
2 Nov to 28 Feb: 9.30am–5.45pm
Last admission 1 hour before closing time.
www.palais-des-papes.com

① Palais Nouveau
The lower part of the massive façade of the New Palace of Clement VI is a row of large Gothic arches. Two octagonal towers grace the entrance (Porte des Champeaux).

② Palais Vieux
The Old Palace of Benedict XII with the Tour de la Campane and the Tour de Trouillas (to the rear). The chimney of the latter marks the kitchen.

③ Grande Trésorerie
The treasury in the lower portion of the Tour des Anges housed and protected the movable wealth of the popes, the basis of their power. The treasurer was the highest dignitary of the papal court.

④ Tour des Anges
Completed in 1335, the Angels' Tower (Papal Tower) with its Gothic arcades displays the characteristics of a donjon: windowless lower floors, crenellation and machicolations. The bedroom of the popes in the tower was decorated around 1336 with a tracery of oak leaves and vines on a painted blue background.

⑤ Chambre du Cerf
Adorned with fine animal frescoes and hunting scenes, the Deer Room on the 4th floor of the Tour de la Garde-Robe, where the Old Palace and New Palace adjoin, was the study of Pope Clement VI. The floor tiles were manufactured in 1963 to match the original tiles which have survived in the study of Benedict XII.

⑥ Grande Chapelle
Mass and other liturgical ceremonies were held above the Grande Audience in the Grande Chapelle (Chapelle Clémentine), 52m/170ft long, 15m/50ft wide and 20m/65ft high. The grandest occasions were the papal coronations.

The Consistory Hall was the backdrop for the pope and his court's religious and secular affairs; princes and envoys were received here. The pope sat at the south wall, the cardinals on wooden benches. Remnants of frescoes by Simone Martini from the cathedral of Notre-Dame-des-Doms are displayed here.

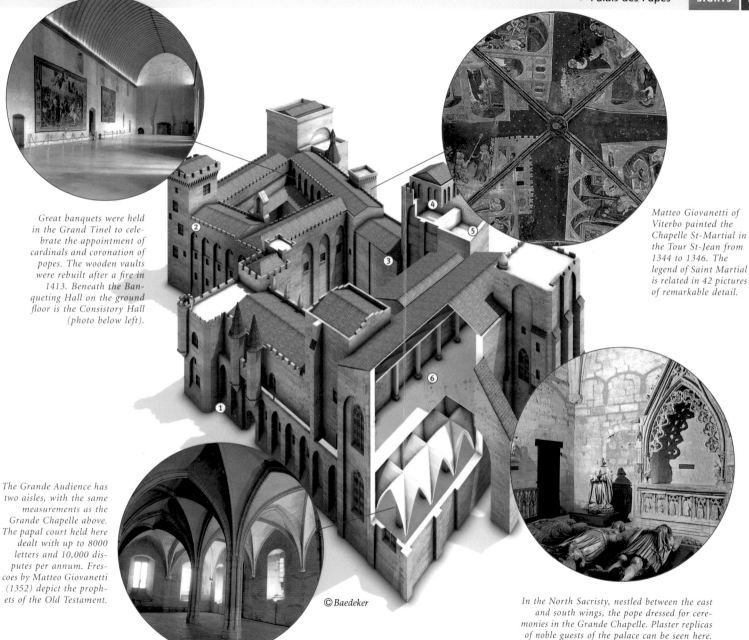

Great banquets were held in the Grand Tinel to celebrate the appointment of cardinals and coronation of popes. The wooden vaults were rebuilt after a fire in 1413. Beneath the Banqueting Hall on the ground floor is the Consistory Hall (photo below left).

Matteo Giovanetti of Viterbo painted the Chapelle St-Martial in the Tour St-Jean from 1344 to 1346. The legend of Saint Martial is related in 42 pictures of remarkable detail.

The Grande Audience has two aisles, with the same measurements as the Grande Chapelle above. The papal court held here dealt with up to 8000 letters and 10,000 disputes per annum. Frescoes by Matteo Giovanetti (1352) depict the prophets of the Old Testament.

© Baedeker

In the North Sacristy, nestled between the east and south wings, the pope dressed for ceremonies in the Grande Chapelle. Plaster replicas of noble guests of the palace can be seen here.

Musée Vouland

Collection Lambert

stone sculpture of a Tarasque from Noves (3rd century BC) is notable. In the western part of the old town, close to the Porte St-Dominique (Rue V. Hugo), the Musée Louis-Vouland presents French furniture from the 18th century, as well as paintings, tapestries and ceramics (closed Mon). Art of the 1960s to 1990s – Cy Twombly, Sol LeWitt, Anselm Kiefer, for example – can be found in the 18th-century **Hôtel de Caumont** on Rue Violette (closed Mon except July–Aug).

Around Avignon

Villeneuve-lès-Avignon

A bridge crosses the Barthelasse island to Villeneuve-lès-Avignon (11,800 inhabitants; Région Languedoc-Roussillon), which Philip the Fair, at the end of the 13th century, made into a border stronghold against Provence, which belonged to the Holy Roman Empire. In the papal era in Avignon, many cardinals lived here in splendid palaces. The quiet district is still an excellent location today. On the bank of the Rhône, a bulwark secured the northern end of the Pont St-Bénézet; the surviving Tour Philippe-le-Bel (1293–1307) serves as a reminder. The daunting Fort St-André, constructed by John the Good and Charles V up to 1368, reveals remnants of a Benedictine abbey and a Romanesque chapel. Both fortifications command wonderful views of Villeneuve, Avignon, Mont Ventoux, the Lubéron and the Alpilles. A visit to the Musée Municipal (Rue de la République, closed Mon) with the »**Coronation of the Virgin«, a painting by Enguerrand Quarton** (1453) and works by Nicolas Mignard (mid-17th century) is a must. The neighbouring church of Notre-Dame (1333) to the south also has an interesting treasury and collection of art. Further north, the **Chartreuse du Val de Bénédiction**, founded in 1356 by Pope Innocent VI, then rebuilt and extended in the 17th and 18th centuries, is most impressive. It contains three cloisters. The resplendent tomb of the pope is in the chapel; a monk's house has been faithfully restored to allow an insight into daily life in the Charterhouse. Today, the monastery is a cultural centre, where exhibitions, concerts, readings etc. are held in summer.

Saint-Michel-de-Frigolet

Fragrant herbs scent the air of Montagnette, approx. 12km/7.5mi southwest of Avignon. St-Michel-de-Frigolet Abbey, founded in the 10th century is hidden here. After 1858 it was rebuilt in medieval fashion by Premonstratensians, who have returned to reside here since 1918. The 11th-century Chapelle de Notre-Dame-du-Bon-Remède is still preserved within the church. Inside, the **gilded wood panelling** with paintings from the studio of Nicolas Mignard (1606–70) are of interest. They were a generous gift from Anne of Austria, who prayed here for an heir – the result was none other than Louis XIV, the Sun King. In one wing of the cloister, beautiful santons (nativity figurines) carved from olive wood can be admired.

Besançon

O 5

Région: Franche-Comté
Département: Doubs

Altitude: 250m/820ft
Population: 122,000

Besançon, the capital of ▶ Franche-Comté, is the centre of the French clock and watch industry: the impressive old town lies in a loop of the river Doub, watched over by a mighty citadel, a work of the famous fortress builder Vauban.

In ancient times, Vesontio was capital of the Gallic Sequani, and from the Middle Ages Besançon was, for a long time, the main town of Franche-Comté (Free County of Burgundy). In 1032–34 it fell into the hands of the German kings, and in 1157 Emperor Frederick Barbarossa held an Imperial Diet here. From the 13th century, as Bisanz, it was a city of the Holy Roman Empire, until in the Treaty of Nijmegen of 1678 it became part of France and seat of the provincial administration, as well as of a university. In this period that the town gained the character it still possesses today: **Vauban**, Louis XIV's military engineer, had the upper town torn down, including the ca-

Besançon then and now

Besançon Map

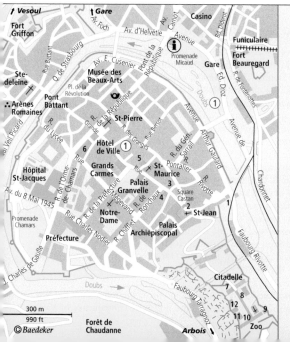

1 Porte Rivotte
2 Porte Noire
3 Maison Natale des Frères Lumières
4 Maison Natale de Victor Hugo
5 Bibliothèque Municipale
6 Palais de Justice
7 Musée Comtois
8 Espace Vauban
9 Noctuarium
10 Musee de la Résistance
11 Climatorium, Insectarium
12 Aquarium

Where to eat
① Le Chaland

Where to stay
① Nord

Besançon in a loop of the Doubs, with the citadel watching over the approaches

thedral, to make space for the citadel. The clock and watch industry was founded during the French Revolution by immigrants from the Swiss Jura. The modern industries of microtechnology and precision technology have continued this tradition. The author **Victor Hugo** (1802–85) was born in Besançon, as were the brothers Auguste and Louis Lumière (1862 and 1864), the inventors of cinema. The young feel of the town owes much to the presence of the university with its 19,000 students.

What to See in Besançon

✶
Citadel

The neck of the river loop to the south of the old town is secured by the citadel, which was built from 1674 to 1711 a good 100m/330ft above the Doubs. The **museums** within its walls are Espace Vauban (history of the citadel), Musée Comtois (regional folklore, with a large collection of marionettes) and the Musée de la Résistance et de la Déportation (Second World War, Vichy Government). Nature studies, with an aquarium, zoo and nocturnal animal reserve, all are also on offer. There is a wonderful view of the old town and river from the restaurant terrace. The Porte Rivotte to the east, part of the 16th-century fortifications, leads into the old town. Next to the cathedral stands the Porte Noire, an archway erected around AD 175 in honour of Marcus Aurelius. The cathedral of St-Jean (12th–13th century) has an east and **west choir**, probably going back to Carolingian times. The east choir, rebuilt in 1729 in Baroque style, contains valuable paintings (Van Loo, Natoire and others). The *Madonna and Child with Saint* by Fra Bartolomeo (1512) is next to the organ. An astronomical clock by A.-L. Vérité (1860), made up of some 30,000 parts, is in the tower.

✶
St-Jean

✶
Grande Rue

The Grande Rue has been the main axis of the town since ancient times. The sober appearance of the houses, a consequence of Vauban's influence, is alleviated by the imaginative design of the court-yard entrances and staircases (no. 67 in particular). The spectacular centrepiece of the old town is the **Palais Granvelle**, built 1534–42 for Cardinal Nicolas de Granvelle, chancellor to King Charles V; the Musée du Temps here invites visitors to explore the mysteries of time and the history of its measurement (closed Mon–Tue). The Théâtre of 1778 on Rue Mégévand is the work of Ledoux, architect of the revolutionary period (▶Franche-Comté, p.415. Next to the beautiful town hall (1573) stands the 16th-century Palais de Justice, former seat of justice (Parlement) for Franche-Comté.

Close to the river Doubs, a former granary (1835) houses the Musée des Beaux-Arts et d'Archéologie, the oldest in France, founded in 1694. It displays archaeological finds, primarily from Gallo-Roman times, as well as paintings by L. Cranach the Elder, Bronzino, Tintoretto, Rubens, Goya, Courbet, Picasso and more (closed Tue).

✷
Musée des Beaux-Arts et d'Archéologie

From the Pont Battant, look back towards the impressively coherent front of Quai Vauban (16th century). On the right bank of the Doubs lies the attractive **Quartier de Battant**, once the district of the winegrowers, who cultivated their vines on the slopes. Large cellar doors on the houses here are the only reminders of this era. Take a walk east along Promenade de Micaud, one of the parks on the Doubs, for another fine view of the citadel.

Quartier de Battant

The best view of Besançon and the Jura heights as far as the Vosges is from the 460m/1509ft hill of Notre-Dame-de-la-Liberation (3km/2mi southeast, with a statue of the Virgin Mary, 1945) and from the Belvédère de Montfaucon (617m/2024ft, another 2km/1.25mi northeast).

Vantage points

 VISITING BESANÇON

INFORMATION

Office du Tourisme
2 Place de la 1ᵉʳᵉ Armée Française
F-25000 Besançon
Tel. 03 81 80 92 55, fax 03 81 80 58 30
www.besancon.fr

WHERE TO EAT

▶ Inexpensive / moderate
① *Le Chaland*
Pont Bregille / Parc Micaud
Tel. 03 81 80 61 61
The old barge is a rare place to dine. Regional fare.

WHERE TO STAY

▶ Budget
① *Nord*
8 Rue Moncey,
tel. 03 81 81 34 56
www.hotel-du-nord-besancon.com.
19th-century house in the town centre. Comfortable rooms, friendly service, good value for money.

FESTIVALS AND EVENTS

July–Sept: various music, jazz and other festivals. Christmas market during Advent.

✷✷ Blois

Région: Centre   **Altitude:** 72m/236ft
Département: Loir-et-Cher   **Population:** 52,000

Blois, in a picturesque spot on the northern bank of the ►Loire between Orléans and Tours, was a royal residence in the 15th and 16th centuries. A splendid castle and cathedral stand tall over the old town.

History In the 11th and 12th centuries the Counts of Blois were amongst the most powerful lords in France. The county was sold to Louis d'Orléans in 1391, his son Charles commencing with the alteration and reconstruction of the castle in 1440. His son, in turn, became king in 1498 as Louis XII and declared Blois to be his residence; his son-in-law, François I, continued work on the splendid building.

What to See in Blois

✷✷
Castle The Place du Château is dominated by the castle, or rather by the Louis XII wing (1498–1503) a Flamboyant Gothic edifice of red brick and grey ashlar (open April–June and Sept 9am–6.30pm, July–Aug until 7pm, Oct until 5pm; rest of the year 9am–12.30pm, 1.30pm–5.30pm). Above the archways is the crowned **porcupine**,

A splendid staircase tower influenced by the Italian Renaissance

Louis XII's emblem, above the portal an equestrian statue of Louis (replica, 1857). Inside, the wing is supported by an arcade flanked by stair towers. To the right, the Salle des Etats constitutes the remnants of the medieval castle (13th century); the adjoining **François I Wing** (early Renaissance, 1515–24) features a famous octagonal staircase (the salamander and the »F« are the symbols of François). Opposite the entrance stands the southwest wing, built in 1635–38 for Gaston d'Orléans, Louis XIII's brother, one of the earliest works of neo-classical French Baroque, with a library and stately banquet hall. In the southeast, the **Louis XII Wing** ends at the Galerie Charles d'Orléans, with the castle chapel of St-Calais. The terrace of the medieval Tour de Foix offers a wonderful view of the town.

The François I Wing boasts a series of majestic rooms, their contents, however, are largely in 19th-century Romantic style. On the first floor, a huge fireplace bears the emblems of François I (salamander) and Anne de Bretagne (ermine). The chambers of Catherine de Medici adjoin; most interesting is the completely wood-panelled **chambre de secrets** with 237 separate compartments in which, according to Dumas the elder, she hid poison. The Salle des Etats-Généraux (30×18m/98×59ft, 12m/39ft high), where the Estates-General met in 1576 and 1588, were redesigned around 1870. The huge tapestries (17th and 18th centuries) designed by Rubens depict episodes from the lives of Louis XIV and Constantine the Great. On the upper level of the Louis XII Wing, the Musée des Beaux-Arts exhibits paintings from the 16th to 19th centuries, including works by Boucher, Ingres, David and Fromentin, as well as ceramics and musical instruments. The chapel was consecrated in 1508; the façade and interior are the result of 19th-century restoration. M. Ingrand crafted the stained glass windows (1957).

◄ François I Wing

◄ Musée des Beaux-Arts

◄ St-Calais Chapel

Blois Map

Préfecture   8
Rue de la Paix
École des Beaux-Arts
LA GARENNE
R. d'Angleterre
École d'Angleterre
Centre de Congrès
Palais de Justice
Kathedrale
Tour Beauvoir
Rue du Palais
Hôtel de Ville
4   5   6
Rue Denis Papin
Gare
Rue Jean Moulin
St-Vincent
R. Porte Côté
Rue du Commerce
7
R. de Lattre-de-Tass.
Pl. V. Hugo
1
Avenue Jean Laigret
Gambetta
Jardin des Simples et des Fleurs Royales
2
Schloss   2
Place Louis XII
Avenue Gambetta
Rue des Lices
3
2
St-Nicolas
Quai de la Saussaye
Pont Jacques Gabriel
Quai Villebois Mareuil
Loire
200 m
660 ft
© Baedeker
1

1 Pavillon Anne de Bretagne
2 Couvent des Jacobins
3 Marché
4 Hôtel d'Alluye
5 Maison des Acrobates
6 Maison Papin
7 Maison de la Magie
8 Haras National

Where to eat
① Rendez-vous des Pêcheurs
② Le Triboulet

Where to stay
① Hotel de France
② Le Savoie

Pavillon Anne de Bretagne	On Place Victor-Hugo and the Jardin du Roi, what is left of Louis XII's gardens, stand the Jesuit church St-Vincent-de-Paul (1655) and the Pavillon Anne de Bretagne (*c*1500; now a tourist office). From here, the **façade of the loggia** can be seen in front of the medieval castle. It was commissioned by François I and marked by the influence of the Italian Renaissance.
St-Nicolas	Between castle, cathedral and the Loire lies the old town with its interesting bourgeois houses. South of the castle stands the Benedictine church St-Nicolas (12th–14th century) in Anjou style; the capitals in the choir and the retable (15th century) are worth examining. The **Couvent des Jacobins** (15th–16th century) is adjacent to the market hall and now serves as a museum for religious art and natural history. Just a short walk away, the Loire-Quai offers a beautiful view of the Pont J. Gabriel.
Jacobin convent	
St-Louis cathedral	Go past the Fontaine Louis-XII and on to the cathedral of St-Louis up on high, largely rebuilt in Gothic fashion between 1678 and 1702 after severe hurricane damage. The crypt dates back to the 10th and 11th centuries. The apse points the way to the bishop's palace (18th century, town hall). There is a marvellous view from the gardens east of the palace.
Hôtel de Ville	

▶ VISITING BLOIS

INFORMATION

Office de Tourisme
3 Av. J. Laigret, F-41000 Blois
Tel. 02 54 90 41 41
www.bloispaysdechambord.com

FESTIVALS AND EVENTS

Mid-April to 20 Sept: Son et Lumière every evening in the castle courtyard (Wed in English); July–Aug: music on the streets; June–Sept: Fêtes de Louis XII in the castle; 2nd Sun in the month: flea market

WHERE TO EAT

▶ **Moderate / expensive**
① *Au Rendez-vous des Pêcheurs*
27 Rue Foix, tel. 02 54 74 67 48
Closed Sun/Mon lunchtime. A wonderful little bistro with excellent but down-to-earth cooking, emphasis on fish.

② *Le Triboulet*
18 Pl. du Château, tel. 02 54 74 11 23
Closed Sun–Mon. Small, pleasant inn with regional specialities, terrace in the summer months.

WHERE TO STAY

▶ **Budget**
① *Hotel de France et de Guise*
3 Rue Gallois, tel. 02 54 78 00 53
www.franceetguise.com
Little old hotel with 50 rooms opposite the chateau. Single and family rooms available.

▶ **Budget**
② *Le Savoie*
6 Rue Ducoux
Tel. 02 54 74 32 21
www.hotel-blois.com. Small, convivial hotel, off the tourist track.

Among the fine houses of the Middle Ages and the Renaissance, these deserve mention: the Gothic Maison Denis Papin; the Maison des Acrobates, named after its 15th-century carved figures; Hôtel d'Alluye, built in 1508 with courtyard arcades for Florimond Robertet, treasurer to three kings and a Renaissance enthusiast who spent time in Italy. In the Maison de la Magie Robert-Houdin on Place du Chateau, explore the worlds of magic and illusion.

Horse lovers should not miss the **National Stud** (Haras National, 62 Avenue Maunoury; closed Sun).

Further sights

> ## ❗ *Baedeker* TIP
>
> ### Loire from the air
>
> The gentle Loire valley landscape is even more beautiful from a bird's-eye view, either by hot air balloon, light aircraft or helicopter. Such pleasure comes at a considerable price, determined by whichever »carrier« is chosen, and the length of flight, with anything from 50–250 possible. The Loire valley tourist offices have more information on the subject.

✳ Bordeaux

F 8

Région: Aquitaine	**Altitude:** 5m/16ft
Département: Gironde	**Population:** 230,000

Bordeaux, centre of the most famous wine region of the world, impresses with its classical 18th-century grandeur. Its status as an important harbour and university city adds to the enjoyable atmosphere.

Sited on the left bank of the wide Garonne – which is roughly 500m/1600ft wide here and joins the Dordogne some 20km/12mi downstream to form the Gironde – Bordeaux is the sixth most important harbour in France and the centre of the Bordelais, whose wines are in demand the world over. Wine growing and the wine trade were vital sources of income as far back as Roman times, when the town was called Burdigala. Following Eleanor of Aquitaine's marriage to Henri Plantagenet in 1152, the town was in English possession for three centuries, from 1154 to 1451–53; at this time, and again in the 18th century, the wine trade with Britain proved a catalyst for Bordeaux's growing economic and cultural significance. In the 18th century, the town was radically reshaped and gained the appearance it still has today. It has recently had a major facelift. During the Franco-German War of 1870–71, in World War I and for two weeks in 1940, Bordeaux was the capital of France. As stages on the Way of St James (►Baedeker Special p.792), the cathedral of St-André and the basilicas St-Seurin and St-Michel are on the list of **UNESCO World Heritage**. As well as the wine trade, the wider region, numbering 735,000 inhabitants, concentrates on shipbuilding, the chemical and foodstuff industries and crude oil processing.

Old wine-trading town

Magnificent panoramic view and the Pont de Pierre

What to See in Bordeaux

✱
Pont de Pierre
The best route of approach is from the east, traversing the 486m/ 530yd-long Pont de Pierre (1821); this permits a view of a more than 1km/0.5mi-long stretch of houses, a marvellous example of 18th-century urban architecture, accentuated by the second-highest spire in France. The imperial Porte de Bourgogne (around 1755) marks the entrance to the town centre.

Quartier
St-Pierre
North of the Porte de Bourgogne, sections of an old district have survived. In the late Gothic Porte Cailhau (1494) visitors not only learn about the town's history, but also have an excellent view. A vegetable market is held on Thursday mornings at St-Pierre (14th–15th century). The beautiful Place du Parlement was once the royal market

✱
Place de la
Bourse
place. Place de la Bourse opens onto the Garonne. It was developed from 1728 to 1755 based on plans by the elder and younger Gabriel, with the exchange (Palais de la Bourse, 1749) and the Hôtel des Fermes du Roi (French customs museum; closed Mon).

Place de la
Comédie
Grand Théâtre
On the site of the former Roman forum, the Grand Théâtre (1780) is not the most attractive of buildings from the outside; the interior is a different matter, with lavish staircases and foyers, as well as the grand auditorium with a gigantic crystal chandelier (tours possible). Opposite stands the spectacular **L'Intendant**, a wine shop with 15,000 wines in stock (www.intendant.com). To the north, opposite the tourist office, the Conseil Interprofessionel du Vin de Bordeaux

Maison du Vin
(CIVB) resides in the Maison du Vin de Bordeaux with information at the ready. Wine seminars in different languages and excursions into the Bordelais are part of the service (www.ecole.vins-bordeaux.fr).

The most elegant district of the city, with chic boutiques, delicatessens and bistros, is the **Golden Triangle** around the Place des Grands Hommes, formed by the Cours de l'Intendance, Cours Clemenceau and Allées de Tourny. Rue Ste-Catherine and Rue Porte Dijeaux are the shoppers' favourite streets; the splendid Galerie Bordelaise (19th century) stands at their intersection. The Spanish artist Goya lived at no. 57 Cours de l'Intendance (open to visitors) from 1824 until his death in 1828. The church of Notre-Dame was built from 1684 to 1707 on the model of Il Gesú in Rome. On Place des Grands Hommes stands the glass »culinary emporium« Marché des Grands Hommes. Continue to the wonderful Place Gambetta, also influenced by the Louis-Quinze style. The Porte Dijeaux was erected in 1748.

★
Triangle d'Or

Place des Grands Hommes
Place Gambetta

To the south of Place Gambetta, the Hôtel de Lalande (1779) houses the museum of arts and crafts, displaying furniture, jewellery, porcelain and pottery, as well as luxury items and everyday objects from the 16th to 18th centuries (closed Tue).

Musée des Arts Décoratifs

Further south is the grand ensemble of the Place Pey-Berland / Place Rohan with the Palais Rohan (town hall, formerly the archbishop's palace; 1781) and cathedral. Palais Rohan is home to the **Museum of Art** (open Wed–Mon 11am–6pm) with works of major painters from the 15th to the 20th century, including Titian, Perugino, Veronese, Van Dyck, Brueghel, Rubens, Delacroix (the famous *Greece Expiring on the Ruins of Missolonghi*), Renoir and Corot, as well as sculptures by Rodin.

Hôtel de Ville

★ ★
Musée des Beaux-Arts

The resplendent cathedral of St-André is reminiscent of Notre-Dame in Paris, not only due to its size (124×44m/136×48yd). Rebuilding work in the 14th and 15th centuries replaced just the transept and

★
St-André cathedral

Highlights Bordeaux

choir. There were insufficient funds to renew the nave of 1096, in which Louis VII and Eleanor of Aquitaine were wed. Flying buttresses and ribbed vaults were added in the 13th and 15th centuries. The west façade is plain, due to its proximity to the city wall; the north side is the showpiece with the main portal and 13th-century Porte Royale, above which is a gallery of bishops. In front of the cathedral choir stands the 47m/154ft Tour Pey Berland (1446), with a Madonna of 1863 (tower staircase accessible).

Tour Pey Berland

★

Musée d'Aquitaine

The excellent museum of archaeology and folklore (20 Cours Pasteur) documents the history of the region from antiquity up to the 19th century (closed Mon). On Cours V. Hugo stands the mighty gateway to the town, the 15th-century **Grosse Cloche** (»big bell tower«).

Bordeaux Map

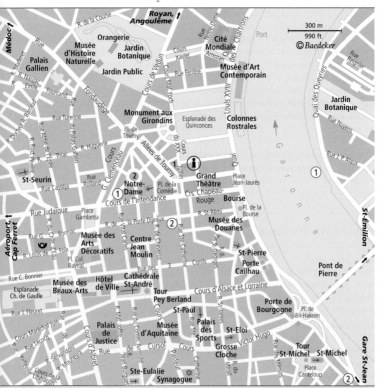

1 Maison du Vin de Bordeaux
2 Marché des Grands Hommes

Where to eat
① L'Estacade
② La Tupina

Where to stay
① Continental
② Hotel de la Presse

The Place du Parlament in the style of Louis XV is a popular place to meet

Further east near the river, a 114m/374ft tower (1492) – at 47m/154ft there is an excellent panorama of the town – marks the location of the basilica (14th–15th century; modern stained glass windows by Max Ingrand). A flea market is held on the square at weekends.

Basilique St-Michel

The largest square in Europe (12.6ha/31 acres) sweeps across the northern perimeter of the old town. Developed from 1818 to 1828, its centrepiece is the **monument** (1902) commemorating the **Girondistes** who were executed in Bordeaux in 1793. The bronze statues, melted down by the Germans in 1943, were subsequently reconstructed. Statues of Montaigne and Montesquieu, who both studied in Bordeaux, decorate the square. Further to the northwest is the beautiful municipal park with botanical gardens and a natural history museum. West of the Jardin Public the last remains of ancient Burdigala may be seen: the impressive gateway to a 3rd-century amphitheatre with a capacity of 15,000.

Esplanade des Quinconces

Jardin Public

Palais Gallien

North of the Esplanade des Quinconces is the district of Les Chartrons, named after the 14th-century Carthusian monastery which stood here. Outside the city walls, Protestant merchants from Germany, Holland and England settled in the 17th century and soon took control of the colonial trade and wine markets. Today it is a peaceful residential area with attractive bourgeois houses and shopping streets (especially Rue Notre-Dame with its antique shops). The **Entrepôt Lainé** (Rue Ferrère), is a warehouse, built in 1824 and now converted into the architecturally and artistically excellent Museum of Contemporary Art (closed Mon; good restaurant). The cruiser and former museum ship *Colbert*, which previously had a mooring place on Quai des Chartrons, has been scrapped. Further north (41 Rue Borie) is a splendid wine merchant's depot dating back to 1720, its storerooms now open as a museum (closed Sun–Mon).

Les Chartrons

★
Musée d'Art Contemporain

Musée des Chartrons

▶ VISITING BORDEAUX

INFORMATION

Office de Tourisme
12 Cours du 30 Juillet
F-33080 Bordeaux
Tel. 05 56 00 66 00, fax 05 56 00 66 01
www.bordeaux-tourisme.com
Maison du Vin de Bordeaux
3 Cours du 30 Juillet
F-33075 Bordeaux
Tel. 05 56 00 22 66, fax 05 56 00 22 82
www.vins-bordeaux.fr

TRANSPORT

Gare St-Jean 1.5km/1mi southeast of
the centre (tram C, Place des Quinconces). Merignac airport 10km/6mi
to the west, Jet'Bus to Gare St-Jean,

tourist office and Pl. Gambetta. Buses
and TBC trams. Information offices:
Gare St-Jean, Pl. Gambetta, Cours du
30 Juillet; travel pass (»tickarte«) for
1–3 or 7 days. River excursions depart
north of the Pont de Pierre.

FESTIVALS AND EVENTS

End of June in even-numbered years
(alternating with the): 4-day Fête le
Vin, gigantic »wine bar« with concerts, procession of the wine broth-
erhoods, fireworks and much more.
End of June in odd-numbered years:
4-day Fête le Fleuve with tall ships.
2nd half of June in odd-numbered
years Vinexpo; July/Aug: Estivales de

Bordeaux with all kinds of distrac-
tions. Oct: Fête du Vin Nouveau.
Events listed in *Spectaculaire* and
Bordeaux Plus

CARTE PASS

The reasonably priced Carte Pass is
valid in seven municipal museums.

WHERE TO EAT

▶ Moderate

L'Estacade
Quai des Queyries, tel. 05 57 54 02 50
Dine with a wonderful view: an
elegant but informal restaurant, built
on piles in the river. Fish and regional
cuisine.

La Tupina
6 Rue Porte de la Monnaie
Tel. 05 56 91 56 37
Very well-known, countrified but
stylish tavern. Delve into the specialities of the southwest. Don't go
without a bon appetit.

WHERE TO STAY

▶ Budget / mid-range

Continental
10 Rue Montesquieu
Tel. 05 56 52 66 00
www.hotel-le-continental.com
Lovingly restored 18th-century urban
palais in the Triangle d'Or. Excellent
value for money, but breakfast is
better taken elsewhere.

Hotel de la Presse
6 Rue Porte Dijeaux
Tel. 05 56 48 53 88
www.hoteldelapresse.com
Small, well-kept hotel in the pedestrian zone. Rooms 320 and 207 have a
view of the Grand Théâtre; the rooms
facing the courtyard are quieter, but
lack the view.

Approx. 500m/550yd northwest of Place Gambetta, the church of St-Seurin is worth a visit (12th–15th century, 19th-century façade). The porch dates back to an 11th-century building and has interesting capitals. There is a richly sculpted figure portal on the southern side (13th–14th century). In the choir, a 14th-century stone bishop's throne stands to the left. On the right is a great late Gothic reredos impressively with twelve alabaster reliefs of the life of St-Seurin and a 14th-century Madonna. In the crypt (11th century; early Christian spolia) reliquary shrines and sarcophagi from the 6th–7th centuries can be seen.

✳ **St-Seurin**

Around Bordeaux

The Bordelais can lay claim – although other regions would dispute this – to being the most famous wine-growing area in the world. Its top wines fetch astronomical prices: a bottle of 2000 Mouton-Rothschild goes for something like 500 €, a 2000 Pétrus for approx. 2000 €. On the occasion of the Paris Exposition Universelle (International Exhibition) in 1855, the so-called **Classement** for Médoc wines was introduced, classifying the 60 best tiers in five categories (Grands Crus). This method of classification has barely been altered until this day (in 1973, Mouton-Rothschild was bestowed the honour of Premier Cru), although it is not without controversy. Vintners excluded from the »crème« set up the Cru Bourgeois system in 1932, in which the upper categories are titled Cru Supérieur and Cru Exceptionnel. The remaining areas of grape cultivation in the Bordelais have their own classification. Many of the »Château« vineyards can be traced back to noble families of the 17th and 18th centuries; more recently, financiers and companies from outside the wine business have acquired many domains.

Wine growing in the Bordelais

The vineyards begin in the western and southern areas of Bordeaux, although many of the Graves have since been built upon. Here is an overview of the main regions, their wines and grape varieties, and some of the most important producers (starting from Bordeaux):

South bank of the Gironde: Haut-Médoc, Médoc (red: Cabernet Sauvignon, Cabernet Franc, Merlot; e.g. Lafite, Latour, Margaux).
South bank of the Garonne: Pessac-Léognan, Graves (white: Sémillon, Sauvignon Blanc; red: Cabernet Franc, Cabernet Sauvignon; e.g. Haut-Brion, Domaine de Chevalier, Fieuzal, Rahoul); Barsac, Sauternes (dessert wine from Sémillon, Sauvignon Blanc and Muscadelle; e.g. Climens, Yquem, Rieussec, Raymond-Lafon).
Southeast (between the Garonne and Dordogne): Entre-Deux-Mers with a series of appellations including Côtes de Bordeaux, Cadillac, Loupiac (mostly fresh white wines, good quality).
North bank of the Dordogne: Fronsac, Pomerol, St-Emilion (red: Merlot, some Cabernet Sauvignon and Malbec; e.g. Pétrus, Trotanoy, Evangile, Latour-Pomerol; Ausone, Gaffelière, Angélus).

Appellations and chateaux

One of the most famous and expensive vineyards of the world: Château Lafite-Rothschild. It dates back to the 17th century and has belonged to the Rothschilds since 1868.

North bank of the Gironde: Côtes de Bourg, Côtes de Blaye (red: Merlot; white: Sauvignon, Colombard).

Médoc
A trip along the D 2 / D 204 to the north leads through a range of famous wine addresses. Most of these **vineyards** are not open to the public, however. Those extending a welcome to visitors (prior reservation is necessary) include the chateaux Mouton-Rothschild, Lafite-Rothschild, Beychevelle, Kirwan, Margaux and Palmer. The tourist office and Maison du Vin in Bordeaux, as well as the Maison du Tourisme in Pauillac provide information on tickets, visiting hours and organize excursions to the chateaux (in English and French). The following are also worth a mention: Château Siran (wonderfully appointed), Château Maucaillou (with wine museum), Fort Médoc (erected by Vauban in 1689) and Vertheuil (Romanesque church, 11th–15th centuries with a beautiful portal).

★
Côte d'Argent
(northern part)
The Atlantic coast between Pointe de Grave on the Garonne estuary in the north and Biarritz in the south is a 250km/150mi stretch of

flat, straight coastline: the Côte d'Argent, with wide, sandy beaches bordered by pine forests and lakes. This a unique landscape enjoys great popularity as a holiday destination for the French. The best-known resorts include Soulac-sur-Mer, Montalivet and Lacanau. An array of campsites and innumerable holiday homes complete the tourist infrastructure. A description of the northern stretch from Pointe de Grave to Cap Ferret opposite Arcachon follows here; for the southern part ►Gascony and ►Côte Basque.

Verdon-sur-Mer

The northernmost point of the Médoc is **Pointe de Grave**, site of the modern harbour of Verdon-sur-Mer (ferry to Royan, ►p.697) and a fortress. The lighthouse offers wonderful views and also contains a small museum about the Phare de Cordouan, a 66m/216ft-high Renaissance lighthouse 9km/5.5mi west of the Pointe, erected in the late 16th century and reconstructed in 1788. The tourist office in Verdon organizes boat trips to the lighthouse.

Phare de Cordouan

Soulac (2800 inhabitants) is an attractive seaside resort with a pretty 10th-century church in Poitevin Romanesque style, Notre-Dame-de-la-Fin-de-Terres, which disappeared completely into the sand in the 18th century. Ancient Noviomagus was here, and today there is an archaeological museum. Le Gurp and Montalivet are nudist beaches. Lacanau-Océan, also very popular, is a surfers' paradise and venue for world championship events. The coast continues to the 20km/12mi-long, flat peninsula of Cap Ferret with its endless sandy Atlantic beaches, and the **Bassin d'Arcachon** (►Gascony, Côte d'Argent), a vast holiday camp. A 53m/170ft lighthouse on Pointe de Cap Ferret has splendid views.

Soulac

Lacanau-Océan

Cap Ferret

Famous the world over for its red wine, this utterly charming little town (2400 inhabitants, UNESCO World Heritage Site) lies approximately 40km/25mi east of Bordeaux on the slopes above the Dordogne, surrounded by ramparts from the 13th–15th centuries. The lovely Place du Marché with its cafés is notable for the **Eglise Monolithe**, a church built in the rock in the 8th–12th centuries (14th-century portal; guided tours). The Romanesque and Gothic tower (12th–15th centuries; open to visitors) rises above the church. High up to the northwest of the market square stands the collegiate church (12th–15th century) with a fine Last Judgement on the north door, 12th-century murals and choir stalls; entry to the transept is via the tourist office.

Saint-Emilion

The view of the town from the south side is marvellous. Below the Porte de la Cadène (15th century) lie the ruins of the 14th-century Franciscan monastery, where Crémant de Bordeaux is produced in the cellars (tasting possible). To the southwest stands the **Château du Roi**, a 13th-century castle founded by Henri III Plantagenet with a 32m/104ft-high donjon, from where the Jurade de St-Emilion proclaims the beginning of the vintage. There are, of course, many wine merchants; the Maison du Vin at the collegiate church offers a good overview of the various vineyards.

Blasimon — From St-Emilion it is worth heading 25km/15mi south to visit the ruins of the Benedictine monastery at Blasimon (12th–13th century) with impressive sculptures, particularly in the portal.

Château La Brède — 15km/9mi southeast of Bordeaux, amidst beautiful scenery, stands the moated castle of La Brède (12th–15th centuries), birthplace in 1689 of Charles de Segondat, Baron Montesquieu, who wrote *De l'Esprit des Lois* here.

Cadillac — Some 30km/20mi southeast of Bordeaux on the right bank of the Garonne lies Cadillac, a bastide founded in 1280 and famous for fine dessert wine. In the Château des Ducs d'Epernon (16th–17th century with vast fireplaces), the Maison du Vin and a wine brotherhood have their headquarters. From Langon, 15km/9mi to the south, two sites of interest can be reached. The highly acclaimed **Château d'Yquem** at Sauternes (not open to the public) produces the most expensive and possibly finest dessert wine in the world. The little river Ciron provides the climatic conditions for noble rot, the autumnal morning mist. 7km/4.5mi south of Langon stands the mighty Roquetaillade

Château Roquetaillade — Castle, completed in 1306 for Cardinal de la Mothe.

Bourges

K 5

Région: Centre	**Altitude:** 130m/426ft
Département: Cher	**Population:** 76,000

The old ducal town of Bourges is the centre of the county of Berry, the »granary« at the heart of France. As well as an attractive old quarter, it also has a cathedral which is one of the most important works of French High Gothic architecture.

The centre of France — The wide loop of the middle reaches of the Loire encloses the fertile territory of Berry. Its centre is Bourges, capital of the département of Cher with a university and important branches of industry: aviation and armaments (Aérospatiale), mechanical engineering, vehicle construction and tyres (Michelin). From 1360 Bourges was the residence of the Dukes of Berry, who were responsible for the town's boom years and the founding of the university in 1463, where Jean Caulvin, better known as the reformer John Calvin, studied from 1530. Duke Jean (1340–1416), brother of King Charles V made a name for himself as a patron; amongst other projects, he commissioned the famed Book of Hours by the Limburg brothers (**Les Très Riches Heures**, ▶ p. 80). Charles VII (»King of Bourges«) relocated his court here after 1422, as large parts of the Crown land were occupied by England and Burgundy; with the support of Jeanne d'Arc and Jacques Cœur, he succeeded in crowning himself king.

The cathedral of St-Etienne is one of the finest Gothic churches in France

What to See in Bourges

The old town sits atop a hill, with a UNESCO World Heritage Site, the cathedral of St-Étienne, as its landmark. The choir was built from 1198 to 1215, the nave and main façade completed by 1266 and consecration took place in 1324. The grand west façade, flanked by mighty towers, features five deep, richly sculpted entrances. The tympanum of the centre door boasts a wonderful depiction of the Last Judgement (around 1250). Following its collapse in 1506, the 65m/213ft north tower was rebuilt in Flamboyant style, as were the two portals to the left. The view from the top is magnificent. Above the south portal is a Majestas Domini (Christ in Majesty), surrounded by the symbols of the evangelists and, on the central pillar, Christ giving a blessing (13th century). The interior, 124m/136yd long and 41/45yd wide, has no transept and is divided into a 37m/121ft-high nave and two lower aisles, which continue into a double ambulatory. The **stained glass windows** dating from 1215–25 in the radiating chapels of the choir (take binoculars!) are splendid; the other windows date back to the 12th–17th centuries. The figures of Jean de Berry and his wife, fashioned around 1425 by Jean de Cambrai, stand in front of the middle choir chapel; note also the marble Madonna (late 14th century) and the astronomical clock of 1424.

St-Étienne
cathedral

◄ Interior

It is worth looking into the Gothic crypt of 1200, above ground, which contains parts of the rood screen and the **marble tomb of Duke Jean de Berry** by Jean de Cambrai, 1422–38. The design for the rose window of the main façade, which was made here, is etched into the floor.

◄ Crypt

South of the cathedral stands the bishop's palace of 1680, later the town hall and now, amongst other things, a museum of lace-making.

Bishop's palace

▶ VISITING BOURGES

INFORMATION

Office de Tourisme
21 Rue Victor Hugo, 18000 Bourges
Tel. 02 48 23 02 60, fax 02 48 23 02 69
www.ville-bourges.fr
www.bourges-tourisme.com

FESTIVALS AND EVENTS

Late April: Printemps de Bourges (six days of high-class pop and jazz); book hotel rooms well in advance. 1st weekend in Sept: Fête des Marais.

WHERE TO EAT

► Moderate / expensive

① *Jacques-Cœur*
3 Place Jacques-Cœur
Tel. 02 48 26 53 01. Traditional French fare served in princely, historical atmosphere.

► Inexpensive

② *D'Antan Sancerrois*
50 Rue Bourbonnoux
Tel. 02 48 65 96 26
Attractive, friendly establishment under medieval beams. Very intimate. »Cuisine du terroir« on the menu, with wines from the upper Loire (Sancerre, Menetou, Pouilly).

WHERE TO STAY

► Mid-range / Luxury

① *Hotel de Bourbon*
Boulevard de la République (on Carrefour de Verdun)
Tel. 02 48 70 70 00
www.hoteldebourbon.fr
A 17th-century abbey with modern comforts. Fine restaurant Abbaye St-Ambroix (tel. 02 48 70 80 00) in the former church, traditional cuisine.

The adjacent pretty Jardins de l'Archevêché park, probably laid out by Le Nôtre in the 17th century, has an exceptional good view of the cathedral. People come here to dance on Sunday afternoons.

Maison de la Culture A sculpture by Alexander Calder on Place du 8 Mai 1945 marks the Maison de la Culture (exhibitions, concerts, theatre); the cafe is a popular meeting place.

Hôtel Lallemant This beautiful merchant's house from the late 15th century with its ornately painted coffered ceilings houses the Musée des Arts Décoratifs (furniture, tapestries and paintings, primarily from the 17th century; closed Mon). The emblems of Louis XII and Anne de Bretagne, **Hôtel Cujas** porcupine and ermine, can be seen on the fireplaces. The Hôtel Cujas, a beautiful Renaissance building from 1515, is home to the **Musée du Berry** (closed Tue) with prehistoric and Roman relics, local artefacts and marble statues (»pleurants«) from the tomb of Jean de Berry.

✶ ✶ Palais Jacques-Cœur The Palais Jacques-Cœur was built between 1443 and 1453 on the remains of the Gallo-Roman town ramparts. The office and living quarters are grouped around an arcaded courtyard and represent one of the finest examples of a grand bourgeois Gothic town residence (open all week). **Jacques Cœur**, born in 1395 as son of a fur trader, grew to be a powerful entrepreneur in coal mining, shipbuilding and trade, as well as minister of finance to King Charles VII in 1440. Forced to flee to Rome due to a plot against him, he was later made captain of a fleet in an expedition against the Turks. He died in 1456 on Chios. His coat of arms, heart and scallop (»cœur«, »coquille St-Jacques«), and motto »A vaillan cœur rien impossible« (»To the brave, nothing is impossible«) decorate the building in many places. The ceiling of the marvellous private chapel with brightly coloured frescoes painted in 1488 depicts an angelic choir in starry heavens.

The Hôtel des Echevins (closed Tue), completed in 1489 for the mayor and his magistrates, has an attractive courtyard, a staircase tower in Flamboyant style and a Renaissance gallery. Inside, 20th-century paintings and drawings are on display, with particular attention given to the compelling works of the artist M. Estève (1904–2001). A pleasant walk leads to the Marais, the canalized marshes of the Yèvre to the east of town, where people tend their gardens.

Further attractions

★
Marais

Around Bourges

In the area around the small town of St-Amand-Montrond (13,000 inhabitants), which lies 43km/27mi to the south of Bourges, the

Saint-Amand-Montrond

Bourges *Map*

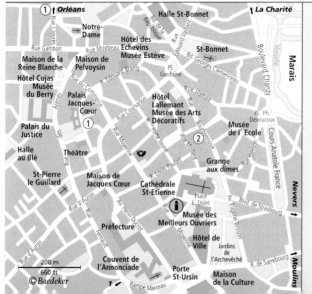

1 Muséum d'Histoire Naturelle

Where to eat
① Jacques-Cœur
② D'Antan Sancerrois

Where to stay
① Hotel de Bourbon

Orléans · La Charité · Halle St-Bonnet · Notre-Dame · Hôtel des Echevins · Musée Estève · St-Bonnet · Rue Gambon · Rue Mirebeau · Maison de la Reine Blanche · Maison de Pelvoysin · Pl. Gordaine · Bd. Georges Clemenceau · Boulevard Chanzy · Marais · Hôtel Cujas · Musée du Berry · Palais Jacques-Cœur · Hôtel Lallemant · Musée des Arts Décoratifs · Rue Joyeuse · Pl. Ph. Devoucoux · Musée de l' Ecole · Palais du Justice · Halle au Blé · Théâtre · Porte Jaune · Grange aux dîmes · Cours Anatole France · St-Pierre le Guillard · Maison de Jacques Cœur · Cathédrale St-Etienne · Place E. Dolet · Musée des Meilleurs Ouvriers · Nevers · Préfecture · Hôtel de Ville · Jardins de l'Archevêché · Blvd. de Strasbourg · R. de Sarrebourg · Moulins · Couvent de l'Annonciade · Porte St-Ursin · Maison de la Culture · Rampe Marceau

200 m
660 ft
© Baedeker

famed white **Charolais cattle** are bred. The 12th-century Romanesque church of St-Amand is worthy of note. 3km/2mi northwest at

✳
Noirlac

Cher stands the Abbey of Noirlac, an excellent example of the simple, yet perfect architecture of the Cistercian Order. Concerts are
staged in the church.

Château de
Meillant
Bruère-
Allichamps

7km/4.5mi north of St-Amand-Montrond, the Château de Meillant
is worth a visit. It is opulently appointed and similar to the castles of
the Loire. Right at the heart of the idyllic Bruère-Allichamps (6km/
3.5mi west of Meillant), a Roman milestone marks the **middle of**
France. (20km/13mi away at Saulzais-le-Potier and 30km/19mi further south at Vesdun, the locals claim the same honour for themselves.)

Nohant

Some 50km/30mi southwest of St-Amand lies La Châtre, and 6km/
3.5mi north from there, the village of Nohant with the manor house
of 1760 in which the author Georges Sand (Aurore Dupin, 1804–76)
grew up, lived for many years and ultimately died. Now it is a museum, with the family graveyard in the park.

Brest

C 4

Région: Bretagne	**Altitude:** 35m/114ft
Département: Finistère	**Population:** 156,000

Brest, at the northwestern tip of France, has a great history as a
port. After the Second World War it was rebuilt, albeit less attrac-
tively. Its marvellous location and marine atmosphere make it well
worth visiting.

Historic port

The second-largest town in Brittany possesses the second-largest
military harbour (after Toulon) and a commercial harbour with large
dockyards. The **Rade de Brest**, separated from the Atlantic by an
1.8km/1mi-wide channel (Goulet), forms an ideal natural harbour,
which explains the strategic significance of Brest and its eventful past.
The Romans exploited Beg Rest (Breton for »edge of the wood«) as a
military base as long ago as the 3rd century. In 1342 the castle was
captured by the English and in 1532 passed into the hands of the
French Crown. Richelieu initiated expansion into a military harbour
in 1631. Under Colbert, the infamous **Bagno** was commissioned, a
prison for up to 3000 inmates which was in operation until the 19th
century. From 1683 the town was remodelled by the military architect
Vauban. In the Second World War, Brest was occupied by the German
Wehrmacht and reduced to ashes and rubble by Allied bombs in the
summer of 1944, with the exception of the fort. Reconstruction up to
1961 lent the town a less than inviting uniform appearance.

Strategically important for centuries: the citadel and naval port of Brest

What to See in Brest

Rue de Siam, the main street, leads from the Place de la Liberté (town hall) to the Recouvrance Bridge. A visit to the Musée des Beaux-Arts (Place Sadi Carnot) is a must. It has paintings by Dutch, Italian and French artists of the 17th to 20th centuries, particularly works of the **Pont-Aven School** and the Impressionists. Open Tue–Sat 10am–noon, 2pm–6pm, Sun 2pm–6pm. The best view of the commercial harbour (Port de Commerce), the Plougastel peninsula and Pointe des Espagnols can be obtained from Cours Dajot (map in front of the prefecture).

Rue de Siam

✴

Musée des Beaux-Arts

Cours Dajot harbour

The impressive fortress at the mouth of the river Penfeld was constructed in the 15th and 16th centuries on the foundations of the Roman castrum. The marine museum in the keep deals with the history of the arsenal, the French navy and the harbour (open April–mid-Sept 10am–6.30pm, otherwise closed Tue). The Tour Madeleine offers a lovely view across the bay of Brest.

✴

Château

Erected in 1954, the 22m/72ft-high and 87m/95yd-long Recouvrance Bridge over the Penfeld is, at a weight of 530 tonnes, **Europe's largest lift bridge** and provides good views of the fort, Penfeld estuary and naval port. The Motte-Tanguy Tower (14th century, now a municipal museum) was a part of the town's defences. To the west of

Pont de Recouvrance

Tour de la Motte-Tanguy

▶ VISITING BREST

INFORMATION

Office de Tourisme
Pl. de la Liberté, F-29200 Brest
Tel. 02 98 44 24 96, fax 02 98 44 53 73
www.mairie-brest.fr

SHIPPING TRAFFIC

Boat excursions and ferries to Molène
and Ouessant and to the Crozon
peninsula (Le Fret, Camaret) depart
from the Port de Commerce and also
from the yacht marina Océanopolis.

FESTIVALS AND EVENTS

Mid-July to end of Aug: Thursday
evenings »Jeudis du Port« (music,
street theatre etc.). Every four years
(next: 2012) some 2000 old sailing
ships congregate at the Rade de Brest.

WHERE TO EAT

▶ Inexpensive

① *La Pensée Sauvage*

13 Rue Aboville, tel. 02 98 46 36 65
An institution in Brest that serves
hearty rustic French dishes in a
simple and friendly atmosphere.
Good value for money, reservation
recommended.

WHERE TO STAY

▶ Budget / mid-range

① *Hotel de la Corniche*

1 Rue Amiral Nicol
Tel. 02 98 45 12 42
www.hotel-la-corniche.com
Pretty little house in old Breton style,
east of the centre and close to the
marina. Pathways along the coast.

Brest Map

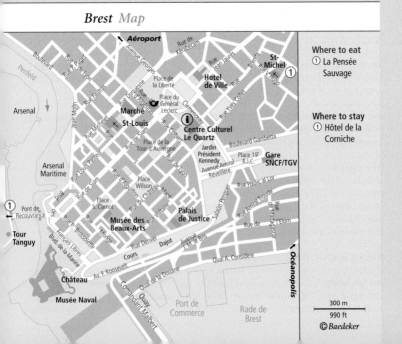

Where to eat
① La Pensée
Sauvage

Where to stay
① Hôtel de la
Corniche

300 m
990 ft
© Baedeker

the Penfeld estuary, the naval port extends over 4km/2.5mi to the old German submarine base. Visits (passport required) from Easter to mid-September from the Porte de la Grande Riviere.

naval port

One of the major attractions of Brittany is Océanopolis, 3km/2mi east at Port de Plaisance Moulin-Blanc, a research institute containing one of Europe's largest aquariums. Man's relationship to the sea in terms of science, technology and industry is illustrated here. Visitors can navigate a model ship from a fascinating command bridge simulator. Open May–June 9am–6pm, July–Aug 9am–7pm, otherwise 10am–5pm or 6pm, closed Mon during school term.

★
Océanopolis

★ ★ Bretagne · Brittany

C–E 4 / 5

Dramatic rocky coastline and beaches of fine-grained sand, old fishing villages, a lonely hinterland with pastures and hedges, remnants of a mysterious megalithic culture and lively Celtic traditions all contribute to the appeal of Brittany, for many the most beautiful peninsula and most attractive holiday destination in France.

Brittany, reaching out into the Atlantic at the northwestern corner of the country, has two sides to its character. »Ar Mor«, »land on the sea«, is the name given to this stretch of coast by the Gauls. Rocky cliffs dominate the coastline, broken by sandy bays, picturesque fishing villages and seaside resorts, popular for their mild climate and healthy iodine-filled air. »Argoat«, »land of the woods«, describes the hinterland, once lonely heaths, moors and woodland, now merely the »land of meadows and hedges«. The peninsula is crossed by the Massif Amoricain, with the peaks of the Monts d'Arrée reaching 384m/1259ft (Roc Trévézel), 330m/1082ft (Ménez-Hom) on the Crozon peninsula and in the Montagnes Noires 326m/1069ft (Roc de Toullaëron). The capital is ► Rennes, as the historic capital of ►Nantes was annexed to the Pays de la Loire region in 1981. Brittany is the second most popular holiday region in France after the Côte d'Azur. Most aim for the coast, but hikers, houseboat holidaymakers and thalassotherapy enthusiasts will also find much to suit their tastes.

France's most beautiful peninsula

The region has a rich, living **tradition of myth and legend**, with Percival and the Holy Grail, Merlin the Magician and the fairy Viviane, the town of Is which sank into the sea, and the drama of Tristan and Isolde. The connection between the world of myth and Christianity led to a heartfelt **veneration of saints**: 7777 patrons and saints make the list of Breton festivals and days of celebration a rather long one. Among the highlights are the »pardons« in honour of local saints, from May to September (dates available from the tourist offices).

Breton culture

Breton costumes and music at the Festival de Cornouaille in Quimper

Holy celebrations are usually staged in the **enclos paroissiaux** (parish close or churchyard), which comprise church or chapel, ossuary, cemetery, triumphal arch, calvary (calvaire) and surrounding wall; the theme is the life and Passion of Christ, with scenes from the life of the Virgin Mary and local history alongside. The most famous enclos can be found in Tronoën, Pleyben, Guimiliau and St-Thégonnec. Further proof of how regional culture is alive in these parts is the continuing tradition of the Breton language, spoken today by some 600,000 inhabitants who have Brezhoneg either as their first or second language. Countless music, dance and folklore festivals take place all year round.

History The impressive remnants of **Megalithic culture**, a civilization which remains a mystery even today, date back to the New Stone Age (approx. 5000–1800 BC; ▶ Baedeker Special p.306). Around 500 BC, Celts settled in Brittany. Caesar's victory in the Gulf of Morbihan in 56 BC heralded the beginning of Romanization. Around AD 450, Christian **Celts** fleeing from the heathen Anglo-Saxons in Ireland and Britain settled here and christened their new home Bretagne (Little Britannia). Immigration from these parts continued into the 7th century, prompting the Christianization of the land and a revival of the Celtic language, related to Gaelic. In 799, Bretagne fell to Charlemagne's Frankish kingdom, yet retained a degree of independence, as a duchy (from 826) and later as a kingdom (from 851), under Norman or English suzerainty. In 1491, Anne de Bretagne, daughter and heir to the last Breton duke, was compelled to marry

King Charles VIII, with the duchy passing irrevocably into royal hands in 1532. In the 16th and 17th centuries Brittany thrived financially, with the cloth trade and commercial shipping reaping particular benefits from its accession to the French kingdom. The enclos paroissiaux were established in that era as an expression of the great piety of the people. In 1675, the so-called Stamp Duty Revolt, an uprising of the poor against the States, was brutally suppressed. The French Revolution initially met with enthusiasm in Brittany, and yet the republicans at the helm of the state did not see fit to grant political autonomy to the province. On the contrary, the peninsula was divided into five départements and the Breton language forbidden. From 1793, the royalist **Chouans** desperately resisted the Parisian central government; their leader, Georges Cadoudal, was shot in 1804. In the 19th century, Brittany was sidelined both politically and economically; burgeoning industrialization bypassed the region and many labourers moved further afield. It was not until the early 1960s that the government took steps to end its isolation. Since then, industrial development has been promoted. Alongside shipbuilding, electronics and car manufacture, food processing has taken on an important role, infrastructure has been modernized (for example, a TGV connection) and agriculture brought up to date. Today, the peninsula is the **centre of the French fishing industry** and accounts for over 50% of the national catch. It is also an important agricultural region, breeding beef cattle and pigs, and producing milk, cheese and vegetables. Roughly 30% of oysters and 25% of mussels nationwide come from the region. Tourism, however, remains the number one industry.

Highlights Bretagne

Dinard
Enjoy the atmosphere of an old »British-style« seaside resort
► page 293

Côte du Granit Rose
Sandy beaches between huge, rounded cliffs of pink granite.
► page 295

Calvary
Scenes from the life and Passion of Christ set in stone.
► page 297, 300

Côte des Abers
Marvellous rocky coast and vast estuaries reaching inland.
► page 299

Le Folgoët
The red granite rood screen is a highlight of Breton stone carving.
► page 299

Festival de Cornouaille
The oldest and most significant festival on the Breton calendar is staged in Quimper.
► page 301

Concarneau
Well-fortified old town on an island, with beautiful beaches on the south side.
► page 302

Carnac
The massive ancient stones of Brittany are still something of an unsolved mystery.
► page 303

⏵ VISITING BRITTANY

INFORMATION

CRT Bretagne
1 Rue R. Ponchon, F-35069 Rennes
Tel. 02 99 28 44 30, fax 02 99 28 44 40
www.tourismebretagne.com

WHERE TO EAT

▶ Expensive

Relais Gourmand Roellinger
Rue Duguesclin, F-35260 Cancale
Tel. 02 99 89 64 76, closed Tue–Wed.
One of the best restaurants in a fine
building. A postprandial bed can be
found in the Richeux Castle, the Les
Rimains guest house or in the taste-
fully appointed holiday apartments
Gîtes Marins.

▶ Moderate

La Côte
Kermario, F-56340 Carnac
Tel. 02 97 52 02 80, closed Mon
Stylish rustic atmosphere near the
menhirs of Kermario, with a veranda.
Creative cuisine. Make sure to book.

▶ Inexpensive / moderate

Auberge des Terres Neuvas
25 Rue du Quai, F-22100 Dinan
Tel. 02 96 39 86 45, Closed Wed and
Sun evenings except July and Aug.
Fish and seafood on the Rance in
elegant but cosy surroundings with a
pretty terrace.

La Voilerie
7 Quai G. Toudouze
F-29750 Camaret-sur-Mer
Tel. 02 98 27 99 55, Excellent fish
restaurant in the town centre.

WHERE TO STAY

▶ Luxury

Villa Reine Hortense
19 Rue Malouine, F-35800 Dinard
Tel. 02 99 46 54 31, www.villa-reine-
hortense.com. Elegant villa from the
turn of the 19th/20th century, beautifully situated on the beach.

Diana
21 Boulevard Plage, F-56340 Carnac
Tel. 02 97 52 05 38, www.lediana.com.
On the Grande Plage, the best address
in Carnac: Boulevard de la Plage.
Choose from sea view balcony (less
quiet) or facing mini-golf course.
Restaurant terrace facing the sea.

▶ Mid-range

D'Avaugour
1 Pl. du Champ Clos, F-22100 Dinan
Tel. 02 96 39 07 49. Finest hotel in
town, above the city ramparts with a
beautiful flower garden. Stylish rooms,
breakfast served on the terrace.

▶ Budget / mid-range

Hostellerie de la Pointe St-Mathieu
F-29217 Plougonvelin
Tel. 02 98 89 00 19, www.pointe-
saint-mathieu.com. Unique location,
next to the lighthouse and monastery
ruins where the road comes to an end.
Beautifully modernized 14th-century
house with a good restaurant, bar and
swimming pool.

Armoric
3 Rue Penfoul, F-29950 Bénodet
Tel. 02 98 57 04 03, www.armoric-
benodet.com. Between the beaches
and marina. Heated pool.

St-Christophe
Place Notre-Dame, F-44500 La Baule
Tel. 02 40 62 40 00, www.st-christo-
phe.com. (July–Aug half-board only).
An enchantingly intimate atmosphere
pervades the three villas from the
early 19th century. Approx. 100m/
110yd to the beach.

Places to Visit in Bretagne

This description is a round trip around the peninsula from ► Mont St-Michel in an anti-clockwise direction.

A lively place (4600 inhabitants) on the N 176, with the memorable **cathedral of St-Samson**, a huge, fortified granite construction in Norman Gothic style (13th–14th century); the finest elements are the stained glass windows (13th century) and the choir stalls (14th century), as well as the tomb of Bishop James, crafted by the Florentines Antoine and Jean Juste (16th century). Recommended sites close by are the 65m/213ft hill of Mont-Dol (2km/1.25mi north) and the 9.5m/31ft-high Menhir de Champ-Dolent (2km/1.25mi south).

Dol-de-Bretagne

The attractive little fishing town and seaside resort of Cancale (5000 inhabitants), a centre for oyster farming since the 17th century, lies 15km/9mi east of ► St-Malo on the bay of Mont St-Michel. The St-Kerber oyster farms and oyster museum on the southern edge of town (Route de Corniche) are well worth a visit.

Cancale

► St-Malo

St-Malo

Cross the 2km/1.25mi-wide Rance estuary on the dam of the **tidal power station** (Usine Marémotrice, ► Baedeker Special p.752) to reach Dinard (10,000 inhabitants), one of the most elegant seaside resorts of Brittany. The Gulf Stream allows mimosa and camellia to blossom. The Grande Plage, a beautiful beach for swimming, with casino and luxury hotels, stretches to the north; close to the southern end of the »Moonlight Promenade« (Clair du Lune) stands the Villa Eugenie (1868) with the Musée du Site Balnéaire. A boat trip up the fjord-like Rance to Dinan is enjoyable.

★ Dinard

The walled town of Dinan (12,800 inhabitants) stands high above the left bank of the Rance. A mix of 15th- and 16th-century houses in Rue du Jerzual and the castle of the Duchess Anne de Bretagne with a 14th-century fortified tower and historical museum lend the old town a charming complexion. The Basilica St-Sauveur (12th–16th centuries) merits a visit; the 15th-century Tour d'Horloge is adjacent on the western side, with wonderful panoramic views.

★ Dinan

On the »Emerald Coast« between Pointe du Grouin north of Cancale and St-Brieuc lie numerous attractive seaside resorts. Among the highlights are the medieval Fort La Latte, 40km/25mi west of Dinard, and, accessible via a coastal path 5km/3mi away, **Cap Fréhel**, with cliffs rising 72m/236ft above the sea (lighthouse, excellent view). The cape can also be reached by boat from St-Malo and Dinard.

★ Côte d'Emeraude

★ ★ Cap Fréhel

Saint-Brieuc Some 4km/2.5mi inland, above the deep incisions of the valleys of Gouët and Gouëdic, spanned by viaducts, the town dates back to the foundation of an oratory by Saint Brieuc in the 6th century. The Gothic cathedral of St-Etienne on Place du Général de Gaulle was erected from 1170 to 1248 and reinforced on several occasions to serve as a fortress church. The Baie de St-Brieuc is famed for its **scallops**. Key ports are St-Brieuc, St-Quay-Portrieux and Erquy.

✳

Quintin In the 17th and 19th centuries, the little town of Quintin, 18km/11mi southwest of St-Brieuc, found fortune with the cloth industry. Beautiful old timber-frame houses and town houses recall the golden era. Tuesdays are especially lively here when the market is in full swing.

Guingamp Guingamp (8000 inhabitants), just 30km/19mi to the west of St-Brieuc, lies on the dividing line between the Breton west and Gallic east of Brittany. The Basilica Notre-Dame-de-Bon-Secours (13th century to 1535) with its three towers thoroughly deserves a visit and is, indeed, an important site of pilgrimage. The Black Madonna is carried through town on the first Saturday night in July in the **Pardon**; on the following Sunday the lively Festival des Danses Bretonnes takes pride of place.

✳

Côte du Goëlo From St-Brieuc, the highly varied Côte du Goëlo stretches 50km/30mi as far as the Ile de Bréhat in the northwest: cliffs some 70m/230ft high, secluded sandy bays, picturesque river estuaries. Until 1935 the coastal dwellers lived chiefly from fishing the waters off Newfoundland and Iceland. Today mussel farming plays an important role, as does tourism in resorts such as Binic and St-Quay-Portrieux. It is worth making time to see the Chapelle de Kermaria-an-Isquit (4km/2.5mi west of Plouha) with its impressive 15th-century Danse Macabre fresco. 8km/5mi west of Kermaria, in the small hamlet of Lanleff stands a circular ruin (**Temple de Lanleff**, 11th century), thought to be a replica of the Church of the Holy Sepulchre in Jerusalem.

Kermaria

Lanleff

Paimpol The small harbour town of Paimpol around a deeply indented bay is characterized by charming thatched houses and Mediterranean vegetation. Its heyday as a harbour was from 1852 to 1935 in the days of Icelandic fishing. The voyages lasted six months and over 2000 Paimpolais lost their lives, as the »perdu en mer« inscriptions on many commemorative plaques illustrate. The old town and two museums conjure up the atmosphere of days gone by.

✳

Ile de Bréhat Via Ploubazlanec continue to Pointe de l'Arcouest, from where boats depart for the 15-minute crossing to the Ile de Bréhat, known as »flower island« by virtue of its subtropical vegetation. Daytrippers come to the island to visit local sights including lighthouses and a mill, and to enjoy its natural beauty.

Wonderful contrasts of colour on the Côte du Granit Rosé

★ ★
Côte du Granit Rose

From Pointe de l'Arcouest the granite coast reaches westwards as far as St-Michel-en-Grève. The reddish granite cliffs, mild climate, broad sandy beaches and numerous bathing spots make this one of the most beautiful coastlines of the region. Visible in the hinterland as well as on the coast, stone colossi date back 300 million years, formed by lava flows from beneath the earth's surface. The Pointe du Château north of Tréguier and the stretch of coast to the west of Perros-Guirec are particularly striking.

Tréguier

A former diocesan town 15km/9mi west of Paimpol on a hill at the confluence of the Jaudy and Guidy. In 1253 **Saint Yves**, one of Bretagne's greatest patron saints, was born close by; a celebrated pilgrimage takes place in his honour on the third Sunday in May. The 14th- and 15th-century cathedral built from Caen stone (Jurassic limestone) is one of the most beautiful in Bretagne. The carved figures of »Saint Yves between a poor man and a rich man«, the mausoleum of Duke Jean V and the 15th-century transept are noteworthy.

Plougrescant

★
Pointe du Château

7km/4.5mi north of Tréguier, Plougrescant is marked by the leaning tower of the Chapelle St-Gonéry, its wooden vaults brightly decorated with imaginative paintings (late 15th century). The Pointe du Château lies 3km/2mi to the north, where the waves have cut a deep rift in the jagged cliffs.

Perros-Guirec

Situated on a peninsula, this small town is one of the most popular holiday destinations of the northern Bretagne, along with the neighbouring Ploumanac'h. It boasts lovely sandy beaches, a marina unaffected by the tides and a casino, and is a starting point for excursions to the offshore Sept-Iles. A toll path approximately 6km/3.5mi long,

Ploumanac'h	»a way between sea and clouds«, connects Perros with Ploumanac'h. In and around this small harbour are the most bizarre stone colossi. The castle of **Costaéress** (1892) stands on an island. Its illustrious guests have included Henryk Sienkiewicz, who is said to have written his famous novel *Quo Vadis* here.

*

Corniche Bretonne
Trégastel
Pleumeur-Bodou
Trébeurden

The Corniche Bretonne begins in Perros-Guirec, following the Côte de Granit Rose to Trébeurden and offering wonderful views. Trégastel, another popular resort, is famous for its rock formations, a dozen sandy beaches, a large thermal baths complex and an aquarium. Pleumeur-Bodou is visible from a great distance, thanks to the white dome of the space communications centre (with the interesting museum Cité de Télécoms). It is worth taking time to head southeast from Penvern on the D 21 to see the 8.1m/26ft-high **Menhir de St-Uzec**, erected here between 4500 and 2000 BC. Trébeurden is a busy little seaside resort (the tiny Le Goéland bistro is the best place to eat lobster); there are beautiful views from the Castel headland and Pointe de Bihit.

Lannion

This old, typically Breton town (18,300 inhabitants) – with modern electronics companies – has a lovely site on the river Léguer and equally fine medieval timber-frame houses, especially on Place du Gén. Leclerc. 142 steps lead up to the Eglise de Brélévenez, built around 1200 by the Knights Templar, and an excellent view from the top.

*

Corniche d'Armorique

The coast between St-Michel-en-Grève and Roscoff is called the »Ceinture Dorée« (golden belt) by virtue of its importance for agriculture, **artichokes in particular**. The especially charming Corniche d'Armorique stretches for 13km/8mi from the resorts of St-Michel-en-Grève and Locquirec, the latter with a church featuring 18th-century paintings and a wonderful carved 16th-century altar screen.

St-Jean-du-Doigt

*

Enclos paroissial ►

The small place at Plougasnou owes its name to a finger reliquary of John the Baptist, which has pride of place in the Flamboyant-style church, built in the 15th century. The parish close with a beautiful Renaissance fountain, chapel (1577) and two ossuaries is the setting for a grand »pardon« on the last Sunday in July. From the resort of Primel-Trégastel the 48m/157ft-high Pointe de Primel can be reached, a shimmering red sea of rock.

* *

Cairn de Barnenez

The roughly 7000-year-old burial mound on the headland of Kernéléhen, on the bay of Morlaix, is one of the largest and oldest of its kind in Europe (around 70m/230ft long, 25m/82ft wide).

Morlaix

Morlaix lies in a narrow valley on the little rivers of Jarlot and Queffleuth, which become the Dosse, flowing into the English Channel

5km/3mi further on. A 285m/310yd-long railway viaduct (1861) towers over the town. Of especial interest in the old town, with its lovely timber-frame houses, are the **lantern houses** from the 15th–17th centuries; take a look at the Maison de la Reine Anne (33 Rue du Mur). The beautiful bay of Morlaix is known for its rich variety of bird life. Beyond Château du Taureau (1552), which once served as a prison, is the resort of Carantec.

Château du Taureau

A tour of parish closes leads west from Morlaix to Landerneau and back across the Montagnes d'Arrée. First stop is St-Thégonnec, 15km/9mi to the southeast, with possibly **the most famous church-yard of all**, bequeathed by wealthy drapers and horse breeders. A splendid triumphal arch (1587) leads to the calvary of 1610 with its expressive statues. The ossuary dates back to 1682 and is one of the finest in Brittany; the crypt contains a life-size carved Entombment (1702) and a fine treasury. The church of Notre-Dame was re-modelled on several occasions and has some surprisingly playful Baroque features.

★★
Saint-Thégonnec

Guimiliau, 8km/5mi to the south-west, can boast the **second-largest calvary** in Brittany (1581–88). With over 200 figures hewn from granite, it represents 25 scenes from the Passion of Christ. The 16th-century church of St-Miliau has a wealth of intricate carvings. The small ossuary in Renaissance style (1648) merits attention, as does the round sacristy of 1683.

Typical dress of the Pays Bigouden: tall bonnets of starched lace

The small town of Lampaul-Guimiliau, 3.5km/2mi to the west, features the next parish close, the main attraction being the extremely decorative church itself. A brightly coloured triumphal beam (16th century) spans the nave, and two of the six altars (17th century) are amongst the most elaborate in Brittany.

★
Lampaul-Guimiliau

One of the oldest calvaries (1521) stands in Pencran, 2km/1.25mi southeast of Landerneau. La Martyre, 6km/3.5mi east of Pencran, was the site of an important fair from the 14th to 18th century, with the churchyard a tangible reminder. The ossuary features a strange

Pencran

★
La Martyre

Storm-lashed cliffs and smalls plots of pasture for cattle and sheep: Ile d'Ouessant

sculpture or caryatid dating from 1619; the porch of the church of St-Salomon (1455) is also noteworthy for its fine decorative sculptures.

✱
Montagnes d'Arrée
Forêt de Huelgoat

The tour continues via Sizun to Commana at the foot of the Montagnes d'Arrée, part of the Parc Naturel Régional d'Armorique. The highest points are the Roc'h Trévézel at 384m/1259ft and the Montagne St-Michel at 382m/1253ft. In the 600ha/1482-acre forest of Huelgoat on the eastern edge of the Montagnes d'Arrée, hiking trails are marked through a sea of bizarrely formed granite colossi.

Saint-Pol-de-Léon

Back on the coast, St-Pol-de-Léon is a market for the fertile landscape of Léon, with two-thirds of French artichokes harvested here. The 77m/252ft bell tower of the **Chapelle du Kreisker** can be seen from afar, even rising above the towers of the former cathedral (1431). It was built in the 15th century, modelled on St-Pierre in Caen (►Normandy).

Roscoff

From here, it is just 5km/3mi to the tip of the Léon peninsula and the seaside resort of Roscoff, with ferry connections to Ireland and England. The Renaissance tower of the church of Notre-Dame-de-Kroaz-Baz rises above the quaint commune. The centre for oceanography with an aquarium is certainly worth a visit. 2km/1.25mi from the mainland lies the fertile **Ile de Batz**, also called the »vegetable island«.

Château de Kerjean

Not far from Plouescat to the south, the Renaissance Château de Kerjean, built from 1553 to 1590, houses a museum for Breton folklore. Theatrical and musical performances take place in summer.

Le Folgoët is the scene of a »grand pardon« on the first Sunday in September. According to legend, a pious eccentric lived here in the 14th century; after his death, a white lily grew on his grave. It was on this very spot that Jean V had the church built in 1422. The red granite rood screen in Flamboyant style is a fine achievement of 15th-century Breton stonework.

✱
Le Folgoët

A trip along the Breton northwestern coast is most impressive. The so-called Abers Land (Côtes des Légendes) is a magnificent rocky coastline with small beaches (»grèves«) and numerous lighthouses. The **abers** are fjords that cut far into the valleys, though less deep and with less steep banks than the vast estuaries of the north coast. The Aber Wrac'h to the west of Plouguerneau is one of the most impressive spots. Off Portsall, the wrecked oil tanker *Amoco Cadiz* caused an environmental disaster in 1978. From Portsall, scenic roads lead south via Porspoder and Brélès. **The westernmost point of the French mainland** is the 50m/164ft-high cliff line of Pointe de Corsen. From the small bathing resort of Le Conquet, ferries cross to the islands of Molène and Ouessant.

✱
Côtes des Abers

Portsall

Pointe de Corsen
Le Conquet

8km/5mi long and 4km/2.5mi wide, the Ile d'Ouessant can be reached by ship from Brest in 2½ hours or 1½ hours from Le Conquet. The waters between the Atlantic and English channel are riddled with dangerous reefs, hence the seafarers' saying: »He who sees Ouessant, sees his own blood.« Some 1000 inhabitants live from sheep rearing and tourism. The island belongs to the Armorica regional nature park and is home to an impressive array of plant life and wildlife.

✱
Ile d'Ouessant

On the headland 4km/2.5mi south of Le Conquet, 30m/100ft high, a monastery is thought to have been founded as early as the 6th century. The extensive ruins date from the 13th–16th centuries. As well as a signal station, the 54m/177ft St-Mathieu lighthouse offers excellent all-round views, from the Ile d'Ouessant in the northwest, via the harbour of Brest to the Crozon peninsula.

✱
Pointe de St-Mathieu

►Brest

Brest

Famed for its **strawberries**, the fertile peninsula of Plougastel reaches far into the bay of Brest. The main settlement is Daoulas, site of the largest calvary in Bretagne (1604, destroyed in 1944 and later rebuilt) with 180 figures.

Presqu'Ile de Plougastel

Passage to the Crozon peninsula, which is shaped like a cross, is either by ferry (Brest – Camaret / Le Fret) or the 272m/298yd-long Térénez suspension bridge. On the western side, the scenery is characterized by promontories with majestic cliffs and romantic sandy bays, whilst the east features the fjord-like estuary funnel of the

✱
Presqu'Ile de Crozon

Aulne and the **Menez-Hom** mountain, dwarfing everything else with its 330m/1080ft. The pleasantly undulating hinterland of grain fields and small woods is less typical of the »Breton look«. The sights here include – in addition to the natural beauty of the Pointe de Penhir and Pointe des Espagnols – the remnants of a 5th-century abbey at Landévennec, the commune of Crozon with a wonderfully carved altar in the church of St-Pierre and the fishing village of Camaret, as pretty as a picture.

Head east via Châteaulin to **Pleyben**, famous for its »galettes« (biscuits) and churchyard; the calvary dates to somewhere between 1555 and 1650. On the first Sunday in August, this is the scene for a »grand pardon«.

Impressive churchyard in Pleyben

✶
Locronan
Douarnenez

✶ ✶
Pointe du Raz

The small artisan town of Locronan has granite houses dating from the 16th–18th centuries decorated with flowers, and the late Gothic church of St-Ronan. Continue to **Douarnenez**, a lively harbour town with a maritime museum and the gateway to Le Cap Sizun, which culminates in the magnificent, 70m/230ft-high headland Pointe du Raz (photo p. 15). The famous little Hotel de l'Iroise, landmark of the Pointe, was demolished in 1997, ostensibly due to a lack of planning permission. The view from here extends over the cliffs of the Raz de Sein to Ile de Sein (ferry from Audierne). Every other year (2010, 2012 etc), hundreds of splendid **old sailing ships** muster off Douarnenez at the end of July.

Cornouaille-
coast

From the Pointe du Raz, follow the Cornouaille coast with its beaches of fine sand, punctuated by rocky reefs and steep inclines. The places of interest here are St-Tugen (3km/2mi west of Audierne), the »Cathédrale des Dunes«, as the chapel of Notre-Dame-de-Tronoënis known, with one of Bretagne's oldest calvaries (around 1460), the fishing port of St-Guénolé with craggy cliffs and the **Phare d'Eckmühl**, the lighthouse on the point of Penmarc'h.

✶
Quimper

The capital of the département of Finistère (67,000 inhabitants) lies on the river Odet, which flows into the Atlantic at Bénodet. In spite of some industry, the former ducal town has retained its character as one of the »most Breton« settlements. At its heart lies the Gothic ca-

▶ VISITING QUIMPER

INFORMATION

Office de Tourisme
Pl. de la Résistance
F-29000 Quimper
Tel. 02 98 53 04 05
Fax 02 98 53 31 33
www.mairie-quimper.fr

FESTIVALS AND EVENTS

3rd week of July: Cornouaille Festival
with participants from all the Celtic
regions of Europe (photo p.290)

WHERE TO EAT

▶ Moderate / expensive

① *L'Ambroisie*
49 Rue E.-Fréron
Tel. 02 98 95 00 02
Closed Sun evenings, also closed Mon
in winter. Good, straightforward
Breton cuisine, modern ambience.

▶ Inexpensive

② *Crêperie St-Marc*
2 bis Rue St-Marc
Tel. 02 98 55 53 28

Tiny, charming crêperie, claiming to
be the oldest in Quimper. The
temptation is to sample the whole
menu.

WHERE TO STAY

▶ Mid-range

① *Gradlon*
30 Rue de Brest
Tel. 02 98 95 04 39
www.hotel-gradlon.fr
Elegant, plushly furnished hotel with
attractive garden where breakfast is
served. No restaurant.

▶ Budget / mid-range

② *Mercure*
21 bis Av. de la Gare
Tel. 02 98 90 31 71
www.accorhotels.com
By the TGV station, on the edge of the
old quarter. Traditional hotel with
modern comforts of the Mercure
franchise.

Quimper Map

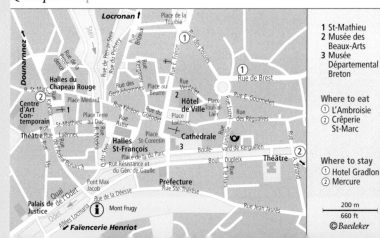

thedral of St-Corentin, built from 1239 to the 15th century. Between the 76m/249ft-high towers (completed in 1856) a statue of King Gradlon on horseback, the legendary founder of the town, stands tall. Adjacent is the 15th-century bishop's palace with the Musée Départemental Breton (archaeology, local history, ceramics from Quimper). North of the cathedral is the Musée des Beaux-Arts with an excellent collection of paintings, including works of the **Pont-Aven School**. The centre features attractive timber-frame houses and stretches west of the cathedral between the small rivers Odet and Steïr. In Locmari, two faience workshops may be visited, as well as an interesting ceramics museum. In Ergué-Gabéric, 7km/4.5mi to the east, the Chapelle de Kerdévot displays a marvellous Flemish polyptych, carved and gilded in the 15th century.

✳
Chapelle de Kerdévot

Concarneau

✳ ✳
Ville Close ▶

From Bénodet and Fouesnant, famous for its cidre, go on to Concarneau (20,000 inhabitants), the third-largest fishing port in France after Boulogne and Lorient. The old town on an island of the Moros estuary is enclosed by towered ramparts from the 14th–17th centuries. A Musée de la Pêche in the former arsenal illustrates the history of Concarneau and fishing.

Pont-Aven

The old commercial town lies in a picturesque wooded valley on the river Aven, which flows into the Atlantic 8km/5mi further downstream. Its claim to fame is **Paul Gauguin** (1848–1903), who came here between 1886 and 1894, with other artists following. The renowned Pont-Aven School, founded by Gauguin and others, was inspired by the landscape and people (museum on the town hall square).

Old town and fishing harbour of Concarneau

The Grande Plage is Quiberon's main attraction

In the old town of Quimperlé stands one of the finest Románesque churches of Brittany, the 11th-century **Ste-Croix** modelled on the Church of the Holy Sepulchre in Jerusalem. From this point, it is worth travelling 20km/12mi north to Le Faouët. A remarkable number of beautiful chapels are in the area, such as **St-Fiacre** with its unusual tower and wonderful, colourful wooden rood screen (circa 1480), and in Kernascléden (10km/6mi southeast) Notre-Dame with marvellous frescoes from 1469–70.

★ ★
Quimperlé

Le Faouët

The town (62,000 inhabitants) at the mouth of the Scorff and Blavet rivers was, like Brest und St-Nazaire, heavily bombed in the Second World War as the German Wehrmacht had established an important submarine base here; it was rebuilt in the 1950s and 1960s. Naval, commercial and fishing ports plus a marina characterize the townscape. The citadel in the old harbour of Port-Louis houses museums, one of which is the Museum of the French East India Trade Company. At the exit to the bay are Port-Louis and the resort Larmor-Plage.

Lorient

Carnac on the Bay of Quiberon is a popular holiday destination with long, sandy beaches and a **mecca of Megalithic culture**. Not far from the 17th-century church of St-Cornély is the Musée de Préhistoire Miln-Le-Rouzic, one of the most important of its kind (open daily except Tue, June–Sept). Northeast of Carnac, in Le Ménec, Kermario and Kerlescan, some 3000 menhirs testify to a largely unknown civilization (▶Baedeker Special p.306). Megaliths can also be found in the surrounding area, in Crucuno, for example, at Erdeven (a field at Kerzerho) and on the Locmariaquer peninsula.

Carnac

★
◀ Musée Miln-Le-Rouzic

★
Locmariaquer

Presqu'île de Quiberon

The narrow peninsula of Quiberon was once an island, before sand built up to connect it to the mainland. The east coast, the lee side, is blessed with ideal sandy beaches, while the virtually uninhabited Atlantic coast to the west is rockier and altogether wilder, as the name suggests: Côte Sauvage. **Quiberon** (photo p.303) is the main commune or town in the area, on the southern tip of the peninsula. It is not only a popular health and seaside resort, but also an important sardine harbour. Ferries depart from here to the offshore islands of Houat, Hoëdic and Belle-Ile.

※ **Belle-Ile-en-Mer**

The »beauty in the ocean«, the largest Breton island, has become something of the »place to be« for the French, thanks to its wonderfully varied landscape of fertile fields, wooded valleys, pleasant beaches and rocky coastline. The 17th-century citadel built by Vauban above the capital of the island, Le Palais (museum), serves as a reminder of English and Dutch attacks.

※ **Golfe du Morbihan**

※ **Ile de Gavrinis**

»Morbihan«, meaning the »little sea«, an inland water with many islands and islets, is connected to the Atlantic only by means of a canal. The landscape is not the only attraction for visitors, as there is so much more to discover; numerous menhirs, dolmen and tumuli, for example. On the Ile de Gavrinis there is an impressive burial mound (access by boat from Larmor-Baden).

Atmospheric spot in Vannes

Vannes (54,000 inhabitants) is, like Auray, a point of departure for boat trips in the Gulf of Morbihan. It was here that Brittany became a part of France in 1532. In the historic centre, with parts of the town ramparts still standing, the cathedral of St-Pierre was constructed between the 13th and 19th centuries. The archaeological museum in Château Gaillard (15th century) contains the most interesting prehistoric in Brittany collection after Carnac. The Musée des Beaux-Arts La Cohue – a former market hall and court of justice (13th century) – displays religious art and works from the 19th and 20th centuries. The Jardins de la Garenne have a fine view of the old town and the washhouses on the Marle.

The little town of **La Roche-Bernard** is the gateway to the Grande Brière, the third-largest marshland in France after the Camargue and Marais Poitevin. From the Ile de Fédrun with its attractive village, boat trips take visitors to the marshes. Guérande is worth visiting to see the medieval centre within the town walls. »Gwen ran«, the »white town«, owes its wealth to trade in salt from the area's salt marshes (marais salants). Today, tourism plays a more significant role, although there are also some popular fishing and bathing spots such as Piriac, Le Croisic (the aquarium is well worth a look) and Batz-sur-Mer, as well as the elegant **La Baule**. Founded in 1879 and considered, along with Biarritz, one of the most important seaside towns on the French Atlantic coast, it claims to possess the most beautiful beach in Europe (9km/5.5mi long).

★
Guérande-
peninsula

La Baule

The important harbour and industrial town of St-Nazaire (68,000 inhabitants) can be found where the Loire flows into the Atlantic. It was almost completely destroyed in World War II. The platform between the St-Nazaire basin and the river provides a fine view across the harbour and the erstwhile submarine base, now the excellent shipping museum **Escal'Atlantic**, where the atmosphere on board a luxury liner is recreated (April–Sept daily, otherwise closed Mon–Tue). Further north at the Chantiers d'Atlantique (tours available), the world's biggest passenger ship, the Queen Mary 2, was built. A 3356m/2mi-long and 61m/200ft-wide road bridge opened in 1975 sweeps across the Loire estuary. Close to the road to Guérande lies the prehistoric burial mound of Dissignac.

Saint-Nazaire

★
◀ harbour

Vannes Map

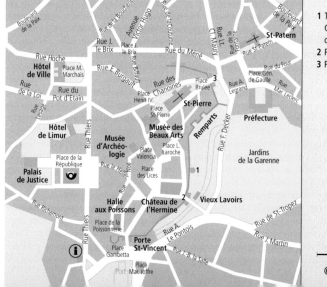

1 Tour du Connétable de Richemont
2 Porte Poterne
3 Porte Prison

150 m
495 ft
© Baedeker

The menhir in St-Uzec, »baptized« with a cross and symbols of the Passion

RIDDLES OF THE STONE AGE

In the Second World War, American G.I.s mistook the menhirs for German »dragon's teeth«, anti-tank defences. Over the centuries, various theories have sought to explain the meaning of these groups of stones, but they remain a mystery to this day.

Since time immemorial Brittany has been home to some of the most famous stone monuments in western and southern Europe. Some 4500 dolmens, 56 stone avenues and 58 stone circles are dotted across the region; they are so numerous at Morbihan on the Atlantic coast that this part of the peninsula has been declared an open-air museum.

Monuments of stone

Megalithic culture (from the Greek »megas« meaning »large« and »lithos« meaning »stone«) in Brittany is evident in the **menhirs** (from »men«, the Breton word for »stone«, and »hir«, which means »long«) and dolmens (from »taol«, meaning »table«). A menhir is a vertical monolith. It can stand alone or as a **cromlech** in circles, semi-circles or squares. Stretching on occasion for miles, as in Carnac, such a line is termed an **»alignement«**. **Dolmens**, meanwhile, are flat, horizontal slabs supported on vertical stones. Burial chambers of this design usually stood below artificial mounds, beneath either a tumulus (Latin for hill) or a cairn (Breton for stone monument, i.e. a hill constructed from rubble). An allée couverte (gallery grave) is a gallery comprising several dolmens.

Who, how and why?

The search to discover the origin of the megaliths began far back in the mists of time. Who erected the stones? When, how and why? In medieval times they were considered the work of the devil, or of magicians or giants who dwelled on the earth before the Flood. There is no end to the legends and sagas surrounding them. »Petrification as a punishment« is a recurring theory as far as the 3000 menhirs of Carnac are concerned: this was said to be the fate of Roman soldiers who were persecuting Saint Cornély.

The locals grew attached to the stones and invested them with all sorts of superstitions. The vertical stones were said to have healing properties and, above all, the power of fertility. Small wonder, then, that priests saw the stones as »devil's work« and believed

The Alignements du Ménec at Carnac comprise no less than 1099 stones

it their duty to destroy them. They added crosses to some of the menhirs and engraved Christian symbols to indicate the triumph of Christianity: others were simply smashed to pieces. Their success was limited: even today, young women rub their bellies against a menhir if they want to become pregnant. A traditional feature of Breton weddings is for the happy couple to kiss as they pass through a dolmen and dance around a menhir.

In more enlightened times, particularly the Romantic age, the megaliths were attributed to the time-honoured Celtic priests, the druids. Vivid imaginations made them scenes of bloody sacrifice. Up until the 1960s, the 50,000 or so stone monuments along the west coast of Europe – from Sweden and the Orkney Isles in the north via Brittany and Spain in the west to Malta in the south – were thought to be emulations of megalithic constructions in the east (Egypt, the Levant and Greece). With the help of radiocarbon dating, however, it was revealed that some megalithic monuments in Brittany were **almost 2000 years older than the pyramids** in Egypt! Today, the general consensus is that the megaliths of western Europe were erected between 5000 and 1500 BC, at a time when western Europe and the eastern Mediterranean had virtually no contact with

each other. They are older than similar structures in Tibet, Japan, Africa and on the Easter Islands. Who were their makers? – Stone Age peoples who lived in coastal areas before the Celts and left no trace save for the roughly hewn stone blocks. The question of how they built the monuments is equally a matter for speculation. Possibly they used wooden rollers and levers, with belts made of animal skins. Calculations suggest that some 15 to 20 labourers were required to shift one ton. A 3–4m/ 10–13ft menhir weighs 10–12 tons; the largest menhir in the world, the Men er Hroec'h of Locmariaquer, is 20m/65ft long weights 350 tons. It is also possible that the stone blocks were already on site and did not have to be transported very far, as all the menhirs are made of local granite.

Of the questions left unanswered, the most tantalizing is: why? What purpose did the menhirs serve? For astronomical measurements? As a calendar, a meeting place or religious site? All manner of theories, plausible and far-fetched, have been advanced, but none can be conclusively proved. The dolmens, however, are generally accepted to have been burial sites.

★ ★ Burgundy · Bourgogne

L–N 5–6

Enchanting scenery, impressive art treasures from a glorious past, world-famous wines and gastronomic addresses revered both at home and abroad make Burgundy *the* region for connoisseurs and bons vivants.

A landscape for bons vivants
»Bourgogne, l'art et le plaisir de vivre« – Burgundy, art and pleasure, this is how the historic province and latter-day Région Bourgogne – with ▶Dijon as its capital – in eastern France chooses to present itself. As a transitional land between north and south, it is not unified geographically, but takes in parts of the Paris Basin, the Rhône-Saône trench and the Massif Central. In the north, Burgundy shares a border with Champagne, in the south the hills of the Charolais mark the beginning of Beaujolais, and in the west it opens into the Paris Basin. To the east, the Saône roughly follows the border to the French Jura and Franche-Comté. Burgundy is a largely hilly region, mountainous in Morvan, an extension of the Massif Central. It is also a region of rivers and canals which connect it with virtually all of France. Along with the Seine, Loire and Rhône, the main waterways include the Canal de Bourgogne, the Marne-Saône Canal and the Loire Lateral Canal, barely in use for commercial shipping but still an extremely attractive proposition for boating holidays (▶Baedeker Special p.192).

Economy
Agriculture comes first in Burgundy. The timber industry also has a long tradition; over 30% of the land is covered by woodlands. Tilling the land and breeding white Charolais cattle are also key activities, as is wine production. Precision engineering and metalwork are the main fields of industry. The industrial museum in Le Creusot serves as a reminder of the earlier importance of mining and heavy industry. Dijon is famed for production of foodstuffs, particularly cassis and mustard.

Burgundian wines
In Burgundy, three of the most famous French wine regions can be found: Chablis deep in the northwest, Côte d'Or in the centre, divided into the northern Côte de Nuits and the southern Côte de Beaune, and the Chalonnais and Mâconnais regions in the south. (Beaujolais lies almost completely in the département of Rhône and is not included in Burgundy's wine region – the same goes for the region on the Loire around Pouilly). The four main grape varieties are Pinot Noir, Gamay, Chardonnay and Aligoté, although red Burgundy is synonymous with Pinot Noir and the great white wines are made from Chardonnay. Aligoté is cultivated in areas where the ground is not really suitable for Chardonnay. Passe-Tout-Grain (as the name says, »anything goes here«) is an uninspiring blend of Pinot Noir and Gamay.

Highlights Burgundy

Vézelay
Spirituality and marvellous Romanesque architecture in the pilgrimage basilica
▶ page 312

Auxerre, Tournus, Paray-le-Monial
Splendid church architecture, both Romanesque and Gothic
▶ page 314, 319, 322

Côte d'Or
Destination for wine pilgrims and other connoisseurs from all over the world
▶ page 316

Beaune
Residence of Burgundian dukes and the wine centre of Côte d'Or
▶ page 317

Cluny
The centre of monastic reform possessed the largest church of Christendom.
▶ page 319

Panoramic view
Excellent views from the famous rock of Solutré
▶ page 321

The earliest traces of mankind can be found in the Grottes d'Arcy dating back 100,000 years, whilst finds at the rock of Solutré date from around 25,000 BC. The end of Celtic Gaul was signalled in 52 BC when Caesar invaded Burgundy and defeated the Gauls of Vercingetorix at Alesia. In 443 the East Germanic Burgundians moved into the Saône plateau and gave their new home its name. When the Frankish Empire was divided in 843 in the Treaty of Verdun, Burgundy was split into an eastern and western half along the river Saône. In the east, two kingdoms were created, united as the Kingdom of Burgundy and annexed to the Holy Roman Empire under Conrad II in 1032. The western half became part of the West Frankish kingdom and developed into the independent **Duchy of Burgundy**, today known as Bourgogne. In medieval times, **Bernard of Clairvaux** (1091–1153) was victorious in his battle against the ostentation of Cluny and affirmed his position as reformer of the monasteries – with effects that were felt throughout Europe – and as proclaimer of the Second Crusade.

History

In 1363 Burgundy fell to Philippe le Hardi (Duke Philip the Bold) of the house of Valois, fourth son of King Jean II. Under his rule and that of the three dukes who succeeded him – John the Fearless (Jean sans Peur, 1404–19), Philippe le Bon (Philip the Good, 1419–67) and Charles le Téméraire (Charles the Rash, 1467–77) – Burgundy enjoyed a glorious period of ascendancy and expansion. It stretched from Switzerland to Flanders and was, for a time, **France's greatest rival**. In 1477 Charles the Bold met his death in battle at Nancy at the hands of the united armies of Louis XI, the Swiss and the Duke of Lorraine. His 20-year-old daughter married Emperor Maximilian I. The fight of the French monarchy to inherit Burgundy dragged on until 1493. Later Artois and Franche Comté finally passed into

► VISITING BURGUNDY

INFORMATION

CRT Bourgogne
BP 20623, F-21006 Dijon Cedex
Tel. 03 80 280 280 (in France, 0825 00
21 00), fax 03 80 280 300
www.bourgogne-tourisme.com

WHERE TO EAT

► Expensive

Troisgros
Place de la Gare, F-42300 Roanne
Tel. 04 77 71 66 97, fax 04 77 70 39 77
Closed Tue–Wed and 2 weeks in Aug.
The Troisgros restaurant, in the
family since 1930, is one of the most
highly reputed in all France. Its
neighbour Central is the less expensive version. Those reluctant to leave
after dinner can check into the small
but exquisite hotel in Bauhaus style.

Jardin Gourmand
56 Bvd Vauban, F-89000 Auxerre
Tel. 03 86 51 53 52. Closed Tue–Wed.
Elegant restaurant in the centre, with
shady garden terrace. Innovative cuisine, good selection of Chablis wines.

► Moderate

Relais des Gourmets
47 Rue Paris, F-89200 Avallon
Tel. 03 86 34 18 90. North of Place
Vauban. Good regional cuisine in an
atmosphere more reminiscent of the
south. Terrace outside and good value

for money. Advance booking recommended.

Hostellerie des Clos
18 Rue J. Rathier, F-89800 Chablis
Tel. 03 86 42 10 63, www.hostellerie-
des-clos.fr
Perfectly suited to learning more
about Chablis, the styles and producers, whilst enjoying Burgundian
cuisine with a star to its name. Many
wines served in half bottles. The
historic building also contain 32
charming rooms for the night (mid-
range price category).

► Inexpensive / moderate

Chez Jules
11 Rue Strasbourg, F-71100 Chalon-
sur-Saône, tel. 03 85 48 08 34, closed
Sun and 1–20 Aug. Intimate, friendly
restaurant on the island of St-Laurent,
serving regional dishes.

WHERE TO STAY

► Mid-range

Parc des Maréchaux
6 Avenue Foch, F-89000 Auxerre
Tel. 03 86 51 43 77, www.hotel-
parcmarechaux.com
Distinguished 1850s house, friendly
atmosphere, beautiful salons, large
rooms in Imperial style. The quieter
rooms face towards the park.

La Lucarne aux Chouettes
Quai Bretoche
F-89500 Villeneuve-sur-Yonne
Tel. 03 86 87 18 26, www.lesliecaron-
auberge.com. 14km/8.5mi south of
Sens. The actress Leslie Caron had
four 17th-century houses remodelled.
Lovely views of the Yonne from the
terrace. The idyllic Auberge has a
good restaurant.

Monasteries, such as this one at Fontenay, have left their mark on Burgundy for centuries

French hands. Today, a wealth of impressive buildings, religious and secular, as well as art treasures, bear witness to the erstwhile importance of Burgundy as a territorial power in Europe.

Beginning from Cluny and Cîteaux, a reform movement was set in motion in the 10th and 11th centuries which not only renewed the Catholic Church, but also had a huge impact on architecture, sculpture and painting, producing an array of great masterpieces. Burgundy has close to 350 **Romanesque churches**, so that even the keenest architectural enthusiasts can only view a selection. Cluny, Vézelay, Tournus and Paray-le-Monial should make the shortlist. The Gothic style came in gradually from the Ile-de-France around the middle of the 12th century, initially only taking hold in the northern half of the region, as in Dijon and Auxerre. The late Gothic Flamboyant style made even fewer inroads in the 14th century. Even the Renaissance, spread by Italian artists, only had limited influence; castles like those of the Loire valley can be found in Ancy-le-Franc, Sully and Tanlay.

Art

The North: From Dijon to Sens

Semur-en-Auxois (5000 inhabitants), approx. 60km/35mi northwest of Dijon, beautifully located in a loop of the river Armançon, has managed to retain its **medieval townscape**. At its highest point, the Gothic church of Notre-Dame (13th–16th centuries) stands tall. Note the tympanum of the north door, and inside a tomb of 1490 and the lovely 14th-century windows. The library and the municipal museum are located in the 17th-century Jacobin monastery. The 44m/144ft Tour de l'Orle d'Or, what is left of the castle, houses a local museum. Some 12km/7mi west is Epoisses, famous for its cheese, with a castle dating largely from the 14th century.

★
Semur-en-Auxois

Epoisses

Flavigny-sur-Ozerain

✸ Flavigny, one of the best-preserved medieval villages of Burgundy, sits on a hilltop 17km/11mi east of Semur-en-Auxois. The chapel and crypt, remnants of the Benedictine abbey founded around 720, are worth inspection.

Alise-Ste-Reine

The neighbouring Alise-Ste-Reine is said to be **Alesia**, where Caesar's Roman armies and the Gauls of Vercingetorix waged battle in 52 BC. The Gallic prince was forced to surrender after six weeks of siege. In 1865, on the 407m/1335ft-high Mont Auxois, a monument visible from far and wide was erected to the long-haired, moustachioed Vercingetorix. Excavations from the Gallo-Roman town of Alesia can also be seen here.

Avallon

Avallon (9000 inhabitants) lies 35km/22mi west of Semur-en-Auxois on a promontory above the Cousin. The attractive old heart of the town is still enclosed by walls from the 14th–15th century. The church of St-Lazare (12th century; fine sculptures on the west portal) and Tour de l'Horloge, a clock tower from 1460, are definitely worth a look. The Musée de l'Avallonnais displays historical exhibits and a small collection of art.

✸✸ Vézelay

Vézelay (550 inhabitants) is 14km/8.5mi west of Avallon, picturesquely located on the northern edge of the Morvan on a hill above the Cure. Its basilica Ste-Madeleine, one of the largest abbey churches in the land, is rightfully acclaimed as a great Romanesque masterpiece (UNESCO World Heritage Site). Ostensibly the final resting place of the remains of Mary Magdalene, it became one of the most important sites of pilgrimage in Christendom and departure point of the Via Lemoviciensis on the Way of St James. Here, in 1146, Bernard of Clairvaux proclaimed the **Second Crusade** as the pope's envoy. In the 13th century, the authenticity of the relics was called into question and Vézelay lost its significance, the abbey closing in 1537. During the French Revolution, »only« the sculptures of the west façade were destroyed. The existing tympanum is the work of Viollet-Le-Duc, who began restoring the church in 1840. Work on the abbey church commenced in 1096 in the east,

Vézelay, place of pilgrimage on the Way of St James

and the porch followed from 1140 to 1160. The sculptures of the three portals, dated 1125–30, as well as the capitals in the Romanesque nave and aisles, are among the finest achievements of Romanesque art. There is a beautiful crypt beneath the early Gothic choir, and an excellent view from the terrace behind the choir apse. 12th-century ramparts, the Porte Neuve with two formidable towers (14th–16th century) and the quaint old town add up to a delightful walk.

✔ DON'T MISS

- Mass in the basilica of Vézelay resounds to the splendour of a four-part choir. It is celebrated in the morning, afternoon and early evening – times vary slightly during the week.

Cure valley ✱

The Cure valley is one of the scenic highlights of Lower Burgundy; it is well worth taking a trip from the beautiful Pierre-Perthuis south of Vézelay to Auxerre. The coral reef limestone contains a system of caves, of which the Grande Grotte at Arcy can be accessed (wrap up warm!).

Abbaye de Fontenay ✱✱

The abbey of Fontenay at Montbard, approx. 20km/12mi north of Semur, was founded in 1118 by Bernard of Clairvaux – hidden away at the end of a wooded valley, as Cistercian custom preferred (photo p.311). Built from 1139 to 1147, it is one of the most important witnesses to the early architecture of the order (UNESCO World Heritage Site), conveying a picture of how the **Cistercians** lived in the 12th century. Church, dormitory, transept, chapter house, parlatorium and scriptorium, as well as smithy and jail – the monastery had judicial power – all still exist today. Open to visitors daily from 10am to 5pm or 7pm (Nov–March closed noon–2pm).

Châtillon-sur-Seine

✱ ✱

◀ Trésor de Vix

The main attraction of this pretty old town (6200 inhabitants), 33km/20mi northeast of Montbard, is the archaeological museum in the Maison Philandrier, a resplendent Renaissance structure (open daily in July–Aug, otherwise closed Tue). The **Vix treasure** refers to valuable finds from the burial site of a Celtic princess who died in the 6th century BC. Her grave was found in 1953 at Vix, 6km/3.5mi north of Châtillon. Pride of place goes to a bronze krater from Magna Graecia (southern Italy). With a height of 1.64m/ 8ft 6in and a weight of 208kg/458lb it is the largest vessel to have survived from antiquity (6th century BC). A walk up to the summit leads to castle ruins and the church of St-Vorles. The latter was largely built in the 10th century, and contains a beautiful tomb (1527).

Ancy-le-Franc ✱

One of the most important **Renaissance chateaux** in France is at Ancy-le-Franc, 27km/17mi northwest of Montbard, completed in 1622 and probably based on plans by Sebastiano Serlio from Bologna, who worked on Fontainebleau in 1540 by invitation of King François I. Its design is rich in Italian Renaissance detail (Primaticcio, Niccolò

Renaissance chateau at Tanlay

dell'Abbate, School of Fontaine-bleau). Old cars and coaches are displayed in the farm buildings.

In **Tanlay**, a few miles down the Canal de Bourgogne from Arma-nçon, boasts a magnificent Ren-aissance chateau. The ceiling fres-co in the dome of the Tour de Ligue – probably painted by ar-tists of the Fontainebleau school in 1569 – reflects the spirit of the age by depicting the parties of the Wars of Religion as Olympic gods and goddesses.

✱
Tonnerre

The commercial town of Tonnerre (6000 inhabitants) stands 10km/ 6mi west of Tanlay. Here, in 1293, Marguerite de Bourgogne founded the Hôpital Notre-Dame des Fontenilles, the model on which the Hôtel-Dieu in Beaune would be constructed (June–Sept, closed Mon, otherwise only open at weekends for guided tours). The 91m/ 100yd-long ward with wooden barrel vaults contains important works of art, including a tomb of 1454 and an exhibition. The neigh-bouring Hôtel d'Uzès (16th century) and the Fosse Dionne, below the church of St-Pierre, are also worth seeing. The source was once dedicated to the Celtic fertility goddess Divona, later serving as a washing place. The pretty washhouse dates back to 1758.

Chablis

The small wine village (2400 inhabitants) with a famous name lies 15km/9mi west of Tonnerre on the Serein. To the north of the river lie the seven **Grand Cru terroirs**, the viticulture sites of the Chardon-nay grape from which Chablis is pressed: Blanchots, Les Clos, Val-mur, Grenouilles, Vaudésir, Preuses, Bougrot. The Premier Cru ter-roirs cover some 750ha/1850 acres on both sides of the river. Great wine festivals take place at the beginning of February (St-Vincent), on the first weekend in May (Pastorales) and on the fourth weekend in November (Fête des Vins).

Auxerre

Auxerre, a lively commercial town and département capital (38,000 inhabitants), stands on two hills roughly 150km/95mi northwest of Dijon, on the left bank of the Yonne. A circular boulevard surrounds the medieval town; a fine view of the churches of St-Germain, St-Eti-enne and St-Pierre may be enjoyed from the Paul Bert bridge. The
✱
St-Etienne ►
most noteworthy features of the Gothic cathedral of St-Etienne (11th–16th century, southern tower unfinished) are the sculptures adorning the west façade and the choir (1234) with outstanding stained glass windows. The crypt below dates back to the 11th-cen-tury Romanesque predecessor, with frescoes equally old. North of the cathedral stands the church of **St-Germain**, the remains of an ab-bey founded in the 6th century. Of paramount interest in this Ro-

manesque and Gothic church (12th–15th century) are the crypts, built in the 9th century around the grave of Saint Germain from Auxerre (378–448) and decorated with frescoes. They belong to the archaeological museum of St-Germain in the monastic buildings. On the town hall square stands the 15th-century Tour de l'Horloge, although the town hall itself dates from 1733 and the timber-frame houses from the 16th century. Further west stand the oldest existing civic building in stone (Hôtel du Cerf-Volant, 14th–15th centuries) and the Musée Leblanc-Duvernoy, an 18th-century town house (Rue d'Eglény) with furnishings, faiences, tapestries from Beauvais and an art collection (17th–20th century). The church of St-Eusèbe has an octagonal Romanesque stone spire (15th century).

Auxerre on the Yonne

In Pontigny (800 inhabitants) 20km/12mi northeast of Auxerre the abbey church, built around 1150 and 108m/118yd in length, is the largest remaining Cistercian church in France following the destruction of Cîteaux and Clairvaux. The choir stalls and organ date from the 17th century.

★
Pontigny

Sens (28,000 inhabitants), in the northwest corner of Burgundy, 57km/35mi north of Auxerre, was an important spiritual centre in the Middle Ages, hosting councils, the trial and condemnation of Abelard in 1140 and the marriage of Louis IX, also known as Saint Louis, in 1234. **St-Etienne Cathedral** (1140–80, transept 1516), one of the oldest and finest Gothic buildings, serves as a reminder. The decoration of the west doors (12th century) was largely destroyed in the French Revolution, but the statue of Saint Etienne on the central column is amongst the objects that survive. The treasures inside the cathedral include the windows of the choir (12th–13th century) and the nave (16th century), the choir grille (1762), the high altar by G.N. Servandoni (18th century) and the tomb of the Dauphin Louis, son of Louis XV and father of Louis XVI. (G. Coustou, 1777). Adjacent to the cathedral is the 13th-century archbishop's palace with a municipal museum; as well as archaeological exhibits, the valuable cathedral treasure is housed here. The cathedral square is dotted with cafés and also home to the 19th-century market hall; the old quarter

Sens

★
◄ St-Etienne

★
◄ Cathedral treasury

features 16th-century houses, the most attractive of which is the Maison d'Abraham with a Tree of Jesse on a corner pier.

The South: From Dijon to Mâcon

** Côte d'Or The heart of Burgundian viniculture is the Côte d'Or, the narrow western strip of the Saône valley, beginning south of Dijon and ending 60km/35mi to the southwest at Santenay. The northern part is called the **Côte de Nuits**, the southern part the **Côte de Beaune**. Charming villages lie here, with names inspiring the greatest respect in the world of wine, such as Gevrey-Chambertin, Chambolle-Musigny, Vougeot, Nuits-St-Georges, Aloxe-Corton, Volnay, Meursault and Puligny-Montrachet. The gentle landscape at the meeting point of the Hautes-Côtes and Saône valley is as pretty as a picture. The »Route des Grands Crus« leads through the Côte de Nuits (D 122 to-Vougeot); signposts indicate the whereabouts of so-called combes, small, picturesque gorges, e.g. from Gevrey-Chambertin to Combe Lavaux.

The chateau in **Clos de Vougeot**, one of the most famous vineyards in Burgundy, is seat of the Confrérie des Chevaliers du Tastevin (daily guided tours); part of the Trois Glorieuses takes place here in November (see below, Beaune). Meursault, in the Côte de Beaune and famed for its excellent white wine, also takes part in the Trois Glorieuses with the »Paulee« (wine-growers' banquet).

A popular place to visit is the castle of **La Rochepot** on a rocky peak northwest of Chassagne-Montrachet, reconstructed at the end of the 19th century on the basis of earlier plans.

Abbaye de Cîteaux 11km/7mi east of Nuits-St-Georges, Saint Robert of Molesme founded the **original monastery of the Cistercian Order** in 1098. Only fragments remain to recall the former importance of the abbey, including a 12th-century chapel, a 15th-century library and arcades of the Gothic cloister. The abbey has been in use again since 1898.

 VISITING CÔTE D'OR

WHERE TO EAT

► **Inexpensive / moderate**
Chez Guy
3 Place de la Mairie
F-21220 Gevrey-Chambertin
Tel. 03 80 58 51 51, closed Wed and in Feb. Fine Burgundian cuisine in surprising combinations, a good selection of wines from the region at attractive prices. Cosy atmosphere.

WHERE TO STAY

► **Luxury**
Château Ziltener
F-21220 Chambolle-Musigny
Tel. 03 80 62 41 62, www.chateau-ziltener.com, closed Dec–Feb.
One of the finest manor houses in Burgundy (17th century) with luxuriously appointed, spacious chambers, antique furniture and marble bathrooms.

Aloxe-Corton on the Côte d'Or produces renowned red wines

Beaune (23,000 inhabitants), 38km/24mi south of Dijon, is one of the finest destinations in Burgundy, thanks to its quaint townscape, medieval buildings and, last but not least, omnipresent wine. From the 14th century it was, like Dijon, a seat of the dukes. The main attraction is the **Hôtel-Dieu** (open daily from end of March to mid-Nov. 9am–6.30pm, otherwise 9am–11.30am, 2pm–5.30pm), a hospice built in Burgundian-Flemish style from 1443 to 1451 to plans by Jacques Wiscrère. It was commissioned by Nicolas Rolin, advisor to Duke John the Fearless and chancellor to King Philippe III, and his wife, Guigone de Salins. The simple outer façade does not hint at the splendour within. High roofs with colourfully glazed tiles and timber galleries surround a beautiful courtyard. The 50m/164ft-long ward features a painted and carved pointed barrel vault and was in use until 1971. Chapel, washroom, kitchen and pharmacy can all still be seen. In the museum stands the famous altar polyptych by Roger van der Weyden (1443) of the *Last Judgement*. A festival of Baroque music is held in July in the hospital and in Notre-Dame.

The hospital is on the Place de la Halle with the tourist office and many shops guaranteed to whet the appetite; in the impressive market hall, during the **Trois Glorieuses** (3rd weekend in November), an auction of wine from the hospice takes place. Somewhat further north, a residence of the dukes houses the Musée du Vin de Bourgogne. A few paces further is the church of Notre-Dame (12th–14th century); the most important decorative items are the tapestry in the choir (1474–1500) and a 12th-century Madonna with Child. The

Beaune

◀ Hôtel-Dieu

◀ Old town

The splendid roof of the Hospice de Beaune with colourfully glazed tiles

adjacent **Place Monge** marks the centre of the old town, site of the beffroi (belfry or tower), the remains of an abbey church from the 14th century. Wonderful old houses line Rue de Lorraine, leading to the town hall, formerly an Ursuline convent (17th century); a museum here presents a son of Beaune, the scientist E. J. Marey (1830–1904) who invented chronophotography, a forerunner of cinema. The Porte Marie de Bourgogne in the south houses the Musée des Beaux-Arts (primarily Flemish and French painting of the 17th–19th centuries). 6km/3.5mi south of Beaune on the A6, the **Archéodrome** illustrates human development up to the end of the Roman era.

! *Baedeker* TIP

Vin de Bourgogne

Important ports of call for wine enthusiasts are the Office de Tourisme and the Bureau Interprofessionel des Vins de Bourgogne (BIVB, 12 Blvd. Bretonnière, tel. 03 80 25 04 80, www.bivb.com) in Beaune. In addition to all kinds of information on vineyards, opening hours and addresses, much more is on offer, such as tastings and seminars, excursions with bus or bicycle. Relevant literature may be browsed in the Beaune Athenaeum (5 Rue de l'Hôtel-Dieu).

Chalon-sur-Saône Chalon-sur-Saône (52,000 inhabitants), an industrial town 28km/17mi south of Beaune, at the confluence of the Canal du Centre and the Saône, was an important trading post in the Middle Ages. On the town hall square, the church of St-Pierre, one of the few Baroque churches in Burgundy (17th century), stands alongside the river along with the Musée Denon and its laudable archaeological collection. On the banks of the Saône, the town dedicated a museum to its most famous son, **Nicéphore Niepce** (1765–1833); in 1827 he was the first to create a durable photograph. The old town reaches north from here, with the former cathedral of St-Vincent (13th–15th century) at its northeastern perimeter. Burgundian wines can be sampled and purchased in the Maison des Vins in the Parc G. Nouelle. The remains of a 16th-century municipal hospital and the Tour du Doyenné (15th century) can be seen on the island of St-Lauren. 4km/2.5mi east, the rose garden (Roseraie St-Nicolas) is an ideal spot to take a break.

The attractive little town of Tournus (6200 inhabitants) lies 25km/16mi south of Chalon, on the right bank of the Saône. Its former abbey church of St-Philibert is one of the most important Romanesque buildings in France. Monks from the Atlantic island of Noirmoutier founded a monastery here in 875. The church as it stands today incorporates a narthex dated around the year 1000 to the west, an 11th-century nave and a choir and crossing completed in 1120. The space **is unusual in structural terms** – massive brick columns bear transverse barrel vaults over lateral arches – and is best viewed from the St-Michel Chapel in the upper level of the narthex. Two relief panels in the Arch of Gerlanus facing the nave are amongst the oldest examples of Romanesque sculpture in France. In the choir stands Saint Philibert's reliquary shrine and in the south aisle a 12th-century cedar wood Madonna with Child. Only fragments remain of the other monastery buildings. Both the Musée Perrin-de-Puycousin (folklore, 3 Rue du Collège) and the Musée Greuze in the 18th-century Hôtel-Dieu are worth visiting.

Tournus

✶ ✶

◀ St-Philibert

Southwest of Tournus extends the hilly landscape of the Mâconnais, with vineyards, small villages and Romanesque churches. A picturesque drive along the D 14 and D 981 to Cluny passes through medieval Brancion, with castle ruins and the Romanesque church of St-Pierre, and Chapaize with the church of St-Martin, built in the early 11th century, one of the finest early Romanesque structures in Burgundy. If the exterior is relatively plain, then the interior of the Baroque chateau built from 1605 to 1616 in Cormatin is all the more splendid. 4km/2.5mi south lies Taizé, where the **ecumenical community** founded in 1940 attracts people from all over the world (www.taize.fr).

Mâconnais

Brancion
Chapaize

✶
Cormatin
Taizé

Cluny (4800 inhabitants) was the medieval centre of a monastic institution with over 2000 monasteries across western Europe. The monastery was dissolved in the 1789 Revolution and sold to a demolition company which destroyed most of it by 1823. Cluniacum had been founded in 910 by Duke William the Pious to revive the crisis-ridden monastic world. The rapid rise of the abbey led to the first church (Cluny I) being replaced in 981 by a second (Cluny II). The

✶
Cluny

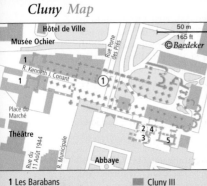

Cluny Map

Hôtel de Ville
Musée Ochier
Rue Porte des Prés
©Baedeker
R. Kenneth J. Conant
Place du Marché
Théâtre
Rue du 11 Août 1944
R. Municipale
Abbaye

1 Les Barabans
2 Clocher de l'Eau-Bénite
3 Chapelle St-Etienne
4 Chapelle St-Martial
5 Chapelle Bourbon

Cluny III
present plan

Where to stay
① Hotel Bourgogne

foundation stone for the gigantic church of St-Pierre-et-St-Paul (Cluny III) was laid in 1088, the final consecration taking place in 1130. It remained the **largest church in Christendom** (187.3m/205yd long) until the building of Saint Peter's Basilica in Rome. Little now remains of the original: part of the main gate of the abbey, the foundations of the porch, pieces of the 14th-century west towers and the vaulted southern arms of both transepts. A small clock tower forms the southwest corner, and on the transept an octagonal tower stands 62m/203ft high.

In the **Musée Ochier**, housed in a late 15th-century palais, artefacts from the abbey are on display.

Some of the church's capitals, made between 1088 and 1130, as well as models of the monastery complex, have been collected as exhibits in the granary (13th century) at the southern edge of the abbey garden. In the 19th century, the **National Stud** was established here.

▶ VISITING CLUNY

WHERE TO EAT
► **Moderate**
Moulin du Gastronome
540 Route de Cluny
F-71850 Charnay-lès-Mâcon (2.5km/1.5mi west of Mâcon), www.moulin-dugastronome.com, tel. 03 85 34 16 68. Regional delicacies, imaginatively prepared. 8 rooms (lower to medium category).

WHERE TO STAY
► **Mid-range**
Bourgogne
Place Abbaye, F-71250 Cluny
Tel. 03 85 59 00 58, www.hotel-cluny.com. Attractive house built from 1817 with Empire furniture, garden and courtyard. Restaurant with Burgundian specialities (closed Tue–Wed).

In Berzé-la-Ville 12km/7.5mi southeast of Cluny, the Cluniacs maintained a priory from the end of the 11th century. The chapel (open April–Oct 9am/10am–noon, 2pm–5.30/6pm) contains marvellous **Romanesque frescoes** dating from the mid-12th century; in the centre, almost 4m/13ft high, is a Christ in the Mandorla, flanked by the apostles. Close by in Berzé-le-Châtel, an imposing castle from the 10th to 12th centuries stands guard over the road to Cluny.

✶ ✶
Berzé-la-Ville

Berzé-le-Châtel

Mâcon (34,500 inhabitants) on the right bank of the Saône is a famous name in the wine trade. A lovely view of the town can be enjoyed from the St-Laurent bridge. The cathedral of St-Vincent (13th century) was torn down in 1799; the remainder is used as a lapidarium. The Musée des Ursulines documents the history of the town and surrounding area. In the Hôtel-Dieu (1770) in the northern part of the old town an old pharmacy can be seen. The poet Alphonse Lamartine, born in Mâcon in 1790, is remembered in a museum in the Hôtel Sénecé. On the Place aux Herbes towards Saône, a grotesquely decorated wooden Renaissance house (from around 1500) is difficult to miss. The recommendable **Lamartine tour** takes in places to the west of Mâcon (further information at the tourist office).

Mâcon

12km/7.5mi southwest of Mâcon, the famous rock of Solutré and its Vergisson »twin« rise above the vineyards of Pouilly-Fuissé, where coveted Chardonnays are produced. At the foot of the Solutré rock, which is named after an era of the Stone Age (Solutréen), a 2m/6ft layer of bones of horses and other animals some 25,000 years old was discovered. A museum explores the finds in detail. It is well worth climbing the rock to enjoy the magnificent **view** across the Saône valley as far as the Alps.

✶
Roche de Solutré

The Bresse region between the Saône and French Jura (► Franche-Comté) owes its reputation to famous agricultural produce, namely poultry with Appelation d'Origine Contrôlée (AC) and blue-mould cheese. Timber-frame farmhouses with »Saracen« chimneys are characteristic of the area. Bourg (43,000 inhabitants), the old capital of the county and département of Ain (Région Rhone–Alpes), 35km/22mi east of Mâcon, is famous for the **monastery of Brou**, a late Gothic jewel in the southeastern suburb of the same name (open daily). The abbey church commissioned by Margaret of Austria (daughter of Maximilian I) and designed by Louis van Bodeghem from Brussels, was constructed from 1513 to 1532. The ornate portal is outstanding, as are the rood screen, beautiful windows and magnificent choir stalls in oak (1530–32). The most notable sights are the tombs of Margaret of Austria († 1530), her husband Philibert the Handsome († 1504) and his mother Marguerite of Bourbon († 1483). In the monastery buildings (from 1506) there are French, Flemish and Italian paintings of the 16th–20th centuries, sculpture of the 15th–17th centuries and old furniture from the region.

Bresse

Bourg-en-Bresse
✶ ✶
Monastère Royal de Brou

The West: From Dijon through the Morvan

Châteauneuf-en-Auxois

This pretty little spot (60 inhabitants) 35km/22mi northwest of Beaune is dominated by a castle whose origins date back to the 12th century. It was expanded by Philippe Pot from 1457, who also owned La Rochepot (►Côte d'Or, p.316).

✳ Saulieu

Situated 65km/40mi northwest of Beaune on the northeastern border of the Morvan and numbering 2800 inhabitants, Saulieu is renowned for the 52 **Romanesque carved capitals** in the church of St-Andoche (1130), which are thematically and stylistically related to those of the cathedral in Autun. Saulieu is also the birthplace of the famous French animal sculptor François Pompon (1855–1933). A room is dedicated to him in the local museum, which has Gallo-Roman artefacts and religious sculptures on display.

✳ Morvan

The Morvan (»black mountain« in Celtic), is an extension of the Massif Central lying in the middle of the region to the west of Autun. Thick forests and enchanting lakes, such as the Lac des Settons, a network of bridle paths and hiking trails, along with an array of sporting opportunities, make this a popular holiday destination. In the north it reaches a mere 600m/2000ft, whilst the south is mountainous in character, the highest peaks being the Haut-Folin (901m/2956ft) and Mont Prénelay (855m/2805ft). From the year 2 BC, on

Mont Beuvray

the 821m/2693ft Mont Beuvray, stood a Gaulish oppidum named **Bibracte**, capital of the Aedui; it was here that Vercingetorix assumed high command of the Gaulish troops in the battle against the Romans in 52 BC. In spite of his defeat at Alesia (►p.312), the French celebrate this year as the birth of the »Gallic people«. The Morvan provided wood for the city of Paris for centuries, for which purpose the 174km/108mi Canal du Nivernais with 110 locks and three tun-

Château-Chinon

nels was built in 1842. The main town of the Morvan is Château-Chinon (3000 inhabitants). The Musée du Septennat exhibits gifts which François Mitterrand received as president, and the Musée du Costume shows French clothing from the 18th to the 20th century.

Sully

Madame de Sévigné christened the castle 15km/9mi northeast of Autun the »Fontainebleau of Burgundy«. In 1808 Mac-Mahon, later marshal and president of France, 1873–79, was born here.

Autun

Autun (16,500 inhabitants, 48km/30mi west of Beaune), the »southern gateway to the Morvan«, was founded in the 10 BC by the Romans as Augustodunum and developed into the »Rome of Gaul«. Two town gates are all that remain from this time (Porte St-André, Porte d'Arroux), along with fragments of the largest Roman theatre in Gaul and the ruins of the Temple of Janus. The town experienced a second boom during the Middle Ages through a pilgrimage to the shrine of Saint Lazarus. The most important edifice is, thus, the **ca-**

thedral of **St-Lazare**, built from 1120 in the Cluniac Romanesque style. The renowned figures which adorn the church are masterpieces of Romanesque sculpture, thought to have been fashioned around 1135 by Master Gislebertus. Inside, it is worth admiring the 101 capitals. Some have been replaced by replicas; the originals are in the chapter house. The neighbouring Musée Rolin (in two 15th-century palais) houses further works from the cathedral, including the *Temptation of Eve*, as well as Gallo-Roman exhibits and a valuable medieval collection.

✶ ✶
◄ St-Lazare

Musée Rolin

Le Creusot (28km/17mi south of Autun, 26,700 inhabitants) and its neighbour Montceau-les-Mines (21,200 inhabitants) are at the heart of an important industrial region. The iron that has been extracted here since the Middle Ages, together with the coal deposits discovered in the 17th century, forms the basis of the metal industry. History is brought to life in the Ecomusée de l'Homme et de l'Industrie, housed in the Château de la Verrerie, a glassworks founded in 1787 (open daily). At the southern edge of town stands the defining landmark, a **100-ton steam hammer** built in 1876.

Le Creusot

Paray-le-Monial (9200 inhabitants), some 70km/45mi northwest of Mâcon, is a magnet for art aficionados and pilgrims. In 973 a Benedictine monastery was founded here, subordinated to the abbey of Cluny in the year 999. The abbey church of Notre-Dame (now Sacré-Cœur) with a mighty crossing tower was built in the 12th century as a smaller version of the Cluny III mother abbey and is one of the most important Romanesque churches in Burgundy. The eastern section, both inside and outside, is particularly beautiful. To the right of the façade, the classical buildings of the monastery adjoin. In the neo-Romanesque Chapelle de la Visitation lie the remains of the nun M.-M. Alacoque (1647–90 canonized in 1920); her revelations led to the cult of the Sacred Heart, which spread through France after the lost war of 1870–71. It is worth taking a look at the Renaissance town hall (1525) with its splendid façade and the Tour St-Nicolas, a bell tower of a ruined church. The Musée du Hiéron (north of the Chapelle de la Visitation) presents

✶
Paray-le-Monial

The choir pyramid of Notre-Dame in Paray

Charolais cattle on idyllic pastures close to Semur-en-Brionnais

religious art and Italian, French and Flemish paintings from the 16th to 18th centuries.

Digoin Digoin, 10km/6mi west of Paray at the confluence of several rivers and canals, was once an important point for the transportation of coal, wood and wine. Today, holiday houseboats moor here. The 243m/266yd **canal bridge** across the Loire (1834) is a lovely sight to behold.

Brionnais Paray is a fine place to start a tour of the hills of the Brionnais, famous for the white **Charolais cattle** that graze there. In St-Christophe-en-Brionnais a cattle market is held early on Thursday mornings in October and November. The 11th century priory church in Anzy-

✳
Anzy-le-Duc le-Duc is a key work of Burgundian Romanesque. Its capitals display the oldest cycle of sculpted figures in Burgundy. Further highlights are the Romanesque church of St-Hilaire in Semur-en-Brionnais, the centre of the Brionnais, and the remains of the abbey of St-Fortunat in Charlieu. The surviving **portal sculptures** of the Benedictine ab-

✳
Charlieu bey founded in 872 are among the most important testimonies to Burgundian Romanesque art. Automobile enthusiasts would do well to visit the museum at the 1380 moated castle of La Clayette, 7km/4.5mi southwest of Bois-Ste-Marie. In Charolles (19km/12mi north

Charolles of La Clayette), everything revolves around the breeding of Charolais cattle, from the weekly market to the festival held on the first weekend in December; the Institut Charolais on the N 79 explains all there is to know about the breed. A museum in the 15th-century Prieuré displays ceramics from the region from 1836 up to the present day, along with works by local painters.

✳ Caen

G 3

Région: Basse-Normandie   **Altitude:** 2m/6ft
Département: Calvados   **Population:** 117,000

Caen, close to the Normandy coast, was largely destroyed by the Allied landings in 1944 and is now a lively, modern town. Impressive reminders of the medieval seat of William the Conqueror have been preserved.

Caen (pronounced »kã«), 16km/10mi from the English Channel on the Orne, is the capital of Basse ►Normandie and the département of Calvados. In the 12th century, the town was the residence of **William the Conqueror** (1027–1087), Duke of Normandy and subsequent King of England, and his wife Matilda of Flanders. The ruling couple founded two monasteries, now amongst the most important Romanesque structures in Normandy, to procure dispensation from the pope for their marriage, as they were cousins. In June and July 1944, 80% of the town was destroyed during the Allied landings and the weeks of fighting that ensued on the Calvados coast; part of the old quarter was painstakingly rebuilt. The harbour, connected to the sea by the Orne and the Canal de Caen, has an important economic

History

▶ VISITING CAEN

INFORMATION

Office de Tourisme
Place St-Pierre, F-14000 Caen
Tel. 02 31 27 14 14
fax 02 31 27 14 18
www.caen.fr

SHIPPING LINES

Boats to Ouistreham from the Quai Vendeuvre (July–Aug several times a day, otherwise Sun only). Ferry to Portsmouth from Ouistreham.

WHERE TO EAT

► Moderate / expensive
Le Pressoir
3 Av. H. Chéron, tel. 02 31 73 32 71
Closed Sat lunch, Sun evening and Mon. Modern style within old walls, excellent »cuisine du marché« with a regional touch, at fair prices.

► Inexpensive / moderate
② *Le Carlotta*
16 Quai Vendeuvre
Tel. 02 31 86 68 99, closed Sun.
A typical »Parisian« brasserie of the belle époque with marvellous meat and fish dishes, and tripes of course, at reasonable prices.

WHERE TO STAY

► Budget
① *Hotel des Cordeliers*
4 Rue des Cordeliers
Tel. 02 31 86 37 15
Fax 02 31 39 56 51
18th-century house in a quiet location, very pleasant, simply designed rooms overlooking the inner garden or pedestrian zone. No restaurant, but a cellar bar.

role, as do heavy industry, electronics, chemicals, mechanical engineering and automobile manufacture. The lively cultural scene is boosted by some 25,000 students.

What to See in Caen

Chateau

Duke William had a castle built around 1060 on the river bank in the centre of the town. The foundation walls of the keep date back to the 12th century, the Salle de l'Echiquier (treasurer's chamber) is a remnant of the 14th-century ducal palace; the Chapelle St-Georges (12th–15th century) was rebuilt. Two museums (both closed Tuesdays) are worth visiting: the **Musée des Beaux-Arts** with international works from the 16th century onwards (including pieces by van der Weyden, Perugino, Dürer, Ruysdael, Tintoretto, Rubens, Courbet, Boudin, Monet and Dubuffet) and faiences from Rouen, Nevers and Strasbourg. The **Musée de Normandie** in the former governor's lodge (17th–18th century) relates the history of the town and region.

✶ ✶
Musée des Beaux-Arts

✶
Musée de Normandie

✶
St-Pierre

The centre of the town is Place St-Pierre, marked by the reconstructed 78m/255ft tower of the church of St-Pierre (13th–16th century), on which many Breton and Norman spires and towers were modelled. Opposite, on the west side, the Hôtel d'Escoville, a beautiful Renaissance house from 1538, is now a tourist office. Just a few steps away, the Maison des Quatrans (around 1400) has an impressive timber-frame façade.

Caen Map

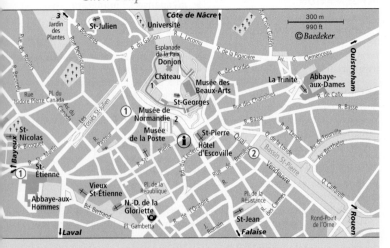

	Where to eat	Where to stay
1 Salle de l'Échiquier	① Le Pressoir	① Hotel des Cordeliers
2 Maison des Quatrans	② Le Carlotta	
3 Le Memorial		

The Abbaye aux Hommes is the striking centrepiece of Caen

Old town
The tiny district to the northeast of St-Pierre, with houses from the 16th–18th centuries, draws many visitors. The St-Sauveur district also survived the Second World War reasonably intact. On Rue St-Pierre there are two fine timber-frame houses at no. 52, the Musée de la Poste et des Techniques de Communication, and no. 54.

Abbaye aux Hommes
The magnificent Norman Romanesque »Men's Abbey«, dwarfed by the 82m/269ft and 80m/262ft towers of the church of St-Etienne, was established between 1066 and 1077. The plans were probably the work of the first abbot, Lanfranc, later archbishop of Canterbury. The spires and the Gothic choir with four towers were added in the 13th century. The impressive interior is 115m/125yd long and 24m/79ft high. A stone in front of the high altar marks the spot where the grave of William the Conqueror lay († 1087) before it was destroyed by Calvinists in 1562. During the 1944 bombings the abbey served as a refuge for thousands of townsfolk. On the south side of the church, the adjoining buildings were added in 1704. The town hall and Musée d'Initiation à la Nature are housed here today, the latter a nature museum aimed specifically at children.

> ✔ **DON'T MISS**
>
> - »Tripes à la mode de Caen« is famous among gourmets. Sceptics should overcome their inhibitions to try tripe in the traditional manner with cidre, Calvados, vegetables and a bouquet garni, stewed in the oven for at least eight hours.

St-Nicolas	Northwest of St-Etienne, close by, the former church of St-Nicolas (1083–93) stands in an atmospheric graveyard; the Romanesque porch and choir apse merit a look.
✳ Abbaye aux Dames	The counterpart to the men's abbey is the women's abbey, east of the centre, founded by Matilda of Flanders in 1062. Its Romanesque church of La Trinité, 50m/164ft long and 9m/30ft wide, is modest in comparison to St-Etienne. Inside is the queen's tomb and an impressive crypt. Since 1823, the 18th-century abbey buildings have been used as a hospital. The pretty Parc d'Ornano is adjacent.
✳ Mémorial	Hardly any other region in France was so deeply scarred as Normandy by the horrors of the Second World War. The Mémorial, a modern **peace museum** northwest of the town centre (www.memorial.fr), documents not only the Allied landings, but also draws attention to the threat facing peace and to the work of the UN. It also organizes bus trips to D-Day sites such as **Omaha Beach**.

✳ ✳ Camargue

M 9

The Camargue is a rare landscape indeed: the Rhône delta with its saline swamps and sandy beaches is as flat as a pancake. The famed semi-wild horses and bulls and mounted herdsmen have almost been consigned to the past, however.

Ever changing landscape

The Camargue – named after the Roman Senator Camar from Arles – comprises the roughly 750 sq km/290 sq mi of the Grande Camargue between Grand Rhône and Petit Rhône, the river dividing at ▶Arles, and the approximately 200 sq km/77 sq mi Petite Camargue belonging to Languedoc, west of the Petit Rhône. Between the Grand Rhône and the Etang de Berre lies the Crau, a plateau of glacial brash from the Durance (▶Arles). For centuries, the Rhône has been washing up scree and earth, edging the land ever further into the sea; Aigues-Mortes, founded as a port, is now 6km/3.5mi from the sea. Other sections of the coast are breaking up: Stes-Maries-de-la-Mer was well inland in medieval times and now stands directly on the coast. The part of the Etang de Vaccarès lagoon close to the sea consists primarily of arid salt flats and dunes, where umbrella pines, juniper bushes and tamarisk grow. Flat lakes and reed-covered swamps in between are the habitat of a wide variety of waterfowl, especially the thousands of flamingos.

The idea of an »untouched natural landscape« is over-optimistic. Since the Middle Ages, the Camargue, above all in the north, has been used for agriculture, nowadays aided by vast irrigation systems. Arabs most likely introduced rice cultivation from Spain, intensified since 1980 to peg back salination. Apart from the traditional horse

Great flocks of flamingos and thatched farmhouses are characteristic of the Camargue

and cattle breeding and viniculture (»vin de sable«), tourism is the most important source of income – the black bulls and white horses of the Camargue are nothing more than peacefully grazing stage sets or reserved for tourists (»promenades à cheval«).

A Tour through the Camargue

St-Gilles (11,000 inhabitants), a centre of fruit-growing and viniculture 16km/10mi west of ► Arles on the edge of the Camargue, has the fine church of **St-Gilles** (late 11th century, destroyed in 1562 and renewed in the 17th century, albeit half the size of the original), with a façade featuring three portals of around 1150, one of the major works of Romanesque sculpture in Provence. Note in the tympana (from left to right) the Three Magi, Christ in the Mandorla, the Crucifixion (vividly realistic); the friezes below depict the Passion; in the portal area the apostles; right at the bottom, at the sides of the main entrance are Cain and Abel to the left, a centaur spanning his bow and Balaam with his donkey. The crypt with the 11th-century tomb of St-Gilles (Aegidius) was an important pilgrimage site in medieval times, and a point on the journey along the Way of St James. In the ruins of the choir stands the »Vis de St-Gilles«, a stone spiral staircase (1142) crafted from complex elements hewn with unbelievable precision. The Maison Romane, where Pope Clemens IV (1265–68) was born, houses a small museum of local history.

Saint-Gilles

✴

 St-Gilles

Aigues-Mortes (5000 inhabitants) owes its »town of dead waters« moniker to the swamps which surround it on the western edge of

Aigues-Mortes

Bull run in front of the medieval walls of Aigues-Mortes

the Camargue; two canals now connect it to the sea, 6km/3.5mi away. Its foundation can be traced back to Louis IX, who started out on the First Crusade from here in 1248. Up to the end of the 13th century he and his son Philip the Bold developed the town's defences – it was the kingdom's only harbour on the Mediterranean – with a vast ring of ramparts and towers (accessible). The imposing, 37m/121ft-high **Tour de Constance** at the northern corner served for several centuries as a jail for Templars, Huguenots and other political opponents. At the centre, the shaded Place St-Louis is home to a plain Gothic church, Notre-Dame-des-Sablons, with modern windows by C. Viallat.

✳
Ramparts ▶

Le Grau-du-Roi

Port-Camargue

La Grande-Motte

8km/5mi southwest of Aigues-Mortes lies Le Grau-du-Roi, a former fishing village turned holiday destination, welcoming over 200,000 visitors per year. Adjoining to the south is the gigantic marina of Port-Camargue, developed from 1969. Northwest of Le Grau-du-Roi lies **La Grande-Motte**, where pyramid-style apartment blocks mark the era of tourism which began in 1974. A total of 18km/11mi of sandy beaches are equipped with all the usual facilities.

Pont de Gau

Musée des
Roulottes

From Aigues-Mortes take the D 58 heading east to reach the 14th-century Tour Carbonniere and its panoramic view after 3km/2mi. The D 570 leads to Pont de Gau with an information centre for the **Camargue nature reserve** (www.parc-camargue.fr) and bird sanctuary. At Pioch Badet, 8km/5mi north of Stes-Maries, the Musée Tsigane reveals the history of the Sinti and Roma gypsies.

▶ VISITING CAMARGUE

INFORMATION

CDT Bouches-du-Rhône
13 Rue Roux des Brignoles
F-13006 Marseille
Tel. 04 91 13 84 13
www.visitprovence.com

Office de Tourisme
Boulevard des Lices
F-13200 Arles
Tel. 04 90 18 41 20, fax 04 90 18 41 29
www.ville-arles.fr

TIPS

The main attractions in summer are
Stes-Maries, Aigues-Mortes and the
heavily populated beaches. Some
parts of the landscape are nature
reserves, protected from tourists by
fences. Those visiting in summer
should be on their guard against
mosquitoes and car break-ins.

FESTIVALS AND EVENTS

Aigues-Mortes: around 20 Aug, Fête
St-Louis (medieval fair); 1st half of
Oct: Fête Votive (many spectacles
with bulls and horses: Abrivados,
Courses de Taureau, Vachettes, Ban-
didos). Stes-Maries: Easter–Oct bull-
fights; 24th/25th May and around 20
Oct: Sinti gypsy pilgrimage; end of
July: Festo Vierginienco; 11 Nov:
Festival d'Abrivado.

WHERE TO EAT

▶ Moderate
Salicorne
9 Rue Alsace-Lorraine
F-30220 Aigues-Mortes
Tel. 04 66 53 62 67
Behind Notre-Dame-des-Sablons
church. Rustic design with stone,
beams and wrought iron. Good
southern cuisine, attractive terrace.

WHERE TO STAY

▶ Budget / mid-range
St-Louis
10 Rue Amiral Courbet
F-30220 Aigues-Mortes
Tel. 04 66 53 72 68
www.lesaintlouis.fr
Attractive 18th-century house be-
tween the Tour de Constance and
Place St-Louis (open April–Oct).
Shady terrace. Restaurant serves
Provençal specialities.

Mirage
14 Rue C. Pelletan
F-13460 Stes-Maries-de-la-Mer
Tel. 04 90 97 80 43
www.lemirage.camargue.fr
Comfortable, friendly house in a
former cinema with pretty salon.
Garden terrace, ideal for picnics.
200m/200yd to the beach.

The most popular destination in the Camargue is Saintes-Maries-de-
la-Mer (2400 inhabitants). The name is derived from the legend in
which the three Marys (Marie Jacobe, sister of the Virgin Mary; Mar-
ie-Salome, mother of John the Apostle; and Mary Magdalene, the
penitent) came ashore here from Palestine, in AD 40. They were accompanied by Maximin and Sidonius (►Aix-en-Provence, St-Maximin) and the black servant Sara-la-Kali, who became patron saint of
the Sinti. The fortress-like church at the heart of the patently com-

★
Stes-Maries-
de-la-Mer

»Sara the Black« at the May pilgrimage

mercial tourist spot was built in the 10th, 12th and 15th centuries; it is served by a well in case of siege. A chapel above the apse contains the remains of the first two Marys, the crypt contains the reliquary of their servant. The reliquaries are the goal of colourful **Sinti pilgrimages** in May and October. From the roof of the church there is a splendid view, particularly at sunset. The 19th-century former town hall is home to the Musée Baroncelli for local history. Beyond the beach, developed in 1984 and secured by a dyke, stands the arena for the bullfights held in summer.

Between Albaron and Arles on the D 570, the **Mas du Pont de Rousty**, a sheep farm from 1812, is today the Musée Camarguais. A 3.5km/2mi nature trail explains the history of the landscape and its inhabitants.

Etang de Vaccarès At Albaron (13th-century tower; pumping station for irrigation) the D 37 branches off. Beyond Méjanes it follows the on average 50cm/20in-deep Etang de Vaccarès, the largest lagoon in the Camargue, covering approx. 6000ha/14,800 acres. At Villeneuve the charming D 36 B diverts southwest; an information centre for the nature reserve with nature trail can be found at La Capelière. From Paradis, the lighthouse Phare de la Gacholle is within reach (the last leg on foot). From here, a path leads across the digue à la mer, a dyke constructed around 1860, to Stes-Maries-de-la-Mer.

Salin-de-Giraud At Salin-de-Giraud, salt is extracted from seawater. An artificial hill provides a fine view of the evaporation basins, brightly coloured with algae, the white salt piles – and of the vast industrial plants beyond the Grand Rhône. The D 36 d leads to the **Plage de Piémanson**, the **Plage de Piémanson** »beach of Arles«, its fine sands awash in summer with campers, trippers and – on one stretch – nudists, despite the complete lack of facilities.

Cannes

Région: Provence – Alpes – Côte d'Azur **Altitude**
Département: Alpes-Maritimes **Population:** 68,000

Nowhere on the ▶Côte d'Azur can boast more exclusive hotels, eccentric restaurants or chic boutiques than Cannes, meeting place of the rich and the beautiful. As if the town, wonderfully sited on the Golfe de la Napoule, needed further confirmation of its attractiveness, international congresses and media festivals underline its appeal.

The rise to fame of this resort followed its »discovery« by the British **History** chancellor of the exchequer, Lord Brougham, who had to stay in Cannes in 1834 due to an outbreak of cholera in Nice. The harbour was established in 1838, and 30 years later work was begun on the promenade. An exceedingly mild climate, lush subtropical vegetation and a beautiful beach – a largely artificial development – have made Cannes a first-rate holiday destination of considerable popularity.

What to See in Cannes

The old town Le Suquet covers the 67m/219ft-high Mont Chevalier. **Old town** Right at the top is a 12th-century watchtower, built by the abbots of Lérins, offering marvellous views. It belongs to the Musée de la

Cannes Map

1 Notre-Dame de l'Espérance	7 Marché Forville
2 Ste-Anne	8 Hôtel de Ville
3 Tour du Mont-Chevalier	9 Marché aux Fleurs
4 Musée de la Castre	10 Notre-Dame de Bon Voyage
5 Gare Routière	11 Centre Administratif
6 Eglise de la Miséricorde	12 Centre Sportif Montfleury

Where to eat
① Fouquet's
② La Cave

Where to stay
① Carlton
② America

► VISITING CANNES

INFORMATION

Office de Tourisme
Palais des Festivals, F-06400 Cannes
Tel. 04 92 99 84 22, fax 04 92 99 84 23
www.cannes.fr

EVENTS

May: film festival (accommodation for these 12 days must be booked in advance, exorbitant prices).
July–Sept Été à Cannes: mainly music, various genres

WHERE TO EAT

► Moderate / expensive

① *Fouquet's*
10 La Croisette
Tel. 04 92 98 77 00
In the Hôtel Majestic. With his brilliant and unconventional manner of cooking, Bruno Oger is considered one of the best French chefs. Elegant but relaxing brasserie atmosphere.

► Inexpensive / moderate

② *La Cave*
9 Blvd. de la République

Tel. 04 93 99 79 87
Cosy bistro with open kitchen, where hearty Provençal fare is prepared.

WHERE TO STAY

► Luxury

① *InterContinental Carlton*
58 La Croisette
Tel. 04 93 06 40 06, www.ichotels-group.com
Pure luxury in a world-famous hotel palace on the promenade, open since 1912. Three restaurants with different layouts. Private beach with many opportunities for water sports. Room prices according to views.

► Mid-range

② *Hotel America*
13 Rue St-Honoré, tel. 04 93 06 75 75, www.hotel-america.com.
Well-kept establishment a stone's throw from the promenade, with nicely furnished modern rooms and friendly service. Excellent value for money considering the location and facilities.

La Croisette, catwalk and bathers' paradise

Castre, displaying ancient artefacts and art from the Far East and Central America. Further north stands the late Gothic church of Notre-Dame-de l'Espérance, erected as late as 1521–1648; the 18th-century Madonna and the wooden statue of Saint Anne (from around 1500) are worthy of note.

Boulevard du Midi

Boulevard Jean-Hibert runs westwards along the ocean to the beautiful Square Mistral; here it is met by the 3km/2mi-long Boulevard du Midi, with a public shingle beach and above it the grand villas of the Quartier Anglais, and the Corniche de l'Esterel (Corniche d'Or).

✱ Vieux Port

From the Old Port (Port Cannes I), ships depart for the Iles de Lérins (see below). The Gare Maritime (harbour railway station, 1957) is on the northern side with the pretty Allées de la Liberté, lined by plane trees and site of a flower market in the mornings, and the town hall of 1876 in the northwest corner. The shopping centre with the **market hall** (Marché Forville, 1870) can be found to the north of the town hall. Luxury boutiques are liberally spread along Rue Félix-Faure/Rue d'Antibes.

✱ La Croisette

Heading eastwards from the impressive Palais des Festivals, opened in 1982, is the pride of Cannes, the Boulevard de la Croisette, developed around 1860, with its luxurious hotels, shops and beaches. Doing nothing here can cost 10–40 € per day. The stretches of beach at the western and eastern edges are open to the public. Home to the 1929 Palm Beach Casino, the La Croisette headland closes the bay to the east. North of La Croisette is the charming district **La Californie**, where Picasso purchased a villa in 1955; the Russian Church (1894) on Boulevard Alexandre-III is worth seeing. A marvellous view can be savoured from the Observatoire de Super-Cannes, at a height of 325m/1066ft.

Around Cannes

Some 4km/2.5mi southeast lie the Lérins Islands. The largest of these is the Ile Ste-Marguérite, thick with eucalyptus and pinewoods. The Fort Royal, built in the 17th century and expanded by Vauban in

Evening in Le Suquet, the old town of Cannes

1712, stands to the north; for many years it served as a prison. It was here that the »man in the iron mask« was held captive towards the end of the 17th century, his identity a mystery to this day. Roman finds can be examined in the Musée de la Mer.

Ile Saint-Honorat Approximately 700m/0.5mi further south lies the smaller Ile St-Honorat. The Abbaye de Lérins on the south coast was one of the most important abbeys in Europe in medieval times; the Cistercian monks who live here today produce excellent wine and an exquisite cordial. The church (around 1870) and museum are open to visitors. The Château St-Honorat stands in the water, built in 1073 as a place of refuge from the Saracens, with a beautiful two-storey cloister (14th–16th century). There is an excellent vista from the abbot's lodge at the top.

✱
Vallauris Some 5km/3mi to the northeast lies Vallauris (26,000 inhabitants), a famous pottery town. 70 potter families from Genoa settled here in 1501, and Picasso lived here from 1946 to 1948. The finest pottery is Madoura, also licensed for ceramics based on Picasso's designs. The unostentatious Romanesque chapel (c1220) of the »Chateau« contains Picasso's monumental *War and Peace*, on which he worked from 1952 to 1959; the castle also houses a ceramics and modern art museum. A Picasso sculpture, *Man with Sheep*, stands in the church square; in Rue Sicard is a ceramics museum.

Mougins Approx. 5km/3mi north of Cannes, first class restaurants grace the erstwhile fortified mountain village of Mougins (13,000 inhabitants). Picasso lived here from 1961 until his death in 1973; the Musée de le Photographie displays old cameras and famous photographers' portraits of Picasso. Further north on the motorway, at the Bréguières service station, the automobile museum is worth stopping for.

✱ ✱ Carcassonne

K 9

Région: Languedoc-Roussillon	**Altitude:** 111m/364ft
Département: Aude	**Population:** 46,000

Carcassonne is famous the world over as the most impressive fortified town of medieval Europe – even if not everything is originally from that period, but a product of the romantic imagination of the 19th century.

History In the year 1 BC, the Romans fortified the market of Carcasso on the way to the Atlantic. In the 6th century it fell into the possession of the Visigoths, then the Arabs (725) and the Franks (759). In 1209, the town, a **Cathar** stronghold, was conquered by Simon de Montfort; he went on to use it as his base for a brutal war on the Cathars

The fortress town of Carcassonne appears like a mirage above the Aude

(►Baedeker Special p.452). In 1229 the town and county fell to the French Crown. The fortifications were extended by the Counts of Béziers (1130), Saint Louis (from 1240) and Philip the Bold (around 1280) and were, at last, considered unassailable. From 1240, the Ville Basse was developed along the lines of southern French bastides, in which the citizens expelled from the fortress could settle. The 1659 Treaty of the Pyrenees rendered the fortress redundant. It fell into disrepair until it came to the attention of Prosper Mérimée; restoration work began in 1843 under Viollet-le-Duc and was completed in 1910.

What to See in Carcassonne

The capital of the département of Aude lies at the southern foot of the Montagne Noire on the ancient route from the Mediterranean, through the Garonne valley – today along the Canal du Midi – to the Atlantic. Beyond the Aude it extends into the flat grid layout of the **Ville Basse**, where life continues as normal without too many tourists. The circular boulevard traces the circumference of the town walls, demolished in the 18th century. At the heart is Place Carnot with a Neptune fountain (1770). A **market** is held here on Tuesdays, Thursdays and Saturdays. The main sights are the church of St-Vincent (14th century, Languedoc Gothic) with a beautiful main portal in the north, and in the south the cathedral of St-Michel (around 1250) with 14th-century windows, a treasury and a 19th-century

Cavaille-Coll organ. The art museum in Rue de Verdun displays works by Flemish and Dutch painters of the 17th–18th centuries and local artists, as well as a ceramics collection.

★ ★
Cité

Two bridges south of the 13th-century Pont Vieux lead up to the 150m/490ft-high **fortified town**, with a double curtain wall (about 1300m/1400yd and 1700m/1850yd in length) and 52 towers. The fortifications had decayed to half their height before Viollet-le-Duc had them rebuilt to 19th-century aesthetic ideals. The similarity to **Disneyland** is no coincidence; Disney found inspiration for cartoon films in Carcassonne, and the Kevin Costner Robin Hood movie (1991) was filmed here. The charm of the romantic alleyways is, sad to say, considerably diminished by the mass of souvenir kitsch on offer. To avoid the heaviest crowds, aim to visit in the morning or evening.

The only points of access are the twin-towered Porte Narbonnaise in the east and Porte d'Aude in the west. From the former, Rue Cros-Mayrevieille leads to the Château Comtal (around 1125, extended in

▶ VISITING CARCASSONNE

INFORMATION

Office de Tourisme
28 Rue de Verdun
F-11890 Carcassonne
Tel. 04 68 10 24 30, fax 04 68 10 24 38
www.carcassonne.org

TRANSPORT

Municipal buses (Agglo'Bus), information at the Square Gambetta (Ville Basse). Shuttle bus in summer between Bastide St-Louis and Cité.

EVENTS

14 July: illumination of the Cité with fireworks; July: Festival de Carcassonne (music, theatre, dance); Aug: historical spectacles.

WHERE TO EAT

▶ Inexpensive / moderate

① *L'Ecurie*
43 Bvd Barbès, tel. 04 68 72 04 04
In 18th-century stables on the southern edge of the Ville Basse. Good local cuisine and wines.

▶ Inexpensive

② *Auberge de Dame Carcas*
3 Pl. du Château, tel. 04 68 71 23 23
Located in the Cité, unpretentious restaurant with hearty fare and a good selection of regional wines.

WHERE TO STAY

▶ Mid-range

① *Donjon*
2 Rue du Comte Roger
Tel. 04 68 11 23 00
www.hotel-donjon.fr
In historic buildings at the heart of the Cité. Nice, small and comfortable rooms. Brasserie serves local specialities.

La Rode
F-81700 Lempaut
Tel. 05 63 75 51 07, http://pagespersonorange.fr/larode. Chambre d'hôte in a 16th-century monastery, 18km/11mi southwest of Castres (past the D 622). Well-kept rooms with old furniture; accessible kitchen for self catering. Ideal for families.

13th century), a self-contained fortress with fine, broad views from the battlements. Of the many »museums« keen to entice tourists, the Im@ginarium, a multi-media show on the war against the Cathars, is the only one to be recommended.

The east section of the former cathedral of St-Nazaire, with wonderful **stained glass windows**, was erected from 1269 to 1330 on the model of St-Denis in Paris as a symbol of the Crown's victory over the south. The nave was consecrated in 1096, the west façade crenellated by Viollet-le-Duc. 22 remarkable statues and tombs, including that of Simon de Montfort, can be seen in the choir.

✱ St-Nazaire

Around Carcassonne

The Montagne Noire, an extension of the Cevennes, climbs gradually up to the 1210m/3969ft Pic de Nore. The steep northern face over the Thoré and the south face enjoy different climates and vegetation: the first is very rainy and features dense pinewood and deciduous

Montagne Noire

Carcassonne Cité *Plan*

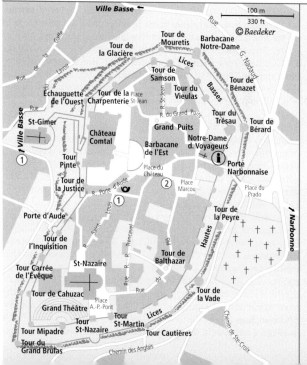

© Baedeker

Ville Basse →

100 m
330 ft

Where to eat
① L'Écurie
② Auberge de Dame Carcas

Where to stay
① Donjon

Tour de Mouretis
Barbacane Notre-Dame
Tour de la Glacière
Lices
Tour de Samson
Tour du Vieulas
Tour de Bénazet
Échauguette de l'Ouest
Tour de la Charpenterie
Place St-Jean
R. du Grand Puits
St-Gimer
Tour du Trésau
Tour de Bérard
Château Comtal
Grand Puits
Barbacane de l'Est
Notre-Dame d. Voyageurs
Porte Narbonnaise
Tour Pinte
Place du Château
Place Marcou
Place du Prado
Tour de la Justice
R. Porte d'Aude
Porte d'Aude
Tour de la Peyre
Tour de l'Inquisition
Tour Carrée de l'Évêque
St-Nazaire
Tour de Balthazar
Tour de la Vade
Tour de Cahuzac
Grand Théâtre
Place A.-P.-Pont
Tour St-Martin
Tour St-Nazaire
Tour Cautières
Tour Mipadre
Tour du Grand Brûlas
Chemin des Anglais
Chemin de Ste-Croix
Hautes
Lices
Narbonne
Ville Basse

forest, whilst the latter has more Mediterranean garrigue, chestnut and olive trees, and vines. 16km/10mi north of Carcassonne (accessible via Conques-sur-Orbiel) lie the Châteaux de Lastours, **four castles** of the Cathar Pierre de Cabaret, who resisted the siege of Simon de Montfort. The view is best from the eastern belvedere. The D 112 leads to the Pic de Note (broad panorama).

Châteaux de Lastours

Minervois

✳ Minerve

An excursion to the Minervois wine-growing region to the northeast of Carcassonne is warmly recommended. The name derives from the beautifully situated old village of Minerve (100 inhabitants), a stronghold conquered by Simon de Montfort in 1210; 180 Cathars who refused to renounce their beliefs were burned here. The Romanesque church of St-Etienne (11th–12th century, some parts 6th century) with an altar from 456, an archaeological museum and the Musée Hurepel on the history of the Cathars deserves a closer look. Southwest of the village, the **ponts naturels** are natural tunnels which the Cesse has bored into the limestone rock. North of Siran (12km/7.5mi southwest of Minerve), the 13th-century Chapelle de Centeilles features beautiful frescoes from the 14th and 15th centuries; wonderful views across the vineyards.

Chapelle de Centeilles

Castelnaudary

Castelnaudary stands on the Canal du Midi, 37km/23mi west of Carcassonne (11,000 inhabitants). It is known as the capital of **cassoulet**, although both Carcassonne and Toulouse stake a similar claim to be the home of this hearty ragout of white beans, pork and duck or goose. The canal harbour is a particularly attractive spot, with the 17th-century Pont Vieux. The church of St-Michel (14th century) has a striking 56m/183ft tower and a beautiful 18th-century organ. A fine view over the Laurageais may be enjoyed from the restored windmill looking north across town.

Castres

✳ ✳ Musée Goya ▶

At the edge of the Sidobre hills, a good 60km/35mi north of Carcassonne, lies Castres (45,000 inhabitants), for centuries one of the most important sites of the woollen industry in France. Developing from a Benedictine abbey founded around 810, the 16th and 17th centuries witnessed scenes of atrocity in the Calvinist town. A visit to the **Musée Goya**, with the most important collection of Spanish painting in France after the Louvre, is an absolute must. It can be found in the town hall, the former bishop's palace (by J. Hardouin-Mansart, 1669; garden by Le Nôtre) and is open daily July–Aug 9am–noon, 2pm–6pm, otherwise Tue–Sun until 5pm. Most prominent are works by Francisco de Goya (1746–1828), including the series of etchings entitled *Los Caprichos*, *Desastres de la Guerra*, *Tauromaquia* and *Disparates*. The Baroque cathedral of St-Benoît (1677–1718) replaced the 9th-century abbey church. The colourful medieval houses on the river Agoût are a beautiful tableau. The philosopher and socialist politician **Jean Jaurès** was born in Castres in 1859 (he was murdered in 1914); a museum in the north of the old town is dedicated to him.

✴ Cevennes · Cévennes

L 8

A delight for nature lovers and those seeking remote and peaceful landscapes, the Cevennes are a range of mountains between the Massif Central and the coastal plains of the Mediterranean.

The Cevennes are a low mountain range of slate and granite at a height of some 1500m/4900ft; the highest peaks are Mont Lozère (Sommet de Finiels, 1699m/5574ft) and Mont Aigoual (1567m/5141ft). To the east, towards the Rhône valley, it drops away sharply; to the west it meets the steppe-like 1000m/3300ft-high karst plateau of the Grands Causses. The barren, extremely **sparsely populated upland** – the Lozère département, to which the lonely Monts d'Aubrac belong, has just 14 inhabitants per sq km (36 per sq mi) – is one of the poorest regions of France due to its lack of natural resources; sheep rearing, the only activity of significance, does, however, produce the famous Roquefort cheese, which matures in the cellars of Roquefort-sur-Soulzon.

Landscape

The Cevennes mark the climatic divide between the harsh Massif Central and the Mediterranean. Cold winters and hot summers, strong winds and rainfall seek out the thinly vegetated plateaux; oaks grow on the slopes and in the gorges, with sweet chestnuts the next most prevalent vegetation. Over-exploitation of the beech forests for the numerous glassblowing workshops was curtailed in the mid-19th century; since then, coniferous trees have been intensively planted. In the south, Mediterranean garrigue, olive groves and vineyards reach into the highlands.

Climate and vegetation

Cevennes and Causses are home to a fascinating **flora and fauna** with many rare species. The aims of the approx. 300 sq km/115 sq mi Parc National des Cévennes and the similarly sized Parc Naturel Régional des Grands Causses are, apart from nature conservation

National parks

Highlights Cevennes

Natural experience
Whether with a rucksack or donkey, the Cevennes National Parks are best discovered on foot.
▶ page 343

Corniche des Cevennes
Breathtaking panoramas on a military road established by Louis XIV
▶ page 344

Gorges du Tarn
Up to 600m/2000ft deep gorges in the Causses, perfect for kayakers and climbers
▶ page 346

Roquefort
In cellar caves, the famous cheese made from Cevennes sheep's milk matures.
▶ page 347

Paragliders have discovered an ideal spot at Millau

and the preservation of traditional peasant culture, the organization of environmentally sustainable holiday activities. The harsh landscape with woods, coarse pastures, barren plateaux and deeply incised valleys is a refuge for nature lovers and hikers, with many gîtes ruraux offering accommodation. Information on all relevant matters can be obtained at the national park offices in Florac and Millau.

History   The pathless upland takes its name from the Latin »mons Cebenna« and offered refuge to the Huguenots, called **Camisards** due to their white shirts, during the Wars of Religion in the 16th century. The Camisard revolt broke out in 1702. The bloodiest phase of the Cevennes War, in which the troops of Louis XIV destroyed most of the villages, endured until 1704. It was not until 1787 that Louis XVI guaranteed religious freedom with an edict of toleration. The population of the Cevennes is still predominantly Protestant, and the descendants of the Huguenots meet at the beginning of each September at Mas Soubeyran, the house of the former leader »Roland« (see below).

Places to Visit in the Cevennes

Mende   In the upper reaches of the Lot lies Mende (730m/2395ft, 12,000 inhabitants), a provincial town of surprising elegance and the main locality of the Lozère département. To the south of the town rise the steep slopes of the Causse de Mende, over 300m/980ft high (Mont Mimat, 1067m/3500ft; wonderful view of Mende). The cathedral of Notre-Dame was begun in 1368 and gained its towers in the 16th century. It was then largely destroyed by the Huguenots in 1579 and rebuilt in the 17th century. Inside note the tapestries from Aubusson (1708), an 11th-century Black Madonna from the Orient and the clapper of the bell »Nonpareille«, said to have been the largest in existence: it weighed 25 tons and was destroyed in 1579; the clapper alone is 2.15m/7ft long and weighs 470kg/1036lb. The 13th-century Pont de Notre-Dame across the Lot is also a work of beauty. In Rue Notre-Dame, the synagogue is the oldest building (13th century); a 17th-century house contains a regional museum, the Musée Ignon Fabre.

Southwest of Mende, the granite massif of Mont Lozère looms large with its harsh moorlands. From Le Bleymard the 1548m/5078ft **Col de Finiels** pass leads south, with the Sommet de Finiels (1699m/5574ft) two hours away via a sheep trail (wonderful view of the Cevennes). Beyond the pass lies Le Pont-de-Montvert, whose castle saw the outbreak of the Cevennes War, and is the site of the Ecomusée du Mont Lozère (open air museum, with Gîte d'Etape).

★
Mont Lozère

Le Pont-de-Montvert

This quaint little town (2100 inhabitants) is a good base for excursions into the Cevennes, the Causses and the Tarn Gorge; the tourist office offers information concerning all outdoor activities. The 17th-century castle houses the centre of the **Parc National des Cévennes**, with a wide range of information and maps.

Florac

▶ VISITING CEVENNES

INFORMATION
CRT Languedoc-Roussillon
Acropole, 954 Avenue Jean Mermoz,
F-34960 Montpellier Cedex 2
Tel. 04 67 20 02 20, fax 04 67 64 47 48
www.sunfrance.com
CRT Midi-Pyrenees
54 Bvd de l'Embouchure, BP 52166
F-31022 Toulouse Cedex 2
Tel. 05 61 13 55 48, fax 05 61 47 17 16
www.tourisme-midi-pyrenees.com

**WHERE TO EAT /
WHERE TO STAY**

▶ **Mid-range / luxury**
Château de la Caze
La Malène, F-48210 Ste-Enimie
www.chateaudelacaze.com
Tel. 04 66 48 51 01, closed mid-Nov
to end of March.

Enchantingly located on the riverbank, this defiant castle has retained its atmosphere as a hotel, appointed with simple elegance.
The restaurant (with a terrace) serves up regional delicacies.

▶ **Budget**
Hostellerie Chantoiseau
F-48220 Vialas
Tel. 04 66 41 00 02
www.chantoiseau-vialas.fr
 Cosy hotel 20km/12mi east of Le Pont-de-Montvert in a 17th-century coaching inn with much wood and stone. Small, simple rooms, vaunted regional cuisine. Cellar with over 1000 wines, the emphasis on southern French grapes (tasting and purchase possible).

Corniche des Cévennes

Saint-Laurent-du-Trèves

Mas Soubeyran

The 53km/33mi-long Corniche des Cévennes, which follows the ridge from Florac southeast to St-Jean-du-Gard, was constructed for the troops of Louis XIV in the war against the Huguenots, providing breathtaking views across the mountains. In the limestone rock at St-Laurent-du-Trèves, traces of dinosaurs 190 million years old were discovered; it is also a wonderful vantage point for views of Causse Méjean and Mont Lozère. From St-Jean-du-Gard the D 50 leads to **Mas Soubeyran**, now the Musée du Désert, in which the history of the Huguenot Wars is documented.

Anduze

Situated to the southeast of St-Jean-du-Gard, the small town of Anduze (3000 inhabitants) was the main stronghold of the Duke of Rohan's Protestant uprising of 1622. Following the Treaty of Alès, only the clock tower (1320) survived. The remainder of the fortifications were razed to the ground. Close to the Protestant church of 1829, the curious fountain on Place Couverte dates back to 1649. 2km/1.25mi north (D 129) lies the astounding **Bambouseraie de Prafrance**, established in 1855, a bamboo forest with many more exotic plants; H.-G. Clouzot filmed the classic thriller *The Wages of Fear* here.

Delicious Roquefort matures in cool, damp cellars

On the southeast edge of the Cevennes, across the border in Languedoc, lies **Alès** (41,000 inhabitants), centre of a coal-mining region. South of the Vauban fortress, which towers above the old town in a bend of the Gardon, stands the cathedral of St-Jean-Baptiste (western section Romanesque and Gothic, the remainder 17th–18th century) with paintings from the 18th and 19th centuries in the nave. Well worth a visit is the Musée du Colombier with paintings of the 16th–20th centuries, notably by Brueghel the Elder, Van Loo and other Dutch artists. 3km/2mi west of the town a coal mine has been made into a museum. An excellent place to eat is Auberge de St-Hilaire in St-Hilaire-de-Brethmas (6km/3.5mi southeast of Alès, tel. 04 66 30 11 42).

Mont Aigoual

The granite and slate massif of the Aigoual (1567m/5141ft) rises to the south of Florac, where clouds from the Atlantic and Mediterranean cast their precipitation. From 1875, the deforested mountains were replanted with beech forests. The meteorological station, established in 1887, provides a **magnificent panoramic view** – on a clear day, from the Pyrenees to Mont Blanc.

Picturesque rock faces and castle ruins: the Tarn at Castelbouc →

✴ ✴ Grands Causses · Gorges du Tarn

Landscape
The Grands Causses, vast, desolate, infertile karst plateaux, ravaged by wind and weather, to the east of Millau (see below), are separated by impressive gorges – Gorges du Tarn, Gorges de la Jonte – into the Causse de Sauveterre, Causse Méjean and Causse Noir. South of the Vallée de la Dourbie, the Causse du Larzac adjoins.

✴ ✴
Gorges du Tarn
The Gorges du Tarn are among the most impressive natural sites in France. From its source on Mont Lozère, the river Tarn has dug its way 600m/2000ft deep into the limestone. These **canyons** can be experienced on foot, by boat or from the road, which make the D 907 B along the riverbank look like an overcrowded car park in the summer months. Canoes and kayaks can be hired in Ste-Enimie and La Malène to paddle down to Pas de Souci.

✴
Sainte-Enimie
From Florac, the D 907 B leads via Ispagnac (11th–12th century church), the Quézac bridge (14th century) and the ruins of Castelbouc to Ste-Enimie (500 inhabitants), built in a part of the gorge above a loop in the Tarn. It is worth seeing the 12th-century Romanesque church, the museum of local history in the Vieux Logis, the Place au Beurre with an old granary, the remains of a monastery founded around 630 by Sainte Enimie, a Merovingian princess, and the town walls.

La Malène
Beyond the Château de la Caze (15th century) is La Malène (200 inhabitants); a wonderful view of the place can be enjoyed from the snaking route up the southern side. From here it takes about an hour to sail through the narrow Détroits to the **Cirque des Baumes**. The route continues through the Pas de Souci, a sea of cliffs through which the river splashes and foams (vantage point). Les Vignes is a good spot from which to reach the most impressive viewpoint, the Point Sublime, 400m/1310ft above the Cirque des Baumes.

✴ ✴
Point Sublime

Le Rozier
At the confluence of the Tarn and Jonte lies Le Rozier, the name a reminder of the roses cultivated by monks in the 11th century. A one-hour hike to the Rocher de Capluc is a worthwhile undertaking to see castle ruins and enjoy a view of the Méjean, though the ascent to the summit requires a head for heights. Between Meyrueis and Le Rozier are the somewhat less striking, but romantic gorges of the Jonte, which rises in the Aigoual. The best vantage points are the Terrasses du Truel 1.5km/1mi below the village of the same name.

✴
Gorges de la Jonte

✴
Aven Armand Grotte de Dargilan
Two impressive, sizeable stalactite caves are within reach of Meyrueis. North of the Jonte lies the Aven Armand (11km/6.5mi on the D 986), with up to 30m/100ft high stalagmites, south of the Jonte the Grotte de Dargilan (9km/5.5mi via the D 39). It is well worth taking the D 29/110 from Le Rozier over the Causse Noir to Millau. Branch

off after another 10km/6mi the bizarre dolomite labyrinth of Montpellier-le-Vieux; this natural monument has been completely tailored to tourists. Higher viewing points provide beautiful views across the Causses.

✱ Montpellier-le-Vieux

A southern atmosphere is already noticeable in the lively town of Millau (379m/1243ft, 21,400 inhabitants) on the confluence of the Tarn and Dourbie. Famous since the 12th century for leather goods, the manufacture of gloves in particular, it is now a base for climbers and paragliders and very busy in July and August (information office of the National Park of the Grands Causses: 71 Bvd de l'Ayrolle). On the pretty Place du Maréchal-Foch, bordered by arcades, stands the 18th-century **Hôtel de Pégayrolles** with the Musée de Millau (mineralogy and palaeontology, archaeology, 1st-century ceramics from Graufesenque, which lay 1km/0.5mi to the east, leather and gloves) as well as the Gothic church of Notre-Dame-de-l'Espinasse (1582), where there are fine views from the 42m/137ft Gothic belfry (12th–17th centuries). Some 4km/2.5mi west of Millau, a **cable-stayed viaduct** designed by Norman Foster and completed in 2004, spans the Tarn. The A 75 crosses the valley at a height of 270m/885ft, the tallest pylon measuring a gigantic 343m/1125ft – the highest road bridge in the world.

Millau

Approx. 22km/misouthwest of Millau lies the little town of **Roquefort**, home of the famous blue cheese made from sheep's milk. As long ago as 1407, King Charles VI granted exclusive production rights to the locals. The maturing cellars set in limestone are an attraction; the air is consistently moist and cool, creating favourable conditions for the fungus *penicillium roqueforti*.

Looking down into the Cirque de Navacelles

In the south of the Causse du Larzac, some 33km/20mi southwest of Ganges, the small river Vis cut a loop into the limestone, subsequently cutting it off altogether. The best view of this dried-out valley with the village of Navacelles can be enjoyed from the D 130.

✱ Cirque de Navacelles

★★ Chamonix · Mont Blanc

07

Région: Rhône-Alpes
Département: Haute-Savoie

Altitude: 1037m/3402ft
Population: 9700

Chamonix, in the magnificent mountainous landscape of Mont Blanc, is the ultimate name for mountain climbers and winter sports enthusiasts in the Alps. An absolute »highlight« is a ride on the longest and highest cable car in the world.

On Mont Blanc Nothing can compare to the marvellous location of Chamonix-Mont-Blanc – the official name – at the heart of breathtaking mountain scenery at the foot of the highest massif of the Alps. For many mountain enthusiasts, the ascent of the 4808m/15,774ft high Mont Blanc is a lifetime's dream. Skiers and the less active can savour the best of the mountains with the aid of spectacular cable cars. Chamonix also has a casino and caters for sports and leisure pursuits of all kinds.

From the year 1091, the valley of the Arve was known as »campus munitus« and belonged to a Benedictine priory. In the 18th century it became more widely known through the English adventurers Pococke and Windham, along with the natural scientists Saussure and Bourrit from Geneva. The first Winter Olympics were held here in 1924.

▶ VISITING CHAMONIX

INFORMATION

Office de Tourisme
85 Place du Triangle d'Amitié
F-74400 Chamonix
Tel. 04 50 53 00 24
Fax 04 50 53 58 90
www.chamonix.com

TIPS

From mid-July to mid-August, Chamonix is completely overrun. Those intent on coming during this period are well advised to book accommodation early, or look slightly further afield. It is a good idea to leave the car in, for example, St-Gervais-Le-Favet (rail connection). The cable car to the Aiguille du Midi is in operation from 6.30am in July and August, but lengthy queues develop as early as 8am.

WHERE TO STAY

▶ Luxury
Le Hameau Albert 1er
38 Route du Bouchet
Tel. 04 50 53 05 09, www.hameaualbert.fr. Founded in 1903, the hotel is named after the Belgian king who stayed here on many occasions. A chalet and Savoy farmhouse with twelve outstandingly beautiful rooms belong to the hotel. The restaurant is one of the finest in the region; Maison Carrier is less pricey.

▶ Budget / mid-range
Hôtel de l'Arve
60 Impasse des Anemones
Tel. 04 50 53 02 31, www.hotelarve.chamonix.com
Small, cosily rustic house in a peaceful spot on the Arve.

The main street (Rue Dr-Paccard/Rue J.-Vallot) runs right through the town. To the west of the crossroads with Avenue M.-Croz stands the Hôtel de Ville (town hall), the church (1709, façade 1864) and the Maison de la Montagne (mountain guide office and information), a former vicarage. A memorial to Dr. Paccard, one of the first Mont Blanc climbers, stands on the Arve. Further downstream a monument (J. Salmson, 1887) commemorates the first scientific ascent in 1787 by the scientist Horace-Bénédict de Saussure and Balmat, his guide. The Musée Alpin relates the history of the valley and its development.

Chamonix

Built from 1959 to 1965, the 11.6/7.2mi-long Mont Blanc Tunnel (toll) begins above the hamlet of Les Pèlerinsat a height of 1274m/4179ft and ends at 1370m/4494ft at Entrèves. It is open all year round.

Mont Blanc Tunnel

Mountain Transport and Hikes

The tours recommended here are easy, but proper mountain equipment is still recommended. Warm clothing is also advisable for cable car trips, such as the one to the Aiguille du Midi, reaching chilly heights of almost 4000m/13,123ft. Please note: the rapid climb to these heights can be hard work for the cardiovascular system! IGN maps offer the best navigational assistance.

Tips

A cable car built in 1926–1930 leads up to the Brévent (2526m/8287ft) northwest of Chamonix. From 1090m/3576ft, the upper terminus with a restaurant at 2505m/8218ft, just below the summit, is reached in 15 minutes, with **glorious views** of the Mont Blanc range, the Bernese Alps and the Dauphiné mountains. One hike well worth recommending leads from Planpraz to Brévent (1¾ hours, return leg 1¼ hours, descent to Chamonix another 1½ hours).

✶ ✶
Brévent

Up to the Flégère (1877m/6158ft) north of Chamonix, a cable car ascends from Les Praz. Approx. 800m/0.5mi above the church of Chamonix, the way up to the Flégère takes a left turn towards Argentière, arriving at the Chalet de la Floriaz (1337m/4517ft, marvellous view) around one hour later. Some 1½–2 hours further is the Croix de la Flégère (1877m/6158ft; hotel; similarly excellent panorama). From Croix de la Flégère, a cable car takes visitors up to the Index (2385m/7824ft). The hike from here to Lac Blanc (2352m/7716ft, inn; 1¼ hours, return leg to the hotel 45 minutes) is pleasant and without steep climbs. Traditionally, the most attractive time to undertake a hike from La Flégère to Planpraz (see above, Brévent), or vice versa, is the late afternoon.

✶ ✶
Flégère

Opened in 1908, a cog railway (starts opposite the railway station; May–Oct) takes 20 minutes to reach Montenvers at 1913m/6276ft. From here, enjoy the wonderful view across the **Mer de Glace**, a con-

✶
Montenvers

Balmat and Saussure point the way to Mont Blanc

fluence of three glaciers 7km/4.5mi long and at some points 1–2km/ 0.5–1.25mi wide. Opposite is the overhanging western face of the Aiguille du Dru, behind it to the left the Aiguille à Bochard, to the right the Aiguille du Moine, to the southeast the Grandes-Jorasses, to the far right the Aiguille des Grands Charmoz. A cable car leads to a tunnel bored into the glacier. Those with sufficient experience of the mountains will be tempted by a return journey over the Chapeau: across the Mer de Glace in 45 minutes to the right lateral moraine, a further 45 minutes up to the Chapeau (1601m/5252ft; cafe), a rock outcrop at the foot of the Aiguille à Bochard; another 45 minutes to the Hôtel Beau Séjour (1243m/4078ft) and 20 minutes to Les Tines.

The 5.4km/3.25mi-long suspension cable railway leads from Praz-Conduit (1040m/3412ft) in approx. 20 minutes via the Plan de l'Aiguille station (2308m/7572ft) to the northern peak of the Aiguille du Midi (3790m/12,434ft), with a lift to the main summit (3842m/12,600ft). From the upper station, a cable car takes 20 minutes to cover the 5km/3mi over the Gros Rognon (3533 m) to the Punta Helbronner. A further cable car (3462m/11,358ft) continues to the Rifugio Torino (3371m/11,059ft) below the Col du Géant (3365m/11,040ft); from here, another cableway heads down via the Pavillon del Monte Frety (2130m/6988ft) to Entrèves-La-Palud in Italy (1370m/4494ft). Return to Chamonix by bus. The entire trip from Chamonix to Entrèves (approx. 15km/9.5 mi) takes around 1½ hours and is an absolutely fantastic experience. From the station at Plan de l'Aiguille, take a jaunt to the Lac du Plan de l'Aiguille with a marvellous panoramic view of Mont Blanc, before descending the Henry-Vallot path to Montenvers (approx. 2½ hours).

★★
Aiguille du Midi

From Les Houches (5km/3mi west of Chamonix) a cable car leads up to the Pavillon de Bellevue (1794m/5885ft). Here, the **Tramway du Mont-Blanc** (cog railway) connects St-Gervais to the Nid d'Aigle (2386m/7828ft). It is part of a normal route up Mont Blanc (see below) and is accordingly well frequented.

Bellevue

Nid d'Aigle

From Les Bossons 4km/2.5mi southwest of Chamonix a 45-minute walk (or chair lift) leads to the Pavillon des Bossons (1298m/4258ft, restaurant) on the left lateral moraine of the Glacier des Bossons. The views take in the glacier, with Mont-Blanc du Tacul (4248m/13937ft) towering above; to the left, the Aiguille du Midi (3790m/12,434ft) and the Aiguille du Plan (3673m/12050ft). The ascent to the Chalet des Pyramides (1845m/6045ft) takes 1¾ hours.

Glacier des Bossons

Mont Blanc (ice peak 4808m/15,774ft, rock peak 4792m/15,721ft) was conquered for the first time in 1786 by the doctor Michel Paccard and the hunter Jacques Balmat, both from Chamonix, and then in 1787 by the scientist Horace-Bénédict de Saussure, again with Balmat. For experienced climbers, the ascent with a guide should not present any great problems, although the considerable height does mean ideal weather conditions are necessary, a fact which is underestimated by many. The regular ascent, depending on capability, requires 8–12 hours. Take the Tramway du Mont-Blanc to the Nid d'Aigle (2386m/7769ft) from the Glacier de Bionnassay and ascend to the Refuge Tête-Rousse (3167m/10,390ft, 2 hours). From here, the Refuge de l'Aiguille du Goûter (3817m/12,522ft, accommodation) is 3 hours away, the summit a further five hours.

★★
Mont Blanc

✴ Champagne–Ardenne

M 3–4

Champagne, an idyllic landscape in the northeast of France, produces the most famous and elegant sparkling wine in the world. Old towns with magnificent Gothic churches as in ▶ Reims are a reminder of an important past.

✴
Land of the famous sparkling wine

The Région Champagne–Ardenne stretches from the Belgian frontier in the north to the sources of the Seine in Burgundy in the south, and from Lorraine in the east to the Ile-de-France in the west; the main town is Châlons-en-Champagne. Champagne owes its worldwide celebrity status to the luxurious drink of the same name. Gourmets will also be familiar with Ardennes ham and typical varieties of cheese such as Langres and Chaource, all with the AC seal. The region is not one of the more popular tourist destinations, but has much to offer. Castles and fortresses in the north bear witness to the strategic significance of its borders over long periods; outstanding monuments and beautiful medieval timber-frame houses can be seen in ▶ Troyes, ▶ Reims, Charleville-Mézières, Châlons-en-Champagne and Chaumont. The landscape guarantees variety and tranquillity: from the dense woods of the Ardennes and Argonnes through vast plateaux of cornfields and gentle chains of hills laced with vineyards, to a lake district in the south with oak woods and gently flowing rivers.

Champagne crayeuse

The western region taking in Reims, Épernay, Châlons, Ste-Ménehould and Vitry-le-François represents the »Champagne crayeuse«, or »chalk Champagne«, also called »Champagne pouilleuse« (»dry«, »miserable«), with meagre earth of porous chalk. The undulating plateau is largely used as sheep pasture, as the agricultural potential of the land is poor. On the sunny slopes, the deep roots of the vine give forth a sour wine, basis for the famous champagne. East of Ste-

---

Highlights Champagne and Ardenne

Champagne
No journey through Champagne would be complete without a visit to one of the wine producers in Épernay or Reims.
▶ page 354, 728

Troyes
Timber-frame houses, churches full of treasures and modern art in the old capital of Champagne
▶ page 786

The Champagne Route
The Route Touristique du Champagne takes in the main producers in seven delightful steps.
▶ page 359

Fortifications
The Ardennes, a much-contested strip of land – Rocroi, Mézières and Sedan recall periods of war.
▶ page 360/361

Early morning in the vineyards on the Marne

Champagne humide

Ménehould and Vitry in a concentric arc is »Champagne humide«, consisting of layers of sand and clay of the lower-lying chalk. Here are many small stock-breeding farms in a landscape rich in water and woods. Iron ore deposits located where Champagne meets Lorraine gave rise to heavy industry.

Ardennes

The Ardennes, an undulating, well-wooded upland with elevations of approx. 500m/1640ft, run through the northeast of Champagne, with the Maas and Semois dividing them. Primarily known for their beech and fir forests, and rich in game, the Ardennes can be explored on foot, on horseback or by bicycle.

History

When Caesar conquered Gaul in 57 BC, he declared Durocortorum (Reims) the capital of »Campania«, as eight roads met here. In 451, the unified army of the Romans, Visigoths, Burgundians and Franks defeated Attila, King of the Huns, at Troyes, some 20km/12mi to the north. When the archbishop of Reims baptized Clovis I, King of the Franks, in the year 496, Reims became a holy **royal town of France**. In medieval times, sought-after luxury goods such as spices, silk and Flanders cloth were exchanged here at famous **trade fairs**. This period of prosperity has left a legacy of marvellous buildings. In 1328, Champagne fell to the French throne through the marriage of its last heiress with Philip VI; in 1429, Jeanne d'Arc led Charles VII to be crowned in Reims. The philosopher Denis Diderot (1713–84) hailed from Champagne, as did G.-J. Danton (1759–94), a key figure in the French Revolution. At Valmy, the revolutionary troops registered their first victory against the Prussian and Austrian army in 1792. The Battle of Sedan was a famous incident in the Franco-German War of 1870–71.

Places to Visit in the Champagne Region

Forêt d'Argonne ✴ The Argonnes, a chain of hills with picturesque valleys and forests, lie between ►Reims and ►Verdun on the border with Lorraine. A small tour of the most interesting sites begins in Clermont-en-Argonne on the N 3, where it is worth looking at the 16th-century church of St-Didier and St Anne's Chapel with a tomb thought to be the work of Ligier Richier. On the Butte de Vauquois (14km/8.5mi north) the scars of First World War battles can still be seen. In **Varennes-en-Argonne** (4km/2.5mi northwest) in 1791, Louis XVI and Marie-Antoinette were arrested as they fled (see local museum). Continue southwest on the D 38 / D 2 via Lachalade with its impressive Cistercian abbey to reach Les Islettes, once famous for faiences and tiles. 14km/8.5mi southeast, high up in Beaulieu-en-Argonne, the ruins of a Benedictine abbey with a huge 13th-century grape press can be viewed.

Verzenay In Verzenay, 13km/8mi southeast of ►Reims in the vineyards at the edge of the Montagne de Reims, stands a lighthouse (1909) with a museum of champagne.

Épernay ✴ Épernay (27,000 inhabitants, 27km/17mi south of Reims), the second **centre of Champagne production** after Reims, lies in the middle of the wine-growing region on the Marne. In the chalk subsoil are 100km/60mi-long tunnels, in which some 200 million bottles

Jiggling boards in Epernay: Champagne is produced here

are stored at temperatures of 9–12°C (48–53°F). The most important manufacturers opening their doors to the public include Moët & Chandon (founded 1743), Mercier, Pol Roger and De Castellane (cellars and bottling), as well as a dozen of smaller names. The tourist office adjacent to the 1858 town hall (also worth a look) provides all the relevant information. Acts of destruction throughout the ages have left few historic structures. Rows of houses built by champagne companies in the 19th century in diverse styles adorn the Avenue de Champagne east of the town hall; this is also the location of the **Château Perrier** (municipal museum), with a champagne department that reveals everything there is to know about the famous bubbly. The De Castellane (57 Rue de Verdun) house with an imposing tower (vantage point) also features a museum of champagne. In Hautvillers, a quaint village 6km/3.5mi northwest of Épernay, stands the abbey in which **Dom Pérignon** was a cellar master; his tombstone can be seen in the church.

✳ **Hautvillers**

Elegant bourgeois palais and beautiful timber-frame houses are typical features of this wine merchants' town (50,000 inhabitants) 48km/29mi south of Reims. In the cathedral of St-Etienne (13th century, façade from 1634), the marvellous stained glass windows from the 12th–16th centuries (especially the rose window in the south transept) and the church treasury are worth a look. One of the most beautiful churches of the Champagne region is the collegiate church of Notre-Dame-en-Vaux (1157–1217) with four towers and splendid Troyes windows in the choir (16th century). In the adjacent Musée du Cloître, sculptures and capitals are on display. Literary enthusiasts should visit the **Musée Schiller-et-Goethe** (Rue L. Bourgeois, July–Aug Wed–Mon 2pm–4pm, otherwise only at weekends), a foundation of the last descendant of Schiller, Baroness von Gleichen-Russwurm. The late 19th-century market hall to the south of the town hall and municipal museum has culinary and architectural merit. The Porte-Ste-Croix in the south of the town was erected in 1770 for the arrival of Marie-Antoinette, the future wife of Louis XVI. The basilica of Notre-Dame-de-l'Epine, visible from afar 6km/3.5mi northeast of Châlons (N 3), is a popular place of pilgrimage. It was constructed between 1406 and 1527 in glorious Flamboyant fashion with splendid gargoyles.

Châlons-en-Champagne
✳
◄ St-Etienne

✳
◄ Notre-Dame-en-Vaux

✳
Notre-Dame-de-l'Epine

Standing above the Marne, 32km/20mi south of Chalons-en-Champagne, the town (16,700 inhabitants) was founded by François I in the mid-16th century as a fortification on a grid system. It was rebuilt after being almost completely destroyed in 1940. The church of Notre-Dame in the centre on Place d'Armes (17th–18th century) represents French classicism. Several champagne cellars extend an invitation to visitors. 10km/6mi to the north, St-Amand-sur-Fion is worth a visit. It is a **typical Champagne village** with numerous timber-frame houses and an elegant, pink Gothic church from the 13th

Vitry-le-François

✳
Saint-Amand-sur-Fion

century, featuring elements from its predecessor (centre portal, sections of the nave). The choir, porch and some of the decorated capitals date from the 15th century.

Lac du Der-Chantecoq Covering an expanse of 48 sqkm/19 sq mi, this is the largest artificial lake in France, regulating the water level of the Marne. The most interesting buildings of the flooded villages were reconstructed in the Ste-Marie-du-Lac museum village. With boat harbours, bathing spots and many other sporting facilities, it is a popular place for excursions. Waterfowl and migratory birds can be seen here – Scandinavian storks in particular. The Ferme de Berzillières farming museum is also worth a visit.

Brienne-le-Château An 18th-century castle (closed to the public) towers over the small town (3300 inhabitants, 40km/25mi east of Troyes) close to the Aube. Napoleon was a student at the military academy here (now with a museum) from the ages of 10 to 15. The main French region for **sauerkraut** after Alsace celebrates the »Fête de la choucroute en champagne« on the third Sunday in September.

Bar-sur-Seine Beautiful timber-frame houses (15th–17th centuries) are the dominant feature in the old centre of Bar-sur-Seine, one of the key sites of the Côte des Bar region of Champagne. The church of St-Etienne (1505–1616) unifies Flamboyant, Renaissance and classical styles, with beautiful 16th-century Troyes windows. There is a fine view from the remains of the castle where Joan I de Navarre was born in 1273. 17km/11mi to the east, Essoyes on the river Ource was a fa-

Essoyes

▶ VISITING CHAMPAGNE

INFORMATION
CRT Champagne-Ardenne
15 Avenue du Maréchal Leclerc
F-51013 Châlons-en-Champagne
Tel. 03 26 21 85 80, fax 03 26 21 85 90
www.tourisme-champagne-ardenne.com

WHERE TO STAY
▶ Mid-range
Les Berceaux
13 Rue Berceaux
F-51200 Épernay, tel. 03 26 55 28 84
www.lesberceaux.com Restaurant closed Mon–Tue and 2nd half of August; wine bar closed Sat–Sun.

A wonderful small hotel in the middle of Épernay in a side road off Place République, boasting an elegant restaurant with classic French cuisine and pleasant wine bar with fair prices.

WHERE TO EAT
▶ Budget
Vieux Puits
18 Rue Roger Sondag, F-51160 Ay
Tel. 03 26 56 96 53
A pretty and welcoming country inn in Ay, seat of the Institut des Vins de Champagne, with an outstanding wine cellar.

vourite subject of the painter **P.-A. Renoir**. His studio is open to visitors; he and his family are buried in the graveyard.

Chaource (21km/13mi southwest of Troyes) is well known to gourmets for its cheese. As well as 15th-century timber-frame houses, the church of St-Jean-Baptiste with a gilded wooden polyptych of a crib is notable; the crypt contains the impressive entombment of the Master of Chaource (1515).

Chaource

Situated between Troyes and Chaumont on the Aube, the »other« Bar (6200 inhabitants) held a famous fair in the Middle Ages and now offers tours and tastings in a number of champagne cellars. The wooden galleries on the west and south sides of the church of St-Pierre (12th–16th centuries) served as market halls; the high altar previously stood in Clairvaux Abbey (see below). The colourful 15th-century statue of the Virgin Mary is a product of the Troyes school. On the 2nd weekend of September, a champagne market takes place. 13km/8mi southeast stands the famous **Clairvaux Abbey**, founded in 1115 by the Cistercian monk Bernard de Fontaine, aged just 25, who would become one of the most important figures of the Catholic Church as Bernard de Clairvaux. The church of 1140 was torn down by 1819, as the complex was turned into a state prison. The monastery buildings can still, in part, be explored (May–Oct Saturdays, mid-July to mid-Aug daily at 4.15pm).

Bar-sur-Aube

Abbaye de Clairvaux

The small village 16km/10mi east of Bar-sur-Aube was home to **Charles de Gaulle** (1890–1970) from 1933. His house La Boisserie is open to visitors (June–Sept). The pink granite, 43m/141ft-high Cross of Lorraine – the symbol of the Résistance – on the hilltop is a reminder of the French general and president.

Colombey-les-Deux-Eglises

Chaumont (28,000 inhabitants), 85km/52mi southeast of Troyes on a plateau between the Marne and Suize, was the seat of the counts of Champagne until 1329. The 11th- and 12th-century keep survives from their castle, whilst 16th–18th-century houses can be seen in the town. There is a splendid view from the 52m/170ft-high, 654m/2145ft-long **railway viaduct** (1856). As well as the Musée d'Art et d'Histoire in the castle and the Maison du Livre et de l'Affiche in a former grain silo, exhibiting over 10,000 posters, the church of St-Jean-Baptiste (12th–16th centuries) merits a visit; look out for the coloured tomb of 1471 and a relief of the Tree of Jesse (16th century).

Chaumont

 Baedeker TIP

Vélosolex

This most French of transportation methods shows what it can do in Chaumont in early June – in a 24-hour race. Bicycles with auxiliary motors compete in five categories, from production models (almost 1000km/620mi circuit!) to custom-built versions. Further information: http://solexclub.free.fr.

WINE OF KINGS, KING OF WINES

The most noble of sparkling wines has largely been »democratized« today. What has been preserved is its worldwide protection as a brand, for only the produce of the northernmost wine region of France, made by a specified process, is permitted to call itself »champagne«.

This was a condition of the Treaty of Versailles in 1919 and an EU decree in 1994 – and the name is also internationally protected. The cretaceous terrain around Reims and Épernay and the grapes of the red Pinot Noir and Pinot Meunier, as well as the white Chardonnay (usually blended, except for Blanc des Blancs) are decisive factors in its character. The legally restricted areas of cultivation and the climate, as well as measures to reduce the grape harvest and the yield in the pressing process also play important roles.

A brief history

Wine has been produced in the Champagne region since Gallo-Roman times. Saint Remigius, archbishop of Reims, referred expressly to the vineyards in his testament in 553. Cultivation in medieval times was predominantly controlled by the monasteries, the reputation of wine spreading through trade fairs. Towards the end of the 17th century,

the cellar master of the abbey of Hautvillers, **Dom Pérignon**, perfected a natural method of fermentation which caused the wine to effervesce without losing its clarity. Succeeding Malmsey and sherry, champagne became the preferred festive tipple of the European aristocracy. Storage and transportation, however, presented considerable problems. Only about half of the champagne produced actually made it as far as the table. It was not until the Napoleonic era that pressure-resistant bottles and suitable corks were developed.

The heyday of champagne export began after the Napoleonic Wars. Today, production of the brand has reached 350 million bottles per year – this although the area of cultivation covers just 30,000 hectares/74,000 acres. The largest supplier, with a market share of over 20%, is the luxury goods company LVMH (Louis Vuitton Moet-Hennessy), with the houses of Moet & Chandon, Veuve Cliquot, Piper-Heidsieck, Krug,

The rise of the House of Pommery began in 1858, when Louise Pommery took over the reins. It was she who created brut champagne.

Mercier and Ruinart. Pommery was taken over by the Vranken Group in 2002.

Méthode champenoise

Champagne is produced according to a special process. Most basic white wines from white and black grapes ferment in steel tanks at low temperatures (12–25°C/53–77°F). After the first fermentation, they are combined with wine from previous years in a **cuvee** (wines from a single year are termed **Millésimé**, vintage champagne), which determines the style and character. Herein lies the secret of competing champagne houses. The wine is now bottled, then sugar and yeast are added (liqueur de tirage) so that a second fermentation takes place in the bottles. As a rule, this lasts for 15–18 months, although great champagnes can mature out of the yeast for up to 15 years. Remuage – the gradual turning and regular jiggling of the tilted bottles – allows the sediment to settle in the neck so that it can be disgorged later. This is achieved by freezing the neck of the bottle in an ice bath. On opening the bottle, the frozen deposit shoots out. The negligible loss is balanced by a solution of sugar in wine (dosage), the concentration of which determines the character of the end product: from brut, sec and demi-sec (dry) to doux (sweet). Following recorking, the champagne has to be stored for a lengthy period before it can be sold. The chalk substratum of the Champagne region provides the ideal environment for champagne to mature. Over 250km/150mi of caves, known as **crayères**, can be visited in Reims, Épernay and elsewhere.

Route du Champagne

The wine lands of Champagne are joined in the seven sections of the 700km/450mi Route Touristique du Champagne. Five of these are in the »Triangle Sacré du Champagne« between Épernay, Reims and Château-Thierry with the main areas of cultivation Montagne de ►Reims, Côte des Blancs and Vallée de la Marne, making up 80% of the vineyards. The other two sections wind their way through the Côte des Bars.

✱
Langres

Denis Diderot, who was born in the attractive town of Langres (9500 inhabitants), 35km/22mi south of Chaumont, in 1713, is commemorated by a statue by Bartholdi on the square of the same name. The cathedral of St-Mammès (1141 to approx. 1195) was given a classical façade in the 18th century. The town's 4km/2.5mi of ramparts, with twelve towers and seven gates, are the ideal route to walk around the town and enjoy the splendid surrounding scenery.

Places to Visit in the Ardennes

Charleville-Mézières
✱
Place Ducale ▶

The commune of Charleville-Mézières (56,000 inhabitants) lies close to the Belgian border on the river Meuse. At the heart of classical Charleville in the north is the Place Ducale, developed in the early 17th century and based on the Place des Vosges in Paris. A statue stands in memory of the town's founder, Charles of Gonzaga (1580–1637). The southeast corner of the square features the modern Musée de l'Ardenne (archaeological and ethnological history of the Ardennes). As the birthplace of Arthur Rimbaud (1854–91), a museum in the Vieux Moulin (north of the centre on the riverbank) has been dedicated to the poet. In medieval Mézières, further south at the narrowest stretch of the Meuse loop, remains of the 16th-century fortifications can still be seen. The church of Notre-Dame-de-l'Espérance, in late Gothic Flamboyant style, contains beautiful modern windows (1955–79). Every three years in October (2009, 2012 etc), the town is transformed into a giant stage for the International Marionette Festival.

Mézières ▶

✱
Vallée de Meuse

Revin

Rocroi

North of Charleville-Mézières, the Meuse winds its way through the lonely Ardennes, sometimes through deep gorges, to the pretty spot of **Givet**, last stop before the Belgian border, where there is a fort built in 1555. Wonderful views of the town of Revin, nestled between two loops of river, can be enjoyed from the 400m/1312ft-high Mont Malgré Tout. 14km/8.5mi west of Revin stands the famous star-shaped fortress town of **Rocroi** (2400 inhabitants), constructed in 1675 by Vauban.

The beautiful loop of the Meuse at Monthermé

The old fortress town **Sedan** (21,000 inhabitants) lies 23km/14mi southeast of Charleville-Mézières on the Meuse, at the edge of the Ardennes. Here Marshall Mac-Mahon surrendered in the Franco-German War in 1870, with Napoleon III taken prisoner. From 1424, a castle was established here, which would become the **largest fortress in Europe** through repeated stages of expansion. To the west of the

complex is the Palais des Princes de Sedan (Château-Bas, 1613). The
Musée du Château illustrates the history of town and castle; the
15th-century roof in the Grosse Tour is worth a closer look. Textiles
have played an important role in Sedan since the Middle Ages, as recorded in the Musée des Anciennes Industries at the Le Dijonval royal cloth factory, founded in 1646.

✱
◄ Château Fort

From Bazeilles with its mighty castle (1750), continue to the pretty
little town of Mouton, 18km/11mi southeast of Sedan. The impressive church of Notre-Dame was consecrated in 1231 (15th- and
16th-century towers); the interior is a particularly beautiful example
of early Gothic architecture. A neighbouring museum (Musée du
Feutre) explains all there is to know about felt.

Mouzon

Chartres

Région: Centre
Département: Eure-et-Loir

Altitude: 142m/465ft
Population: 42,000

**Chartres lies on the route between Paris and the Loire, visible from
a distance with its magnificent cathedral, one of the finest examples of Gothic architecture.**

The Frankish county of Chartrain passed into the hands of the
House of Blois in the 10th century and was sold to the Crown in
1286. Charles the Bald bequeathed to the cathedral the veil of the
Virgin Mary in 876 from the reliquary treasures of Charlemagne,
since which time it has been a popular destination for pilgrims. In
memory of Henri IV, crowned in Chartres in 1594, »chicken in the
pot« (poule au pot) is a regular fixture in the local restaurants –
Henri had expressed the wish that every citizen should have such a
bird in the pot on Sundays. Chartres is capital of the département
and centre of **Beauce**, a fertile plateau which stretches between Paris
and Orléans; it is considered the bread basket of France. 70% of the
Eure-et-Loir département is given over to agriculture, producing 1.8
million tons of wheat for the nation's baguettes, plus 0.3 million tons
of peas. Other important industries include engineering (car parts),
pharmaceuticals and chemicals, electronics, cosmetics and perfume
industries. Over 180 firms between Chartres, Orléans and Blois con-
stitute Cosmetic Valley.

**Chartres now
and then**

✱ ✱ Notre-Dame Cathedral

A Gallo-Roman sanctuary or religious structure probably stood on
the hill of the town and was built upon in Christian times. In the 9th
century a Carolingian church stood here until it burnt down in

History

1119. Its crypt was incorporated into the new Romanesque church, the main façade of which was constructed from 1134. A town fire in 1194 again saw it engulfed in flames, although the main façade and veil of the Virgin Mary miraculously survived. In the 13th century the cathedral was rebuilt, even more magnificent than before: the nave was completed between 1195 and 1220, then the choir and transepts. The cathedral was consecrated in 1260. The destruction associated with the French Revolution passed the cathedral by, as the bureaucrats deliberated for too long as to how to manage the overwhelming task.

Exterior The cathedral, a UNESCO World Heritage Site, is recognized as one of the finest Gothic monuments of the nation, »the Acropolis of France, a **palace of styles**« (A. Rodin). Constructed approximately between 1145 and 1165, the simple south tower (106m/347ft) and the 115m/377ft north tower (upper half 1507–13) flank the austere early Gothic façade. Work commenced in 1145 on the three doors of the **Portal Royal**, a masterpiece of Romanesque and early Gothic

✶ ✶
Portal Royal ▶ sculpture. The rigid figures have heads that breathe an expression of individual life; the tympana are marked by similar rigour. The central tympanum portrays Christ as judge of the world, the tympanum to the right scenes from the life of the Virgin Mary, the one on the left Christ's ascension to heaven and the proclamation of his return. The **stiff, elongated figures on the jambs** are prophets, priests and so forth. A splendid 13th-century rose window, 13.35m/44ft in diameter, stands above three high windows, and higher still the Gallery of Kings with 16 large statues. The three doors of each of the two transepts are also richly sculpted, in the south with the theme of the Last Judgement, the north with scenes from the life of the Virgin Mary and figures from the Old Testament.

Cathedral *Plan*

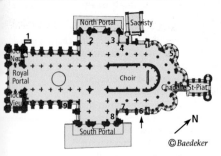

©Baedeker

1 Staircase to the Clocher Neuf
2 Entrance to the north tower
3 Peace Window (1971)
4 Our Lady of the Pillar
5 Chapelle du Saint-Sacrament
6 Entrance to the crypt
7 Notre-Dame-de-Belle-Verrière
8 Saint Fulbert Window
9 Chapelle Vendôme

Interior The interior is impressive not only for its scale. The nave and transepts have aisles, and a double ambulatory surrounds the inner choir. The dimensions are: length 130m/426ft, height 37m/121ft and width

✶ ✶
Windows ▶ 16.4m/54ft, the transept 64.5m/212ft. The cathedral's greatest treasures are the **stained glass windows** (take binoculars!). 184 windows covering 2600 sq m/29,000 sq ft and containing countless lead-cased

Contrasting towers flank one of the earliest Gothic rose windows

panes (*c*400 per sq m/35 per sq ft), with the famous and enchanting
bleu de Chartres, portray holy legends and (in the ambulatory) 22
scenes from the life of Charlemagne. The three wonderful lancet
windows of the west front survive from the previous Romanesque
cathedral. From left to right, they depict the Passion, the life of Mary
and the Tree of Jesse. Other items worthy of note are the Notre-
Dame-de-la-Belle-Verrière window at the right-hand entrance to the
choir (pre-1119), the late Gothic rood screen with Renaissance elements (1514–29) portraying scenes from the life of the Virgin Mary
and the Gospels, as well as 41 groups of sculptures from the 16th to
18th centuries. The Black Madonna (around 1510) at the left-hand
entrance to the choir is the **Notre-Dame de Chartres**. The Chapelle
Vendôme is dedicated to the Sainte Voile, the Holy Veil of silk which
the Byzantine Empress Irene gave to Charlemagne in the year 802.
The floor of the nave is a labyrinth, a common symbol in medieval
pilgrimage churches; the 262m/287yd path is negotiated by pilgrims
on their knees. A white slab with a metal button on the floor of the
southern transept serves as a timekeeper: on 21 June, the day of the
summer solstice, between 12.45pm and 12.55pm (noon in solar
time) a ray of sunlight illuminates the slab.

Crypt	Beneath the choir and nave lies the 110m/120yd-long crypt dating
Treasury	from the 9th/11th century, the largest in France. The Chapelle St-Piat (14th century) contains ornate liturgical artefacts.

Other Sights in Chartres

Musée des Beaux-Arts

Grenier de Loëns

Centre International du Vitrail

From the terrace behind the choir, the view of the medieval lower town on the river is beautiful. The adjacent bishop's palace (17th–18th century) houses an art museum displaying valuable cembali and a good collection of art (including works by Vlaminck, Soutine and Zurbarán). A museum of stained glass is housed west of the cathedral in the Grenier de Loëns, a tithe barn with a beautiful timber-frame façade and 13th-century wine cellar.

What else to see

In the old town along the Eure, which has protected heritage status, the 15th-century Maison du Saumon (a restaurant) southeast of the cathedral is one of a number of beautiful old houses. From here, go down to a 16th-century timber-frame house with stone staircase (Escalier de la Reine Berthe) and the Gothic church of St-Pierre (12th–13th century) with beautiful windows dating from the late 13th century. A picturesque path with views of old **washhouses and mills** leads along the east bank of the Eure. Next to the railway station, an engine shed has been transformed into a museum for old agricultural equipment (COMPA).

Around Chartres

Châteaudun

✳ A castle (12th–16th century) with a proud round tower above the Loir dominates the medieval town (14,500 inhabitants) 44km/27mi

▶ VISITING CHARTRES

INFORMATION

Office de Tourisme
Pl. de la Cathédrale, F-28000 Chartres
Tel. 02 37 18 26 26, fax 02 37 21 51 91
www.chartres-tourisme.com

WHERE TO STAY

▶ **Mid-range**
Grand Monarque
22 Place des Epars, tel. 02 37 35 60 32
www.bw-grand-monarque.com.
Conversion of a Baroque post-coach station into a high-class hotel with an equally good restaurant (closed Mon) and a cosy bistro.

WHERE TO EAT

▶ **Moderate**
Moulin de Ponceau
21 Rue Tannerie, tel. 02 37 35 30 05
A romantic spot on the Eure. The old mill with a terrace is a rustic but elegant setting for fine French cuisine.

FESTIVALS AND EVENTS

Summer evenings: illuminations in the town. Late June: Fête de l'Eau, the town's big celebration; July/Aug: Soirées Estivales; 15 Aug: Procession with »Notre-Dame de Chartres«.

southwest of Chartres. In the Ste-Chapelle (1464) next to the tower, 15 life-size, originally painted, statues of saints – including the mysterious **Ste-Marie-l'Egyptienne**, completely covered by her flowing locks – and murals can be seen. In the old town note the church of Mary Magdalene (partly Romanesque) and various old houses, especially on Rue St-Lubin and Rue des Huileries. The new town around the town hall square was developed after the fire of 1723 by Jules Hardouin, nephew of the famous architect of Versailles, Hardouin-Mansart. Just a few steps to the north of the town hall, on the beautiful Proménade du Mail above the Loir, the Musée des Beaux-Arts et d'Histoire Naturelle exhibits prehistoric, Egyptian and medieval artefacts, as well as a large ornithological collection.

Clermont-Ferrand

L 7

Région: Auvergne
Département: Puy-de-Dôme

Altitude: 401m/1315ft
Population: 141,000

The old capital of the ►Auvergne lies close to the Puy de Dôme, one of the most beautiful volcanic peaks of the Massif Central. This is the home of Michelin, the biggest tyre company in the world; the lively university town features intriguing old districts and an excellent museum of art in Montferrand.

The Celtic oppidum Nemessos on the cathedral hill developed into the thriving town of Augustonemetum in Roman times. In the 3rd century it was converted to Christianity and from the 8th century became known as Clair-Mont. In 1095 Pope Urban II preached the **First Crusade** to a gathering of over 300 bishops and abbots; here they uttered the fatal cry »Deus lo vult«, »God wills it«. The philosopher and mathematician Blaise Pascal was born in Clermont in 1623 († 1662). In 1731 the northeastern neighbour of Montferrand, seat of the counts of Auvergne, was amalgamated with Clermont. The rubber industry began here in 1832, with the **Michelin** tyre company founded in 1886.

History

What to See in Clermont

The lively centrepiece of the town is Place de Jaude with an equestrian statue of the Gallic hero Vercingetorix by F.-A. Bartholdi (1902). In the church of St-Pierre-des-Minimes (17th century), fine panelling can be seen in the choir (1736), whilst the théâtre opposite was created in 1894 in a converted textile hall. From Rue du 11 Novembre, take a right into Rue des Gras to see fine old houses of volcanic rock. A changing programme of art exhibitions is run in the Hôtel

Place de Jaude

▶ VISITING CLERMONT-FERRAND

INFORMATION

Office de Tourisme
Place de la Victoire
F-63000 Clermont-Ferrand
Tel. 04 73 98 65 00
Fax 04 73 90 04 11
www.clermont-fd.com

EVENTS

Early February: international short
film festival. End of May: Fêtes
Médiévales

WHERE TO STAY

► Mid-range

① *La Radio*
43 Avenue P.-et-M.-Curie
F-63400 Chamalières
Tel. 04 73 30 87 83
www.hotel-radio.fr. Beautiful Art
Deco ambience of the 1930s, large,
modern rooms. Situated in the suburb
of Clermont, its restaurant is also
famous for fine French and Auvergnat
cuisine (closed Sun).

► Budget

② *Dav'Hotel Jaude*
10 Rue Minimes
Tel. 04 73 93 31 49
www.dav-hotel.fr
Set in a quiet side street off Place de
Jaude. Modern, spacious rooms, good
service and big breakfast. No restaurant.

WHERE TO EAT

► Moderate

① *Cinq Claire*
5 Rue Ste-Claire, tel. 04 73 37 10 31
Closed Sun–Mon. Honest, regional
fare served under vaults. Wide range
of cheeses.

Clermont-Ferrand *Map*

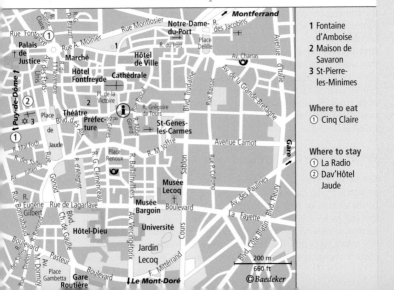

1 Fontaine
  d'Amboise
2 Maison de
  Savaron
3 St-Pierre-
  les-Minimes

Where to eat
① Cinq Claire

Where to stay
① La Radio
② Dav'Hôtel
  Jaude

200 m
660 ft

© Baedeker

Clermont with its cathedral of volcanic stone, with the Puy-de-Dome in the background

Fontfreyde (16th century, attractive courtyard). To the north stands the market hall.

At the centre of the old town, the dark form of the cathedral rises above a sea of houses. Crafted in near-black stone from Volvic, the only large structure built with this intractable material, it was designed in the Gothic style of northern France. The foundation stone was laid in 1248. By the end of the 13th century choir, transept and a section of the nave were completed. The towers and west façade were replaced from 1865 in neo-Gothic style by Viollet-le-Duc. The 30m/98ft-high interior is adorned by magnificent stained glass windows from the 13th–15th centuries, inspired by those of Notre-Dame in Paris. On the left of the first choir chapel, 13th-century frescoes have survived, whilst a Romanesque Madonna stands in the Lady Chapel. The 10th-century crypt contains a beautiful 4th-century marble sarcophagus. To the left of the north portal is the entrance to the Tour la Bayette (marvellous panoramic view) and the treasury.

✶ Cathedral of Notre-Dame-de-l'Assomption

✶ ◀ stained glass windows

The picturesque alleys around the cathedral have retained elements from the 12th–13th centuries and houses with beautiful courtyards from the 15th–18th centuries, for example in Rue des Chaussetiers (Maison de Savaron, 1513), Rue Pascal (»Rue noble«) and Rue du Port.

Old town

South of the cathedral on the Place de la Victoire, tourist information is not all that is on offer: the Espace Art Roman is devoted to Romanesque art treasures and the Espace Massif Central offers guidance on the natural sites in the mountains.

Maison du Tourisme

North of the town hall on the Place de la Poterne stands the Fontaine d'Amboise, a beautiful Renaissance fountain built from lava (1515). There are good views of the Puys from here.

Fontaine d'Amboise

Notre-Dame-du-Port ✶

The church of Notre-Dame-du-Port (11th–12th century) is a fine example of Auvergne Romanesque in light sandstone. The choir, with radiating chapels and crossing towers, is particularly impressive. A richly sculpted south portal features a Moorish-influenced horseshoe arch and a Christ in Majesty with seraphim (12th century) in the tympanum. The door lintel depicts, from the left, the Three Magi, Christ in the temple, the baptism of Christ. Inside, the capitals are worth a look, especially those in the ambulatory (from around 1150). A Black Madonna, copied from a Byzantine original in the 17th century, can be seen in the 11th-century crypt.

Baedeker TIP

Trianon

Be sure to sample bittersweet »Pascalines« with raspberry flavour and »Volcanias«, truffle volcanoes, at Trianon in Rue 11 Novembre. The shop itself, a listed Art Nouveau jewel from 1909, is no less of a delicacy.

More museums

A visit to the Jardin Lecoq is recommended, home to the Musée Lecoq (mineralogy, botany, zoology, calculating machines of Pascal) and the Musée du Bargoin (prehistory, Gallo-Roman finds, magnificent rugs from the Near and Far East).

What to See in Montferrand

Townscape

Approximately 2km/1.25mi northeast of the centre of Clermont, via the Avenue de la République, lies Montferrand, established in the 13th century as a bastide, with two crossing main thoroughfares. Many noble and bourgeois houses from the Gothic and Renaissance periods have survived, often with attractive courtyards.

Carrefour des Taules

At the Carrefour des Taules, centre of the old town, Rue de Rodade (tourist office), Rue des Cordeliers and Rue du Séminaire all converge, each with noteworthy houses. The latter leads past the Halle

Notre-Dame-de-Prospérité

aux Toiles and Hôtel Pradal to the collegiate church of Notre-Dame-de-Prospérité, built from 1304 (Flamboyant Gothic, 16th-century façade). Rue du Séminaire continues to the **circular Place M. Sembat**, where the castle of the counts of Auvergne once stood, and to the excellent museum of art, a conversion of an Ursuline convent

Musée des Beaux-Arts Roger Quillot ✶

(Fainsilber and Gaillard, 1992). The different levels are reached via a ramp similar to that in the New York Guggenheim museum; art and crafts from the Middle Ages to the 19th century are on display (closed Mon).

Around Clermont-Ferrand

Plateau de Gergovie

The Celtic oppidum **Gergovia**, where Vercingetorix repelled Caesar in 52 BC, is thought to have been discovered on the Plateau de Gergovie approx. 7km/4.5mi south of Clermont. A small museum offers details of the battle and accompanying research, as well as a fine view of the surrounding area.

★ ★ Colmar

P 4

Region: Alsace
Département: Haut-Rhin

Altitude: 190m/623ft
Population: 67,000

Colmar is regarded as the prettiest town in ► Alsace after Strasbourg. Its old centre is characterized by carefully restored timber-framed houses and a Renaissance palace, while its impressive museums contain works of art which are famed throughout the world.

Colmar is the capital of the Haut-Rhin (Upper Rhine) département, and lies in the Rhine plain at the end of the Münstertal valley. Its first mention in documents dates from 823 when it was named »Columbarium« (»pigeon loft«). When the Hohenstaufen dynasty controlled the Holy Roman Empire, the town developed into the most important trading centre in the Upper Alsace region. In 1226 Emperor Friedrich II elevated Colmar to the status of a free imperial city, and in 1354 it joined the Alsatian »Décapole« league and was made the headquarters of that union. From 1679 the town was under French sovereignty, and the religious freedom that had existed there since the Reformation was overturned. Between 1871 and 1918, the town came back under German aegis as the capital of the Upper Alsace region in the German territory of Elsass-Lothringen (Alsace and Lorraine). Despite ferocious fighting in the battle of the »Poche de Colmar« (the Colmar Pocket) in February 1945, the town was left largely unharmed. Colmar was the birthplace of Martin Schongauer (1450–91), a famous creator of paintings and etchings, and also provided a workplace for Matthias Grünewald (Mathias Gothart Nithart from Würzburg, c1460/70–1528), a great master of late Gothic art. Sculptor Frédéric Auguste Bartholdi (1834–1904), who fashioned New York's Statue of Liberty, also came from Colmar.

History

»Petite Venise«, a picturesque gem

Colmar's most famous work of art, the Isenheim Altar by Matthias Grünewald

What to See in Colmar

✷ ✷
Musée d'Unterlinden

This museum, one of the richest and most famous in France, is located in a Dominican convent that was founded in the early 13th century (open May–Oct daily 9am–6pm, Nov–April Wed–Mon 9am–noon, 2pm–8pm). Its finest treasures are exhibited in the chapel: a set of works painted by Martin Schongauer for the monastery of Isenheim near Gebweiler in around 1470 plus four altar panels depicting the Passion from Schongauer's workshop and the magnificent winged **Isenheim altarpiece**, painted by Matthias Grünewald in around 1515, also for the Isenheim monastery. His depiction of Christ suffering on the cross is just as breathtaking today as when it was created. Originally the altarpiece could be reconfigured for different dates in the church year, so it could show the Crucifixion flanked by Saint Anthony, the Nativity with choirs of angels, the temptation of Saint Anthony or his meeting in the desert with the hermit Paul. Nowadays the panels are displayed separately to aid their conservation. Several altar models hang on the walls, however, for demonstration purposes. The carved shrine from the central section contains figures of Saint Augustine, Saint Anthony and Saint Jerome and is attributed to Nicholas of Hagenau. In the rooms around the Gothic gallery fragments from various stages of building can be seen, as well as examples of ecclesiastical art (Romanesque and Gothic sculptures, stained glass and goldsmith work). Discoveries from prehistoric and early historic eras as well as from the Gallo-Roman and Merovingian periods are displayed on the ground floor. There are also examples of modern art there (e.g. Renoir, Picasso, Léger, Rouault, Vasarely, Braque). The first floor features local Alsatian folk art.

Town center

The historic town centre with its numerous town houses from the 16th–17th centuries is a jewel of its kind. The Maison des Têtes hotel

A horse-drawn coach on the Grand'Rue

and restaurant, a Renaissance building from 1609, is named after the 106 heads and other statues that adorn it. There are some more picturesque, timber-framed buildings a little further south on Rue des Boulangers and Rue des Serruriers.

The **Eglise des Dominicains** (Dominican church, 13th and 15th centuries, now deconsecrated) is a fine example of Rhenish early Gothic architecture. Notable features inside include the remarkably slender columns, the stained glass (14th–15th centuries) and altars from Marbach near Eguisheim. Another highlight is *The Virgin in a Bower of Roses*, another masterpiece painted by Martin Schongauer (1473).

Collégiale St-Martin

The collegiate church of St-Martin (»the cathedral«, 13th–14th centuries) is highlighted by its 72m/236ft tower. The St Nicholas door at the southern end of the transept is richly decorated, and there are some fine stained glass windows in the choir as well as a Crucifixion tableau from the 14th century.

Ancien Corps de Garde

The southern perimeter Place de la Cathédrale is lined with several medieval buildings. The fabulously decorated oriel of the former courthouse (Ancien Corps de Garde, 1575) was once used for announcing judgments and sentences. To the left of that building is Maison Adolph (1350), one of the oldest private dwellings preserved in the city. On the picturesque corner of Rue Mercière/Rue des Marchands is the absolutely magnificent **Maison Pfister**, built for a milliner in 1537. Across the road is Maison du Cygne, part of which is believed to have been home to Martin Schongauer. Next door to it the birthplace of Frédéric Auguste Bartholdi has been made into a museum.

Maison Pfister

Bartholdi museum

Ancienne Douane

The Ancienne Douane (1480), also called the Koifhus (old market hall), was formerly the economic and political centre of the town. Its ground floor was used for storing goods and for the payment of duties, while the upper floor was the headquarters of the Décapole league. Behind the market hall a fountain by Bartholdi commemorates Captain Lazarus von Schwendi (1522–84), the man said to have brought the Tokay vine back from Hungary upon his return from a war against the Turks. The Pinot Gris vine that is known as Tokay in Alsace is, however, unrelated to any of the vines used to make Hungarian Tokay wine.

► VISITING COLMAR

INFORMATION

Office du Tourisme, 4 Rue des Unterlinden, F-68000 Colmar Tel. 03 89 20 68 92, fax 03 89 41 34 13, www.ot-colmar.fr

FESTIVALS AND EVENTS

International Music Festival, early–mid July; Foire Régionale des Vins d'Alsace, 10-day wine festival in August; jazz festival early September, a famous Christmas market in December

WHERE TO EAT

► Moderate / inexpensive
Caveau St Pierre
24 Rue de la Herse, tel. 03 89 31 99 33, closed Mon. An outdoor restaurant right next to the river Lauch with a superb view of Colmar's delightful Little Venice. A rustic setting with moderate prices.

WHERE TO STAY

► Mid-range / luxury
Maison des Têtes
19 Rue Têtes, tel. 03 89 24 43 43 www.la-maison-des-tetes.com In Colmar there is no more up-market place to stay than this tastefully renovated Renaissance building. The rooms facing the pretty courtyard are larger and quieter. Its cosy, rustic restaurant serves excellent Alsace cuisine.

► Mid-range
St-Martin
38 Grand'Rue
Tel. 03 89 24 11 51
www.hotel-saint-martin.com
These two Renaissance buildings around a courtyard and tower in the shadow of the cathedral are lovely and comfortable.

Colmar *Map*

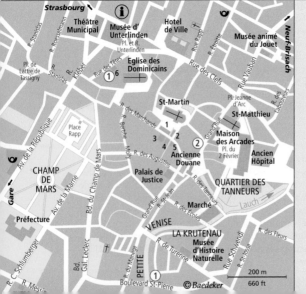

1 Ancien Corps de Garde
2 Maison Pfister
3 Musée Bartholdi
4 Maison du Cygne
5 Maison Schongauer
6 Maison des Têtes

Where to eat
① Caveau St-Pierre

Where to stay
① Maison des Têtes
② St-Martin

© Baedeker

200 m
660 ft

The main street, **Grand'Rue**, has some notable buildings such as Maison des Arcades (a Protestant rectory from 1609) and the former Franciscan church of St-Mathieu with its valuable stained glass windows from the 14th–15th centuries. The pretty **tanners' quarter** (quartier des tanneurs) stretches to the southwest of the old market hall, while further downstream the Lauch loops around the formerly fortified suburb of Krutenau, once the greengrocers' district. A walk down the eastern bank of the Lauch leads to the Pont St-Pierre bridge, from which there is a fine view of the picturesque **Petite Venise** (»Little Venice«) quarter with its tall but narrow houses along the river. Children of all ages should not miss the toy museum (Musée du Jouet on Rue Vauban), which features a collection of dolls and a large model railway.

Other sights

★ ★ Côte d'Azur

O–P 9

Ever since well-to-do British travellers discovered the »French Riviera« and started to take winter holidays there, it has been seen as a playground for the rich and famous from all corners of the world. The coast of ►Provence still has plenty to offer ordinary visitors, with its fabulous beaches, pretty old villages and awe-inspiring coastal landscape. It remains an outstanding place for a holiday.

The Côte d'Azur (French Riviera) is a strip of coastline running 250km/150mi along the shores of the Ligurian Sea, a region of the Mediterranean that runs eastward of Marseille from Cassis as far as the Italian border. The name Côte d'Azur was coined by the French novelist Stephen Liégard in 1887 and is now a byword for a holiday region par excellence: sunshine, sandy beaches and azure sea. Every year some 10 million holidaymakers of every class and nationality visit the area. It is not only the coast itself which is exquisite. The hilly inland scenery that grows increasingly mountainous further eastward is also a delight with its precipitously sited villages. From the end of the 19th century a whole range of famous artists settled along the Côte d'Azur, including Renoir, Signac, Matisse, Chagall and Picasso. This is one of the prime reasons why there are so many excellent museums and galleries. The Côte d'Azur does, of course, get very crowded during the high season of July–August despite the higher prices at that season. For that reason, it is probably better to go there in spring or autumn when the temperatures, too, are lower and more pleasant. Even the mild and sunny winters are lovely.

★ ★ Holiday region

The great abundance and variety of geographical features around the Côte d'Azur is due to the geological structure of the region, starting

Landscape and climate

The »Azure Coast« – view across the Esterel massif to Nice and the Maritime Alps beyond

in the west with a riven and karstified limestone massif pocked with deep narrow bays (calanques), followed by the Massif des Maures, an ancient granite, gneiss and slate massif, and the Massif d'Esterel, primarily gneiss but with many streaks of red porphyry, especially near the coast, creating a delightful effect against the blue of the sea. Then, at the eastern end, come the chalk and Jurassic limestone foothills of the Maritime Alps that plummet sharply downward at the coast, leaving little room for human settlement (e.g. the village of Eze is less than 1km/0.5mi from the coast but has an elevation of 427m/1400ft). The climate is very stable due to the sheltered location. The sun shines 300 days a year, but it does not get too hot in the summer and remains very mild and sunny during the winter with daylight temperatures ranging from 6°C/43°F to 15°C/59°F. The mistral wind can sometimes be felt in the west, and warm sirocco winds can blow during the summer.

Flora The native flora has suffered badly from human encroachment and forest fires. Evergreens such as the aleppo or maritime pine and deciduous trees like holm oaks, cork oaks, common oaks and sweet chestnuts have been seriously depleted. The plants that typify the landscape nowadays come from all corners of the world. Some were introduced as early as the colonization by the Greeks, who brought vines and olive trees, and some arrived in the 19th century when palms, mimosas and eucalyptus were introduced. Other imports include planes, cypress, pines, orange and lemon trees, agaves and opuntia from America. The Mediterranean maquis (garrigue) shrubland consists of kermes oaks, mastic, myrtle, strawberry bushes, gorse, thistles, rockrose and tree heath as well as many fragrant herbs such as lavender, sage, thyme and rosemary.

Economy Since the 19th century, flower growing has been a key activity. The plants are either exported as cut flowers or used as raw material for the renowned perfume industry. The traditional hub of the perfume trade is the town of Grasse, where thousands of tons of flower petals and raw materials, both natural and synthetic, are used every year. About a third of the workforce is employed in tourism. However, the turnover from that is still exceeded by service companies, the electronics and computer industries as well as chemical and biotechnological research and production. Cultivation of fruit and vegetable and the production of sea salt are other important industries.

History

The Ligures, a Celtic tribe who settled the coast, are still recalled in names such as »Golfe du Lion«. The Greeks established a colony called Massalia (Marseille) in around 600 BC. It soon became the main centre of trade in southern France and had further outposts to the east at Nikaia (Nice) and Antipolis (Antibes). After Caesar's conquest of Gaul, he established the first Roman settlement at **Forum Iulii** (Fréjus) in 49 BC. In the first half of the 8th century the Saracens established a base in the Massif des Maures and represented a threat to the entire coastal region during the 9th and 10th centuries (the name of the mountain range is not derived from the Moors but from the Provençal word »maouro« meaning »dark forest«). As of 1486 the Riviera and all of Provence became part of France, whereas Nice allied itself to Savoy in 1388. With the peace settlement of 1815 Nice was granted to the kingdom of Sardinia-Piedmont, but became part of France in 1860 after a referendum. The Allies landed on the Côte des Maures on 15 August 1944.

Places to Visit on the Côte d'Azur

Bandol

The port and tourist resort of Bandol (7500 inhabitants) is situated in a pretty bay and has a casino, a yacht marina and beautiful beaches. It also produces excellent wines (Bandol AC). It is worth taking time to visit **Ile de Bendor**, owned by pastis manufacturers Ricard and featuring a holiday centre and a museum of wines and spirits, or heading 3km/2mi north to the Jardin Exotique zoo, to the Romanesque chapel of Notre Dame du Beausset Vieux with its Madonna created in Puget's studio (and a marvellous view), to **Le Castellet**, a fortified village high on a hill (11th-century castle, 12th-century church), or the Paul Ricard racing circuit. 4km/2.5mi to the east is the town of (14,800 inhabitants) and there is an interesting museum of sports cars on the way. The town itself has a pretty fishing harbour and yacht marina. The Hotel de la Tour exudes an aura of genteel luxury.

Sanary-sur-Mer

Ollioules (5km/3mi northeast of Sanary), famous for its flower growing, is a pretty village with arcades in front of its houses and a ruined castle. To the north lie the Gorges d'Ollioules, a canyon carved out by the river Reppe that features some startling rock formations. High above the gorge in the village of Evenos a ruined castle is built of the same dark basalt stone as the houses.

Ollioules

★
Gorges d'Ollioules
Evenos

▶ VISITING CÔTE D'AZUR

INFORMATION

CRT Riviera-Cote d'Azur
400 Promenade des Anglais
F-06203 Nice Cedex 03
Tel. 04 93 37 78 78, fax 04 93 86 01 06
www.guideriviera.com

MUSEUM PASS

The Carte Musées Côte d'Azur ticket
can be obtained from tourist offices,
from any of the participating museums or from FNAC stores. The best
version of the card is one that is valid
for any 7 days out of 14.

WHERE TO EAT

▶ Expensive
Josy-Jo
2 Rue du Planastel
F-06800 Haut de Cagnes
Tel. 04 93 20 68 76, closed Sat lunch
and Sun.
First-class and thoroughly tempting
regional cuisine with no unnecessary
trimmings, served inside a charming
house that was once home to Soutine
and Modigliani or in the garden
under vines.

▶ Moderate
La Jarrerie
8 Av. Amiral de Grasse
F-06620 Le Bar sur Loup
Tel. 04 93 42 92 92. Traditional
Provençal and modern cuisine is
prepared in this 17th-century build-
ing. Its cosy but elegant dining room

features a fireplace and oak beams. In
summer, meals can be enjoyed in the
shady garden.

▶ Moderate / inexpensive
Les Potiers
135 Rue des Potiers, F-83600 Fréjus
Tel. 04 94 51 33 74, July–Aug closed
lunchtime. Tiny little establishment
near Porte des Gaules. Classic recipes
like mussel soup, duck, saddle of
lamb. A reservation is required.

WHERE TO STAY

▶ Budget / mid-range
Oasis
Impasse Charcot, F-83600 Fréjus
Tel. 04 94 51 50 44, www.hotel-
oasis.net. Nice little hotel with garden,
100m from the beach.

La Bellaudière
78 Av. P. Ziller, F-06130 Grasse
Tel. 03 93 36 02 57, www.logis06.com
15 comfortable rooms in a town
house from the 16th–19th centuries
on the road to Nice. Restaurant
terrace with a fabulous view.

Auberge des Seigneurs
1 Rue du Dr Vinet, F-06140 Vence
Tel. 04 93 58 04 24, www.auberge-
seigneurs.com. Situated in the
Château de Villeneuve where many
renowned figures have resided. Provençal atmosphere, rustic, cosy and
quiet. Good local cuisine.

Toulon ▶Toulon

Hyères Hyères (53,000 inhabitants) lies at the foot of the hill of Castéou
(204m/670ft high). It is the oldest of the winter health resorts on the
Côte d'Azur and has some magnificent villas, hotels and a casino.
Nowadays its fine long beaches (Hyères Plage in particular) have re-

Even though they are now firmly part of the tourist trail, old villages like St-Paul-de-Vence still have a lovely atmosphere

sulted in it being overrun with tourists. Its **old town centre** around Place Massillon is a pearl with its flower market, the Tour St-Blaise and the remnants of a 12th-century Knights Templar commandery. The square in front of the church of St-Paul (12th–16th centuries) offers a fabulous view. In Parc St-Bernard above the town it is possible to see the ruins of a medieval castle as well as the Villa de Noailles cultural centre (Robert Mallet-Stevens, 1923). The newer part of the town includes the Musée Municipal (archaeology, folklore and natural history), while the Jardin Olbius Riquier, a lovely park featuring exotic plant life, lies south of the N 98.

Notre-Dame-de-Consolation

The chapel of pilgrimage Notre-Dame-de-Consolation (1955, the view is splendid) is situated on the Costebelle hill about 3km/2mi south of Hyeres. From there it is worth taking the path up to Mont des Oiseaux, which rises to a height of 306m/1004ft (the walk takes about an hour and a half). Beyond Toulon-Hyères airport, the sandy beaches of **Hyères-Plage** stretch away to the south. Two causeways lined by beaches, the westerly of which can only take traffic in the summer, link **Presqu'Ile de Giens** to the mainland. The salt flats between the causeways are a habitat for some fascinating birdlife. The wooded Iles d'Hyères are geologically part of the Massif des Maures. Both Porquerolles and Port-Cros are nature reserves. Their steep, rugged coastlines peppered with coves make lovely places for a swim. The islands are great for rambling. Porquerolles, (7×3km/4.5×2mi) the largest island, produces a fine wine. On the south coast (45 minutes from the village) a lighthouse rises to 96m/315ft above the cliffs. To the east of Porquerolles is the sparsely populated Ile de Port-Cros and the rocky Ile du Levant, where the Héliopolis naturist colony was founded in 1932, the first of its kind in the world. The rest of the island is off-limits except to the military. Ferries run from Toulon, La Tour-Fondue, Hyères-Plage, La Lavandou and Cavalaire.

★ ★
Iles d'Hyères

Massif des Maures

Between Hyères and Fréjus lies a mountain range forested with holm oaks, firs and chestnut woods. It reaches a height of 779m/2556ft at Sauvette. The **Corniche des Maures** runs along a gloriously scenic coastline from Le Lavandou past St-Tropez to Fréjus, taking in a series of smaller resorts with fabulous beaches. It is possible to undertake some fascinating tours through the massif. The following route

Away from the bustle St-Tropez is just another pretty fishing port

through the western section covers some 85km/55mi: from Le Lavandou along the D 41 past Arboretum de Gratteloup to Col de Babaou (414m/1358ft) and on to Collobrières, the main town on the Massif des Maures and a centre for chestnut processing. From there carry on further east along the ridge and take a right turn towards the remnants of Chartreuse de la Verne (founded in 1170 although its buildings are mostly 17th–18th century, closed Tuesdays). The next place on the tour is the somewhat touristy Grimaud, a picturesque »village perché« (with its ruined castle and St-Michel church both dating from the 11th century). Consider a short diversion to La Garde-Freinet (10km/6mi), formerly the main settlement of the Saracens (there are some remains of a castle northeast of the village) and later a centre for the production of cork. Cogolin is known for the **manufacture of pipes** from the roots of the bruyère (erica) bush. St-Sauveur church (11th–16th centuries) has a Renaissance portal made of the green serpentine that is common in the area. Continue southwest over the Col du Canadel (268m/879ft) and down to Canadel-sur-Mer.

Collobrières

✴
Grimaud

Cogolin

✴
Ramatuelle

The ancient, but now very tourist-oriented, village of Ramatuelle (northeast of La Croix Valmer, 2000 inhabitants) has a most impressive shape, being virtually round. The outer houses once formed part of a circular wall. The Romanesque church has a serpentine portal built in 1620. The grave of a notable former inhabitant, actor **Gérard Philipe** († 1959), can be found in the cemetery.

✴
Saint-Tropez

✴
Musée de
l'Annonciade ▶

The 5500 inhabitants of St-Tropez – actually a perfectly »normal« little town – do very well (at the considerable expense of tourists) from the myth that the fishing port gained in the 1950s and 1960s from the Paris intelligentsia, rich devil-may-cares and the film industry. In summer it attracts 100,000 visitors a day and can consequently be pretty chaotic. There is a large car park at Nouveau Port, where the biggest attraction is situated in the former Chapel of the Annunciation (1558). The **Musée de l'Annonciade** (closed Tue) has an outstanding collection of Impressionist and modern art, including works by Signac, who »discovered« St-Tropez in 1892. During the off-season it is easier to enjoy the charms of the harbour and an old town that extends as far as its citadel. The church (Italian Baroque, 1784) features a bust of St Torpes, from whom the town gets its name. To celebrate his feast day, the town holds a great »Bravade« (originally meaning an act of defiance), a festival and parade which lasts from 16 to 18 May. The 17th-century **citadel** (don't miss the great view) houses a museum of seafaring and local history. One of the prettiest sights in the town is Rue de la Misericorde with its charming arcades. There is a chapel of the same name with a fine serpentine portal at the point where it joins the main shopping street, Rue Gambetta. The nearest **beaches** are to the west and east of the town and extend beyond the Cap de St-Tropez. The sandy beaches around the Bay of Pampelonne southeast of St-Tropez, 8km/5mi long and fully equipped, are the main attraction, although everything costs money from car parking to beach umbrellas. In the very depths of the bay of St-Tropez lies Port-Grimaud, a resort for yachting holidaymakers which was built in 1966 but in olde-worlde style.

◀ Beaches

Port-Grimaud

▶ VISITING ST TROPEZ

WHERE TO STAY

▶ Luxury

① *La Ponche*
Port des Pêcheurs
F-83990 St-Tropez
Tel. 04 94 97 02 53
www.laponche.com
A hotel composed of 17th-century houses with a view of the fishing harbour, which has boasted some famous guests. Not all the rooms have balconies. The ambience is cosy, the restaurant very good.

WHERE TO EAT

▶ Moderate

① *Petit Charron*
6 Rue Charrons, tel. 04 94 97 73 78
Closed 1–15 Aug
No-frills bistro with a family atmosphere serving excellent local fare.

St-Tropez Map

Where to eat
① Petit Charron

Where to stay
① La Ponche

200 m
660 ft
©Baedeker

Sainte-Maxime　The Corniche des Maures continues to the northeast. Amid the family atmosphere of Ste-Maxime (9600 inhabitants), the casino bears witness to a more glamorous past. The church has a fine marble altar (18th century, from La Verna in Italy) and there is an exhibition of mechanical musical instruments at the Musée du Phonographe et de la Musique Mécanique.

Fréjus　Fréjus (48,000 inhabitants) is situated on the edge of the agricultural district around the estuary of the river Argens at the foot of the Esterel Massif. It and neighbouring St-Raphaël (see below) have now have now practically merged into a single conurbation. The fine sandy beach of Fréjus-Plage and its marina are very attractive. Fréjus is also well known for its Roman past. Founded by Caesar as Forum Iulii, it became a military harbour under Augustus and featured a lagoon connected to the sea by a canal some 500m/550yd long and 30m/100ft wide. By 1774 the harbour had silted up and was eventually filled in. The most important Roman relic is the **amphitheatre**
▶ Roman buildings
(Arènes, c AD 100), which was used for various events. It measures 114×83m/125×91yd and had room for 10,000 spectators. The city gate, Porte des Gaules, is situated at Place Agricola, and at the northeastern edge of the town (N 7) there are remnants of a viaduct with the theatre remains not far to its west. An archaeological museum is included in the **cathedral complex**, which is the other main attraction in the town. Enter the early Gothic cathedral (around 1200) through the southern entrance with its carved Renaissance doors (1530), and on the left note the 5th-century baptistery containing spolia from the forum. The cathedral proper has no aisles to its nave: the aisle to the north is actually a separate church in its own right. Notable features are an altarpiece in 16 sections by Jacques Durandi († c1470) and the choir stalls (c1440). The cloister (13th century) has a coffered ceiling that includes a cycle of paintings of the Apocalypse (15th century).

✳
Cathedral complex ▶

Saint-Raphaël　St-Raphaël (31,000 inhabitants) has pretty promenades alongside its old harbour and a beach lined by palm and plane trees. It is dominated by its casino and the neo-Byzantine church (1889). Here Napoleon landed in 1799 after his Egyptian campaign (hence the pyramids by the harbour), and from here too he retreated to Elba in 1814. The old centre of the town includes the fortified Knights Templar church of St-Pierre from the 12th century, next to which is the Musée d'Archéologie.

Massif de l'Esterel　The Esterel Massif runs for about 20km/12mi before dropping steeply into the Mediterranean. The coast road between St Raphaël and La Napoule, the **Corniche d'Or** (Corniche de l'Esterel, N 98), was only built in 1903, at last providing access to some fabulous scenery with red fields of porphyry and green flora set against the azure of the sea. The forests that once covered the massif have vanished as a

One of the loveliest beaches on the Côte d'Azur: Plage de Pampelonne near St-Tropez

result of forest fires. The N 98 passes though Boulouris and Cap du Dramont (where you can walk to the lighthouse, 1 hour there and back), Agay (with the road to Pic de l'Ours, 496m/1627ft high; 1½ hours there and back from the car park), Anthéor and the mighty Pic du Cap Roux (453m/1486ft; 2 hours there and back from the car park), Le Trayas, Miramar with its little coves and Théoule sur Mer.

Alternatively take the N 7 to drive inland around the massif. Upon leaving Fréjus some exotic buildings (pagoda, mosque) recall the days when colonial troops were stationed in Fréjus. After about 11km/7mi a small road leads off to the right towards **Mont Vinaigre**, the highest peak in the massif (618m/2028ft, for a fantastic panorama of the surrounding landscape 15 minutes from the car park).

Via Aurelia

★ ★
Mont Vinaigre

Popular sand and shingle beaches run from Théoule to Cannes. La Napoule Plage has a large marina and a medieval castle (14th century) with a gallery.

La Napoule Plage

Vallauris is included under ►Cannes.

Cannes

The old town of Grasse (48,000 inhabitants, 17km/11mi north of Cannes) seems to be boxed in by steep cliffs leading up to Roquevignon on the hill. The town is famous for its **perfume industry**, which has been in existence since the 16th century. Catherine de' Medici popularized perfumed gloves (leatherwork has been flourishing in Grasse since the 13th century). Some 30 perfume companies are based here, although the lion's share of the flowers used in the industry now come from abroad. It is fascinating to visit the salesrooms and exhibitions of Fragonard (see below), Galimard (73 Route de Cannes) or Molinard (60 Blvd. Victor Hugo), and a bottle of pure flower distillate makes a wonderful souvenir (information from the tourist office, Place du Cours). There is also a marvellous view from

Grasse

Place du Cours. Further down the hill is the Musée de la Parfumerie, next to Fragonard's own lovely museum and salesroom. The Musée d'Art et d'Histoire de Provence is situated in the Hôtel de Clapiers Cabris (1771) and concentrates on the town's history, furniture and ceramics. Villa Fragonard was once home to the Rococo painter **Jean-Honoré Fragonard**, who lived there from 1791 to 1806 having been born in Grasse in 1732. The town was seat of a bishop from 1244 until 1790. Its cathedral, Notre Dame du Puy, (12th–13th centuries with extensions from the 17th–18th centuries) displays Lombard influences and looks decidedly archaic inside. Three works of art in the church are notable, a Rubens (1602), a triptych ascribed to Ludovico Brea and *Washing of the Feet* by Jean-Honoré Fragonard (1755), one of his few religious images. The 13th-century bishop's palace next door now houses the town hall. A little further north by the northern perimeter of the magnificent palace of Gerbers Isnard (1781) is the very atmospheric Place aux Aires, where a flower market takes place in the mornings.

Gorges du Loup   ✴ It is well worth taking a round trip from Grasse through the Loup Gorge (about 40km/25mi). The trip takes in the fabulously situated (and rather touristy) **Gourdon**. Its 13th-century castle has a history museum and a museum of naive painting. In **Le Bar**, another lovely spot, the church of St-Jacques contains a *Dance of Death* from the late 15th century and an altar polyptych by Ludovico Brea.

Antibes   ►Antibes for Juan-les-Pins and Biot.

Grasse Map

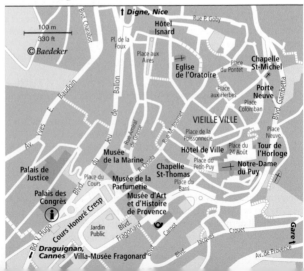

To the west of the Var estuary, the town of Cagnes-sur-Mer (44,000 inhabitants) is, like Gaul, split into three parts. The former fishing harbour of Cros-de-Cagnes is now a beach resort (boasting the giant pyramids of **Marina Baie des Anges**). Behind that is the modern town Cagnes-Ville and the picturesque old quarter of Haut-de-Cagnes with its Grimaldi castle (14th–17th centuries, with a marvellous Renaissance courtyard), housing a museum on the cultivation of olive trees, a collection of portraits of famous painters donated by cabaret singer Suzy Soulidor and a gallery featuring works by Chagall, Matisse and Renoir among others. On the first floor there is a notable ceiling fresco painted by the Genoese artist Giovanni Carlone (1584–1630). Frescoes in the Chapelle Notre-Dame-de-Protection just outside the walls of the old town to the northeast date to around 1525. Maison Les Colettes (1km/1100yd to the east) was the home of **Pierre-Auguste Renoir** from 1908 until his death in 1919 and is now an interesting museum.

Cagnes sur Mer

Overlooked by its castle, Villeneuve-Loubet (2km/1.25mi southwest) has the Musée d'Art Culinaire, housed in the building where the famous cook **Auguste Escoffier** (1846–1935) was born.

Villeneuve-Loubet

A little way inland the pretty medieval village of St-Paul (3000 inhabitants) is perched picturesquely upon a hill. Since its discovery by painters such as Modigliani and Picasso in the 1920s, the town has lost something of its innocence. The hotel restaurant Colombe d'Or became world famous because the painters were known to pay their bills with the donation of a painting. Boutiques, studios, galleries and souvenir shops now dominate the scene. The well preserved 16th-century circle of walls incorporates a sizeable keep. The treasures in the church (13th–17th century) are well worth viewing, and on Place de la Castre there is a museum of local history. Marc Chagall († 1985), a former resident of St-Paul, is buried in the cemetery. The famous **Fondation Maeght** is 1km/1100yd northeast of St-Paul. The establishment, endowed by the art dealers Aimé and Marguerite Maeght, combines a very beautiful natural landscape with modern architecture and art. It is open July–September 10am–7pm, 10am–12.30pm, 2.30pm–6pm otherwise. Note that when a special exhibition takes place, the gallery's own works are not on display.

✶
Saint-Paul-de-Vence

A Miró sculpture at Fondation Maeght

Teetering above the coast, there is no other village like Eze

Vence

Vence (18,000 inhabitants) 3km/2mi to the north was made seat of a bishop in 439. At the centre of its pretty old quarter stands the cathedral Nativité-de-Notre-Dame (11th–17th century) with fine 15th-century choir stalls. A Roman sarcophagus serves as the altar, and the baptismal chapel features a mosaic by **Marc Chagall** (1979), who was resident in Vence up till his death in 1985. The palace of the barons of Villeneuve (13th–17th century) at the western edge of the old town now houses a museum of art and a hotel. To the north of the town (D 2210) a rosary chapel belonging to a Dominican convent was designed by Henri Matisse in 1947–51, even though he described himself as an »atheist seeker after truth«.

✳
Chapelle du Rosaire ▶

Nice

▶Nice

✳ ✳
Corniches

Three stretches of coast road, each about 30km/20mi long, link Nice to Menton on the Italian border. The Corniche du Littoral (N 98), also dubbed the Corniche Inférieure, hugs the shore and passes through several villages, most of which are very busy with traffic. The Moyenne Corniche (N 7) follows the coast at a higher elevation, passing over many bridges and overhangs, while the Grande Corniche (D 2564), built in the reign of Napoleon, runs along the top of the cliffs. Both the higher roads offer fantastic views.

Villefranche-sur-Mer

Villefranche (8000 inhabitants) is situated in a beautiful bay. The natural harbour sheltered by Cap Ferrat was an important military harbour from the Middle Ages until quite recent times. The US Mediterranean fleet was stationed here until 1962. One notable feature of the picturesque old town is its Rue Obscure, covered over with dark arches. Next to the fishing harbour stands the chapel of St-Pierre, which was decorated by Jean Cocteau in 1957. The citadel (1580) houses the Musée Volti (a local sculptor), the Musée Goetz Boumeester (abstract art) and a collection of archaeological finds.

The charming Cap Ferrat, with its sandy beaches and lovely walks, emerged as a colony of villas for the rich and famous at the beginning of the 20th century. The magnificent villa of Baroness **Ephrussi de Rothschild** (1912), now open to the public as a museum, shows furniture, tapestries, porcelain items and Impressionist paintings, and is worth visiting for its café-restaurant alone.

✷ **Cap Ferrat**

This belle époque resort (4000 inhabitants) with its casino and marina has a particularly balmy climate. Its sights include the magnificent **Villa Kerylos** on the Baie des Fourmis, which was built for the archaeologist Théodore Reinach in 1902.

Beaulieu-sur-Mer

Eze (2500 inhabitants) is split into two sections. The famous Eze-Village is accessed via the Moyenne Corniche. It is perched dizzyingly 427m/1400ft above the sea. A 14th-century gate guards the entrance to the village. The finest views are to be had from the castle ruins. The Jardin Exotique park around the castle is also worth a visit, as is the Chapelle des Pénitents Blancs (14th century with enamel images by J. M. Poulain outside, and a Nice-school *Crucifixion* and a Catalonian crucifix from 1258 inside) or the perfumeries of Fragonard and Galimard. In 1883 Nietzsche devised the third part of his magnum opus *Thus Spoke Zarathustra* on the path leading down to the sea that now bears his name. The other part of the town is the coastal resort of Eze-Bord-de-Mer.

✷ ✷ **Eze**

The commune of La Turbie (2600 inhabitants), on the Grande Corniche 480m/1575ft above the sea, is the site of a Roman monument, the **Trophée des Alpes** (Trophy of Augustus). Formerly 50m/164ft in height, the monument was dedicated by the Roman senate in 6 BC to honour Caesar Augustus' conquest of the Alpine peoples. In the 14th century it was converted into a fortress, but was blown up in 1705 during the War of the Spanish Succession. The nearby church of St-Michel-Archange (18th-century Italian Baroque) is richly decorated and features a communion rail made of agate and onyx, paintings by Jean-Baptiste van Loo plus a Pietà from the Brea school. There is fantastic view down to Monaco from the Tête de Chien promontory to the south of the town.

✷ **La Turbie**

There are two fascinating examples of Provençal **nids d'aigle** (»eyries«) to the north of La Turbie in Peillon (with the chapel of Notre-Dame-des-Douleurs from the 15th–16th centuries and its magnificent frescoes painted by Giovanni Canavesio in around 1485) at an elevation of 376m/1234ft, and Peille 630m/2067ft overlooking the river Peillon. The latter has a collegiate church with a Lombard tower (12th–13th century) and a retable by Honoré Bertone (1579).

✷ **Peillon**

✷ **Peille**

►Monaco

Monaco

Roquebrune-Cap-Martin

Roquebrune-Cap-Martin (13,000 inhabitants) is another town with two distinct districts. Old Roquebrune with its arched alleys is built on the hillside. The castle was constructed in 970 as a defence against the Saracens, and there is a fine view from its 13th-century keep. Cap-Martin to the east of the cape itself has expanded into Menton. The walk to Monaco can take as little as two hours (coming back by bus or train). On a footpath just outside Roquebrune is a building called the Cabanon, a tiny shack that was built by the architect **Le Corbusier** in 1952. He often resided there in the years preceding his death in 1965. Indeed it was here that he suffered a fatal heart attack while taking a bath. His grave is in the cemetery here. Next door is Villa E-1027, created by the Irish designer Eileen Gray.

Menton

The town of Menton (29,000 inhabitants) is almost in Italy. Both in appearance and lifestyle it leaves little doubt as to its proximity and shared history with the neighbouring country. From 1346 to 1848 it was controlled, with a brief hiatus or two, by the Principality of Monaco but subsequently became a free town under the protection of the Kingdom of Piedmont-Sardinia until a referendum in 1861 brought it under the aegis of France. Its mild climate, which even allows oranges and lemons to ripen (there is a lemon harvest festival in February), made it a winter resort for the rich and nouveau riche as well as for various artists. Nowadays it is an unassuming holiday resort with little glamour. The beach is small and stony. The Parvis St-Michel square, the centrepiece of the old town, hosts concerts in the summer. The fabulously decorated parish church (1619–75 with a tower on the left dating from the 15th century) is situated here, while the Eglise de la Conception (1689) is further up the hill. The wedding reception suite of the Hôtel de Ville (Rue de la Republique) was decorated by Jean Cocteau in 1957 (open Mon–Fri). The 17th-century bastion in the harbour includes a museum to Cocteau. The Promenade du Soleil leads from the bastion past the 1896 market hall to the Casino Municipal (1932) and the glorious Jardin Biovès. The main shopping street, Rue St-Michel, runs parallel to the promenade. Further to the southwest on Av. Carnot, Palais Carnoles (1717) houses the Musée des Beaux-Arts, featuring early French and Italian masters as well as modern art.

! **Baedeker TIP**

Rail adventures

The **Train des Pignes** (»Pine Cone Express«) runs along a 150km/95mi length of track built between 1890 and 1911 via Entrevaux to Digne. A guide book with walks can be obtained from the Chemins de Fer de Provence station in Nice. Steam trains ply the stretch from Entrevaux to Puget-Théniers on Sundays from May to October. Reservations: C.F.P., tel. 04 97 03 80 80, www.trainprovence.com. The building of the 119km/74mi **Tenda line** was a daring endeavour. Starting in 1920, the line linked Nice to Cuneo via the Roya valley and the Col de Tende tunnel. Several trains run every day from the SNCF station in Nice and the 80km/50mi journey as far as Tende takes about 1¾ hours.

Inland from Nice · Massif du Mercantour

At the far eastern end of the Côte d'Azur the Maritime Alps descend steeply to the Mediterranean. The main peak of the **Massif du Mercantour** (Cime du Gélas, 3143m/10,312ft) is only 50km/30mi away from Nice. Hairpin roads with splendid views wind through some staggering mountain terrain with picturesque gorges. There is also a surprising abundance of artistic treasures, primarily from the Nice school of art. The following routes are organized from east to west. For the Route des Grandes Alpes ►Tours.

Digest

The N 202 runs north from Nice airport through the lower Var valley, which is hemmed on both sides by mountains almost 1000m/3300ft high. From Pont Charles Albert it is worth making a short diversion to Gilette and Bonson, where the church has paintings by Antonio Brea and Jacques Durandi, on account of the stupendous view. At Plan du Var the D 2565 turns off into the impressive Gorges de la Vésubie carved by the Vésubie river. There is another great view from the pilgrimage chapel of Madone d'Utelle (1806) in the village of Utelle at an elevation of 1174m/3852ft. As far as Lantosque the landscape retains a Mediterranean character but the terrain thereafter is Alpine. At Roquebillière take a look at the church of St-Michel-du-Gast (12th–16th centuries with a 16th-century retable of Saint Anthony). Venanson's St-Sébastien chapel has frescoes painted in 1481 by Giovanni Baleison relating the legend of the chapel's patron saint.The pretty village of St-Martin-Vésubie (1000 inhabitants, 960m/3150ft) is the starting point for tours of the Parc National du Mercantour. The park is well furnished with hiking paths (including GR 52; information in St-Martin). Among the pretty old houses on the narrow Rue du Dr Cagnoli stand the Chapel of the White Penitents (late 17th century), the parish church (17th century) with its altar panels by Ludovico Brea and the house of the Comtes de Gubernati.

Var/Vésubie

✱
Gorges de la Vésubie

Saint-Martin-Vésubie

The 40km/25mi of road leading from St-André northeast of Nice to the 1604m/5262ft peak of Col de Turini (D 2204/2566) is well known as the closing stage of the **Monte Carlo Rally**. The 16th-century church of St-Pierre in L'Escarène is worth a look for its Renaissance façade, as is the church of Ste-Marguerite (post 1483), wonderfully situated in Lucéram, with its beautiful Nice-school altars: a retable of St Margaret (Ludovico Brea, 1500), one of St Anthony (attributed to Giovanni Canavesio, 1480) and various other retables by Antonio Brea (1510) and Franscisco Brea (1560).

Col de Turini

L'Escarène

✱
Lucéram

The D 2566 leads from Menton through the delightful Carei valley past Castillon to **Sospel** (2600 inhabitants), where the suburbs on the east and west of the river Bevera are linked by an 11th-century tower bridge, in which the tourist office is also located. The church

Carei valley
Sospel

Tende, the last village in the upper valley of the Roya, has an unmistakeably Ligurian look

of St-Michel, which was a cathedral at the time of the Papal Schism, has a Baroque façade (1641) and an outstanding polyptych by Francisco Brea from about 1530. Above the village is Fort St-Roch. The fort is completely underground and is like a town in its own right (guided tours available).

Breil-sur-Roya The road then leads over the 879m/2884ft Col de Brouis (named after the wild heather that is so common here) into the valley of the river Roya. The old town of Breil-sur-Roya (2000 inhabitants) has a lovely location between the river and a spur of the 1610m/5282ft Mount Arpette. The church of Sancta Maria in Albis (17th century with an altar panel from 1500 and a magnificent 17th-century organ front) on Place de Brancion and the railway museum Ecomusée du Haut-Pays are worth visiting. Follow the Gorges de Saorge to the old **Saorge** hamlet of **Saorge** itself (350 inhabitants), clinging precariously to the mountainside. The heritage-listed marketplace is particularly attractive. Unfortunately the 11th-century church of Madonna del Poggio to the south of the village is not open to the public. It is an outstanding example of the Lombard Romanesque style. At St-Dal-**La Brigue** mas-de-Tende a minor road turns off towards La Brigue (600 inhabitants) in the lovely Levense valley. Its collegiate church, St-Martin (late 15th century), contains a number of altarpieces of the Nice school. An outstanding art treasure can be found 4km/2.5mi to the **★ ★** east in the pilgrimage chapel of **Notre-Dame-des-Fontaines**, in the **Notre-Dame-des-** vicinity of which there are a number of healing springs. The 12th- to **Fontaines** 14th-century building is plain but every inch of it – an area of some 320 sq m/3500 sq ft –is decorated with dramatic frescoes painted by Giovanni Canavesio and Giovanni Baleison in 1491–92. Information: www.labrigue.fr.

St-Dalmas forms the starting point for hikes through the region surrounding Mont Bego (2872m/9423ft) and the **Vallée des Merveilles**
(Valley of Marvels), famous for the pictures scratched into its rock
during the early Bronze Age (*c*2800–1500 BC). Due to the sheer
number of visitors, visits are strictly controlled and certain areas may
only be accessed in the company of an official guide. The tourist office in Tende (www.tendemerveilles.com) provides information, and
tours are offered from both Tende and St-Dalmas. Cabins are available for overnight stays. Mountain climbing equipment is essential.

★
Vallée des
Merveilles

The small town of Tende (816m/2677ft, 2000 inhabitants) has only
been part of France since 1947. It had been a **border town in the
Kingdom of Piedmont** since the Middle Ages. Above the reddish and
green slates of the town, part of which dates back to the 15th century, remains of a castle of the Lascari family destroyed in 1692 still
linger. The Musée des Merveilles provides information on the rock
drawings found in the **Valley of Marvels**, and the Lombard-Gothic
church of Notre-Dame-de-l'Assomption (1462–1506, the burial place
of the Lascaris) is distinguished by its fine portal. The **Tenda Pass**
(1871m/6138ft) was fortified by Italy from 1882 onwards. Its southern side, mostly not asphalted, is one of the most hair-raising passes
of the Alps. The N 204 leads to Limone Piemonte through a tunnel,
3182m/3480yd long, which was opened in 1882.

Tende

★ Côte Basque

F 9

**Since Biarritz became a renowned seaside resort in the mid-19th
century thanks to the patronage of Empress Eugénie, the Côte Basque and the verdant hills inland at the western edge of the Pyrenees have been popular with holidaymakers. Nowadays its Atlantic
breakers make the coast a Mecca for surfers, too.**

The most southerly stretch of France's Atlantic coastline, between Bidassoa on the Spanish border and Biarritz, is called the Côte Basque.
It is a continuation of the Gascon Côte d'Argent ►Gascony. The Basques, who call themselves »Euskaldunak« and their nation »Euskadi«,
live in an area that stretches from the eastern Pyrenees as far as Bil-
bao, with about 200,000 Basques living on the French side of the
border in the regions of Labourd, Lower Navarre, Soule and nearly
two million on the Spanish side. The origin of the race is not known.
The language is definitely not Indo-European in origin. Spanish Basques have campaigned fiercely for autonomy, with some elements
even resorting to terrorism, but France experienced little unrest until
the 1980s, and even then to a much lesser degree then on the other
side of Bidassoa. Even in the Basque lands of France, however, cultural roots are emphasized. Theatre and music groups that highlight

The Basque
country

local solidarity are highly popular, as are language schools and academies for pelota, a game involving hitting a ball against a wall, or fronton, with hand or bat and catching it again. Basque folklore includes other sports in addition to pelota, mainly contests of strength pursued by men only, such as tug-of-war, tree-sawing competitions or rock lifting, as well as acrobatic dancing, music and singing. The Basques are particularly fond of singing but not, for some reason, in public. Spanish-style bullfighting is pursued here as »course de vaches«, although these bulls are spared the sword, instead being used by the bold, amateur fighters more as a kind of »gymnastic hurdle«.

Places to Visit on the Côte Basque

★
Biarritz

Biarritz (31,000 inhabitants) was once among the most famous seaside resorts in the world. It is beautifully situated on the rugged, windswept Atlantic coast. Fine, sandy beaches, mineral springs and a mild climate all contributed to the transformation of the former fishing village. The villa built here in 1854–55 for Empress Eugénie was replaced in 1900 by the luxurious Hôtel du Palais. More splendid **villas** from the belle époque still bear witness to the atmosphere of bygone days but otherwise the charm of Biarritz has been rather swamped by modern-day plastic and concrete. The visitors are eclectic, ranging from the »haute volée« to young surfers, since the best **surfing waves** in Europe are said to break here. The stand-out events in the calendar are the Fêtes Musicales (late April), the Surf Festival (one week in mid-July) and Le Temps d'Aimer (a mid-September festival of ballet). The town's central square is Place Georges-Clemenceau. The route to the sea leads via Place Bellevue, with the Bellevue Casino (1887) on the left and Casino Municipal on the right. The **Grande Plage** stretches as far as Pointe St-Martin, where a lighthouse 44m/138ft high offers a fine view. Next comes Plage de la Chambre d'Amour, a lovely beach – but be careful when swimming on account of the high waves and strong currents. Blvd. Maréchal-Leclerc leads away from Casino Bellevue past the neo-Gothic Ste-Eugénie church and the picturesque fishing harbour to the Esplanade de la Vierge. A small iron bridge designed by Gustave Eiffel himself leads to the rocky outlier **Rocher de la Vierge** and its statue of the Virgin Mary, where there is a marvellous panoramic view from the Adour estuary as far as the Spanish coast. It is worth paying a visit to the Musée de la Mer and its aquaria across from the rock. A Romano-Byzantine imperial chap-

! *Baedeker* TIP

Basque confectionery

Marranos – Jews expelled from Spain – are said to have brought with them the secret of manufacturing chocolate. Other Basque specialities include »muxus« (literally »kisses«, almond macaroons) and »kanouga« (soft caramels). Good places in Biarritz to savour these tempting confections include Miremont, Henriet and Pariès on Place Clemenceau as well as St-Charles on Rue Pellot.

el, also featuring Moorish influences, was built in 1864 for Empress Eugénie, whose forefathers originally came from Spain. Two other museums are interesting: the Museum of Oriental Art (Rue G. Petit) and the chocolate museum (Av. Beaurivage).

Bayonne

Bayonne (42,000 inhabitants), about 5km/3mi from the Atlantic coast on the river Adour, has retained its Gascon and Basque identity in a way that Biarritz has not. Its main importance is as a trans-shipment centre for bulk goods (maize and chemical raw materials from Lacq). Bayonne is famed for its ham and chocolate. As the gateway to the passes of the western Pyrenees, the town used to be heavily fortified, and the site of the former walls is now given over to pretty promenades that ring the town. With the Nive flowing into the Adour at this point, rivers split the town into three sections. The suburb of St-Esprit lies north of the Adour and includes the citadel erected in 1674–79 by Vauban and the 15th-century St-Esprit church. The area to the west of the Nive is called Grand Bayonne and includes the old town centre, stretching from the Nive confluence and the lively Place de la Liberté with its theatre and town hall to the cathedral of **Ste-Marie**. The edifice was built in a northern French Gothic style in stages from 1213 to 1544, but the façade, the north tower and the pyramid spires are 19th century. The Renaissance windows are of note, especially in the chapel of St-Jerome from 1531, as is the 13th-century door to the sacristy.

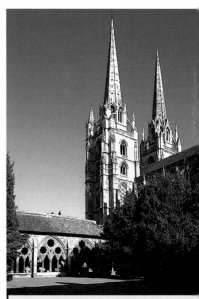

The cathedral of Ste-Marie in Bayonne

To the north of the cathedral stands Château Vieux. The Petit Bayonne suburb on the other side of the Nive has a very Basque feel to it. The excellent **Musée Basque** is situated on the north bank of the Nive in a building dating from the 15th century. Cross Rue Bourg-Neuf – the heart of the suburb – to the **Musée Bonnat**, which houses includes works by Botticelli, Van Dyck, Rubens, Hals, El Greco, Turner, Goya, Constable and others along with a major collection of graphic works. In late August a big Basque festival takes place, with a »bull drive«, bullfights, music and rugby matches.

Bidart Guéthary

Two villages to the south of Biarritz are especially charming. Bidart is situated atop steep cliffs and its delightful village square with fronton wall and town hall also has a typical Basque church with a wood-

▶ VISITING CÔTE BASQUE

INFORMATION

CDT Béarn–Pays Basque
4 Allée des Platanes, F-64100 Bayonne
Tel. 05 59 46 52 52, fax 05 59 46 52 46
www.tourisme64.com
Biarritz Tourisme
1 Square d'Ixelles, F-64200 Biarritz
Tel. 05 59 22 37 10, fax 05 59 24 14 19
www.biarritz.fr

WHERE TO EAT

▶ Expensive
Café de Paris
5 Place Bellevue, Biarritz
Tel. 05 59 24 19 53. In the hotel of the same name. Excellent, classical cuisine, including regional specialities.

▶ Moderate
Kaïku
17 Rue République, F-64500 St Jean de Luz, tel. 05 59 26 13 20, closed Tue. Basque-style restaurant in the town's oldest building. Generous dishes that change with the seasons. In summer, you can eat on the terrace.

▶ Inexpensive
Bistrot des Halles
1 Rue du Centre, Biarritz
Tel. 05 59 24 21 22, closed Mon. This bistro to the south of the market hall provides inexpensive, down-to-earth delights. The seafood is excellent.

WHERE TO STAY

▶ Luxury
Hotel du Palais
1 Avenue Impératrice
F-64200 Biarritz
Tel. 05 59 41 64 00, fax 05 59 41 67 99
www.hotel-du-palais.com. Former seaside palace belonging to Empress Eugénie. Luxurious, antique-furnished rooms and a heated swimming pool. The restaurant Villa Eugénie is held to be among the best in town (open every day). Less expensive options include La Rotonde and L'Hippocampe.

▶ Budget / mid-range
Le Grand Hôtel
21 Rue Thiers, F-64100 Bayonne
Tel. 05 59 59 62 00
www.bw-legrandhotel.com. Situated to the north of the cathedral, recent renovation has not ruined its charm. The rooms facing the courtyard tend to be quieter.

▶ Budget
Maïtagaria
34 Av. Carnot, Biarritz
www.hotel-maitagaria.com, tel. 05 59 24 26 65. This friendly, family-run hotel in a smart 19th-century mansion has large, elegant rooms and is just 500m/550yd from the beach.

en ceiling, galleries and a magnificent 18th-century altar. Guéthary, a seaside resort that extends up the hillside, still retains something of its original character. Its 17th-century church across the main N 10 road is worth seeing.

★
Saint-Jean-de-Luz

Saint-Jean-de-Luz (13,000 inhabitants) an important fishing village, was a base for whalers who sailed as far as Newfoundland, Greenland and Spitzbergen as early as the 13th and 14th centuries. Nowadays it concentrates on catches of tuna and sardines. St-Jean is also an elegant and atmospheric seaside resort, which some prefer to Biarritz, featuring a long beach with a promenade, a casino, villas, and a well-kept old town. Next to the harbour is **Château Lohobiague** (1643), where Louis XIV celebrated his wedding to Maria Theresa, daughter of Spain's King Philip IV (now a museum). The neighbouring Place Louis-XIV has a music pavilion. Further west stands the Maison de l'Infante, where Maria Theresa once lived. The wedding itself took place in **St-Jean-Baptiste** (13th century), the biggest and most beautiful of the Basque churches, impressively decorated with multi-storey galleries, a ship's keel ceiling and a giant gilded retable (1679). The entrance can still be seen, although it was bricked up after the wedding.

Ciboure

Across the river Nivelle from St-Jean-de-Luz is Ciboure with its old-world streets and timber-framed houses. The 16th-century St-Vincent church has an interesting bell tower. House number 12 on the harbour quay is where composer Maurice Ravel was born in 1875.

✳
Corniche Basque
Hendaye

The Corniche Basque coast road runs from St-Jean-de-Luz, offering fabulous views of the wild and rocky coastline, especially at Socoa. Its destination is the resort of **Hendaye** (11,500 inhabitants) with its verdant gardens and the attractive Boulevard de la Mer. In the river Bidassoa, which forms the border with Spain, the Isle of Pheasants is the place where in 1659 the Pyrenean peace treaty and a year later the marriage contract between Louis XIV and Maria Theresa were signed. Hendaye station was the venue for a meeting between Hitler and Franco on 23 October 1940.

St-Jean-de-Luz, a pretty and lively Basque fishing port

✳✳ **Dauphiné**

O 8

Dauphiné, the land east of the Rhône, has a long and varied history as well as boasting some impressive mountain scenery and the highest passes in the Alps. Dramatic gorges sever the Vercors plateau and Chartreuse is famous for its eponymous monastery.

Landscape   The historic landscape of Dauphiné, which borders ▶Savoy to the southwest, consists of the départements Isère, Hautes-Alpes and Drôme. They closely follow the borders set in 1349 when the region first became part of France. The main town is ▶Grenoble. The natural border to the west and partly to the north is the river Rhône. The eastern limit is the French-Italian frontier. The northeastern border is a line running from a bend in the Rhône at St-Genix-sur-Guiers as far as Galibier. The area south of a line from Montelimar to Gap belongs to ▶Provence. The central section of Dauphiné is the immense Massif des Ecrins (Massif du Pelvoux) to the southwest of Grenoble, which reaches a height of 4102m/13,458ft. This high Alpine region of Upper Dauphiné adjoins the more agricultural foothills of Lower

Route des Grandes Alpes   Dauphiné (including Chartreuse and Vercors) in the west. The Route des Grandes Alpes, which links Lake Geneva with Menton on the Côte d'Azur, is a wonderful route through the high Alps and is described in the suggested tours section of this book. The Route Napo-

Route Napoléon   léon, which opened in 1932 and is marked by signs bearing a small eagle, leads through the lower slopes of the Alps from Grenoble via Gap, Sisteron, Digne and Castellane to Cannes.

History   Dauphiné is known to have been settled by Celts, who were subdued in 121 BC after 60 years of war with the Romans. In 933 it became part of Lower Burgundy in the Burgundian kingdom, and thus part

---

Highlights Dauphiné

La Meije
Unforgettable views of the crevassed, glaciated Meije Massif
▶ page 397

Briançon
Ancient fortified town on the route to Piedmont
▶ page 398

Col du Galibier
A delight for connoisseurs of mountain passes
▶ page 398

Embrun
Lombard Romanesque architecture under Provençal skies in the Queyras valley
▶ page 399

Canyons of Vercors
Breathtaking roads lined by stone cliffs hundreds of metres high
▶ page 399

Grande Chartreuse
Nucleus of the Carthusian monastic order in a remote forested landscape
▶ page 401

of the Holy Roman Empire in 1033. As of the 10th century, the counts of Albon claimed large swathes of Dauphiné. Guigues VI added his nickname »delphinus« (meaning dolphin, »dauphin« in French) to the territory in the 12th century. In 1349 the land was sold to the French Crown, whereafter it was traditionally granted as a fiefdom or appanage to the royal heir, who then took the title **Dauphin**. During the religious wars of the 16th century, Dauphiné was a bastion of Protestantism. 200 years later, it triggered the French Revolution when the courthouse in Grenoble refused to carry out instructions from the king in 1788. On 21 July 1788 an assembly in nearby Vizille demanded personal freedom for all French citizens. By 1815 the region was enthused by the return from Elba of Napoleon and the people of Grenoble opened up the city gates for his entry, as Napoleon himself recognized in his memoirs: »Before I reached Grenoble I was just an adventurer; in Grenoble I became a prince.«

Around the Massif des Ecrins

►Grenoble

Grenoble

The Massif de Chamrousse rises to the southwest of Grenoble and reaches a height of 2257m/7405ft at the Croix de Chamrousse (there is a cable car and a view point). From the thermal springs at Uriage les Bains a roads hairpins up to the not particularly attractive winter resort of Chamrousse (1650–1750m/5400–5750ft).

Massif de Chamrousse

Vizille is a small industrial town (7000 inhabitants) 17km/11mi southeast of Grenoble, known for a mansion (1619) that belonged to François de Bonne, leader of the Huguenots who was made a duke and also connétable of Lesdiguières. Its Salle du Jeu de Paume, where the world-changing demands of 1788 were made, no longer exists, although there is an excellent museum of the French Revolution (closed Tue).

Vizille

Beyond the industrial Romanche valley, the small convalescent resort of Bourg-d'Oisans (2900 inhabitants) can be found 720m/2360ft up in the mountains. It is the main settlement in the Oisans district. A mineral museum is located in one transept of the church.

Bourg d'Oisans

A hair-raising route leads up to Alpe d'Huez (1860m/6100ft), a sunny winter resort and famous as a regular stage finish on the Tour de France. Its impressive modern church Notre-Dame-des-Neiges (1970) possesses a renowned organ (concerts Thu 8.45pm). Various cable cars ascend the mountains to an altitude as high as the 3300m/10,800ft **Pic Blanc**, where there is a stunning view.
In summer it is possible to take some spectacular walks in the Grandes Rousses. Magnificent views can also be seen from Pic du

✶ Alpe d'Huez

▶ VISITING DAUPHINÉ

INFORMATION

CRT Rhône-Alpes
104 Route de Paris
F-69260 Charbonnieres-les-Bains
Tel. 04 72 59 21 59, fax 04 72 59 21 60
www.rhonealpes-tourisme.com CDT
Isère, 14 Rue de la République
F-38019 Grenoble
Tel. 04 76 54 34 36, fax 04 76 51 57 19
www.isere-tourisme.com

WHERE TO EAT

► Budget
Le Rustique
36 Rue du Pont d'Asfeld
F-05100 Briançon
Tel. 04 22 21 00 10
A genuinely rustic restaurant in the
capital city. Good Savoy cuisine such
as apple tart with foie gras.

WHERE TO STAY

► Budget
Edelweiss
32 Avenue de la République
F-05100 Briançon
Tel. 04 92 21 02 94
www.hotel-edelweiss-briancon.fr
Opposite Théatre du Cadran near the
haute ville. Quiet rooms, some with a
view of the town. Family atmosphere
in a 19th-century house.

Le Clos
20 ter Av. Cdt. Dumont
F-05000 Gap
Tel. 04 92 51 37 04, www.leclos.fr
Well-kept Logis de France by a large
park on the N 85 to Grenoble. Good
restaurant with traditional local cuisine and a nice terrace.

Lac Blanc (2623m/8606ft) and Dôme des Petites Rousses (2813m/
9229ft, 30 minutes from Lac Blanc).

The popular ski district of Les Deux-Alpes lies south of the Romanche valley where the lifts and cable cars go as high as 3568m/
11,706ft. There is a fine view of the **Meije** and other peaks of the
Massif des Ecrins as far as Mont Blanc.

Les Deux-Alpes

The glacier-covered Massif des Ecrins (Massif du Pelvoux) is the
most impressive mountain outcrop in the French Alps outside Mont
Blanc itself and was declared a national park in 1973 (office in Briançon). Its highest peaks are Barre des Ecrins (4102m/13,458ft), Meije
(3983m/13,068ft), Ailefroide (3953m/12,969ft) and Mont Pelvoux
(3946m/12,946ft).

✷✷
Massif des Ecrins

La Grave (1526m/5007ft) in the upper Romanche valley has a family
atmosphere and is the starting point for mountain climbs through
the breathtakingly beautiful **Meije group**. It is also worth taking a cable car to Col de Ruillans (3211m/10,535ft), while skiers can ascend
even further to Dôme de la Lauze.

La Grave

← *La Grave and the Meije mountain range as seen from Oratoire de Chazelet*

★ ★
Col du Lautaret
Col du Galibier

The N 91 climbs up the Col du Lautaret (2058m/6752ft, viewpoint and Alpine garden), from where the **Col du Galibier** (2646m/8681ft, closed from October till late May) stretches across the peaks to Valloire in ► Savoy. This is one of the most gruelling stages of the Tour de France. At the southern end of the old tunnel, there is a memorial to Henri Desgranges, who established the race in 1903 (► Baedeker Special p.160). From here it is possible to reach a height of 2704m/8871ft and one of the most beautiful Alpine panoramas. Advanced mountain trekkers will be rewarded by the climb to Pic Blanc du Galibier (2955m/9695ft, 3 hours up and back).

La Salle

In La Salle, 8km/5mi outside Briançon, the church of St-Marcellin is a notable attraction. In spite of its Romanesque appearance, the south porch actually dates from the 16th century. The church and its tower were built in the 13th century.

★
Briançon

Europe's highest town Briançon (11,000 inhabitants, 1200–1320m/3900–4300ft altitude) occupies a picturesque location above the confluence of the Durance and Guisane rivers. For years it was a border outpost against Savoy, although it was only fortified by the French in 1590 and by Vauban from 1692 onwards. In 1815 it withstood an attack by Austrian forces that outnumbered the defenders by 20 to 1, and in 1940 held out against Italian assaults. The new suburb of Ste-Cathérine spreads up the hillside towards Haute Ville, the triple-walled old town. A walk through the west of the town will pass by Notre-Dame church, built by Vauban from 1703 to 1726. The tourist office is directly opposite.

Briançon: view of the Porte d'Embrun gate on Pic de Peyre Eraute

The Maison des Têtes (façade 1907), Maison Jean Prat (Renaissance), a museum of horology and the Maison du **Parc des Ecrins**, where all kinds of information concerning the national park can be obtained, are all situated on the Grande Rue, the town's main street. The Pont d'Asfeld was built from 1729 to 1731 across the Durance gorge to the east of the Ville Haute. Its arch spans some 40m/130ft and is 56m/184ft high.

Col de Montgenèvre

To the east of Briançon the N 94 ascends to the Col de Montgenèvre at 1854m/6083ft (open all year), a pass leading to Piedmont that was vital in both military and economic terms. It was carved out in 1807.

At Argentière-la-Bessée (15km/9mi southwest of Briançon with the 12th-century chapel of St-Jean and a silver-mining museum) the road forks and turns off down towards Vallouise along the Gyronde valley into the heart of the Ecrins Massif with its carpets of green under bizarre peaks and typical peasant houses. There are notable buildings in Les Vigneaux (St-Laurent, 15th-century Lombard Romanesque and murals), Puy-St-Vincent (St-Vincent, 15th-century with late medieval frescoes) and Vallouise (St-Etienne, 15th–16th century, purgatory chapel with frescoes). From Ailefroide (1510m/4954ft) at the foot of Mont **Pelvoux** it is possible to drive as far as the Pré de Madame Carle, a popular staring point for hikes in the high Alps.

Vallouise

The journey from Briançon to Château Queyras takes a genuinely impressive route across the 2360m/7743ft Col d'Izoard, also a notorious stage of the Tour de France (there is a small museum). To the south of the summit, the road crosses the **Casse Déserte**, a barren and eroded wilderness.

✶
Col d'Izoard

The landscape of **Queyras** in the east of Dauphiné, close to the Italian border, includes the valley of the river Guil, which flows for 40km/25mi from its source on the 3841m/12,602ft Monte Viso. This is one of the least spoiled regions of Dauphiné and gets plenty of sunshine in both summer and winter. The main town is Château Queyras with its huge castle (13th century, expanded in the 16th–17th centuries). A geological display is housed in the church crypt. Scenic hikes can be enjoyed starting from Abriès, Molines en Queyras and **St-Véran** (290 inhabitants, 2042m/6699ft, the highest settlement in Europe). The Col Agnèl pass (2744m/9003ft) leads into Piedmont with a fantastic view. The two-hour climb to the Pain du Sucre (3208m/10,525ft) is very rewarding.

✶
Queyras

Château Queyras

Col Agnèl

The Route des Grandes Alpes runs though the Combe de Queyras to the market town of Guillestre (Notre-Dame-d'Aquillon, 16th-century church with a lovely 14th-century portico), past the impressive fortifications on Mont-Dauphin, which were built from 1692, as far as Durance (N 94). The route then continues further south down the Col de Vars (2111m/6926ft) to Barcelonnette (►Provence).

Guillestre

Embrun (6000 inhabitants, 870m/2854ft) is situated on a rocky plateau high above Durance. It is a popular holiday resort in both summer and winter. In the Middle Ages it was the territory of a prince-bishop who was empowered to mint coinage and administer justice. The town's cathedral, **Notre-Dame-du-Réal** (12th–13th century), is testimony to this past. It is considered the finest church in Dauphiné, an outstanding example of the Lombard style. The most notable features are the northern portal »Le Réal«, the rose window, one of the oldest organs in France (late 15th century) and the church

Embrun

✶
◄ Cathedral

treasury. A portion of the fabulous murals in the Chapelle des Cordeliers (15th century; where the tourist office is situated) is attributed to Giacomo Jaquerio. At no. 6 Rue de la Liberté, the main street alongside Rue Clovis-Hugues, there is a lovely Renaissance doorway.

Barrage et Lac de Serre-Ponçon

The Lac de Serre-Ponçon to the west of the town is open for swimming. It is a reservoir formed by a dam built from 1955 to 1961, measuring 600m/650yd in length and 120m/400ft in height. One other recommended diversion is from Crots (4km/2.5mi south of Embrun) up to the monastery of Boscodon, which was founded in 1142. The location and the strict lack of adornment in the church is reminiscent of the Cistercian monasteries in Provence.

Gap

Gap (39,000 inhabitants), capital of the départément Hautes-Alpes, is delightfully situated against the backdrop of the Alps. Repeated destruction of the town has meant that few old buildings are left to testify to its long history. However, the **Musée Départemental** with its archaeological and folklore collections is fascinating to visit, as is the 17th-century tomb of the Duc de Lesdiguières (see Vizille above). To the northwest of the town stands the former bishop's residence Château de Charance, now the main offices of the Parc National des Ecrins.

Champsaur

From Gap the Col Bayard (1248m/4094ft) leads to the high valley of Champsaur, where cereal and cattle farming are practised. The bocage landscape is most unusual for the Alps. The Barrage du Sautet is situated 40km/25mi north of Gap, while the pilgrimage chapel

✳ Notre-Dame-de-la-Salette

of Notre-Dame-de-la-Salette can be reached from Corps. It was built amid fabulous scenery at an elevation of 1760m/5774ft, after the Virgin Mary was said to have appeared to two children in 1846. During the six summer months it attracts thousands of pilgrims, who are accommodated in a large hostel.

Matheysin Plateau

The Matheysin Plateau stretches northward from La Mure. Coal was extracted from the plateau until 1997; there is a mining museum in La Mure. A journey on the **metre-gauge railway** (www.trainlamure.com), opened in 1988 to run from La Mure alongside the Drac as far as St-Georges-de-Commiers, is a delight. The line includes a variety of man-made features needed to cope with a 565m/1854ft difference in elevation along the route. The road is also recommendable.

✳ Chartreuse

Scenery

The D 512/D 912 (65km/40mi) from Grenoble to Chambéry leads through the massif of Chartreuse, which reaches a height of 2082m/6837ft at Chamechaude and was declared a nature reserve in 1995. Its dark forests and rugged limestone cliffs alternate with pasture. Along the way, it is worth making a diversion down the gorges of

Guiers Mort and Guiers Vif. At Col de Porte the road turns off to Charmant Som (1867m/6125ft; 30 minutes from the car park there is a magnificent view, taking in Grande Chartreuse). Before the resort of St-Pierre-de-Chartreuse, a road leads off left towards the famous **Grande Chartreuse** monastery, mother house of the Carthusian order founded by St Bruno in 1084. Since 1940 it has once again been home to several monks. It is

> ## Baedeker TIP
>
> ### Green and yellow Chartreuse
> The legendary liqueurs of Chartreuse Verte, with 55% alcohol, and Chartreuse Jaune (40%), are said to have been manufactured for the first time in 1605. 130 herbs are used in the recipe, along with honey. Nowadays the liqueurs are made in Voiron 25km/16mi west of Grande Chartreuse (guided tours every day; www.chartreuse.fr).

not open to the public but there is a museum at La Correrie (daily early Feb to early Nov). Once the route has crossed the Col du Granier beneath the towering cliffs of Mont Granier (1933m/6342ft), the tunnel exits onto the Pas de la Fosse, with a stunning view of Chambéry and Lac du Bourget (►Savoy).

★ Grande Chartreuse

★ ★ Vercors

The Vercors range, stretching southwest from Grenoble as far as the Drôme valley, is a karst mountain formation peppered with crevasses and caves. Its highest point is at Grand Veymont, where the summit is 2341m/7680ft high. It is a popular region for skiing and hiking, an official nature reserve since 1970. The »Vertacomiriens«, as the inhabitants call themselves, make a living from agriculture (cattle and sheep farming) and tourism. From 1942 to 1944 the region was a key battleground for the French Resistance.

Scenery

Its key attractions are best described in the form of a round trip starting at ► Grenoble. Passing the Tour-sans-Venin (a ruin with a fine view), head for St-Nizier-du-Moucherotte (600 inhabitants; 12th-century church; cable car to Moucherotte, 1901m/6237ft). Beyond Lans-en-Vercors, where the main office for the **Parc Naturel Régional du Vercors** is located, the route comes to **Villard-de-Lans** (1043m/3422ft, 3300 inhabitants), a resort for winter and summer holidays and the starting point for tours to Côte 2000, for example, (cable car, 1 hour on foot) or Grande Moucherolle (cable car from Corrençon). 8km/5mi southwest (D 215 c) the Calvaire de Valchevrière is a memorial recalling the destruction of the village in 1944.

From Villard the D 531 runs through the spectacular Bourne gorge, initially cut boldly into steep cliffs but levelling out into the bottom of the valley beyond Choranche. Northward of Choranche, the Grottes de la Choranche cave system features startling stalactites and stalagmites as well as an underground lake. After Pont en Royans (880 inhabitants), where the houses appear to be glued to the rocks

★ ★ Gorges de la Bourne

★★
Grands Goulets

above the river, take the D518 through the Petits Goulets and Grands Goulets gorges, the most spectacular stretch of road in Vercors, chiselled into the rock and wending through tunnels and over galleries to Barraques-en-Vercors, where it opens out into the verdant high valley of Vernaison. Continue past the two small resorts of La-Chapelle-en-Vercors (destroyed in July 1944 but later rebuilt) and St-Agnan-en-Vercors to the Grotte de la Luire. Until it was discovered by German troops, this acted as a field hospital for the French Resis-

Col de Rousset

tance. The road then carries on southward to the Col de Rousset (1254m/4114), beyond which the Alpine air gives way to the Mediterranean climate over the Diois district (around Die).

Vassieux-en-Vercors

Before reaching the Col de Rousset the route takes the D 76 north west to Vassieux, which also suffered destruction at the hands of German troops in 1944. A memorial in the form of the national cemetery of Vercors and a small museum recall the atrocity. As it passes the Memorial du Vercors (Resistance museum), the D 76

Forêt de Lente

climbs towards the pine and beech forest of Lente, which provided raw materials for shipbuilding and charcoal burning in the 19th century. As of 1897 a road was built over the Col de la Machine and

★★
Combe Laval

through the **Combe Laval**. It is one of the most breathtaking routes in Vercors, running through near-vertical cuttings in rocks that are as high as 600m/2000ft.

★
Col de la Bataille

If preferred, an alternative route to take from Vassieux-en-Vercors leads to ▶Valence, taking the D199 southwest from the intersection of Les Trois Routes in the direction of Col de la Bataille (1313m/4308ft, closed in winter). This is another hairy stretch of Alpine road. At Léoncel there is an interesting monastery, founded by the Cistercians in 1137. Its typically unadorned church was consecrated in 1188. A Gite d'Etape (hostel) has been set up in one of the monks' dormitories.

★★ Dijon

Région: Bourgogne	**Altitude:** 245m/804ft
Département: Côte d'Or	**Population:** 154,000

With its historic skyline, handsome buildings and outstanding artistic treasures, Dijon is one of the most fascinating and attractive towns in ▶Burgundy.

History

In Roman times Dijon was the site of a Roman camp on the road from Lyon to the Rhine and called Divio. As of the 11th century, the city became part of the Duchy of Burgundy. It experienced its first golden age under Philip the Bold (1342–1404), the first of the »great

Forty »pleurants« mourn around the tomb of John the Fearless

dukes«, when Dijon became the capital of one of the most important territorial states in Europe and glittered with fine new buildings. After Charles the Bold died in 1477, Burgundy became a royal province with Dijon as its capital. From 1631 until the French Revolution all »gouverneurs de Bourgogne« came from the Condé family. During this era the city experienced its second cultural heyday, as the innumerable palaces in the town still testify. **Gustave Eiffel**, architect of the famed tower in Paris, was born here in 1832 († 1923). The city is the capital of the Côte d'Or département and a university town attracting some 24,000 students. Among its best-known traditional culinary offerings are crème de cassis (blackcurrant liqueur) and mustard.

What to See in Dijon

The heart of the old town is the semi-circular, colonnaded Place de la Libération, laid out at the same time as the **Ducal Palace** by Jules Hardouin-Mansart, one of the builders of Versailles, between 1682 and 1701. The west wing of the palace is now used as the town hall. There is a magnificent view from the 15th-century Tour Philippe le Bon, which is 46m/151ft in height. The palace's east wing is now occupied by the Musée des Beaux-Arts, one of France's most important art museums (open May–Oct Wed–Mon 9.30am–6pm, and 10am–5pm the rest of the year). The ground floor houses the 15th-century palace kitchens, and in the 14th-century chapter hall some fine examples of ecclesiastical craftsmanship are on view. The first and second floors are dedicated to painting and sculpture: Burgundian and Flemish paintings from the 15th century, Italian and Flemish art from the 16th–18th centuries, French pieces from the 19th century and works by German, Swiss and Italian painters from the Middle Ages and the Renaissance (including Conrad Witz), as well as 19th- and 20th-century art. The most interesting room is the Salle des Gardes with its masterpieces from the Burgundian school of the 14th–15th centuries, some of which come from the Carthusian monastery of Champmol (see overleaf), in particular the magnificent **tombs** of two Burgundian dukes, the aforementioned Philip the Bold

★
Palais des Ducs

★ ★
◀ Musée des Beaux-Arts

★ ★
◀ Tombs of the dukes

Dijon Map

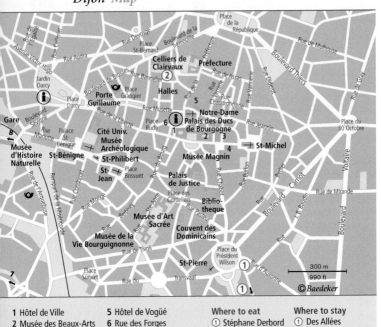

1 Hôtel de Ville	5 Hôtel de Vogüé	**Where to eat**	**Where to stay**
2 Musée des Beaux-Arts	6 Rue des Forges	① Stéphane Derbord	① Des Allées
3 Théâtre	7 Musée Amora	② Bistrot des Halles	
4 Musée Rude	8 Chartreuse de Champmol		

(† 1404), fashioned by Jean de Marville, Claus Sluter and Claus de Werve (1381–1408), and the dual tomb of John the Fearless († 1419) and Margaret of Bavaria, by Claus de Werve, Jean de la Huerta and Antoine Le Moiturier (1419–70). The two altars carved by Jacques de Baerze for Philip the Bold in 1390 were also originally located in the Carthusian church. Melchior Broederlam was the artist responsible for the superb paintings on the wings. The famous **portrait of Philip the Good** with the Order of the Golden Fleece is attributed to Rogier van der Weyden (*c*1445).

Notre-Dame ✳

To the north of the palace stands the church of Notre-Dame, a fine example of Burgundian Gothic (1220–50) style. Its façade is very unusual, being **purely for show**, with arcades of fine columns and pretend water spouts shaped like monsters. The clock tower (1382) to the right originally only had the statue of a man but in the course of time a woman and two children were added (the last in 1881). The figures around the portal behind the vestibule were destroyed in 1794 along with much of the interior decoration. Nevertheless the church's greatest treasure remains: Notre-Dame-de-Bon-Espoir (Our

Lady of Good Hope), one of the oldest remaining wooden Madonnas in France (late 11th century).

The district around the Ducal Palace includes many of the finest »hôtels«, i.e. former aristocratic homes from the Middle Ages and Renaissance. The most interesting streets are Rue de la Chouette with the elegant Hôtel de Vogüe (c1614), Rue Verrerie, Rue Chaudronnerie, Rue Vannerie and Rue des Forges (Hôtel Morel-Sauvegrain, nos. 52–56 from 1435, 13th-century Hôtel Aubriot, no. 40, Hôtel Milsand, no. 38 from 1561 and Hôtel Chambellan, no. 34 from the late 15th century, which houses the tourist office).

✱ **Old quarter**

The church of St-Michel (1499–1529) features a combination of late Gothic and Renaissance architecture. Its façade is unique. The towers were added later in 1667. Copies of works by the Dijon sculptor François Rude (1784–1855) are on display in the deconsecrated church of St-Etienne.

✱ **St-Michel**

Musée Rude

The Gothic cathedral of St-Benigne was built between 1271 and 1325 to replace an unusual 11th-century building which had suffered a

St-Benigne cathedral

▶ VISITING DIJON

INFORMATION

Office de Tourisme, Place Darcy
F-21000 Dijon
Tel. 08 92 70 05 58
(0.34 € per minute)
fax 03 80 42 18 83,
www.dijon-tourism.com

PASS DIJON - CÔTE DE NUITS

The Dijon Card (1–3 days) covers museums, guided tours and use of public transport in the Dijon area.

FESTIVALS AND EVENTS

End of May to end of June: Les Enchantés, a wide variety of musical events. Late Aug/early Sept: Fêtes de la Vigne. Early November: Foire Internationale et Gastronomique.

WHERE TO EAT

▶ **Moderate / expensive**

① *Stéphane Derbord*
10 Place Wilson, tel. 03 80 67 74 64, closed Sundays and 1–20 Aug. The best restaurant in Dijon alongside Le Pré aux Clercs. Served amid its modern ambience, the elegant cuisine combines regional and exotic flavours.

▶ **Budget**

② *Le Bistrot des Halles*
10 Rue Bannelier, tel. 03 80 49 94 15, closed Sun and Mon. Popular bistro with a family atmosphere, dating from 1900 and opposite the market hall. An institution in Dijon and a guarantee of outstanding Burgundian fare. Reservation required.

WHERE TO STAY

▶ **Budget**

① *Des Allées*
27 Cours Gén. de Gaulle
Tel. 03 80 66 57 50, fax 03 80 36 24 81
Small, modern hotel close to the city centre but located in a quiet park. No restaurant.

collapse. The remains of the previous church can be seen in the **crypt**, including the undercroft and a rotunda with two rings of columns, which were destroyed in 1794 but have been largely reconstructed. Saint Benigne himself, one of Burgundy's most important missionary figures, is buried here. In the preserved monastery buildings an archaeological museum displays finds from the Roman era, medieval sculptures and exhibits from prehistory and early history.

Other sights   In a fine 17th-century building (4 Rue des Bons Enfants) the Magnin Collection shows works of painters from France and abroad from the 15th–19th centuries. The Palais de Justice was built in 1572 to house the Burgundian law courts. A Bernardine convent houses two interesting museums: the Musée d'Art Sacré in a splendid Italian Baroque church of 1709 exhibits ecclesiastical art from the 12th–19th centuries, while in the actual nuns' quarters the Musée de la Vie Bourguignonne covers local folklore (both museums closed Tue).

! **Baedeker TIP**

Moutarde Dijon – Pain d'Épice de Dijon

Amora Maille is the leading manufacturer of Dijon's tasty pâté, 75,000 tons of which are eaten in France every year. At no. 32 Rue de la Liberté, next to the charming shopping street of Rue du Bourg, Maille has a lovely old shop, which also functions as a museum. Another jewel in the city's crown is the Mulot et Petitjean shop (13 Place Bossuet), which is famous for its pain d'épice.

★ ★
The Well of Moses at Champmol

The Carthusian monastery was founded under Philip the Bold to accommodate the graves of the Dukes of Burgundy. It was destroyed in 1793 and its remains can be found in the grounds of the psychiatric clinic around 1km/1100yd to the west (accessible Mon–Sat on tours organized by the tourist office). What can still be seen there includes the church consecrated in 1388, the chapel door with its decorative statues, one stair tower and the **Well of Moses**, a hexagonal pedestal almost 8m/26ft high created by Claus Sluter from 1395 as the base for a Calvary and restored in 2003. The six hugely impressive prophets and the mourning angels blazed a trail for the development of sculpture in Burgundy during the 15th century.

Disneyland Resort Paris

K 4

Walt Disney's American dream factory created this gigantic fairy-tale and adventure park to the east of Paris, which attracts 12 million visitors a year.

At Marne la Vallée, just about 30km/12mi east of Paris, a whole world of magic and illusions spreads over an area of 20 sq km/8 sq mi – one fifth the size of Paris itself. It includes the Disneyland Park, Walt Disney Studios Park, Disney Village pleasure centre, various hotels, two conference centres and a 27-hole golf course. There are a large number of eating places ranging from fast food cafés to deluxe restaurants, some catering to a number of specialist tastes: King Ludwig's Castle, for example is not to be missed by connoisseurs of Bavarian cuisine, and English food can be enjoyed in the Toad Hall Restaurant. A few interesting facts: 12,000 people are employed here, speaking 19 languages and doing 700 different jobs, among them 700 actors, 100 technicians and 50 musicians. The seven hotels have more than 5800 rooms to accommodate more than 20,000 guests per night. The restaurants purvey around 30 million meals per annum including about 150,000 a day at peak times. Visiting the Disneyland resort during the holidays takes a lot of patience. The children may love it but some disappointed visitors think everything is too expensive and the time could be better spent discovering the delights of the real France. The **Disneyland Park** has more than 40 attractions, plus shows, parades and other events. Main Street, U.S.A. is a trip back to a small American town at the end of the 19th century. The Disneyland Railroad gives the best overall impression of the site, while Frontierland is made to look like the Wild West, complete with paddle steamers, gold mines and more. In Adventureland pirates do their foul deeds and in Fantasyland you can find Sleeping Beauty's castle or meet Snow White and the Seven Dwarfs. Discoveryland lets you admire mankind's greatest inventions or conquer outer space. **Walt Disney Studios Park** offers a look behind the scenes of Disney's dream factory and includes a massive film studio, stunt action, tours amid some fantastic props, plus a backstage glimpse of various film and television productions. **Disney Village** is »America live« with plenty on offer, even for night owls. It includes restaurants and discos, boutiques and shops, a children's theatre and a cinema complex. **Buffalo Bill's Wild West Dinner Show** (costs extra) is a highlight of the entire site, featuring horses, cowboys, Annie Oakley and Sitting Bull, and even the menu has a western touch.

Did you know?

Disneyland Park

A colourful parade at Disneyland

▶ VISITING DISNEYLAND

INFORMATION

Information and booking at any travel agent or www.disneylandparis.com

OPENING TIMES AND ADMISSION

Early July–late Aug 10am–11pm, otherwise dependent on season and day of the week closing between 6pm and 10pm.

Day ticket for 1 park, adult/child €49/41, 2-day ticket (2 parks, valid 1 year) €108/92. Children 12 and over count as adults, children 3 and under come in free. Certain attractions are limited to people/children above a certain height.

Ticket sales via internet, at the park entrance, from the tourist office in Paris, at airports, large Metro and RER stations and certain chain stores (FNAC, Virgin Megastore Champs Elysées). Apart from normal tickets there is also a large selection of special offers (travel to and from, hotels, restaurant reservations, special events etc.).

HOW TO GET THERE

A4 motorway (junction 14, Parcs Disney). Car park for people not staying at the hotel €8/day. SNCF/TGV connections or RER line A from Paris to Marne la Vallée/Chessy station. Buses from Roissy and Orly airports.

✳ Franche-Comté · Jura

N/O 6

The remote Jura region between Burgundy and Switzerland with its terrain of wide-ranging uplands and pretty rivers primarily attracts visitors who love nature and fine scenery. Its cultural and gastronomic delights are equally numerous.

Scenery   The former »Free County of Burgundy«, the present French region of Franche-Comté, is situated between the tourist magnets of Alsace in the north, Burgundy in the west and Switzerland in the east. Its own charms seem to have escaped all but a few connoisseurs. The rural scenery and natural beauties, including romantic waterfalls and streams, are integrated into an extensive network of paths and cycle routes, along with cross-country ski runs and other winter sport facilities. The major feature of Franche-Comté is the **French Jura**, a 200km/125mi-long, 60km/40mi-wide section of a hard limestone mountain system that stretches from the upper Rhône as far as the Czech Republic. The highest summit of the range is close to Geneva (Crêt de la Neige, 1718m/5636ft). The eastern part is dominated by rough, windswept plateaux and mountains with broad meadows and dark evergreen forests. Between the parallel-running mountain ridges (monts) there are wide valleys (vals), which are linked by narrower valleys running across the peaks (cluses). Towards the west the

Jura range descends gently over rolling plateaux with woods, fields and lakes. Due to the mild climate of the upper Saône valley, formerly known as »Bon Pays«, it has always been a scene of agriculture and cattle breeding. Life was easier there than in the mountains, where there was said to be, »eight months of snow, two months of wind, but the rest of the year is wonderful.« On the western slopes of the Jura, opposite Burgundy's Côte d'Or, wine is produced on a strip about 10km/6mi wide known as »Côte« or »Vignoble«.

Due to its abundance of trees – two fifths of Franche-Comté is covered in forest – there is a long tradition of logging in the region. In the rest of the area, agriculture and primarily cattle raising play the major role. Wine and fruit are cultivated in the foothills. Long-established industrial centres include ► Besançon, Montbéliard, Belfort, Morez and St-Claude. One key industry is **watch making**: Besançon has been the hub of the French watch industry since the late 18th century. **Economy**

Morbier, Bleu de Gex, Vacherin (Mont d'Or) and Comté are all well-known cheeses. They are the culinary epitome of the region, being produced from the milk of the bright red Montbéliarde cattle. The wine of the Jura region has its own distinct character. About 1800 hectares/4500 acres are cultivated, producing not only Pinot Noir, Pinot Blanc and Chardonnay but also local specialities such as Poulsard and Trousseau (both for somewhat less appealing red wines) and Savagnin, a variant of the Traminer grape. This is used to make gold-coloured vin jaune, which is allowed to ferment for six years in small oak barrels. One other speciality is the sweet vin de paille made from currant-like dried grapes. **Cheese and wine**

Highlights *Franche-Comté*

Notre-Dame-du-Haut
Powerful architecture and a meditative atmosphere amid the rolling scenery
► page 411

Montbéliard
Like part of Germany in France – appropriately, with a big car factory not far away
► page 411

Doubs valley
Gorges, waterfalls and lakes along the winding river Doubs, the region's main waterway
► page 412

Arc-et-Senans
The royal salt works, designed by Ledoux, architect of the revolutionary period
► page 415

Réculées and cirques
Deep valleys carved through the rock along with precipitous basins amid the limestone of the Jura range
► page 416

A view all the way to Switzerland
The highest of the Jura peaks with views over Lake Geneva
► page 417

Striking architecture: Corbusier's Notre-Dame-du-Haut in Ronchamp

The independent spirit of the Celtic Sequani tribe is still reflected in the region's modern name: »Franche«, meaning »free«. Their defeat in Alesia in 52 BC (► Burgundy) led to Burgundy becoming part of the Roman empire. The Romans built roads and towns like Besançon, Salins, Dole, Lons le Saunier and Pontarlier. In 442 the area passed into the hands of the east Germanic Burgundians and its history was then linked to the new Duchy of Burgundy (Frankish as of 534). After 843 two separate kingdoms emerged but were united in a new kingdom of Burgundy in 934. The part east of the Saône was known as the Free County of Burgundy from 1032 and was linked to the Holy Roman Empire. After many years of conflict with the French king, the region was annexed to the Habsburg dominion under Emperor Maximilian I in 1493. Louis XIV took it back in 1674, and it was finally ceded to France by the peace treaties of Nijmegen in 1678. Two great Frenchman were born in the Jura: the biologist Louis Pasteur (1822–95) came from Arbois, and the painter Gustave Courbet (1819–77) was born in Ornans.

Places to Visit in Franche-Comté and Jura

Belfort
The capital of the Territoire de Belfort has 52,000 inhabitants. Due to its location at the northern tip of the »Burgundian Gate« – »Trouée de Belfort« – it has always had strategic importance. Nowadays it possesses lucrative textile, machinery, electrical and electronics industries. Alstom, builders of the TGV trains, is based here. One testimony to this earlier strategic importance is the mighty **citadel**, built after 1687 by Vauban, Louis XIV's military architect. It was extended from 1822 onwards but part was razed in 1871. The barracks houses a historical museum and an art gallery, which includes works by Signac, Vlaminck, Utrillo, Courbet and Rodin, among others. There is a marvellous view out over the Jura and Vosges mountains. A walk along the wall fortifications leads to Belfort's landmark, a statue of a **lion** 22m/72ft long and 11m/36ft high, carved from Vosges sandstone by Colmar's Frédéric-Auguste Bartholdi (1880). The Porte de Brisach (1687), to the northeast of the old town, was also part of Vauban's fortifications. The town itself is split into two sections. The old town on the left bank of the river Savoureuse centres on Place de la République with its Monument des Trois Sièges, also by Bartholdi, the Palais de Justice (1901) and the Préfecture. Further east on Place d'Armes is the parish church of St-Christophe (1727–50, with its lovely interior) and the town hall (1724–89).

★
Lion of Belfort ►

A trip out to Ronchamp (20km/12mi northwest) is a must – and not only for architecture enthusiasts. The former mining town is overlooked by the chapel of Notre-Dame-du-Haut. It is a pivotal work of modern architecture, built from 1950 to 1955 by **Le Corbusier** and dedicated to peace. Apart from the powerful and individual design of the reinforced concrete exterior (the walls and roof have a dual shell), the inside too is fascinating thanks to the treatment of space and play of light entering through openings glazed with coloured glass. There is also a fine view over the scenery of the **Trouée de Belfort**. In Ronchamp itself, the mining museum (Musée de la Mine) is worth a visit.

Ronchamp

★ ★

◄ Notre-Dame-du-Haut

Luxeuil-les-Bains (about 50km/30mi northwest of Belfort, 8800 inhabitants) is famous as a spa and for its abbey, which was founded by the Irish monk Saint Columban at the end of the 6th century. The town's centrepiece, amid its lovely old red sandstone houses, is the **basilica of St-Colomban** (13th–14th centuries), although only one of its three towers now remains (rebuilt 1527). The basilica's finest features are its Baroque organ front (1617–80) and the pulpit (1806), originally from Notre-Dame in Paris. The cloisters house a museum dedicated to the pretty Luxeuil lace. Conspicuous buildings on the main street include Hôtel du Cardinal Jouffroy and, opposite that, the Musée de la Tour des Echevins (both 15th century). The latter has an exhibition of Gallo-Roman archaeological finds as well as paintings by Adler, Vuillard and others. A thermal spa from the 18th century situated in a park to the north of the town has now been fully modernized.

Luxeuil-les-Bains

Gray (6700 inhabitants), 45km/28mi northwest of Besançon on the Saône river, was once an important river port. Nowadays it is a waystation for boating tourists. Notable buildings in the centre of town include the church of Notre-Dame (late 15th century), the splendid Renaissance town hall (1568) and the palace of the Comtes de Provence (18th century), housing a fine collection of paintings in the Musée Baron Martin. The palace at Champlitte (20km/12mi north of Gray, 16th–18th centuries) houses a museum of Haute-Saône folklore (closed Tuesdays).

Gray

Champlitte

A memorial sporting the coats of arms of Württemberg and Montbéliard is on view in front of the palace. Made of Swabian travertine, it recalls the marriage alliance between Count Eberhard of Württemberg and Henriette d'Orbe, heiress of the County of Montbéliard, on 13 November 1397, which initiated a fruitful relationship between the two domains. Until 1793 Montbéliard, then called **Mömpelgard**, was part of Württemberg, as the ubiquitous rampant stags of the Württemberg arms testify. The very appearance of the town also betrays that heritage: some of its main buildings are the work of the »Swabian Leonardo da Vinci«, Heinrich Schickhardt. The Reforma-

Montbéliard

tion was brought to the town in 1556, and many Huguenots fled here at the end of the 16th century. Modern Montbéliard (29,000 inhabitants), about 15km/9mi south of Belfort on the Rhine-Rhône Canal, forms along with Audincourt and Sochaux part of a large industrial conurbation that boasts a population of 123,000 and is dominated by the **Peugeot car factory**, which employs 13,000 people. Montbéliard lies beneath a castle with towers named Henriette (1424) and Frédéric (1595), home to a small museum of nature and archaeology. During Advent a **Christmas market** is held on Place St-Martin, site of a few interesting buildings including the town hall (1778), Hôtel Beurnier-Rossel (1773) and historical museum, Maison Forstner (late 16th century) and Temple St-Martin, the **first Protestant church in France** (Schickhardt, 1607). Further west is the imposing complex of the Halles (16th century), once the headquarters of the regional council. The Peugeot museum in Sochaux to the

✹
Peugeot museum ▶

northeast of Montbéliard (Musée de l'Aventure Peugeot, open daily) is not to be missed. It is also possible to visit the factory, the largest in France (minimum age 12, Fri 8.30am, information from Montbéliard tourist office and Peugeot Communication, tel. 03 81 33 27 48).

Besançon ▶Besançon

✹
Vallée du Doubs

The valley of the river Doubs is a scenic highlight of the French Jura. The river's source is close to Mouthe at an altitude of nearly 900m/2950ft. It flows into the Saône at Verdun-sur-le-Doubs, 90km/56mi away, although over that distance the river itself winds so much that it actually covers 430km/267 mi. For much of its length, the Doubs marks the border to Switzerland. Good starting places for trips into the Doubs valley include **St-Hippolyte** (380 inhabitants, 30km/19mi south of Montbéliard) and **Morteau** (6700 inhabitants, 31km/19mi northeast of Pontarlier), a centre for the watch industry and known for its smoked sausages and the »gâteau de ménage« made at Boulangerie Lucas. Among the most impressive sights are the **Corniche de Goumois** (southeast of St-Hippolyte) with its gorgeous panorama, then Echelles de la Mort further upstream, Belvédère de la Cendrée, the 28m/92ft waterfall of **Saut du Doubs** and Lac de Chaillexon (boat trips from Villers-le-Lac and Les Brenets in Switzerland, www.nlb.ch). Other places to see include the watchmaking museums at Morteau and Villers-le-Lac.

Romantic trip down the Doubs

Roche du Prêtre (»Priest's Rock«) 12km/7mi north of Morteau is 350m/1148ft high and has the loveliest view of the Cirque de Consolation, a rock caldera in which the former monastery of Notre-Dame-de-Consolation, now a mission centre, is sited. This is the source of the river Dessoubre, which flows through a lovely valley and into the Doubs near St-Hippolyte.

The village of Montbenoît (17km/11mi southwest of Morteau) is in the self-declared **»Republic« of Saugeais**. There are customs guards at the »frontier«. Inside the village are some charming remnants of an abbey founded around 1150. The nave dates from the 12th century, the choir from the 16th century, and the tower only came into being in 1903. The carved choir stalls (1527) with curious and lively scenes are sadly quite badly damaged.

Montbenoît

Ornans (4000 inhabitants, 26km/16mi south of Besançon), the main town in the Loue valley, was the birthplace of **Gustave Courbet** (1819–77). The house where he was born is now a museum and even

★
Ornans

 VISITING FRANCHE-COMTÉ

INFORMATION

CRT Franche-Comté
La City, 4 Rue Gabriel Plançon
F-25044 Besancon Cedex Tel. from abroad 00 800 2006 2010
Tel. in France 08 10 10 11 13
www.franche-comte.org

WHERE TO EAT

► Moderate / inexpensive
Le Pot au Feu
27 bis Grande Rue
F-90000 Belfort
Tel. 03 84 28 57 84. Nice bistro near the Porte de Brisach serving traditional cuisine. Its specialities are the stews, »pots au feu«, after which it is named.

Balance Mets et Vins
47 Rue Courcelles
F-39600 Arbois
Tel. 03 84 37 45 00
Closed Tue evenings and Wed, July–Aug only Wed.
Enjoy the wines of the Jura – by the glass if you want – and excellent regional cooking with modern dishes for variation. The terrace is very pretty.

WHERE TO STAY

► Mid-range/luxury
Château de Germigney
F-39600 Port-Lesney
Tel. 03 84 73 85 85, www.chateaude-germnigney.com
Charming country house 12km/7mi north of Arbois, tastefully furnished in the style of Napoleon III. Very good restaurant with dishes from Jura and Provence, reasonably priced bistro.

► Budget / mid-range
Le Lac
Grande Rue, F-25160 Malbuisson
Tel. 03 81 69 34 80, www.hotel-le-lac.fr
High standard in the Swiss style, antique furniture, right on the shores of Lac de St Point (and the main street).

The Saline Royal at Arc-et-Senans, one of Ledoux's outstanding works

has some of his paintings. The Loue, a frequent motif for Courbet, flows through the village, where the old houses make for a lovely, dainty appearance. Anglers should not miss the Maison Nationale de la Pêche et de l'Eau.

★ ★
Source de la
Loue

The Loue starts out as an underground stream. Close to 20km/12mi southeast of Ornans it splashes to the surface through a rock cliff 100m/330ft high, the most vigorous of the »fontaines jurassiennes«, before passing through the impressive Nouailles gorge. On the D 67 past Mouthier there are several scenic viewpoints. The Belvédère du Moine north of Renédale is tremendous.

Pontarlier

Pontarlier (18,000 inhabitants), close to the Swiss border, was and is once again the capital of **absinthe**. The history of the liqueur is depicted in the town's museum. Centre Espera (on the edge of the town heading towards Besançon, www.espera-sbarro.com.fr) exhibits creations of the car designer Franco Sbarro, but is currently closed. South of the town, the Doubs has carved a 200m/660ft-deep gorge (cluse), one of the loveliest in the Jura. It is guarded by the **Château de Joux**, a rugged fortification that dates back as far as 1034 and was once a prison housing such inmates as Mirabeau, Toussaint Louverture (the national hero of black Haiti who died here in 1803) and Heinrich von Kleist (1806). There is a beautiful view down the cluse from Le Frambourg.

★
Cluse de
Pontarlier

Métabief

Métabief (18km/11mi south of Pontarlier) is a Mecca for hikers in the Jura, for mountain bikers as a venue for European and world championships, and for winter sports enthusiasts. Mont Morond (1419m/4656ft, cable car) and Mont d'Or (1463m/4800ft, 10 mins from car park) have a fantastic view taking in Lake Geneva and Mont Blanc. The making of the famous Vacherin cheese, which takes its name from the mountain, can be viewed in various places including the Fromagerie du Mont d'Or.

★
Mont d'Or

Dole

Right in the west of Franche-Comté, 46km/29mi southwest of Besançon, on the Doubs river lies Dole (26,000 inhabitants). It was the capital of the Free County until 1674, as the magnificent 15th- to 18th-century houses testifies. The best view of the old town and the collegiate church of Notre-Dame with its solid tower (16th century) can be seen from Place aux Fleurs. Things to look out for in the church include its polychrome marble decoration and the 18th-century organ. The biologist and chemist **Louis Pasteur** was born in Dole in 1822 († 1895). The house where he was born on Canal des Tanneurs (Rue Pasteur) is open to the public and there is a museum next door.

The architect **Claude-Nicolas Ledoux** (1736–1806) was the most important exponent of French Revolutionary architecture, which toed a strictly classical line. Ledoux developed ideas that sometimes seem to foreshadow the madness of the Fascists. One of his main buildings can be seen in Arc-et-Senans about 40km/25mi southwest of Besançon. From 1775 to 1778 a salt factory, the Saline Royale, was established at the behest of Louis XVI. It was intended to form the core of a model industrial town. Since it failed to make a profit, only one semi-circle was completed. It closed in 1895. Salt was extracted here from brine brought through a wooden pipeline from Salins-les-Bains (see below) 21km/13mi to the southeast. The plant is now a UNESCO World Heritage Site and includes the fascinating Ledoux Museum with plans and models as well as a salt museum (open daily).

Arc-et-Senans

★
◄ Saline Royale

The health spa of Salins-les-Bains (3300 inhabitants) lies in the narrow valley of the Furieuse. Its salt deposits were known in Roman times, but today are used solely for medicinal purposes (Les Thermes, with a nice spa). A circuit of the tunnels 250m/800ft under the ground is most impressive. There are still some remnants of the town fortifications. The 13th-century church of St-Anatoile is a fine example of Burgundian Gothic style. The 17th-century chapel of Notre-Dame-de-la-Libératrice inside the 18th-century town hall is also worth a look.

Salins-les-Bains

The name »Source du Lison« refers to the source of the Lison, the Sarrazine grotto and the Creux Billard, attractive karst phenomena 15km/9mi east of Salins-les-Bains.

★
Source du Lison

Levier about 10km/6mi east of Source du Lison is the starting point for the Route des Sapins (Pine Route) that leads 55km/34mi to Champagnole. It runs through the 10,000ha/40 sq mi of the Forêt de la Joux, France's most attractive evergreen forest. The **Sapin Président** is a famous fir tree 45m/148ft high and more than 200 years old.

★
Forêt de la Joux

The picturesque little town of Arbois (3700 inhabitants, 14km/9mi southwest of Salins-les-Bains, nestling between vine slopes on the

Arbois

river Cuisance, is the focal point for the **wines of the Jura**. A wine festival is celebrated on 20 July. This is where Louis Pasteur (see above, Dole) spent his early years. His parents' home and his labora-

! *Baedeker* TIP

Wine and chocolate
The Arbois and its wines have a fine reputation, mainly due to Henri Maire, who took over his parents' estate in 1939 (visitor centre on Place de la Liberté). Other renowned wines include those of Foret, La Pinte, Tissot and Fruitière Vinicole. The Hirsinger Pâtisserie at Grande Rue 38 is among the best of France's »chocolatiers«.

tory are open to the public. Starting from the church of St-Just (12th–13th centuries) with its chunky, 60m/200ft tower, built in the 16th century, take the bridge over the river past the town hall (and tourist office) to Place de la Liberté. To the east an 18th-century mansion houses the Musée Sarret de Grozon (furniture, pottery, painting). Further north is the fascinating wine museum in Château Pécaud, a remnant of the town fortifications. From the Pont des Capucins (upstream from St-Just) near Tour Gloriette (16th century) there is a splendid view. It is also worth taking a walk up to Pupillin (2.5km/1.5mi), which has its own appellation controllée vineyard.

★ ★
Reculées

Between Arbois and Lons-le-Saunier there are a few unusually charming V-shaped valleys. These »reculées« frequently end in a caldera (»cirque«) with craggy rock walls. The Reculée des Planches 5km/3mi southeast of Arbois contains the sources of the Cuisance and the fascinating Grotte des Planches. The D 469 leads 200m/660ft higher to the Cirque du Fer à Cheval. The Cirque de Ladoye (9km/6mi south of Poligny) is just as good, but the real highlight is the Cirque de Baume (see below).

Cirque de Ladoye

Poligny

The small town of Poligny (5000 inhabitants) 9km/6mi south of Arbois is the »capital« of **Comté**, the region's famous cheese. A demonstration of how the cheese is made can be seen at Maison du Comté. The church of St-Hippolyte has some fine Burgundy-school statues from the 15th century. Behind the church is a convent of the Poor Clares, originally dating back to 1415.

Lons-le-Saunier

The capital of the Jura département (18,500 inhabitants) is a popular thermal spa, where the salt springs have been used since Roman times. It is well known, however, as the home of »Laughing Cow« cheese spread (»La Vache Qui Rit«), made by the Bel company. **Claude-Joseph Rouget de Lisle** (1760–1836) was born here. He composed the music and lyrics of the Marseillaise, later to become the French national anthem. Arcade-fronted houses from the 17th century line Rue de Commerce (no. 24 is Rouget's birthplace, now a museum). There is also a small art museum in the town hall with several notable paintings (Courbet, Pointelin, Brueghel the Younger), while the neighbouring Hôtel Dieu (1740) has an old pharmacy. Other buildings worth checking out include the Romano-Gothic church of St-Désiré with its 11th-century crypt, the archaeology museum, the Puits Salé (salt deposits) in a nearby park as well as the Eglise des Cordeliers with its lovely 17th-century carvings in the choir.

The hamlet of Baume-les-Messieurs (200 inhabitants) northeast of Lons-le-Saunier has a picturesque location between precipitous cliffs. It grew up around an abbey founded by St Columban in around 580. Its monks were responsible for founding of Cluny Abbey in 909 (► Burgundy). The monastery church (12th–15th centuries) has a fine 16th-century Flemish altar in colourful framing (guided tours available). To the south of the village is the **Cirque de Baume**. A steep path leads down to the caves beneath, which were formed by a source of the river Dard. When there is heavy rain the stream emerges in a waterfall. South of the cirque, the Belvédère des Roches de Baume can be accessed from the D 471, where there is a fantastic view of the rock caldera. The Creux de Révigny, southeast of Lons-le-Saunier, is another impressive feature.

Baume-les-Messieurs

✳ ✳
Cirque de Baume

Creux de Révigny

To the east of Lons-le-Saunier between Champagnole, Clairvaux-les-Lacs and the Pic de l'Aigle, there are many lakes, the most beautiful of which is Lac de Chalain. South of there, the river **Hérisson** forms the Lac de Chambly and Lac du Val. The Hérisson flows from Lac de Bonlieu at an altitude of 805m/2640ft and descends via various waterfalls down to the 520m/1706m-high Plateau de Doucier. The Cascade de l'Eventail falls southeast of Lac du Val (from Doucier by the D 326 to Moulin Jacquand, rest of the way on foot), and the Cascade du Grand-Saut is also impressive.

Région des Lacs

✳
Cascades du Hérisson

The area is close to Switzerland. A day trip in the direction of Lake Geneva offers some marvellous scenery, here among the highest peaks of the Jura mountains, from which there are views of the Swiss Waadtland and French Chablais as far as Mont Blanc. From Champagnole the N 5 runs southward over the region around Morez and Les Rousses to the Col de la Faucille (1320m/4331ft) with the winter and summer sports resort of the same name. A cable car leads up to the 1534m/5033ft summit of **Petit Mont Rond**, from where there is a magnificent view. One definite recommendation is the easy walk up to the 1689m/5541ft summit of Colomby de Gex (2½ hours there and back). From there it is even possible to see Geneva's famous landmark, the Jet d'Eau, on a clear day. Hiking the entire route from Col de la Faucille over the highest Jura peak, the **Crêt de la Neige** (1718m/5636ft), to Fort de l'Ecluse by the Rhône gap (see below) takes 2 days (8 hours + 5½ hours). One place for the overnight stop is in the chalet at Le Gralet (not serviced).

Lake Geneva

✳
Mont Rond

✳
Colomby de Gex

The wonderfully romantic Valserine valley, also called the Valmijoux, stretches away to the west of the ridge from Mijoux (lovely view)

✳
Valserine

Typical karst terrain in the Jura Mountains at Cirque de Baume

near the Col de la Faucille in the north as far as Bellegarde in the south. The Crêt de Chalam (1545m/5069ft) overlooks the valley in the west and offers a great view as far as Mont Blanc.

Crêt de Chalam ✳

Bellegarde Bellegarde-sur-Valserine is at the confluence of the Valserine and the Rhône. It is the main town and the industrial centre of the valley (11,000 inhabitants). Approaching the town from the Geneva side means passing through the Défilé de l'Ecluse, the dramatic gap where the **Rhône bisects the Jura** , guarded by a fort built in 1820–40. Fit walkers can climb the 1100 steps to the upper part of the town.

Défilé de l'Ecluse ✳

Seyssel From Bellegarde follow the Rhône southward to Lac de Bourget (▶Savoy). Seyssel is an important centre of **wine production** in Savoy, primarily making white wine from the Altesse grape. A rope bridge connects the two old parts of the village, which was once split between France and Savoy (now the départements of Ain and Haute-Savoie). For those who favour difficult mountain roads, by car or by bike, the round trip westward over the 1531m/5023ft Grand Colombier is not to be missed. The mountain has some of the most marvellous views in the Jura mountains (from Seyssel to Culoz via Brenaz, approx. 55km/35mi)

Grand Colombier ✳✳

Nantua Nantua (3900 inhabitants) is west of Bellegarde and delightfully located on a lake 2.5km/1.5mi long. The town is famous for Nantua sauce, a light-brown crab sauce. It can trace its history back to a Benedictine abbey founded in the 8th century, of which only the 12th-century church of St-Michel and its damaged Romanesque portal still remain in existence. Inside the church is the painting of *St Sebastian Tended by the Holy Women* by Eugène Delacroix (1836). Northward opposite the church is the regional museum for the history of the Résistance and deportation (closed Mon). From Nantua it is about 40km/25mi to Bourg-en-Bresse (▶Burgundy).

Gascogne · Gascony

F–J 7–9

With its long sandy beaches, the southwest of France seems made for family holidays. However, it is also possible to discover a lovely hinterland of old villages with a vivid atmosphere and an impressive artistic heritage.

Gascony covers the major part of southwest France between the Atlantic, the Pyrenees and Garonne. Its biggest attraction is its **coastal plain** with broad, sandy beaches that stretch in an almost straight line along the Atlantic bordered by pine forests and lagoons. It covers the southern part of the **Côte d'Argent** (► Bordeaux) and extends 125km/80mi between Arcachon in the north and the mouth of the Adour in the south (►Côte Basque). Resorts such as Arcachon, Biscarosse and Mimizan and a large number of camping sites and holiday homes are available. Beyond the coast the region is separated into **Landes**, areas of wood and heather which were formerly primarily moorland. To the southeast it adjoins the **Armagnac** uplands, part of an alluvial fan that spreads out to the north from the central Pyrenees. The area is known for its excellent Armagnac brandy.

Scenery

The name of Gascony comes from the Basques, who fled from the Visigoths in Spain over the Pyrenees at the end of the 6th century and settled in the Garonne basin. In the Frankish era, Vasconia was an independent duchy from 768. The Armagnacs were reputed to be highly courageous, and King Charles VII used them as mercenaries against the Swiss, who won a victory against them near Basle in 1444. Survivors moved into Alsace and Swabia. Gascony also has partial administrative responsibility for the regions of Aquitaine und Midi-Pyrénées.

History

Highlights Gascony

Land of the bastides
Fortified villages such as Gimont, Fleurance, Montréal and Mirande testify to a turbulent past.
► page 420–422

Auch cathedral
Splendid oak carvings and magnificent Renaissance stained glass
► page 420

Jazz festival
First-class jazz music in Marciac makes for a great festival for all.
► page 423

Rural culture of the Landes
Farmhouses, orchards, workshops, sheep barns – a trip into the past
► page 424

Atlantic beaches
Endless sand from Arcachon and the dunes of Pilat to Hossegor
► page 425

Places to Visit Inland

Auch

The lively provincial town of Auch (23,500 inhabitants) is on the river Gers. In the Middle Ages it was the capital of Armagnac County. The focal point of the old town, higher up the hill is the **cathedral of Ste-Marie** (UNESCO World Heritage Site), which was constructed between 1489 (choir) and 1662 (façade). It is one of the last Gothic churches. Its superb feature is its carved oak choir stalls, which took some 50 years to complete after about 1500. The 113 seats are decorated with more than 1500 figures. The choir chapels have fabulous Renaissance windows (16th century) by Arnaud de Moles. The organ (1694) can be heard in special concerts, e.g. third weekend in May. The 40m/131ft Armagnac Tower adjoins the choir. A monumental outdoor stair (1864) leads down to the D'Artagnan monument on the Gers. To the north lie the former bishop's palace (c1750, Préfecture) and the Jacobin chapel with the outstanding Musée des Jacobins (archaeology, folklore, ethnology of North and South America).

★ ★
Choir stalls ►

Gimont

The pretty country around Auch is dotted with fortified villages. 24km/15mi eastward is the **bastide** of Gimont, founded in 1266. Its 16th-century market hall bridges the main street. The church is an example of the Mediterranean Gothic style (15th–16th centuries). Gimont is known for its foie gras and bullfights. **Foie gras** is also the product from which Samatan lives. 19km/12mi south of Gimont, it is possibly the most important market town for this luxury foodstuff in all France (Halle au Gras; sales Monday mornings, peak season Oct–Dec). Information from the tourist office.

Samatan

Simorre

Simorre (700 inhabitants), 24km/15mi southwest of Gimont (D 12), has an interesting fortified church (14th–15th centuries, »beautified«

From Auch the Pyrenees seem almost close enough to touch

by Viollet-le-Duc) with splendid choir stalls and stained glass windows.

Fleurance Fleurance (6300 inhabitants), 24km/15mi north of Auch in the Gers valley, was established in 1280 on a triangular plan as a **bastide**. The main square with the market hall is lined by arcades. The church was built of brick and ashlar during the 14th and 15th centuries in the southern French Gothic style (13th-century choir). The Renaissance stained glass windows in the apse are by Arnaud de Moles.

Lectoure The former bishop's seat of Lectoure (10km/6mi north of Fleurance) is beautifully situated on a mountain spur above the Gers valley. The view from the promenade around its old bastion extends as far as the Pyrenees. The 12th-century Romanesque church was partially destroyed in 1473, then rebuilt. The tower was once 90m/295ft tall, but half of it was knocked down in 1782. The town hall was formerly a bishop's palace. The excellent good museum in its basement covers the town's Gallo-Roman past and features more than 20 **taurobolia**, altars for the pagan sacrifice of bulls.

 VISITING GASCONY

INFORMATION

CRT Aquitaine
Cité Mondiale
23 Parvis des Chartrons
F-33074 Bordeaux Cedex
Tel. 05 56 01 70 00, fax 05 56 01 70 07
www.tourisme-aquitaine.fr
CRT Midi-Pyrenees
54 Boulevard de l'Embouchure
F-31000 Toulouse
Tel. 05 61 13 55 48, fax 05 61 47 17 16
www.tourisme-midi-pyrenees.com

WHERE TO EAT AND STAY

Due to the popularity of the Way of St James, it can be very difficult to find accommodation along the main pilgrimage route in July and August.

▶ Luxury

Les Loges de l'Aubergade
52 Rue Royale, F-47270 Puymirol
Tel. 05 53 95 31 46
www.aubergade.com
Puymirol is a pretty little town on a hill 17km/11mi east of Agen. A medieval residence of the Comte de Toulouse became a hotel with a restaurant regarded as one of the best in southwestern France (closed Mon and Tue midday).

▶ Budget / mid-range

Trois Lys
38 Rue Gambetta, F-32100 Condom
Tel. 05 62 28 33 33
www.lestroislys.com
Pretty 18th-century building near the cathedral. Unassumingly elegant interior. Swimming pool, shady terrace and a good restaurant.

Le Dauphin
7 Avenue Gounod, F-33120 Arcachon
Tel. 05 56 83 02 89
www.dauphin-arcachon.com
Charming 19th-century house, 300m from the town centre and beach, swimming pool and rooms for 1–4 persons.

La Romieu ✱

This »village of cats« (500 inhabitants) about 14km/9mi northwest of Lectoure was part of a 13th–14th century collégiale with two beautiful towers (there is a fabulous view from Tour Est). Tour du Cardinal is what remains of a palace built for Bishop Arnaud d'Aux (1318).

Agen

Amid the fertile Garonne plain, surrounded by vegetable farms and orchards, Agen (32,000 inhabitants) is the capital of the département Lot-et-Garonne. The old town spreads out from the right bank of the Garonne, which is crossed by a canal over an aqueduct. Interesting features in the cathedral of St-Caprais (11th–16th centuries) include the choir and the capitals of the pillars of the crossing. The town hall (1666) is situated on the market place along with the four beautiful palais that house the Musée des Beaux-Arts (archaeology, art, paintings). Among its notable possessions are the **Venus of Mas** (1st century BC), faience pottery by **Bernard Palissy** (16th century) and works by artists including Goya, Corot and Sisley.

> ! **Baedeker** TIP
>
> **Pruneaux d'Agen**
>
> Agen is well known for its plums, which are used in all sort of ways – from liqueurs to cakes and other confectionery. A range of shops offer tastings of their products. One good place is Confiserie Bosson (20 Rue Grande Horloge), in existence since 1835.

Condom

40km/25mi southwest of Agen on the river Baïse, Condom (7700 inhabitants), was a bishopric until 1789. It is a pretty town distinguished by the cathedral of St-Pierre (1506–21) and its cloister, now the town hall. A stone's throw further north is the Musée de l'Armagnac (local folklore). The signs showing the place name are embedded in concrete, as its inescapable associations meant they were repeatedly stolen. Even though the town has nothing to do with the article in question, recent times have nevertheless seen the opening of a condom museum (Musée du Préservatif).

Abbaye de Flaran ✱

The abbey 8km/5mi south of Condom, in spite of destruction in the religious wars and the loss of its Baroque elements, is still regarded as the best-preserved **Cistercian monastery** in Gascony. The 13th-century church is particularly fine, and unusual in that the transept is longer than the nave.

Larressingle

Larressingle, 5km/3mi west of Condom, is a tiny **fortified village** dating from the 13th century. The church is incorporated into the keep. It was almost inevitable that a pleasure park should have built here featuring medieval siege engines to entertain the hordes of pilgrims on the Way of St James.

Montréal ✱ **Séviac**

Montréal, 15km/9mi west of Condom, is thought to be the oldest bastide in Gascony (established 1255). Near Séviac remains of a luxurious 4th-century villa boasting some fantastic mosaics has been excavated.

The Marciac festival is a cornerstone of the French jazz scene

24km/15mi southwest of Condom the castle of Cazeneuve, which was formerly owned by Henri IV, stands on a mountain spur (11th–14th centuries, redesigned in the 17th century). It possesses a magnificent interior and a lovely park.

★ **Cazeneuve**

Mirande (3500 inhabitants), 25km/16mi southwest of Auch, is the archetypal **bastide** (established 1281) with its grid layout, a main square with arcades and a 15th-century church with a fortified tower. The Musée des Beaux-Arts exhibits porcelain from some of France's famed potteries and paintings from the 15th–19th centuries. In mid-July a country music festival attracts plenty of visitors.

Mirande

Marciac for jazz and foie gras! For the first two weeks of August this little bastide, 22km/14mi west of Mirande, becomes a **Mecca for jazz fans**. Huge marquees host concerts by the likes of Wynton Marsalis as well as French accordionists or bands from Africa. All day visitors can enjoy plenty of other groups at Festival Off in the open-air restaurants of Village Gourmand. Jazz in Marciac, BP 23, F-32230 Marciac, tel. 0892 69 02 77, fax 05 62 09 38 67, www.jazzinmarciac.com.

Marciac

This particularly fine **bastide** 29km/18mi northeast of Mont de Marsan was built by the English in 1291. 3km/2mi to the southeast is the chapel of Notre-Dame-de-Cyclistes (11th century), while to the south lies the fascinating Ecomusée de l'Armagnac (agriculture and manufacturing in Armagnac).

Labastide-d'Armagnac

Mont-de-Marsan (32,000 inhabitants), capital of the Landes département, nestles between the Midour and Douze rivers, which come together to form a waterway called the Midouze at a nice spot with old buildings. Musée Despiau-Wlérick, housed in 14th-century buildings, exhibits an archaeological collection as well as works by the

Mont-de-Marsan

Course Landaise in the arena at Dax: a perfectly executed »Angel's Leap«

sculptors Charles Despiau (1874–1946, born in Mont-de-Marsan) und Robert Wlérick (1882–1944) and other artists like Ossip Zadkine. In mid-July the feast of Mary Magdalene is celebrated with flamenco dancing, bullfighting and a procession.

Saint-Sever St-Sever 14km/9mi south of Mont-de-Marsan is the site of the most beautiful Romanesque abbey churches of southern France. It was founded in 988 and is famed for its capitals.

Ecomusée de la Grande Lande ✳ A steam railway runs from Sabres (35km/22mi northwest of Mont de Marsan) to the **Ecomusée de la Grande Lande**, an agricultural museum at the centre of the local nature park (open end of March to early Nov, daily 10am–6pm). Many events celebrating rustic tradition are held in summer. The Auberge des Pines in Sabres provides accommodation and opportunities to enjoy the local delicacies (http://aubergedespins.fr).

Dax Even in Roman times Dax (20,500 inhabitants, 50km/30mi southwest of Mont de Marsan) was a well-known **thermal spa** (Aquae Tarbellicae) and remains one of the most important in France to this day. There is a lovely promenade along the Adour, and the remains of the 4th-century Roman walls in the neighbouring park. In the centre the arcade-lined Fontaine Chaude spouts water at 64°C/147°F. Further south are the remains of 2nd-century temple with the Musée de Borda (archaeology and folklore) opposite. The cathedral with its classical interior (17th–18th century) still has some elements from its predecessor (11th–14th centuries), including the Gothic door to the left aisle. During the day it is possible to enjoy the waters at Thermes de Borda and Calicéo, while evenings can be spent at the Atrium, the Art Deco casino built in 1928. The great **Feria** takes place in mid-August. On the other side of the Adour is the church of St-Paul-lès-Dax (11th century) with its noted reliefs and interesting capitals in the apse.

Côte d'Argent

Landes

For centuries the sands of the coast were blown eastward by winds. The »Landes« (heaths) thus developed into a mixture of sandy steppes, heathland and swamps. It was only at the end of the 18th century that people began to bind the dunes by planting fir trees. This led to a green belt of pines and oaks. The area is now increasingly used for agriculture, primarily for the cultivation of maize.

Bassin d'Arcachon

The Bassin d'Arcachon, the one large bay on the Côte d'Argent, is famous for its **oyster cultivation** (15,000 tons p.a.). In the middle of the bay is the Ile aux Oiseaux with its picturesque houses on stilts. Boat trips start from Arcachon and other villages. It is also worth taking a trip around the Bassin through the oyster fishing villages to Cap Ferrat (►Bordeaux). At the southeast corner of the Bassin there is a bird reserve called Le Teich (museum and walks).

Arcachon

This popular lakeside town and thermal spa (12,000 inhabitants) grew up out of a fishing village from 1860. The so-called **Ville d'Eté** (summer town) on the Bassin d'Arcachon is a resort with a marina and casino as well as sandy beaches that stretch around the cape as far as Pyla. Its other attractions include an aquarium and a museum of model ships. To the south on the wooded dunelands is the **Ville d'Hiver** (winter town) with its pretty old villas.

An abundance of sand on the Dunes of Pilat, the highest in Europe

Access to Parc Mauresque is provided by an antique lift. Anyone interested in finding out more about oysters and their culinary qualities, or in taking a trip with an oyster fisherman, should visit **Maison d'Huitre** in Port de Larros on the eastern fringe of Arcachon (tel. 05 56 66 23 71, closed Sundays outside the oyster season). Near Pyla, southwest of Arcachon, the Dune du Pilat (Pyla), some 120m/394ft high and 2.5km/1.5mi long, attracts hordes of visitors in the summer months. The exquisite sunsets here are not to be missed.

★ ★
Dune du Pilat

Biscarrosse

Biscarrosse Plage is rather ugly but nevertheless popular with surfers. The old town of Biscarrosse itself lies between the étangs some 10km/6mi inland. It has a **seaplane museum** as well as a lovely late Gothic church (14th century). Near Mimizan the coast is off-limits to the public.

Mimizan

Mimizan and its beach, Mimizan Plage (photo p.114), have also been colonized by tourists. An important harbour in the Middle Ages, it was submerged under sand in the 18th century. The tower of the 12th-century abbey is still visible, and there is a somewhat eccentric museum opposite it.

Hossegor
Capbreton

These two popular family resorts are only separated by the Boudigau Canal. Their aesthetic qualities have not benefited from the building boom, even though a few older houses still remain in the town centres. Hossegor was once an elegant spa, while Capbreton was an important fishing port. Its fisherman are said to have reached Newfoundland as early as 1392. Here, too, the coast is excellent for surfing.

Grenoble

Région: Rhône-Alpes		**Altitude:** 210m/689ft	
Département: Isère		**Population:** 156,000	

On any trip through the mountainous scenery of ► Dauphiné it is worth stopping in Grenoble, its capital. A mixture of old and new, the town is impressively situated at the meeting point of three deep valleys and possesses some excellent museums.

Grenoble then and now

The name of the town goes back to AD 379, when it was dubbed Gratianopolis in honour of the Roman emperor Gratian. It became a bishopric as early as 375. Its university was founded in 1339. In 1968 the Winter Olympics were held here. Now capital of the Isère département, its traditional industry is glove making but its research facilities, along with the electrochemical and metals industries, are also of importance. Hydroelectric power and the presence of coal helped the development of industry in the 19th century. Grenoble was also

Cable cars sway across the Isère up to the citadel

the home town of the novelist **Stendhal**, whose full name was Marie-Henri Beyle (1783–1842).

What to See in Grenoble

Place Grenette forms the lively nexus of the town. Maison Stendhal was home to the eponymous author during one phase of his childhood. The palace of the Duke of Lesdiguières (1543–1626) acted as the town hall until 1967 but now houses the **Musée Stendhal** (closed Mon). It is adjoined to the east by the church of St-André, built up to 1236 as a chapel for the Dauphin's palace. The tower was added in 1298. The left-hand part of the transept houses the 17th-century tomb of the famed chevalier Bayard, »the knight without fear and without reproach«, who courageously served three kings during the 15th and 16th centuries.The northern side of Place St-André is occupied by the former court and government building, the Parlement de la Dauphiné (15th–16th centuries) with its beautiful early Renaissance façade. The splendid **panelling** in the Chambre de la Cour des Comptes was created by the Swabian artist Paul Jude in 1521–24.

Place Grenette

✷
Parlement de la Dauphiné

Fort de la Bastille (16th century, cable car from Quai Stephane-Jay) has the best view of the city from a height of some 250m/820ft above the valley. There are lovely walks back down to the Isère, either to the west through the Parc Guy Pape or eastwards towards the church of St-Laurent, which was erected over a **Merovingian crypt** from the 6th–7th centuries and is one of the city's most important archaeological attractions (closed at present). The Musée Dauphinois (history and culture of Dauphiné, closed Tue) is another interesting museum housed in a fine 17th-century monastery.

✷
Fort de la Bastille

✷
St-Laurent
✷
Musée Dauphinois

This modern museum of art features works from the 13th–20th centuries and is one of the most important in France. Its collection ranges from old masters through to the 19th century (e.g. Courbet, Renoir, Monet) plus modern (Matisse, Chagall, Picasso, Magritte etc.) and contemporary art. The Egyptian and graphics collections are noteworthy. Open Wed–Mon 10am–6.30pm.

✷✷
Musée de Grenoble

▶ VISITING GRENOBLE

INFORMATION

Office de Tourisme
14 Rue de la République
F-38000 Grenoble
Tel. 04 76 42 41 41
www.grenoble-isere.info

EVENTS

Early March: jazz festival. 1st–2nd
week in July: festival of short films

WHERE TO EAT

▶ Inexpensive / moderate
Le Petit Paris
2 Cours J.-Jaurès, tel. 04 76 46 00 51

First-rate bistro cuisine at very reasonable prices highlighting regional
specialities. Friendly service in an Art
Deco ambience.

WHERE TO STAY

▶ Budget
Hotel de l'Europe
22 Place Grenette
Tel. 04 76 46 16 94
www.hoteleurope.fr
The longest established hotel in town
is right in the middle of the old
quarter (pedestrian zone). Modern
furnishings and soundproofed rooms.

Grenoble Map

1 Musée de la Résistance
2 Musée des Troupes de Montagne

Where to eat
① Le Petit Paris

Where to stay
① Europe

Notre-Dame cathedral (12th–15th centuries) possesses a tabernacle of 1457 that is more than 14m/46ft high, though it has been robbed of its statuary. St-Hugue's chapel was once the nave of a 13th-century church. The Musée de l'Ancien Évêché in the bishop's palace exhibits ecclesiastical art. Remnants of an early Christian baptistery can also be seen.

Notre-Dame cathedral

Musée de l'Ancien Évêché

Several important buildings were erected within the Parc Paul-Mistral in the southeast of the city for the Winter Olympics of 1968, including the town hall (M. Novarina, 1967), the 70,000-seater stadium and the ice rink. To the south (Av. Gén. Champon) is the unusual Maison de la Culture, popularly known as **Le Cargo** (A. Wogenscky, 1968), which serves as an opera house and theatre. A factory built in 1900 to plans by Gustave Eiffel (Le Magasin, Cours Berriat 155) has now been made into a centre for contemporary art.

Parc Paul-Mistral

Centre d'Art Contemporain

⋆ ⋆ Ile-de-France

The Ile-de-France, the area surrounding Paris, has been called the »cradle of France«, as the language, art and civilization of the country all have their roots there. The history of the region is reflected in many splendid palaces and gardens, in magnificent churches and cathedrals, some of which are among the nation's greatest treasures.

The Ile-de-France consists of eight départements: ► Paris, Seine-et-Marne (capital: Melun), Yvelines (Versailles), Essonne (Evry), Hauts-de-Seine (Nanterre), Seine-St-Denis (Bobigny), Val-de-Marne (Créteil) and Val-d'Oise (Beauvais) and is home to almost 11 million people. In terms of industry, too, the Ile-de-France plays a key role, with administrative and service industries predominating. Its thousands of miles of footpaths, cycle routes and bridleways, as well as numerous water sport facilities, attract many Parisians at weekends. Visitors to Paris will also be well rewarded by taking a trip to any of the many attractive spots in the Ile. This description covers the major sights in a clockwise direction, starting with St-Denis just north of central Paris.

The heart of France

From the time of the Merovingian king Clovis I, who ruled France from 481 to 511, Paris was the capital of the Frankish kingdom, and Reims the place where its kings were crowned. In the 10th century the Capetian dukes united various French counties into a duchy called Francia. Along with its capital at Paris, the duchy became the focus of the entire French kingdom. The name »Ile-de-France« is first documented in the 15th century and refers to an »island« north

History

of Paris enclosed by the Marne, Seine, Oise, Thève and Beuvronne rivers. Later, in the 16th century, it was expanded to form a province and was established as a région in 1976.

Places to Visit in the Ile-de-France

Saint-Denis The Parisian suburb of St-Denis (132,000 inhabitants, about 10km/6mi north of the city centre) is famed for its basilica, where the kings of France were buried for more than a thousand years – from Dagobert I to Louis XVIII. More recently it has become known as the site of the modern football and rugby stadium, Stade de France, where France won the FIFA World Cup in 1998. There was once a powerful Benedictine abbey here. Its abbot, Suger, ordered construction of the

★ ★ current basilica from 1137 onwards. It was **the first large church in**
Basilica ▶ **the Gothic style** (photo p.17). It is consecrated to the martyr Saint Denis (or Dionysius), the first bishop of Paris, who was beheaded in about AD 250. Legend has it that Denis picked up his severed head at Montmartre, where he was killed, and walked from there to the cathedral site. The vestibules, choir and crypt (12th century) clearly illustrate the transition from Romanesque to Gothic. The rest of the building dates from the 13th century when construction was supervised by Pierre de Montreuil. During the French Revolution in 1793, the church was damaged and its tombs robbed. Viollet-le-Duc, however, restored the basilica to its former glory from 1858. The interior is 108m/118yd long, 29m/95ft high and 39m/43yd wide in the transept. Its towering pillars and the 37 windows, each 10m/33ft high, are highly impressive, even if the windows themselves are mostly

★ ★ modern. The tombs represent a veritable **museum of French funer-**
Tombs ▶ **ary sculpture**. The tombs of Louis XII († 1515) and Anne of Brittany († 1514), which were constructed between 1517 and 1531, are particularly notable, as are those of Henri II († 1559), completed in 1573, and Catherine de Medici († 1589) by Primaticcio. The tomb of Dagobert I (7th century) is embedded in the wall to the right of the high altar. The tomb of François I in the transept to the south was designed by Philippe de l'Orme. The 18th-century abbey buildings alongside the church are the work of Robert de Cotte. In 1809, Napoleon established a girls' college for the daughters of holders of the Légion d'Honneur. The museum of the Carmelite convent (22 bis

Tomb of Louis XVI and Marie Antoinette in the cathedral at St-Denis

Rue Gabriel Péri) exhibits some relics from the Paris Commune of 1871 alongside examples of modern art. The museum of the famous cutlery manufacturers **Christofle** (112 Rue A.-Croizat, open Thu–Fri) is also worth a visit.

Le Bourget, 16km/10mi northeast of the centre of Paris, is the site of the airport, founded in 1914, where Charles Lindbergh landed at the end of his trans-Atlantic flight in 1927. The massive **Paris Air Show** (mid-June in 2010, 2012 etc.) is an El Dorado for aircraft spotters, as is the Musée de l'Air et de l'Espace (www.mae.org).

Le Bourget

Anne de Montmorency, a field marshal under several monarchs, had a palace built in the charming little town of Ecouen, some 20km/12mi north of Paris, between 1538 and 1555. For the most part it retains its original furnishings. Apart from paintings, tapestries and a 16th-century interior, it also features some magnificent fireplaces. The town church, St-Acceul, has some fine windows dating from the 16th century.

Ecouen

◄ Musée de la Renaissance

Abbaye de Royaumont, a Cistercian abbey in pretty surroundings about 30km/19mi north of Paris, was established in 1228 by Louis IX (Saint Louis). It was one of the richest abbeys in France until the time of the Revolution and is now a cultural centre (concerts Sept–Oct). Remains of the 13th-century church, which measured more than 100m/330ft in length, can still be seen along with the cloisters, refectory, kitchens and the palace built by Le Masson for the last abbot in the 18th century.

★
Abbaye de Royaumont

Saint Denis *Plan*

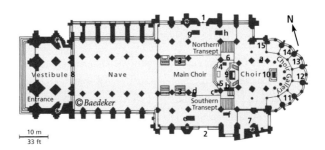

1	Porte des Valois
2	Southern portal
3	Choir seating (Gaillon)
4	Bishops' throne
5	Madonna with Baby Jesus (from St Martin des Champs)
6	Entrance to crypt
7	Treasury
8	Cavaillé-Coll organ

ALTARS

9	High altar
10	St Denis
11	Crucifixion
12	Childhood of Christ
13	St Pérégrin
14	St Eustache
15	The Evangelists (with remnants of mosaics)

TOMBS (selection)

a	Chlodwig
b	Dagobert I/Nantilde
c	Pepin III (the Younger)
d	Charles Martel
e	François I/Claude de France
f	Charles V
g	Louis XII/Anne de Bretagne
h	Henri II/Catherine de' Medici

▶ VISITING ILE-DE-FRANCE

INFORMATION

CRT Paris-Ile-de-France
11 Rue Faubourg-Poissonière
F-75009 Paris
Tel. 01 73 00 77 00

Espace du Tourisme de l'Ile de France
99 Rue de Rivoli
(Carrousel du Louvre), F-75001 Paris
Tel. 01 44 50 19 98; www.pidf.com

PARIS MUSEUM PASS

Admission to a whole range of
attractions in the Ile-de-France region
(www.parismuseumpass.com)

TRANSPORT

Many places in Ile-de-France are
easily reached by RER and SNCF
trains from Paris.

Ile de France *Map*

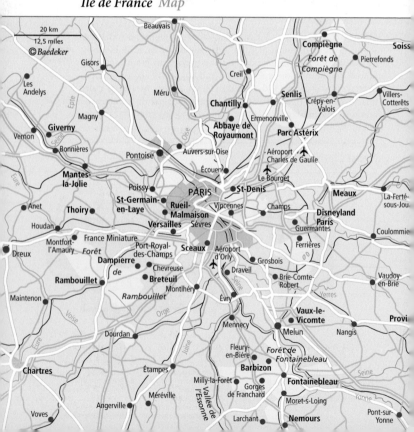

A jewel of the French Renaissance: Petit Château in Chantilly

The stylish town of Chantilly (11,500 inhabitants), 50km/30mi north of Paris, and actually part of ► Picardy, was the residence of the counts of the Princes of Bourbon-Condé in the 17th and 18th centuries. Their palace is situated on an island at the eastern edge of the town. Pierre Chambiges built the palace from 1528 on the site of an old castle for Connétable Anne de Montmorency. It became the residence of the Condé family, an offshoot of the Bourbon dynasty, during the 17th and 18th centuries. Only the **Petit Château** (1560) now remains in its original condition. The Duc d'Aumale, fifth son of the »Citizen-King«, Louis Philippe, had the **Grand Château** rebuilt before 1881 in the fashionable neo-Renaissance style. Both buildings now make up the Musée Condé (22 March to Oct open Wed–Mon 10am–6pm, otherwise 10.30am–5pm). The Grand Château houses the major collection of paintings assembled by the Duc d'Aumale, including works by Memling, Raphael, Lippi, Fouquet, Poussin and Delacroix. The library in the Petit Château possesses one of France's finest art treasures, the **Très Riches Heures du Duc de Berry** (photo p.80) with its superb miniatures fashioned by the Limburg brothers from 1410 to 1416 and by Barthélemy d'Eyck 30 years later. The parkland, including the Grandes Ecuries (stables, 1719–40), and the surrounding woods, as well as the palace itself, all make this a major tourist attraction. Chantilly is also a **Mecca for French horse racing enthusiasts**, being home to more than 2500 thoroughbred horses. The Grandes Ecuries house a museum (Musée Vivant du Cheval) and the Hippodrome is a venue for horse jumping in April and September. The town is also famous for lace and porcelain as well as giving its name to crème Chantilly (whipped cream).

Chantilly

◄ Palace

◄ Musée Condé

Senlis   10km/6mi northeast of Chantilly, Senlis (14,000 inhabitants), also part of ▶Picardy, has a pretty, walled old quarter. The nave of the **cathedral of Notre-Dame** was built in 1184, its Flamboyant-style transept replaced after a fire in 1504. The tympanum of its richly sculpted main entrance (1170) was the first to depict the coronation of the Virgin. Pierre Chambiges' 16th-century façade for the south transept is also noteworthy. The town's museums are worth a visit: Musée de la Vénerie (hunting) in the former priory, Musée d'Art et Archéologie (Roman heritage and early Gothic art), Musée des Spahis (French soldiers in North Africa), Musée de l'Hôtel Vermanois (local museum).

Parc Astérix   Parc Astérix, some 10km/6mi south of Senlis on the A1, offers the chance to relive scenes from the adventures of Asterix and Obelix, to experience their endless battles with the Romans and to enjoy all kinds of attractions. Information: Parc Astérix, BP 8, F-60128 Plailly, tel. 08 26 30 10 40, www.parcasterix.fr. From Paris: RER line B 3 to Roissy, then by CIF bus.

Ermenonville   **Jean-Jacques Rousseau** died in this village 13km/8mi southeast of Senlis in 1778. The 18th-century palace of his host is now a hotel, but its lovely parkland is open to the public. Ermenonville is at the edge of extensive woodland with delightful walks through the trees. The **Mer de Sable**, a »sea of sand« with dunes and a pleasure park, is well worth a visit.

Chaalis   Near Ermenonville, on the other side of the N 336, are the impressive remains of the Cistercian abbey of Chaalis, founded in 1136. One wing of the cloisters (13th century), the chapel (13th century) with frescoes by Primaticcio and a wing of the abbot's palace (1739) have survived the ages. In the latter, an ostentatious building, there is a museum exhibiting furniture, paintings by Giotto and others, religious statuary and a collection relating to Rousseau.

Villers-Cotterêts   This small town 37km/23mi east of Senlis (8400 inhabitants) is known for the edict in which François I declared French to be the official language of the country instead of Latin and ordered the registration of births. There is an interesting palace with a fine Renaissance stairway (1535) and audience room. Alexandre Dumas Senior (1802) and Junior (1824) were both born in the village (there is a small museum).

Compiègne   ▶Picardy Nord – Pas de Calais

✳   The town of Meaux, almost 50km/30mi east Paris on the river
Meaux   Marne (51,000 inhabitants), a bishopric since 375, gained fame through the preacher and historian Bossuet (1627–1704). Its Gothic **cathedral** (12th–16th centuries) has uncompleted towers and an im-

pressive interior. The museum in the bishop's palace (17th century) is mainly dedicated to Bossuet.

In Champs-sur-Marne 30km/19mi east of central Paris is the Rococo palace (1708) of **Madame de Pompadour** (►Famous People), where *Dangerous Liaisons* was filmed by director Steven Frears. Its fantastic furnishings, including wonderful panelling, and Salon Chinois give a splendid impression of the era of Louis XIV. The park was designed by Claude Desgots, a nephew of Le Nôtre.

✳ **Champs**

►Disneyland

Disneyland Paris

The abbey of Jouarre (23km/14mi east of Meaux) was founded in 630. Its **Merovingian crypt** (actually two chapels) has survived and is France's oldest ecclesiastical building. One tower of the 12th-century Romanesque church is also still standing.

Jouarre

About 90km/55mi southeast of Paris, Provins (11,600 inhabitants) held one of the most important **fairs of the ► Champagne region** during the Middle Ages (UNESCO World Heritage Site). Several important medieval buildings lie within its walled upper town, including the church of St-Quiriace (1160) with its fine Gothic choir and 17th-century dome, the 44m/ 144ft Tour de César (defensive tower, 12th–16th centuries), the Porte St-Jean and Grange aux Dîmes, a 13th-century tithe barn which houses the town's museum. In the lower town there are several old churches, such as the Romanesque and Gothic St-Ayoul (12th–16th centuries, with 16th-century alabaster statues and the

✳ **Provins**

! **Baedeker TIP**

The roses of Provins
The red rose, emblem of the English House of Lancaster, is derived from the roses that the troubadour Thibaud brought back from the Orient and cultivated in Provins. In June the roses are in full bloom in Roseraies Vézier (Rue des Prés).

Tour Notre Dame du Val (16th century) to the north. The church of St-Loup-de-Naud 8km/5mi southwest belongs to a Benedictine monastery. Its outstanding portal, reminiscent of Chartres, is highly noteworthy.

This chateau, 55km/35mi southwest of Paris took only four years to build (1657–61). The most important palace in the land until Versailles came into being (photo p.15), it was constructed for **Nicolas Fouquet**, who as finance minister had amassed (or embezzled) a vast fortune. When Louis XIV visited the chateau for its opening in 1661, he was so impressed that he employed the same designers – architect Le Vau, painter Le Brun and garden designer Le Nôtre – for his own palace at Versailles. Fouquet's lack of tact in flaunting his avarice while trying to dupe the king was to prove his downfall. Three weeks

✳ ✳ **Vaux-le-Vicomte**

later he was stripped of all offices and spent the last 19 years of his life in prison. Open mid-March to early November 10am–6pm; the fountains are turned on April to early October, 2nd and 4th Saturdays of the month, 3pm–6pm. On Saturday evenings from May to early October the palace is enchantingly lit by hundreds of candles.

Evry   Evry, 22km/14mi south of Paris, has the only 20th-century cathedral in France (consecrated 1995). The design of its cylindrical structure and museum of religious art are unmistakeably the work of architect **Mario Botta** from Ticino in Switzerland.

✷ ✷
Fontainebleau

The small town of Fontainebleau (15,500 inhabitants) 64km/40mi south of Paris is a popular destination for day trippers from the capital: the **Forest of Fontainebleau** is said to be the most beautiful in France and its famous **chateau** is a UNESCO World Heritage Site. The Capetians had a small hunting lodge here as of the 12th century. Starting in 1528, François I built a Renaissance palace on the site,

A chateau with a long history: Fontainebleau with the Cour des Adieux

which was further extended by Henri II, Henri IV and Louis XIII. The chateau was Napoleon I's favourite retreat. During the Second World War it served as a headquarters, first for the German then later for the American forces. From 1945 to 1965 it was the headquarters of NATO. The extensive complex of mostly two-storey wings is organized around five courtyards. The outer courtyard in the west (Cour du Cheval Blanc or Cour des Adieux) is where Napoleon took leave of his guard regiments upon his abdication in 1814. The chateau proper is entered via the wing that now houses the Napoleon museum. The building was

grandly furnished under François I by both French and Italian artists, including Rosso Fiorentino, Primaticcio and Niccolò dell'Abate. Under Henri IV Flemish influences came to the fore. The real highlight is the **Galerie François I** (1528–30), the corridor leading to the Cours Ovale, which was decorated with panels, frescoes and stucco by Rosso Fiorentino. Napoleon had his bedroom in one of the rooms along the gallery, which was only added in 1786. The subsequent royal chambers are adorned with ceiling paintings and stucco by Primaticcio as well as with fine tapestries. The southern wing of the Cour Ovale is entered via the Escalier du Roi (1749), which features scenes from the life of Alexander the Great by Rosso and Primaticcio. The ballroom, added by François I, was redecorated by Primaticcio under Henri II for the royal mistress Diane de Poitiers. The gardens are glorious as well: the Jardin Anglais, laid out under Napoleon, the »parterre« of Le Nôtre with its ponds, fountains and statues, and the carp pond with a pavilion between them.

Magnificent woodland, canyons, rocks and barren heath make impressive scenery in the 200 sq km/77 sq mi of hilly terrain around Fontainebleau. Footpaths were signposted here as early as the 1830s, the first to be so marked anywhere in the world. Nowadays the walkers are joined by joggers, cyclists and climbers. Guides and maps can be obtained from tourist offices. Barbizon (1400 inhabitants) northwest of Fontainebleau has attracted many painters, such as Millet, Corot and Daumier, seeking to capture the landscape. The Auberge du Père Ganne, where they stayed, has now been made into the **Musée de l'École de Barbizon**. Rousseau's studio is also open to the public.

**★ ★
Forêt de Fontainebleau**

**★
Barbizon**

In 1630, the medieval fortress in Courances, 10km/6mi west of Barbizon was turned into a pretty chateau with a fine park laid out by Le Nôtre. Milly (5km/3mi south) was home to novelist, painter and director **Jean Cocteau** (►Famous People) until he died in 1963. He is buried in Chapelle St-Blaise-des-Simples, which he himself decorated. Herbs from the surrounding countryside are offered for sale in the market hall of 1479. Amid the forest to the west of the village stands the 22m/72ft tall *Cyclops*, a bizarre construction by Swiss artist Jean Tinguely (guided tours available).

**★
Courances
Milly-la-Forêt**

▶ VISITING FONTAINEBLEAU

TRAVEL / OPENING TIMES
SNCF from Paris Gare du Lyon to Fontainebleau Avon, then bus AB to the chateau. Open April–Sept 9.30am–6pm, until 5pm at other times, closed Tue; gardens 9am–6/7pm.

WHERE TO STAY
▶ **Mid-range**
Hotel de Londres
1 Place Gén. de Gaulle
F-77300 Fontainebleau
Tel. 01 64 22 20 21
www.hoteldelondres.com
For anyone wishing to feel a little like one of the kings at Fontainebleau, this 150-year-old building with its appropriate furnishings, right next to the chateau, is just the place. Some rooms have a view of the chateau.

▶ **Budget**
Hôtel Victoria
112 Rue de France
Tel. 01 60 74 90 00
www.hotelvictoria.com
Nicely renovated old building close to the chateau. Comfortable and cosy rooms with parquet flooring, some with fireplaces. Breakfast on the terrace opening out into the large garden. Dedicated car park.

✳
Nemours

Victor Hugo described the small town of Nemours (12,000 inhabitants), on the river Loing about 80km/50mi south if Paris as »charming«. In the centre, where a canal marks the line of the former fortifications, the proud castle and the 16th-century church of St-Jean-Baptiste are both worth seeing. Along the road to Sens (▶Burgundy) is the modern **Musée de Préhistoire** de l'Ile de France. Hiking routes lead through the impressive sandstone rock formations

Larchant

Larchant (550 inhabitants), 8km/5mi northwest of Nemours, is another old fortified town. In the 12th and 13th centuries a large pilgrims' church was built for the remains of St-Mathurin (3rd century), who was born here. It possesses some fine Romanesque and Gothic works of art, including murals from the 12th century. 3km/2mi to the north the great sandstone Massif de la Dame Jouanne is highly popular with climbers.

✳
Etampes

This small town (22,000 inhabitants), about 50km/30mi south of Paris was where the **royal mistresses** lived in the 16th century, among them Anne of Brittany, Diane of Poitiers and Gabrielle d'Estrées. Many fine palaces and churches recall this era: Notre Dame du Fort (11th–13th centuries) with its unusual floor plan and noteworthy statuary around the southern entrance, St-Martin (12th–16th centuries), St-Basile (12th, 15th–16th centuries) and St-Gilles (12th–13th, 16th centuries). From Tour Guinette, all that remains of a castle built in 1150, there is a fine view. The Parisian suburb of **Sceaux**, 12km/7mi southwest of the city centre, is picturesquely located atop a hill. Colbert had a chateau built for himself here starting in 1670. Although only its **park**, laid out by Le Nôtre, remains in existence, it is one of loveliest in the Paris district. There is another palace (1856), of little importance except that it now houses the Musée de l'Ile de France (porcelain, paintings, interior design). L'Haÿ-les-Roses, 6km/3.5mi east of Sceaux, is famous for its rose park.

> **!** **Baedeker TIP**
>
> **Music in the park**
> On a balmy summer evening after a visit to Paris, the perfect place to be is the park at Sceaux. Saunter and admire the fountains, then go to the orangery of 1685 and listen to a classical concert. Information: Saison Musicale de Sceaux, http://festival.orangerie.free.fr, tel. 01 46 60 07 79.

Châtenay

Voltaire was born in 1694 in neighbouring Châtenay. Its church of St-Germain-l'Auxerrois (11th–13th centuries) has a notable choir. From 1807 to 1818 Villa La Vallée-aux-Loups was home to the writer and statesman François-René de Châteaubriand (1768–1848), who gave his name to the famous fillet steak with sauce Béarnaise.

Meudon

Another Parisian suburb, Meudon (44,000 inhabitants), about 10km/6mi southwest of the centre, was home to Rabelais, Balzac, Céline,

Richard Wagner (the libretto for the *Flying Dutchman* was written at 27 Av. du Château) among others, who are commemorated in the Musée d'Art et d'Histoire. Once, a large 15th-century chateau overlooked the town centre, which was owned by the Dukes of Guise and the Grand Dauphin, the heir apparent of Louis XIV. It was largely destroyed by Prussian forces in 1871. Its pavilion was rebuilt as an observatory. There is still a fine view of Paris and the Seine valley from the **Grand Terrace**. The sculptor Auguste Rodin lived in Villa des Brillants (19 Avenue Auguste-Rodin) on the northwestern edge of the town from 1895 until his death in 1917. The building is now a branch of the Paris Musée Rodin.

The neighbouring town of Sèvres (23,000 inhabitants) on the left bank of the Seine is famous for its **porcelain factory**, which was founded in Vincennes in 1738 and was moved to Sèvres in 1756 by Madame de Pompadour. It has occupied its current building near the bridge since 1876 (guided tours available). The neighbouring Musée National de Céramique (with shop) illustrates the history of porcelain manufacture, primarily in the Near East and Far East, in France and particularly in Sèvres itself.

Sèvres

✷
◀ Pottery museum

About 10km/6mi south of Versailles there are some remnants of a 13th-century **Cistercian abbey**. Louis XIV ordered this centre of Jansenism, a Catholic reform movement opposed to the Jesuits, to be destroyed in 1710. The building, which goes by the name of Petites Écoles, houses the Musée National des Granges, with various exhibits on the history of Jansenism.

Port-Royal-des-Champs

6km/3.5mi southwest of Port Royal, in the river valley of the same name, there is a splendid **chateau**, built from 1675 to 1683 by Jules Hardouin-Mansart for Duke Honoré de Chevreuse. Painting of the (Salle de la Minerve) was undertaken by Dominique Ingres in 1843, while the parkland was laid out by Le Nôtre.

✷
Dampierre

About 50km/30mi southwest of Paris, the road to Chartres passes through Rambouillet, where the palace has been the **summer residence of the French president** since 1896 (tours permitted when the president is not in residence, closed Tue). A 14th-century chateau was reconstructed in 1706 by the Comte de Toulouse, son of Louis XIV and Comtesse Montespan. Louis XVI had a dairy built in the form of a Greek temple for Marie Antoinette in 1783. The English Garden has an enchanting seashell pavilion from 1775. Children of all ages will be delighted by the Musée Rambolitrain with its old model railways (closed Mon–Tue). There is some delightful woodland around the town (Forêt d'Yvelines).

Rambouillet

Françoise d'Aubigné, governess to Louis XIV's illegitimate children with the Comtesse Montespan, supplanted the comtesse as the king's

Maintenon

favourite mistress. The monarch made her **Marquise de Maintenon** and presented her with the fine chateau 23km/14mi southwest of Rambouillet. In the park it is still possible to see the remnants of an uncompleted aqueduct, which was to have been 4.5km/3mi long and formed part of a gigantic project to divert water more than 80km/50mi to supply the gardens at Versailles.

Montfort-l'Amaury The small town of Montfort-l'Amaury (2600 inhabitants), on the edge of the Rambouillet forest and 19km/12mi north of Rambouillet itself, was home to **Maurice Ravel** from 1921 until his death in 1937. A museum is dedicated to him. Some town walls can also be seen along with the church of St-Pierre (15th–17th centuries, beautiful Renaissance windows), the Ancien Charnier (charnel house, 16th–17th century) and the ruins of a castle high up on the hill with a good view.

✶ Anet This small village (2700 inhabitants) 15km/9mi north of Dreux in the Eure valley is famous for the Renaissance chateau of Diane de Poitiers. The building work, starting in 1546 to plans by Philibert de l'Orme, involved some of the greatest artists of the period, including **Benvenuto Cellini** and the tapestry makers of Fontainebleau. Unfortunately only the left-hand wing, the gatehouse and the chapel have been preserved. The patroness can be seen in many places in the guise of the goddess Diana, but there are no realistic portraits of her.

Versailles ▶Versailles

France Miniature At Elancourt 10km/6mi southwest Versailles it is possible to view France on a **scale of 1:30**. Along a path 3km/2mi in length are some of the typical scenery and peasant villages, the most beautiful Loire chateaux, strategic castles and forts, famous cathedrals and many attractions of the capital. Information: www.franceminiature.fr. From Paris via SNCF trains (combined train and admission tickets available) from La Défense or Montparnasse to La Verrière, then bus 411.

Saint-Cloud St-Cloud (28,500 inhabitants) is a suburb of Paris on the left bank, 12km/7mi west of the city centre. Its palace, built for Philip d'Orléans, was destroyed by the Prussians in 1870 and the land was later cleared. There is still a lovely park, designed by Le Nôtre and stretching 450ha/1100 acres southwards as far as Sèvres. The fountains, the **Grande Cascade** (by Lepautres and Hardouin-Mansart, 1734) and the 42m/138ft Grand Jet are famous.

✶ Rueil-Malmaison Rueil-Malmaison (75,000 inhabitants), 15km/9mi west of central Paris, has two chateaux. **Joséphine**, wife of Napoleon Bonaparte as of 1796, purchased Château Malmaison (1620, closed Tue) in 1799 and lived here till she died in 1814, even after her divorce from the emperor. From 1861 it became the residence of Empress Eugénie, wife of Napoleon III. The furnishings of Joséphine's era have been partially restored. Articles from the time of Napoleon's exile to St Helena and other documents relating to Napoleon are on display in the Château de Bois-Préau, which also belonged to Joséphine. In the church of St-Pierre-et-St-Paul (c1600) note for the late 15th-century organ, brought here from Santa Maria Novella in Florence by Napoleon III.

In Bougival, 5km/3mi west of Rueil Malmaison, a plaque by the Seine commemorates the **Marly machine**, a giant pumping engine built in 1681–84 that raised 5000 cu m/1 million gallons of water by 150m/500ft every day to supply Versailles and Marly. It is also worth looking at the house where Russian novelist Ivan Turgeniev lived and died in 1883 (Musée Tourgueniev).

Bougival

In Marly-le-Roi, 3km/2mi further west, Louis XIV commissioned Hardouin-Mansart to build a summer residence with pavilions, parks and fabulous fountains. The buildings have sadly disappeared but the lovely park remains, along with a small museum. **Alexandre Dumas** had the Château de Monte-Cristo built at Port Marly in 1846, incorporating all the oriental splendour the name evokes (museum).

Marly-le-Roi

Before Louis XIV moved his court to Versailles in 1682, the neighbouring town of St-Germain-en-Laye (40,000 inhabitants) had been a **residence for the kings of France** since Louis the Fat in the 12th century. The palace that can still be seen today, Château Vieux, was built for François I from 1539 by Pierre Chambiges, retaining the Ste-Chapelle built for Louis IX in 1230 (the template for the Ste-Chapelle in Paris). Henri II expanded it from 1556 by adding the Château Neuf, and two more pavilions from his time are still preserved, one of them being the birthplace of Louis XIV, now the luxurious Hotel Henri IV (www.chateauxhotels.com). The chateau houses the national archaeological museum, (closed Tue), exhibiting finds from the earliest settlements until the era of Roman Gaul. The lovely palace gardens, laid out by Le Nôtre in around 1670, include the Petite Terrace and the Grande Terrace, which stretches for 2.4km/1.5mi across the Seine, from where there is a marvellous **view over the loop in the river to La Défense** and Paris. Other attractions in the town include the birthplace of Claude Debussy (tourist office), the 17th–18th century pharmacy in the municipal library and the museum in the Prieuré, featuring important paintings from the Pont-Aven school and the Symbolist Nabis group. The famous organist Marie-Claire Alain (b. 1927) plays at the parish church of St-Germain. The neighbouring town of Poissy, to the northwest, is where **Le Corbusier** completed his Villa Savoye in 1932. It is considered to be a veritable manifesto for modern architecture.

★
Saint-Germain-en-Laye

★
◄ Musée des Antiquités Nationales

★
◄ Musée Prieuré

◄ Poissy

Maisons-Laffite   Maisons-Laffite (22km/14mi northwest of Paris city centre) is known for its large **chateau**, one of the most elegant and harmonious in all of France, built from 1642 to 1651 by François Mansart. Its 17th–18th century furnishings include tapestries and paintings.

Mantes-la-Jolie   Mantes-la-Jolie (44,000 inhabitants, 54km/36mi west of Paris) on the left bank is where King Henri IV converted to Catholicism in 1593 with his famous comment »Paris is worth going to mass for«. The Gothic collegiate church of Notre-Dame (12th–14th centuries) is of

✷
Notre Dame ►   importance, taking as it does the eponymous cathedral in Paris as its template. The design of the choir apse is unusual. The museum in the 17th-century Ancien Hôtel Dieu is dedicated to neo-Impressionist painter Maximilien Luce (1858–1941).

Giverny   ►Normandy

Auvers-sur-Oise   The small town of Auvers-sur-Oise (6200 inhabitants) is wedged into a strip several miles long between the river Oise and the edge of the Plateau du Vexin some 33km/21mi from Paris and was a haunt of various artists in the 19th century, including Cézanne, Corot, Daubigny, Renoir and **Vincent van Gogh**. Van Gogh rented a room at Auberge Ravoux opposite the Mairie, which he also painted. The inn is still worth recommending with its cosy atmosphere and hearty food (advance booking recommended, tel. 01 30 36 60 60). It was in Auvers that Van Gogh committed suicide in 1890. He and his brother Theo are both buried in the cemetery here. At the Château de Leyrit (1632) visitors can take a virtual tour through the Impressionist era.

✷ Languedoc-Roussillon

L–M 9

The region of Languedoc-Roussillon extends over 200km/125mi of coast between the Pyrenees and the mouth of the Rhône. It has plenty to offer, including France's oldest vineyards, precipitous Cathar fortresses, atmospheric old towns and endless beaches.

Départements   The two provinces that form the region, Languedoc and Roussillon, comprise the départements Lozère, Gard, Hérault, Aude and Pyrénées-Orientales. The capital is ► Montpellier. The most northerly département, Lozère – otherwise known as ►Cevennes – is the most sparsely populated part of France. The precipitous fortresses in the Corbière Mountains, built in the 10th–11th centuries as part of a belt of defences against Aragon, were then used as havens by the Cathars

Coasts and   (Albigensians) in the 13th century. The swampy coastline, sprinkled
resorts   with numerous lagoons (étangs), originally had few seaside resorts. Not until after 1963 did the transformation of the whole west coast

Highlights *Languedoc-Roussillon*

St-Guilhem-le-Désert
Medieval village on the edge of the Cevennes with a monastery from the time of Charlemagne
► page 444

Sète
The »Venice of Languedoc«: atmosphere of a genuine Mediterranean port and fishing harbour
► page 445

Narbonne
Impressive historic artefacts dating back to the province of Gallia Narbonensis
► page 447

Cathar forts
The breathtakingly situated havens of the »pure ones«
► page 450

Collioure
The prettiest little town on the Côte Vermeille, famous for the »Fauves«
► page 451

---

of the Golfe du Lion begin: marshes were drained, beaches opened, old towns like Sète, Agde and Perpignan were expanded and dozens of holiday settlements of greater and lesser degrees of nastiness were built. The oldest and best known, La Grande Motte, opened in 1974 and was followed by many more, such as Port Barcarès, Port Leucate, Gruissan, Cap d'Agde and Port Camargue.

Towards the end of the 6th century BC, the coast was settled by Phoenicians and Greeks. It was later occupied by the Romans. In 214 BC Hannibal crossed the Pyrenees and in 719 the Arabs took the Perthus pass and conquered Narbonne. The Franks regained the region in 759 under the leadership of Pepin the Younger. The county of Roussillon – more or less corresponding to the modern département of Pyrénées Orientales – came under the control of relatives of the counts of Barcelona in 1172. During the crusade against the Cathars, Simon de Montfort took Carcassonne and Béziers in 1209, their populations being expelled or murdered. (► Baedeker Special p.452). In 1229 Raymond VII, Count of Toulouse, ceded portions of his dominion to the Crown, and in 1258 Louis IX gave Roussillon to the Kingdom of Aragón. This began a golden age for the area, and especially for ► Perpignan, capital of the Kingdom of Mallorca from 1276 to 1344. The desire for independence remained, however. Roussillon rebelled in 1640 and was joined by the Catalans. They declared the French king Louis XIII Count of Barcelona. The peace treaty of 1659 did not fulfil the desire for a united Catalonia, however, since the main ridge of the Pyrenees was declared the border between France and Spain. **History**

Initially Vulgar Latin mutated into a language called »langue d'oc« (including the dialects of Languedoc itself, Provençal, Gascon, Lim- **Occitan and Catalan**

ousin and Auvergnat), which attained a literary peak in the work of the troubadours of Aquitaine in the 10th and 11th centuries. As the French monarchy asserted its primacy, the languages of the south were suppressed and in 1539 the **Edict of Villers-Cotterêts** made »langue d'oil« the official language. When universal education was introduced in 1882, use of Occitan was forbidden in schools. Only since 1951 has the language, now at least understood by some 10 million people, been allowed as a subject in the classroom. A similar story applies to Occitan's linguistic relative Catalan, which is used as both a common and official language in Spanish Catalonia and can still be heard in Roussillon. This Romance language had its first heyday in the 13th century with the unification of Aragón and Castile. In 1479, however, Castilian became the dominant language in Spain.

Wine cultivation

Boasting a third of the cultivated area and 40% of French production, Languedoc is the most important wine-growing area in the country. A whole range of excellent table wines and outstanding fine wines are produced here, most of them red wines. The most important labels are Coteaux du Languedoc, Faugères, St-Chinian, Minervois, Corbières, Limoux (including the highly regarded Blanquette, France's oldest sparkling wine), Côtes du Cabardès, Côtes de la Malepère and Fitou. The dessert wines of Rivesaltes, Maury and Banyuls are also renowned.

Places to Visit in Languedoc und Roussillon

The following description points out the most interesting places on the coast between ► Montpellier and ► Perpignan, followed by the Corbières mountains and the Côte Vermeille. The region also includes the Cevennes, Nîmes and Carcassonne, and portions of the Pyrenees and the Camargue (see the relevant entries below).

★
Saint-Guilhem-le-Désert

The village of Saint-Guilhem-le-Désert, impressively situated at one end of a gorge some 45km/28mi northwest of Montpellier, grew up around **Gellone Abbey**, founded in 804. Its founder, William of Orange, was a cousin and friend of Charlemagne. The church apse (1076) contains William's reliquary and a splinter of the True Cross, donated by Charlemagne himself. This made the abbey an important staging post on the Way of St James. The cloisters were plundered after the Revolution and the treasures later found their way to The Cloisters museum in New York. The fine organ is by Jean-Pierre Cavaillé (1789).

The pools on the beach by the ugly concrete towers of Palavas les Flots 10km/6mi south of Montpellier conceal a unique variety of flora and fauna (tours are organized by the tourist office). The **ancient port of Maguelone** is on the spit to the west. It was initially destroyed in 737 by Charles Martel. A new fortified cathedral (1060) remained more or less intact when the village was crushed again by Richelieu in 1633; its western entrance from 1178 is very beautiful. In June concerts featuring ancient and Baroque music are given.

Palavas

Marseillan, 7km/4.5mi north east of Agde, is where the famous vermouth **Noilly Prat** is made (tours May–Sept).

Marseillan

Entirely surrounded by water and bisected by canals, Sète (40,000 inhabitants) is the most important fishing port and the second most important freight harbour of Mediterranean France after Marseille. The old harbour was constructed under Louis XIV as of 1666 when the Canal du Midi was built to link the Mediterranean to the Atlantic. The lively town is at its prettiest alongside the **Canal de Sète** under the 183m/600ft peak of Mont St Clair. There is a fish auction house at Vieux Port, and boats make trips round the harbour from Quai Général Durand further to the north. Around 25 August the Fête de Saint Louis is celebrated with a sea jousting competition. It is very pleasant to take a walk over Mont St-Clair with its splendid view. In the mariners' cemetery Sète-born poet **Paul Valéry** (1871–1945) is buried. At the top end of the cemetery the Musée Paul Valéry features documents and items from the town's history. At the western foot of Mont St-Clair is the cemetery of Le Py, last resting place of the chanson singer (1921–81), **Georges Brassens** who grew up in Sète (Espace Brassens at the cemetery).

Sète

★
◄ Mont St-Clair

Cross the spit alongside Bassin de Thau bay to reach Agde (20,000 inhabitants) at the mouth of the river Hérault. Amid its picturesque, if somewhat gloomy streets under the volcano of Mont St-Loup (115m/377ft) can be found the cathedral of St-Etienne (started 1173), an interesting fortified church with lava walls 2–3m/7–10ft thick and a splendid 17th-century marble altar. Musée Agathois is located in a Renaissance palace and covers aspects of the local folk culture. 4km/2.5mi away, the resort of Cap d'Agde has several marinas and plenty of amusements. It is also a well-known centre for nudism.

Agde

Cap d'Agde

VISITING LANGUEDOC-ROUSSILLON

INFORMATION
CRT Languedoc-Roussillon
CS 79507
F-34960 Montpellier Cedex
Tel. 04 67 22 81 00
www.sunfrance.com

WHERE TO EAT
▶ Inexpensive / moderate
La Palangrotte
1 Rampe P. Valéry, F-34200 Sète
Tel. 04 67 74 80 35, closed Mon and
Sun evening (except July–Aug). The
leading restaurant in the town is near
the canal, a true institution featuring
excellent cuisine, primarily fish.

Chez Philippe
20 Rue Suffren, F-34340 Marseillan
Tel. 04 67 01 70 62, closed Sundays
and Mondays except July–Aug. Culinary highlight near the Bassin de
Thau. A varied Mediterranean menu
(3–4 courses with plenty of choice) is
served in friendly atmosphere inside
or on the terrace.

WHERE TO STAY
▶ Mid-range
Grand Hôtel
17 Quai de Lattre de Tassigny
F-34200 Sète
Tel. 04 67 74 71 77
www.legrandhotelsete.com
A genuinely grand hotel built in 1882
and centrally located by the canal.
Nice, comfortable rooms with antique
furniture and a fabulous view.

▶ Budget
Hotel des Poetes
80 Allées Paul Riquet, F-34500 Béziers
www.hoteldespoetes.net
Old, attractively modernized building
in the town centre by a romantic
park. Extremely friendly and good
value for money.

The northern French Gothic style at the cathedral of St-Juste in Narbonne

The Musée de l'Éphebe features the magnificent **Ephebe of Agde** (4th century BC).

Béziers (71,500 inhabitants) is beautifully located about 12km/7mi inland on a small bluff alongside the river Orb, which the Canal du Midi crosses here by means of a viaduct built in 1857. The town developed from a colony of Roman veterans called Biterrae Septimanorum but was destroyed in 1209 in the course of the Albigensian Crusade (►Baedeker Special p.452). Mid-August sees the grand **Feria de Béziers**, when bulls are driven through the streets. The city's landmark is the fortified cathedral of St-Nazaire (12th–14th centuries), with its remarkable rose window measuring 10m/33ft in diameter as well as a Romanesque choir with frescoes from the 14th century and a 17th-century organ. The jumble of alleys in the old town spreads out to the east of the cathedral. Hôtel Fayet and Hôtel Fabrégat house the excellent Musée des Beaux-Arts. Rue Viennet leads to the superb **Allée Paul-Riquet**, dedicated to the engineer who built the Canal du Midi (statue by David d'Angers). The fascinating Musée du Vieux Biterrois is housed in a 1702 barracks in the south of the city. It covers archaeology, folklore and features the **treasure of Béziers**). The church of St-Jacques, partly dating back to the 12th century, with its richly decorated choir is next door.

Béziers

✳
◄ St-Nazaire

✳
◄ Musée des Beaux-Arts
✳
◄ Musee du Vieux Biterrois

From Roman times until the silting of the harbour in the 14th century Narbonne (48,000 inhabitants) was an important trading centre. Founded in 118 BC as Narbo Martius, it developed into the magnificent capital of the province **Gallia Narbonensis**. Its present-day wealth is based on wine cultivation in the Corbières mountains (► p.449). Narbonne is bisected by the Canal de la Robine, which opened to 1789 to connect the river Aude to the Mediterranean. The city's centrepiece is the **Place de l'Hôtel de Ville** with the archbishop's palace, a complex comprising the Palais Vieux (12th century) and Palais Neuf (14th–18th centuries). Between the massive 13th-century towers Viollet-le-Duc built the neo-Gothic façade of the town hall, which was completed in 1850. The palace houses the interesting Musée d'Art et d'Histoire (paintings from the 16th to 20th centuries, furniture and pottery) and the Musée Archéologique, one of the **most important museums of Roman times** in France (both open July–Sept 11am–6pm, otherwise 9am–noon, 2pm–6pm). On the square next to the town hall, remnants of the Roman Via Domitia (c120 BC) have been unearthed. The cathedral of **St-Just** adjoins the palace to the north. It consists solely of a single wonderful choir, at 41m/135ft the tallest in France, built 1272–1332 in pure northern French Gothic style. The 14th-century windows, the 18th-century choir stalls, the great organ (1741) and the church's marvellous treasures (including 15th-century tapestries from Brussels and illuminated manuscripts) are all of note. There is a fine view from the terraces and the northern tower. To the north of St-Just there is a

Narbonne

✳
◄ Palais des Archevêques

✳ ✳
◄ Musée Archéologique

✳
◄ St-Just

horreum (underground warehouse), Narbonne's only remaining Roman building. The early Gothic church of St-Paul-Serge (12th–13th centuries) is situated in the southwest of the city. It has an elegant choir (begun in 1224) and a stoup for holy water carved in the shape of a frog. Further east lie the splendid belle époque market hall and the church of Notre-Dame-de-la-Mourguié (13th century), which exhibits archaeological finds from classical and medieval times.

Narbonne Plage

Gruissan

About 16km/10mi east of Narbonne beyond the 214m/702ft limestone massif of **Montagne de la Clape**, where there are some pleasant walks, is the unattractive Narbonne Plage, ugly in spite of its miles of sandy beach. Gruissan (10km/6mi to the south), however, is a pretty old fishing and salt-producing village clustered around a rocky hill topped by the ruin of a medieval fort. Gruissan Plage has some holiday chalets set on stilts, which are 100 years old.

Fontfroide

The abbey of Fontfroide (photo p.446) was founded in 1093 in a romantic valley 15km/9mi southwest of Narbonne and by 1145 had become the most important abbey in Languedoc. It played a major role in the war against the Cathars. Its simple, late 12th-century Romanesque church survives, along with a notable cloister, the chapter house, refectory and some dormitories. The monastery's sheep barns have undergone a fantastic transformation into a restaurant, Les Cuisiniers Vignerons, where an imaginatively varied regional menu can be enjoyed (moderate prices, lunchtimes only, tel. 04 68 41 86 06).

Salses

The impressive bastion of Salses (2000 inhabitants) was erected by Ferdinand II of Aragón from 1497, when this was border territory, and modernized by Vauban in 1659 even though the Pyrenean peace treaty had rendered it superfluous. The village is situated on the **Etang de Leucate**.

Rivesaltes is at the centre of a large wine-growing area, where some well-known sweet wines, in particular Muscat de Rivesaltes (vin doux naturel, VDN), are made.

Tautavel

20km/12mi northeast of Rivesaltes is the village of Tautavel, made famous by the discoveries of prehistoric humans (»Tautavel Man« from about 450,000 BC) in the Caune de l'Arago cave. There is a museum in the European Centre for Prehistory and Early History.

Perpignan ► Perpignan

Thuir

Bages

The wine village of Thuir 15km/9mi southwest of Perpignan is where the popular aperitif **Byrrh** is made (tours available). The Musée International d'Art Naïf in Bages, 10km/6mi south of Perpignan, exhibits so-called »primitive art« from around the world.

The names »Salanque« or »Côte des Perpignanais« refer to the rather monotonous flat coast with its fine sandy beaches between the Etang de Leucate and Argelès-Plage (▶ Côte Vermeille). Various **resorts** with marinas and a full range of amusements as well as water sports facilities are dotted along the way, some of them on the spits that separate the lagoons from the sea. They include Port-Leucate, Port-Barcarès, Canet-Plage and St-Cyprien Plage (museum with works by Matisse, Cézanne, Miró etc.). Amid them are the surprisingly pretty La Franqui and Leucate-Village; the latter well known for its shellfish farms.

Côte des Perpignanais

Elne (6000 inhabitants) is situated on a hill rising from the coastal plain. In the 5th–6th centuries it was the capital of Roussillon and remained a bishopric for more than 1000 years until 1602. The cathedral of Ste-Eulalie (1042–62, one of France's finest Romanesque buildings) remains as a testimony to that era. Inside are an 11th-century Romanesque marble altar, a 14th-century Catalonian altarpiece and a font dating back to Roman times. The cloister with its richly sculpted capitals (12th–14th centuries) is outstanding.

Elne

★

◀ Ste-Eulalie

Places to Visit in the Corbières

Inland from the coast around Narbonne and Perpignan the Corbières stretch away to the north. The rolling landscape is used for **wine cultivation** and rises gradually from the Aude valley towards the south to a height of 1231m/4039ft at its highest point, Pic de Bugarach east of Quillan. In the prevailing Mediterranean climate vineyards, cedars, cypress and garrigue scrub characterize the scenery.

Countryside

In Lézignan-Corbières, a small wine-trading town 20km/12mi west of Narbonne, it is well worth seeing the Musée de la Vigne et du Vin (wine museum) in the old manor house.

Lézignan-Corbières

▶Carcassonne

Carcassonne

Lagrasse (700 inhabitants, 20km/12mi southwest of Lézignan), one of the »prettiest villages in France«, was dominated for many centuries by the **Benedictine abbey** of Ste-Marie-d'Orbieu, which dates back to at least 778. The tower (1537), church (13th century, with earlier parts), two cloisters (11th–13th centuries and 1760) and the 18th-century abbot's house can still be seen. The abbot's house is still used by a Catholic Byzantine order. The central square with its market hall and the bridges over the river Orbieu (one of which dates to the 11th century) are very pretty.

★

Lagrasse

Limoux (9500 inhabitants, 24km/15mi southwest of Carcassonne) is known for **Blanquette**, a sparkling wine, and its Grand Carnaval from the middle of January until late March. The Place de la République in

Limoux

Collioure: small beach by the church of Notre-Dame-des-Anges

the centre is lined by medieval arcades with restaurants and cafés. At carnival time it throngs with the »Fécos«, dancers dressed as pierrots in strange, expressionless masks. Information on Limoux Blanquette and visits to the local wine cellars can be obtained from the Syndicat des Vins on Av. du Pont-de-France (www.limoux.aoc.com).

✸ ✸
Cathar forts

The main fort in the ring of defences that was directed against Spain was ►Carcassonne, but it had »**five sons«**: Puilaurens, Peyrepertuse, Quéribus, Aguilar and Termes. Termes (22km/14mi, with a view of the Gorges du Terminet,) is accessed from Lagrasse via the D 212. Aguilar is near Tuchan (27km/17mi northwest of Perpignan), while the others line up in breathtaking locations on the hillsides along the D 117 between Perpignan and Quillan: Quéribus near Maury, Peyrepertuse (»pierced rock«, 6km/3.5mi northwest) and Puilaurens, east of Axat. West of Quillan there are two more famous castles, Puivert and Montségur (next page).

Gorges de Galamus

North of St-Paul-de-Fénouillet the river Agly runs through a 300m/1000ft-deep gorge carved through the mountains. It takes five minutes to get from the D 7 down to the hermitage of St-Antoine.

Quillan

Quillan (3800 inhabitants) makes a good base for day trips. It has a 13th-century ruined castle, and its church of Notre-Dame dates from 1677. West of Quillan, already beyond the borders of the Corbières region, the D 117 passes the supposed **Troubadour castle** of Puivert (12th–14th centuries). From Bélesta the D 5 and D 9 lead to the massive ruins of the castle of Montségur, located on a steep hill at an altitude of 1215m/3986ft (30 minutes' climb; photo p.453). In 1244, 207 so-called Albigensians were burned alive on the Prat dels Cremats, at the bottom of the mountain, at the end of a ten-month siege. Montségur is equated by many with the legendary **Montsalvat**, where the Holy Grail, the chalice used at the Last Supper, was reputed to be hidden. The village is now considered the symbolic focus for those seeking Occitanian autonomy.

Puivert

✸
Montségur

Places to Visit on the Côte Vermeille

Scenery

The »Purple Coast« stretches from Collioure, southeast of ►Perpignan, to the Spanish border. Here outliers of the Pyrenees descend impressively to a windswept coast, with the reddish cliffs from which the region gets its name rising from the deep blue of the Mediterranean. Vines have been grown on the hillsides here since the 7th century BC. Various pretty towns in the bays have become popular resorts.

The medieval town of Argelès-sur-Mer is situated where the plain meets the Pyrenees. In its 14th-century Gothic church some panel paintings from the late Renaissance period are on view. The Casa de les Albères (museum of Catalan folklore) is also interesting. The adjoining Argelès Plage is a sandy beach 6km/3.5mi in length, with dozens of campsites, holiday apartments and everything needed for a beach holiday.

Argelès-sur-Mer

For art enthusiasts, the monastery of St-Génis (8km/5mi west), founded in 819, is a must. Its door lintel, dating from 1020, is the **oldest definitely dated sculpture of its kind in France** (Christ in a Mandorla, flanked by the apostles). The church was built around 1150, while the cloister was reassembled from original stones in 1983.

★
Saint-Génis-des-Fontaines

The picturesque and well frequented little town of Collioure (2700 inhabitants) has been a well-known port since ancient times and was later the harbour for Perpignan. It was »discovered« in 1905 by the painters Matisse and Derain, whose vivid experiments with colour led them being dubbed the »Fauves« (»wild ones«). Some of their paintings can be seen in 20 places along a trail called the **Chemin du Fauvisme**. The Templar castle on the bay was the summer residence (Château Royal) of the kings of Mallorca and the queen of Aragón from 1276 to 1344. Alongside the northern beach stands Collioure's landmark, the church of **Notre-Dame-des-Anges** (1684), the tower of which was once used as a lighthouse. It is beautifully decorated with a massive gilded altar in the Catalan Baroque style (Joseph Sunyer, 1695–1701) and a carved altar screen. In mid-August the four-day festival of St-Vincent is celebrated with fireworks.

★
Collioure

Port-Vendres (6000 inhabitants), formerly Portus Veneris, a fishing port, marina and freight harbour in a deep bay, was expanded into a military harbour from 1772 to plans by Vauban. Its Fort du Fanal is

Port-Vendres

! *Baedeker* TIP

Banyuls

Banyuls is a red or topaz-coloured vin doux naturel (dessert wine) made from Grenache Noir, Grenache Blanc and Macabeu grapes. Its fermentation is stopped by adding extra alcohol. »Banyuls Rancio« is matured for two years, partially in glass demijohns or barrels in the open air. A visit to the wineries of Cellier des Templiers or the Cooperative L'Etoile in Banyuls is very interesting.

Banishment of Cathars from Carcassonne from a contemporary book illustration

THE FREED SOULS

Who were the Cathars, who were so ruthlessly exterminated by the Church and the French Crown in the 13th century? There are still reminders of them in the dramatically located ruins in the foothills of the eastern Pyrenees, where they made their last stand.

The origin of the Cathars, one of the biggest movements for religious renewal in the Middle Ages, can be traced to Bulgaria. Their preaching spread rapidly westward into Italy, France, Catalonia and the German Rhineland. With the support of the local aristocracy, the movement also took root in Occitania during the 12th century, particularly around Toulouse, Carcassonne and Albi (where a church council took place which instituted a crusade against the sect, such that they were thereafter also known as **Albigensians**). The French monarchy was greedy for more control over these independent counties. The later Albigensian crusade decimated the population; local rulers were no longer able to resist the French Crown. The aristocratic courts close to the border with Aragon were at that time a magnet for travellers from all over the world. Philosophers exchanged ideas here, troubadours sang of the beauty of women and of virtuous knights, and the Cathars (from the Greek word »katharoi« meaning »pure ones«) preached here.

Good and evil

Their message was based on an assumption that two powers controlled the universe: the God of the New Testament, the embodiment of goodness; and Satan or Rex Mundi, king of the world, whom they equated with the God of the Old Testament and held responsible for all that was evil. The body and the flesh they held to be the domain of Satan, while all that was truly holy would be the spirit and the soul. The Cathars made a distinction between common followers (»credentes«), who could marry and could follow worldly pursuits, and their »perfect ones«, who did not use the name »katharoí« but called themselves »good Christians (boni Christiani)«. These latter individuals lived in strict poverty and were forbidden meat, cheese, eggs, milk or wine. They eschewed marriage and sexuality altogether. The boni Christiani would wander the country as monks, dressed in black and begging for food and shelter. Using the »langue d'oc«, the language of the people of southern France, they would preach poverty

Montségur seems closer to heaven than to earth

and asceticism, fraternity and the rejection of violence. They railed against the godless lifestyles of the church's leaders in Rome, calling them whoremongers and gluttons. The feudal hierarchy, oaths of allegiance and the church tithe were »of the devil«. In their place, the Cathars preached poverty for priests and the church as a whole. At the beginning of the 13th century, almost a third of the congregation had left the Catholic church and it is estimated that there were as many as a hundred thousand devotees of the Cathar ideal, including four to five thousand »boni«.

God knows his own

As early as 1028, the church had announced a campaign against »falsehood« at the Council of Charroux. When attempts at conversion, ranging from theological debates to fierce threats, failed, the murder of papal legate Pierre de Castelnau in 1208 gave Pope Innocent III an excuse to declare a crusade against the Cathars (a second was ordered in 1228). **Simon de Montfort**, until then an unimportant nobleman from the Ile-de-France, set to work. In 1209 his army of fanaticized, greedy knights and infantry poured into Languedoc, first to Beziers. When the city refused to hand over 22 Cathars, Simon attacked the city and had the entire populace (about 18,000 people) cut to pieces. The Abbot of Citeaux gave permission: »Kill them all; God will know his own!« After Beziers came Narbonne, then Carcassonne. Castle by castle the land was conquered. Bonfires of the condemned burned in Castres, Minerve, Lavaur and Cassès. The persecuted people fled to the castles in the Corbière Mountains: Aguilar, Termes, Peyrepertuse, Quéribus, Puilaurens and Montségur. The last of these became legendary. It was besieged in 1243 by 10,000 men. After ten months, 207 Cathars surrendered and were burned at the stake. According to legend, a small group of »perfect ones« managed escape, bearing a mysterious treasure. The fall of Quéribus in 1255 ended the resistance. The country was laid waste, the local nobles were stripped of their titles, impoverished or killed. Rome re-established the pre-eminence of the church between the Southern Alps and the Pyrenees. When Raymond VII, Comte de Toulouse, surrendered in 1229, he was compelled to plea for forgiveness in a humiliating ceremony and forced to marry off his only daughter and heir to the king's brother, ensuring that the Capetians had secured full control of the south. More can be learned about the Cathars at their (French) website, www.cathares.org.

open to the public. On Place d'Obélisque there is an obelisk dedicated to Louis XIV and a war memorial by Maillol (1923). To the east of the village Cap Béar stretches out into the sea; south of it are several nice bays with beaches for swimming.

Banyuls-sur-Mer   Banyuls (4600 inhabitants) is the main centre of a wine-growing region that stretches from the coast deep into the Albères mountains. Around 20 October a big, colourful harvest festival takes place. Banyuls is not so attractive as a holiday resort, although the aquaria of the oceanographic research station are interesting. The war memorial on Ile Grosse (east of the marina) was designed by **Aristide Maillol**, who was born here in 1861 († 1944). The sculptor's summer residence is situated some 4km/2.5mi to the southwest. To get back to Collioure the route over the 652m/2139ft summit of Tour Made-

✳
Tour Madeloc   loc is recommended, as there is a fantastic view of the coast.

Cerbère   The last village before the Spanish border is Cerbère, dominated by a massive complex of railway sidings. Southeast of the village the black rocks of the rugged Cap Cerbère offer a fine view of the coast. Finally, the border between France and Spain runs over the high pass

Col des Balitres   of Col des Balitres (173m/568ft). The cemetery of the Spanish border
Portbou   town ofPortbou, on the border, is the last resting place of German philosopher Walter Benjamin, who committed suicide here in 1940 rather than face deportation back to Nazi Germany.

✳ # La Rochelle

Région: Poitou – Charentes	**Altitude:** Sea level
Département: Charente-Maritime	**Population:** 80,000

La Rochelle, in the middle of west coast, is a popular holiday destination with its lovely old town, picturesque Vieux Port and a multitude of beaches in the vicinity. Its harbour fortifications and wood-panelled arcade houses still project an atmosphere of the Huguenot era.

Port and university town   The old centre of the Aunis region and capital of the Charente-Maritime département has a large harbour in its western suburb of La Pallice, where ocean-going ships are loaded (6 million tons of freight p.a.). A fishing port and an ultra-modern auction hall are also located there. Since 1993 La Rochelle has been a university town. The surrounding areas, including the islands of Ile de Ré and Ile d'Oléron, are described under ▶Poitou – Vendée – Charentes.

History   La Rochelle was one of France's most important sea ports from the 14th to the 18th century. At the end of the 16th century settlers set

Two towers guard the harbour at La Rochelle

out from here for Canada, and the town's ship owners had trading links with North America. Its citizens' spirit of entrepreneurship and liberty – it had been a free city since 1199 – made La Rochelle one of the **bastions of Protestantism**. After the St Bartholomew's Day massacre of 1572, La Rochelle was besieged without success until 1573. In a year-long siege ordered by Richelieu in 1627–28, however, the city was cut off from the sea by an earthwork 12km/7mi in length and starved into submission. Of 28,000 inhabitants, only 5000 survived. With the repeal of the Edict of Nantes in 1683 and the loss of Canada in 1763, the importance of the town waned. In the Second World War La Rochelle was used as a base for the German U-boat fleet and therefore bombed regularly. The German soldiers garrisoned there only gave themselves up on 8 May 1945, a day after the German surrender had been signed in Reims.

What to See in La Rochelle

The town's premier attraction is its **old harbour**, lined by cafés and restaurants. The northwest corner is guarded by the imposing Porte de la Grosse-Horloge (14th–15th centuries; tower 1746), the only one of the city gates to have been preserved. The entrance to the Vieux Port is flanked by the 42m/138ft Tour St-Nicolas (1345, port museum and viewpoint) in the east and the Tour de la Chaîne (c1385) in the west. The latter is named after the chain that barred the entrance to the harbour in the Middle Ages. The exhibits in the tower itself include a model of the town as it was in medieval times. From here the remainder of the medieval walls run westward to the 70m/230ft Tour de la Lanterne, built from 1445 to 1476 as a lighthouse. It too has a fine view. The attractive **Gabut quarter** near Tour St-Nicolas between the flood basins was constructed in 1858 on the site of earlier fortifications.

From Vieux Port the city's main shopping street, lined with arcades (16th–18th centuries) leads northward. It passes the Hôtel de la

Vieux Port

Rue du Palais Rue Chaudrier

St-Louis

Bourse with its pretty courtyard (1785) and the Palais de Justice (1789). On the side street Rue des Augustins stands Maison Henri II, an aristocratic mansion from 1555. The sober, classical cathedral of St-Louis was built from 1742 to 1762 by Gabriel Senior and Junior. The tower is 15th century. To the north of Place Verdun, Rue du Minage turns off to the right. It too has some picturesque arcades and old houses.

✳ Hôtel de Ville

The centre of town is Place de l'Hôtel de Ville. The castle-like, late Gothic façade of the town hall was completed in 1498, and its magnificent **Renaissance courtyard** dates from around 1600. To the east of the town hall the Protestant church (1708) houses an exhibition of the city's Protestant history. Rue des Merciers with its lovely old houses leads to a colourful square bordered by timber-framed buildings.

Temple Rue des Merciers

✳ Musée des Beaux-Arts

Between the market place and Place Verdun the 18th-century bishop's palace houses the city's collection of paintings. Hôtel Fleuriau, formerly a ship-owner's house, can be accessed from the street that

▶ VISITING LA ROCHELLE

INFORMATION

Office de Tourisme
2 Quai Georges Simenon, Le Babut
F-17025 La Rochelle
Tel. 05 46 41 14 68, Fax 05 46 41 99 85
www.larochelle-tourisme.com

BOATS

»Bus de Mer« services run to the aquarium and Port des Minimes from Cours des Dames, and ferries also sail from there to the islands of Ré, Aix and Oléron.

EVENTS

Late June to early July: international film festival. In the week around 14 July: Francofolies, popular music from rock and rap to jazz, featuring hundreds of concerts.

WHERE TO EAT

▶ Expensive

① *R. et C. Coutanceau*
Plage de la Concurrence

Tel. 05 46 41 48 19, closed Sun.
The best restaurant in town is on the shoreline southwest of the harbour. Classical, creative cuisine in simple modern surroundings.

WHERE TO STAY

▶ Mid-range

① *La 33 Rue Thiers*
33 Rue Thiers, tel. 06 82 6897
Centrally located chambre d'hôte in an 18th-century shipowner's house on the market place. Idyllic guest rooms with antique furniture. Breakfast is served in the walled garden.

▶ Budget

② *Hotel François I*
13/15 Rue Bazoges, tel. 05 46 41 28 46
www.hotelfrancois1er.fr
In the 15th and 16th centuries even kings stayed here. Nowadays it is a very pleasant hotel in the centre of town that would be worth an extra star. Private car park.

runs parallel to the south. It contains the Musée du Nouveau Monde (history of Canadian colonization and overseas trade).

Musée du Nouveau Monde

The botanical gardens are situated on Rue Albert along with the Fleuriau museum (natural history) and Muséum d'Historie Naturelle (ocean fauna, folklore). The **Cabinet des Curiosités Lafaille** with its natural history collection amid furnishings dating back to 1770 is delightful.

Jardin des Plantes

The upmarket district west of Rue du Palais was once home to wealthy Huguenots. Musée d'Orbigny-Bernon on Rue St-Côme (local history, pottery from La Rochelle and the Far East) is also worth seeing. East of the museum on Rue de l'Escale is the 17th-century Maison Venette. A pretty city park runs alongside the former walls. Adjoining to the southwest is the Mail, a popular promenade with a beach and casino.

Huguenot quarter

Interesting places for a trip in the district south of Vieux Port include the aquarium (with 65 separate tanks) and the naval museum **Neptunea** with its old wooden ships, frigates, fishing cutters and model boats.

La Ville en Bois

La Rochelle Map

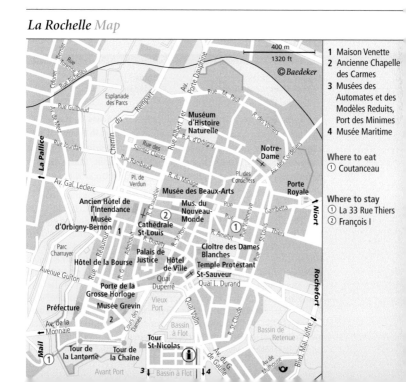

400 m
1320 ft
©Baedeker

1 Maison Venette
2 Ancienne Chapelle des Carmes
3 Musées des Automates et des Modèles Reduits, Port des Minimes
4 Musée Maritime

Where to eat
① Coutanceau

Where to stay
① La 33 Rue Thiers
② François I

! *Baedeker* TIP

Café de la Paix
A wonderful brasserie from the belle époque, Café de la Paix Verdun (54 Rue Chaudrier, tel. 05 46 41 39 79, very reasonable prices) opened in 1900. The building with its beautiful façade has an even longer history. As of 1709 it was a hospital, and it was used as a theatre in revolutionary times.

Port des Minimes 3km/2mi to the southwest the suburb of Port des Minimes has the largest marina on the Atlantic coast of Europe.

La Pallice The suburb of La Pallice, 5km/3mi to the west, was the site for a new harbour, built 1883–90. The **toll bridge leading from here to the Ile de Ré** is 3km/2mi long (see Poitou – Vendee – Charente).

Le Havre

H 3

Région: Haute-Normandie	**Altitude:** 3m/10ft
Département: Seine-Maritime	**Population:** 193,000

The Seine estuary is 9km/5.5mi wide when it reaches Le Havre, the »gateway to the ocean« – the second-largest port in France. It was almost entirely destroyed during the Second World War but has been expansively, if not always attractively, rebuilt. Places to visit include the art museum and the Espace Culturel Oscar Niemeyer.

History King François I was the founder of Le Havre. He had it built in 1517 to replace the harbours of Harfleur and Honfleur, which had silted up. The first warship sailed as early as 1518. Later, France's ocean trade with North America sailed from here. During the American War of Independence, the harbour shipped weapons and aid to the Confederates in return for cotton, coffee etc. In the 1920s Le Havre developed into Europe's biggest terminal for luxury liners. 146 separate Allied air raids virtually levelled the town at the end of the Second World War, when it was a German base, but between 1945 and 1960 it was totally rebuilt. One of the key architects was **Auguste Perret** (1874–1954), a major exponent of steel reinforced concrete architecture. The **Pont de Normandie**, opened in 1995, is the second-largest cable-stayed bridge in the world (total length 2141m/

2340yd, span 856m/936yd, pylons 215m/705ft high), linking Le Havre with the Côte Fleurie (►Normandy).

What to See in Le Havre

From Place de l'Hôtel de Ville where the town hall and its 70m/230ft tower are situated, the broad Avenue Foch leads westward to the two tall buildings of the Porte Océane. An octagonal tower 106m/348ft in height is the hallmark of **St-Joseph** church (Perret, 1957), which is definitely worth visiting. The beach and leisure park stretch northward beyond the villas of the Ste-Adresse suburb as far as Nice Havrais (or Little Nice) 4km/2.5mi away. The marina has more than 1100 berths.

Hôtel de Ville

Marina

The excellent modern Musée des Beaux-Arts André Malraux (closed Tue) exhibits European art of the 17th–20th centuries. Artists from the local region are well represented, including Boudin, Dufy, Monet, Pissarro, Braque and Dubuffet.

★
Musée des Beaux-Arts

Opposite Notre-Dame cathedral (built from 1575, tower 1540, fine 17th-century organ) the former Palais de Justice houses the Muséum d'Histoire Naturelle. The **cultural centre**, opened in 1982, is named after the architect who designed it, Brazilian Oscar Niemeyer (its Café-Musique L'Agora is very popular).

Other attractions

The footbridge over the Bassin du Commerce with its cultural centre and the tower of St-Joseph in the background

Musée de l'Ancien Havre	The history of the port since 1517 is presented in the Musée de l'Ancien Havre, which occupies a 17th-century house.
Docks	To see the modern docks, take a **trip around the harbour** starting from the marina. At Docks Vauban the history of the port is the topic of the Espace Maritime museum.
Prieuré de Graville	The former abbey church of Ste-Honorine de Graville (11th–13th centuries) houses an archaeological museum (1 Rue Elisée Reclus; Rue G. Lafaurie, signposted on the way out of town, closed Mon–Tue).
Harfleur	Harfleur, now an eastern suburb of Le Havre, is a pretty spot at the mouth of the river Lézarde. Its dominant feature is the 83m/272ft tower of St-Martin (Flamboyant Gothic, 12th–16th centuries). The Musée du Prieuré relates the history of the town.

Le Havre Map

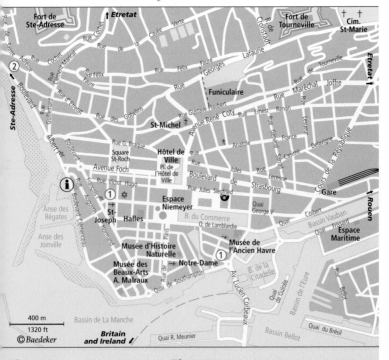

Where to eat		Where to stay
① L'Odyssee	② Les Trois Pics	① Vent d'Ouest

▶ VISITING LE HAVRE

INFORMATION
Office de Tourisme
186 Blvd. Clemenceau
F-76600 Le Havre
Tel. 02 32 74 04 04, fax 02 35 42 38 39
www.lehavretourisme.com

BOATS
Ferries to and from Portsmouth from the Terminal de la Citadelle, Avenue L. Corbeaux; bus links to the railway station and tourist office; harbour trips from the marina on Blvd. Clemenceau.

FESTIVALS AND EVENTS
April and Nov: Marché au Foie Gras Normand. Early Sept: Mèr en Fête.

WHERE TO EAT
▶ **Inexpensive**
L'Odyssee
41 Rue Gén. Faidherbe
Tel. 02 35 21 32 42, closed Mon. This friendly establishment is one of the best places in town to go for fish. Very good fare at an excellent price.

Les Trois Pics
Sente A. Karr, tel. 02 35 48 20 60, closed Mon. On Promenade Regates in the northerly suburb of Ste-Adresse, the restaurant has a fine view of the Seine estuary. The menu includes fish as well as Norman foie gras.

WHERE TO STAY
▶ **Mid-range**
Vent d'Ouest
4 Rue Caligny, tel. 02 35 42 50 69, www.ventdouest.fr. Quiet, centrally located hotel close to the sea with a stylish, English maritime feel. There is a garage but no restaurant.

✴ Le Mans

Région: Pays de la Loire
Département: Sarthe

Altitude: 80m/262ft
Population: 151,000

The »Le Mans 24-hour race« is famous the world over, but art enthusiasts will be drawn by the magnificent cathedral. Situated in northwest France, half-way between Paris and Nantes, the town also has a lovely old centre.

In the Middle Ages Le Mans was the capital of the county of Maine.   **History**
Nowadays it is the administrative centre for the Sarthe département and a university town. In 1873 Amédée Bollée built his first steam automobile here and thus laid the foundations for the French car industry (Renault). The first 24-hour car race was held in 1923. The lovely old town has formed the backdrop for many historic films, including *Cyrano de Bergerac*.

What to See in Le Mans

St-Julien

Beyond Place des Jacobins, where markets are held on Wednesdays and Sundays and a flea market on Fridays, the 134m/440ft-long Romanesque and Gothic cathedral of St-Julien (11th–15th centuries) towers above the town. Its wonderful 12th-century **south entrance** is reminiscent of the royal portal of Chartres. The **choir**, built between 1217 and 1254, is a fine example of Gothic architecture that features a double ambulatory, double and triple flying buttresses, and a ring of conspicuously protruding chapels. The interior is lit by magnificent **stained glass windows** from the 12th–15th centuries, especially in the 34m/112ft-high choir. The baptismal chapel off the northern transept has the Renaissance tombs of Charles IV of Anjou and Guillaume du Bellay. The central choir chapel (Chapelle de la Vierge) is decorated with fantastic Gothic frescoes (*Concert of Angels*, 15th century).

Old town

The old town high up on the hill lies southwest of the cathedral. Its centre with pretty old timber-framed houses and narrow streets is surrounded by a Gallo-Roman wall (3rd–4th centuries), the best-preserved example outside Rome itself. The best view of the fortifications is from the Quai Louis-Blanc and the Pont Yssoir, where eleven towers reinforce the defences parallel to the Sarthe. A tunnel runs under the old town towards Place des Jacobins. **Rue de la Reine-Bérengère** and its continuation, Grande Rue, are highly picturesque. The **Musée de la Reine Bérengère** is dedicated to folklore and re-

▶ VISITING LE MANS

INFORMATION

Office de Tourisme
Rue de l'Etoile, F-72000 Le Mans
Tel. 02 43 28 17 22, fax 02 43 28 12 14
www.ville-lemans.fr

EVENTS

April–May: Europa Jazz Festival. Mid-June: 24-hour race, tickets from the Office de Tourisme or the Automobile Club de l'Ouest (ACO), tel. 08 92 697 224, fax 02 43 84 47 13www.lemans.org

WHERE TO EAT

▶ **Moderate / expensive**
Le Pantagruel
Place St-Pierre

Tel. 02 43 24 87 63
Closed Mon. In the old town near the Hotel de Ville. High-class cuisine concentrating on fish and seafood, served by the large fireplace in the winter and on the terrace in summer.

WHERE TO STAY

▶ **Mid-range / luxury**
Domaine de Chatenay
F-72650 Saint-Saturnin
Tel. 02 43 25 44 60
www.domainedechatenay.com
A delightful 18th-century manor house in a large park. Rooms and suites with antique furnishings, dinner for residents in the elegant salon.

The choir of the cathedral, one of the finest examples of Gothic architecture

gional history. Maison d'Adam et d'Eve on Grande Rue (no. 71) is a lovely Renaissance house from 1525.

The Musée de Tessé is housed in the bishop's palace. As well as a fine collection of paintings, including Italian masters of the 14th–15th centuries and classic French works, it also possesses an enamel plaque of 1145–50 for the grave of Geoffroy de Plantagenet in Verdun.

✱ **Musée de Tessé**

The town hall was built in 1760 on the site of the former palace of the Comtes de Maine. The palace's Romanesque windows are still preserved. Here Geoffroy de Plantagenet was born, to be followed in 1133 by his son, the future Henry II of England. Bérengère, the widow of Richard the Lionheart, Henry's son, also lived here for many years.

Hotel de Ville

The geographical centre of Le Mans is the huge Place de la République south of the old town. The Palais de Justice, built on the remains of a monastery, and the Baroque Eglise de la Visitation (1730) are both situated on the western side of the square.

Place de la République

Further south, the former abbey church of Notre-Dame-de-la-Couture is also worth a look. Originally built in the 10th century, the present building dates from the 13th–14th centuries. Its façade has **many splendid sculptures around the entrance**. Inside tapestries and paintings are on display, including the *Dream of Elijah* by Philippe de Champaigne (17th century) and a fine marble Madonna opposite the pulpit by Germain Pilon (1570). In the 10th-century crypt with its remarkable capitals a relic of Saint Bertrand is kept.

Notre-Dame-de-la-Couture

Around Le Mans

Circuit de la Sarthe
The 13.6km/8.5mi **racing circuit** is about 6km/3.5mi south of Le Mans. Other than on race days, the circuit is open for normal traffic. The museum has more than 150 historic racing cars on display, and visitors can experience driving the circuit for themselves on a simulator.

Abbaye Notre-Dame-de-l'Epau
Queen Bérengère founded Epau Abbey, 4km/2.5mi southeast of Le Mans, in 1229. Some of the surviving buildings go back as far as the 15th century. The 13th-century tomb of the queen can be seen inside the church. A music festival is held here in May.

✳ Le Puy-en-Velay

L 7

Région: Auvergne
Département: Haute-Loire
Altitude: 630m/2067ft
Population: 22,000

The volcanoes of the ► Auvergne give Le Puy its unique appearance. Two extinct volcanic craters, Rocher Corneille with its massive statue of the Virgin Mary and the rocky peak of St-Michel, dominate the town. Since the Middle Ages Le Puy has been the starting point of the Via Podiensis, part of the Way of St James.

History and economy
In the 5th century Le Puy became the bishop`s seat for the diocese of Velay. Since the 10th century it has been a goal for pilgrims to the Black Madonna. A tradition of lace-making goes back to the 15th century, while the major industries in the modern-day capital of the Haute-Loire département are engineering and foodstuffs. The lintels of Le Puy, grown in Velay and sold under the AC label, are famed among gourmets.

What to See in Le Puy

Place du Breuil
South of the old town, Place du Breuil is the site of a theatre and the Préfecture, behind which the **Musée Crozatier** in the Jardin Vinay covers the history and culture of the region. From Place du Breuil head to Place du Plot (18th-century fountains) then turn left onto **Rue Panessac** with its lovely houses from the 15th–17th centuries. From there go along Rue Chamarlenc (note no. 16 Maisin des Cornards) and Rue Raphaël up to Place des Tables and up the wide steps to the cathedral. To the left of the cathedral is the Gothic façade of Hôtel Dieu.

✳✳ Notre-Dame
The cathedral of Notre-Dame-du-Puy (11th–12th centuries) displays a mixture of architecture from Auvergne and southwestern France along with Byzantine influences. The arcades, their façades built with

▶ VISITING LE PUY

INFORMATION

Office de Tourisme
Place du Clausel
F-43000 Le Puy en Velay
Tel. 04 71 09 38 41, fax 04 71 05 22 62
www.ot-lepuyenvelay.fr. Information
for pilgrims from the tourist office.

WHERE TO EAT

► Inexpensive

① *Au Poivrier*
69 Rue Pannesac
Tel. 04 71 02 41 30, closed Sun
(except in Aug).
Nice bistro in a lovely narrow street in
the old town. French cuisine highlighting local dishes.

WHERE TO STAY

► Budget

① *Le Régina*
34 Bd. Maréchal-Fayolle
Ttel. 04 71 09 38 41
www.hotelrestregina.com Very pleasant and comfortable hotel with modern rooms. Good but reasonably
priced, popular restaurant.

FESTIVALS AND EVENTS

July–Aug: various music festival, from
folk to classical.
14th–15th Aug: pilgrimage to the
Black Madonna.

*A panorama of Le Puy with the statue of Our Lady on the Rocher Corneille,
St-Michel and the cathedral*

colourful volcanic stone, lead to a porch underneath the cathedral's 12th-century bays. Note the 12th-century doors decorated with reliefs, Byzantine-influenced 13th-century frescoes on the vaults and the floor containing fragments of the supposedly miraculous »Stone of Visions«, which dates back to pre-Christian times. The ceremonious atmosphere is emphasized by the dark stone, the heavy transverse arches and high domes above the six bays. To the left is the Chapelle des Reliques (with 15th-century murals of the *Seven Liberal Arts*). Inside the Baroque high altar of 1723, the **Black Madonna** is displayed. The statue was brought back from a crusade by Louis IX (Saint Louis) in 1254 and may have been made originally as an image of the Egyptian goddess Isis. It was damaged in 1794 and replaced by a copy. In the left-hand transept there are Romanesque frescoes (12th–13th century) and a stairway leading to a fresco of St Michael that dates from the 12th century. From the right-hand transept, the Porche du For opens out onto Place du For, where there is a fine view of the town. The sacristy holds the church's remarkable treasury, including a Theodulf bible from the 9th century. The cloister adjoining the left-hand aisle features beautifully sculpted capitals, where the influence of the Moors in Spain can be clearly seen. The adjoining chapter house has a large 13th-century mural, while the assembly room above the cloister includes a collection of ecclesiastical art.

◀ Interior

✹
◀ Cloister

✹
Rocher Corneille

The peak of Rocher Corneille (Mont d'Anis) rises north of the cathedral to a height of 140m/460ft. The 16m/52ft tall, red-coloured statue of **Notre-Dame-de-France** was cast in 1860 from iron melted

Le Puy-en-Velay Map

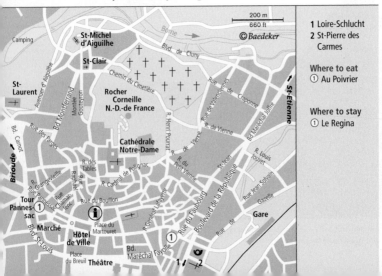

200 m
660 ft
© *Baedeker*

1 Loire-Schlucht
2 St-Pierre des
   Carmes

Where to eat
① Au Poivrier

Where to stay
① Le Regina

down from 213 cannons that were captured during the Crimean war. A stairway winds up inside the statue and a superb view from the top.

The chapel of Aiguilhe-St-Michel seems almost to grow out of the 85m/279ft volcanic cone of the same name (»aiguilhe« meaning »needle«). It was built in 962 on the site of what was probably a Temple of Mercury. It exhibits oriental influences, particularly on the magnificent entrance wall. There are 10th-century frescoes in the choir. At the foot of Mount Aiguilhe the 12th-century chapel of St-Clair is in typical Velay style.

★ Aiguilhe-St-Michel

At the northwestern edge of the old town it is worth looking at the Dominican church of St-Laurent (14th century). Its Gothic style is rare in Velay. The choir includes the tomb of Constable Du Guesclin (14th century). Close by at Rue Du Guesclin 2, the studio of the Conservatoire National de la Dentelle has an exhibition on how lace is made. An adjoining building shows a collection of lace since the 17th century.

St-Laurent

Lace museum

Around Le Puy

About 6km/3.5mi northwest of Le Puy, the impressive ruins of Château de Polignac (12th–15th century, although some remains date back to Roman times) cluster on top of a basalt plateau 100m/330ft high with a great view. In the village itself, the Romanesque and Gothic church is interesting.

Château de Polignac

East of Le Puy, the Loire winds through a narrow valley in the direction of St-Etienne. In Chamalières there is a unique church in the Auvergne Romanesque style.

★ Gorges de la Loire

Heading south away from Le Puy on the N 88 there is a great view of a **loop in the Loire** beyond Taulhac. Another 16km/10mi southwest past Cayres, Lac du Bouchet is a circular lake inside a volcanic crater at an altitude of 1208m/3963ft.

Lac du Bouchet

Westward of Lac du Bouchet are the magnificent Gorges de l'Allier. The route from Le Pont d'Alleyras through Monistrol to Langeac is lovely by car or **by train**, as the railway line runs through parts of the valley where no roads reach.

★ Gorges de l'Allier

About 40km/25mi southeast of Le Puy, the mountains of Gerbier de Jonc and Mont Mézenc are two rewarding places to visit. The first (1551m/5089ft), cone-shaped and only sparsely covered with vegetation, is in the Vivarais region and belongs to the eastern portion of the Massif Central. The foot of the mountain is where the **Loire has its source**. Wild daffodils, orchids and pansies bloom here in late

Gerbier de Jonc

spring. From the car park and restaurant, a walk of about 30 minutes up steep, narrow paths leads to the summit. In good weather it is possible to see as far as the Alps from the small plateau at the top.

★ ★
Mont Mézenc

The view from Mont Mézenc (1753m/5751ft, from the Croix de Boutières pass on the D 400, 30 minutes on foot) is even better. On clear days the view encompasses practically all of southeast France, from Mont Ventoux to Mont Blanc.

Lille

L 2

Région: Nord – Pas de Calais
Département: Nord

Altitude: 21m/69ft
Population: 191,000

Lille, near the Belgian border, forms the centre of France's fourth-biggest economic region, along with Roubaix and Tourcoing. In the wake of profound structural changes, Lille now comes over as a self-confident city with a lively cultural scene and one of the most important art museums in France.

Commercial metropolis of the north

85 communes in the region, including Roubaix, Tourcoing and Ville-neuve d'Asc, have joined with Lille to form the »Communauté ur-baine Lille Métropole«, which boasts some 1.1 million inhabitants. Since the decline of older industries such as coal, steel, shipbuilding and textiles – which has left scars that are still visible – the capital of French Flanders (► Picardie) and the Région Nord is coming back to life. Contributory factors to this include new businesses such as mail-order shopping, electronics and services. The new transport links however, including a station on the TGV network which connects the city to Paris, London (via the channel tunnel) and Brussels, have not provided the hoped-for boost to the economy. The university, based in Villeneuve d'Ascq to the east, has 100,000 students.

The centre of Lille, Grand'Place with the tower of the Nouvelle Bourse

The city's name used to be written L'Isle (an »island« between the rivers Lys and Deûle). It became part of Burgundy in 1349 through the marriage of Margaret of Flanders to Philip the Bold and for many years was the capital of the county of Burgundy and the residence of its rulers. After an interlude of Spanish Habsburg rule starting in the 16th century, Louis XIV occupied the town in 1667, with the quite indefensible justification that it was part of the legacy of his wife, Maria Theresa of Spain. The city was eventually ceded to France by the Treaty of Utrecht in 1713. Lille owed its wealth to the medieval wool industry, later to mining, iron and steel, and cloth manufacture. **Charles de Gaulle**, the near legendary general and later president of France (1958–69), was born in Lille in 1890.

What to See in Lille

The lovely Baroque old quarter gains its character from the contrast between brick and worked stone. It centres on **Place du Général-de-Gaulle** (Grand' Place). A column on this square commemorates a siege by the Austrians during the revolutionary war of 1792. The beautiful Vieille Bourse (1652) is a complex of 24 two-storey mansard houses in Flemish Baroque style. The exquisite **inner courtyard** is a popular public space, where various activities from tango dancing to chess games and book fairs take place. To the south of Place de Gaulle is the Grand' Garde (1717), while Furet du Nord, reputedly the largest bookshop in the world, occupies the western side.

✱
Vieux Lille

✱
Vieille Bourse

Place du Théâtre boasts an opera house (1914) and the Nouvelle Bourse with its mighty tower, constructed from 1918 in Flemish Renaissance style. The row of houses opposite the building (Rang de Beauregard) is typical of the architecture of Lille in the 17th century.

Place du Théâtre

 VISITING LILLE

INFORMATION

Office du Tourisme
Place Rihour, F-59000 Lille
Tel. from abroad 03 59 57 94 00
Tel. in France 0891 56 2004
www.lilletourisme.com

LILLE METROPOLE CITY PASS

The pass (1–3-days) includes admission to many attractions as well as public transport in the region.

WHERE TO EAT

► **Expensive**
① *À l'Huîtrière*
3 Rue des Chats-Bossus
Tel. 03 20 55 43 41

The best restaurant in Lille serves fish and see food in Art Deco surroundings. The accompanying fish shop with its beautiful ceramic decoration is a feast for the eyes. Closed Sun evening and end of July to end of Aug.

WHERE TO STAY

► **Mid-range**
① *Hôtel de la Paix*
46 bis, Rue Paris, F-59800 Lille
Tel. 03 20 54 63 93
www.hotel-la-paix.com.
A charming hotel right in the centre of town with a 19th-century stairway and lots of paintings. The rooms are pretty and have all mod cons.

Lille Map

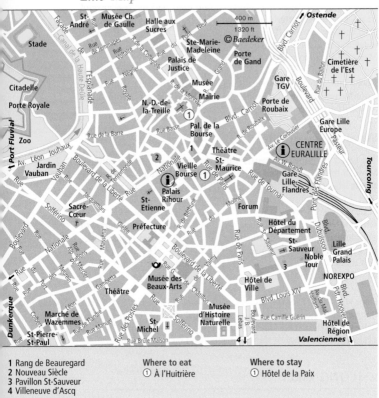

1 Rang de Beauregard
2 Nouveau Siècle
3 Pavillon St-Sauveur
4 Villeneuve d'Ascq

Where to eat
① À l'Huitrière

Where to stay
① Hôtel de la Paix

Palais Rihour Place Rihour adjoins Place de Gaulle to the southwest. A gigantic war memorial towers in front of the **residence of the dukes of Burgundy**, built from 1454–1473, which houses the tourist office. Rue de la Grande Chaussée leads away on the left-hand side of the Nouvelle Bourse towards its junction with **Rue des Chats Bossus** (»street of the hunch-backed cats«). Beyond Place du Lion d'Or on Rue de la Monnaie stands the Hospice Comtesse, which dates back to a hospi-

✱
Hospice Comtesse tal founded in 1237. Its current buildings (15th–18th century) house a fascinating museum of the city (closed Tue). The neo-Gothic cathedral of Notre-Dame de la Treille (1850) was furnished with a new façade in 1999.

✱ ✱
Musée des Beaux-Arts The museum of fine arts in a magnificent palais of 1892 is regarded as the most important in France after the Louvre. Its famous **collection of paintings** includes works by Rubens, Van Dyck, Goya, Dela-

croix, Courbet, Monet, Renoir and Toulouse Lautrec. The ground floor displays French sculpture from Houdon and David d'Angers to Rodin and Bourdelle alongside European and Far Eastern china, while the basement features items from the Middle Ages and Renaissance. Among the most interesting exhibits are the **models of the Flemish cities of northern France**. Open Mon 2pm–6pm, Wed–Sun 10am–6pm.

Eastward of the Porte de Paris, a triumphal arch built between 1682 and 1695 to honour Louis XIV, stands the **town hall** (1924–32). There is a great view of the city from its 106m/348ft tower.

> ! **Baedeker** TIP
>
> ### Braderie de Lille
>
> On the second weekend in September a huge flea market called the Braderie takes place. It is said to be the largest of its kind in the world. Over two days visitors can traverse its 200km/ 125mi of passages lined with both bric-a-brac and quality antiques. To recharge the batteries, the traditional sustenance is mussels and chips (»moules-frites«).

Maison de Gaulle

The house where Charles de Gaulle was born, north of the centre at Rue Princesse 9, has been made into a museum (closed Mon–Tue).

Citadel

West of the centre beyond the Deûle Canal is a citadel built by Vauban for Louis XIV between 1687 and 1690. Until the First World War it was one of France's most important forts and is still used by the military today. The parkland around it is popular with walkers and joggers.

Wazemmes

The **market hall** in the southwestern suburb of Wazemmes is well worth a visit, as all the delights of northwest France are on offer. There is also a flea market on Sundays.

Euralille

The Baroque old town merges into the late 20th century to the east, where the Euralille development surrounds Lille Europe station. This »exhibition of contemporary architecture« was planned by Rem Koolhaas, who also designed the concert and congress hall, Lille Grand Palais. Others contributors include Claude Vasconi (Tour Lilleurope WTC), Christian de Portzamparc (Tour du Crédit Lyonnais) and Jean Nouvel (the office, hotel, shopping and residential complex Centre Euralille).

★ ★
Musée d'Art Moderne Lille Metropole

In **Villeneuve d'Ascq**, 8km/5mi to the east, the world-famous Musée d'Art Moderne Lille Metropole (1 Allée du Musée) exhibits 200 works from the early 20th century, including pieces by Braque, Kandinsky, Klee, Laurens, Léger, Mirò, Modigliani, Picasso, Rouault and Van Dongen. To get there take Metro line 1 to Pont de Bois, then no. 41 bus to Parc Urbain Musée. (Closed for building work, probably until autumn 2009).

Limoges

J 7

Région: Limousin　　　　　　　　**Altitude:** 290m/950ft
Département: Haute-Vienne　　　**Population:** 137,000

**Limoges, the capital of ▶Limousin, is the centre for porcelain and
enamel in France. Along with the national porcelain museum and
various factories, the old quarter is also well worth a visit.**

Limoges past and present
The city developed out of two settlements which can still be distinguished today. The oldest part is called (Haute) Cité, atop a hill by
the river Vienne. The Bas Cité grew up at the base of the hill. Its picturesque alleys then stretch away as far Pont St-Etienne. Adjoining it
to the west is the Ville (or »Château«) district which grew up later
around the abbey of St-Martial and has effectively been the centre of
the city since the 14th century. The economic focal points in the capital of the Haute-Vienne département are government, the university
with its 17,000 students, and the footwear industry.

History
Limoges was converted to Christianity in around 250 by Saint Martial, whose grave was to become a major pilgrimage destination on
the (▶Baedeker Special p.792). The hill by the river became a fortified settlement during the migrations that followed the demise of the
Roman empire. Later the city was made seat of a bishop. The abbey
of St-Martial (destroyed 1792) and a castle were built there, and fi-

Limoges Map

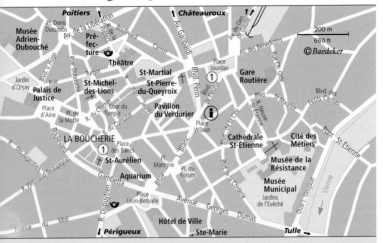

1 Gare des Bénédictins

Where to eat
① Petits Ventres

Where to stay
① Hotel de la Paix

The square in front of the neo-Renaissance town hall is adorned, fittingly in Limoges, with a magnificent porcelain fountain

nally in 1792 the two sections of the town were combined to form the city of Limoges.

Enamel and porcelain

The art of enamel working, which emerged due to the deposits of metal ore in the vicinity, had already reached its peak before the end of the 12th century (in the abbey of St-Martial among other places). Another golden age came in the 16th century with the mosaic painter, Léonard Limosin. The first porcelain factory was established in 1771 after the discovery in nearby St-Yrieix of very fine china clay. During the 19th century, Limoges developed into France's porcelain capital. The Impressionist painter **Pierre-Auguste Renoir** (1841–1919), who was born in Limoges, started his career as a painter of porcelain.

What to See in Limoges

✱ St-Etienne

The Cité quarter, distinguished by its timber-framed buildings and Gothic arcades, is also the site of St-Etienne cathedral, one of the few Gothic buildings of this size in southern France. Work began in 1273 but the church was not finished until 1888, although adherence to the original plans assured a uniform building style. Parts of a former Romanesque church on the site remain in the form of a section of crypt and the lower storeys of the tower (62m/203ft). The church is entered through the spectacular portal of St-Jean in the northern transept (Flamboyant, 1516–30) and the Renaissance doors, which date from the time the portal was built, depict the legends of St Martial and St Stephen. The elegant interior has impressive features such as a **Renaissance rood screen** (1534) beneath the modern organ front and three tombs grouped around the choir.

▶ VISITING LIMOGES

INFORMATION

Office de Tourisme
12 Boulevard de Fleurus
F-87000 Limoges Tel. 05 55 34 46 87,
fax 05 55 34 19 12
www.tourismelimoges.com

WHERE TO EAT

► Inexpensive
Petits Ventres
20 Rue Boucherie
Tel. 05 55 34 22 90, closed Sun–Mon.
Good, classic fare in a rustically

furnished timber-framed building in
the old butchers' quarter.

WHERE TO STAY

► Budget
Hôtel de la Paix
25 Place Jourdan
Tel. 05 55 34 36 00, fax 05 55 32 37 06
Not just a hotel but a veritable
museum of old gramophones. The
rooms are a bit old-fashioned but
comfortable. Pleasant service but no
restaurant.

Musée Municipal

The **city museum** in the 18th-century bishop's palace exhibits Limousin enamel work from the 12th–19th centuries as well as Egyptiana, French paintings from the 17th–20th centuries and architectural sculpture from classic antiquity to the Middle Ages, including mosaics from the grave of St-Martial. From the choir of the cathedral, picturesque narrow streets lead down to the river Vienne, which is crossed by Pont St-Etienne (1210) and Pont St-Martial (1215) further south. The Cité des Métiers demonstrates bygone crafts with interesting **large models**.

River Vienne

Cité des Métiers

St-Martial

Place de la République occupies a spot in the northeast of the Château quarter with remains of the abbey of St-Martial, which was started in 848 by Benedictine monks but changed over to Cluniac rule in 1063. Three churches grew up around the grave of St Martial himself, the largest of which was the 102m/112yd-long basilica of St-Sauveur (demolished 1791). In the 4th-century necropolis various crypts with sarcophagi are on view.

St-Pierre-du-Queyroix

Not far to the southwest the church of St-Pierre-du-Queyroix (13th–14th centuries) has an impressive tower (13th century). Notable features include the choir stalls (1513), a 16th-century Pietà, a statue of Christ (late 14th century) and the stained glass window to the right of the choir (1510).

St-Michel-des-Lions

The church of St-Michel-des-Lions (1364 to 16th century) is in the western part of the quarter. The bright interior of this hall church contains some late Gothic stained glass (15th century), a 15th-century Pietà and the 19th-century shrine that houses the relics of St Martial.

To the south of St-Michel the route takes in the **market hall** (1889), decorated with a ceramic frieze. Behind that is the well-frequented butchers' quarter, where some of the timber-framed buildings date back as far as the 13th century. The Chapelle St-Aurélien (1475, 17th-century façade and shingle-clad tower) was and remains the chapel for the butchers' guild. The **Musée National Adrien Dubouché**, established in 1845, is the most important museum for ceramics in France after that in Sèvres (closed Tue). Its 12,000 exhibits encompass locally produced items as well as pieces from all over Europe, China, Japan and Persia. In the old quarter of Les Casseaux it is possible to an admire a massive **kiln** dating from 1884 (Four Rond) in an old factory. Beautiful and technically elaborate, the Art Nouveau railway station (1925–29) has a distinctive 60m/200ft tower.

La Boucherie

> ! **Baedeker** TIP
>
> **Porcelain & enamel**
> A range of porcelain and enamel factories are open to visitors. Some 40 businesses in and around Limoges have their own sales show-rooms. Information is available from the Office de Tourisme. In July and August every two years (2010, 2012), the Biennale d'Email Contemporain takes place.

Limousin

H–J 6/7

The very centre of France's hexagonal borders is occupied by Limousin, the least populated part of France. With its green and hilly bocage scenery, its picturesque villages and castles, it could be seen as the very epitome of the French landscape.

In spite of its beautiful scenery Limousin – the region is named after its capital ►Limoges – is apparently off the beaten track for tourists. Indeed there are few conventional attractions in the usual sense, but its abundance of lakes and rivers makes the region good for anglers, canoeists and sailors. The Vézère, Corrèze, Vienne and Creuse rivers rise in the mountainous east (Plateau de Millevaches, Monts des Monédières), where peaks reach a height of some 1000m/3300ft. In the départements of Creuse, Haute-Vienne and Corrèze there are only 42 people per sq km/109 per sq mi, and agriculture forms the basis of the economy. Manufacture of porcelain and wallpaper, as well as leatherworking, are key trades in the region. Every seven years (2009, 2016) some 20 towns (including ►Limoges, Le Dorat, St Junien, Nexon, Aureil) stage colourful processions between May and July called »ostensions«.

Facts on Limousin

Romanesque art predominates, as the Gothic style made few inroads into these rural areas. Distinctive aspects of Limousine Romanesque are the use of granite, which means there is little architectural deco-

Architecture

ration; framing of windows with rounded beading; and towers with octagonal upper sections, the transition from the square lower storeys being masked by gables.

History A human skeleton dating back to the early Stone Age some 100,000 years ago was found near La Chapelle-aux-Saints (Corrèze). Prehistoric megaliths and barrows are dotted all over the countryside. In Celtic and Roman times, the history of Limousin was linked to that of ►Auvergne. Here Vercingetorix tried to repel the invasion of Julius Caesar but was defeated in the famous battle of Alesia. After southwest France fell to the English Crown under King Henry II in 1154, Philip II was able to regain first Auvergne then Limousin in 1223. In the 14th century three different men from Limousin were elected pope: Clement VI, Innocent VI and Clement's nephew Gregory XI. They were all resident in Avignon and ensured that the church in Limousin had about 40 cardinals and over 300 bishops. During the Second World War, Oradour-sur-Glane and Tulle witnessed bloody massacres of the civil populace.

Places to Visit in Limousin

Places to visit in Limousin are described here in a clockwise direction around a circle centred on ►Limoges and starting in the west. The Dordogne crosses the most southerly part of Limousin between the Barrage de l'Aigle and Beaulieu. The river valley is described in detail under ►Périgord.

Saint-Junien St-Junien (30km/19mi west of Limoges, 10,600 inhabitants) produces more than half of the **gloves** made in France. Its notable Romanesque church (12th–13th century) is in typical Limousin style and the tomb of St Junien, a local saint who died in 540, is a masterpiece of 12th-century sculpture. Numerous houses date from the 14th–17th centuries and the Notre-Dame-du-Pont chapel (Flamboyant, 1451) on the right bank of the Vienne is interesting too.

Highlights Limousin

Oradour-sur-Glane
Wiped out by the SS on 10 June 1944
► page 477

St-Léonard-de-Noblat
Pure Romanesque forms in Limousin
► page 478

Aubusson
Home of the famous tapestries
► page 479

Moûtier-d'Ahun
Medieval church with beautiful Baroque panelling and oak choir stalls
► page 479

Uzerche
»Home owners of Uzerche, palace dwellers in Limousin«
► page 482

Oradour (13km/8mi northeast of St-Junien) has become a symbol of Nazi terror in France. On 10 June 1944, in a retaliatory raid seeking to suppress the French Resistance, all 642 inhabitants, including 246 women and 213 children, were murdered by 160 SS soldiers, including 14 from Alsace, one of whom was a volunteer. The village was obliterated and has been left in ruins with a memorial in the graveyard. A new village with the same name has been built nearby.

Oradour-sur-Glane

Bellac (44km/27mi northwest of Limoges, 4900 inhabitants) village occupies a picturesque spot on the border with Poitou and was home to dramatist Jean Giraudoux (1882–1944, birthplace 4 Av. Jaurès, memorial on the town hall gardens). A **theatre and music festival** is held in his honour every July. Notre-Dame church has both a 12th-century Romanesque and a 14th-century Gothic nave. On the northern wall is a wonderful 12th-century reliquary shrine made of gilded copper with gemstones and cloisonné medallions.

Bellac

St-Pierre in Le Dorat (12km/7mi north of Bellac, 2200 inhabitants), one of the most important **Romanesque churches** of Limousin, is a massive building some 77m/84yd long that dates from the early 12th century. The entrance with its fan-shaped archivolts is remarkable. Its Spanish or Moorish appearance exhibits the influence of the Way of St James. The notable features inside are a baptismal font from pre-Romanesque times, the 11th-century crypt and the church treasure in the sacristy.

✶ Le Dorat

Ambazac (4200 inhabitants) is 21km/13mi northeast of Limoges among the Monts d'Ambazac, which ascend to a height of 700m/2300ft. In the church of St-Antoine (12th century) a number of valuable items on view are linked with St Etienne de Muret. They include 11th-century liturgical vestments which were donated to the saint by Empress Mathilde in 1121, and a fantastic **reliquary shrine** of 1123, which was made at Grandmont Abbey 8km/5mi to the north, formerly an abbey of some importance but no longer in existence.

Ambazac

La Souterraine (5400 inhabitants) is 52km/32mi northeast of Limoges (A 20/N145). Its name, »the underground«, comes from a 10th-century crypt, above which Notre-Dame church was built from 1017. The present building was started in 1120 but has been damaged and rebuilt on several occasions. On the outside, the head corbels above the Mozarabic-influenced west door and the Romanesque Madonna by the south door are of interest, while inside the dual transept with its oval dome, the capitals of the nave and the 12th-century altar are the highlights. The crypt has a granite Madonna as well as remains of a Gallo-Roman well. The St-Jean town gate (14th century) was a prison until 1860. The former convent Saint-Bernard-de-Soeurs-de-Saveur is also interesting; it is now the hostel for St James Way pilgrims.

La Souterraine

Charming scenery around the medieval bridge at Moutier d'Ahun

Creuse valley Crozant
The river Creuse descends from the Massif Central and runs through a picturesque valley between Fresselines and Argenton to the dam that forms the Chambon reservoir. At the southern end in **Crozant** (31km/19mi northeast of La Souterraine) there are remains of a 13th-century castle built by the Comte de Marche on the ridge between Creuse and Sédelle, and destroyed or abandoned after 1588.

Guéret

✱

Musée de la Sénatorerie ▶
The capital of the département of Creuse (14,700 inhabitants, 33km/21mi east of La Souterraine) was capital of the county of Marche in the 13th century. The **local museum** housed in the Hôtel de la Sénatorerie (17th–18th centuries) has a fascinating collection of goldsmith and enamel work, particularly reliquary shrines and works by Léonard Limosin; French, European and Chinese pottery; Aubusson tapestries; and local archaeological finds (closed Tue except July–Aug).

Saint-Léonard-de-Noblat
St-Léonard-de-Noblat (5000 inhabitants), 21km/13mi east of Limoges above the Maulde valley, is famous for its marzipan. It has a charming old town dating from the 13th–16th centuries and was formerly a stops on the Way of St James. It was also the birthplace of physicist Joseph-Louis Gay-Lussac (1778–1850; there is a museum). The biggest attraction is the **collegiate church** (11th–13th centuries). Its tower is one of the finest examples of Limousin Romanesque architecture. There are some remarkable capitals on the western façade and the portico of the tower. Inside the choir stalls (1480) are lovely and the main altar (18th century) has relics of St Leonard, whose feast is celebrated with a huge horse fair on the Sunday following 6 November.

Bourganeuf
Bourganeuf, on a hill some 28km/17mi northeast of St-Léonard where three valleys meet, was the French headquarters of the Knights of St John (Knights Hospitallers) from 1227 to 1750. The commandery, now the town hall, possesses Aubusson tapestries from the late 18th century. Next door **Tour Zizim** (1486) is named after the Otto-

man pretender Cem or Djem, son of Mehmed II, who was held here by the grand master of the Knights Hospitallers, Pierre d'Aubusson, from 1486 until he was handed over to Pope Innocent VIII in 1489. Nothing remains of the luxurious oriental furnishings in which he lived, although the oak beams are impressive. The Knights Hospitallers' church of St-Jean (12th–15th century) could be directly accessed from two of the knights' dormitories.

The hamlet of Moutier d'Ahun (200 inhabitants) seems to have been transported directly out of the Middle Ages. A bridge leads across to the abbey, which dates from 1000. The 12th-century church has been seriously damaged on several occasions and the nave no longer exists. Its splendid Gothic portal was built as of 1489. The magnificent **oak seating** was made between 1673 and 1680 by Simon Bauer, who hailed from Auvergnat in spite of his German-sounding name. His signature is on the first misericord at the left of the top row.

★
Moutier d'Ahun

The town of Aubusson (5000 inhabitants), 39km/24mi east of Bourganeuf in the Creuse valley, is world famous for the tapestries that were made there from the 14th century. Even now it possesses several manufacturers of »**gobelins**«, some of which offer tours (www.ot-aubusson.fr). In the summer both old and new creations

Aubusson

 # VISITING LIMOUSIN

INFORMATION

CRT Limousin
30 Cours Gay-Lussac, C.S. 500 95
F-87003 Limoges Cedex
Tel. 05 55 11 05 90
Fax 05 55 05 07 56
www.tourismelimousin.com

WHERE TO EAT/ WHERE TO STAY

► Mid-range / luxury
Château de Castel Novel
F-19240 Varetz (5km/3mi north of Brive), tel. 05 55 85 00 01
www.castelnovel.com
Live like a king in this 13th–15th-century palace, where the writer Colette (wife of the owner) once lived. There is a large park with a pool and the restaurant serves superb, classic regional dishes.

► Budget
Grand St-Léonard
23 Av. du Champ de Mars
F-87400 St Léonard de Noblat
www.hotelrestaurantlegrandsaintleonard-limousin.com, tel. 05 55 56 18 18. The old post office on the eastern edge of St-Léonard could be a throwback to the earliest days of tourism. What you save on the accommodation can be spent in the excellent restaurant.

Hôtel de la Gare
25 Avenue Churchill
F-19000 Tulle
Tel. 05 55 20 04 04, http://hotel-restaurantdelagarefarjounel.com
Tulle's classic hotel opposite the station. Lovely rooms clustered around a courtyard and furnished in Provençal style. The restaurant serves classic cuisine in generous portions.

✷

Musée de la
Tapisserie ▶

are exhibited in the town hall. The Centre Jean-Lurçat houses the tapestry museum, featuring works from the 17th to 20th centuries along with a workshop where weaving can be viewed. From Pont de la Terrade there is a lovely view of the old houses along the narrow river valley, dominated by the 13th-century church of Ste-Croix (with 19th-century modifications).

Chambon-
sur-Voueize

At the extreme north east corner of Limousin (39km/24mi northeast of Aubusson) the beautifully situated little town of Chambon-sur-Voueize (1100 inhabitants) possesses one of the most important Romanesque churches in Limousin: Ste-Valérie (12th century). It is 87m/95yd long, its transept 38m/42yd wide. The portico in front of the entrance is typical for Limousin. Above it is the 13th-century Tour des Bourgeois. At the other end of the church, the final bays before the crossing are overshadowed by the Tour des Archives, under which there are lovely 17th-century choir stalls. Among the valuables in the treasury is a reliquary shrine with a 15th-century bust of Saint Valérie.

Evaux-les-Bains

The resort of Evaux-les-Bains, 2km/1.5mi from Chambon, was revered for its healing potential as early as Roman times and includes some **30 springs** (14–60°C). The more recent baths date from 1831–58 and the turn of the 19th to the 20th century. The abbey of St-Pierre-et-St-Paul was founded in the 9th century and has an unusual tower. In the 13th century both a Romanesque and an early Gothic storey were built on top of the Carolingian base. A day trip down the dammed valley of the Tardes (to the northwest) is lovely.

Plateau de
Millevaches

The Plateau de Millevaches in the eastern part of Limousin is a lonely, barren and very sparsely populated mountain plain dominated by pine forests, heath and cattle fields. Puy Pendu and Mont Bessou both reach an altitude of 977m/3205ft. Heavy rainfall makes the area a source of many rivers, such as the Vezère, Vienne, Creuse and Cher. The name »Millevaches« does not refer to cows (»vaches«); theories about its origin range from corruption of the Celtic word »batz« meaning »source« to the Latin »moles vacua«, »empty land«. Its picturesque **reservoir lakes** (Vassivière, Vaud-Gelade, Monceaux-la-Virolle and Chammet) are inviting places for bathing or water sports. One place that is certainly worth a visit lies on an island in the middle of Lac de Vassivière (35km/22mi east of St Léonard de Noblat): the **Centre d'Art Contemporain**, designed by architect Aldo Rossi.

✷

Lac de Vassivière

Felletin

The people of Felletin were weaving tapestries even before those of Aubusson, 11km/7mi to the north. The world's largest tapestry, measuring 22.8×11.6 m/75 ft×38 ft and now gracing the walls of the new **Coventry Cathedral**, was made here. Eglise du Moûtier (1122, rebuilt from 1451) has a very unusual Gothic portal.

Charmingly situated at the southern edge of the Plateau de Mille-vaches (17km/11mi west of Ussel), Meymac is a pretty old market town. The church of the abbey that was founded in 1085 not only has some very fine capitals but also a 12th-century Black Madonna. A museum of archaeology and folklore and a centre for contemporary art are housed in the former cloister buildings. It is well worth taking a trip to **Mont Bessou** and its tower for a fantastic view towards the volcanic craters of Auvergne.

Meymac

★
Mont Bessou

The Plateau de Millevaches is bordered to the southwest by the Monts des Monédières, a crystalline massif with extensive heathland and many granite foundlings. From the 911m/2989ft summit of **Suc-au-May** there is a fine view.

Monts des Monédières

Ussel (11,400 inhabitants) is at the southern edge of the Plateau de Millevaches. Its pretty old town has many houses dating from the 15th–17th centuries. The palais of the Comtes de Ventadour is also worthy of mention. The 12th-century church of St-Martin gained a new nave in the 15th–16th centuries (18th-century choir stalls). The Chapelle des Pénitents Blancs in Rue Pasteur is now an art and folklore museum, while Hôtel Bonnot de Bay houses a regional and craft museum. On Place Voltaire there is a granite **Roman eagle** weighing some 800kg/three quarters of a ton, which was found near the mill of Peuch to the south of the town.

Ussel

This old town (1300 inhabitants) 10km/6mi south of Limoges is famous for the abbey that was founded here by Saint Eligius (St-Eloi) in around 630. Eligius was a goldsmith who became a minister under King Dagobert and was made bishop of Noyon. The abbey church of St-Pierre (1143) has bays vaulted with pendentive domes, characteristic of Périgord Romanesque. The choir stalls date from the 15th century.

Solignac

St-Yrieix (800 inhabitants) is situated in a fertile cattle-rearing district 40km/25mi south of Limoges. China clay was discovered here in 1768 and spurred the development of the porcelain industry in ► Limoges. Its collegiate church (12th–13th centuries) was built on the site of a 6th-century abbey. It bears the nickname »Moûtier« (»mustard pot«). The reliquary of Saint Yrieix is in the choir. Other attractions include the Tour du Plô (13th century) and town houses from the 15th–16th centuries.

Saint-Yrieix-la-Perche

11km/7mi east of St Yrieix (1500 inhabitants), Coussac-Bonneval is the lovely setting for **Château Bonneval** (14th–17th centuries). In its beautifully furnished rooms, an exhibition documents the life of Ahmet Pasha, who was born in 1675 as Claude Alexandre de Bonneval, fought with Prince Eugene of Savoy, modernized the Ottoman army and died in Constantinople. The lamp for the dead (12th century) was formerly placed at the entrance to the cemetery.

Coussac-Bonneval

Ségur-le-Château

Arnac-Pompadour

Ségur (15km/9mi southeast of St Yrieix) is among the most beautiful villages in France. Its 12th-century castle, now in ruins, was the birthplace of Jean d'Albret, later King John III of Navarre, and Jeanne d'Albret, mother of France's Henri IV. Pompadour (24km/15mi southeast of St Yrieix) was made famous by Jeanne Le Normant, lover of Louis XV, who granted her the impressive palace and the title of **Marquise de Pompadour** (►Famous People). The king established a stud in 1761, which is now the national stud of France (Haras). It is open to the public and various riding events take place there in summer.

✱
Uzerche

Thanks to its location in a loop of the Vézère and its old castle-like houses, Uzerche (30km/19mi northwest of Tulle, 2800 inhabitants) is one of the **loveliest towns in Limousin**. The old town is approached from the south through the Bécharie Gate, the only gate that remains of the old fortifications, and is overshadowed by the Romanesque church of St-Pierre (11th–14th centuries). There are some particularly nice capitals in the choir; the holy water stoups at the south and west entrances were once capitals too. On Rue Pierre-Chalaud, there are houses from the 12th–16th centuries, and on its continuation (Rue de la Justice) stands the seneschal's palace, which now houses a regional archaeology centre. There is a great view of the town from the D 3.

Naves

From Uzerche the N 120 runs southwest towards Tulle (30km/19mi). It is worth taking a detour to Naves for its 14th-century church with a huge, carved walnut Baroque altar (1650–1704).

Collonges-la-Rouge lives up to its epithet

The capital of Bas Limousin and the département of Corrèze (17,000 **Tulle** inhabitants), seat of a bishop since 1317, stretches for 3km/2mi along the narrow valley of the Corrèze. Apart from its pretty Renaissance houses, the cathedral of Notre-Dame (12th–14th centuries) and its 75m/246ft tower are also of note. To the south it is adjoined by a cloister that houses a museum. Northward of the cathedral on Place Gambetta is Maison Loyac, a splendid town house (15th–16th centuries). Its neighbour to the south is a **museum of the Résistance** that recalls the atrocities committed by German troops on 8 June 1944. Tulle is France's **Accordion City**. The one remaining accordion workshop, Maugein, is open to the public and a festival on the 3rd weekend in September attracts lots of visitors.

Close to the wonderfully situated village of Gimel (650 inhabitants) ✱ the 140m/460ft Gimel Falls cascade down from the mountain (1 **Gimel Falls** hour there and back from the centre of the village). Gimel's church has a fabulous treasury including a 12th-century reliquary fashioned in Limousin enamel, the **shrine of Saint Stephen**. Another notable example of the goldsmith's craft, a 15th-century reliquary for the head of St Fortunata, can be seen in the church at Ste-Fortunade **Ste-Fortunade** (6km/3.5mi south of Tulle).

From Tulle the N 89 runs along the Corrèze valley to Brive-la-Gail- ✱ larde. About half way along, a little to the south, is the Cistercian ab- **Abbaye de** bey of Aubazine, founded in the 12th century by St Etienne. His **Aubazine** superb **tomb** (c1250) is situated in a church (started in 1156) that is typically plain according to the Cistercian custom. Its first six bays were destroyed in 1757. The unusual feature of the tower is the handling of the transition from a square to an octagonal plan. Other highlights include the graves from the neighbouring convent of Coyroux, which previously had colourful framing, a Pietà (15th century) and an oaken sacristy cupboard which actually dates from the 12th century.

25km/16mi southwest of Tulle on the banks of the Corrèze, Brive-la- **Brive-la-** Gaillarde (49,700 inhabitants) gets its appellation, meaning »Brive **Gaillarde** the Bold«, from its brave resistance to many a siege. The concentric layout of the old town, where the ring of boulevards follows the line of the old city walls, features the interesting collegiate church of St-Martin (12th–14th centuries, 18th-century choir) with its large 12th-century font. Next to the south side of the church take note of the Maison des Tours St-Martin (15th–16th centuries). To the southwest is the Tour des Echevins (16th century). There is a regional museum in the Hôtel de Labenche (c1540) in the eastern part of the old town.

This hamlet of 400 inhabitants 21km/13mi southeast of Brive is en- **Collonges-** tirely built of **red sandstone** and is regarded as one of the prettiest in **la-Rouge** the land. From the old station go past the old Mermaid House (16th century, open to the public) to the Hôtel des Ramades des Friac then right to the Relais (a stop on the Way of St James) and the Château de Benge, turning left past the granary towards the church of St-Pierre (11th–12th centuries). Its white stone tympanum (pre-1140) is outstanding. Further east, Castel de Vassinhac dates from 1583. From Castel de Maussac return to the station.

✶✶ Loire Valley

F–L 5/6

The Loire, or more precisely the central section of its course, is one of the major tourist destinations in France. In the course of the centuries, kings and aristocrats built fabulous chateaux and palaces, which blend in beautifully with the gentle, charming landscape. This is indeed the »Garden of France«, as Rabelais expressed it.

The River of Kings
The Loire, the longest river in France, not only flows through the heart of the country but, historically and in terms of character, is its main artery. It is said that France is at its most French here. Apart from the gorgeous scenery, the mild climate, the navigability of the Loire and its proximity to Paris contributed to the fact that aristocrats and nouveaux riches alike continually sought to settle along the most beautiful section of the valley. **More than 600 chateaux and palaces** can be counted along the stretch from Sully to Chalonnes, which was declared a World Heritage Site by UNESCO in 2000. This also means that during the peak tourist season, visitors have to share the area with a myriad other tourists.

Highlights Loire

Pouilly and Sancerre
Two of the country's finest wines are made here.
► page 490

Sully
Medieval craftsmanship and the splendour of the Renaissance
► page 491

St-Benoît-sur-Loire
The tomb of St Benedict and one of the finest Romanesque churches
► page 491

Chambord
François I built this massive and bizarre

Renaissance palace
► page 493

Chenonceau
The »ladies' chateau«, built overlooking the Cher
► page 497

Azay-le-Rideau
Balzac called this charming chateau a »diamond on the Indre«
► page 499

Fontevraud-l'Abbaye
Once a powerful abbey and burial place of a royal dynasty
► page 502

River and chateau amid verdant scenery at Chaumont

Course of the river

The Loire is 1020km/634mi long and rises in the Cevennes on Gerbier de Jonc (1408m/4619ft), only 150km/95mi from the Mediterranean Sea. The river then flows northwards, cutting through the central Velay mountain range, before flowing past Le Puy into the basin around St-Etienne and Roanne. Until shortly before Briare it forms much of the border between Burgundy and Auvergne. At Nevers it joins the Allier, and the resulting broad river forges northward in a wide arc between Bourbonnais and Nivernais to its most northerly point at ►Orléans. The Loire then flows west through extensive flood meadows through the silt plain of the Varennes and finally through the Armorican Massif into the Atlantic. The estuary, a great funnel stretching for 50km/30mi, takes it as far as southern Brittany. The term »Loire valley« is usually applied more restrictively to the segment between Giens and Ancenis near Nantes. A large number of the »Loire chateaux« and the historic villages which attract tourists are not actually on the Loire itself, but nestle alongside its tributaries: the Allier, Cher, Indre and Vienne, which flow from the south, and the Loir, Sarthe and Mayenne, which combine to form the Maine just before Angers and flow into the Loire from the north.

Tributaries

In the flood plain of the Loire and its tributaries, the fertile loam soil and the mild climate, influenced by the Atlantic to the west with an ameliorating effect from the river itself, make the country excellent for growing fruit and vegetables. About 60% of the land is given over to agriculture. There are large cereal-growing areas around Orléans and, in the old limestone quarries between Saumur and Tours, mushrooms are cultivated. Massive market gardens also produce flowers. Not the least of its charms is that the Loire is home to some excellent wines; the well-known names include Sancerre and Pouilly-Fumé downstream and Loire, Vouvray, Chinon, Bourgueil, Savennières and Muscadet de Sèvre-et-Maine further upstream. The cities,

Economy

◄ Loire wines

▶ VISITING LOIRE-TAL

INFORMATION

CRT Centre – Val de Loire
37 Avenue de Paris, F-45000 Orleans
Tel. 02 38 79 95 28, fax 02 38 79 95 10
www.visaloire.com

CRT Pays de la Loire
2 Rue de la Loire, BP 20411
F-44204 Nantes Cedex 2 Tel. 02 40 48
24 20, fax 02 40 08 07 10
www.westernloire.com

WHERE TO EAT
▶ Moderate / expensive
Les Ménestrels
11 Rue Raspail, F-49400 Saumur
Tel. 02 41 67 71 10, closed Sun. One
of the best restaurants in Saumur,
situated between the palace and the
Loire. Tuff stone and wooden beams
lend atmosphere to the dining rooms
their flair. The terrace is lovely.

WHERE TO STAY / WHERE TO EAT
▶ Budget / Moderate
George Sand
39 Rue Quintefol
F-37600 Loches
www.hotelrestaurant-georgesand.
com, tel. 02 47 59 39 74
This 15th-century building on the
shore of the Indre has rooms with the
feel of home even if the furniture is a
tad old-fashioned. Restaurant with
fine, traditional cooking and a terrace
with a view of the river.

Manoir de la Giraudière
Route de Savigny
F-37420 Beaumont en Véron
Tel. 02 47 58 40 36, www.giraudiere.com
Pretty 17th-century aristocratic residence, 5km/3mi northwest of Chinon,
surrounded by woods and meadows,
with its own swimming pool. Comfortable rooms and a good restaurant.

▶ Mid-range
Hôtel Rivage
1 Quai de Nice, F-45500 Gien
Tel. 02 38 37 79 00, fax 02 38 38 10 21.
The best hotel in Gien, with a terrace
next to the Loire. Some of its elegant
rooms offer a splendid view of the
river. Excellent, modern classic cuisine in a pretty dining room.

▶ Luxury
Domaine de Beauvois
F-37230 Luynes, tel. 02 47 55 50 11
www.grandesetapes.fr
Idyllic 16th-century manor 4km/2.5mi
northwest of the village with stylish
rooms, elegant dining room with a
magnificent fireplace. Excellent food
with emphasis on regional specialities.

key industrial centres, are supplied with power by four nuclear
plants. The main industries are machine engineering and car manufacture, electronics and other high-tech offshoots, pharmaceuticals
and cosmetics, textiles, glass, ceramics and food processing. River
shipping, which was vital for centuries, largely disappeared with the
coming of the railway. Only the final section of the Loire, downstream of Nantes, is still used by trading barges. The canals, however,
(Canal de Roanne à Dijon, Canal latéral à la Loire and other feeder
canals) are still popular for holiday boating.

Nevers Map

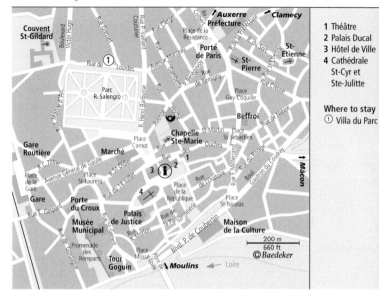

1 Théâtre
2 Palais Ducal
3 Hôtel de Ville
4 Cathédrale
  St-Cyr et
  Ste-Julitte

Where to stay
① Villa du Parc

the unadorned architecture at its best, are remarkable. The **convent of the Sœurs de la Charité** with the glass sarcophagus of **Saint Bernadette Soubirous** draws a great many pilgrims. She entered the convent after seeing visions of the Virgin Mary at ►Lourdes in 1866 and died here in 1879 (there is a small museum).

Magny-Cours

Since 1991 Formula 1 star drivers have battled for the laurels in the **French Grand Prix** at Magny-Cours (13km/8mi south of Nevers). Information and tickets: www.magnyf1.com. The Musée Ligier F1 is open during race meetings.

La Charité-sur-Loire

The pretty little town of La Charité-sur-Loire (6500 inhabitants) 24km/15mi north of Nevers gained prominence through the Cluniac priory that was built here from 1059 and became a stage on the Way of Saint James. From Pont de Pierre (1520) there is a view of the impressive collegiate church of Ste-Croix-Notre-Dame, which once measured 122m/133yd in length and was modelled on Cluny. Building work began in 1059 and the church was consecrated in 1107. Extensions continued to be built until 1135, but in 1559 the building was largely destroyed. The sculptural decoration in the choir remains notable. The Musée Municipal in Hôtel Adam (18th century) possesses examples of Art Nouveau and Art Deco works as well as folklore exhibits. A walk around the old defences (»Promenade des ramparts«) offers some fine views of the town.

Bourges	▶Bourges
Pouilly-sur-Loire	Pouilly-sur-Loire (12km/7mi north of La Charité) and Sancerre, 16km/10mi northwest on the other side of the Loire are both famous **wine centres**. The Sauvignon grape, as grown in this chalky soil, brings forth elegant wines with a vigorous and often typically flinty bouquet (Sancerre, Pouilly-Fumé). Pouilly (1700 inhabitants) has a number of good restaurants. From neighbouring St-Andelain there is a tremendous panoramic view of the Loire and its surrounding vineyards as far as Morvan.
Sancerre	Sancerre, a small, old-world town (2200 inhabitants), perches in picturesque fashion atop a hill. There is a fortified tower (beffroi) from 1509 right in the middle of town, which is now used as a bell tower for the neo-Romanesque church of Notre-Dame. There is a great view from the chateau gardens, especially the Tour des Fiefs (14th century). A wine trail traces a loop around Sancerre. The famous Crottin goat's-milk cheese is made in the nearby village of **Chavignol**.
Cosne-sur-Loire	In the small industrial town of Cosne, 11km/7mi north of Sancerre on the right bank of the Loire, both the parish church of St-Agnan, along with the remains of a Cluniac priory (11th century), and the **Musée de la Loire** (including paintings by Dufy, Utrillo, Chagall, Derain) are well worth seeing.
Puisaye	Take a trip out from Cosne into the hills of Puisaye, which stretch from the right bank of the Loire as far as Auxerre. Lakes and woodland characterize the peaceful scenery. Some of the most interesting places to go are St-Amand with stoneware typical for the Puisaye region, Château Ratilly (with four wings and a moat; 12th–17th centuries), the five-winged palace of St-Fargeau (built for Anne-Marie-Louise d'Orléans, niece of Louis XIII), St-Sauveur, birthplace of the novelist Colette (museum), and Guédelon, where a medieval castle has been rebuilt using old techniques (www.guedelon.fr).
Briare	Briare is famed for its aqueduct, 664m/762yd long and 11m/36ft wide, which takes the **Loire lateral canal** over the Loire. The iron structure was built from 1890 to 1894 by Gustave Eiffel's company.
Gien	The small town of Gien (17,000 inhabitants) marks the start of the »true« Loire valley. Gien was largely destroyed in June 1940 as forces battled for its bridge, but is still very attractive. The plain **chateau**, built between 1494 and 1500 for Anne de Beaujeu, daughter of Louis XI, houses a hunting museum. There is a lovely view from the terrace. The bell tower of the church of Jeanne d'Arc was originally part of Anne de Beaujeu's collegiate church. The ceramics factory at the northwestern edge of the town near the river was established in 1821 and made Gien famous for pottery (tours, museum, shop).

On the way to Sully the road passes one of the four nuclear power stations situated along the Loire (with information centre). Sully itself (6000 inhabitants, market day Monday) occupies a picturesque spot with an impressive **chateau**, situated in a lake dammed off from the Loire (open daily). Originally built before about 1360, it was purchased and extended in 1602 by Maximilien de Béthune, Duke of Sully and finance minister to Henri IV. Voltaire, banished from Paris on account of his sharp wit, wrote and staged his first plays here at the age of 22. The highlight is the top room in the residential wing with its keel-shaped roof construction, made from oak in 1363. In June and July a festival of classical music, folk and jazz takes place.

Sully-sur-Loire

✶ ✶
◀ Ceiling throne

St-Benoît-sur-Loire (1900 inhabitants) possesses a famous Benedictine abbey, which dates back to the 7th century. It gained its repute as the burial place of **St Benedict of Nursia**, founder of the Benedictine order. His remains were brought here, along with those of his sister, Saint Scholastica, from the ruins of Monte Cassino Abbey in around 660. The abbey became a spiritual centre under brilliant abbots such as Theodulf, Odo, Abbo and Gauzlin. The large **basilica** (daily 6.30am–10pm), one of the finest neo-Romanesque churches in France, was built from 1026 to 1218. Its entrance tower, featuring some wonderful capitals depicting the Apocalypse, the life of Jesus and the life of Mary, was built around 1030 under Abbot Gauzlin. The impressively bright and clearly structured interior of the basilica clearly shows the transition from the Romanesque to the Gothic style and is a worthy setting for masses with Gregorian chants (Mon–Sat noon, Sun 11am). Concerts take place here from time to time, too. The ambulatory around the choir is a characteristic of pilgrimage churches. The lovely choir stalls date from 1413, while the floor is from the late Roman period (4th–5th centuries),

✶ ✶
Saint-Benoît-sur-Loire

The unusual entrance tower of St-Benoît

having been brought here from Italy in 1531. The **relics of St Benedict** lie in the 11th-century crypt in a modern shrine.

About 5km/3mi to the northwest in Germigny-des-Prés, the chapel built for Abbot Theodulf before 806 is regarded as **the oldest church in France**. The early Romanesque/Byzantine form of the building is outstanding. According to contemporary documents it was based on

✶ ✶
Germigny-des-Prés

the palace chapel in Aachen, and has been compared with the famous church at Echmiadzin in Armenia. The **mosaic** under the conch arch in the choir (Angel with Ark of the Covenant; c800) is linked to the mosaics of Ravenna. The horseshoe-shaped arches of Spanish-Moorish art are also conspicuous. A concert here is the chance to experience the fantastic acoustics.

Châteauneuf -sur-Loire In the small town of Châteauneuf-sur-Loire (7000 inhabitants) 5km/ 3mi west of Germigny there are remnants of the so-called »**little Versailles«**, which was built for the secretary of Louis XIV. Its octagonal stables now house the Musée de la Marine de Loire, and there is a **Tigy** fine English-style park. In Tigy 8km/5mi to the south the Musée de l'Artisanat Rural Ancien exhibits old rural crafts (Easter–Oct Sun only, July–Aug Wed–Mon).

Orléans ►Orléans

Cléry- Saint-André Cléry-St-André (2700 inhabitants, 15km/9mi southwest of Orléans) has a late Gothic basilica in a cool Flamboyant style (late 15th century), where **King Louis XI** (1423–83) and his wife Charlotte of Savoy are buried. There is a marble statue of the king made in 1622. Since the 13th century an oak Madonna with Child on the high altar has been revered as miraculous.

Beaugency Although the 14th-century bridge of Beaugency (7100 inhabitants) has often been the scene of battle, it has survived to the present day. The **chateau** was built from 1439 for Comte Jean de Dunois, »Bastard of Orléans«, who had gone to war with Joan of Arc. Inside the Musée Vannier displays antique furniture and fashions worn by Orléanais citizens. Alongside the chateau is the 36m/118ft Donjon de César, remains of an 11th-century fortress. The Romanesque Notre-Dame church (12th century) is part of an abbey. In 1152, it was the venue for a **council** which annulled the marriage of Louis VII and Eleanor of Aquitaine so that she could marry Henry II of England. This lay at the root of the long war between England and France. The triangular tower on Place St-Firmin, the pretty centrepiece of the town, is all that remains of a church built in the 15th century. To the northwest of the chateau is the **old town** with the Maison des Templiers (Templar house), the 17th-century Hôtel de Ville featuring some fine tapestries, and the Tour de l'Horloge, formerly a gate tower in the town walls. There are some lovely promenade walks along the Loire. 7km/4.5mi downstream on its own man-made island stands the St-Laurent nuclear power station (information centre, observation tower).

Saint-Dyé- sur-Loire Saint-Dyé-sur-Loire had its heyday when the building materials for Chambord were being quarried here. The town's roots go back to the hermit Deodat (Dié, Dyé), who lived in the 6th century. Nowadays it has an enchanting, old-fashioned atmosphere. Things to see include the church (9th century to late 15th century) with the sarcophagus of Saint Dyé himself. The Maison de la Loire in Hôtel Fontenau (17th century) stages exhibitions about the Loire.

Chambord, the largest, most famous and **most splendid of the Loire chateaux**, is 5km/3mi south of St-Dyé-sur-Loire on the river Cosson, a tributary of the Loire. It possesses no fewer than 440 rooms as well as 365 chimneys and towers. The whole building is 117×156m/ 128×171yd in size. François I started building work here on a Renaissance hunting lodge in 1519. His insignia, an »F« and a salamander, can be seen in many places. Leonardo da Vinci, who was resident at Amboise between 1516 and 1519, is said to have contributed to the plans, in particular those of the dual stairway. Up to 1800 workers were simultaneously active on the site. In 1559 construction finished for the time being, but Henri II and Louis XIV continued the expansion. Louis XV granted use of the chateau to his father-in-law, the exiled king of Poland, Stanisław Leszczyński, and in 1746 it was gifted to Maurice of Saxony, who lived here from 1748 to 1750.

★ ★
Chambord

The French Revolution inflicted little damage on the building itself, but all the furnishings were sold. Since 1930 the chateau has been in state ownership. Its extensive **surrounding parkland** covers some 55 sq km/21 sq mi, of which 80% is wooded. It is encircled by the longest wall in France, 32km/20mi in length and built between 1542 and 1645. Six gates and avenues provide access to the chateau itself. The western section of the park is criss-crossed by footpaths and mountain bike trails, and there are viewpoints for observing wildlife.

> **!** *Baedeker* TIP
>
> ### Accommodation near Chambord
>
> For a place to stay go to Bracieux, 8km/5mi south of the chateau. The Bonnheure offers rustic accommodation in a family atmosphere and concentrates on the cycling clientele (www.hoteldelabonnheur.com, tel. 02 54 46 41 57, budget prices). Fantastic cuisine by Bernard Robin is on offer at Relais de Bracieux (tel. 02 54 46 41 22, www.relaisdebracieux.com, closed Tue and Wed, and Mon and Sun evenings in Jan–Feb, expensive).

►Blois

Blois

The elegant **Château Villesavin** about 11km/7mi south of Chambord (near Bracieux) was built between 1527 and 1537 for Jean Le Breton, chamberlain to François I and architect of Chambord. Among its interesting features are a Italianate fountain (16th century) in the courtyard, a collection of carriages, a huge pigeon loft accommodating some 1500 birds and a charming museum of marriage. A number of rooms are open to the public.

Villesavin

The classical chateau of Cheverny (near Cour Cheverny 12km/7mi southeast of Blois), still owned by the heirs of Comte Henri de

★
Cheverny

CHÂTEAU DE CHAMBORD

✳ ✳ The extravagant Renaissance king François I built himself a grandiose folly, two days' travel from Paris. His dream of diverting the Loire so that that he could enter »on foot« was, however, not to be.

⏱ Opening times:
Open daily. 12 July to 17 Aug: 9am–7.30pm; 22 April to 11 July and 18 Aug to 30 Sept until 6.15pm; Jan to 21 March and Oct–Dec until 5.15pm.
Events:
May–Sept 11.45am (July–Aug also 4.30pm): Spectacle d'Art Equestre (equestrian show in historical costume).
July–Sept 9.30pm/10.30pm: Son et Lumière (sound and light show).
June–Oct every 2nd Sunday of the month at 4pm: concerts, times vary.
Stag rutting season (mid-Sept–mid-Oct): guided stag watches.
Other events at other times of year.
Information: Domaine National de Chambord, F-41250, tel. 02 54 50 40 00,
Tel. (inside France only) 0825 826 826 080,
Fax 02 54 20 34 69, www.chambord.org

① Donjon

The core of the estate is the donjon (keep) with its four circular towers at the corners. Designed by Domenico da Cortina, who was resident in Blois from 1512 to 1531, its symmetrical floor plan exemplifies modern architectural thinking of the period. Its four squares, each with a corner tower, contain enclosed and virtually identical living quarters.

② Chambers of King François I

François I resided on the top floor of the northeastern tower. The exquisite furnishing with velvet embroidered in gold has been reconstructed. The king's barrel-vaulted cabinet, which is outside the tower, was later used by Catherine Opaliska, ex-queen of Poland, as a chapel.

③ Apartments of Louis XIV

In accord with his Absolutist ideals, Louis XIV, who stayed at Chambord many times between 1660 and 1685, moved his apartments to the middle of the main façade, as he also did at Versailles. The whole space between the northern towers was included so that there were two antechambers in front of his quarters.

Above: The salamander, which appears on François I's coat of arms, can be seen in more than 800 places around the building.
Below: Regal splendour is relived at the historic horse shows.

A dual staircase leads to the roof terrace from which the royal court could watch tournaments, military parades, festivals and other diversions. To stand here is to be encircled by a veritable forest of chimneys, domes, turrets and roofs.

The Chambre Royal was the bedroom of Louis XIV. It was furnished in 1681 and later served as an audience room for Stanislav Leszczyński and Maurice of Saxony.

With his central ground plan Domenico da Cortona developed concepts that were later taken up by Palladio in his famous villas in Veneto.

The famous staircase, alleged to have been designed by Leonardo da Vinci, consists of two separate spiral staircases circling a common axis so that they never meet.

©Baedeker

Hurault, who built it from 1604 to 1634, stands out due to its simplicity and outstanding furnishings, including original furniture and tapestries. The trophy room has some 2000 stag antlers. One particular attraction is the large **pack of hounds** (feeding time Apr–Sept daily 5pm). Cheverny was immortalized in comic fiction as Château Millhouse (»Moulinsart«) where Tin Tin and Snowy had many adventures (exhibition). The woodlands of the Forêt de Cheverny extend to the southeast of Cheverny. They are part of the Sologne forest.

Beauregard

Château Beauregard, about 8km/5mi northwest of Cheverny at Cellettes (signposted) in the Forêt de Russy, was built from 1522 and extended after 1545 by secretary of state Jean du Thier. Its **Galerie des Illustres** (1646) is famous. It includes 327 portraits of important figures in the history of France from 1328 to 1643. The Cabinet des Grelots with its coffered ceiling and Delft floor tiles is also splendid.

Valençay

Another **Loire chateaux** is at Valençay (55km/34mi south of Blois, open April–Oct). The huge estate, built from 1540 by Philippe de l'Orme, architect of Fontainebleau, fully displays the riches of its original owner, Jacques d'Estampes. The features recalling a medieval castle are in this case solely for decoration. The main wing with its massive entrance pavilion (1599) is in Italian Renaissance style, while the two-storey west wing is Baroque (Louis Seize). The west wing also features a portrait gallery with ancestors of the Talleyrand family, Empire furniture (including a table from the Congress of Vienna), porcelain and a Talleyrand museum; there is a park and a good restaurant in the orangery.

Chaumont-sur-Loire

The simple and typical village of Chaumont-sur-Loire (1000 inhabitants) on the left bank of the Loire, about 20km/12mi southwest of Blois, is overlooked by a **chateau** which once had some very famous residents: none other than Catherine de Medici, Diane of Poitiers and Madame de Staël. A building with four wings was built here on the site of a medieval castle from 1466 to 1510, although the north wing was demolished in the 18th century. The eye-catching frieze on the outer wall depicts a burning (hot) mountain (»chaud mont«; although the name is more likely to derive from »mons calvus«, »bare mountain«) and two intertwined Cs, which stand for Charles II of Amboise, one of the original owners, and his wife Catharine de Chauvigny. There is a great view from the terrace. Horse-drawn coaches travel through the park with its mighty cedars from the stables (1877) in summer. Chaumont is also famous for a large and magnificent **garden show**.

Festival des Jardins ▶

Amboise

▶Amboise

Chenonceau, the »Château des Dames« in Cher

The hamlet of Chenonceaux (400 inhabitants) on the north bank of the Cher, about 14km/9mi south of Amboise, is famous for **Château Chenonceau**, situated right in the middle of the river (open daily, July–Aug 9am–8pm). On the terrace, accessed via an avenue of plane trees, there is a donjon, all that remains of an earlier building from 1432. In 1512 the estate came into the possession of Thomas Bohier, master of the royal household for kings from Charles VIII to François I, who had the main building erected. Henri II granted the chateau to his mistress Diane of Poitiers in 1547, but after his death Catherine of Medici exiled her to Chaumont. Catherine not only held extravagant festivities here, but also had the 60m/200ft linking building constructed from 1570 to 1576. Since 1913 the chateau has been owned by chocolate manufacturers Menier. From 1940 to 1942, when the Cher formed the border between occupied France and the Vichy domain, the gallery was used by many escapees. The chambers of the queens and mistresses are fascinating and the delightful orangery has a fine restaurant, which is slightly out of the way of the tourist hordes (March to 20 Nov). The magnificent gardens are illuminated in the evenings in July and August (9.30pm–11pm), with Baroque music for entertainment.

8km/5mi east of Chenonceaux, pretty Montrichard (3600 inhabitants) nestles alongside the Cher. It is famed for its **wine and champagne cellars**. The town museum is housed in the massive donjon (12th–13th centuries). Next door is the chapel of Ste-Croix, where the Duke of Orléans, later to become Louis XII, married Louis XI's daughter Jeanne in 1476. Sights include the triple-gabled Maison de l'Ave Maria (16th century; with the tourist office) and 12th-century Maison du Prêche. In Bourré, 3km/2mi to the east, many of the underground quarries of the region are now used as dwellings or wine cellars, or for rearing mushrooms or silkworms (guided tours available).

✱
Loches
Loches (6300 inhabitants), picturesquely situated on the Indre some 30km/19mi southwest of Montrichard, is a historic gem. Its **castle hill** and medieval town are still encircled by walls 2km/1.5mi in length. This »town within a town« is entered from the northwest via the Porte Royale (11th–13th centuries), a defensive barbican with a local museum. On the left is the Musée Lansyer (Emile Lansyer, landscape painter, 1835–93) and the church of St-Ours (c1150) with its two unusual pyramid-shaped vaults between the towers and the Romanesque portal, which has no tympanum but three rows of finely decorated arches. A 14th–15th-century chateau to the north of the church, the residence of Charles VII, became notorious for the decadent feasts the king held for his mistress Agnès Sorel. Other sights include the alabaster tomb of Sorel herself (1422–50), a diptych by Jean Fouquet (copy) with a bare-breasted Madonna based on a portrait of Agnès Sorel, a triptych of the Passion (1485) by Fouquet and a chapel dedicated to Anne of Brittany. South of St-Ours is the strong 11th-century **keep** which, along with the neighbouring buildings, forms the southern entrance to the upper town. From the top there is a great view. From the Martelet tower, in which Duke Ludovico il Moro of Milan was imprisoned for eight years (he died almost immediately after his release), walk around the Cité Médiévale: leftward to the north in the direction of the Porte des Cordeliers on the banks of the Indre, then towards the vegetable market with the Tour St-Antoine (1575), Porte Picois and the town hall (1543) before returning to Porte Royale.

! | **Baedeker TIP**

Tomatoes fit for a king

Château La Bourdaisière offers accommodation fit for a king (tel. 02 47 45 16 31, www.chateaulabourdaisiere.com, expensive). More than 400 varieties of tomato are cultivated in the gardens before being made into such succulent delights as jam and liqueurs.

Montlouis
Montlouis, between ▶ Amboise and ▶ Tours on the shores of the Loire, is a wine-making centre and twin to Vouvray on the other side of the river. Take a look at the 12th-century Romanesque church, the Maison de Loire (geography of the river) and **Château de Bourdaisière** (c1520), where King François I dallied with the beautiful wife of the castle owner Philippe Babou and Henri IV had an affair with her granddaughter, Gabrielle d'Estrées. There is a wine festival on 15 August and jazz in September at the Jazz en Touraine festival. The **Vouvray** gravelly soil of Vouvray produces some famous **white wines** and sparkling wines from the Chenin vine. The museum at Château Moncontour is well worth a visit. Tastings are also on offer at Maison du Vouvray and many other vineyards. There is a wine festival on 15 August.

Luynes
The pretty township of Luynes, about 10km/6mi west Tours some way back from the Loire, is dominated by a 13th-century castle,

which has been owned by the Ducs de Luynes for centuries (guided tours April to Sept). The village has a beautiful 15th-century market hall amid its timber-framed buildings. 1.5km/1mi to the north there is a Roman aqueduct.

DON'T MISS

- The Nuits de Mille Feux at the start of July are unforgettable as thousands of candles light up the gardens of Villandry. In mid-August the palace courtyard is given over to Baroque music, and during the Journees de Potager in mid-September the gardeners are available to answer questions about the estate.

Villandry (800 inhabitants, about 15km/9mi west of Tours) is also well known, not so much for its large chateau, built from 1536 by Jean le Breton (see Villesavin above), as for the palace's **Renaissance gardens**. They were restored to their original appearance by their owner, Nobel prize-winning doctor Ramon y Cajal, in 1906 (the Garden of Love is particularly celebrated). In the chateau itself, tapestries and furniture from the 18th century are on display as well as paintings by Italian and Spanish masters from the Renaissance and Baroque periods. The Moorish ceiling made of gilded cedar wood comes from a mosque built in Toledo in the 13th century, and was incorporated into the fabric of the castle by its owner after 15 years of work.

Langeais

The **chateau** in the township of Langeais (3800 inhabitants, 21km/13mi west of Tours) – a rugged castle on the outside but inside, facing the courtyard, an elegant country house – was built during the reign of Louis XI in just four years, starting in 1465, and never altered. Along with the 15th- and 16th-century furnishings inside, it presents that rare thing, an authentic look at the world of a bygone age. The Flemish tapestries are wonderful. The grounds around the castle also contain the ruins of the oldest defensive tower in France, built some time around 950 by Foulques Nerra. In 1491 Charles VIII married Anne of Brittany in this chateau, an alliance that brought to an end the Breton threat to Touraine.

★ ★
Azay-le-Rideau

This small town on the Indre (3000 inhabitants), 10km/6mi south of Langeais is famed for its **Renaissance chateau**, situated on an island in the middle of the river (open July–Aug 9.30am–7pm, April–June and Sept closes 6pm, Oct–March 10am–12.30pm, 2pm–5.30pm). It was built from 1518 to 1529 on the site of an old fortress guarding the ford for the king's chamberlain Berthelot, who was forced to flee in 1527 after being indicted for embezzlement. Notable features include the inward-leaning staircase (with a salamander and ermine, the insignia of François I and his wife Claude de France), the kitchens, the dining hall with its tapestries and a chimney fashioned by Rodin (cast from another chimney in Montal-en-Quercy), the great hall with its ceiling beams and the exquisitely furnished chambers. The church of St-Symphorie, on the market place north of the Indre, is in Romanesque and Gothic style (11th–12th centuries). The right-hand aisle still exhibits the remains of an earlier, 6th-century building.

✱
Indre
No visit would be complete without a boat trip along the idyllic river Indre (information about the »**Circuit des moulins et belles demeures**« is available at tourist offices). Honoré de Balzac (1799–1850) wrote several of his novels at the chateau of Saché, where his study has been preserved as it was. The village market place is adorned by a sculpture made by Alexander Calder, who settled here in 1962. **Montbazon**, with the keep of a castle built by Foulques Nerra, has some excellent restaurants and hotels. In Cormery it is still possible to see the remains of an abbey founded by Alcuin, Charlemagne's teacher, in 791. The cemetery has a lanterne des morts tower dating from the 12th century.

Ussé
The palace at Ussé, which overlooks the Indre about 14km/9mi west of Azay, is the most romantic of all the Loire chateaux and is said to have served poet Charles Perrault (1628 –1703) as the model for **Sleeping Beauty's palace**. It was built from the 15th to the 17th century, although the north wing was demolished in 1659. Antique furniture, magnificent tapestries and coats of arms are all on display. The chapel in the park (1535) has splendid Renaissance furnishings and a terra-cotta Madonna, which has been attributed to Luca della Robbia.

✱
Chinon
In the enchanting township of Chinon (8600 inhabitants, 20km/12mi southwest of Azay-le-Rideau) the Middle Ages seem to come to life. The old town on the banks of the Vienne, the ruins of the château and the medieval market held on the first weekend of August all testify to this. From 1154 to 1205 Chinon was at the centre of the duchy of Anjou. Here Joan of Arc met Charles VII on 9 March 1429 and convinced him to let her undertake the reconquest of the parts of France that remained in English hands. The mighty **fortress**, 400m/440yd in length, is surrounded by a wall dating from the 10th century. The central castle is entered via a clock tower (13th century) 35m/115ft high, where there is a small museum dedicated to Joan of Arc. The Grande Salle, where she met Charles VII, was demolished by Richelieu in 1699; only the front wall with the fireplace was preserved. 140 Knights Templar were imprisoned in the Donjon du Coudray in 1308, and the accusation of heresy against them was not lifted until 1312. The **old town** stretches between the lower slopes of the castle hill and the river Vienne. Among the most interesting attractions are the 15th- and 16th-century houses of Rue Voltaire, running southeast under the fortress, and the main square Place du Grand Carroi. Here the Hôtel des États Généraux is said to have been the place where Richard the Lionheart died in 1199. Nowadays it is the local museum, the Musée du Vieux Chinon. Chinon is at the centre of an important wine-growing region and its fine, fruity red

The fortified town of Chinon gives its name to a renowned wine

wines from the Cabernet and Cabernet Franc grapes are presented at the **Maison du Vin de Chinon** (Impasse des Caves-Painctes). The Caves Painctes of the »Bons Etonneurs Rabelaisiens« that extend beneath the castle can be viewed on guided tours. The Musée Animé du Vin is a somewhat kitschy affair with mechanical figures, but also a place to enjoy fouées garnies, filled rounds of flatbread.

Alongside the Loire about 12km/7mi north of Chinon is the nuclear power station of Chinon. Block A, built in 1963, was the first in France, but was shut down in 1973 (information centre, tours available). **Avoine-Chinon**

It is worth making a diversion to Tavant (about 14km/9mi east of Chinon, on the left bank of the Vienne) if only for the church of St-Nicolas (c1120). In its crypt, some Romanesque frescoes from the mid-12th century have been preserved. They are among the most important such remains in France. **✷ Tavant**

The small town of Richelieu, some 20km/12mi south of Chinon, only exists on account of Armand-Jean du Plessis, **Duke of Richelieu**, cardinal and politician (1585–1642), who had it built along with the accompanying chateau from 1630. The axis of the park is continued along the main street (Grande Rue), passing through spectacular gates to the market place with the Baroque church of Notre-Dame, the wooden market hall and the town hall, where there is a museum. Lovers of old trains come to see the railway between Richelieu and Ligré (10km/6mi to the north), which has an uncertain future. **Richelieu**

Loudun Loudun (19km/12mi west of Richelieu, 7700 inhabitants) is across the border in Poitou. In 1634 the young and free-spirited priest Grandier was accused of having bewitched some nuns and was burned alive. An opera, *The Devil of Loudun*, was written about it by Penderecki. All that remains of the Foulques Nerras fortress is the **Tour Carrée** dating from 1040, which has a great view of the town and its surroundings. The 14th-century church of St-Hilaire has a lovely portal (16th century); the collection of the neighbouring Musée Charbonneau-Lassay concentrates on local history. The church of St-Pierre-du-Marché (established 1215) has a Renaissance door. Murals dating back to the 13th century have been discovered in the 11th-century church of Ste-Croix.

! *Baedeker* TIP

Enjoying the river

It is delightful to experience the Loire and its tributaries aboard a houseboat (available on the Loire between Angers and Nantes) or one of the pleasure boats that ply the waterways. It is also possible to travel on a replica of the traditional Loire boats, such as a gabare. Information from local tourist offices or CRT Val de Loire.

Bourgueil The pleasant township of Bourgueil (4100 inhabitants) 5km/3mi north of the Loire between Tours and Saumur is famed for its **red wine** (Maison du Vin on Place de l'Eglise). Opposite the church of St-Germain (11th century) is the 19th-century market hall. Another interesting attraction on the eastern edge of town is the ruin of an abbey founded here in 990, where a local museum has been set up. **Chevrette** 2km/1.5mi north in Chevrette, the main attractions are the Moulin Bleu, a 15th-century windmill with a fine view of the Loire valley and Bourgueil, and the cool cellars that house a wine museum offering tastings (Cave de la Dive Bouteille).

★ ★
Fontevraud l'Abbaye The small town of Fontevraud (1200 inhabitants), about 4km/2.5mi south of the Loire between Chinon and Saumur, is famous for its abbey, founded in 1099 (open 9am–6.30pm June–mid-Sept, 10am–12.30pm and 2pm–6pm otherwise). Both monks and nuns lived here according to the Benedictine rule, but the establishment was always headed by an abbess, born of an influential aristocratic family. This explains the immense wealth and political importance of the abbey, expressed in the fact that even members of the royal house were buried here. Nowadays the abbey is the main headquarters of the Centre Culturel de l'Ouest (featuring concerts and exhibitions, www.fontevraud.com) and site of a fine hotel with reasonable prices (www.hotelfp-fontevraud.com). The large, plain **church** is in two parts: the choir with ambulatory and transept were consecrated in 1119, while the nave dates from 1150. **Tombs of members of the house of Plantagenet** can be seen in the right-hand part of the transept: from left to right the reclining figures of Isabella of Angoulême (wife of King John; identification not certain), Richard the Lion-

The tomb of Henry II of England and Eleanor of Aquitaine at Fontevraud

heart, Eleanor of Aquitaine (died here in 1204) and King Henry II of England. From here a passage leads to the **cloister of Our Lady**, the largest in France (dating from about 1520 to 1560) and the chapter house (1543). The buildings of St Benedict's cloister (c1600) were formerly used as a hospital. The octagonal **kitchen** at the southwestern corner of the cloister of Our Lady (c1060) is spectacular. A low door leads through to the 45m/49yd-long refectory (12th century, reconstructed 1515). West of the abbey stands the parish church of St-Michel (c1180), where valuable treasures from the abbey, including a tabernacle cover of 1621, can be viewed.

Candes-St-Martin, where the Vienne flows into the Loire, and neighbouring Montsoreau across the border in Anjou are two of the »prettiest villages in France«. The main attraction in the former is the impressive Gothic church, which was erected between 1175 and 1225 at the place where **St Martin of Tours** is said to have died in 397. Château Montsoreau was primarily built around 1455 and formerly stood right on the banks of the Loire. Concerts are held here in July and August. It is worth climbing up from the chateau to enjoy the view over the confluence between the Vienne and Loire rivers (signposted). About 1.5km/1mi to the west are some former cave dwellings and a 16th-century windmill, Moulin de la Herpinière. There were once several hundred mills of this design in the region. Their conical bases remain a distinctive feature of the countryside.

★
Candes-Saint-Martin

★
Montsoreau

Brézé, 9km/6mi south of Saumur, also has an elegant Renaissance chateau, ringed by sloping vineyards. Its distinctive feature is an **underground complex** including, kitchens, a bakery, stables and more. These facilities have gradually been being carved out of the tuff rock since the 9th century.

Brézé

Medieval Saumur (32,000 inhabitants), on the left-bank of the Loire, makes an attractive impression with its rugged castle and pretty

Saumur

waterfront. Since 1763 the **National Cavalry School** has been based here. The khaki uniforms of its alumni are a distinctive feature of the town. Since 1972 the National Riding School has been here, too. Its celebrated **Cadre Noir** can be seen at occasions like the Carrousel de Saumur around 20 July. Saumur's wines are also renowned, especially **Mousseux**. At the edge of town whole rows of cellars are carved out of the rock.

✴
Chateau ▶

One of the most beautiful Loire chateaux was built here by Louis I of Anjou in about 1370. Around 1590, the proud castle was rebuilt as a major fortress by the Protestant town governor, Duplessis Mornay. The three wings of the building feature a fine late Gothic stairway of 1371. There is a wonderful view from the Tour du Guet. The chateau houses the Musée des Arts Décoratifs (tapestries, pottery) and the Musée du Cheval (equestrian museum).

Old town ▶

Place de la République is right on the river bank. It has the Hôtel de Ville (left-hand side 16th century) and the classical theatre (with tourist office) in its western half. Towards the castle lies the Romanesque church of **St-Pierre** (12th–16th centuries) with its massive tower above the crossing. Notable features include the portal, marvellous 16th-century tapestries and the Baroque organ, which is used for concerts. The church square is the heart of the old town and features timber-framed houses along with the market hall of 1982. To the south of the castle there is a botanical garden, while the church of Notre-Dame-de-Nantilly is to the west. It is lovely Romanesque building (12th–14th centuries) with a Flamboyant south aisle added around 1480. A rather stern, coloured 12th-century Madonna is venerated here. There are also splendid Aubussons from the 15th–17th centuries. The Combier orange liqueur factory (Rue Beaurepair) and the **cavalry school** with its museum (Av. Foch) are situated in the west of the town.

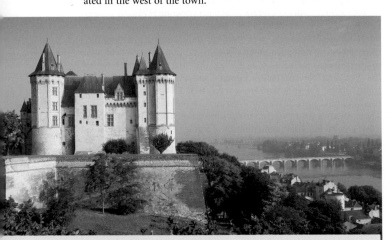

A fairy-tale castle overlooking the Saumur and the Loire

1km/1100yd upstream from the Loire bridge is the extensive complex of the abbey **Notre-Dame-des-Ardilliers** (1628–1693, in Baroque style), formerly an important place of pilgrimage with a miraculous statue of Our Lady. The cellars hewn into the tuff stone of St-Hilaire-St-Florent   (2km/1.25mi west) are now occupied by producers of sparkling wines and mushrooms, including France Champignon, France's biggest mushroom supplier (museum). **St-Hilaire** is also the site of the École Nationale d'Equitation (National Riding School) (www.cadrenoir.fr; guided tours April–Sept Tue–Sat). Things to see in **Bagneux**, 2km/1.25mi further south, include one of the biggest and most impressive

◄ Outskirts

> ## ! Baedeker TIP
>
> ### Saumur Brut
>
> Saumur's excellent sparkling wine can be tasted in various cellars, which also provide for guided tours. They include the cellars of Ackerman, Bouvet-Ladubay, Veuve Amiot, Langlois Château and Gratien-Meyer. The Maison du Vin next to the tourist office provides information and wine to taste (Quai Gautier, May–Sept closed Mon pm, otherwise Sun–Mon).

megalithic burial places in Europe as well as a vintage car museum. 2km/1.25mi south of the centre, east of the Thouet, there is a museum of tanks, the biggest in the world, with some 700 exhibits (Musée des Blindés, 1043 Route de Fontevraud). The village of Montreuil-Bellay (4100 inhabitants, 17km/11mi south of Saumur) is fabulously situated on the Thouet and has an **imposing castle**, which was transformed between the 12th century and the early 16th century from a fortress into a mansion. The new chateau (1484–1505) is notable, featuring as it does a chapel with 15th-century frescoes, a kitchen like the one in Fontevraud, residential buildings (actually four separate houses) for the choirmasters, which even have their own bathrooms, and the collegiate church of Notre-Dame (c1480), featuring the coats of arms of the families buried here.

★
Montreuil-Bellay

Doué-la-Fontaine (7500 inhabitants), 19km/12mi southwest of Saumur, is famous for its roses. What was once parkland belonging to the former chateau is now a **magnificent rose garden** (May–Sept; for events see www.cheminsdelarose.fr). In Mid-July the Journées de la Rose festival takes place in the Arènes. All that is left of the chateau itself are the stables, in which a charming museum of old-fashioned shop and workshop equipment is housed (Musée des Commerces Anciens, see signposts). There are also numerous ancient cave dwellings in the surrounding region (e.g. Village Troglodytique in Rochemenier, 6km/3.5mi northwest).

Doué-la-Fontaine

12km/7mi northwest of Saumur at a pretty spot on the Loire is the impressive former **abbey church** of Cunault (12th–13th centuries). The 11th-century bell tower is a lovely example of Loire Romanesque style. The building, some 65m/71yd long, is characterized by its elegant simplicity, contrasted by the 223 beautifully decorated

★
Cunault

capitals (some are modern replacements; take binoculars). On the tympanum of the west portal there is an enthroned Madonna, and the domes of the apse have Romanesque and Gothic frescoes. In the choir ambulatory there is a 13th-century shrine of very rare painted wood with the relics of St Maxentiolus.

Brissac-Quincé Brissac, about 16km/mi southeast of Angers, has a compact 48m/157ft-high **chateau** built from the 13th to 15th centuries (these sections were partially destroyed in the religious wars) and then from 1606 to 1621. The two old towers at the corners are not in keeping with the rest of the building. Even though the chateau is occupied – by the same family for the last 500 years – its magnificently furnished rooms are open to public. Highlights include the Veuve Clicquot painting in the Grand Gallery and the theatre added in 1883. The vintners' cooperative is also worth visiting.

Baugé The **chateau** of Baugé (3600 inhabitants, 37km/23mi northeast of Angers) was built for Good King René of Anjou from 1454. Points of interest are the elegant spiral staircase with its palm vault and a small museum with faiences, weapons and coins (and the tourist office, too). The Chapelle des Filles-du-Cóur-de-Marie south of St-Laurent is where the famous **Croix d'Anjou** is kept. Allegedly made from a piece of the True Cross, the relic was brought from Constantinople by crusaders. Its beautiful setting dates from the late 14th century. Its shape with two crosspieces inspired the Cross of Lorraine after soldiers under René II of Lorraine made it their emblem at the Battle of Nancy. Other things to see include the pharmacy of the Hôpital St-Joseph, established in 1643. Among the curious features of the Baugeois landscape are the church towers with the pointed, twisting spires. There is a particularly impressive one in Le Vieil-Baugé.

Angers ►Angers
Nantes ►Nantes

Lorraine

Lorraine, in the northeast of France between Alsace and Champagne, is steeped in history. Though it has a reputation as an ugly industrial region, in fact it possesses extensive areas of largely unspoilt nature and its attractive towns such as Nancy, Toul and Metz are more than worthy of a visit.

Geography Lorraine has no obvious natural borders. In the southwest it adjoins the Vosges mountains (►Alsace) and in the north the Ardennes lowlands. To the west is the Paris basin while the Plateau de Langres lies to the south. The most important rivers are the Meuse (Maas), the

Highlights Lorraine

Moselle and their tributaries the Sarre (Saar) and the Meurthe. Encompassing the départements of Meurthe-et-Moselle (capital ►Nancy), Moselle (►Metz), Meuse (Bar le Duc) and Vosges (Épinal), Lorraine is home to some 2.3 million people.

The treaty of ►Verdun in 843 divided the Frankish empire between the three sons of Louis the Pious, Lothair I, Ludwig the German and Charles the Bald. Charles inherited the western kingdom (West Francia), Ludwig the eastern one and Lothair the one in the middle. In 855 this middle dominion was further divided among the sons of Lothair, Ludwig, Charles and Lothair II. The latter named his region »Lotharii regnum«, which became **Lotharingia** or **Lorraine**. In 1552 the French crown took possession of the bishoprics Metz, Toul and Verdun. Stanisław Leszczyński, the deposed king of Poland and Louis XV's father-in-law, became Duke of Lorraine in 1738 and when he died in 1766 the land came under French rule. During the 19th and 20th centuries it was said that everyone of note in Europe, »toute l'Europe«, would meet at the hot spas around the fringes of the Vosges, in Bains les Bains, Plombières, Vittel and Contrexéville. After the Franco-German war of

Lorraine, yesterday and today

Inside the ceramics museum in Sarreguemines

▶ VISITING LORRAINE

INFORMATION

CRT Lorraine
Abbaye des Prémontrés, BP 97
F-54704 Pont à Mousson Cedex
Tel. 03 83 80 01 80, fax 03 83 80 01 88
www.tourisme-lorraine.fr

WHERE TO STAY

► Budget

Fontaine Stanislas
F-88370 Plombières les Bains
www.fontaine-stanislas.com
Tel. 03 29 66 01 53, open April–Oct
4km/2.5mi outside town (D 20)
overlooking the valley. Located in
thoroughly peaceful surroundings,
this hotel boasts a pleasant atmosphere and a garden.

WHERE TO EAT

► Expensive

Château d'Adomenil
Rehainviller, F-54300 Lunéville

Tel. 03 83 74 04 81
www.adomenil.com
closed Mon, Tue–Fri open evenings
8km/5mi southwest of Lunéville
An 18th-century ducal palace provides an appropriate backdrop to the
exquisite, locally inspired cuisine
(reservation required). Fine rooms
and suites also available.

► Inexpensive / moderate

Cap Sud – À la Belle Marée
144 Route de Bresse
F-88400 Gerardmer
Tel. 03 29 63 06 83
Fax 03 29 63 20 76;
closed Mon (except school holidays)
Tucked away in the Vosges mountains, this restaurant is furnished in
the style of a luxury cruise liner. It is
famous for its Mediterranean and
Atlantic fish dishes.

1870–71 a large part of Lorraine including Metz, much of which was
already German-speaking, was annexed by the new German Empire,
where it was linked with Alsace to become part of the administrative
district of Elsass-Lothringen. After the First World War, in which
Lorraine was the scene of some ghastly bloodshed – the **Battle of
Verdun** alone cost the lives of 700,000 soldiers in 1916 – the land
was restored to France and has remained French ever since, apart
from the brief interregnum of 1940–44. The strength of the economy
has been based on the mining of coal and iron ore as well as on the
steel, chemicals and textile industries, which were particularly characteristic of northern Lorraine. Production of salt was also a key factor and a major impetus for the establishment of the chemicals industry here. At the beginning of the 1960s, these industries provided
jobs for more than 200,000 people, but nowadays the number has
dropped to just 35,000. The last iron mine closed in 1993 and the
last colliery went in 2004 (and with it the last remnant of the coal industry in France). Since the mid-1960s attempts have been made to
regenerate the region. Lorraine now has the largest concentration of
foreign companies in France and its factories include Daimler's Smart
plant in Hambach. Due to the lack of fertility of the chalky soil, agri-

culture is mainly confined to cereals, dairy farming, and fruit grow-ing (the Mirabelle plums are of importance internationally).

Places to Visit in Northern Lorraine

Sarreguemines (German Saargemünd, 23,800 inhabitants), 18km/11mi south of Saarbrücken, is famous for its **faience factory**, which has been in existence here since 1790.The directors' building has a tremendous collection on display, while the Musée des Techniques Faiencières demonstrates how faience pottery is made. There is a great view from the ruins on top of the castle mound. For those with an interest in the 6000-year history of human settlement in the re-gion, the excavations at **Bliesbruck-Reinheim**, which span the border (about 10km/6mi east of Sarreguemines) are not to be missed.

Sarreguemines

✶ ✶

◄ Pottery museum

Parc Archéologi-que

In St-Avold (17,000 inhabitants), 45km/28mi east of Metz, the mighty Benedictine church of **St-Nabor**, built in Baroque style in 1755–69, is well worth stopping for. It is considered to be the most important 18th-century ecclesiastical building in Lorraine. In terms of style it features a unique mix of classicist ideas around the basis of a Gothic-style hall church.

Saint-Avold

Phalsbourg (German: Pfalzburg, 4000 inhabitants) 16km/10mi east of Sarrebourg (► see below) grew up after 1568, when a castle was built there. In 1662 it was conquered by France and as of 1679 Vau-ban laid out a fortress to protect the Rhine crossing (it was levelled in 1871). The Porte de France and Porte d'Allemagne gates are rem-nants of those fortifications. A museum in the Hotel de Ville pro-vides information on the garrison town and on the **Erckmann-Chatri-an** writing team, whose novels (including *L'Ami Fritz*) are highly re-vered in Alsace and Lorraine. Émile Erckmann was born in Phalsbourg in 1822.

Phalsbourg

The little resort of Dabo (German: Dagsburg; 3200 inhabitants), 18km/11mi southeast of Sarrebourg, is situated among some lovely scenery on the mountain of Rocher de Dabo (664m/2175ft), which can be seen for miles around. Until 1679 it was topped by a castle called the Dagsburg. Nowadays the site is occupied by the chapel of St-Léon, built in 1890 in honour of Pope Leo IX (1049–54), who was born in the castle.

Dabo

✶
Rocher de Dabo

The small industrial town of Sarrebourg (13,300 inhabitants) 70km/43mi east of Nancy lies at the edge of the Vosges mountains on the upper Sarre. The Chapelle des Cordeliers – a remnant of a 13th-cen-tury church that was demolished in 1970 – now houses the tourist office. At one end there is a huge stained glass window by **Marc Cha-gall**. The exhibits at the Musée du Pays de Sarrebourg include pot-tery from Sarrebourg and Niderviller as well as Gallo-Roman finds.

Sarrebourg

Fort Schoenenbourg near Wissembourg in Alsace is largest of the Maginot-Line installations open to the public

AN EXPENSIVE MISTAKE

After the First World War, northern France saw the building of the most extensive and fearsome line of fortifications in the world. Construction devoured one third of the state budget, 5000 million gold francs, the equivalent of 3000 million today.

Once it had been decided in 1919 that the borders needed to be secured, plans were made by ambitious defence minister **Andre Maginot** (1877–1932) for a massive bulwark. The defences came into being between 1929 and 1932, the most extensive fortification being concentrated on the 300km/200mi of the Alsace and Lorraine border between Mulhouse and Sedan, where 35 small forts and 23 large ones were built, along with around 400 individual bunkers. This required digging up whole sections of land, with well over 200km/125mi of tunnels and shafts being excavated underground. For the fortifications above the surface alone, enough concrete was used to have rebuilt the Cheops pyramid. The steel used for the turrets and other armour could have built the Eiffel Tower six times over. Its underground cities for the army were equipped with miles of railways, with lifts, casement defences, magazines, power stations, hospitals, bakeries and kitchens. The whole enterprise sucked in so much money that it was no longer possible to finance a modern tank infantry or an air force. In the end, the Maginot Line was of no use. In 1940, Hitler's panzer divisions simply drove around it. The invasion came as a total surprise, across neutral Belgium and through the Ardennes into the heart of France. The Nazi tanks simply followed a great arc, taking in Paris and penetrating back to the Swiss border. Only one of the forts, la Ferté, was actually taken. The French army maintained the »Ligne Maginot« until 1970. Several of the large forts are still used for military purposes. Some of the installations in northern Alsace and Lorraine, though, have been restored and opened to the public (others are used for private cultivation of mushrooms). The most imposing of the publicly accessible facilities are Fort Schoenenbourg and Fort Four à Chaux (the »lime oven«), both near Wissembourg in Alsace, and Fort Hackenberg (p.511). When visiting them, bear in mind that the temperature in these giant mole holes remains constant – at a rather chilly 12–15°C/54–59°F.

Pont-à-Mousson (14,600 inhabitants), on the Moselle between Nancy and Metz, is surrounded by heavy industry but the **arcade houses** that line Place Duroc (including no. 7, »the house of the seven deadly sins«) at its centre, which date from the 16th–18th centuries, are well worth a look, as is the church of St-Martin (14th–18th centuries) with one outstanding late Gothic tomb. The Premonstratensian (Norbertine) abbey to the north on the bank of the Moselle came into being in the early 18th century and now serves as a cultural centre.

Pont-à-Mousson

▶Metz

Metz

Amnéville (or Hagondange) lies about 18km/11mi north of Metz. A major spa complex, **Thermapolis** (www.polethermal.com), opened here in 1996 after drilling encountered a source of mineral water heated to a temperature of 41°C/106°F. In the meantime it has become a major leisure and recreational site. Parc Walygaytor (www.walgatorparc.com) near Maizières offers visitors the usual list of leisure park attractions.

Amnéville-les-Thermes

Fort Hackenberg (near Veckring 23km/14mi east of Thionville) was the biggest fort on the **Maginot Line** (▶ Baedeker Special p.510). 1200 men could survive here without the delivery of supplies for three months and the guns could deliver 4 tonnes of shells per minute. Tours around 20 March–mid-Nov Sat–Sun 2pm–3.30pm, Wed 3pm, 15 June–15 Sept also Mon, Wed, Thu 3pm; otherwise Sat 2pm.

✶
Fort Hackenberg

▶Verdun

Verdun

The small fortified town of Montmédy (2300 inhabitants) lies on the Belgian border 47km/29mi north of Verdun. Subsequent to the Peace of the Pyrenees in 1659 it was further reinforced by Vauban (citadel in the upper town and walls around the lower town). 8km/5mi to the north, the tiny commune of **Avioth** has a surprise in store in the shape of the magnificent and elegant Gothic basilica of Notre-Dame, which was built for pilgrims in the 13th and 14th centuries. Their destination was the lime wood Madonna, which according to legend had been found in a thorn bush at the start of the 12th century.

Montmédy

Toul (17,000 inhabitants), 24km/15mi west of Nancy in the upper Moselle valley, was highly important in the Middle Ages, when it was a bishopric and a free town of the Holy Roman Empire (until 1648). The fortifications, built by Vauban in 1698–1712, feature four gates and have been preserved almost in their entirety. The **cathedral** of St-Etienne (1221–1507) is a testament to the importance of the bishopric with its impressive late Gothic façade, two incomplete towers rising to a height of 65m/213ft, and a large gallery (13th–14th centuries). The majestic **episcopal palace** (1753) has been in use as the

✶
Toul

The cathedral of St-Etienne in Toul

town hall since 1789. To the west, beyond Rue Michâtel with its fine Renaissance house at no. 16, is the church of St-Gengoult (13th–16th centuries), a small disbursement of the cathedral. There are some lovely stained glass windows in the choir (*c*1260), while the gallery (*c*1515) has some elegant Flamboyant carvings and some very pretty sculpted capitals. On Rue Général-Gengoult there are some old houses, some of which date back to the 14th century. The museum in a 13th and 18th-century hospice (Rue Gouvion St-Cyr) is also worth a look. 15km/9mi to the north, near **Andilly**, is the largest German military cemetery from the First World War, with more than 33,000 graves.

Commercy Poland's ex-king Stanisław selected the village of Commercy (7000 inhabitants), situated 32km/20mi northwest of Toul on the Maas, as his residence and had the **Baroque chateau** of the counts of Vaudemont rebuilt from 1745–47 by Héré (the building is now used by the municipal council). The town's former swimming pool from 1930 now houses the Musée de la Céramique et de l'Ivoire.

Saint-Mihiel The small village of Saint-Mihiel (5300 inhabitants) on the Meuse, 18km/11mi north of Commercy, grew up around a Benedictine abbey founded in 709. It was also home to the sculptor **Ligier Richier** (1507?–67), whose representations of the human form still owe allegiance to the Gothic style, although his decorations are definitely Renaissance. In the village's churches there are several superb works of his, including the walnut-carved tableau *John Supporting Mary as She Falls* (1531) in St-Michel (18th century; vestibule and tower 12th century) and a tomb sculpture (1554–64) in St-Etienne. It is also worth visiting the library and museum of ecclesiastical art in the 17th-century convent of St-Michel.

Bar-le-Duc The former capital of the duchy of Bar (17,000 inhabitants), 35km/22mi southwest of St-Mihiel, is set amid some charming scenery. The centrepiece of the upper town is Place St-Pierre, lined as it is with beautiful houses dating from the 14th–18th centuries. In the late Gothic church of St-Etienne (14th–17th centuries) there is a crucifixion group (1530) as well as a tomb for Prince René de Châlon, who died in 1544; with its famous »skeleton« figure. These too were masterpieces by **Ligier Richier**. Across the former main street of Rue des Ducs-de-Bar – with its lovely houses from the Renaissance and Baroque periods – stands the new chateau, built as of 1567 and now housing the Musée Barrois, which features a large archaeological collection as well as paintings by French and Flemish masters. On the way down to the lower town, the road passes the Collège Gilles de Trèves (1574) with its beautiful Renaissance courtyard. Cross Pont Notre-Dame, which has its own chapel, to the church of Notre-Dame (11th–14th centuries). The nave contains a notable crucifix by Richier (1530), while the southern transept has a relief of the Assumption of Mary (1500).

Places to Visit in Southern Lorraine

The age-old bishopric of St-Dié (23,700 inhabitants, 75km/47mi southwest of Strasbourg) was largely burned to the ground in the Second World War and nowadays has a very modern appearance. It was here that Martin Waldseemüller published the first work of geography to mention »America« in 1507 (a copy of *Cosmographiae Introductio* is kept in the town library). In 1945 Le Corbusier was given the task of planning a new city, but all that came of it was a single sock factory built in the north of town. In the centre, a group of church buildings survived the devastation. The Romanesque-Gothic **cathedral** was furnished with its classical façade in the 18th century; while the Romanesque nave boasts some fabulous capitals. An incomplete cloister (15th–16th centuries) links the cathedral to the church of Notre-Dame-de-Galilée, a fine example of Rhineland Romanesque from the 12th century. Musée Pier-Noël next to the cathedral features finds from La Bure (► see below), a collection of birdlife exhibits and memorabilia related to Minister Jules Ferry (1832–93) as well as modern art (including Léger, Dalí, Miró). 8km/5mi further north, a Celtic settlement (Camp celtique de la Bure), which existed during a period from 2000 BC till the 4th century AD, has been excavated.

Saint-Dié

✶
◄ Church buildings

◄ Celtic settlement

Baccarat, about 25km/16mi northwest of St-Dié, has been a centre for the manufacture of **crystal glass** since 1764. The production hall of the old factory now houses the Musée du Cristal, highlighting innumerable aspects of the manufacturing process and exhibiting many fine examples of work. Crystal glass has also been used alongside concrete in the design of the church of St-Rémy (1957).

Baccarat

Lunéville (21,000 inhabitants) 37km/23mi southeast of Nancy was the residence of the dukes of Lorraine from 1702 to 1737. In 1801 it provided the setting for the signing of a peace treaty between France and Austria. Its heyday came under the aegis of Stanisław Leszczyński, who had the **chateau** redesigned in Rococo style by a student of Mansart in 1723. The chateau houses exhibits of faience work from Lunéville itself, an apothecary from the 18th century, leather wall coverings and Art Nouveau glass. The Baroque church of St-Jacques in the pretty old town was built between 1730 and

Lunéville

1747 by Boffrand and Héré. The carvings inside on the pulpit, the choir stalls and the organ, as well as some paintings, were created by Lunéville's own Jean Girardet (1708–88). The Musée du Vélo et de la Moto has more than 200 old bicycles and tricycles on display.

Nancy ▶Nancy

Gérardmer ✴ The western slopes of the high Vosges mountains, with their wooded peaks and lakes dating back to the Ice Age, are popular with tourists in both summer and winter. Gérardmer (9500 inhabitants; 666–1100m/2185–3609ft) lies at the centre of the region. It is set in pretty surroundings on the shore of the largest of the lakes beneath

the Col de la Schlucht pass leading to ▶Colmar. Countless hotels, restaurants, leisure and sport facilities etc. are at the disposal of visitors. The town's textile factories concentrate on **linen products** and indeed occupy the top position in the French market (there are guided tours and factory shops to visit). One important date for the diary is the **Festival of the Narcissus** (Fête de la Jonquille), which takes place biennially in the second half of April in odd years. The end of January is given over to the Festival of Fantasy Film (Fantastic'Arts). There is also the chance to take some great day-trips into ▶Alsace.

Gérardmer, »Pearl of the Vosges«, is also a popular place for a day trip

Épinal Épinal (38,000 inhabitants), capital of the Vosges département, is situated on the Moselle amid an extensive forest. Among its most famous legacies are the **Images d'Épinal**, colourful pages that were printed in the town as of 1796 and, for a while, were sold throughout the world. Some of the finest examples can be seen in the Imagerie d'Épinal and its Musée de l'Image (42 Quai de Dogneville). The Mu-

Musée d'Art Ancien et Contemporain ▶ ✴ sée d'Art Ancien et Contemporain (1992; closed Tue), situated at the southern tip of the island in the middle of the Moselle, exhibits several Gallo-Roman finds, ecclesiastical art and some outstanding paintings (by Claude Lorrain, La Tour, Brueghel, Rembrandt; Arte Povera and various pop artists, among others). The old town is on the right bank of the Moselle where the basilica of St-Maurice (12th–14th centuries) is well worth a visit. Its main entrance is the truncated Portail des Bourgeois at the northern end of the building. In the interior, the Burgundian influence is clear to see. The park to the east that overlooks the old town also has the ruins of a castle, which was destroyed in 1670.

Remiremont (8500 inhabitants), 26km/16mi south of Épinal at the foot of Mount Parmon (613m/2011ft) on the upper reaches of the Moselle dates back to the founding in the 11th century of a religious establishment for women of the aristocracy, which was once rather famous. The collegiate church of St-Pierre, built in the 13th century above an 11th-century crypt (the façade and tower are 18th century), dominates the town along with the foundation houses and the late Baroque **Abtisse Palais** (1752, now used for various purposes including as the town hall). Some lovely arcade houses from the 17th–18th centuries line Rue Charles de Gaulle. There are two museums dedicated to the culture and history of the town and the surrounding region.

★
Remiremont

This **health spa** (1900 inhabitants) in the narrow Augronne valley, 30km/19mi south of Épinal, was already well known in Roman times. Its 28 springs with temperatures ranging from 13–74°C/55–165°F was a magnet for politicians and high society in the 18th and 19th centuries. The imposing Thermes Napoléon complex was built after 1857. To the southwest lie the lovely Parc Impérial and the casino. In the northwestern part of the old town there is a museum (with works by painter Louis Français, who was born in Plombières, along with others by von Corot, Courbet etc.), the Bain National (a tavern dating back to 1818), Roman baths, the pretty Maison des Arcades (1762) and Bain Stanislas.

Plombières les Bains

One nice place to go for a day trip from Plombières is Bains les Bains (1600 inhabitants), reached via a zig-zagging route along the valley of the Semouse. The village's hot springs are still used by two health establishments going back to the 19th century.

Bains les Bains

Vittel (6100 inhabitants, 42km/26mi west of Épinal) is set in a beautiful location and has been **Lorraine's most famous health spa** since the 19th century. Its cold mineral water bubbles from four separate springs. There are lovely parks, plenty of sports facilities, a golf course, race track and casino that all contribute to the entertainment of visitors. The late Gothic church of St-Rémy (c1500) is also worth seeing. At the edge of the village stands the factory where more than 5 million bottles of the famous water are filled every day (guided tours available). The health spa of Contrexéville, set in gorgeous scenery about 8km/5mi southwest of Vittel, is also famous for its mineral water. Health establishments built in Byzantine style back in 1910 still give the village some high-class flair.

★
Vittel

Contrexéville

28km/17mi northwest of Contrexeville overlooking the river Meuse is the old town of Neufchâteau (7500 inhabitants). In the Middle Ages it enjoyed major importance as a free town in the duchy of Lorraine. Some pretty old buildings are still preserved in the upper town, including the Hôtel de Ville with its magnificent stairway

Neufchâteau

(1597). The two-storey church of St-Nicolas (12th–15th centuries, rebuilt 1704) is splendidly furnished in Baroque style and possesses a notable group of tombs from the 15th century.

Domrémy-la-Pucelle

Perhaps the most famous village in all Lorraine is Domrémy-la-Pucelle, 9km/6mi north of Neufchâteau. **Joan of Arc** was born here on 6th January 1412, since when the town has gained its appellation »La Pucelle« (»the virgin«). It was here that the 17-year-old Joan began her quest against English forces during the Hundred Years' War. Her birthplace near the church is open to the public and there is a small museum next door.

★ ★ Lot Valley · Vallée du Lot

G–J 8

The scenic delights of the Lot valley are equal to those of the nearby and more famous Dordogne. The character of this stretch of the river alternates between picturesque charm and the wildness of nature. The river bank is dotted with enchanting villages and towns.

The river and its scenery

★ ★

Gorges du Lot ▶

The Lot rises in the ▶Cevennes on the 1497m/4911ft Montagne du Goulet. It then flows westwards along the edge of the Massif Central, across the Quercy region and into the Garonne some 480km/300mi from its source. The canyons downstream of Estaing are the highlight. Some are 300m/1000ft deep and are comparable to the Gorges du Tarn in the ▶Cevennes. In bygone days the Lot was an important transport artery, linking the Auvergne and the wine trading centre of Cahors with Bordeaux. Nowadays, kayakers and climbers seek adventure between Espalion und Conques. From St Cirq-Lapopie it is possible to navigate a houseboat as far as Luzech. The red wines of AC Cahors are famous. They are mainly made from Malbec grapes, an old variety.

Places to Visit in the Lot Valley

These attractions in the Lot valley are described following the river downstream from Espalion to Villeneuve-sur-Lot (upper reaches of the ▶ Cevennes, Mende), then down through Rodez and Villefranche-de-Rouergue south of the Lot.

Espalion

Espalion (4400 inhabitants), with its old **tanners' houses** on the Lot and its Vieux Pont (11th century) is a beautiful sight. The 16th-century Vieux Palais was formerly the residence of the governor. The former church of St-Jean now houses the Musée Joseph Vaylet (local folklore and deep-sea diving). Another local museum, the Musée du Rouergue, is housed in a former prison. The small Romanesque Eglise de Perse (11th century, 1km/0.5mi southeast) has an interesting

St-Cirq-Lapopie rises up the slopes high above the Lot valley

south door depicting the Pentecost. From the medieval **Château de Calmont** (accessed via the D 920), which guards the valley there is a tremendous view. About 10km/6mi south of Espalion it is also worth seeing **Bozouls**, situated above a deep and narrow canyon cut by a loop of the river.

Estaing

This old-world little village (600 inhabitants) is charmingly placed where the Lot valley opens out. A 15th-century Gothic bridge spans the river. The imposing **chateau** (15th–16th centuries) was formerly the home of the aristocratic d'Estaing family and there is a lovely view from the terrace. The relics of Saint Fleuret are kept in the 15th-century church.

★
Gorges du Lot

From Estaing the D 920 runs past the Golinhac Dam, beyond which lies the deepest and narrowest part of the Lot valley.

Entraygues-sur-Truyère

At the confluence with the Truyère, flanked by slopes of orchards and vineyards, is the small and delightfully medieval town of Entraygues-sur-Truyère (1300 inhabitants), characterized by its »cantous«, **covered alleyways**. For a small tour, start from Place Castanié and take Rue Basse, Rue du Collège and Rue Droite. A lovely 13th-century Gothic bridge spans the Truyère.

★★
Conques

Conques (300 inhabitants) is situated in the narrow, verdant valley of the Ouche. Its abbey was an important stop on the Way of St James between the 11th and 13th centuries (▶ Baedeker Special p.792). Old houses cluster around the church of **Ste-Foy** (11th–12th centuries). The saint was martyred in 303 at the age of 13 for her faith. The **church treasury** (open daily), combining superb craftsmanship from the 9th to 16th centuries, also contains a famous relic statue of the saint herself, made of gold and seated on a throne (9th century, with numerous additions, but the head is thought to date back to the 4th century). The other great masterpiece is the tympanum of the **west portal** (c1130), which has 124 colourfully painted figures and is among the best and biggest in France. The 12th-century wrought-iron choir screen is also notable.

Figeac
North of the Lot, on the river Celé, Figeac (9500 inhabitants) grew up around an abbey founded in the 9th century, which was also a station on the Way of St James. This ensured the prosperity of the town, as can be seen from its remaining medieval districts. On Place de la Raison, which opens onto the river, are the former abbey church of St-Sauveur (the oldest parts are 11th century) and an obelisk recalling Jean-François Champollion (1790–1832), a son of the village who was the first to decipher Egyptian hieroglyphics at the beginning of the 19th century (▶ Famous People). About 200m/200yd west of there is the Gothic **Hôtel de la Monnaie** (late 13th century), a typical Figeac building with arcades, Gothic windows and an open attic storey (tourist office and local museum). Head northeast along Rue Gambetta with its Knights Templar commandery (12th–15th centuries) and past the market hall to the Musée Champollion. In front of the museum a **replica of the Rosetta stone** is set into the ground. The church of Notre-Dame-du-Puy (12th–14th century), which has a carved retable (late 17th century), towers over the town. St-Cirq-Lapopie (190 inhabitants) is beautifully located on top of a cliff above the Lot. Its houses have been lovingly restored by

✳ Saint-Cirq-Lapopie

▶ VISITING LOT-TAL

INFORMATION
CRT Languedoc-Roussillon
CS 79507
F-34960 Montpellier Cedex
Tel. 04 67 20 02 20
www.sunfrance.com
CRT Midi-Pyrenees
54 Blvd. de l'Embouchure
F-31000 Toulouse
Tel. 05 61 13 55 48, Fax 05 61 47 17 16
www.tourisme-midi-pyrenees.com

WHERE TO EAT/WHERE TO STAY
▶ Budget
La Chartreuse
Chemin de Chartreuse
F-46000 Cahors
Tel. 05 65 35 17 37
www.hotel-la-chartreuse.com Modern hotel on the river Lot with a fantastic view of the town. Large, well-furnished rooms and a restaurant.

La Garissade
Place de la Mairie
F-49240 Labastide-Murat
www.restaurant-garissade.fr,
tel. 05 65 21 18 80, 35km/22mi northeast of Cahors.
A chateau dating from 1226 with tasteful modern rooms, good rural cooking.

La Puce à l'Oreille
5 Rue St Thomas, F-46100 Figeac
Tel. 05 65 34 33 08
A restaurant in the old town brimming with character. Housed in a 15th-century former stable; it serves good and lovingly prepared local dishes.

Even today Conques is still an important stop on the Way of St James

artists and craftsmen. The church dates from the 15th century. There is a great view from the rocky promontory with the ruins of a castle.

Take a little detour northward to the valley of the Célé. The **Grotte de Pech-Merle** cave near Cabreretsis famous for its animal paintings (▶Baedeker Special p. 662). The Amédée-Lemozi museum has plenty of information about the discoveries. Close to Cuzals, 6km/3.5mi northeast of Cabrerets, the open-air farmhouse museum, Musée de Plein Air du Quercy, presents a picture of rural life in the 19th century.

Célé valley

Cahors (21,500 inhabitants), former capital of the county of Quercy, is prettily situated in a loop of the Lot. Here it is already possible to smell the lighter air of the Midi region. In the Middle Ages, as a trading post of Lombard bankers, it was an important commercial and financial centre for the whole of Europe. Pope John XXII, who was born in Cahors, founded a university here as early as 1332. In the west of the town the Lot is spanned by the Pont Valentré (1308–80). Its three massive towers 40m/130ft high, defied the English during the Hundred Years' War. Blvd. Gambetta leads north from the southern bridge, and the old town is to the east of it. East of Place Mitterrand (tourist office) is the Romanesque cathedral of St-Etienne (1117, 14th-century façade), one of the oldest and largest domed churches in southwest France. Its calotte domes, 32m/105ft high and 18m/60ft in diameter, were painted in the 14th century. The magnificent **north door**, formerly the main entrance, was built around 1140 and depicts the Ascension of Christ. A lovely late Gothic cloister (1509) adjoins to the south. It is worth making a **tour** of the town, starting at the cathedral and taking in Rue Nationale, Rue Lastié and Rue St Urcisse to the Maison de Roaldès (late 15th

Cahors

✶
◀ Pont Valentré

✶
◀ St-Etienne

century) on the river Lot. Head north from there to the 34m/112ft Tour Jean XXII (a remnant of a former palace) and the church of St-Barthélemy (14th–16th centuries). Further north are Tour St-Jean and the Barbican (the town's 15th-century watchhouse), part of the fortifications. Beyond Pont Valentré there is a reconstructed floating mill and 400m/440yd further south along the river the Fontaine des Chartreux, a spring which was sacred to the Gauls and is still used to supply drinking water.

Puy-l'Evêque
Below Cahors the Lot meanders amid tall rocky cliffs as far as Puy-l'Evêque. Places to see include the Chateau de Mercuès (13th–15th centuries, a Relais & Châteaux hotel), Luzech and Grézels with the Château de la Coste. It is worth taking a day trip out from Duravel

Château de Bonaguil
or Fumel to the fearsome Château de Bonaguil, which evokes the spirit of the Middle Ages but was not in fact built until 1477–1520 in order to impress the English and the local peasants.

Villeneuve-sur-Lot
Villeneuve-sur-Lot (24,000 inhabitants) was established as a **bastide** in 1253. There are still remnants of the fortifications in the form of the Porte de Pujols south of the river, and Porte de Paris north of it (Place de la Libération). Pont Vieux was built in the 13th century by the English, while the chapel that extends over the water dates from the 16th century. The Musée de la Vallée du Lot (history of the Lot and its bastides) is located in an old mill.

Rodez
Rodez (23,700 inhabitants), capital of the Aveyron département, is 28km/17mi southwest of Espalion on a hill overlooking the river Aveyron. Place d'Armes is dominated by its fortified **cathedral of Notre-Dame** (13th–15th centuries), the façade of which presents a less than satisfying contrast between the Flamboyant part and the Renaissance gable. The 87m/285ft tower on the northern side has some magnificent Flamboyant carving (16th century). The interior is rather unimaginative but richly furnished. To the right there is a stone lattice (15th century) and a tomb (16th century), while the transept has a superb lectern (1470) and a carved organ front (17th century). The choir stalls are late Gothic (15th century). To the north of the cathedral are the bishop's palace and a remnant of the former fortifications known as the Tour de Corbières (1443). The

Laguiole

The pocket knives, which have been made in Laguiole (pronounced »layól«), 25km/16mi northeast of Espalion, since 1829 are now cult objects for the style conscious. At Forge de Laguiole, run by Philippe Starck, and in the Musée du Couteau visitors can see them made and even try their own hand. Information: www.forge de laguiole.com, www.tourisme-aveyron.com. Further towards Aubrac in the spectacular modern hotel and restaurant of Michael Bras at an altitude of 1225m/4019ft, both the architecture and the food seek to be at one with nature (www.michel-bras.com, tel. 05 65 51 18 20, closed Nov–March).

Romanesque church of St-Amans (12th–18th centuries; with fine capitals and 16th-century tapestries), the Musée Fenaille (archaeological discoveries, medieval sculpture, arts and crafts) and Musée Denys Puech are all worth a visit too.

Villefranche-de-Rouergue (12,000 inhabitants, 36km/22mi south of Figeac) is an old bastide, with a fine example of the typical **arcaded squares** in the centre (market on Thursdays). The collegiate church of Notre Dame adjoins it to the east. Though building began in 1260, the 56m/184ft tower was never finished. The choir stalls (1487) have several amusing carved figures. To the south of the main square is another pretty piazza with fountains dating from 1336. The Musée Urbain Cabrol has a nice, colourful collection (early history, ecclesiastical art, folklore etc.). | Villefranche-de-Rouergue

✶ ✶ Lourdes

G 9

Région: Midi-Pyrénées
Département: Hautes-Pyrénées

Altitude: 410m/1345ft
Population: 16,300

Every year more than 5 million people come from all over the world to Lourdes in its beautiful setting at the northern edge of the Pyrenees. More than half of those visitors are pilgrims, many thousands of whom come in the hope of being healed from illnesses or afflictions.

Lourdes, some 40km/25mi southeast of Pau (►Pyrenees, p.726), is a famous place of pilgrimage but the sometimes exaggerated kitsch of its devotionalism can certainly create a slightly mixed impression. Even sceptics, though, could not fail to be impressed by the atmosphere of profound belief that has been known to move mountains. | Famous place of pilgrimage

Lourdes Map

1 Basilique Supérieure
2 Basilique du Rosaire, Crypte
3 Musée du Gemmail
4 Musée Grévin
5 Moulin de Boly
6 Moulin Lacade
7 Grottes du Loup
8 Grottes de Bétharram

Where to stay
① Majestic

History Its status as a magnet for pilgrims goes back to an appearance of the Virgin Mary to the shepherdess, **Bernadette Soubirous** (1844–79) in the grotto of Massabielle in 1858 and the reputation of the waters that have bubbled from a spring in the grotto she is said to have brought forth at that time. Bernadette, who lived at the Couvent St-Gildard in Nevers (►Loire Valley) from 1866 until her early death, was declared a saint in 1933. The first national pilgrimages had started as early as 1873. Alleged cures are verified by a commission of doctors. The last healing to have been recognized by medicine and by the church took place in 1976.

What to See in Lourdes

Cité Religieuse The Cité Religieuse is situated in a loop of the Gave de Pau. From the bridge the Esplanade des Processions leads to Esplanade du Rosaire (rosary square). The underground church of **St-Pie X** (1958) is 201m/660ft long and 81m/266ft wide, providing room for a congregation of 20,000, making it one of the larges places of worship in the world. The sacramental processions that start out from the grotto come to their end at Esplanade du Rosaire and afterwards there is a blessing of the sick. The neo-Byzantine **Basilique du Rosaire** (basilica of the rosary, 1889) holds 2000 people. Ramps lead up from here to the Basilique Supérieure (1871) with its 70m/230ft tower atop the cliffs of the grotto.

 VISITING LOURDES

INFORMATION

Office de Tourisme
Place Peyramale, F-65100 Lourdes
Tel. 05 62 42 77 40, fax 05 62 94 60 96
 www.lourdes-france.com

ETIQUETTE AND CUSTOMS

Smoking is forbidden within the grounds of the Cité Religieuse. People are also advised to wear appropriate clothing.

EVENTS

Between Palm Sunday and the middle of October every day a sacramental procession leaves from the grotto of Massabielle at 4.30pm and there is another torch-lit procession at 8.45pm. The Festival de la Musique Sacrée takes place during the fortnight around Easter.

WHERE TO STAY

In spite of there being some 260 hotels in town, it can still be hard to find a room around Easter or the feast of the Assumption, indeed throughout the months of May, August (especially 12–17) and October. It is essential to book early.

► Budget

Majestic
9 Avenue Maransin, tel. 05 62 94 27 23
www.majesticlourdes.fr
Only 10 minutes from the pilgrimage sites, this pretty hotel offers excellent value.

To the north, nestling beneath the basilica, is the Massabielle grotto (Grotte Miraculeuse) itself, measuring just 12m/39ft wide and 10m/33ft deep. In the niche where Our Lady is said to have appeared there is a Madonna statue, made from Carrara marble in 1863 to match the descriptions given by St Bernadette herself. Further to the west there are 17 pools, in which thousands of sick people immerse themselves in the hope of being healed.

Grotte Massabielle

The **Notre-Dame pavilion** houses the **Musée Bernadette** and the **Musée d'Art Sacré du Gemmail**. North of the Gave is the **Espace Ste-Bernadette**, a church that holds some 7000 people, and an adjoining hospital station. Also there is the **Accueil Notre-Dame**, one of the two large hospitals in the town.

The town's central square is **Place Peyramale**. To the east stands the main church, the neo-Romanesque **Sacré-Cœur** (1877–1903). What is known as the »**Cachot**« (hole) was home to the six members of the Soubirous family from 1856 to

The Basilica of the Rosary in Lourdes

1863. On Rue Bernadette-Soubirous stand the **Moulin de Boly**, where Bernadette was born, and **Moulin Lacade**, where the family lived after Bernadette's visions. The imposing **castle** (13th–17th centuries) 80m/262ft above the town is accessed via a ramp from Rue du Bourg or by a lift (on the eastern side). There is a fine view from the terrace. The castle houses the museum of the Pyrenees (local folklore). An aquarium on the road to Tarbes offers an interesting look at the wildlife of the Pyrenean rivers.

◄ Fort

Around Lourdes

There are lovely views from **Béout** (791m/2595ft), southeast of the town, and **Pic de Jer** (948m/3110ft), accessed by a funicular railway (lower station in the valley on the N 21 to Argelès; also climbable on foot, 2½ hours there and back).

Viewpoints

16km/10mi west of Lourdes are the Grottes de Bétharram (open February–mid-October), an extensive system of caves with an underground river on which boat trips take place.

Grottes de Bétharram

★ Lyon

Région: Rhône-Alpes **Altitude:** 175m/574ft
Département: Rhône **Population:** 466,000

The business metropolis of the upper Rhône valley and the third biggest city in France after Paris and Marseille, Lyon has a wonderful old town dating back to the Renaissance, a lively cultural life and first-class museums – not to mention the fact that it is a veritable Mecca for gourmets.

Metropolis on the Rhône

Lyon, a former trading centre and now a modern industrial metropolis, lies at the centre of an urban district that is home to 1.3 million people at the confluence of the Rhône and Saône rivers. In addition to the traditional silk processing industry, the economic drivers of the region are banks, chemicals and pharmaceuticals, textiles and machine engineering, as well as several research establishments. As capital of its région and département, service industries also play a key role. Lyon also has three universities, innumerable colleges and is home to the headquarters of Interpol. Its culinary delights are positively endless, from exclusive five-star temples to cosy »bouchons« (bistros), small but renowned for their high quality. Paul Bocuse started his career in the city. After serving an apprenticeship with the legendary Mère Brazier, he started out to create his own new cooking revolution. The city also has a wealth of legacies to reflect a history going back more than 2000 years. The quartiers of Vieux Lyon, La Croix-Rousse and parts of Presqu'Ile have been added to the list of **UNESCO World Heritage Sites**. East of the Rhône an (ultra)-modern suburb has arisen with buildings by many renowned contemporary architects.

View of Lyon in the loop of the Saône, overlooked by the Colline de Fourvière

History

In 43 BC the Romans founded the city of Lugdunum on the hill inside the bend in the Saône where there had previously been a Celtic settlement. The city grew quickly and in the time of Emperor Augustus it was appointed as the capital city of a province called Gallia Lugdunensis. By AD 177 there was a Christian community in the city. Lyon gained its city charter as early as 1320 and soon became a centre for banking, for cloth and silk weaving, at the introduction of Louis XI, and for the printing of books. From the beginning of 15th century, Lyon hosted important fairs but there was a setback with the repeal of the Edict of Nantes in 1685, since it meant that the mainly Protestant silk factory owners were forced to leave the city. Revolt against the revolutionary Jacobites 1793 ended with the destruction of large swathes of Lyon and the execution of some 6000 citizens. The turn of the 19th century brought a new economic dawn with the invention of the Jacquard loom. Lyon was occupied by Ger-

Highlights Lyon

Vieux Lyon
The city as it looked in Renaissance times

Musée des Beaux-Arts
Exquisite art treasures from ancient Egypt to gems of Art Nouveau

Colline Fourvière
Roman remains, a magnificent pilgrimage church and a terrific view

L'Arc-en-Ciel
Eat in style at the »pencil« tower with its marvellous view.

Traboules
Hidden Lyon

In der stimmungsvollen Rue du Bœuf

man forces during the Second World War and the crimes of the city's commandant, Klaus Barbie, the »Butcher of Lyon«, still linger in the memory. Dozens of important figures were born in or lived in Lyon, including Rabelais, who was a doctor at the city hospital and published his novels about Gargantua and Pantagruel while resident here. Other notables include André-Marie Ampère, novelist Antoine de St-Exupéry, Joseph-Marie Jacquard who invented the eponymous loom, and the inventors of cinema, Lumière brothers Louis and Auguste.

What to See in Lyon

★ ★
Vieux Lyon

Vieux Lyon is the heart of the city, nestling at the foot of the Colline Fourvière at the bend in the Saône. To be precise the area consists of three separate suburbs, St-Paul in the north, St-Jean in the middle and St-Georges in the south. With its narrow alleys and more than 300 lovingly restored restaurants and buildings from the 15th–17th centuries, it forms one of the best preserved and most comprehensive **Renaissance complexes** in all of Europe. Among its most picturesque streets are Rue du Bœuf, Rue de la Juiverie (centre of the Jewish community in the Middle Ages), Rue St-Jean and Rue des Trois Maries.

Traboules

Among the typical features of old Lyon are the narrow passages where balls of silk where taken to dry and which were often used as escape routes by fleeing citizens. More than 300 of them cover a total length of more than 50km/31mi. There are some nice examples between 1 Rue du Bœuf and 24 Rue St-Jean and in the Croix-Rousse quartier between 9 Place Colbert and 29 Rue I. Colomès. Frequently the entrances are hidden behind courtyard doors. The guided tours offered by the tourist office take in several of these secret passages.

Hôtel de Gadagne

Hôtel de Gadagne (15th century), the largest of the city's Renaissance buildings, houses the Musée Historique de Lyon and the Musée International de la Marionnette (closed Tue). The latter has dolls and puppets from all over the world on view, including **Guignol** puppets, invented by Lyon's Laurent Mourguet at the beginning of the 19th century. Maison du Soleil, in the St-Georges quartier, was formerly a venue for Théâtre Guignol performances.

St-Jean

The construction of the cathedral of St-Jean lasted from 1192 until well into the 15th century, so that it exhibits both Romanesque and

Gothic aspects. Inside there is a magnificent **astronomical clock** made by clockmaker Nicholas Lippius (1598) of Basle. The early Gothic stained glass work is also noteworthy.

Colline Fourvière, the 130m/427ft hill at the centre of town, derives its name from »Forum Vetus« (old forum). Two funicular railways lead up to its summit from Place St-Jean. Crowning the top is the not entirely tasteful, but somehow all the more splendid, basilica of **Notre-Dame-de-la-Fourvière**, built in a Romanesque-Byzantine style in 1896. There is a lovely view from the terrace and from the Tour de l'Observatoire: on clear days it is possible to see as far as Mont Blanc. Next to the basilica stands a 17th-century pilgrimage chapel and the accompanying Musée de Fourvière. About 400m/440yd further south are the remains of the **Roman city**, including the ruins of two theatres (one of which is still used for various events). The outstanding Musée de la Civilisation Gallo-Romaine (17 Rue Cléberg, closed Mon) relates the history of the region up until medieval times.

Colline Fourvière

Musée Gallo-Romain

The narrow spit between the Rhône and the Saône to the north of the confluence of the rivers was not built up until the 19th century. **Place des Terreaux**, the former market place, was built over the former course of the Rhône, which had been filled in with soil (»terre«). The statues of the imposing fountains by Frédéric-Auguste Bartholdi symbolize the Rhône and Saône rivers. The town hall (1646–72) and its 40m/131ft tower were rebuilt in Baroque style after a fire in around 1700 by court architects Jules Hardouin-Mansart and Robert de Cotte. In 1992, the **opera house** from 1831 gained a new glass and black steel dome, which was designed by Jean Nouvel (there is a good restaurant inside it). One nice gimmick is the way in which the density of the crowds in the foyer is indicated on the roof.

Presqu'Ile

▶ VISITING LYON

INFORMATION

Office de Tourisme
Place Bellecour, F-69 000Lyon
Tel. 04 72 77 69 69, fax 04 78 42 04 32
www.lyon-france.com

TRANSPORT

Metro plus TCL tram and bus information bureau: Gare Routière de Perrache.
Car parks are signposted »P Lyon Parc Auto«.
Saint Exupéry Airport 25km/16mi east of town, Satobus to the stations.

LYON CITY CARD

The Lyon City Card provides admission to museums, guided tours, a boat trip down the river and free travel on local public transport.

FESTIVALS AND EVENTS

June–Aug: Nuits de Fourvière (concerts etc. in the amphitheatre).
Around 8 Dec: Fête des Lumières (city illuminations with lanterns, torch-lit procession to Notre-Dame de Fourvière. Times and dates can be found in *Lyon Poche* and *Le Petit Bulletin*.

Lyon's »Bouchons« – »corks« in English – offer hearty food at reasonable prices

WHERE TO EAT

► Expensive

① *Auberge de L'Ile*
Ile Barbe, Place Notre-Dame
Tel. 04 78 83 99 49, closed Sun–Mon and for three weeks at the start of August.
A 16th-century house in an idyllic spot on the Saône island at the northern edge of the city with exquisite, creative and varied French cuisine.

② *Paul Bocuse*
40 Rue de la Plage
Collonges (about 10km/6mi north on the banks of the Saône)
Tel. 04 72 42 90 90
This restaurant, run by the eponymous and world famous chef, is a veritable showpiece. The chef usually allows his subordinates to do the cooking but the dishes are his creations.

► Inexpensive / moderate

③ *Les Adrets*
30 Rue du Bœuf, tel. 04 78 38 24 30, closed Sat–Sun and all of August.
Homely little bistro with roof beams and a terra-cotta floor. Excellent traditional cuisine at very reasonable prices.

④ *Brasserie Georges*
30 Cours de Verdun
Tel. 04 72 56 54 54.
No visit to Lyon should miss this local institution, a gigantic but still cosy dining hall from the 1920s with red-upholstered seats, chandeliers and drapes. Jazz on Saturday evenings.

⑤ *Café des Fédérations*
8 Rue Major Martin
Tel. 04 78 28 26 00, closed Sun.
One of the best bouchons: hearty delicacies such as andouillette in mustard sauce, terrines, pork rump ragout, poulet au vinaigre – a reservation is essential.
Also recommended: La Meunière, 11 Rue Neuve, tel. 04 78 28 62 91; and Chez Mounier, 3 Rue des Marroniers, tel. 04 78 37 79 26.

WHERE TO STAY

► Mid-range

Beaux Arts
75 Rue Prés. E. Herriot
Tel 04 78 38 09 50
www.accorhotels.com
This traditional hotel from around 1900 stands on the main street of the spit. Some of the rooms are decorated in Art Deco style while others are fashioned by modern designers. The hotel has its own restaurant.

► Budget / moderate

Hôtel des Artistes
8 Rue G. André, tel. 04 78 42 04 88
www.hotel-des-artistes.fr
Next door to the Théâtre des Célestins, this hotel exhibits plenty of 19th-century charm but has pleasant modern rooms (try to get one facing the theatre or the square, not the courtyard).

Bayard
23 Place Bellecour, tel. 04 78 37 39 64
www.hotelbavard.fr
Another 19th-century building with individually furnished rooms, featuring brass beds and marble fireplaces. Room 2 has a four-poster bed and a fabulous view of Place Bellecour.

Lyon Map

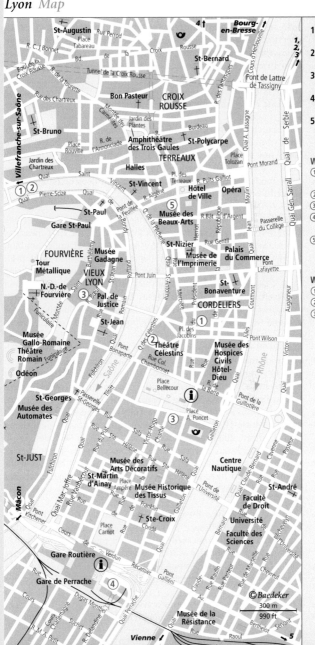

1 Parc de la Tête d'Or
2 Musée d'Art Contemporain
3 Musée d'Histoire Naturelle
4 Maison des Canuts
5 Aéroport St-Exupéry

Where to eat
① Auberge de l'Ile
② Paul Bocuse
③ Les Adrets
④ Brasserie Georges
⑤ Café des Fédérations

Where to stay
① Beaux-Arts
② Artistes
③ Bayard

© Baedeker
300 m
990 ft

★★
Musée des
Beaux-Arts

Palais St-Pierre was built as a Benedictine abbey between 1659 and 1685 and now houses a **museum of art**, the second biggest in France after the Louvre. It contains important works dating from Roman times, through the old masters up till the modern day (open Wed–Mon 10am–6pm). The former cloister is a great place for a picnic.

Fresque des
Lyonnais

To the northwest, on Rue de la Martinière near the Saône, there is a huge and rather amusing mural caricaturing famous Lyonnais figures.

St-Nizier

The church of St-Nizier with its two distinctive towers was formerly Lyon's cathedral. Rebuilt in Gothic style in the 15th century, it also has a fine Renaissance doorway (16th century). Beneath the choir there is a crypt dating back to the 6th century, which also features some modern mosaics. The printing museum depicts the history of printed works as it developed in late 15th-century Lyon.

Musée de
l'Imprimerie

Hôtel-Dieu

Hôtel-Dieu on the Rhône, a former hospital, was built in the 17th–18th centuries. The long main façade facing the river measures 325m/355yd in length. Work upon it started in 1741 under Soufflot, builder of the Pantheon in Paris, but it was not finished until 1842. It now houses the **Musée des Hospices Civils** (history of nursing care). Place Bellecour covers an area of 310 × 200m/340 x 220yd and is graced by an equestrian statue of Louis XIV by Lyonnais artist François-Frédéric Lemot (1800). The façades of the buildings on the east and west sides of the square date from around the same time.

★
Place Bellecour

St-Martin-
d'Ainay

West of Place Ampère stands the church of St-Martin-d'Ainay (11th century), the oldest church in Lyon (four columns dating back to Roman antiquity and some 12th-century mosaics in the choir), built on the site of an old Roman temple. On the opposite side of Place Ampère stand two interesting museums incorporated into an aristocratic town house built in 1739, the (furniture, tapestries, coins etc.) and the Musée Historique des Tissus with its outstanding collection drawn from 2000 years of art in textiles (34 Rue de la Charité). Southward beyond the Rhône, a centre for the history of the Résistance and deported French citizens has been opened in the former **Gestapo headquarters** (closed Mon–Tue), which no visitor to Lyon should miss.

Musée des Arts
Décoratifs

★
Centre d'Histoire
de la Résistance

La Croix-Rousse

On a hill that adjoins Presqu'Ile to the north lies the working class district of La Croix-Rousse. Its houses were built in the 19th century for **canuts** (weavers) resettled from the old town. They would then work in their new homes with the recently invented Jacquard looms. The Maison des Canuts museum (10–12 Rue d'Ivry, closed Sun–Mon) offers a fascinating look at life as it was then

Maison des
Canuts

Parc de la Tête
d'Or

The newer parts of the city stretch away to the east of the Rhône. The Parc de la Tête d'Or with its zoo and botanical gardens, rosarium and lake is situated to the north on the banks of the river. Italian architect Renzo Piano was responsible for the complex beside the Rhône. It includes a congress centre, a multiplex cinema, a museum of contemporary art (with changing exhibitions) and the headquarters of the international police organization Interpol. Adjacent to the south is the **Les Brotteaux** quarter, characterized by its Art Nouveau houses. The modern quartier of La Part-Dieu is marked by the 142m/466ft **»Pencil«** (Le Crayon) building of the Crédit Lyonnais bank (built 1977, with Hotel Radisson SAS at a height of 100m/330ft and restaurants). The area includes the TGV station, a massive shopping centre and the Maurice Ravel Auditorium, a venue for cultural events.

Cité Internationale

Les Brotteaux La Part-Dieu

The town planner **Tony Garnier** (1869–1948) was highly active in Lyon. His housing estate in the 8th arrondissement (Rue des Serpollières) is very interesting, as is the abattoir (7th arrondissement, Place A. Perrin), now used for exhibitions and similar events. Maison du Livre, de l'Image et du Son, is a media centre (Villeurbanne, 247 Cours E.-Zola) designed by Mario Botta (1988). On the southern edge of the town is a new mosque, which opened in 1994 (Ballandras/Mirabaud; open to the general public Sat–Thu 9am–11pm). The latest feature is the new railway station for Lyon-St-Exupéry airport, designed by Santiago Calatrava.

Tips for architecture enthusiasts

Around Lyon

About 25km/16mi northwest of Lyon (D7) at L'Arbresle (5300 inhabitants) there is another piece of modern architecture worth seeing, Le Corbusier's Ste-Marie-de-la-Tourette convent (1959).

L'Arbresle

Another place worth visiting on a day trip is the Musée Automobile Henri Malartre, 10km/6mi north of Lyon. Owned by a scrap dealer with a love of old cars, it offers a collection of more than 150 antique vehicles, 50 motorbikes, bicycles and even trams (closed Mon).

Rochetaillée

✷✷ Marseille

N 9

Région: Provence – Alpes – Côte d'Azur   **Altitude:** 160m/525ft
Département: Bouches-du-Rhône   **Population:** 826,000

Marseille, on the shores of the Mediterranean east of the Rhône estuary, is France's oldest city, second only to Paris in size and certainly its most important trading port. Even its reputation as the »Chicago of the Mediterranean« is no reason to steer clear of the city. Its mixture of pulsating, south European metropolis, Provencal atmosphere and a colourfully eclectic population is unique in France.

The Marseille melting pot Since it was founded, Marseille – capital of the Bouches-du-Rhône département and home to 1.3 million people in its surrounding urban district – has been a multi-cultural city. Its economic well-being has always been dictated by the harbour and docks, which is now the second largest port facility in Europe after Rotterdam. A large pro-

portion of the goods are loaded and unloaded in Fos-sur-Mer and Lavéra at the mouth of the Grand Rhône, both of which opened in 1965. Marseille is also France's third biggest passenger harbour with 1.2 million travellers per annum. The airport in Marignane is also the third biggest in the country after Paris and Nice and handles some 5 million passengers a year. All this is indicative of the economic importance of the region, which is now also switching over to high-tech industries. The traditional industries (shipbuilding, edible oils, petrochemicals and steel) are in now decline, and as a consequence Marseille has the highest unemployment rate in France. The situation is heightened

Notre-Dame-de-la-Garde above the old harbour of Marseille

by the presence of Arab, African and Asian immigrants. More than 50% of residents are either foreign or French citizens of foreign extraction, including some 100,000 Arabs, many living in the Belsunce quarter north of the Canebière.

History The city was founded under the name Massalia by Greeks from Phocaea in Asia Minor in around 600 BC. During the struggles between Caesar and Pompey, it took the side of the latter, leading Ceasar to besiege and conquer the city in 49 BC. After the decline of the Roman Empire, the city lost its importance and fell to the Visigoths, then to the Franks and to the Arelate kingdom. The harbour's importance was massively revitalized during the era of the crusades and, over the course of time, a variety of defensive installations were built. A plague that raged during 1720 and 1721 cost the lives of some 50,000 people from a population of 90,000. Nevertheless the booming and lucrative trade with the colonies that had begun in the 16th century and the industries that had grown up to exploit products such as sugar, coffee, cocoa and spices soon swung Marseille back to rapid growth. In July 1792, 500 revolutionary soldiers marched from Marseille to aid the defence of the capital, Paris, bringing with them their own anthem, the *Marseillaise* (actually composed in Strasbourg). With France's influence increasing in

North Africa after 1830 (Algeria was occupied in 1847) and the opening of the Suez canal in 1869 the city's importance as both harbour and trading centre burgeoned still further. There was some extensive expansion of building after 1848 (e.g. Rue de la République, Notre-Dame-de-la-Garde). During the Second World War, Marseille was heavily bombed, first by the Germans and Italians in 1940 then by the Allies in 1943–44. In 1943 German troops demolished much of the old town with explosives, sparing only some of the more historic buildings. Reconstruction was led by Auguste Perret (1874–1954), the significant »concrete and steel« exponent.

What to See in Marseille

The picturesque **old harbour**, which still occupies practically the same spot as originally settled by the Greeks, is frequented by yachts and fishing boats. As of 1844 the main trading harbour was relocated northward to the Joliette district. The restaurants and cafés in this part of town are rather touristy but usually offer good fare, such as bouillabaisse, indisputably the finest (and dearest) fish soup in the world. There is a fish market every morning on the Quai des Belges. The Hôtel de Ville was built at the northern tip of the harbour in 1663–83 following a Genoese model. There is a fine view from Fort St-Nicolas (12th century, extended *c*1670) at the mouth of the harbour.

★
Vieux Port

Hôtel de Ville

The main artery of the city centre is the Canebière boulevard, which starts from the old harbour. Its whole proud length is lined with shops and businesses, hotels and cafés. Its name comes from »cannabis«, hemp being the raw material that was formerly transformed here into rope. It is the city's only high-class boulevard, and was once compared with the Champs-Elysées in Paris. Nowadays it forms a border between the »Arabic« north (Belsunce) and the wealthier southern parts of town.

La Canebière

Highlights Marseille

Vieux Port
The heart of the city since Roman antiquity
▶ page 533

Vieille Charité
Noble contrast to the working class district
▶ page 538

Musée des Beaux-Arts
Perugino, Rubens, Daumier and much more
▶ page 539

Quartier de l'Arsenal
Going out in the old military district
▶ page 539

Notre-Dame-de-la-Garde
Marseille's major landmark dominates the scenery for miles around
▶ page 540

Grande Étoile
A viewing platform far above the Mediterranean metropolis
▶ page 541

Marseille Map

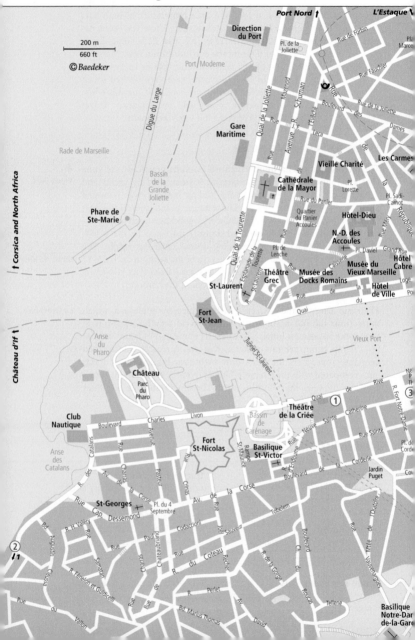

200 m
660 ft
©Baedeker

Port Nord ↑   L'Estaque

Direction du Port
Pl. de la Joliette
Rue de Forbin
Rue Fauchier
Rue de la Joliette

Port Moderne

Gare Maritime

Rade de Marseille

Bassin de la Grande Joliette

↑ Corsica and North Africa

Phare de Ste-Marie

Vieille Charité
Les Carmes
Cathédrale de la Mayor
Pl. Lorette
Pl. Sadi-Carnot
Rue du Panier
Quartier du Panier Accoules
Hôtel-Dieu
N.-D. des Accoules
Pl. Daviel
Hôtel Cabre
Pl. de Lenche
Théâtre Grec
Musée des Docks Romains
Musée du Vieux Marseille
Hôtel de Ville
St-Laurent

Château d'If ↑

Fort St-Jean

Vieux Port

Anse du Pharo
Tunnel St-Laurent

Château Parc du Pharo

Club Nautique
Boulevard Charles Livon
Bassin de Carénage
Théâtre de la Criée
Quai de Rive
Rue Sainte Catherine
Rue Sainte

Anse des Catalans

Fort St-Nicolas
Basilique St-Victor
Rue Neuve Sainte
Pl. de Corde
Corderie
Jardin Puget

St-Georges
Pl. du 4 Septembre
Av. de la Corse
Boulevard de la Corderie

Bd. Marius Thomas

Basilique Notre-Dame de-la-Gard

↑ Aix-en-Provence
Aéroport

† St-Lazare

Jardin
Publique

Musée des
Beaux-Arts
Palais
Longchamp
Musée d'Histoire
Naturelle
Musée
Grobet-
Labadié

Blvd. G. Desplaces
Place V. Hugo
Av. Gén. Leclerc
Rue Honnorat
Camille
Flammarion
Rue d'Isoard
Bernard
Longchamp

Gare St-Charles
ⓘ

Arc de
Triomphe

Blvd. Ch. Nédelec
Blvd. M. Bourdet

Av. P. Sémard

Blvd. Voltaire
Blvd. National
Rue de

Pl. J.
Guesde

Rue d'Aix

Place des
Marseillaises

Liberté

Place A.
Labadié

Rue
Boulevard
de
Consolat
la
Liberation

St-Théodore

Rue des Dominicaines
Rue Convalescents
Nationale
Boul. de la
Rue St-Bazile
Cours J. Thierry

Cours Roosevelt
Rue Monte-Cristo
Rue
du
Camas

BELSUNCE

Cours Belsunce
Capucins
Rue Tapis Vert
Allées L. Gambetta
Blvd. Dugommier
Canebière
Blvd. Garibaldi
La
St-Vincent-
de-Paul
Rue Adolphe Thiers
Rue St-Saumin
Boul. Eugène Pierre

Centre de
la Bourse
St-
Cannat

Jardin
des
Vestiges

Musée
d'Histoire
de Marseille

St-Ferréol

Musée de
la Marine

Bourse
ⓘ Place
Général
de Gaulle

Canebière
Place
Carli
Rue des Trois Mages
Place
J. Jaurès
Rue de Terrusse
St-Michel
Chave
Boulevard
de l'Olivier

Quai des Belges
R. Vacon
Rue de
Rue d'Aubagne
Cours Lieutaud
Cours Julien
Rue
Rue
Ferrari
Rue
St-Pierre
Ferrari

Opéra

Ste-
Trinité
Calvaire

R. Estelle
Rue des
3 Frères Barthélemy
Rue A. Blanqui
Rue Château
Rue Fongate
Rue des Vertus

Rue F. Davso

St-Charles

Palais
de Justice

Pl.
Monthyon

Rue Ferréol
Paradis
Rue Grignan
Rome
R. Dieudé
Pl. F.
Baret
B. Salvator

Pl.
Cézanne

Notre-Dame
du-Mont

Rue
de Tilsit
Rue Paravin
Rue Loubière
Rue d'Alger

Musée
Cantini

Préfecture

Sylvabelle
St-Sacrement

Rue Perrin
Rue
Boulevard
Baille
Cécile
Sainte

ierre
Puget
Rue

N. D. de
Lourdes

St-Joseph
St-Nicolas
Dragon
Rue de
Lieutaud
Rue Melchion
Boulevard
Baille
R. Antoine Maille

Rue du Breteuil
Synagogue ✡
Paradis
Eglise des
Dominicains
Rue Ste-Victoire
Rue Sainte
Rue Suffren
Boulevard Baille
Gouffé
St-Jean
Baptiste
R. R. Brun

Prado Tunnel (toll)
② ↘2
Crs.

Where to eat	Where to stay	
1 Corniche Kennedy	① Les Mets de Provence	① St-Ferréol's	---○--- Métro
2 Cité Radieuse	② Bistro Gambas	② Le Corbusier	
	③ Chez Fonfon		

⏵ VISITING MARSEILLE

INFORMATION

Office du Tourisme
4 La Canebière, F-13001 Marseille
Tel. 04 91 13 89 00, fax 04 91 13 89 20
www.marseille-tourisme.com
Another office in Gare St-Charles.

TRANSPORT

Marignane airport, 28km/17mi
northwest of the city, is linked via bus
from Gare St-Charles. Metro, trams
and buses are run by the RTM
(Espace information: 6 Rue de Fa-
bres). Ferries also ply across the old
harbour between the Hotel de Ville
and Place aux Huiles and there are
also services further afield to Corsica,
Sardinia and North Africa, which
leave from Gare Maritime. Other
ferries go to Château d'If, the Calanques and Cassis from the Quai des
Belges.

CITY PASS

A City Pass entitles the holder to
admission to 14 museums plus guided
tours, the boat trip to Château d'If,
the use of all public transport facilities
and also shopping discounts.

FESTIVALS AND EVENTS

2 Feb: Pélérinage de la Chandeleur in
St-Victor. March: carnival. End of
June to mid-July: Festival de Marseille
(music, dance, cinema and theatre).
15 Aug: Fête de l'Assomption in the
Cathedrale de la Major. December:
Foire aux Santons (a market for clay
nativity statues). Events are listed in
L'Hebdo, Sortir, Vox Mag and *L'Officiel
des Loisirs* as well as at www.marseil-
lebynight.com.

MARKETS

Quai des Belges, daily fish market.
Cours Julien, Mon–Sat: vegetables,
Wed also other foods. Chemin de la
Madrague Ville, Sat–Sun: flea market,
antiques. Avenue du Prado, Mon–Sat:
huge colourful market.

SAFETY AND SECURITY

Even though safety in Marseille has
improved, it is advisable to carry as
few valuables as possible and not to
leave anything behind in the car. The
Belsunce quartier between Cours
Belsunce, Canebière and the station
should be avoided at night.

WHERE TO EAT

▶ Moderate / expensive

① *Les Mets de Provence*
18 Quai de Rive-Neuve
Tel. 04 91 33 35 38, closed Sun and
three weeks in Aug. An institution
since 1937, with a cosy Provencal
atmosphere on the first floor of the
»Maurice Brun« building. The menu
is only offered verbally. (Those with
an eye on the purse strings should try
the nearby Bar de la Marine.)

② *Chez Fonfon*
140 Rue Vallon des Auffes
Tel. 04 91 52 14 38, closed Sun.
One of the best places to get authentic
bouillabaisse – though it can cost up
to €50 – and other seafood delicacies,
on a small bay under the Kennedy
Corniche. The rather expensive
L'Epuisette on Vallon des Auffes is
excellent too.

▶ Inexpensive / moderate

③ *Bistro Gambas*
29 Place aux Huiles
Tel. 04 91 33 26 44
A classic establishment for shellfish in
every variation, with a large selection
of (white) wine. Pleasant atmosphere.

WHERE TO STAY

► Mid-range

① *Saint Ferréol's*
19 Rue Pisançon, tel. 04 91 33 12 21
www.hotel-stferreol.com
A very pretty and comfortable hotel in a pedestrianized zone just a stone's throw from the Vieux Port and La Canebière. No restaurant.

► Budget / mid-range

② *Hôtel Le Corbusier*
280 Blvd. Michelet
Tel. 04 91 16 78 00
www.hotellecorbusier.com
One of the most unusual places to stay in all of France, in the Unite d'Habitation designed by Le Corbusier (21 bus from Vieux Port). Plain but nice rooms and a fantastic view, whether inland or out to sea (the latter is more costly). Guests have access to all facilities of the »city in one building« (pool on the roof, café, shops etc.).

Bourse

The bourse or stock exchange is just a stone's throw from the harbour. Its imposing structure, built in 1854, now houses the **Musée de la Marine**, a naval museum, which also possesses the art collection of Marseille's chamber of commerce. Next door on La Canebière is **Musée de la Mode** Espace Mode Méditeranée, where the Musée de la Mode Haute exhibits fashions dating back to the 1930s. In the basement of the massive Centre de la Bourse shopping centre the Musée d'Histoire de ★ **Musée d'Histoire de Marseille** Marseille (closed Sun) has an exhibition of archaeological finds dating from prehistory until the Middle Ages, which includes a whole **Roman ship** from the 3rd century. In the »Jardin des Vestiges« there are some remnants of a Greek fort (2nd–3rd century BC).

Old town

The hill to the north of the old harbour has been settled since the time of the ancient Greeks. The old town, **Le Panier**, with its steep and winding streets, stretches over its slopes. Redevelopment work has been underway since the end of the last war, and after years as a North African slum the quarter has now blossomed into an appealing area for going out with numerous attractive shops.

Musée du Vieux Marseille

Behind the Hôtel de Ville (1653) stands Maison Diamantée (1570), named after the styling of its façade, which houses the Musée du Vieux Marseille (history of the city, Provencal furniture and dress). Further west there is another museum, the Musée des Docks Romains, built over an excavation of Roman dock facilities and warehouses, which is also well worth seeing. The lively Place de Lenche **Place de Lenche** marks the site of the **Greek agora**. There is a fine view across the harbour. A little further south it is possible to see some remains of a Greek theatre.

Fort St-Jean

In Fort St-Jean, built under Louis XIV, the **Musée des Civilisations de l'Europe et de la Méditerranée** (MuCEM) should open in 2010. The Romanesque church of St-Laurent (with 15th–16th century **St-Laurent** chapels and an octagonal tower from the 18th century) is nearby. There is a lovely view of the city from its terrace.

Port Moderne

To the north of Fort St-Jean is the area where the new harbour was built as of 1844. It covers an area of more than 200ha/500 acres, and has some 25km/16mi of quays. Most of the passenger ships, which ply to destinations that include Corsica and North Africa, dock at the Bassin de la Grande Joliette. At present the whole docklands area is undergoing major rebuilding work: office complexes for large companies are being created as are shopping arcades for cruise ship and ferry passengers.

Cathédrale de la Major

✳

Ancienne Cathédrale de la Major

The gigantic neo-Byzantinie Cathédrale de la Major (1852–93) towers up beyond the modern docks: At 141m/154yd in length, it is the largest church building of the 19th century (cf. Cologne Cathedral at 135.6m/148yd). There is some rich furnishing with plenty of marble and mosaics. The older cathedral nestles in the new church's shadow to the east. It lost its earlier five bays when the present four were being built. The choir and transept (11th century) are fine examples of Provencal Romanesque. Inside there is a terra-cotta relief (1073) by Luca dell Robbia as well as a Romanesque reliquary from 1122.

✳

Vieille Charité

✳

Museums ►

Vieille Charité is a hospital for the poor built in 1671–79 by the important Marseille architect and sculptor Pierre Puget (1620–94). It includes one of the **most impressive Baroque churches in Provence** – totally in contrast to its surroundings. It now houses a cultural centre and various museums (closed Mon): the Musée d'Archéologie Méditerranéenne (with an Egyptian collection and finds from Etruscan, Greek, Celtic and Roman excavations); the Musée d'Art Africain, Océanien, Amérindien. The café L'Art et les Thés in Vieille Charité is a nice spot to take a break.

Hôtel-Dieu

Vieux Palais de Justice

Hôtel de Cabre

The imposing Hôtel-Dieu (hospital) was built by Portal and Hardouin-Mansart (late 18th century). As an institution it can claim to have been founded as long ago as the 12th century. In the courtyard there is a memorial to the Marseille artist and lithographer Honoré Daumier by Emile Antoine Bourdelle. One other building on the same square, Place Daviel, is the beautiful old Palais de Justice (1747). Its **wrought iron balcony rails** (»à la marguerite«) are typical for Marseille. To the south the Chapelle du Calvaire (19th century) sits beneath the Clocher des Accoules, a remnant of an 11th-century church. A little further east on Grand'Rue the late Gothic Hôtel de Cabre from 1535 can be seen. It was spared demolition in 1943 but in 1954 was rotated through 90°.

Palais Longchamp

Boulevard Longchamp leads up to the Longchamp Palais, built from 1862 to 1869 as a commemorative monument and water tower at the end of a canal conveying water to Marseille from the Durance,

Place aux Huiles in the Quartier de l'Arsenal

which had been finished in 1849. To the left of the pillared edifice is
an **art museum** with paintings from the 16th and 17th centuries (Perugino, Rubens) and works by French painters of the 18th and 19th
centuries (including Courbet, Corot, Millet, Ingres) along with some
by Pierre Puget and Honoré Daumier, who were both born in Marseille. To the right is the Musée d'Histoire Naturelle (natural history
of the Provence/Côte d'Azur region, also featuring an aquarium exhibiting Mediterranean fauna). The Musée Grobet-Labadié occupies
a large town house from 1873 and has musical instruments, medieval
sculptures, lovely tapestries, faience lace and furniture from the 18th
century on display.

★
**Musée des
Beaux-Arts**

**Musée Grobet-
Labadié**

A building built in the 17th century for the Compagnie du Cap
Nègre (southeast of the harbour, 19 Rue Grignan, closed Mon) now
houses the Musée Cantini, which concentrates on some of the 20th
century's most important artists, from the Fauves to abstract works
by Matisse, Dufy, Kandinsky, Picasso and others.

★
Musée Cantini

The **classical warehouses** around Place Thiars south of the old harbour were built in about 1780. Nowadays they have become a popular meeting place with plenty of fine restaurants, bars and cafés. Two
of the buildings that comprised the naval arsenals, built over a period
spanning 1488 to 1749, have managed to survive (Cours d'Estienne-
d'Orves 23 and 25). Close by to the east is the Art Deco opera
house. The Criée des Poissons is a **fish auction hall** built in 1909,
which has been the home of the Théâtre National de Marseille since
1981.

**Quartier de
l'Arsenal**

La Criée

St-Victor's basilica was part of a monastery founded in AD 416 by St
Cassius, one of Europe's first monasteries. The current castle-like
building with walls up to 3m/10ft thick was built in 1040, although it
underwent several alterations lasting into the 15th century. The crypt
of the earliest church and the **catacombs**, including some sarcophagi
going back to Roman times, are highly impressive. On 2 February
the landing of the three Marys of the sea is celebrated (see ► Camargue, Stes-Maries-de-la-Mer). The speciality of Marseille's oldest
baker, »Four des Navettes« (east of the church), also refers back to
that event.

St-Victor

Parc du Pharo Parc du Pharo on the hill south of the harbour entrance is a popular place for a walk or a picnic. The big chateau was built by Napoleon III for his wife Eugénie. The park offers a great view of the harbour and the town.

Notre-Dame-de-la-Garde Atop a rocky outcrop at an elevation of 154m/440ft, the Basilique Notre-Dame-de-la-Garde gazes out across the city from the site of a former pilgrimage chapel. It was built in 1853–64 in Byzantine style. Its 60m/200ft tower is topped by a gilded Madonna from the studio of Christofle, which itself measures nearly 10m/33ft in height. Inside the church, which is frequented by pilgrims all year round and not only during its feast day of 15 August, there are many decorative votive offerings. There is a **magnificent view** from here and on 10 February and 28 October it should be possible see the summit of Pic du Canigou (►p.720) in the eastern Pyrenees some 250km/150mi away, directly in front of the setting sun.

Hôtel du Département About 700m/750yd east of Palais Longchamp (Metro 1, St-Just) stand the administrative buildings for the département. Its three blue wings (»Vaisseau Bleu«) are an outstanding example of modern architecture (Alsop and Störmer, 1994).

Suburbs of Marseille

✷ Corniche J. F. Kennedy

Parc Borély

The Corniche Kennedy runs southwards along the coast from Parc du Pharo. On the way it passes the picturesque port of Vallon des Auffes as well as many beaches, restaurants and holiday homes. After 5km/3mi it arrives at Plage du Prado, signalled by a vast copy of Michelangelo's *David*, erected in 1903. Beyond it, the lovely Parc Borély surrounds a chateau of the same name dating from the 18th century. Another 8km/5mi from here lies Cap Croisette.

✷ Unité d'Habitation

About 1.3km/1400yd south of Rond Point du Prado there is another icon of modern architecture, **Le Corbusier's** Unité d'Habitation (Cité Radieuse) built in 1947–1952. It is 165m/180yd long, 57m/187ft high and its 18 floors contain 337 apartments and a hotel ►p.537.

Around Marseille

Château d'If The rocky island in the middle of the Bay of Marseille was made famous by **Alexandre Dumas'** (Père) novel *The Count of Monte Cristo* (1845). For a while the fortress, dating from 1524, was used as a prison. From the summit of the rocks there is a wonderful view. Ferries ply there from the old harbour (Quai des Belges).

Chaîne de l'Estaque L'Estaque, on the northwestern edge of Marseille, is famed as the subject of a painting by Cézanne. In spite of the many changes it has undergone since then, it is still a popular place for a day trip. The

Chaîne de l'Estaque, a picturesque limestone massif, stretches away to the east past a whole series of pretty seaside resorts from Niolon as far as Cap Couronne. Martigues (44,000 inhabitants) is situated on the canal leading to **Etang de Berre**, which has been transformed from a little fishing harbour to an industrial town and port (with several oil refineries). Ile Brescon, with the Pont St-Sebastien and the 17th-century church of Ste-Madeleine, is very pretty. Musée Ziem exhibits works by landscape painter Félix Ziem (1821–1911) as well as some items of local history. Swimming, surfing etc. are to be avoided around Etang de Berre, since the lagoons are badly polluted with industrial effluent.

Martigues

Northeast of Marseille **Château Gombert** (the suburb bears the same name) houses the Musée des Arts et Traditions Populaires. The Technopole underneath it is an important scientific centre. Grande Étoile (651m/2136ft), highest peak in the Chaîne de l'Étoile, can be reached in two and a half hours from Grotte Loubière, 2km/1mi west of Château Gombert (there is a fabulous view from the top).

Château Gombert
★
Grande Étoile

Southeast of Marseille, the Calanques form narrow bays cut deep into the white chalk cliffs. Some of them can be accessed on foot or by boat from Cassis. With the exception of the paths that lead directly to Calanques de Sormiou, Morgiou and En Vau, access is forbidden between 1 July and 15 Sept due to the risk of fire.

★ ★
Calanques

The fishing town of Cassis (22km/14mi southeast) overflows with people in the summer. Along with its castle (14th century, not open to the public), it is beautifully located in a bay surrounded by spectacular rocky cliffs. White wine from Cassis is renowned and goes beautifully with the seafood that is landed here. There is a big wine festival on the first Sunday in September. Ferry boats also ply from here to the Calanques. The narrow and winding **Corniche des Crêtes** runs from Cassis along the Falaises, the highest cliffs in France, as far as Cap Canaille (416m/1365ft). There is a breathtaking view of the coast from the Calanques as far as Cap Croisette. Crossing the summit at Grande Tête (399m/1309ft) it is then another 19km/12mi down the hill to La Ciotat.

Cassis

The port of La Ciotat (32,000 inhabitants) has a pretty town centre with houses from the 17th–18th centuries, the heyday of shipbuilding. The once important wharf was closed in 1986. Alongside the old harbour are the church of Notre-Dame-de-l'Assomption (17th century) and the local museum, in the former town hall (1864). On Blvd. Clemenceau the **oldest remaining cinema in the world**, the Eden Théâtre (1889), was once visited by the Lumière brothers, who showed some of their films here in 1895. To the south the jagged peaks of the Bec de l'Aigle (155m/509ft) overlook the town, while the beach of Clos-les-Plages stretches away to the north.

La Ciotat

Flower market in front of the cathedral in Metz

Metz

Région: Lorraine **Altitude:** 173m/568ft
Département: Moselle **Population:** 127,000

**Metz, the historic capital of ▶Lorraine, is virtually a gigantic muse-
um in itself, with its rich legacy of old churches, palaces and town
houses. Its atmosphere is charming, a mixture of provincial France
and Italian flair.**

History Metz, capital of the Moselle département, is situated at the foot of
the hills that flank the rivers at the confluence of the Moselle and the
Seille. The city has twenty bridges. It has been a university town
since 1971 as well as being the headquarters of the European Centre
for Environmental Protection. It has been an important trading
centre since time immemorial. Due to its location, Metz was made
capital of eastern Gaul back in Roman times, when it was known as
Divodurum. As of the 6th century it came to be called Mettis and
was the residence of the Merovingian and Carolingian kings (Charlemagne had his own wife Hildegard buried here) before becoming a
bishopric and a free town of the Holy Roman Empire. In 1552 the
three dioceses of Metz, Toul and Verdun were ceded by the German
electors to the French king Henri II. Metz was absorbed back into
Germany in the period between 1870 and 1918 and again, briefly,
during the Second World War.

What to See in Metz

★ ★
St-Etienne The monumental cathedral of St-Etienne was built over a period
starting in about 1220 until 1522 and came to assimilate an older
church. The 90m/295ft Tour de Mutte contains an 11 ton bell cast in

1605. The church is entered via the 13th-century Portal of the Virgin. Some of the original sculptures have survived to this day. The interior is breathtaking, with its high ceiling rising to 42m/138ft (although the church is only 13.5m/44ft wide) and the magnificent **stained glass windows** (covering 6500 sq m/7800 sq yd). The oldest of them date back to the 13th century, but modern times are also represented with works by Villon, Bissière and Chagall. The swallow's nest organ can be traced back to 1537, while the episcopal throne made of so-called Cipollino marble to the left in the choir goes back to Merovingian times. The crypt and the church treasury are also worth seeing.

Place d'Armes

The lovely Place d'Armes next to the cathedral came into being along with the town hall in the 18th century on the site of an old cloister. The architect was Jacques-Francois Blondel of Paris. The palace in front of St-Etienne was erected for one of the bishops but was never finished. Since 1831 it has served as a market hall.

★ **Musées de la Cour d'Or**

A 17th-century Carmelite monastery and a corn hall dating back to 1457 now house museums exhibiting archaeological finds from the Gallo-Roman era and the Merovingian period. In addition, there are religious artworks from the Middle Ages, as well as German, Flemish and French paintings by Delacroix and Van Dyck (closed Tue). To the east of the museum (Rue des Trinitaires), Hôtel Livier (12th cen-

Hôtel Livier

Metz *Map*

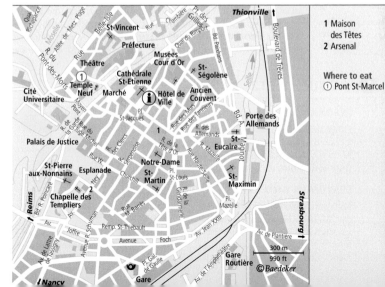

1 Maison des Têtes
2 Arsenal

Where to eat
① Pont St-Marcel

tury) was the most important stronghold of the rich and acquisitive patricians of Metz, who were known as »Paraiges«.

Moyen Pont
From Moyen Pont there is a wonderful view of one arm of the Moselle and of the Protestant church **Temple Neuf** (1904). Beyond it on Place de la Comédie stands a theatre, the oldest still in use in France, and the préfecture building (both from around 1739).

✳ Esplanade
Further south, the Esplanade leads along the banks of the Moselle. It is a belt of parkland between the old town and the former citadel. The Palais de Justice (1776) is situated on the northern side of it.

✳ St-Pierre-aux-Nonnains
The now deconsecrated church of St-Pierre-aux-Nonnains in the south may contain remnants of the oldest church in France. The foundations go back to about AD 390. In the 7th century it was part of a Benedictine abbey while the 16th century saw it integrated into the city's defences (cultural events are also held here). The arsenal from 1863 was transformed into a modern **cultural centre** (and concert venue) by Ricardo Bofill. The neighbouring Knights Templars' chapel, a centrally constructed octagonal building, dates from the 12th century.

Arsenal

Knights Templars' chapel

St-Martin
Beyond St-Martin (1202), with its old windows (15th, 16th, 19th centuries), a moving epitaph with an image of Mary in labour (15th century) and a Baroque organ (1771), the route leads to Place St-Louis. With its arcade houses from the 14th–16th centuries, it is one of the last remaining examples of how the town must have looked in the Middle Ages.

✳ Place St-Louis

✳ Maison des Têtes

Porte des Allemands
East of the Hôtel de Ville on En Fournirue, do not miss the Renaissance Maison des Têtes (no. 51). Rue des Allemands continues towards the **Porte des Allemands** (German gate), a mighty defensive installation that leans out over the Seille. Southward beyond the

▶ VISITING METZ

INFORMATION
Office de Tourisme
2 Place d'Armes, F-57000 Metz Tel. 03 87 55 53 76, fax 03 87 36 59 43
www.mairie-metz.fr

FESTIVALS AND EVENTS
May: spring festival. July/Aug every day: Metz en Fête (jazz, classical museum and street theatre; Fri–Sun fountains with musical accompaniment). End of Aug: Mirabelle Festival. Dec: Christmas market. Events are listed in *Carnet de Rendez-Vous* (in tourist office).

WHERE TO EAT
▶ **Inexpensive / moderate**
① *Pont St-Marcel*
1 Rue du Pont St-Marcel
Tel. 03 87 30 12 29
Diners in this very colourfully designed restaurant are served hearty Lorraine cuisine by smartly dressed staff.

Porte des Allemands, the church of St-Maximin (11th–12th centuries) is also worth a look. Its stained glass windows were designed by Jean Cocteau (1962–70). **St-Maximin**

Quartier ImpérialAround 1900 under **Kaiser Wilhelm**, a quarter dating back to the Middle Ages was cleared to make place for a **new town**. Emblems of the new era included the huge central station, the water tower and the main post office. Today the Quartier Impérial, long unpopular, has found its place and is even being considered as a UNESCO World Heritage Site. To the south beyond the station a new cultural quarter is being created. Alongside the Arènes hall (2001), used for sporting and other events, the spectacular **Centre Pompidou Metz**, a subsidiary of the famous institution in Paris, is due to open its doors in 2009 (www.centrepompidou-metz.fr).

✳ **Monaco**

P 9

Area: 1.95 sq km/0.75 sq mi
Altitude: 0–65m/0–213ft

Citizens: 6100
Population: 32,000

The principality of Monaco, on the ► Côte d'Azur near the border between France and Italy, is the second smallest state in Europe. It has a reputation as a chic oasis for tax refugees but it has seldom been out of the tabloids since the actress Grace Kelly became its princess.

Prince Albert II followed his father Rainier III as the sovereign of the Principauté de Monaco in 2005. His dominion covers just 1.95 sq km/0.75 sq mi of land, making it smaller than any other European state other than the Vatican. Monaco's population is 19% native Monegasque (speaking Monegasco, a Provencal-Ligurian dialect), along with French citizens (32% approx.), Italians (20% approx.) and other foreigners. **State and populace**

National flag

Archaeological finds in Monaco-Ville itself point to the cliffs having been settled since the Stone Age. Greeks from Massalia (Marseille) set up a trading station here called Herakleia Monoikos, which was later taken over by the Romans. After periods when it was controlled by the Lombards and the Saracens, Monaco was granted to Genoa in the 8th century. In 1215 it was furnished with a fortress, remains of which still exist, but in 1297 it was claimed by the baron Francesco Grimaldi, who had been driven out of Genoa and who took the town by disguising himself and his men as monks. In 1308 another of the Grimaldis purchased deeds granting the entire town to his family. After a period of Spanish sovereignty from 1524 to 1641 (during which the title of prince was granted to the rulers in 1612), Monaco **History**

No false modesty among the yachts in Monte Carlo harbour

was inherited by a French line of the family, Goyon de Matignon-Grimaldi, and in 1731 and 1793 it was absorbed into France. However, in 1814 the domain was granted back to the Grimaldi »prince« Honoré IV. As of 1815 it was maintained under the protection of the kingdom of Piedmont-Sardinia, but this role was passed on to France in 1860. Prince Charles III, who had been against the treaty, ceded Menton and Roquebrune to France in 1861 in exchange for the granting of independence to the state. The country's first casino was opened in 1856, but it was only with the establishment of the Société des Bains de Mer (S.B.M.) in 1861 and the building of the Grand Casino that the principality started its rise to become the meeting place of the rich and famous. Albert I decreed a constitution in 1911. Rainier III of the Polignac line (1923–2005) ascended the throne in 1949 and caused a stir in 1956 when he married the American film actress Grace Kelly (Princess Gracia Patricia, †1982). Today, the principality is governed by his son Albert II. Monaco has been a member of the United Nations since 1993. During the 1980s, new suburbs were built on land reclaimed from the sea, increasing the land area to nearly 2 sq km/0.75 sq mi.

Administration Since the constitution of 1962, the state has been set up as a constitutional hereditary monarchy. Power lies officially with the prince himself but is delegated to a state minister. The government is formed by the state minister (Ministre d'Etat) and a ruling senate (Conseil de Gouvernement) which has three members, responsible for home affairs, finance and the economy, and social and public works. The elected body consists of a national parliament (Conseil National) voted on a five-yearly cycle and a communal council (Conseil Communal), which is elected every four years. Both internal government and foreign policy are closely tied to France. Unions of currency and customs institutions were passed in 1865 and 1925 and tax law has been unified since 1963. Since 1885 the principality has issued its own stamps and it produces its own euro coins.

Economy Monaco gained wealth and fame thanks to gambling. Nowadays the casinos contribute only 4% of the state income; over half of the amount is collected as a result of the high rate of VAT (25–40%). On the other hand, there is no income tax, no capital gains tax and no inheritance tax. 10% of the working population of 41,000 (of which 30,000 are commuters) are employed in industry (electronics, electrical engineering, chemicals, pharmaceuticals, etc.). Another 11% work in the hotel trade. The most lucrative branch of the economy, though, is banking, employing 7% of the workforce but contributing 18% of gross national product. Monaco is also an important venue for conferences and festivals.

What to See in Monaco

The oldest part of the town is Monaco Ville, its narrow streets capping a narrow peninsula that rises to 60m/200ft above sea level. The **royal palace** is in the west. The oldest parts of the building go back to around 1215. Guided tours (April–Oct) offer access to rooms of elaborate magnificence, including the Renaissance throne room, the York bedroom (18th century) and the Italian Gallery with frescoes by 16th-century Genoese painters. The Musée des Souvenirs Napoléoniens et Collection des Archives Historiques covers the history of the principality and the era of Napoleon I (closed Nov). At 11.55am each day, the spectacle of the **changing of the guard** takes place outside the palace. The cathedral was built in 1875–84 in Romano-Byzantine style and is where Monaco's princes and bishops are interred, including **Princess Grace**, whose grave has become something of a target for pilgrims. The great organ from 1976 can be heard in various concerts. Next door to the cathedral is the Palais de Justice, built in 1930.

Monaco-Ville
✳
◄ Palais du Prince

✔	DON'T MISS

- The cathedral possesses an outstanding polyptych of St Nicholas by Ludovico Brea (◁1500) as well as other works of art that emerged from the Nice school. From September to June the boys choir can be heard singing at the 10am Mass every Sunday.

✳
Cathedral

To the east of the Jardins St-Martin is the renowned **sea-life museum** (open daily), which was founded as early as 1910. The façade facing the sea sits atop a massive building underneath. It contains valuable scientific collections including some specimens from the submarine expeditions of Prince Albert I and diving equipment used by Jacques Cousteau. Its aquaria feature more than 4000 species and there is also a laboratory with its own library, plus model ships and technical equipment. There is a fantastic view from the roof terrace (and café). A car park adjoins the museum to the east and its roof provides the venue for an audio-visual presentation, the »Monte Carlo Story«. Next door there is an open-air cinema, which claims to have the largest screen in Europe and shows films in their original language (with French subtitles on occasion).

✳ ✳
Musée Océanographique

Monte Carlo Story

On the back way up to the palace, try to visit the Chapelle de la Visitation with its fascinating Piasecka Johnson collection (ecclesiastical art), the Historial des Princes (cabinet of wax effigies) and the Chapelle de la Miséricorde (1639), which has one wooden statue of Christ carved by François Joseph Bosio, dubbed »Napoleon's sculptor«, who was born in Monaco in 1769.

Chapelle de la Visitation

Monaco Map

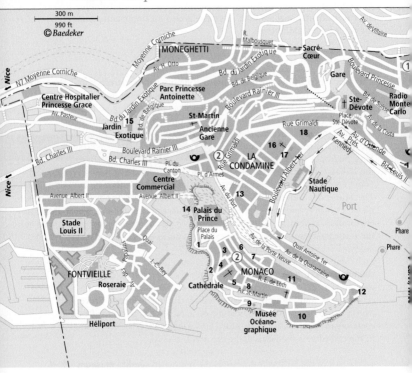

Jardin Animalier

Alongside the palace and away to the west is the suburb of Fontvieille, the creation of which involved reclaiming some 30ha/160 acres of land. The city zoo, the Jardin Animalier, is situated on the steep slope leading down from the old town and has a variety of tropical fauna. The **Complexe Commercial** houses the car museum, which includes more than 100 fabulous old vehicles, as well as a museum of stamps and coins and a naval museum (featuring model ships).

Marina

The marina was built up between 1901 and 1926 and is crowded with luxury yachts. A new pier measuring 352m/385yd in length was opened in 2003. The entire length of it was constructed in Spain and shipped to Monaco by sea. It weighs some 163,000 tons. Beyond the harbour is the suburb of **La Condamine**, which in places has the air of an independent small town with its shops and cafés, the market hall (1880) on the lively Place d'Armes and the old railway station (behind which is an entrance to the modern station, situated under-

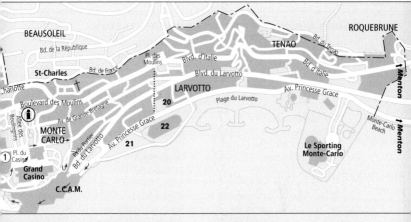

Promenade Ste-Barbe
Conseil National
Musée du
Vieux Monaco
Palais de Justice
Évêché
Historial des
Princes de Monaco
Chapelle de la Misericorde
Mairie
Prince Albert 1er

10 Parking des Pêcheurs/
   Monte Carlo Story
11 Ministère d'Etat
12 Fort Antoine (Théâtre)
13 Marché
14 Jardin Animalier
15 Musée
   d'Anthropologie
   Préhistorique
16 Église Réformée
17 Bibliothèque Louis Notari

18 Automobile Club
   de Monaco
19 Centre de Rencontres
   Internationales
20 Musée National
   de Monaco
   (Automates et
   Poupées d'Autrefois)
21 Jardin Japonais
22 Grimaldi Forum

Where to eat
① Polpetta
② U Cavagnetu
Where to stay
① Hotel de Paris
② Helvetia
·········· State border
·········· Lift
→ · → · → Course
   of the Monaco
   Grand Prix

Ste-Dévote

ground in its own tunnel and opened in 1999). The little church of Ste-Dévote (1870) with its beautiful marble altar (18th century) is situated in a valley entrance at the northeast corner of the marina. There is another entrance to the railway station on Place Ste-Devote.

Moneghetti

★
Jardin Exotique

The eastern slopes of the Tête de Chien are ascended via innumerable stairways and sharply winding roads that lead up to the **Moyenne Corniche** (N 7, ►p.384) and run through the terrace-like district of Moneghetti, characterized by its villas and gardens. Tropical plants are grown in the Jardin Exotique, while the Grotte de l'Observatoire has some gorgeous stalactites and stalagmites. The park also includes the Musée d'Anthropologie Préhistorique, which exhibits some of the prehistoric finds excavated in the region.

Monte Carlo

The suburb of Monte Carlo itself stretches away to the north of the harbour. Higher up, the slope is criss-crossed with shopping streets: Blvd. Princesse-Charlotte, Avenue de la Costa with its countless

▶ VISITING MONACO

INFORMATION

Monaco Tourist Authority
7 Upper Grosvenor Street, London
W1K 2LX
Tel. (020) 7491 4264

Direction du Tourisme
2 a Blvd. des Moulins
MC-98 000 Monaco
Tel. (00 377) 92 166 166
www.visitmonaco.com

FESTIVALS AND EVENTS

End of Jan: Monte Carlo rally. 27 Jan:
Feast of Ste-Dévote, the city's patron
saint. 23–24 June: Feast of St-John
with folk events and a big firework
display. Around 20 May: Formula 1
Grand Prix (tickets available from the
Automobile Club de Monaco, 23
Blvd. Albert 1er, fax 92 258 008,
www.acm.mc). 19 Nov: national holiday. All year round there are plenty
of cultural, sporting and other events,
including a circus festival (Jan) and
the Masters tennis tournament
(April). Events are listed in the free
paper *Bienvenue*.

CASINOS

Casino Garnier, Le Sporting, Café de
Paris, Sun Casino, minimum age 18,
www.casino-monte-carlo.com

WHERE TO STAY

▶ Luxury

① *Hôtel de Paris*
Place du Casino, tel. 92 16 30 00
www.montecarloresort.com
Luxurious accommodation with the
spirit of the belle époque in the most
exclusive hotel in Monaco. Two
gourmet restaurants.

▶ Budget

② *Helvetia*
1 Rue Grimaldi, tel. 93 30 21 71
Affordable hotel in attractive and
lively surroundings near the Place
d'Armes. The comparable Hôtel de
France nearby (6 Rue de la Turbie) is
quite nice as well.

WHERE TO EAT

▶ Expensive

① *Louis XV*
Part of the Hotel du Paris
Tel. 98 06 88 64
Mediterranean cuisine, prepared
under the aegis of Alain Ducasse, one
of the country's most celebrated chefs.

▶ Inexpensive

② *U Cavagnetu*
14 Rue Comté-F.-Gastaldi
Tel. 93 30 35 80. One of the few
affordable places to eat, this restaurant
serves good Monegassian food.

★ ★
Casino

luxury stores and its continuation, Boulevard des Moulins (where
the tourist office is located). The »heart« of Monaco is situated on a
terrace to the north of the harbour. The **Grand Casino** was built in
1877–79 by the architect of the opera house in Paris, Charles Garnier, and houses the legendary tables of the Société Anonyme des
Bains de Mer. The east wing is occupied by Salle Garnier, the opera
hall ostentatiously decorated in red and gold. The famed **Hotel de
Paris**, opened in 1864 (including one 3-star restaurant and the Pan-

orama restaurant as well), makes up a fabulous complex of belle-époque buildings along with the casino and Café de Paris opposite, where the terrace is among the most popular viewing points in town. Below the casino, the **C.C.A.M. congress centre** (1978), a huge building with a hexagonal floor plan, has Blvd. Louis II running right underneath it (forming the »tunnel« section of the legendary Grand Prix circuit). It contains the Rainier III auditorium, the Monte Carlo Grand Hotel and the Sun Casino. The roof is adorned by a Victor Vasarely mosaic (1979) using coloured tiles. There is a **Japanese garden** on Av. Princesse-Grace, which was designed by Yasuo Beppu and makes for a peaceful oasis amid the Monte-Carlo bustle. Neighbouring

The casino, still the hub of Monte Carlo life

it to the east are the **Grimaldi Forum**, another conference centre (Notari and Genin, 2000), and the man-made gravel beaches. In one villa built by Charles Garnier there is a museum of puppets and automatons with over 100 puppets, more than 80 automatons and in excess of 2000 miniature items from the 18th and 19th centuries. The rose garden features sculptures by Zadkine, Maillol, Rodin and Bourdeille.

Montpellier

L 9

Région: Languedoc-Roussillon
Département: Hérault

Altitude: 119m/390ft
Population: 244,000

Montpellier, metropolis of the ▶Languedoc-Roussillon region, has been developing truly dynamically since the immigration of French Algerians in the 1960s, with whole suburbs having been built and new industries attracted. That is not to say that the old Montpellier and its lively old town have been lost. The city is home to more than 60,000 students and boasts a first-rate cultural scene.

The city came into being after the destruction of Maguelone (▶ p.445) by Charles Martel (737). In 1204 it fell into the hands of Aragón by marriage before passing to the kings of Majorca. It was purchased by the French crown in 1349. The university, established

History

Place de la Comédie, the lively hub of the city

in 1289, boasted Petrarca and Rabelais among its students. The medical faculty is the oldest in Europe and still enjoys a superb reputation to this day. When Provence came over to the French monarchy in 1481, Montpellier lost its importance as a trading port in favour of Marseille. At the end of the 16th century it was the main bastion of the Hugenots, who were defeated by Louis XIII in 1622.

What to See in Montpellier

Antigone Approaching the city from the autoroute in the east, the road passes through the suburb of Antigone, its 2200 homes having been designed by **Ricardo Bofill** using copious quantities of ochre-coloured concrete. Work began in 1980 and it is considered a prime example of postmodern architecture. The two shopping centres, Polygone and Triangle, lead to the Place de la Comédie, the centrepiece of the

Place de la Comédie city with its cafés and its fountain, the Fontaine des Trois Grâces built in 1776. The Opéra Comédie (1888) is on the western edge. It is loosely modelled on the opera house in Paris.

The old town centre stretches away to the northwest of the square. Its splendid houses were built for both aristocrats and rich com-

Esplanade Charles de Gaulle moners. To the north Place de la Comédie opens onto the Esplanade de Gaulle, with the conference centre and opera house, **Corum**, at the end. Eastward of the Esplanade there is a **citadel**, erected by Richelieu to stand guard over the Protestant city. Musée Fabre is di-

✳

Musée Fabre rectly opposite. It is one of the most important **art museums** in France. Major works on display include pieces by Italian and Dutch artists (17th–18th centuries) as well as French artists of the 19th–20th centuries, among them Ingres, Courbet, Dufy and Matisse (Rue Montpelliéret, open Tue, Thu, Fri, Sun 10am–6pm, Wed 1pm–9pm, Sat 11am–6pm).

✳

Promenade du Peyrou Promenade du Peyrou was created from 1688 to 1773 and takes the form of various terraces. The equestrian statue of Louis XIV (1828) replaced an earlier version from 1692, which was destroyed during the French Revolution. There is a great from view from there, reaching as far as the Cevennes and the Mediterranean. At the western end there is an **island château**, prettily built in the shape of a pillared temple. It is supplied with water along a 14km/9mi canal, which came into operation in 1766. The final stretch runs over an aqueduct 800m/880yd long and 21.5m/71ft high. The Jardin des Plantes, north of the Promenade du Peyrou, was the first botanical garden in France when it opened in 1593.

Botanical garden

East of the promenade stands a 15m/50ft-high triumphal arch dating from 1693, when it was built in honour of Louis XIV. Beyond the Palais de Justice is the university's medical faculty, housed in the former abbey of St-Benoît (1364). Also in the building is Musée Atger, which exhibits drawings by such great artists as Carraccio, Brueghel, Rubens, Van Dyck and Fragonard (open Mon, Wed, Fri

Arc de Triomphe

Musée Atger

 VISITING MONTPELLIER

INFORMATION

Office de Tourisme, 30
Allée de Lattre de Tassigny
F-34 000 Montpellier Tel. 04 67 60 60
60, fax 04 67 60 60 61,
www.ot-montpellier.fr
Extra offices are opened at the station and at 78 Av. du Pirée in summer.

TRANSPORT

The airport lies 8km/5mi southeast of the centre, bus connection. Trams and buses operated by TaM, information bureau: 6 Rue Jules Ferry (tram station Gare St-Roch).

FESTIVALS AND EVENTS

Early Feb: the town's French populace get together for the Swing Dance Festival. June: Printemps des Comédiens (theatre and circus). June–July: International Dance Festival (ballet).

WHERE TO EAT

► Expensive

Le Jardin des Sens
11 Avenue St-Lazare, tel. 04 99 58 38 88, closed Sun. Lavishly decorated restaurant noted for its trailblazing combinations, e.g. offal with seafood

or poultry and cocoa. The elegant designer interior makes for an appropriate backdrop. With cookery school and hotel. Located north of the city, access via the N 113.

► Moderate

Les Bains
6 Rue Richelieu, tel. 04 67 60 70 87. A little out of the way but with a wonderful inner courtyard and excellent everyday fare. The bar and the salon de thé are very pleasant too.

► Inexpensive

Caves Jean Jaurès
3 Rue Collot, tel. 04 67 60 27 33. This comfortable wine tavern near the market hall serves good, hearty food (e.g. duck in white wine sauce).

WHERE TO STAY

► Budget

Hotel du Palais
3 Rue du Palais, tel. 04 67 60 47 38
www.hoteldupalais-montpellier.fr.
Pretty 19th-century building in the centre of town with cheerful rooms, »antique« furniture and a familial atmosphere. No restaurant.

! *Baedeker* TIP

Modern Montpellier

You can experience modern Montpellier by taking a no. 1 blue-line tram on the ultra-modern tramway that opened in 2001 and runs from the Corum conference centre to the railway station, then through the Antigone estate to the city's latest addition, the futuristic Odysseum leisure park with its multiplex cinema, 3D planetarium and ice rink.

1.30pm–5.45pm, closed Aug). Adjoining it to the east is the Gothic cathedral of **St-Pierre** with its remarkable entrance portico.

The **Hôtel des Trésoriers de France** was home to the rich merchant Jacques Cœur (► Bourges) for ten years in the 15th century. Nowadays Musée Languedocien uses the building for its collection of archaeology and local folklore. Rue d'Embouque-d'Or leads to the Hôtel de Varennes, which houses **Musée Fougau** (folk art, everyday life in Montpellier) and the Musée du Vieux Montpellier. On Place Jaurès there are remnants of the 12th-century Romanesque church of Notre-Dame-des-Tables. Its 10th-century crypt is now home to the Musée de l'Histoire de Montpellier. Not far to the west beyond the préfecture on Rue Ballalerie, the **mikwe** (a Jewish ritual bathhouse of the 12th century) can still be seen and the public can gain access to it as part of the guided tours organized by the local tourist office.

Montpellier Map

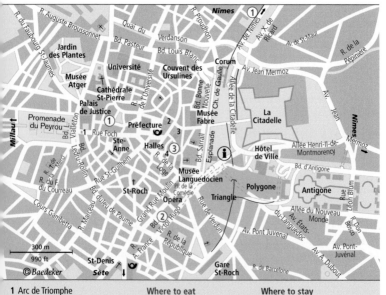

1 Arc de Triomphe
2 Hôtel de Mirman
3 Hôtel de Varennes
4 Notre-Dame-des-Tables

Where to eat
① Le Jardin des Sens
② Les Bains
③ Caves Jean-Jaurès

Where to stay
① Palais

★ ★ Mont Saint-Michel

F 4

Région: Basse-Normandie
Département: Manche

Altitude: 3–78m/10–256ft
Population: 50

A »pyramid rising from the sea« is how Victor Hugo described the famous Mont Saint-Michel. It rises impressively out of the mud flats in the Gulf of ►St-Malo. The monastery is one of the most important works of medieval architecture and one of the most popular attractions in France.

The hill with the abbey on top is at its prettiest when it completely surrounded by water, but nowadays this only occurs about 15 times a month when the tides reach a height of some 12m/40ft. The best chance of seeing it like this is on days when the moon is either full or new (information available from tourist offices). Be there approximately 2 hours before high tide. Because the bay is silting up, the Couesnon river is to be dammed by 2010; this will hold back the water at high tide and then release it rapidly at low tide, washing away silt deposits. The current causeway is to be replaced by a bridge set on pillars, and visitors will then be able to take an electric train to the mount.

Tides

The Abbey of Mont Saint-Michel

According to legend it was the Archangel Michael himself who told the Bishop of Avranches to build a chapel on what was then called Mount Tombe in 708. In 966, Benedictine monks from St-Wandrille founded an abbey there and built the church of Notre-Dame sous-Terre (Our Lady under the Earth). In the 11th century a massive **Romanesque church** was built, with the earlier buildings being incorporated as »crypts«. The three-storey convent to the north is accessed from there. In 1154–86 the buildings were expanded, the church gained its two towers, the platform was extended to the west with new living quarters and a hostel was built to the southwest. The Gothic complex of **La Merveille** followed in 1212–28. The abbey was fortified even before the outbreak of the Hundred Years' War in the 14th century and it withstood all attacks by the English. In 1421 the Romanesque choir of the church collapsed and was rebuilt in the late Gothic Flamboyant-style. In 1446–50 the »crypt of the broad pillars« was erected. The abbey went into decline after 1516, when the abbots started to be appointed by the king and were permitted to keep all income for themselves. After a fire in 1776 the first three bays of the abbey church broke away and the **western terrace** was built in their place. By the end of the 18th century there were only a dozen monks still resident at Mont St-Michel. During the French Revolution they were expelled and the complex was used as a prison (which it re-

History

ABBAYE DU MONT ST-MICHEL

✶ **St Michael himself is said to have commissioned the building of this abbey on a rocky island in the Wadden Sea. When the cone atop the tower of the abbey church rises out of the mist from the horizon, you are inclined to believe it.**

Opening times for the abbey:
May–Aug 9am–7pm, otherwise 9.30am–6pm
Last admission 1 hour before closing
Sung Masses, Tue–Sat 12.15pm, Sun 11.30am
Evening visits to abbey illuminations:
July–Aug Mon–Sat between 6pm and 10.30pm
(last admission)

① Romanesque church

The nave survives from the original Romanesque design. The division of the walls into three levels with arcades, double triforia and clerestory windows follows a scheme that was common in Normandy.

② Crypts

Underneath the arms of the abbey church's transept there are two crypts. The northern one is called Notre-Dame-des-Trente-Cierges while the southern one is dedicated to St Martin. The former is inside the enclosure and has an intimate atmosphere, while the latter has massive barrel vaulting and performed a ceremonial function.

③ Crypte des Gros-Piliers

The Romanesque choir collapsed in 1421. 25 years later building work started on a new church in the late-Gothic Flamboyant style. The choir was not completed until 1513. Its foundations are formed by the »crypt of the great pillars«. Each of the pillars is some 2m/6ft 6in thick and supports one of the pillars of the choir while the double column supports the high altar. The space is used as a waiting room for the neighbouring courtroom.

④ La Merveille

In the early 13th century after partial destruction of the abbey during the conquest of Normandy by the French King Philippe II Auguste, no expense was spared in the rebuilding. Three storeys, each with two large and impressive rooms, each individually furnished, were towered upon one another to make up the monastery buildings.

⑤ Crossing tower

The tower, which tops the pyramid of the abbey mount so effectively, was completely rebuilt by Victor Petitgrand, a pupil of Viollet les Duc from 1890 to 1897. He kept close, though, to the condition as it was in 1390, as reported in the diary of the Duke of Berry. The statue of the Archangel Michael by E Frémiet is 4m/13ft high and weighs 450kg/0.44 tons. It was placed on its pedestal in 1897.

Mont St-Michel *Map*

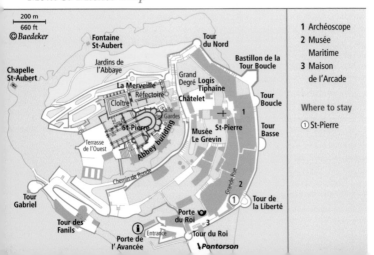

200 m
660 ft
©*Baedeker*

Fontaine St-Aubert
Tour du Nord
Jardins de l'Abbaye
Bastillon de la Tour Boucle
Chapelle St-Aubert
Grand Degré
Logis Tiphaine
La Merveille
Réfectoire
Châtelet
Cloître
Salle des Gardes
Tour Boucle
St-Pierre
Musée Le Grevin
St-Pierre
Tour Basse
Abbey building
Terrasse de l'Ouest
Chemin de Ronde
Tour Gabriel
Tour des Fanils
Porte du Roi
Grande Rue
Tour de la Liberté
Porte de l'Avancée
Entrance
Tour du Roi
Pontorson

1 Archéoscope
2 Musée Maritime
3 Maison de l'Arcade

Where to stay
① St-Pierre

The cloister with
slender columns
and arcades made of
...en stone seems to float between
...aven and earth.

Marvellous illuminated
manuscripts were created in
the scriptorium. Some of them
are on view at the town hall in
Avranches (p.605).

The late Gothic choir is distinguished by its lightness and elegant proportions.

© Baedeker

Under the western terrace is the crypt of
Notre-Dame-sous-Terre, originally a small
church dating from the Carolingian era.

mained till 1863). A causeway was built to link the island to the mainland in 1879. Since 1966 it has again become home to several Benedictine monks.

Entrance hall and outer buildings
From Grand'Rue a long stairway (Grand Degré) leads up to the main gate of the fortress (Châtelet, late 14th century), which is also the east entrance to the abbey. A 13th-century portal opens into the guardroom with its pointed arches and large fireplace (ticket office). Between the abbot's quarters and the church, there is a 90-step stairway up to the **terrace** in the west. There is a lovely view from there across the bay, taking in the island of La Tombelaine and sometimes reaching as far as Cancale. The design of the complex can be seen very well from the northwest corner of the terrace. The abbey church occupies the summit of the rock (atop the 156m/512ft tower is a statue of St Michael fighting a dragon); while the west has the Romanesque abbot's quarters and the north is occupied by the Gothic »Merveille«.

Church
Inside the church, the huge Romanesque nave (11th–12th centuries) and the tall, elegant Gothic choir (15th–16th centuries) make for an impressive contrast. The three so-called crypts, originally earlier churches, can be visited as part of a guided tour.

La Merveille
The Gothic building »La Merveille«, to the north of the church, has two three-storey wings to the east and west. The older eastern section (1211–18) contains, from top to bottom, an alms chamber, a hall for guests and a refectory. The west wing (1218–28) includes cellars, the so-called Hall of Knights and a cloister. The **cloister**
Cloister
(cloître) features slim pillars in two offset rows, rising to pointed arches and carrying arcades, each decorated with leaves and ornamental creatures in the Norman tradition of the 13th century. The open book in the garden is a reference to the abbey's reputation as
Refectory
the »Cité des Livres«. The single-aisled **refectory** has beautiful panelled vaulting and astonishing acoustics. The so-called **Hall of**
Hall of Knights
Knights (Salle des Chevaliers) has four aisles and measures 26 × 18m/85 × 60ft. Louis XI is said to have instituted the order of the Knights of St Michael here. It was used as a »scriptorium«, i.e. for writing books. The ceiling is supported by three rows of chunky
Cellar
columns with ornamented capitals. Two rows of columns supported the cross-ribbed vaulting of the cellar pantry (cellier). Various models of the island are on display here. The long **alms**
Alms chamber
chamber (dating back in part to the 12th century) was used to house poor pilgrims and is now used as a book shop (librairie).

Other attractions
Half way up the **Grand'Rue** on the left-hand side stands the parish church of St-Pierre (11th century, later much altered). It houses the Archéoscope where audio-visual techniques are used to simulate a journey back through the abbey's past. The Musée Maritime

▶ VISITING MONT ST-MICHEL

INFORMATION

Office de Tourisme
BP 4, F-50170 Mont St-Michel
Tel. 02 33 60 14 30, fax 02 33 60 06 75
www.ot-montsaintmichel.com
www.monuments-nationaux.fr
Information office on the A84 at
St-Aubin-de-Terregatte.

TIPS

More than 1 million people visit
Mont St-Michel (UNESCO World
Heritage) every year. It can get very
crowded between May and the start of
September. Things only calm down
when the abbey is closed or during
the off-season. The unique atmosphere is best experienced in the
course of an overnight stay, when
gorgeous sunsets can be seen from the
square in front of the abbey church.

WHERE TO EAT / WHERE TO STAY

▶ Moderate
Saint Pierre
Grande Rue
Tel. 02 33 60 14 03
www.auberge-saint-pierre.fr
One of the best hotels on the island.
Comfortable and tastefully furnished
guest rooms. There is a good crêperie
in the rustic, nicely designed dining
rooms.

covers the maritime habitat, the changing of the tides and the silting
of the bay. The wax museum (Musée Grevin) can be enjoyed too.

About 3km/2mi north of Mont St-Michel is the granite cone of La   **La Tombelaine**
Tombelaine, a bird sanctuary 56m/184ft high and 950m/1040yd
wide. A tramp across the mud flats is exciting but can be dangerous
due to the tides, so trips to the island should only be taken in the
company of a guide.

Mulhouse

P 5

Région: Alsace
Département: Haut-Rhin

Altitude: 240m/787ft
Population: 112,000

**Mulhouse, the second biggest city in ▶Alsace, is surrounded by in-
dustry. That, however, makes it no less worthy of a visit. The city's
historic centre is being painstakingly refurbished, and with some success, but the main attractions are the technical museums, which pay
tribute to an industrial heritage dating back to the 18th century.**

Mulhouse is located 30km/19mi northwest of Basle between the   **History**
Rhine basin and the hilly Sundgau region. Textiles, engineering and
car manufacture, chemicals, printing, leather goods and the food in-

dustry all have a long tradition here, which is why it has been dubbed the **»Manchester of Alsace«** and »city of 120 chimneys«. The city was first mentioned in documents in 803 and was declared a city under the Hohenstaufen dynasty. In 1308 it became a free city of the Holy Roman Empire and joined the Alsatian Décapole league in 1354. From 1515 to 1648 Mulhouse was an »associate member« of the Swiss cantons. With the coming of the Reformation, and especially after the revocation of the Edict of Nantes in 1685, the city became a bastion of Calvinism, which was accompanied by an economic boom. In 1746 four of its citizens opened a textile factory to make »Indiennes«, named after the printed fabrics of India, which were highly popular at the time. When the region was absorbed into France in 1792, it further boosted industrial development.

What to See in Mulhouse

Place de la Réunion

The centrepiece of the city is the marketplace (Place de la Réunion), which features the **city hall**, a beautiful Renaissance building from 1552 entirely covered in trompe-l'œil paintings. Its magnificent council hall formerly served as a meeting place for the city's republican council. Hanging from the right-hand gable is a replica of the »Klapperstein«, from which blasphemers would once be suspended as a punishment. The stairs to the right are the entry to the historical museum (closed Tue). The neighbouring neo-Gothic Protestant **Temple St-Etienne** (1858–68) has some lovely stained glass windows rescued from an earlier building built in the 14th century. Rue du Sauvage (Wildemannsgass), to the northeast beyond the town hall, is the main artery of the city centre. To the north it opens out onto Place d'Europe with the ghastly 100m/330ft-high Europa tower (1972). There is a great view of the town and its environs from the revolving restaurant. A more attractive building is the huge cultural centre of **La Filature**, opened in 1993 to the east of the city centre (Allée Nathan Katz; music, theatre, exhibitions).

Rue du Sauvage

La Filature

Musée des Beaux-Arts

The Musée des Beaux-Arts is located in Villa Steinbach (Place Guillaume Tell, south of Place de la Réunion) and exhibits works from the Middle Ages up till the 20th century, including examples by von Brueghel, Boucher and Cranach and by the Sundgau painter Jean-Jacques Henner (closed Tue).

✴

Musée de l'Impression sur étoffes

As of 1827 the Nouveau Quartier came into existence to the southeast of the city centre. The museum of fabric printing in the suburb shows the technique and how it developed in Alsace (14 Rue Jean-Jacques Henner, closed Mon).

✴ ✴

Musée National de l'Automobile

The Musée National de l'Automobile, north of the city centre, is an absolute must and not just for car fans. Its collection was originally put together by the Schlumpf brothers, who financed their passion

▶ VISITING MULHOUSE

INFORMATION
Office du Tourisme
9 Avenue Foch
F-68100 Mulhouse
Tel. 03 89 35 48 48
Fax 03 89 45 66 16
www.tourisme-mulhouse.com

WHERE TO STAY
► Mid-range
① *Bristol*
18 Av. de Colmar
Tel. 03 89 42 12 31
Fax 03 89 42 50 57,
www.hotelbristol.com
A short distance north of the old town
in a building from the early 20th
century. Large, comfortable rooms
with modern furnishings.

► Budget
② *Le Clos du Mûrier*
42 Grand Rue
F-68170 Rixheim

www.closdumurier.fr
Tel. 03 89 54 14 81
Chambre d'hôte, 6km/4mi southeast
of town in a magnificent 16th-century
building featuring modernized rooms
in which guests can self-cater,
although who would want to when it
is possible to dine in style in Rixheim
at the »Manoir« (expensive, tel. 03 89
31 88 88, closed Sun, open holidays)?

WHERE TO EAT
► Inexpensive
① *Winstub Henriette*
9 Rue Henriette
Tel. 03 89 46 27 83, closed Sun.
This typically Alsatian wine tavern is
named after the first individual to
adopt French citizenship in 1798.
Good, hearty local cuisine. In summer
the terrace adjacent to the pedestrian
zone is opened. Reservation is required.

from the profits of the textile factory they owned. Around 500 vintage and not so vintage vehicles, including practically every model issued by **Bugatti**, reflect the entire history of vehicle production (192
Av. de Colmar, open daily April–Oct 10am–6pm, otherwise till 5pm;
in Jan Mon–Fri from 1pm).

The **railway museum** in the western suburb Dornach is every bit as
impressive. More than 100 steam and electric locomotives, plus carriages and goods wagons from 1844 to the present day, are on display, as well as a large model railway (2 Rue Alfred de Glehn, open
daily April–Oct 10am–6pm, otherwise till 5pm; in Jan Mon–Fri from
1pm). The neighbouring Musée EDF Electropolis offers an experience explaining the history and applications of electricity (55 Rue du
Pâturage, open Tue–Sun 10am–6pm).

★ ★
Cité du Train

Electropolis

As a change from all the technology, the zoo and botanical gardens
cover 25ha/62 acres in the southeast of the city. There is also a tower
with a great view of the vineyard slopes close to the zoo.

★
Parc Zoologique
et Botanique

Around Mulhouse

Musée du Papier Peint

The **wallpaper museum** in Rixheim, 5km/3mi east of Mulhouse, is housed in an 18th-century building with three wings that was once the commandery of the Teutonic Knights. It was converted into a wallpaper factory by Jean Zuber in 1790 and is now used as the city hall. The old printing presses in the museum are as impressive as the fabulously designed wallpapers themselves (open June–Sept daily 10am–noon, 2pm–6pm, Oct–May Wed–Mon 10am–noon, 2pm–6pm).

Peugeot Citroën

The factories and facilities of Peugeot Citroën extend out in all directions along the D 39 northeast of Mulhouse. 13,000 people are employed there. Tours are organized by Mulhouse's Office du Tourisme.

Ottmarsheim

In Ottmarsheim, about 10km/6mi northeast of Rixheim, it is possible to see a »copy« of the Palatinate chapel in Aachen, an unusual centrally built octagonal building from the rule of Emperor Otto, which was consecrated in 1049. The Rhine here is made navigable by means of man-made canals and the cut with its lock and power station (1948–52) is very interesting. Further north are the premises of chemicals giant Rhodia (formerly Rhône-Poulenc).

✷✷ Nancy

04

Région: Lorraine	**Altitude:** 212m/696ft
Département: Meurthe-et-Moselle	**Population:** 106,000

Nancy, the historic capital of ▶Lorraine, is worth breaking a journey for. Its unusual, not to say unique, character is built around its splendid Baroque centre, a legacy of the former Polish king Stanisław I, as well as by many fine examples of Art Nouveau, which spawned a separate school of its own in Nancy.

Nancy past and present

Nancy is the capital of the Meurthe et Moselle département, a university town nestling on the left bank of the Meurthe and also served by the Rhine-Marne canal. In the 12th century the city was the residence of the dukes of Lorraine. Charles the Bold, last duke of Burgundy, occupied the area in 1475 because it lay between his own Burgundian and Flemish possessions. In the 15th century a new town was built to the south of the original centre, adopting a rectangular street grid. The city gained its magnificent Baroque appearance in the 18th century when Stanisław Leszczyński, deposed king of Poland and as father in-law of Louis XV the last duke of Lorraine, took up residence in the town as of 1737. Local specialities include Mirabelle plums, macarons and, in particular, baba Stanislas, a yeast gugelhupf (upside-down cake) flavoured with rum.

Is there any lovelier place to drink a coffee than at Place Stanislas in Nancy?

What to See in Nancy

In the very year he took residence, Stanisław (Fr. Stanislas) set about creating an unforgettable monument to himself. He linked the old and new towns of Nancy with a corridor 500m/550yd long, made up of **Place Stanislas, Place d'Alliance and Place de la Carrière**. All the most important public buildings lie along this axis. The ensemble has now been declared a UNESCO World Heritage Site.

Named after its sponsor, Place Stanislas was designed and built by architects Emmanuel Héré and wrought-iron artist Jean Lamour between 1751 and 1760. The square covers 124 × 106m/136 × 166yd and is enclosed by five magnificent palaces. In the middle there is an 1831 monument to this last independent ruler of Lorraine. Lamour's stupendous gilded wrought iron grilles adorn all the road junctions as well as surrounding the statues of Neptune and Amphitrite, both created by sculptor Barthélémy Guibal. The largest of the palaces is the **Hôtel de Ville** (city hall, 1752–55; with some superb banisters on the stairs by Lamour).

Baroque city centre

★ ★
Place Stanislas

Musée des Beaux-Arts

Housed in one of Héré's pavilions and a modern annexe, Nancy's **art museum** (closed Tue) exhibits European paintings from the 14th century till the present day as well as etchings by Nancy's own Jacques Callot (1592–1635) and some brilliant Art Nouveau items made by the glassmakers Daum.

Place de la Carrière

Palais du Gouverneur

Pass under the triumphal arch, erected in honour of Louis XV in 1757, to reach Place de la Carrière, which was designed by Héré. Héré was also the designer of the governors' palace (Palais du Gouverneur, 1760) and the colonnade-lined square in front of it. Adjoining it to the east is the pretty Pépinière, a park including a rose garden and menagerie. The statue of painter Claude Gellée, a.k.a. Claude Lorrain (1600–82), who was born near Nancy, was created by Auguste Rodin.

Palais Ducal

The **dukes' palace**, the most important non-ecclesiastical building of the late Gothic period in Lorraine, was built in 1502–44 on the site of a castle that had been destroyed in 1475. Later on, it was largely rebuilt. Its finest feature is the »Porterie« (1512) on Grande Rue

▶ VISITING NANCY

INFORMATION

Office de Tourisme
Place Stanislas, F-54 000 Nancy
Tel. 03 83 35 22 41, fax 03 83 35 90 10
www.ot-nancy.fr

TRANSPORT

Trams, buses and trolley buses are operated by STAN; information at the main hub »République« to the south of the main railway station.

WHERE TO EAT

▶ Inexpensive / moderate

① *Brasserie Excelsior*

50 Rue H. Poincaré, tel. 03 83 35 24 57
A »monument historique« with a rich interior forming a perfect backdrop to the excellent cuisine. Even a snack with a cake and a glass of wine, though, is an unforgettable delight.

② *La Mignardise*

28 Rue Stanislas, tel. 03 83 32 20 22, closed Sun evenings. Popular bistro a

stone's throw from Place Stanislas, furnished with a mix of Louis Seize and the hyper-modern. The solid yet creative cuisine compares well with the backdrop. There are several other good spots on Rue Stanislas.

WHERE TO STAY

▶ Luxury

① *Grand Hôtel de la Reine*

2 Place Stanislas, tel. 03 83 35 03 01
www.hoteldelareine.com
Wonderful 18th-century palace with a beautiful staircase and guest rooms in Louis XV style. The service leaves nothing to be desired. Including gourmet restaurant (closed Sat midday and Sun evening).

▶ Budget

② *Portes d'Or*

21 Rue Stanislas, tel. 03 83 35 42 34
www.hotel-lesportesdor.com
Very pleasant hotel with modern, if relatively small, rooms and upholstered doors.

(equestrian statue of Duke Anton from 1851). To the left of the entrance there is a door with a monkey dressed as a Franciscan friar. Inside the palace the **Lorraine Museum** (closed Mon) displays archaeological finds, medieval sculpture and collections covering local history and folklore. The first floor features the 55m/60yd long **Galerie des Cerfs** with exhibits from the era of the dukes, tapestries, rubbings by Jacques Callot, etchings by Jacques Bellange and paintings by Georges de la Tour (including the famous *Woman Catching a Flea*) and Claude Deruet.

★
Musée Lorrain

Heading north, the next important building is the Eglise des Cordeliers (Franciscan church) from 1487, which was the last resting place of the dukes of Lorraine and is now a wing of the Musée Lorrain. Apart from the tombs in the crypt a whole range of important gravestones is on view, including that of René II (1509), his second wife Philippe de Gueldre (of Ligier Richier †1547) and cardinal Charles de Vaudémont (†1587). The octagonal Chapelle Ducale (1607) guards the sarcophagi of those dukes from the Baroque period. The abbey next door houses the Musée Régional des Arts et Traditions Populaires featuring folk art, furniture, costumes and handcrafted objects.

★
Eglise des Cordeliers

Lined by old houses, Grande Rue leads on to the Porte de la Craffe (1436, although the inscription has otherwise), a double gate to the

Porte de la Craffe

Nancy Map

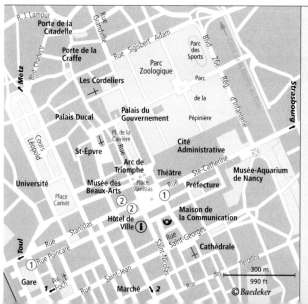

1 Musée de l'Ecole de Nancy
2 Notre-Dame-de-Bon-Sécours

Where to eat
① Brasserie Excelsior
② La Mignardise

Where to stay
① Grand Hôtel de la Reine
② Portes d'Or

© Baedeker

Another unmissable delight in the Art Nouveau city: Brasserie Excelsior, est. 1910

city guarded by two huge round towers. Until the French Revolution there was a prison inside but the now the gatehouse is part of the Musée Lorrain (with implements of torture on display).

Quarter around the dukes' palace The Palais Ducal is surrounded by notable town houses, including Hôtel Ferrari (29 Rue Haut-Bourgeois 29, 18th century) and Hôtel d'Haussonville (Rue Mgr.-Trouillet 9, *c*1550). The giant neo-Gothic church of **St-Epvre** (1865–71) is marked out by its 87m/285ft tower. Interesting buildings on Rue de la Source include no. 12, Hôtel de Lillebonne, and Hôtel du Marquis de Ville (no. 10, façade 1747).

✷✷
Musée de l'École de Nancy An Art Nouveau villa in Nancy's southwest houses the marvellous **School of Nancy Museum** (Rue du Sgt-Blandan 36, closed Mon–Tue). Its collection exhibits all aspects of turn-of-the-century (1900) style: glass, furniture and jewellery by Emile Gallé, founder of the École de Nancy, as well as examples by Prouvé, Daum, Majorelle, Lurçat, Vallin and others. **Cristalleries Daum** (Rue des Cristalleries 17) has its own shop, where it is possible to buy fine crystal glass.

! *Baedeker* TIP

Art Nouveau tour
There are examples of Art Nouveau all over Nancy. A small guide with a map of the nicest buildings can be obtained from the tourist office.

The **Muséum Aquarium**, the only natural history museum in Lorraine, is dedicated to the world of tropical fish and coral reefs, though it also possesses a fine palaeontological section. The **Maison de la Communication** brings the 200-year history of telecommunications to life.

✷
Notre-Dame-de-Bon-Secours The southeastern part of the city is graced by the small but beautifully appointed Baroque church of Notre-Dame-de-Bon-Secours (Av. de Strasbourg), designed by Emile Héré in 1741, which also contains the tomb of Stanisław Leszczyński and a mausoleum for his wife Catherine Opalinska. Behind the altar stands the **Virgin of Mercy** by

Mansuy Gauvin (1505), commissioned by Duke René II and now an important object of pilgrimage. Further southeast (turning off to the right under the bridge) the Musée de l'Histoire de Fer illustrates the story of iron, the raw material which played such a key role in the Lorraine economy.

Musée de l'Histoire de Fer

Around Nancy

The basilica of St-Nicolas (15th–16th century) in St-Nicolas-de-Port is one of the most important buildings of the late Gothic Flamboyant style in France. It was built from 1480 to 1560 as a church for pilgrims to the highly revered **relics of St Nicholas**, which were brought back from Bari in southern Italy by a knight of Lorraine in 1090. The stained glass work (early 16th century) is also noteworthy. The **Musée Français de la Brasserie** is housed in a former brewery which closed in 1985.

★ Saint-Nicolas-de-Port

Nantes

`F 5`

Région: Pays de la Loire
Département: Loire-Atlantique

Altitude: 8m/26ft
Population: 282,000

Lying 60km/37mi from the Atlantic on the banks of the Loire, Nantes was formerly the capital of Brittany. Its legacy of buildings – especially the chateau and cathedral – an outstanding museum of art and other cultural facilities make the sixth biggest city in France an essential place to visit.

For centuries Nantes served as the capital of the Duchy of Brittany and was a hub of French overseas trade. Nowadays, Nantes and St-Nazaire on the Atlantic share a common harbour of great industrial importance, which makes the area one of the key economic centres in France. The Nantes stock exchange is second in size only to the one in Paris. Increasingly too, new industries are emerging in place of traditional economic pillars (agriculture and food industries, electronics, insurance). The city hardly makes a typically Breton impression, but it has its own youthful flair, to which the university and its 40,000 students make a key contribution. Not least among its charms, though, is the excellent yet affordable food, which makes any stay enjoyable.

Economic centre of the west

Up till the end of the 15th century, the town's inhabitants had fought to uphold its independence against Romans, Normans, the English and the French. It was capital of the Duchy of Brittany in the Middle Ages and residence of Brittany's dukes until it fell to the French crown in 1532. It was here in 1598 that Henri IV of France signed

History

the famous edict granting certain religious freedoms to the Protestant minority. Thanks to the ocean-going harbour, the 16th century had seen the start of an economic boom. The true heyday of Nantes came, though, in the 18th century, when it was the centre of the slave trade in Europe. Between 1715 and 1775 no less than 787 ships sailed from Nantes to Africa and from there, laden with »ebony«, on to the Antilles, to return carrying coffee, tobacco and indigo. The boom years ended with the terror of the Revolution. In 1793 Jean-Baptiste Carrier, emissary of the National Convention, had more than 10,000 aristocrats, priests and other »useless deadweights« executed, some tied together in pairs and drowned in the Loire, a procedure recorded in history under the name »mariage républicain«. A new upswing came with the opening of a new harbour at St-Nazaire in 1856 and the establishment of various new industries. In 1981, Nantes was separated from Brittany to become capital of the Loire-Atlantique département, part of the Pays de la Loire région, although Breton legal rights were to be maintained. Nantes was the birthplace of various notables including Anne of Brittany (1477–1514), writer Jules Verne (1828–1905) and caricaturist Claire Brétécher (born 1943).

Nantes Map

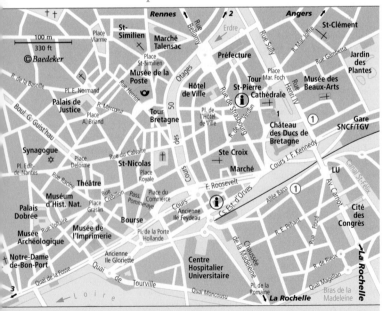

1 La Psalette
2 Quai de la Motte-Rouge
3 Musée Jules Verne

Where to eat
① Lou Pescadou

Where to stay
① L' Hôtel

Tomb of King François II and Marguerite de Foix in the exquisite cathedral

What to See in Nantes

Old Nantes sits to the north of the Loire. Visitors emerging from the station are greeted by an unusual tower, which formerly belonged to the well known **LU biscuit factory** at the start of the 20th century, but which has been used as a cultural centre since 1999. The initials »LU« stood for »Lieu Unique« (unique place).

Lieu Unique

In spite of being built over a period lasting more than five hundred years, from 1434 to 1891, the cathedral leaves a uniform impression. Its limestone construction makes the interior bright, if sober, and allowed it to be built to a great height (37.7m/124ft) above the 102m/112yd central aisle. The bas-reliefs of the portal on the northern side depict the passion of the martyrs Rogatianus and Donatianus. The transept on the right has the tomb of Brittany's last duke François II (†1488) and his wife Marguerite de Foix, which is a Renaissance masterpiece by **Michel Colombe** (1507). Four large statues in the corners represent the cardinal virtues of Justice, Fortitude, Prudence (the statue has two faces looking in both directions) and Temperance.

✱ Cathédrale St-Pierre-et-St-Paul

The **château of the dukes** was built as of 1466 in the reign of François II, Duke of Brittany, on the site of former Gallo-Roman and medieval fortifications. His daughter Anne (queen of France 1491–1514) and subsequent rulers continually expanded it. The Grand Gouvernement was rebuilt in 1684 after a fire. A graceful stair tower (Tour de la Couronne d'Or) adjoins it to the south. In front of

✱ Château des Ducs de Bretagne

Palais des Ducs Plan

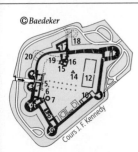

© Baedeker

1 Entrance	**12** Harnachement
2 Tour du Pied de Biche	**13** Tour du Fer à Cheval
3 Tour de la Boulangerie	**14** Remnants of the
4 Tour de Jacobins	original castle
5 Grand Gouvernement	**15** Loge du Concierge
6 Tour de la Couronne d'Or	**16** Vieux Donjon
7 Puits (Well)	**17** Bastion Mercoeur
8 Grand Logis	**18** Tour au Duc
9 Tour du Port	**19** Vieux Logis
10 Petit Gouvernement	**20** Tour des Espagnols
11 Tour de la Rivière	(destroyed 1800)

the tower is a fountain also dating from François II's reign, which has a wrought iron canopy representing the crown of the Breton duchy. The Grand Logis and Grand Gouvernement now house a museum for the history of Nantes (open daily July–Aug, otherwise closed Tue).

Musée des Beaux-Arts

The **art museum**, one of the most important provincial museums in France, possesses paintings from the 13th to the 20th centuries, including masterpieces by D'Ingres, de la Tour, Courbet, Chagall, Picasso, Dubuffet, Tinguely and Kandinsky (open Wed–Mon 10am–6pm, Thu till 8pm).

● VISITING NANTES

INFORMATION

Office de Tourisme
Cours de Clisson/Rue Kergévan
F-44 000 Nantes Tel. 08 92 46 40 44,
fax 02 40 89 11 99
 www.nantes-tourisme.com

TRANSPORT

Buses and trams are run by TAN.
Information: Espace Transport, 2 Allée
Brancas. Nantes-Atlantique Airport,
bus link via TAN Air.

PASS NANTES

The Pass Nantes (valid 1–3 days)
includes entrance to more than 20
attractions as well as free travel on
buses and trams.

WHERE TO EAT
► Moderate
① *Lou Pescadou*
8 Allée Baco, tel. 02 40 35 29 50, closed
Sun. An El Dorado for lovers of fish
and seafood, from lobsters to loup de
mer in a salty crust pastry. Opposite
the chateau.

WHERE TO STAY
► Mid-range
① *L'Hôtel*
6 Rue Henry IV, tel. 02 40 29 30 31
www.nanteshotel.com
A very fine establishment opposite the
chateau with a garden but no restaurant, though an outstanding breakfast
is served. It also has its own car park.

! **Baedeker** TIP

La Cigale

Nantes possesses, with no fear of exaggeration, the finest brasserie in the world. The »Cicada« (lit.) dates from 1895 and reveals the full splendour of the belle époque. Good food. 4 Place Graslin, tel. 02 51 84 94 94, open daily 7.30am–12.30am.

The area around the church of Ste-Croix still has some lovely old houses. **Place du Bouffay** is especially picturesque. A vegetable market takes place there every morning (except Mon–Tue), as it has done since the 15th century.

★ Old town

In the 1920s, a side arm of the Loire and its tributary the Erdre were filled in to connect the island of Feydeau to the northern section of the city. In the 18th century, ship-owners and slave traders had a number of classical residences built here. No. 4 Cours Olivier de Clisson is the birthplace of Jules Verne.

Ile Feydeau

West of the Cours des 50 Otages – named after 50 hostages who were shot by German troops for the sake of retribution in 1941– the 144m/472ft **Tour de Bretagne** (1976) makes for a rather ugly eye-catcher. South of it is Place Royale, established in 1790. The shopping street Rue Crébillon links the square with Place Graslin. Close to the junction with Rue Santeuil is the entrance to **Passage Pommeraye**, dating from 1843, a wonderful retail store (open Sun 9am–7pm, otherwise 8am–8pm). Place Graslin is modelled on the Odéon in Paris and its northern side is graced by the Grand-Théâtre, built in 1783–88.

Place Royale

★ Passage Pommeraye

Not far to the west there are three interesting museums: the Muséum d'Histoire Naturelle with its vivarium, Musée Dobrée with the art treasures of ship-owner Thomas Dobrée (including a gold and ivory shrine containing the heart of Anne of Brittany) and the Musée Archéologique. Southwest of the city centre, on a northern arm of the Loire, a naval escort vessel has been opened as a museum. Further upstream, above the harbour, is the **Jules-Verne-Museum**, dedicated to the science fiction writer (3 Rue de l'Hermitage, closed Tue).

Museums

Musée Naval Maillé-Brézé

Around Nantes

Boat trips down the valley of the Erdre, which runs into the city from the north, are highly popular. A trip lasting about two hours starts from the Quai de la Motte-Rouge. Along the river there are a series of elegant mansions, including the 15th-century Château de la Gâcherie on the west bank.

Boat trip on the Erdre

Clisson A trip to Clisson, 24km/15mi southeast of Nantes at the confluence of the Sèvre Nantaise and the Moine, leads right into the wine-making region of **Muscat de Sèvre-et-Maine**. Clisson occupied a highly strategic location, a fact to which the romantic 13th-century castle and other buildings bear witness. The whole place was destroyed in 1793 during the Vendée revolt and was rebuilt in Italian style.

Ancenis Ancenis, about 40km/25mi east of Nantes on the north bank of the Loire, is another wine town. It was formerly one of the fortifications along the southern border of Brittany; its first castle was built in 980. The remains of fortifications and of the palace, which can still be seen, date from the 16th century. The centre of town has a lot of houses made from slate (16th–17th centuries). The church of St-Pierre-et-St-Paul (15th–16th centuries) is notable for its 15th-cen-
Champtoceaux tury fresco. About 10km/6mi outside Ancenis, in Champtoceaux on the south bank of the river (with the ruin of a castle destroyed in the 15th century), there is a magnificent **view along the Loire**.

✶✶ Nice

P 9

Région: Provence – Alpes – Côte d'Azur	**Altitude:** Sea level
Département: Alpes-Maritimes	**Population:** 383,000

Its fabulous location on the ▶ Côte d'Azur and its mild climate make Nice one of the oldest and most important winter health resorts on the Côte d'Azur, and even today it is a place where the beau monde meet. The Italian-influenced city has, however, still managed to retain a »normal« and laid-back atmosphere.

Metropolis of the Riviera »Fashionable« Nice, nestling beautifully between the Maritime Alps and the »Bay of Angels«, is the fifth biggest city in France and the metropolis of the French Riviera. It has the busiest airport in the country after Paris and the most important harbour for ferries, to Corsica for example. As the capital of the Alpes-Maritimes département and a university town with 35,000 students, it has a vigorous cultural scene and some outstanding museums. Even though they are not that attractive, the beaches are very busy.

History The oldest traces of settlement date back 400,000 years and have been found in the eastern suburb of Lympia (**Terra Amata**). In 350 BC Greeks from Massalia (Marseille) established the trading post of Nikaia Polis on what is now the castle hill. The Romans settled on the hill of Cimiez in 154 BC. In the early part of the Middle Ages Nikaia belonged to the county of Provence, passing to the duchy of Savoy in 1388, which fell to Sardinia in 1720. It was at that time that the harbour and fortifications were built. A referendum in 1860

The catwalk on which to see and be seen: Promenade des Anglais in Nice

brought Nice under French sovereignty. One of the city's sons is the hero of the Italian struggle for freedom, **Giuseppe Garibaldi** (1807–82). The mild climate in Nice led in the 19th century to its becoming one of the first winter convalescence resorts for the upper classes. This had started as early as 1776 when Scottish physician Tobias Smollett recommended it for those with lung ailments. In more recent times, key historical figures have included Jean Médecin, mayor as of 1928, and his son Jacques, mayor from 1966 (†1998). The latter oversaw the development of Nice into the so-called »Chicago of the Mediterranean« (evoking the gangster period of the 1920s), in spite of which he still has many devotees. Even today press reports still highlight »massive corruption« and the arrival of the Russian »nouveau riche« is being accepted with mixed feelings. Nice is also a city with serious social problems, resulting from the huge gulf between rich and poor, and has a radical right-wing mayor who has already ordered expulsion from the town of several »undesirable elements«.

What to See in Nice

The 92m/302ft hill, where a castle stood until 1706, offers an impressive view of the city. Remains have been unearthed here of two churches, built one on top of the other (11th and 15th centuries), as well as the foundations of Greek buildings. On the way to the promenade along the beach stands the Tour Bellanda (1880), which houses the Musée de la Marine (seafaring museum, closed Mon–Tue).

Colline du Château

Tour Bellanda

● VISITING NICE

INFORMATION

Office du Tourisme et des Congrès
5 Prom. des Anglais, F-06000 Nice
Tel. 0892 70 74 07, fax 04 89 06 48 03
www.nicetourisme.com
Additional offices at the railway station
(Avenue Thiers) and at the airport.

TRANSPORT

The airport lies 6km/3.7mi west, 98/98
bus to the centre. Buses and trams run
by Ligne d'Azur, information offices: 3
Place Masséna, 29 Avenue Malausséna.

FESTIVALS AND EVENTS

12-day carnival culminating on Shrove
Tuesday with fireworks and the great
»flower battle«. July: jazz festival. 14
July: Fête Nationale with fireworks.
June–Aug numerous concerts includ-
ing the Festival de Musique Sacrée.

MUSEUMS

Entry to the city's official museums is
always free; free admission to national
museums on the 1st Sunday of the
month. For information on the Carte
Musées Côte d'Azur see ▶p.376)

SHOPPING

Fashion: Rue Paradis, Av. de Suède,
Rue A. Karr, Rue du Mal. Joffre.
Delicatessen including confiserie
Niçoise: Rue St-François de Paule and
Quai Papacino (at the harbour).

WHERE TO EAT
▶ Moderate / expensive
① *Château des Ollières*
39 Av. des Baumettes, tel. 04 92 15 77 99
Restaurant in a bizarre belle-époque
chateau, which was built by a Russian
prince for his paramour (now a dream
of a hotel with 9 rooms, with its own
small park). Outstanding, high-class
local cuisine, with friendly service.

▶ Moderate
② *La Merenda*
4 Rue Raoul Bosio, no telephone,
closed Sat–Sun and 3 weeks at the
beginning of Aug
With the excellent local cuisine, it is no
wonder that La Merenda is always full.

▶ Inexpensive
③ *Cantine de Lulu*
26 Rue Alberti, tel. 04 93 62 15 33,
closed Sat–Sun. Apart from some
French classics (and some unusual
dishes from the late-Victorian/Edwar-
dian era) the food served here is firmly
part of the Niçoise tradition.

WHERE TO STAY
▶ Luxury
① *Négresco*
37 Promenade des Anglais
Tel. 04 93 16 64 00
www.negresco-nice.com
Legendary hotel with antique furnishings from the 17th–18th centuries and
the belle époque. Private beach. The
restaurant, Le Chantecler, is equally
high class and top quality (tel. as hotel).

▶ Mid-range
② *Windsor*
11 Rue Dalpozzo, tel. 04 93 88 59 35
www.hotelwindsornice.com
Attractive, slightly off the wall building
about 150m/160yd from the beach:
every room has been designed by a
different contemporary artist. Tropical
garden with small swimming pool plus
a restaurant.

▶ Budget
③ *St-Georges*
7 Avenue G. Clémenceau, tel. 04 93 88
79 21, www.hotelsaintgeorges.fr. Small,
pleasant hotel. Breakfast is served in
the garden.

During the day there is a market on Cours Saleya, but in the evening it becomes a place to eat

The labyrinthine old town extends to the west of the castle hill. At its heart is the lengthy **Cours Saleya**, the lively and colourful market-place where flowers and food are sold, except on Mondays when antiques take precedence. At the eastern edge of the square is the magnificently decorated Chapelle de la Miséricorde (1736), including a Vierge de la Miséricorde (Virgin of Mercy) by Jean Mirailhet (1430) and a Madonna attributed to Ludovico Brea (c1510).

North of Cours Saleya is the Palais de la Préfecture (1613), built for the princes of Savoy, with the palais de justice next door (1892). The **cathedral of Ste-Réparate** on Place Rossetti was built from 1650 to 1757 in early Baroque Romanesque. Notable features of the marvellous furnishings include the beautiful choir seating and a Madonna in a coloured frame (16th century). The magnificently furnished Jesuit church of St-Jacques (Gesú) was also built to a Romanesque template (17th century). Where Rue Rossetti crosses Rue Benoît-Bunico, there was a Jewish ghetto as of 1430. The magnificent **Palais Lascaris** (1650) on Rue Droite was the residence of the Lascaris-Ventimiglia family, the counts of Castellar. Inside it there is an immense stairway and an apothecary dating back to 1738 (closed Tue). Further north, beyond Place St-François and its fish market, is Nice's first parish church, St-Martin-St-Augustin, where Martin Luther is said to have held masses in 1510 and where Garibaldi was baptized. There is an impressive **pietà** by Ludovico Brea (1489). The route ends up at Place Garibaldi, a square laid out in the 17th century with arcades in Piedmontese style.

Across the river Paillon, a cultural assemblage has been put together, including a theatre and a museum for modern and contemporary art (Yves Bayard, Henri Vidal, 1990; closed Mon). The museum displays a good cross-section of artistic images from the 1960s and 70s (with an emphasis on works by **Yves Klein**. There is a nice view from the roof. To the north of the museum is the long complex of the **Acropolis** congress and exhibition centre, while opposite it to the east is the

Vieille Ville

Chapelle de la Miséricorde

Palais de la Préfecture

St-Martin-St-Augustin

Paillon site

★
Musée d'Art Moderne et d'Art Contemporain

Nice Map

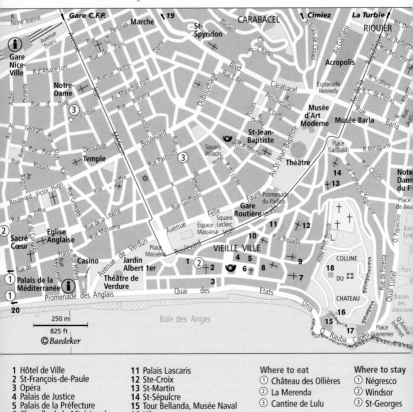

© Baedeker

1 Hôtel de Ville
2 St-François-de-Paule
3 Opéra
4 Palais de Justice
5 Palais de la Préfecture
6 Chapelle de la Miséricorde
7 St-Suaire
8 St-Jaume
9 St-Jacques (Eglise du Gésu)
10 Cathédrale Ste-Réparate

11 Palais Lascaris
12 Ste-Croix
13 St-Martin
14 St-Sépulcre
15 Tour Bellanda, Musée Naval
16 Lift
17 Monument aux Morts
18 Map of the view
19 Musée Chagall, Cimiez
20 Musées Masséna, des Beaux-Arts, d'Art Naïf

Where to eat
① Château des Ollières
② La Merenda
③ Cantine de Lulu

Where to stay
① Négresco
② Windsor
③ St-Georges

Jardin Albert I

science museum, Musée Barla. Across Place Masséna, whose red colour has been preserved and on which stands the Fontaine du Soleil, the route leads to Jardin Albert I and the Promenade des Anglais.

★
Promenade des Anglais

It is difficult to imagine that the 6km/4mi of the Promenade des Anglais were laid and between 1822 and 1824 as a path just 2m/6ft wide. Nowadays it is distinguished by luxurious buildings in belle époque and Art Deco styles: the Palais de la Méditerranée (1929), Palais Masséna (1898) and the famous **Hotel Negresco** (1912). Palais

Musée d'Art et d'Histoire

Masséna now contains the Musée d'Art et d'Histoire (closed Tue), which exhibits a selection including Roman discoveries, works of art by the Nice school artists and a collection reflecting local history.

Les Baumettes

The university quarter is in the west of the city. On Av. des Baumettes a palazzo from 1878 houses the fascinating **Musée des Beaux-Arts** (closed Mon), with works by Fragonard, Braque, Chagall, Rodin, Picasso and many more. Further west (Av. Val-Marie) is the Musée International d'Art Naïf Anatole Jakovsky, which takes a look at primitive art from all over the world (closed Tue).

Eglise Russe

Like San Remo, Nice too has a splendid Russian church in the Moscovite style (St-Nicolas, 1912). It is situated on Boulevard Tsarevich to the west of the main station near Boulevard Gambetta.

Carabacel

The **Musée National Message Biblique Marc Chagall** can be found in the northern suburb of Carabacel on the boulevard leading to Cimiez (closed Tue). It is the most important exhibitor of works by painter Marc Chagall (1887–1985).

★ Cimiez Roman town

The suburb of Cimiez, which was the most popular area for the villas of the rich in the 19th century, also possesses the relics of the **Roman town** of Cemenelum. The amphitheatre (with space for more than 5000) and hot baths are both well preserved. The Musée d'Archéologie (closed Tue) has an exhibition of some of the finds. Next door in a magnificent Genoese villa (1670) are numerous works by **Henri Matisse**, who lived in Nice from 1917 until his death in 1954 (closed Tue).

★ Musée Matisse

Notre-Dame-de-Cimiez

Above the Roman ruins stands the monastery of Notre-Dame-de-Cimiez, founded in the 9th century. The church possesses one fine early work by Ludovico Brea, a triptych from 1475 (pietà, Saints Martin and Catharine), as well as a Crucifixion (1512) and Jesus being taken down from the Cross, which may be by either Ludovico or Antonio Brea. The cemetery is the last resting place of both Matisse and Dufy.

Harbour quarter

At the foot of the 178m/584ft Mont Boron, which marks the eastern edge of the Baie des Anges, nestles the harbour quarter with its unadorned residential buildings in Italian style. The suburb of Riquier, which was established in the years after 1780, adjoins it to the north. In 1965, 21 layers of a 400,000-year-old refuge used by members of the species Homo erectus was found the premises of the Terra Amata Museum (25 Blvd. Carnot, closed Mon).

Musée de Terra Amata

Around Nice

Observatory

At the edge of Mont Gros (375m/1230ft) in the northeast of Nice, there is an observatory built by Charles Garnier (dome by Gustave Eiffel, 1885). To get there, take the Grande Corniche (D 2564).

CAP 3000, Parc Phénix	In the southwest, near the airport, is the huge **CAP 3000** shopping centre, which is worth a visit. Northeast of the airport, visitors can take a rest in Parc Phénix (Parc Floral) with its lake, birdhouses and huge greenhouse. On the lake there is a delight for devotees of both modern architecture and Far Eastern culture in the form of the Musée Départemental des Arts Asiatiques (405 Promenade des Anglais; closed Tue), designed by **Kenzo Tange** and opened in 1998.
✱ **Musée des Arts Asiatiques**	

Maritime Alps The country inland from Nice, between the valley of the Var and the French-Italian border, is described in the section on the ▶Côte d'Azur. Trains also run from the SNCF station through the **Tende Pass** to Cuneo, while the Gare C.F.P. on Rue A.-Binet is the terminus for the **Train des Pignes**, which runs via Entrevaux to Digne (▶Baedeker Tip p.386).

✱ ✱ Nîmes

M 9

Région:	Languedoc-Roussillon	**Altitude:**	39m/128ft
Département:	Gard	**Population:**	138,000

Nîmes nestles charmingly amid the foothills of the Cevennes. When it comes to classical buildings, it is the richest town in France. It is, however, a lively and youthful town, as demonstrated in its Whitsun celebrations and cultural scene.

History Nemausus, on the road from Rome to Hispania, submitted to the Romans in 121 BC and quickly became one of the most important towns in Gaul. Under Augustus veterans from Egypt were settled in »Colonia Augusta Nemausus«. Coins with crocodiles and palm trees (part of the city's coat of arms) are indicative of this fact. Antoninus Pius, the emperor as of 138 AD, was born in Nîmes. During the religious wars of the 16th century, there were bloody battles here between Catholics and Reformists, as three quarters of the population were Huguenots. The textile industry instituted a new economic boom in the 18th century and retains its importance to this day. The blue serge »de Nîmes« (or denim) has been famous the world over since Levi Strauss, Franconian by birth, used it to make his »blue jeans« (from »bleu de Gênes«) in the USA.

What to See in Nîmes

✱ ✱ **Arènes** The main attraction in Nîmes is its **amphitheatre** dating from the end of the 1st century (open June–Aug 9am–7pm, otherwise shorter opening hours). At 133 × 101m/145 × 110yd in area and 21m/69ft in height, it had space for 24,000 spectators. It is not the biggest but it is the best preserved of the 70 Roman amphitheatres known to have survived. Its richly decorated main entrance is on the northwestern side. Its 124 exits (vomitories) meant that visitors could vacate the building in a matter of minutes. In the Middle Ages the arena was used as a fortress and later became a residential estate housing some 2000 people. Its rebuilding and restoration were initiated in 1809. A roof allows the stadium to be used even in winter. Apart from sport and music events it is also a venue for **bullfighting**. The Musée Taurin (museum of bullfighting, Rue A. Ducros) is a stone's throw from Les Arènes.

The Roman arena is the centrepiece of Nîmes

To the east of the arena runs the busy **Esplanade Charles de Gaulle** with the Fontaine Pradier (1848), which bears a personification of Nîmes. Rue Notre-Dame leads from there to the Abribus bus station, designed by Philippe Starck. North of the arena is Place du Marché with the Fontaine au Crocodile, designed by Martial Raysse (evoking the crocodile in the city's arms). Further east, Rue de l'Aspic has some lovely old houses.

Place de la Maison Carrée (photo p.581) is dominated by the **Roman podium temple**, which was built as of AD 4 in honour of Augustus's grandchild. It is one of the best preserved Roman buildings anywhere. Over the years it has served as a church, a consul building, a stable, an archive and a museum, among other things. Opposite stands the Carrée d'Art (Norman Foster, 1993) with its **museum of contemporary art**, which exhibits works post-1960 (open Tue–Sun 10am–6pm).

★
Maison Carrée

Musée d'Art Contemporain

The atmospheric Jardin de la Fontaine was created in 1750 in the region of a spring, which was a shrine in Celtic times. The so-called **Temple of Diana** was probably part of a Roman thermal baths. Towering 114m/374ft over the park is Mont Cavalier with its tropical flora. It is topped by the 32m/105ft, which dates back to Celtic times and was incorporated into the city's defences by the Romans. There is a great view from its lookout platform.

★
Jardin de la Fontaine

Tour Magne

Underneath the fort, built in 1687 on Rue de Lampèze, are the remains of a Gallo-Roman pump house, which distributed the water carried into the town over the Pont du Gard (▶see below). Ten lead pipes lead from its circular basins out to the various parts of town.

Castellum Divisorium

⏵ VISITING NÎMES

INFORMATION

Office de Tourisme
6 Rue Auguste, F-30000 Nîmes
Tel. 04 66 58 38 00, fax 04 66 58 38 01
www.ot-nimes.fr

FESTIVALS AND EVENTS

Corridas in the Arena. Whitsun: Féria
de Pentecôte, with »Pégoulade«. 3rd
weekend in Sept: Féria des Vendanges.
Information and tickets: Bureau de
Location des Arènes, 4 Rue de la
Violette, tel. 0891 70 14 01
July/Aug: rock, folk, jazz etc.

MUSEUM PASS

For all museums plus the Arena,
Maison Carrée and Tour Magne.

WHERE TO STAY

▶ Mid-range

① *New Hôtel La Baume*
21 Rue Nationale
Tel. 04 66 76 28 42, www.new-hotel.com
Renaissance palais with a lovely inner
courtyard. Inconspicuously elegant,
modern furnishings in warm colours –
a place to feel comfortable. (Significantly more expensive during the
Férias.)

▶ Budget

② *Hôtel Amphithéâtre*
4 Rue des Arènes
Tel. 04 66 67 28 51, fax 04 66 67 07 79
A 300-year-old building, charmingly
furnished. Some of the rooms have a
nice view of the marketplace.

48 Grand'Rue

F-30420 Calvisson (15km/9mi)
Tel. 04 66 01 23 91, fax 04 66 01 42 19
www.bed-and-art.com
This hotel in a small 15th-century
building southwest of Nîmes is run by
an art historian/painter couple who
also offer painting lessons. Very tastefully furnished, quiet rooms and a
fabulous courtyard.

Saint-Géniès

Route de St-Ambroix, F-30700 Uzès
Tel. 04 66 22 29 99
www.hotel-saintgenies.com
For those in search of peace and quiet,
this hotel 1.5km/1mi outside Uzès is
ideal. Very good value for money.
Breakfast includes home-made jam.
There is a swimming pool but no
restaurant.

WHERE TO EAT

▶ Inexpensive

① *Les Olivades*
18 Rue Jean Reboul
Tel. 04 66 21 71 78, closed Sun–Mon.
Elegant and comfortable atmosphere
in the old vault. Very good cuisine at a
fair price and a corresponding selection of wines – it is adjoined by a
»vinotheque«.

② *Le Ménestrel*
6 Rue École Vieille, tel. 04 66 67 54 45
Somewhat plush and over-decorated
restaurant, but famed as the best place
for local cuisine.

Notre-Dame et St-Castor The cathedral is situated on the pretty **Place aux Herbes**. It was established in 1096 but destroyed in the 16th century, then rebuilt in
the 19th century in Romano-Byzantine style. On the gable of the
western façade a Romanesque relief is preserved showing scenes

Ancient and modern come face to face on Place de la Maison Carrée

from the creation story. In the former episcopal palace next door, the Musée du Vieux Nîmes (history of the region and its textile industry; closed Mon) is most interesting. The large market hall is not to be missed either.

★ **Musée du Vieux Nîmes**

On Blvd. Amiral Courbet, which bounds the old town to the east, a former Jesuit college houses the remarkable archaeological museum (Celtic and Roman finds, sculptures from up till the Middle Ages, coins, pottery and more; closed Mon).

★ **Musée Archéologique**

The Porte d'Auguste gate, named after the Roman emperor Augustus, who commissioned the first walls surrounding the city, was the starting point for the Via Domitia, the other end being in Rome. In the 14th century it was incorporated into a fortress and was only rediscovered in 1752. The line of another wing, destroyed during the French Revolution, is marked out on the ground.

Porte d'Auguste

The art museum (Rue Cité-Foulc, closed Mon) displays numerous works, primarily by old masters from the 16th–18th centuries). There is also a large Roman mosaic, which was unearthed at this very spot.

Musée des Beaux-Arts

Since the mid-1980s, renowned architects have **reshaped** Nîmes in a fascinating way at a number of sites. Apart from the Musée d'Art Contemporain, the Abribus and the fountain on Place du Marche, noteworthy new developments include Place d'Assas (Raysse, 1989), the Nemausus council housing complex (Nouvel, 1987) on Route d'Arles, and the École des Beaux-Arts (Balmassière, 1987).

New Nîmes

Around Nîmes

The famous mineral water – a brand owned by Nestlé – is bottled in Vergèze, 13km/8mi southwest of Nîmes (tours daily, pre-booking recommended, tel. 04 66 87 61 01).

Perrier

Nîmes Map

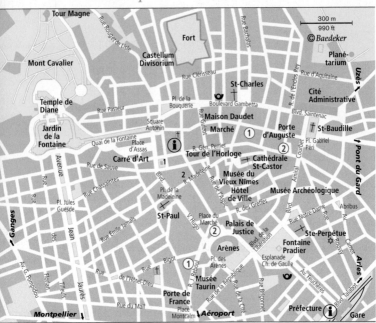

300 m
990 ft
© Baedeker

Tour Magne

Rue Rouveyrie de Lisle

Fort

Castellum Divisorium

Mont Cavalier

Rue Clérisseau

Plané-tarium

Rue Bacheils

Rue d'Aquitaine

Uzès

St-Charles

Cité Administrative

R. de l'Enclos Rey

Blvd. Saintenac

Temple de Diane

Rue Pasteur

Pl. de la Bouquerie

Boulevard Gambetta

Maison Daudet

Marché ①

Porte d'Auguste

† **St-Baudille**

Pl. Gabriel Péri

Jardin de la Fontaine

Quai de la Fontaine

Place d'Assas

Square Antonin

Carré d'Art

R. Gén. Perrier

Tour de l'Horloge

Cathédrale St-Castor

②

Courbet

Rue Guiton

Avenue

Rue de Sauve

Rue Chassaintes

Rue de la Madeleine

R. Madeleine

Musée du Vieux Nîmes

Hôtel de Ville

Musée Archéologique

Blvd. Amiral

Abribus

Pont du Gard

Pl. Jules Guesde

Rue

Jean

Rue Émile Jamais

Pl. de la Madeleine

St-Paul

V. Hugo

Place du Marché

②

Palais de Justice

R. des Greffes

Rue Notre-Dame

Rue

Av.

Carnot Rousey

Ste-Perpétue ✡

Ganges

Av. R. Pompidou

Florian

Tilleuls

Jaurès

Bigot

Rue

de l'Hôtel-Dieu

Rue

Papauté

Arènes

Pl. des Arènes

① †

Musée Taurin

Blvd. de la Libération

Fontaine Pradier

Esplanade Ch. de Gaulle

Av. Feuchères

Blvd. Talabot

Arles

Rue du Mail

Porte de France

Rue de la République

Rue Briçonnet

Préfecture ①

Gare

Montpellier

Place Montcalm

▶ **Aéroport**

1 **Maison Carrée**
2 **Opéra**

Where to eat
① Les Olivades
② Le Ménestrel

Where to stay
① New Hôtel La Baume
② Amphithéâtre

★ ★
Pont du Gard

About 25km/16mi northeast of Nîmes, the deep valley of the Gardon river is bridged by the Roman aqueduct, the 49m/16ft-high and 275m/290yd-long Pont du Gard. This mighty building work with three levels of arches was built in around AD 50 employing no mortar and using solid blocks hewn from the rock. It was part of a waterway stretching some 50km/31mi, by which water was transported to Nîmes from the river Eure (to the northwest near Uzès), although this is at an elevation only 17m/66ft higher than Nîmes itself. Every day about 20,000 cubic m/4.4 million gallons of water flowed along the stone-paved canal along the top row of arches, and that continued for as many as 500 years according to the lime deposits left behind. The Pont du Gard has, in spite of all the interventions of time, been so well preserved that even in the 19th century it was proposed that it once more be included as part of a water distribu-

Water for Nîmes: a purely functional construction, but now one →
of the most impressive examples of Roman architecture

tion network. It even survived severe flood waters in September 2002 with no damage. This miracle of Roman architecture is a **UNESCO World Heritage Site** and attracts 2 million visitors a year. On hot days many people like to swim in the river. There is a large pay car park and a modern **visitor centre** at the northern edge of the site with a good museum and audio-visual presentation. There is no avoiding the »historic« guides and animations for children, but the illumination of the bridge every evening between June and September is impressive (July–Aug daily, June/Sept Fri–Sat; www.pontdugard.fr).

Uzès Uzès (7800 inhabitants), 25km/16mi north of Nîmes overlooking the valley of the River Alzon, is another place worth visiting. Its arcade-lined **Place aux Herbes** is highly atmospheric. The chateau of the dukes of Uzès (Duché, 11th–17th centuries) has a Renaissance inner courtyard dating from 1565. There is a lovely view from the Tour Bermonde (11th century). The episcopal palace now houses the Musée Georges Borias (art, folklore, memorabilia of novelist André Gide, whose father came from Uzès). The circular **Tour Fenestrelle** (12th century), 42m/138ft high and based on a Lombard model, is unique in France. It is all that remains of a Romanesque cathedral, the successor of which, St-Théodorit, was consecrated in 1652 (façade 1873, organ 1685). In the second half of July, the »Nuits Musicales« festival takes place featuring both classical and traditional music. Connoisseurs of Haribo sweets will not want to miss the **Musée de Bonbon** on the D 981 to Avignon (open daily July–Sept, otherwise closed Mon).

The round tower of the Romanesque church is the distinctive emblem of Uzès

* * Normandy

The »Land of the Normans« corresponds to that area of northern France between the Paris basin and the English Channel. Along the varied coast, 600km/370mi long, lie some of the best-known resorts in France, milk and cream, cider and calvados are produced on the verdant fields inland. Castle, chateaux and gorgeous little towns are all reminders of the region's ever-changing history.

The name Normandy conjures memories of the Norsemen, who plagued the coasts of the western Frankish kingdom from the 7th century on, of the Norman ruler William who successfully conquered England in 1066 and of the biggest invasion force in history, the Allied landings which opened the final phase of the Second World War. For local government purposes Normandy is split into the regions of Haute Normandie (to the east) and Basse Normandie (to the west), names which simply refer to their distance from Paris. The great charm of Normandy lies in the highly varied coastline, which stretches 600km/370mi between Le Tréport in the northeast and ►Mont St-Michel in the southwest. Sections of the coast bear evocative names like the Alabaster Coast (Côte d'Albâtre), the Flower Coast (Côte Fleurie) and the Mother of Pearl Coast (Côte de Nacre). The chalk cliffs of the Côte d'Albâtre are famous – they are at their most spectacular at Étretat. The Cotentin Peninsula, part of Armorican Massif, stretches far out into the English Channel. Inland, though, Normandy has a quite different look. The Bocage Normand district is a land of woods and meadows and includes the romantic »Switzerland of Normandy«. Hedges divide fields and meadows where apple and pear trees grow and dairy cows graze. Right in the middle of Normandy is the fertile Pays d'Auge, which is the origin of products such as cider, calvados and camembert cheese. There are also stirring reminders of history, especially in the old capital of ►Rouen and at ► Mont St-Michel (St Michael's Mount). The Atlantic climate is mild, damp and changeable. The peak periods for visiting are in the summer months of July and August. Inland, it is particularly lovely around the time that the fruit trees blossom in April and May.

Landscape of Normandy

The main centres of industry are Rouen and Le Havre, Dieppe and Caen. The nuclear industry is not only of local importance, as the reprocessing facility at Cap de la Hague near Cherbourg is used by many European countries. Visitors from abroad are a major factor. The key tourist destinations include the resorts of Deauville, Trouville, the Cotentin Peninsula and the two pilgrimage centres of Lisieux and Mont St-Michel. Normandy is mainly reliant on agriculture, though. Its most familiar products, apart from cream and butter, include numerous varieties of cheese, such as Pont l'Evêque, Livarot and Camembert, as well as the alcoholic drinks cider and

Economy

Highlights *in Normandy*

calvados. **Cider**, apple juice fermented to a refreshing wine-like beer with 3–5% alcohol, has been made here since the 13th century. Served cold, it is a popular thirst quencher. **Calvados** is distilled from cider and has more than 40% alcohol. The best calvas are made from 2 to 3-year-old cider, which is then mulled two or three times and the distillate allowed to ferment in oak barrels, from which the amber colour and bouquet come. For more information, visit the region's many Musées des Cidres, e.g. in Valognes on the Cotentin Peninsula.

History   From the 7th century onwards, Scandinavian plunderers, the **Norsemen and Vikings**, began to appear along the coasts of the Frankish kingdom ruled by the Merovingians. They attacked and plundered towns, villages and monasteries. They sailed up the Seine and conquered Rouen in 841, then Paris itself in 845. Barely a century later, the invaders had settled in the country. King Charles the Simple of the western Frankish kingdom (West Francia) ceded about half of what is now Normandy to the Viking Rollo in 911 in return for his vow of allegiance and his baptism to Christianity. This was not enough to stop him and his sons continuing their conquests, expanding Normandy to the extent it still occupies today. Duke William (»**William the Conqueror**« expanded the dominion still further with his victory at Hastings in 1066, which led to him being crowned king of England. The consequence was that when Henry Plantagenet became Henry II of England in 1153, he inherited a kingdom which initially stretched from Aquitaine to the borders of Scotland. It was King John who lost Normandy to France's King Philippe II in 1204. During the Hundred Years' War, Normandy came back into English hands between 1417 and 1450. In 1431, the trial of **Joan of Arc** took place in Rouen, ending with her being burned at the stake as a witch and a heretic. The religious wars between Huguenots and Catholics

The chalk cliffs of the »Alabaster Coast« are particularly impressive near Étretat, as here at Falaise d'Aval

from 1562 to 1598 and the repeal of the Edict von Nantes in 1685 led to Protestants fleeing from France en masse. On D-Day, 6 June 1944, the **Allied landings** started along the coast of Normandy (►Baedeker Special p.600).

The Normans adopted Christianity quite early on. Their brilliant architects would stamp their mark on the country for centuries to come, as reflected in Normandy's magnificent cathedrals, monasteries and castles. In addition, the Normans were expert in the rearing of cattle and horses; Norman cows are descended from the Norwegian Telemark breed, and Normandy remains a centre for the breeding of horses till this day. In the 19th century, many artists were attracted here by the light and colour of the region and the Honfleur and Impressionist schools were established. The most famous of these painters, Claude Monet, grew up in Le Havre and lived in Giverny from 1883 till his death in 1926. His house and garden are among the top attractions in the region. Victor Hugo, André Gide and Marcel Proust also liked to stay in Normandy. Eric Satie was born in Honfleur in 1866.

Culture

⏵ VISITING NORMANDY

INFORMATION

CRT Normandie
Le Doyenné, 14 Rue Charles Corbeau
F-27 000 Evreux
Tel. 02 32 33 79 00, fax 02 32 31 19 04
www.normandie-tourisme.fr

WHERE TO EAT

▶ Moderate / expensive

Spinnaker
52 Rue Mirabeau, F-14800 Deauville
Tel. 02 31 88 24 40, closed Mon–Tue
Pascal Angenard is considered the
most creative cook in Deauville. A
pleasant modern ambience in a pretty
old building.

▶ Moderate

Ferme de la Ranconnière
Route d'Arromanches, Crépon
F-14480 Creully, tel. 02 31 22 21 73
www.ranconniere.fr
Those who fancy a spot of hearty
Norman cuisine in a fabulous old fort
should try this hotel and restaurant
13km/8mi east of Bayeux. Ideally, stay
over in one of the 42 very stylish
rooms (budget / mid-range).

WHERE TO STAY

▶ Luxury

Normandy-Barrière
38 Rue J. Mermoz
F-14800 Deauville, tel. 02 31 98 66 22
www.lucienbarriere.com
Deauville's classic luxury hotel next to
the Royal Barrière (Boulevard E. Cor-
nuché) is built in Norman style. It has
an indoor swimming pool and a garden.

▶ Mid-range / luxury

Le Donjon
Chemin de St-Clair, F-75790 Étretat
Tel. 02 35 27 08 23, fax 02 35 29 92 24
www.hoteletretat.com
Small, high-class hotel located in an
old fort above the town, with a great
view of the rocks at Étretat. Romantic
rooms, all individually styled. Some
have their own whirlpool baths. There
is a swimming pool in the park and a
very good restaurant (closed Mon and
lunchtimes).

L'Absinthe
10 Quai de la Quarantaine
F-14600 Honfleur
Tel. 02 31 89 23 23, www.absinthe.fr
A 16th-century presbytery near the
harbour at Honfleur provides comfortable, charming rooms of under-
stated luxury and a good restaurant.

▶ Budget / Mid-range

Hôtel d'Argouges
21 Rue St-Patrice, F-14400 Bayeux
Tel. 02 31 92 88 86, fax 02 31 92 69 16,
www.hotel-dargouges.com
Small, elegant 18th-century mansion
with large rooms to feel at home in.
The lovely courtyard is like a park. It is
easy to get to the centre of Bayeux on
foot.

Le Chantilly
120 Av. de la République
F-14800 Deauville
Tel. 02 31 88 79 75, fax 02 31 88 41 29,
Nicely renovated middle-class residence in Deauville near the La Touques race track. The rooms facing the
courtyard are quieter. No restaurant.

Château de la Roque
F-50180 Hébécrevon
Tel. 02 33 57 33 20
www.chateau-de-la-roque.fr
Fine Chambre d'Hôte, 7km/4mi west
of St-Lô, in an aristocratic residence
from the 16th–17th centuries, surrounded by ponds and furnished for
comfort.

✳ ✳ Côte d'Albâtre

The gravelly beaches of the »Alabaster Coast« between Le Tréport and Le Havre are lined for long distances by tall, white **chalk cliffs**, rising in places to more than 100m/330ft in height. Wind, rain and waves have been eroding them since prehistoric times. The characteristic banding of the cliffs is due to darker deposits of flint.

Picturesque cliffs

The small port of Le Tréport (6000 inhabitants), at the northern tip of Normandy, nestles at the foot of some impressive cliffs. The 15th-century church of St-Jacques above the harbour has a fine Renaissance doorway. The hill known as Calvaire des Terrasses offers a tremendous view, as does the terrace of the Le Trianon hotel.

Le Tréport

Dieppe (36,000 inhabitants) is an important passenger port and since the 1820s has been a **popular seaside resort** framed by picturesque chalk cliffs. It is worth visiting the municipal museum in a fort dating from 1433 (history of the mariners' town, arts and crafts and art including ivory carvings made in Dieppe between the 16th and 19th centuries). The hub of the lovely town centre is the small square of Place du Puits Salé with the church of St-Rémy (16th–17th centuries) to the west and the beautiful Gothic cathedral of St-Jacques (13th–16th centuries) to the northeast. Adjoining the atmospheric fishing harbour is the Avant-Port (with ferries to England). To the east lies the very old suburb of Le Pollet, formerly the fishermen's quarter. There is a great view from the chapel of Notre-Dame-de-Bon-Secours (1876). The Cité de la Mer provides a wealth of information about the underwater world (in its aquaria), shipbuilding and fisheries.

Dieppe

> ! **Baedeker** TIP
>
> ### Let's go fly a kite
>
> On the meadows between the beach and Boulevard de Verdun in Dieppe the sea breezes waft many a brightly coloured kite through the air. For one week in September (in even years) kite enthusiasts from all over the world hold a meeting here.

►Rouen

Pays de Bray

The prettily situated seaside resort of Varengeville (1200 inhabitants) possesses France's **biggest pigeon loft** in the Manoir d'Ango, which is well worth seeing. The rich ship-owner Jehan d'Ango had the Renaissance mansion built by Italian architects in 1533–45. Other places worth a visit include Park Le Bois des Moutiers, part of an English-style stately home. There is a fine view from the church of St-Valery (11th–15th centuries); painter Georges Braque (1882–1963) and composer Albert Roussel (1869–1937) are buried in its cemetery. Braque was the creator of the deep blue window inside the church, while its counterpart to the left of the choir was produced by the Belgian, Raoul Ubac. There is another great panoramic view from the Phare d'Ailly lighthouse, 2km/1.5mi to the west.

Varengeville-sur-Mer

Saint-Valery-en-Caux

The history from the 13th century till the present day of the small port of Saint-Valery-en-Caux, now a busy seaside resort, is documented in Maison Henry IV, a fabulous half-timbered building.

Fécamp

The fishing port of Fécamp (21,500 inhabitants) does a lively trade. Beautifully located at the end of Valmont valley, it is framed by its beach and by the tallest cliff in Normandy (126m/413ft). Guy de Maupassant spent some time in the popular seaside resort and some of his stories are set there. In the Middle Ages, Fécamp was an important place of pilgrimage, where drops of Christ's blood were revered. This explains the large size of the **abbey church of Ste-Trinité**. At 128m/140yd in length, it is almost as long as Notre-Dame in Paris. This gem of the Norman school was built from 1175 to 1220 (façade 18th century). The choir has a fine screen (1868) and seating from 1748. The relics are kept in the Lady Chapel. Opposite the church are the ruins of the ducal castle (10th–11th centuries). **Bénedictine** liqueur has been distilled in Fécamp since 1863. More can be learned about the product at the definitively splendid Palais Bénédictine from 1892 (110 Rue Alexandre-Le-Grand), where visitors can sample the wares and enjoy the remarkable collection of medieval art. The pilgrims' chapel of Notre-Dame-du-Salut (13th–14th centuries) is situated atop 114m/374ft-high chalk cliffs to the north of the town.

★ ★ Étretat

This popular resort nestles between chalk cliffs rising to 90m/295ft. To the north is the Falaise d'Amont, while the west is marked by the spectacular Falaise d'Aval, which resembles an arch. Off the coast the Creuse d'Étretat rises to 70m/230ft above sea level. Among the other things worth seeing are the market hall (1926) and the church of Notre-Dame (11th–13th centuries). Maurice Leblanc, creator of gentleman thief, Arsène Lupin (►Rouen), bought a fine house here in 1918. Nowadays visitors are invited to relive the climax to the *Riddle of the Aiguille Creuse* (hollow needle).

Le Havre

►Le Havre

★ ★ Vallée de la Seine

Scenery

The Seine has its source in Burgundy and flows through Champagne, the Ile-de-France and Normandy, reaching the sea some 775km/482mi later at Le Havre on the English Channel. It was and remains the most important transport artery of northern France. Its valley is the scenic core of Haute-Normandie. The **long meanders** of the river between Paris and the sea contribute to its great length, triple the distance as the crow flies, even though the actual gradient is very small (only 16m/52ft between Vernon and the estuary). The lower reaches are spanned by three large bridges: Pont de Brotonne, Pont de Tancarville and Pont de Normandie (a toll is payable on the latter

Richard the Lionheart had Château-Gaillard built above Les Andeleys

two). One particularly impressive stretch is the 110km/68mi Route des Abbayes between ▶Rouen and ▶Le Havre, although the section between Giverny and Les Andelys is also very beautiful.

★
Giverny

Giverny (500 inhabitants), some 70km/43mi northwest of Paris, was home to the painter **Claude Monet** from 1883 till his death in 1926. His house and the beautiful garden he had laid out to his own specifications, expressed in numerous pictures, are a major attraction (open April–Oct Tue–Sun 9.30am–6pm). The nearby Musée d'Art Américain is also interesting, featuring works by American impressionists and possessing a nice terrace café.

Vernon

Vernon (25,000 inhabitants), opposite Giverny, has some lovely half-timbered buildings and there is a fine view of the town from its bridge. Inside its imposing Notre-Dame church (12th–16th centuries), take note of the organ (15th–16th centuries), the stained-glass windows (16th century) and the high altar. Musée Poulain (12 Rue du Pont) has an archaeological and local history collection on view, as well as paintings by Monet, Sisley, Bonnard and others. Upon a rocky promontory over the Seine are the ruins of the **Château de Gaillon**. At the western edge of the town, it is worth visiting the splendid Château de Bizy (1740). A **boat trip** from Vernon to Pressagny-l'Orgueilleux (mid-May–mid-Sept Sun, July–Aug also Wed–Fri and Sat) or Les Andelys (July–Aug Fri) is also not to be missed.

! **Baedeker TIP**

Hôtel Baudy

It is wonderful to take a break in this old café and restaurant, where the contemporaries of Monet once ate and painted. Meals are served under the lime trees or in the rose garden (81 Rue Claude Monet, Giverny, tel. 02 32 21 10 03).

Les Andelys
Around Les Andelys (8500 inhabitants) the Seine valley is flanked by high chalk cliffs. The magnificent ruin of **Château Gaillard** overlooks the town. It was built in 1197 by Richard the Lionheart to deny the French king access to Rouen (although the French did nevertheless conquer it in 1204). In the suburb of Grand Andely the church of Notre-Dame (nave 13th century, Flamboyant façade 16th–17th centuries) has 16th-century stained glass windows and a Renaissance organ. There is a great view from the bridge over the Seine.

Gisors
Gisors (9600 inhabitants), 30km/19mi east of Les Andelys, is the former capital of Vexin. It looks down over the valley of the river Epte on the border of the former Norman duchy. The magnificent 11th–12th-century **Norman fortress** is one of the finest examples of medieval architecture and there is a great view to boot. The church of St-Gervais-et-St-Protais (13th–16th centuries) is also worth seeing for its marvellous sculpture.

✷
Evreux
Evreux (54,000 inhabitants), the pleasant capital of the Eure département, has suffered destruction on countless occasions, most recently during air raids between 1940 and 1944. It centres on the cathedral of Notre-Dame (12th–17th centuries), notable features of which include the beautiful stained glass windows from the 13th–16th centuries and Renaissance cabinets in the chapels around the choir. The episcopal palace (1481) houses the Musée Municipal (archaeology, art and local crafts). The former **abbey church of St-Taurin** (11th–15th centuries) in the west of the town has a 13th-century shrine containing the relics of St Taurin himself, a masterpiece of French goldsmithery. Pâtisserie Auzou (Rue Chartraine) is famous for its own works of art including »Caprices des Ursulines« and »Pavés d'Evreux«.

A little beyond Rouen in **St-Martin-de-Boscherville** the D 982 passes the abbey church of St-Georges, built in 1080–1125, a gem of late Romanesque architecture. The abbey itself still has the 13th-century vaulted chapter hall, where there is an exhibition of beautiful pillar statuary and capitals. Concerts are held in the summer months.

In **Jumièges** (1500 inhabitants), two mighty 46m/151ft-high towers mark the **magnificent ruins** of an **abbey**, which was established in 654 and de-

Notre-Dame cathedral in Evreux

stroyed in 1790. They lie at the centre of an enchanting park. The church was consecrated in 1067 in the presence of William the Conqueror. The remaining doorway from the church of St-Pierre is a fine example of the Norman architecture of the 10th century.

Norman Seine Regional Nature Park

The Parc Naturel Régional des Boucles de la Seine Normande covers some 500 sq km/200 sq mi along the river from near Duclair to the estuary. The core of the park is the 74 sq km/30 sq mi Forêt de Brotonne. Information about footpaths, the diverse museums etc. can be obtained from the Maison du Parc in Notre-Dame-de-Bliquetuit.

Saint-Wandrille

North of the Seine on the D 982 is the abbey of St-Wandrille, founded in 649. Over the centuries it has been razed and rebuilt many times. Since 1931 it has once again been in the possession of the Benedictine order. The present-day buildings were originally built from the 14th–18th centuries. The 13th–16th-century abbey church only exists now as a picturesque ruin.

Caudebec-en-Caux

Caudebec (2300 inhabitants), on the west bank of the Seine, is the main town of the Pays de Caux. A lively market takes place every Saturday. The late Gothic church of **Notre-Dame** (1426–1534) is noteworthy. Henri IV deemed it the most beautiful in his kingdom, and it boasts three wonderful doorways in the west and an organ from the early 16th century. The Musée de la Marine de Seine displays boats used for shipping along the Seine in bygone days.

Villequier

The tiny village of Villequier (750 inhabitants) occupies a pretty location on the banks of the Seine, overlooked by a chateau. The daughter of Victor Hugo, Léopoldine, died here along with her husband, Charles Vacquerie, in a boat accident in 1843. A museum in the house where the Vacqueries lived recalls the writer and his family (closed Tue). 6km/4mi to the southwest beyond Norville, **Château Ételan** (Flamboyant Gothic, late 15th century) dominates the valley. There is a great view from the terrace.

Lillebonne

Even in Roman times Lillebonne was an important harbour, as testified by the ruins of an amphitheatre (2nd century). In the 11th century William the Conqueror had a castle built here and its 34m/112ft keep is still in existence.

Tancarville

The little town of Tancarville (1100 inhabitants), at the mouth of the Seine, boasts the ruins of an 11th-century castle as well as a 1410m/1542yd-long **suspension bridge** across the Seine, with 125m/410ft pylons (1959). The former swampland of Marais Vernier extends south of the river. The village of Marais Vernier still has the look of a medieval settlement.

★
Marais Vernier

►Le Havre

Le Havre

The seafaring era still leaves its mark at the old harbour in Honfleur

✳ Côte Fleurie

The beautiful »Flower Coast« (Côte Fleurie) stretches for 32km/20mi between Honfleur in the east and Cabourg in the west. Along its length are some of the best known and most fashionable resorts in northern France.

✳ Honfleur

Opposite ► Le Havre at the mouth of the Seine, the old seafaring town of Honfleur (8200 inhabitants) is linked to Le Havre via the Pont de Normandie. With its 1684 harbour and countless pretty houses, it is one of the most charming towns in Normandy. Many an expedition once set out from here, including one that reached Brazil in 1503 and another that led to the founding of Quebec in 1608. In the 19th century **a multitude of artists** flocked to the town, including the painters Boudin, Courbet, Sisley, Pissarro, Renoir and Cézanne. They would meet at Ferme St-Siméon, west of the Seine-estuary (now a luxury hotel; www.fermesaintsimeon.fr). Musée Boudin (Place Erik Satie) exhibits paintings by the eponymous artist, who was born in Honfleur, along with those of some of his contemporaries. The square itself is named after a most unusual composer, who was born in Honfleur in 1866 (Maisons Satie, 67 Blvd. Charles V). North of the Vieux Bassin is the astonishing late Gothic church of **Ste-Cathé-rine**, made entirely of wood by local shipbuilders, as was the free-standing bell tower from 1468. In the church of St-Etienne (14th–15th centuries) the Musée de la Marine covers the history of seafaring from the town. The neighbouring prison now houses the Musée d'Art Populaire (Norman folk art). About 1km/1000yd north-west of the centre, to the south of the road to Trouville, there is a hill with the pilgrimage chapel of Notre-Dame-de-Grâce (1615), the final destination of the **seamen's procession**, which takes place at Whitsun. Further southeast, Mont Joli offers an even clearer view of the town.

The **Corniche Normande**, with many fine vantage points along its length, links Honfleur with the popular resort of Trouville (5400 inhabitants). Trouville has a fine sandy beach and is slightly quieter than its posh neighbour, Deauville (4500 inhabitants – but many more in high season) on the other side of the Touques. Deauville, which has only existed since 1861, is considered to be France's polo capital. At the start of September the **Festival du Cinéma Américain** even attracts celebrities from Hollywood. An illustrious clientèle meets here for horse racing, yachting regattas, golf and equestrian events as well as for the horse fair for one-year-old colts and mares. The town also has an attractive promenade along the beach, a large yachting marina, a casino and various other leisure attractions, and there are plenty of film, concert and other events.

✱ **Trouville**

✱ **Deauville**

The Côte Fleurie takes in a variety of popular resorts before it ends, including Villers sur Mer, Houlgate and Dives sur Mer. The small town of Cabourg (3500 inhabitants), established in the 1880s, owes its fame to the Romanticist **Marcel Proust** (1871–1922), who often resided at the Grand Hôtel, which, along with the casino, lies at the centre of the semi-circular layout of the town. It is even possible to stay overnight in Proust's room.

Cabourg

✱ Pays d'Auge

The Pays d'Auge, the verdant country inland from the Côte Fleurie, is home to the three culinary »Cs«: camembert, cider and calvados.

Fun on the beach by the casino in Deauville

The land where milk and cider flow

The Calvados département is filled with meadows and rows of apple plantations. The **Route du Cidre** runs through attractive places like Cambremer, Beuvron en Auge (the »capital« of cider), Bonnebosq and Beaufour Druval. It is possible to visit many a cellar to taste or buy cider, calvados or camembert.

✱ **Lisieux**

The capital of the Pays d'Auge (24,000 inhabitants), about 30km/19mi south of the Seine estuary, is an important place of pilgrimage. Born in Alençon in 1873, Thérèse Martin grew up in Lisieux and entered the Carmelite convent there when she was just fifteen with special dispensation from the pope. She died in 1897 and was canonized in 1925. People make pilgrimage in her honour to the Ste-Thérèse basilica (1924–54, one of the largest churches to be built in the 20th century) and the Chapelle du Carmel. After the ravages of the Second World War, the town has been rebuilt in less than attractive fashion, but the cathedral of St-Pierre (1170–1250, south tower 1579) is still worth seeing. St Thérèse herself would go to Mass in the main chapel in the choir.

✱ **Bernay**

Situated between Evreux and Lisieux, Bernay (11,000 inhabitants) is a gem of Norman architecture (Saturday is market day) and boasts the **oldest Romanesque church in Normandy** (begun 1013). It belonged to an abbey, the buildings of which are still used for the town hall and a museum (with some good paintings, ceramics and Norman furniture).

✱ **Le Bec Hellouin**

An abbey was established in this idyllic village on the Risle (35km/22mi southwest of Rouen) in 1034 and during the Middle Ages it was one of the most important in the country. The buildings that remain today date from the 17th–18th centuries, with only the separate Tour St-Nicolas coming from any earlier (15th century). During Masses held late in the morning, the Benedictine monks sing Gregorian chants.

Château de Beaumesnil (1640), 13km/8mi southeast of Bernay, is certainly not to be missed. Dubbed the **Norman Versailles**, it also features a museum of bookbinding.

Château de Beaumesnil

Since the village of Camembert has been officially amalgamated into Vimoutiers (4700 inhabitants) 4km/2.5mi away, the latter has been styling itself »the capital of cheese«. Musée du Camembert (10 Av. de Gaulle) covers all aspects of the eponymous cheese's manufacture (there is also a Route du Camembert.) In Camembert itself, the Maison du Camembert recalls Marie Harel, who gave succour to a fleeing priest in 1790. The priest, in gratitude, then told her the recipe for the making of the famous cheese.

Vimoutiers

✳ ## Côte de Nacre

It was along the coast known as the Côte de Nacre between Ouistreham/Riva Bella at the mouth of the Orne and Grandcamp Maisy, that the Allied landings took place in the Second World War. The so-called »mother of pearl coast« is a stretch of flat sand and gravel beaches. On 6 June 1944 (D-Day), the Allied forces established their bridgehead in Europe here. Nowadays this peaceful stretch of land is dotted with reminders of the fighting. The **Circuit du Débarquement** is a tour taking in all the historic places. An insight into the events can be gained at the Mémorial in ►Caen. Omaha Beach, to the west of the fishing port of Port-en-Bessin, saw some of the heaviest fighting along the coast.

Upon the sandy beach of this little resort (550 inhabitants, photo p.601) the Allies established their floating harbour, »Mulberry B«, by submerging massive pontoons off the coast. Huge quantities of armaments, supplies and soldiers were put on land here. At low tide, remnants of the facility can still be seen. The Musée du Débarquement offers an introduction to the events and the 360° cinema »Arromanche 360°« shows a semi-documentary film.

Arromanches-les-Bains

Bayeux (15,000 inhabitants, 27km/17mi northwest of Caen) is the capital of Bessin, as the area of meadows and fields inland from there is known. Almost unbelievably, the town survived the Second World War undamaged. The pretty old town with its fine town houses from the 14th–18th centuries centres upon the Gothic **cathedral of Notre-Dame**, a masterpiece of Norman Gothic (13th–15th centuries). Inside, the high altar and the Baroque choir screen are noteworthy. In around 1070–80, Bishop Odo, brother of William the Conqueror, made a bequest for the decoration of the church. This was the famous **Bayeux tapestry** (Telle du Conquest), a frieze 70m/77yd long and 50 cm/2ft wide depicting his brother's conquest of England in 1066. There are 58 scenes, some featuring written text, 623 figures, 759 animals, and 37 buildings and ships, culminating with William's

Bayeux

✶ ✶
◄ Tapisserie de Bayeux

coronation in Westminster (photo p.50). The tapestry is now on view at the Centre Guillaume le Conquérant (Rue Nesmond, May–Aug 9am–7pm, 15 March–April and Sept–15 Nov till 6.30pm, otherwise 9.30am–12.30pm, 2pm–6pm). The Musée Baron Gérard in Hôtel Doyen, near the cathedral, is an interesting place to visit as is the Conservatoire de la Dentelle (6 Rue du Bienvenu), which even offers courses in lace making. The large war museum (Musée Mémorial de la Bataille de Normandie) lies at the southwestern edge of town, 200m/220yd from the British military cemetery.

Inland from the Côte de Nacre

✱
Suisse Normande

The lovely valley of the Orne, about 40km/25mi south of Caen, is flanked with impressive rock formations and proudly calls itself **Suisse Normande** or Normandy's Switzerland. It is indeed reminiscent of the Thurgau region of the Alpine state. Fans of all types of sport, from canoeing to rambling and from mountain biking to climbing, have made the territory their own. The main centres are Thury Harcourt (1800 inhabitants) and **Clécy** (1200 inhabitants). The cafés of the latter, with their terraces by the river, are highly popular. The scenic highlights are the stretch of the Orne between Thury-Harcourt and Pont d'Ouilly, the **Roche d'Oëtre**, south of Pont-d'Ouilly over the Rouvre gorge (fantastic view) and the valleys of the Orne's tributaries, the Vère and Noireau.

> ### ! Baedeker TIP
>
> **Moulin du Vey**
>
> One beautiful place to spend a few days holidaying on the Orne is the former mill in Clecy (12 rooms, moderate prices, tel. 02 31 69 71 08, www.moulinduvey.com). The restaurant, in a Norman-style aristocratic garden lodge, serves fine regional cuisine.

Falaise

Falaise (8300 inhabitants), 35km/22mi south of Caen, is dominated by its solid castle, where **William the Conqueror** was born in 1027 as the illegitimate son of Duke Robert and his pretty mistress, Arlette. The keep and one 35m/115ft-high round tower (13th century) are still standing as are the churches of Ste-Trinité and St-Gervais (11th–16th centuries).

✱
Haras du Pin

Horse lovers should not miss Haras du Pin (15km/9mi east of Argentan), a **national stud**, founded in 1715, which now possesses 70 stud stallions of various breeds. From June to September a horse and cart parade takes place every Thursday at 3pm.

Parc Naturel Régional de Normandie-Maine

Château de Carrouges

The Normandie-Maine Regional Nature Park covers some 2350 sq km/900 sq mi of southern Normandy, roughly bounded by Mortain in the west and Alençon in the east. 450 sq km/175 sq mi of the area is wooded, while numerous rivers and lakes offer opportunities for canoeing or sailing. The Maison du Parc in the attractive Château de

View from Croix de la Vaverie over a loop in the Orne

Carrouges (15th century), 26km/16mi northwest of Alençon, has information on footpaths, bridleways and cycle routes etc.

Alençon

Alençon (30,000 inhabitants), 120km/75mi south of Caen, was a famous **lace making** town (»points d'Alençon«) in the 17th and 18th centuries. The Musée des Beaux-Arts et de la Dentelle (Cour Carree de la Dentelle, open daily in summer, otherwise closed Mon; guided tours in summer) recalls this fact. There are some astoundingly complex examples of lace making on view here, as well as Flemish, French and Italian paintings from the 15th–20th centuries (including Boudin, Buffet, Courbet).The church of Notre-Dame was built in 1444 in the Flamboyant style (tower and choir 18th century). Its delicate **portico** (1506) is a real gem. It is almost like lace itself. Next to the church is the lovely Maison d'Ozé (15th century, tourist office). The centrepoint of the attractive old suburb of St-Léonard – look out for the wrought iron balconies – is the eponymous church (15th century).

◀ Notre-Dame

Domfront

Domfront (4300 inhabitants, 19km/12mi west of Bagnoles) picturesquely overlooks the Varenne from a rocky ridge 135m/443ft above the river. There is a great view from the 11th-century watchtower that remains from the medieval border fortress that once stood here. 13 of the 24 towers of the town's walls remain, too. Things to see include the old centre with its neo-Byzantine church (1924, interesting design) and the late 11th-century church of Notre-Dame-sur-l'Eau on the river. There is a lovely view of the latter from the bridge over the Varenne.

OPERATION OVERLORD

The weather forecast for 5 June 1944 was actually pretty miserable. Nevertheless Allied meteorologists spotted a brief window of high pressure. The overall commander of the Allied forces, General Dwight D. Eisenhower, saw his chance and ordered the invasion of Normandy for the following day. The next opportunity would not have occurred for another two weeks due to the vagaries of the tides.

6 June 1944 saw the beginning of the largest military invasion of all time. It would signal the decisive phase of the Second World War. Although German signallers had indeed monitored all the Allied radio traffic, they nevertheless assumed that the invasion was a feint, believing there would be plenty of time before the Allies were ready to act in earnest. The Germans had been preparing their defences for years but their expectation was that the Allies would land at the Pas de Calais, where the English Channel is at its narrowest. In fact, the Allies planned to mount their assault between the mouth of the Orne and the Cotentin Peninsula. In the night of 5–6 June, the navies and air forces of the Allies set the Germans under fire, while a massive landing fleet assembled in the middle of the Channel. Three paratroop divisions leap-frogged the ships to drop at landing points inland. Despite heavy losses, 23,000 of the paratroopers managed to penetrate back to the coast, a British division in the east and two American divisions in the west. Between 6.30 and 7.30 in the morning some 175,000 soldiers from nine nations arrived at the French beaches, bringing with them around 20,000 vehicles. The British and Canadians landed at beaches in the east codenamed **Gold**, **Juno** and **Sword**. The Americans disembarked in the west at **Utah Beach** and **Omaha Beach**. To help get their heavy machinery onto the land they brought pre-fabricated concrete pontoons, called Mulberries, which were sunk off the coast of Arromanches and at Omaha Beach.

The beginning of the end

The Germans had been surprised by the force of the bombing and maritime bombardment, but it was still astonishing that the Allies managed to unite their five bridgeheads into a single front some 80km/50mi in length. By 26 June they had taken

The remains of some »Mulberries« can still be seen off Arromanches

Cherbourg, and Caen fell on 9 July, meaning that both the key German bases had been overcome. The battle for Normandy ended on 21 August at Tournai sur Dives. The Germans had lost a quarter of a million soldiers and their divisions were largely obliterated. The British and Canadian armies pressed further north, crossed the Seine and pushed on towards Belgium, while the Americans headed for **Paris**. The Germans there capitulated without a fight and handed over the city undamaged, even though this was in contravention of Hitler's orders. Eisenhower gave the honour of entering the city to a French armoured division under General de Gaulle and they marched in triumphal procession through the capital on 25 August 1944.

Nowadays the Normandy coast between Cabourg in the east and the Cotentin Peninsula in the west gives an impression of being one great open-air museum, peppered with individual museums, wartime exhibitions, memorials and defensive remnants. There, information of greater or lesser quality about the D-Day landings (or »Jour J« or »Tag X«) is passed on to new generations. Each village, though, has its own story contributing to the mythology of the rescue and liberation of France. Some 4 million visitors a year engage in »battlefield tourism«, making it a major earner for the local economy. Eight tourist routes have been established, which lead through the once embattled territory, signposted as **Normandie – Terre Liberée**, to their final destinations at the military cemeteries. Detailed information can be obtained from tourist offices at regional and local level.

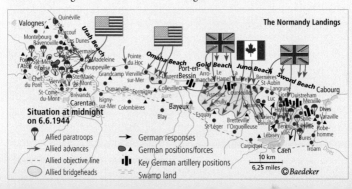

✳ Cotentin Peninsula

Scenery

The headland of Presqu'Ile du Cotentin reaches far out into the English Channel and marks the western border of Normandy. Its appearance is dominated by the **steep coastline** with picturesque cliffs and bizarre rock formations, often reminiscent of Brittany. The lonely inland region with its grassy landscape crossed by hedges (bocages) is highly charming, too.

Parc Naturel Régional des Marais du Cotentin et du Bessin

The Cotentin and Bessin Regional Nature Park, covering more than 1500 sq km/580 sq mi around Carentan, encompasses hedgerow scenery (bocage) and marshes (marais) crossed by canals. The maison d'accueil in St-Côme du Mont (3km/2mi north of Carentan) provides information and excursions as well as accommodation in its »Gîtes Panda«.

Isigny-sur-Mer

Isigny-sur-Mer, west of the Vire, is one of the centres of Norman dairy farming. Cream (often made into caramels), butter, Camembert cheese and Pont l'Evéque from here have AC certification. You can taste or buy the goods at the Coopérative Laitière.

Utah Beach

Ste-Mère-Eglise

The first place to go on the Cotentin coast is Utah Beach. Numerous monuments here recall the D-Day invasion, which started on 6 June 1944 at about 12.30am with a wave of American paratroopers. In Ste-Mère-Eglise, the first village to be captured, a stained glass window in the church and a nearby museum, the Musée Airborne (closed Dec–Jan), relate the events of the battle. Another interesting spot is the Ferme Musée du Cotentin, where rural life in Normandy unfolds before your very eyes.

Cherbourg, naval base and ferry port to England

Valognes (7200 inhabitants) has been dubbed »the Versailles of Normandy« due to its many mansions, built as winter residences for the rural aristocracy. A vision of luxury is supplied at the Hôtel de Beaumont. The **Musée Régional du Cidre et du Calvados** offers its visitors plentiful information on the manufacture of alcoholic beverages from apples.

Valognes

The pretty little town of Saint-Vaast-La-Hogue (2100 inhabitants) is a popular holiday destination on the east coast. It is famed for its oyster cultivation. Boats ply to the island of Tatihou, which Vauban fortified in the 17th century (interesting maritime museum) and where many species of birds can be viewed (reserve).

Saint-Vaast-La-Hogue

Even the Vikings used the natural harbour of Barfleur (600 inhabitants). The road through Gatteville leads from there to the promontory of **Pointe de Barfleur**, where the 76m/250ft lighthouse from 1835 can be climbed.

Barfleur

Cherbourg (27,000 inhabitants) on the north coast possesses the largest artificial harbour in the world, protected by a dyke 3700m/4000yd long. It came into being in 1853 as a military harbour but quickly became important for trans-Atlantic crossings. Ferries also sail from here to England and Ireland. There is an excellent view of the town and its harbour from Fort du Roule, at an elevation of 110m/361ft in the southeast of town. The Musée de la Guerre et de la Libération is also there.
The town is not all that attractive but the **Musée Thomas-Henry** (Italian and Dutch painters, including Fra Angelico, Filippo Lippi, Jean-François Millet, Camille Claudel), the church of Ste-Trinité (1423–1504) and the E. Liais Park are all worth a visit. The arsenal and the military harbour, the third largest in France (from where France's first atomic submarine set out in 1967), are only accessible on certain days. It is possible, though, to visit **Cité de la Mer** (in the old Gare Maritime Transatlantique station, daily), and marvel at the submarine *Redoutable* and a giant aquarium.

Cherbourg

From Hameau-de-la-Mer it is possible to drive around the wild and romantic Cap de la Hague on some pretty country roads. One side road leads from Dannery to the **Nez-de-Jobourg**, a 127m/417ft-high promontory with rugged clefts that stretches far out into the Atlantic (fantastic view). The peninsula also possesses a well known atomic waste reprocessing plant, which has been known to release even contaminated water into the sea (the guided tours have been halted).

★
Cap de la Hague

Barneville-Carteret's long sandy beaches have made it a popular seaside resort. The protected harbour is a base for fishing boats and yachts. There is a fine view from atop the promontory of Cap de Carteret.

Barneville-Carteret

Lessay Lessay (1800 inhabitants), between Carteret and Coutances, has a monastery founded in 1050 with an impressive frugal, early Romanesque church. Since the 12th century the famous **Foire Sainte Croix** has taken place here on the second weekend of September, a massive agricultural market where horses, donkeys, dogs, cattle and poultry are traded and hundreds of lambs are eaten.

Coutances Coutances (9500 inhabitants), on a hill about 10km/6mi from the busy beaches at Agon Coutainville, is the town after which the whole Cotentin Peninsula is named. Its highest point is occupied by the Notre-Dame cathedral (1251–74), one of the finest examples of

✷
Notre-Dame ▶ **Norman High Gothic**. In its elegant interior, notable features include the stained glass windows from the 13th–14th centuries. Musée Quesnel-Mórinière and the Jardin des Plantes are worth a visit, too. The »Jazz sous les Pommiers« festival takes place around the feast of the Ascension.

Saint-Lô Saint-Lô (20,000 inhabitants), between Coutances and Bayeux and overlooking the idyllic Vire valley, was largely destroyed during the Second World War and its reconstruction has not been particularly attractive. Its fame rests on the **national stud** (haras), which has 80 breeding stallions from seven different breeds (tours daily June–Sept). From both outside and inside the church of Notre-Dame (13th–16th centuries) the external pulpit and the large stained glass windows by Max Ingrand are the most interesting features. The Musée des Beaux-Arts owns paintings by Corot, Millet and Boudin, among others.

✷
Abbaye de Southeast of Coutances in the valley of the Seine there are some rem-
Hambye nants of Hamnye Abbey, founded in 1145, including parts of the abbey church (1120–1200, with lovely Gothic vaulting) and some of the monastic buildings.

Granville The location of this walled town upon a rocky ridge, along with its casino, contributed to this popular seaside resort (12,600 inhabitants) being dubbed the »Monaco of the north«. A museum in the villa called »Les Rhumbs«, where **Christian Dior** (1905–57) was born, documents the creations of the fashion czar. At Place de l'Isthme, from which there is a marvellous view, the Musée R.-Anacréon features paintings from the 20th century; meanwhile, inside the Grande Porte, the Musée du Vieux-Granville illustrates the history of the region. Pass the Gothic church of Notre-Dame (15th–16th centuries,

---

! **Baedeker** TIP

Where France and Britain meet

From Barneville Carteret and Granville it is possible to take a ferry to the channel island of Jersey (without a car and arriving at either Gorey or St Helier). Although it is not exactly inexpensive, the trip is nevertheless to be recommended. To get around on the island, use the bus services, take a taxi, or rent a car.

The character of Grand Ile in the Chausey archipelago is unmistakeably English

with a 14th-century Madonna statue) to get to the lighthouse on the Pointe du Roc. It is also possible to take a day trip to the **Grande Ile Chausey** and the channel island of **Jersey**, both known for their splendid plant life.

Avranches (9500 inhabitants) on the Baie du Mont St-Michel was in 1172 the scene of a church council, which acquitted Henry II of England after the murder of Thomas Becket. The cathedral was destroyed during the French Revolution. From the spot on which it stood, the »Plate-forme«, and from the Jardin des Plantes there are wonderful views of the Sélune estuary and ▶**Mont St-Michel**. The late 19th-century basilica of St-Gervais-et-St-Protais with its 74m/243ft tower is also worth a visit, as is the Musée du Trésor. The old episcopal palace (Musée Municipal) has works of art dating back to the Middle Ages as well as a folklore collection on display. The Hôtel de Ville displays precious **medieval manuscripts produced at Mont St-Michel**.   **Avranches**

Orange

Région: Provence–Alpes–Côte d'Azur   **Altitude:** 46m/151ft
Département: Vaucluse   **Population:** 29,000

Orange, a quiet town in the lower Rhône valley, is known for its opera festivals and its impressive monuments from the Roman era, which have given it UNESCO World Heritage status.

In 105 BC, the first confrontation between Roman troops and the Cimbri and Teutons took place outside the gates of the Roman town of Arausio. 100,000 Romans were killed there. During the period of the Pax Romana, Orange, settled by veterans, had four times as many inhabitants as it does today. In 1544 the town was the capital of a small principality but came under the control of the Dutch line of the house of Nassau. It was on account of this that members of the Dutch royal family gained the titles of Prince or Princess of Orange-Nassau (and is the reason that the town is very popular with Dutch tourists).   **History**

What to See in Orange

✱
Arc de Triomphe

On the N 7 to the north of the town stands a 22m/72ft triumphal arch, built around 20 BC, the finest example of its kind in France (the western section has been almost entirely reconstructed). A bronze quadriga (four-horse chariot) and four statues once topped the top attica, where a relief depicts a Gaulish battle. To the left and right underneath Gaulish naval trophies can be seen, while the eastern side depicts Gallic prisoners.

✱ ✱
Théâtre Romain

The **Roman theatre** is situated to the south of the old town. It is the best preserved of all such classical examples (open April–Sept 9am–6.30pm, otherwise 9am–12 noon, 1.30pm–5pm). Established in the early days of the Roman emperors but probably rebuilt in the 2nd century AD, it had room for some 10,000 spectators. The acoustics are superb. The massive wall of the stage (103m/113yd wide, 36m/118ft tall) still has remnants of some brilliant decoration and it is the only such theatre to possess a statue of an emperor (Augustus, 3.55m/11ft 8in high). A variety of cultural events are held here in the summer, including the famous **Chorégies** (operas).

Adjoining the ruins to the west stands a Roman temple, which forms the end point of a 400m/440yd-long stadium. Opposite, the local museum (Musée Municipal) shows archaeological discoveries from antiquity (the Roman land registry documents are of great importance).

Hôtel de Ville
Notre-Dame

In the middle of town is the 1671 town hall, with the Romanesque cathedral of Notre-Dame (1083–1126) a little further north. It was badly damaged in the Wars of Religion but was later reconstructed.

Colline St-
Eutrope

From the Colline St-Eutrope, where the ruins of Orange's castle stand, there is a great view of the town and the environs as far as Mont Ventoux.

Orange Map

Where to eat
① Parvis

Where to stay
① Arène

© Baedeker

Around Orange

Châteauneuf-du-Pape (2000 inhabitants, about 10km/6mi south of Orange) is one of the **most famous wine-producing villages in France**. Its name is synonymous with a vigorous red wine made from up to 13 different types of grape, all of which thrive on the gravelly banks east of the Rhône between Orange and Avignon. It was from here that the concept of monitoring the quality of wine was initiated in 1923, which culminated in the adoption of origin labelling (AOC). In the Caves Brotte-Père Anselme, a museum provides information on wine cultivation in the region. Information about vintners, tastings etc. is available from the tourist office on Place du Portail. The village clusters around a hill, itself decked with vines; the ruins of a castle, which was built for Pope John XXII and completed in 1333 (it was blown up by German troops in 1944), stand here. The castle's cellars serve as the headquarters of »Échansonnerie des Papes« (exhibitions etc.). On the other side of the Rhône, the castle of Roquemaure can be seen, where Pope Clement V died in 1314.

Châteauneuf-du-Pape

Pont-St-Esprit (9200 inhabitants), 23km/14mi northwest of Orange, is named after its **Rhône bridge**, built in 1265–1309 and almost 1000m/1100yd long with 25 arches (19 of which are ancient). There is a good view of it from the terrace between the churches of St-Saturnin and St-Pierre (17th century). From Place St-Pierre, Rue St-Jacques heads southwards. There the Maison des Chevaliers houses an interesting museum of ecclesiastical art and the equally fascinating apothecary of an old hospice.

Pont-Saint-Esprit

North of Pont-St-Esprit the Ardèche, which rises on the edge of the Massif Central, flows into the Rhône. Between Vallon-Pont-d'Arc

✷ ✷
Gorges de l'Ardèche

 VISITING ORANGE

and the confluence (about 60km/37mi) the river has carved impressive gorges up to 300m/100ft deep. The D 290 runs partly along the gorge and partly above it, offering some fine views. The river is protected as a nature reserve and in summer it is very popular with canoeists (kayaks for hire). In the region around the gorges there are some splendid caves containing stalactites and stalagmites, such as Aven d'Orgnac to the south near Orgnac and Aven de Marzal to the north between Bidon and St-Remèze. In 1995 the Chauvet cave was discovered at Vallon-Pont-d'Arc; it contains some of the oldest known pictures in the world (►Baedeker Special p.662).

Orléans

J 5

Région: Centre
Département: Loiret

Altitude: 110m/361ft
Population: 116,000

At Orléans the ► Loire reaches its most northerly point. The university town and lively trading hub is famous for Joan of Arc, the »maid of Orléans«, who initiated the turning point of the Hundred Years' War against the English.

Orléans is the second biggest town on the middle stretch of the Loire after Tours. It lies between the fertile Beauce basin and the Sologne region with its many forests and lakes. In this capital of the Centre région and the Loiret department, horticulture and industry (food, electronics, machinery, pharmaceuticals) play a key role.   **Economy**

In the 3rd century Orléans was known as Aurelianum and was an important transport intersection. In 498 it was conquered by the Frankish king Clovis, who made it the capital of his kingdom. Its university was established as early as 1305. During the Hundred Years' War, Orléans was France's last bastion against the English. Then 17-year-old **Joan of Arc** took control of the army and liberated the besieged town on 7–8 May 1429. In the Wars of Religion, Orléans was an important Protestant centre. John Calvin studied here. After 1563 the town was largely destroyed. It became prosperous in the 17th century thanks to sugar and textiles. In 1940 part of the old town was obliterated by German bombing.   **History**

What to See in Orléans

The most distinctive feature is the massive Holy Cross cathedral, which Marcel Proust described as the ugliest in France. The western façade, the 81m/266ft towers of which dominate the grandiose but   **Cathédrale Ste-Croix**

← Pont d'Arc on the upper Ardèche, more than 30m/100ft high and just as wide

rather dull Rue Jeanne d'Arc, was not built until 1767–93, which explains the oddness of the building (including its Baroque decor and the crowns topping the towers). The 114m/374ft central tower was finished in 1858. The history of the construction work is thus highly varied: the building's Romanesque predecessor collapsed in the 13th century and work ensued on a new cathedral from 1278 until well into the 16th century. In the religious fighting of 1568, though, it was largely destroyed. It was rebuilt from 1601 to 1829. The sterile and uniform interior is still impressive, thanks to its size (136m/149yd long). Notable features include the 17th-century organ, the superb **choir stalls** (1706) and the Baroque marble pietà by Bourdin (1623) in the central chapel of the choir. In the transept on the left, a statue of **St Joan** (1912) triumphs over English leopards, while next to the altar is a tomb sculpture for Cardinal Touchet (1927), who motivated for her canonization. In the crypt some remnants of the earlier buildings can be seen, as well as the church treasury.

Musée des Beaux-Arts

The fine arts museum (closed Mon) next to the cathedral has some outstanding works from the 15th–19th centuries, including examples by the masters of Siena and by Tintoretto, Van Dyck, Boucher, Wat-

Orléans Map

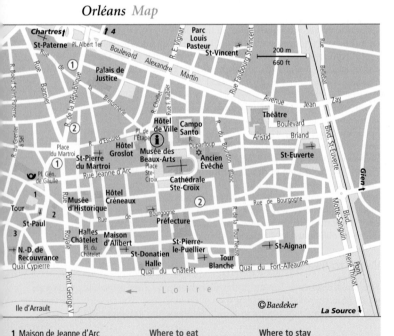

© Baedeker

1 Maison de Jeanne d'Arc
2 Centre Péguy
3 Hôtel Toutin
4 Muséum d'Histoire Naturelle

Where to eat
① La Chancellerie
② La Petite Marmite

Where to stay
① Hôtel d'Arc
② Hôtel d'Orléans

teau, Gauguin (the well-known *Fête Gloanec*), Soutine and Dufy, as well as sculptures by Maillol, Zadkine and others.

Hôtel Groslot (town hall), a pretty brick and worked stone building adorned in rich decoration, was built in 1549–55 for the governor of Orléans. It was here that King François II died in 1560, having just turned 17 years old. He was visiting the general council with his wife, Mary Stuart of Scotland. Other kings also spent time here. The statue of Joan of Arc in front of the steps is the work of Marie d'Orléans, daughter of the »Citoyen Roi« Louis-Philippe. In the park there are some remnants of the late 15th-century Chapelle St-Jacques.

Hôtel de Ville

The popular Place du Martroi, centrepoint of the old town, is appropriately adorned by a heroic equestrian statue of Joan of Arc (Denys Foyatier, 1855). Reliefs featuring scenes from her life appear on the pedestal. Houses from the 17th century stand on Rue d'Escures (to the east). Rue Royale, heading south, was built in 1760 (though most

Place du Martroi

 VISITING ORLÉANS

INFORMATION

Office de Tourisme
2 Place de l'Etape, F-45000 Orléans
Tel. 02 38 24 05 05, fax 02 38 54 49 84,
www.tourisme-orleans.fr

FESTIVALS AND EVENTS

End of April/beginning of May: festivities in honour of Joan of Arc featuring concerts, a historic procession and celebratory Masses in the cathedral. Second half of June: Orléans Jazz. Penultimate week of Sept in odd years: Festival de la Loire with 100 traditional river boats, cultural events, concerts and illuminations. Event dates can be found in *Orléans Poche*.

WHERE TO EAT

► **Inexpensive**

① *La Chancellerie*
27 Place du Martroi, tel. 02 38 53 57 54. Best-known brasserie in Orléans, housed in an aristocratic dwelling from the 18th century at the most attractive spot in town. A terrace is opened in summer. Large choice of

meals and wine. The »Martroi« is also inexpensive and equally pleasant.

② *La Petite Marmite*
178 Rue de Bourgogne, tel. 02 38 54 23 83. This cosy restaurant with a wooden beamed ceiling has a good reputation for its traditional local cuisine, including foie gras, truffles and andouille sausage.

WHERE TO STAY

► **Mid-range**

① *Hôtel d'Arc*
37 Rue de la République, tel. 02 38 53 10 94, www.bestwestern.com
Traditional Art Nouveau hotel. Simple, modern rooms with sound insulating windows and friendly service. The old lift is a real gem.

► **Budget**

② *Hôtel d'Orléans*
26 Rue A. Crespin, tel. 02 38 53 35 34, http://hoteldorleans.fr. Simple, pleasant establishment in a quiet side street. No restaurant.

At the centre of everything in Orléans: the Joan of Arc statue on Place du Martroi

of the buildings have been reconstructed since 1945). It runs down to the 330m/360yd-long Pont George V, built in 1755. There is a great view of the town from here.

In the elegant Hôtel Cabu from 1550, the **historical museum** displays archaeological discoveries from Orléans going back to Gallo-Roman times (including the **treasure of Neuvy-en-Sullias**) and extending into the Middle Ages (open May–Sept Tue–Sat, otherwise Wed and Sun only).

A half-timbered building in which Joan of Arc lived back in 1429 has been faithfully reconstructed and now contains a museum dedicated to the saint. The church of St-Paul (15th century) possesses a black Madonna (16th century). Hôtel

Other sights Toutin (1540), which once belonged to François I's chamberlain, has a fine courtyard. In the church of Notre-Dame-de-Recouvrance (1519) the sights include some Renaissance sculptures in the choir and some beautiful glass windows (11th century). St Aignan was a bishop of Orléans noted for his courage; the 15th–16th-century church that bears his name possesses a crypt, completed in 1029 and belonging to an earlier building on the site, which is one of the earliest and largest vaulted hall-type crypts in France.

Around Orléans

✳
**La Source
Parc Floral**
Orléans' university was established in 1959–63 in the La Source district (8km/5mi south of the centre). There is a fabulous advert for the local gardening industry in the 35ha/85 acres of flower gardens around the source of the **Loiret**, a 12km/7mi-long tributary of the Loire, from which the département takes its name.

Forêt d'Orléans

✳
**Château
Chamerolles**
Large areas of woodland and heath stretch north of the town. 25km/16mi northeast of Orléans and 3km/2mi east of Chilleurs-aux-Bois is the elegant **Château Chamerolles**, which was built in the 16th century in place of a 12th-century island castle. The south wing houses an interesting perfume museum, while spice-bearing plants are grown in the lovely Renaissance garden. On the way back to Orléans it is possible to take a swim in the idyllic Etang de la Vallée or travel along the **Canal d'Orléans**, built in 1692.

✶ ✶ Paris

Région: Ile-de-France
Département: Ville de Paris

Altitude: 27–129m/89–423ft
Population: 2.2 million

The Eiffel Tower, the Champs-Elysées, the Louvre, Montmartre, the Quartier Latin, Notre-Dame, the list goes on. Paris is a Mecca for savoir-vivre, a multi-cultural metropolis with an immortal mythos and a unique atmosphere. For many, the capital of France is the loveliest city in the world.

Paris, seat of government, all the key authorities and numerous international organizations, is situated in northern France in the ▶Ile-de-France région. In spite of the advancing regionalization of bodies, which exceeds that of any other European nation, the capital city remains, as ever, *the* political, administrative, spiritual, cultural and economic centre of the country – with 11 million people living in greater Paris. The city extends on either side of the Seine and is overlooked by the three hills of Montmartre (129m/423ft), Buttes Chaumont (101m/331ft) and Montagne de Ste-Geneviève (60m/197ft). The charms of Paris are truly outstanding and UNESCO has declared the magnificent buildings along the banks of the Seine between Pont de Sully and Pont d'Iéna – Notre-Dame, Pont Neuf, the Louvre, the Dôme des Invalides, Ste-Chapelle and the Eiffel Tower – along with the Ile St-Louis to be a World Heritage Site. In addition, Paris's parks, its quiet streets of the old residential districts, its cafés and bistros, its colourful markets, the classic elegance or mayhem of its fashion studios, its cuisine and the virtually endless scope of its cultural life all contribute to the unique flair of France's metropolis, which is enjoyed annually by more than 15 million visitors.

The centre of France

A Brief History of Paris

The Ile de la Cité was the site of a Gallic fortress called **Lutetia Parisiorum**, which was conquered by the Romans in 52 BC. They established a colony on the left bank of the Seine but it was abandoned in the 3rd century after attacks by the Franks and Alemanni. Under the Merovingian dynasty, Paris became the capital of the Frankish empire and emerged as the core of a new French kingdom under the Capetians in the 10th century. As early as the 13th century, Paris, with its famous **university**, was a focal point of western culture. The city had long since spread beyond the walls built in around 1200 under Philippe II when Étienne Marcel – head of the chamber of commerce, who had taken over government of the city – started new fortifications in 1356. These extended from the Seine to what are now the Grands Boulevards and Porte St-Denis.

Antiquity and the Middle Ages

Paris Map

Tour 1
Tour 2
Tour 3
Tour 4

Clichy

La Défense

Palais des Congrès
Place de la Porte Maillot
Place St-Ferdinand

Espace Wagram

Av. des Ternes
Pl. des Ternes

Boulevard
Parc Monceau

Musée Nissim de Camondo

Salle Pleyel

Musée Jacquemart-André

St-Augustin
Pl. St-Augustin

Place Charles-de-Gaulle

Arc de Triomphe de l'Étoile

Av. Friedland
Chambre de Commerce

Chambre de Commerce

Salle Gaveau

St-Philippe-d.-R.
Min. de l'Intérieur

Avenue Foch

Bois de Boulogne

Musée Dapper

Musée Arménien
Musée d'Ennercy

St-Honoré d'Eylau

Marché

Place de Mexico

Centre de Conférences Internationales

Rond-Point des Champs-Élysées

Théâtre Marigny

Palais de l'Élysée
Ste-Madelei

Pal. de la Glace

Espace P. Cardin

Place de la Concorde

Musée Guimet
Place d'Iéna

Palais de Tokyo

Théâtre des Champs-Élysées

Grand Palais

Petit Palais

Orangerie
Paul

Place du Trocadéro

Palais de Chaillot

Seine

Pont d'Iéna
Port de la Bourdonnais

Musée du Quai Branly

Min. d. Aff. Etrangères

Palais Bourbon

Min. de la Défense

Institut Géogr.
Ste-Cloti

Tour Eiffel
Champ

Pl. des Invalides

Maison de Radio France

Boulogne

Hôtel des Invalides

Musée Rodin

Hôtel Matigr

de Mars

Ecole Militaire

St-Léon

St-François-Xavier

Sécrétariat d'Outre-Mer

Imprimerie Nationale

UNESCO

UNESCO

Place de Breteuil

MONTPARNASSE

250 m
825 ft

©Baedeker

250 m

Tour Montparnasse

▶ **VISITING PARIS**

INFORMATION

Office de Tourisme
25 Rue des Pyramides, F-75001 Paris
Tel. 08 92 68 30 00, fax 01 49 52 53 00
www.parisinfo.com, www.paris.fr
Information offices:
Carrousel du Louvre, 25 Rue des
Pyramides, Gare de Lyon, Gare du
Nord, 21 Place du Tertre (Mont-
martre)
Espace du Tourisme de l'Ile-de-France
Carrousel du Louvre, F-75001 Paris
Tel. 08 26 16 66 66
(from abroad +33 1 44 50 19 98)
www.paris-Ile-de-France.com

GETTING THERE

Motorways from all corners of France
converge on the Paris ring road, the
Boulevard Péripherique. The airports,
Roissy Charles de Gaulle (CDG) and
Orly (www.aeroportsdeparis.fr) are
connected to the city centre via the
RER as well as both RATP (Roissybus,
Orlybus) and Air France buses. The
main SNCF terminus stations face out
to various points of the compass: Gare
du Nord services not only head to
northern France but also extend to
Belgium and northern Germany; Gare
de l'Est runs services eastward out to
and beyond the borders of Germany
and Switzerland; while Gare de Lyon
serves points south.

TRANSPORT

It is advisable to use local public
transport. The RATP (www.ratp.fr)
runs the underground railway network (the Métro) as well as bus
services and the suburban RER rail
lines. The Métro and RER run
between 5.30am and 12.30am, while
the last bus service is at 8.30pm.
Métro services run every 90 seconds
during rush hour and 2–7 minutes

apart otherwise. Maps of the lines are
available from Metro and RER stations. The RATP's »Carte Orange«
ticket (requiring a passport photo) is
valid Monday to Sunday for all public
transport and is well worth buying for
a three-day visit. The more expensive
»Paris Visite« (1–5 day) ticket covers
services in Paris itself and in certain
parts of the Ile-de-France (e.g. Versailles, Fontainebleau) and offers discounts at some attractions. Taxis,
identified by a light on top, can
simply be hailed on the street.

CITY TOURS

L'Open Tour, Cityrama and RATP
(Balabus) buses, Seine boat services run
by Bateaux Parisiens, Bateaux Mouches,
Canauxrama and Vedettes de Paris.

FESTIVALS AND EVENTS

21 June: Fête de la Musique. Late
June/early July: Course des Garçons et
Serveuses de Café (8km/5mi run by
tray-bearing waiters and waitresses).
National holiday: on the evening of 13
July there is dancing at fire stations all
over the town; on 14 July itself a
military parade takes place on the
Champ Elysées at about 10am and at
around 11pm there is a fireworks
display at the Champ de Mars. From
about 20 July till 20 Aug: during Paris
Plage the north bank of the Seine is
turned into a sandy beach 2km/1.5mi
long with music and dancing in the
evenings. Late July: last stage of the
Tour de France finishes on the
Champs-Elysées. Sept–Dec: Festival
d'Automne with art, music and theatre. 31 Dec: New Year's celebrations,
especially at the Eiffel Tower and the
Champs-Elysées. Events are listed in
*L'Officiel des Spectacles, Pariscope,
Time Out* and local newspapers.

MUSEUMS

Most museums are closed on Mon, while the Louvre closes Tue. The Carte Musées-Monuments ticket (for 1, 3 or 5 days, available from tourist offices, stations, Métro stations and FNAC shops) includes admission to more than 60 museums and artistic monuments in Paris and in the ►Ile-de-France. It rarely pays off financially, but it does render queuing for tickets unnecessary.

SHOPPING

Fashion: Rue du Faubourg St-Honoré, the area of Av. Georges V/Avenue Montaigne/Champs-Elysées, around Place des Victoires, St-Germain-des-Près, Marais (Pl. des Vosges/Rue des Rosiers). Shoes: Rue de Grenelle, Rue de Cherche-Midi, Rue de Rennes. Jewellery: Marais, the district between Garnier-Opera, Rue Royale and Place Vendôme. Delicatessen: Place Madeleine, around Rue Montorgueil, Rue Poncelet.

WHERE TO EAT

► Expensive

① *Jules Verne*
Eiffel Tower (2nd platform)
Tel. 08 25 56 66 62
www.restaurants-toureiffel.com
The most impressive restaurant in town with all of Paris in view. The interior is plain but the food is by no means overshadowed by the stunning view.

② *Spoon*
12 Rue Marignan (8th arr.)
Tel. 01 40 76 34 44, closed Sat–Sun and approx. 25.7– 25.8.
Ambitious bistro run by Alan Ducasse with imaginative cross-over cuisine.

► Moderate

③ *Chez Georges*
1 Rue du Mail (2nd arr.)

Tel. 01 42 60 07 11, closed Sun and Aug. This picture-book bistro near Pl. des Victoires is a treasure chest of traditional cuisine – not recommended for calorie counters.

④ *Thoumieux*
79 Rue St-Dominique (7th arr.)
Tel. 01 47 05 49 75. Authentic Parisian brasserie from the 1930s with long tables, red benches and simple dishes. Hearty cuisine from the southwest. Rooms available.

⑤ *Les Caves Solignac*
9 Rue Decrès (14th arr.)
Tel. 45 45 58 59, closed Sat–Sun
A little out of the way in Montparnasse, but well worth a visit: this cosy little restaurant serving unpretentious traditional fare is a place in which to feel at home.

► Inexpensive

⑥ *Chartier*
7 Rue du Faubg-Montmartre (9th arr.)
Tel. 01 47 70 86 29.
A gem of the belle époque, this restaurant has served the same succulent dishes since 1896 including stew, veal blanquette and black pudding. Waiters do their work in the station-like dining room wearing long white aprons, black waistcoats and bow ties.

⑦ *Ambassade d'Auvergne*
22 Rue du Grenier St-Lazare (3rd arr.)
Tel. 01 42 72 31 22, open daily
A down-to-earth establishment near the Marais serving authentic Auvergne cuisine in appropriate, perfectly suitable surroundings. Good wine list with inexpensive options.

⑧ *Brasserie de l'Isle St-Louis*
55 Quai de Bourbon (4th arr.)
Tel. 01 43 54 02 59, closed Wed and Aug. Very well-located place with a view of

Notre-Dame's buttresses. Despite its narrow confines, people have been enjoying the Alsatian food here since 1870. Reasonably priced wines.

WHERE TO STAY

▶ Luxury

① *Crillon*
10 Place de la Concorde (75008)
Tel. 01 44 71 15 00, www.crillon.com
One of the most exclusive (and expensive) hotels in the world. The Les Ambassadeurs restaurant is of equally high quality (brunch on Sun, closed Mon).

② *Relais Christine*
3 Rue Christine (75006)
Tel. 01 40 51 60 80
www.relais-christine.com
This elegant and charming mansion, which is part of a 13th-century Augustine monastery, is located in the midst of St-Germain-des-Prés but is still quiet and even secluded.

▶ Mid-range

③ *Lenox St-Germain*
9 Rue de l'Université (75007)
Tel. 01 42 96 10 95
www.lenoxsaintgermain.com
Prettily furnished in English style. The surrounding area offers many opportunities for browsing through bookshops and antique stores.

④ *Place des Vosges*
12 Rue Birague (75004)
www.hotelplacedesvosges.com
Tel. 01 42 72 60 46.
Quiet 17th-century building, beautifully situated at Place des Vosges with friendly service. Its salon is in the style of a French Renaissance chateau but the rooms are more modern.

⑤ *Vieux Marais*
8 Rue du Plâtre (75004)

Tel. 01 42 78 47 22
www.vieuxmarais.com
In a quiet side street near the Centre Pompidou, this hotel is designed in plain, modern style with no flowery wallpaper or brocade. Very good value for money.

⑥ *Hameau de Passy*
48 Rue de Passy (75016)
Tel. 01 42 88 47 55, fax 01 42 30 83 72,
www.paris-hotel-hameaudepassy.com
The 16th arrondissement between the Trocadéro and the Bois de Boulogne is considered particularly chic. This hotel is quiet and hidden away. Small, modern rooms.

▶ Budget

⑦ *Avre*
21 Rue de l'Avre (75015)
www.hoteldelavre.com, tel. 01 45 75 31 03. In a relatively quiet side street off the Blvd. de Grenelle south of the Champ de Mars. Friendly rooms facing the street or the garden, which is also used for serving breakfast.

⑧ *St-André des Arts*
66 Rue St-André des Arts (75006)
www.francehotelguide.com, tel. 01 43 26 96 16. Wonderfully old-fashioned hotel in the heart of St-Germain with a very friendly atmosphere. Comfortable rooms for 1–4 people.

▶ Bed & breakfast, apartments

Alcove & Agapes
Tel. 01 44 85 06 05
www.bed-and-breakfast-in-paris.com

France apartments
Tel. 01 56 89 31 00
www.rentapart.com

Bed and breakfast
www.parisbandb.com

In the 15th century, the Hundred Years' War put a block on any further expansion. Under **François I**, however, new building work was started (Louvre, Tuileries, Hôtel de Ville), although the real boom only came after the Wars of Religion had ended under **Henri IV**. In the reign of Louis XIII, the expansion of the walls on the right bank, which had been started under Valois, was extended to the full extent of the Grands Boulevards and to the west of Porte St-Denis. As of 1614 the Isle de St-Louis was created and built up. **Louis XIV** provided Paris with many of its monumental buildings (Louvre colonnades, Hôtel des Invalides, churches, Place Vendôme). Shortly before the Revolution, new quarters were added to the jurisdiction of city tax collectors under the »Enceinte des Fermiers Généraux«. These extended on both sides of the river as far as the line of the outer boulevards from the Arc de Triomphe in the west to Place de la Nation in the east. During and after the **Revolution** most of Paris's monasteries, which occupied large amounts of land in prime locations, were dissolved and vanished from existence.

Renaissance and Absolutism

French Revolution

The first imperial period (1804–14) saw Paris become the hub of all Europe. What **Napoleon I** plundered on his campaigns was used for the benefit of his capital. He started work on the Rue de Rivoli, the stock exchange (Paris Bourse), and the Madeleine church among other things, although most work was incomplete when he fell from power, including the Arc de Triomphe. The July Monarchy (1830 to 1848) determinedly continued the building work initiated under Napoleon. More than 100 million gold francs were spent on streets, churches, civic buildings and bridges. Paris was once again ringed by a wall, with 13 village parishes incorporated into the city.

First empire

July Monarchy

All the building undertaken so far was overshadowed by the construction work which took place under Napoleon III, who appointed **Georges-Eugène Haussmann** to be prefect in 1853. He was instrumental in making Paris, which till then had retained its narrow medieval character apart from a few older boulevards, into the city we know today. About 25,000 buildings were demolished, 70,000 new ones being built. The Boulevard de Strasbourg and Boulevard de Sébastopol on the right bank and Boulevard du Palais and Boulevard du St-Michel were all begun. Boulevards Haussmann and Magenta on the right bank were added next. St-Germain took form on the left bank, the Rue de Rivoli was extended, the Avenue de l'Opéra and the whole area of the Champs-Elysées all came into being. Public building projects included a new wing for the Louvre and the opera house.

Napoleon III

During the Third Republic, more streets were carved out of the old layout. Transport was improved enormously, in particular with the construction of the Métro. The land that had once been occupied by walls was given over to residential housing and parkland; the Parc

Third Republic

Four tours of Paris (►city map)

Tour 1 (8km/5mi)

The impressive features of the Ile de la Cité include the cathedral of Notre-Dame and the Sainte-Chapelle. Head from there to the southern bank of the Seine and cross the Pont de Carrousel to the Louvre. Continue through the Tuileries to Place de la Concorde. Next, walk up the Champs-Elysées to the Arc de Triomphe (and look at the view from the top). Head back down to Avenue Georges V, one of the fashion world's »main arteries«, and then to Place d'Alma. Walk through the Palais de Tokyo to come out at Place du Trocadéro with its Palais de Chaillot; then cross the Seine to the Eiffel tower, which is brightly illuminated at night. From Port du Bourdonnais it is then possible to take a Bateau-Mouche back to the Ile de la Cité.

Tour 2 (5km/3mi)

Visit the Louvre early in the morning (on days when it is closed, try the Musée d'Orsay instead). Then head through the Louvre des Antiquaires to the Palais Royal and continue along Rue St-Honoré to Place Vendôme. Rue de la Paix is another luxurious street leading to Opéra Garnier. On Blvd. Haussmann, make a flying visit to the Galeries Lafayette. The grandeur of the Grand Boulevards can be experienced on Blvd. Montmartre. After taking in Musée Grevin on Passage Jouffroy, go on to Montmartre. From Notre-Dame-de-Lorette head up Rue des Martyrs to Blvd. de Rochechouart and climb the famous hill (by stairway or by rail). Sunset from Sacré-Cœur is a beautiful sight to see.

Tour 3 (7km/4mi)

From the Champs-Elysées go past the Grand Palais and Petit Palais across the Seine to the monumental Hôtel des Invalides and Dôme des Invalides (with the tomb of Napoleon). The neighbouring Musée Rodin offers a stark contrast. On Blvd. St-Germain – and with a brief detour southward to Rue Grenelle – it is possible to take in the atmosphere in the famed quarter of artists and intellectuals. Boutiques, bookshops, bars and cafés all invite shopping and enjoyment. Around the church of St-Germain-des-Prés, the oldest in Paris, there are some famous names: Brasserie Lipp, Café de Flore, Les Deux Magots, and the oldest coffee house in Paris, the Procope on Rue de l'Ancienne Comédie. The Musée Hôtel de Cluny has magnificent medieval artistry on show. Take a break in the Jardin du Luxembourg before the final stage at the Sorbonne and the Panthéon. The evening can then be pleasantly whiled away on the Ile-St-Louis.

Tour 4 (5km/3mi)

After spending the morning at the Musée d'Orsay (or the Louvre), cross the Pont Royal and wander through the Tuileries to Rue de Rivoli with its arcades of galleries, boutiques and cafés. Further north is the Forum des Halles, where the city market halls once stood, and St-Eustache. The earlier atmosphere that the quarter once possessed can still be sensed on and around Rue Montorgueil. Passage Colbert and Passage Vivienne, west of Place des Victoires, are also very nice. The Centre Pompidou is an attraction in its own right and its museum of modern art is well worth a stop (as is a brief pause in the roof restaurant). Next, ride the Métro from Rambuteau and take a trip to the famous cemetery, Cimetière du Père Lachaise (or Parc des Buttes Chaumont). Returning to Rambuteau, take a walk through the Marais and visit Musée Picasso. The tour ends at the lovely Place des Vosges.

Other sights:

La Défense, Bois de Boulogne, Montparnasse with the Tour Montparnasse and Cimetière, a boat trip on Canal St-Martin to Parc de la Villette. Further out of town (► Ile-de-France): St-Germain-en-Laye, St-Denis, Giverny, Vaux-le-Vicomte, Fontainebleau, ►Versailles.

Paris is even more beautiful by night – Ile de Cité and Notre-Dame

First and Second World Wars

des Expositions and Cité Universitaire were also brought into being here. Some spectacular buildings were created for **World's Fairs** (in 1889 the Eiffel Tower and in 1937 the Palais de Chaillot and Musée d'Art Moderne). During the First World War, Paris was saved from German occupation by the »Miracle of the Marne«. Paris was occupied by German troops in the Second World War, though, between 1940 and 1944. It was nevertheless spared major damage.

Fourth and Fifth Republics

After 1945, some extraordinary buildings were created: in 1958 the UNESCO building, in 1959 CNIT in **La Défense**, in 1963 Maison de la Radio, in 1974 Tour Montparnasse and the Centre International de Paris, in 1977 the Centre Pompidou. In 1971 the famous **Les Halles market was demolished** and the site was transformed into the Forum des Halles, which opened in 1981. The building of fast roads along the banks of the Seine, along with a circular motorway, has relieved some of the ever-increasing traffic since the early seventies. In 1977, Jacques Chirac became the city's first elected mayor in place of the appointed prefects who had run the city until that time.

Bicentenaire

In 1989 major efforts were put into the celebration of the **two-hundredth anniversary of the French Revolution**. This involved a great deal of building work, including the glass pyramid in the courtyard of the Louvre, the opera building on Place de la Bastille and the Grande Arche in La Défense. In 1997 the massive national library opened in the Tolbiac quarter, while the first new Métro line since 1935, the fully automatic line 14, was built in 1997 to link the reconstructed districts in the southeast (Bercy, Rive Gauche) to the centre.

Projects

The constant expansion of the city has seen some major projects brought to life and, during the Mitterand era, many of them verged

← *The Eiffel Tower, the emblem of Paris,*
as seen from the terrace of the Palais de Chaillot

on gigantomania. With the increasingly vociferous protests of the populace, though, it appears that such projects will have to be designed with a »gentler« hand in future. Priority is being given to domestic building and the creation of an **infrastructure for the people**, primarily concentrating on factory and working class districts, which have traditionally had a poor reputation. These include Rive Gauche between Gare Austerlitz and Porte d'Evry, Bassin de la Villette around Place Stalingrad in the northeast, Gouttes d'Or north of Montmartre (one of the poorest parts of Paris) and Billancourt to the south of the Bois de Boulogne (formerly the site of the Renault plant).

✶ ✶ Ile de la Cité

The Ile de la Cité is the oldest part of Paris. A **castle** was built at the Pont au Change, the site of the huge present-day premises of the Palais de Justice, and the installation was expanded to became a magnificent royal residence. Even after the building of the old Louvre, the site remained the official residence. Nowadays though, apart from Sainte-Chapelle and part of the foundations, only the three outer towers, Tour de César, Tour d'Argent and the crenellated Tour St-Louis (Bon-Bec), remain in existence. All date from the time of Philip the Fair (1285–1314). The Tour de l'Horloge at the northeastern corner (early 19th century) has a clock, which has been renewed several times over the years (including in 1370 by Henri de Vic). The greater part of the **Palais de Justice** was built around the turn of the twentieth century. Its marvellous wrought iron gates (1785) open onto the Cour de Mai, where a maypole once stood. The neo-classical palace hall measures 73m/80yd in length, is 28m/30yd wide and 10m/33ft high, and in 1871 replaced the great hall of the royal palace.

✶ **Palais de Justice**

Sainte-Chapelle, the **holy chapel** (open March–Oct 9.30am–6 pm, otherwise 9am–5pm), is a wonderful gem of the Gothic style. The two-storey palace chapel was built under Louis the Pious in 1246–48, probably by Pierre de Montereau, in order to house a thorn from Jesus's crucifical crown of thorns and other relics that had been brought back to France in 1239 (now kept in Notre-Dame). It was deconsecrated in 1791, during the Revolution, and is now used as a concert hall (concerts March–Nov almost daily 7pm/8.30pm, www.archetspf.asso.fr). The vaulting in the lower chapel is only 6.6m/22ft high. The building was originally intended for the use of palace servants, while the upper chapel was reserved for members of the royal family. The 20m/66ft walls of the chapel are almost entirely occupied by windows 15m/49ft high and 4m/13ft wide. Some of their stained glass work dates back to the time of Louis the Pious. The late Gothic rose window with its depiction of the Apocalypse was completed in 1493–98 during the reign of Charles VIII. The statues on the buttresses of the nave represent the Twelve Apostles.

✶ ✶ **Sainte-Chapelle**

NOTRE-DAME DE PARIS

✦ ✦ **A veritable jewel on the Seine, this masterpiece of French Gothic towers above the Ile de la Cité. For more than 800 years the cathedral has borne witness to the history of France and its capital.**

🕑 Opening times:
Mon–Fri, 8am–6.45pm, Sat–Sun till 7.15pm (last admission 45 min before closing), high Mass Sun 10am, organ recitals Sun 4.30pm
Crypte Archéologique: Tue–Sun, 10am–6pm
Towers: April–Sept, 10am–6.30pm, July–Aug Sat–Sun till 11pm (last admission 45 min before closing)

① Gallery of Kings
This collection, huge in terms of both numbers and the size of the statues, was created in an entirely new style from 1220 onwards by a workshop of sculptors. The statues were originally colourfully painted.

② Arcade gallery
The delicate arcades, with columns only 20cm/8in thick, conceal the ground storeys of the towers as well as the gable of the nave. They were erected in around 1230.

③ Organ
The instrument of the famed Aristide Cavaillé-Coll (1867) with its 8500 pipes and 110 stops is the largest in France.

④ Notre-Dame de Paris
In front of the southwestern pillar at the centre of the church is a statue of the cathedral's patron saint, made around 1330.

⑤ Choir railings
The 23 reliefs on the choir railings were made as of the late 12th century. They bear depictions of scenes from the life and death of Christ, but these date from an »over-restoration« in the 19th century. The lovely carved choir stalls date from the 17th century.

⑥ Buttresses
The cathedral gained its high Gothic appearance around 1220–30. This involved the enlarging of the upper windows and the construction of the fine buttresses.

⑦ Church treasury
The sacristy, added in 1845–50, houses the Trésor, where the important relics are kept: a thorn from Jesus's Crown of Thorns as well as splinters and a nail from the True Cross. Open Wed, Sat, Sun 2.30pm–6pm.

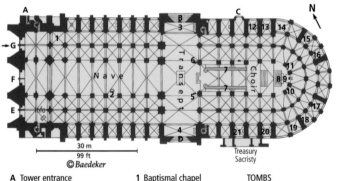

© Baedeker

30 m
99 ft

A Tower entrance	1 Baptismal chapel	TOMBS
B Portail du Cloître	2 Pulpit	12 de Beaumont
C Porte Rouge	3 Northern rose window	13 de Juigné
D Portal	4 Southern rose window	14 de Noailles
Saint Etienne	5 Notre Dame	15 de Quelen
E Portal	6 St Denis	16 de Belloy
Sainte Anne	7 Choir seating	17 Morlot
F Portal of the	8 High altar	18 Darboy
Last Judgement	9 Pietà	19 d'Harcourt
G Portal of the	10 Louis XIII	20 Sibour
Virgin Mary	11 Louis XIV	21 Affre

the splendid contents of the **choir chapels**, the tomb of the Duc d'Harcourt († 1718) by Jean-Baptiste Pigalle is a highlight.

★
◄ Choir chapels

★ Ile St-Louis

The idyllic Ile St-Louis, which neighbours the Ile de la Cité to the east, was constructed between 1614 and 1630 by linking the islands Ile Notre-Dame and Ile aux Vaches. Its beautiful **palais** – like Hôtel de Lauzun (Le Vau, 1657) and Hôtel Lambert (Le Vau, 1640) – help it retain its 17th-century aura. Nowadays, art galleries, antiques shops and purveyors of outlandish fashion have made the area their own. The narrow main street is the site of the richly furnished church of St-Louis-en-l'Ile (1664–1726). But it is not only cosy cafés, nice hotels and charming restaurants that the Ile St-Louis has to offer, it also has the **best ice cream parlour** in Paris: Berthillon (Rue St-Louis-en-l'Ile) has a choice of more than 30 flavours.

Hôtel Lauzun and Hôtel Lambert

★ ★ Louvre

The Louvre houses one of the biggest and most famous collections of art in the world and attracts more than 6 million visitors every year. The oldest of the buildings on the site was a **castle** erected under King Philippe II at the end of the 12th century, which was fabulously furnished by Charles V in about 1365 (remnants are preserved in the Cour Carrée and Cour Napoléon). During the 15th century it was used as an arsenal and a prison. In 1546 François I employed Pierre Lescot, the most outstanding architect of the early French Renaissance, to create a new building. The main legacy of this is the southern part of the main façade. Subsequent kings made changes to the »old Louvre« and it was largely completed by Claude Perrault, who oversaw the building of the magnificent colonnades of the eastern façade between 1667 and 1674. After Louis XIV transferred his court to Versailles in 1682, the unfinished buildings became neglected and decaying. It was only under Napoleon that the Louvre, which had been transformed into a museum as early as 1793, was restored. It was reconfigured again between 1981 and 1999, with the new 22m/72ft glass pyramid (Ieoh Ming Pei) forming a new highlight in the Cour Napoléon.

History

Before or after or even while taking in the art: the café in the Louvre

Works of art   The contents of the Louvre are immense in scope: of more than 350,000 works of art, about 30,000 are on display at any time. Here is a brief summary of the eras of art featuring outstanding, world fa-

Antiquity ►   mous exhibits. Etruscan art: Sarcophagus from Cerveteri (6th century BC). Mesopotamia, Iran, Phoenicia and Assyria: stele of Naram-Sin, king of Agde (*c*2270 BC); Assyrian winged bull (8th century BC); laws of Hammurabi. Egypt: stele of the snake god Zet (*c*3000 BC); seated scribe from Saqqara (*c*2500 BC); stele of Antef (courtier under Thutmos III); bust of King Amenophis IV; sarcophagus of the chancellor Imeneminet (7th century BC). Greece: pieces of the Parthenon from Athens (447–438 BC); metopes from the temple of Zeus in Olympia (5th century BC); Venus de Milo (Aphrodite statue from the isle of Me-

A magnet for all lovers of art, the »Mona Lisa«

los, 2nd century BC); »Lady of Auxerre« (*c*630 BC); Nike of Samothrake, a Greek victory goddess (*c*200 BC); Apollo Saurochthónos and Aphrodite of Knidos, copies of Praxiteles (4th century BC), Athlete's head from Bénévent; L'Ephebe d'Agde; Roman sarcophagi, 2nd–3rd century AD, sculpted ends 12th–19th centuries: Michelangelo, *Bound Slaves*; Donatello, *John the Baptist, Madonna and Child*; Tilman Riemenschneider, *The Virgin Annunciate*; Tomb of Philippe Pot (15th century); Bouchardon, Amor statue.

▶ VISITING LOUVRE

INFORMATION . ADMISSION

Tel. 01 40 20 51 51, www.louvre.fr
Main entrance in the glass pyramid.
Other entrances: Carrousel du Louvre, Porte des Lions, Richelieu-Passage, Cour Carée

OPENING TIMES . TICKETS

Open Wed–Mon from 9.00am, Wed and Fri until 10pm (reduced admission after 6pm), otherwise 6pm. Free admission on the first Sunday of each month.
Tickets are available from various places, including the following:

FNAC, Virgin, Carrefour and Auchan. Buying tickets from one of these is a good way to avoid queuing at the ticket office (the same applies to the Paris Museum Pass). It is advisable to obtain a museum guide first and a listing of when the various sections are open before planning out what you want to see, as various sections are only open on certain days of the week. It is possible to exit and re-enter the Louvre. You are advised to wear comfortable shoes and a supply of drinks and snacks would not go amiss.

Spanish paintings from the 14th–18th centuries: El Greco, Zurbaran, Murillo, Ribera, Velázquez, Goya. German and Dutch masters of the late Gothic and Renaissance (15th–16th centuries): Dürer, self-portrait; works by Hans Holbein the Younger and Lucas Cranach. Flemish and Dutch paintings of the 16th–17th centuries: Peter-Paul Rubens, Jan van Eyck, Hieronymus Bosch, Brueghel the Elder, Frans Hals; Rembrandt, *Supper at Emmaus*; Van Dyck, *Portrait of Charles I of England*. Italian masters of the 13th–17th centuries: Giotto, Filippo Lippi, Botticelli, Mantegna, Tiepolo, Carracci, and the great highlight, the *Mona Lisa* and *Madonna of the Rocks* by Leonardo da Vinci, *Marriage at Cana* by Veronese, *Portrait of a Courtier (Baldassare Castiglione)* by Raphael, *Death of the Virgin* by Caravaggio. French masters of the 16th–19th centuries: Clouet, Lebrun, Poussin, La Tour; *Liberty on the Barricades* by Eugène Delacroix; *Les Glaneuses* by Jean-Francois Millet; *The Turkish Bath* by Jean Auguste Dominique Ingres. Among the craft items the riches of the abbey at St-Denis and remnants of the **French crown jewels** stand out.

◄ Paintings

◄ Craft items

The west pavilion of the north wing contains the museum of decorative art featuring interiors and day-to-day items from the Middle Ages to the start of the 20th century. The fashion museum in the Rohan wing exhibits clothing from the 16th century to the present day, including dresses by Chanel, Dior, Cardin and other couturiers. Both of these museums are closed on Mondays.

**Musée des Arts Décoratifs
Musée de la Mode**

Rue de Rivoli runs to the north of the Tuileries and the Louvre. Built from 1811 to 1856, it is one of the finest streets in Paris. It boasts simply everything from high-class boutiques and shops for unusual gifts to cosy cafés and colourful souvenir shops.

✳
Rue de Rivoli

Place de la Concorde · Tuileries

The glittering Place de la Concorde, built in 1836–54 by Cologne's Jacques Ignace Hittorff, is particularly effective thanks to its axes of view: up the Champs-Elysées to the Arc de Triomphe in the west, the Tuileries to the east, the Madeleine on Rue Royale to the north and Palais Bourbon across the Seine to the south. The granite **Obelisk** of Luxor, almost 23m/75ft tall and weighing 250 tons, formerly belonged to a temple at Thebes in Egypt from the 13th century BC and was dedicated to Louis Philippe in 1831. The two fountains (representing Agriculture, Industry, Seafaring and Fisheries) were all created by Hittorf, as were the female figures representing Frances eight biggest cities.

✳ ✳
Place de la Concorde

At the eastern edge of Place de la Concorde, Baroque winged horses with Mercury and Fama (by Coysevox) guard the entrance to the Jardin des Tuileries, formerly a pleasure garden for the monarchy, which was created as of 1664 by Le Nôtre. To the left on the Terrasse

✳
Jardin des Tuileries

★ ★
Musée
del'Orangerie ▶

des Feuillants is a real tennis court (Jeu de Paume), and theMusée de l'Orangerie opposite has a collection of **famous paintings** by Cézanne, Renoir, Matisse, Picasso, Modigliani and others, including the almost 100m/110yd-long frieze *Nymphéas* (*Water Lilies*) by Claude Monet.

Arc de Triomphe
du Carrousel
Carrousel du
Louvre

Towering 14.6m/48ft high alongside the Place du Carrousel is the Arc de Triomphe du Carrousel (1808), built to celebrate Napoleon's victories over the Austrians. Underneath the square there is a huge shopping centre (1993) including a tourist office for the Ile-de-France as well as restaurants and galleries. An upside-down pyramid funnels light into the malls.

Champs-Elysées · Arc de Triomphe

★ ★
Champs-Elysées

This is where the heart of France beats. 2km/1.5mi long and built at the end of the 17th century, the Avenue des Champs-Elysées (»Elysian fields«) is said to be the most beautiful boulevard in the world. Top-notch hotels and restaurants, luxury shops, cafés and fast food establishments, theatres and cinematic palaces – the street offers everything possible to pass the time away.

★
Petit Palais

The two superb neo-Baroque palaces, Grand Palais and Petit Palais, were built for the World's Fair of 1900. Petit Palais (to the east) con-

The Arc de Triomphe hails the victories of the emperor Napoleon

tains the **Musée des Beaux-Arts** de la Ville de Paris, possessing outstanding collections of paintings and sculptures from classical times into the 20th century (including Rembrandt, Van Dyck, Delacroix, Millet, Cézanne, Monet), as well as tapestries, furniture, porcelain and craft items. The magnificent glass and iron palace, the Grand Palais, is used for exhibitions.

Grand Palais

The Champs-Elysées climbs the hill to Place Charles-de-Gaulle (known as Place de l'Etoile till 1970). There the eye is drawn remorselessly to the stunning Arc de Triomphe de l'Etoile, 49m/161ft high and 45m/49yd wide by 22m/24yd deep. The awesome building, a **national monument** and one of the finest works of Classicism to emerge from the imperial era, was completed in 1836 under Louis Philippe. The pillars are decorated with colossal images: to the right from the east *Revolt of the Volunteers Against Prussia in 1792* (*Marseillaise*) by Francois Rude, to the right *The Coronation of Napoleon* (Treaty of Vienna 1810) by Cortot; to the right from the west, the revolt of the French people in 1814 is depicted, and to the left the blessings of peace in 1815. The reliefs above them and on the narrow ends depict battles from the time of the republic and the imperial age. A relief under the eaves (*Departure and Return of the Troops*) and the names inside of 172 battles and 386 generals (those who died in battle are underlined) complete the military memorials. In 1921 the **first tomb for the unknown soldier** was initiated (ceremonies daily at 6.30 pm). From the platform on top of the arch there is a staggering **view** of Paris. A museum exhibits documents covering the history of the monument along with reminders of Napoleon I and the First World War (open daily, tickets from the passages beneath the square).

★ ★
Arc de Triomphe de l'Etoile

! Baedeker TIP

Open doors

On »Journées du Patrimoine« over the weekend nearest to the 20th September many cultural monuments can be viewed for free or for a nominal price, in particular some that would otherwise be closed to the public, such as the Elysée Palace (1718, residence of the state president), Palais Royal and Hôtel de Matignon (home of the prime minister). Information: tel. 01 56 06 50 21, www.jp.culture.fr.

Grands Boulevards

The Madeleine church north of the Place de la Concorde was begun under Napoleon in 1806 as a temple of glory but it was not completed until 1842. In 1837 Marochetti produced the marble group called the *Assumption of Mary Magdalene* for the high altar. The huge fresco by Jules-Claude Ziegler above the altar depicts figures of history (including Constantine the Great, Dante, Napoleon I, Pius VII). To the right of the entrance to the church stand what are **probably the nicest public toilets** in Paris, an example of Art Nouveau from

Sainte-Marie-Madeleine

1905. The Fauchon and Hédiard **delicatessen establishments** on Place Madeleine provide for an abundance of irresistible delicacies.

✶
Grands Boulevards

The Madeleine is also the start of the 30m/100ft-wide Grands Boulevards, built during the expansion of the city under Louis XIV. They run in a great 4.3km/2.7mi-long arc to Place de la Bastille. With their elegant shops, theatres, cinemas, discotheques, restaurants and terrace cafés they are second only to the Champs-Elysées itself as the main thoroughfares of the city north of the Seine.

Boulevard des Capucines

From the Madeleine church, Boulevard de la Madeleine and Boulevard des Capucines (with the legendary temple of French chanson, the Paris **Olympia**, rebuilt in 1998) lead to Place de l'Opéra, one of the busiest intersections in Paris. To the left, the Grand-Hôtel building contains the famous **Café de la Paix**, which is a listed building.

✶
Opéra Garnier

Paris Story

The Théâtre National de l'Opéra, built in 1862–75 by Charles Garnier, is one of the biggest and **most splendid theatres** in the world (open daily 10am–5pm, guided tours www.operadeparis.fr). Adjoining its 54m/177ft-long Foyer du Public there is a balcony with a wonderful view. Nearby the »multivision show« Paris Story provides a journey through 2000 years of the city's history (11 bis, Rue Scribe, open daily; www.paris-story.com).

Boulevard des Italiens

Musée Grévin

The most elegant shops along the route can be found at the eastern end of the Blvd. des Capucines and along its continuation, Blvd. des Italiens. The junction of Blvd. Haussmann is the start of Blvd. Montmartre. In Musée Grévin, established 1882, you can come face to face with large (wax) figures of personages from the history of France, from Charlemagne to Zinedine Zidane.

Porte St-Denis

Porte St-Martin

At the crossroads of Blvd. de Bonne-Nouvelle and Rue du Faubourg-St-Denis/Rue St-Denis – one of the city's oldest streets – Porte St-Denis (Blondel, 1673) celebrates the victories of Louis XIV in Holland. The eastern end of Boulevard St-Denis is marked by Porte St-Martin, also built to honour Louis XIV, in this case for the conquest of Besançon and Limburg and victories over the Spanish, Germans and Dutch (Bullet, 1675).

✶
Musée des Arts et Métiers

The Conservatoire National des Arts et Métiers, housed in the monastery of St-Martin-des-Champs since 1798, possesses a museum (closed Mon), which grew out of a collection of machines and tools used for teaching the working class. It is now one of the most important **technical museums** in Europe.

Place de la République

Place de la République, built in 1888, is adorned by an imposing statue of »The Republic« (1883). In front of the monument there is a lion with an urn, symbolizing universal suffrage.

Baedeker TIP

Cathedrals of luxury

If the Louvre is the apotheosis of all museums, then Galeries Lafayette (40 Boulevard Haussmann), with its beautiful Art Nouveau atrium under the glass dome, enjoys the same status among department stores. Whether shopping or just looking, those with tired legs can take a break in the roof restaurant. The nearby Printemps store (64 Boulevard Haussmann) also has a fine restaurant under its own glass dome and is well worth a visit.

From Place de la République the avenue of the same name leads eastward to the biggest (44ha/109 acres) and most famous of Paris's three **main cemeteries**, opened in 1804 and named after the confessor of Louis XIV. Maps are free at all the entrances so that anyone can choose which of the 70,000 graves, flamboyant or simple, they want to see, be it Abelard and Heloïse, Balzac or Oscar Wilde, Chopin, Rossini or Bizet, Yves Montand, Simone Signoret or Maria Callas. Graves of some like Edith Piaf, the »Paris Sparrow«, and Doors singer Jim Morrison have become veritable »places of pilgrimage«. The **Mur des Fédérés** (wall of the Communards) is where 147 members of the famous commune were shot on 28 May 1871. There is also a memorial to victims of Nazi concentration camps.

★
Cimetière du
Père-Lachaise

From Place Vendôme to Opéra Bastille

The harmoniously designed Place Vendôme was conceived in 1686–1708 by J. Hardouin-Mansart, the most important architect of the Grand Siècle. The 43.5m/143ft **Vendôme column**, emulating Trajan's column in Rome, was cast from the metal of 1200 Austrian and Russian cannons. Its relief depicts the 1805 war against Austria and Russia. At the top stands Napoleon garbed in Roman imperial regalia. Composer Frédéric Chopin died in no. 12 in 1849. The legendary **Hotel Ritz** has had an eminent list of guests and was the final residence of Princess Diana. The elegant shops on the square are among the most celebrated in Paris.

★
Place Vendôme

Rue St-Honoré passes the church of St-Roch, one of the finest Baroque church buildings in Paris (Lemercier, 1653–1740). There are numerous graves here, some of them assembled here from other destroyed churches, as well as notable paintings. Concerts are given on Sundays at 10am.

St-Roch

Palais Royal	Palais Royal is one of Paris's most important buildings. For a long time it was used as a residence by members of the royal family and it was from here that the masses made their way to the Bastille on 14 July 1789. Of the original building, Palais Cardinal (built for Richelieu by Lemercier in 1639), only the Galerie des Proues on the eastern side of the courtyard remains (it is named after the ships' prows that decorate it). The square, **Place du Palais Royal**, is dominated by the »Colonnes«, black and white striped columns by Daniel Buren,
Jardin du Palais Royal	and is also a popular place for skaters. The Jardin du Palais Royal is surrounded by colonnades from 1786.
Louvre des Antiquaires	Between Palais Royal and the Louvre, shoppers can positively revel in glorious antiques. The former Grands Magasins du Louvre (2 Place du Palais Royal) now boast **250 luxury shops** offering everything possible to enhance any home, from sumptuous Baroque and exquisite Art Deco to Tibetan craft items.
✴ **St-Eustache**	The towerless church of St-Eustache was built between 1532 and 1637, so that it displays elements of both Gothic and Renaissance styles. The façade (1754–88) is one of the primary works of French Baroque. From 1795 to 1803 the church was transformed into the Temple de l'Agriculture. In its elegant interior (88m/96yd long, 34m/112ft high) there are innumerable works of art on view, including a Madonna by Jean-Baptiste Pigalle (18th century), the *Apostles on the Road to Emmaus* by Rubens, the *Martyrdom of St Eustace* by Vouet and a tomb piece for Jean-Baptiste Colbert († 1683), finance minister under Louis XIV (Coysevox to a design by Le Brun). The magnificent **organ** can be heard at 11am and 5.30pm Sunday Masses. The lively quarter around St-Eustache has numerous long established bars and shops offering everything from bric-a-brac to haute couture.

> ! **Baedeker** TIP
>
> **Rue Montorgueil**
>
> North of the Forum des Halles, the area around Rue Montorgueil, in spite of a certain »gentrification«, still exhibits some of the atmosphere of the Les Halles market district. Among its bars and appetizing food shops, try out Patisserie Stohrer (51 Rue Montorgueil), founded in 1725 by the confectioner to the Polish king Stanisław Leszczyński, especially the pithiviers or the apricot tart.

✴ **Forum des Halles**	Where the Forum des Halles now stands, there was formerly a central market hall dating from 1854–59 and called **Les Halles**, known as the »belly of Paris«. It was demolished in the years before 1971 and the market was relocated to the southern suburb of Rungis near Orly. The site now has one of the biggest interchanges between Métro and RER lines. The four floors above the stations of Les Halles and Châtelet-Les Halles have more than 300 shops, restaurants, cafés, cinemas, museums and theatres. More than 800,000 people stream

Once dubbed a »monstrosity«, the Centre Pompidou is now a successful centre of culture

through these passages every day. Nowadays a few »undesired developments« are starting to emerge, such as the drug trading that goes on here, and there are plans to remodel the site again, though with no results as yet. The royal parish church of St-Germain l'Auxerrois (13th–16th centuries) has a late Gothic façade, a vestibule decorated with statues (1439), a sumptuous Flemish altar and a triptych in the left-hand aisle (both 16th century). The seating for the royal family was made by **Le Brun** (1684). Many artists who served the monarchs of the 17th–18th centuries are buried here.

St-Germain l'Auxerrois

Pont Neuf (1578–1603), even though its name means »new bridge«, is actually the oldest of the bridges in Paris. There is a marvellous view of the city centre from it. (The La Samaritaine department store has been converted into a hotel by the LVMH conglomerate.) Upstream from here, as far as Pont Louis Philippe, both banks of the Seine are lined by the stands of the Paris **bouquinistes** (book sellers).

✷ Pont Neuf

At Place du Châtelet the Fontaine de la Victoire (1808) recalls Napoleon's Egyptian campaign. The western side of the square is occupied by the Théâtre Musical de Paris, while the eastern side has the Théâtre de la Ville. Cross the northern channel of the Seine via the Pont au Change from here (where there is a great view) to get the Ile de la Cité (►p.623). **Tour St-Jacques**, a remnant of the church of St-Jacques la Boucherie which was razed in 1797, rises up above the Rue de Rivoli. It is now used as a meteorological station.

Place du Châtelet

The **Centre National d'Art et de Culture Georges Pompidou**, known as the Pompidou Centre or Beaubourg for short, is a top-notch temple of culture (open Wed–Mon 11am–10pm). Still startlingly unusual,

✷ ✷ Centre Pompidou

Place des Vosges, a gorgeous set of 36 almost identical buildings

★ ★
Musée d'Art
Moderne ▶

the 166m/182yd-long, 60m/66yd-wide »refinery« was designed in steel and glass by Richard Rogers and Renzo Piano and opened in 1977. It attracts up to 25,000 visitors daily. The Musée National d'Art Moderne within the building is France's flagship of classic modern art. There is a tremendous view from the **6th-floor restaurant**.

Hôtel de Ville

The Hôtel de Ville on its eponymous square (where official executions were held between 1310 and 1832) is the residence of Paris's mayor. The magnificent neo-Renaissance building with some 200 statues was built in 1874–82 to plans conceived by Ballu and Deperthes.

★
Marais

The Marais district extends east of Boulevard Sébastopol (3rd and 4th arr.). It was once an expensive residential quarter and still includes houses of the aristocracy from the 16th–18th centuries, but nowadays it has become the one of the most delightful places for **a night out in Paris**. Rue des Rosiers is famous as the hub of the city's Jewish community, but – not least because it is so attractive – is increasingly becoming a run of the mill shopping area; the famous Jo Goldenberg restaurant closed in 2006. Places to see include Hôtel Amelot de Bisseuil (47 Rue Vieille du Temple), Hôtel d'Aumont (7 Rue de Jouy), built by Le Vau circa 1650, Hôtel Beauvais (68 Rue F.-Miron), where a 7-year-old Mozart was a guest of the Bavarian ambassador in 1763, and Hôtel de Lamoignon from 1598 (24 Rue Pavée), containing the Bibliothèque Historique de la Ville de Paris. The Musée d'Art et d'Histoire du Judaïsme in Hôtel St-Aignan (1647) is dedicated to the history of Jews in France (71 Rue du Temple, closed Sat).

★
Musée d'Histoire
du Judaïsme

One of the »fathers« of the Picasso museum in Hôtel Salé (5 Rue de Thorigny) was André Malraux, who as Minister of Culture introduced a law by which inheritance taxes could be paid off with art treasures. This enabled the French state to amass a huge collection from Picasso's heirs, with works from all phases of his development. Open Wed–Mon, April–Sept 9.30am–6pm, otherwise till 5.30pm.

★ ★
Musée Picasso

In a Renaissance building from 1544, Musée Carnavalet (23 Rue de Sévigné) provides a summary of Paris's history. In the late 17th century the palais was the residence of **Madame de Sévigné**, whose exchange of letters with her daughters is one of the most impressive legacies documenting life at the court of the Sun King.

Musée Carnavalet

Place des Vosges dates from 1607–12, when as Place Royale it was the glittering **centre of an aristocratic suburb**. It was used for state receptions and weddings as well as being a popular place for fighting duels. Only the earliest of the façades are »genuine«. Most of the buildings are half-timbered edifices for which frontices have been faked with stucco and paint to look like worked stone and brick. In the middle of the square there is an equestrian statue of Louis XIII dating from 1819. Cafés, restaurants and quality shops have all established themselves beneath the arcades. L'Ambroisie has three Michelin stars and the Coconnas restaurant is also very good. Madame de Sévigné, who succeeded in capturing the times in her letters, was born at no. 1; no. 6, Hotel de Rohan-Guéménée, was home to Victor Hugo from 1832 to 1848 (museum).

★ ★
Place des Vosges

Not far southeast of Place des Vosges at the end of the Grand Boulevard is Place de la Bastille, usually shortened just to La Bastille. The years 1370–83 saw the building here of the notorious city prison, the **Bastille St-Antoine**, which on 14 July 1789 was stormed by the people of Paris and later razed to the ground. On the square the 51m/167ft Colonne de Juillet honours those who fought in the July Revolution. The mausoleum beneath the column houses the fallen from the wars of 1830 and 1848. There is a wonderful view from the observation platform (283 steps to the top).

★
Place de la Bastille

Colonne de Juillet

The Opéra de la Bastille was opened in 1989. It is a less than exciting glass building by Uruguayan-Canadian architect Carlos Ott but the café there is a popular place to meet. With the construction of the opera building, the whole area began to change. On Rue du Faubourg St-Antoine and neighbouring streets old-time crafts are now mixing with art traders, and workshops have been transformed into exclusive loft studios, boutiques, stylish bars and galleries.

Opéra de la Bastille
★
Bastille quarter

The **disused railway line** along Av. Daumesnil (southeast of the Opéra de la Bastille) has become a green belt running for 3km/2mi through the Reuilly quarter. Under the arches of the viaduct at the

Viaduc des Arts

! *Baedeker* TIP

Train Bleu

At the Gare de Lyon with its 64m/210ft tower from 1900, the »Train Bleu« restaurant keeps alive the luxurious atmosphere of travel from a bygone age. The cuisine in the giant eatery is no better than average but the ambience is unique.

start of Av. Daumesnil visitors can potter around the designer shops and studios. The café at no. 43 offers a jazz brunch on Sundays.

Canal St-Martin
Houseboats and yachts, old locks and romantic tow paths in the middle of Paris? Yes, a canal from Port de l'Arsenal opened in 1808, although parts of it were built over later. Canal St-Martin runs 4.5km/3mi northward to the Bassin and Parc de la Villette (▶p.649) and Canal de l'Ourc. The best time to come is on Sunday afternoons when the roads along the banks are closed to traffic. Boat trips down the canal are also very enjoyable.

Northern Suburbs

✳
Musée Jacque-mart-André
In its aristocratic place (158 Blvd. Haussmann) Musée Jacquemart-André (open 10am–6pm) displays works by Flemish masters of the 17th century, English paintings from the 18th century, and French paintings by Boucher, Fragonard and others, as well as the **finest collection of Italian Renaissance works** in France. There is a wonderful café-restaurant in the courtyard (open 11.45am–5.30pm).

✳
Parc Monceau
✳
Musée Nissim de Camondo
Duke Philippe d'Orléans had Parc Monceau laid out off Boulevard de Courcelles in 1778 as a meeting place for the beau monde. Its palms and artificial ruins give it a special charm. Musée Nissim de Camondo (63 Rue de Monceau) possesses a combination featuring an outstanding collection of furniture, art and tapestries from the 18th century.

✳
Montmartre quarter
The Montmartre quarter extends up the slopes of the 129m/423ft Butte Montmartre and across its summit. The area gained fame as the **Bohemia of the 19th century** with artists like Toulouse-Lautrec, Manet and Apollinaire. Around the Boulevard de Clichy it is possible to find everything the erotic goods industry can offer, while **Place Pigalle** lives up to its bawdy reputation with numerous cabarets and

bars, as well as the Moulin Rouge on Place Blanche. The Musée de l'Erotisme (72 Blvd. de Clichy, open 10am–2pm) is not to be missed by devotees either. However, it is also worth visiting the Musée de la Vie Romantique (16 Rue Chaptal), the studio of the contemporarily successful artist Ary Scheffer (1795–1858).

Musée de l'Erotisme

Steps, promenades and even a funicular railway lead up the slopes of the Butte Montmartre from Place St-Pierre. The basilica of Sacré Cœur at the top, one of Paris's premier landmarks, can be seen for miles around. The gigantic neo-Romanesque-neo-Byzantine building with its 83m/272ft dome was built after the war of 1870–71 and the Communards' revolt as an act of atonement to the city's Catholic population. Begun in 1873, it was consecrated in 1919. The 94m/308ft tower contains a bell weighing almost 19 tons called »La Savoyarde«. The awe-inspiring gold mosaic work in the choir (1923) glorifies the »Sacred Heart of Jesus«. From the terrace in front of the church, and even more so from its dome, there is a staggering view of Paris.

✷ ✷ Montmartre

✷ Sacré-Cœur

The streets and squares around the church have, in spite of the bustle of souvenir shops, cabarets and amusement arcades, not entirely lost their pleasant village-style character. This includes Place du Tertre with its perennially well frequented cafés and restaurants and its famous while-you-wait portraitists. Other places worth a visit are Espace Dalí (11 Rue Poulbot) and the Musée de Montmartre (12 Rue Cortot).

Place du Tertre

Place du Tertre with Montmartre's emblem, the Sacré Coeur, in the background

✳ Cimetière de Montmartre

The cemetery opened in the west of the quarter in 1795 is the last resting place of many well-known figures, including Heine, Berlioz, Offenbach, Alexandre Dumas fils, Degas, Dalida and Truffaut.

Marché aux Puces de St-Ouen

Between Porte de Clignancourt and Porte St-Ouen north of the Boulevard Périphérique, the St-Ouen **flea market** has been taking place from Saturday to Monday since 1885. It actually consists of ten markets; the best known of which is the Biron antique market, while the most impressive is probably the Marché Vernaison with its stylish furniture and bric-a-brac.

✳ Parc des Buttes-Chaumont

In the working class quarter of the 19th arrondissement Haussmann took a former quarry and laid out the Buttes-Chaumont, finishing in 1867. In its pond there is a little temple, which offers a fine view of Montmartre and the plain of St-Denis. An even better view is to be had from a hill (101m/331ft) and its café at the southern edge of the park.

From the Pont de l'Alma to the Bois de Boulogne

Pont de l'Alma

Pont de l'Alma crosses the Seine and the new road tunnel, where Princess Diana, the ex-wife of the heir to the British throne Prince Charles, was killed in a car accident on 31 August 1997. The torch of freedom on Place d'Alma has become a place of pilgrimage for her devotees.

Palais de Tokyo

Palais Galliera

✳ Musée Guimet

In the Palais de Tokyo (11 Av. Prés. Wilson) the Musée d'Art Moderne de la Ville de Paris displays works from post-impressionists, cubists and Fauves up to the latest figurative artists (closed Mon). Its café is a nice place to take a break. The magnificent Palais Galliera, a stone's throw to the north, is the place to go to revel in **fashion** at the Musée de la Mode de la Ville de Paris (closed Mon). Musée Guimet (Place d'Iena) is considered the most important museum in France for **art from the Middle East and Far East** (closed Tue). It has a lovely Japanese garden.

✳ Palais de Chaillot

The finest view of the Eiffel Tower (photo p.621) can be had from the terraces of the Palais de Chaillot, built for the World's Fair of 1937 and very often simply called the Trocadéro. Its west wing contains the Musée de la Marine, documenting the history of the French merchant and military navies. The **Cité de l'Architecture et du Patrimonie** in the east wing contains important French buildings and frescoes in model or copy form (both closed Tue). The Cinémathèque Française, once housed here, has moved to the Bercy quarter (building by Frank Gehry 2006, 51 Rue de Bercy, www.cinemathque-francaise.fr).

✳✳ Musée Marmottan-Monet

The Musée Marmottan at the edge of the Bois de Boulogne (2 Rue L. Boilly) possesses not only empire furniture and medieval miniatures

Across Pont Alexandre III, named after a Russian tsar, towards the Hôtel des Invalides

but also the **largest Monet collection in the world** with more than 100 of his works, as well as paintings by other important impressionists, open Tue–Sun 10am–6pm.

Eiffel Tower · Hôtel des Invalides

The premier Paris landmark, the totally useless but wonderful Eiffel Tower, was built starting in 1887 by **Gustave Eiffel** for the World's Fair of 1889. At the time it was the tallest building on earth (open mid-June–Aug 9am–0.45am, otherwise 9.30am–11.45pm). Constructed from some 16,500 pieces of iron and 2.5 million rivets, the tower is 320.75m/1052ft 4in high including the television aerial on top. The lowest stage has a breadth of 129.22m/424ft, while the first storey, 58m/190ft up, is 65m/213ft wide. The second storey platform is at 116m/381ft and the third is 276m/906ft above the ground. From there, a stairway leads up 24m/79ft to a balcony just 5.75m/19ft in diameter. For normal visitors, the first and second stages are accessible via lift or stairs, while the third can only be reached by lift. On rare clear days the view from the platform at the top stretches some 90km/56mi and is at its best just before sunset. There are restaurants at the top and on the first storey (►p.617).

✶ ✶
Tour Eiffel

The Champs de Mars once served as a parade ground for the École Militaire, but were later used as a park for grand national celebrations and the World's Fairs that took place in Paris. The mighty **École Militaire** was built in 1751–74 for the newly established cadet school according to plans drawn up by the famous Jacques-Ange Gabriel. Since 1880 it has been the seat of the French military college.

Champs de Mars

The Hôtel des Invalides, a complex covering some 12.7ha/31 acres, was begun in 1671 under Louis XIV and was intended to house

Hôtel des Invalides

about 6000 veterans. Nowadays, though it still does house a few invalids of war, it is now home to several government bodies. In front of the 210m/230yd-long north façade are the 18 riflemen statues of the »Batterie triomphale«, 20 plundered bronze cannons from the 17th–18th centuries and two Panther tanks from the Second World War. From the great courtyard it is possible to enter the famous army museum, which contains exhibits from all over the world. Anyone interested in history can also see the models of the city from the 17th–19th centuries at the Musée des Plans-Reliefs. Inside the frugal church of St-Louis des Invalides hang captured flags from the wars of the 19th century, while Chapelle Napoléon to the right of the choir has remains of the emperor's tomb from St Helena and the coffin used to transport him back to France.

✳ Musée de l'Armée

St-Louis des Invalides

Louis XIV had the monumental Dôme des Invalides built (Jules Hardouin-Mansart 1677–1706, Robert de Cotte till 1735) as a ceremonial backdrop to his visits to church. Its »highlight« is the dome (97m/318ft high or 107m/351ft including its crucifix) with its gilded lead roof. Beneath the dome is theporphyry (a type of granite) sarcophagus with the mortal remains of **Emperor Napoleon I** and the lead coffin of Napoleon II, his only legitimate son (Duke of Reichstadt, 1811–32). In the cross aisles can be found the graves of Marshall Turenne (1611–75) and the fortress architect Le Prestre de Vauban (1633–1707), while the chapels in the corner have tombs for Joseph Bonaparte, Napoleon's eldest brother (1768–1844, king of Naples), his younger brother Jérôme (1784–1860, king of Westphalia) and the heart of his wife Catharina of Württemberg († 1835) plus those of Marshall Foch (1851–1929) and Marshall Lyautey († 1934).

✳ Dôme des Invalides

✳ Crypt of Napoleon

For many the Musée Rodin in Hôtel Biron is their most favoured among all of Paris's art museums, as the works of **Auguste Rodin** (1840–1917) and the woman in his life **Camille Claudel** (1864–1943) are some of the most moving sculptures ever created: *The Thinker*, *The Gates of Hell*, *The Kiss*, *The Burghers of Calais*, among many others (open Tue–Sun April–Sept 9.30am–5.45pm, Oct– March till 4.45pm). Its **garden**, where there is a lovely terrace café, is a wonderful place to relax.

✳✳ Musée Rodin

From the Eiffel Tower to Montparnasse

Since 2006, the superb ethnological collections of the Musée de l'Homme and Musée National des Arts d'Afrique et d'Océanie have been on display in this elegant building designed by Jean Nouvel (Tue–Sun from 11am, Tue–Wed and Sun till 7pm, otherwise till 9pm).

Musée du Quai Branly

From Place de la Résistance (opposite 93 Quai d'Orsay) it is possible to descend into the underground world of the **Paris sewers**. Beyond

Égouts de Paris

the Aérogare (buses going solely to Orly Airport) on the Quai d'Orsay stands the foreign ministry (1853), which like Scotland Yard is best known by its (former) location and is usually called simply the **Quai d'Orsay**. Since 1795 the prestigious Palais Bourbon at the Pont de la Concorde has been the venue for meetings of the **national assembly** (guided tours Sat).

Quai d'Orsay

✱

Palais Bourbon

The former Quai d'Orsay railway station, a huge glass and iron construction, was built for the World's Fair of 1900 by Victor Laloux but was only transformed into a museum of art in 1986 (open Tue–Sun 9.30am–6pm, Thu till 9.45pm). A visit there is a must as it possesses a large number of truly famous works dating from 1848 to 1916, covering styles ranging from Realism, Impressionism and Symbolism to Art Nouveau. It also has a good café-bistro.

✱ ✱

Musée d'Orsay

The **Académie Française** was founded by Cardinal Richelieu in 1635. Its 40 members are termed »Immortels«. The academy has the task of encouraging the French language and maintaining its purity. Along with other scientific institutes it has been based since 1805 in the **Institut de France** (23 Quai de Conti), which Le Vau completed in 1672 at the commission of Cardinal Mazarin. Guided tours (Sat–Sun 10.30am–3pm) allow access to the great assembly hall beneath its dome, where the grave sculpture of the cardinal himself (by A. Coysevox) is also on view. The three court-

Art in a railway setting at the Musée d'Orsay

yards make for a picturesque route through to Rue Mazarine. From the École des Beaux-Arts, Rue Bonaparte leads to the 11th-century church of St-Germain-des-Prés, the oldest in Paris. Formerly this was the site of a church belonging to the abbey of »St Germain (Germanus) of the Fields«, consecrated (by St Germain as St Vincent's) in 558, and was where the Merovingian kings had their tombs. The present church was painted in 1850 and contains several beautiful pictures and tomb pieces, as well as the burial slab of philosopher René Descartes († 1650).

✱

St-Germain-des-Prés

Boulevard St-Germain, built in 1855–66, is 3km/2mi long and forms the main thoroughfare of the **quarter of artists and intellectuals**, St-Germain-des-Prés. Its cafés and brasseries are legendary: Lipp (no. 151), Deux Magots (no. 170), Flore (no. 172). The Procope (Rue de l'Ancienne Comédie) is the oldest coffee house in Paris and is now a café and restaurant. Its second-hand bookshops and antique dealers, fine boutiques, delicatessen establishments and jazz bars leave no time for boredom.

Boulevard St-Germain

In St-Germain-des-Prés there is always something going on

Palais du Luxembourg

The palace built by Salomon de Brosse from 1615 to 1621 for Marie de' Medici, widow of Henri IV and mother of Louis XIII, is now the home of the senate, the second house of the French parliament. The **Jardin du Luxembourg**, which is part of its estate, is one of the most popular parks in Paris and is a paradise for children, too. There they can learn to steer a boat (for hire), ride a pony or enjoy puppet theatre. There are all sorts of opportunities for play. There is even a beekeeping school and there are plenty of orange and other fruit trees. The romantic **Fontaine des Médicis** recalls the first owner of the palace.

Montparnasse quarter

From Carrefour de l'Observatoire, the Boulevard du Montparnasse runs through the quarter of the same name, which supplanted Montmartre as the centre for artistic life after the First World War. Nowadays it is an **entertainment quarter** with plenty of cinemas, cafés and good restaurants. The 1970s saw the construction of huge office and residential buildings between Boulevard du Montparnasse and Boulevard de Vaugirard, including the 209m/686ft **Tour Montparnasse** (1974), which offers a great view Paris from its roof terrace (open daily until 10.30pm/11.30pm).

Cimetière du Montparnasse

✳

Fondation Cartier

East of Gare Montparnasse station is the third biggest **cemetery** in Paris. Opened in 1824, those who are buried here include Baudelaire, Maupassant, Sartre and de Beauvoir, Jean Seberg and Serge Gainsbourg. A free map is available from the office (3 Blvd. E. Quinet). A stone's throw away (261 Blvd. Raspail) Fondation Cartier invites visitors to view its collection of contemporary art (Jean Nouvel, 1995).

Catacombes

From Place Denfert-Rochereau (with its version of the Lion of Belfort in bronze) it is possible to enter the grisliest place in Paris. Former underground quarries have been used since 1810 for stacking skeletons exhumed to make space in Paris's cemeteries (closed Mon).

From the Quartier Latin to Place d'Italie

The Quartier Latin, the oldest part of Paris after la Cité and the **site of its universities, colleges** and scientific institutes over a span of centuries, stretches between the Jardin du Luxembourg and Gare d'Austerlitz as far as the Boulevard de Port-Royal. Its main thoroughfare is Boulevard St-Michel, often abbreviated to »Boul-Mich«, one of Haussmann's most important roads. With its fashion and bookshops, restaurants and snack bars, it is the hub of student life during the school and university year (Oct–June).

Quartier Latin

Boulevard St-Michel

Burgundy's Cluny abbey built a city residence for its abbots on the site of a Roman spa in around 1330. From 1485 to 1510 this was replaced by the Hôtel de Cluny, the only **late medieval apartment palace** left in Paris other than the Hôtel de Sens in the Marais. It contains a superb museum of medieval art and European culture (open Wed– Mon 9.15am–5.45pm, www.musee-moyenage.fr). Among its many unique exhibits, the outstanding highlights are the »Tapisseries de la Dame à la Licorne« (c1500) and the golden altar antependium from the Minster in Basle, a gift of the German emperor, Heinrich II († 1024). The late Gothic **chapel** with its canopies is highly impressive. Under the tremendous vaulting of the frigidarium (cold baths), the best preserved part of the old **Roman baths**, concerts now take place. The »medieval« garden is very nice too.

✶ ✶
Hôtel de Cluny

✶
◀ Chapel

From the Boul-Mich, Rue des Écoles leads to the Sorbonne, the old **university of Paris**. Robert de Sorbon, chaplain to Louis IX, opened a school for impoverished theology students in 1253 and this developed into the theological faculty of the Paris university, which had been established in 1215. It was to play a key role in the history of French thinking. The present building was erected in 1624–42 under Cardinal Richelieu, then the rector, and was extended in 1885–1901. It houses the philosophy faculty. The Grand Amphithéâtre, the biggest lecture hall (2700 seats), is adorned with a mural by Puvis de Chavannes (*Allegory of the Sorbonne*). The distinctive dome belongs to the Sorbonne church, built between 1635 and 1642 by Lemercier. Its north façade is particularly beautiful. Inside the naked interior, the imposing tomb (1694) of **Cardinal Richelieu** (1585–1642) by Le Brun stands out.

Sorbonne

Eglise de la Sorbonne

The Collège de France east of the Sorbonne was established by François I in 1530 as a college for Latin, Greek and Hebrew. What was to be a haven for French humanism was built in 1610. Here, **lectures** are given on every possible subject, and even today they are open **to anybody** at no cost.

Collège de France

Southeast of the Sorbonne, Rue Soufflot runs up the Montagne de Ste-Geneviève to the Panthéon. What was once the near derelict site

✶
Panthéon

of a church above the grave of St Genevieve (6th century) was given over between 1758 and 1789 to the building of a highly impressive church building (122m/133yd long, 84m/92yd wide, 91m/299 m high, indeed the highest point is 117m/384ft above the ground) as a result of an oath by Louis XV. In 1791 it was rededicated to house the tombs and **memorials to the outstanding men** of the Revolution. In the gable of its vestibule an 1837 relief by David d'Angers shows *France (La Patrie) Distributing Laurels to Her Sons*. Inside the dark interior there are frescoes depicting the life of St Genevieve. The depictions of her childhood (1877) on the right-hand side of the transept are particularly notable as is *Saint Genevieve Watching Over the Besieged City of Paris* (1898), on the left of the choir. Both are by Puvis de Chavannes. It is possible to climb up to the dome from the northern transept. To the left of the choir there is an entrance to the crypt, where such men as Mirabeau, Rousseau, Voltaire, Victor Hugo, Emile Zola, resistance fighter Jean Moulin and culture minister André Malraux are all buried.

✳
Frescoes ▶

Crypt ▶

✳
St-Etienne-du-Mont

The church of St-Etienne-du-Mont (1492–1626), where Pascal and Racine are interred, is famed for its extraordinarily fine rood screen by Philibert de l'Orme (1535). Other things to note include the 1640 pulpit and the stained glass work (16th century) in the right-hand transept. A modern reliquary in the choir gallery contains parts of St Genevieve's sarcophagus.

Rue Mouffetard

Place de la Contrescarpe south of St-Etienne is where the narrow Rue Mouffetard begins. The quarter around it was once dominated

Weekend fun on the Seine and alongside it

by foul-smelling tanners (»mofette« = »skunk«). Nowadays it is lined by shops, snack bars and arcades. A colourful **market** is held on the lower part each morning from Tuesday to Sunday. Unfortunately it is increasingly descending into a »tourist attraction«.

✴
Institut du Monde Arabe

At Pont de Sully the Institut du Monde Arabe (Jean Nouvel, 1988) catches the eye. It has been created to encourage cultural exchange between the French and Arabic worlds. Behind the 1600 glass panes of the southern façade, metal shutters control the amount of daylight entering the building. An outstanding **museum** (access on 7th floor, closed Mon) illustrates Islamic art and science since the 9th century. On the roof there is a »fine« restaurant and a self-service cafeteria. There is also a great view.

✴
Arènes de Lutèce

Northwest of the Jardin des Plantes, the remains of a Roman **amphitheatre** from the 2nd century AD were excavated in 1869. It once accommodated some 15,000 spectators.

Mosquée de Paris

On the western edge of the Jardin des Plantes (39 Rue Geoffroy-St-Hilaire) is the **central mosque** of Paris with its 33m/108ft minaret. Built between 1922 and 1926, it was the first mosque in France. Visitors should be discreetly dressed and shoes are to be removed. Inside the complex, you can immerse yourself in the **world of the orient**, as it also contains a hammam (bath), a café, a restaurant with a shady courtyard and a bazaar.

✴
Jardin des Plantes

A 1635 garden for growing medicinal herbs has now developed into a magnificent park and zoo (including rose gardens with 350 breeds of rose). Among its fascinating attractions are the natural history collection in the **Muséum National d'Histoire Naturelle** (Rue Buffon), in existence since 1793, and the Grande Galerie de Zoologie. Gardens (free) and zoo are open daily, while the museums are closed on Tuesdays.

Bibliothèque Nationale

In 1997 the national library was opened on the southern bank of the Seine, the last in a series of exorbitantly expensive projects (»Grands Travaux«), with which President Mitterrand strove to write his name into history. As an actual library, though, this »Babel of books« with its four 80m/260ft-high magazine towers designed by Dominique Perrault is seen as catastrophically ill-advised.

✴
Manufacture Royale des Gobelins

Rue Mouffetard (see above) runs into the Avenue des Gobelins. The unassuming no. 42 actually conceals the famous **Gobelin factory**, established in 1601 by King Henri IV and transferred to the factory of the dye-making family Gobelin in 1667. The family name has become synonymous with the word for tapestry in France. The museum here displays French, Flemish and Italian tapestries, among others (open Tue–Sun 12.30pm–6.30pm).

The »Grande Arche« at La Défense, conceived as a window on the world

Place de l'Italie

Avenue des Gobelins runs southward to Place d'Italie, the transport hub of southeastern Paris. The **Grand Écran** (architect: Kenzo Tange), which opened in 1992, is situated here. The area south of Place d'Italie, dominated by tower blocks, has developed into the »Chinatown« of Paris since the 1970s and has the largest **East Asian community** in Europe. Avenue d'Ivry, in particular, is a great place to shop or to eat, including as it does the giant Tang Frères supermarket and the »Olympiades« with the Chez Tang restaurant. One other attraction is the Chinese new year festival in late January and early February.

Chinatown

Butte-aux-Cailles

The charming and still village-like district southwest of Place d'Italie was the centre of the Communards revolt of 1871. Nowadays it is possible to take a swim in the **1924 Piscine** (Place Paul-Verlaine), which is fed by warm waters (28ºC/82ºF) from an artesian well, and rest later in a café or restaurants such as the rustic Chez Gladines (30 Rue des 5 Diamants) or the somewhat higher class L'Avant-Goût (26 Rue Bobillot, closed Sun–Mon).

Places to Visit on the Edge of the City

★ ★
La Défense

The 8km/5mi-long **Axe Historique** – the Champs-Elysées, Av. de la Grande Armee and Av. Charles de Gaulle – leads from the Louvre to Pont de Neuilly and beyond to the overwhelmingly futuristic sky-scraper suburb of La Défense, built at the end of the 1950s. The confusingly martial tone to the name refers to a statue recalling the defence of Paris in 1871, which was erected in 1883 (now located at the Bassin Agam). The first brilliant architectural accomplishment here was the Centre des Nouvelles Industries et Techniques (CNIT), which has a canopy with a surface area of 90,000 sq m/100,000 sq yd supported at three corners. The most eye-catching feature, though, is the **Grande Arche**, a »triumphal arch for humanity«, an open cube with sides 110m/120yd long, designed by Dane Johann Otto von Spreckelsen (1989). The brasserie on the top floor offers a tremendous view. Of the other buildings, which provide offices for more than 3600 companies –including a dozen of the biggest companies in France – the 190m/623ft twin towers of the Coeur Défense (Cobb & Pei, 2001), diagonally opposite the EDF tower, stand out.

From the Arc de Triomphe the 120m/130yd-wide Avenue Foch runs to Porte Dauphine, the main access point for the Bois de Boulogne. With its woods, ponds, waterfalls and an open-air theatre, it is a popular **local leisure spot** for Parisians (boat and cycle hire). There are also two famous race courses here, the steeplechase course at **Auteuil** and the flat course of **Longchamp**), as well as the **Roland Garros** tennis stadium, in which the French Open is held at the end of May. In the northwest is theChâteau de Bagatelle, a miniature palace built in 1777 for the Comte d'Artois (later Charle͘s X) in the space of just 64 days in order to comply with a bet. In June an international competition for new sorts of rose takes place in the charming rose garden, in existence since 1905. The national folklore museum on Avenue du Mahatma Gandhi documents traditional arts, crafts and agriculture.

✳ Bois de Boulogne

✳ Bagatelle

Musée des Arts et Traditions Populaires

The Bois de Vincennes at the southeastern edge of the town is the largest **English park** in Paris, established by Haussmann and completed in 1867. Apart from its romantic lakes, there is the Parc Floral – in the Les Magnolias restaurant near the chateau brunch is served on Sundays – a flower park with attractions for children, a butterfly garden and a tropical garden as well as the largest zoo in Paris. In summer jazz concerts are held. At the entrance to the park the Musée d'Afrique et d'Océanie displays weapons, jewellery, pottery and paintings from Africa and the Pacific islands.

✳ Bois de Vincennes

Musée des Arts d'Afrique et d'Océanie

The Château de Vincennes, at the southern edge of the suburb of the same name, has a long and important history as a **royal residence** and as a prison for personal or political enemies of France's kings. Philippe II had what was originally a royal hunting lodge expanded into a residence during the 12th century. The rugged fortifications were completed in 1337. In the 52m/170ft residential keep, a museum covers the history of Vincennes. Other things worth seeing are the royal chambers, the treasury and the collection of weapons. The chapel was built from 1387 to 1552 and was based on the Sainte-Chapelle. It features some fine Renaissance stained glass work. Le Vau created the Pavillon de la Reine and Pavillon du Roi from 1654 to 1661. Louis XIV and Maria Theresa spent their honeymoon there.

✳ Château de Vincennes

Parc de la Villette in the northeast corner of Paris, built on the former battle site, attracts 3 million visitors a year. The **leisure park** has

✳ ✳ La Villette

something for everybody. In the **Cité des Sciences et de l'Industrie** visitors (no younger than 3) are introduced to the world of science. Children can have fun in theme parks and there is a »moving« cinema experience for all in the **Cinaxe**, where flight simulator technology is used. In the reflecting steel sphere of **Le Géode** documentary films are shown on a 172° screen covering 1000 sq m/1200 sq yd. South of the Canal de l'Ourc the lovely cast iron **Grande Halle** (1867), formerly the »Halle aux Bœufs«, now provides space for exhibitions, concerts and other cultural events. On Avenue Jean-Jaurès music lovers are well catered for. Alongside the renowned **Paris Conservatoire** (where concerts and ballets are held all year round) there is also the Cité de la Musique (Christian de Portzamparc, 1995), where the concert hall plays host to music of all kinds from all over the world. (In 2012 the new Philharmonie de Paris, which is being built according to plans by Jean Nouvel, should be complete.) The Musée de la Musique exhibits musical instruments from the 16th century to the present day. The park is free and open every day although the attractions charge admission. On Mondays the facilities are closed. During the school holidays it wise to contact the Cité des Sciences several days before any potential visit (tel. 01 40 05 80 00, 08 92 69 70 72; www.villette.com, www.cite-sciences.fr). From about 15 July to 15 Aug from Tue–Sun there is **open-air cinema**, and a **jazz festival** is held in the first half of September.

Around Paris

Ile-de-France A region of around 50km/31mi radius about the capital boasts a huge number of interesting and important attractions, as listed under ▶Ile-de-France.

Fun for big and small alike in Parc de Villette

✶ ✶ Périgord · Dordogne Valley

Périgord and the Dordogne are two names that conjure up images of some of the finest scenery in France. The latter is derived from the name of the river which forms the region's main attraction along with its picturesque valley and the beautiful old towns and villages along its length.

Périgord has a truly picture-book landscape, replete with castles and bastides, chateaux and abbeys. The caves and other prehistoric sites with their relics of Stone-Age man (Cro-Magnon, Lascaux) are world famous. The cliff-lined rivers provide any number of opportunities for climbing, cycling, canoeing or angling. For gourmands, the name of Périgord is synonymous with liver and pickled meats (confit) from duck or goose, and also with walnuts and truffles. Some 4000 tons of black truffles (*Tuber melanosporum*) are »harvested« each year with the aid of pigs and dogs. The area's best known wines are the red Côtes de Bergerac and the fine dessert wine Monbazillac.

Land of geese and truffles

The historic bounds of Périgord largely correspond to those of the Dordogne département with its capital ► Périgueux. The Dordogne itself rises upon Puy de Sancy in the central massif and covers 472km/293mi up to its confluence with the Garonne. It flows through the Quercy region as far as Souillac. The nucleus of Périgord, between the Vézère and Dordogne rivers, is Périgord Noir (»Black Périgord«), which owes its name to the extensive forest of dark-leaved holm oak. It is adjoined to the northwest by Périgord Blanc, which includes the town of Périgueux. This »White Périgord« region consists of a hilly limestone plateau with cereal fields, meadows and chestnut forests. West of the confluence between the

Scenery

Highlights in *Périgord*

Vézère and Dordogne lies Périgord Pourpre (»Purple Périgord«), a wine-growing area centred on Bergerac. Périgord Vert (»Green Périgord«) is the section north of Périgueux between Excideuil and Nontron crossed by the Auvézère and Dronne rivers.

In the Vézère valley, various discoveries have come to light dating back to the early Stone-Age Cro-Magnon people, named after the village where their fossils were first identified. These people displaced Neanderthal man from Europe around 35,000 BC. Finds include fireplaces, artistically designed artefacts, tools, human skeletons and the famed cave paintings (► Baedeker Special p.662). During the Middle Ages, the region was a borderland between areas of French and English influence and was the scene of heavy fighting over several centuries. From the 13th century onwards, large numbers of castles and bastides, i.e. fortified villages, were built. It was not until 1607 that the region finally came under the lasting control of the French crown. **History**

Places to Visit in Southern Périgord

These destinations in southern Périgord are listed as if they were part of a single trip down the Dordogne starting below the Gorges de la Dordogne. The upper reaches of the river are described under ►Auvergne.

The old bargees' village of Spontour is located in a loop of the Dordogne cutting deep through the surrounding scenery. There it is possible to see one of the old barges (gabares). From here the road does not follow the river closely, but from one point southwestward on the D 29 there is a good view of the Barrage de Chastang, with the largest hydro-electric power plant on the Dordogne. **Spontour** **Barrage de Chastang**

The picturesque old town of Argentat (3200 inhabitants) is seen to best effect from its **stone bridge**. Quai Lestourgie, dating from 1844, once handled the loading and unloading of barges. The drive along the river to Beaulieu is very beautiful. **Argentat**

Beaulieu (1200 inhabitants) literally means »beautiful place« and this village certainly lives up to its name. It is here that the Dordogne valley in its truest sense begins. The magnificent abbey church of St-Pierre (choir and transept from 1100–40 with the rest being added up until the 14th century) owes its appearance to the Auvergne Romanesque style. The southern portal from 1125 is among the finest examples of Romanesque sculpture, comparable with Moissac and Souillac. There is a lovely **spot by the river** where the 12th-century Chapelle des Pénitents stands; the local museum is here. Beaulieu is **★** **Beaulieu-sur-Dordogne**

← *Spectacular place of pilgrimage above the river Alzou: Rocamadour*

famed for its strawberries and on the second Sunday in May a big **strawberry festival** is celebrated with a giant strawberry tart, made using some 800kg/16cwt of the sweet fruit.

Château de Castelnau

11km/7mi to the south, the 14th-century chateau of the barons of Castelnau towers over the confluence of the Ceré and Dordogne. From the rugged red stone castle, there is a marvellous view of the scenery around the river and of the Quercy region to the south.

✱

Gouffre de Padirac

Southwest of Castelnau, the Gouffre de Padirac (open end of March–mid-Nov; come before 10am in summer), one of the biggest karst cave systems in France, can be accessed via a natural vertical shaft (gouffre). Visits include a boat trip on the underground river for which warm clothing is recommended.

Causse de Gramat

The market town of Gramat marks the centre of the **barren limestone plateau** which stretches away south of the Dordogne as far as ▶Lot and is mainly used as sheep pasture. The colours in autumn are particularly gorgeous. 2km/1mi south of Gramat, Parc de Vision de Gramat« provides information on the flora and fauna of the region.

✱ ✱

Rocamadour

Situated in a narrow gorge on the Alzou, the village of Rocamadour (600 inhabitants) is one of the most unusual places of pilgrimage in France (although it unfortunately turns into a tourist nightmare in the high season). Pilgrims have been flocking here since the Middle Ages, many a crowned sovereign amongst them, in order to view the **Black Madonna of Rocamadour** (12th century) in the Chapelle Notre-Dame. This is part of a church complex which can only be reached by lift or by a stairway with 233 steps. It also includes the church of St-Sauveur (11th–12th centuries) and the Musée d'Art Sacré Francis Poulenc (ecclesiastical art). On top of the high cliffs stands a 14th-century castle, accessed via a way of the cross from the complex of churches. The goat's cheese named after the village was granted AC status in 1996.

✱

Carennac

Carennac, to the west of Castelnau, is one of the »prettiest villages in France« and is famous for its priory, founded in the 10th century. The main entrance of the 12th-century church of St-Pierre has a wonderful tympanum. The cloister and the chapter hall with its 15th-century life-size tomb sculpture are also well worth seeing.

Martel

According to legend, the atmospheric township of Martel (1450 inhabitants), 5km/3mi north of the Dordogne, grew up around a church which Charles Martel had built after his victory over the Arabs in 732. Of the walls that once encircled the village, the 12th-century Tour de Tournemire is still in existence. The centre is very pretty with the **Hôtel de la Raymondie** (13th–14th centuries, housing the town hall, local museum and tourist office), Maison de la Monnaie (13th-century mint), a market hall (18th century) and Maison Fabri (12th century). To the east, outside the village of Gluges on the Dordigne, the **Belvédère de Copeyre** offers a superb view of the river.

Gluges

Passing the photogenic Château de la Treyne (17th century, now a hotel) the road leads to Souillac (3500 inhabitants), the lively hub of the region. Its outstanding feature is the 12th-century church, which belongs to an abbey founded in 7th century and features three high domes and a **fabulous doorway**, the remains of which were moved inside the building after the end of France's religious wars. The tympanum features a bas-relief depicting the legend of Theophilus. The Musée National de l'Automate features exhibits of mechanical toys dating back as far as 1860.

✷ Souillac

Gourdon (4800 inhabitants), on the border between Périgord and Quercy was once fortified. A market is held under the arcades of the town hall (13th–17th centuries). The church of St-Pierre dates from the 14th century. There is a splendid view from the castle hill. In the caves of Cougnac (about 3km/2mi north), Stone-Age paintings dating back to the Magdalénien period (17,000–15,000 BC) have been discovered.

Gourdon

Caves of Cougnac

From the D 703 west of Carsac there is a great view of Château Montfort and the **loop of the river** that has also come to bear its name.

Cingle de Montfort

The old town of Sarlat (10,400 inhabitants), the capital of Périgord Noir situated about 7km/4mi north of the Dordogne, is said to be one of the most beautiful places in France. The **Saturday market** is a culinary highlight of the region. Sarlat grew up around an abbey founded in the 9th century. After the Hundred Years' War, when much of the town was destroyed, it re-emerged with the pretty looks it has retained to this day, featuring many fine **Renaissance town houses**. The town is bisected by the 19th-century Rue de la République (»la Traverse«). Most of the attractions are to be found to the east of the road. The cathedral of St-Sacerdos (14th–16th centuries) is found towards the south of the old town. The tower of its main façade dates back to an earlier Romanesque building. The 18th-century Baroque organ is still used for concerts. The old episcopal palace adjoins the cathedral to the southwest. To the east stands a so-called **lanterne des morts**, an unusual tower made of volcanic rock with a conical roof (12th century). It is not known what the tower was used for. From there Passage Ségogne

✷ ✷ Sarlat

This lovely house is where writer Étienne de Boëtie was born in 1525

Castelnaud with Beynac et Cazenac in the background – Dordogne par excellence

or Rue de la Liberté lead to the luxurious 16th-century Hôtel de Maleville (tourist office) and Place de la Liberté with the 17th-century town hall. Markets are held here on Wednesdays and Saturdays. Behind the church of Ste-Marie – now a market hall – Hôtel Plamon (15th–17th centuries) on Rue des Consuls once belonged to a rich cloth-making family.

Domme

Philip the Bold founded this **bastide** or fortified village on the edge of an escarpment high above the Dordogne in 1283. The **view** of this most beautiful part of the river valley is wonderful to behold, although it is inevitably enjoyed in the company of a great many other tourists. Large parts of the former fortifications still remain in existence (in particular the Porte des Tours in the east). The market hall, reconstructed in the 19th century, stands on Place de la Halle with the 16th-century Maison des Gouverneurs (tourist office) facing it to the east and the Musée d'Art et de Traditions Populaires to the west. The market hall also includes an entrance to a cave system, which the citizens used as a refuge during the Hundred Years' War and the subsequent religious wars.

La Roque-Gageac

La Roque-Gageac (380 inhabitants, photo p.174–175), squeezed between the river and the cliffs, is one of the prettiest and most typical villages along the Dordogne with its workers' houses and impressive mansions, as well as the 20th-century Château La Malartrie. Above the church, the 15th-century Manoir de Tarde stands in front of the cliffs with their ancient cave dwellings.

Beynac-et-Cazenac

Beynac-et-Cazenac is another pretty village (480 inhabitants) sandwiched between the river and the vertical cliffs. The castle on the cliffs was built in the 13th century and, as of 1368, it was France's bastion against the English fortification of Castelnaud across the river. The path that circles it offers a great view of the valley and the other chateaux along its length. On the way up to the castle (Caminal des Panieraies) there is a 15th-century church, formerly the castle church, as well as houses from the 15th–17th centuries.

Castelnaud across the Dordogne is a »real« medieval castle. It was an English bastion from the 13th century until 1442. Nowadays it houses a **museum of medieval warfare**. On summer evenings historic Son et Lumière displays are given. There are some great views taking in the valleys of both the Dordogne and the Céou.

✳ **Castelnaud**

The valley of the Vézère, which rises on the Plateau de Millevaches, is at its most charming between Montignac and Limeuil at the confluence with the Dordogne. From Montignac, it is worth taking a day trip to

✳ **Vézère**

St-Amand-de-Coly with its unusual 12th-century church, the western part of which is formed by a fortified tower with a huge spire.

Saint-Amand-de-Coly

The world-famous **Grotte de Lascaux**, 2km/1mi south of Montignac, features more than 1500 cave paintings dating back to the Neolithic Magdalénien period (17,000–15,000 BC). For reasons of conservation, it is not possible to visit the original caves, a fact that has led to the opening of Lascaux II, an effective simulation, which even uses the same pigments as the original (open July–Aug 9am–8pm, April–June and Sept 9.30am–6.30pm, Oct–March 10am–12.30pm, 2am–5.30pm; closed Mon in Nov–Dec and Feb–March, closed Jan). Between mid-April and September tickets are only available from next door to the tourist office in Montignac after 9am and the number of visitors is limited to 2000 per day, so that tickets sell out quickly during the high season (www.semitour.com). In Le Thot, 5km/3mi southwest of Montignac, the Espace Cro-Magnon museum introduces visitors to the styles and techniques of Stone-Age painting (► Baedeker Special p.662).

✳✳ **Lascaux**

The valleys of the Vézère and Beune come together at the confluence of the rivers in the famous village of Les Eyzies-de-Tayac (960 inhabitants). Much of their lengths are made up of narrow gorges with tall overhanging cliffs (abris) and caves, which were used as dwellings in prehistoric times. The site of the discoveries at Lascaux, along with others along the river Vézère, have been named a **UNESCO World Heritage Site**. In 1868 at Cro-Magnon, part of Les Eyzies, a skeleton belonging to a 30,000-year-old human, now known as Cro-Magnon man, was found behind the hotel of the same name. A good insight into the discoveries and the latest research can be gained from the Musée National de la Préhistoire (open daily July–Aug 9.30am–6.30pm, June/Sept 9.30am–6pm, otherwise Wed–Mon 9.30am–12.30pm, 2pm–5.30pm), located in an important modern building below the chateau of the barons of Tayac, and the Musée de Spéléologie in the Tayac cliffs. Museums and tourist offices also pro-

✳✳ **Les Eyzies-de-Tayac**

vide information on other cave systems and prehistoric dwellings in the region. At Tursac, 6km/4mi north of Eyzies, Préhistoparc shows how people of those times used to live.

Saint-Léon-sur-Vézère

Situated in a loop of the river Vézère, St-Léon is particularly lovely with its Châteaux de la Salle and Clérans as well as its plain and very ancient-looking **church**, which has a nave dating from pre-Romanesque times (nice place for a picnic). In August, St-Léon (along with St-Amand-de-Coly) becomes the centre of the **Festival Musical du Périgord Noir**.

Cadouin

The abbey in Cadouin (380 inhabitants), to the south of the Dordogne, was established in 1115. Even in the Middle Ages it was an important **place of pilgrimage** due to its »shroud of Christ«, which was first documented in 1214 and has been dated to around 1100 on account of its Kufi script. The church was consecrated in 1154 and still exhibits the austere form favoured by the Cistercians. The cloister (15th–16th centuries) does display some Flamboyant Gothic and Renaissance elements, though. In one of the neighbouring buildings there is a large bicycle museum.

✱
Monpazier

16km/10mi further south is Monpazier (500 inhabitants), one of the prettiest and best preserved **bastides** in Périgord. It was built in 1284 by the Duke of Aquitaine, England's King Edward I. At the centre of its rectangular street grid is the Place des Cornières with its 16th-century market hall and bulky arched streets.

Place des Cornières in Monpazier

At Tremolat, where the 12th-century church is a good example of the ecclesiastical architecture of Périgord, the **meanders** of the Dordogne curl particularly beautifully through cliffs and gentle fields.

✳ **Cingle de Tremolat**

At Lanquais (with its impressive cuisine) on the left bank of the Dordogne, there is a veritable »fairy-tale castle«, which was built in stages from the Middle Ages until the Renaissance. This is the start of the wine-growing region distinguished by the **Appellation Bergerac** label. In conditions similar to Libournais, grapes are grown to make elegant white wines (Montravel), dense reds (Côtes de Bergerac, Pécharmant) and Monbazillac, a famous sweet wine.

Lanquais

Bergerac (27,000 inhabitants), capital of Périgord Pourpre and centre of a wine and tobacco-growing region, has a particularly attractive **old town** stretching from the docks to Rue de la Résistance (tourist office on Place de la République). A former Recollect monastery now houses the Maison du Vin (museum with wine tasting). East of there, in Maison Peyrarède (1603), is a tobacco museum. On Place Cayla/Place de la Myrpe there is a memorial to Cyrano de Bergerac, even though he actually had nothing to do with the town. Other interesting places include the local folklore museum (wine, barrel-making, shipping) and the museum of ecclesiastical art. Surprisingly, pictures by the Venetian Pordenone and by Gaudenzio Ferrari (16th century) are on view in the church of Notre-Dame. 7km/4mi south of Bergerac, amid the vineyard slopes, is the chateau of **Monbazillac**, built in around 1550 and the emblem of the eponymous sweet wine (daily visits with wine tasting, closed Mon Nov–March).

Bergerac

Brantôme and its abbey

Places to Visit in Northern Périgord

North of ▶ Périgueux the Dronne flows through **Périgord Vert**, Green Périgord, which certainly lives up to its name. The stretch between Bourdeilles and Brantôme is especially beautiful. In Bourdeilles (800 inhabitants) the chateau (with a medieval section dating back to the 13th century and a Renaissance building with a beautiful interior from the 16th), **the Gothic bridge and the old mill** – which houses a superb restaurant – make up a glorious ensemble.

✳ **Bourdeilles**

Brantôme (2100 inhabitants) is situated in a loop of the Dronne. A 16th-century bridge leads across to an **abbey**, which was founded by

Brantôme

▶ VISITING PÉRIGORD

INFORMATION

CRT Auvergne
La Pardieu, 7 Allee P. de Fermat
F-63178 Aubière Cedex
Tel. 04 73 29 49 49, fax 04 73 34 11 11
www.auvergne-tourisme.info

CRT Limousin
30 Cours Gay-Lussac, C.S. 500 95
F-87003 Limoges Cedex 1
Tel. 0 55 11 05 90, fax 05 55 05 07 56
www.tourismelimousin.com

WHERE TO EAT / WHERE TO STAY

▶ Mid-range / luxury

Les Glycines
Route Périgueux
F-24620 Les Ezyies de Tayac
Tel. 05 53 06 97 07
A pretty building from 1862 with garden, swimming pool and restaurant terrace. High-class salons. Enchantingly designed rooms; the ones at the at the rear are quieter than the ones facing the busy street.

Moulin du Roc
F-24530 Champagnac de Belair
www.moulinduroc.com
Tel. 05 53 02 86 00
6km/4mi northeast of Brantôme, this lovingly rebuilt 17th-century oil mill is a dream come true. First-class cuisine. It is particularly pleasant to

sit in the garden alongside the Dronne.

Moulin de l'Abbaye
F-24310 Brantôme, tel. 05 53 05 80 22
www.moulinabbaye.com
The old mill on the Dronne is a wonderfully romantic spot, especially the shady garden of its superb restaurant. The »Au Fil de l'Eau« is an inexpensive alternative.

▶ Inexpensive

La Grange du Mas
Le Mas de Sireuil
F-24620 Les Eyzies-de-Tayac
Tel. 05 53 29 66 07
www.grange-du-mas.com
Closed Oct–Easter. Outstanding rustic cookery is served in this ferme-auberge east of Les Eyzies. The foie gras, rillettes, pâté etc are homemade. With very pleasant rooms and apartments.

Les Charmilles
20 Blvd. St-Rodolphe
F-19120 Beaulieu sur Dordogne
www.auberge-charmilles.com
Tel. 05 55 91 29 29.
This charming country house (with restaurant) is situated in the immediate vicinity of an arm of the river Dordogne.

Charlemagne in 769 and rebuilt as of 1075. Only the tower remains in its original condition. Its wimperg gables in front of the bell chamber are patterned on the Limousin Romanesque style. One of the old capitals is now used as a font. Among the monastery buildings (16th century, altered in the 19th) are a dormitory, with a ship's keel roof truss, and the Musée Fernand-Desmoulin, which displays archaeological discoveries as well as the unusual works of the eponymous artist.

Château de Puyguilhem, 12km/7mi northeast of Brantôme, was built at the beginning of the 16th century and is patterned on the chateaux of the Loire valley. Its beautiful interior decoration is its finest attraction.

Puyguilhem

This pretty village 8km/5mi east of Puyguilhem has a chateau and a church from the 12th century, which consists only of a choir and three apses. The vaulting collapsed in 1787 and was replaced by a wooden roof in 1850. A market hall is built onto the church.

Saint-Jean-de-Côle

Roughly 40km/25mi east of Périgueux, the **largest Baroque chateau in southwestern France** can be found. It was built in around 1650 in place of a medieval castle, which had belonged to the famed troubadour Bertran de Born in the 12th century. The chateau was totally destroyed by fire in 1968 but has been rebuilt and furnished in the original style. Apart from the chestnut roof seating atop the southwest tower, the gardens count among its special attractions.

✶ Hautefort

Périgueux

H 7

Région: Aquitaine
Département: Dordogne

Altitude: 85m/279ft
Population: 32,000

Périgueux, capital of the ►Périgord region, has a pretty old town which is under a preservation order and spreads along the river Isle either side of the large and unusual cathedral.

Beyond its ugly modern suburbs, Périgueux centres on an old town made up of two parts. The entire cathedral quarter »Puy-St-Front« is a listed area. It grew up between the 5th and 11th centuries around an abbey. A second, separate section is the »Cité« quarter in the west of town. This was the area where the earliest settlement took place and dates back to the era of the Celtic Petrocori tribe, who became known as »Vesuna« to the Romans and for whom this was the second most important Gallic colony after Burdigala (Bordeaux). The town of Périgueux itself was established in 1251.

City layout

What to See in Périgueux

Périgueux is centred around Place Bugeaud. The Puy-St-Front quarter extends from there as far as the river. The cathedral, built from 1125 to 1173, was »restored« between 1852 and 1901 by Paul Abadie, who was later to design the Sacré-Cœur in Paris. It was at that time that the cathedral's domes acquired their bizarre shutters and lanterns. The building itself, a Byzantine four-pillared church with four domes laid out in a cross, is modelled on **San Marco in Venice**. The bell tower above the narthex was part of an earlier building. The fru-

✶ Cathedral of St-Front

STONE AGE ART GALLERIES

In southeastern France, amateur spelunkers exploring the gorges of the Ardèche came across the oldest murals known to the world. The paintings were made with stunning skill – more than 30,000 years ago.

On 18 December 1994, archaeologist and caver Jean-Marie Chauvet was paying another visit to the karst hills near **Vallon Pont d'Arc** with two of his colleagues. The Ardèche has, over the course of centuries, carved out gorges up to 200m/650ft deep through the rocky massif. Water has seeped through the stone to create innumerable caves and, during the Stone Age, these were used by people as temporary dwellings. A cold breeze from a rocky cleft caught the attention of the three and together they scrabbled out an entrance to a shaft. A few hours later they found themselves in an unusually large cave system with four chambers. On the walls, though, were more than 300 red and black images of animals, both individual and in groups. Hand prints and abstract carvings accompanied them. The bestiary included rhinoceroses, wild horses, various big cats, buffalo, mammoths, bears, stags, an owl and a hyena. The prehistoric artist or artists had fully mastered the art of drawing and perspective. The animals are depicted with life-like realism with the artists cleverly using natural contours and cracks in the rock beneath. Dating of the finds caused a sensation; the paintings had apparently come into being around 31,000 BC, long before the great cultures of the Nile or in Greece and Italy. They were thus the oldest cave paintings yet known.

In 1868, human remains had been excavated in the Vézère valley. They were named after the place they were found, **Cro-Magnon**. It is now believed that the Cro-Magnon people were hunters and gatherers who had fled from the prevailing ice age in northeastern Europe some 25,000 to 35,000 years ago to the glacier-free southwest of France. In 1879 cave paintings were discovered in a cave at **Altamira** in Spain, which were dated to a period from 20,000 to 9000 BC. Most of the places in Europe where such finds have been discovered are in France (150 locations), Spain (128) and Italy (21). The most important of these are the aforementioned Altamira site (discovered 1879) and others at **Pech Merle** (1922 near Cabrerets in the Celé valley, see ▶Lot Valley), **Lascaux** (1940, near Montignac in Périgord), **Grotte Cosquer** (in a bay east of Marseille) and **Grotte Chauvet**.

The two »speckled horses« and mysterious hands in the cave of Pech Merle

Hidden splendour

Unfortunately some of the wonders of these caves will have to remain hidden from the public. What the centuries have failed to achieve can be accomplished by hordes of visitors in a matter of years. In 1948 the caves at Lascaux were opened to the public. As early as 1963, though, it became essential to close them again. The breath and sweat of all those bodies had caused fungus, bacteria and algae to grow in the caves and attack the paintings. Since 1983 Lascaux II has been opened, a perfect copy, which even uses the same pigments.

Those **pigments** were composed of soil and ores containing iron oxides and hydroxides. Red iron oxide gave red, goethite and clay were used for yellow and brown iron oxide provided the brown. Black pigment was obtained from manganese ores, from coal, from bone, horn, jawbones or wood. To help the paint adhere better to the rough surface of the rocks, the artists mixed them with lime and water. The lime formed crystals that still protect the paintings to this day. Paint was applied either by hand or with simple brushes. A spray technique was also used, whereby the pigment was crushed to a fine powder and blown by mouth or with a blow pipe onto the wall. Commonly, drawings are also carved into the rock. The works are **dated** by means of the carbon 14 method with support from X-ray and laser irradiation, chemical analysis and electron microscopy. These methods and the paintings found in the Chauvet cave have altered our perception of the chronology. Hitherto it had been assumed that the development had begun with the primitive so-called Aurignac style (35,000–28,000 years BC) and led then to the high-point of the Magdalénien style (13,500 BC – as at Lascaux). The paintings at Chauvet, however, show that the later degree of perfection had already been achieved 20,000 years before the Lascaux artists.

What remains obscure is the **meaning** of these paintings. It seems certain that the people did not live permanently in the caves but kept returning to decorate their walls over a period of centuries. For some time the prevalent thesis was that of Abbé Breuil, who proposed that the artists were spirit conjurors seeking to assist the hunt by conjuring animals. In the mid-20th century, André Leroi-Gourhan discovered that bison and horses were often drawn in specific combinations. His interpretation was that the animals represented the human sexes, the bison being the female and the horse the male. Evaluation of the Chauvet finds has also cast this theory aside, since the bison there are mostly shown as decisively and robustly masculine.

▶ VISITING PÉRIGUEUX

INFORMATION

Office de Tourisme
26 Place Francheville
F-24000 Périgueux
Tel. 05 53 53 10 63, fax 05 53 09 02 50
www.ville-perigueux.fr

MARCHÉ DES GRAS

Nov–March Wed and Sat: market for
foie gras, pastries, truffles etc. Mid-
Nov: Salon du Livre Gourmande.

WHERE TO EAT

▶ Moderate

Le Clos St-Front
5 Rue de la Vertu
(entrance Rue St-Front)
Tel. 05 53 46 78 58.
Fine restaurant in a beautiful old
building, renowned for modern Peri-
gord cuisine. The menu is short but
contains such delights as superb hot
foie gras with caramel sauce. There is
a pretty inner courtyard lined with
palm trees.

WHERE TO STAY

▶ Budget

La Charmille
Laurière, F-24420 Antonne
(12km/7.5mi)
Tel. 05 53 06 00 45, fax 05 53 06 30 49
www.hotel-lacharmille-perigord.com
Unobtrusive elegance is what distin-
guishes this fine old mansion with a
familial atmosphere. The rooms facing the garden are quieter. There is
also a restaurant.

The cathedral of St-Front on the Isle near Périgueux

gal interior has interesting chandeliers in Byzantine style and a 17th-century walnut altar. The Romanesque-Gothic cloister (with tombs of Merovingian royals) is all that remains of a monastery, which was demolished in the 19th century.

The quays along the river are lined by houses from the 15th–16th centuries. There is a great view of the old town from the Pont des Barris bridge. North of the cathedral, by the charming Cours Tourny, is the Musée du Périgord, which features archaeological finds from prehistory and from the Gallo-Roman period. **Rue Limogeanne** (the main shopping street) leads from there to the market place and town hall (17th–18th centuries). Place St-Louis – which becomes the culinary centre of Périgord at the time of its winter market – is the site of the Maison du Pâtissier.

✶
Vieux Périgueux

✶
Musée du Périgord

West of Place Francheville is the Cité, the second old quarter. St-Etienne, one of the **oldest domed churches** in Aquitaine, served as a cathedral until 1669. Its two western bays were destroyed in 1577 and pulled down. What remains is the square of the 12th-century choir and one 11th-century west bay. Inside there is a Baroque altar made of oak and walnut and the tomb of J. d'Astide, the bishop of Périgueux in the 12th century. To the northeast are the **Arènes**, remnants of an arena 153 × 122m/167 × 133yd in size, which accommodated some 20,000 spectators. In front of the arena, to the southwest, is the Porte Normande gate, thought to date back to the 3rd century, as well as a Roman house and the so-called Château Barrière, part of the medieval fortifications. Further southeast are the Tour de Vésone, the remains of one of Vesuna's temples (2nd century) and the Musée Gallo-Romain, housed in the remnants of a Roman building.

Cité
✶
St-Etienne

✶ Perpignan

K 10

Région: Languedoc-Roussillon
Département: Pyrenées-Orientales

Altitude: 60m/197ft
Population: 107,000

Perpignan (Perpinyà), the former capital of Roussillon, has a distinctively Catalonian character. In the Middle Ages it was actually the capital of the kingdom of Mallorca. This pleasant city is a good starting point for tours of the eastern Pyrenees and the Côte Vermeille.

Perpignan, just 10km/6mi from the Mediterranean and 30km/19mi from the border with Spain, was the administrative centre of the Balearic kingdom of Mallorca from 1278 to 1344. Roussillon, Cerdagne and the coast as far as Montpellier were all ruled from here. It was not until the Pyrenean peace treaty of 1659 that Rousillon and the city were ceded to France. Nowadays Perpignan is the prefectorate

Capital of Rousillon

▶ VISITING PERPIGNAN

INFORMATION

Office du Tourisme
Place A. Lanoux, F-66000 Perpignan
Tel. 04 68 66 30 30, fax 04 68 66 30 26
www.perpignantourisme.com

FESTIVALS AND EVENTS

Good Friday: Procession de la Sanch
(Catalonian procession). Around 21
June: seven-day festival, Festa Mayor
St-Joan, featuring music, midsummer
bonfire and a market, the Marché
Médiéval. Mid-Oct: three-week jazz
festival and a festival for the wine
harvest.

WHERE TO EAT

▶ Moderate / expensive

① *Casa Sansa*
4 Rue Fabrique Couverte
Tel. 04 68 34 21 84. This bistro is an
institution in the world of Catalonian
cuisine. It has been situated in its
present medieval building since 1846.
Inexpensive lunchtime menu and an
excellent choice of (open) wines.

② *Côté Théâtre*
7 Rue du Théâtre

Tel. 04 68 34 60 00
One of the most favoured places in
Roussillon, inconspicuous from the
outside but all the more exquisite
inside. Classic cuisine with a local
touch.

WHERE TO STAY

▶ Mid-range

① *Park Hôtel*
18 Boulevard J. Bourrat, tel. 04 68 35
14 14, www.parkhotel-fr.com
Modern luxury hotel with an ugly
façade but air-conditioned, sound-
insulated rooms, furnished the style of
the Spanish Renaissance. The elegant
restaurant, Au Chapon Fin, serves
classic gourmet cooking.

▶ Budget

② *Hôtel de la Poste*
6 Rue des Fabriques Nabot
Tel. 04 68 34 42 53, fax 04 68 52 75 77,
Charming hotel from 1832. Most of
the rather old-fashioned rooms have a
small balcony. There is an inexpensive
restaurant serving local cuisine. Hôtel
de la Loge on the same street is also to
be recommended.

for the département of Pyrénées Orientales. The city does not number among France's great tourist attractions, as the low prices here
indicate, but it is certainly worth a visit all the same.

What to See in Perpignan

Le Castillet
The northern entrance to the old town is guarded by **Le Castillet**,
the one remaining city gate (1368) and the city's major landmark.
There is a great view from the top and the tower also contains a museum of Catalonian culture (Casa Païral). The centrepiece of the old
town is the **Loge de Mer** (built from 1397 onwards), former cham-
Loge de Mer
ber of commerce and court of maritime law. It was rebuilt in Gothic
style in the 16th century (café and restaurant). The neighbouring

Hôtel de Ville (13th–17th centuries) has some lovely 18th-century wrought iron railings, while the courtyard features the Maillol sculpture *Méditerranée*. Adjoining it to the west is the Palais de la Députation, a council building from 1447.

The cathedral of St-Jean is an impressive example of **Catalonian Gothic**. Building work started in 1324 and, although the façade remained unfinished, the church was consecrated in 1509. Things to note include the winged altar in the right-hand chapel off the choir (16th century) and the gilded altar of St Peter (15th century) in the left-hand chapel. The high altar (Claude Perret, 17th century) is made of marble and there is a font that dates back to pre-Roman times. Underneath the organ there is an entrance leading to the Chapelle Notre-Dame-dels-Correchs, which features a supine figure of King Sancho. The southern doorway leads to the Chapelle du Dévot Christ with its impressive **crucifix**, carved in the Rhineland in 1307. The Campo Santo was established in 1302.

✱ St-Jean

✱ Dévot Christ

South of the Hôtel de Ville lies the lively Place de la République with its market hall and theatre. The **Musée Hyacinthe Rigaud** exhibits works by the eponymous Perpignan-born artist (1659–1743; ►p.99), who was a highly famous painter during the reigns of Louis XIV and XV. It also features work by Spanish and Catalan masters of the 14th–16th centuries along with modern artists such as Picasso, Maillol, Dufy and Calder. In the »oriental« quarter around **Place de Puig** – populated by North Africans and Roma Gypsies – the church of

Place de la République

St-Jacques

Perpignan *Map*

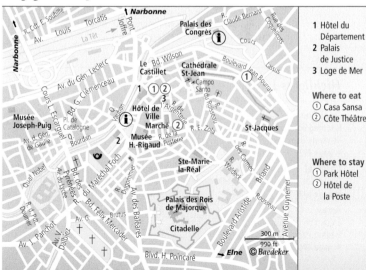

1 Hôtel du Département
2 Palais de Justice
3 Loge de Mer

Where to eat
① Casa Sansa
② Côte Théâtre

Where to stay
① Park Hôtel
② Hôtel de la Poste

300 m
990 ft
→ Elne   © Baedeker

St-Jacques (1245, rebuilt in Catalonian style in the 14th century) is the headquarters of the »Confrèrie de la Sanch«, which organizes the impressive Good Friday procession.

Citadel
✳
Palais des Rois de Majorque

The mighty citadel was built from the mid-15th century, being extended by its respective owners until well into the 17th century. At the heart of the city is the palace of the Mallorcan kings, built in 1276 as a residence for King Jaime I, although none of the furnishings of his day remain. The Gothic chapel of Ste-Croix is well worth a look; there is a fine view from the fortified tower.

Picardy · Nord-Pas-de-Calais

J–M 1–3

»Le Nord« is the name given to the area north of the Ile-de-France that includes the regions of Picardy, Artois and Flanders. The coast along the English Channel, with its endless sandy beaches, is a magnet for tourists, while the broad, flat country inland is an El Dorado for those seeking peace and quiet. The ancient and noble cities of the region contain some of the most beautiful cathedrals in France.

Holiday destinations in the north

»Le Nord«, northern France between the Parisian metropolis and the English Channel or the Belgian border, is particularly popular with day-trippers from England and Belgium (attracting nearly 60 million a year) but is now being discovered by longer term holidaymakers. The Côte d'Opale, the »Opal Coast« between Calais and Berck, has mile upon mile of broad, sandy beaches, ideal for relaxation or sport. The northeast, including the built-up region around ▶Lille is highly industrial, whereas the broad and largely flat hinterland remains sparsely populated but is well catered for in terms of cycle paths, footpaths and waterways.

Highlights Le Nord

Opal Coast
Dazzling light and salty winds across miles of sandy beaches
▶ page 672

Carnival
Giving the lie to »northern reticence« …
▶ page 672

Arras
Enjoy the atmosphere of an old Flemish trading centre
▶ page 674

Lewarde coal mine
Monument to another age
▶ page 675

La Coupole
German wartime weapons installations now used as a space museum
▶ page 676

Beauvais and Laon
Find out what »Northern Gothic« means here.
▶ page 678, 680

Picardy has some 1.85 million inhabitants and incorporates the départements of Aisne, Oise and Somme, The capital is ►Amiens. The geology is that of a chalk layer some 100–200m/300–650ft deep, crossed by the river Somme in the west and the Oise in the east. The region is heavily cultivated.

Picardy

Lille is the capital of a region taking in the Nord and Pas-de-Calais départements. In Artois, which occupies most of the Pas-de-Calais département, the key industries are agriculture and cattle. The coal deposits of northern France stretch through much of the northeast between Douai and Béthune. Mining of coal from the late 19th century brought a major economic boom to the region. French Flanders corresponds to the Nord département. Most of Flanders lies in what is now Belgium, to the north. The area, mostly flat and largely used for agriculture, is speckled with typical Flemish villages; Flemish is sometimes still spoken. The central section, south of Lille, overlaps the French coal basin and is much more heavily industrialized than Artois. The area has been famous down the centuries for the manufacture of linen and cotton textiles. An extensive system of canals across the whole of the north facilitated the transport of mass cargo.

Nord-Pas-de-Calais

◄ Artois

◄ Flanders

In the Middle Ages, Picardy was split into numerous dominions. These gradually came under control of the French crown during the 12th–14th centuries. It was thanks to the textile industry, which was of importance all over Europe, that the region enjoyed its earliest heyday. The marriage Margaret of Flanders to Philip the Bold inaugurated the rule of the dukes of Burgundy. Among the richest aristocrats in Europe, they encouraged architecture and painting. In Noyon, Laon, Senlis, Soissons, Amiens and Beauvais, magnificent Gothic cathedrals were built. With the death of Charles the Bold in 1477, these possessions passed into the hands of the Habsburg king, Maximilian I. In the 16th century they came under Spanish control and were only returned to French hands in the 17th century. The discovery of coal deposits brought industrialization to the area. The two World Wars left deep scars and the post-war years were marked by the decline of heavy industry and thoroughgoing reconstruction. The

History

A Rodin sculpture in front of the town hall in Calais recalls a heroic episode from the Hundred Years' War

▶ VISITING LE NORD

INFORMATION

CRT Nord – Pas-de-Calais
Place Mendès-France, BP 99
F-59028 Lille Cedex
Tel. 03 20 14 57 57, fax 03 20 14 57 58
www.tourisme-nordpasdecalais.fr
www.nordfrankreich-tourismus.com
CRT Picardie
3 Rue Vincent Auriol
F-80011 Amiens Cedex 1Tel. 03 22 22
33 66, fax 03 22 22 33 67
www.picardietourisme.com

WHERE TO STAY

▶ Budget

Bannière de France
11 Rue F. Roosevelt,
F-02000 Laon
Tel. 03 23 23 21 44, fax 03 23 23 31 56,
www.hoteldelabannieredefrance.com
17th-century post office in the middle
of the upper town near the cathedral.
Large rooms with uneven floor-
boards. The traditionally furnished
dining room offers excellent cuisine.

Résidence
24 Rue L. Borel, F-60000 Beauvais
Tel. 03 44 48 30 98, fax 03 44 45 09 42,
www.hotellaresidence.fr. In a quiet
street at the edge of town. Familial
atmosphere, plain and simple rooms.

▶ Mid-range

Bristol
17 Rue Monnet, F-62520 Le Touquet
Tel. 03 21 05 49 95, www.hotelbristol.fr
Very pretty, well-kept establishment
between the market and the sea,
offering excellent value for money.

WHERE TO EAT

▶ Moderate

La Petite Auberge
45 Blvd. P. Brossolette
F-02000 Laon, Tel. 03 23 23 02 38.
The best hotel in town, situated in the
lower town near the station. Traditional cuisine in modern surroundings. The Bistrot St-Amour is more
inexpensive.

channel tunnel to England and connection to France's TGV rail network have not brought the hoped-for economic upturn, but have
contributed to making the region more attractive in a general sense.

The Channel Coast

Dunkerque The important port of Dunkerque (Engl: Dunkirk; 72,000 inhabitants) is situated on the North Sea coast some 14km/9mi from the
Belgian border. At the end of May in 1940 it witnessed the **evacua-
tion of the Allied troops** to England, when the forces became encircled by the German army. 80% of the town was destroyed at that
time. It is still centred on Place Jean-Bart, where there is a monument by David d'Angers to the famous privateer of the 17th century,
who is buried in the church of St-Eloi (16th–19th centuries). A 58m/
90ft fortified tower (13th–15th centuries; now housing the tourist office) was once the church tower. The **Musée des Beaux-Arts** exhibits
Dutch, French and Italian paintings of the 16th–19th centuries.

North of the town hall (1900; with a 75m/246ft tower), Place du Minck is the starting point for boat tours of what is the **third largest harbour** in France. The east harbour can also be toured from there on foot. The Tour de Leughenaer (»Liar's Tower«) looks down upon the town from the north of Place du Minck. Once part of the town's fortifications, it is now used as a lighthouse. Other interesting features are the port museum on the Bassin du Commerce, a fire ship and the Duchesse Anne, a German sailing vessel from 1901, which was used as a training ship. To the north stands the lighthouse, at 63m/207ft the tallest in France. The town is famed for its **carnival**, which takes place on weekends in February/March, particularly the Sundays before and after Ash Wednesday.

★
Bergues

Bergues (4200 inhabitants) is still surrounded by 17th-century walls and moats, punctuated by impressive gates. Situated 9km/6mi south of Dunkerque, it is distinctively Flemish. In 2007 Dany Boon shot his wonderful film *Bienvenue chez les Ch'tis* here. The 54m/177ft **tower** (with tourist office) was, like most of the town, reconstructed after 1944 in the local ochre bricks. The local museum in the Mont de Piété (pawnbroker from 1633) exhibits French and Flemish painters (including La Tour, Van Dyck, Massys). Interesting places in the surrounding region include the church at **Quaëdypre** (5km/3mi southeast) and Hondschoote, 11km/7mi to the east, a former centre of the worsted trade with a Renaissance town hall and the Noordmeulen windmill, thought to have been in existence since 1127.

Hondschoote

Calais

Calais (78,000 inhabitants), located at the point where the Strait of Dover is at its narrowest, is the main transit port to England. Every

Wimereux, one of the traditional resorts on the Côte Opale

year more than 20 million people pass through the town. It was badly damaged during the Second World War but has been quite skilfully rebuilt. In front of the imposing **town hall**, built in Flemish Renaissance style in 1922, stands a famous monument, the *Burghers of Calais* (Auguste Rodin, 1895). It recalls the English siege of 1346–47 and the heroic decision by six of its men to sacrifice their lives for the sake of the remaining population. In Parc St-Pierre opposite, a war museum has been opened in a former German bunker. The Pont George V bridge leads north to the **Musée des Beaux-Arts et de la Dentelle** (closed Tue). As well as items from the history of the town, it has sculptures from the 19th and 20th centuries, a fine collection of paintings and examples of Calais' important lace industry. Passing Notre-Dame church (13th–14th century), built in the English »Perpendicular style«, continue to Place d'Armes and Tour Guet (13th century). Crossing Pont Henon by the marina the route then leads past Fort Risban to the never-ending beach that stretches from the north of the town. On clear days it is possible to see the **White Cliffs of Dover** 36km/22mi away. There is a fine view of the town and the harbour from the 58m/190ft lighthouse (1848).

米 米
Burghers of Calais ►

米
Musée des
Beaux-Arts ►

Eurotunnel
The Eurotunnel, which crosses the English Channel from Sangatte near Calais to Folkestone in Kent, was opened in 1994 and has now brought Paris to within 3 hours travel from London. The 50.5km/ 31.5mi length of the tunnel passes through a limestone bed, totally impervious to water, some 40–115m/130–380ft under the sea. It consists of two main tunnels of 7.6m/25ft diameter and a service tunnel. The French terminal is situated at the southwestern edge of Calais (►p.169).

米
Côte d'Opale
The prettiest section of coast between the Belgian border and the bay of the Somme is the so-called Opal Coast between Calais and Berck sur Mer. Numerous footpaths, including the **GR Littoral**, criss-cross the landscape (brochure *Randonées en Côte d'Opale* from tourist offices). Two distinctive points that stand out from the windblown scenery, with its hues of green, white and blue, are the rocky promontories of **Cap Blanc Nez** (134m/440ft) and **Cap Gris Nez** (45m/ 148ft). The first offers a breathtaking view of the coast and the English Channel. On neighbouring

? DID YOU KNOW ...?

■ The north of France likes its festivals. The carnival celebrations are particularly loud and colourful. One key aspect of the celebrations involves the *géants*, massive figures whose heritage dates back centuries and who also appear in local parades and processions etc., sometimes dancing. In Douai there is a whole family of the creatures *(la famille Gayant)*. The head of said family is represented by a figure 8.5m/28ft high and weighing some 370kg/816lbs, which takes 6 men to carry it. Dunkerque, Aire sur la-Lys, Bailleul and Cassel and others also have their own »géants«. Information about them and the dates when they appear can be found in the brochure *L'Année des Géants*, available from tourist offices.

Grand'Place in Arras exudes Flemish flair

Mont d'Hubert (151m/495ft) there is a panorama restaurant called Thomé de Gamond, which houses the Musée du Transmanche (history of the channel tunnel). Cap Gris Nez has a lighthouse and the remains of a German bunker. A large bunker of the German artillery unit »Batterie Todt« at nearby **Audinghen** now houses a museum of German Second World War coastal defences, the Atlantic Wall. Underneath the fortifications there is a rail-mounted K 5 gun with a calibre of 28cm/11in.

The important fishing harbour of Boulogne (45,000 inhabitants) is perhaps the most interesting town on the Strait of Dover. The Channel here is crossed by a catamaran car ferry in 50 minutes. Boulogne's historic attractions can be found within the 13th-century walls of its upper town, which occupies a rectangle covering 410 × 325m/450 × 355yd. The western part of the area contains the town hall (1734) with its 47m/154ft beffroi (12th–18th centuries, with a good view). A dome 102m/335ft in height dominates the church of Notre-Dame. Built in Greco-Roman style in 1827–66, it has a notable 11th-century crypt and a treasure chamber. The 13th-century chateau of the counts of Boulogne next door has exhibits from Gallo-Roman antiquity as well as examples of local culture and artworks by French artists of the 19th century on view. Another place worth a visit is the **Nausicaä** maritime centre (www.nausicaa.fr) at the entrance to the harbour. More than 6,000 species of fish live in its aquaria. 3km/2mi north of the town the 54m/177ft Colonne de la Grande Armée, built in 1841, is a memorial to Napoleon Bonaparte's planned invasion of England (it offers a great view). On the last weekend in August the **Calvaire des Marin** (sailors' procession) takes place, which commemorates to the »landing« of a black Madonna statue in the 7th century.

Boulogne-sur-Mer

◀ Upper town

✳
Le Touquet

Le Touquet (5600 inhabitants) at the mouth of the Canche is one of the best known **seaside resorts** on the Opal Coast. It has been popular with both Britons and Parisians since the 1880s. Among its many attractive buildings in a diverse range of styles, the Hotel Westminster (1930), still the finest hotel in town, and the town hall (1931) deserve special mention.

Montreuil

The town of Montreuil, 10km/6mi southeast of Le Touquet above the valley of the Canche, is a pretty spot for a day trip. It is still ringed by walls dating from the 17th century. The collegiate church of St-Saulve (11th–12th centuries) has some lovely capitals and paintings (18th century). On the opposite bank of the Canche stands the Carthusian monastery of Notre-Dame-des-Prés (1314), which was reconstructed by a pupil of Viollet le Duc in 1870.

Other Places to Visit in Nord-Pas-de-Calais

✳
Arras

Arras (43,500 inhabitants), once the capital of the county of Artois, was famed for its **Gobelin tapestries**. Indeed the Italian word for such tapestries is »arazzi«, i.e. »from Arras«. In the town centre there are two squares lined with uniform arcaded houses from the 17th and 18th centuries, which exude the character of a Flemish trading centre. Place des Héros is the site of the reconstructed **late Gothic town hall** (tourist office); it has a 75m/246ft beffroi, from which there is a fine view. The tourist office is also the starting point for visits to the **boves**, underground passages which have been used by the citizens as quarries or wine cellars as well as places of refuge since the 10th century. Rue de la Taillerie leads from Place des Héros to the equally beautiful Grand'Place. The former abbey church of St-Vaast, further to the west, was built in the 18th century. A convent houses the Musée des Beaux-Arts, which has exhibits including tapestries, medieval sculpture, paintings from the 16th–18th centuries and French masters from the 19th century. Close by to the south is a house in which Maximilien de Robespierre lived from 1787 to 1789. The society of **Compagnons**, wandering artisans, has set up an interesting museum there. During the First World War, the environs of

War memorials

the town were the scene of heavy fighting, as the numerous military cemeteries, war memorials and craters speckling the landscape testify. One example is the Canadian monument near Vimy 8km/5mi to the north and the cemetery (with museum) on the mountain ridge of Notre-Dame-de-Lorette, 10km/6mi northwest of Vimy.

Cambrai

Cambrai (35,000 inhabitants) is at the centre of an agricultural region on the banks of the Schelde. From its Porte de Paris (14th century), at the southern edge of the old town, head past the 18th-century **Notre-Dame cathedral** (tomb of Archbishop Fénelon by David d'Angers, 1826) to Maison Espagnole, built in 1595 (tourist office). Continuing straight on from here leads to the town hall, which has a clock tower from 1512 where »Martin« and »Martine« strike the hours. The church of St-Géry (1698–1745) has a beautiful interior featuring red and black marble, as well as *The Entombment*, a grave sculpture by Rubens. Beyond Place Fénelon, Rue Vaucelette leads to the Musée des Beaux-Arts with its veritable kaleidoscope of exhibits (archaeology, medieval sculpture, and Dutch and French art spanning the 16th to the 20th centuries, including works by Utrillo, Rodin, Claudel and Zadkine. Head east to get back to Maison Espagnole.

Le Cateau-Cambrésis (7700 inhabitants), 24km/15mi southeast of Cambrai, was the birthplace of the painter **Henri Matisse** in 1869 († 1954). Musée Matisse in Palais Fénelon provides an overview of his work (closed Tue). Other sights include the Baroque church of St-Martin from 1635, the archbishops' palace and the underground passage beneath the town. The town once boasted many **breweries**, and Brasserie Lefebvre Scalabrino has now been put back into action. In Caudry (8km/5mi to the west), a centre for lace making, the Musée de la Dentelle covers all aspects of the delicate material. Its modern church houses the valuable relics of St Maxellende.

Le Cateau-Cambrésis

Caudry

About 40km/25mi south of ►Lille, at the edge of the coal field which stretches from the Ruhr region of Germany as far as Artois, lies the industrial town of Douai (45,000 inhabitants). Its last colliery was closed in 1990. The town is centred around Place d'Armes and the Hôtel du Dauphin (tourist office). Alongside the town hall (15th/19th centuries) is a 64m/210ft **bell tower** or beffroi (1380–1475), which possesses the biggest glockenspiel in Europe (guided tours available). On the other side of the river Scarpe there is a Carthusian monastery from the 16th–17th centuries with a museum displaying works by French and Dutch artists, including the **winged altar of Anchin** (Jean Bellegambe, 1513), as well as paintings from the Italian Renaissance, Dutch-Flemish masters (including Jan Massys) and a Venus by **Giambologna**, who was born in Douai in 1529. In **Lewarde**, 8km/5mi southeast of Douai, a disused colliery has been made into the biggest **mining museum** in France (Centre Historique Minier, open daily).

Douai

The town hall and beffroi express the civic confidence of Douai

The era of coal mining in France has come to an end.
This shaft winding in Lewarde is a museum

Lille

►Lille

Saint-Omer

This dignified little town (15,000 inhabitants), situated between Calais and Lille amid countryside laced with canals, is dominated by the beautiful cathedral of Notre-Dame (13th–16th centuries.), whose valuable possessions include the 13th-century tomb of St Omer himself and the 16th-century tomb of Bishop Eustache de Croy. The **Musée des Beaux-Arts** in Hôtel Sandelin (1777) has exhibits of exquisite furniture, artistic craftwork of the Middle Ages, Delft faiences, Flemish tapestries and notable paintings. In the east of town near the canal there are still some remnants in existence of the abbey of St-Bertin, built in 1640. These include one tower that rises to a height of 58m/190ft as well as nine arcades belonging to the former church.

✱ **Musée des Beaux-Arts** ►

✱ **La Coupole**

The immense underground **V 2 rocket base** established for the German army near Helfaut (5km/3mi south of St-Omer) is now open to the public every day. Apart from the wartime military hardware, including one real V 2 rocket, there is also an audio-visual presentation, which describes how rocketry developed from the V2 to the moon landing in the space of two and a half decades. About 12km/7mi northwest of St-Omer, another bunker installation is still in existence (Le Blockhaus).

Le Blockhaus

Cassel

The pretty little settlement of Cassel (2300 inhabitants), 23km/14mi northeast of St-Omer and nestling on a wooded hillock nearly 180m/590ft high, is very Flemish in character. It still possess a large number of town houses from the 16th–18th centuries. The Musée de Flandre is housed in the Hôtel de la Noble Cour. **A fine view of the Flanders countryside** can be seen from the highest point of the village; an 18th-century wooden windmill has also been reconstructed here.

Aire-sur-la-Lys

The small town of Aire-sur-la-Lys (10,000 inhabitants), 19km/12mi southeast of Cassel has retained much of its appearance from the 17th–18th centuries, especially around the Grand'Place. The pretty

Flemish Renaissance Bailliage (1604) was once the headquarters of the town militia. The late 15th-century church of St-Pierre is among the most important Flamboyant-Renaissance churches in Flanders. Its portico and 62m/203ft-high tower were completed at the end of the 17th century.

Places to Visit in Picardy

The Somme rises to the northeast of St-Quentin, meanders westwards through Picardy and flows into the English Channel some 245km/152mi later near St-Valery-sur-Somme. With its lakes and islands, the section between Peronne and ► Amiens boasts the most charming scenery. During the First World War in 1916, a murderous battle took place to the east of Amiens, in the area around Albert. Many memorials and military cemeteries recall the fighting.

✳ **Vallée de la Somme**

The Historial de la Grande Guerre in Péronne (open daily) provides a host of information on the First World War. After Abbeville the Canal de la Somme branches off the river to the harbour and resort of **St-Valery-sur-Somme**.

Péronne

The **Bay of the Somme** with its endless sandy beaches and surprising absence of tourists, is a paradise for birdlife. Other places of interest for bird lovers are Maison de l'Oiseau in Lanchères le Hourdel and the Parc Ornithologique Marquenterre between Authie and the mouth of the Somme.

✳ **Baie de la Somme**

Rue (3000 inhabitants) is the capital of a region of the same name. In the Middle Ages it had its own harbour. The fortified upper town is pretty and boasts a few interesting attractions such as the 15th–16th-century Chapelle du St-Esprit, which was erected to house a crucifix said to have the power to do miracles, and the 15th-century watchtower (beffroi), which towers over the town hall. The Eco-musée Picarvie in the lower town illustrates life in the Picardy of old.

✳ **Rue**

Abbeville (25,000 inhabitants), 20km/12mi from the sea on the banks of the Somme, was the former capital of the Ponthieu region. The town was badly damaged by German air raids in May 1940 and has been rebuilt in modern style. In the middle of the town, though, there is still the church of St-Vulfran (started in 1488 and with a 17th-century choir), the façade of which is a prime example of **late Gothic Flamboyant**. The Musée Boucher de Perthes is housed inside a 13th-century watchtower and various other buildings (15th century) and boasts exhibits of prehistoric finds, medieval sculpture and other works of art. One interesting place southeast of the town is **Château Bagatelle** (1754), which was built for the Abbeville textile magnate Abraham Van Robais.

Abbeville

✳ ◄ St-Vulfran

The village of Saint-Riquier (1200 inhabitants), 9km/6mi northeast of Abbeville, grew up around a Benedictine abbey. The abbey church

✳ ◄ Abbey church

(13th/15th–16th centuries) is built in purest Flamboyant style and has an unfinished tower 50m/164ft in height. Its 17th-century interior is fabulously appointed. The monastery buildings now house a museum of rural life (Musée de la Vie Rurale).

✳
Rambures

The **castle** at Rambures (14km/9mi southwest of Abbeville) is the best example of the defensive architecture of the 15th century in Picardy. A true bulwark with walls 3.5–6m/10–20ft thick, its three-storey tunnel system had space for a whole garrison. It also has a fine park.

Amiens

►Amiens

Beauvais

Located between Amiens and Paris on the left bank of the river Thérain, Beauvais (57,000 inhabitants) was once an important bishopric and is renowned for the manufacture of Gobelin tapestries. The Galerie Nationale de la Tapisserie near the cathedral has a display of tapestries from the 15th– 20th centuries. It is also possible to visit a **Gobelin factory** established by Colbert in 1664. The other major attrac-

✳ ✳
St-Pierre ►

tion in the town is the magnificent Gothic **cathedral of St-Pierre**, a highlight of French Gothic architecture. The building, which was to put all before it in the shade, was started in 1227, although only the choir and transept were completed (in conjunction they measure 72.5m/80yd in length) because erroneous calculations had led to the collapse of the vaulting in 1247 and 1284. The vaulting was rebuilt in the years up to about 1320 and at a height of 48.2m/158ft the cathedral is still amongst the highest in existence. The astonishing 153m/500ft tower in the middle also collapsed in 1573 due to lack of support in the absence of a nave and has never been reconstructed. The marvellous **façade of the southern part of the transept**, built in pure Flamboyant style, was designed by Martin Chambiges, Michel Lalye and Jean Vast (1500–48), while the doors were made by Jean Le Pot (1535). The astronomical clock (1886, made with more than 90,000 components) in the breathtaking interior is a copy of the one in Strasbourg. Take note, too, of the 16th-century stained glass windows, which were made in local factories. The modest nave of the **Carolingian church** (»Basse Œuvre«, 998) still stands in front of the cathedral. The episcopal palace (14th–16th centuries) now accommodates the Musée de l'Oise, which exhibits archaeological finds, medieval sculpture, Gobelin tapestries and paintings. The spacious Place Jeanne-Hachette and the local festival, which takes place at the end of June, are dedicated to Jeanne Laîné, who defended the town against Charles the Bold of Burgundy (1472). The 18th-century town hall stands on the southern side of the square.

✳ ✳
Compiègne

Located 60km/37mi east of Beauvais on the Oise, Compiègne (43,000 inhabitants) was a popular residence for monarchs dating back to the Merovingians and today its glorious 150 sq km/60 sq mi of **woodland** remain a popular place to go. In 1430 Joan of Arc was captured here by the Burgundians and handed over to the English. In the forest around Compiègne, 6km/4mi east of the town, stood the railway carriage in which the **ceasefire** with Germany was signed on 11 November 1918, ending the First World War. On 22 June 1940, another signing was held in the same carriage at the same place to symbolize that the boot was now on the other foot. Hitler's forces later brought the carriage back to Germany but it was destroyed in a bombing raid in 1943. Nowadays a similar carriage of the same design has been placed at the spot to take its place (Clairiére de l'Armistice, closed Tue). The **classical chateau** is austere but its 200m/220yd frontage is still impressive. It was built for Louis XV by Ange-Jacques Gabriel from 1751 to 1788 and still has its sumptuously furnished chambers, as well as a museum of coaches and automobiles and a museum dedicated to the imperial German era of 1815–71. Equestrian enthusiasts should not miss the extensive **stud** in the historic stables. The exhibits in the Musée Vivenel, in Hôtel Songeons on the Oise, include vases from Etruria and the Hellenic realms.

Morienval

Morienval, 16km/10mi south of Compiègne, is the first stop on a charming day trip. The late Gothic **abbey church**, Notre-Dame de Morienval, has three towers as well as one of the earliest examples of Gothic vaulting (*c*1125) in the gallery around the choir. Continuing on, Pierrefonds (10km/6mi northeast) dates back to a castle, construction of which began in 1390. The building was razed by Richelieu but would be replaced from 1857 onwards by a building representing the romantic ideal of a medieval stronghold of knights, as designed by Viollet le Duc.

Pierrefonds

The early Gothic cathedral of Notre-Dame in Laon has seven towers

✴ Laon

The lovely old town of Laon (28,000 inhabitants), capital of the Aisne département, is 37km/23mi south of St-Quentin on a rocky plateau amid a fertile plain. In the Middle Ages it was the capital of the Western Frankish empire (West Francia) and was also a bishopric. A funicular railway (POMA) leads up from the railway station to the **Ville Haute** (upper town). The cathedral of Notre-Dame (1155–1235) is one of the most important early Gothic churches in France. The immense building (121m/132yd long outside and 110m/120yd inside, 30.5m/100ft wide and 53.3m/175ft high in the transept) became a template for many a cathedral church. One unusual feature is the squared-off end of the choir. Notable features in the interior include the beautiful 13th-century stained glass windows, the 18th-century choir screen and the cathedral treasury. To the right of Notre-Dame's main façade stands Hôtel Dieu (1177, housing the tourist office), in which it is still possible to see some of the old Gothic invalids' hall. There is a great view from the promenade around the 16th-century citadel in the east, which also leads further east along the southern ramparts to the former abbey of St-Martin (12th–13th centuries) and the Porte de Soissons (13th century).

✴ ✴ Notre-Dame ►

Noyon

The small town of Noyon (14,000 inhabitants) 24km/15mi north of Compiègne, renowned as a cherry-growing centre (festival on the first Sunday in July), has been a bishopric since the 6th century. **Notre-Dame cathedral** (1150 –1290) is a fine example of the transition between Romanesque and Gothic styles. Its chapter hall, the cathedral's chapter library (16th century) and the episcopal palace (16th century, Musée du Noyonnais) are all interesting. Reformer John Calvin (1509–64) was born in Noyon – the rebuilding work on the house of his birth was completed in 1930 and it is now a museum (closed Tue). On the edge of a forest 6km/4mi to the south is Ourscamps abbey, built in 1129 (with 18th-century extensions). The church is a ruin but, with its three 30m/33yd-long vaulted aisles, the splendid **invalids' hall from 1260**, now used as a chapel, is well worth seeing.

✴ Notre-Dame ►

✴ Abbey Ourscamps ►

Saint-Quentin

The industrial town of St-Quentin (61,000 inhabitants) is 47km/29mi northwest of Laon. The centre of the town is upon a hill on the right bank of the Somme canal and is dominated by the massive collegiate church of St-Quentin (12th–15th centuries) with its magnificent choir end. Inside, the choir, the stained glass window (1230) and the organ front (1703) are all particularly notable. Building work on the **town hall** began in 1331 but it was in 1509 that it gained its marvellous Flamboyant façade. The town possesses several **béguinages**, some dating back to the 13th century, and many an **Art Deco façade**. Places to visit include the Musée d'Entomologie, which has more than 600,000 butterflies, and Musée Lécuyer with its portraits of Maurice Quentin de la Tour, who was born in St-Quentin in 1704 and died here in 1788.

✴ Musée Lécuyer ►

Situated 38km/24mi east of Compiègne on the River Aisne, Soissons (31,000 inhabitants) was the very first capital of France after Clovis's victory over the Roman general Syagrius in 486. At its centre is the **Gothic cathedral** of St-Gervais-et-St-Protais. The oldest part of the church is the southern transept (*c*1177). The interior, 116m/127yd long, is distinguished by its plain elegance. The church's riches include the stained glass windows in the 13th-century choir and the *Adoration of the Shepherds* by Rubens in the northern transept. The St-Jean-des-Vignes monastery in the southern part of town was founded in 1076 and once very rich; of the 13th–14th-century buildings, the Gothic façade of the church with its two 15th-century towers 70 and 75m/230 and 246ft high, some parts of the cloister and the refectory are still in existence. The remainder was used for restoration work on the cathedral from 1805 onwards. The 13th-century collegiate church of St-Léger now houses the Musée d'Archéologie et d'Art (Gallo-Roman and medieval periods, paintings). On the opposite bank of the Aisne is the abbey of St-Médard, which has a crypt from the 11th century.

Soissons

◄ St-Gervais-et-St-Protais

◄ St-Jean-des-Vignes

✷ Poitiers

Région: Poitou-Charentes   **Altitude:** 120m/394ft
Département: Vienne   **Population:** 87,000

Poitiers, the former capital of ►Poitou , is a lively university town. It is prettily located on a rocky plateau, encircled by the valleys of the Clain and Boivre rivers. As the centre of the Poitevin Romanesque style, it is particularly interesting to art lovers.

Already of importance in Celtic and Roman times, when the city was called Limonum, Poitiers quickly became a centre of Christianity. The **first major bishop** was St Hilarius (Hilaire, † 368), teacher to St Martin of Tours; it was under him that the baptistery of St-Jean, France's oldest Christian building, was built. In 732, Poitiers (Moussais-la-Bataille) was the venue for the Battle of Poitiers (also known as the Battle of Tours), in which Charles Martel defeated the Moors. After the marriage in 1152 of Eleanor of Aquitaine to Henry Plantagenêt, later to become king of England, Poitiers was her primary residence. Jean de Berry, count of Poitou from 1369 to 1416, wrote himself into history with the marvellous novella *Les Très Riches Heures* about the Limburg brothers (►Bourges). The university was founded in 1432, at a time when Paris was in English hands and Poitiers was capital of France. In 1569 the city was conquered by the Huguenots, while 1579 saw a grand council meet in Poitiers with the objective of putting an end to the religious warfare.

History

● VISITING POITIERS

INFORMATION
Office de Tourisme
45 Place Ch. de Gaulle
F-86000 Poitiers
Tel. 05 49 41 21 24, fax 05 49 88 65 84
www.ot-poitiers.fr

WHERE TO EAT
▶ **Inexpensive / moderate**
① *Antipodes (Cellier St-Hilaire)*
65 Rue T. Renaudot
Tel. 05 49 42 02 93
Restaurant in a listed medieval wine
cellar belonging to the church of St-
Hilaire. Good traditional cooking.
Closed Sun, jazz on Thu.

WHERE TO STAY
▶ **Budget**
② *Château de Vaumoret*
Le Breuil-Mingot
Tel. 05 49 61 32 11
Fax 05 49 01 04 54
Very friendly chambre d'hôte in a
17th-century manor house 8km/5mi
east of Poitiers. Five rooms for 2–4
people. A kitchen is available so that
guests can prepare small snacks.

What to See in Poitiers

★ ★
Notre-Dame-la-Grande

In spite of its name, Notre-Dame-la-Grande is actually rather small.
It was built from the end of the 11th century until the mid-12th century and is one of the **finest examples of Poitevin Romanesque**. The
mid-12th-century west façade, with tiled conical roofs topping its
two flanking towers, is divided into four sections and is spectacularly
decorated with sculptures. The actual portal has dummy portals on
either side. Above them there are scenes from the Bible (including
Adam and Eve, the Annunciation, the Nativity). The arcades to the
top left and right feature bishops and apostles, and right at the top is
Christ in a Mandorla. On summer evenings the façade is lit by a variety of bright laser illuminations, including one version representing
the original colour scheme. The semi-dome above the choir has a
12th-century fresco. The rather ghastly painting work elsewhere was
perpetrated in the 19th century in the name of »reconstruction«.

Palais de Justice

Hôtel de l'Échevinage

Hôtel de Ville

Musée Chièvres

The early 12th-century Tour Maubergeon and parts of the counts'
chateau are preserved in the Palais de Justice. Inside, the magnificent
Grande Salle dates from the time of Eleanor of Aquitaine and has an
open roof structure along with a gigantic Gothic chimney. Rue Gambetta passes by the former assessors' office, the 15th-century town
hall and the 16th-century church of St-Porchaire with its distinctive
Romanesque tower above the portico (11th century). The city's central square is Place Maréchal-Leclerc, site of the town hall (1876). A
little further to the west stands an 18th-century palace, which houses
the Musée Rupert de Chièvres, mainly exhibiting furniture, porcelain, enamel and Dutch paintings from the 16th–17th centuries.

Rue de la Chaîne, the town's main thoroughfare lined by half-timbered buildings and the town palais, leads past the late Gothic Hôtel Fumé (early 16th century; with half-timbered arcades in its courtyard) towards the church of St-Jean-de-Montierneuf, featuring an 11th-century choir and a Renaissance doorway.

Hôtel Fumé

Montierneuf

The Romanesque church of St-Hilaire-le-Grand (11th–12th century) has a lively history of building work, as testified by the rows of columns that have been incorporated inside the building. The crypt underneath the raised choir houses the relics of St Hilaire himself and has been an important place of pilgrimage since the Middle Ages.

★
St-Hilaire-le-Grand

The lively Grand'Rue with its pretty shops leads eastward from Notre-Dame-la-Grande. The huge cathedral of St-Pierre is about 100m/110yd long inside and 27m/89ft high. Built in the years 1166–1271, it has the typical Anjou shuttered arcade and layered towers. The upper part of the western façade with the rose window dates from the 14th–15th centuries. The portals depict Death and the Crowning of the Virgin Mary, the Last Judgement and scenes from the life of St Thomas. Statues of prophets, Apostles and saints adorn the arched passages. The choir has some magnificent windows and the choir stalls date from the building of the church (making both among the oldest in France). There is also a Clicquot organ from 1778.

Grand'Rue
◄ Cathedral of St-Pierre

The neighbouring Espace Mendès-France is dedicated to the sciences (exhibitions and a planetarium). Musée Ste-Croix has an exhibition of prehistoric and Gallo-Roman finds, plus collections of folklore and art (including Camille Claudel, Bonnard, Sisley). In front of the Musée Ste-Croix, below street level, is the baptistery of St-Jean, the **oldest preserved Christian building** in France. Built between 356 and 368 on foundations that were even older, and extended in the

Espace Mendès-France
Musée Ste-Croix

★
Baptistère St-Jean

Poitiers Map

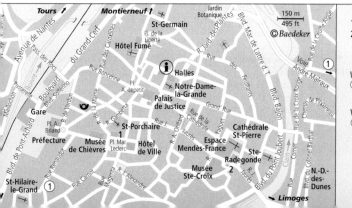

1 Théâtre
2 Baptistère St-Jean

Where to eat
① Antipodes

Where to stay
① Château de Vaumoret

*Notre-Dame-la-Grande is the ultimate example
of Poitevin Romanesque*

7th and 11th centuries, it boasts a large pool for fully immersed baptisms, frescoes from the 11th–14th centuries and the sarcophagi of Merovingian royals.

The church of **Ste-Radegonde** on the eastern edge of the city was built from the 11th century onwards on the site of a chapel in which the city's patron saint had been buried. The nave and western doorway date from the 13th–15th centuries. The crypt contains the tomb of St Radegund herself († 587), who was the daughter of the Thuringian king Berthar, wife of Chlothar (Clotaire) I and legendary vanquisher of the dragon Grand

View Goule. The best **view of the city** is to be seen from the observation platform of Notre-Dame-des-Dunes east of the Clain.

Around Poitiers

Abbaye de
Ligugé
The abbey of Ligugé, 8km/5mi south of Poitier, was established in 361 by St Martin of Tours, which makes it the **oldest monastery** in France. The ancient building was destroyed by marauding Arabs but a new one was built in the 11th century. The church (Flamboyant/ Renaissance) is the result of early 16th-century rebuilding work. Archaeological excavations around the abbey have brought to light sections of buildings dating back to the 6th century. The Benedictine monks here still produce some delightful enamel work.

Nouaillé-
Maupertuis
In a wooded valley 10km/6mi southeast of Poitiers there is another **Benedictine abbey**, which was fortified with walls and moats during the Hundred Years' War. The transept and choir of the 11th–12th-century Romanesque church was partially rebuilt in the 17th century. Notable features inside include the rood screen, the choir stalls, a 17th-century lectern and what is alleged to be the sarcophagus of St Junius (9th century).

✱
Futuroscope
Aficionados of cinematic spectacle must not miss Futuroscope, about 10km/6mi north of Poitiers, a leisure park with 16 **superlative cinemas** (plus hotel, restaurants, attractions for children): a 360° screen, 3 D, Cinéma Dynamique (a simulator), the »Crystal Palace« (with a screen covering 600 sq m), interactive cinema and much more. It centres around a pond, which is transformed by night into a fascinating world of images. Open daily from 10am, closing times vary (up to approx. 11pm in summer). Information: www.futuroscope.-com. Directions: autoroute A 10, no. 9 and E line bus from Poitiers (station/town hall), TGV station.

✳ ✳ Poitou - Vendée - Charentes

The fabulous variety of the Atlantic coast between the mouth of the Loire and Gironde rivers makes for a popular tourist destination with 2600 hours of sunshine per year. Inland, in the regions of Poitou, Vendée and Charentes, there is much for those who delight in culture to see and experience, for example in Poitiers and in the Charente valley with the wine-growing area around Cognac, home of the famous brandy.

The area south of the Loire between Touraine and the Atlantic is a fertile plateau rising to some 150m/500ft, which links spurs of the Armorican Massif with the Collines Vendéennes, themselves rising to as high as 285m/935ft. The eastern part is occupied by Poitou, while the western section near the coast is Vendée. This is made up of the Bocage Vendéen, a landscape of rolling hills and fields bordered by hedgerows, and a coastal plain guarded from the ocean by dunes. For administration purposes, Poitou is separated into the départements of Vienne (capital at Poitiers) and Deux-Sèvres (capital Niort) along with the southern part of Maine et Loire (Angers). Vendée has its own eponymous département (centred on La Roche sur Yon). **Poitou and Vendée**

The Charentes border Poitou to the south and are primarily made up of the départements Charente (in the east) and Charente-Maritime (in the west). ▶La Rochelle is surrounded by the countryside of Aunis, which sometimes descends into swampland, while to the south the neighbouring Saintonge territory stretches as far as Gironde. It too contains much boggy terrain but consists largely of fertile coastal plain and makes up most of the département Charente-Maritime. Between Aunis/Saintonge and Limousin, the old county of Angoumois centres on Angoulême. This corresponds largely to the modern département of Charente. **Charentes**

Highlights in the Poitou-Charentes region

Saint-Savin
A large-scale Romanesque »illustrated Bible«
▶ page 687

Marais Poitevin
Punting in the »green hell of Poitou«
▶ page 690

Islands of lights
The Ile de Yeu, Ile de Noirmoutier, Ile de Ré or Ile d'Oléron all have everything you

need for a relaxing holiday.
▶ page 690 – 692

Angoulême
Old ducal residence with atmosphere and a gem of Poitevin Romanesque
▶ page 693

Cognac
This is where the world famous brandy is made.
▶ page 695

The Vieux Château on the »wild side« of Ile de Yeu

Côte de la Lumière

As the crow flies, the **coast** between Ile de Noirmoutier and Gironde extends some 170km/106mi, but with all its nooks and crannies it actually stretches for 500km/300mi. It is no coincidence that this area is dubbed the »Coast of Light«. It has as many hours of sunshine in a year as the Côte d'Azur. Unlike the Côte d'Argent in the south, though, the Côte de la Lumière is much more varied. Rocky cliffs alternate with duneland and exquisitely long, flat, sandy beaches. Off the coast there are several islands, large and small. With its pleasant seaside resorts, the resulting character is both familiar and casual. There is a happy lack of concrete bastions while the natural atmosphere and absence of bustle, along with the moderate prices, all contribute to a list of positives. Large parts of the coast are made up of protected bays (especially the Bassin de Marennes between Ile d'Oléron and the mouth of the Gironde), ideal for the **cultivation of oysters and mussels**.

History

Between the Loire and Garonne, the territory of Aquitaine, one of the four provinces of Roman Gaul, dissolved into a series of counties, some of which were later elevated to duchies. Charles Martel defeated the Arabs at the Battle of Tours (also called the Battle of Poitiers) in 732, but after 820 the area was plagued by Norman raids, resulting in the building of numerous defensive towers. Many monasteries and collégiales were built from the 9th century onwards along the **Way of St James** to Santiago de Compostela. The most westerly route of the pilgrimage trail, the Via Turonensis, led through Poitiers, Aulnay and Saintes to Bordeaux (►Baedeker Special p.792). The marriage of Eleanor of Aquitaine to Henry Plantagenêt (Henry II of England) in 1152 brought Poitou under English control until the end of the Hundred Years' War (1337–1453). The Reformation quickly picked up devotees here. Both Angoulême and La Rochelle were key centres for the Huguenots and provided important economic impetus. The French Wars of Religion, which lasted until

1598, were at their most intense here. By 1627, though, La Rochelle was once again under siege from Catholic royalists and the town was conquered. Vendée remained true to the crown during the Revolution and revolted against the republic in 1793. The revolt lasted until 1796 and more than 150,000 people were killed in the numerous intervening battles.

Places to Visit in Poitou and Vendée

The small town of Montmorillon (7000 inhabitants), 50km/31mi southeast of Poitiers, is known for its Romano-Gothic church of Notre-Dame, where the crypt is decorated with some fabulous **frescoes** (the life of St Catherine, the Apocalypse). The square in front of the church offers a splendid view down the valley. Maison Dieu is a hospice dating from the late 11th century and both the 12th-century Chapelle St-Laurent (where concerts are sometimes given) and the 12th-century Octogone, thought to have been a charnel house, belong to it. The complex of buildings now also houses the Musée de La Tour and the 17th-century tithe barn has the Musée de Préhistoire.

Montmorillon

40km/25mi east of Poitiers on the river Gartempe, the small town of Saint-Savin (1100 inhabitants) has an 11th-century abbey church containing France's largest (412 sq m/500 sq yd) and possibly its most beautiful **Romanesque cycle of frescoes** (UNESCO World Heritage Site; open July–Aug daily 10am–7pm, otherwise Mon–Sat 10am–noon, 2pm–6pm and Sun 2pm–6pm, in winter till 5pm; closed Jan). The nave features four strips of images – one atop another on both walls – the Creation, Cain and Abel, Noah and the Ark, the crossing of the Red Sea, Moses, the Tower of Babel, Abraham and Isaac and the story of Joseph in Egypt. They start on the left-hand side and extend from the crossing towards the entrance on the right. Paintings also cover the narthex (Apocalypse), the vaulting of the nave, the gallery (from which everything can be viewed) and the crypt. The church measures 76m/83yd in length and is a fine example of Poitevin Romanesque. The passage around the choir marks it out as a church for pilgrims. There are also some outstanding capitals and a notable Romanesque altar. Beyond the **Vieux Pont** bridge (13th–14th centuries) over the river Gartempe, there is a great view of the giant complex with its 77m/253ft tower and 17th-century monks' quarters.

Saint-Savin

 ✶ ✶

◀ Romanesque frescoes

Chauvigny (6600 inhabitants), 20km/12mi east of Poitiers on the river Vienne, is dominated by no less than **five chateaux**. In addition there is also the Poitevin Romanesque church of St-Pierre (11th–12th centuries), famous for its capitals. Next door is the Musée de Chauvigny and a few steps further north the Donjon de Gouzon (11th century), now housing an industrial museum (and offering a great view from the terrace).

✶
Chauvigny

St-Hilaire in Melle was once a stop on the Way of St James according to Santiago de Compostela

Poitiers ▶Poitiers

Châtellerault Châtellerault, 30km/19mi northeast of Poitiers (36,000 inhabitants) is noted for its leather industry and because Descartes spent several years of his youth here (small museum, 126 Rue Bourbon). To the south on Rue Bourbon is the former priory church of St-Jacques (12th–13th centuries, façade 19th century). Head west from there to Hôtel Sully (17th century), which houses the local museum (arts and crafts, paintings, sculpture, history of the French Acadian colonies in Canada) and Pont Henri IV (1575 –1611). On the left bank there is a former munitions factory now used as a cultural centre. **La Manu** contains a veteran car and motorcycle museum and two chimneys, which have been incorporated into a work of art.

Parthenay Parthenay (10,500 inhabitants, 45km/28mi west of Poitiers) is the lively centre of the cattle rearing region of Gâtine and thus features a cattle market and meat processing factories. According to legend, the town owes its establishment to the sorcery of the mermaid Melusine. Historically it was one of the way stations on the and is therefore well catered for in terms of hospices and churches. Ideally the town should be entered from the north along the old pilgrims' route, crossing the **bridge and passing through the St-Jacques gate** (13th century), and then heading along Rue de la Vaux St-Jacques up to the citadel (walled in the 12th century), from where there is a lovely view of the loop in the river. In Parthenay-le-Vieux (2km/1.5mi to **Parthenay-le-Vie-** the west) the Romanesque church of St-Pierre with its Poitevin **ux** façade is interesting. To the right it features Samson and the lion, while the left-hand side has a typical equestrian figure with crown and falcon, thought to represent Constantine the Great. The figure which frequently appears in the bathtub is supposed to be Melusine.

Lusignan Lusignan (2600 inhabitants, 25km/16mi southwest of Poitiers) is picturesquely situated on the ridge of a hill alongside the Vonne river.

The lovely Melusine is said to have built the castle here (now a ruin) in one night. There is a great view down the river valley from the terrace. Other things to see include a Romanesque church (11th century, late Gothic portal), the market hall and some pretty old houses (some dating back as far as the 15th century).

Melle (4000 inhabitants, 32km/20mi southwest of Lusignan) was highly important in the Middle Ages for its silver mines. It has no less than **three churches in the Poitevin Romanesque style**, all of which are worth taking a look at.The first is St-Hilaire on the bridge over the Beronne, a most harmonious 12th-century building with a very nice choir section. On its northern transept it features the equestrian figure that appears so frequently in Poitou, dedicated to Constantine the Great and therefore signifying the victory of Christianity over the heathens. There are some magnificent capitals inside. The oldest church is the frugal St-Savinien, where chamber music concerts take place in May and June. The most recent church, St-Pierre (mid-12th century), has a notable southern doorway. In July the festival for the local goat's cheese of **Chabichou** is not to be missed. In Le Loubeau, about 1km/1100yd further south, it is possible to visit the royal silver mines.

Melle

★

◄ St-Hilaire

In Celles, 6km/4mi northwest of Melle, the abbey church of Notre-Dame, rebuilt in the 17th century by Francois Leduc, has an unusual **doorway** inherited from a Romanesque predecessor. Nine archivolts are arranged in small concentric arcs, the seams decorated with grimacing faces. It is thought that oriental influences were in play.

Celles-sur-Belle

The forest of Chizé, 20km/12mi south of Niort, has been set aside as a reserve for rare European wildlife (the entrance to Zoorama Européen is near Villiers en Bois).

Forêt de Chizé

Niort (59,000 inhabitants) is the gateway to the Marais Poitevin (► see below). It is also capital of the Deux-Sèvres département. Along the Sèvre Niortaise there is a **double donjon**, remnants of a castle initially started by Henri II and completed under Richard the Lionheart (museum of local folklore and archaeology, fine view from the top). Next door is a market hall with a fantastic array of goods. To the south, the 15th–16th-century church of **Notre-Dame** has an elegant 15th-century bell tower some 76m/250ft in height. Notable features inside include tapestries from Aubusson and the red marble tombs of a governor and his family (1684). Rue St-Jean leads northeast through a district with some lovely old houses (some dating from the 15th century) to the Pilori, a 16th-century fortified tower. The Logis d'Hercule displays archaeological finds from the town. Musée Bernard d'Agesci (near the station) combines the museums of natural history and art (arts and crafts, Italian, Flemish and Dutch masters, even a Corot).

Niort

★ ★
Marais Poitevin

At one time a bay stretched from the Atlantic as far inland as Niort. It is still possible to trace the old coastline where the land rises steeply up to the surrounding limestone plateau. The bay silted up and, with the help of Dutch dyke builders, centuries of work starting in the 11th century allowed the land to be drained and made available for cultivation. This created a charming green landscape some 80 sq km/31 sq mi in size, crossed by canals large and small, and lined with poplars, alders and meadowland. From many places it is possible to **take out a punt** (on your own or with a boatman). The main town, **Coulon**, has a number of attractions including the 11th-century church, an aquarium and the Maison des Marais Mouillés. The »port« of Arçais is a pretty spot.

! *Baedeker* TIP

Festival des Abbayes

In May and June the ruins of Maillezais abbey make an atmospheric backdrop for concerts by renowned orchestras playing both classical and ecclesiastical music. Concerts are also held at the abbeys of Nieul sur l'Autise (about 8km/5mi northeast of Maillezais) and Chassay-Grammont (about 15km/9mi southwest of Pouzauges; ▶p.693). Information at www.vendee.fr and http://abbayes.vendee.fr.

★
Maillezais

On the northern edge of the Marais, upon limestone cliffs that once descended to the ocean, there are some impressive ruins belonging to the **abbey** of Maillezais, founded in 989. The buildings were built between the 11th and 15th centuries but after the Revolution they were cannibalized for stone. In Maillezais itself, the church of St-Nicolas is interesting. The central doorway sports a frieze of acrobats.

La Rochelle ▶La Rochelle

Ile de Ré

The Ile de Ré, 28km/17mi long and 7km/4mi wide (15,000 inhabitants), is completely flat and lined with sandy beaches, which means it is very crowded in summer with families and youngsters. Amid a varied landscape, featuring dunes, oyster pools, woods, vegetable fields and vineyards, there are some pretty villages with whitewashed houses decorated by flowers. The island is connected to the mainland at **La Pallice** near La Rochelle via a 2930m/3200yd-long toll bridge and by boat. Beyond Rivedoux Plage are the Fort de la Prée (1625) and remains of the Abbaye des Châteliers (12th century, destroyed 1623). La Flotte is a pretty, peaceful fishing village with an old market hall. **St-Martin**, the charming administrative centre, is ringed by fortifications from the 15th–17th centuries. A citadel dating from the same period is still used as a prison. At the centre of town stands the fortified church of St-Martin (15th century, but badly damaged by English artillery in 1692). The sailors' quarter sits like an island in the midst of the harbour. East of the harbour, the tourist office and a museum of seafaring are both housed in the late 15th-century Hôtel de Clerjotte. **Ars** is another charming spot. The tower of its 12th-century church of St-Etienne is painted black and white as a signal to shipping. The western tip of the island is occupied by the 57m/187ft-high Phare des Baleines lighthouse, built in 1854. The best beaches are near the lighthouse and along the southern coast.

Pretty Luçon (9300 inhabitants), 45km/28mi north of La Rochelle in Vendee, was established as a port in the 10th century. The 12th-century abbey church of Notre-Dame was elevated to cathedral status in 1317 and rebuilt in Gothic style during the 14th century. Cardinal Richelieu was bishop here between 1607 and 1624. After the façade was destroyed in the religious wars, it was replaced in the 17th century by Francois Leduc in the prevalent classical style (85m/279ft tower 1829). The **episcopal palace** has a lovely Renaissance façade which, like the cloister, dates from the 16th century. Another charming spot is Jardin Dumaine from the time of Napoleon III. **Luçon**

Life in this popular seaside resort (15,500 inhabitants) mainly revolves around the **3km/2mi-long beach** (even though it gets very narrow at high tide). The beach is lined with hotels, shops, restaurants and bars. Casino de la Plage is at the western end, while at the eastern end there is a zoo. Beyond the seafront, Les Sables itself, which also has a large fishing harbour, remains very pretty in its own right. The church of Notre-Dame-de-Bon-Port was commissioned by Richelieu in 1646. The Musée de l'Abbaye Ste-Croix is housed in a 17th-century Benedictine abbey and exhibits both folklore and modern art. Beyond the canal the old **fishermen's quarter, La Chaume**, clusters around the 12th-century Tour d'Arundel and Fort St-Nicolas. North of the town, 12km/7mi of coastline with sandy **Les Sables d'Olonne**

What counts in Les Sables is sunshine and sand

beaches is flanked by the **Forêt d'Olonne**, a pine forest with a wealth of footpaths for ramblers. Such scenery continues beyond the fishing villages and resorts of Bretignolles, St-Gilles-Croix-de-Vie and St-Jean-de-Monts as far as the Ile de Noirmoutier.

About 18 km off the coast is the charming island of Yeu (10km/6mi long, 4km/2.5mi wide, 4900 inhabitants), which presents two faces to the world. To the southwest is the »wild« **Côte Sauvage**, reminiscent of the ruggedness of Brittany, while the northeast has the familiar Vendée coastline of sandy beaches and pine forests. Ferries ply from Fromentine and St-Gilles-Croix-de-Vie to the fishing harbour **★ Ile de Yeu**

▶ VISITING POITOU-VENDÉE-CHARENTES

INFORMATION

CRT Poitou-Charentes
8 Rue Riffault, BP 56
F-86002 Poitiers Cedex
Tel. 05 49 50 10 50, fax 05 49 41 37 28
www.poitou-charentes-vacances.com
CRT Pays de la Loire
2 Rue de la Loire, BP 20411
F-44204 Nantes Cedex 2
Tel. 02 40 48 24 20, fax 02 40 08 07 10
www.loiretalatlantik.com

WHERE TO STAY / WHERE TO EAT

▶ Mid-range

Atlantic
5 Promenade Godet
F-85100 Les Sables d'Olonne
Tel. 02 51 95 37 71
www.atlantichotel.fr
A family-run hotel right next to the
beach with generously sized rooms
(those facing the sea are more expensive). Restaurant and roofed
swimming pool.

Château du Pélavé
9 Allée de Chaillot, Bois de la Chaize
F-85330 Noirmoutier en l'Ile
www.chateau-du-pelave.fr, tel. 02 51
39 01 94, fax 02 51 39 70 42
Enchanting belle-époque villa, nestling quietly in the woods between the
beach and the harbour. Very good
restaurant with local cuisine, naturally
including fish and seafood.

Relais du Lyon d'Or
4 Rue d'Enfer
F-86260 Angles sur l'Anglin
Tel. 05 49 48 32 53, www.lyondor.com
This royal storage facility from the
15th century is situated in one of the
»prettiest villages in France« (16km/
10mi north of St-Savin). There are
open fires in cosy rooms, some of
which have a terrace. The restaurant
serves regional specialities.

of Port Joinville. A museum here is dedicated to Marshall Pétain,
who was imprisoned from 1945 to 1951 in Fort Pierre Levée and is
buried in the village cemetery. The **Vieux Château** (11th–16th centuries) sits romantically upon the wild western coast. To the southeast
is the deeply sheltered harbour of Port de la Meule, used by sailors
fishing for Langusten and lobster. One of the many legacies of megalithic culture is the dolmen of La Planche à Puare at the northwest
tip (►Baedeker Special p.306).

✴
**Ile de
Noirmoutier**

This popular seaside paradise with some 40km/25mi of sandy beach
is in the northeast of the coast of to the south of the Loire estuary.
19km/12mi long and up to 7km/4mi wide, the island can be reached
at low tide via the **Passage du Gois** causeway or by a bridge to the
south. Apart from tourism, vegetable farming, fisheries, oyster cultivation and salt manufacture are all key to the island economy. Over
the dunes of Barbâtre lies the main town of **Noirmoutier-en-l'Ile**
(4800 inhabitants) with a castle dating from the 11th–15th centuries.
There is a small museum of local history in the keep (with some no-

table Staffordshire faiences from the 18th–19th centuries and a lovely view from the roof extending to La Baule in the north and Ile de Yeu in the south). The Romanesque-Gothic church of St-Philibert has an 11th-century crypt with the cenotaph of St Philibert himself. The saint's actual relics were taken by monks to Tournus in ►Burgundy during the 9th century. Other interesting places are the aquarium at the canal docks and the museum for hand-made boats. To the east of the town there are 60ha/148 acres of woodland, the **Bois de la Chaize**, which have a decidedly Mediterranean look with pines and mimosas (blossoming in late February). Adjoining this to the north are the fine sand of the Plage des Dames and the Promenade des Souzeaux, from which the coast of Pornic can be seen. In La Guérinière there is another nice folklore museum.

The Collines Vendéennes are a range of hills dominated by **heathland**, which stretch from Les Herbiers (25km/16mi southwest of Cholet) to south of Parthenay. The area was formerly dotted with a great many windmills. North of Les Herbiers, Mont des Alouettes (231m/758ft) has three restored mills and a chapel from 1823. It also has a great view taking in Nantes, the sea and the Bocage scenery. To the southeast (D 755/D 752), past the Moulin de Justice, is St-Michel-Mont-Mercure the highest point of the range (285m/935ft); the church tower, from which there is a great view, is topped by a 9m/30ft-high statue of St Michael (1898). It is also worth taking detours to the 270m/886ft peak of **Puy Crapaud** near Pouzauges and to the church of Pouzauges le Vieux (13th-century frescoes).

Collines Vendéennes

East of Les Herbiers is the 15th-century chateau of Le Puy du Fou, which has been made into a huge leisure park with a Roman and a medieval village, Viking longships, falconry demonstrations and much more. Between mid-June and early September (Fri and Sat evenings) the chateau forms the backdrop for the Cinéscénie festival, a vast **historic spectacle** incorporating every imaginable effect and featuring more than 1200 actors performing for over 13,000 spectators (www.puydufou.com).

Le Puy du Fou

Places to Visit in the Charentes

The river Charente rises near Rochechouart on the western edge of Limousin and meanders 360km/224mi through the Angoumois and Saintonge scenery to the Atlantic coast. Between Angoulême and Saintes it forms a pleasant valley some 100km/60mi long, lined with cognac vineyards and charming old towns.

Charente

Angoulême (46,000 inhabitants), capital of Angoumois and the département of Charente, is charmingly situated on a plateau above the river Charente. Walking around the whole city on its ramparts can be quite impressive. In the town itself there are some fine mansions

★
Angoulême

from 17th–18th centuries, while the centrepiece is the great **town hall** (1858–66), built on a site formerly occupied by the chateau where the dukes of Angoulême resided. All that is left of the actual chateau are the 13th-century Tour de Lusignan (open to the public) and the 15th-century Tour de Valois. From the town hall, Rue de la Cloche-Verte leads past Hôtel St-Simon (1540) to the Gothic church of St-André (with some beautiful seating from 1692). The highlight

★ ★
St-Pierre ►

of the Romanesque cathedral of St-Pierre (built in 1105–28, destroyed by Huguenots in 1562 and rebuilt in 1634) is its western façade, one of the **major works of Poitevin Romanesque**, with Christ in a Mandorla presiding over more than 70 figures at the Last Judgement. In the episcopal palace (12th–15th centuries) next door, the Musée des Beaux-Arts exhibits old artistic craftwork, including the wonderful Celtic **Helmet of Agris** (4th century BC), paintings (from the Barbizon school and others) and art from overseas. For comic-freaks the Musée de la Bande Dessinée (Rue de Bordeaux 121) is a veritable place of pilgrimage. Its Mediatheque offers the chance to read **practically every comic issued in France** since 1946 (the International Comic Festival takes place here every January; www.bdangouleme.com). Other places to see include the »Le Nil« paper museum north of the town alongside the Charente (near the comic centre) and the archaeological museum.

La Rochefou-
cauld ►

About 22km/14mi northeast of Angoulême, La Rochefoucauld (3500 inhabitants) possesses a chateau from the 11th–16th centuries, which forms a fine ensemble with the 17th-century bridge over the Tardoire. The village is named after the aristocratic family which still owns the chateau to this day, and which also gave us the officer and author of *Réflexions ou sentences et maximes morales*, François de La Rochefoucauld (1613–80). The hospital across the river has an interesting 17th-century apothecary. About 30km/19mi north of Angou-

Lichères ►

lême in the fields near Lichères stands the small Romanesque church of St-Denis with its Byzantine-inspired tympanum and interesting apse design.

Confolens ►

Roughly 40km/25mi northeast of La Rochefoucauld, the town of Confolens (3100 inhabitants) occupies a picturesque spot at the confluence of the Vienne and Goire rivers. The lovely 15th-century **Pont Vieux** bridge over the Vienne formerly boasted fortified towers. Beyond half-timbered houses from the 15th–18th centuries and the 15th-century church of St-Maxime is an 11th-century donjon, all that remains of the town's defences. On the left bank of the Vienne stands the Romanesque church of St-Barthélemy (11th century) with its fascinating doorway. The **International Folklore Festival** in August is well known.

Charroux ►

The important abbey of Charroux, 25km/16mi northwest of Confolen, was provided with relics by **Charlemagne**. They are said to include to include part of the True Cross and even of the »body of Christ«, making the abbey an important destination for pilgrims. Councils also took place here. In 989 the »treuga Dei« (Peace of God) was declared. Of the 126m/138yd-long church consecrated in 1096 by Pope Urban II, only the massive central tower remains in existence. Inside the chapter hall, though, there are some marvellous figures around the main doorway, and the church treasury is also worth a look.

In Civray, 11km/7mi west of Charroux on the Charente, the church of St-Nicolas is worth seeing for its interesting façade, an outstanding work of Poitevin Romanesque. The colourful interior is modern apart from the fresco in the southern part of the transept (14th century). ★ **Civray**

In the northern part of the Charentes region (about 45km/28mi northeast of Saintes), Aulnay (1500 inhabitants) was once a stop on the Way of St James and its church, St-Pierre, has some finely sculpted archways (prayers to the Lamb of God, cardinal virtues and cardinal sins, zodiac signs and months of the year). The dummy portals depict the crucifixion of the Apostle Peter and Christ enthroned in heaven. The sculptures around the magnificent **southern portal** feature the Elders of the Apocalypse (31 instead of 24) along with a musical instrument and a perfume flask, figures of legend such as Melusina, and a harp-playing donkey. There are also some splendid capitals inside. ★ **Aulnay** ★ ◀ St-Pierre

From Angoulême, take the narrow roads **to the right of the Charente**, which pass by a range of attractions in some idyllic locations. **Trois Palis** has a Romanesque church with fine capitals as well as the Letuffe chocolate factory. There is a great view from the bridge below St-Simieux. In **Châteauneuf-sur-Charente** the façade of the church of St-Pierre has an interesting large equestrian statue (probably Constantine the Great). The 12th-century abbey of Bassac is dominated by an imposing tower. The little town of **Jarnac**, birthplace and final resting place of **Francois Mitterrand** (1916 –96), is on the edge of the Grande Champagne, the core region for cognac production (centred on Segonzac). Apart from the 11th-century abbey church, places to visit include the famous **cognac producers** of Courvoisier and Royer. A little outside Cognac itself, slightly north of the river, are the chateau and dolmen of Garde-Epée and, in its lonely spot, the stark and frugal Augustine abbey church of Notre-Dame-de-Châtre (11th century). ★ **Charente valley**

In the 17th century a method was developed to make 10 litres of the region's somewhat thin wine into 1 litre of good spirits. Thus in the 18th century expatriates from the British Isles – like Jean Martell of Jersey, Irish soldier Richard Hennessey, Scotland's Baron Otard – de- **Cognac**

● VISITING COGNAC

WHERE TO EAT

▶ **Inexpensive**

La Courtine

Allée Fichon, Tel. 05 45 82 34 78
It is not so much the traditional cuisine which makes this comfortable bistro a must, but rather its fantastic location in Parc François I. Its terrace is on the bank of the Charente. Jazz from time to time.

WHERE TO STAY

▶ **Budget**

Résidence

25 Avenue V. Hugo, F-16100 Cognac
Tel. 05 45 36 62 40, fax 05 45 36 62 49,
www.hotellaresidence-cognac.com
This plain and simple but charming hotel near Place François I offers friendly service. There is no restaurant.

cided to take advantage of this. This was how **cognac** liqueur came into being. The raw materials are obtained from a cultivated area covering some 700 sq km/270 sq mi around the town of Cognac itself (19,500 inhabitants). The companies Otard, Hennessy, Camus, Rémy Martin and Martell all keep large cellars (»chais«) around Cognac, in which the spirit is aged, and these are open to visitors. They also have shops of course (information from the tourist office, 16 Rue du XIV Juillet). The chais belonging to the company Otard have been located in the 13th–16th-century **Château de Valois** on the Charente since 1795. King François I was born in the same chateau in 1494. The Musée de l'Art et d'Histoire (local history, folklore, arts and crafts and works by Gallé) is housed in Hôtel Dupuy d'Angeac in the park around the town hall. The old town has many buildings from the 16th–17th centuries, especially on Grande Rue and Rue Saulnier. The widespread black coating is a fungus which thrives on the vapour from alcohol, »the angels' portion«.

◀ Cognac cellars

Saintes (28,000 inhabitants) on the Charente was an important stop along the Way of St James in the Middle Ages. The capital of Saintonge was where Doctor Joseph Ignace Guillotin (1738–1814) was born, the man incorrectly believed to have invented the guillotine. At the centre of the **old town** (west of the Charente) is the 15th-century cathedral of St-Pierre. Its transept was begun in 1117 for an earlier building. Notable features include the Flamboyant portal and the chunky 72m/236ft-high portal tower (15th century), which is reminiscent of Limousin Romanesque. In the Présidial, a 17th-century palace, the Musée des Beaux-Arts exhibits French, Dutch and Flemish paintings as well as porcelain from Saintes itself. Southwest of the old town, the church of St-Eutrope was consecrated by Pope Urban II in 1096. Its nave was destroyed in 1803 but the choir (with its fine capitals) and crypt housing the sarcophagus of St-Eutrope, first bishop of Saintes, still remain. The bell tower and northern transept date

Saintes

from 1496. About 300m/330yd northwest is a Roman arena, which accommodated 20,000 spectators (126 × 102m/138 × 112yd, 1st century AD). **On the right bank of the Charente**, a triumphal arch for Germanicus (19 AD) has stood at its present location since 1842. Nearby to the south, there is an archaeological museum with some Roman architectural relics and sculptures. The abbey of Ste-Marie-aux-Dames was established in 1047. Here pilgrims on the Way of St James were cared for and daughters of aristocratic families were educated. The typical Saintonge façade has a famous portal (which includes 24 elders making music at the Apocalypse).

✳
◄ Ste-Marie-
aux-Dames

About 20km/12mi north of Saintes (D 127), Fenioux possesses a Carolingian Romanesque church, which has an interesting portal and bell tower. The 12th-century **lanterne des mortes tower**, the largest in Poitou, is designed as a set of columns with a stairway leading up inside.

✳
Fenioux

Rioux, about 12km/7mi southwest of Saintes (D 129), has one of the most unusual Romanesque churches in Poitou. The single-aisled building from the 12th century has a polygonal choir with a complex design and no statuary except for the corbels under the roof. It recalls the Norman architecture of Italy. The church of St-Trojan in Rétaud (5km/3mi northwest) is similar.

✳
Rioux

The »beautiful coast« is the name given to the **northern bank of the Gironde estuary** between Mortagne-sur-Gironde and the Pointe de la Coubre, and with good reason. Along the mainly rocky coast, from which it is possible to see the northern tip of the Médoc (► Bordeaux), there are several pretty fishing ports and resorts with nice beaches. The Gironde is the only river in western Europe in which sturgeon breed (it has been forbidden to catch them since 1982).

✳
Côte de Beauté

The tiny village of Talmont-sur-Gironde is known for its 12th-century Romanesque church of St-Radegonde, with lovely capitals on the central pillars, which rises up from the Gironde. The caves in the limestone cliffs of Meschers, further to the northeast, were dwellings for prehistoric people. One is now a bar and crêperie, and another (with animations) is open to the public. The stretch of coast between here and Pointe de Suzac is particularly beautiful.

Talmont-sur-
Gironde

Meschers

Royan (17,500 inhabitants) developed into an elegant seaside resort in the 19th century. In 1847 **the first casino** in a French resort opened its doors here. Although it was almost totally destroyed in 1945, it has now been nicely restored. The old town is mostly comfortably somnolent but in the western part, Teil Pontaillac, it is still lively. It is pleasant to take a walk along the **Corniche de Pontaillac**. The concrete and steel church of Notre-Dame (1958) is 65m/213ft tall, but not much of an eye-catcher. The same material was used for

Royan

the dome of the Marché Central at the end of Blvd. A. Briand (1955). There is harbour in the bay to the east (Grande Conche), from which boats ply to the lighthouse, Phare de Cordouan, ▶Bordeaux) and there is also a beach 2km/1.5mi long. The car ferry to **Verdon-sur-Mer** (▶ p.281) on the other side of the Gironde runs every 30–45 minutes in summer.

Pointe de la Coubre

At St-Palais the coast starts to take on a **duneland** character, accompanied by pine and holm oak woods (with plenty of footpaths) as far as Ronce les Bains at the mouth of the Seudre. Another recommendation is to start out from St-Palais along the Sentier de la Corniche footpath to Pont de Diable (signposted, 45 minutes there and back) In La Palmyre there is a zoo, and there is a fine view from the 64m/210ft **Phare de la Coubre** lighthouse. The coast to the north (Côte Sauvage) is a protected natural landscape and, at certain times, it has some severe breakers.

Seudre

The Seudre has given rise to a **lagoon landscape** to the northwest of Saujon. Along with the coast north of Marennes and the east coast

Oyster harvesting between Marennes and the isle of Oléron with Fort Louvois in view

of the Ile d'Oléron, it forms the biggest oyster farming region in France. The »Marennes-Oléron« brand of shellfish are famous. On certain days from June–Sept a steam train (Train des Mouettes) runs between Saujon and La Tremblade. The medieval market hall in **Mornac-sur-Seudre** is interesting, too. From Tremblade it is possible to take a boat to explore the oyster beds. The 85m/279ft-high St-Pierre de Sales' church (15th century; viewing terrace) in **Marennes** stands out from quite a distance. The 4km/2.5mi-long Damm La Cayenne, south of the village, is a centre of oyster cultivation. About 8km/5mi northeast of Marennes, the fortifications of Brouage (500

✳ Brouage

inhabitants), established in 1630–40, stand out amid the swampland. Among the remaining structures are the powder magazine, the barrel-making workshop and the smithy (tourist office).

✳ Ile d'Oléron

The Ile d'Oléron covers 180 sq km/70 sq mi (30km/19mi long, 6km/4mi wide, 18,000 inhabitants), making it France's second biggest island after Corsica. It is popular place for a summer holiday. It is flat and has some **wonderful beaches** with fine sand, as well as wide areas of pine and holm oak woodland. The longest viaduct in France

(3027m/3310yd) connects it to the mainland. The hub of life of the island is the little town of **St-Pierre-d'Oléron** (5400 inhabitants). There is a lovely view from the tower of its 18th-century church. On neighbouring Place Camille-Memain, an old cemetery, there is a 30m/98ft-high lanterne des mortes tower, dating from the 13th century. Musée Oléronais, located in a typical farmhouse, illustrates the history and folklore of the island. **Château d'Oléron** can be found on the east coast along with a fort and a pretty fishing harbour. To the north, the Route des Huîtres runs past an oyster-farming region as well as a nature park and bird sanctuary called **Marais aux Oiseaux** before reaching Boyardville, which came into existence with the building of Fort Boyard. The latter was built at the mouth of the Charente in 1804–59 and in 1871 was used as a prison for the members of the Paris Commune. Sandy beaches line the Forêt des Saumonards. St-Georges and St-Denis both have lovely Romanesque churches. The **Phare de Chassiron** lighthouse (1836) at the northern tip of the island is 50m/164ft tall and it is possible to climb the steps to the top. The quieter and less accessible west coast of the island, with the fishing port of La Cotinière (famous for its prawns), has long sandy beaches, but the waves are often heavy. **St-Trojan-les-Bains** (1500 inhabitants) is known for its Mediterranean flora and for the Fête des Mimosas in February.

◀ Tours

Rochefort (26,500 inhabitants), southeast of La Rochelle about 8km/5mi inland from the coast on the river Charente, is virtually a huge open-air museum. It was established by Colbert as of 1666 as a **naval base**, which grew to rival Toulon on the Mediterranean in importance. Up to 10,000 men were employed within its huge facilities. The arsenal was not closed until 1926. Following the Charente down from the north, first there is a dry dock from 1669 (Vieille Forme, the oldest in the world), a food warehouse (magasin aux vivres) and the 374m/409yd long ropemaking plant (corderie, with a museum). Further south are the Porte du Soleil (1830), the entrance to the arsenal, where the *Hermione*, a three-masted sailing ship in which Lafayette sailed to Boston in 1780, is currently being reconstructed. Next to the gate is the Hôtel des Cheusses, which houses the Musée de la Marine and the tourist office. To the west (Rue P. Loti) stands an eccentrically oriental styled house, which was the birthplace and childhood home of Pierre Loti (1850–1923), a naval officer and author of adventure novels. Some 200m/220yd to the north are the Musée d'Art et d'Histoire and Place Colbert with its fountain from 1750, then come the town hall and the church of St-Louis (1672). At the southern edge of town, the **transporter bridge** over the Charente is an interesting iron construction. 176m/192yd long and 50m/164ft high, it was built in 1900.

Rochefort-sur-Mer

Fouras, which has been fortified since the time of the Norman incursions, was expanded by Vauban as an outpost of Rochefort in the

Fouras

17th century. Inside the fort, a 15th-century donjon has been preserved (local museum, good view). There is a very lovely walk from the resort and fishing port (3900 inhabitants) to the **Pointe de la Fumée**. From the point, a ferry goes across to the Ile d' Aix (200 inhabitants, no cars allowed), which also has a Vauban fort as well as good sandy beaches. The speciality of the island is prawns. It was in the commandants' house here that **Napoleon** spent the days before his banishment to St Helena (9–15 July 1815). Opposite the house there is a museum dedicated to Africa. The church of St-Martin is a remnant of a Benedictine abbey and possesses an 11th-century crypt.

Ile d'Aix

✴ ✴ **Provence**

N–O 8/9

A whole spectrum of scenic delights awaits between the Rhône, the Alps and the Mediterranean: the enchanting old towns, dazzling light and gentle lifestyle combine to make Provence one of the most popular holiday destinations in France. Add the warm and sunny climate and the beaches of the ▶ Côte d'Azur, and the stage is set for a wonderful holiday.

Provence in brief

The borders of Provence (the name comes from the Roman province of »Provincia Gallia Narbonensis«) are not precisely defined, since they have changed so often over the course of history. The core of Provence (Basse-Provence) is seen as the triangle between Montélimar, Aigues-Mortes and Toulon, although its territory could be seen as extending over all of eastern France between the lower Rhône and the Italian frontier, thus including Haute-Provence, the maritime Alps and the Côte d'Azur. For local government purposes, the Provence – Alpes – Côte d'Azur (PACA) district covers the départements of Vaucluse (capital Avignon), Bouches du Rhône (Marseille), Var (Toulon), Alpes de Haute-Provence (Digne), Hautes-Alpes (Gap) and Alpes-Maritimes (Nice). This area also surrounds the independent coastal principality of ▶ Monaco.

Scenery

With the exception of the Rhône delta (Camargue), Provence is hilly territory. The stony limestone soil can only be cultivated with the aid of irrigation. The first canal channelling water from Durance was completed as early as 1554. In the hills, sheep and goats are kept, while the lowlands are cultivated with vineyards, fruit and olive trees. The fertile valleys are also used for cultivating vegetables, fruit and wine. In Haute-Provence, especially around Verdon, lavender is grown and this plant has become the regional symbol for Provence as a whole. Stretches of land unsuitable for agriculture often have garrigue landscapes, consisting of Mediterranean macchia flora with holm and kermes oaks and shrubland, cistus plants, thistles, weeds, elderberries and broom shrubs. The typical cypress trees were only

Highlights Provence

Vaison-la-Romaine
A trip back to Roman times
► page 704

Mont Ventoux
The »windy mountain«, emblem of Provence
► page 705

Fontaine-de-Vaucluse
The refuge of Petrarcas with a fantastic spa
► page 707

Ganagobie
The biggest and most beautiful Roman mosaic in France
► page 710

Senanque
Pure Cistercian monastic life
► page 707

Lubéron
A Provencal microcosm of its own
► page 708

Grand Canyon du Verdon
Spectacular scenery flanked by rocky cliffs 700m/2300ft high
► page 711

Sisteron
The gateway to Provence between the Rocher de la Baume and the citadel
► page 713

introduced at the end of the 19th century. The vegetation, which resembles that of latitudes south of Rome, is due to Provence being sheltered by the protection of the Alps in the north with the open sea to the south, leading to a warm and dry climate.

The mistral wind is often felt in the Rhône valley and Provence – especially between Avignon and Marseille. A cold, dry wind, often of gale force, the mistral blows from the Cevennes and the Alps through the Rhône valley when there is low pressure over the Golfe du Lion. As a measure against the mistral, settlements are often protected by stands of cypress or stone walls, and vegetable fields and vineyards are surrounded by hedges and rushes.

Mistral

Provence entered history with the founding of Massalia (Marseille) by Greeks from Asia Minor in around 600 BC. The Greeks appealed for help to the Romans when conquered by the Celts, resulting in the Romans taking over and forming a province called **Provincia Gallia Narbonensis** in 122 BC. Narbonne and Aix were the main military bases of the province. A heyday for the province began under Augustus, as recalled even today in many places, for example at Vaison la Romaine, Orange and Arles. As of 536, Provence became part of the French kingdom but from the 8th–10th centuries it suffered at the hands of the Saracens who mounted pillaging raids in the area. The Treaty of Verdun of 843 granted Provence to Lothair I, who established a kingdom here in 855 for his son Charles. As of the 10th century Provence was part of the Holy Roman Empire, although its

History

▶ VISITING PROVENCE

INFORMATION

CRT Provence - Alpes - Cote d'Azur
10 Place de la Joliette, BP 46214
F-13567 Marseille Cedex 2
Tel. 04 91 56 47 00, fax 04 91 56 47 01
www.decouverte-paca.fr
CRT Rhône-Alpes
104 Route de Paris
F-69260 Charbonnieres-les-Bains
Tel. 04 72 59 21 59, fax 04 72 59 21 60
www.rhonealpes-tourisme.com

WHERE TO STAY

▶ Budget / moderate
L'Evêché
Rue de l'Evêché
F-84110 Vaison-la-Romaine
Tel. 04 90 36 13 46, fax 04 90 36 32 43,
www.eveche-vaison.com
Chambre d'hôte in a 500-year-old
episcopal residence in the upper
town. Pleasant, prettily furnished little
rooms and a lovely view from the
terrace.

▶ Mid-range
La Ferme Rose
Hameau des Bassacs
F-04360 Moustiers-Sainte-Marie
Tel. 04 92 75 75 75, fax 04 92 73 73 73
http://lafermerose.free.fr
Situated about 1km/1100yd in the
direction of Ste-Croix-du-Verdon,
this pretty country house in Italian
style offers very pleasant, large rooms,
named after the colour of the bathroom. No restaurant.

▶ Luxury
Abbaye de Ste-Croix
Route du Val-de-Cuech, F-13300 Salon-de-Provence, tel. 04 90 56 24 55
www.hotelsprovence.com
5km/3mi northeast of Salon-de-Provence. Luxury hotel in a 12th-century
Cistercian monastery with a lovely
view of Salon. Very tastefully designed
rooms (those in the monks' cells are
very small). Excellent restaurant and
pool.

Séguret, a pretty wine-making village near the Dentelles de Montmirail

counts were largely independent. In 1178 Frederick Barbarossa had himself crowned king of Provence in Arles. Charles of Anjou became count of Provence by marriage in 1246. During this Anjou period, Avignon became the headquarters of the papacy, or of the papal pretenders (1309–1403).

Another boom came in 1434–80 under the rule of »Good King« René, who took up residence in Aix in 1442. In 1481 Provence was inherited by the French monarchy. The Wars of Religion saw many atrocities, principally the massacre of the Waldensians of Lubéron in 1545. In 1720 Nassau-ruled Orange fell to the king. Avignon became French in 1791 along with Venaissin, which had until then been a dominion of the pope. In the Second World War, Provence was occupied by German troops in 1942 but was freed by the Allies in 1944. Even today, Provence nurtures its cultural independence, especially the Provençal language. Its most eminent proponent in modern times was **Frédéric Mistral** (1830–1914), who won the Nobel Prize for literature in 1904.

Places to Visit in Provence

Montélimar (33,000 inhabitants) on the Rhône is famous for its **white nougat**. Above the old town stands the 12th-century **chateau** of Adhémar, from which there is a fine view. To the north, the cooling towers of the Cruas nuclear power plant can be seen. Attractions on Rue Pierre Julien, the main street, include Place du Marché, the 15th-century collegiate church of Ste-Croix and the fascinating Musée de la Miniature in Hôtel Dieu. There is a great view of the town, of Mont Ventoux and the Alpine foothills from the ruins of the chateau of **Rochemaure** across the Rhône.   *Montélimar*

Viviers, located west of the Rhône 11km/7mi south of Montélimar, has been a bishopric since the 5th century. The ecclesiastical precinct on its rocky plateau is dominated by the **cathedral of St-Vincent** (12th–15th centuries). Its notable characteristics include a choir with Flamboyant vaulting (c1500) and Gobelin tapestries. There is a wonderful view from the terrace, taking in Mont Ventoux and the Rhône valley. The free-standing bell tower was once part of the town's defences (12th–14th centuries). In the lower town, apart from Maison des Chevaliers (1546), there are several other charming houses to be seen on Grande Rue. The town hall and the Hôtel de Roqueplane, the episcopal palace (both 18th century) are both on Place Latrau.   *Viviers*

The Tricastin, the hill country to the east of the Rhône valley, is famed for its **truffles**. At its northwest corner, Grignan (1300 inhabitants) clusters around an imposing 16th-century chateau, from the terrace of which there is a fine view. This was home to the famous correspondent **Madame de Sévigné**, who also died here in 1696. She is buried in the church of St-Sauveur (1539).   *Grignan*

St-Paul-Trois-Châteaux 16km/10mi southwest in St-Paul-Trois-Châteaux (the name is a corruption of »Tricastin«, there are no chateaux here), the cathedral (11th–12th centuries) is an impressive of example of Provencal Romanesque. The building with the tourist office also has a **truffle museum**. The pretty wine-making village of St-Restitut nearby is another good place to visit.

Valréas 10km/6mi east of Grignan, Valréas (9400 inhabitants) was once the capital of the papal lands of **Venaissin**. The pretty little town is encircled by a boulevard, which follows the line of the old fortifications. Its most notable features are the Hotel de Ville (15th–18th centuries) and the 12th-century church of Notre-Dame-de-Nazareth with its imposing south portal. On 23 June a huge **St John's Eve festival** is celebrated.

Nyons Famed for its **olives and truffles**, the old town of Nyons (6700 inhabitants) lies 14km/9mi east of Valréas at the end of the narrow Eygues valley. Sheltered by mountains, it has its own microclimate, in which even olive trees, which are highly susceptible to cold, can thrive. From the arcade-lined Place du Dr. Bourdongle, take the Rue de la Résistance (with its 14th-century buildings) to the early Gothic church of St-Vincent and the local museum. From there climb the hill of Calvary, topped by the 13th-century Tour Randonne, in which there is a bizarre neo-Gothic chapel (1863). Beneath it Rue des Grands Forts runs into a covered stretch through a large gate, a remnant of an old castle. A 14th-century packhorse bridge spanning 40m/130ft crosses the Eygues. Next to it are the Vieux Moulins, olive oil mills from the 18th–19th centu-

Roman excavations in Vaison

ries, which are still in use today. At the foot of Mont Ventoux is the **★ Vaison-la-Romaine** lively little town of Vaison-la-Romaine (5600 inhabitants), noted for its **Roman remains**. Former capital of the Celtic Vocontii tribe, it was declared an »allied city« in 58 BC and as of 30 BC it was rebuilt with a luxurious new town plan. Roman districts extend to both sides of the main square. The Quartier de Puymin in the east has an interesting museum and a theatre (1st century AD), while the Quartier de la Villasse to the west has shopping streets, baths and remains of foundation walls with mosaics. The cathedral of Notre-Dame was built in **★ Notre-Dame ▶** the 11th–12th centuries, expanding a large Merovingian church. Take a look at of the pre-Romanesque altar and the cloister (12th century). At the northwestern edge of town, the chapel of St-Quénin has a three-sided Romanesque choir, also from the 12th century. Heading south of the main square, the shopping street, Grande-Rue, leads to the River Ouvèze, spanned by a massive Roman bridge. From there, ascend to the **upper town**, which originated in the 14th century and developed in the shelter of a 12th-century castle belonging to the counts of Toulouse. The **castle ruins** stand on a rocky plateau from which there is a great view as far as Mont Ventoux.

◀ Upper town

Mont Ventoux (Provencal: »ventour«, meaning »windy mountain«) is a limestone ridge towering as high as 1909m/6263ft. The mistral blows particularly fiercely on the mountain but, even in its absence, the slopes are 10–20 C colder than in the valley. As of the 16th century its trees were cut down to provide timber for the wharves of Toulon, so that the peak is now utterly barren and, with its limestone geology, also dazzlingly white. To explore the mountain it is advisable to wake up early on a summer morning before any clouds have formed. In July–Aug or at weekends it gets very busy. For anyone interested in Alpine flora, though, the first fortnight in July is a fascinating time of year. The peak was conquered by **Petrarca** in 1336 and nowadays is home to an observatory and radio antennae. On clear days, there is a magnificent **view** of Provence as far as the Alps and the Pyrenees. To return to Vaison la Romaine, descend the southern flank of the mountain via Bédoin and Le Barroux to **Beaumes-de-Venise**, famed for its eminent red and rosé wines and for its vin doux naturel. The route continues around the Dentelles de Montmirail (»the lace peaks«), a rugged limestone massif and a popular place for walkers and climbers. Passing the 12th-century chapel of Notre-Dame-d'Aubune, the road leads through the renowned wine-growing area of Vacqueyras and Gigondas (red wines), Sablet, Seguret (where there is a fine view from the castle ruins) and Rasteau (sweet wine).

✳ ✳
Mont Ventoux

◀ Tour

✳
Dentelles de Montmirail

**Vacqueyras
Gigondas**

In order to continue from Mont Ventoux to Carpentras, take the route via Sault in the east, which is lined with **lavender fields**, then continue on the D 942 through the picturesque Gorges de la Nesque. At the exit from the gorge, there is an impressive view of the intensively farmed plain around Carpentras.

✳
Gorges de la Nesque

The Ardèche, Pont-St-Esprit and Châteauneuf-du-Pape are all described in the section on ▶Orange.

Orange

Carpentras (27,000 inhabitants), 20km/12mi southeast of Orange, is where the agricultural wares of the Auzon plain are brought to market and refined. Friday is market day. The high season for truffles is between November and March. From 1320 to 1791 Carpentras was capital of the papal domain, the **Comtat Venaissin**, previously the

Carpentras

Along with Le Thoronet and Silvacane, Sénanque is one of a triad of impressive Cistercian monasteries in Provence

headquarters of Pope Clement V. From 1342 its important Jewish community was granted protection (i.e. they paid protection money) by the popes. In the centre stands the Gothic cathedral of St-Siffrein (1405–1519). Its south doorway, late Gothic Flamboyant in style, is known as the **Porte Juive** (Jews' entrance, 1480); it was the means by which Jewish converts could enter to be baptized. Among the attractions inside are some panel paintings by Mignard and Parrocel and the church treasury; it possesses a horse bridle said to have been donated by Constantine the Great and allegedly containing a nail from the True Cross. On the northern side of the church are some remains of a Romanesque cathedral and a Roman triumphal arch (1st century AD) with pictures of prisoners. Adjoining St-Siffrein to the north, the Palais de Justice was formerly an episcopal palace (1640, ostentatious rooms). Rue d'Inguimbert leads from there to **France's oldest synagogue** (1367, rebuilt 1741–43). In the west of the old town are the famous Bibliothèque Inguimbertine (1745), the Musée Comtadin (folklore) and the Musée Duplessis (paintings). It is planned that the imposing **Hôtel Dieu** (*c*1750) in the south of town (tourist office) will become a cultural centre. It already has a brilliant old apothecary with faiences from Moustiers on view. The **Art-Deco lido** (Piscine couverte, 1930) is also worth visiting.

Pernes-les-Fontaines
The idyllic medieval township of Pernes-les-Fontaines (10,000 inhabitants), 6km/4mi south of Carpentras, was the capital of the Comtat Venaissin from 968 to 1320. It takes pride in its **36 fountains**. The area by the River Nesque with the 16th-century Porte Notre-Dame, the bridge and the chapel of Notre-Dames-des-Graces is very pretty.

The Gothic frescoes of battle scenes in the Tour Ferrande are interesting (they probably show Charles of Anjou against the Hohenstaufen kings in around 1285; bookings at the tourist office).

11km/7mi further south is the lively little town of L'Isle-sur-la-Sorgue (15,500 inhabitants), where the Sorgue splits into **several channels**. A series of water wheels once provided power for industry (wool, silk, paper and tanners' mills) and six of them have survived to the present day. Baroque works of art from five different monasteries were assembled in the 17th-century church of Notre-Dame-des-Anges during the French Revolution. There are lots of antique shops and a big, attractive market on Sundays (food and bric-a-brac).

L'Isle-sur-la-Sorgue

The key attraction in the little village of Fontaine-de-Vaucluse (600 inhabitants), 7km/4mi east of l'Isle, is the river Sorgue itself. The village gets overrun with crowds in the summer. The river issues forth from beneath a 200m/650ft cliff at the end of the valley (»vallis clausa«) and, particularly when the waters are high, especially in spring, it bubbles with crystal-clear water. A cave museum, a paper mill, a museum of law and the impressive »Musée d'Histoire 1939–1945« (closed Tue) all line up along the route between the village and the river's source. The village itself, overlooked by the ruin of a chateau that once belonged to the bishops of Cavaillon, was for 16 years a retreat for the Italian humanist and poet **Francesco Petrarca** (1304–74). A column on Place de la Colonne and a museum recall him. The tomb of St Véran, bishop of Cavaillon in the 6th century, is to be found in the crypt of the 11th-century Romanesque church of St-Véran.

✹ **Fontaine-de-Vaucluse**

► Avignon

Avignon

The chic and exemplary mountain village of Gordes (2000 inhabitants) lies just 5km/3mi east of Fontaine de Vaucluse as the crow flies (25km/16mi by road) at the edge of the Plateau de Vaucluse. At one stage it was almost abandoned, until it was discovered by both authentic and »wannabe« artists. Right at the top of the village is a **Renaissance chateau** (1525) with a wonderful fireplace, along with the unassuming Musée Pol Mara. 3km/2mi south is an open-air museum, **Village des Bories**. Bories are windowless dry-stone cabins. This building technique dates back to the Stone Age but its use continued in Provence until the early 20th century.

✹ **Gordes**

Village des Bories

Very much off the beaten track, 4km/2.5mi north of Gordes, is the important Cistercian abbey of Sénanque, which was established in 1148 and has once again been inhabited by Cistercian monks since 1988. Some of the monastery buildings (c1180–1210) and the church (started 1160) are open to the public. The unadorned frugality and

✹ **Sénanque**

clear lines of the Romanesque buildings reflect the uncompromising spirituality and sober lifestyle of the Cistercians. In high summer, the blooming lavender makes the sight particularly attractive.

✱
Roussillon

Roussillon (1200 inhabitants) is prettily situated 10km/6mi east of Gordes on a plateau above the Imergue valley. It is famous as the **Town of Ochre**. The whole village is fashioned from strikingly coloured ochre, which was formerly quarried here in an extremely high quality form. There is a great view from the chateau at the north of the village. Throughout the surrounding countryside there is an impressive amount of information about ochre itself. Be careful about getting too close – ochre can very easily leave bright and intense stains.

Cavaillon

The provincial town of (25,000 inhabitants), 27km/17mi southeast of Avignon, has the biggest fruit and vegetable market in southern France. It is famed for its **melons**. Take a look at the 12th-century Romanesque church of St-Véran with its pretty cloister, the wonderful **synagogue** (Rococo, 1772), where there is a small museum, and the Musée de l'Hôtel Dieu (local archaeology). At the western edge of the town it is possible to see a small arch dedicated to the city's founder, Cabellio. Behind it, from the Colline St-Jacques, there is a good view.

✱
Montagne du Lubéron

A mountain range decked with oak and beech forests and garrigue vegetation stretches east of Cavaillon. The highest point at Mourre Nègre is at 1125m/3691ft. The range is divided into Petit Lubéron and Grand Lubéron by the Combe de Lourmarin. Most of it is included in the Parc Naturel Régional du Lubéron, which is very popular with ramblers.The beautifully situated **Oppède le Vieux** has

Petit Lubéron ►

gained a whole new population of artists and novelists. Its ruined castle was once owned by Baron Maynier d'Oppède, who ordered the massacre of more than 2000 Waldensians from 24 villages in 1545. Other beautifully located villages include **Ménerbes** (familiar from the novels of Peter Mayle), **Lacoste**, whose ruined chateau was once owned by the Marquis de Sade, and **Bonnieux**, where 15th-century panel paintings by a German master can be seen in the lower church. Bonnieux also features a bakery museum and, above all, the Eglise Vieille (12th–15th centuries), from the terrace of which there

Grand Lubéron ►

is an expansive view as far as Mont Ventoux. The narrow **Combe de Lourmarin** needs to be negotiated to get to **Lourmarin**, where there is a large Renaissance chateau (15th–16th centuries, now owned by the Academy of Art in Aix). Albert Camus († 1960) is buried in the cemetery here. A road via **Ansouis** with its fine chateau (12th–17th centuries) and La Tour d'Aigues, with the ruins of its own Renaissance chateau, leads right over the Grand Lubéron to Apt; the route passes Castellet (and its lavender distilleries) and Auribeau, the starting point for ascents of **Mourre Nègre** (3–4 hours there and back).

The lower church of Bonnieux in enchanting Lubéron

Apt (11,200 inhabitants) is known for its candied fruits. The former cathedral of St-Anne (12th–17th centuries) has two crypts one on top of the other (the lower one probably dating back to Merovingian times). Chapelle St-Anne was built as of 1662 after Anne of Austria, Louis XIII's wife, made a pilgrimage to visit the relics of her saintly namesake in order to pray for children. Those relics and several others are still revered here. Other interesting places include the archaeological museum and the museum of the Lubéron national park. 10km/6mi northeast of there at Rustrel, it is still possible to see ochre-bearing rocks (»Colorado de Rustrel«).

Silvacane abbey, south of the Montagne du Lubéron near La Roque Anthéron, was established in 1144 to care for travellers at a busy intersection and represents the most impressive example of **Cistercian Romanesque in Provence** (basilica 1175–1230, dormitory 1210–30, cloister late 13th century; the delightful refectory was redesigned in 1420).

The pretty town of Salon de Provence (38,000 inhabitants), north of the Etang de Berre, was the birthplace of Adam de Craponne (1527–76), the initiator of the important canal system between the Durance and the Rhône. The region known as Crau (▶Camargue) extends to the west. Known in Roman times as Castrum Salonense, the town was reconstructed under Charlemagne after the salt marshes were drained. At the **Château de l'Empéri** (10th–15th centuries), one of the biggest fortresses in Provence, it is worth taking a look at the 12th-century chapel of St-Cathérine and the military museum there. To the east of the chateau is the 13th-century church of St-Michel, where the Romanesque portal has an unusual tympanum composed of relief panels (12th century). To the northeast are the

Porte d'Horloge (17th century) in Salon

town hall (1655) and the Porte Bourg-Neuf, part of the 13th-century fortifications. There is a museum in a house that was once home to the astrologer **Nostradamus** (Michel de Nostredame, 1503–66), who lived here as of 1547. He is buried in the church of St-Laurent (14th–15th centuries), a fine example of Provencal Gothic.

Manosque, on the mid-section of the River Durance, is a centre for high-tech industry and has grown from 5000 inhabitants in the 1960s to 20,000 today. Thanks to the noted writer **Jean Giono** (1895–1970), who was born here and spent much of this life in the town, much of Manosque's old legacy has been retained. Centre Giono near the imposing Porte Saunerie gate, which guards the southern entrance to the old town, recalls him. Other things to see include the churches of St-Sauveur (13th–14th centuries, with a tower extension from 1725) and Notre-Dame-de-Romigier (originally 10th century, where a 4th–5th-century sarcophagus made of Carrara marble is used as an altar). Take a look, too, at the 17th-century Hôtel de Ville. On Saturday mornings a market is held on Place du Terreau. The company l'Occitane refines lavender oil here into perfume essence, soap and other products.

Sauvan   The **Château de Sauvan**, about 6km/4mi south of Forcalquier, was built in 1719–29 and is one of the most beautiful classical buildings in Provence (»Trianon de Provence«, guided tours July–Aug Sun–Fri 3.30pm, April–June and Sept–mid Nov Thu and Sun, Feb–March Sun).

★   Ganagobie   About 27km/17mi northeast of Manosque, 350m/1150ft over the Durance, is the **Abbaye de Ganagobie**, built by monks from Cluny in the 12th century and reoccupied by Benedictines since 1897. One unusual feature of the Romanesque/early Gothic complex is its doorway, which has decoration in the form of rounded teeth. The pointed barrel vaulting in the nave and the double aisled transept are uncommon too. The **floor mosaic** (1135–70) is exquisite. There are also great views to the east and west. Further north across the Durance are the »Pénitents des Mées«, pudding stone cliffs some 100m/330ft high, which erosion has carved into picturesque shapes.

✳ ✳
◄ Floor mosaic

Thoronet Abbey (22km/14mi southwest of Draguignan) is the oldest of the three **Cistercian monasteries** in Provence (established in 1136, built in 1160–90). The church with its two side aisles and five apses is characterized by its plain but dignified architecture. Among the abbey buildings, the impressive cloister and the chapter hall are the highlights. The capitals that top the columns of the latter are the only decorations in the entire abbey. Masses with Gregorian chanting are held every Sunday at 12 noon and a festival, the »Rencontres de Musique Médiévale«, takes place in the second half of July.

✳
Le Thoronet

This typical Provence village north of Le Thoronet (6km/4mi as the crow flies, 20km/12mi by road) is listed as a protected site. It possesses a large **chateau** (17th century; large kitchen, furnishings, art) with parkland laid out by Le Nôtre.

✳
Entrecasteaux

The picturesque old town of Draguignan (34,800 inhabitants) nestles around a rock topped by a clock tower. The avenues in the west and south of the old town were built in the 19th century by Baron Haussmann, who had redesigned much of Paris. In the 16th-century **Ursuline convent** the fascinating local museum features exhibits of pottery, furniture and both French and Flemish painters (including Rembrandt, Van Loo, Frans Hals). A stone's throw to the east is the Musée des Arts et Traditions de Moyenne Provence (folklore, mainly agriculture and crafts.)

Draguignan

The river Verdon is 175km/190mi long and is the most important tributary of the Durance. Between Castellane and Lac de Ste-Croix it flows through **awe-inspiring gorges**. For 21km/13mi of its length it has carved chasms up to 700m/2300ft high but as little as 6m/20ft wide through limestone banks rich in fossils. The river attracts canoeists, the cliffs are a magnet for climbers, and walking through the canyon is a real experience. The **Sentier Martel** footpath from the Châlet de la Maline to Point Sublime can be covered in 4 hours, but is only suited to those who are very fit. Mountain footwear, torches and supplies of water are all essential. Taxis plying between La Palud, the Auberge du Point Sublime and La Maline return tired walkers to their cars. The roads are very busy in summer so tours are best undertaken early in the morning or in early evening.Good places to start a tour covering some 150km/93mi would be either Moustiers or Castellane. From Castellane go southwest on the D 952, which follows the twists and turns of the river. At Pont de Soleils turn left on-

✳ ✳
Grand Canyon du Verdon

◄ Tour

to the D 955 and later right onto the D 90 (past Trigance) and the D 71. The **Balcons de la Mescla** offer a fabulous view of the confluence with the river Artuby some 250m/800ft below. Continue by crossing the Pont d'Artuby (popular with bungee jumpers) to the Falaises des Cavaliers (there is a viewing platform next to the restaurant). The road then follows the raging river in a canyon 400m/1300ft deep. After rounding the rock bowl of Cirque de Vaumale and broaching the 964m/3162ft summit of the Col d'Illoire the road descends to the shimmering turquoise Lac de Ste-Croix reservoir, a popular place for holidaymakers and water sports enthusiasts. To get back to Moustiers along the north bank of the Verdon, take the D 952 past Belvédère de Galetas and over the Col d'Ayens (1032m/3386ft) to La Palud-sur-Verdon. Those wishing to take in a 23km/14mi loop of the Route des Crêtes should turn right a little later onto the D 23 (the loop should be followed in a clockwise direction to return to Palud). Continue along the D 952, which eventually passes the place with what is probably the most beautiful view of all, **Point Sublime** (about 10 minutes on foot from the car park). To complete the tour, do not fail to drive up to the village of **Rougon**.

Moustiers-Sainte-Marie

The pretty village of Moustiers-Sainte-Marie (600 inhabitants) is impressively situated in front of a rocky cliff. The pilgrimage church of Notre-Dame-de-Beauvoir (12th–16th centuries) nestles in a gap in the cliff. In 1249 a crusader, happy to be returning, ran a 227m/248yd-long **chain with a gilded star** across this gap. After 20 minutes' climb, the way of the cross leads up to a fantastic view. Production of the gorgeous **faience pottery**, for which the spot is fa-

Grand Canyon du Verdon Map

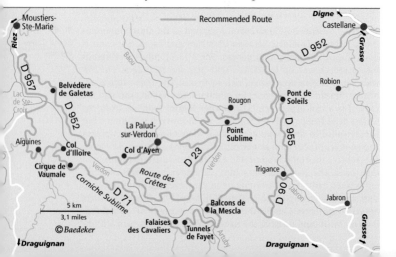

Straight from the geology textbook: Rocher de Baume in Sisteron (see below)

mous, was introduced in 1679 from Faenza in Italy (museum, closed Tue). Notre-Dame church has a sturdy tower in Lombard Romanesque, a 12th-century Romanesque nave and a 14th-century Gothic choir with seating from the 16th–18th centuries, which was added at a crooked angle. The traditional local festival takes places between 31 August and 8 September. The »Les Santons« restaurant (Place de l'Eglise, tel. 04 92 74 66 48, closed Tue, in July–Aug also closed Mon) is excellent.

A 325km/200mi-long road taking in a beautiful and varied landscape with a summit at Col Bayard (1248m/4094ft), north of Gap, the Route Napoléon runs from Cannes via Grasse, Castellane, Digne, Sisteron and Gap to Grenoble. It follows the route Napoleon took after he landed in Golfe Juan on 1 March 1815 after leaving Elba (signposted with small eagles).

★ Route Napoléon

The thermal spa of Digne (16,700 inhabitants) is in the foothills of the Alps. It is the capital of the Alpes-de-Haute-Provence département and centre of the Réserve Géologique de Haute-Provence (famous fossil discoveries, especially around Barles and Barrème). The pretty old town with its narrow alleys and stairways is clustered around the hill upon which the **cathedral of St-Jérôme** stands (1490, rebuilt in neo-Gothic style in 1851). To the north on Blvd. Gassendi is the Musée de Digne (natural history, 17th-century Italian and Flemish paintings, folklore). The Romanesque cathedral of Notre-Dame-du-Bourg (1200–1330) has the remains of some 14th–16th-century murals and a Merovingian altar in the crypt (both 5th century). Along the road to Nice is the house, now a museum, where Asian explorer **Alexandra David-Néel** (1868–1969) lived from 1927. 2km/1.5mi north of the town is the Centre de Géologie with its museum (15 minutes' walk from the car park, great view).

Digne-les-Bains

This small town (6900 inhabitants) is gloriously located where the river Durance cuts through the »Gateway to Provence« (or to Dauphiny). Since Roman times it has been an important transport hub

★ Sisteron

and a location of strategic importance. There is a spectacular view from the citadel (12th–16th centuries) of the **Rocher de la Baume** and Dauphiny. Interesting places in the old town include the **cathedral of Notre-Dame-des-Pommiers** (1160–1220) with altar paintings by Mignard (1643), Van Loo, Coypel and others, narrow streets (»andrônes«) with pretty houses from the 16th–18th centuries and towers from the town walls (*c*1370). East of the cathedral, the modern Musée Terre & Temps is housed in an old Visitationist convent. It covers the measurement of time and time zones on Earth.

Mercantour and Ubaye

The mountain ranges that rise beyond Haute-Provence, the Alpes de Haute-Provence and the northern part of the Maritime Alps enclose the countryside of Mercantour and Ubaye. Inland from Nice the land ascends to the Massif du Mercantour (▶ Côte-d'Azur). The Ubaye, valley of the eponymous Durance tributary, forms the northern edge of Mercantour and thus of the Provencal Alps. The splendid mountain terrain between the upper reaches of the Verdon and the Italian border is peppered with impressive gorges (Gorges de Daluis, du Cians, de la Vésubie) and breathtaking passes: Col d'Allos (2240m/7349ft), **Col de la Cayolle** (2326m/7631ft) and **Col de la Bonette**, at 2802m/9193ft the highest pass in the Alps. The area is also of interest for its architecture and artistic history, as it was influenced by Italian-Alpine culture. Primarily, there are numerous Romanesque churches from the 11th–14th centuries, which were built by architects and craftsmen from Lombardy.

Entrevaux

This fortified village on the middle section of the Var (800 inhabitants) is overlooked by a spectacular rocky outcrop topped by a **fortress**, which Vauban erected in 1692–1706. The town is entered via the Porte Royale (1658–90) and its attractions include the magnificent cathedral (1627) with its high altar painting and choir seating from the 16th century.

Colmars

This village (360 inhabitants) on the upper reaches of the Verdon bordered Savoy from the Middle Ages. Its walls from 1528 and the **Forts de Savoie and de Francs** (1695) testify to this fact. The church is in early Gothic style but dates from the 16th–17th centuries. In the second week of August there is a medieval festival, and in mid-October sheep pass through the village as they are taken down from the summer pasture.

Barcelonnette

Barcelonnette (2900 inhabitants), capital of the Ubaye, is known for its magnificent villas, which were built in the years following 1880 for the **Mexicains**, valley dwellers who had emigrated to Mexico and become rich before returning to their homeland. They can mostly be seen on Av. de la Libération, Av. des Trois-Frères-Arnaud and Av. Porfirio-Diaz. The centre of the village is the lively Place Manuel, adorned by the 15th-century Tour Cardinalis. For Col de Vars see ▶p.399.

✦ ✦ Pyrenees · Les Pyrénées

The Pyrenees, the mountains that divide France and Spain, offer spectacular scenery from the verdant foothills with their idyllic valleys to the dramatic wilderness of the rocky massifs. This is a paradise for lovers of nature and sport enthusiasts.

The Pyrenees mountain range is 80–130km/50–80mi wide and stretches for a length of some 430km/267mi between the Atlantic and the Mediterranean. Some of its peaks rise as high as 3400m/11,000ft. The border with Spain mostly runs along the main ridge, such that only a third of the range belongs to France. Due to geological and climatic conditions, the French side, unlike the Spanish portion, gets plenty of water, and there are brooks and lakes all over the place. Hikers and climbers are supremely well catered for here. The long-distance hiking path GR 10 runs the entire length of the Pyrenees. There is also a whole range of resorts and winter sports venues – often with a lengthy tradition. Plenty of reason, then, to make the long journey.

Scenery

Due to the more southerly location of the range, the sun reaches a similar degree of intensity a good month earlier than in the Alps. That means that during the winter sports season in the Pyrenees, January is much like February would be in the Alps. If skiing is not the reason for your visit, then mid-May is when conditions start to get very pleasant, even though there can still be some snow in the higher reaches. The summer months of July and August are best avoided, partly because this coincides with the holiday season in

Climate and when to go

Highlights Pyrenees

Céret
Small town with some great art
▶ page 718

Pic du Canigou
Classic walks over the »Pyramid of the Pyrenees«
▶ page 720

Grotte de Niaux
Stone-Age paintings in all their splendour
▶ page 722

St-Bertrand-de-Comminges
Important relics of the Middle Ages and of the Romans
▶ page 723

Pic du Midi de Bigorre
The most marvellous view in the Pyrenees
▶ page 725

Pau
Former capital of Béarn and birthplace of Henri IV
▶ page 726

St-Jean-Pied-de-Port
Picturesque stop on the Way of St James at the crossing point to Roncesvalles
▶ page 729

Espelette
A typical Basque village
▶ page 730

▶ VISITING PYRENEES

INFORMATION

CRT Languedoc-Roussillon
CS 79507, F-34960 Montpellier Cedex
Tel. 04 67 20 02 20
www.sunfrance.com

CRT Aquitaine
23 Parvis des Chartrons
F-33074 Bordeaux Cedex
Tel. 05 56 01 70 00, fax 05 56 01 70 07
www.tourisme-aquitaine.fr

CRT Midi-Pyrenees
54 Boulevard-de-l'Embouchure
F-31000 Toulouse
Tel. 05 61 13 55 48, fax 05 61 47 17 16
www.tourisme-midi-pyrenees.com

WHERE TO EAT
▶ Moderate
Pyrénées
Place Royale
F-64000 Pau, Tel. 05 59 27 07 75.
This restaurant is very popular with
the locals and serves delicious local
cuisine. When the weather is fine, it is
possible to eat outdoors. Closed Sun.

Au Temps de la Reine Jeanne
44 Rue Bourg-Vieux, F-64300 Orthez
Tel. 05 59 67 00 76, fax 05 59 69 09 63
Rustic restaurant with good food in
an historic building right opposite the
tourist office.
Also a hotel with 20 tastefully furnished rooms (www.reine-jeanne.fr).

▶ Inexpensive
Euzkadi
Rue Principale, F-64250 Espelette
Tel. 05 59 93 91 88, fax 05 59 93 90 19
This typically Basque establishment in
the centre of town is one of the best
places to go to taste the velvety sweet
savour of piments d'espelette. Reservations are essential. There is also

affordable accommodation available
(the rooms at the rear are quieter).

WHERE TO STAY
▶ Mid-range / luxury
La Terrasse au Soleil
Route-de-Fontfrède, F-66400 Céret
Tel. 04 68 87 01 94, fax 04 68 87 39 24
www.terrasse-au-soleil.com
open March–Oct.
Old Catalan house in a beautiful
location with a view of the Roussillon
and the Pic du Canigou. Elegant,
sometimes very large rooms with a
comfortable atmosphere. Pool, golf
and the La Cérisaie restaurant with its
lovely terrace (moderately priced).

Grand Hôtel Vignemale
F-65120 Gavarnie, tel. 05 62 92 40 00
www.hotel-vignemale.com
Open May–Oct. Quality mountain
hotel dating from 1907, just off the
main street with a fantastic view into
the rocky crater. Very nice terrace.

▶ Budget / mid-range
Hôtel Montpensier
36 Rue Montpensier, F-64000 Pau
Tel. 05 59 27 42 72, fax 05 59 27 70 95
www.hotel-montpensier-pau.com
Pretty, old English building, all in
dainty pink and possessed of old-
fashioned charm. Good level of
comfort at moderate prices.

▶ Budget
Biker's Paradise
49 Route de Ria, F-66500 Prades
http://bikers-paradise.de, tel. 04 68 05
36 79. This holiday guest house, run
by a German couple, is not just for
bikers. Beautifully situated at the foot
of the Pyrenees with a wonderful
view. Nice apartments and studios,
parking, swimming pool.

The Cirque de Gavarnie is the great natural wonder of the central Pyrenees

France – and the Pyrenees are a very popular place for a holiday – but also because the heat that far south can be uncomfortable. September and October are also very favourable times of year to travel.

Two passes cut deep through the range, separating it into the Eastern Pyrenees (Pyrénées Orientales), Central Pyrenees (Pyrénées Centrales) and Western Pyrenees (Pyrénées Occidentales, a.k.a. the Pyrénées Basques or Pyrénées Atlantiques). The Eastern Pyrenees rise up steeply from the Mediterranean Sea (►Côte Vermeille) to the Col de Perche (1610m/5282ft) and Col de Puymorens (1915m/6283ft). The highest peak in the region is Puigmal (2912m/9554ft) on the Spanish side. The valley of the Tech, which leads southwest into the mountains, separates the Albères range in the south from the Canigou Massif (2785m/9137ft). The Central Pyrenees form a self-contained ridge between Col de Puymorens and Col du Somport (1631m/5351ft) and reach their highest altitude amid the Maladeta group in Spain (Pico de Aneto, 3404m/11,168ft). The Western Pyrenees resemble some of the mountain ranges further north, dominated by deciduous forests and mountain pasture. They descend gently from Pic d'Anie (2504m/8215ft) through the Basque country to the shores of the Atlantic (►Côte Basque). **Structure**

In spite of the serious transport difficulties, the Pyrenees never formed a truly impenetrable barrier. The Basque country, Navarre **History** and Catalonia all included regions on both the north and south sides of the mountains. The present frontier between France and Spain was primarily set by the Peace of the Pyrenees, signed in 1659. Prehistoric settlement of the Pyrenean foothills has been demonstrated by various discoveries in cave systems such as at Tautavel (approx. 450,000 years old) and Aurignac, which has given its name to the early Stone Age Aurignacian period. In the 2nd millennium BC, the Ligurians settled the Pyrenean foothills, and the Iberians followed in the 6th century BC. From about 125 BC southwestern France as far as the Pyrenees was conquered by the Romans. The city of Lugdunum Convenarum (St-Bertrand-de-Comminges), founded in 72 BC, quickly became an important centre. In the 6th century AD the Basques, who do not belong the Indo-European group of peoples and are of unknown origin, spread over the mountains into Aquitaine. In around 720 the Arabs crossed over the Pyrenees, with Charlemagne crossing in the opposite direction in 778. The heavy losses incurred during the return from that campaign inspired the old French *Song of Roland*.

Historic landscape

The French **Basque country** occupies the western part of the French département of Pyrénées-Atlantiques (with its capital at Pau). The eastern part corresponds to the former Merovingian county of **Béarn**, which became part of Gascony in the 7th century before being amalgamated with Foix and Navarre in modern-day Spain in 1290. Adjoining it to the east is the county of **Bigorre**, which was independent from the 9th century to the end of the 13th, when it was taken over by the counts of Foix (département Hautes-Pyrénées, capital Tarbes). Further still to the east, the former county of **Foix** itself (département Ariège, capital Foix) came under the French crown in 1589 along with Béarn and the northern part of Navarre, having been the homeland of Henri IV who was born in Pau. The most easterly part of the Pyrenees was occupied by the county of **Roussillon**, which had been part of Spain from the 12th century until the Peace of the Pyrenees of 1659, but now makes up the département Pyrénées-Orientales with a capital at ►Perpignan.

Places to Visit in the Eastern Pyrenees

Céret

The pleasant little town of Céret (7300 inhabitants), situated at the entrance to the Tech valley, became well known thanks to the artists drawn to the spot by Catalan sculptor Manolo Hugué (1872–1945), including Gris, Braque, Picasso and Chagall. The Musée d'Art Moderne, founded in 1950, therefore possesses an outstanding collection of classical modern works –including **53 by Picasso alone** (open 15 July–15 Sept 10am–7pm, otherwise till 6pm; Oct–15 Feb closed Tue). The 14th-century Vieux Pont, northwest of the town, crosses the river Tech with a span of 45m/49yd. There is a lovely view from the bridge to Canigou in the west and the Albères in the south. Céret's **festival season** is not to be missed. At the end of May there

★ ★
Musée d'Art Moderne ►

is a great cherry festival, mid-July sees several days of »Féria« with bullfighting, and the Festival de la Sardane takes place around 20 July.

The **thermal spa health resort** of Amélie-les-Bains (3400 inhabitants), named after the wife of »citizen king« Louis-Philippe, enjoys a particularly mild and sunny climate. Its sulphurous springs were already in use in Roman times. The Thermes Romains has some surviving remains of the Roman baths. Many visitors come to the Masquerade on Shrove Tuesday, to the Blessing of the Mules on 25 June and to the International Folk Festival in the second week of August. The Catalan village of **Palalda** is very pretty, with its 10th-century church, a museum of folklore and another covering the history of the post office. A day trip out to the Gorges de Mondony is to be recommended, as is the ascent of the Roc de France (1450m/4757ft; 3 hours from Montalba).

Amélie-les-Bains

Mondony valley, Roc de France

Further up the Vallespir – as the Tech valley is also known – lies Arles-sur-Tech (2800 inhabitants) where there is an abbey founded in 900. The main entrance of the 11th-century church of Ste-Marie, which unusually opens to the east, has a notable tympanum. To the left of the main entrance there is a sarcophagus (4th century) out of which water flows, a phenomenon that some take to be a miracle (www.pseudo-sciences.org). To the northwest Puig de l'Estelle towers 1778m/5833ft over Arles. Iron ore is mined on the mountain's southern slopes. A little further upstream along the D 115 there is a right turn leading into the Gorges de la Fou, a very narrow canyon with walls up to 100m/330ft high.

Arles-sur-Tech

★
Gorges de la Fou

The fortified Catalan town of Prats-de-Mollo (1100 inhabitants, 745m/2444ft) sits at the head of the valley. Entered via the Porte de France, its narrow streets and stairways then lead up to the 17th-century church of Ste-Juste (tower 13th century). Its gilded high altar is most impressive and on the right-hand wall there is a votive offering made from the rib of a whale. The village is overlooked by Fort Lagarde (1692).

Prats-de-Mollo

The D 618 takes a winding route with many a hairpin bend from Amélie up to Col Xatard (752m/2467ft), where there is a tremendous view from Canigou to the sea. 17km/11mi further is the remote priory of **Serrabone** (11th–12th centuries), outside a frugal building of dark slate, but inside adorned with some fabulous sculpture and a superb rood screen made of pink marble.

The small town of **Prades** (5800 inhabitants) at the foot of Mount Canigou is also dominated by pink marble in the façades of its buildings. The 17th-century church of St-Pierre has a 12th-century Lombard-Romanesque bell tower and a magnificent altarpiece (1696–99) by Catalonia's Josep Sunyer. Another important building in terms of

Col Xatard

★
Prieuré de Serrabone

art and the history of the church is the beautifully situated abbey of **St-Michel-de-Cuxa** 3km/2mi south of Prades, which was formerly the religious hub of Roussillon. After the Revolution it was sold and plundered. In 1889 one of the towers collapsed. The Metropolitan Museum in New York obtained some fragments of the cloisters in 1925 (The Cloisters Museum) but it was possible to use what remained to reconstruct at least half of the building. The tower exhibits Lombard influence, while the pre-Romanesque church (974) possesses a 12th-century pulpit rostrum as in Serrabone. The Visigothic horseshoe arches are a conspicuous feature.

✱
Villefranche-de-Conflent

Squeezed into the narrow valley of the river Têt, Villefranche, **a fortified town founded in 1090** (435m/1427ft, 230 inhabitants), was once a stage on the Way of St James. Previously an outpost of the kingdom of Aragón, after the Peace of the Pyrenees of 1659 the fortifications were extended by Vauban and the mighty **Fort Liberia** was constructed. Within its impressive rectangle of walls there are some lovely houses from the 15th–17th centuries. The two-aisled St-Jacques (12th–13th centuries) boasts a retable by Sunyer (left-hand aisle) and equally notable 15th-century Spanish choir stalls. Ville-

Cerdagne railway

franche is the starting point for the narrow-gauge **train jaune** leading up into the Cerdagne as far as Latour-de-Carol (62km/39mi). The prettiest stretch is between Olette and Mont-Louis.

Corneilla

The 11th-century church of Notre-Dame, with its Lombard bell tower, has an unusual tympanum with the Virgin Mary seated on a throne. To the left of the choir there is a 12th-century Catalonian statue of Our Lady.

Vernet-les-Bains

The pleasant valley of the Cady leads through orchards to Vernet-les-Bains (650m/2132ft, 1500 inhabitants), a small thermal spa at the foot of the Pic du Canigou, the »sacred mountain of the Catalans«,

✱
Pic du Canigou

and the starting point for climbing this magnificent pyramid. There are two main ways to ascend the peak: the first is by car on the road up to the mountain chalet of Mariailles (1718m/3500ft), from where there are gentle but somewhat long paths to the top (8 hours there and back); the second is to use an off-road vehicle or taxi to Châlet des Cortalets, from which it takes 3–4 hours to get to the summit and back. It is also possible to combine the two. The summit is 2784m/9134ft high and there is a **fantastic view** (but only on the sadly rare days of clear weather). On 22–23 June a midsummer festival is celebrated at the peak with a large bonfire, which is lit on 22 June at midnight.

Picturesquely perched on rocks at an elevation of 1094m/3589ft above Casteil, the abbey of **St-Martin-du-Canigou** was built between 997 and 1026 and has two churches. It is accessed on foot from Casteil and the trek talks a good hour there and back.

St-Bertrand-de-Comminges and the basilica of St-Just were of great importance in bygone days

The **Cerdagne** is a protected mountain valley with a mild climate. It plays a major role in history as the nucleus of Catalonia. Its capital **Llivia** is still a Spanish enclave in France. On the eastern edge of the base at an elevation of 1600m/5250ft lies the fortified village of Mont-Louis (200 inhabitants), which has a citadel built in 1681 by Vauban. A **solar power station** built in 1953 provides power to the parish (daily guided tours).

Mont-Louis

This summer and winter resort (1900 inhabitants) was established at an elevation of 1750m/5740ft in the years after 1910. It is considered to be particularly sunny but is otherwise not very attractive. Northeast of the village is the important Ermitage (hermitage) pilgrims' chapel with the »Vierge de l'Invention«, which is revered as being miraculous. The retable (1707) and the »Camaril« in charming Baroque style were both made by Sunyer. Between Odeillo and Via the well-known **solar furnace** of the research centre for solar energy has been in operation since 1969 (visitor centre open daily).

Font-Romeu

One walk worth recommending leads from the mountain village of Dorres (with its hot sulphurous springs) about 15km/9mi to the west to the Ermitage de Belloch (about one and a half hours there and back, although – unfortunately – it is also possible to drive there).

Ermitage de Belloch

►Andorra

Andorra

Places to Visit in the Central Pyrenees

The pass of Col de Puymorens at 1920m/6300ft is one way of getting from the Cerdagne to the valley of the **Ariège**, where the tiny Mérens horses live in a semi-wild state. The other is to use the 4.8km/3mi-long tunnel.

Col de Puymorens

Ax-les-Thermes (1500 inhabitants, 720m/2362ft), a traditional **convalescent spa**, attracts plenty of visitors in both summer and winter. The hot springs, flowing at temperatures of 18–78 C/64–172 F, were already in use in Roman times. During the Middle Ages, crusaders infected with leprosy would seek a cure at the Bassin des Ladres on

Ax-les-Thermes

Place du Breilh. There are plenty of opportunities for hiking in the mountains and cable cars ascend to the **ski pistes** Ax 1400 and Ax 2300.

Tarascon-sur-Ariège
✱
Grotte de Niaux

In the small town of Tarascon-sur-Ariège (3400 inhabitants, 480m/ 1575ft), take a look at the 14th-century tower of St-Michel and the Gothic church with its 14th-century doorway. The Grotte de Niaux, 4km/2.5 to the southwest, has some wonderful **cave paintings** (▶ Baedeker Special p.662; in July–Aug bookings need to be made several days in advance, tel. 05 61 05 10 10). At Surba, northwest of Tarascon, the Parc de la Préhistoire has been opened. In the region there are several other caves, including at Bédeilhac, Lombrives and Vache). Between Tarascon and Foix, the **Pont du Diable** bridge spans the river Ariège.

Foix

Foix, the capital of the former county (9100 inhabitants, 380m/ 1247ft) of the same name, and now of the Ariège department, is beautifully situated in a triangle formed by the Ariège and Arget rivers. It is overlooked by a castle on a mighty cliff (12th–15th centuries; Musée d'Ariège). The last count of Foix was the art-loving but unscrupulous Gaston III (1331–91), who called himself **Phoebus** and wrote the famous *Livre de la Chasse*. Things to see in the abbey church of St-Volusien (12th–15th centuries) include the 15th-century choir and its seating. In the old town with its half-timbered houses the original well can still be seen. It is possible to go rafting along an underground river from Labouiche to the northwest of the town from April to the beginning of November (daily).

Labouiche

✱
Mas d'Azil

The Mas d'Azil cave about 30km/19mi northwest of Foix is a natural tunnel, more than 400m/440yd long and as much as 50m/54yd wide, through which the nascent river Arize and the road both run. In its side galleries there are cave paintings on view and finds have been made from a period ranging from 30,000 to 10,000 BC. The adjoining Musée de la Préhistoire has further exhibits.

St-Girons
St-Lizier

North of St-Girons (7000 inhabitants, Romanesque church with a unique façade), in a picturesque setting on a hill above the river Salat, lies the small town of St-Lizier (1600 inhabitants), which was a bishopric back in the Middle Ages. Remains of the Roman walls and **two cathedrals** can still be seen. The cathedral of St-Lizier in the lower town (10th–15th centuries) has Romanesque frescoes in the choir as well as a lovely gallery and treasury. The upper town meanwhile has the Cathedrale de la Sède (12th–15th centuries) with its 17th-century episcopal palace (now a museum of local folklore).

Aulus-les-Bains

Between the two passes of Col d'Agnes and Col de Latrape (33km/ 21mi southeast of St-Girons) at an altitude of 760m/2500ft lies the small spa and winter sports resort of Aulus les Bains; where four springs provide a mineral water containing calcium and iron. In the vicinity there are some lovely waterfalls such as the Cascade d'Arse [*sic*].

Saint-Bertrand-de-Comminges

The half-abandoned village of St-Bertrand-de-Comminges (230 inhabitants) over the Garonne was highly important in the past. The Roman town of **Lugdunum Convenarum** had up to 60,000 inhabitants and, according to Flavius Josephus, it was to here that Herodes Antipas, the king who ordered the beheading of John the Baptist, was later exiled. Excavations have unearthed the forum, temples, baths and theatres, amongst other buildings. In the Galerie du Trophée, a former Benedictine abbey, statues from the 1st and 2nd centuries are on display. After the city was destroyed by Vandals in 408, it did not re-emerge until the Middle Ages. The **cathedral of Notre-Dame** was started in 1120 and completed in 1352 by Bertrand de Got – later to become Pope Clement V. It features choir stalls from 1535 and a Renaissance organ. In its small Romanesque cloister, which is open to the north, there is a famous column depicting the four Evangelists. In the Musée de Comminges there is an exhibition of Roman finds. Visitors should not miss the causeway to the 11th–12th-century **basilica of St-Just** near Valcabrère. The noteworthy north portal of the basilica stands amid an atmospheric cemetery.

> **!** **Baedeker TIP**
>
> **Festival du Comminges**
> In the months of June and August, classical music concerts are given in Notre-Dame cathedral, the basilica of St-Just, in the collegiate church of St-Gauden as well as the Romanesque church of Martres-Tolosane. Information: tel. 05 61 88 32 00, fax 05 61 97 04 75, www.festival-du-comminges.com.

Bagnères-de-Luchon

This elegant **thermal spa** (3200 inhabitants, 630m/267ft), the most important in the Pyrenees, is in a charming spot at the confluence of the Pique and One rivers, surrounded by mountains rising to more than 3000m/10,000ft. The spa has been known since Roman times – three of its thermal baths have been excavated – and came back into fashion when Marshall Richelieu, nephew of the famous cardinal and governor of Languedoc, came here in 1760. The sulphur-bearing and radioactive springs with water at temperatures from 18–72 °C/64–162 °F are used mainly by people with bronchial complaints. The house where Richelieu stayed houses the tourist office and the Musée du Pays de Luchon. A cable car leads up to the winter sports facilities of Superbagnères at an elevation of 1800m/5900ft.

Around Bagnères

About 5km/3mi west, in the One valley, the 11th-century Romanesque church of St-Aventin with its two bell towers is interesting. To the east of the entrance there is a 12th-century Madonna and Child. Another 2km/1.5mi to the west at Castillon, a small road leads to Granges d'Astau, from where there is a lovely footpath to **Lac d'Oô**

Col du Tourmalet is one of the loveliest passes through the Pyrenees

(1504m/4924ft, two and a half hours there and back). Another recommended day trip starts from Luchon and heads south into the **Vallée du Lys**, at the end of which the highlights are a wild canyon called theCirque d'Enfer (Circle of Hell) and the magnificent Cascade d'Enfer waterfall.

Cirque d'Enfer

Bagnères-de-Bigorre

Bigorre is the name of the country between Lourdes and the frontier. The thermal spa resort of Bagnères-de-Bigorre (9000 inhabitants) is 20km/12mi southeast of Tarbes in the midst of the Adour valley. In its picturesque **old centre** west of the river Adour, the 15th-century Tour des Jacobins is very interesting, as are a lovely half-timbered building on Rue Victor-Hugo, the remains of the St-Jean cloister and the church of St-Vincent (15th–16th centuries). The convalescent park includes a casino, the Musée Salies (Italian, Flemish and French paintings, as well as porcelain) and the hot spa itself. Inside a mill alongside the Adour, the Musée du Vieux Moulin exhibits folk implements and artworks. Southwest of the town is an older convalescent home in the Parc Thermal du Salut. To the west rises the peak of Mont du Bédat (881m/2890ft, one and a half hours there and back), from which there is a great view. About 2km/1.5mi south of the town in the park around Château de Médous there is an entrance to the cave system of Grotte de Médous with its underground river (navigable by pleasure boat) and some splendid stalagmites and stalactites.

Mont du Bédat
Grotte de Médous

Vallee d'Aure

South of Campan (where there is a church and a market hall from the 16th century) a road turns off south to Tourmalet. To the east the **Col d'Aspin** (1489m/4885ft, magnificent view) provides a route to the Vallee d'Aure. St-Lary-Soulan, another thermal health spa, can be used as a starting point for tours of the Néouvielle Massif; in winter it is a ski resort. **Lac d'Oredon** (1849m/6066ft) can be accessed by car so gets very overcrowded in summer. Nevertheless, it does offer some very nice mountain tours (Col d'Aubert, Pic-de-Néouvielle).

Saint-Lary-Soulan

Col du Tourmalet (2115m/6939ft) has become notorious as a stage finish on the Tour de France. The mountain scenery is superb. From winter sports resort La Mongie (1800m/5906ft), cable cars ply up to the **Pic du Midi de Bigorre** (2877m/9439ft), the emblem of the Central Pyrenees. The peak is occupied by an observatory as well as the Musée des Etoiles astronomical museum. The view, though, is breathtaking and that alone is worth the cable car fare.

✶
Col du Tourmalet

✶ ✶
Pic du Midi de Bigorre

Located in the friendly Gave de Pau valley, the resort of Luz-Saint-Sauveur (thermal spa) was made famous in 1860 by Napoleon III and his wife Eugénie. The church was built in the 12th century but in the 14th century it was transformed into a fortress by the Knights of St John. Notable features include a doorway with an image of Christ enthroned and panelling from the 18th century. In the Chapelle Notre-Dame-de-la-Pitié a museum for religious art has been set up. To the south of the town is the Pont Napoléon bridge, built in 1860 and spanning a distance of 47m/51yd.

Luz-St-Sauveur

The valley south of Luz-St-Sauveur leads towards three **magnificent rocky bowls**, the Cirques de Troumouse, d'Estaube and de Gavarnie. The latter is practically a national treasure and was a declared a UNESCO World Heritage Site in 1997. Tours set out from the mountain village of Gavarnie (1365m/4478ft, 200 inhabitants), although it gets very overcrowded in summer. Its 14th-century church also has World Heritage status. The tours involve a one-hour walk or pony trek to Hôtel du Cirque (1570m/5151ft) where 1500m/5000ft-high cliffs enclose a crater of 2km/1.5mi in diameter. Another 30 minutes from there on foot is the Grande Cascade. At 420m/1378ft, this waterfall is the highest in Europe and is fed by an underground stream. As of mid-July an open-air festival is held here. Although much less frequented, the Cirque de Troumouse, a little further to the east, is almost as spectacular (toll road, open from about May–Oct).

✶ ✶
Cirque de Gavarnie

✶
Grande Cascade

✶ ✶
Cirque de Troumouse

A road leads from Gavarnie up to the Col de Tente (2208m/7244ft), from where a hike of medium difficulty leads across the glaciers (4 hours there and back, climbing equipment and suitable clothing required) to the **Brèche de Roland**, a 100m/330ft-deep natural gap in the cliffs located at an altitude of 2807m/9210ft, which according to legend was cut by the hero Roland using the sword Durandal.

✶ ✶
Brèche de Roland

Situated in the fertile valley of the Adour, Tarbes (49,000 inhabitants) was once the capital of Bigorre county, and now fulfils that role for the département of Hautes-Pyrénées. The cathedral of Notre-Dame-de-la-Sède dates from the 12th–14th centuries (furnishings 18th century). The park to the south of it is now occupied by a stud (haras). The beautiful **Jardin Massey** with its 40m/130ft observation tower stretches away to the north, where the cloister of the abbey of St-Sev-

Tarbes

er-de-Rustan (15th–16th centuries, reconstructed) and Musée Massey (paintings, folklore, history of horse breeding in Tarbes) both stand. Tarbes was also the birthplace of Marshall Ferdinand Foch (1851–1929); the house in which he was born is now a museum.

Lourdes

►Lourdes

Argelès-Gazost

The little thermal spa resort of Argelès-Gazost (463m/1519ft, 3200 inhabitants) 13km/8mi south of Lourdes consists of the old village up the hill and the 19th-century health resort amid its pretty parkland. There is a great view from the 17th-century Tour Mendaigne (with a plaque showing what can be seen). On the northern edge of the town the Parc Animalier des Pyrénées provides an opportunity to experience some of the native wildlife species.

✳ **Pic de Pibeste**

Although Pic de Pibeste to the north of Argelès is only 1349m/4426ft high, the **view** is still superb. To the south are the 3000m/10,000ft peaks, including Pic du Midi de Bigorre in the southwest, while Lourdes, Tarbes and Pau are all in the north. The mountain can be climbed starting from Ouzous; it will take four and a half hours for the ascent and the return journey. In St-Savin, 3km/2mi south of Argelès, the church of the Benedictine abbey of St-Savin (11th–12th centuries, fortified in the 14th century) is well worth taking a look at. It was formerly the religious hub of Bigorre. Its Romanesque portal shows Jesus in priests' vestments, which is unusual. The casing of the organ is decorated with masks that roll their eyes while the instrument is being played.

St-Savin

✳ **Cauterets**

Deep in the high Pyrenees, the appealing, old-fashioned health resort of Cauterets (932m/3058ft, 1300 inhabitants) is one of the gateways to the Pyrenees National Park (information at the Maison du Parc). **Thermes César** is a great place to get over all those strenuous sporting exploits. The ski pistes on the high **Lys plateau** (1850–2400m/ 6000–8000ft) are safe for skiing into the spring and can be accessed via cable car. One popular destination for a day trip from the Pont d'Espagne is Lac de Gaube (1725m/5659ft); it can be reached by car or bus or in 45 minutes on foot. Alternatively there is a cable car from which the walk only takes 15 minutes. Continuing further for another two hours to the Refuge des Oulettes brings the awesome Mount **Vignemale** (3298m/10,820ft) into view.

✳ **Lac de Gaube**

Places to Visit in the Western Pyrenees

✳ **Pau**

Pau (207m/679ft, 80,000 inhabitants), capital of the Pyrénées-Atlantiques département, has been a popular resort in summer or winter since its mild climate was discovered by British travellers in the 19th century. The economy of the town, which has even had its own university since 1970, is based on high-tech industries and the natural gas fields around Lacq. In 1464 it became the capital of the county of Béarn. Jeanne d'Albret, the queen of Navarre, who had converted to Protestantism, resided here. Her son was to become Henri IV, king of France, in 1589. The town's proudest feature is the **Boulevard des Pyrénées**, which stretches for 1km/1100yd between Château Beaumont and its park, from where there is a magnificent view (the most conspicuous peak is Pic du Midi d'Ossau). The **chateau** was erected in the 13th–14th centuries as a fortified castle, but was rebuilt in the 16th century as a Renaissance palace. Visitors can view the rooms of Jeanne d'Albret and Henri IV with his tortoiseshell crib as well as the Musée du Château (furniture, tapestries from the 16th–18th centuries, art from the Henri IV era) and the Musée Béarnais (history, folklore). The **art museum** is highly important, with works by Tintoretto, El Greco, Rubens and Degas (closed Tue). Jean-Baptiste Bernadotte came from Pau. Under Napoleon, he became a general and in 1818 he was made king of Sweden. The house where he was born is now a museum. Various English villas can be seen in the area of Rue Monpensier; leading to Parc Lawrence and also in the eastern part of town. Beyond the Gave de Pau is Jurançon, which is virtually a suburb of Pau and the centre of the eponymous wine-growing region. It specializes in a tangy **white wine** made from local grapes (Jurançon sec) and an outstanding, highly aromatic late vintage (Moelleux).

✱
◄ Musée des Beaux-Arts

Jurançon

The small town of Lescar, 8km/5mi north of Pau, was the original capital of Béarn (until 841). Its cathedral of Notre-Dame (started in 1120) housed the tombs of the kings of Navarre. The capitals in the eastern part of the building are highly notable, as are the mosaics in the choir (12th century).

Lescar

Orthez (62m/203ft, 10,000 inhabitants), 40km/25mi northwest of Pau on the Gave de Pau, was Béarn's capital from 1194–1460 and later became a bastion of Protestantism, boasting its own Calvinist university. Its emblem is the 13th-century **Pont-Vieux** bridge, guarded by a massive tower. Take a look at the 13th–14th-century Tour Moncade, the remains of a castle built by Gaston Phoebus, the house of

Orthez

? DID YOU KNOW ...?

■ The familiar old Basque beret, which traditionally epitomizes »French« headwear, is not native to the Basque country, but in fact comes from Béarn. Apart from Nay (15km/9mi southeast of Pau) Oloron-Ste-Marie is considered the effective capital for the woollen caps, which were originally worn by shepherds to protect them from the elements.

Jeanne d'Albret (*c*1500), the 14th-century Hôtel de la Lune and the fine town houses. The 13th-century church of St-Pierre was part of the town's defences and its 14th-century doorway is in the Languedoc Gothic style.

★★
Col d'Aubisque

Gourette Les Eaux-Bonnes

From Argelès-Gazost (▶p.726) the D 918 leading westward over the Col d'Aubisque pass (1709m/5607ft) to Laruns (35km/22mi south of Pau) is one of the loveliest stretches of road in the Pyrenees. The oldest winter sports venue in the mountains, Gourette (1385m/4544ft, pistes on the Pic de Ger, 2613m/8573ft), and Les Eaux Bonnes (400 inhabitants, 750m/2461ft), an old-fashioned health spa, are located along the pass.

Pic du Midi d'Ossau

Gabas, the last spot along the Ossau valley before the Col du Pourtalet, is situated at the foot of the »Matterhorn of the Pyrenees«, the Pic du Midi d'Ossau (2884m/9462ft, a highly weathered volcanic spout). It is also possible to reach the Lac de Bious-Artigues (1417m/4649ft) by car, from where hikes around the **Lacs d'Ayous** (4–5 hours) and the circumnavigation of the Pic du Midi (7 hours) can be undertaken. East of Gabas, a cable car leads up the **Pic de la Sagette** (2031m/6663ft), while trains with open carriages run through breathtaking scenery to the **Lac d'Artouste** (1989m/6526ft).

Oloron-Sainte-Marie

The lively Oloron-Ste-Marie (11,000 inhabitants), at the confluence of the Gave d'Aspe and Gave d'Ossau, came into being in 1858 with the amalgamation of two smaller settlements. In the western part of the town, a former bishopric, the cathedral of **Ste-Marie** (12th–13th centuries, choir 14th century) with its splendid Romanesque portal is worth a look (archivolts from outside: 24 Elders of the Apocalypse, scenes from pastoral life; tympanum: Christ taken down from the cross and lions over the doors representing the persecution and eventual triumph of the church). It was commissioned by Gaston IV of Béarn after his return from the First Crusade. To the east of town on the **castle hill** between the Gave d'Aspe and Gave d'Ossau stands the church of Ste-Croix, built in around 1080 (the Moorish dome dates from the 13th century). There is a lovely view from the terrace to the west of the church.

Rolling Basque scenery around Sare

An impressive mountain backdrop surrounds the village of **Lescun** a little way away from the Vallee

d'Aspe. The **Col du Somport** (1632m/5354ft) was in medieval times
the route taken by pilgrims on the Way of St James to Santiago de
Compostela. The modern N 134 road uses a two-lane tunnel 8.6km/
9400yd long, which was opened in 2003 despite protests from inhabitants of the valley and nature protectionists. It is primarily used by
heavy freight vehicles. The railway tunnel that runs parallel to it has
been closed since 1970.

13km/8mi further west is Mauléon-Licharre (3500 inhabitants), a
town which flourished thanks to the production of espadrilles and
cheese. The castle was the headquarters for the governors of Soule.
Château d'Andurain (*c*1600) has a shingle roof with a very nice
chestnut truss. The countryside of Soule extends south of Mauléon-
Licharre. The southwestern part of it is formed by a heavily wooded
massif. In **Gotein** there is a church featuring one of the »bell walls«
(clocher-calvaires) that are typical hereabouts. Tardets-Sorholus
(with its fascinating arcade houses) is the starting point for at trip
down the Gorges de Kakouetta, the prettiest gorge in the Basque
country (about 1.5km/1mi long, 260m/150ft deep and narrowing to
as little as 3m/10ft wide).

Mauléon Licharre

Soule

★
**Gorges de
Kakouetta**

St-Jean-Pied-de-Port (1400 inhabitants) is characterized by the red
sandstone of its buildings. It was formerly the capital of Lower Navarre and used to be an important port of call on the Way of St James
on the way to Roncesvalles (►see below). »Pied-de-Port« means »at
the foot of the pass«. The **upper town** is ringed by walls dating from
the 15th century. The right bank of the river Nive is crossed by the
main boulevard, Rue de la Citadelle, with its houses from the
16th–17th centuries. A gate in the tower of the church of Notre-
Dame-du-Pont leads to the bridge. The boulevard continues on the
other side. Under the bridge are the old hospital and Maison Jassu,
where the ancestors of Far-East missionary Francisco de Jassu y Jav-
ier lived. There is a lovely view from the bastion in front of the
citadel. **Irouléguy**, 6km/4mi west of St-Jean, has the only vineyards
anywhere in the Basque country (white wine made mainly from the
old grape variety Tannat).

★
**Saint-Jean-Pied-
de-Port**

Across the Spanish border the road leads up to a pass 1057m/3468ft
above sea level called **Puerto de Roncesvalles**. In 778 this was the
scene of a battle between the Franks under Charlemagne and the
Basques, which was the source of the 12th-century poem about the
hero Roland. After 21km/13mi the road reaches the Augustinian abbey, Colegiata de Roncesvalles, founded in 1130 and including an interesting 13th-century church (gilded retables, Virgen de Roncesvalles) and a museum.

Roncesvalles

The mountain health resort of Cambo-les-Bains (4100 inhabitants),
about 20km/12mi southeast of Biarritz overlooking the valley of the

Cambo-les-Bains

Nive, is divided into two parts: Bas Cambo is a typical-looking Basque village, while Haut Cambo is dominated by villas. The Art-Nouveau style Villa Arnaga (1.5km/1mi west, museum) was home to dramatist Edmond Rostand (1868–1918). A memorial to him has been erected in the town centre.

✱

Espelette

Espelette (6km/4mi southwest, 1600 inhabitants) is famed for its hot, red **chilli peppers** (»piments«, festival on the last Sunday in October), which hang from September onwards on the walls of the red and white half-timbered houses. The cemetery next to the hilltop church (Renaissance doorway) has some typical circular gravestones, whose round shape symbolizes the sun. **Ainhoa** (11km/7mi southwest, 540 inhabitants) also has half-timbered houses that are typically »picture-book Basque country«. The church boasts some beautiful gilded panelling. The path to Notre-Dame-de-l'Aubepine with its double gallery (one hour's walk) is very nice too.

✱

Ainhoa

Sare

The pretty village of Sare also has an interesting church (three galleries, magnificent Baroque altars). From there the Col de St-Ignace leads down to St-Jean-de-Luz on the ►Côte Basque.

✱

La Rhune

Col de St-Ignace also boasts an electric **funicular railway from 1924** which leads to the 900m/2950ft peak of La Rhune, emblem of the French Basque land. There is a terrific view from here, taking in the coast, the surrounding land and the Pyrenees. The walk down to the valley station takes two hours (information: www.rhune.com).

✱ ✱ Reims

L/M 3

Région: Champagne-Ardenne	**Altitude:** 83m/272ft
Département: Marne	**Population:** 191,000

Reims was where the kings of France were crowned from the 10th century until 1825. Nowadays it is the capital of the ►Champagne-Ardenne region and renowned, of course, for champagne wine, as well as for its cathedral, which is one of the masterpieces of the Gothic era.

History

Capital for the Celtic Remi tribe and later the Roman town of Durocortorum, Reims was one of the most prosperous towns in all of Gaul. The high regard in which the bishops of Reims were held, due to their role in Christianizing the Franks, led to their being granted by the Carolingian dynasty the privilege of anointing the kings of the Franks. Reims was where the kings of France were crowned from 988 till 1825, and on 17 July 1429 Joan of Arc led Charles VII to his coronation in the cathedral. Reims was largely destroyed during the

First World War. The surrender of the Germans at the end of the Second World War was signed here on 7 May 1945. The cathedral, the episcopal palace and the monastery of St-Remi are all on the list of UNESCO World Heritage Sites.

✱ ✱ Notre-Dame Cathedral

The cathedral is considered a **masterpiece of High Gothic** due to its consistency, the harmony of its layout and the abundance of sculpture. It was built on the site of a 5th-century church, where Clovis, king of the Franks, was baptized in 496 by bishop Remigius. As the site where most of the kings of France were crowned, it enjoys particular reverence. Building started in 1211 under Jean d'Orbais and was essentially finished by 1294 (further storeys of

The façade of the cathedral has an impressively harmonious look

the towers in 1428). The tower over the cross, which had been built in 1485, was destroyed along with much of the rest of the cathedral in 1914. Unlike the rest, though, it has not been rebuilt.

Above the three magnificent pointed arches of the entrance portal is a superb rose window 12m/39ft in diameter, along with other windows featuring fine tracery, over which 56 4.5m/15ft statues, the so-called Gallery of the Kings, is situated. The towers, even without spires, are 82.5m/271ft tall. The 2300 pictures and bas-reliefs that adorn the whole of the building are some of the finest products of medieval sculpture (although many have had to be replaced by copies). The depictions at the middle entrance concentrate on the life of the Virgin Mary with the visit of the Archangel Gabriel and the Annunciation of Christ's birth to the right and images of Anna, Zachariah Mary, Joseph and a magnificent statue of Solomon to the left. By the left-hand portal next to the door, there is a smiling angel, known as the **Sourire de Reims** (a reconstruction). The northern façade of the transept has statues of bishops and others around its middle portal, while the side portal on the left has a huge Christ in a gesture of blessing, beneath which there is a depiction of the Last Judgement featuring the most important relief work known to have been done by the Reims masonry workshop (13th century). The 138.5m/ **Interior**

Main façade

151.5yd-long interior, accessible daily 7.30am–7.30pm, makes the cathedral the longest in France (it is 38m/125ft high, and 49.5m/162ft in the transept). It saw fewer alterations in later eras than did most cathedrals and makes a very serious, almost stern impression. One unique feature is the **west wall** with its 120 figures, each an important testimony to the development of French sculpture in the 13th century. The communion scene on the bottom row to the right of the main entrance is particularly notable. Most of the old stained glass work has been lost, although some has been restored. The windows in the lower part of the chapel at the apex of the choir were created by Chagall in 1974.

Reims Map

1 Hôtel des Comtes de Champagne	3 Palais de Justice	Where to eat	Where to stay	▨ Champagne cellars
2 Préfecture	4 Théâtre	① Les Charmes	① Hôtel Crystal	
		② Les Crayères		

⏵ VISITING REIMS

INFORMATION

Office de Tourisme
2 Rue Guillaume-de-Machault
F-51100 Reims
Tel. 0892 701 351, fax 03 26 77 45 27
www.reims-tourisme.com

FESTIVALS AND EVENTS

Mid-June: Les Sacres du Folklore, the biggest event of its kind in northern France featuring groups from all over the world. Mid/end of June: Fêtes Johanniques, medieval spectacle dedicated to Joan of Arc (the procession on Sunday attracts 2000 participants). In summer »musical walks« take place, with music played in odd places, and there is a big picnic in the park at Pommery. Nov: jazz festival in Pommery.

WHERE TO EAT
▶ Expensive
② *Château Les Crayères*
64 Boulevard Vasnier
Tel. 03 26 82 80 80
www.lescrayeres.com
Closed Mon and Tue. Magnificent manor house from the end of the 19th century in Louis XVI style, formerly owned by Pommery, set in extensive parkland. Top-class restaurant – Didier Elena won his spurs under Alan Ducasse. Early reservation recommended. 19 large and beautifully furnished rooms and an English-style bar.

▶ Inexpensive
① *Les Charmes*
11 Rue Brûlart, Tel. 03 26 85 37 63
Closed Sundays and four weeks in July/Aug. Small, charming bistro close to St-Rémi and champagne cellars with quality French cuisine. Superb fare for the price.

WHERE TO STAY
▶ Budget
① *Hôtel Crystal*
86 Place Drouet d'Erlon, tel. 03 26 88 44 44, www.hotel-crystal.fr
Old-fashioned charm on the lively (pedestrianized) main square with pleasant, functional rooms and a very nice inner courtyard. Various other 2 and 3 star establishments on Place Drouet can also be recommended.

Other Attractions in Reims

The episcopal palace, redesigned up to 1690 by Jules Hardouin-Mansart and Robert de Cotte – both architects who worked on Versailles – now houses the cathedral museum (closed Mon), which has many of the original statues, chambers of the kings who dwelt in the palace during the coronation proceedings, and 15th-century tapestries made in Arras.

★
Palais-du-Tau

In front of the Palais de Justice (1846) on the square in front of the cathedral stands a bronze statue of Joan of Arc mounted on her horse (Paul Dubois, 1896). The 18th-century Abbaye de St-Denis houses the Musée des Beaux-Arts (closed Tue), displaying a fine selection of paintings, sculptures, antiquities and other works of art.

Place du Cardinal-Luçon
★
Musée des Beaux Arts

Among the most noteworthy are those of **Lucas Cranach the Elder and Lucas Cranach the Younger**, mainly depicting the electors of Saxony and their wives, along with paintings by Corot and the »Toiles peintes« (»painted linen«) from the 15th and 16th centuries.

Place Drouet d'Erlon
The elongated Place Drouet d'Erlon with its arcades of shops, restaurants and cafés forms the heart of the city. At its southern end stands the church of St-Jacques (12th–16th centuries) featuring modern windows by da Silva and Sima. At the northern end it opens out into Square Colbert. A bronze statue there is an 1860 memorial to Reims' own Jean-Baptiste Colbert (1619–83), the finance minister under Louis XIV.

Porte de Mars
The Place de la République is dominated by the Porte de Mars, a 3rd-century Roman triumphal arch 33m/108ft in height, which was still used as a city gate as late as 1544. At the Collège Technique behind the railway station, the room occupied by the American High Command where **German surrender** was signed on 7 May 1945 is open to the public (Musée de la Reddition, closed Tue). Chapelle Foujita, opened in 1966, was decorated by the Japanese artist Leonard Foujita (1886 –1968).

Hôtel le Vergeur
From the Hôtel de Ville (1630), Rue Colbert leads to the Place du Forum with its cryptoporticus, formerly the entrance to the **Roman forum** (2nd century AD). At the northeastern corner is Hôtel le Vergeur (13th–16th centuries), which houses the city's museum of local history. Fans of vintage cars will not want to miss the **Musée Automobile** de Reims-Champagne and the over 200 »jewels of the past« kept there (closed Tue).

✳ St-Rémi
The abbey church of St-Rémi is considered to be one of the finest early Romanesque churches in northern France. It was built from 1005 to 1049 on the site of a Carolingian building. The oldest part of the building is the southern tower. Between 1162 and 1182 the church was remodelled in Gothic style. Notable features inside include the (reconstructed) tomb of St Remigius, the inlaid stone tiles (13th century) and the Altar of the Three Baptisms (Christ, Constantine, Clovis; 1610). In the monastery buildings, the **Musée Abbaye St-Rémi** exhibits some of the city's works of art dating from Roman times to the Middle Ages, a collection of items from the city's military history and ten magnificent tapestries depicting scenes from the legend of St Remigius (1523–31).

> **! Baedeker TIP**
>
> **Champagne**
>
> Any visit to Reims simply must take in the champagne companies, such as Pommery, Mumm, Taittinger and Ruinart. The huge cellars in the chalk subsoil are also open to the public. The tourist office can provide comprehensive information.

Rennes

F 4

Région: Bretagne
Département: Ille-et-Vilaine

Altitude: 30m/98ft
Population: 212,000

Rennes is the capital of ▶Brittany as well as being its social and economic hub. It is, however, a long way from the coast and, since it was newly established after a serious fire in 1720, does not give a typical »Breton« impression.

Some of the streets around the cathedral of St-Pierre still exude something of a medieval atmosphere. The city is dominated by the presence of some 50,000 students at its two universities and more than two dozen colleges. Learning is a major factor in Rennes. In 1982 the »Triangle d'Or« was established, which set up close cooperation between teaching establishments, research institutes and practical industry, so that more than 4000 people are now working in research – in spheres from electronics to biotechnology and medicine. Major economic contributors include cars (Citroën), printing and publishing (local newspaper *Ouest France*) and the food industry.

Learned city

In the early Middle Ages, Rennes was one of France's key border outposts against Breton insurgents. Until Brittany was officially annexed to the French crown in 1532 (14-year-old Anne of Brittany had already married King Charles VIII in 1491), the city was at the core of a large duchy, but it took its place as the venue for the Breton »parlements« (law courts) in 1561. On 22 December 1720 the centre of the city was decimated by fire. The famous royal architect J. Gabriel (1666–1742) redesigned the city on a chessboard grid and in the new classical style.

History

What to See in Rennes

The river Vilaine, which divides that part of the old city centre which survived the 1720 fire from the new southern city, has been diverted into canals and part of it now runs underground. Typical features of its houses include the jutting upper storeys and carved figures on top of the balcony balustrades. The chapel of St-Yves from 1494 now houses the tourist office and an exhibition covering the history of Rennes. The **Hôtel de Blossac** (1728) marks the western edge of the area destroyed by fire and is considered a very fine testimony to the rebuilding of the town. It was formerly the residence of the governor of Brittany and now houses Brittany's version of the National Trust, the Centre de Documentation sur le Patrimoine. There are more interesting houses on Rue de la Psallette, which leads around the choir of the cathedral of St-Pierre (nos. 1, 1609; no. 8, formerly a school for the cathedral's vocal choir). The crooked half-timbered house **Ty**

★
Old town

◉ VISITING RENNES

INFORMATION

Office du Tourisme
11 Rue St-Yves, F-35000 Rennes
Tel. 02 99 67 11 11, fax 02 99 67 11 10
www.tourisme-rennes.com

TRANSPORT

Metro and buses operated by STAR,
whose office is in the main post office
(12 Rue du Pré Botté).

FESTIVALS AND EVENTS

First half of July: Tombées de la Nuit,
music and theatre in the old town.
In Oct or Nov the Breton »Yaouank«
festival takes place from Saturday
evening till Sunday morning.

WHERE TO EAT

▶ Moderate / expensive

① *Le Saison*
1 Impasse Vieux Bourg, St-Grégoire
(3km/2mi north), tel. 02 99 68 79 35
www.le-saison.com, closed Mon
»Cuisine gourmande«, imaginatively
repackaged in a modern atmosphere.
Lovely terrace.

▶ Moderate

② *Taverne de l'Ecu*
12 Rue Baudrairie, F-35500 Vitré
Tel. 02 99 75 11 09. Take a day trip to
Vitré with its 16th-century masonry
near the chateau with large fireplaces
in the dining rooms. Breton and
Provencal cuisine.

▶ Inexpensive

③ *La Réserve*
38 Rue-de-la-Visitation
Tel. 02 99 84 02 02, closed Sun
Fine French and Breton fare at a nice
price in a pretty old bistro.

④ *Quatre B*
4 Place Bretagne, tel. 02 99 30 42 01
Closed Sun and Mon lunchtime
Small, modern restaurant with informal atmosphere and classic cuisine
presented with a modern flavour.

WHERE TO STAY

▶ Budget

① *Hôtel des Lices*
7 Place des Lices, tel. 02 99 79 14 81
www.hotel-des-lices.com
Close to the lively market halls.
Modern, comfortable rooms, some
with a balcony. Lovely view from the
upper floors.

*Place Champs Jacquet with its half-
timbered buildings from the 17th century*

Koz (Rue St-Guillaume 3) from the 16th century is richly adorned with sculptures and is one of the prettiest buildings in the city.

The imposing cathedral of St-Pierre was said by Hippolyte Taine to be »the ugliest building I have ever seen«. Prosper Mérimée, though, claimed it »justified praise«. The interior of the church, built in 1787–1844 by Mathurin Crucy of Nantaiser, seems gloomy in spite of its magnificent decoration with plenty of stucco and gilt. The gilded altar with its **Flemish carvings** (1520) depicting scenes from the life of the Virgin Mary is well worth seeing, though. The nearby Portes Mordelaises are remains of the city's fortifications which were built in the 15th century.

Cathédrale St-Pierre

Portes Mordelaises

In St-Sauveur (1703–28), the gilded wrought-iron pulpit (1781), a carved canopy, also gilded (1768), and the statue of Notre-Dame des Miracles are all worthy of mention.

St-Sauveur

In the Middle Ages, Place des Lices was a tournament venue. Nowadays it is the scene of a large market held every Saturday morning in and around the two 19th-century **market halls**. The northern part of the square is lined by magnificent aristocratic residences, while the west is marked by the Tours des Horizons skyscrapers (G. Maillol, 1960).

Place des Lices

Rennes Map

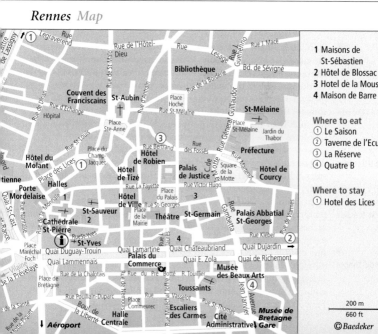

1 Maisons de
   St-Sébastien
2 Hôtel de Blossac
3 Hotel de la Moussaye
4 Maison de Barre

Where to eat
① Le Saison
② Taverne de l'Ecu
③ La Réserve
④ Quatre B

Where to stay
① Hotel des Lices

200 m
660 ft
©Baedeker

La Grande Chambre, court chamber at the Palais de Justice

Palais de Justice ✴ The most famous building in the town is the Palais du Parlement, headquarters of the **Breton government**, built in 1618–55 by Salomon de Brosse. It is surrounded by elegant houses from the 17th and 18th centuries. The design of the interior and furnishings was undertaken as of 1709 by the most famous painters, carpenters and sculptors of the Louis XVI era. In 1726, when the city was being rebuilt, Jacques Gabriel created a new façade. Part of the palais was damaged in a riot by Breton fisherman in 1994, but it has been restored and is once again open to the public (open mid-July–mid-Aug Sun; otherwise guided tours available, apply at the Office de Tourisme). One room that is furnished with particular pomp is the 20 × 10m/66 × 33ft **Grande Chambre**, with a 7m/23ft-high ceiling. The boxes were designed so that the aristocracy could follow the court trials.

Place de la Mairie

Théâtre ✴ Place de la Mairie in the centre of the classical district is the site of the city hall (Jacques Gabriel, 1743) and opposite it, the theatre. The city hall features a ballroom and a pantheon for the fallen of the First World War. Brittany's own Jean-Julien Lemordant painted the roof of the hall with scenes of Breton dancing in the gleaming white neo-classical theatre (Claude Millardet, 1831). There is a great view from the middle of the square outside the city hall southward down Rue d'Orléans to the Palais de Commerce (►see below).

Palais St-Georges

St-Mélaine

Jardin du Thabor ✴ At one end of Rue St-Georges, which survived the fire and has many splendid **half-timbered buildings**, stands the Palais St-Georges, built in 1670 for the abbess Madeleine de la Fayette (it is now a government building). The parish church from 1672 previously belonged to the Benedictine abbey of St-Mélaine. The crossing with its horseshoe arches and some of the columns in the 11th-century nave are rare examples of the Romanesque style, rarely seen in Brittany. There is a fine cloister (1663) next to the episcopal palace (1672). A beautifully wrought door leads into the Jardin du Thabor, formerly an orchard belonging to the abbey. The present park with its bandstand pavilion and birdhouse came into being around 1866. The botanical gardens have 3000 species of plant and a lovely rose garden.

The old Rue St-Mélaine leads down to Place Ste-Anne with its neo-Gothic church and pretty half-timbered houses (16th century). The Couvent des Franciscains is where the union of Anne of Brittany and King Charles VIII took place in 1491.

St-Aubin

The river Vilaine was diverted into canals in 1840 but still forms the east-west axis of Rennes. The Place de la République was built directly on top of the river itself. The view of the lower parts of town, probably seen as disreputable in those days, populated as it was by tanners, dyers and butchers, is blocked by the monumental **Palais de Commerce** (1886–1932, now the main post office). The university building (1856) houses the **most important art museum in Brittany**. It has paintings from the 14th to the 20th century on display, including works by Rubens (a tiger hunt painted for Schloss Schleissheim near Munich), La Tour and from the Pont Aven school, as well as drawings (by Da Vinci, Dürer, Botticelli and others) and archaeological exhibits. Open Wed–Mon 10am–noon, 2am–6pm.

Place de la République

✶ ✶
Musée des Beaux-Arts

The Museum of Brittany has an abundance of riches that document the history and development of the region from prehistoric times until the present day. It is housed in the Les Champs Libres cultural centre near the station (Cours des Allies, open Tue noon–9pm, Wed–Fri noon–7pm, Sat–Sun 2pm–7pm).

✶ ✶
Musée de Bretagne

Around Rennes

The Ferme de la Bintinais open-air museum (closed Mon) is situated along the road to Noyal-Châtillon. It offers an insight into the region's agriculture and retains both useful flora and domestic animals of breeds used in former times. There are some interesting demonstrations, too, which take place according to the time of year.

✶
Ecomusée du Pays de Rennes

Châteaugiron (4000 inhabitants), 16km/10mi southeast of Rennes, was one of Brittany's most important towns in the Middle Ages. In the 16th century the town vouched for the Protestant cause and was destroyed by the Catholic League in 1589. It flourished again later as a centre of sailcloth manufacture. Its pretty old **half-timbered houses** from the 16th–19th centuries are reminders of that period, as is its castle. The Tour de l'Horloge and the 38m/125ft donjon both date from the 13th century.

✶
Châteaugiron

Vitré (15,300 inhabitants), 35km/22mi east of Rennes, is an old fortified township on the former Breton border. Its highest point is occupied by its **powerful castle** (14th–15th centuries.), which exhibits examples of medieval art, furniture and tapestries. Below it, the picturesque streets of the old town and especially Rue Baudrairie, formerly occupied for both work and dwelling by saddle makers, are a very interesting sight. The Gothic church of Notre-Dame

✶
Vitré

(15th–16th centuries) has a most unusual exterior pulpit. Opposite the church stands Hôtel Ringues, built in the 16th century for a rich merchant and now used as a community centre.

Château des Rochers-Sévigné
The chateau of Les Rochers, almost 7km/4mi south of Vitré, was from 1654 to 1690 the residence of Madame de Sévigné, famous chronicler of life in the royal court in the time of Louis XIV.

La Guerche-de-Bretagne
The pretty little town of La Guerche-de-Bretagne (4000 inhabitants), 22km/14mi south of Vitré, was formerly part of a chain of fortified outposts guarding the eastern border of Brittany. From here a route leads to one of the most important **megalithic monuments** in Brittany (15km/9mi west of La Guerche, between Retiers and Essé). La

✴ La Roche-aux-Fées
Roche-aux-Fées, »the Fairy Rock«, is a megalithic structure 22m/24yd in length, 6m/20ft wide and 4m/13ft high and is though to have been erected in around 2500 BC (▶Baedeker Special p.306).

Fougères
Fougères (23,000 inhabitants), about 50km/31mi northeast of Rennes in a loop of the Nançon river, is known for its footwear industry but it is also aligned towards agriculture. The largest **cattle market**

Twilight in Josselin: Château des Rohans

in Europe takes place here. The town was formerly fortified and has a massive **castle** (11th–15th centuries), the courtyard of which is now used as an open-air theatre. The late Gothic church of St-Sulpice (14th–18th centuries) to the south of the castle has a unique tower above its intersection and the chapels around the choir have some beautiful granite retables. Musée E. de la Villéon is housed in a half-timbered building next to the town hall (both 16th century) and is dedicated to the impressionist painter of that name (1858 –1944), who was born in Fougères.

The small medieval town of **Josselin** (2400 inhabitants) about 35km/22mi southwest of the Forêt de Paimpont has a large **chateau next to the River Oust**, the Château des Rohans (14th–16th centuries). Place Notre-Dame features some fine half-timbered houses and the 12th-century church of Notre-Dame-du-Roncier with its magnificent stained glass windows from the 15th–16th centuries. On the national holiday a big medieval festival is held here.

Rouen

Région: Haute-Normandie
Département: Seine-Maritime

Altitude: 10m/33ft
Population: 109,000

Rouen, capital of ► Normandy, has long been of major economic importance thanks to its situation between Paris and the coast. Possessing more than 2000 half-timbered buildings, magnificent Gothic churches and outstanding museums, it is one of the top places to visit in all of northern France.

Rouen, capital of the Haute-Normandie région and the Seine-Maritime départements, is about 130km/81mi from the Seine estuary and the English Channel. It is one of the most important sea and river ports in France; the Seine is navigable by ocean-going vessels up to this point. The conurbation around Rouen is home to nearly 400,000 people.

Important harbour

Rouen, known as Rotomagus when the Celts were here, was attacked several times by the Normans in the 9th century. In 911 their leader Rollo became the first Duke of Normandy. After William the Conqueror was crowned king of England in 1066, Rouen remained an English possession until 1204. It also returned to English hands in 1419–49 during the Hundred Years' War. It was here that the **trial of Joan of Arc** took place in 1431, which ended with her being burned as a witch. The struggles between Catholics and Calvinists hindered the development of the town in the 16th and 17th centuries, in spite of its important textile industry. After the lifting of the Edict of Nantes in 1683, more than half the population left the city. Rouen suffered serious damage during the Second World War. It was also the birthplace of writers Pierre Corneille (1606–84) and Gustave Flaubert (1821–80).

History

What to See in Rouen

The city's kernel is Place du Vieux Marché, the square where Joan of Arc was burned on 30 May 1431. A crucifix and plaque mark the spot. Inside the church of Ste-Jeanne-d'Arc, built in 1979, it is possible to see windows from the 16th-century church of St-Vincent, which was destroyed in 1944. The southern edge of the square is lined by lovely half-timbered buildings. The magnificent **Hôtel du Bourgtheroulde** to the south of the old marketplace was built in 1486–1531 for the judge Guillaume Le Roux and is presently occupied by a bank.

**★
Place du Vieux Marché**

Rue du Gros Horloge, the main thoroughfare of the old town, runs from the old marketplace to the cathedral and is flanked by old half-

Rue du Gros Horloge

Rouen, the former capital of Normandy on the Seine

timbered buildings from the 15th–17th centuries. The city's unique landmark is the **Gros Horloge** (a clock with a single hour hand dating from 1389), which is now part of a Renaissance gatehouse. The fortified tower next door was completed in 1398. Nos. 60–66 make up a building which was formerly the old town hall, designed by the famous Jacques Gabriel (1607).

Palais de Justice

The Palais de Justice northward of the Gros Horloge is a masterpiece of Gothic architecture. It was completed in 1509 according to designs by Rémi Leroux as the headquarters for Normandy's main law courts (Echiquier). Underneath the courtyard, excavations have uncovered the oldest known Jewish building in France, the **Monument Juif** from around 1100. Guided tours are provided by the Office de Tourisme.

Notre-Dame cathedral

The Gothic cathedral of Notre-Dame, one of the biggest and most spectacular in the country, was built primarily between 1201 and 1220 (transept 1280). The Flamboyant façade (1509–30), the full 56m/61yd breadth of which has now been restored to gleaming white, was immortalized in more than 30 pictures by **Claude Monet**. The works count among the founding works of Impressionism. In July–Aug the façade is illuminated by colourful lights. In the tympanum of the central portal there is a fine Tree of Jesse (1524). To the left can be seen the façade of the Tour St-Romain, the lower part of which dates back to an earlier Roman building, while to the right stands the 77m/253ft Tour de Beurre (1485 to 1507), the building of which was financed by a tax paid by citizens to allow them to eat butter during times of fasting. The black cast-iron spire above the intersection (1876) tops a tower which at 151m/495ft is the **highest church tower in France**. The side entrances, especially the Portail des Libraires in the north, are also very appealing. The interior is 135m/148yd long and 51m/167ft high under the tower and exhibits impressive amounts of elegance and unity. The wonderful **choir gallery** is the last resting place of such important figures as Rollo, first Duke of Normandy, and the heart of King Richard the Lionheart of England (whose body is in Fontevraud, ▶Loire). The highlight is the **tomb of the Cardinal of Amboise** (1520) in the central Chapelle de la Vierge. The heart of King Charles V is interred in the 11th-century crypt.

The building opposite the cathedral is the attractive Bureau des Finances (1509; with the tourist office). Adjoining the cathedral to the east is the archiepiscopal palace (15th–18th centuries), in which the city's archbishops still reside to this day.

Place de la Cathédrale

Archevêché

The church of St-Maclou (1437–1521, crossing tower 1868) is a veritable **jewel of the late Gothic period**. Behind its delicate vestibule with its quintuple axis are three doorways, of which the centre and left ones exhibit some splendid wooden relief carvings (scenes from the Bible) apparently by Jean Goujon. The organ cabinet in the otherwise plain interior is also by Goujon. Along the northern side of the church runs Rue Martainville, lined with half-timbered houses

✱
St-Maclou

 ## VISITING ROUEN

INFORMATION

Office de Tourisme
25 Place-de-la-Cathédrale
F-76000 Rouen
Tel. 02 32 08 32 40, fax 02 32 08 32 44
www.rouentourisme.com

TRANSPORT

Buses and Metro operated by TCAR. Information: Espace Métrobus, 9 Rue Jeanne D'Arc
Trips around the harbour March–Oct, Sat 2.30pm (bookings in tourist office).

FESTIVALS AND EVENTS

End of May: Joan of Arc festival. Start of July (every 4–5 years, last one in 2008): Armada, largest meeting for sailing ships in the world, featuring concerts, boat trips, fireworks etc. (book a hotel a year before). Events are listed in *L'Agenda Rouennais*.

WHERE TO EAT
► Moderate
① *La Couronne*
31 Place-du-Vieux Marché
Tel. 02 35 71 40 90. Whether or not its claim to be the oldest tavern in France is true, its half-timbered building from 1345 makes it one of the nicest, and the duck, prepared to Rouen's

own recipe, is superb. On the same square, other places worth recommending are the high-class bistro P'tit Zinc and the popular and inexpensive Les Maraîchers.

► Inexpensive
② *Brasserie Paul*
1 Place-de-la-Cathédrale
Tel. 02 35 71 86 07. Very popular thanks to its outstanding location and atmosphere. The bistro cooking is good and very reasonably priced.

WHERE TO STAY
► Budget
① *De-la-Cathédrale*
12 Rue St-Romain, tel. 02 35 71 57 95
www.hotel-de-la-cathedrale.fr
17th-century building near the cathedral with a wonderful atmosphere. The rooms facing the courtyard are recommended.

② *Le Vieux Carré*
34 Rue Ganterie, tel. 02 35 71 67 70
www.vieux-carre.fr
Half-timbered building from 1715 with an enchanting inner courtyard and pretty rooms at nice prices – the perfect ingredients for an enjoyable stay.

Aître St-Maclou ✱

with many an antique shop among them. An alley at no. 186 leads toAître St-Maclou, a plague cemetery dating from 1348. It is surrounded by **wooden galleries** (from about 1530) decorated with carved scenes from the Dance of Death.

Saint Ouen ✱

St-Ouen was formerly one of the most powerful Benedictine abbeys in Normandy. Its church, built from 1318–39 and another beautiful example of late Gothic building, is no less than 137m/150yd in length. It is topped by a fabulous **crossing tower** (1515), appropriately dubbed the »Crown of Normandy«. The west portal and the towers were only built between 1846 and 1851. Take a look at the

Rouen Map

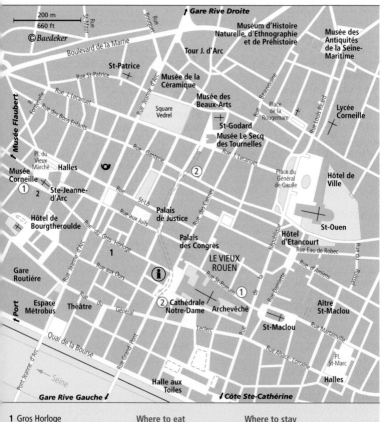

| 200 m |
| 660 ft |
©Baedeker

Gare Rive Droite
Rue St-Maur
Rue Bouquet
Rue
Muséum d'Histoire Naturelle, d'Ethnographie et de Préhistoire
Musée des Antiquités de la Seine-Maritime
Boulevard de la Marne
Tour J. d'Arc
St-Patrice
Rue St-Patrice
Musée de la Céramique
Rue J. Lecanuet
R. Fontenelle
Rue des Bons Enfants
Rue Jeanne d'Arc
Square Vedrel
Musée des Beaux-Arts
Place de la Rougemare
Lycée Corneille
Rue Louis Ricard
Beauvoisine
Musée Flaubert
St-Godard
Rue Gantere
Musée Le Secq des Tournelles
Rue J. Lecanuet
Pl. du Vieux Marché
Halles
Musée Corneille
Ste-Jeanne-d'Arc
St-Lô
Rue aux Juifs
Rue des Carmes
Place du Général de Gaulle
Hôtel de Ville
Hôtel de Bourgtheroulde
Rue du Gros-Horloge
Palais de Justice
Palais des Congrès
Hôtel d'Etancourt
St-Ouen
Rue Eau de Robec
Rue de la République
Rue du Ruissel
Rue d'Amiens
Gare Routière
Rue Jeanne d'Arc
Rue aux Ours
LE VIEUX ROUEN
Rue St-Romain
Rue Damiette
Espace Métrobus
Théâtre
Rue du Général
Cathédrale Notre-Dame
Archevêché
St-Maclou
Aître St-Maclou
Rue Marrainville
Port
Quai de la Bourse
Rue Grand Pont
Leclerc
Rue
Rue Alsace-Lorraine
Pl. St-Marc
Halle aux Toiles
Halles
Pont Jeanne d'Arc
Seine
Gare Rive Gauche
Côte Ste-Catherine

1 Gros Horloge
2 Musée Jeanne d'Arc

Where to eat
① La Couronne
② Brasserie Paul

Where to stay
① De la Cathédrale
② Le Vieux Carré

Le Gros-Horloge in the lively old town

Portail des Marmousets in the southern transept, where the tympanum features depictions of Death, the Ascension and the Assumption of Mary. The highlights inside include stained glass windows from the 13th–16th centuries and a splendid **choir screen** (1747). The organ front from 1630 surrounds a famous 19th-century Cavaillé-Coll instrument. The monks' quarters have been used as the city hall since the French Revolution.

Around Square Vedrel, a pleasant park, there is a group of interesting **museums** (all closed Tue). The Gothic church of St-Laurent houses the Musée Le Secq des Tournelles, which exhibits a unique collection of artworks in wrought iron. Opposite stands the **Musée des Beaux-Arts**, one of the best provincial museums in France, with paintings from the 15th to the 20th centuries (including examples by Caravaggio, Velázques, Géricault, Boudin, Dufy and Monet, with *Façade of the Cathedral in Rouen* among the works of the latter). The Musée de la Céramique in Hôtel d'Hocqueville (1657) has an extensive collection of ceramic works.

A modern housing district stretches from the cathedral southward as far as the Seine. The only remnant of the old town is the market hall and the adjacent Fierté St-Romain, both from the Renaissance period (1542). In 1860 a new road, Rue Jeanne d'Arc, was built through the old town, and it now forms the city's north-south axis. On Rue du Donjon there is a remnant of a **castle** built in around 1200 by King Philippe II called the Tour Jeanne d'Arc (closed Tue). Joan of Arc was held here in 1431 for trial and torture by her judges.
Tour Jeanne d'Arc

Hôtel-Dieu in the west of the city was where **Gustave Flaubert** was born in 1821. His father worked as a physician there. Nowadays it houses Musée Flaubert and another museum covering the history of medicine.
Musée Flaubert

Around Rouen

The D 982, running roughly parallel to the Seine between Rouen and ▶ Le Havre is signposted as the Route des Abbayes (»Abbey Road«). The varied scenery and the multitude of cultural monuments make it one of the most exciting experiences in ▶Normandy.
★ Route des Abbayes

Pays de Bray, to the northeast of Rouen on the border with Picardy, is characterized by an image of verdant meadows. Its most important town is **Neufchâtel-en-Bray**, famous for its cheese. The health resort of Forges-les-Eaux (17km/11mi to the south) has experienced such luminary guests as Louis XIII and Cardinal Richelieu. The casino is very chic.
Pays de Bray

Forges-les-Eaux

Saint-Étienne

M 7

Région: Rhône-Alpes	**Altitude:** 517m/1696ft
Département: Loire	**Population:** 183,000

St-Étienne, southwest of Lyon, is an important industrial town, even if it is hardly a must-see tourist destination. The museum of modern art, though, is not something« to be ignored so easily.

Industrial centre in the process of change

St-Étienne, capital of the Loire département, has been an important centre of industry since the Middle Ages thanks to the coal deposits in the upper Loire region. Its main business has been metalworking, armaments, glass and textiles. The first railway line in France was opened between St-Étienne and Andrézieux in 1827. When coal mining came to an end in the 1980s, the traditional industries were supplemented by electronics, agricultural chemicals and plastics. In recent times, the town has presented a much more open face to the world.

What to See in St-Étienne

Rue de Gaulle, Rue Gambetta

The whole town is bisected by a set of roads running for some 6km/4mi in a dead straight line along a north-south axis: Rue Bergson, Rue Charles-de-Gaulle, and Rue Gambetta (the latter also has a tram line). **Place Jean Jaurès** with the Préfecture, the 1882 city hall and the church of St-Charles lies in the centre.

St-Étienne

South of Place Jaurès is the Place du Peuple, the medieval marketplace with its tower and one lovely 16th-century half-timbered building. To the west is the 15th-century church of St-Étienne, known as the Grand'Eglise (tower 17th century), where there is a lovely colourful tomb (16th century). The square in front of the church has some interesting buildings from the 15th and 16th centuries A little further west is the **Comédie de St-Étienne**, founded in 1947 and now an important institution in France's theatrical scene.

Musée du Vieux St-Étienne

Musée d'Art et d'Industrie

✳ **Site Couriot**

Further south along the »main axis«, the 17th-century Hôtel-de-Villeneuve contains a **museum of local history**. The district to the left of the tramway is the old quarter of Faubourg d'Outre Furan (»the other side of the Furan brook«). An **industrial museum** covers the subjects of coal mining, armament manufacture and textile production, and there are also some old motorcycles on display (closed Tue). From the Hôtel de Ville, Rue A. Briand leads westward to the Couriot coal mine, which operated from 1913 to 1973 (Musée de la Mine, closed Tue).

✳ ✳ **Musée d'Art Moderne**

The **museum of modern art** in the northern suburb of La Terrasse (4.5km/3mi from the centre) was designed by Didier Guichard and built in 1987. Its cladding of black tiles is intended to recall the »era of coal«. With its works from the classical modern period (Picasso, Léger, Miró, Picabia etc.) and from late 20th century (Klein, Stella, Warhol, Baselitz and others), it is one of the most important art museums in France (open Wed–Mon 10am–6pm).

Around St-Étienne

The small town of Firminy lies 11km/7mi southwest of St-Étienne. Other than Chandagar in India, it was the only urban planning project to be conducted by **Le Corbusier** and includes his Unité d'Habitation estate, the stadium etc. – the church was completed in 2005, and its addition to the list of World Cultural Heritage Sites is pending (www.ville-firminy.fr).

✷
Firminy

Southeast of St-Étienne the Massif du Mont Pilat ascends and separates the Loire valley from the Rhône. At **Crêt de l'Œillon** it reaches an elevation of 1370m/4495ft, while **Crêt de la Perdrix** is at 1432m/4698ft. Both summits are accessible by road (with a short walk to the top). Leaving St-Étienne on the D 8 (at Rochetaillée there is a right turn to the fantastic Gouffre d'Enfer), take the D 8A or D 63 after Bessatto the Crêt de l'Œillon, where there is a stunning panorama encompassing the Rhône valley, the Alps, Mont Ventoux in the east and Puy-de-Sancy in the west.

Mont Pilat

✷ ✷
Crêt de l'Œillon

The springs of St-Galmier (4200 inhabitants), 16km/9mi north of St-Étienne, produce the well known mineral water, **Badoit**. In the church (15th–17th centuries, Flamboyant Gothic) there is a tremendous Madonna pillar from the 16th century and a 15th-century Flemish triptych.

Saint-Galmier

▶ VISITING ST-ÉTIENNE

INFORMATION

Office de Tourisme
16 Av. de la Libération
F-42000 Saint-Étienne
Tel. 04 77 49 39 00, www.saint-etienne.fr

WHERE TO EAT

▶ **Inexpensive**
Du Musée D'Art Moderne
Tel. 04 77 79 24 52, closed Mon
A visit to the outstanding art museum can be rounded off in appropriate culinary style. The museum restaurant offers modern, light cuisine that shows an eagerness for experimentation (especially fish) at very nice prices.

WHERE TO STAY

▶ **Budget**
Terminus du Forez
31 Av. Denfert-Rochereau
Tel. 04 77 32 48 47
www.hotel-terminusforez.com
Classical hotel with all mod cons opposite the railway station. In spite of its size it has quite a familial atmosphere. With restaurant.

Montbrison Montbrison (14,000 inhabitants), about 35km/22mi northwest of St-Étienne between the Loire basin and the Forez mountains, was the former capital of Forez county. The **chateau of the counts** once stood on the volcano around which the town houses are now grouped. The circular boulevard traces the line of the former defensive walls, passing the Musée d'Allard (dolls and marionettes, minerals) in the west. In the south, near the river Vizézy, stands the Gothic church of Notre-Dame-d'Espérance (1226), whose 15th-century doorway has a Madonna with Child on the tympanum from the 14th century. To the east of the church is the so-called Diana (1296), formerly a meeting hall for the Decapolis league (from which the name derives), which has wooden vaulting from the 14th century, nearly all of whose 1700 beams are decorated with paintings.

Lac de Grangent To the west of St-Étienne lies Lac de Grangent, one of the dammed reservoirs along the upper reaches of the Loire, surrounded by thick **St-Victor-** woods. St-Victor-sur-Loire with its Romanesque church and medie-**sur-Loire** val castle is one of the prettiest villages in the vicinity. At the northern end of the reservoir is another idyllic spot with the ruins of the Château de Grangent, which have stood on their own island since the damming of the river.

★ ★ Saint-Malo

E/F 4

Région: Bretagne   **Altitude:** Sea level
Département: Ille-et-Vilaine   **Population:** 53,000

Flaubert called it a »stony crown on the waves«; Chateaubriand dubbed St-Malo's fortified old town »a granite citadelle«. Since the end of the 19th century, this important port in the east of ▶Brittany has also been a popular seaside resort.

Old mariners' The fortress-like old town of St-Malo (»Ville Close«) was originally **port** on an island but is nowadays connected to the mainland by two causeways. Since the 17th century, this harbour the Emerald Coast has of course grown enormously. In 1967 both Paramé (east of the Ville Close) and St-Servan (to the south) have been amalgamated into the urban district. Many lovely old villas, the »Malouinières«, testify to the fact that St-Malo has been a popular summer holiday destination since the 19th century.

The threatening Ville Close of St-Malo rises out of the waters

In the 6th century the Welsh monk MacLow settled Aleth spit (now St-Servan) and became one of the seven holy founders of Brittany. His name became »Maclou« in French and »Malo« in Breton. Norman incursions in the 9th century forced the inhabitants to move to the island, which could be better defended than the mainland. In the course of time some vast **defensive walls** were built. They were most recently bolstered in 1693–95 using plans by Simon Garangeau, a pupil of Vauban. The town has never been taken from the sea. St-Malo's wealth was based on seafaring from very early on. It was the Malouin **Jacques Cartier** who discovered Canada in 1534. St-Malo's rise to become the centre for the »Corsairs« took place at the end of the 17th century and the start of the 18th century, when Malouine pirates made the seven seas a danger for all honest men. When piracy declined, St-Malo switched over to the slave trade and deep sea fishing. In August 1944, Allied air raids destroyed 80% of the city centre, but in the years that followed the old town was once more rebuilt in the classical style of the 18th century. In 1768 St-Malo was the birthplace of writer and French foreign minister **Francois-René de Chateaubriand** († 1848).

✳ Ville Close

The best way to start a tour of Vieux Malo – also called »Intra Muros« or »inside the walls« – is by doing a round trip of the walls themselves. Depending on the tides – high tide and low tide can differ by as much as 8–13m/26–43ft (►Baedeker Special p.752) – there may be some fantastic views of the harbour, the islands, the town itself and out to sea. The masonry presently on view dates mainly from the start of the 18th century, when the town was spreading out to cover an area of some 24ha/59 acres. The main entrance gate, Porte St-Vincent (1709), is at the southernmost fortified tower. The **Grande Porte** from 1582 is a particularly ferocious looking bulwark. North of the Ville there is a chain of islands off the coast, which once made for an important defensive line. Some of them had their own fortifications. Inside the walls at Place Vauban an aquarium has been opened; in the Exotarium, reptiles are on view.

Tour des Remparts

Aquarium

The fortified **castle** was mainly built in the 15th–16th centuries on the orders of the dukes of Brittany in order to defend the port, but also to control it. The oldest part is the Petit Donjon (14th century). The Grand Donjon (to the south) was built in 1424. In 1475 the

✳ **Château**

Municipal museum	Tour Générale was erected. The **Musée de la Ville et du Pays Malouin** is housed in the towers and documents deep sea fishing, everyday life in the region and early tourism. In 1498 the Tour Quic-engroigne was appended to the Petit Donjon. Its name derives from a quote by Anne of Brittany: »Qui qu'en groigne, ainsi sera, car tel est mon plaisir.« (»If anyone grumbles, then so it shall be and I shall take pleasure in it.«) The Tour des Dames and Tour des Moulins in the courtyard both date from the early 16th century. The town hall is housed in the former barracks (18th century).
Tour Quic-engroigne	

In the 16th century the »Galère« was added to the eastern side of the castle facing Esplanade St-Thomas. It was later expanded into a three-sided fort by Vauban.

Other attractions	The building at 2 Place Chateaubriand was home to the Chateaubriand family for five years (he was actually born in no. 3). One of the official tours devised by the municipal authorities starts from the square. The **cathedral of St-Vincent** (12th–13th centuries) with its stained glass windows by von Max Ingrand and Jean Le Moal is said to stand on the site of the original St Malo's actual grave. At 13 Rue de Toulouse there is a doll and toy museum.

 VISITING ST-MALO

INFORMATION

Office de Tourisme
Esplanade St-Vincent, F-35400 St-Malo
Tel. 08 25 13 52 00, fax 02 99 56 67 00
www.saint-malo-tourisme.com

FERRIES

Boats ply to the outlying islands as well as to Dinard / Dinan / St-Servan from the southern side of Ville Close.

WHERE TO EAT

► **Moderate / expensive**

① *À la Duchesse Anne*
5 Place Guy La Chambre
Tel. 02 99 40 85 33
Closed Sun evenings, Mon lunchtimes and all day Wed
Fine restaurant with a lengthy tradition incorporated into the city wall of the Ville Close. French cuisine of the old school, primarily outstanding fish dishes.

② *St-Placide*
6 Place Poncel, St-Servan
Tel. 02 99 81 70 73
A building dating from 1907 with a terrace on a pretty square. Regional cuisine, i.e. fish and seafood, especially fish soup.

WHERE TO STAY

► **Mid-range**

① *Hotel Central*
5 Grande Rue, tel. 02 99 40 87 70
www.hotel-central-stmalo.com
In the Ville Close, with well tended if plain rooms. With seafood restaurant »La Pêcherie«.

② *Ascott Hotel*
35 Rue du Chapitre, St-Servan
www.ascotthotel.com, tel. 02 99 81 89 93. Wealthy citizen's villa from the 19th century with an interesting mixture of old-time ambience and modern furnishings.

Suburbs and Surroundings of St-Malo

In order to defend St-Malo, especially from English attack, the islands off the coast in front of the town were fortified during the 17th century. In 1689, the Fort National was built on the cliffs of the **islet**, which is accessible on foot at low tide. The site had previously been used for official executions. **Grand Bé**, where Chateaubriand is buried, can also be reached on foot. 300m/330yd further west lies the smaller island of Petit Bé. In 1692 and 1756 the **Ile de Cézembre**, 4km/2.5mi northwest, was fortified; it now attracts visitors thanks to its fine beach. 1.5km/1mi further northeast is the fort of La Conchée (Vauban/Garangeau, *c*1700).

Islands off the coast

It is pleasant to take a walk around the Cité d'Aleth, situated on the eponymous peninsula south of the Ville Close. Start from Place St-Pierre with its ruins of **Aleth cathedral**. To the northwest stands a fort built in 1759, which was extended by German occupying forces during the Second World War. South of Place St-Pierre, **Tour Soulidor** (1369 –82), actually composed of three distinct towers, rises up from the water's edge. Its interesting museum (Musée International du Long Cours Cap-Hornier) is dedicated to the exploration of Cape Horn. The pretty resort of St-Servan south of the Cité d'Aleth has one of the biggest sporting marinas in Brittany.

Cité d'Aleth

Saint-Servan

St-Malo Ville Close Map

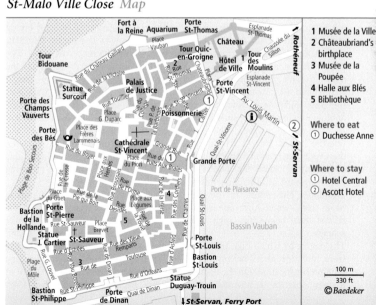

1 Musée de la Ville
2 Châteaubriand's birthplace
3 Musée de la Poupée
4 Halle aux Blés
5 Bibliothèque

Where to eat
① Duchesse Anne

Where to stay
① Hotel Central
② Ascott Hotel

100 m
330 ft
© *Baedeker*

The tidal power station on the Rance near St-Malo

THE PULL OF THE TIDES

The movement of the tides provides a fascinating natural spectacle on the Atlantic coast. Twice a day the beauty and riches of the beach are revealed, only to be concealed again later.

The rise and fall of the sea arises from the pull of the moon and the sun (the nearby moon having twice the effect of the distant sun). Their gravity means that there are always two peaks running around the surface of the oceans, separated from one another in time by a period averaging 12 hours and 25 minutes. For this reason the sea level rises and falls twice a day, with the time of the high and low tides changing by 50 minutes per day. When there is a new moon or a full moon, the sun, moon and earth are all aligned and the gravitational forces of the sun and moon reinforce one another, giving rise to **spring tides**. At half-moon periods, the three celestial bodies form a triangle and the overall gravitational effect reaches a minimum, since the waters are drawn upward at different points on the globe. This results in the lower **neap tides**, when high tide can be several feet below the high water average.

The degree by which high tide differs from low tide varies heavily depending on the location. On the open sea it may only be a few decimetres,

barely a foot, whereas in narrow bays and funnel-shaped river estuaries it can be several metres. On the shores of the Baltic Sea the rise and fall is only about 11cm/4in, while the North Sea rises by about 4m/13ft on the German coast, for example. On the southwest coast of England, the difference between high and low tides can be up to 11.5m/40ft, while at Fundy Bay in Canada it reaches 16m/53ft, the biggest difference on earth. The tides of northwestern France are the strongest in Europe. The height difference in the bay of St-Malo is as much as 14m/46ft and in the neighbouring bay around Mont St-Michel it is 15m/49ft, so that the sea goes out some 15km/9mi at low tide. When the tide comes in at Mont St-Michel, it is said to rush to shore »like galloping horses«.

Even though the tides are not quite as high in other places along the Atlantic coast, they are certainly perceptible everywhere in France. Even inland their effect can be seen, as at Abers, a funnel-shaped river estuary reaching up to 30km/19mi inland northwest of Brest. At high tide, the river Odet

Fun for all: looking for interesting things in the flats at low tide

hurtles through the Breton town of Quimper, 16km/10mi from the sea. At low tide, it is barely a trickle.

Fishing on foot

The tides make for an ever-changing picture at the coast. Where boats had, hours earlier, been rocking on the waves, suddenly they are teetering on their sides in the silt. Rocks and reefs seem to appear from nowhere. Sand banks and islands are briefly joined to the mainland and can be reached without even getting wet feet. Damp sand, sometimes grey-white, sometimes glittering gold, gleams in the sun, along with dozens of algae-decked rocks that have suddenly come to light. They smell of ozone and iodine, these newly uncovered beaches, with only a few little pools to echo the breakers that once laid claim to them, breakers that now crash miles away in the distance. This is a time to go fishing on foot, »pêche à pied«. Amateurs in the art of beach fishing carefully poke out mussels, crabs and other delicacies of the sea from their hiding places and collect them in plastic buckets. But others are hunting too: silver gulls, sea swallows, wading herons, curlews etc. Yet then the sea returns to re-conquer its former land for the next six hours.

The monks at Mont St-Michel made good use of high tide with a clever scheme. When building began in the 10th century, the only stone that could be used to build their abbey came from the island of Chausey, 30km/19mi out in the sea. Therefore they built huge wooden rafts and loaded the quarried rock onto them at low tide, then allowed the sea to lift them and carry them to their eventual destination as it came in. Even as early as the 12th century, inhabitants of the region were already using the tides to do work for them. They built artificially dammed basins to collect seawater at high tide in order to drive their water wheels.

Nowadays the big differences in tidal levels are used to produce electricity. In the funnel-shaped estuary at Rance near St-Malo, where the rise is up to 14m/46ft and high tide reaches 22km/14mi inland, the world's first **tidal power station** (usine merémotrice) opened in 1966. It consists of a dam 750m/820yd long with 24 horizontal tube turbines, the vanes of which can be adjusted to the direction of flow. Every year this station produces some 550 million kWh, almost 10% of the energy requirements of Brittany.

The ebb and flow of the tides are a central part of life on the Atlantic coast. In newspapers, in hotels at harbours or resorts, the times are published every day for all to see.

Paramé
Rothéneuf

✱
Rochers Sculptés

The **Grande Plage** begins in the vicinity of Ville Close. The beach stretches for 2km/1.5mi as far as Paramé, a popular seaside and health resort (Thalasso therapy centre, casino). Rothéneuf adjoins St-Malo to the east amid rocky cliffs and coves. On Rue David Macdonald Stewart the home of Cartier, discoverer of Canada can be seen (museum). Take a look at the »scurrilous pirates« made by Abbé Fouré (1839–1910), known as the Ermite de Rothéneuf (Hermit of Rotheneuf). When he was thirty years old, one side of his body was paralysed by a stroke and he could longer speak. He retired to this beautiful spot on the coast and spent the next 25 years carving the rocky cliffs till he had made more than 300 pirates, sea monsters and other figures.

Usine
marémotrice

Between St-Servan and Dinard a 750m/820yd dam across the Rance is part of a **tidal power station** producing energy from sea currents (guided tours can be arranged via the Office de Tourisme in Dinard; ►p.293).

✱ ✱ Savoy · Savoie

N/O 6–8

Savoy stretches from the rolling landscape alongside Lake Geneva and Lac d'Annecy to the dramatic peaks and glaciers around Mont Blanc. Testaments to its historic legacy and, not least, its superb food make it a worthy tourist destination in both summer and winter.

Scenery

The French Alps are part of the landscapes of Savoy, ► Dauphiné, Haute-Provence (►Provence) and the ►Côte d'Azur. Historic Savoy, the 1860 borders of which corresponded almost precisely with the modern-day départements of Haute-Savoie and Savoie, is bounded in the north by Lake Geneva (Lac Léman), in the northwest by the Rhône as far as the bend at St-Genix-sur-Guiers and in the south by a line over the Col de la Croix de Fer to Galibier and extending northeast to the Cime de la Planette. The northern (Chablais) and western parts of Savoy are made up of delightful Alpine foothills. The high Alpine region is defined by three rivers and their valleys, the Arve (Faucigny), the Isère (Tarentaise) and the Arc (Maurienne). The Arve and the Isère are split by the Aravis Massif (Pointe Percée, 2752m/9029ft) and that of Mont Blanc, the highest mountain in the Alps at 4808m/15,774ft (►Chamonix). Between the Isère and the Arc is the Massif de la Vanoise (Grande Casse, 3855m/12,648ft), which has been a national park since 1963 (and continues into Italy's Parco Nazionale del Gran Paradiso). In 1995 the Massif des Bauges south of Lac d'Annecy was also declared a nature park for the region.

Passes and
tunnels

The 11.6km/7.2mi-long Mont Blanc tunnel links ►Chamonix with the Aosta valley (Courmayeur) in Italy, from where a return trip can

Contrasts of Savoy: view of Mont Blanc from Combloux

be made over the 2188m/7178ft Petit Saint-Bernard into Tarentaise (this »Tour de Mont Blanc« is rounded off by taking in Beaufort and Megève). The D 902 leads from Bourg-St-Maurice to the Col d'Iseran (2770m/9088ft), the second-highest pass in the Alps, which is closed between about November and June. Further south, just before Lanslebourg, a road leads off to Mont Cenis (2083m/6834ft), while the motorway to Turin can be joined at Susa. Finally the 12.9km/8mi Fréjus tunnel starts from Modane and emerges at Bardonecchia in Piedmont.

Agriculture is the main contributor to the region's wealth, with cattle farming, milk and cheese production supplemented by fruit and wine cultivation in the Alpine foothills. The Alpine rivers have been used to supply hydro-electric power since 1869. Nowadays the plants of Alpes du Nord supply a quarter of France's hydro-electric power. The electro-chemical and metallurgical industries go back nearly as far, their massive factories blots on the landscape of the Alpine valleys. In more recent times, machine engineering and fine mechanics (watch making) have also been added as these are less affected by the transport difficulties of the region. **Economy**

Since England's Pococke and Windham »discovered« the valley of Chamonix in 1741, and even more since the first ascent of Mont Blanc by farmer Jacques Balmat and doctor Michel Paccard, the Savoy Alps have been a popular holiday destination. Winter sports venues such as Chamonix, Megève, Les Arcs, La Plagne, Val d'Isère and **Tourism**

Tignes are internationally known and the range of mountains from Dent du Requin to the Grandes Jorasses provide the most beautiful and technically difficult climbs in the Alps. Those with less sporting intent can enjoy health spas such as Aix-les-Bains, Thonon and Evian as well as the renowned cuisine and superb wines of Savoy.

History Savoy was the original homeland of Italy's Sardinia-Piedmont royal house, whose kingdom remained in existence until 1945. The Celtic Allobrigian tribe migrated to the area in the 6th century BC. When Hannibal crossed the Alps in 218 BC it may possibly have been over Mont Cenis. As of 121 BC, 60 years of war finally led to occupation by the Romans and the region became part of the Roman province Gallia Narbonensis. The Burgundians settled here after 443 and they called their new domain »Sapaudia«, from which »Savoy« has derived. After a period of Frankish rule, control passed to the German Holy Roman Emperor Conrad II in 1032. The counts of Savoy controlled the Alpine passes and were able to extend their dominion as far as Bourg-en-Bresse, Turin and Nice by the mid-15th century. However an invasion by François I in alliance with the Swiss led to defeat for Savoy in 1536 so that Geneva, Waadt and Wallis had to be ceded to Switzerland. After 24 years of French occupation, Duke Emanuel Philibert 1560 moved his capital from Chambéry to Turin in Piedmont. Louis XIV occupied Savoy several times before the Utrecht peace treaty of 1713 granted the country to the kingdom of Sicily. Five years later it was swapped for Sardinia. After the unification of Italy, in which it had played a key role, Sardinia-Piedmont granted Savoy and Nice to the French in 1860 in reparation for French military support in the war against Austria. A referendum of the people then confirmed the change of sovereignty. The Winter Olympics have been held on Savoy territory three times: Chamonix in 1924 (the very first Winter Olympics), Grenoble in 1968 and Albertville in 1992.

Highlights Savoy

Places to Visit in Savoy

Lake Geneva (also called Lac Léman) is 72km/45mi long, 14km/9mi wide, 310m/1000ft deep and covers an area of 582 sq km/225 sq mi. It is surrounded by delightful countryside and atmospheric villages. The influence of the lake ensures that the climate is very balmy so that it is worth a visit at any time of year. A boat trip on the lake is, of course, an essential part of any such visit, ideally on one of the authentically restored paddle steamers.

★ ★
Lake Geneva

The fortified medieval outpost of Yvoire, about 25km/16mi northeast of Geneva, has defensive walls dating from the 14th century. The chateau by the lake is not open to the public but its **gardens** (Jardin des Cinq Sens) are an enjoyable experience. The pretty neighbouring village of Excenevex, noted for the manufacture of gold leaf, has a nice, large sandy beach.

★
Yvoire

Excenevex

Thonon (425m/1394ft, 30,000 inhabitants), a popular health spa, is prettily located on a terrace above the lake. From the fortifications on the edge of the escarpment there is a wide-ranging view reaching as far as the Jura mountains. Place du Château was where the castle of the dukes of Savoy stood until 1589. West of there is the 17th-century Château de Sonnaz containing the Musée du Chablais (folklore). In the old town centre there are two adjoining churches, Şt-François-de-Sales (neo-Gothic, 1889–1930) and St-Hippolyte (12th–17th centuries), where Francis of Sales himself once preached. Hôtel Dieu (to the south) occupies a former Minorite monastery from 1636.

Thonon

> **!** **Baedeker TIP**
>
> ### Château de Ripaille
>
> The palace of the Dukes of Savoy, situated to the north of Thonon above the lake, is one of France 100 »Sites Remarquables du Goût«. The renowned wine can be savoured in the lodge. From mid-June to mid-September the noted Le Prieuré restaurant of Thonon runs a subsidiary here, which makes a pleasant spot to relax after a tour of the building and its walls.

Evian-les-Bains (375–500m/1230–1640ft, 7000 inhabitants), the »Pearl of Lake Geneva«, has been an **internationally renowned health resort** since the end of the 18th century. The treaty granting independence to Algeria was signed here in 1962. The casino (1912), the Hôtel de Ville (Villa Lumière, late 19th century), the thermal spa facilities (1900) and the tavern (1903) make up a fabulous belle-époque ensemble, enhanced by some huge hotels. Parc Thermal is where the latest spa facilities are located. The church of Notre-Dame-de-l'Assomption (13th–15th centuries) was extended in 1926. The 19th-century choir stalls inside are beautiful.

Evian-les-Bains

One good to place to go for a day trip from Evian is the valley known as the **Dranse d'Abondance** (D 22). Its name comes from

Abondance

▶ VISITING SAVOY

INFORMATION

CRT Rhône-Alpes
104 Route-de-Paris
F-69260 Charbonnieres-les-Bains Tel.
04 72 59 21 59, fax 04 72 59 21 60
www.rhonealpes-tourisme.com

WHERE TO EAT

▶ Moderate / expensive

Belvédère
7 Chemin du Belvédère
F-74000 Annecy, tel. 04 50 45 04 90
www.belvedere-annecy.com
The view from here, 2km/1.5mi
southeast of Annecy on the Boulevard
de Corniche, is truly fabulous. The
same can be said for the excellent and
unusually imaginative menu (closed
Sun evenings, Wed). It is possible to
spend the night here in the comfortable rooms (moderate prices).

WHERE TO STAY

▶ Mid-range

L'Abbaye
15 Chemin de l'Abbaye, F-74940
Annecy-le-Vieux, tel. 04 50 23 61 08
www.hotelabbaye-annecy.com
Imposing Savoy estate in the northern
suburb of Le Vieux. The wooden
galleries around the courtyard provide
access to the stylishly furnished rooms.

Le Manoir
37 Rue Georges 1er, F-73100
Aix-les-Bains, tel. 04 79 61 44 00
www.hotel-lemanoir.com
Pretty Relais-de-Silence hotel in a
former subsidiary of the old palatial
hotels, Splendide and Royal. Comfortable rooms, a terrace leading to
the garden, swimming pool, sauna
and restaurant with classic cuisine.

Frescoes ✱ Abondance abbey, founded here in the 11th century. Its 14th-century cloisters are particularly beautiful, with frescoes by the Piedmontese artist Giacomo Jacquerio (1420, *Life of Mary*). Another village well worth seeing is **La Chapelle d'Abondance** with its »swiss-style« wooden chalets.

Morzine The D 902 leads from Thonon through the Dranse de Morzine valley, past the impressive **Gorges du Pont de Diable** and the remains of the abbey, Notre-Dame-d'Aulps (12th–13th centuries) up to Morzine (1000m/3280ft, 3000 inhabitants), which in summer is a base camp for tours through the mountains and in winter makes a pleasant ski resort, along with Avoriaz and Les Gets. A tour over the **Col de la Joux Verte** pass (1760m/5774ft) takes in the waterfall at Ardent, particularly magnificent when the snows are melting, and Lac Montriond, nestling at an elevation of 1049m/3442ft.

Faucigny The beautiful valley of the Arve, so-called Faucigny country, runs southeast from Geneva, growing ever narrower as it cuts into the region around Mont Blanc. Comfortably unassuming Megève (1113m/ **Megève** 3652ft, 4700 inhabitants) is nevertheless a renowned winter sports venue. One nice diversion is to take the road east from Taninges to

Samoëns and the **Cirque du er à Cheval**. St-Gervais-les-Bains (900m/
2953ft, 5100 inhabitants), a thermal spa with a fantastic view of the
Mont Blanc Massif, is another great place to spend a winter. St-Gervais (with its eponymous church built around 1700) is the prime
starting point for tours of Mont Blanc, but even regular Joes can take
the **Mont Blanc tramway** to Nid d'Aigle (2372m/7782ft), a marvellous experience. Another place to go on a day trip is up to Ass, where
the modern church was designed with the help of Braque, Matisse
and others.

To get from Megève to Lac d'Annecy, the best recommendation is to
take the Col des Aravis (1498m/4915) route (other routes go via La
Clusaz or the Col de la Croix-Fry). Amid the superb Alpine scenery
there is a wonderful view of the Mont Blanc Massif.

Nestling amid stunning mountain scenery, the Lac d'Annecy is
14km/9mi long, 3km/2mi wide and 82m/269ft deep. The pretty old
town of Annecy (52,000 inhabitants) is currently undergoing a facelift with various modern buildings. From the bridge near the church
of St-François (1645) there is a picture-book view of the 12th-cen-
tury **Palais de l'Isle** (subsequently the home of the counts of Geneva,
as well as its mint and law courts), located on an island in the middle
of the café-lined Thiou river. It houses a historical museum. A
stone's throw further to the north stands the late Gothic Dominican
church of St-Maurice (15th century), where the chapels were bestowed by wealthy families. Further to the west comes the 16th-
century **cathedral of St-Pierre**, where Saint Francis of Sales was once
active. Next door is the episcopal palace from 1784. The massive
tower rising up in the north (c1550) is part of the neo-classical
church of Notre-Dame-de-Liesse (1851). Heading west of the episcopal palace and across the bridge leads to **Rue St-Claire**, the main
street of old Annecy with its avenues of trees and houses from the
16th–18th centuries. A cheese market takes place here on Tuesdays.
In the rugged **castle** high over the town (Tour de la Reine 12th century, otherwise 14th–16th centuries), the counts of Geneva once
ruled. It now houses a local museum and its beautiful Grande Salle
is used for concerts. South of the castle are the Conservatoire d'Art
et d'Histoire and the basilica of the Annunciation (1930), where
relics of Francis of Sales and Joan of Chantal, who founded the order
of Salesian nuns in 1610, are kept.

A trip around Lac d'Annecy is not to be missed. In **Sévrier** there is
not only an interesting museum for the national dress of ladies in Savoy, but also the Musée de la Cloche, established by the Annecy bell
makers Paccard, who made the famous »Savoyarde« bell for the Sacré-Cœur in Paris. **Duingt**, its Savoy houses twined with grapevines, is
overlooked by a castle from the 11th century. On the opposite bank
of the lake is the idyllically situated **Talloires**, where the Benedictine

On Col de la Forclaz, Lac d'Annecy is at your feet

abbey (17th century, although the original dated back to around 1000) has now been made into a hotel. The inn, Auberge du Père Bise, is also famous. Another worthy place for a day trip is the Ermitage de St-Germain. 2km/1.25mi beyond Menthon the storybook **Château de Menthon** (13th–15th century) looks down from its mountain perch. From Veyrier (where there is a famous but exorbitantly expensive hotel and restaurant) a path leads up the slopes of **Mont Baron** (1252m/4108ft, 5 hours there and back). There is a wonderful view from the summit.

Massif des Bauges To get from Lac d'Annecy to Lac du Bourget means travelling through the 2000m/6500ft massif of Les Bauges (a nature park) with its distinctive wooden chalets. From Sévrier, first head south over the **Col de Leschaux** (897m/2943) to La Charniaz (19km/12mi); then either go west on the D 911 through Chéran gorge and over the spectacular **Pont de l'Abime** (another 21km/13mi), or take the longer and tougher route (45km/28mi) southwest via the Col de Plainpalais (1173m/3848ft), **Mont Revard** (1537m/5043ft, wonderful view) and the Col de la Cluse (1184m/3885ft) to Aix-les-Bains (45km/28mi, see below).

✳ ✳
Mont Revard

✳
Lac du Bourget Lac du Bourget is the **largest and deepest lake in France** (18km/11mi long, 3km/2mi wide, 145m/475ft deep) and is great for fishing. Squeezed between Mont de la Charvaz in the west and the steep, towering Mont de Corsuet in the east (catch the view from the rocks of La Chambotte) it is only separated from the Rhône flowing past it to the north by 2km/1.25mi of swampland. The two are connected by a canal, in which the flow of water changes direction depending

on the water level in the lake. One nice boat trip plies to the Abbaye de Hautecombe, which is the last resting place of 42 Savoy princes and princesses leading up to the last of the Italian kings, Umberto II († 1983). The church (1824–43) of the abbey, which was founded in the 12th century, has been decorated with great enthusiasm (it has more than 300 statues), but not necessarily the greatest of taste. Also to be seen is an unusual 12th-century »water mill«. **Le Bourget-du-Lac** (2900 inhabitants), after which the lake is named, was the residence of the counts in the Middle Ages. Its church (13th–15th centuries) and the monastic buildings (11th–15th centuries) of the Clunian priory are well worth seeing.

Abbaye de Hautecombe

Le Bourget-du-Lac

Aix-les-Bains (26,000 inhabitants), nestling under Mont Revard, is known the world over as a health resort with a mild climate. The Romans, too, built baths here (Aquae Domitianae). The two nationally run spas (Thermes Nationaux, 1849–1934, 1972), including the **Roman remains**, are open to the public. Other Roman relics include the 9m/30ft arch, erected by Lucius Pompeius Campanus, and the temple of Diana (now an archaeological museum). The town hall is located in the 16th-century chateau of the Marquis d'Aix. The Renaissance stairway of the building is built with stone taken from Roman buildings. Rue Davat leads north from the Thermes Nationaux past the neo-Byzantine church of Notre-Dame to the notable **Musée Faure** (Impressionist works, the second biggest collection of Rodin sculptures in France; closed Tue).

Aix-les-Bains

◄ Musée Faure

Chambéry (270m/886ft, 57,000 inhabitants) was from 1232 to 1562 the capital of independent Savoy and since 1860 it has filled that role for the département of Savoie. It lies in a fertile river valley between Chartreuse (► Dauphiné) and the Bauges Massif. The **castle** (14th–15th century, prefecture) of the counts and dukes of Savoy overlooks the city. It is accessed via Porte St-Dominique, formerly part of a Dominican monastery. The Gothic Ste-Chapelle (1408, façade 17th century) has some marvellous vaulting in the choir, 16th-century stained-glass windows and trompe-l'œil paintings by Vicario (1831). East of the castle is the **cathedral of St-François-de-Sales** (15th–16th centuries). Its façade is incomplete but the decorative painting inside was done by Vicario (1835). The episcopal palace next door houses the Musée Savoisien (prehistory, folklore, ecclesiastical art). Blvd. du Théâtre is adorned by the unusual **Elephant Fountain** from 1838. To the northwest is the outstanding **Musée des Beaux-Arts** (in an old granary, closed Tue), with works by Uccello, Titian, Preti and Watteau, among others. Rue Croix-d'Or south of the cathedral is lined with aristocratic houses. Alongside Carré Curial (a former barracks, 1802) on Rue de la République is the modern cultural centre Espace A. Malraux (Mario Botta, 1987). 2km/1.5mi further east (on a continuation of Rue de la République) is Les Charmettes, where Jean-Jacques Rousseau lived from 1736 to 1742.

Chambéry

◄ Musée des Beaux-Arts

◄ Les Charmettes

Combe de Savoie The section of the Isère between Montmélian and Albertville is called the Combe de Savoie and is used extensively for agriculture. The **most important wine-growing area of Savoy** (Apremont, Abymes, Chignin, Arbin) runs from Chambéry to Fréterive. There is a lovely view from picturesque Château Miolans (14th–15th century).

Albertville Albertville (345m/1132ft, 17,400 inhabitants), venue for the 1992 Winter Olympics, is situated at the confluence of the Arly and the Isère rivers. It came into being in 1835 with the amalgamation of L'Hôpital and Conflans under King Charles-Albert of Sardinia. Albertville has the Winter Olympics to thank for the somewhat sterile Place de l'Europe (Le Dôme cultural centre) and its trompe-l'œil façades. The »Maison des 16es Jeux Olympiques« museum is very popular. Old **Conflans**, on a mountain ridge above Albertville, is a

Conflans testament to earlier times with its gates, rugged walls and 18th-century Baroque church with a carved pulpit. Maison Rouge, a 14th-century convent, now houses a local museum.

Moûtiers The Tarentaise area, the valley of the Isère, is cattle country. Its capital is **Moûtiers** (4100 inhabitants, 480m/1575ft), which for a long time was an archbishopric. The cathedral of St-Pierre goes back to the 11th century (although it has undergone frequent modification).

It has some expressive tombs and crucifixion groups from the 16th century. The old episcopal palace has exhibitions covering the Baroque and the history of the Tarentaise region. The famous ski slopes of **Les Trois-Vallées**, Les Menuires/Val-Thorens, Méribel and Courchevel are accessed from Moûtiers. Like the pistes of Pralognan, La Plagne, Les Arcs, Tignes and Val d'Isère, they are located upon the **Massif de la Vanoise**, which occupies about a third of the land in Savoy and rises to height of 3855m/12,648ft at Grande Casse. The Vanoise National Park offers plenty of wonderful mountain treks and tours of the glaciers at all levels of difficulty.

Passing the impressive 11th-century priory church of St-Martin in Aime on the way, the road then leads to **Bourg-St-Maurice**

Winter wonderland in Méribel

Autumnal scene in the upper Val d'Isère

(6700 inhabitants, 840m/2756ft) at the foot of Little St Bernard. Around 10 July a major **international folk festival** is held here (Fêtes de l'Edelweiss).

Tignes

The well-known winter sports venue of Tignes (2000 inhabitants) lies at an elevation of between 1550 and 2100m (5000–7000ft) above the Lac du Chevril reservoir. Its concrete skyscrapers from the 1960s and 70s have been supplemented by smaller, more appealing hotel buildings in Alpine style. 48 ski-lifts open up 150km/100mi of piste at all degrees of difficulty, including the **Grande Motte** (mountain station 3456m/11,339ft, summer skiing). The 180m/590ft dam – adorned with a huge painting – is associated with a power station producing some 750 million kilowatt hours of power every year. Val d'Isère (1850m/6070ft, 1600 inhabitants) is linked with Tignes to

Val d'Isère

make up the **Espace Killy**. The centre of the old village disappeared behind concrete blocks in the 1970s. Newer architecture with raw stone, wooden balconies and slate roofs is making its present felt here too, though. Mountain railways and lifts lead to various peaks including Rocher de Bellevarde (2827m/9275ft), Tête du Solaise (2560m/8399ft) and Pointe du Montet (3300m/10,827ft).

Col d'Iseran

A road opened in 1937 rises steeply towards the Col de l'Iseran (2764m/9064ft). It passes Belvédère deTarentaise (2528m/8294ft) and, beyond the summit of the pass, **Belvédère de la Maurienne** (2503m/8212ft), where there is an orientation plaque for the magnificent view (experienced mountaineers should consider climbing Pointe des Lessières, 3041m/9977ft, two and a half hours there and back). The old village of Bonneval (200 inhabitants), at an elevation

✶

Bonneval-sur-Arc

of 1835m/6020ft, preserves its attractive looks with its stone-covered houses by **prohibiting modern building materials**. It lies in the valley

Lanslevillard

of the Arc, called Maurienne. From there pass through Bessans (Notre-Dame-des-Graces, 17th century; Chapelle St-Antoine, 1526, with murals) to get to Lanslevillard (the 15th-century Chapelle St-Sébastien has some brilliant murals) and Lanslebourg (Espace Baroque in the old church) at the foot of **Mont Cenis** (2083m/6834ft).

Avrieux

The road to Italy was built between 1803 and 1811. Avrieux, where Charles the Bald died in 877 on a return trip from Italy, has a 17th-century church dedicated to St Thomas Becket with fabulous Baroque furnishings. Modane is at one end of a railway tunnel built as early as 1857–1872 (13.6km/8.5mi) as well as the Fréjus road tunnel to Italy (12.9km/8mi, toll), opened in 1980.

Modane

Valloire

A steep road winds through many a hairpin from St-Michel-de-Maurienne up to the high **Valloirette** valley. Here lies Valloire (1430m/4692ft, 1200 inhabitants), a popular holiday resort in both summer and winter with a richly furnished church from the 17th century (carved high altar 1652). The 2646m/8681ft-high **Col du Galibier** pass leads to the **Col du Lautaret** (N 91) between Grenoble and Briançon (▶Dauphiné).

Saint-Jean-de-Maurienne

The historical capital of Maurienne (8900 inhabitants) was a bishopric until 1906. The cathedral of St-Jean-Baptiste is remarkable. Built in 1040–70 and altered into the Gothic style in the 15th century (classical vestibule from 1771), it has some splendid **Gothic choir stalls** inside (1498) and a fine Flamboyant-style tabernacle. The interesting Musée des Traditions Mauriennais and Musée Opinel (a knife manufacturer well known in France; closed Sun) are housed in the 18th-century episcopal palace.

✶✶ Strasbourg

P 4

Région: Alsace	**Altitude:** 143m/469ft
Département: Bas-Rhin	**Population:** 267,000

Strasbourg justifiably calls itself the »Carrefour de l'Europe«, the »meeting point for all of Europe«. The magnificent old capital of ▶Alsace has roots in both French and German cultures and, as the headquarters of numerous European institutions, it is now a political and cultural go-between for the united Europe.

European city with a long history

Strasbourg is not only the capital of ▶Alsace and the département of Bas-Rhin, but it is also at the very centre of the European Union. The Council of Europe, the European Court of Justice, the Human Rights Commission and the European Parliament (alternating with Luxembourg) all have headquarters here. In addition, its three universities, the European School of Governance, various museums, theatres and opera houses, along with the Franco-German TV broadcaster Arte make it the cultural metropolis of the whole region. Visitors, though, primarily think of Strasbourg as the lovely old free city of the Holy Roman Empire. With its cathedral, the Minster, its half-timbered buildings from the 16th–17th centuries and prestigious buildings of the 18th century and the Wilhelminian period, UNESCO has now declared the old city to be a World Heritage Site. Strasbourg is, too, the centre for the culinary tradition of Alsace – no wonder that the city is as popular with tourists as it is with its »Eurocrats«.

Economy

Until 1871 Strasbourg was a garrison town at the centre of an agricultural region. Thanks to the good transport links arising from its location on the Rhine, it experienced a massive boom as of that time. Coal and ore deposits encouraged development of chemicals and metal industries and, to add to these, the food industry, wood production and more recently electronics and clothing manufacture have all been represented in the city. Even today its docks retain their importance as the second biggest on the Rhine after those of Duisburg and the second biggest in France after Paris. International conventions and trade fairs are also drawing a growing number of participants to the town.

History

In the year 16 AD, the Romans established a fort on the Ill called Castrum Argentoratum, which was later to become an important trading centre. In 498 the settlement came into possession of the French crown. Its first documented mention as »Strataburgum«, »a fort or burgh on the road (strasse)« was in the 6th century. In 842 Charlemagne's grandsons, Louis the German and Charles the Bald, signed a pact against their brother Lothair I here. What are called the »Strasbourg oaths« are the oldest surviving documents written in

Highlights *Strasbourg*

Minster
Gothic architecture reaches for the heavens in an expression of metropolitan self confidence.
▶ page 766

Palais Rohan
Magnificent demonstration of the new »French« age
▶ page 771

Petite France
Half-timbered idyll on the Ill canals
▶ page 772

Musée d'Art Moderne
Contemporary art presented in sleek modern style
▶ page 772

Wilhelminian new town
The other Strasbourg of Prussian pomp after 1870
▶ page 772

European Parliament
Where Europe is being »created«
▶ page 773

Notre-Dame Cathedral

both Old High German and Old French. Under the Hohenstaufen dynasty, Strasbourg was granted a city charter in 1150 and it became a free city of the Holy Roman Empire in 1262. For a while it was the richest and most brilliant city of the empire and saw a blossoming of art and science. Mystics such as Meister Eckhart and Johannes Tauler were followed by humanists, such as Geiler von Kaysersberg and Sebastian Brant. It was here in 1434–44 that Johannes Gutenberg developed printing with movable type. After the Reformation was initiated in 1520, satirist Johann Fischart (1546–90) and teacher Johannes Sturm (1507–89) were resident here; the latter founded a theological academy which was to be a forerunner of the city's university and boasted such students as Goethe and Herder. Subsequent to the Peace of Westphalia of 1648, in which all of Alsace had been granted to France with the exception of Strasbourg and Mulhouse, the city was nevertheless annexed by Louis XIV in 1681. In the 18th century French culture gradually ousted the Germanic roots in Alsace. During the 1870–71 war between France and Germany, Strasbourg was besieged and bombarded in August 1871, finally being absorbed, with the rest of Alsace, into the new German Empire. This remained the case only until the end of the First World War, although Strasbourg would also come under German rule again in 1940–44. It became the seat of the Council of Europe in 1949.

✶ ✶ Notre-Dame Cathedral

History of construction The historic centre of the city includes the Grande Ile between the Ill and the Fossé du Faux rampart. It centres on the **Minster**, one of the most important legacies of western architecture. Work first started in 1176 to renew a Romanesque building on the site, which had been damaged by fire. By around 1225 the choir and the central section were finished with both sides of the transept following in 1230 and the nave being completed some time around 1275. The west façade (as of 1277) was initially planned as a classic French double-towered frontage but only the north tower was completed. When the architect Erwin von Steinbach died in 1318, the more than 13m/43ft rose window was already complete. The central section of the third storey came into being as of 1384, as planned by Michael Parler. Ulrich von Ensingen, who had been responsible for Ulm Minster, started work on the 142m/466ft north tower in 1399 and it was completed by Cologne's Johannes Hültz in 1439. In 1793 some 235 statues and countless ornaments fell victim to the Revolution. Plans were made to demolish the tower as it towered over the other buildings and thus violated the concept of equality. Instead, though, it was only covered with a lead Jacobin dome. 329 steps lead up to the observation platform 66m/217ft above the ground.

The portal sculptures, which dated from the 13th century, have largely had to be replaced with newer copies. Some of the originals, now to be seen in the Musée de l'Œuvre Notre-Dame, formed a pattern, in terms of content and style, for many other buildings. The tympana of the main portal and the side portal on the left depict scenes from the life of Christ. The right-hand side portal is flanked

Sculptures

Strasbourg Cathedral Plan

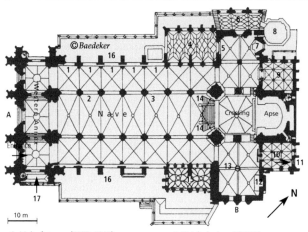

© Baedeker

A Main doorway (1277–1298)
B Clock entrance (c1220)
1 Emperor's windows (12th–14th C.)
2 Organ (André Silbermann, 1716; shell 1385/1489)
3 Pulpit (Hans Hammer, 1487)
4 St Martin's chapel (1515–20), altars 1698
5 Group set on the Mount of Olives (15th century)
6 St Laurence's chapel (1495–1505)
7 Font stone (Josse Dotzinger)
8 Sacristy

9 St John's chapel (c1240, with chapter hall above it)
10 St Andrew's chapel
11 To exhibition hall
12 Astronomical clock (1539–84)
13 Pillar of Angels (1230–40)
14 Steps to crypt
15 St Catherine's chapel (1331, vaulting 1563)
16 Kiosk barriers
17 Entrance to tower

► VISITING STRASBOURG

INFORMATION

Office du Tourisme
17 Place de la Cathédrale
F-67000 Strasbourg Tel. 03 88 52 28
28, fax 03 88 52 28 29
www.strasbourg.com
Centre d'Information sur les
Institutions Européennes
Tel. 03 88 15 70 80, fax 03 88 15 70 89
www.strasbourg-europe.com

TRANSPORT

Through traffic is prohibited in the
inner city. The centre is quickly
reached, though, via the modern tram
system from the Relais Tram park-
and-ride car parks along the access
roads to the city (Mon–Sat price
includes trip into the city and back).
Delightful boat trips can be taken on
the Ill canals.

FESTIVALS AND EVENTS

There are many events in summer, e.g.
June's Festival International de Musique. Since 1570 there has been a
Christmas market during Advent primarily centred on the square in front
of the cathedral, the station forecourt
and Kléber and Broglie squares.

WHERE TO EAT
► Expensive
① *Au Crocodile / Buerehiesel*
Culinary art in a class of its own can
be savoured at Au Crocodile (10 Rue
Outre, Tel. 03 88 32 13 02, closed Sun
and Mon) and Buerehiesel (Parc de
l'Orangerie, Tel. 03 88 45 56 65,
closed Sun and Mon). The latter
emphasizes its Alsatian heritage.

► Moderate / expensive
② *La Cambuse*
1 Rue Dentelles, tel. 03 88 22 10 22
Small, comfortable spot in Petite

France, serving only fish and other
seafood.

③ *Maison Kammerzell*
16 Place de la Cathédrale
Tel. 03 88 32 42 14
In spite of the uniqueness of the
location and the building, this is no
tourist trap. Excellent cuisine at
reasonable prices. The moderately
priced hotel in the same building is
also recommended (www.maison-
kammerzell.com).

► Inexpensive / moderate
④ *Caveau Gurtlerhoft*
13 Place de la Cathédrale
Tel. 03 88 75 00 75
Cosy, rustic restaurant serving Alsatian specialities.

Traditional »Winstubs«
Munsterstuewel, 8 Pl. du Marché-
aux-Cochons-de-Lait
Chez Yvonne, 10 Rue-du-Sanglier
Le Clou, 3 Rue Chaudron
Hailich Graab, 15 Rue des Orfèvres
Ami Schutz, 1 Rue Ponts Couverts

WHERE TO STAY

During sittings of the European
parliament (Mon–Fri, precise times
can be obtained from the tourist
office) and in December it can be
difficult to find a room. Timely
booking is essential.

► Luxury
① *Regent Petite France*
5 Rue des Moulins
Tel. 03 88 76 43 43, www.regent-
hotels.com
A dream hotel in a former ice-cream
factory between the Ill canals with a
view of Petite France and the cathedral. Avant-garde design with furni-

ture by Philippe Starck. Comparatively inexpensive restaurant (especially lunchtimes).

► Mid-range

② *Europe*
38 Rue Fossé des Tanneurs
Tel. 03 88 32 17 88
www.hotel-europe.com
Half-timbered building in a side street off the Grand Rue with large, comfortable guest rooms. The hotel has

had many famous guests, including Voltaire and Goethe.

► Budget / mid-range

③ *Gutenberg*
31 Rue des Serruriers
Tel. 03 88 32 17 15
www.hotel-gutenberg.com
Classy, pleasant and large rooms in a palais from 1745. Excellent price for the service. If possible try to get room 34 or one of the Mansarde rooms.

Strasbourg Map

1 Maison Kammerzell	4 Maison Pasteur
2 Pharmacie du Cerf	5 Musée Alsacien
3 Hôtel de la Chambre de Commerce	6 Cour du Corbeau

Where to eat
① Au Crocodile
② La Cambuse
③ Maison Kammerzell
④ Gurtlerhof

Where to stay
① Regent Petite France
② Europe
③ Gutenberg

by figures dressed as the foolish virgins in the company of the tempter and the wise virgins with Christ as their bridegroom. The southern entrance to the transept depicts the death of Mary in its left-hand arch, while the right-hand one shows her coronation. The female figures by an unknown master mason (*c*1220) to the left and right of King Solomon represent Ecclesia (Christendom) and Synagoge (Jewry).

★ ★
Interior

At 103m/113yd long and 41m/135ft wide the interior looks immense. Narrow clustered piers support vaulting which reaches a height of 31.5m/103ft above the nave. The superb **stained glass windows** from the 12th–14th centuries consist of half a million individual pieces of glass. The northern side aisle has 21 images of German **emperors and kings**. At the beginning of spring and autumn, a greenish beam of sunlight picks out the canopy over the statue of Christ on the pulpit. The southern transept also boasts a masterpiece of Gothic sculpture in the form of the Angel Pillar or **Pillar of the Last Judgement** (1230–40). The famous **astronomical clock** was built by Tobias Stimmer (1539–84). At approximately 12.30pm, the mechanism causes the Apostles to start moving. Also noteworthy are the late Gothic pulpit (1486) and the Andreas Silbermann organ (1716), which is enclosed in a housing largely dating back to 1489.

On Place du Marché-aux-Cochons-de-Lait, the suckling pig market, there is an abundance of Alsatian half-timbered buildings

The building for the masons' lodge (14th–16th centuries) is now home to the cathedral museum (Ger: »Frauenhausmuseum«; closed Mon), which possesses the original Gothic plans, innumerable original sculptures and medieval stained glass work, including the **Head of Christ** from the abbey church in Wissembourg, the oldest example of occidental stained glass (c1070).

✷ **Musée de l'Œuvre Notre-Dame**

Other Sights in Strasbourg

The **square before the cathedral** boasts two of the loveliest half-timbered buildings in the city. Maison Kammerzell is at the northern corner (ground floor 1467, half-timbered upper storey 1589) with bull's-eye panes and exaggerated wood carving. Then on the corner facing Rue Mercière (Krämergasse) is an apothecary building (1567), which has been in existence since 1268.

✷ **Maison Kammerzell**

Pharmacie du Cerf

The archiepiscopal palace, Palais Rohan, was built in 1728–42 on the site of an earlier medieval episcopal residence. It was designed by court architect Robert de Cotte and is an excellent example of the new French tastes of the 18th century. No less than three museums are housed in the building (all closed Tue): the Musée Archéologique, the **Musée des Beaux-Arts**, with its outstanding paintings by Italian, Spanish and French masters from the Gothic era up to the 18th century, and the Musée des Arts Décoratifs, featuring Alsatian handcrafted art and one of the finest collections of ceramics in France.

Palais Rohan

✷ ✷ ◀ Museums

Southwest of the palais behind the Musée de l'Œvre Notre-Dame, the picturesque pig market stretches away towards the Ill. It is adjoined to the northeast by the Place du Marché-aux-Poissons (fish market). On Saturday mornings a market for all kinds of foodstuffs is held here. The Grande Boucherie, built in 1586 as an abattoir, contains the museum of the city's history (closed Tue). Opposite stands the Ancienne Douane (former customs and chamber of commerce building), which hosts various changing exhibitions.

Place du Marché-aux-Cochons-de-Lait

Grande Boucherie

Next, cross the Ill by the Pont du Corbeau. The entrance to the **Cour de Corbeau**, one of the loveliest courtyards in the city, is here. It used to belong to a guesthouse that remained in existence until 1854 and entertained guests including Voltaire, Casanova and King Frederick the Great of Prussia. Further upstream, three buildings dating from the 17th–18th centuries now accommodate the Musée Alsacien with its exhibits pertaining to everyday customs, handicrafts and folk art.

✷ **Cour de Corbeau**

✷ **Musée Alsacien**

Crossing the Ill again, the route leads past St-Thomas' church on the way to Petite France. It is the only **Gothic hall-type church** in Alsace (9th–14th centuries). Now a Protestant church, in 1521 it hosted sermons by reformer Martin Bucer. Other things to see include the huge and moving tomb of Field Marshall Moritz of Saxony († 1750)

St-Thomas

by Jean-Baptiste Pigalle (1777) as well as the Baroque Silbermann organ (1740), upon which Mozart himself once gave a concert in 1778 and which was often played by Albert Schweitzer.

✴✴
Petite France
Ponts Couverts
Barrage Vauban

The former **tanners' quarter** (Quartier des Tanneurs) of Petite France is outstandingly picturesque with its half-timbered houses and narrow streets. At the edge of the area four towers still stand that were part of the **medieval defences** of the city, which also included the Ponts Couverts, covered wooden bridges over the channels of the Ill (the present-day bridges date from 1860). There is a great view from the terrace of the Barrage Vauban. This great dam was a part of the city fortifications erected in 1686–1700 under Louis XIV.

✴✴
Musée d'Art
Moderne et
Contemporaine

The museum of modern and contemporary art was opened on the other side of the Ill in 1998. Designed by Adrien Fainsilber, its collection ranges from Impressionism to the present day, with particular emphasis on the work of Strasbourg-born **Hans Arp**. There is a lovely view of the old town from the sculpture terrace and the chic café.

Northern old
town

Place Gutenberg west of the cathedral is dominated by the **Hôtel du Commerce**, the most important Renaissance building in Lower Alsace. It was built from 1582 to 1585 as a town hall. The northern part of the old town grew up in the 18th century. Its focus is Place Kléber, named after a general who was born in Strasbourg in 1753. The northern side of the square is occupied by the former central police station (L'Aubette, 1772). To the northeast of Place Kléber is the elongated Place Broglie, set out in 1742. The **town hall** was built here in 1736 under the name of Hanauer Hof for the benefit of the counts of Hessen. The eastern side of the square is occupied by the Opéra du Rhin (1822, with its »theatrical« café). The Banque de France is on the site of the building where Claude-Joseph Rouget de Lisle is said to have first performed the song that would become the *Marseillaise* on 26 April 1792.

✴
Wilhelminian
quarter

Northeast of the island on which the old town stands, a quarter that was built when the city was under German sovereignty under Kaiser Wilhelm spans both sides of the Ill. Its magnificent buildings emulate the Florentine Renaissance (the station west of the old town was also created in 1880). The **Place de la République** features an expressive memorial entitled »Mother Alsace holds her sons, who fell for France and for Germany« (1936) and also has the **Palais du Rhin**, completed in 1889 as a residence for Wilhelm I. The **Musée Tomi Ungerer** opposite the national theatre attracts fans of this satirist with a cruel pen (closed Tue). Avenue de la Liberté leads past the post office across the Ill to the university (1884). A park behind it includes the botanical gardens, the planetarium and the zoological museum. Further south along the Boulevard de la Victoire there is a stunning **Art Nouveau building with the city baths**.

The European Parliament building, erected to follow the curve of the Ill

Allée de la Robertsau leads northeast from the university to the popular and idyllic Parc de l'Orangerie, laid out in 1804 to plans by Le Nôtre and including the small palace of the Empress Joséphine (1805). The park is also where »Buerehiesel« can be found, one of the finest restaurants in France, located in an old half-timbered building moved here brick by brick from Molsheim and rebuilt in 1885 (►p.768).

Parc de l'Orangerie

To the west of the park is the impressive »**Eurotown**«, first the square aluminium and glass building of Palais Europe (Bernard, 1977), where the Council of Europe meets, then behind that on the other side of the Ill the European parliament (Architecture Studio Europe, 1998). The European Court of Justice (Richard Rodgers, 1994) is on the other side of the Rhine-Marne canal. Information on tours or visits to the meetings of the various bodies can be obtained from the tourist office and the Centre d'Information sur les Institutions Européennes (►p.768).

EU buildings

It is also worth visiting the northern part of Port Autonome between the city centre and the Rhine (north of the Europa bridge to Kehl). A retired tugboat is now used to house the museum of shipping in the Rhine (**Naviscope**, Rue du Général Picquart).

Port Autonome

Toulon

Région: Provence – Alpes – Côte d'Azur   **Altitude:** 1–10m/3–33ft
Département: Var   **Population:** 166,000

Toulon, situated at the most southerly point of the ▶Côte d'Azur, is not exactly one of those must-see destinations, but as France's most important military harbour it has a lively atmosphere, especially in the old town centre, which has been rebuilt since its destruction in the Second World War.

Important Mediterranean harbour

Thanks to its position on a bay sheltered by the St-Mandrier peninsula, Toulon, the capital of the Var département and centre of an urban district with more than 500,000 inhabitants, has always been an important harbour for traders, ferries and fishing. However, it is the navy that is the major employer here, providing work for more than 6000 people. Other industries include shipbuilding, armaments and flower cultivation.

History

In ancient times, Greek Telonion and later Roman Telo Martius was not only of importance as a harbour but also for the extraction of purple dye from sea snails. The first mention of the city as a bishopric dates from 441. Toulon became part of France in 1487 and became a major bastion of the French naval fleet. During the Revolution in 1793 the royalists delivered the city into the hands of Britain's Admiral Hood, but it was taken back by the revolutionary army, whereby a certain 23-year-old lieutenant by the name of Bonaparte was mentioned in despatches for his valour. In the Second World War, Toulon was the base for the French Mediterranean fleet. The city was bombarded by the Germans in November 1942 and the fleet was sunk on 27 November. Further destruction was wrought by Allied air raids in 1943–44. Extensive suburbs grew up in the 1960s but the inner city fell into decay. Since then the city has regained a busy but comfortable »Provencal« atmosphere, especially in the new »Vieux Toulon«.

In the harbour at Toulon

What to See in Toulon

Quai Cronstadt

The city's main boulevard, Quai Cronstadt, runs along the **Darse Vieille** (old harbour basin), overlooked by the tower of the new town hall. The Préfecture Maritime is at the western end of the street and

Musée de la Marine

behind that is the fascinating naval museum. The Atlanteans of

Pierre Puget (1657), which once adorned the old town hall, destroyed in the Second World War, can be seen at the Mairie d'Honneur.

From here the narrow but lively Rue d'Alger runs northward into Rue Hoche, ending at the pretty **Place Puget** with its Fontaine des Trois Dauphins (1782). Rue Landrin then provides access to the Cours Lafayette, where markets are held on Tuesday and Sunday mornings, and the **Musée du Vieux Toulon** (city history, ecclesiastical art; closed Sun). Next door is the early Gothic cathedral of Ste-Marie-Majeure (11th–12th centuries, rebuilt in the 17th century; tower 1740), where France's gold reserves were hidden during the war of 1870–71. South of the cathedral is Place de la Poissonnerie (fish mar-

Old town

Ste-Marie-Majeure

Toulon Map

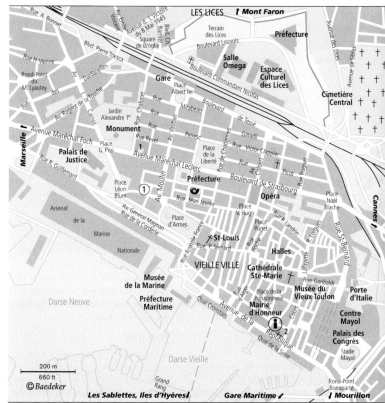

1 Musée d'Art et d'Archéologie
2 St-François-de-Paule

Where to stay
① Le Jaurès

ket). At the eastern edge of the old town the Porte d'Italie has survived, a remnant of Vauban's city fortifications.

Other attractions Adjoining the old town to the north, a suburb dating from the 19th century contains the magnificent **opera house** (1864). To the northwest is Place de la Liberté with its Monument de la Fédération. The Musée d'Art is a little further west and features art from the 13th–20th centuries along with prehistoric and antique finds from archaeological excavations. The Musée d'Histoire Naturelle (geology, palaeontology) is also housed here. After visiting the museum, spend a little time in the neighbouring Jardin Alexandre I.

Military harbour The Darse Neuve was built in 1680–1700 and is lined by docks and naval arsenals (not open to the public). This was also the site of the notorious Bagno, a prison which was opened in 1748 to house prisoners formerly sentenced to be galley slaves and remained in existence until 1874. Up to 4000 were incarcerated there and set to work on the wharves and docks. The lovely **Porte de l'Arsenal** dates from 1738.

Mourillon The imposing **Tour Royale** (1514, impressive view) is at the southern end of the spit in the southeastern suburb of Mourillon. Adjoining it
✱ to the east is Toulon's beach along with Fort St-Louis (1707). The
Corniche Mistral Corniche Mistral runs along the Grande Rade heading east, passing the Jardin d'Acclimatation (botanical gardens) on the way to the charming housing district of **Cap Brun** (103m/338ft, nice view). Below the coast road, the »Sentier des Douaniers« (»path of the customs men«) winds among the romantic coves.

▶ VISITING TOULON

INFORMATION

Office du Tourisme
334 Av. de la République
F-83000 Toulon
Tel. 04 94 18 53 00, fax 04 94 18 53 09
www.toulontourisme.com

WHERE TO EAT

▶ **Moderate / expensive**
Bernard
Plage de Magaud, Cap Brun
Tel. 04 94 27 20 62.
Slightly hidden away on the seashore, but a marvellous place to enjoy seafood. Bouillabaisse by order, reservations essential. Closed Oct–March and Sun evenings/Mon.

WHERE TO STAY

▶ **Budget**
① *Le Jaurès*
11 Rue J. Jaurès, tel. 04 94 92 83 04
www.hoteljaures.fr
Located near the Palais de Justice, this pleasant hotel is worthy of another star. The rooms facing the courtyard are nice and quiet.

FERRIES

Boats leaving for trips round the harbour and to the Iles d'Hyères, La Seyne and St-Mandrier all ply from Quai Cronstadt. The ferries to Corsica and Sardinia cast off from the southeastern basin of the harbour

A very steep and narrow road and a cable car (from Av. Amiral-Vence) lead up to the 584m/1916ft summit of Mont Faron, which overlooks the city to the north. The Musée Mémorial du Débarquement covers the landing of Allied forces in August 1944. There is a superb view from its roof.

★ Mont Faron

★ Toulouse

`J 9`

Région: Midi – Pyrénées
Département: Haute-Garonne

Altitude: 146m/479ft
Population: 398,000

Toulouse, the fourth biggest city in the country, is the biggest economic metropolis of southwest France. The friendly »ville rose« with its Mediterranean atmosphere is, however, not only the centre of the French space and aerospace industry, but also a city of art with important buildings, museums and cultural establishments.

As there are no quarries around Toulouse, brick is the prime building material. It is for that reason that Toulouse has the nickname »la ville rose«. »Tolosa« was the Romans' name for the city, then a way station on the road from Narbonne to Bordeaux. From 419 to 506 Toulouse was the capital city of the Visigoths' domain. Under the Franks it became the main city of Aquitaine. Between 845 and 1249 the town was governed by the counts of Toulouse, who held spectacular court here. At the time of the Cathar) crisis, Toulouse was the leading city for the so-called Albigensians. Count Raymonde VI was excommunicated in 1207 and church forces laid siege to the city on several occasions. The Cathar wars were ended by the Treaty of Paris of 1229 (► Baedeker Special p.452), which brought Languedoc and Toulouse under the sovereignty of the French crown. During the 15th century, the town became prosperous from the trade in dye, and it quickly adopted influences from the Florentine Renaissance. It suffered a setback around 1560, though, when importation of in-

Toulouse then and now

The Toulouse Romanesque of St-Sernin

▶ VISITING TOULOUSE

INFORMATION

Office de Tourisme
Donjon du Capitole, F-31000 Toulouse
Tel. 05 61 11 02 22, fax 05 61 23 74 97
www.toulouse-tourisme.com

TRANSPORT

Metro and buses operated by Tisseo.
Information: Place Esquirol, Station
Capitole.
Blagnac Airport 8km/5mi northwest,
bus link to the city centre. Boat trips
on the Garonne and the Canal du
Midi from Quai de la Daurade.

EVENTS

July/Aug: »Toulouse d'Été«, Tue–Fri
there are concerts in various attractive
locations in the city, from chamber
music to gospel. Oct: »Octobre Bleu«
in and around Toulouse with internationally famous musicians.

WHERE TO EAT

▶ Expensive

① *Michel Sarran*
21 Blvd. A.-Duportal
Tel. 05 61 12 32 32. Closed Aug.
Michel Sarran calls his cooking style
»italo-espano-gasconne«. For what it
has to offer, this establishment with
its simple modern furnishings is
relatively inexpensive, but that makes
it very popular.

▶ Inexpensive / moderate

② *Les Halles Victor Hugo*
From Tue to Sun it is possible to a
enjoy a superb and very cheap meal
on the first floor of the market hall in
the plain and simple ambience of six
restaurants.

③ *Brasserie Flo Les Beaux Arts*
1 Quai de la Daurade
Tel. 05 61 21 21 12

Magnificent brasserie from the 1930s
on the Garonne with a view of the
Pont Neuf bridge and its nightly
illuminations. Traditional cuisine.

④ *La Bohème*
3 Rue Lafayette, tel. 05 61 23 24 18
Simple restaurant with a familial
atmosphere in a 17th-century building near the Capitole. Hearty regional
cuisine based on goose and duck.

WHERE TO STAY

▶ Luxury

① *Grand Hotel de l'Opéra*
1 Place du Capitole, tel. 05 61 21 82 66
www.grand-hotel-opera.com
The city's premier hotel occupies a
prime location and is based around a
former abbey. The atmosphere does
indeed have something of the »oper-
atic«. The restaurant, »Les Jardins«, is
first class and serves a menu inspired
by local recipes (closed Sun and
Mon). The brasserie is well priced
(closed Sun).

▶ Mid-range

② *Hôtel des Beaux-Arts*
1 Place Pont-Neuf, tel. 05 34 45 42 42
www.hoteldesbeauxarts.com
Small but pleasant hotel with unobtrusive modern furnishings. Some
rooms on the first floor include a
patio with superb views of the
Garonne. Restaurant ▶Brasserie Flo.

▶ Budget

Chapon Fin
Place Récollets, F-82200 Moissac
Tel. 05 63 04 04 22, fax 05 63 04 58 44,
www.lechaponfin-moissac.com
Classic hotel on the marketplace, a
stone's throw from the famous abbey
of St-Pierre. Comfortable rooms and
a good restaurant and brasserie.

Toulouse Map

1 Hôtel-Dieu
2 Musée de la
Médicine

Where to eat
① Sarran
② Les Halles
③ Brasserie Flo
④ Bohème

Where to stay
① Grand Hotel de l'Opera
② Beaux-Arts

digo caused a drop in popularity of the Toulouse dyestuffs. After the First World War, Toulouse developed into a major hub for the national armaments and aerospace industries. Concorde made its maiden flight from here in 1969. Nowadays, the Airbus company has its headquarters in Toulouse and Ariane rockets are built here, too. Even though it is historically the main metropolis of Occitania and thus of ▶ Languedoc, reorganization of national boundaries in the 1960s meant that it is no longer part of the region now bearing that name. Toulouse has had its own university since as long ago as 1233 and, in addition, it now possesses 14 grandes écoles as well as other educational establishments, so that as many as 80,000 students live in the city.

What to See in Toulouse

Capitole

The focal point of the city is the atmospheric **Place du Capitole** with its pretty arcades. The cheery but dignified Capitole building itself is 128m/140yd long. Built in 1753, it gets its name from the »Capitouls«, former appellation for the city's mayors. The building is occupied by both the town hall (with its magnificent Salle des Illustres) and the theatre, where the famed orchestra is based. Behind the Capitole, the tourist office is located inside the 1529 donjon, while to the north stands the interesting 14th-century church of Notre-Dame-du-Taur. Its façade was the inspiration for many of the churches in the region.

Notre-Dame-du-Taur

★ ★
St-Sernin

The basilica of St-Sernin was one of the way stations for the pilgrims on the Way of St James and is one of the most beautiful Romanesque buildings anywhere (open July–Sept Mon–Sat 8.30am–6.15pm, Sun till 7.30pm, Oct–June Mon–Sat 8.30am–11.45am, 2pm–5.45pm, Sun 8.30am–12.30pm, 2pm–7pm). A basilica was in existence from the 4th century and housed the grave of St Sernin (Saturninus), who had been martyred in 250. After Charlemagne had bequeathed a number of important relics (including relics of six of the Apostles), the floods of pilgrims meant that a new building became essential. The brick construction was started in 1080, the earliest section being the choir (consecrated 1096), and was largely completed by 1118 (it was restored in the 19th century by Viollet le Duc and the main façade dates from 1929). The most beautiful part of the building is the **choir with its nine chapels** and the 65m/213ft octagonal tower above the centre of the intersection of nave and transept (mid-13th century), which brought forth many imitations in Languedoc and Gascony. The **Porte Miégeville** entrance (von »mieja vila«, centre of town) to the southern side aisle is quite outstanding with its 12th-century Romanesque sculptures (tympanum: Ascension of Christ; lintel: the Apostles; left-hand console: King David), as is the Porte des Comtes in the south transept (capitals with the story of the poor man Lazarus). The building was modelled on the pilgrims' churches

Interior ▶

of Limoges and Conques. The impression inside is almost like being in a deep, narrow canyon (115m/126yd long, 21m/69ft high. With a nave and four aisles, it is 32.5m/107ft wide, while the transept measures 64m/70yd). The magnificent altar was made by Bernardus Gelduinus (1096). The gallery around the choir is peppered with gilded relic shrines and the grave of St Sernin himself (18th century) is behind the altar along with some reliefs by Gelduinus. The choir screen (16th–17th centuries) and choir stalls (1670) are beautiful too.

In the arcades on Place du Capitole, the pretty heart of the city

Musée St-Raymond

The city's archaeological museum is in a college building from 1523 and exhibits not only archaeological finds from Roman times and prehistory, but also works of art from the Middle Ages and the Renaissance.

✱ Eglise des Jacobins

This Gothic Dominican church (1235) – the Dominicans were in the forefront of the war against the Cathars – has a magnificent interior: a bright hall, divided into two aisles by a row of columns 28m/92ft high. The vaulting develops above the choir into a **palm-like fan**. As of 1368 and in recent times since 1974 the remains of St **Thomas Aquinas** (1225–74) have been kept here. The nearby Hôtel de Bernuy was built from 1509 to 1534 for a Spanish dye merchant. Further southwest on the quay of the Garonne river is the Baroque church of Notre-Dame-de-la-Daurade (1790).

Hôtel de Bernuy Notre-Dame-de-la-Daurade

The lovely Hôtel Dumay (16th–17th centuries) houses the local historical museum. On Rue St-Rome (a pedestrianized zone featuring several luxury shops) there are not only some impressive Renaissance houses, but also the Gothic Tour Séguy and Tour de Sarta further south.

Musée du Vieux Toulouse

The richest domicile in the city was built in 1555–57 by Nicolas Bachelier for dye merchant and capitoul (municipal officer of Toulouse) Pierre d'Assézat. Its courtyard is lovely. **Fondation Bemberg** inside it is well worth a visit with its collection of art from the 16th–20th centuries (including Tintoretto, Gauguin, Dufy; closed Mon). The 14th–15th-century Augustine monastery has its own collection of ecclesiastical sculptures (early Christian sarcophagi, medieval sculptures) and paintings by famous artists from the 15th–20th centuries on view.

Hôtel d'Assézat

✱ Musée des Augustins

St-Étienne

At the eastern edge of the old town, a huge tower marks the cathedral of St-Étienne, the somewhat grotesque, piecemeal look of which is down to the lengthy period over which the building work was carried out (11th–17th centuries). The nave was the first building in all of southern France to feature Gothic elements and the 19m/62ft span of its vaulting was the widest in Europe in its time. The rose window was added to the western façade in 1230. The dual-aisled choir was begun in 1272 and was originally intended as the core of a different church entirely, whereby the transept was to have been demolished. The windows in the choir (15th–17th centuries) are highly noteworthy, as are the choir stalls (1611), organ (17th century) and tapestries (16th–18th centuries).

Old town south

Rue Perchepeinte, renowned for its antique shops, leads from the cathedral to the Musée Paul Dupuy (arts and crafts from the Middle Ages onwards). Then take Rue Ozenne, with its beautiful 15th-century buildings, towards Hôtel Béringuier-Maynier, built in 1517–27, when it was the first »Renaissance import« in Toulouse. Beyond Place des Carmes and its market hall stands the church of Notre-Dame-de-la-Dalbade (1503–45) with a Renaissance portal from 1537 (tympanum 20th century). **Rue Dalbade** is also worth a look with its fine palaces, especially the 16th-century Hôtel de Clary, the façade of which was made in the 17th century entirely out of (expensive) stone. The Musée d'Histoire Naturelle and the botanical gardens both lie to the south of Allée J.-Guesde.

West of the Garonne

Pont Neuf (1544–1632) spans the Garonne leading to a pumping station from 1823 (Château d'Eau, an exhibition venue). Opposite stands the Hôtel Dieu St-Jacques with the Musée de la Médicin. Rue Viguerie then leads to the large Dôme de la Grave complex. Further west is the 1831 **abattoir**, which has now been made into a museum of modern art and counts Picasso's *Minotaur in Harlequin Costume* among its possessions (closed Mon). Its pretty café offers good food at a reasonable price. Finally, cross the Garonne once again via the St-Pierre bridge to take a look at the **EDF Bazacle**, a power station from 1889 (open Tue–Fri 2pm–7pm; exhibitions). The fish passage is interesting too.

✳
Les Abattoirs

EDF Bazacle

Around Toulouse

Airbus

The guided tour through the world of Airbus begins in Blagnac (about 5km/3mi west). Bookings with Taxiway (www.taxiway.fr, tel. 05 34 39 42 00) or in July–Aug at the Toulouse tourist office.

Montauban

Montauban (52,000 inhabitants), capital of the Tarn et Garonne département, lies 50km/31mi north of Toulouse. It was founded in 1144 as the second of Aquitaine's bastides and is well known as a **centre for jazz** (July–Aug Festival de Jazz, Jazz en Tarn-et-Garonne).

The elegant cloister at Moissac with its 76 different capitals

The town is almost entirely built of brick and there is a great view of it from the Pont Vieux (1348) bridge. The episcopal palace (1664) at the eastern end of the bridge houses the Musée Ingres, featuring works (including 4000 drawings) by Montauban's own **Jean-Auguste-Dominique Ingres** (1780–1867) and sculptures by Antoine Bourdelle (1861–1921). Opposite that museum, the 17th-century Cour des Aides contains a folklore museum. Head east past St-Jacques' church (14th–15th centuries) with its distinctive tower to Place Nationale where there are some fine 17th-century arcades and a market. The tourist office is located in the 17th-century Collège des Jesuites at the northeastern edge of the old town (Place Prax Paris). At the southern end the Notre-Dame cathedral from 1732 is built in a rather cold classical style but its left-hand transept contains the *Vow of Louis XIII* by Ingres.

★
◀ Musée Ingres

Moissac (12,000 inhabitants) 31km/19mi northwest of Montauban is famous for its **Benedictine abbey**, founded in the 7th century and deconsecrated in 1790. The 1120 **south doorway** of the abbey church of St-Pierre (11th–12th centuries) is one of the finest works of Romanesque sculpture anywhere. The imagery of the tympanum shows the second coming of Christ and the Last Judgement, while the doors are flanked by pictures of St Peter (left) and Isaiah. The fantastic central column features two pairs of lions that cross over one another along with St Paul and the prophet Jeremiah. The 12th-century Romanesque crucifix in the nave is also noteworthy. The 11th–13th-century cloister features alternating single and double columns, although the faces that once adorned the capitals were destroyed during the French Revolution. The tourist office arranges visits to the cloister (open July–Aug 9am–7pm, April–June, Sept–Oct 9am–12.30pm, 2pm–6pm (Sat–Sun from 10am), Nov–March 10am–noon, 2pm–5pm (Sat–Sun afternoons only). The abbots' palace houses the Musée Moissagais (folklore). From its tower there is a great view of the old town and of the vineyards in the neighbouring territory. The white **Chasselas grapes** from Moissac (AOC) are well known.

Moissac

★ ★
◀ Doorway

★ ★
◀ cloister

Tours

H 5

Région: Centre
Département: Indre-et-Loire

Altitude: 55m/180ft
Population: 137,000

The Touraine is famed as the »garden of France«, and most of the Loire chateaux (▶Loire Valley) are to be found there. The region centres on Tours at the confluence of the Loire and Cher, a modern city slightly reminiscent of Paris but with a cheerful southern French atmosphere and boasting some important testimonies to its history.

History
By the 4th century Tours was already the capital of four Roman provinces when it was known as Urbs Turonum (after the Gallic Turons). St Gatian had already preached Christianity here in the 3rd century, but it was only with the famous **St Martin**, who was bishop of Tours from 372 onwards, that the religion became established. St Martin's tomb became a place of pilgrimage and a national monument for the Franks. The town of Martinopolis grew up, with a basilica and monastery. It was amalgamated with the Cité district, which is based on the Roman town, in the 14th century. In 573 Gregor, who wrote the *History of the Franks*, became the bishop here, while in 732 Charles Martel defeated the Moors in the battle of Tours and Poitiers. Charlemagne despatched Alcuin to the city in 796 and he established a university and an important college of scripture. From the reign of Louis XI until that of François I, Tours was capital of the kingdom. It was Louis who introduced the city's silk industry, which flourished until the mid-17th century. The rich city was one of the earliest to switch to Protestantism, which inevitably drew it into the religious warfare of the period. The Calvinists plundered the monastery of St-Martin in 1562, but vengeance came ten years later when Tours too experienced its own version of the St Bartholemew's Day massacre. German bombardment in 1940, 1942 and 1944 destroyed large areas of Tours. **Honoré de Balzac's** birthplace (1799 –1850) is now an important centre of industry (textiles, pharmaceuticals, foodstuffs, printing), a trading centre for agricultural produce and wine, while its university caters for 30,000 students.

What to See in Tours

City centre
The centre of the city is bisected by the **Rue Nationale**, a lively shopping street with stores and chic boutiques which dates back to 1763. The impressive town hall (1905) is situated on Place Jaurès along with the Palais de Justice (1843). The old town lies to the west of

Place Plumereau
Rue Nationale and centres on Place Plumereau, with its half-timbered buildings from the 15th century. Among its interesting streets

Rue Briçonnet
is Rue Briçonnet, which leads away northward from the northwest-

ern corner of Place Plumereau. The façades of its houses range from
Romanesque up to the 18th century. At the northern end stands the
late 15th-century Maison de Tristan. Musée du Gemmail (gemmail is
a kind of glass enamel) in Hôtel Raimbault (Rue de Mûrier) has
works by artists including Picasso
and Braque. One of the finest
houses is Hôtel Goüin (photo
p.81), built in 1510 and modelled
on an Italian forerunner. It now
houses the Touraine Archaeological
Society's collections (prehistoric
and Gallo-Roman finds, art from
the Middle Ages to the 18th
century).

Until 1802 **St-Martin's basilica**
stood to the south of Place Plumereau. There are remnants of the

110m/361ft-long church with a nave and four aisles, built over the
grave of St Martin between the 11th and 13th centuries: these are the
Tour d'Horloge, formerly part of the west façade, and Tour Charlemagne, which marked the end of the northern transept. Rue des
Halles roughly follows the line of the old nave. The new basilica was
built from 1886 to 1902 in Romanesque-Byzantine style by Victor
Laloux, who was also responsible for the Gare d'Orsay in Paris. The
apse has an altar with the relic of St Martin's skull and in the crypt –
in its original location – is **St Martin's tomb**. The Musée St-Martin
on Rue Rapin has an educational exhibition concerning both the
saint and the basilica. To the south of the 434m/475yd-long Pont Wilson (1774) lies the church of St-Julyen (1259), formerly part of a
Benedictine abbey. **Musée des Vins-de-Touraine** is an interesting museum located in the abbey's wine cellar, while the chapter hall houses
the **Musée du Compagnonnage**, which covers the life and works of
France's workers. A courtyard with the remains of the Hôtel de
Beaune-Semblançay (a palais built for the finance minister of Louis
XII and François I) and the Fontaine de Beaune (1511) can be accessed from Rue Nationale.

Quartier
St-Julyen

Hôtel de Beaune

The ancient city, the Cité, occupies the area around the cathedral
with Rue Colbert as its main axis (nice buildings from the 15th–16th
centuries). The Tour de Guise, a remnant of a castle built in around
1260, still stands alongside the Loire. The chateau contains the Historial de Touraine (wax museum) and an aquarium, while there is a
historical display in the Logis du Gouverneur.

Cité

Chateau

The cathedral (photo p.787) is consecrated to the first bishop of
Tours. The choir of this basilica was completed in around 1260,
while the nave dates from about 1440 and the late Gothic west façade

★
St-Gatien's
cathedral

▶ VISITING TOURS

INFORMATION

Office de Tourisme
78–82 Rue B. Palissy, F-37000 Tours
Tel. 02 47 70 37 37, fax 02 47 61 14 22
www.ligeris.com, www.ville-tours.fr

FESTIVALS AND EVENTS

Last Sat in July: garlic and basil
market. June/July: Fetes Musicales de
Touraine. Sept: Jazz en Touraine.

WHERE TO EAT

► Inexpensive / moderate

① *La Deuvalière*

18 Rue de la Monnaie
Tel. 02 47 64 01 57, closed Sun and
Mon
Cosy eatery in a lovely 15th-century
building with outstanding cuisine that
changes with the seasons. Advance
booking essential.

WHERE TO STAY

► Budget

① *Du Manoir*

2 Rue Traversière, tel. 02 47 05 37 37
http://site.voila.fr/hotel.manoir.tours
A very pretty hotel both inside and
out, with some old furnishings.
Breakfast served in the vaulted cellar.

② *Moderne*

1–3 Rue V. Laloux, tel. 02 47 05 32 81,
www.hotelmoderne37.com
Pleasant and comfortable family-run
hotel near the town hall.

Tours Map

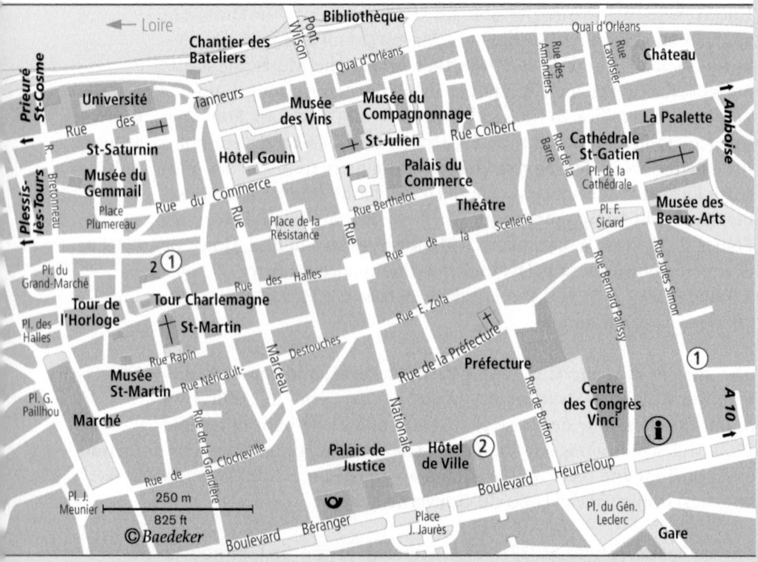

1 Hôtel Beaune-Semblançay
2 Logis des Ducs de Touraine

Where to eat
① La Deuvalière

Where to stay
① Moderne
② Du Manoir

from 1484. The 16th-century towers already exhibit aspects of Renaissance architecture (there is a great view from the south tower). The **stained glass windows** (1260) in the choir are the cathedral's magnificent highlight (bring binoculars!). In the first chapel off the choir to the right there is a wonderful marble grave sculpture for Charles Orland and Charles, son of Charles VIII (early 16th century). Organ recitals are given on Sundays and Wednesdays in August. A three-sided cloister (15th–16th centuries) adjoins the cathedral to the north. It is called »La Psalette« after the choral school that was once housed there. The stair tower is modelled on the one in Blois.

The cathedral of St-Gatien and the archiepiscopal palace

A museum of art in the episcopal palace, built in the 17th and 18th centuries, exhibits furniture, paintings and sculptures from the same period. Apart from the Barbizon artists and Impressionists such as Monet and Dégas, noteworthy works include some by Rembrandt and Mantegna (the latter having been looted by Napoleon from San Zeno in Verona). In the courtyard stands a Lebanese cedar which was planted in 1804 as well as Fritz the Elephant from Barnum & Bailey's circus, who was stuffed after he had to be put down in 1904. Blvd. Heurteloup has »monuments« of two epochs right opposite one another, the **railway station** (Victor Laloux, 1898) and the **Centre de Congrès Vinci** (Jean Nouvel, 1993; used for cultural events). Next to the »Vinci« is the tourist office.

★
Musée des
Beaux-Arts

Suburbs and Environs of Tours

At the eastern edge of the town, on the right bank of the Loire between the motorway and the N 152, there are still some remnants of **Marmoutier abbey** (closed to the public), founded in 372 by St Martin and once among the most powerful abbeys in France. Its impressive portal dates from 1220. **Grange de Meslay** from 1220, 6km/4mi to the north, was formerly in the possession of Marmoutier. The farm's barn is 60 × 25m/200 × 80ft in size and has open chestnut roof seating from the 15th century.

Another pretty spot with a lovely rose garden is the ruin of the priory of St-Cosme, founded in 1092 in what is now the western suburb

Priory of
St-Cosme

of La Riche. Pierre de Ronsard (1525–85), the most important member of the »Pléiades« group and one of France's greatest poets, was prior here and is buried in the choir. Apart from sections of the 11th–12th-century church, the refectory, the house of the prior and various other monastic buildings are still in existence.

Plessis-lès-Tours About 1km/1100yd south of Prieuré St-Cosme there remains one unadorned wing of a chateau King Louis XI had built from 1474 and in which he died in 1483. There is a reconstruction of Louis' bedroom. Guided tours are organized by the tourist office in Tours.

✶ ✶ Troyes

M 4

Région: Champagne-Ardenne	**Altitude:** 113m/371ft
Département: Aube	**Population:** 63,000

Troyes, the old capital of ►Champagne, has a bewitching old town, which is one of the most beautiful half-timbered quarters in France. Innumerable beautifully furnished churches and museums testify to the traditional prosperity of the city.

Capital of Champagne Troyes – in the southern part of Champagne on a section of the Seine where the river splits into a number of separate channels – was a key meeting place for people from all over Europe in the Middle Ages. The cloth and wool industry, which still employs some 15,000 people, has been in existence since the 15th century.

History Once the capital of the Tricasse Gauls, the city was called Augustobona by the Romans. The Catalaunian fields north of Troyes were the scene of a battle in 451, in which the western Roman legions, in alliance with Burgundians, Franks and Visigoths, defeated the »Scourge of God« Attila. In the 10th century the city came under control of the counts of Champagne, who built churches and hospitals and instituted the fair that is still held to this day. In 1284 the county passed to the French through marriage. The Treaty of Troyes in 1420 marks a key date in the Hundred Years' War. Isabeau of Bavaria, wife of King Charles VI, whose ability to rule fluctuated wildly, chose to name her son in law, Henry V of England, as heir to the throne. In 1524 the city was ravaged by fire.

! **Baedeker TIP**

Factory outlets

Bargain hunters come to Troyes by the bus-load to shop at its factory-outlet shops. The key areas are Marques Avenue in St-Julyen-les-Villas, 3km/2mi to the southwest (N 71) plus McArthur Glen and Marques City in Pointe Ste-Marie, 3km/2mi to the northeast (N 77/D 960). On Sunday and Monday mornings the shops are shut. More information can be obtained from the Office de Tourisme.

By then the textile industry had already come into being with the bonnetiers, manufacturers of caps and stockings, being mentioned in documents dating from 1505.

Troyes' importance as an artistic centre goes back to the establishment of studios as long ago as the 13th century, which created a style of their own during the Renaissance, the so-called **Troyes school**. The most outstanding members of this school were the sculptors Jean Gailde and Jacques Julyot (15th–16th centuries). Troyes also had an excellent reputation for stained glass work between the 14th and 17th centuries and examples can be seen in churches all over the city. Among the most important artists were Jean Soudain (16th century) and Linard Gontier (1565–1642). Troyes was also the birthplace of Pierre Mignard

An elegant harmony pervades the cathedral of Saints Peter and Paul

(1612–95), a competitor of Le Brun, and sculptor François Girardon (1628–1715).

What to See in Troyes

The old town, bounded by Boulevard Gambetta, Boulevard Victor Hugo and Boulevard 14 Juillet and a bend of the Seine, is reminiscent of the cork in a champagne bottle: the quarter where the bishops and aristocrats lived (the »cité«), is its head and the merchants' quarter (»bourg«) is the stopper. Most of the buildings are half-timbered, the prettiest being in the area around St-Jean. The narrow Ruelle des Chats has a truly medieval feel.

★★
Old town

The church of St-Nicolas, built after the fire of 1524, has a lovely southern doorway with statues fashioned by local-born François Gentil (16th century) and an unusual balcony with the Chapelle du Calvaire and *Christ at the Pillar*, also by Gentil. The choir seating dates from the 17th century.

St-Nicolas

In the late-Gothic church of St-Pantaléon there are numerous sculptures from the 16th century on view, all works from the Troyes school. In the magnificent 16th-century Hôtel Vauluisant across the way there are two museums, the Musée de la Bonneterie (history of

St-Pantaléon

Hôtel Vauluisant

▶ VISITING TROYES

INFORMATION

Office de Tourisme
16 Boulevard Carnot, F-10000 Troyes
Tel. 03 25 82 62 70, fax 03 25 73 06 81
www.tourisme-troyes.com

PASS'TROYES

The Pass'Troyes ticket includes admittance to various museums, a city tour, tastings of local products and discounts at factory-outlet shops.

FESTIVALS AND EVENTS

End of June–end of July.: »Ville en Musiques« with all kinds of music. Late Oct/early Nov: »Nuits de Champagne«, music festival.

WHERE TO EAT

▶ Moderate / expensive

① *Le Valentino*
35 Rue Paillot de Montabert
Tel. 03 25 73 14 14, closed Sun evenings and Mon as well as the second half of Aug.
Located in a picturesque 16th-century building in the middle of the old town and featuring a lovely terrace. Fine French cuisine with some interesting new ideas.

▶ Inexpensive

② *Bistrot du Pont*
5 Place Ch. de Gaulle
Pont-Ste-Marie (3km/2mi northeast)
Tel. 03 25 80 90 99, closed Sun evenings and Mon. The food in this bistro on one arm of the Seine is as nice as the surroundings.

WHERE TO STAY

▶ Mid-range / luxury

① *Champ des Oiseaux*
20 Rue Linard-Gonthier
Tel. 03 25 80 58 50
www.champdeoiseaux.com
Something really special. Three half-timbered houses from the 15th–16th centuries, restored using old-fashioned techniques but equipped with all mod cons. Very good breakfast served in a salon with its own fireplace or in the enchanting courtyard during summer.

Troyes Map

1 St-Pantaleon
2 St-Jean
3 Pharmacie de l'Hôtel-Dieu
4 Musée d'Art Moderne

Where to eat
① Le Valentino
② Bistrot du Pont

Where to stay
① Champ des Oiseaux

knitted garments from Troyes) and the Musée Historique de Troyes et de la Champagne (art from the 13th–16th centuries, coins and costumes).

In Hôtel de Mauroy, a lovely aristocratic residence from the Renaissance period (1560), there is a marvellous collection of tools from centuries gone by on view, which is run by the **Compagnons du Devoir**, a society of wandering artisans (open daily).

Maison de l'Outil

The basilica of St-Jean, built between the 14th and 16th centuries, was in 1420 the venue for the wedding of Catherine, daughter of Charles VI and Isabeau, to Henry V of England. The nave is Gothic, while the much taller choir dates from the 16th century. Take note of the sumptuous **high altar** (1667) and the 16th-century visitation group along the right-hand side aisle. The town hall on Place du Maréchal Foch is in Louis-Treize style (1624–70, extended in 1935).

St-Jean

Hôtel de Ville

Ste-Madeleine is the oldest church in the city. Its Gothic nave and transept date from the 12th century, while the tower and choir are from the Renaissance (16th century). The magnificent stone **rood screen**, with its rich Flamboyant decoration, is the work of Jean Gailde (1508–17). Other notable features are the 15th-century statue of St Martha dressed in folk costume in the right-hand side aisle and the lovely windows in the choir (late 14th–early 15th century).

Ste-Madeleine

The church of St-Urbain, one of the finest Gothic buildings in Champagne, was built in 1262–86 for Troyes-born Pope Urban IV. In the choir, a delicate stone »frame« supports the 13th-century stained glass windows. Below the statues, take a look at the *Madonna with Grape*, a key work of the Renaissance in Troyes (16th century).

★
St-Urbain

Hôtel-Dieu-le-Comte is used by the university but also preserves a lovely apothecary from the early 17th century. A superb wrought iron grille fences off the courtyard.

Hôtel-Dieu

The cathedral, one of the key Gothic buildings in Champagne, was built from 1208 to 1638. The west façade and the northern transept, with its splendid **Beau Portail** (1546), were designed by Martin Chambiges, who was also a key contributor to the cathedrals in Beauvais and Sens. The interior, with a nave and four aisles, is lit by some wonderful **windows** from the 13th, 15th and 16th centuries. The left-hand side aisle features a window depicting *Christ in the Mystic Winepress* (Leonard Gontier, 1625). The cathedral treasury with its enamel, ivory, gold and embroidery from the 11th to 19th centuries is also worth seeing.

★
St-Pierre-et-St-Paul

The episcopal palace (16th, 17th, 19th centuries) next door now houses the museum of modern art, featuring works from the period

★
Musée d'Art Moderne

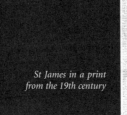

*St James in a print
from the 19th century*

THE PILGRIM'S STAFF AND SCALLOP SHELLS

Since the early Middle Ages, pilgrims have been making their way through France. They still do, along a route marked by the emblem of St James, scallop shells. Their destination is northwest Spain, the legendary grave of the Apostle James the Elder in Santiago de Compostela.

According to the Acts of the Apostles (12.1), King Herod had St James beheaded in AD 44. There are many legends as to how his body came to be found on the Campus Stellae (the field of stars) and many more regarding the **discovery of the grave around 830**. One story incorporates the Spanish campaign of King Charlemagne, who was attacked by Moors on the return journey near Roncesvalles, losing his lieutenant Roland in the process. This gave rise to the famous *Song of Roland*, which became part of the French national epic. In about 1140 the *Song of Roland* was incorporated into a larger work, which was to make the pilgrimage to Santiago famous. The Codex Calixtinus, in which the tale appears, incorporates, among other things, a detailed description of the Way of St James along with numerous practical tips. Some of the accommodations mentioned here are still in use. All over Europe people set out for Santiago. The pilgrimage was inspired by two decisive events, the **conquest of Jerusalem** by the

Arabs in AD 637 and a conflict between the HolyRoman emperor and the pope, which culminated in the **investiture controversy** of the 11th century. Since the Holy Land itself was too far away for most people, the journey was too dangerous and too expensive, and the fact that there were sometimes obstacles that prevented a pilgrimage to Rome, a large number made a pilgrimage to to Spain instead. The pilgrimage first flourished in the 12th century when it is estimated that up to 300,000 pilgrims arrived at Santiago every year. Apart from the purely religious reasons, such as salvation from material or spiritual troubles, many were driven by a sense of adventure, difficulties at home (epidemics, war) or existential fears. Many financed the trip by taking jobs along the way as workmen or builders. For instance, a certain »Juan de Colonia« (Hans of Cologne) is known to have built the 84m/276ft cathedral tower in Burgos and the Capilla del Condestable, among other things before arriving at Santiago.

The distant objective: the cathedral in Santiago de Compostela

Old ways

West Francia had several saints' graves and celebrated **places of pilgrimage**, e.g. the graves of St Martin (Tours), Mary Magdalene (Vézelay), Saint-Gilles (Ägidius) and Le Puy (Fides), one of the earliest destinations for pilgrims of Our Lady. These pilgrimage destinations already possessing an important infrastructure, became key stages on the Way of St James. Eventually a whole network of monasteries was established; each could be reached within a day's travel and offered accommodation, repose and medical help to pilgrims. The pilgrims' guide, the Codex Calixtinus, identified all the key pilgrimage destinations along with four main routes to Santiago. One route via Paris, the **Via Turonensis** – called »La Grande Route«, goes through Orléans, Tours, Poitiers, Saintes and Bordeaux. The Vézelay route, **Via Lemovicensis**, takes in Limoges, St-Léonard and Perigueux. The **Via Podiensis**, via Le Puy, also covers Conques, Rocamadour and Moissac. The Arles route via Toulouse (**Via Tolosana**) includes Arles, St-Gilles, and St-Guilhem-le-Désert. The first three join together at Ostabat to cross the Ibaneta Pass (1057m/3468ft) into Spain. The Arles route takes the Somport Pass (1562m/5125ft) then on to Puente La Reina, where all the routes meet as the »Camino de Santiago«.

New ways

Since the late 1980s the Way of St James has undergone a Renaissance, not to say a boom. Whereas 5000 pilgrims made their way to Santiago in 1990, in 2003 it was 75,000. In »holy years«, when the feast of St James (25 July) falls on a Sunday, the numbers have been even higher (around 160,000 in 2004). The first pope to follow the route was Pope John Paul II, in 1982. The pilgrims' equipment and the infrastructure makes for a quite different degree of comfort these days; the motives for the journey, too, have changed. Instead of fulfilling an oath, atoning for sins or similar reasons, people now highlight the spiritual experience of the journey, which has become a way to enlightenment. The experience of nature and culture – medieval towns with superb churches, monasteries and bridges all appear in abundance along the routes – is another important reason. Everyone feels part of a whole family of brothers and sisters in St James. In many countries there are St James societies to support the pilgrims with information at home and along the route. For information contact Secretary, Confraternity of St James, 27 Blackfriars Road London SE1 8NY; tel. +44 (0)20 7928 9988, fax +44 (0)20 7928 2844 www.csj.org.uk.

1850 to 1950 (Bonnard, Cézanne, Degas, Gauguin, Matisse, Modigliani, Picasso and others) as well as a collection of art from Africa and Oceania (closed Mon).

Abbaye St-Loup In the abbey of St-Loup (17th–18th centuries), take a look at the library, which possesses more than 300,000 volumes, 8000 manuscripts and 700 incunables and thus one of the largest in the country.

Musée des Beaux-Arts The building also houses the Musée des Beaux-Arts, which has antiques and paintings by French, Flemish and Dutch old masters.

Valence

M 8

Région: Rhône-Alpes	**Altitude:** 123m/404ft
Département: Drôme	**Population:** 67,000

Valence is the centre of the mid-section of the Rhône valley, functioning as its economic nexus and as a transport link between Burgundy and Provence, the Alps and the central massif. The lively capital of the département also has a university.

History Valence dates back to the Roman colony of Valentia, founded in the 2nd century BC. The university was established in 1452 and its students included Rabelais. During the religious wars, Protestant leader François de Beaumont ordered the murder of Catholics in Vienne in 1562 after the governor there had three Protestants executed. In 1785, 16-year-old Napoléon Bonaparte enrolled as a cadet in Valence's artillery college.

▶ VISITING VALENCE

INFORMATION

Office de Tourisme
11 Blvd. Bancel
F-26000 Valence
Tel. 0892 70 70 99
Fax 04 75 44 90 41
www.valencetourisme.com

WHERE TO EAT

► Moderate / expensive

L'Epicerie
18 Place St-Jean
Tel. 04 75 42 74 46
Closed Sat lunchtimes/Sun and 1–20

Aug Outstanding local cuisine in pleasant unpretentious surroundings. 16th-century building, some vaulted ceilings.

Bistrot Le 7 par Anne Sophie Pic
285 Av. V. Hugo
Tel. 04 75 44 53 86
www.pic-valence.com
The famous first-class hotel restaurant Maison Pic (same address) has a less expensive subsidiary that is just as elegant. Pretty terrace.

The central section of the Rhône is flanked by renowned vineyards such as L'Hermitage

What to See in Valence

Whether approaching the town from the north or south on the N 7, it is possible to park in Parc Jouvet on the Champ du Mars. The small kiosk here (1880) became famous in a painting by the »painter of lovers«, **Raymond Peynet**.

Champ du Mars

The art museum in the episcopal palace displays works by Flemish, Dutch, French and Italian masters from the 16th–19th centuries. The sanguine chalk drawings by Hubert Robert (1733–1808) are interesting too, as are the paintings of the Barbizon school and some Gallo-Roman mosaics.

Musée des Beaux-Arts

The 12th-century Romanesque cathedral was rebuilt in the 17th century after collapsing, but in a manner true to the original design. The choir and its gallery and chapel roof were inspired by Auvergne Romanesque. To the north of the cathedral stands the so-called Pendentif, the tomb of the cathedral master Mistral and his family (1548).

St-Apollinaire

On Grande Rue, the main shopping street, no. 57 is fascinating. It is called the Maison des Têtes (1532) after the heads under the roof, which represent the four winds. Further north is the 19th-century church of St-Jean with its Roman capitals in the portico.

Grande Rue

Located north of the Pendentif (Rue Pérollerie 7), Maisón Dupré Latour has a Renaissance courtyard. A little further north, Rue St-Martin leads to the church of Notre-Dame-de-Soyons (façade 17th century).

Maison Dupré Latour

Around Valence

From St-Péray across the Rhône, a climb lasting some 75 minutes leads up to the castle of Crussol, 230m/755ft above the valley. There

★
Château de Crussol

is a great view from here down the Rhône valley to Valence and the outliers of the Massif Central.

Tain l'Hermitage ✳ About 20km/12mi north of Valence, on a granite hill rising up from a loop in the Rhône, is one of France's most famous vineyards, **Hermitage**. Here, the Syrah grape is used to make some rich red wines. The red wines of AC Crozes Hermitage, which adjoins the vineries to the north and south, also have an excellent reputation.

Romans sur Isère Romans (17km/11mi northeast of Valence, 34,000 inhabitants) owes its prosperity to the guild of cobblers that has existed here since the 15th century. This is recalled at the interesting Musée International de la Chaussure. The collegiate church of St-Barnard (12th–14th centuries) with its Flemish tapestries from 1555 is also worth a visit.

Vendôme

J 5

Région: Centre
Département: Loir-et-Cher

Altitude: 82m/29ft
Population: 17,500

Vendôme, to the north of the mid-section of the Loire, is an idyllic gem. Its old town centre is cradled between two arms of the Loir and crossed by narrow canals. Its fascinating history has left it with several important and attractive buildings.

History What in Roman Gaul had been known as Vindocinum (»white mountain«) developed into a county in the 10th century. Count Geoffrey Martel bestowed a Benedictine abbey, which was consecrated in 1040, and donated relics he had brought from Constantinople, a tear of Christ and an arm of St George. This made the town an important stop on the Way of St James (the relics have been kept at the Vatican since 1803). Balzac was a pupil at the Oratorian college from 1807 to 1813. Nowadays Vendôme is known for the manufacture of gloves, electrical goods and machinery. Until a few years ago, the books published by the well-known **Presses Universitaires de France** were printed here. The publishing house brought out important books at low prices.

What to See in Vendôme

Castle ruins On the limestone rocks to the south of the town there was once a castle dating back to the 9th century, of which some 13th–14th-century towers and walls still remain in existence. The Tour de Poitiers was rebuilt in the 15th century. The garden of rest at the collegiate church of St-Georges has the tombs of the rulers of Vendôme. There is a great view from Promenade de Montagne.

An abbey dedicated to the Holy Trinity is marked out by its 83m/ ✳
272ft 12th-century tower, which stands apart from the remaining   **La Trinité**
buildings. The church (12th–16th centuries) is 72m/79yd long and
has a **magnificent façade** in Flamboyant Gothic style. Notable features inside include the stained glass windows in the choir (16th century), the Mary window in the eastern chapel from 1140 – the oldest
window anywhere with this motif – choir rails and seating (16th century), as well as the painted Romanesque statues on the columns of
the crossing. The monks' quarters next to the cloister house a museum (history, folklore, ecclesiastical art).

From the **bridge over the Loir** in the east there is a fine view of La   **Tour of the town**
Trinité church and the Porte d'Eau. Head back along Rue de l'Abbaye
to reach Place St-Martin and St Martin's tower, all that remains of a
Renaissance church which was demolished in 1857. There is also a
statue of Rochambeau. From the northeastern corner of the square,
Rue du Change leads to the former Chapelle du Lycée (St-Jacques,
1452). To the west of the chapel is the Oratorian college, founded in
1623 and now used as the town hall. The pretty **Parc Ronsard** starts
here. It contains the 15th-century Hôtel du Saillant (tourist office)
and an old washhouse. To the west of the town hall (on Rue St-Jacques) stands the church of St-Madeleine (1474) with its wooden barrel vaulting. Follow **Rue Poterie** southward to the 14th-century gate
of Porte St-Georges (extended 1807). Cross the Loir and turn left to
the car park or head north of the Loir past the 1892 market hall,
where markets still take place on Fridays, to Rue St-Bié.

The valley of the Loir is a little off the beaten track but is worth dis-   ✳
covering. Cycle paths are signposted along the river as far as the con-   **Loir valley**

 VISITING VENDÔME

INFORMATION
Office de Tourisme
47 Rue Poterie, F-41100 Vendôme Tel.
02 54 77 05 07, fax 02 54 73 20 81
www.vallee-du-loir.com

WHERE TO EAT / WHERE TO STAY

► **Inexpensive**
Auberge de la Madeleine
Place de la Madeleine
Tel. 02 54 77 20 79, fax 02 54 80 00 02
This lovely, accommodating and fam-
ily-friendly hotel shares an excellent
reputation with its restaurant. Lovely
terrace on the Loir. Closed Wed.

Le Vendôme
15 Faubourg Chartrain, tel. 02 54 77
02 88, www.hotelvendomefrance.com
Modern, somewhat showy hotel in an
old building. The La Cloche Rouge
restaurant is considered one of the
best in town.

► **Moderate**
Moulin Frabault
116 bis Faubourg St-Bienheuré
www.vendome41.com, tel. 02 54 73
16 58. The old mill on the Loir is an
enchanting place. The food is outstanding, the rooms cosy.

fluence with the Sarthe at ►Angers. On the way there are pretty villages, idyllic natural scenery, wine cellars, chateaux and other fascinating historical legacies to offer variety to the journey. Information is available from the Office de Tourisme in Vendôme. About 20km/12mi southwest of Vendôme, two particular gems stand out. The first

Lavardin of them is Lavardin (250 inhabitants), where there is a ruin of a castle built in the 12th–15th centuries, a 13th-century medieval bridge and the frugal early Romanesque church of St-Genest (11th–13th centuries, featuring important frescoes from the 12th–16th centu-

Montoire ries). There is a pretty view from the bridge in Montoire (4500 inhabitants), where Hitler met with Marshall Petain, head of the Vichy government, in October 1940, marking the beginning of the »collaboration«. Documents relating to the event are on view in the railway station. The chapel of St-Gilles can be found south of the bridge. It once belonged to a Benedictine priory and possesses some outstanding frescoes from the 12th–13th centuries.

Verdun

N 3

Région: Lorraine   **Altitude:** 119m/390ft
Département: Meuse   **Population:** 21,000

The name Verdun is now associated with the murderous battle that raged in the countryside around it during 1916–17, in which some 800,000 people lost their lives. It has since declared itself a town dedicated to peace and reconciliation and huge numbers visit it every year.

History Even before the First World War, Verdun, in the valley of the Meuse (Maas) in northwest ►Lorraine, played a key role in the history of both France and Germany. In 843 the **Treaty of Verdun** split Charlemagne's empire into three dominions, a western kingdom under Charles the Bald, a middle kingdom (under Lothar I) and an eastern kingdom under Louis the German. These lands would form the core of modern-day Germany and France. Verdun, as part of the middle kingdom, became part of the Holy Roman Empire in 925, with bishops given the status of earthly rulers. Later, Verdun was declared a free city of the empire. In 1552 it was occupied by Henri II and it finally became part of France in 1648. Thereafter fortifications were built, primarily by Vauban (as of 1675). After 1871 the bastions were strengthened still further and two belts of forts were established around the town.

Battle of Verdun, 1916 In the First World War the town became a key pillar of the French defences. Between 21 February 1916 and August 1917 the front ran some 4–15km/2.5–10mi north of the town and merciless attacks were carried out by both sides. The embattled town was kept in supplies via a route now called the »Voie Sacrée« (Sacred Way) running from Bar-le-Duc. After early successes for the Germans, the resistance of the French bolstered and within a small area a furious war of attrition ensued, which resulted in the death of some 800,000 men, not including the many soldiers lost, wounded or captured.

What to See in Verdun

Verdun consists of an old **upper town**, with the citadel and cathedral, plus a lower town with the business quarters. The highest point is occupied by the cathedral of Notre-Dame. Between 990 and 1024 the first church followed the pattern of the cathedrals of the empire in the Rhineland, namely a pillared basilica with two transepts and two apses. From 1136 to 1140 the eastern section was rebuilt in Burgundian style. More modifications and extensions were added in the 14th–16th centuries and after 1755 (including the west towers). Other notable features include the choir stalls, the organ (1762), the crypt and the church treasury. A 14th–15th-century cloister adjoins the southern side of the cathedral. The episcopal palace was built in 1725–54 by court architects Robert and Jules-Robert de Cotte. It now houses the **Centre Mondial de la Paix** (World Centre for Peace), which is mainly aimed at young people.

✱ Notre-Dame

Palais Episcopal

Vauban built the citadel on the site of the abbey of St-Vanne, which had been established in 952. Its 12th-century Tour de Vanne still remains. 7km/4mi of passages linked the multitude of facilities, from a huge bakery to operations rooms and munitions depots (guided tours on small trains, closed Jan).

Citadel

Ossuaire de Douaumont, a memorial and burial place for 130,000 soldiers

Battlefields of Verdun Map

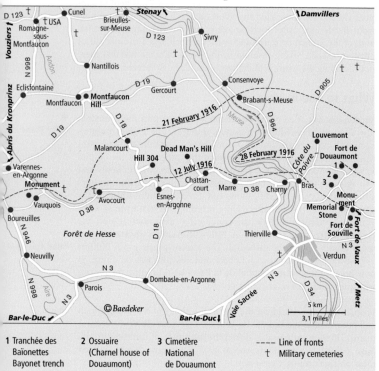

1 Tranchée des Baïonettes Bayonet trench	2 Ossuaire (Charnel house of Douaumont)	3 Cimetière National de Douaumont	---- Line of fronts † Military cemeteries

Hôtel de la Princerie
The 16th-century Hôtel de la Princerie houses the city museum whose exhibits range from prehistoric items to Renaissance pieces. The huge victory monument nearby was built in 1929 and recalls the fallen soldiers of the first war.

Fortifications
Porte Chaussée with its two rugged round towers (14th century, on the left bank of the Meuse) and Porte Châtel (15th century; north of the Palais Episcopal) were once part of the city walls.

Battlefields and Memorials

The battlefields, which retain their oppressive, eerie quality to this day (although quite a number of tourists mistake them for a leisure park), are situated either side of the Meuse to the north of the town.

Right of the Meuse
The memorials are closed in January. Leaving Verdun on the N 3 towards Etain, the road passes the French military cemetery of Faubourg-Pavé. 6km/3.5mi along the D 112 to Dieppe there is a monu-

▶ VISITING VERDUN

INFORMATION

Verdun Tourisme
Place de la Nation
F-55106 Verdun
Tel. 03 29 84 14 18, fax 03 29 83 99 93
www.verdun-tourisme.com

WHERE TO EAT

▶ **Inexpensive**
Le Clapier
34 Rue des Gros Degrés
Tel. 03 29 86 20 14, closed Sun

Hearty, unpretentious restaurant
serving Lorraine cuisine.

WHERE TO STAY

▶ **Budget**
Hôtel Le Montaulbain
4 Rue de la Vieille Prison
Tel. 03 29 86 00 47, fax 03 29 84 75 70,
This pleasant hotel near the cathedral
(pedestrian zone) offers well kept,
plain rooms. No restaurant.

ment to the builders of the Maginot Line (▶Baedeker Special p.510)
and Fort de Souville. At the crossroads near the chapel of Ste-Fine a
stone lion marks the most southerly point reached by the front, just
4km/2.5mi from Verdun. Further east, a side road off the D 913 leads
to Fort de Vaux (museum), where there is an expansive view from
the hill. Returning to the D 913 and heading northwest, an obelisk
beyond the Mémorial de Verdun recalls the village of Fleury-devant-
Douaumont, which was captured and regained some 16 times and
after its destruction was never rebuilt.

Passing the French national cemetery, the road comes to the monu- **Ossuaire de**
mental charnel house of Douaumont, an eerie place where the re- **Douaumont**
mains of 130,000 unknown French and German soldiers are interred. France's most important memorial to the First World War, its
hall is 137m/150yd long and the tower is 46m/151ft high.

Northwest of the ossuaire there is another memorial, Fort de Douau- **Fort de**
mont. It was built in 1885 and fell on 25 February 1916. The **Tran- Douaumont**
chée des Baïonettes, a First World War trench between the ossuaire
and the fort, has been roofed over. Here, French infantrymen, their
bayonets ready for an attack, were totally buried. The mass grave was
left as it was.

On the left bank of the Meuse, too, northwest of Verdun towards **Left of the**
Charny, there were also many hard-fought spots, including the dual **Meuse**
hills of **Mort Homme** (295 and 265m/968 and 869ft), Hill 304 and
Montfaucon Hill (Butte de Montfaucon, 336m/1102ft), which is topped by a 70m/230ft monument erected by the USA. From the monument's platform there is a good view of the northwestern part of the
battlefield. Further northwest lies the huge American military cemetery of Romagne-sous-Montfaucon.

● VISITING VERSAILLES

INFORMATION

Office de Tourisme
2 bis Avenue de Paris
F-78000 Versailles
Tel. 01 39 24 88 88, fax 01 39 24 88 89
www.mairie-versailles.fr
www.versailles-tourisme.com
Chateau: tel. 0810 81 16 14
www.chateauversailles.fr

GETTING THERE FROM PARIS

Approx. 20km/12mi west (A 13, N 10). SNCF: trains from La Défense, Montparnasse and St-Lazare. RER: line C 5 to Versailles-Rive Gauche (600m/660yd)from the chateau, C 8 to Versailles-Chantiers (1.2km/1mi from the chateau). RATP 171 bus from Pont de Sèvres.

TIPS FOR THE VISIT

Opening times ▶p.804. It is advisable to plan an entire day for a visit to the chateau. The crowds are at their thickest on Sat, Sun and Tue, when the Paris Louvre is closed. It is worth arriving early in the morning. For those who only want to see the Grands Appartements, 3.30pm–4pm is a good time. Visitors can have a picnic or rent bicycles in the park.

ADMISSION AND ACCESS

Tickets are best bought before your visit at a SNCF-Transilien counter or in a FNAC shop. Information and tickets in the forecourt on the left. The »passeport« allows admission to the chateau, the Trianons and the Grandes Eaux Musicales; in addition tickets are available for the chateau or the Trianons only. An audio guide is included in the price. Entrances: A (Cour Royale right) main entrance, C (Cour Royale left) guided tours for groups and individuals. Holders of a

Paris Museum Pass ▶Paris may use entrance C without queuing.

WHERE TO EAT

▶ Moderate

① *Le Limousin*
1 Rue de Satory, tel. 01 39 50 21 50
Classy bistro in the style of the early 19th century. Nomen est omen: a lot of meat is on the menu here, and the house speciality is leg of lamb with herbs. Open seven days a week.

▶ Inexpensive

② *À la Ferme*
3 Rue Maréchal Joffre
Tel. 01 39 53 10 81
Next to the well known but somewhat faded »Potager du Roy«, diners here can eat in less formal surroundings and at more affordable prices. On the menu are grilled meat and dishes from southwestern France.

WHERE TO STAY

▶ Luxury

① *Trianon Palace*
1 Blvd. Reine
Tel. 01 30 84 50 00
www.starwoodhotels.com
Here at the edge of the Trianon park you can truly live like a king in the elegant ambience of the early 20th-century. The Gordon Ramsay restaurant serves the finest cuisine, while La Veranda is more moderately priced.

▶ Budget

② *Le Cheval Rouge*
18 Rue André-Chenier
Tel. 01 39 50 03 03
25 rooms. A plain but well-kept hotel with historical flair 10 minutes from the chateau. Very good service and value for money. The car park in the hotel's own courtyard is an advantage.

vate chambers (cabinets intérieurs) are accessed via the bedroom. They too were furnished at the time of Marie Antoinette (1770–81) and feature a golden cabinet, library and billiard room etc.

Salons

The Hall of Mirrors was enclosed by two salons, in evocation of classical symmetry. The salon adjoining the queen's chambers is the **Salon de la Paix** (Salon of Peace), while the northern salon is the **Salon de la Guerre** (Salon of War). The painting on the ceiling of the Salon de la Paix was created by Le Brun, while the painting of Louis above the fireplace is by Lemoyne. In the 17th century, mirrors were exorbitantly expensive. In the Hall of Mirrors at Versailles (73m/80yd long, 10.5m/12yd wide, 12.3m/40ft high) courtiers and courtesans wait on their royal charges. Its 17 arches, each with a mirror inside, face 17 windows with rounded arches opening onto the park. The furnishings have been reconstructed true to the originals. The paintings in the barrel vaulting tell the story of Louis XIV's reign.

Galerie des Glaces

The Salon de l'Œil de Bœuf, named after the oval window (»bull's eye«), served as a vestibule for the king's »coucher et lever« ceremonies. It contains paintings by Veronese as well as a noteworthy frieze, 53m/58yd in length and depicting children at play.

Salon de l'Œil de Bœuf

The thoroughly gilded **bedroom** of the king was furnished in 1701. It was here that Louis XIV died on 1 September 1715. One notable aspect is that the room is at the very centre of the whole palace complex. Among the paintings preserved here are examples by Valentin de Boulogne, Carracci, Domenichino and Van Dyck. The next room, **the council chamber** (Cabinet du Conseil), is where all affairs of state were decided in the time of Louis XV and XVI. The white-gold furnishings of the masterful French Rococo were fashioned by Ange-Jacques Gabriel. From here it is possible to enter the Cabinets Intérieurs du Roi, the private chambers of the king, also designed by Gabriel.

Chambre du Roi

Cabinet du Conseil

The **king's own apartments** come next: the Salon d'Apollon (ceiling painted by Ch. D la Fosse); the Salons de Mercure, de Mars, de Diane, de Vénus and de l'Abondance and – extending into the north wing – the Salon d'Hercule. The ceilings of all seven rooms are painted with mythological scenes. By this evocation of classic themes, Louis XIV sought to highlight his own greatness.

Grand Appartement du Roi

The adjoining chapel in the north wing (1699–1710) was started by Hardouin-Mansart but the interior was designed by Robert de Cotte. Ange-Jacques Gabriel designed the opera hall at the end of the north wing for Louis XV, although it was not completed until 1770.

La Chapelle

Opéra

Various rooms in the north and south wings have now been given over to the **museum of French history**, established in 1837 by the

Musée de l'Histoire de France

»Roi Citoyen«, Louis-Philippe. Its bombastic paintings and sculptures seek to evoke the glory of France (no hint of a defeat appears anywhere). Almost all of the south wing is occupied by the 120m/131yd-long, 13m/14yd-wide **Galeries des Batailles** (battle gallery), which has 36 giant paintings, including some by Delacroix. In the assembly room on the ground floor, an exhibition celebrates the »golden moments of parliament«.

★ ★
Parc de Versailles

The park at Versailles is the ultimate example of 17th-century French garden design. **André Le Nôtre** (1613 to 1700), son of one of the gardeners at the Tuileries in Paris, created his masterpiece here. Symmetry and nature, enhanced by geometric forms, exemplified the ideal of the French classical period, namely the mastery of nature by man. As far as the Allée d'Apollon the gardens, with their fountains and ponds, along with hundreds of statues and vases, have been retained in their original condition. The best view is from the upper terrace when the fountains are turned on. The **Bassin de Neptune** in the north was created by Le Nôtre (1684), its sculptures being added by Adam, Bouchardon and Lemoyne (as of 1740). From the

! *Baedeker* TIP

Royal feasts

On summer weekends from Easter to the end of October, fountain displays are accompanied by Baroque music (»Grandes Eaux Musicales«, several times daily, with fireworks at night). The »Grandes Fêtes de Versailles« provide an idea of how Louis celebrated his own festivals in the gardens, with opera, theatre or ballet. Information and tickets: tel. 01 30 83 78 89, fax 01 30 83 78 90, www.chateauversaillesspectacles.fr.

Parterre du Midi, marble stairways lead southward down to the **Orangerie** (Mansart, 1686). Behind that, the Pièce d'Eau des Suisses pond is a lovely place for a picnic. Along the main axis of the estate, the **Axe du Soleil** (axis of the sun), the Allée Royale, also called the »Tapis vert« (carpet of green), links the ponds of Leto (Apollo's mother) and Apollo himself. The statues at the Bassin d'Apollon, showing Apollo upon his chariot of the sun behind an impetuous team of horses (Jean-Baptiste Tuby, 1670), is supposed to be an image of Louis XIV.

Tapis vert

Bassin d'Apollon

Grand Canal
Petit Canal

A waterway with real ships to remind people of France's naval might, where sunsets could be witnessed across the sparkling surface, was also an unmissable part of any display. The Grand Canal is 1588m/1mi long and 62m/68yd wide. It is crossed by the smaller Petit Canal. Nowadays it is possible to take to the waters in a rowing boat.

Les Trianons

Trianon was the name of a village that Louis XIV bought and levelled to make himself a refuge from strict protocol and a place to be with his family. The **Grand Trianon** (or »Marble Trianon«) which can be seen today was Hardouin-Mansart's 1687–88 replacement for the original »Porcelain Trianon«. Marie-Antoinette adapted it to the fashion of her day as did Napoleon and Louis-Philippe. The miniature **Petit Trianon** palace, with its pretty English garden, was commissioned from Gabriel by Louis XV for the delight of Madame Pompadour. Later, Louis XVI gifted it to his queen, Marie-Antoinette.

In 1784 a »hamlet« was built – a farmhouse around a lake with a dairy, a mill and a pigeon loft. Here the ladies of the court, dressed as farm wenches, would amuse themselves.

Le Hameau

What to See in the Town

Place d'Armes is the starting point for the main axes of the town. The eastern side of the square is occupied by the **royal stables** (Hardouin-Mansart, 1679–85). The Grande Ecurie (to the north) could accommodate up to 2500 horses. Nowadays, in the Musée des Carrosses, royal carriages from the Baroque era are on display (open April–Oct, Sat–Sun: 12.30pm–6.30pm). Students of the equestrian academy still demonstrate the noble art of dressage here (Matinales des écuyers, Sat–Sun 11.15am; Opus 2008, Sat 6pm and 8pm, Sun 3pm; www.acadequestre.fr).

*Place d'Armes
Ecuries Royales*

Not far south of the Av. de Sceaux is the royal tennis court, the Salle du Jeu de Paume (1686), where the national assembly took place in 1789. Further south is the **cathedral of St-Louis** (1754) and west of there the Carrés St-Louis, a »centre of commerce« from 1755. To the east is the Potager du Roi (royal vegetable garden), which still supplies vegetables to restaurants to this day. On Rue de l'Indépendance-Américaine is the Grand Commun, the former foreign ministry (Mansart, 1682), which now contains the Bibliothèque Municipale with all the books that once graced the royal library. To the north of Av. St-Cloud – in the lively commercial quarter – it is worth taking a look at the church of Notre-Dame (Mansart, 1686), the **Marché Notre-Dame** and Musée Lambinet (1750), which combines all sorts of exhibits illustrating the history of Versailles.

Other attractions

Vienne

M 7

Région: Rhône-Alpes
Département: Isère

Altitude: 158m/518ft
Population: 30,000

Vienne, located south of Lyon on the Rhône, has a certain southern flair that makes it almost Provencal in character. Visitors are drawn to its legacy of Roman monuments, and gourmets make pilgrimages here to eat at one of the best restaurants in the country.

History The capital city of the Celtic Allobrogian tribe was transformed under Roman emperor Diocletian into the centre of the Dioecesis Viennensis, which encompassed most of southern France. In the 3rd century Vienne became a bishopric and under the self-confident secular rule of the bishops it experienced another heyday. Boso, Count of Vienne, became king of Lower Burgundy in 879, and by the 12th century Vienne had become the capital of Dauphiny. In 1450–51 the town came under the dominion of the French crown.

What to See in Vienne

St-André-le-Bas On the banks of the Rhône, the primarily Romanesque 12th-century abbey church of St-André-le-Bas also exhibits some Provencal influences. The sub-structure and the apse go back as far as an earlier Carolingian building (9th century). In the 12th -century cloister, where northern influences are apparent, there are several Christian sarcophagi from the 5th century as well as a lapidarium.

Temple d'Auguste et de Livie Hôtel de Ville Rue des Clercs leads to Place du Palais, site of the town's premier monument, the **temple of Augustus and Livia** (*c*20 BC). To the east lies Place de l'Hôtel de Ville, the hub of the town and site of its town hall.

St-Maurice The twin-towered cathedral of St-Maurice was built over a period from the 12th to the 16th centuries, so that it combines Romanesque and Gothic elements (Flamboyant façade). The interior is 97m/106yd long and has no transept. Its notable features include Romanesque capitals, 16th-century Flemish carpets and beautiful windows, also from the 16th century.

✳ St-Pierre Musée Lapidaire Southwest of the cathedral, near the Rhône, is the church of St-Pierre, where tombs of the bishops are housed. It is one of the oldest churches in France (5th–10th centuries, tower and portal 12th century). It also contains a lapidarium.

Musée des Beaux-Arts et d'Archéologie East of St-Maurice, the Musée des Beaux-Arts et d'Archéologie displays Roman finds (the **silver from the 3rd century** is particularly fine), French porcelain, paintings from the 16th–19th centuries and antique furniture. Nearby to the northeast there is an archaeological park with a double arch from the forum and foundations of a shrine to the goddess Cybele.

Roman theatre On the slopes of Mont Pipet, further to the east, there is a 1st-century Roman theatre. Within its 130m/142yd diameter 13,500 spectators could be accommodated. At times of the year when the weather is fine many concerts etc. take place here. There is a lovely view from **Mont Pipet**, which is topped by a 19th-century chapel and a statue of the Virgin Mary.

In the Jardin Public park south of the Rhône, a piece of Roman road from the 4th century has been preserved. Another 500m/550yd or so further south stands the »Pyramide« (»Aiguille«), an obelisk 26m/85ft in height that served to mark the turning point during chariot races in the Roman circus. West of the Rhône, a huge **Gallo-Roman settlement** has been discovered (St-Romain-en-Gal), which is thought to have been part of a conurbation including Ste-Colombe and Vienne. There is a highly informative museum at the entrance. In the neighbouring suburb of Ste-Colombe there are more Roman excavations. The tower, Tour Philippe de Valois (1353), stands next to the river.

Other classical remains

★
St-Romain-en-Gal

Around Vienne

The steep vineyards of the Côte Rôtie start to appear just a few miles south of Vienne. The grapes grown here (primarily Syrah) are used to make some outstanding red wines. Condrieu is famed for its highly aromatic white Viognier, which until a few years ago was exclusive to this region.

Côte Rôtie Condrieu

Situated some 40km/25mi south of Vienne in ► Dauphiny, Hauterives is famed for its **Palais Idéal**, the dream of former postman Ferdinand Cheval (1836–1912) realized in stone. From 1879 until he died, Cheval worked on his fabulous »palace«. His tomb in the cemetery was also self-built and it, too, is well worth taking a look at.

Hauterives

 VISITING VIENNE

INFORMATION

Office de Tourisme
3 Cours Brillier, F-38200 Vienne
Tel. 04 74 53 80 30, fax 04 74 53 80 31
www.vienne-touisme.com

EVENTS

Late June–mid-July: jazz festival with a great line-up in the Roman theatre (www.jazzavienne.com).

WHERE TO EAT / WHERE TO STAY

► Expensive
Beau Rivage
F-69420 Condrieu, tel. 04 74 56 82 82, www.hotel-beaurivage.com
One lovely place to enjoy the classic cuisine is this hotel restaurant with a beautiful garden on the river.

La Pyramide
14 Blvd. Fernand Point,
Tel. 04 74 53 01 96, closed Tue and Wed and 1 week in mid-Aug. Virtually a Mecca for gourmands, as this was where the legendary Fernand Point was chef until the 1950s. The kitchen and hotel still do honour to his name.

► Inexpensive / moderate
Le Bec Fin
7 Place St-Maurice
Tel. 04 74 85 76 72, closed Mon, Wed evenings and 10 days at the beginning of July. For those wishing to delight in the local delicacies, this spot between the Rhône and the cathedral is just the place.

INDEX

LIST OF MAPS AND ILLUSTRATIONS

PHOTO CREDITS

PUBLISHER'S INFORMATION

Illustrations etc: 371 illustrations, 85 maps and diagrams, one large map
Text: Dr. Bernhard Abend, Anja Schliebitz, with contributions by Achim Bourmer, Dr. Madeleine Reincke und Walter Rottiers
Editing: Baedeker editorial team (John Sykes, Robert Taylor)
Translation: Simon Clay, Gareth Davies, Robert Taylor
Cartography: Franz Huber, München; MAIRDUMONT, Ostfildern (map)
3D illustrations: jangled nerves, Stuttgart
Design: independent Medien-Design, Munich; Kathrin Schemel

Editor-in-chief: Rainer Eisenschmid, Baedeker Ostfildern

1st edition 2009

Based on Baedeker Allianz Reiseführer »Frankreich«, 13. Auflage 2009

Copyright: Karl Baedeker Verlag, Ostfildern
Publication rights: MAIRDUMONT GmbH & Co; Ostfildern

Printed in China

DEAR READER,

We would like to thank you for choosing this Baedeker travel guide. It will be a reliable companion on your travels and will not disappoint you.

This book describes the major sights, of course, but it also recommends the best bistros, as well as hotels in the luxury and budget categories, and includes tips about where to eat or go shopping and much more, helping to make your trip an enjoyable experience. Our authors Dr. Bernhard Abend and Anja Schliebitz ensure the quality of this information by making regular journeys to France and putting all their know-how into this book.

Nevertheless, experience shows us that it is impossible to rule out errors and changes made after the book goes to press, for which Baedeker accepts no liability. Please send us your criticisms, corrections and suggestions for improvement: we appreciate your contribution. Contact us by post or e-mail, or phone us:

▶ **Verlag Karl Baedeker GmbH**
Editorial department
Postfach 3162
73751 Ostfildern
Germany
Tel. 49-711-4502-262, fax -343
www.baedeker.com
www.baedeker.co.uk
E-Mail: baedeker@mairdumont.com

BAEDEKER GUIDE BOOKS AT A GLANCE

Guiding the World since 1827

◄ Andalusia	◄ Florence	◄ Egypt
◄ Austria	◄ Florida	◄ Dubai
◄ Bali	◄ France	◄ Dresden
◄ Barcelona	◄ Greece	◄ Cologne
◄ Berlin	◄ Iceland	◄ Budapest
◄ Brazil	◄ Ireland	◄ Brazil
◄ Prague	◄ Italy	◄ South Africa
◄ Rome	◄ Japan	◄ Spain
◄ South Africa	◄ London	◄ Thailand
◄ Portugal	◄ Mexico	◄ Tuscany
◄ Paris	◄ New York	◄ Venice
◄ Norway		◄ Vienna

Baedeker **Dresden**

Baedeker **France**

Baedeker **Greece**

Baedeker **Iceland**

Baedeker **Norway**

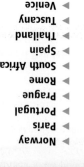